Using Educational Psychology in Teaching

Paul Eggen
University of North Florida

Don Kauchak
University of Utah

 Pearson

Director and Publisher: Kevin M. Davis
Content Producer: Janelle Rogers
Sr. Development Editor: Jeffrey Johnston
Media Producer: Lauren Carlson
Portfolio Management Assistant: Maria Feliberty
Executive Field Marketing Manager: Krista Clark
Executive Product Marketing Manager: Christopher Barry
Manufacturing Buyer: Carol Melville
Full Service Project Management: Thistle Hill Publishing Services, LLC
Cover Designer: Carie Keller
Cover Image: Mareen Fischinger/Westend61/OFFSET
Composition: Pearson CSC
Text Font: Palatino LT Pro 9.5/13

Credits and acknowledgments for material borrowed from other sources and reproduced, with permission, in this textbook appear on the appropriate page within the text.

Every effort has been made to provide accurate and current Internet information in this book. However, the Internet and information posted on it are constantly changing, so it is inevitable that some of the Internet addresses listed in this textbook will change.

Library of Congress Control Number: 2018959885
Library of Congress Cataloging-in-Publication Data is available upon request.

10 9 8 7 6 5 4 3 2 1

ISBN 13: 978-0-13-524054-0
ISBN 10:   0-13-524054-9

To Judy and Kathy,
teachers who have changed many lives.

Brief Contents

Contents

9   Knowledge Construction and the Learning Sciences   384

10   Motivation and Learning   414

11   A Classroom Model for Promoting Student Motivation   462

15 Standardized Testing and Learning

About the Authors

Paul Eggen

Paul has worked in higher education for nearly 40 years. He is a consultant for public schools and colleges in his university service area and has provided support to teachers in 12 states. Paul has also worked with teachers in international schools in 23 countries in Africa, South Asia, the Middle East, Central America, South America, and Europe. He has published several articles in national journals, is the co-author or co-editor of six other books, and presents regularly at national and international conferences.

Paul is strongly committed to public education. His wife is a middle school teacher in a public school, and his two children are graduates of public schools and state universities.

Don Kauchak

Don has taught and worked in schools and in higher education in nine states for over 40 years. He has published in a number of scholarly journals, including the *Journal of Educational Research, Journal of Experimental Education, Journal of Research in Science Teaching, Teaching and Teacher Education, Phi Delta Kappan,* and *Educational Leadership.* In addition to this text, he has co-authored or co-edited six other books on education. He has also been a principal investigator on federal and state grants examining teacher development and evaluation practices, and presents regularly at the American Educational Research Association. He currently volunteer-tutors first, second, and third graders in a local elementary school. These students have taught him a lot about educational psychology.

Preface

Welcome to the eleventh edition of our text. As in all fields, educational psychology rapidly advances, and our goal in this edition is to capitalize on these advances to produce a book that meets three goals: to provide the most conceptually sound theory possible, to include up-to-date research, and to prepare a text that provides the most concrete and specific suggestions in the field for applying the content of Educational Psychology in PreK–12 classrooms. Upon the advice of Kevin Davis, our editor, to reflect the third goal and symbolize an essential thrust of our text, we have changed its name to *Using Educational Psychology in Teaching*. Many students can describe and explain the topics included in an educational psychology text, but far fewer know how, as teachers, to apply these topics to increase their students' learning.

The Most Applied Text in the Field

Applications in Classrooms

We attempt to reach our third goal above in several ways. First, we introduce each chapter with a case study in which a teacher is applying the content of the chapter to increase student learning and development.

We then integrate the case studies throughout the chapters in attempts to make the content of each meaningful for readers and further illustrate how educational psychology can be used in teaching to increase student learning.

We expand on this process by including one or more sections in each chapter titled "Using Educational Psychology in Teaching: Suggestions for Applying . . . with Your Students." In these sections we include specific suggestions for applying, for instance, Vygotsky's theory of cognitive development, social-emotional learning, culturally responsive teaching, universal design for learning, social constructivist views of learning, theories of motivation, formative assessment, and so on, in classrooms. We then illustrate each of these suggestions with concrete examples taken from the real world of PreK–12 teaching. As a further illustration, the video episodes on which the case studies integrated throughout chapters 2, 9, 11, 13, and 14 are based are included with the MyLab Education component that accompanies this text. These episodes show the actual classroom lessons and provide students with authentic, real-world insights into learning and teaching, and they will hopefully make the written case studies and chapter content more meaningful for readers.

In addition to these specific suggestions we include *Classroom Connections*, which provide additional suggestions for applying the content of each section at the elementary, middle school, and high school levels, and we include *Developmentally Appropriate Practice* sections in each chapter that offer suggestions for adapting the content for different developmental levels.

Also, in each chapter we include two, three, or four Application Exercises, placed throughout the chapter, that ask readers to apply the chapter content to the real world of teaching. A total of 47 exercises are included in the book's 15 chapters, 38 of which are based on video episodes of approximately five minutes or less, leaving 9 that are based on written case studies. Feedback for all the Application Exercises is included.

In the eText we include Video Examples, ranging from approximately 40 seconds to 2 minutes in length, that provide brief, concrete illustrations of the chapter content. The Video Examples are placed next to the topics they illustrate.

Finally, at the end of each major section of every chapter, we include Self-Check Practice and Quiz-Me exercises designed to help readers acquire a deep understanding of the content in the chapters. The exercises are all written at higher cognitive levels, they focus on classroom application, and readers can respond to the practice exercises as often as they want. Feedback is provided for all the exercises.

As authors, we continue to spend a great deal of time in PreK–12 classrooms, working directly with teachers and students, and we believe this experience helps us provide the most realistically applied textbook in educational psychology. If you want a book that is truly applied, we believe this is the book for you.

Applications in Today's World

In addition to our attempts to help readers apply the content of educational psychology in their teaching, we also provide short sections throughout the text titled *Ed Psych and You,* which ask one or more questions about personal experiences that can be explained with topics in educational psychology. For instance, we ask questions such as:

Are you bothered when something doesn't make sense? Are you more comfortable in classes where the instructor specifies the requirements, outlines the grading practices, and consistently follows through? "Yes" is the answer for most people. Why do you think this is the case?

Theories of cognitive development help answer this question.

Think about some of your friends and acquaintances. Are those who seem happiest and have the greatest sense of well-being also the most intelligent or academically successful? If not, why do you think that's the case?

These questions can be answered with research examining social-emotional development.

Do you like to play games? Do you like playing all games or only certain ones? Why do you enjoy some and not others? Is succeeding in some games more important to you than succeeding in others?

We can answer these questions with theories of motivation.

We discuss and explain questions such as these in each chapter. This feature is our attempt to remind readers that educational psychology, in addition to providing essential applications in PreK–12 classrooms, can be applied in our daily lives. It is one of the most attractive aspects of the field.

Conceptually Sound Theory and Up-to-Date Research

Educational psychology has enormous implications for the way we teach and help students learn. To capitalize on these implications and reach the first two goals we identified at the beginning of the preface, we are including much new and updated content. We outline it below.

In Every Chapter

Top 20 Principles from Psychology—The American Psychological Association has identified 20 principles that are particularly applicable for PreK–12 teaching and learning. We describe the principles in Chapter 1; at the beginning of each chapter we identify the principles that are particularly emphasized in that chapter, and we specify the location in the chapter where the principle is applied with a callout.

The National Council on Teacher Quality (NCTQ)—The NCTQ has identified six essential teaching strategies that all new teachers need to know. As with the top 20 principles from psychology, we discuss the strategies in Chapter 1, identify those that are particularly emphasized at the beginning of each chapter, embed examples of their applications in the chapters, and identify the example with a callout.

Diversity

Diversity and immigration—Our students are the most diverse in the history of our nation, and immigrant students are making up an increasing proportion of school populations. We devote Chapter 4 to the topic and we include sections in each of the other chapters that examine the implications of diversity for our work with students. Unlike some representatives of today's political world, we sincerely believe that diversity enriches us all, and we express this optimistic view throughout the text.

The theoretical framework for culturally responsive teaching—Research indicates that "Culturally Responsive Teaching" can increase achievement for all students and particularly members of cultural minorities. We significantly expand our discussion of culturally responsive teaching in Chapter 4 of this edition, and we include new content that offers a theoretical framework that supports the practice.

Discriminatory classroom management policies—Research consistently indicates that racial disparities exist in teachers' classroom management practices. We examine this research in detail in Chapter 12 and offer specific suggestions for developing equitable classroom management policies.

Are members of cultural minorities over- or underrepresented in special education? Research indicates that, in contrast with popular beliefs, members of cultural minorities are underrepresented in special education, which deprives them of services that can help them succeed and thrive. We examine this issue in detail in Chapter 5.

Learning, Development, and Motivation

Critical thinking and the Internet—Critical thinking has become a major issue in today's world of "conspiracy theories," "post truth," and "fake news." Research indicates that today's students have difficulty separating fake news from real news and conspiracy theories from facts. In our discussion of critical thinking in Chapter 8, we examine these issues in detail, and we offer suggestions for what we, as teachers, can do to help students develop the critical thinking abilities that will help them deal effectively with these issues.

Technology, learning, and development—Technology is ubiquitous, and the impact of technology/social media/smartphones on learning and development is widely discussed in the research literature. We provide detailed discussions of both the positive and negative influences of technology on learning and development, and particularly social-emotional development, throughout the text.

The cognitive neuroscience of learning and development—Neuroscience is expanding our understanding of learning and development, and this understanding has important implications for our teaching. We examine these implications in detail, and provide suggestions for what we, as teachers, can do to capitalize on our increasing understanding of neuroscience to improve learning for all students.

Executive functioning—Executive functioning is essential for both learning and daily living. It is so important that strategies for measuring it are included on tests of intelligence and school readiness. We include a detailed description of this important process in our discussion of cognitive views of learning in Chapter 7, and we offer suggestions teachers can use to help students develop their executive functioning abilities.

Universal design for learning (UDL)—UDL designs instructional materials and activities to make content accessible to all learners. UDL is the process designed to ensure that inclusion is successful for learners with exceptionalities. We examine UDL in detail in our discussion of learners with exceptionalities in Chapter 5.

Should students be taught to code?—A move to teach middle and high school students to *code*—learn to use the language programmers employ to design apps, websites, and software—is now sweeping through our nation's schools. The goal is to, in the language of Timothy Cook, CEO of Apple, help solve a "huge deficit in the skills that we need today." This initiative is controversial. We examine the initiative, its implications for learning and teaching, and the controversies involved in Chapter 8.

Grit: Sustained commitment to achieving long-term goals—Grit is an essential motivation concept associated with growth mindsets, mastery goals, high levels of perseverance, delay of gratification, and an absence of pleasure seeking. It has come into widespread prominence as the result of work by psychologist Angela Duckworth. We significantly expand our discussion of this important concept in our study of motivation, and we offer suggestions for developing "grit" in students.

Social-Emotional Learning and Development

Social-emotional development—Social-emotional development is receiving a great deal of research attention, and some experts believe it's even more important than cognitive development. We devote a major section to this topic in our discussion of personal, social, and moral development in Chapter 3, and we refer to the topic at various locations throughout the chapters.

LGBTQ students—Research consistently indicates that LGBTQ students have a myriad of problems in both school and life outside of school. And their issues have been exacerbated by the political controversies surrounding transgender youth. We examine the issues involved and what teachers can do to promote the social-emotional development of these young people and help them overcome the many challenges they now face.

School shootings—In the wake of an increase in school shootings and particularly the massacre at Marjory Stoneman Douglas high school in Parkland, Florida, teachers and students across our country have been traumatized, and the trauma is impacting teaching, learning, and students' social-emotional development. We examine the issue, its implications for learning and teaching, and the political controversies surrounding the idea that teachers be armed.

Sexual assault and sexual harassment in schools—Sexual harassment has a long history, but the "Me Too" movement, which gained prominence in late 2017, gave it widespread publicity. Sexual harassment and sexual assault are more common than would be expected in schools. We discuss this issue and what can be done to prevent both in our discussion of gender and gender issues in Chapter 4.

The opioid crisis—The opioid crisis is ravaging our country, it's impacting our schools, and it has important implications for teachers and schools. We examine this topic in detail together with the implications it has for learning, teaching, and social-emotional development.

Instruction and Assessment

Backward design—Backward design is a prominent approach to planning for instruction. We use this conceptual framework in our discussion of instructional planning in Chapter 13 and classroom assessment in Chapter 14, and we offer specific suggestions for ways teachers can capitalize on this planning approach to increase learning in their students.

Case studies linked to standards—Learning standards are now a part of teachers' lives, and many new teachers are uncertain about how to plan and implement instruction designed to help students meet the standards. In a further commitment to our emphasis on application, we link many of our case studies throughout the text to standards, and we provide a detailed discussion of instruction grounded in standards.

Data-driven instruction—Data-driven instruction is a teaching approach that relies on information about student performance to inform teaching and learning. It emphasizes clear objectives, baseline data, frequent assessment, and instruction grounded in assessment data. We examine data-driven instruction in our discussion of assessment in Chapter 14.

Personalized learning—Personalized learning refers to instruction in which the pace of learning and the instructional approach are optimized for the needs of each learner. Commonly linked to technology, this approach to learning has both strong proponents and equally strong critics. The approach has important implications for teaching, and we examine both the implications and the controversies in our discussion of instruction in Chapter 13.

Formative assessment—Formative assessment is the process of gathering information about student learning with the goal of informing next steps in teaching. It is one of the most powerful learning tools we have. We significantly expand the discussion of this process and its counterpart, summative assessment, in our discussion of classroom assessment in Chapter 14.

ESSA—The Every Student Succeeds Act (ESSA) is the most recent federal effort to improve education in our country. Accountability remains its central component, but the definition of achievement goes beyond standardized test results to include other measures of student learning, such as motivation and self-regulation. We describe the act in our discussion of standardized testing in Chapter 15, together with its implications for teaching and learning in our nation's schools.

The backlash against high-stakes testing—High-stakes testing and particularly value-added modeling are highly controversial. We discuss these controversies, and the implications they have for teaching and learning, in detail in our examination of standardized testing in Chapter 15.

edTPa—edTPa (Educational Teacher Performance Assessment) is a high-stakes pre-service assessment process designed to answer the question, "Is a new teacher ready for the job?" As its use becomes more widespread, it will have increasingly important implications for teacher preparation. We examine this assessment process in our discussion of accountability in Chapter 15.

This new content adds to our detailed descriptions of traditional theories combined with the latest research. Our goal is to make the content in this text as comprehensive and up-to-date as any in the field. Combined with our emphasis on application, we believe this is a text that can help prepare teachers who are truly professionals.

MyLab Education

One of the most visible changes in the eleventh edition, and also one of the most significant, is the expansion of the digital learning and assessment resources embedded in the eText and the inclusion of MyLab Education in the text. MyLab Education is an online homework, tutorial, and assessment program designed to work with the text to engage learners and to improve learning. Within its structured environment, learners see key concepts demonstrated through real classroom video footage, practice what they learn, test their understanding, and receive feedback to guide their learning and to ensure their mastery of key learning outcomes. Designed to bring learners more directly into the world of K–12 classrooms and to help them see the real and powerful impact of educational psychology concepts covered in this book, the online resources in MyLab Education with the Enhanced eText include:

- Video Examples. About 3 or 4 times per chapter, an embedded video provides an illustration of an educational psychology principle or concept in action. These video examples most often show students and teachers working in classrooms. Sometimes they show students or teachers describing their thinking or experiences.

- Self-Checks. In each chapter, self-check quizzes help assess how well learners have mastered the content. The self-checks are made up of self-grading, multiple-choice items that not only provide feedback on whether questions are answered correctly or incorrectly, but also provide rationales for both correct and incorrect answers.

- Application Exercises. These exercises give learners opportunities to practice applying the content and strategies from the chapters. The questions in these exercises are usually constructed-response. Once learners provide their own answers to the questions, they receive feedback in the form of model answers written by experts.

Supplementary Materials

This edition of *Using Educational Psychology in Teaching* provides a comprehensive and integrated collection of supplements to assist students and professors in maximizing learning and instruction. The following resources are available for instructors to download from www.pearsonhighered.com/educator. Enter the author, title of the text, or the ISBN number, then select this text, and click on the "Resources" tab. Download the supplement you need. If you require assistance in downloading any resources, contact your Pearson representative.

Instructor's Resource Manual

The Instructor's Resource Manual includes chapter overviews and outcomes, lists of available PowerPoint® slides, presentation outlines, teaching suggestions for each chapter, and questions for discussion and analysis along with feedback.

PowerPoint® Slides

The PowerPoint® slides highlight key concepts and summarize text content. The slides also include questions and problems designed to stimulate discussion, encourage students to elaborate and deepen their understanding of the topics in each chapter, and apply the content of the chapter to both the real world of teaching and their daily lives. The slides are further designed to help instructors structure the content of each chapter to make it as meaningful as possible for students.

Test Bank

The Test Bank provides a comprehensive and flexible assessment package. The Test Bank for this edition has been revised and expanded to make it more applicable to students. To provide complete coverage of the content in each chapter, all multiple-choice and essay items are grouped under the chapters' main headings and are balanced between knowledge/recall items and those that require analysis and application.

TestGen®

TestGen is a powerful test generator available exclusively from Pearson Education publishers. You install TestGen on your personal computer (Windows or Macintosh) and create your own tests for classroom testing and for other specialized delivery options, such as over a local area network or on the web. A test bank, which is also called a Test Item File (TIF), typically contains a large set of test items, organized by chapter and ready for your use in creating a test, based on the associated textbook material. Assessments may be created for both print and testing online.

The tests can be downloaded in the following formats:

TestGen Testbank file—PC

TestGen Testbank file—MAC

TestGen Testbank—Blackboard 9 TIF

TestGen Testbank—Blackboard CE/Vista (WebCT) TIF

Angel Test Bank (zip)

D2L Test Bank (zip)

Moodle Test Bank

Sakai Test Bank (zip)

Acknowledgments

Every book reflects the work of a team that includes the authors, the staff of editors, and the reviewers. We appreciate the input we've received from professors and students who have used previous editions of the book, and we gratefully acknowledge the contributions of the reviewers who offered us constructive feedback to guide us in this new edition:

Amy Sedivy-Benton, University of Arkansas at Little Rock; Kym Buchanan, University of Wisconsin–Stevens Point; Rory B. Dippold, George Mason University; Natasha Araos, Florida Atlantic University; and E. Michael Nussbaum, University of Nevada, Las Vegas.

In addition, we acknowledge, with our thanks, the reviewers of our previous editions:

Patricia Barbetta, Florida International University; David Bergin, University of Toledo; Elizabeth Levine Brown, George Mason University; Scott W. Brown, University of Connecticut; Kay S. Bull, Oklahoma State University; Barbara Collamer, Western Washington University; Jerome D'Agostino, University of Arizona; Betty M. Davenport, Campbell University; Brenda M. Davis, Randolph-Macon College; Ronna F. Dillon, Southern Illinois University; Oliver W. Edwards, University of Central Florida; Thomas G. Fetsco, Northern Arizona University; Leena Furtado, California State University, Dominguez Hills; Newell T. Gill, Florida Atlantic University; Claire Gonzalez, University of North Florida; Charles W. Good, West Chester University; Amy Hogan, Ottawa University; Robert L. Hohn, University of Kansas; Joel B. Judd, Adams State College; Pamela K. Kidder, Fort Valley State University; Dov Liberman, University of Houston; Jeffrey Liew, Texas A&M University; Hermine H. Marshall, San Francisco State University; Tes Mehring, Emporia State University; Luanna H. Meyer, Massey University–New Zealand; Michelle Morris, Northwestern State University; Nancy Perry, University of British Columbia; Evan Powell, University of Georgia; Anne N. Rinn, Western Kentucky University; Jay Samuels, University of Minnesota; Gregory Schraw, University of Nebraska, Lincoln; Dale H. Schunk, Purdue University; Serena Shim, Ball State University; James A. Shuff, Henderson State University; Douglas W. Smith, Coastal Carolina University; Rozanne Sparks, Pittsburgh State University; Rayne A. Sperling, Pennsylvania State University; Robert

J. Stevens, Pennsylvania State University; Julianne C. Turner, Notre Dame University; Nancy Vye, University of Washington; Steven Whitney, University of Missouri; Glenda Wilkes, University of Arizona; Dylinda Wilson-Younger, Alcorn State University; and Karen M. Zabrucky, Georgia State University.

In addition to the reviewers who guided our revisions, our team of editors gave us support in many ways. Kevin Davis, our publisher, guided us with his intelligence, insight, and understanding of the field. Jeffrey Johnston, our development editor, was available whenever we had questions or needed help and provided us with invaluable support. Angela Urquhart and Andrea Archer, our project managers, have been thoroughly professional in their efforts to make the content of the book clear and understandable.

Our appreciation goes to all of these fine people who have taken our words and given them shape. We hope that all of our efforts will result in increased learning for students and more rewarding teaching for instructors.

Finally, we would sincerely appreciate any comments or questions about anything that appears in the book or any of its supplements. Please feel free to contact either of us at any time. Our e-mail addresses are: peggen@unf.edu and don.kauchak@gmail.com.

Good luck and best wishes.

Paul Eggen

Don Kauchak

Using Educational Psychology in Teaching

Chapter 1
Educational Psychology: Understanding Learning and Teaching

Learning Outcomes

After you've completed your study of this chapter you should be able to:

1.1 Describe expert teaching and explain how expert teaching influences student learning.

1.2 Describe the types of professional knowledge that expert teachers possess.

1.3 Describe different types of research and explain how research contributes to teachers' professional knowledge.

1.4 Identify factors that influence teaching in today's classrooms.

You've just opened your book, and you're probably wondering what this class will be like and how it will make you a better teacher. To introduce you to the content of this text, we begin by looking at three brief classroom lessons—one from elementary, another from middle school, and a third from high school—taken from the real world of teaching.

Sophia Perez, a first-grade teacher, is working with her 18 students to help meet the following standard:

> Use singular and plural nouns with matching verbs in basic sentences (e.g., He hops; We hop). (Common Core State Standards Initiative, 2018a).

She has the children sitting on a carpet at the front of the room as she displays the following on her document camera:

> <u>Owen runs</u> around the corner to find his ball. <u>Olivia and Emma run</u> after him. After getting his ball, <u>he walks</u> back to where they are playing. <u>They walk</u> back right behind him.

She has the students read the short paragraph aloud in unison and then points to the underlined portions. "What is the difference between these two?" she asks, pointing at *Owen runs* and then *Olivia and Emma run.*

With guidance from Sophia, the students conclude that *Owen* refers to one person, and *Olivia and Emma* refer to two people, and *runs* is used with one person, and *run* is used with two people. She does the same with *he walks* and *they walk.*

She then displays the following sentence:

> **Kelly skips rope, and sometimes we skip together.**

She continues by asking, "Now, why did we use 'skips' here, but 'skip' here?" She points to the sentence in each case, and she guides the students to conclude that "skips" was used because Kelly was one person, whereas "skip" was used because "we" represents more than one person.

For practice, she then gives the students three additional sentences and has them determine if the sentences are written correctly.

Now, let's look at Keith Jackson, a middle school math teacher.

Keith is working with his 26 students on decimals and percents, to help meet the following standard.

> **Find a percent of a quantity as a rate per 100 (e.g., 30% of a quantity means 30/100 times the quantity); solve problems involving finding the whole, given a part and the percent (Common Core State Standards Initiative, 2018b).**

He begins the lesson by showing his class a 12-ounce soft drink can from a machine, a 20-ounce bottle, and a six-pack with price tags on them.

To help his students meet the standard, he organizes them in pairs and assigns the task of using their understanding of decimals and percents to determine which is the best buy.

As the students work, Keith moves around the room, asking questions and guiding their efforts, and when the groups conclude that the six-pack is the best buy, he asks, "So, how do you know?"

"The cost per ounce is the lowest for them," Savannah responds, pointing to the six-pack.

Now, let's turn to Kelsey Walsh, a high school social studies teacher with 32 students in her class.

Kelsey is beginning a unit on assessing conclusions with evidence as she focuses on the following standard:

> **Assess the extent to which the reasoning and evidence in a text support the author's claims (Common Core State Standards Initiative, 2018c).**

"Our goal," Kelsey begins, pointing to the standard, "is to be able to determine how well writers and speakers support the claims they make with evidence. This will help us learn to think critically about what we hear and read, and ultimately, it will make us more informed citizens and will help us avoid problems on the Internet, such as fake news or getting scammed."

She then displays the following for the students:

> **Because our broadcasting companies are for-profit organizations dependent on advertisers, their news broadcasts are superficial and meaningless. For instance, the NBC nightly news, scheduled for a half hour, only has, on average, about 20 minutes of actual news, with the rest advertising. The total broadcast is only 28 minutes long. A recent newscast covered four major topics, the last three of which took a total of about 7 minutes.**

"Now," Kelsey continues after giving the students time to read the display, "what's the author's claim here?"

With her guidance, they decide that the author is claiming that news broadcasts are shallow and superficial and perhaps even meaningless.

Kelsey then asks them what the author provides as evidence supporting the claim, and the students note that the author provides the number of minutes of actual news and the number of topics in a typical half-hour newscast.

After additional discussion, the class agrees that newscasts are at least somewhat superficial.

"But, I don't think the author supported his assertion that the telecasts are meaning-less . . . superficial maybe, but not meaningless," Olivia asserts toward the end of the discussion.

"Why do you say that?" Kelsey probes.

The class continues the discussion, debating whether newscasts are actually meaningless.

Helping students learn and develop is the goal of all teaching, so consider the following question. In each of the examples above, which of the following factors had the most impact on students' learning?

- *Curriculum and the available materials*—the content students study, such as subject–verb agreement in Sophia's case, decimals and percents in Keith's, and claims and evidence in Kelsey's, together with the examples that each teacher used.
- *Standards*—statements describing what students should know or be able to do at the end of a period of study. Each teacher's lesson focused directly on a standard.
- *Class size*—Sophia has 18 students in her class, Keith has 26, and Kelsey has 32.
- *The teacher*—Sophia, Keith, and Kelsey.

While each of the factors, as well as others, such as adequate facilities and leader-ship—the principal and other school leaders—will influence students' learning, the unequivocal answer to our question is: the TEACHER! The quality of teachers is, with-out question, the most important factor influencing our students' learning (Araujo, Carneiro, Cruz-Aguayo, & Shady, 2016; Chetty, Friedman, & Rockoff, 2014; Houkes-Hommes, ter Weel, & van der Wiel, 2016).

Expert Teaching and Student Learning

1.1   Describe expert teaching and explain how expert teaching influences student learning.

Interestingly, the importance of teachers hasn't always been obvious to educational leaders and policy makers. In efforts to improve schooling, reformers have tried a num-ber of strategies, including different organizational structures, such as open classrooms, a variety of curricular and instructional approaches, such as Whole Language and what was commonly called "New Math," and more recently, the infusion of support systems, such as technology. However, none of them proved to be the hoped-for panacea (Kunter et al., 2013).

The key to increasing student learning is simple, but admittedly not easy. Find and prepare the highest quality teachers possible. No organization, system, or enterprise is any better than the people in it, and the same applies to schools. Research consistently confirms that expert teaching is the primary factor influencing student achievement (Araujo et al., 2016; Kunter et al., 2013). Additional research suggests that the quality of a school is determined by the quality of its teachers (Goldhaber, 2016), and a compel-ling review of research found that students taught by expert teachers are more likely to attend college and earn higher salaries, and are less likely to have children as teenagers (Chetty et al., 2014).

Similar results have been found in educational systems around the world, sug-gesting that the success of a nation depends on the development of its **human capital**, people's professional knowledge and skills, social abilities, and personality attributes that contribute to a nation's cultural and economic advancement. "Advances in dis-covering the most important inputs of the human-capital production function have led to the conclusion that teacher quality is crucial for building a country's human-capital stock" (Houkes-Hommes et al., 2016, p. 358).

Some people, including many educational leaders, once believed that expert teaching is essentially instinctive, a kind of magic performed by born superstars. And, as is the case with other domains, such as athletics, music, or art, some teachers do indeed have more natural ability than others. However, research dating back to the 1960s and 1970s indicates that expert teachers possess knowledge and skills that are not purely instinctive. Rather, they are acquired through study and practice (Fisher et al., 1980), and more recent work corroborates these earlier findings (Kunter et al., 2013; Lemov, 2015). This is true in all domains. For example, many athletes, through hard work and training, perform better than their counterparts with more natural ability.

Experts—we've referred to "expert" teachers throughout this discussion—are people who are highly knowledgeable and skilled in a particular domain, such as music, architecture, medicine, or teaching. Expert teachers' professional knowledge and skills are what set them apart from their less effective colleagues. This knowledge and these skills help them promote more learning in students than is possible by less capable teachers. This is why you're taking this course and studying this book. Your goal is to begin acquiring the knowledge and skills that will lead to expertise, and our goal is to help you in this process.

MyLab Education Self-Check 1.1

Educational Psychology, Professional Knowledge, and Expert Teaching

1.2:   Describe the types of professional knowledge that expert teachers possess.

Educational psychology is the academic discipline that focuses on the scientific study of human learning and teaching (Berliner, 2006). The content of educational psychology focuses on the professional knowledge you will acquire as your teaching expertise develops. We discuss this professional knowledge in the following sections.

Professional Knowledge

Professional knowledge refers to the knowledge and skills unique to an area of study, such as law, medicine, architecture, or engineering. The same applies to teaching. In this section we focus on how educational psychology can increase your professional knowledge, and with it, your expertise.

Ed Psych and You

How much do you know about teaching and learning? To test your knowledge, complete the following *Learning and Teaching Inventory*. It will introduce you to the kinds of knowledge you'll need to become an expert teacher.

Learning and Teaching Inventory

Look at each of the 12 items below and decide if the statement is true or false.

1. The thinking of children in elementary schools tends to be limited to the concrete and tangible, whereas the thinking of middle and high school students tends to be abstract.
2. Students generally understand how much they know about a topic.
3. Experts in the area of intelligence view knowledge of facts, such as "On what continent is Brazil?" as one indicator of intelligence.

4. Expert teaching is essentially a process of presenting information to students in succinct and organized ways.

5. Preservice teachers who major in a content area, such as math, are much more successful than nonmajors in providing clear examples of the ideas they teach.

6. To increase students' motivation to learn, teachers should praise them liberally and as much as possible.

7. The key to successful classroom management is to stop classroom disruptions quickly.

8. Preservice teachers generally believe they will be more effective than teachers who are already in the field.

9. Teachers learn by teaching; in general, experience is the primary factor involved in learning to teach.

10. Students learn most effectively when they receive information consistent with their **learning styles**, their preferred approaches to thinking and problem solving.

11. Criticizing students damages their self-esteem and should be avoided.

12. Because some students are left-brained thinkers and others are right-brained thinkers, teachers should make an effort to accommodate these differences in their students.

Let's see how you did. The correct answers for each item are outlined in the following paragraphs. As you read the answers, remember that they describe students or people in general, and exceptions will exist.

1. *The thinking of children in elementary schools tends to be limited to the concrete and tangible, whereas the thinking of middle and high school students tends to be abstract.*
   False: Research indicates that middle school, high school, and even university students effectively think in the abstract only when they have considerable prior knowledge and experience related to the topic they're studying (Berk, 2019a). When you study the development of students' thinking in Chapter 2, you'll see how understanding this research can improve your teaching.

2. *Students generally understand how much they know about a topic.*
   False: Learners, in general, and young children in particular, often cannot accurately assess their own understanding (Hacker, Bol, Horgan, & Rakow, 2000). Students' awareness of what they know and how they learn strongly influences understanding, and cognitive learning theory helps us understand why. (You will study cognitive learning theory in Chapters 7, 8, and 9.)

3. *Experts in the area of intelligence view knowledge of facts, such as "On what continent is Brazil?" as one indicator of intelligence.*
   True: The Wechsler Intelligence Scale for Children—Fourth Edition (Wechsler, 2014), the most popular intelligence test in use today, includes several items similar to this example. We examine theories of intelligence, including controversies involved in these theories, in Chapter 5.

4. *Expert teaching is essentially a process of presenting information to students in succinct and organized ways.*
   False: The better we understand learning, the more we realize that simply explaining information to students is often ineffective (Kunter et al., 2013; Pomerance, Greenberg, & Walsh, 2016). Learners construct their own knowledge based on what they already know, and their emotions, beliefs, and expectations all influence the process (Bruning, Schraw, & Norby, 2011; Schunk, Meece, & Pintrich, 2014). You will study knowledge construction in Chapter 9.

5. *Preservice teachers who major in a content area, such as math, are much more successful than nonmajors in providing clear examples of the ideas they teach.*

False: One of the most pervasive misconceptions about teaching is the idea that knowledge of subject matter is all that's necessary to teach effectively. In a study of teacher candidates, researchers found that math majors were no more capable than nonmajors of effectively illustrating math concepts in ways that learners could understand (U.S. Department of Education, 2008). Knowledge of content is obviously important, but teaching expertise requires additional understanding, understanding how to make that content meaningful to students (Ayers, 2018; Buchholtz, 2017). (You will study ways of making knowledge accessible to learners in Chapters 2, 6–9, and 13.)

6. *To increase students' motivation to learn, teachers should praise them liberally and as much as possible.*

   False: Although appropriate use of praise is effective, overuse detracts from its credibility. This is particularly true for older students, who discount praise if they believe it is invalid or insincere. Older students may also interpret praise given for easy tasks as indicating that the teacher thinks they have low ability (Schunk et al., 2014). Your study of motivation in Chapters 10 and 11 will help you understand how teachers can increase students' motivation to learn.

7. *The key to successful classroom management is to stop disruptions quickly.*

   False: Research indicates that classroom management, a primary concern of beginning teachers, is most effective when, instead of responding to problems after they occur, teachers prevent management problems from occurring in the first place (Emmer & Evertson, 2017; Evertson & Emmer, 2017). (You will study classroom management in Chapter 12.)

8. *Preservice teachers generally believe they will be more effective than teachers who are already in the field.*

   True: Preservice teachers (like you) are often optimistic and idealistic. They believe they'll be effective with young people, and they generally believe they'll be better than teachers now in the field (Ingersoll & Smith, 2004). They are also sometimes "shocked" when they begin work and face the challenge of teaching on their own for the first time (Grant, 2006; Johnson & Birkeland, 2003). Teaching is complex and challenging, and the more knowledge you have about learners, learning, and the teaching process, the better prepared you'll be to cope with the realities of your first job.

9. *Teachers learn by teaching; in general, experience is the primary factor involved in learning to teach.*

   False: Experience is essential in learning to teach, but it isn't sufficient by itself (Depaepe & König, 2018; König & Pflanzl, 2016). In many cases, experience results in repeating the same actions year after year, regardless of their effectiveness (Staub, 2016). Knowledge of learners and learning, combined with experience, however, can lead to high levels of teaching expertise.

10. *Students learn most effectively when they receive information consistent with their learning styles, their preferred approaches to thinking and problem solving.*

    False: Research consistently indicates that attempts to accommodate students' different learning styles fail to increase achievement, and in some cases even detract from learning (Howard-Jones, 2014; Masson & Sarrasin, 2015; Pashler, McDaniel, Rohrer, & Bjork, 2008). Further, "There is no credible evidence that learning styles exist" (Riener & Willingham, 2010, p. 22). We examine the concept of learning styles in Chapters 2 and 5.

11. *Criticizing students damages their self-esteem and should be avoided.*

    False. Under certain circumstances, criticism can increase motivation and learning. For instance, criticism, such as a teacher saying, "Come on, you can do better work than this," communicates high expectations to students and the belief that they are capable learners. We're not suggesting that you make criticizing students a habit, but periodic and well-timed criticism can enhance motivation (Deci & Ryan, 2008).

12. *Because some students are left-brained thinkers and others are right-brained thinkers, teachers should make an effort to accommodate these differences in their students.*
    False. The idea that we tend to be right-brained or left-brained is a myth (Im, Cho, Dubinsky, & Varma, 2018; Staub, 2016). "This popular myth, which conjures up an image of one side of our brains crackling with activity while the other lies dormant, has its roots in outdated findings from the 1970s . . . " (Boehm, 2012, para. 1).

These items introduce you to the professional knowledge base of teaching, and we now examine this knowledge in more detail. Research indicates that four related types of knowledge are essential for expert teaching (Darling-Hammond & Baratz-Snowdon, 2005; Kunter et al., 2013; Shulman, 1987). They're outlined in Figure 1.1 and discussed in the sections that follow.

Knowledge of Content

We obviously can't teach what we don't understand. To effectively teach about the American Revolutionary War, for instance, a social studies teacher needs to know basic facts about the war and also how the war relates to other historical events and factors, such as the French and Indian War, the colonies' relationship with England before the Revolution, and the unique characteristics of the colonies. The same is true for any topic in any other content area, and research confirms the relationship between what teachers know and how they teach (Bransford, Brown, & Cocking, 2000).

Pedagogical Content Knowledge

Knowledge of content is necessary but not sufficient for expert teaching. We must also possess **pedagogical content knowledge (PCK)**, an understanding of how to represent topics in ways that make them understandable to learners, as well as an understanding of what makes specific topics easy or difficult to learn (Ayers, 2018; Buchholz, 2017).

This dimension of teacher knowledge increases both achievement and learner motivation. "Teachers' PCK affects not only students' achievement but also their motivation, specifically their enjoyment of the subject. . . " (Kunter et al., 2013, p. 815). Expert teachers understand the content they teach, and they also know how to make it understandable and interesting to students.

So, as you study specific topics in your content area, such as math, social studies, science, or any other, ask yourself, "How can I illustrate this topic so students can understand it?" The ability to do so will reflect your pedagogical content knowledge, and it is one of the most important aspects of teaching expertise.

Developing Pedagogical Content Knowledge.   Developing our ability to illustrate topics—our PCK—need not be extremely difficult. With practice, experience, and a mindset where we commit ourselves to providing our students with examples and other representations that are understandable to them, ideas will come to mind.

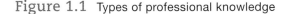

Figure 1.1   Types of professional knowledge

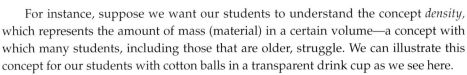

For instance, suppose we want our students to understand the concept *density*, which represents the amount of mass (material) in a certain volume—a concept with which many students, including those that are older, struggle. We can illustrate this concept for our students with cotton balls in a transparent drink cup as we see here.

Then, when we compress the cotton in the cup, students can see that the same amount of cotton (mass) takes up less space (occupies less volume), so the cotton is more dense.

Illustrating the concept this way is much more meaningful for students than using the formula $D = m/v$, which is the way *density* is usually represented, and which many students memorize with little understanding.

As a second example, suppose you're a language arts teacher and you want your students to understand the concept *gerund*, a verb form that behaves as a noun, and *participle*, a verb form that behaves as an adjective. To illustrate these concepts you might display the following short paragraph for your students.

Running is a very good form of exercise, and athletes, such as running backs in football, have to be in very good physical shape. I'm running a three miler this afternoon.

Here students can see that "running" is first used as a noun: (*Running* is a very good form of exercise); then as an adjective: (. . . such as *running* backs in football); and finally as a verb: (I'm *running* a three-miler this afternoon). Represented this way, students can see how the verb forms are used. They don't have to try and understand the concepts based on abstract and often confusing definitions. The ability to represent topics in this way again illustrates pedagogical content knowledge.

Finally, suppose you're a geography teacher and you want to illustrate the concepts *longitude* and *latitude* for your students. You might draw lines on a beach ball as you see here.

As with the language arts example, students can see that the latitude lines are parallel to each other, and the longitude lines meet at the poles. Then, during discussion, we can guide our students to recognize that lines of longitude are farthest apart at the equator, but lines of latitude are the same distance apart everywhere, and that longitude measures distance east and west, whereas latitude measures distance north and south.

Sophia, Keith, and Kelsey, the teachers in the case studies at the beginning of the chapter, each demonstrated pedagogical content knowledge in their instruction—Sophia wrote a short paragraph illustrating subject–verb agreement for her 1st-graders, Keith brought real-world examples of using decimals and percents with his middle schoolers, and Kelsey used a written clip as an example of an author who did and did not provide evidence for a claim. Their ability to represent their topics in these ways is part of the professional knowledge that contributes to teaching expertise.

These are merely examples, and you will find and develop many others when you teach. Depending on the content area, you can represent the topics you teach in several ways:

- *Examples.* Examples, such as the illustrations of *equivalent fractions, density, gerund, participle,* and *longitude* and *latitude,* are useful when we're teaching well-defined topics (Pomerance et al., 2016).

- *Case studies and vignettes.* We use case studies, lessons, and other classroom events taken from the real world of teaching to illustrate the topics we discuss. Sophia's, Keith's, and Kelsey's lessons at the beginning of the chapter are examples of these case studies. They're designed to provide you with concrete instances of teachers in actual classrooms working with real students. Together with vignettes—shorter case studies—they're intended to make the complex topics you'll study understandable and meaningful. For instance, an English teacher might illustrate the concept *internal conflict* with this brief vignette:

Andrea didn't know what to do. She was looking forward to the class trip, but if she went, she wouldn't be able to take the scholarship-qualifying test.

- *Simulations.* **Simulations**, imitations of real-world processes or systems, can be effective for representing topics difficult to illustrate directly (Li, Dai, Zheng, Tian, & Yan, 2018). For instance, an American government teacher creates a mock trial to simulate the workings of our country's judicial system, and a world history teacher uses her students' loyalty to their school, their ways of talking, and their weekend activities to simulate the concept *nationalism.* Another history teacher uses her class's "crusade" for extracurricular activities as a simulation for the actual Crusades.

- *Models.* Models allow students to visualize what they can't observe directly. For instance, a science teacher uses a model of an atom to help students visualize the organization of the nucleus and electrons, as you see here.

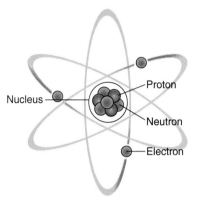

This list helps us understand why knowledge of content and pedagogical content knowledge are related but not identical, and it also helps explain why item 5 in our Learning and Teaching Inventory ("Preservice teachers who major in a content area, such as math, are much more successful than nonmajors in providing clear examples of the ideas they teach") is false. Earning a degree in a content area, such as math, doesn't ensure that someone will be able to create examples—a form of PCK—like the one involving equivalent fractions, nor does majoring in history ensure that a person would be able to think of using a campaign to save a school's extracurricular activities—another instance of PCK—to simulate the Crusades. If we lack either knowledge of content or PCK, we commonly paraphrase information in learners' textbooks or provide abstract explanations that aren't meaningful to our students. We need both kinds of professional knowledge to become expert teachers.

General Pedagogical Knowledge

Knowledge of content and PCK are domain specific, that is, they're related to knowledge of a particular content area, such as the Crusades, multiplying fractions, or the concepts *density, gerund, participle,* or *internal conflict.* In comparison, **general pedagogical knowledge (GPK)** involves an understanding of instructional strategies and classroom management that apply to all subject matter areas and topics (Depaepe & König, 2018). Preservice teachers, such as yourselves, tend to downplay the importance of GPK, and, as a result, reduce their efforts to acquire the skills associated with it (Merk, Rosman, Rueß, Syring, & Schneider, 2017). We urge you to avoid falling into this trap, because research confirms the importance of GPK as a prerequisite for teaching expertise (König, & Pflanzl, 2016). Further, teachers high in GPK are less likely to burn out and more likely to believe that they're capable of promoting learning in their students, regardless of conditions (Lauermann & König, 2016).

Instructional Strategies.   Instructional strategies, one form of GPK, involve abilities such as knowing how to organize lessons, engaging students in learning activities, and checking for understanding. Instructional strategies are important regardless of the grade level, content area, or topic. For instance, careful planning, organizing instruction, and questioning skills are as important if you're teaching 1st-graders, middle school learners, or advanced high school students (Good & Lavigne, 2018; Lemov, 2015). These strategies are essential aspects of general pedagogical knowledge, and you will study them in detail in Chapter 13.

Classroom Management.   Classroom management is a second essential component of GPK. To be effective, we need to create classroom environments that are safe, orderly, and focused on learning (Emmer & Evertson, 2017; Evertson & Emmer, 2017). To meet this goal, we must know how to plan, implement, and monitor rules and procedures, organize groups, and intervene when misbehavior occurs. The complexities of these processes help us see why item 7 in the Learning and Teaching Inventory ("The key to successful classroom management is to stop disruptions quickly") is false. It's impossible to maintain an orderly classroom if we wait for misbehavior to occur. We discuss ways of creating orderly environments to prevent management problems in Chapter 12.

Knowledge of Learners and Learning

Knowledge of learners and learning, an understanding of the learning process and how students learn and develop, is the fourth type of professional knowledge. It is also essential, "arguably the most important knowledge a teacher can have" (Borko & Putnam, 1996, p. 675). Let's see how this knowledge can influence the way we teach.

The following items from the Learning and Teaching Inventory all involve knowledge of learners and learning.

MyLab Education
Video Example 1.1

Professional knowledge is essential for expert teaching. Notice how sixth-grade teacher, Dani Ramsay, demonstrates pedagogical content knowledge in the way she illustrates the concept of *personification*, general pedagogical knowledge in the way she interacts with her students, and knowledge of learners and learning in realizing that students learn more when they're involved in learning activities.

> *Item 1: The thinking of children in elementary schools tends to be limited to the concrete and tangible, whereas the thinking of middle and high school students tends to be abstract.* We know that students need to have abstract ideas illustrated with concrete examples, and this is true for older as well as younger students. Chapter 2 helps us understand how students' thinking develops, and helps us understand how to represent topics in developmentally appropriate ways.

> *Item 2: Students generally understand how much they know about a topic.* Learners often aren't good judges of either how much they know or the way they learn. Chapters 7 and 8 help us understand how to make our students more aware of the way they think and how to become more strategic in their approaches to learning.

> *Item 4: Effective teaching is essentially a process of presenting information to students in succinct and organized ways.* Our increasing understanding of the way people learn helps explain why this item is false. We now realize that learners don't behave like video recorders; we don't simply remember what we hear or read. Rather, in our attempts to make sense of the information, we interpret it in personal and sometimes idiosyncratic ways (Chatera & Loewenstein, 2016; Dubinsky, Roehrig, & Varma, 2013). In the process, meaning can be distorted, sometimes profoundly. For instance, the following statements were actually made by students:

"The phases of the moon are caused by clouds blocking out the unseen parts."
"Coats keep us warm by generating heat, like a stove or radiator."
"A triangle which has an angle of 135 degrees is called an obscene triangle."

Obviously, students didn't acquire these ideas from their teachers' explanations. Rather, they interpreted what they heard, experienced, or read, related it to what they already knew, and attempted to make sense of it.

> *Item 6: To increase students' motivation to learn, teachers should praise liberally and as much as possible.* Item 6 has implications for the ways we interact with our students. Intuitively, it seems that providing as much praise as possible is desirable and effective. However, motivation research, which we examine in Chapters 10 and 11, helps us understand why this isn't always the case.

> *Item 9: Teachers learn by teaching; in general, experience is the primary factor involved in learning to teach.* We now understand why this item is false. Experience is important, but we can't acquire all the knowledge we need to be effective from experience alone (Goldhaber, 2016). Acquiring this knowledge is the primary reason you're studying educational psychology.

MyLab Education Application Exercise 1.1: Demonstrating Professional Knowledge in Classrooms

In this exercise you will be asked to analyze how a teacher demonstrates different types of professional knowledge.

Professional Organizations' Contributions to Professional Knowledge

Professional organizations have also examined a wide range of research, which they have compiled and summarized in attempts to provide guidance for teachers as we work with our students.

Developmentally Appropriate Practice

Using Knowledge of Learners and Learning to Promote Achievement in Students at Different Ages

While much of what we know about learners and learning applies to students of all ages, **developmental differences**, age-related changes in students' thinking, personalities, and social skills, exist.

Because the developmental level of your students affects their learning and your teaching, a feature titled "Developmentally Appropriate Practice" appears in each chapter. **Developmentally appropriate practice** refers to instruction that matches teacher actions to the capabilities and needs of learners at different developmental levels. This feature describes ways to adapt each chapter's content to the different learning needs of early childhood and elementary, middle school, and high school students.

Here's how the feature will appear in subsequent chapters:

FAMILY CIRCUS

"How do they fit so much water in that little spigot?"

Working with Students in Early Childhood Programs and Elementary Schools

Young children's thinking differs from the thinking of older students. As an example, look at the accompanying cartoon. Wondering how all the water could fit in the spigot is characteristic of the thinking of young children. Older students would of course realize that a vast reservoir of water exists that we can't see. Young children's personal and social characteristics also differ from those of older students and influence how they interact and learn in classrooms.

We examine these differences in each of the chapters in the book.

Working with Students in Middle Schools

As a result of maturation and experience, the thinking and social skills of middle school students differ from those of young children. For example, older students are more likely to realize that they don't understand an idea being discussed in class and

raise their hands to ask for an explanation. In addition, middle schoolers are increasingly social and find the opposite sex more interesting. These developmental differences have important implications for how we teach and interact with these students.

Working with Students in High Schools

As with differences between elementary and middle school students, additional differences exist between high school learners and their younger counterparts. For example, many high school students are quite mature, and discussing personal and social issues with them on an adult-to-adult level can be effective. They are capable of more abstract thinking than their younger counterparts, although they still need concrete examples to understand new or difficult topics.

In this section we examine the work of two of these organizations:

- The American Psychological Association
- The National Council on Teacher Quality

The American Psychological Association: Top 20 Principles from Psychology for PreK–12 Teaching and Learning

The American Psychological Association (APA), founded in 1892, now has more than 100,000 members in 54 divisions, one of which is Educational Psychology. APA's stated mission is to advance, communicate, and apply psychological knowledge to benefit society and improve people's lives (American Psychological Association, 2018).

Consistent with this mission, the "Top 20 Principles from Psychology for PreK–12 Teaching and Learning" is APA's effort to help teachers and teacher educators apply psychological knowledge to the teaching–learning process. Researchers have identified a number of principles that provide guidance for us as teachers, and they've found 20 that they believe are particularly relevant for our work with students. These are the "Top 20" (American Psychological Association, Coalition for Psychology in Schools and Education, 2015).

They're grouped into five areas:

- Cognition and learning
- Motivation
- Social context, interpersonal relations, and emotional well-being
- Classroom management
- Assessment

Cognition and learning.   **Cognition** refers to thinking, so when we refer to "cognitive" tasks we're describing tasks that require thought—often careful and sustained thought. Cognition includes beliefs, perceptions, and expectations; it depends on experience and prior knowledge; and it's influenced by practice and feedback.

Cognition and learning are the focus of principles 1–8, and these principles answer the question: How do students think and learn?

- *Principle 1: Students' beliefs or perceptions about intelligence and ability affect their cognitive functioning and learning.* Students who believe that intelligence or ability can be improved with effort learn more and perform better on a variety of cognitive tasks (Aronson & Juarez, 2012; Dweck, 2016).

- *Principle 2: What students already know affects their learning.* Learners make sense of new knowledge and experiences based on their existing knowledge. If students lack prior knowledge, we, as teachers, must provide it (Holding, Denton, Kulesza, & Ridgway, 2014; Johnson & Sinatra, 2014).

- *Principle 3: Students' cognitive development and learning are not limited by general stages of development.* Student thinking and reasoning are more nearly influenced by prior knowledge than chronological age (Bjorklund & Causey, 2018; Rogoff, 2003).

- *Principle 4: Learning is based on context, so generalizing learning to new contexts is not spontaneous but instead needs to be facilitated.* Transfer of learning is very specific, so, for instance, students won't automatically transfer basic skills they've learned in math to word problems involving the same basic skills (Bransford, Brown, & Cocking, 2000; Mayer, 2008).

- *Principle 5: Acquiring long-term knowledge and skill is largely dependent on practice.* A magic solution to learning doesn't exist. As demonstrated by athletes, musicians, academicians, and others, practice with feedback is the primary route to advanced knowledge and skills (Eskreis-Winkler et al., 2016; Panero, 2016).

- *Principle 6: Clear, explanatory, and timely feedback to students is important for learning.* Student learning increases when they're provided with specific information about their current level of understanding (Hattie, 2012; Hattie & Timperley, 2007).

- *Principle 7: Students' self-regulation assists learning, and self-regulatory skills can be taught.* Abilities, such as organization, planning, maintaining attention, and exercising self-control, can increase learning, and these abilities can be increased with expert instruction (Butler, Schnellert, & Perry, 2017; Legault & Inzlicht, 2013).

- *Principle 8: Student creativity can be fostered.* The ability to produce original works and productive solutions to problems are important in today's world and, with teacher support, students can acquire this ability (Binyamin & Carmeli, 2017; Malycha & Maier, 2017).

Motivation. "**Motivation** is the process whereby goal-directed activity is instigated and sustained" (Schunk et al., 2014, p. 5). If we work hard to solve a puzzle or attempt to perfect a golf swing, for instance, we're motivated in each case. Solving the puzzle and perfecting the swing are the goals, and motivation helps us sustain our efforts to reach each one.

Principles 9–12 focus on motivation, and they answer the question: What motivates students?

- *Principle 9: Students tend to enjoy learning and to do better when they are more intrinsically rather than extrinsically motivated to achieve.* Students learn more and find learning more satisfying when they attempt to accomplish tasks for their own sake instead of attempts to receive some reward, such as praise or a high grade (Anderman & Anderman, 2014; Cleary & Kitsantas, 2017).

- *Principle 10: Students persist in the face of challenging tasks and process information more deeply when they adopt mastery goals rather than performance goals.* Learners achieve more when they focus on personal improvement rather than high grades or performing better than others (Chatzisarantis et al., 2016; Shin, Lee, & Seo, 2017).

- *Principle 11: Teachers' expectations about their students affect students' opportunities to learn, their motivation, and their learning outcomes.* Students tend to live "up" or "down" to teachers' expectations (Jussim, Robustelli, & Cain, 2009; Schunk et al., 2014).

- *Principle 12: Setting goals that are short term (proximal), specific, and moderately challenging enhances motivation more than establishing goals that are long term (distal), general, and overly challenging.* Being able to readily monitor progress toward moderately challenging goals increases motivation (Kanfer, Frese, & Johnson, 2017; Schunk et al, 2014).

Social Context, Interpersonal Relations, and Emotional Well-Being. A classroom in which students feel welcome, physically and emotionally safe, and supported by their teachers increases motivation to learn. Principles 13–15 focus on these factors and answer the question: How do social context, interpersonal relations, and emotions influence student learning?

- *Principle 13: Learning is situated within multiple social contexts.* Family, neighborhood, community, and the larger culture all impact motivation and learning (Lee & Stewart, 2013; National Association of School Psychologists, 2013).

- *Principle 14: Interpersonal relationships and communication are critical to both the teaching–learning process and the social-emotional development of students.* The teacher-student relationship provides an essential foundation for both motivation and learning (Archambault, Vandenbossche-Makombo, & Fraser, 2017; Kuhl, 2017).

- *Principle 15: Emotional well-being influences educational performance, learning, and development.* Positive emotions, such as enjoyment, hope, and pride, increase both motivation and achievement (Broekhuizen, Slot, van Aken, & Dubas, 2017; Graziano & Hart, 2016).

Classroom Management. **Classroom management** includes all the actions teachers take to establish an environment that supports academic learning, self-regulation, and social and emotional development. It's much more than maintaining an orderly classroom, and research suggests that students are more motivated to learn and learn more in orderly classrooms (Back, Polk, Keys, & McMahon, 2016).

Classroom management is the focus of principles 16 and 17, and they answer the question: How can classrooms best be managed?

- *Principle 16: Expectations for classroom conduct and social interaction are learned and can be taught using proven principles of behavior and effective classroom instruction.* Student behaviors that promote learning and positive social interactions are best taught at the beginning of the school year and reinforced throughout the year (Joe, Hiver, & Al-Hoorie, 2017; Rispoli et al., 2017).

- *Principle 17: Effective classroom management is based on (a) setting and communicating high expectations, (b) consistently nurturing positive relationships, and (c) providing a high level of student support.* A well-designed system of classroom procedures and rules, positive relationships between teachers and students, and academic support from teachers create a classroom environment that promotes motivation and learning (Emmer & Evertson, 2017; Evertson & Emmer, 2017).

Assessment.   **Classroom assessment** includes all the processes involved in making decisions about our students' learning progress. Using high-quality assessments is one of the most effective ways to increase both motivation and learning (Chappuis & Stiggens, 2017; Gonzalez & Eggen, 2017; Pennebaker, Gosling, & Ferrell, 2013; Schunk et al, 2014).

Principles 18–20 focus on assessment and they answer the question: How can teachers use assessment to promote student learning?

- *Principle 18: Formative and summative assessments are both important and useful but require different approaches and interpretations.* Formative assessments, assessments that provide information used to make instructional decisions, and summative assessment, the process of gathering information used to make conclusions about learner achievement, both increase motivation and achievement (Chappuis & Stiggins, 2017; Popham, 2017).

- *Principle 19: Students' skills, knowledge, and abilities are best measured with assessment processes grounded in psychological science with well-defined standards for quality and fairness.* Assessments must be both valid and reliable to maximize learning (American Educational Research Association, American Psychological Association, & National Council on Measurement in Education, 2014; Wiliam, 2014).

- *Principle 20: Making sense of assessment data depends on clear, appropriate, and fair interpretation.* Educators must be able to interpret assessment results and accurately communicate those results to students and caregivers (American Educational Research Association, American Psychological Association, & National Council on Measurement in Education, 2014; Chappuis & Stiggins, 2017).

These principles are presented and applied throughout this text. At the beginning of each chapter we identify the APA principles that are emphasized in that chapter, and we identify locations in the chapters where the principles are illustrated. For instance, if you look at the beginning of Chapter 2 you'll see the principles that are emphasized in that chapter, and the same is true for each of the chapters that follow.

The National Council on Teacher Quality: Six Strategies that Every New Teacher Needs to Know

The National Council on Teacher Quality (NCTQ) is a Washington, DC-based think tank, founded in 2002, that advocates for improved teacher preparation (Pomerance et al., 2016). A prominent research team commissioned by the NCTQ examined hundreds of research studies focusing on teaching strategies demonstrated to improve student learning, and they identified six that are particularly effective. They're grouped into three pairs:

- Helping students take in new information

- Ensuring that students connect information to deepen their understanding
- Helping students remember what they have learned

Helping Students Take in New Information.   We receive information primarily through two pathways: auditory for spoken words, and visual for written words and graphic or pictorial representations. The first two strategies help capitalize on these pathways.

- *Strategy 1: Pairing graphics with words.* Student learning increases when teachers present content both verbally and visually (Clark & Mayer, 2003).

- *Strategy 2: Linking abstract concepts to concrete representations.* "Teachers should present tangible examples that illuminate overarching ideas and also explain how the examples and big ideas connect" (Pomerance et al., 2016, p. vi). Each of the teachers in the lessons that introduced the chapter built their instruction around concrete examples—Sophia with her short paragraph illustrating subject–verb agreement, Keith with his different containers of soft drinks, and Kelsey with her clipping illustrating an author's claim and evidence.

Helping Students Connect Information to Deepen Their Understanding.   **Meaningfulness** describes the extent to which items of information are linked and related to each other. The more interconnected our information is in memory, the more places we have to connect new information, and the more efficient learning becomes (Radvansky & Ashcraft, 2014). The 3rd and 4th strategies are designed to help students make their understanding meaningful.

- *Strategy 3: Posing probing questions.* Asking students questions such as, "why," "how do you know," and "what if" encourages them to link ideas to each other, which makes the topics they study more meaningful (Pomerance et al., 2016). This strategy is readily applicable. For instance, Sophia displayed the sentence

  "Kelly skips rope, and sometimes we skip together"

  and then asked, "Now, why did we use 'skips' here, but 'skip' here?" Keith asked, "So, how do you know?" when the students concluded that the six-pack was the best buy, and Kelsey asked "Why do you say that?" when Olivia asserted that the author didn't support his claim that telecasts are meaningless.

- *Strategy 4: Alternating problems with solutions provided and problems students must solve.* Using **worked examples**, problems with completed solutions, is a proven strategy for improving problem solving and increasing meaningfulness (Lee & Chen, 2016; ter Vrugte et al., 2017). (We examine worked examples in detail in Chapter 8.)

Promoting Retention.   Efficiently storing information in memory so it can be retrieved when needed is an important goal of all learning. The 5th and 6th strategies help students retain information until it is again needed.

- *Strategy 5: Distributing practice.* Students need a great deal of practice to develop knowledge and skills, and distributing this practice over time makes storage in memory more efficient and boosts retention (McCrudden & McNamara, 2018).

- *Strategy 6: Assessing learning.* Assessment is a learning tool. Assessment and feedback help students effectively store and retain information (Chappuis & Stiggins, 2017; Hattie, 2012).

As with the principles from APA, the strategies that are emphasized in each chapter are outlined in the chapter's introduction, and we identify locations in the chapters where the strategies are illustrated. We hope that our efforts to make the strategies meaningful will help you incorporate them into your teaching skill set when you take your first job.

Professional Knowledge and Reflective Practice

We make a staggering number of decisions in our teaching; some historical research suggests as many as 800 per day (Jackson, 1968). For example, the following are some of the decisions the teachers in our case studies at the beginning of the chapter made. Each:

- Interpreted their standard and made a decision about their specific learning objectives
- Built their lessons around examples designed to help their students reach the objectives
- Decided what students they would call on and the order in which they would call on the students
- Decided on the specific questions they would ask and how they would respond to students if students answered incorrectly

No one is there to help us make these decisions; we're essentially on our own. This leads us to the idea of **reflective practice**, the process of conducting a critical self-examination of our teaching (Butani, Bannister, Rubin, & Forbes, 2017; Dees, Moore, & Hoggan, 2016). Reflection involves "deliberately contemplating one's own experiences and knowledge to regulate one's thinking" (Parsons et al., 2018, p. 229) Every professional decision we make is designed to promote student learning; reflective practice can help us become more sensitive to student differences, and it can make us more aware of the impact of our instruction on learning. "The capacity to reflect on one's work is widely seen as a fundamental component of effective professional practice" (Kovacs & Corrie, 2017, p. 4).

Reflection simply amounts to asking ourselves a series of questions, most effectively when they're specific and immediate, such as at the end of a lesson. For instance, the question: "Were my learning objectives clear?" is more effective than, "What went well, or poorly, in the lesson?"

Additional questions we might use to guide our reflection include the following. Each is grounded in research focusing on effective instruction (Good & Lavigne, 2018; Kunter et al., 2013).

- Was my lesson adequately linked to my preceding lesson? Did my students see the connection?
- Were my students well behaved and engaged? If not, what should I change to better manage my classroom?
- Was I well organized? Did I have my materials ready? Did I begin my instruction immediately and use classroom time efficiently?
- Did I represent my topic clearly? What examples could I have used that would have been more motivating and understandable?
- Did I adequately interact with my students, or did I spend too much time talking?
- Were my interactions with students positive and supportive? Do my students feel safe in my classroom?
- Did my homework assignment provide my students with adequate practice to reinforce their learning?

Many other questions exist, but this list gives us a starting point. As you acquire experience, you will identify questions most effective for your own thinking. Most important is the process. As we said above, the capacity to reflect on one's work is fundamental to effective professional practice.

The Role of Research in Acquiring Professional Knowledge

1.3 **Describe different types of research and explain how research contributes to teachers' professional knowledge.**

To begin this section, we join a conversation between two middle school teachers in the faculty lounge after school on a Thursday afternoon.

"Scoring another quiz, I see," Mike Clark comments to Leah Thompson, a friend and colleague.

"Yes," Leah smiles. "Quiz Thursday, hand it back Friday, and we go over it carefully, so they see what they've done wrong, and they fix it."

"I don't like giving tests. It takes time away from instruction, so they learn less," Mike retorts.

"I used to feel the same way, but I changed my mind. Let me tell you why. I'm working on my masters, I took a course last fall called, 'Research-Based Instruction,' and it changed my life. The instructor built the entire course around research, and assessment was one of the major topics. . . . She, the instructor, shared a bunch of research, indicating that quizzes, tests, and other assessments, if applied correctly, can dramatically increase learning. And, she practiced what she preached—the class met once a week, we had a quiz every class, and I learned more than I have in any class I've taken."

"What does 'applied correctly' mean?"

"Two things; first the quiz or test must be aligned with the instruction, that is, the goals, instruction, homework, and assessment must all be consistent with each other, and second, detailed feedback must be given after the assessment. That was all part of the research she covered. . . . So, now, I teach, give homework on what I've taught, discuss the homework, give the quiz, provide feedback the next day, and we repeat the process. And, the results are clear. I did a study comparing my kids' achievement this year to last year, and the kids this year are ahead; they're learning way more."

This short case study illustrates the importance of **research**, the process of systematically gathering information in attempts to answer professional questions (Gall, Gall, & Borg, 2015; Mills & Gay, 2016). The research Leah referred to answered the question, "What impact does ongoing assessment have on student learning?" and the answer expanded her professional knowledge, improved her teaching, and increased her students' learning. As she commented, "It changed my life."

Research is the foundation of our professional knowledge base in educational psychology. For instance, each answer to the items in our *Learning and Teaching Inventory* are based on research, and both the "Top 20" principles from psychology and the NCTQ teaching strategies that all new teachers need to know are derived from research.

Expert teachers are consumers of research. It's the primary mechanism they use to improve their practice, and this is true of all professionals—physicians, architects, engineers, and others. In addition, teachers are now under increased pressure to ground their instruction in research-based practice (Common Core State Standards Initiative [CCSSI], 2018d; Pomerance et al., 2016).

Research in education exists in several forms, each of which answers different kinds of questions. They include:

- Quantitative research
- Qualitative research
- Mixed methods research
- Action research
- Design-based research

Quantitative Research

Quantitative research refers to the systematic, empirical investigation of phenomena using numerical data and statistical techniques. Many examples relevant to our teaching practices exist, and they all attempt to answer professional questions, one of the most important being, "What can we do to increase our students' learning?" The research Leah cited used quantitative designs. (We examine the impact of assessment on learning in detail in Chapter 14.)

As another example, consider this research question: Should we call on students who do not volunteer to answer, that is, they don't raise their hands? Some teachers argue that we should not, believing that calling on non-volunteers puts them "on the spot" and makes them uncomfortable. This question has been researched, and to answer it, researchers trained teachers of one set of classes to call on all the students as equally as possible, but in classes of comparable ability, the teachers only called on volunteers—students who raised their hands. Then, the researchers compared the achievement of the classes on a posttest. The posttest provided numerical information about the achievement of the two sets of classes, so the studies were quantitative. The results indicated that student achievement in the classes where all students were called on was significantly higher (Good & Lavigne, 2018; Kerman, 1979; Lemov, 2015; McDougall & Granby, 1996).

These research results have important implications for our teaching; they suggest that we should be making an effort to call on all our students in our classes as equally as possible, whether or not they raise their hands (Good & Lavigne, 2018; Lemov, 2015).

This example illustrates the importance of teachers using research to improve their practice. As a result, we're better informed about how we should interact with our students.

Qualitative Research

Qualitative research attempts to describe complex educational phenomena in a holistic fashion using non-numerical data—words and pictures—as an alternative to quantitative research (Creswell & Poth, 2018). It uses methods such as interviews, focus groups, observations, and case studies to describe the phenomena it is investigating. The results of qualitative studies are then published in narrative reports with detailed descriptions of settings and participants, whereas quantitative studies report numerical results and statistical analyses (Creswell & Poth, 2018).

In a classic qualitative study of teaching, Robert Bullough (1989) spent a year observing a first-year, middle school language arts teacher. He also interviewed her and collected artifacts, such as lesson plans, assignments, and assessments, resulting in a realistic account of the triumphs and struggles a beginning teacher experienced in her first year. He didn't suggest that this teacher's experience generalized to the experiences of all first-year teachers; rather, he simply described one teacher's first year in as much detail as possible and then allowed readers to draw their own conclusions about the teacher's experiences.

In a more recent example, researchers used interviews, focus groups, and teachers' artifacts to examine the impact on English language learners (ELLs)—students who speak a native language other than English—of integrating arts, such as literature, music, drawing, and painting, into the curriculum. They found a number of positive results including improved performance on state standardized tests (Ingraham & Nuttall, 2016). They acknowledge, however, that "Because this was a case study, it may not be generalizable" (p. 18). This is true of all qualitative research, but the researchers also suggest that the possible benefits of increased emphasis on the arts in the curriculum for ELL students should be further examined.

As another example, possibly relevant to you at this point in your schooling, researchers conducted in-depth interviews with a selected group of students at different points in a MOOC—Massive Open Online Course—in an attempt to explain why more than 90% of students who take MOOCs never finish the courses. The interviews indicated that students are initially attracted to the MOOCs, substantively because they're free, but they fail to take into account the amount of time required (Eriksson, Adawi, & Stöhr, 2017). This research suggests that you should ask yourself if your schedule allows you to allocate the time needed to complete a MOOC, should you decide to enroll in one.

As we see from this discussion, quantitative and qualitative research provide us with different kinds of information, but they both contribute to our professional knowledge.

Mixed Methods Research

Mixed methods research is a research design that combines quantitative and qualitative methods. For instance, in one study a researcher used a mixed methods design to study the acquisition of mathematical pedagogical content knowledge (MPCK). He used a quantitative design to examine the extent to which preservice teachers acquired MPCK and then used interviews—the qualitative component—to examine their perceptions of their math methods courses. The findings indicated that preservice teachers who scored highest in acquisition of MPCK also perceived their methods courses to be most valuable (Buchholtz, 2017). These results suggest that the more effort you put into your courses, the more professional knowledge you'll acquire, and the more successful you're likely to be when you begin teaching. This all makes sense.

As another example, a mixed methods study used a quantitative design to measure lifelong-learning competencies, such as self-management, information acquisition, and decision making in elementary teachers, and, as with the previous example, used structured interviews to examine teachers' perceptions of the value of lifelong learning. The findings were similar to those in the other study; teachers with high levels of lifelong learning competencies perceived lifelong learning as more valuable and important than those whose competencies were lower (Acar & Ucus, 2017).

These findings have implications for us all at many levels, and particularly motivation. The more competent we become in any domain, such as music, art, athletics, or teaching, the more likely we are to perceive what we study as valuable, and the more motivated we become to acquire even greater competence.

Action Research

To begin this section, let's look back at a portion of Leah Thompson's conversation with her friend Mike Clark, which we used to introduce our discussion of research.

So, now, I teach, give homework on what I've taught, discuss the homework, give the quiz, provide feedback the next day, and we repeat the process. And, the results are clear. I did a study comparing my kids' achievement this year to last year, and the kids this year are ahead; they're learning way more.

MyLab Education

Video Example 1.2

Teachers can use action research to improve their instruction and increase their students' learning. This teacher explains how she used action research to examine the influence of weekly quizzes on her students' test anxiety, motivation to learn, and attitude toward the assessments.

Leah commented, "I did a study comparing my kids' achievement . . . " Her study illustrates **action research**, research conducted by teachers or other school officials designed to answer a specific school- or classroom-related question. The research is conducted with the goals of gaining insight, developing reflective practice, and "improving student outcomes and the lives of those involved" (Mills, 2018, p. 10). Leah gained insight into the role of assessment in learning, and she is improving student outcomes—her students' learning.

When you teach, and as you gain experience, you'll have many additional questions about the effects your actions have on your students' learning. Some might include:

- How much homework should I give?
- Should I systematically grade homework, or merely check to see if students have completed it?
- Am I using group work effectively? What could I do to make it more effective?
- Should I give my students free time to socialize with their classmates? If so, how much?

Many other examples exist, and to answer these questions, you might conduct your own action research studies. This is what Leah did as she investigated the impact of assessment on her students' learning.

Action research can use quantitative, qualitative, or mixed methods approaches, just as used by professional researchers, and if carefully organized and systematically conducted, it can be published in professional journals or presented at conferences just as other researchers do. For instance, one action research study used a quantitative design to examine the impact of efforts to improve the cultural responsiveness of prospective social studies teachers (Tuncel, 2017), and another used a qualitative design to assess teachers' perceptions of the role of action research in professional development (Yigit & Bagceci, 2017). These are but two examples of action research studies published in respected journals. In fact, the movement has expanded to the point that it now has entire journals devoted to the publication of action research studies (Clarke & Bautista, 2017).

Design-Based Research

Educational research has been criticized over the years because of its lack of impact on classroom practice. For instance, many teachers can't cite a single research study that has had an impact on their teaching (Anderson & Shattuck, 2012).

In response to these criticisms, **design-based research (DBR)**, research involving collaborative efforts between researchers and practitioners with the goal of solving real-world problems, has evolved. "DBR is not so much a precise research methodology as it is a collaborative approach that engages both researchers and practitioners in . . . analyzing, designing, and evaluating educational innovations and interventions aimed at solving complex, real-world educational problems" (Ford, McNally, & Ford, 2017, p. 50).

In addition to its emphasis on improving classroom practice, DBR has the following characteristics (Lewis, 2015; McKenney & Reeves, 2014):

- It is conducted in a real-world context, such as a classroom.
- It focuses on the design and testing of educational interventions, which could be a specific learning activity, type of assessment, administrative innovation (such as

starting school later in the morning), or application of some form of technology, among others.

- It typically uses mixed methods designs.
- It involves multiple iterations, that is, it repeats the process with the aim of approaching a desired goal. The result of one iteration is used as a starting point for the next one.
- It involves a partnership between researchers and practitioners.
- It is intended to contribute to theory.

DBR and action research are similar but not identical. For instance, when action research is conducted, the educator, such as a teacher or administrator, is both researcher and teacher, whereas a design-based study involves a partnership between researchers and practitioners. "The partnership in a design-based study recognizes that teachers are usually too busy and often ill trained to conduct rigorous research" (Anderson & Shattuck, 2012, p. 17). It also recognizes that teachers working in the real world of classrooms are essential for a study's validity. Further, design-based research doesn't focus exclusively on a local need, as would be the case with action research; it also attempts to contribute to theories that are applicable to a variety of settings.

From your perspective as someone involved in a teacher-preparation program, its attempt to have a practical impact on classroom practice is the most important characteristic of DBR. When successful, DBR provides us with concrete and practical suggestions for improving our teaching.

As we saw above, contributing to **theory**, a set of related patterns that researchers use to *explain* and *predict* events in the world, is one goal of design-based research. This, in fact, is the goal of all research. For instance, research Leah studied in her "Research-Based Instruction" class indicated that students exert more effort when they know they're going to be frequently assessed (Chappuis & Stiggins, 2017; Schunk et al., 2014), and motivation theory describes increased effort as an indicator of motivation. So, we can explain students' increased achievement when they're frequently assessed using motivation theory—simply, they study harder when they know they're going to be assessed. Similarly, we can predict that students will study more if assessment is an integral part of the teaching–learning process. This example illustrates the relationship between research and theory.

MyLab Education Self-Check 1.3

Teaching in Today's Classrooms

1.4:   Identify factors that influence teaching in today's classrooms.

The world of teaching is rapidly changing, and in many ways it's more challenging than it was only a few years ago. But, at the same time, more potential rewards also exist. To start you on the path toward meeting these challenges and reaping these rewards we want to provide you with an overview of what you will encounter when you move into the real world of teaching. In it we examine:

- Standards and accountability
- Teacher licensure and evaluation
- Learner diversity
- Technology

Standards and Accountability

In 1983 an influential report, called *A Nation at Risk: The Imperative for Educational Reform,* was published (National Commission on Excellence in Education, 1983). This widely read document, considered to be a landmark in American education, argued that our country's schools were failing to meet the national need for a competitive workforce, and since its publication a great deal has been written about American students' lack of knowledge and skills. For instance, the National Assessment of Educational Progress, commonly described as "The nation's report card," found, in 2015, only 36% of fourth-graders and 34% of eighth-graders were "at or above proficient" in reading, and in math the figures were 40% for fourth-graders and 33% for eighth-graders (National Assessment of Educational Progress, 2015).

In response to these concerns, educational leaders have established academic **standards**, statements that describe what students should know or be able to do at the end of a prescribed period of study.

The Common Core State Standards Initiative

The **Common Core State Standards Initiative (CCSSI)** is a state-led effort initiated in 2009 to establish a single set of clear educational standards for all states in essential content areas. "The standards were created to ensure that all students graduate from high school with the skills and knowledge necessary to succeed in college, career, and life, regardless of where they live" (CCSSI, 2018d, para. 2). As of 2018, 42 states, the District of Columbia, four territories, and the Department of Defense schools abroad have voluntarily adopted and are moving forward with the Common Core (CCSSI, 2018d).

Sophia Perez, Keith Jackson, and Kelsey Walsh, in the case studies at the beginning of the chapter, all used Common Core standards to guide their instruction, and we saw how they conducted their lessons to help their students reach the standards.

As with all attempts at educational reform, the Common Core standards are somewhat controversial, and a number of states have revised them. However, a review of the revisions found that the Common Core's most important features have been largely preserved (Sawchuck, 2017). Further, states that haven't adopted the Common Core have developed their own standards, so standards will be a part of your teaching life when you begin your career. This process may initially seem a bit intimidating, but you saw that Sophia, Keith, and Kelsey readily incorporated the standards into their instruction, and you will quickly learn to do the same. We examine the process of planning in a standards-based environment in detail in Chapter 13.

Accountability

Accountability is the process of requiring students to demonstrate that they have met standards as measured by standardized tests. These tests exist in a variety of forms. End of course (EOC) exams, such as biology students taking an EOC, or fourth-graders taking an EOC in math at the end of their school years are examples. In addition, every state has developed or adopted standardized tests that students take at the end of the school year, most commonly in reading, writing, and math, and, in a number of states, science (Time 4 Learning, 2018). The precise schedules and grades vary by state, and you can learn about the state tests for your state simply by searching "Standardized Testing by State" using Google or another search engine.

As with standards, accountability will be a reality throughout your teaching career, and teachers are often evaluated by their students' performance on these accountability measures. Our goal in introducing these topics in this chapter is to help you hit the ground running.

Teacher Licensure and Evaluation

In addition to standards and accountability, teacher licensure and evaluation are part of the reality of teacher-preparation programs and teaching in today's classroom. For you, this process will exist at two levels. The first will occur before you begin teaching and will require you to pass a licensure exam; the second is ongoing evaluation that will be conducted throughout your career.

Licensure Exams

Teacher quality is now a national priority, and, for many, it's synonymous with teacher knowledge. In attempts to ensure that teachers possess adequate professional knowledge, all states now require prospective teachers to pass one or more tests before they receive a teaching license. These tests commonly measure general knowledge, as well as the types of professional knowledge we described earlier in the chapter. It is a virtual certainty that you will be required to pass an exam that measures your professional knowledge before you receive your teaching license.

The Praxis® Series, published by the Educational Testing Service, is the test most widely used for teacher licensure (*praxis* means putting theory into practice). A majority of the states in our country use this series to make decisions about licensing new teachers (Educational Testing Service, 2018c). States that don't use the Praxis series have created their own licensure exams, and these exams are similar to the Praxis in design and content.

The Praxis® tests include (Educational Testing Service, 2018a):

- *Praxis*® Core Academic Skills for Educators (Core). These tests are designed to assess entering teacher candidates' knowledge and skills in reading, writing, and mathematics.
- *Praxis*® Subject Assessments. These tests measure subject-specific content knowledge as well as general and subject-specific teaching skills that you need for beginning teaching.
- *Praxis*® Content Knowledge for Teaching Assessments (CKT). These tests measure subject-specific content knowledge, with a focus on specialized knowledge used in K–12 teaching.

The *Principles of Learning and Teaching (PLT)* tests are important parts of the *Praxis*® Subject Assessments (Educational Testing Service, 2018b). The PLT tests measure your general pedagogical knowledge at one of four grade level ranges: Early Childhood, K–6, 5–9, and 7–12. These tests include selected-response (multiple-choice) questions and short constructed-response items based on information provided in classroom case studies similar to those you saw at the beginning of the chapter. The content of educational psychology makes up much of what is measured on the tests, and in our "Preparing for Your Licensure Exam" feature at the end of each chapter you can practice responding to multiple-choice and short-answer questions similar to those you'll encounter on the PLT tests. In addition, the appendix at the end of this text provides a matrix that correlates the content covered in these pages with the content measured on the Praxis PLT exams.

Teacher Evaluation

Teacher evaluation, the process of assessing teachers' classroom performance and providing feedback designed to increase their expertise, is another reality that you will encounter when you begin your career. Teacher evaluation has become an increasingly important issue in education because evidence suggests that, historically, evaluation procedures have done little to reward good teachers and eliminate those that are incompetent. Current reforms are attempting to remedy this problem by creating more valid and reliable teacher evaluation systems (Rosen & Parise, 2017).

You will be provided with detailed information about the evaluation procedures for your school, district, and state when you take your first job. (We examine teacher evaluation in more detail in Chapter 15.)

Learner Diversity

The demographic trends in our country are changing rapidly, and increasing diversity is one of the most significant. For instance, you probably have friends whose ethnic backgrounds are different from your own, and they may speak a native language other than English. In fact, English may not be your first language.

The following statistics illustrate some of these changes:

- Experts estimate that nearly 300 distinct ethnic groups now live in the United States (Gollnick & Chinn, 2017).
- Of the 15 most common surnames in our country, 6 are now Hispanic, with Garcia and Rodriguez ranked sixth and ninth, respectively (United States Census Bureau, 2016).
- Projections estimate that by 2026, 55% of the students in our nation's schools will be members of cultural minorities, with Hispanic students projected to be the largest minority at slightly less than 30% of the total school population (National Center for Education Statistics, 2017c).
- Nearly 10% of all students in our country speak a native language other than English. In Texas the figure is more than 15%, and in California it's more than 20% (National Center for Education Statistics, 2017b).
- Statistics indicate that nearly 1 of 5 children in our country live in poverty (Federal Safety Net, 2017). And, the percentage of American families below the poverty line is consistently higher than in other industrialized countries (Bradbury, Corak, Waldfogel, & Washbrook, 2016).
- More than 1.3 million homeless students were enrolled in our nation's schools in the 2013–14 school year, an increase of more than 38% from 2009–10 (Jones, 2016).
- Finally, about 13% of all students enrolled in our nation's schools receive special education services (National Center for Education Statistics, 2017a).

This all means that you are virtually certain to have students in your schools and classes with very diverse backgrounds. This will be challenging at times, for example, when attempting to help low income students with limited backgrounds keep up with their more advantaged peers. However, the rewards will far outweigh the challenges. Different cultural habits, attitudes, and values make learning experiences enriching for all students, and when students from different backgrounds work together they find out that we're all much more alike than we are different. We all want to have friends, and to be respected and cared for. And, when people, in general, give each other a chance, the rewards can be huge. This has been our experience as authors. We devote Chapter 4 to the topic and include sections examining diversity topics in each of the other chapters of this book.

Technology

Think about the following questions.

1. When was the last time you went to a print encyclopedia to find some information, or to a print dictionary to find the definition of a word?
2. When was the last time you took a picture with a camera that uses film?
3. How often do you "Google" something?
4. Are you a Facebook user?
5. Do you own a smartphone or tablet?
6. Do you prefer to text rather than talk on the phone?

The answer to the first two questions might be, "Never," or "Can't remember when." "Daily" or even more often might be the answer to the third, and "Yes" is probably the most common answer to the last three. We could ask other similar questions, but you get the idea. Technology is now so much a part of our world that we take it for granted.

As with the other topics we've discussed in this section, technology will be an integral part of your teaching life, and it will have benefits and present challenges. As simple examples, we all have access to a virtually unlimited source of information with the Internet and a variety of search engines. Instead of sending a letter in print form home to parents you will probably e-mail it. You will likely have your students do homework or other forms of practice on computers, and you may even teach a course online. You will store lesson plans and a myriad of examples and other resources in your computer, which you can access and display for your students at the touch of your keyboard. Your classroom will likely be equipped with an **interactive whiteboard**, a device that includes a display screen connected to a computer and projector which allows information displayed on the screen to be manipulated with special pens or hands, stored in the computer, and recovered later for further use. Technology such as this is being used in classrooms across the country at grade levels ranging from early elementary through the university level (Roblyer & Hughes, 2019).

Technology, however, can be a double-edged sword. For instance, an expanding body of research now suggests that people are addicted to technology, and particularly their smartphones (Sapacz, Rockman, & Clark, 2016). In fact, smartphone use has become so ubiquitous that spine surgeons are noticing an increase in patients with neck and upper back pain, likely, they believe, because of poor posture during prolonged smartphone use (Cuéllar & Lanman, 2017). As another example, statistics indicate that pedestrian traffic fatalities have increased, and researchers believe that pedestrian distraction is a cause (Retting, 2018). People are staring at their smartphones and they walk into dangerous situations without paying attention.

Further, surveys suggest that while many people believe excessive use of mobile devices is distracting and harmful to group interaction, they confess that they can't resist the temptation themselves (Rainie & Zickuhr, 2015). Even imagined disconnection from smartphones and social media can trigger stress, anxiety, and depression (Elhai, Hall, & Erwin, 2018). These issues have become so prominent that they're being reported in the popular press (Popescu, 2018).

We examine the impact of technology—both positive and negative—throughout the rest of this text.

Using Educational Psychology in Teaching: Suggestions for Applying Professional Knowledge in Your Classroom

Educational psychology is interesting for its own sake, because it helps us understand how we all learn and develop. Most important for you taking this course, however, are the suggestions for using the content of educational psychology in your teaching. Your professional knowledge will be grounded in the content of educational psychology, but for it to be most useful you must be able to apply it to advance your students' learning and development. This is why the book is titled *Using Educational Psychology in Teaching*, and, consistent with this title, specific suggestions for applying the content of educational psychology in your work with students will appear in one or more sections of each chapter. All sections will use the heading, "Using Educational Psychology in Teaching: Suggestions for . . . ," such as "Using Educational Psychology in Teaching: Suggestions for Applying Piaget's Theory of Cognitive Development with Your Students" in Chapter 2, or "Using Educational Psychology in Teaching: Suggestions for Capitalizing on Cultural Diversity with Your Students" in Chapter 4. These suggestions will help you use theories of learning, development, and motivation, and also use research that provides guidance for best practices in instruction, classroom management, assessment, and working with students having diverse backgrounds. This is why you're taking this course and studying this text—so you can acquire the professional knowledge needed to become an expert teacher and then use this knowledge to increase learning for all your students.

The best of luck.

MyLab Education Self-Check 1.4

Chapter 1 Summary

1. Describe expert teaching and explain how expert teaching influences student learning.
   - Experts are people who are highly knowledgeable and skilled in a particular domain, such as teaching. Students taught by expert teachers learn more than students taught by teachers with less expertise.
   - Expert teachers can produce learning in their students and do so despite challenging circumstances.

2. Describe the types of professional knowledge that expert teachers possess.
   - Expert teachers thoroughly understand the topics they teach, and their knowledge is reflected in their actions when they use their pedagogical content knowledge to illustrate those topics in ways that make sense to learners.
   - Expert teachers apply general pedagogical knowledge to organize learning environments and use basic instructional skills in ways that promote learning for their students.
   - Expert teachers' knowledge of learners and learning allows them to design learning activities that involve students, promote motivation to learn, and use developmentally appropriate practice.

3. Describe different types of research and explain how research contributes to teachers' professional knowledge.
   - Research is the process of systematically gathering information in an attempt to answer professional questions, and it is an important source of the knowledge needed for expert teaching.
   - Quantitative research is the systematic examination of events using numerical data and statistical and mathematical techniques.
   - Qualitative research attempts to describe complex educational phenomenon in a holistic fashion using non-numerical data.

- Mixed methods research uses both quantitative and qualitative designs to gather a more complete picture of educational phenomena.
- Action research is applied research designed to answer a specific school- or classroom-related question. It can use both quantitative and qualitative methods.
- Influencing classroom practice is the goal of design-based research, and it involves collaboration between researchers and teachers, a focus on educational interventions, the use of multiple iterations, and mixed methods. Unlike action research it includes both the solution of local problems and efforts to contribute to theory.
- Theories are sets of related patterns that help explain and predict events in the world. Theories can provide valuable guidance for teaching.

4. Identify factors that influence teaching in today's classrooms.
   - Standards, statements describing what students should know or be able to do after a given period of study, and accountability, the process of requiring students to demonstrate that they have met standards as measured by standardized tests, are a professional reality in today's classrooms.
   - Teachers are required to pass a licensure exam before they're allowed to work full time in today's classrooms, and they will also be regularly evaluated during their teaching careers.
   - Today's schools are now attended by students whose backgrounds are the most diverse in our country's history. In addition to differences in cultural and language backgrounds, large numbers of students from low income backgrounds are now attending our nation's schools.
   - Technology is now an integral part of our lives, and it is becoming an increasingly significant factor in today's classrooms.

Preparing for Your Licensure Exam

Understanding Professional Knowledge

You will be required to take a licensure exam before you go into your own classroom. This exam will include information related to the different types of professional knowledge teachers need to become experts, and the following exercises are similar to those that appear on licensure exams. They are designed to help you prepare for the exam in your state. This book and these exercises will be a resource for you later in your program as you prepare for the exam.

The following episodes illustrate four teachers at different classroom levels working with their students. As you read the episodes, think about the different types of professional knowledge that the teachers demonstrate in their lessons.

Rebecca Atkins, a kindergarten teacher, is talking with her children about planting a garden. She sits on a small chair at the front of the room and has the children seated on the floor in a semicircle in front of her.

She begins, "We had a story about gardening the other day. Who remembers the name of the story? . . . Shereta?"

"'Together,'" Shereta softly responds.

"Yes, 'Together,'" Rebecca repeats. "What happened in 'Together'? . . . Andrea?"

"They had a garden."

"They planted a garden together, didn't they?" Rebecca smiles. "The boy's father helped them plant the garden."

She continues by referring the children to previous science lessons during which they had talked about plants and soil. She then asks them about their own experiences helping their parents plant a garden.

"I helped put the seeds in the ground and put the dirt on top of it," Robert offers.

"What kinds of vegetables did you plant? . . . Kim?"

"I planted lots of vegetables . . . tomatoes, carrots."

"Travis?"

"I planted okra."

"Raphael?"

"I planted beans."

She continues, "Tell us more about the story 'Together.' What did they have to do to take care of the garden? . . . Carlita?"

"Water it."

"Bengemar?"

"Pull the weeds from it."

"Pull the weeds from it," Rebecca smiles. "What would happen if we left those weeds in there? . . . Latangela?"

"It would hurt the soil."

"What's another word for soil?"

"Dirt," several of the children say in unison.

"How many of you like to play in the dirt?"

Most of the children raise their hands.

"So, planting a garden would be fun because you get to play in the dirt," Rebecca says enthusiastically.

"I like to play in the mud," Travis adds.

"You like to play in the mud," Rebecca repeats, attempting to stifle a laugh.

We turn now to Richard Nelms, a middle school science teacher, as he illustrates the concept of symmetry for his seventh-graders.

Richard begins his discussion of symmetry by holding up a sponge as an example of an asymmetrical animal; he demonstrates radial symmetry using a starfish; and he then turns to bilateral symmetry.

"We have one more type of symmetry," he says. "Jason, come up here. . . . Stand up here."

Jason comes to the front of the room and stands on a stool.

"Would you say," Richard begins, "that Jason is asymmetrical—that there is not uniformity in his shape?"

The students shake their heads.

He has Jason extend his arms out from his sides as you see here and then asks, "Would you consider this radial, because he has extensions that go out in all directions? . . . Jarrett?"

"No."

"Why not? Explain that for us."

"There's nothing there," Jarrett says, pointing to Jason's sides.

"There's nothing coming from here, is there, and the arms, legs and head are all different?" Richard adds.

"So, we move to the third type of symmetry," he continues, as Jason continues to stand with his arms extended. "It's called *bilateral* . . . . Bilateral means that the form or shape of the organism is divided into two halves, and the two halves are consistent . . . . If I took a tree saw and started at the top," he says,

pointing at Jason's head as the class laughs, "the two halves would be essentially the same."

"Now, tomorrow," he continues, "we're going to see how symmetry influences the ways organisms function in their environments."

Let's look in now at Didi Johnson, a tenth-grade chemistry teacher, as she attempts to help her students understand Charles's law of gases, the law stating that an increase in the temperature of a gas causes an increase in its volume if the pressure on the gas doesn't change.

To illustrate that heat causes gases to expand, Didi prepares a demonstration in which she places three identical balloons filled with the same amount of air into three beakers of water. She puts the first into a beaker of hot water, the second into a beaker of water at room temperature, and the third into a beaker of ice water, as you see here.

"This water is near boiling," Didi explains as she places the first balloon in the beaker. "This is room temperature, and this has had ice in it, so it is near the freezing point," she continues as she puts the other two balloons into different beakers.

"Today," she continues as she begins writing on the board, "we're going to discuss Charles's law, but before we put it on the board and discuss it, we're going to see what happened to the balloons. . . . Look up here. . . . How is the size of the balloon related to the temperature of the water we placed it in?"

"The balloon in the hot water looks bigger," Chris responds.

"Can you see any difference in these two?" Didi continues, pointing to the other two balloons.

"The one in the cold water looks smaller than the one in the room-temperature water," Shannon adds.

"So, from what we see, if you increase temperature, what happens to the volume of the gas?"

"It increases," several students volunteer.

Didi writes, "Increase in temperature increases volume" on the board, emphasizes that the amount of air and the pressure in the balloons were kept essentially constant, and then asks, "Who can state Charles's law based on what we've seen here?"

"Increased temperature will increase volume if you have constant pressure and mass," Jeremy offers.

Didi briefly reviews Charles's law, writes an equation for it on the board, and has the students solve a series of problems using the law.

Finally, let's look at Bob Duchaine's work with his students. An American history teacher, he is discussing the Vietnam War with his eleventh-graders.

Bob begins by saying, "To understand the Vietnam War, we need to go back to the beginning. Vietnam had been set up as a French colony in the 1880s, but by the mid-1900s, the military situation had gotten so bad for the French that they only controlled certain enclaves like the little city of Dien Bien Phu."

He explains that the French surrendered this city in the summer of 1954, and peace talks followed. The talks resulted in Vietnam being split, and provisions for free elections were set up.

"These elections were never held," Bob continues. "Ngo Dinh Diem, in 1956, said there will be no free elections: 'I am in charge of the South. You can have elections in the North if you want, but there will be no elections in the South.'"

He continues by introducing the "domino theory," which suggested that countries such as South Vietnam, Cambodia, Laos, Thailand, Burma, and even India would fall into communist hands much as dominos tip over and knock each other down. The way to prevent the loss of the countries, he explains, was to confront North Vietnam.

"And that's what we're going to be talking about throughout this unit," he says. "The war that we took over from the French to stop the fall of the dominos soon was eating up American lives at the rate of 12 to 15 thousand a year. . . . This situation went from a little simple plan—to stop the dominos from falling—to a loss of over 53,000 American lives.

"We'll pick up with this topic the day after tomorrow. . . . Tomorrow, you have a fun day in the library."

Questions for Case Analysis

In answering these questions, use information from the chapter, and link your responses to specific information in the case.

Multiple-Choice Questions

1. The two teachers who most nearly demonstrated pedagogical content knowledge were:

   a. Rebecca and Richard.

   b. Richard and Didi.

   c. Richard and Bob.

   d. Didi and Bob.

2. The teacher who least demonstrated general pedagogical knowledge was:

   a. Rebecca.

   b. Richard.

   c. Didi.

   d. Bob.

Constructed-Response Question

1. What type or types of professional knowledge did Bob most nearly demonstrate?

MyLab Education Licensure Exam 1.1

Important Concepts

accountability
action research
classroom assessment
classroom management
cognition
Common Core State Standards Initiative (CCSSI)
design-based research
developmental differences

developmentally appropriate practice
educational psychology (ed psych)
experts
general pedagogical knowledge
human capital
interactive whiteboard

knowledge of learners and learning
learning styles
meaningfulness
mixed methods research
motivation
pedagogical content knowledge (PCK)
professional knowledge

qualitative research
quantitative research
reflective practice
research
simulation
standards
teacher evaluation
theories
worked examples

Chapter 2
Cognitive and Language Development

JGI/Jamie Grill/Getty Images

Learning Outcomes

After you have completed your study of this chapter, you should be able to:

2.1 Describe the concept of *development* and explain how Bronfenbrenner's theory contributes to our understanding of development.

2.2 Explain how neuroscience helps us understand development.

2.3 Use concepts from Piaget's theory of intellectual development to explain events in classrooms and everyday living.

2.4 Use Vygotsky's sociocultural theory to explain how language, culture, and instructional support influence development.

2.5 Explain the relationship between language and cognitive development and what we can do to promote language development in our students.

APA Top 20 Principles

Top 20 Principles from Psychology for PreK–12 Teaching and Learning explicitly addressed in this chapter.

Principle 2: What students already know affects their learning.
Principle 3: Students' cognitive development and learning are not limited by general stages.
Principle 5: Acquiring long-term knowledge and skill is largely dependent on practice.
Principle 13: Learning is situated within multiple social contexts.

National Council on Teacher Quality (NCTQ)

The NCTQ Essential Teaching Strategies that every new teacher needs to know specifically addressed in this chapter.

Strategy 2: Linking abstract concepts with concrete representations

"Life is not a problem to be solved, but a reality to be experienced."
— SOREN KIERKEGAARD, DANISH PHILOSOPHER.

Kierkegaard, who lived in the early 1800s, understood that experience is one of the most powerful influences in our lives, and rich experiences can lead to healthy personalities, advanced social skills, and sophisticated thinking. The development of thinking—cognitive development—is our focus in this chapter.

In the following case study, Jenny Newhall, a 1st-grade teacher, wants her students to understand two properties of air: 1) that air takes up space; and 2) that it exerts pressure.

As you watch the episode and read the case study, focus specifically on the children's thinking as the lesson progresses. We join her lesson now.

Jenny assembles the students on the carpet in front of her and begins by asking them how they know if something is real. She shows the students a spoon, asks them if it's real, and then asks if air is real.

They conclude that air is indeed real, and Jenny then displays a fish bowl, three fourths full of water.

She also holds up a glass as you see here.

The students make observations of the glass, and then, to demonstrate that air takes up space, Jenny tells the students she is going to push the inverted glass down into the water and asks the students to predict what they think will happen.

"What do you think? . . . Samantha?"

Samantha describes an experience she had in a swimming pool with her dad, explaining that they had pushed a glass into the water and if the glass was held straight air stayed in the glass, but if the glass was tipped, water came in.

"How interesting," Jenny responds. "What do you think? . . . Michelle?"

"Water might go in the glass," Michelle concludes.

Jenny then pushes the inverted glass into the water as you see here.

She asks if the inside of the glass is wet or dry.

Terry insists that the inside of the glass is wet, but Samantha says it's dry, so Jenny then pushes a paper towel into the bottom of the glass, again immerses the glass in the water as you see below.

She asks Marisa to come up to check to see if the towel is wet or dry.

Marisa concludes that it's dry, and Jenny asks, "Why did the towel stay dry? . . . What do you think? . . . Jessica?"

"Because it's in the glass," Jessica responds.

"But why didn't the water go in the glass?" Jenny probes.

"Because it's tipped over."

"Anthony?"

"A water seal," Anthony responds.

"A water seal," Jenny repeats. Jenny then reminds the students of Samantha's idea about tipping the glass, asks the students what they think will happen, immerses the glass in the water, and tips it.

The students see bubbles escape from the glass, and after a few comments from students they conclude that the bubbles are air escaping from the glass.

Then, to demonstrate that air exerts pressure, she continues, "Now I've got something else. Wait till you see this one," and she asks the students what they think will happen if she places a card over the full glass of water and turn it upside down, as we see here.

"Whoa, now what's happening?" Jenny asks. "Why is it doing this? . . . Thomas?"

"The water is holding it on," Thomas responds.

"What do you think? . . . Christina?" Jenny probes.

"The water looks like it might be super glue or something and won't let that card go."

We'll return to Jenny's lesson later, but for now, let's think about her activity. Using the fishbowl, water, glass, and paper towel, she concretely demonstrated that air takes up space because the air in the glass kept the water out. The fact that the paper towel remained dry was evidence for this phenomenon. She also demonstrated that air exerts pressure with her demonstration using the water-filled glass and card.

Notice that the students didn't initially react to the air in the glass in her first demonstration, and they also concluded that the water held the card onto the glass in her second. This is consistent with the thinking of 1st-graders, and it's directly related to cognitive development, the focus of this chapter.

We begin with the concept of *development* in general.

What Is Development?

2.1   **Describe the concept of *development* and explain how Bronfenbrenner's theory contributes to our understanding of development.**

Ed Psych and You

Think back to when you were in elementary and middle school. What kinds of abilities do you have now that you didn't have then? How about your high school years? How has your thinking changed since you graduated from high school?

The questions in *Ed Psych and You* relate to the concept of **development**, the changes that occur in all of us as we go through our lives. We see these changes in ourselves, as well as our families and friends. Studying development is valuable for two reasons. First, it helps us better understand ourselves and the people around us, because we all go through developmental processes and will do so throughout our lives. Second, it can make us better teachers, because it gives us insights into our students' thinking.

Different types of development occur. **Physical development** describes changes in the size, shape, and functioning of our bodies and explains why we could, for example, run faster as a high school student than as a 5th-grader. **Personal, social, and emotional development** refer to changes in our personalities, the ways we interact with others, and the ability to manage our feelings.

As we saw above, in this chapter we focus on cognitive development, changes in our thinking that occur as a result of maturation and experience. The question "How has your thinking changed?" in *Ed Psych and You* focuses on this aspect of development, and it was also the focus of Jenny's lesson.

Principles of Development

Three general principles apply to all forms of development (Berk, 2019a, 2019b; Feldman, 2017).

- *Development depends on both heredity and the environment.* **Maturation**, genetically driven, age-related changes in individuals, plays an important role in development. For instance, high school students' thinking is more advanced than the thinking of elementary or middle school students, which helps us understand why we don't teach calculus or physics to younger learners.

- The environment, through the experiences we have, is also a major factor in development, and in some ways, may be even more important than heredity. For instance, children who grow up in supportive families and schools that provide rich experiences consistently thrive, even if their native intellectual ability is only modest.

- *Development proceeds in orderly and predictable patterns.* Development is relatively systematic and predictable. For example, we babble before we talk, crawl before we walk, and learn concrete concepts like *mammal* and *car* before those more abstract, such as *democracy* and *symbolism*. These patterns exist in virtually all human beings.

- *People develop at different rates.* While development is generally orderly, the rate at which individuals progress varies. We've all heard phrases such as "He's a late bloomer" or "She never quite grew up," which describe individual differences in people's rates of development. These differences influence our interactions with our students and the effectiveness of our instruction.

With these principles in mind, we turn now to Bronfenbrenner's Bioecological Systems Theory of Development, which helps explain how the environment interacts with our genes to produce the unique individuals we each become.

Bronfenbrenner's Bioecological Systems Theory of Development

To begin this section, let's look at the profile of Josh, an 8-year-old who lives with his parents and younger brother, Zach, in a suburb of a large, urban area. As you examine his profile, think about the influences on his development.

Josh is in the third grade, and his studies are becoming more academic. For example, he now gets traditional grades, and achievement testing is emphasized more strongly than it was in kindergarten, first, and second grades.

Josh's parents have read to him since infancy, and as a result, his reading fluency—the ability to decode words and pronounce them with ease and expression—is advanced, but he has struggled a bit with comprehension. Realizing this, Nicole, his mom, works with him on reading comprehension every day, and his comprehension is now much improved. She takes a low-key and supportive approach that includes considerable praise for both effort and success, and Josh doesn't resist the work sessions.

"If kids can't read, they can't do anything else," Nicole comments, explaining all the work. "He needs to go to college. You can't make it in today's world without a college degree," she asserts.

Josh is an advanced math student, at least in part because both Nicole and Steve, his dad, have provided him with math-related experiences since he was in kindergarten. Steve works for a large firm in the city, and he has considerable job flexibility, such as being able to work from home whenever necessary. As a result, he attends most of Josh's school and non-school related activities.

Nicole has also conferred with his teachers—he has one for literacy and a second one for math, social studies, and science—to ensure that her efforts are aligned with his school experiences. She also communicates with them by e-mail on a regular basis. His teachers provide extra support in small groups when necessary, and they welcome Nicole's communication.

Josh likes school, and, predictably, he says math is his favorite subject.

Now, let's see how Josh's profile relates to Bronfenbrenner's work. The first principle of development above says that *development depends on both heredity and the environment.* Urie Bronfenbrenner, a Russian-born American developmental psychologist, expanded on this principle with his *bioecological systems theory* of development. The "bio" in the title places the child at the center of the developmental process and reminds us that genetics influence development by determining certain characteristics, such as height and some aspects of both temperament and intelligence. The "ecological" component refers to environmental influences on development, and Bronfenbrenner most strongly focused on these influences (Bronfenbrenner & Morris, 2006; Rosa & Tudge, 2013).

To help you understand his theory, imagine a series of environmental "layers," beginning with influences that most directly affect the child and extending to factors more distant. These environmental layers are illustrated in Figure 2.1.

As we see in Figure 2.1, four systems influence development: the *microsystem, mesosystem, exosystem,* and *macrosystem* (Christensen, 2016). To avoid getting bogged down with strange terminology, think about the prefixes. *Micro* means *small; meso* suggests *middle* or *intermediate; exo* refers to *outside* or *external;* and *macro* means *long* or *large.*

With these prefixes in mind, let's see how the environmental layers are illustrated in Josh's life. We see that Nicole and Steve are both directly involved in Josh's schooling and are providing him with a great deal of both academic and emotional support. His teachers also provide extra help when necessary, and we can readily see how his parents' and teachers' efforts will help Josh develop both academically and emotionally. They are part of the **microsystem** (smallest system), the environmental layer that most directly affects the child, such as family, peers, school, and neighborhood. Josh's parents and teachers are involved and supportive, but, unfortunately, not all children are so fortunate, and we can easily see how their development can be adversely affected.

We also saw that Nicole is in close communication with Josh's teachers. This connection makes up the **mesosystem** (middle system), which is composed of interactions between elements of the microsystem. Development is enhanced if these elements work together. For instance, schools that promote high levels of parental involvement increase learner development to a greater extent than those who don't (Lezotte & Snyder, 2011; O'Connor, Dearing, & Collins, 2011).

Figure 2.1 Bronfenbrenner's bioecological model of human development

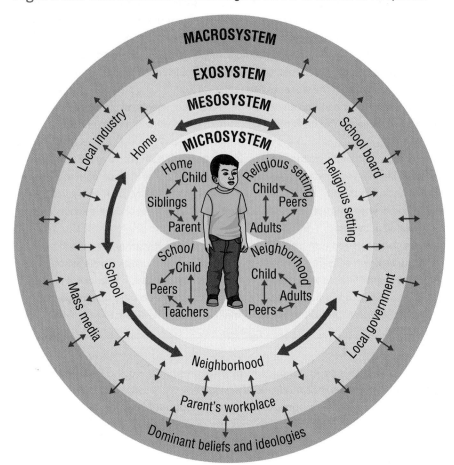

The **exosystem** (external system) includes societal influences, such as parents' jobs, school systems, and workplace conditions, which influence both the microsystem and mesosystem. For example, Steve's job flexibility allows him to be more involved in Josh's activities than is the case for many people. Also, wealthier school systems are more likely to provide nurses, counselors, psychologists, and smaller class sizes, all of which can positively influence development.

The **macrosystem** (large system) is the culture in which a child develops, and it influences all the other systems. Nicole's comments, "If kids can't read, they can't do anything else," and "He needs to go to college. You can't make it in today's world without a college degree," reflect her cultural attitudes and values. As another example, our mainstream culture tends to focus on the individual and emphasize autonomy, whereas others, such as those in parts of Asia, more strongly emphasize social influences and conformity (Goodnow, 2010).

APA Top 20 Principles

This discussion illustrates Principle 13: *Learning is situated in multiple social contexts*—from the *Top 20 Principles from Psychology for PreK–12 Teaching and Learning*.

Implications of Bronfenbrenner's Theory for Our Teaching

So, what does Bronfenbrenner's theory suggest to us as teachers? Actually, a lot. First, as we saw above, we're part of our students' microsystems, so, second only to parents, we are the most important influence on our students' development. This suggests that we should be making every effort to provide the experiences that will contribute to this development (Fond-Harmant & Gavrilă-Ardelean, 2016). As an example, Jenny, our teacher at the beginning of the chapter, provided her first graders with concrete experiences illustrating properties of air. It's likely that the children, at this point in their cognitive development, didn't fully grasp these somewhat abstract ideas, but Jenny's demonstrations nevertheless provided the foundation for more advanced thinking later in their schooling. Jenny was an effective part of the children's microsystem.

Experiences that promote healthy development go well beyond academics. For instance, as teachers we model courtesy, support for those less fortunate than we are, and tolerance for others' opinions. We also model healthy emotions, and through our teaching help develop the social skills needed to succeed in today's world.

And, as we saw with Josh's teachers, we can make an effort to communicate openly and often with parents or other caregivers, so we make a healthy contribution to our students' mesosystems. We can also accommodate exosystems by creating flexible opportunities for parents so they can become even more effective parts of their children's microsystems. Finally, we can communicate healthy cultural attitudes and values that contribute to a healthy macrosystem. From all this, we can see why teaching is some of the most important work in the world.

Analyzing Bronfenbrenner's Bioecological Systems Theory

As with all theories, Bronfenbrenner's bioecological systems theory has both weaknesses and strengths. We begin with some weaknesses.

Weaknesses of Bronfenbrenner's Theory. The theory's primary weakness is its tendency to ignore, or at least downplay, the role that individual's cognition plays in development. The ways children think about themselves, their abilities, and their relationships with others strongly influences their development. To be a comprehensive theory of development, this factor should be included. Further, examining Bronfenbrenner's assertions with research is difficult, so his theory has not been widely assessed.

Strengths of Bronfenbrenner's Theory. Bronfenbrenner's theory helps us better understand the differences we observe in our students, such as why children the same age and even from the same families often think and act differently. It also helps us understand why home–school partnerships are so important and why involving the larger community in our children's education is valuable. For example, research tells us that the children of involved parents are more likely to do their homework, attend school more regularly, and learn more (Kim & Hill, 2015; Kriegbaum, Villarreal, Wu, & Heckhausen, 2016).

His theory also reminds us that our classrooms are embedded within larger contexts, and we must accommodate these contexts to be as effective as possible. And, perhaps most important, his theory has direct implications for the way we work with our students. Bronfenbrenner's theory, including its contributions and criticisms, is summarized in Table 2.1.

MyLab Education Self-Check 2.1

TABLE 2.1 Analyzing theories: Bronfenbrenner's bioecological theory of development

Key question	How do genetics and different levels of environmental influence interact to impact all forms of development?
Key concepts	Microsystem—family, peers, neighborhood, schools Mesosystem—interactions among the elements of the microsystem Exosystem—societal influences, such as parents' jobs and access to health care Macrosystem—culture in which the child develops
Description of development	Development occurs as different levels of environmental influence interact in dynamic systems with each other and with a child's genetic makeup to produce growth.
Catalyst for development	• Genetics • Multiple levels of environmental factors
Contributions	• Provides a detailed description of how genetics and different levels of environmental factors interact to influence children's development • Reminds educators that many factors outside of classrooms have important influences on children's learning and development
Criticisms	• Descriptions of how different levels of the environment interact with each other and with a child's genetics to influence development are somewhat vague. • Theory is difficult to empirically test with research and refine because the components of the theory lack specificity.

SOURCES: Berk, 2013; Bronfenbrenner, 1979, 2005; Bronfenbrenner & Morris, 2006; Feldman, 2014.

The Neuroscience of Learning and Development

2.2   Explain how neuroscience helps us understand development.

Ed Psych and You

We all want to be smart. Is it possible for us to get smarter, or are we stuck with the "smarts" we're born with, and all we can do is maximize what we've been given? Neuroscience helps us answer this question.

Neuroscience is the scientific study of the nervous system, which includes the brain, spinal cord, sensory organs, and the nerves that connect these organs to the rest of the body. The brain is its most prominent component, so, as we would expect, it's the primary subject of neuroscience research. This research is becoming increasingly prominent, and it has implications for the way we teach as we attempt to promote learning and development in our students. To apply neuroscience in our classrooms we first need to understand some basic information about our brains. We begin with what research tells us (Hohnen & Murphy, 2016; Scalise & Felde, 2017).

- The brain is our body's most complex organ. The complexity of any organism's nervous system determines the range of behaviors it's able to produce. For example, worms have simple nervous systems and have only limited options for actions, while frogs have more complex nervous systems and are capable of more complex behaviors than worms. Humans have the most complex nervous systems of all species on earth, which means we have greater options to think and act than any other animal.

- Electrical circuitry is the foundation of the nervous system. The basic wiring of the brain is similar for all members of a species; differences are the result of variations in individuals' brain cells. For example, as humans we're all similarly wired, and variations among us are the result of differences in our individual neural connections.

- The brain is the foundation of the mind and thinking. As the brain is exposed to experiences, intelligence increases.

- The brain makes it possible to communicate by directing language. Language allows the exchange of information and the advancement of knowledge.

- The brain tries to make sense of our experiences by instinctively searching for patterns. For example, small children see some furry animals, hear them go "Woof woof," see them wag their tails, and then construct the concept *dog* based on the similarities—patterns—they see in the animals' characteristics.

- The brain is "plastic," which means that it physically changes in response to events it encounters. The brain's ability to change in structure is called **neuroplasticity**, and it answers the question we asked in *Ed Psych and You*. Yes, with the right kinds of experiences, it's possible for us to literally get smarter! And learning to read is one of these experiences. Research indicates that learning to read, even in illiterate adults, results in neuroplastic changes in individuals' brains (Skeide et al., 2017). Neuroplasticity is arguably the best news that exists about the brain.

Seeing the brain as plastic is a departure from historic views; until about the 1980s scientists thought that the structure of the brain developed during childhood, and that once developed there was little room for change (Pascual-Leone, Amedi, Fregni, & Merabet, 2005). Neuroplasticity is a much more optimistic view.

Unfortunately, neuroplasticity also has a down side. For example, children growing up in extreme poverty produce high levels of cortisol, a hormone released in response to stress. High levels of cortisol in young children impair brain circuits and change the architecture of the brain (McCoy, 2016; Phillips, 2016).

The fact that our brains are plastic—neuroplasticity—has important implications for schools and for all of us as teachers. We examine these implications later in this section of the chapter.

Now, with these basic characteristics of our brains in mind, let's look at the physiology of the brain and how it relates to cognitive development.

The Physiology of the Brain and Cognitive Development

The complexity of the brain is impossible to comprehend. For example, researchers estimate that it is composed of between 100 and 200 billion (yes, billion, not million!) nerve cells, called neurons (Carlson, 2011; Seung, 2012). These **neurons** are the basic learning units of the brain and are central to cognitive development. To help us understand them, how they're structured, and how they work, look at Figure 2.2.

As we see in Figure 2.2, a neuron is composed of a cell body together with **axons**, branches that extend from the cell body and send messages to other nerve cells, and **dendrites**, shorter branches that also extend from the cell body and receive messages from other neurons. The neurons don't actually touch; instead, signals are sent across **synapses**, tiny spaces between neurons that allow messages to be transmitted from one to another. When an electrical impulse is sent down an axon, it produces a chemical that crosses the synapse and stimulates the dendrites of neighboring neurons. Frequent transmission of information between neurons can establish a permanent physical relationship between them. This helps us understand why reading and talking to young children are so important. When parents read to their small children, for example, hearing words and seeing pictures provide experiences that promote synaptic connections in the children's neurons. The more children are read to, the more synaptic connections that occur, and the more permanent the connections become (Pace, Hirsh-Pasek, & Golinkoff, 2016).

Practice promotes the frequent transmission of signals between neurons and helps establish a permanent connection between them. For example, with psychomotor skills,

Figure 2.2 The structure of neurons

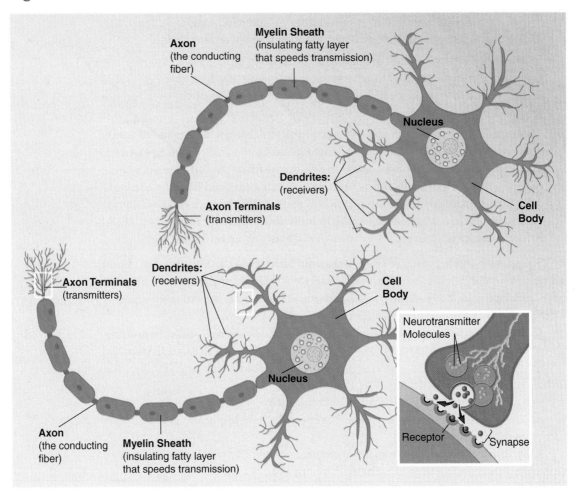

as young athletes shoot jump shots in basketball over and over, neurological connections are formed that result in a smooth and accurate shot.

APA Top 20 Principles

This discussion illustrates Principle 5: *Acquiring long-term knowledge and skill is largely dependent on practice*—from the *Top 20 Principles from Psychology for PreK–12 Teaching and Learning*.

The same applies to cognitive tasks. For instance, when students repeatedly punctuate sentences correctly in their writing, neurological connections are formed that ultimately result in them placing commas accurately—essentially without thinking about it (Dubinsky et al., 2013; Quiroga, Fried, & Koch, 2013; Schunk, 2016).

In other words, "What gets fired gets wired." If synaptic connections are fired often enough, they get permanently wired—sometimes called "hard wired"—into the structure of our brains. As a simple example, once children learn to ride a bicycle, for all intents and purposes, they will always be able to ride. And, once we learn to punctuate sentences correctly, we can—barring a debilitating condition, such as brain trauma—do so for the rest of our lives.

This permanent change in wiring is what we think of as development. For instance, young athletes' physical skills have developed when they become accurate jump shooters, and young writers' cognitive abilities have developed when they use spelling, grammar, and punctuation correctly. These changes are all the result of synaptic connections that have become hard wired into the brain.

Myelination, Synaptic Pruning, and Development

Now, let's look at this firing and wiring process in a bit more detail. For example, when we repeat an activity, such as using a comma correctly in our writing, the same circuit is fired. Every time the circuit fires, a small layer of fat is wrapped around it—similar to the plastic wrapped around the power cord wires we use in our homes—which insulates the circuit, making it work more quickly and efficiently. This process of firing and insulating a circuit is called **myelination**, and the insulating fat layer is called the *myelin sheath*. The more the activity is performed, the more the circuit is fired and myelinated, and the more efficiently the skill is carried out (Hohnen & Murphy, 2016). This again helps us understand why practice is so important.

So, what happens when a circuit is not repeatedly fired? As we would intuitively expect, the synaptic connections disappear. For example, if students get some practice with their writing, synapses are fired, but if the practice isn't sufficient, permanent connections aren't created and they don't become skilled writers.

This process of eliminating synapses that are infrequently used is called **synaptic pruning**. As we saw earlier, our brains instinctively look for patterns, and as it recognizes patterns in our environments, it physically reorganizes through myelination and synaptic pruning, keeping the synaptic connections that are frequently used, and discarding those that aren't. Neuroplasticity allows this physical reorganization, and development is the result; our brains are literally "rewired" (Hohnen & Murphy, 2016; Pace et al., 2016).

This rewiring process also debunks the maxim, "You can't teach an old dog new tricks." Our brains retain the capacity to change and grow throughout our lives (Anguera et al., 2013). It may take more time and effort as we get older, but it is possible. This helps us understand why people are encouraged to learn new skills as they age, such as learning to speak a foreign language. The process results in the formation of new neural connections and helps combat cognitive decline.

The Cerebral Cortex

The cerebral cortex is the part of the brain that rests on its top and sides, and much of human thinking occurs in this area (Hohnen & Murphy, 2016). Not surprisingly, it is proportionately much larger in humans than in other animals, comprising approximately 85% of the brain's total weight and containing the greatest number of neurons and synaptic connections (Berk, 2019b).

The left and right hemispheres of the cortex work together but specialize in different functions. The right controls the left side of our bodies and vice versa. Also, in most people the left hemisphere controls language and logical thinking, and the right deals with synthesizing information—particularly visual images—into meaningful patterns (Staub, 2016).

The Prefrontal Cortex.   As we see in Figure 2.3, the **prefrontal cortex** is a portion of the cerebral cortex that is located near the forehead. It's the area of the brain largely responsible for a range of complex human activities, such as planning, maintaining attention, reasoning, emotional control, and the inhibition of unhealthy thinking and behavior. As development occurs, the prefrontal cortex monitors and guides other parts of the brain's activities (Cartwright, 2012; Casey, Jones, & Somerville, 2011; Kurzweil, 2012).

People develop at different rates is one of the principles of development that we identified at the beginning of the chapter, and this is true for brain development as well (Berk, 2019a, 2019b). For example, the part of our brains controlling physical movement develops first, followed by vision and hearing, and ending with the development of the prefrontal cortex. The prefrontal cortex may not be fully developed until we are in our twenties, and this developmental delay is important because the prefrontal cortex is instrumental for critical thinking and assessing risks. It helps us understand why teenagers may act without thinking and consequently drive teachers up the wall. It also helps us understand why they sometimes display dangerous behaviors, such as drinking and driving, drug use, and

Figure 2.3 The prefrontal cortex

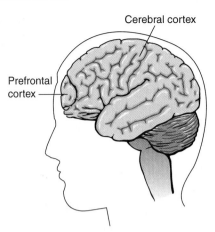

unprotected sex. While equipped with the bodies of adults, their abilities to assess risk and make sound decisions are not fully developed. This helps explain why it's against the law to sell liquor and cigarettes to minors and why firm and consistent home and school environments are so important, particularly for adolescents. Rules and limits that simplify decisions help teenagers through this sometimes confusing period.

Controversies and Myths in Neuroscience

As with most areas, controversies exist in neuroscience. And it may be somewhat unique in that a number of myths have also evolved and have even become part of accepted belief. Let's look at them.

Controversies in Neuroscience

Research in neuroscience has made an important contribution to our understanding of the nervous system, and concepts such as *neuroplasticity* suggest that our learning capabilities are much greater than was once believed. As is often the case with breakthroughs in a field, however, people get caught up in the findings, overreact, and try to use the field—in this case neuroscience—to explain more behavior than is valid. For example, based on brain-scan images, proponents have suggested that they can predict a vast range of behaviors, such as what products people will buy, which political party they'll vote for, and even whether or not they're lying. Critics contend that this is dramatic overreach and well beyond what neuroscience is capable of predicting (Brooks, 2013; Satel & Lilienfeld, 2013; Shulman, 2013).

Controversies also exist in education. For example, we saw earlier how neuroplasticity and the development of synaptic connections contribute to development. Neuroscience research combined with evidence supporting early stimulation in animals have resulted in some "brain-based" advocates recommending specialized instruction during children's early years. Early stimulus deprivation—such as never or rarely reading or talking to children—can indeed impede cognitive development, but evidence doesn't support the application of added stimulation, such as expensive toys or computers. In fact, research suggests that children who watch television or other media extensively have reduced language skills compared to peers who view less media (Lin, Cherng, Chen, Chen, & Yang, 2015; Radesky & Christaskis, 2016).

The existence of critical periods for maximum development is a second controversy. For instance, young children who grow up in bilingual homes learn to speak both languages fluently, but adults attempting to learn a new language struggle to produce sounds that are effortless for native speakers (Gluszek & Dovidio, 2010; Kuhn, 2009). Based on these findings, some advocates suggest designing curricula around these *critical periods*, such as introducing foreign languages to preschoolers.

Critics counter that our brains retain the capacity to benefit from stimulation throughout our lives, and they caution against intensive training for young children. Further, rushing early learning may harm the brain by overwhelming its neural circuits, making it less sensitive to the routine experiences it needs for a healthy start in life (Berk, 2019b).

Controversies also exist with respect to instruction. "Brain-based" instruction advocates emphasize the importance of deliberate practice and active learning strategies such as guided discovery, problem solving, and hands-on learning. Critics note that these strategies have been widely accepted for years, and describing them as "brain-based" adds nothing new to our understanding of expert instruction (Byrnes, 2007).

Neuromyths

A **neuromyth** is a ". . . misconception generated by a misunderstanding, a misreading or a misquoting of facts scientifically established (by brain research) to make a case for use of brain research in education and other contexts" (Howard-Jones, 2014, p. 817).

Two neuromyths are common and enduring. *Students learn most effectively when they receive information in their preferred learning style* is the first. "The most prevalent neuromyth in education is the idea that students have different learning styles" (Masson & Sarrasin, 2015, p. 28). No evidence exists to support the idea that attempts to adapt instruction to students' preferred learning styles increases learning.

Some people are "right brained" whereas others are "left-brained" is a second common neuromyth. We saw earlier that the left and right hemispheres of the cortex have different functions, but the two hemispheres work as an integrated whole, and efforts to teach to the left or right brain are overly simplistic and misguided (Staub, 2016). And, in spite of abundant evidence to the contrary, both of these neuromyths remain widespread and tend to be enduring (Im, Cho, Dubinsky, & Varma, 2018).

Additional neuromyths include the following (Howard-Jones, 2014; Masson & Sarrasin, 2015):

- We use only a fraction of our brains. Evidence indicates that, for the most part, we use all our mental capacity.
- Playing classical music to infants makes them smarter. No evidence exists to support this assertion.
- Adults can't grow new brain cells. Researchers once believed that this is true, but evidence now indicates that we continue to generate neurons throughout our lives.
- Male brains are biologically better suited for math and science than are female brains. Myths about girls and math and science result from cultural beliefs, not neuroscience research, and no evidence exists suggesting that the brains of boys and girls differ with respect to specific academic areas.
- Doing crossword puzzles improves memory. Doing crossword puzzles makes us better at doing crossword puzzles.

The relationship between brain function and physical exercise, and particularly cardiovascular exercise, such as running, biking, or swimming, is not a myth, however (Segalowitz, 2016). Exercise and physical fitness have a positive impact—largely as a result of increased blood flow—on cognitive skills and the way our brains work. This suggests that activities, such as recess, serve a more important function than just letting kids blow off steam. And courses such as P.E. make a contribution to more than physical fitness; they directly contribute to learning (Society of Health and Physical Educators, 2016).

Neuroscience: Implications for Teaching

So, what does neuroscience suggest to us as teachers? Perhaps the most important implication suggests that we change the way we think about students and their capabilities. For example, the concept of *neuroplasticity* suggests that our students, and particularly those viewed as less intelligent than their peers, are actually more capable than we think. And, with the right kinds of instruction and extensive practice, they can become highly functioning adults. The process of changing the hard wiring in these students may take longer, but most can eventually be successful.

A second important implication suggests that we avoid educational fads and purported "brain-based" instruction until we have credible evidence that supports their efficacy. The concept of *learning styles* is a notable example. Attempts to accommodate students, preferred learning styles is wasted effort. First, in a class of 20 or more students, accommodating each student's preferred learning style is impossible. Second, expert teachers typically present their information in visual, verbal, and—when possible—tactile forms anyway. For instance, as we saw at the beginning of the chapter, to demonstrate the properties of air Jenny used concrete examples, and, as she conducted her demonstration, she accommodated verbal learners with her questioning. She also provided hands-on experiences for her students. This is simply good teaching. To suggest that she was somehow using brain-based teaching techniques and attempting to accommodate students' learning styles adds a layer of detail that isn't necessary.

A third implication reinforces the importance of practice for learning. No substitute exists for practice, so sufficient practice, including well-designed homework, is important for learning and development. (We examine homework in detail in Chapter 13.)

Finally, encourage your students to exercise. If your school has eliminated recess, push school leaders to reinstate it. Remind your students of the importance of fitness and try to be a model by developing your own fitness. In addition to the benefits for your students, it will be an investment in your own health.

Having examined the role of neuroscience in understanding development, we turn now to specific theories of cognitive development, beginning with the work of Jean Piaget.

MyLab Education Self-Check 2.2

Piaget's Theory of Cognitive Development

2.3 Use concepts from Piaget's theory of intellectual development to explain events in classrooms and everyday living.

Jean Piaget (1896–1980) was a Swiss developmental psychologist whose research in child development began with the study of his own children's thinking. He then spent his entire professional life examining the thinking of children as they matured, acquired experiences, and attempted to make sense of the world around them. He is one of the most famous and influential psychologists in history.

As an introduction to Piaget's theory, consider the problem that follows on the next page.

The question may seem silly; the amounts are obviously the same. However, when Piaget posed this problem to young children (such as 4- and 5-year-olds), he found that they believed more water was in the taller glass. Older students, on the other hand, note that we simply poured the water into a differently shaped beaker, but the amounts remain the same.

These intriguing differences in children's thinking proved fascinating to Piaget and resulted in one of the most widely studied theories of cognitive development (Inhelder & Piaget, 1958; Piaget, 1952, 1959, 1980). We examine his theory in this section.

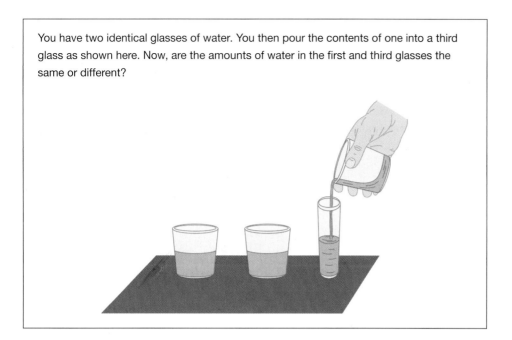

You have two identical glasses of water. You then pour the contents of one into a third glass as shown here. Now, are the amounts of water in the first and third glasses the same or different?

The Drive for Equilibrium

Ed Psych and You

Are you bothered when something doesn't make sense? Do you want, and expect, the world to be predictable? Are you more comfortable in classes where the instructor specifies the requirements, outlines the grading practices, and consistently follows through? "Yes" is the answer for most people. Why do you think this is the case?

As we go through life, we have an enormous number of experiences, and in our discussion of neuroscience we saw that our brains instinctively search for patterns in attempts to make sense of these experiences. This instinct helps answer the question we asked in *Ed Psych and You*. When our experiences make sense and our world is predictable, we arrive at a condition Piaget described as **equilibrium**, which is the state of cognitive order, understanding, and predictability. When we're able to explain a new experience using our existing understanding, we're at equilibrium. For example, if we understand that a gerund is a verb form that acts as a noun, when we see the sentence, "Running is good for you," and conclude that "running" is a gerund, we're at equilibrium. On the other hand, if we haven't had experience with gerunds, and the sentence is confusing to us, our equilibrium is disrupted and we're motivated to reestablish it. Then, when we learn about gerunds, our equilibrium is reinstated, and our understanding of language is more fully developed (Feldman, 2017). Development advances when our knowledge and skills increase as a result of equilibrium being disrupted and restored.

The need for equilibrium is very powerful, so powerful that many people "are motivated to avoid ambiguity, consider little information before reaching judgments, and are reluctant to reconsider existing judgments" (Hillebrandt & Barclay, 2017, p. 741). It also helps explain many common events in our lives. For instance, do you sit in essentially the same seat every time you come to class? Most students do. And if you're married or living with someone, do you have your side of the bed and your partner has his or her side of the bed? Again, most people do. We're all described as "creatures of habit." Following familiar habits and patterns is the result of our need for equilibrium. Teachers are urged to establish classroom routines as early as possible in the school year (Emmer & Evertson, 2017; Evertson & Emmer, 2017). Doing so helps students establish equilibrium by making their school experiences predictable.

The drive for equilibrium can be a double-edged sword, however. To see how, let's look again at Jenny's lesson.

Jenny pushes the paper towel into the bottom of the glass, immerses the glass in the water, and asks Marisa to come up to check to see if the towel is wet or dry. Marisa concludes that the towel is dry.

Jenny:	Why did the towel stay dry? . . . What do you think? . . . Jessica?
Jessica:	Because it's in the glass.
Jenny:	But why didn't the water go in the glass?
Jessica:	Because it's tipped over.
Jenny:	Anthony?
Anthony:	A water seal.

For Jessica, it made sense that the water didn't go into the glass—the towel stayed dry—because the glass was tipped over, and for Anthony, a "water seal" made sense. And, because these explanations made sense to them, they were at equilibrium. Experiences like these help us understand why people retain misconceptions (Sinatra & Pintrich, 2013) and why these misconceptions are so resistant to change (Willingham, 2009).

The drive for equilibrium is the cornerstone of Piaget's theory, and it is the foundation for the rest of his theory. We examine these components next.

The Development of Schemes

To make sense of our experiences and reach equilibrium, people construct **schemes**, mental operations and structures that represent our understanding of the world. Piaget believed that schemes are the building blocks of thinking. For instance, when we learned to drive a car, we had a series of experiences with attempting to start the engine, maneuver in traffic, and make routine driving decisions. As we (cognitively) organized these experiences, they became our "driving" scheme. As suggested by our example with the containers of water, the schemes we construct vary with age. For example, infants develop psychomotor schemes, such as grasping objects and looking for them when they disappear; school-age children develop more abstract schemes like classification and hypothetical thinking.

Piaget used the idea of schemes to refer to a narrow range of operations, such as children's conservation-of-volume scheme (the idea that the amount of liquid doesn't change when poured into a different-shaped container, as you saw in our example) (Piaget, 1952). However, some researchers (e.g., Wadsworth, 2004) find it useful to extend Piaget's idea to include content-related schemes, such as *adding-fractions-with-unlike-denominators*, *gerund*, or *properties-of-air* schemes. As with our driving scheme, each represents our developing understanding based on our experiences, and they are commonly described as *schemas* rather than *schemes*. We use this expanded, content-related-schemes view in our description of Piaget's work.

Responding to Experiences: Assimilation and Accommodation

As we have new experiences, we either interpret them with our existing schemes, if doing so makes sense to us, or we modify our schemes (change our thinking) if we're not able to make sense of the experiences with the schemes we have. For instance, suppose you've learned that adverbs are words that end in "ly," and then you see the following:

Juan and Allison were incredibly excited about going to the football game. They easily maneuvered through the parking lot at the game and quickly found their friends, Jason and Alexandria. The two couples enjoyed the game immensely.

You quickly identify *incredibly*, *easily*, *quickly*, and *immensely* as adverbs. The sentences make sense to you, and you've interpreted the new experience—the short paragraph—with your existing "adverb" scheme. This is an example of **assimilation**, the process of using existing schemes to interpret new experiences.

APA Top 20 Principles

This discussion illustrates Principle 2: *What students already know affects their learning* from the *Top 20 Principles from Psychology for PreK–12 Teaching and Learning*.

Now you have an additional experience, as we see in the following:

Juan and Allison also soon met Jamie and Carla, friends of Jason's. Jamie and Carla were both very friendly, and all three couples had a super time.

Here you see that *soon* and *very* are both adverbs, but they don't end in "ly", and *friendly* ends in "ly" but isn't an adverb. You can no longer interpret this new experience with your adverbs-are-words-that-end-in-ly scheme. You must change your thinking about adverbs, or, in other words, you must accommodate your adverb scheme. **Accommodation** is the process of changing our thinking to create new schemes or adjust existing ones when they can no longer explain new experiences.

How Experiences Advance Development

Now, let's see how experiences advance development. Because you had the experience with the second short paragraph, you now have a more complete understanding of adverbs. This understanding marks an advance in development with respect to parts of speech. If you hadn't had the experience with the second paragraph, you would have continued to think that adverbs are parts of speech that end in "ly" and your understanding of parts of speech would not have developed. This developmental process is potentially never ending. For instance, as you acquire additional experiences, you learn that, in addition to verbs, adjectives, and other adverbs, adverbs can modify noun phrases, prepositional phrases, and whole clauses, and your development with respect to parts of speech is further advanced.

Examples in schools abound. For instance, if young children are given the problem:

and they get 24 as an answer, their subtracting-whole-numbers scheme suggests that they subtract smaller numbers from larger ones. However, if they are then given this problem,

$$43$$
$$\underline{-27}$$

and they also get 24 as an answer, they have—mistakenly—assimilated the new experience into their existing scheme. Their thinking didn't change, and they still subtracted the smaller numbers from the larger ones, ignoring the positioning of the numbers. Now, suppose their teacher models and explains the process for subtracting numbers where regrouping is required, such as with the problem

$$43$$
$$\underline{-27}$$

so they get a correct answer of 16. Then, with guidance and practice they learn to solve a wider variety of problems. The problems, and their teacher's modeling, explaining, guidance, and practice, are experiences that lead to this new capability. Now they can subtract numbers both when regrouping is and is not required. This increased capability represents an advance in development with respect to subtraction.

Social Experience

To this point we've emphasized the role of direct encounters with the physical world, such as the demonstrations Jenny used with her first graders, your experience with adverbs, or the example with subtraction, as a major factor influencing development. However, social experience, the process of interacting with other people, also makes an important contribution to development (Piaget, 1952, 1959, 1970, 1980). Social experiences allow us to test our schemes against those of others. When our schemes match, we remain at equilibrium; when they don't, our equilibrium is disrupted, we are motivated to reestablish it, we adjust our thinking, and our development advances (Howe, 2009, 2010; Siegler & Lin, 2010). As an example, let's look at a conversation between two students.

Devon: (Holding a beetle between his fingers and pointing at a spider) Look at the bugs.

Gino: Yech. . . . Put that thing down. (gesturing to the spider) Besides, that's not a bug. It's a spider.

Devon: What do you mean? A bug is a bug.

Gino: Nope. Bugs . . . actually, insects . . . have six legs. See (touching the legs of the beetle). This one has eight. . . . Look (pointing to the spider).

Devon: So, . . . bugs . . . insects . . . have six legs, and spiders have eight . . . I didn't know that.

Gino: Yeah . . . so, what do you think this is (holding up a grasshopper)?

Piaget would suggest that Devon's equilibrium was disrupted as a result of the social interaction. He then reestablished it by changing his thinking—the process of accommodation—about "bugs" and "spiders," which led to an advance in his development.

Experience and Piaget's Influence on Education

Piaget's emphasis on experience has strongly influenced education in general, and preschool and kindergarten programs in particular (Berk, 2019b; Trawick-Smith, 2014). For instance, in many early childhood classrooms you'll see water and sand tables, building blocks, and other materials that provide young children with the concrete experiences they need to form new schemes. Maria Montessori, an Italian educator who stressed the importance of exploration and discovery, developed what is probably the best-known early childhood program (Feldman, 2017). In her work with children of poverty, Montessori concluded that learning environments in which children simultaneously "worked" on both academic and social activities were needed for development. It wasn't really *work*, however, because children could freely explore learning centers that provided hands-on activities and opportunities for social interaction with other students. Make-believe was encouraged with dress-up costumes and other accessories like play telephones.

Today, however, many early childhood programs, influenced by standards and accountability, emphasize early reading skills, such as knowing the letters of the alphabet, understanding basic concepts such as *left* and *right*, and math skills—counting, number recognition, and even adding to and taking away, for instance. As a result, child-centered programs have decreased in favor of those more academically oriented, and even preschool and kindergarten teachers feel increased pressure to stress teacher-directed, academic training (Berk, 2019b). Despite the influence and popularity of Piaget's emphasis on experience with the physical and social worlds, academically oriented early childhood programs are likely to grow.

Stages of Development

Stages of development—general patterns of thinking for children at different ages or with different amounts of experience—are among the most widely known elements of Piaget's theory. As you examine these stages, keep the following ideas in mind (Miller, 2017):

- Movement from one stage to another represents a qualitative change in thinking—a difference in the way children think, not the amount they know. As an analogy, a qualitative change occurs when a caterpillar metamorphoses into a butterfly, and a quantitative change occurs as the butterfly grows larger.
- Children's development is steady and gradual, and experiences in one stage form the foundation for movement to the next.
- All people pass through each stage in the same order, but at different rates, depending on their experiences and capabilities.

APA Top 20 Principles

These bulleted items illustrate Principle 3: *Students' cognitive development and learning are not limited by general stages* from the *Top 20 Principles from Psychology for PreK–12 Teaching and Learning.*

For example, students at the same age may be at different stages, and the thinking of older children may be similar to that of younger children if they lack experience in a particular area (Kuhn, Pease, & Wirkala, 2009; Siegler, 2012). To illustrate, let's look again at some of the dialogue from Jenny's lesson.

Jenny: All right, now, I'm going to take this empty glass and turn it upside down like this and push it down into the water, just push it, so the whole glass and my hand are under the water . . . Now, what is going to happen?

Terry: It's going to stay at the bottom and it won't come back up.

Samantha: Me and my dad put a glass in the pool once and put it under the water, and kept it straight and no water came in, and if you keep it straight the air will stay in there, but if you tip it, the water will come in.

Jenny: What do you think, Michelle?

Michelle: Water might go in the glass.

Samantha had experiences that Terry and Michelle lacked, so she understood that air was in the glass, and the air kept the water out. Terry and Michelle lacked these experiences so their thinking was not as advanced as Samantha's.

Piaget's stages are summarized in Table 2.2 and described in the sections that follow.

The Sensorimotor Stage (0 to 2 years)

In the sensorimotor stage, children's "thinking" is essentially limited to their senses and motor movements, such as grasping objects and putting items in their mouths. This is how they understand the world, and they don't initially represent the objects in memory; objects are literally "out of sight, out of mind" early in this stage. Later, they acquire **object permanence**, the understanding that objects exist even when out of sight. Children at this stage also develop the ability to imitate, which allows them to learn by observing others. Tremendous growth occurs at this stage, however, and it provides a foundation for the succeeding stages.

The Preoperational Stage (2 to 7 years)

The term *preoperational* derives from the idea of "operation," or mental activity. A child who identifies different animals as dogs, cats, and bears, for example, is performing a mental operation. Perception—what they can see—dominates children's thinking in this stage, and this is where most of Jenny's students are. This is typical for first graders. To illustrate this thinking, let's look again at some of the dialogue from her lesson.

Jenny has pushed the glass with the paper towel in it down into the water, and Marisa has confirmed that the towel stayed dry.

Jenny: Why did the towel stay dry? . . . What do you think? . . . Jessica?

Jessica: Because it's in the glass.

Jenny: But why didn't the water go in the glass?

Jessica: Because it's tipped over.

TABLE 2.2 Piaget's stages and characteristics

Stage	Characteristics	Example
Sensorimotor (0–2)	Goal-directed behavior	Makes jack-in-the-box pop up
	Object permanence (represents objects in memory)	Searches for object behind parent's back
Preoperational (2–7)	Rapid increase in language ability with overgeneralized language	"We goed to the store."
	Symbolic thought	Points out car window and says, "Truck!"
	Dominated by perception	Concludes that all the water in a sink came out of the faucet (the cartoon in Chapter 1)
Concrete Operational (7–11)	Operates logically with concrete materials	Concludes that two objects on a "balanced" balance have the same mass even though one is larger than the other
	Classifies and serial orders	Orders containers according to decreasing volume
Formal Operational (11–Adult)	Solves abstract and hypothetical problems	Considers outcome of WWII if the Battle of Britain had been lost
	Thinks combinatorially	Systematically determines how many different sandwiches can be made from three different kinds of meat, cheese, and bread

Jessica could see that the towel was in the glass, and she could also see that the glass was tipped over, so she concluded that these were the reasons the towel stayed dry. This emphasis on perception is typical preoperational thinking.

The students' preoperational thinking was also demonstrated in their responses to Jenny's demonstration that air exerts pressure. Let's look at some of the dialogue from the example.

Jenny demonstrates that air exerts pressure by placing a card on the glass filled with water, tips the glass over, and the students see that the card doesn't fall and dump the water into the fish bowl.

Jenny: Whoa, now what's happening? Why is it doing this? . . . Thomas?

Thomas: The water is holding it on.

Jenny: What do you think, . . . Christina?

Christina: The water looks like it might be super glue or something and won't let that card go.

Both Thomas and Christina could see that the card didn't fall off the glass, and they could also see the water, so it made sense to them that the water held the card on the glass. Again, this is typical preoperational thinking.

We've seen that perception dominates preoperational thinking, but many important cognitive changes occur in children as they pass through this stage. For example, they make enormous progress in language development, reflecting their growth in the ability to use symbols, and they also learn huge numbers of concepts. For example, a child on a car trip will point excitedly and say, "truck," "horse," and "tree," delighting in demonstrating new knowledge. These concepts are concrete, however, and children in this stage have limited notions of abstract ideas such as *democracy* and *energy*.

The influence of perceptual dominance is also seen in another prominent concept from Piaget's theory: preoperational thinkers' inability to conserve.

Conservation.   **Conservation** refers to the idea that the "amount" of some substance stays the same regardless of its shape or the number of pieces into which it is divided. For instance, at the beginning of our discussion of Piaget's theory, we saw that young children, when faced with the conservation of liquid task, concluded that the amounts of water were no longer the same when the water from one beaker was poured into a larger beaker. For these children, some water could somehow magically appear or disappear without disrupting their equilibrium. They don't "conserve" the amount of water. Older children, however, simply note that the water is poured into a different-shaped beaker, but the amounts remain the same. They "conserve" the amount of water.

A number of conservation tasks exist. The example at the beginning of our discussion of Piaget's theory is one, and two others are outlined in Figure 2.4.

In Figure 2.4 we see that preoperational children don't "conserve," that is, it makes sense to them that the amount of water, the number of coins, or the amount of clay can somehow change without adding or subtracting anything from them.

MyLab Education
Video Example 2.1
Young children's thinking is based on what they can see. Air pushing up on the card holds it on to the cup, but they can't see the air. Instead, because they can see the water, they conclude that the water is holding the card onto the cup.

MyLab Education
Video Example 2.2
Children's thinking at different ages is qualitatively different. Notice the differences in thinking between the younger student and then the older student on the conservation-of-volume task.

Figure 2.4 Conservation tasks for number and mass

Conservation Task	Initial Presentation by Observer	Change in Presentation by Observer	Typical Answer from Preoperational Thinker
Number	The observer shows the child two identical rows of objects. The child agrees that the number in each row is the same.	The observer spreads the bottom row apart while the child watches. The observer then asks the child if the two rows have the same number of objects or if there are more in one row.	The preoperational child typically responds that the row that has been spread apart has more objects. The child centers on the length, ignoring the number.
Mass	The observer shows the child two balls of clay. The child agrees that the amount of clay is the same in each. (If the child doesn't agree that they have the same amount, the observer then asks the child to move some clay from one to the other until the amount is the same.)	The observer flattens and lengthens one of the balls while the child watches. The observer then asks the child if the two have the same amount of clay or if one has more.	The preoperational child typically responds that the longer, flattened piece has more clay. The child centers on the length.

MyLab Education
Video Example 2.3

Centration, or centering, is the tendency in thinking to focus on the most concrete or salient aspect of an object or event while ignoring other features. Here a child centers on the length of the row of coins and ignores the number of coins, because the length of the row is more obvious to her than the number of coins.

Centration (Centering).   **Centration**, the tendency to cognitively—mentally—focus on the most perceptually obvious aspect of an object or event, is another important concept associated with preoperational thinking (Berk, 2019b; Piaget, 1980). Children's thinking in the conservation tasks are examples. For instance, in the conservation of liquid task, they center on the height of the water in the beaker and ignore the fact that they just saw the water being poured from the smaller to the larger beaker.

Similar thinking is demonstrated in the conservation tasks in Figure 2.4. Preoperational thinkers conclude that the longer row has more coins by centering on the length of the row and ignoring the actual number. Similarly, preoperational thinkers tend to center on the shape of the clay ball, so they conclude that the flattened piece has more clay.

Because centration is a characteristic of preoperational thought, we tend to believe that it's limited to the thinking of young children. (Here, we're guilty; we *center* on the age of the children and ignore their actual thinking.) The tendency to "center" goes well beyond the thinking of young children, however. For example, let's look again at our experience with adverbs. If we ask a sample of older students, and even some adults, what an adverb is, they commonly respond, "It's a word that ends in 'ly'." The people center on the "ly" and ignore how the word is used in the sentence.

Examples also exist in our day-to-day world. We hear about "single-issue" voters, meaning they center on one political issue and ignore all others in making their voting decisions. People also tend to make conclusions about others based on a single event, such as whether or not the person passed by them in the hall without saying hello.

Centering is easy to understand. By centering on a single aspect of an object or event, we simplify it, making it easier to remain at equilibrium, a powerful need for all of us. Reminding students that they're centering when we see examples in our classrooms will help contribute to their development and will also contribute to their ability to think critically.

Egocentrism. **Egocentrism** is the inability to see objects and events from others' perspectives (Scaffidi, Boca, & Gendolla, 2016), and it's also a characteristic of preoperational thinking. In a famous experiment, Piaget and Inhelder (1956) showed young children a three-dimensional model of several mountains and asked them to describe how the mountains would look to a doll seated on the opposite side. They described the doll's view as identical to their own. Egocentric thinkers tend to believe that everyone sees the world as they do, and they ignore the possibility that other perspectives exist.

As with centration (centering), egocentrism is considered to be a characteristic of young children, but we see a great deal of it in older students and adults (Thomas & Jacoby, 2013; Scaffidi et al., 2016). For example, laments about the "self-absorption" in our society are common, and the political polarization of our nation is cause for many people's concern. This is all related to people's inability to consider others' perspectives.

So, if you're preparing to teach older students, egocentrism is as relevant for you as it is for teachers of young children.

The Concrete Operational Stage (7 to 11 years)

The concrete operational stage, which is characterized by the ability to think logically when using concrete materials, marks another advance in children's thinking (Flavell, Miller, & Miller, 2002). For instance, when facing the conservation-of-number task, concrete operational thinkers simply say, "You just made the row longer" or "You just spread the coins apart" (so, the number must remain the same). Thinkers at this stage also overcome some of the egocentrism of preoperational thinkers. They are able to understand the perspectives of storybook characters and better understand the views of others, which makes them better able to work effectively in groups.

Classification and Seriation. **Classification**, the process of grouping objects on the basis of common characteristics, and **seriation**, the ability to order objects according to increasing or decreasing length, weight, or volume, are two logical operations that develop during the concrete operational stage. Both are essential for understanding number concepts (Piaget, 1977). For example, before age 5 children can form simple groups, such as separating black and white circles into two sets based on color. When a black square is added, however, they typically include it with the black circles, instead of forming subclasses of black circles and black squares. By age 7 they can form subclasses, but they still have problems with more complex classification systems.

When children are able to order objects according to some dimension, such as length (seriation), they understand **transitivity**, the ability to infer a relationship between two objects based on their relationship with a third. For example, suppose we have three sticks. You're shown sticks 1 and 2, and you see that 1 is longer than 2. Now, stick 1 is removed, you're shown 2 and 3, and you see that 2 is longer than 3.

You demonstrate transitivity when you conclude that 1 is longer than 3, reasoning that since 1 is longer than 2, and 2 is longer than 3, 1 must be longer than 3.

Though concrete operations mark a major advance, thinking at this stage is still limited. For instance, concrete operational thinkers interpret sayings like "Make hay while the sun shines" literally, such as concluding, "You should gather your crop before it gets dark." Let's see how this compares to formal thinkers.

The Formal Operational Stage (Age 11 to Adult)

Although concrete operational learners are capable of logical thought, their thinking is tied to the real and tangible. Formal thinkers, in contrast, can think *abstractly*, *systematically*, and *hypothetically*. For example, formal thinkers would suggest that "Make hay while the sun shines" means something abstract, such as "Seize an opportunity when it exists." The ability to think abstractly allows the meaningful study of topics such as algebra in math or allegory in literature. Formal thinkers also reason systematically and recognize the need to control variables in forming conclusions. For example, consider the following problem:

You're making sandwiches for a picnic. You have rye and whole wheat bread, turkey, ham, and beef for meat, and Swiss and cheddar cheese. How many different kinds of sandwiches can you make?

Formal thinkers attack the problem systematically, such as rye, turkey, and Swiss; rye, turkey, and cheddar; rye, ham, and Swiss; and so on. A concrete thinker attacks the problem haphazardly, forming ad hoc solutions such as rye, turkey, and Swiss; whole wheat, beef, and cheddar; and so on.

Formal operational learners can also think hypothetically. For instance, considering what our country might be like today if the British had won the Revolutionary War requires hypothetical thinking for American history students, as does considering the influence of dominant and recessive genes for biology students. When students can't think abstractly, systematically, or hypothetically, they revert to memorizing what they can, or, in frustration, give up completely.

Piaget's Stages and Research on Students' Thinking

As we've seen so far, age ranges are attached to each of Piaget's stages. Three aspects of these ages and stages are important. First, we know that cognitive development is not limited by general stages. Some students' thinking will be more advanced than would be expected for their ages. For example, as we saw in Jenny's lesson, Samantha commented:

Me and my dad put a glass in the pool once and put it under the water, and kept it straight and no water came in, and if you keep it straight the air will stay in there, but if you tip it, the water will come in.

Samantha had experiences that her classmates lacked, so she was not limited to the pre-operational thinking typically associated with her age. This doesn't mean her thinking will necessarily be beyond preoperations with respect to other topics, however. It will depend on her experiences related to the topics.

Second, because students are in middle, junior high, or high school—within the age range described as formal operational—doesn't mean that their thinking will necessarily reflect this stage. This creates a dilemma, because content areas, such as algebra and more advanced math courses, chemistry and physics, and many concepts in literature, such as *genre, symbolism, satire,* and *foreshadowing,* require formal operational thinking to be meaningful, and many students don't think at this stage. (We offer suggestions for responding to this dilemma in "Using Educational Psychology in Teaching: Suggestions for Applying Piaget's Theory with Your Students" later in our discussion.)

Third, many individuals, including adults, never reach formal operations in a number of content areas. And *centering* and *egocentrism,* though viewed as characteristics of preoperational thought, are common in older students and even adults. So, we should remember that these age ranges are only approximations, and students' thinking will vary widely depending on their background and experiences.

MyLab Education Application Exercise 2.1: Piaget's Theory of Cognitive Development in Fourth Grade

In this exercise you will be asked to use concepts from Piaget's theory to analyze the thinking of fourth-graders.

Neo-Piagetian Views of Cognitive Development

Piaget did his work many years ago, and more recent research has built on and refined his theory. For instance, **neo-Piagetian theories of development** retain Piaget's basic insights into children's construction of knowledge but, instead of describing global stages as Piaget did, these theories focus more on the ways people process information to explain movement from one stage to the next (Siegler, 2000, 2006).

To illustrate this perspective, look at the following list for 15 seconds, cover it up, and see how many items you can remember.

Apple	Bear	Cat	Grape
Hammer	Pear	Orange	Cow
Chair	Sofa	Chisel	Lamp
Saw	Table	Elephant	Pliers

Most adults organize the list into categories such as *furniture, fruit, tools,* and *animals,* and use the categories to remember specific items (Radvansky & Ashcraft, 2014). Young children tend to use less efficient strategies such as repeating the items verbatim. Their ability to gradually begin using strategies, such as forming categories, marks an advance in development.

Neo-Piagetian theory also emphasizes the important role played by *working memory,* the part of our memory system we use to consciously process information as we attempt to make sense of it. The irony of working memory is that it's arguably the most important component of our memory system, but it is also limited; it's capable of holding only small amounts of information for short periods of time (Fougnie, Cormiea, Kanabar, & Alvarez, 2016; Jack, Simcock, & Hayne, 2012). As children develop, their working memory capacity increases, and they learn to accommodate working memory's limitations, which makes their thinking more efficient (Case, 1992, 1998; Marchand, 2012). (We discuss working memory in detail in Chapter 7.)

Neo-Piagetian theorists also suggest that advances in abilities such as maintaining attention and suppressing intuition in favor of conclusions based on evidence marks an advance in development. For instance, some researchers suggest that these abilities help explain why concrete operational thinkers succeed on the conservation-of-number task that was illustrated in Figure 2.4, whereas younger children do not (Houdé et al., 2011). Neo-Piagetian theory suggests that teachers should focus on helping children acquire learning strategies and develop these advanced abilities, which will increase immediate learning and contribute to long-term development (Davidse, de Jong, Bus, Huijbregts, & Swaab, 2011).

Using Educational Psychology in Teaching: Suggestions for Applying Piaget's Theory with Your Students

Now, let's see what Piaget's theory suggests for our work with our students. The following suggestions can help us in our efforts to apply this theory.

1. Provide concrete experiences that represent abstract ideas.
2. Help students link the concrete representations to the abstract idea.
3. Use social interaction to help students refine their understanding.
4. Design learning experiences as bridges to more advanced development.

Provide Concrete Experiences That Represent Abstract Ideas.   As we saw earlier, most of Jenny's students were preoperational with respect to properties of air, so concrete examples were essential for promoting their development. We see this illustrated in Jenny's lesson. For instance, to demonstrate that air takes up space, she immersed the glass in the water and then tipped it so the students could see the air bubbles escape. This was simple, but essential. With respect to air taking up space, it was arguably the most important aspect of her lesson.

Jenny also effectively demonstrated that air exerts pressure, first with her demonstration, as we see here.

Then, she held her hand on the card so the students could see that her hand held the card on the glass, and finally she linked it to air pushing up on the card and holding it on the glass.

Jenny was working with first graders, but, as we saw earlier, students at all levels, including those in middle and high schools, colleges and universities, benefit from concrete experiences. As an example, think about the concept of *negative reinforcement*, a topic taught in courses like this one, and one with which many students like you often struggle. Negative reinforcement, which we discuss in detail in Chapter 6, is defined as an increase in behavior as the result of removing or avoiding an aversive stimulus. This is an abstract concept and often difficult to understand.

Now, look at this example.

You tend to be a bit sloppy and you leave your clothes and dirty dishes on the floor and other places around the house. Your roommate, or significant other, nags on you to be neater, so you pick up your stuff and put it where it belongs, and the nagging stops. Actually, you're doing much better, now often picking up your stuff before your significant other says anything—to prevent the nagging from occurring in the first place.

This short vignette is more concrete than the abstract definition, and it's also much more effective than the definition alone would be. The "nagging" is the aversive stimulus that is removed when you pick up your stuff, and your behavior is increasing; you've gone from not picking up your stuff to picking it up. You even pick it up sooner to avoid the nagging entirely. The vignette provides a concrete example of an abstract concept.

If you're preparing to teaching young children, such as students like Jenny's, you will certainly make every effort to illustrate your topics concretely—just as she did. But older students also need concrete examples, in some ways as much as do younger students. So, asking yourself what you can do to illustrate your topics as concretely as possible is a good foundation for your teaching—regardless of your students' age or grade level.

Link Concrete Representations to Abstract Ideas.   Jenny didn't simply provide the concrete examples; she also linked the examples to the properties of air, which are abstract, particularly for first graders. So, her students had to link the air bubbles escaping from the glass to the idea that air takes up space, so the air kept the water out of the glass. She also held her hand on the card to demonstrate that her hand was exerting the pressure that kept the card on the glass, and then guided the students to the idea that air was holding the card on the glass when the glass was inverted.

Teachers sometimes fail to help students make this connection. For instance, suppose a first-grade teacher is working with her students on the concept of place value.

For this lesson, she wants them to understand that the number 21 represents two 10's and a single one, whereas the number 12 represents one 10 and two ones. She has the students use interlocking cubes to represent the 21 and the 12 as we see here.

The actions she takes next are crucial.

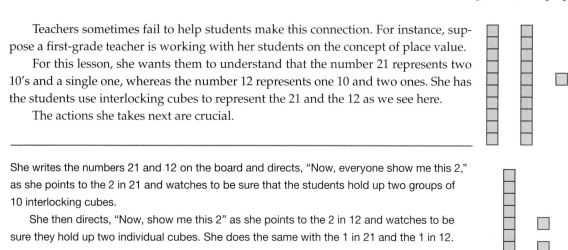

She writes the numbers 21 and 12 on the board and directs, "Now, everyone show me this 2," as she points to the 2 in 21 and watches to be sure that the students hold up two groups of 10 interlocking cubes.

She then directs, "Now, show me this 2" as she points to the 2 in 12 and watches to be sure they hold up two individual cubes. She does the same with the 1 in 21 and the 1 in 12.

If the teacher doesn't make this link explicit, young children often see the experience as two separate learning activities, one with the cubes and the other with the numbers on the board. Neither the experience with the cubes nor the numbers on the board—alone—is sufficient. It's the link between the two that's essential.

National Council on Teacher Quality (NCTQ)

The *National Council on Teacher Quality* describes using examples and linking them to abstract ideas as one of the six essential teaching strategies that all new teachers need to know. "2. Linking abstract concepts with concrete representations. Teachers should present tangible examples that illuminate overarching ideas and also explain how the examples and big ideas connect" (Pomerance, Greenberg, & Walsh, 2016, p. vi).

Use Social Interaction to Refine Understanding.   Concrete representations alone and even links between the concrete examples and the abstract ideas aren't sufficient. To advance development as fully as possible, social interaction is essential. For instance, Jenny's students focused on what was most perceptually obvious, such as Jessica concluding that water didn't go into the glass because it was tipped over and Thomas concluding that the card didn't fall off the inverted glass because the water held it on. Jessica could see that the glass was tipped over, and Thomas could see the water in the glass. In spite of Jenny's demonstrations, without her questioning, the students wouldn't have understood that air takes up space and exerts pressure.

Similarly, the teacher in the example with place value had her students describe their understanding in words, by directing, "Describe this number," as she pointed first to the 2 and then to the 1 in 21, and then guided the students to say, "This is two groups of 10, and this is one all by itself." Without this interaction both learning and development would be incomplete.

Design Learning Experiences as Bridges to More Advanced Development.   It's likely that in spite of her efforts, some of Jenny's students didn't fully understand that water was kept out of the glass because air took up space, and it's even less likely that they understood that air held the card on the glass. The idea that air exerts pressure in all directions—including up—is an abstract and counterintuitive idea that even some adults find hard to understand. However, her demonstrations and questioning provided a foundation for deeper understanding as the students move through school and have additional experiences. For instance, this will help them understand what helps balloons and car tires stay inflated, and eventually what

Classroom Connections

Promoting Cognitive Development in Classrooms Using Piaget's Theory

1. Concrete experiences are essential to cognitive development. Provide concrete examples, particularly when abstract concepts are first introduced.

   - **Elementary:** A first-grade teacher begins her unit on animals by taking her students to the zoo. She uses the visit as a foundation for subsequent lessons which she augments with pictures of the animals they saw.

   - **Middle School:** A geography teacher draws lines on a beach ball to represent latitude and longitude. He initially uses the ball so his students aren't distracted by the detail on a globe.

   - **High School:** An American government teacher involves his students in a simulated trial to provide a concrete example of the American court system.

2. Social interaction contributes to cognitive development. Use interaction to assess students' development and expose them to more advanced thinking.

   - **Elementary:** After completing a demonstration on light refraction, a fifth-grade science teacher asks students to describe their understanding of what they see. He encourages the students to ask questions of each other.

   - **Middle School:** An English teacher has her students discuss different perspectives about a character's motives in a novel they've read.

   - **High School:** A geometry teacher asks students to explain their reasoning as they demonstrate proofs at the chalkboard. She requires the students to clarify their explanations when their classmates are confused.

3. Development is advanced when learning tasks stretch the developmental capabilities of learners. Provide your students with developmentally appropriate practice in reasoning that not only matches their current level of understanding, but also encourages them to advance developmentally.

   - **Elementary:** A kindergarten teacher gives children in pairs a variety of geometric shapes, asks the students to group the shapes, and then has the pairs explain their different grouping patterns while he represents them on a flannel board.

   - **Middle School:** An algebra teacher has her students factor this polynomial expression: $m^2 + 2m + 1$. She then asks, "If no 2 appeared in the middle term, would the polynomial still be factorable?"

   - **High School:** A history class concludes that people often emigrate for economic reasons. Their teacher asks, "Consider an upper-class family in Mexico. Would they be likely to immigrate to the United States?" The class uses this and other hypothetical cases to examine the generalizations they've formed.

concepts, such as *barometric pressure* and *high-pressure* and *low-pressure* weather systems, mean.

As the students' understanding in the lesson on place value develops, they will be more nearly ready to understand what numbers such as 55, 84, 95, and eventually, numbers such as 367 and beyond, mean. These ideas apply to all the topics we teach. Further, as we provide students with experiences, they gradually become more aware of their own thinking, which also represents an advance in development and applies neo-Piagetian views of the developmental process.

MyLab Education Self-Check 2.3

Vygotsky's Sociocultural Theory of Cognitive Development

2.4 Use Vygotsky's sociocultural theory to explain how language, culture, and instructional support influence development.

Piaget viewed developing children as busy and self-motivated individuals who—on their own—form and test ideas with their experiences. An alternative view is offered

Figure 2.5 Learning and development in a cultural context

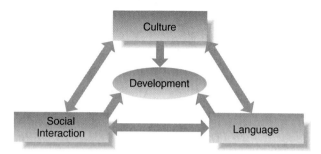

by Lev Vygotsky (1896–1934), whose **sociocultural theory of development** emphasized the role of social interaction, language, and culture on the child's developing mind (Vygotsky, 1978, 1986, 1987, 1997). These relationships are outlined in Figure 2.5 and discussed in the sections that follow.

Learning and Development in a Cultural Context

To begin our study of Vygotsky's theory, let's look at two short vignettes. As you read them, think about the impact of culture, social interaction, and language in each example.

Suzanne is reading The *Little Engine That Could* to her daughter, Perri, who sits on her lap. "I think I can, I think I can," she reads enthusiastically.

"Why do you think the little engine kept saying, 'I think I can, I think I can'?" Suzanne asks as they talk about the events in the story.

"We need to try . . . and try . . . and try," Perri finally says after Suzanne's prompting.

Sometime later, Perri is working on a school project with two of her classmates. "I don't get this," her friend Dana complains. "It's too hard."

"No, we can do this if we keep trying," Perri counters. "We just need to work harder."

Limok and his father look out and see a fresh blanket of snow on the ground. "Ahh, beautiful," his father observes. "*Iblik,* the best kind of snow for hunting, especially when it's sunny."

"What is *iblik*?" Limok wonders.

"It is the soft, new snow; no crystals," his father responds, picking up a handful and letting it sift easily through his fingers. "The seals like it. They come out and sun themselves. Then, we only need the spear. Our hunting will be good today."

Later, as Limok and his friend Osool hike across the ice, Limok sees a fresh blanket of snow covering the landscape. "Let's go back and get our spears," Limok says eagerly. "The seals will be out and easy to find today."

Social Interaction and Development

Vygotsky (1978, 1986) believed that social interaction directly promotes development, and Perri's and Limok's experiences are examples. As she and her mother talked, Perri learned about perseverance, and Limok learned about hunting as he interacted with his father. Vygotsky would say that their thinking developed as a direct result of this interaction. Also important, the exchanges were between the children and a *more knowledgeable other*, Perri's mother and Limok's father. As a result, the children developed understanding that they wouldn't have been able to acquire on their own.

Vygotsky believed that all development occurs in two steps. "Every function in the child's cultural development appears twice: first, on the social level, and later on the individual level. . . . All the higher functions originate as actual relationships between individuals" (Vygotsky, 1978, p. 57).

At the individual level, development is the result of **internalization**, the process of incorporating external, society-based ideas into individual cognitive structures, such as Perri internalizing ideas about perseverance and Limok acquiring an understanding of good hunting conditions (Barrs, 2016). As teachers, helping our students internalize the important ideas in our culture is one of our most important roles.

The ability to apply internalized cultural knowledge in a new context represents an advance in development, such as Perri applying an understanding of perseverance—a concept valued in our culture—by encouraging Dana to keep trying, and Limok recognizing the conditions for good hunting as he and Osool hiked across the ice.

Finally, Perri and Limok were active participants in the social interactions. The concept of *activity* is essential in sociocultural theory, and Vygotsky believed that children learn through active social participation with more knowledgeable people.

Language and Development

Social interaction obviously requires the use of language, and the more skilled we are with language, the more effective our interactions will be. Language also gives us access to a culture's **cognitive tools**, the concepts and symbols that allow us to think, solve problems, and function in that culture. For example, when Limok learned *iblik*, he didn't just learn the word and how to pronounce it; he also learned that it is soft, fresh, crystal-free snow that increases the likelihood of a successful hunt.

As we saw in the example with Limok, these cognitive tools vary among cultures. As another example, we Americans tend to think of *anger* as a unitary concept, but this isn't true in other cultures. For example, the Russian language has two; *serditsia* for anger directed at a person, and the more abstract *zlitsia*, such as anger about politics. German has three angers and Mandarin has five (Barrett, 2016). The Yu'pik people, who live in the Bering Sea just west of Alaska, have 99 different concepts of *ice*, ranging from wavy ice and small cakes of ice to thin ice overlapped like shingles, among many others (Block, 2007). Knowing these differences allows individuals in these cultures to travel and hunt more effectively. In each case these cognitive tools help individuals function in their environments, just as concepts such as *freedom of speech* and *free enterprise* help us function in ours.

Ed Psych and You

Have you ever said to yourself, "I know what I'm trying to say; I just don't know how to say it"? Most of us have. Why do you suppose this is so common?

The role of language relates to the question we asked in *Ed Psych and You*. The ability to put our understanding into words marks an advance in our development; it's a form of application. Language also provides a mechanism for regulating and reflecting on our own thinking. Let's look at this idea in more detail.

Private Speech and Self-Regulation. We all talk to ourselves; we grumble when we're frustrated and we talk ourselves through uncertain situations. Children also talk to themselves. During free play, for example, they mutter to no one in particular, and they talk as they attempt to complete various tasks. Vygotsky believed this free-floating speech is a precursor of internal, **private speech**, self-talk that guides individual thinking and action. Private speech becomes silent as we mature, but it remains important as the topics we study increase in complexity and sophistication. For example, it forms the foundation for cognitive skills such as remembering and problem solving

("Ahh, the problems ask for percent decrease in one case and percent increase in another, so I need to keep in mind where we started.") (Barrs, 2016).

Private speech also helps us control our emotions, which, when combined with thinking and problem solving, forms the beginning of self-regulation. Children who use private speech achieve more than their peers, enjoy learning more, and learn complex tasks more effectively than those who don't (Lidstone, Meins, & Fernyhough, 2010). The absence of private speech may also be a factor in the problems encountered by students with learning disabilities (Friend, 2018).

Zone of Proximal Development

As we saw in the examples with Perri and Limok, children benefit from interacting with more knowledgeable others. Learners, however, benefit most when working in their **zones of proximal development**, a range of tasks that an individual cannot yet do alone but can accomplish when assisted by others (Berger, 2012; Gredler, 2012). Vygotsky (1978) described it as "the distance between the actual developmental level as determined by independent problem solving and the level of potential development as determined through problem solving under adult guidance or in collaboration with more capable peers" (p. 86).

The zone of proximal development was illustrated in Jenny's class in our case study at the beginning of the chapter. For instance, her students didn't understand that air takes up space and exerts pressure, and they wouldn't have developed that understanding on their own. However, with her demonstrations and the guidance she provided with her questioning, they developed an understanding of these properties of air. Jenny's lesson was conducted within their zones of proximal development.

Learners have a zone of proximal development for each task they're expected to master, and they must be in the zone to benefit from assistance. We illustrate this process in more detail in the section "Using Educational Psychology in Teaching: Applying Vygotsky's Theory with Your Students," later in our discussion.

Scaffolding: Interactive Instructional Support

More knowledgeable others, most commonly parents and teachers, play essential roles in helping learners progress through the zone of proximal development for each task they are attempting. For example, as small children learn to walk, their parents walk behind them, holding their hands as they take their tentative steps. As children gain confidence, parents hold only one hand, and later let the children walk on their own. This support illustrates the concept of **scaffolding**, which is assistance that helps learners complete tasks they cannot accomplish independently (Pentimonti & Justice, 2010; Torrez-Guzman, 2011).

We saw scaffolding illustrated in Jenny's lesson. She immersed the glass in the fishbowl, told the students to watch carefully, and tipped the glass so some air bubbles escaped. Let's look again at some of the dialogue.

Jenny:	What do you think is happening, India?
India:	It was bubbles.
Jenny:	What were those bubbles, . . . Sammy?
Sammy:	Coming from the glass.
Jenny:	Brandon, do you know what was coming?
Brandon:	Water.

MyLab Education
Video Example 2.4

Scaffolding is assistance that helps students complete tasks they can't accomplish on their own. Notice how Jenny, the teacher, provides scaffolding with a demonstration together with questioning to help her students understand that air takes up space, an idea they were unable to comprehend without her instructional support.

Jenny: Was it water coming out?

Brandon shakes his head, "No."

Jenny: What do you think, Andrea?

Andrea: They're air bubbles.

Jenny: They're air bubbles.

Jenny then has Christina identify the water line in the glass and guides the students to conclude that air is above the water line.

Jenny was working with first graders, so, as we would expect, they required a great deal of guidance, and Jenny provided it with her demonstration and questioning. This captures the essence of scaffolding (Gredler, 2012; Rogoff, 2003).

It's important to note that effective scaffolding provides only enough support to allow learners to progress on their own. Doing tasks for them can actually delay development. As students' understanding increases, we gradually turn more and more of the responsibility for learning over to them. Let's look at another example.

Karen Patterson, an eighth-grade algebra teacher, is introducing strategies for solving simple linear equations. She writes the following equation on the board.

$$3x + 4 = 10$$

"Now, I first want to get all the unknowns on one side of the equal sign and everything else on the other," Karen says, pointing to the 3x and the 4.

"To accomplish that I'm going to subtract 4 from each side of the equal sign," and she writes the following on the board.

$$3x + 4 - 4 = 10 - 4$$
$$3x = 6$$

She then models dividing both sides by 3, so she is left with x = 2, and she continues to verbalize her thinking as she completes the solution.

She then begins placing more of the responsibility on the students.

Karen now writes the following on the board:

$$4x - 6 = 14$$

"So, what do I need to do first to begin solving this equation? . . . Denise?"

". . . Get the unknowns on one side and the numbers on the other side."

"Good, Denise. So, how will I accomplish that ? . . . Juan?"

" . . . Add 6 to both sides," Juan responds hesitantly.

"Exactly," Karen smiles. "And what do we get?"

Karen then continues guiding her students to the solution.

After guiding the students through a variety of problems, Karen continues to place more responsibility on them by having them solve more complex problems, such as the following:

$$4 + 3x = 6x - 9.$$

Finally, she places complete responsibility on them by having them solve problems on their own.

TABLE 2.3 Types of instructional scaffolding

Type of Scaffolding	Example
Modeling	An art teacher demonstrates drawing with two-point perspective before asking students to try a new drawing on their own.
Think-alouds	A physics teacher verbalizes her thinking as she solves momentum problems at the board.
Questioning	After modeling and thinking aloud, the same physics teacher "walks" students through several problems, asking them questions at critical junctures.
Adapted instructional aids	An elementary physical education teacher lowers the basket while teaching shooting techniques and then raises it as students' skills improve.
Prompts and cues	Preschoolers are taught that "the bunny goes around the hole and then jumps into it" as they learn to tie their shoelaces.
Examples	A language arts teacher displays the statements, "Stars are the windows of heaven," and "You are the light of my life" to illustrate the concept *metaphor.*

In this example, Karen first used modeling—both the procedure and her thinking—as she introduced the strategy for solving linear equations. Then, she shifted to questioning as she began to place more responsibility on the students, and finally she had them solving equations on their own.

Table 2.3 includes some common forms of scaffolding that are used in classrooms.

Diversity: Culture and Development

Piaget and Vygotsky provide very different perspectives on the role of culture in development (Bjorklund, 2012; Miller, 2017). Piaget believed that children in different cultures develop in basically the same way, and he considered his stages of development to be universal and essentially culture-free. In contrast, Vygotsky believed that culture provides the context in which development occurs; we develop by internalizing the cognitive tools embedded within specific cultures. Research supports this view (Cole & Packer, 2011; Morra, Gobbo, Marini, & Sheese, 2008; Rogoff, 2003).

The role of culture was illustrated most concretely in the example with Limok and his father. As they interacted, they used the term *iblik*, a concept unique to their culture that provided a cognitive tool they used for both thinking and communication. The same is true for all learners. Perri's development, for instance, was influenced by Suzanne's work ethic, a factor prominent in our culture. Different cultures emphasize different values and ideas, and children's development is influenced by the culture in which they are immersed.

These factors have implications for our teaching, because, as the diversity of our students continues to increase, they bring different cultures and the cognitive tools within these cultures to our classrooms. So, some may not bring the cognitive tools they need to thrive in our culture, which means we must provide those tools. We examine these ideas in more detail in the next section.

Using Educational Psychology in Teaching: Suggestions for Applying Vygotsky's Theory with Your Students

Vygotsky's theory emphasizes the role of culture, social interaction, and language in development. As with Piaget's work, it has important implications for our teaching. The following suggestions can help us apply his ideas in our classrooms.

1. Embed learning activities in culturally authentic contexts
2. Involve students in social interactions and encourage them to use language to describe their developing understanding.

3. Create learning activities that are in learners' zones of proximal development.
4. Provide instructional scaffolding to assist learning and development.

Embed Learning Activities in Culturally Authentic Contexts. To begin, let's look at the efforts of Jeff Malone, a seventh-grade math teacher, as he works with his students to help them solve problems involving fractions, decimals, and percents.

Jeff begins his math class by passing out two newspaper ads for the same computer tablet. Techworld advertises "The lowest prices in town"; Complete Computers says, "Take an additional 15% off our already low prices." Jeff then asks, "So, where would you buy your tablet?"

Technology is an integral part of our culture, so Jeff built his lesson around the cost of computer tablets, items with which most students are familiar and interested. Embedding learning activities in culturally authentic contexts doesn't have to be difficult; it merely requires a bit of creativity in linking the learning activity to some aspect of our students' culture. For instance, a teacher with several Hispanic students in his class compared the Mexican War of Independence from 1810 through 1821 to our own American revolutionary war with Great Britain and helped his students identify similarities between the two. This simple effort had a double benefit; it made the American Revolutionary War more meaningful to his students with Hispanic backgrounds, and it enriched the experience for all his students, some of whom had no idea that a Mexican war of independence even existed, or confused it with Cinco de Mayo, a widely held celebration of Mexican heritage and pride, but not Mexican independence.

Involve Students in Social Interactions, and Encourage Them to Use Language to Describe Their Developing Understanding. As we saw earlier, Vygotsky believed that social interaction and the use of language are essential for promoting development. To see how Jeff capitalizes on these factors, let's rejoin his lesson.

Jeff shows his students the advertisements, they disagree about which tablet they should buy, and Jeff asks how they might find out.

After a short discussion, the students decide they need to find the price with the 15% discount.

Jeff reviews decimals and percentages and then puts students into groups of three and gives them two problems.

A store manager has 45 video games in his inventory. Twenty-five are out of date, so he puts them on sale. What percentage of the video games is on sale?

Joseph raised gerbils to sell to the pet store. He had 12 gerbils and sold 9 to the pet store. What percentage did he sell?

As he moves around the room, he watches the progress of one group—Sandra, Javier, and Stewart. Sandra zips through the problems; Javier knows that a fraction is needed in each case, but he struggles to compute the decimal; and Stewart doesn't know how to begin.

"Let's talk about how we compute percentages in problems like this," Jeff says, kneeling in front of the group. "Sandra, explain how you did the first problem."

Sandra begins, "Okay, the problem asks what percentage of the video games are on sale. First, I thought, how can I make a fraction? . . . Then I made a decimal out of it and then a percent. . . . So here's what I did first," and she then demonstrates how she solved the problem.

"Okay, now let's try this one," Jeff says, pointing to the second problem. "The first thing," he continues, "I need to find out is what fraction he sold. Why do I need to find a fraction? . . . Javier?"

"... So we can make a decimal and then a percent."

"Good," Jeff smiles. "What fraction did he sell? ... Stewart?"

"... 9 ... 12ths."

"Excellent. Now, Javier, how might we make a decimal out of the fraction?"

"... Divide the 12 into the 9," Javier responds hesitantly.

"Good," and he watches as Javier gets .75.

Stewart also begins hesitantly, beginning to grasp the idea.

After the groups have finished the review problems, Jeff calls the class back together and has some of the other students explain their solutions. When they struggle to put their explanations into words, Jeff asks questions that guide both their thinking and their descriptions.

He then returns to his original computer tablets problem and asks them to apply their knowledge of percentages to it.

Jeff capitalized on social interaction in three ways. First, he had his students discuss where they would buy their tablets, and after they disagreed, instead of simply telling them to find the price of the tablet with the 15% discount, they—with his guidance—made the decision for themselves. This both capitalized on social interaction and also increased the students' motivation because it was their decision rather than his.

Second, Jeff had his students work in groups to solve his review problems; this provided them with opportunities to put their developing understanding into words. And third, he encouraged his students' use of language as they worked. As an example, let's look again at some of the dialogue when he worked with Sandra, Javier, and Stewart.

| Jeff: | Let's talk about how we compute percentages in problems like this. ... Sandra, explain how you did the first problem. |
| Sandra: | Okay, the problem asks what percentage of the video games are on sale. First, I thought, how can I make a fraction? ... Then I made a decimal out of it and then a percent. ... So here's what I did first (and she then demonstrates how she solved the problem). |

And let's look at a bit more dialogue later in the discussion.

Jeff:	Okay, now let's try this one. ... The first thing I need to find out is what fraction he sold. Why do I need to find a fraction? ... Javier?"
Javier:	... So we can make a decimal and then a percent.
Jeff:	Good. What fraction did he sell? ... Stewart?
Stewart:	.. 9 ... 12ths.
Jeff:	Excellent. Now, Javier, how might we make a decimal out of the fraction?
Javier:	... Divide the 12 into the 9.

In both brief sets of dialogue, we see that Jeff had all three students verbalize what they were doing. As we saw earlier, Vygotsky believed that the use of language, such as illustrated here, is essential for development. So, the more language our students use to describe their developing understanding, the deeper that understanding becomes. Initially, they will struggle to put their understanding into words, so we will need to help them. With practice, however, they will gradually become more able to articulate their understanding, and the result will be increased learning and advanced development.

Finally, after he called the groups back together, Jeff had some of the students explain their solutions, which gave them additional practice in using language and presented the rest of the class with modeling that illustrated the students' thinking.

Create Learning Activities That Are in Learners' Zones of Proximal Development.   As we saw earlier, learners can complete tasks within their zones of proximal development with support from someone more knowledgeable—most often a teacher—but they cannot complete the task on their own. To illustrate this idea, let's look again at Jeff's work with Sandra, Javier, and Stewart, each of whom was at a different developmental level. Their different zones of proximal development are illustrated in Figure 2.6.

Sandra could solve the problem without assistance, which is illustrated by the upper right component of Figure 2.6. So, to create a task in her zone of proximal development, Jeff asked her to explain her solution, which is a more advanced task.

The task was within Javier's zone of proximal development, because he was able to solve the problems with Jeff's help. This is illustrated in the middle component of Figure 2.6. But Stewart's zone was below the original task, so Jeff had to adapt his instruction to find the zone for him. Stewart didn't initially know how to attack the problem, but with assistance he found the fraction of the gerbils that had been sold to the pet store. By asking Stewart to identify the fraction, Jeff adapted his instruction to find the zone for this task. This is illustrated in the lower left component of Figure 2.6.

Jeff's instruction seems quite simple, but it is, in fact, very sophisticated. By observing and listening to his students, he assessed their current understanding and then adapted the learning activity so that it was within each student's zone of proximal development.

Provide Instructional Scaffolding to Assist Learning and Development.   As we saw earlier, scaffolding is instructional support that we provide for students that helps them accomplish tasks that are in their zones of proximal development. To illustrate this process, let's look again at dialogue from Jeff's work with Sandra, Javier, and Stewart. They were working on the second review problem, which we see again here.

Jeff's questions provided the scaffolding Javier and Stewart needed to make progress with the problem. He provided only enough support to ensure that they made progress on their own, and gradually released more of the responsibility to them.

Figure 2.6 Scaffolding tasks in three zones of proximal development

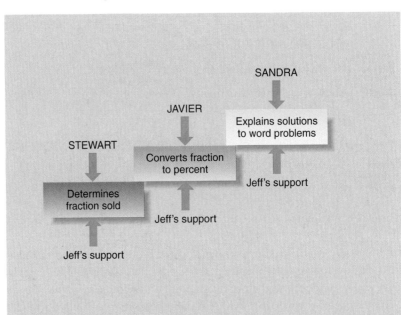

Joseph raised gerbils to sell to the pet store. He had 12 gerbils and sold 9 to the pet store. What percentage did he sell?

Jeff: The first thing . . . I need to find out is what fraction he sold. Why do I need to find a fraction? . . . Javier?

Javier: . . . So we can make a decimal and then a percent.

Jeff: Good. . . . What fraction did he sell? . . . Stewart?

Stewart: . . . 9 . . . 12ths.

Jeff: Excellent. Now, Javier, how might we make a decimal out of the fraction?"

Javier: . . . Divide the 12 into the 9.

Jeff: Good [as he watches Javier get .75. Stewart also begins hesitantly, and then begins to grasp the idea.]

Effective scaffolding adjusts instructional requirements to learners' capabilities and levels of performance, as we saw in Jeff's instruction. We also saw how Jenny adjusted her questioning to scaffold her students. Based on her students' responses, she adjusted her questioning to keep her instruction in their zones of proximal development and ensured that their understanding developed. This is what expert teachers do.

MyLab Education Application Exercise 2.2: Vygotsky's Theory in Language Arts

In this exercise you will be asked to analyze a sixth-grade language arts teacher's application of Vygotsky's theory with her students.

Classroom Connections

Promoting Cognitive Development in Classrooms Using Vygotsky's Theory

1. Cognitive development occurs within the context of meaningful, culturally embedded tasks. Use authentic tasks as organizing themes for your instruction.

- **Elementary:** A second-grade teacher teaches bar graphing by having students graph the different transportation modes that students in the class use to get to school.

- **Middle School:** A science teacher structures a unit on weather by having her students observe the temperature, barometric pressure, and relative humidity; record and graph the data; and compare the actual weather to that forecasted in the newspaper.

- **High School:** Before a national election, an American government teacher has his students poll their parents and students around the school. Students then have a class election, compare these results with their findings at the local and national levels, and discuss differences.

2. Scaffolding is instructional support that assists learners as they progress through their zones of proximal development. Provide enough scaffolding to ensure student success as they progress through each zone.

- **Elementary:** When her students are first learning to print, a kindergarten teacher initially gives them dotted outlines of letters and paper with half lines for gauging letter size. As students become more skilled, she removes these aids.

- **Middle School:** A science teacher helps her students learn to prepare lab reports by doing an experiment with the whole class and writing the report as a class activity. Students then use it as a model for writing their own reports.

- **High School:** An art teacher begins a unit on perspective by sharing his own work and displaying works from other students. As students work on their own projects, he provides individual feedback and asks the students to discuss

(continued)

how perspective contributes to each drawing. Later they can use perspective effectively on their own.

3. Vygotsky believed social interaction to be a major vehicle for cognitive development. Structure classroom tasks to encourage student interaction.

- **Elementary:** After fifth-grade students complete a writing assignment, their teacher has them share their products with each other. To assist them in the process, she provides them with focusing questions that students use to discuss their work.

- **Middle School:** An English teacher uses cooperative learning groups to discuss the novel the class is studying. The teacher asks each group to respond to a list of prepared questions. After students discuss the questions in groups, they share their perspectives with the whole class.

- **High School:** Students in a high school biology class work in groups to prepare for exams. Before each test, the teacher provides an outline of the content covered, and each group is responsible for creating one question on each major topic.

Analyzing Vygotsky's Theory of Cognitive Development

Three important elements exist in Vygotsky's theory of cognitive development. First, Vygotsky held the now widely accepted idea that learners, instead of passively receiving knowledge from others, actively construct it for themselves. However, Vygotsky believed that knowledge is first constructed in a social environment and is then internalized by individuals. Although Piaget also believed that learners construct knowledge, in contrast with Vygotsky, he viewed them as constructing it essentially on their own. Our strong emphasis on interacting with students is grounded in Vygotsky's work.

Second, Vygotsky believed that social interaction and language directly cause development (Rogoff, 2003), whereas Piaget believed that social interaction and language are primarily mechanisms for disrupting equilibrium.

Third, Vygotsky believed that development occurs when learners acquire the cognitive tools needed to function within a particular culture (Bjorklund, 2012; Miller, 2017), whereas Piaget viewed cognitive development as occurring largely outside the boundaries of a particular culture.

Perhaps most important, however, both Vygotsky and Piaget suggest that individuals are cognitively active in the process of constructing knowledge, which suggests we should limit our use of lecturing and explaining as teaching strategies and instead should actively involve students in learning activities. The similarities and differences between Piaget's and Vygotsky's theories, including contributions and criticisms of each, are outlined in Table 2.4.

> **MyLab Education** Self-Check 2.4

Language Development

2.5 Explain the relationship between language and cognitive development and what we can do to promote language development in our students.

A miracle occurs in children in their early years. Born with limited ability to communicate, 6-year-olds know between 8,000 and 14,000 words, and by the sixth grade, their vocabulary has expanded to 80,000 or more (MacWhinney, 2011; Marinellie & Kneile, 2012). More importantly, this expanding use of language makes a major contribution to their cognitive development. Let's look at this idea in more detail.

Language and Cognitive Development

Language and cognitive development are interdependent; the development of either depends on the development of the other. Vygotsky's theory supports this contention. As we saw in our study of his work, he believed that language was integral to cognitive development.

TABLE 2.4 Analyzing theories: Comparing Piaget's and Vygotsky's theories of development

	Piaget	Vygotsky
Key question	How does development occur in all cultures?	How does development occur in a particular culture?
Description of cognitive development	Advances in thinking that result from experiences that disrupt cognitive equilibrium in individuals	Advances in thinking that result from social interactions with more knowledgeable others in a cultural context
	Development is primarily an individual process.	Development is primarily a social process.
Catalysts for cognitive development	Maturation combined with experiences in the physical and social world that disrupt cognitive equilibrium	Language-rich interactions with more knowledgeable others in a social environment
Important concepts	Equilibrium Assimilation Accommodation Schemes Stages of development	Zone of proximal development Scaffolding Internalization Cognitive tools Private speech
Role of social interaction and language	Mechanisms to disrupt equilibrium, which is re-established by the individual	Direct causes of development, which first occurs in a social environment, then is internalized by individuals
Role of peers and adults in development	Promote development by providing experiences and interactions that disrupt equilibrium	Promote development by serving as more knowledgeable others who use language and social interaction to directly cause development
Contributions	• Was first to take a comprehensive look at cognitive development • Made educators aware that children's thinking is qualitatively different from adults' thinking • Helped educators understand that learning is an active process during which learners construct their own knowledge • Has had an enormous influence on school curriculum with his emphasis on the importance of experience in development	• Made educators realize that culture has a powerful influence on cognitive development • Recognized the role that adults and more knowledgeable peers play in cognitive development • Helped educators understand that learning and development are substantively social processes • Provided the theoretical foundation for many of today's approaches to classroom teaching and learning
Criticisms	• Underestimated the abilities of young children and overestimated the abilities of older students • Failed to recognize that students' thinking depends more on their background knowledge and experience than Piaget suggested • Piaget's stages don't adequately describe development for a number of tasks • Piaget's theory doesn't adequately consider the role of culture in development	• Was vague about the specific mechanisms of cognitive growth • Failed to account for the impact of individual experiences and their influence on cognitive development

SOURCES: Berk, 2013; Feldman, 2014; Piaget, 1952, 1959, 1965, 1970, 1977, 1980; Piaget & Inhelder, 1956; Vygotsky, 1978, 1986.

As an example, consider the following problem:

You see a nice T-shirt originally priced at $20, but is now marked down to $15. What is the percent decrease in the price of the shirt?

The shirt is marked down $5, and 5/20 = .25, so it is a 25% decrease.
    Now consider this problem:

You have a temporary, but well-paying job; you're making $15/hour. Because of your good work you get a $5/hour raise. What is the percent increase in your salary?

Your salary has increased $5, and 5/15 = .33, so you have received a 33% increase in salary.
    The results of the two problems don't seem to make sense. How can we go from 20 to 15 and have it be a 25% decrease, but from 15 to 20 and have it be a 33% increase? If 20 to 15 is a 25% decrease, 15 to 20 should be a 25% increase. But it isn't, and this helps us understand why many people struggle with the concepts *percent increase* and *percent decrease*.
    The key to this counterintuitive difference is "where you begin" (to which we briefly alluded in our discussion of private speech). We began with 20 in the first

problem and it was decreased to 15; we began with 15 in the second and it increased to 20.

Becoming comfortable with the concepts *percent decrease* and *percent increase* marks an advance in cognitive development, and the language, "Where you begin" is key to understanding the problems. Without this language, cognitive development would be essentially impossible, and cognitive development makes terms, such as *percent increase* and *percent decrease,* more meaningful. This is what we mean when we say cognitive and language development are interdependent.

Early Language Development

Language development begins in the cradle as adults talk to their newborn infants and encourage their gurgling and cooing (Arnon & Ramscar, 2012). And research suggests that reading to children from the beginning of life promotes language development (Pace et al., 2016).

Children's first words, usually spoken between ages 1 and 2, are **holophrases**, one- and two-word utterances that carry as much meaning for the child as complete sentences. For example, "Mama car" means "That's Momma's car." Children also gradually learn to use intonation and emphasis to convey meaning (MacWhinney, 2011). For example, "Cookie" says "That's a cookie," but "Cookie!" means "I want a cookie." These differences in intonation signal the start of using language to communicate.

Two patterns emerge and continue with the child through later stages. **Overgeneralization** occurs when a child uses a word to refer to a broader class of objects than is appropriate, such as using the word car to also refer to buses and trucks. **Undergeneralization**, which is harder to detect, occurs when a child uses a word too narrowly, such as using "kitty" for her own cat but not for cats in general (Feldman, 2017). Both are normal aspects of language development. In most instances they're corrected through routine interactions, such as a parent saying, "No, that's a truck. See, it has more wheels and a big box on it to carry things," and "Oh, look. There's another kitty."

Young children bring a healthy and confident grasp of language and how it can be used to communicate with others with them to school. The importance of this foundation for learning in general, and particularly for reading and writing, can't be overstated (Tompkins, 2017).

Language Development in the School Years

Cognitive and language development have a hand-in-glove relationship, and two aspects of language development are crucial for cognitive development: vocabulary and the development of syntax and grammar. Let's look at them.

Developing Vocabulary

Before you read this chapter, you may not have understood concepts such as *centration, object permanence,* and *zone of proximal development,* but hopefully you do now. These concepts are part of the knowledge base that helps you understand cognitive development, and the same is true for any area of study. In addition to subject-specific vocabulary, we also want our students to understand abstract concepts, such as *justice, truth,* and *beauty,* which broaden our views of the world and enrich our lives.

We can help our students acquire vocabulary in two ways. The first is explicit instruction that focuses on key sounds, labels, and concepts, and we saw explicit instruction illustrated in our discussion of adverbs earlier in the chapter. For instance, when students see the following example, they often conclude that adverbs are words that end in "ly."

Juan and Allison were incredibly excited about going to the football game. They easily maneuvered through the parking lot at the game and quickly found their friends, Jason and Alexandria. The two couples enjoyed the game immensely.

But then they are given this example.

Juan and Allison also soon met Jamie and Carla, friends of Jason's. Jamie and Carla were both very friendly, and all three couples had a super time.

The second example, combined with discussion, results in them understanding that not all adverbs end in "ly," and some words ending in "ly" are not adverbs. As a result of this explicit instruction, both their language development and their cognitive development have advanced.

Explicit instruction is valuable for learning concepts that are unlikely to be acquired incidentally, and it's particularly important for abstract, complex, and technical terms with precise definitions, such as *monocot* and *density* in science, *binomial* and *imaginary number* in math, and *mercantilism* and *genocide* in social studies, among many others in all content areas (Reutzel & Cooter, 2015). (We use explicit instruction in this text with our "Important Concepts," which identify, define, and illustrate the important concepts in each chapter.)

Ed Psych and You

Look at these sentences:

They were too close to the door to close it.

The wind was too strong to wind up the sail.

The bandage was wound around the wound.

What do these sentences suggest about language development?

Encountering words in context is a second way we acquire vocabulary, and this process relates to **semantics**, a branch of linguistics that examines the meanings of words (Mayor & Plunkett, 2010). *Ed Psych and You* provides an example. For instance, in the sentence, "They were too close to the door to close it," *close* has two different meanings, and the meanings are determined by the context of the sentence. The same is true for the other two sentences. These examples illustrate the complexity of language development and help us understand why it's so challenging for young students.

Syntax and Grammar

Vocabulary is the building block of language, but, just as a house is more than a collection of bricks, language development is more than learning isolated words. It also involves an understanding of **syntax**, the rules we use to create meaningful sentences (Haskill & Corts, 2010). For example, "I do love you." and "Do I love you?" contain identical words, but the meanings are very different because of syntax. **Grammar**, a subcategory of syntax that includes punctuation and capitalization, also aids communication. The development of syntax and grammar proceeds slowly and requires a great deal of practice (Tomasello, 2006, 2011). During the school years children gradually learn more complex language constructions, and this development parallels other aspects of cognitive development. For instance, "Jackie paid the bill" and "She had asked him out" becomes "Jackie paid the bill because she had asked him out." The ability to use more complex sentences reflects the child's developing understanding of cause-and-effect relationships.

Using Language to Learn

Language is the foundation for both learning and communication, and children typically develop the four language skills—*listening, speaking, reading,* and *writing*—in that order (MacWhinney, 2011; Otto, 2018). Regardless of the order, however, they all depend on prior knowledge and experience (Owens, 2016). When children have visited zoos, for example, listening to and reading information about lions, elephants, and giraffes is much more meaningful, as is speaking and writing about them. The same is true for all topics. Now, let's look at these language processes in more detail.

Listening.   We know that "Listening comprehension is a vital skill in all areas of academic life" (Picard & Velautham, 2016). Listening is the first language skill that develops in children, and as all teachers know, students—and especially young ones—are not good at it. They tend to think that good listening means sitting quietly, and they don't realize that it should be a cognitively active process where they think and question themselves about what they're hearing (Barrow & Markman-Pithers, 2016).

Speaking.   Speaking is a naturally occurring process in most students that complements listening and provides a vehicle for organizing thoughts and sharing them with others. As with all language skills, effective speaking depends on background knowledge, but it also requires correct pronunciation and grammar, which is challenging for all students and particularly non-native English speakers (Echevarria, Vogt, & Short, 2018a, 2018b; Peregoy & Boyle, 2017). As with any skill, our ability to speak clearly improves with practice (Otto, 2018). In many classrooms, however, teachers do most of the talking, so students don't have many opportunities to practice speaking.

Reading.   In about second or third grade, the emphasis shifts from *learning to read* to *reading to learn* (Reutzel & Cooter, 2015; Tompkins, 2017). As with listening, many students have a tendency to read passively, not realizing that they understand little of what they've read. They need help in learning to ask themselves questions, such as, "What am I trying to learn here?" and "What parts of this information are most important?"

Writing.   As all of us who have written papers can attest, writing is a cognitively demanding process, which helps us understand why it typically develops more slowly than listening, speaking, and reading (Berk, 2019b). Writing promotes language development in three ways. First, because it involves the organization or reorganization of ideas, it requires us to think carefully about a topic (be cognitively active); it's virtually impossible to write passively. Second, because writing encourages us to think about our audience, it helps develop perspective taking, the ability to consider the thoughts and feelings of the reader, an essential social skill. And third, we can't write about what we don't understand, so it requires us to learn new vocabulary and ideas. Now, before we examine strategies for helping our students develop these important skills, let's consider what impact technology is having on cognitive and language development.

Technology, Learning, and Development: Is Technology Interfering with Cognitive and Language Development?

Throughout the chapter we've emphasized the importance of experience in cognitive development. As we move farther into the 21st century, technology is providing an increasing amount of this experience, and some experts question whether it is interfering with healthy cognitive development. For example, some leaders have asked if our dependence on computers is making us less able to function in the real world (Bauerlein, 2008), and others suggest that we have become more distractible and less able to maintain our concentration as a result of the Internet and social media (Carr, 2010). "With the exception of alphabets and number systems, the Net may well be the single most powerful mind-altering technology that has ever come into general use" (Carr, 2010, p. 116). Carr (2010) argues further that the amount and accessibility of information on the Internet encourage people to examine ideas superficially, and this shallow processing is having negative effects on our cognitive development. "[W]hen we start using the Web as a substitute for personal memory, bypassing inner processes of consolidation, we risk emptying our minds of their riches" (Carr, 2010, p. 192).

Could easy access to computers actually have an adverse effect on our students' thinking and cognitive development? Some research suggests "Yes," and it raises thorny questions. For example, three studies found that the development of computer skills was the only significant educational benefit that resulted from students being supplied with home computers. Achievement in math, language arts, and writing actually declined in some instances, especially for low-income students. Instead of using the computers to access information and provide study aids, students were using them to play video games and socialize (Malamud & Popeleches, 2010; Stross, 2010; Vigdor & Ladd, 2010). International research confirms these findings (Belo, Ferreira, & Telang, 2010). In addition, research suggests that most adolescents view smartphones and other technologies not as a source of new information, but as a vehicle for socialization (Warschauer, 2011). The huge amount of information on the Internet, and students' inability to distinguish between good and bad sites and integrate information from different sources are part of the problem (Afflerbach & Cho, 2010; Manning, Lawless, Goldman, & Braasch, 2011). As educators, we need to do a better job of preparing students for productive use of the Internet.

Not all experts share this pessimistic view of technology's effects on learning and development, however. Steven Pinker (2010), a Harvard psychologist, believes that the Internet, when used wisely, can be a valuable resource for learning and development. Clive Thompson (2013), in his book *Smarter Than You Think*, contends that the Internet augments our memories instead of replacing them, and, he argues, it opens up avenues for us to communicate with and understand other people. In addition, some research suggests that viewing children's educational programming is associated with gains in early literacy and math skills as well as academic success in the elementary grades (Linebarger & Piotrowski, 2010). However, other research suggests that the more time children spend watching prime-time shows and cartoons, the less time they spend reading and interacting with others and the poorer their academic skills (Sisson, Broyles, Newton, Baker, & Chernausek, 2011). In addition, research has also found a link between extensive television viewing and aggression as well as gender stereotyping (Collins, 2011; Hofferth, 2010; Kahlenberg & Hein, 2010).

Technology supporters also point to the *Flynn effect*, named after the researcher who discovered it, which concludes that average intelligence test scores have been rising steadily since intelligence testing first began in the early 1900s (Flynn, 1999). Experts believe that exposure to stimulating environments, including technologies like television and the Internet, contribute to this upward trend (Nettelbeck & Wilson, 2010).

And much-maligned video games, which often have action and violence as their main focus, are also causing researchers to reconsider their stance. Some research suggests that video games can actually have a positive effect on vision, attention, spatial reasoning, and decision making (Denworth, 2013). And other research has found that video games can improve older players' short-term memory and long-term focus, and these brain-changing results were confirmed when researchers found increased activity in the prefrontal cortex, the part of the brain that controls attention (Anguera et al., 2013). However, experts are still cautious about the violence that permeates most video games (Denworth, 2013; Gentile, 2011).

Similar debates exist with respect to language development. For example, the ubiquitous practice of texting by young people has raised questions about its impact on people's ability to use standard language accurately and effectively. Some research suggests that the use of "techspeak" (shortcuts, such as homophones, omissions, nonessential letters, and initials to quickly text messages) hinders people's ability to switch between techspeak and the normal rules of grammar (Cingel & Sundar, 2012). Others go farther, and even the popular media have raised the question, "Is texting killing the English language?" (McWhorter, 2013). Other researchers disagree, and some argue that texting is actually improving language development (Patterson, 2011).

So, is technology interfering with cognitive and language development? You are in the best position to answer this question for yourself. You almost certainly text frequently, and you're likely on Facebook or other forms of social media, such as Twitter, Snapchat, LinkedIn, and others. What effects, if any, do you believe these practices are having on your own cognitive and language development? Only you can answer this question.

In a broader sense, and as with many questions about teaching and learning, questions about the impact of technology on development can't be answered with a simple yes or no. For example, the Internet is, without question, a phenomenal source of information; we often joke, "You can find anything on Google." On the other hand, improper use, such as by playing video games or corresponding on Facebook instead of studying, is indeed likely to detract from learning and development.

One clear message exists. Merely exposing students to technology won't produce learning and may even detract from it. Clear learning objectives and careful planning are essential if students are to derive maximum benefit from technology. And we need to work closely with parents to help them understand that technology must be used appropriately to contribute to learning and development.

Using Educational Psychology in Teaching: Suggestions for Promoting Students' Language Development

Vygotsky believed that language is essential for cognitive development, and simply, to develop language skills, students—and all of us—must practice. And, the more practice we get, the more fully developed we become. We cannot emphasize too strongly the importance of practice.

APA Top 20 Principles

This emphasis on practice is an application of Principle 5: *Acquiring long-term knowledge and skill is largely dependent on practice* from the *Top 20 Principles from Psychology for PreK–12 Teaching and Learning*.

We can provide our students with opportunities to practice in several ways.

Suggestions for Developing Vocabulary. With respect to developing vocabulary, the distinction between *labels* and *concepts* is important. For example, to us, *iblik* is essentially a meaningless label, but *iblik* to Limok is much more; the label is attached to the mental idea (concept) of soft, crystal-free snow that ensures good hunting. This suggests that vocabulary development must include the concepts—mental constructs—attached to the vocabulary (labels). Without the concepts, the labels are meaningless words. This is particularly important for our students who aren't native English speakers, because labels are less likely to be meaningful for them.

So, what do we do? First, when we encounter new vocabulary we provide examples to illustrate the concepts represented by the vocabulary (labels). For instance, suppose in a social studies discussion we encounter the terms *oligarchy* and *hegemony*, concepts that are relevant in today's political world. Without examples, our students will be in the same situation as we were with *iblik*; the terms are meaningless labels.

We can easily provide meaningful examples in this situation with simple vignettes, such as:

In the 19th century, Great Britain was largely ruled by an aristocratic class, a class of people born into families with money and status. This small group of people provided the leadership in both business and government, and they dominated the rest of British society. They were an oligarchy and they had hegemony over the lower classes of the country.

With effort and practice, we can learn to create examples, such as this one, on the spot, so it requires little extra work from us. Then, we can refer to other examples, such as the people close to Russia's president Vladimir Putin forming an oligarchy in present-day Russia, which is exerting hegemony over the vast majority of Russian people. We can even bring the examples closer to home, such as discussing the extent to which bullies have hegemony over less aggressive students.

National Council on Teacher Quality (NCTQ)

This discussion again illustrates the emphasis from the *National Council on Teacher Quality* on using examples and linking them to abstract ideas as one of the 6 essential teaching strategies that all new teachers need to know. "2. Linking abstract concepts with concrete representations. Teachers should present tangible examples that illuminate overarching ideas and also explain how the examples and big ideas connect" (Pomerance, Greenberg, & Walsh, 2016, p. vi).

As another simple example, if students encounter the term *tarmac* in a story, we can show a picture of an airport, point out the location of the tarmac, and ask students to use the term in a sentence. Using examples in this way and encouraging students to use the terms in class discussions and in their lives outside of school provide the practice that is essential for developing vocabulary (Reutzel & Cooter, 2015).

Well-written textbooks assist in the process by putting important concepts in bold print, illustrating them with concrete examples, providing definitions, and listing them at the ends of chapters. This helps learners develop the vocabulary of the content area they're studying.

At the beginning of this section we said that we first provide examples so learners have concepts attached to the vocabulary. Then, we provide students with opportunities to practice the vocabulary in writing and speaking. Let's look at how we can do this.

Suggestions for Developing Writing.   Nowhere in language development is practice more important than in writing. Literally, practice is the only way people learn to write, and this applies to all content areas (Tompkins, 2017). Because we're science or social studies teachers, for instance, doesn't imply that writing is less important. As students write, they get valuable practice using the vocabulary of science, social studies, or any other content area. And, when writing about science, history, or any other content, they also practice using correct grammar and syntax.

We can scaffold our beginning writers by preparing model paragraphs, short essays, and responses to questions, which provide examples of the kind of writing we expect. Once we've prepared these models, we can use them the next time we teach the topic, so the models require little extra work once they're initially prepared. Because classrooms now have document cameras, we can also easily display and analyze examples of student work (covering names to preserve anonymity), which provide additional examples of good (and bad) writing. Short writing assignments integrated into regular lessons also provide students with opportunities to practice.

Suggestions for Developing Speaking Abilities.   In addition to writing, speaking provides another opportunity for students to practice both vocabulary and correct syntax and grammar. And, as with all forms of language development, the more practice students have with speaking, the more fully developed their abilities become (Tomasello, 2011). So, our instruction should provide students with opportunities to practice speaking, and questioning and group work are the primary mechanisms we have for promoting that practice. When we ask questions, we should direct them to the whole class, give all students time to think about a response, and then call on an individual to respond (Good & Lavigne, 2018). When students struggle to put their thoughts into words—and they will inevitably struggle at times—we can provide scaffolding with prompting and even provide our own verbal model responses when necessary. This is particularly important in content areas such as science and math. Using language in these areas is even more important than in other content areas, because the vocabulary is often new and strange to students. Let's look at an example of the kind of support we can provide.

Sonja Weathersbee, a middle school science teacher, holds up a tennis ball for her students to see and then drops it.

"Explain the relative change in potential and kinetic energy of the ball as it drops, . . . Elaine," Sonja directs.

". . ."

"What is potential energy?"

"Energy that's stored."

"Good, . . . so where is the potential energy the greatest?

". . . At the top, where you're holding it."

"So, go ahead and describe that."

". . .The potential energy is the greatest at the top where you're holding the ball," Elaine says finally.

"Excellent. . . . Now, describe what happens to the potential energy as the ball drops, . . . Derek."

". . . The potential energy decreases as the ball drops."

"Good, Derek. . . . Now, let's discuss the kinetic energy."

Here we see that Sonja had to provide Elaine with considerable scaffolding to help her understand the potential energy of the tennis ball. But she didn't stop after she guided Elaine to correct answers to her questions; she encouraged Elaine's use of language by saying, "So, go ahead and describe that," which resulted in Elaine saying, "The potential energy is the greatest at the top where you're holding the ball."

This type of practice has three benefits. First, it gave Elaine additional experience with unfamiliar vocabulary—*potential energy*. Second, it provided her with practice in speaking, and third, using the language promoted her cognitive development. This is another illustration of Vygotsky's belief in the interdependence of cognitive development and language.

Small-group work can also provide students with opportunities to practice that may not exist in whole-group instruction, because the opportunity to talk in a group of three or four is greater than in a class of 25 or more. Group work must be carefully monitored, however, to be sure that students aren't using it as an opportunity to socialize.

As with writing, when students practice vocabulary in their speaking, they should use correct syntax and grammar. For instance, "Tanya and her" is a grammatically incorrect, but common response to the question, "Who went downtown?" When our students use incorrect grammar, we can model the correct response with statements such as, "Oh, you mean, 'Tanya and she went downtown.'" Modeling correct syntax and grammar, without criticism, is particularly important for students who aren't native English speakers.

Suggestions for Developing Reading and Listening Skills.   Once students have developed *fluency*, the ability to correctly decode and pronounce words, comprehension is the essential reading ability we're trying to develop in our students. Comprehension means that students understand the content they're reading, and background knowledge and practice will strongly influence this understanding.

We continually emphasize the importance of examples, and Sonja's simple demonstration with the transfer from potential to kinetic energy is an illustration. After the demonstration, reading about the two forms of energy will be easier and more understandable.

Examples can exist in various forms, such as demonstrations like Sonja's, short vignettes—like the one we used earlier to illustrate *oligarchy* and *hegemony*—video clips, and pictures. For instance, simply showing students pictures of different Native American dwellings, methods of hunting buffalo, and gathering other kinds of food makes listening to or reading about their culture more meaningful (Collins, 2010; Manolitsis, Georgiou, & Parrila, 2011).

In essence, this practice amounts to providing students with experiences, which both Piaget and Vygotsky emphasize in promoting cognitive development, and it again illustrates the hand-in-glove relationship between language and cognitive development.

MyLab Education Application Exercise 2.3: Language Development in Fifth Grade

In this exercise you will be asked to analyze a fifth-grade teacher's efforts to promote language development in her students.

Classroom Connections

Promoting Language Development in Classrooms

1. Language development depends on opportunities to hear and use language. Provide students with activities during which they can practice speaking, listening, and writing in your classroom.

- **Elementary:** A fourth-grade teacher says to a student who has solved a problem involving the addition of fractions with unlike denominators, "Okay, explain to us exactly what you did. Be sure to include each of the terms we've been learning in your description."

- **Middle School:** An eighth-grade history teacher, in a study of the American Revolution, says to his class, "Now, go ahead and take a few moments to put into words the parallels we've discussed between the American, French, and Russian revolutions."

- **High School:** A biology teacher, in a discussion of genetics, says, "Describe in your own words what we mean by the term hybrid. How does it relate to the terms genotype and phenotype we've been discussing?"

2. Language development requires that students practice in emotionally safe and supportive environments. Create an emotional climate in your classroom that makes students feel safe as they practice language.

- **Elementary:** When a third grader struggles to explain how he solved a problem, his teacher says, "That's okay. We all struggle to express ourselves. The more you practice, the better you'll get at it."

- **Middle School:** In response to snickers as a student struggles to describe the parallels in the American, French, and Russian revolutions, the teacher states sternly, "We listen politely when a classmate is trying to explain his or her thoughts. We're here to support each other."

- **High School:** In response to a student who says, "I kinda know what a 'hybrid' is, but I can't quite say it," the biology teacher says, "That's okay. We all struggle. Give it a try, and say as much as you can, and we'll take it from there."

3. Understanding and supportive teachers are an essential component of healthy language development. Provide scaffolding when students struggle with language.

- **Elementary:** When a fifth grader says, "I tried to find for these numbers and . . . " as he struggles to explain how he found a lowest common denominator, his teacher offers, "You attempted to find the lowest common denominator?"

- **Middle School:** As the student hesitates in his attempts to describe differences in the American, Russian, and French revolutions, the history teacher says, "First describe one thing the three revolutions had in common."

- **High School:** In response to the student's struggles, the biology teacher says, "Go ahead and tell us what a hybrid looks like and how it's different from its parents."

MyLab Education Self-Check 2.5

Developmentally Appropriate Practice

Promoting Cognitive and Language Development with Learners at Different Ages

Working with Students in Early Childhood Programs and Elementary Classrooms

Early childhood and elementary students are capable of learning a great many concepts, but they need concrete examples to advance their development. For example, using squares of candy bars to illustrate fractions, real crabs to demonstrate exoskeletons in animals, and experiences in their neighborhoods to illustrate the concept of community can all be effective.

If you're an elementary teacher, language development will be one of your most important goals. Active participation in both whole-group and small-group activities, together with writing about the topics they're learning, provide elementary students with the practice that is essential for their language development.

Sensitivity to individual differences is important when working with young children. For example, boys' language skills develop less rapidly than girls', and some cultural minorities may not be comfortable interacting with adults as conversation partners. Questioning is one of the most useful tools we have for promoting language development. It provides students with access to advanced vocabulary and modeled sentence constructions, and it also provides them with opportunities to practice their own developing language skills. When students struggle, providing prompts and modeled responses to questions are effective forms of scaffolding. Elaborating on responses also provides an opportunity to model correct grammar and syntax. Young students' working memories are still developing, which limits their ability to understand complex directions. Simplifying directions is important for these students.

Working with Students in Middle Schools

Middle school students' cognitive development varies considerably. Some will grasp abstract ideas quickly, whereas others will struggle. Middle school students' thinking remains largely concrete operational, so they still need the concrete experiences that make abstract concepts meaningful. Middle school students need a great deal of scaffolding when working in content areas that are becoming increasingly abstract, such as in pre-algebra and algebra. The more practice they get with putting their ideas into words, the more fully developed both their language development and their cognitive development will become. Frequent assessment will help you ensure that your instruction is within each student's zone of proximal development.

Social interaction becomes increasingly important for middle school students, which presents both opportunities and challenges for us when we teach. When well organized, group work can provide opportunities to expose students to different perspectives and to practice their developing language.

Middle school students' listening skills are still developing, so displaying definitions and other important ideas on the board or document camera is important. Middle school students' skills with complex sentence structures and their understanding of figurative speech and metaphorical language are also developing. Jokes based on double meanings, such as "Hey, did you take a bath today? . . . Why, are you missing one?" provide opportunities to talk about language and its central role in communication (Berk, 2019a).

Working with Students in High Schools

Though high school students are chronologically at the stage of formal operations, the ability to think in the abstract depends on their prior knowledge and experiences. When new concepts are introduced, high school students still need concrete examples. Questioning and class discussions provide students with opportunities to practice language, which makes them more effective teaching strategies than lectures.

The social dimension of learning assumes a powerful role for high school students; how they look and what other people think of them is important. Because high school students like to socialize, periodic small-group work can be effective if it is carefully monitored to prevent it from becoming merely a social experience.

High school students want to appear grown up and are sometimes hesitant to participate in whole-class activities, so explaining why you call on everyone as equally as possible to encourage participation is important. They often want to hide the fact that they don't understand an idea, so they are sometimes reluctant to ask questions. So, the fact that no questions are asked doesn't necessarily mean that students understand what you're teaching. Questioning, particularly as a form of informal assessment, is important with these students, and their ability to answer will give you an indication of their developing understanding.

Providing high school students with practice in writing is important, regardless of your content area. Because of texting and social media, providing high school students with opportunities to practice correctly using grammar, spelling, and punctuation in their writing is even more important than it has been in the past (Pence, Turnbull, & Justice, 2012). As with all of us, the more students write, the more skilled they become, so the more practice, the better.

Chapter 2 Summary

1. Describe development and explain how Bronfenbrenner's theory contributes to our understanding of development.
   - Development describes the physical, cognitive, social, and emotional changes that occur in people as they grow from infancy to adulthood.
   - Principles of development suggest that development depends on both heredity and environment, that it is continuous and relatively orderly, and that learners develop at different rates.
   - Bronfenbrenner's theory of development describes how different aspects of the environment interact with each other and genetics to influence development.

2. Explain how neuroscience helps us understand development.
   - Neuroscience is the scientific study of the nervous system, which includes the brain, spinal cord, sensory organs, and the nerves that connect these organs to the rest of the body.
   - The brain is the most prominent component of the nervous system, and it is the primary subject of neuroscience research.
   - The concept of neuroplasticity reminds us that the brain can physically change in response to new experiences.
   - When we have experiences, messages are sent through electrical impulses from one neuron to another. Repeated experiences can result in a permanent relationship between neurons, literally rewiring the brain. This helps us understand why experience and deliberate practice are so important.
   - A number of controversies and myths have evolved with respect to neuroscience, two of the most common being the importance of learning styles, and the concept of left and right brain dominance.

3. Use concepts from Piaget's theory of intellectual development to explain events in classrooms and everyday living.
   - Concepts from Piaget's theory help explain why people want order and certainty in their lives, and how they adapt their thinking in response to new experiences.
   - According to Piaget, people organize their experiences into schemes that help them make sense of their experiences and achieve equilibrium.

- New experiences are assimilated if they can be explained with existing schemes. Accommodation and a change in thinking are required if new experiences can't be explained with existing schemes.
- Maturation and experiences with the physical and social world advance development.
- As children develop, they progress through stages that describe general patterns of thinking, ranging from perceptual dominance in preoperational thinkers to the ability to think logically and hypothetically for formal operational thinkers.
- Learners are not bound by the general stages; some will demonstrate thinking beyond what would be predicted by their ages, whereas others' thinking will more nearly reflect less advanced stages.

4. Use Vygotsky's sociocultural theory to explain how language, culture, and instructional support influence development.
   - Vygotsky describes cognitive development as the interaction between social interaction, language, and culture.
   - Social interaction and language provide the mechanisms and tools that help children develop understandings that they wouldn't be able to acquire on their own to advance their development.
   - Social interaction and language are embedded in a cultural context that uses the language of the culture as the mechanism for promoting development.

5. Explain the relationship between language and cognitive development and what we can do to promote language development in our students.
   - Children progress from an early foundation of one- and two-word utterances to elaborate language that involves complex sentence structures.
   - Language development during the school years focuses on word meanings (semantics), grammar (syntactics), and using language to learn through listening, reading, and writing.
   - We can promote language development in students by providing them with the experiences and opportunities to practice language that are integral to all forms of development.

Preparing for Your Licensure Exam

Understanding Cognitive and Language Development

You will be required to take a licensure exam before you go into your own classroom. This exam will include information related to cognitive and language development, and the following exercises are similar to those that appear on licensure exams. They are designed to help you practice for the exam in your state. This book and these exercises will be a resource for you later in your program as you prepare for the exam.

In the following case study, Karen Johnson, an eighth-grade science teacher, is attempting to help her students understand basic concepts in science, such as *mass, volume,* and *density.*

"My students are struggling," she laments to a colleague. "These concepts are important in our everyday world. For example, we hear about *dense fog, massive changes, high-volume business,* and so on. . . . But to my kids, mass and density are the same. And if it's bigger, it has more mass and is more dense. . . . I need to do something."

Karen thinks about the issue, and decides to do something different, even if it seems a bit elementary.

So, on Monday, she begins her class by displaying a cup full of cotton balls, as we see here.

She asks the students for observations of the cup and cotton balls, leading them to the idea that *volume* is the amount of space taken up, so the volume of the cotton is the amount of space it takes up in the cup. She continues by leading the students to the idea that mass means the amount of material there is in a substance, such as the amount of cotton.

Karen then compresses the cotton balls, pushing them down into the cup.

"So, is the mass the same as or different from it was before we compressed the cotton? . . . Janine?"

". . . It's the same," she responds hesitantly.

"How do we know?" . . . Zach?"

With some prompting from Karen, Zach concludes, ". . . The total amount of cotton is the same. We haven't taken any cotton balls out or put any in."

"What about the volume? . . . Jacinta?"

"It's less. . . . It's taking up less space," Jacinta says quickly, warming to the task.

"Very good. . . . We now have the same amount of mass in less space, so the cotton is *more dense,*" Karen explains.

Karen then provides some additional examples, such as putting equal volumes of water and vegetable oil on balances. Before doing so, she asks the students to predict which side of the balance will go down. Most predict the oil side will go down, reasoning that it is "thicker" than water.

To the students' surprise, the side with the water goes down, which means it's more dense than the oil.

"Hey, I get it," Ethan nearly shouts. "That's why oil floats on water. It's less dense."

The class then discusses other examples, such as population density, and screens on a window with a tight versus a loose wire mesh.

Karen then asks them what *dense cloud cover* would mean, they discuss the question, and seeing that the period is nearly over, Karen brings the lesson to closure.

Questions for Case Analysis

In answering these questions, use information from the chapter, and link your responses to specific information in the case.

Multiple-Choice Questions

1. Most of Karen's students concluded that the oil side of the balance would go down because the oil was thicker. Of the following, which concept from Piaget's work best explains the students' thinking in this example?

   a. Egocentrism

   b. Centration

   c. Scaffolding

   d. Zone of proximal development

2. Karen's students were eighth-graders. Based on the information in the case study, at which of Piaget's stages of cognitive development were they most likely to be?

   a. Sensor-motor

   b. Preoperational

   c. Concrete operational

   d. Formal operational

Constructed-Response Question

1. Did Karen conduct the lesson in her students' zones of proximal development? Explain why you do or do not think so. What forms of scaffolding did Karen provide? How effective was the scaffolding?

MyLab Education Licensure Exam 2.1

Important Concepts

accommodation
assimilation
axons
centration
classification
cognitive development
cognitive tools
conservation
dendrites
development
egocentrism
equilibrium
exosystem

grammar
holophrases
internalization
macrosystem
maturation
mesosystem
microsystem
myelination
neo-Piagetian theories of
    development
neuromyth
neurons
neuroplasticity

neuroscience
object permanence
overgeneralization
personal, social, and emo-
    tional development
physical development
prefrontal cortex
private speech
scaffolding
schemes
semantics
seriation
social experience

sociocultural theory of
    development
stages of development
synapses
synaptic pruning
syntax
transitivity
undergeneralization
zone of proximal
    development

Chapter 3
Personal, Social-Emotional, and Moral Development

Monkey Business Images/Shutterstock

Learning Outcomes

After you have completed your study of this chapter, you should be able to:

3.1 Describe personality development and explain how it can influence academic success and success in life after the school years.

3.2 Use descriptions of identity development to explain learner behavior.

3.3 Use an understanding of social-emotional development to explain behaviors of students and people beyond the school years.

3.4 Use theories of moral development to explain differences in people's responses to ethical issues.

APA Top 20 Principles

Top 20 Principles from Psychology for PreK–12 Teaching and Learning explicitly addressed in this chapter.

Principle 5: Acquiring long-term knowledge and skill is largely dependent on practice.

Principle 14: Interpersonal relationships and communication are critical to both the teaching–learning process and the social–emotional development of students.

Principle 15: Emotional well-being influences educational performance, learning, and development.

> "Be the change that you wish to see in the world."
>
> — MOHANDAS (MAHATMA) GANDHI

The quote above is particularly relevant to our study of this chapter. We'll see how as the chapter unfolds, so please bear with us.

Let's begin. When we teach, we obviously want our students to acquire knowledge and skills, such as the causes of the Civil War and the ability to solve word problems, but we also want them to learn to manage their emotions, interact effectively with others, and develop a sense of honesty and fair play. These goals are addressed in the study of personal, social-emotional, and moral development, the content of this chapter.

We start with a brief discussion between two middle school teachers as they describe efforts to help one of their students.

"Ahh," Amanda Kellinger, an eighth-grade English teacher, sighs as she slides into a chair in the faculty lounge a half hour after school.

"Tough day?" her friend Bill asks.

"Tough, but rewarding," Amanda answers with a smile. "I've been working with Sean, and he's a challenge. But we're making progress."

"What do you mean?"

"Well, he has a history of jumping on other students for no apparent reason, says they're 'out to get him.' So, I've tried to take him under my wing. Every day after school, he comes in and we talk about what he worked on that day. For instance, he's been practicing being more positive and avoiding lashing out at other students, and today one even complimented him for being so cooperative in group work. He was beaming when he came in."

"Yes, I know Sean," Bill responds. "I had him last year, and when I talked to his mother, she said he's been a handful since birth. And . . . it affected his academic work."

"That's why I'm working with him." Amanda nods. "Life is tough if you can't get along with other people. But kids can practice and improve in these areas, just like they practice academics. That's what we're here for. As I said, demanding but rewarding."

We'll return to this conversation as you study this chapter, but for now, think about Amanda's work with Sean. With her support, he is working on developing the kinds of personal characteristics that will help him function effectively both in school and later life. We focus on these abilities as we examine:

- *Personality development*, changes in our attitudes, emotions, and behaviors in responses to events that occur over time.
- The development of *identity*, growth in our sense of self, including a cognitive assessment of our competence in different areas.
- *Social-emotional development*, the ability to appreciate the perspectives of others, handle interpersonal situations constructively, and manage our emotions.
- *Moral development*, advances in our conceptions of right and wrong and prosocial traits such as honesty and respect for others.

We begin with personality development.

Personality Development

3.1 Describe personality development and explain how it can influence academic success and success in life after the school years.

Ed Psych and You

Have your friends ever set you up with a blind date? If they have, they likely said your date has a "great personality." What does this mean?

Personality is a comprehensive term that describes our attitudinal, emotional, and behavioral responses to experiences in our environment, and *personality development* involves positive changes in those responses. Personality also has a *cognitive* component, meaning that our thinking can influence our attitudes, emotions, and behaviors (Griffin, Guillette, & Healy, 2015). For example, if we realize that we tend to over-react to trivial and unimportant challenges, we can consciously take steps to modify both our attitudes and our behaviors. Amanda, in her work with Sean, is focusing on this cognitive aspect of personality development.

Researchers generally describe personality as composed of five relatively independent traits, often described as the "Big Five" (Barford & Smillie, 2016; van Geel, Goemans, Toprak, & Vedder, 2017):

- *Extraversion*—talkative, assertive, gregarious
- *Agreeableness*—good-natured, tolerant, compassionate

- *Openness*—imaginative, curious, experience seeking
- *Conscientiousness*—thorough, organized, dependable
- *Neuroticism*—emotionally unstable, anxious, insecure

These characteristics help answer the question about "great personality" that we asked in *Ed Psych and You*. In describing your date this way, they were likely suggesting that he or she was extraverted, agreeable, open, and emotionally stable.

Virtually all of us believe that we possess positive personality traits, but it appears that Sean, in the introduction to the chapter, has some issues with respect to them. For example, he appears to be low in agreeableness and openness. He also appears vulnerable to negative emotions, which are unlikely to serve him well in either school or later life if they remain unchanged. This is why Amanda has taken him under her wing.

So, how do we acquire personality traits? Genetics and the environment both play an important role. We begin with the influence of genetics.

Temperament

Temperament describes our inclinations to respond to events in our environment in particular ways. It's largely determined by genetics, and it influences both personality development and the ways children respond to parenting and our actions as teachers (Slagt, Dubas, Deković, & van Aken, 2016). For example, children with irritable and anger-prone temperaments are often low in openness and agreeableness, which can cause negative reactions from others, making it hard to form friendships. Difficult temperaments are also associated with behavioral problems at school and adjustment problems after the school years (Blatný, Millová, Jelínek, & Osecká, 2015).

The influence of temperament follows us throughout our lives. For instance, potential employers consider temperament in hiring decisions, and the temperaments of candidates for public office are carefully scrutinized in campaigns and voters' decision making.

Our temperaments provide the raw materials for personality development, but our environments also play an important role. "A common metaphor for thinking about personality development has been that young children display genetically influenced temperament traits and that life experiences 'layer' personality traits onto the early biological temperament" (Shiner et al., 2012, p. 440). We examine these environmental influences next.

Environmental Influences on Personality Development

Many different environmental factors can influence personality development. Traumatic events, such as the death of a parent, a crippling disease, economic disaster, or divorce, and school factors, such as making new friends, being bullied, and, more positively, the efforts of caring teachers, such as Amanda's work with Sean, can all influence students' developing personalities (Peterson et al., 2014; Schunk, Meece, & Pintrich, 2014).

Parenting is the strongest environmental influence on personality, and a great deal of research has examined different parenting styles. (We saw parental influence illustrated in our discussion of Bronfenbrenner's work in Chapter 2.) We examine this research next.

Parenting and Personality Development

Parents influence personality development in three important ways. First, good parents provide a safe and secure environment that promotes a personal sense of well-being (Berk, 2019a), and second, they give their children their time. We all have 24 hours a day—no more, no less. So, the way we choose to allocate our time is the best measure of caring that exists. Children realize this subconsciously when they're very young, but

Ed Psych and You

What kinds of expectations for your achievement and behavior did your parents have for you? How "strict" were they? How involved were they in your school activities?

with increasing awareness as they mature, and young people strongly react to parents who take the time to talk to them about anything and everything, attend their soccer games when they're 5 years old, their school events throughout the school years, and any other activities in which they're involved. No substitute for this gift of time exists (Dermotte & Pomati, 2016; Ribar, 2015).

Third, effective parents model desirable personality traits, which provide concrete examples the children can emulate (Thompson & Newton, 2010). (This is a first link to our quote from Gandhi at the beginning of the chapter.)

Research suggests that certain **parenting styles**, general patterns of interacting with and disciplining children, positively influence students' development to a greater degree than do others (Baumrind, 2005; Baumrind, Larzelere, & Owens, 2010; Linder Gunnoe, 2013). The most commonly described parenting styles and the general patterns of personality development associated with them include the following (Cipriano & Stifter, 2010; Thompson & Newton, 2010):

- *Authoritative parents* are firm and set high expectations, but at the same time are caring, supportive, responsive, and consistent. They give freely of their time by attending their children's activities, talk to their children, and provide rationales for rules and other behavioral boundaries. Their children tend to acquire desirable personality traits, such as agreeableness, openness, and conscientiousness. As we would predict, their children tend to do well in school, both academically and personally. For example, adolescents with authoritative parents tend to be less aggressive and less likely to be pressured by peers to use alcohol and other drugs (Luyckx, Tildesley, Soenens, & Andrews, 2011).

- *Authoritarian parents* have high expectations but tend to be cold and unresponsive. They expect conformity, they don't explain reasons for rules and restrictions, and they don't encourage verbal give and take. Their children are more likely to become introverted, disagreeable, and may acquire some aspects of neuroticism.

- *Permissive parents* are warm but hold few expectations for their children, who tend to be immature, compulsive, and unmotivated. Used to getting their own way, they may lack conscientiousnees and become disagreeable, which can detract from their success and lead to trouble relating to peers.

- *Uninvolved parents* have few expectations for their children and are unresponsive. Their children tend to be disagreeable, closed, shortsighted, and less able to face life's challenges. Students who characterize their parents as uninvolved are more likely to party, use drugs, and reject adult values (Huesmann, Dubow, & Boxer, 2011).

These parenting styles help answer the questions we asked in *Ed Psych and You* in this section. If your parents had high expectations, established boundaries for your acceptable behavior, talked to you, and were involved in your school activities, they appeared to be authoritative. And, as we saw above, authoritative parenting tends to promote positive personality traits.

On the other hand, we're not suggesting that if your parents were authoritarian, permissive, or uninvolved, you're doomed to a life of incomplete personality development. Though these parenting styles describe general patterns, exceptions exist, and your personal resilience is a powerful factor.

We discuss these parenting styles for two reasons. First, understanding them might result in you becoming a more authoritative parent. And second, a strong parallel exists between authoritative parenting and authoritative classroom management styles of expert teachers (Emmer & Evertson, 2017; Evertson & Emmer, 2017). We examine classroom management in detail in Chapter 12.

Diversity: Cultural Differences in Parenting Styles

The original research on parenting styles was done with European–American, middle-class families. With an authoritative parenting style viewed as desirable, families in the United States and Western Europe tend to encourage independence, competition, and freedom of expression (Chen & Eisenberg, 2012; Spicer et al., 2012). However, many families with Asian, African, Middle Eastern, Native American, and Hispanic backgrounds believe in a more collectivist orientation, valuing obedience, deference to authority figures (especially parents), and the importance of family (Leavell, Tamis-LeMonda, Ruble, Zosuls, & Cabrera, 2012). In these cultures, parents combine high demands for obedience with close, supportive parent–child relationships. They also tend to treat female children more protectively and are less likely to grant autonomy to their daughters (Spicer et al., 2012).

Because of a pattern of high academic achievement in their children, a great deal of research has focused on Asian American families. As a general pattern, these families teach children that obedience is good and devotion to family is more important than individual desires (Calzada, Huang, Anicama, Fernandez, & Brotman, 2012; Chen, Chen, & Zheng, 2012). However, it doesn't suggest that Asian American parents, in general, are strict and harsh with their children (Choi, Kim, Kim, & Park, 2013; Kim, Wang, Orozco-Lapray, Shen, & Murtuza, 2013). And, where authoritarian parenting exists, their children demonstrate higher levels of behavioral problems (Lee et al., 2013).

What patterns exist in this body of research? First, it suggests that the stereotype of Asian American parents being strict, harsh, and cold isn't valid. Research suggests that effective Asian parents have high expectations for academic achievement, but it also indicates strong parental warmth and emotional support (Lee et al., 2013; Wang, 2017).

Similar patterns have been found in other cultures. For instance, in a study of Pakistani parenting practices, researchers found that authoritative parenting was positively associated with emotional regulation in adolescents, whereas permissive parenting had the opposite effect (Jabeen, Anis-ul-Haque, & Riaz, 2013).

These results have implications for parents from all cultural backgrounds. High expectations for children are positive, but they also need the parental involvement, warmth, and emotional support that it takes to meet those expectations. The results make perfect sense. A long history of research suggests that children will rise to meet expectations, but they need the support necessary to do so (Berk, 2019a). Meeting these expectations will result in the increased sense of self-worth valued in Western cultures.

MyLab Education Application Exercise 3.1: Parenting Styles and Personality Development
In this exercise, you will be asked to analyze different examples of parenting styles.

Child Abuse

Denise, one of your students, has been a bright, outgoing, and high-achieving girl historically, but she has abruptly changed. She has become withdrawn, and she looks down and doesn't respond when you call on her. And, although she has typically been well groomed, she is now coming to school looking disheveled. Then you see a welt on her face, and your concern turns to alarm. You go to your assistant principal and report what you've observed.

When we think of parenting, we imagine loving, supportive parents who are involved with their children. Unfortunately, this isn't always true, and while statistically rare, cases such as Denise's do occur. Her changes in behavior, academic performance, appearance, and particularly the welt on her face suggest the possibility of **child abuse**, which, at the federal level, is defined as an act or failure to act by a parent or other caregiver, "which results in death, serious physical or emotional harm, sexual abuse, or exploitation, or an act or failure to act which presents an imminent risk of serious harm" (Child Welfare Information Gateway, 2016, para. 2). *Caregivers* include a variety of people, such as club or organization leaders, coaches, and even teachers. Child abuse includes all forms of physical, sexual, and psychological abuse or neglect, and it can occur in a child's home or in the organizations, schools, or communities with which the child interacts. It goes without saying that abuse has a powerful negative effect on all forms of development, and particularly the development of a healthy personality.

Awareness of child abuse has increased in recent years, likely the result of publicity surrounding high-profile cases of abuse, such as the scandal involving Jerry Sandusky, an assistant football coach at Penn State University who was convicted of 45 counts of sexual abuse in 2012 (Kaplan & Johnson, 2012), and in 2017 his son was arrested on similar charges (Coppinger, 2017). In spite of increased publicity, however, abuse and neglect often remain hidden or unreported, so reliable figures are hard to obtain. However, based on available evidence, some grim statistics exist. For example (American Society for the Positive Care of Children, 2016):

- Over the past 10 years more than 20,000 children have been killed in their own homes by a family member, nearly four times the number of soldiers killed in the wars in Iraq and Afghanistan combined.
- Teens who have been abused are more likely to engage in risky sexual behavior.
- Nearly a third of parents who have been abused will abuse their own children, continuing a heinous cycle.
- Nearly four of five 21-year-olds who were abused as children meet criteria for at least one psychological disorder.
- Nearly 2 of 3 people in treatment for drug abuse reported being abused or neglected as children.
- When sexual abuse occurs, it most commonly involves a family member, relative, or friend.

The probability that you will have abused or neglected children in your classes is low, although it is more likely if you teach in a high poverty area. Child abuse can occur at any level of society, but it tends to be associated with poverty and is often linked to parental substance abuse (American Society for the Positive Care of Children, 2016).

Because you work with children five days a week you are uniquely positioned to identify cases of abuse, and you did precisely what you should have in the example with Denise. Teachers in all 50 states are required by law to report suspected child abuse, and you and your school are protected from civil or criminal liability if the report is made honestly and is documented, such as with descriptions of the welts on Denise's face (Schimmel, Stellman, Conlon, & Fischer, 2015). As teachers, we all need to be aware of the possibility of child abuse—however rare—because it can literally save a life. And perhaps we can make a contribution that will help reduce, in some small way, the negative effects of this abuse on students' development.

Personality and Achievement in School and the Workplace

So what does personality development have to do with academic achievement in schools and workplace success after the school years? A considerable amount of research has examined this question.

First, with respect to schools and learning, a strong link exists between academic achievement and conscientiousness and openness, particularly in adolescents. These results make sense. We would predict, for example, that conscientious students who are open to new ideas would be high achievers. They persist until their learning goals are met, and they respect and appreciate learning and new knowledge (Neuenschwander, Cimeli, Röthlisberger, & Roebers, 2013; Zuffianò et al., 2013).

Personality and workplace achievement have also been thoroughly examined. The relationship between agreeableness, conscientiousness, low neuroticism, and high job performance is one of the best known findings (Avery, Smillie, & Fife-Schaw, 2015; Sackett & Walmsley, 2014). These traits are also linked to workplace motivation and satisfaction (Woods, Lievens, Fruyt, & Willie, 2013). As we might also expect, workers high in extraversion have higher levels of job satisfaction when employed in positions that require social interaction, such as sales (Saksvik & Hetland, 2011).

Using Educational Psychology in Teaching: Suggestions for Supporting Your Students' Personality Development

Two aspects of personality development have important implications for us as teachers. First, we know that the environment strongly influences personality development, and second, school is an important part of that environment. Researchers believe that schooling is a primary influence on the development of positive personality traits, such as agreeableness, openness, and conscientiousness (Bleidorn, 2012; Woods et al., 2013), and research indicates that in many cases conscientiousness can have a stronger influence on success in both school and work performance than cognitive ability (Zyphur, Chaturvedi, & Arvey, 2008).

This research reminds us that our jobs involve much more than teaching math, history, and other content. They also include helping our students develop the positive personality traits associated with both school achievement and success in later life.

The following suggestions can help us meet these goals:

- Learn about our students as people.
- Model positive personality traits.
- Use concrete examples and discussions to teach positive personality traits.
- Use an authoritative classroom management style.

As we discuss these guidelines, we will focus on personality's cognitive component, because awareness and understanding are essential for all forms of development. We turn to the guidelines now.

Learn About Our Students as People.   Our students are unique, and, in order to best promote their development, we need to know about their individual personalities. We can make formal efforts to learn about our students with simple activities such as having them to fill out a short questionnaire that asks about their favorite foods, hobbies, sports, and other aspects of their lives. Doing so takes little effort, merely asking the questions communicates that we're interested in them as human beings, and the process promotes a positive teacher-student relationship. "There is a growing consensus that the nature and quality of children's relationships with their teachers play a critical and central role in . . . teaching them what they need to know to become knowledgeable and productive citizens" (Wentzel, 2010, p. 75). Also, as we interact with our students, we learn a great deal about who is extraverted, agreeable, open, or shy, and we can adapt our instruction accordingly, again without a great deal of extra effort. For instance, during learning activities we can adjust our questions, so students low in extraversion are assured of being able to answer, and, with time, they may overcome some of their shyness. Let's look at an example. Suppose you're an elementary teacher working with your students in math, and you've presented the following problem:

Jeremy has been working on his tablet for 20 minutes, and Cindy has been on hers for 35 minutes. How much longer has Cindy worked than has Jeremy?

You can then call on a student who is reluctant to speak out in class with the directive: "Tell us something about this problem." The student can then offer a variety of answers, such as:

- The students are working on tablet computers.
- It's about a boy and a girl.
- The boy worked on his tablet for 20 minutes. The girl worked on hers longer than the boy.
- The problem asks us to find out how much longer the girl worked.

When students get used to this process (i.e., instead of asking for a specific response, which is typical in classroom activities, you truly are simply asking them to tell you something about the problem), they often become much more willing to respond. Our ability to adapt our instruction in this way is called **goodness of fit**. As another example, goodness of fit exists for energetic and outgoing students when teachers encourage participation in whole-group activities, just as it exists for shy and quiet students in independent seatwork. Goodness of fit again reminds us of how important it is to vary our instruction to try and accommodate our students' different inclinations (Rothbart, 2011; Rudasill, Gallagher, & White, 2010). We can also combine whole-group activities with small-group work to help develop traits such as openness and agreeableness. As we introduce the group work, we can emphasize positive behaviors, such as providing supportive statements and listening politely while group mates are talking, and then monitor groups to ensure that students are demonstrating these behaviors. Using these strategies to develop positive personality traits will take time, and they won't work with every student, but over the course of a school year, they can make a difference. This is what we're trying to accomplish.

MyLab Education
Video Example 3.1
Modeling positive personality characteristics is the most effective action we can take in promoting these same traits in our students. Here, sixth-grade teacher, Dani Ramsay, models openness, agreeableness, and conscientiousness as she explains how she supports her students' academic efforts.

Model Positive Personality Traits. At the beginning of the chapter we offered the quote, "Be the change that you wish to see in the world," and here we see again how it applies. Arguably, modeling positive personality characteristics is the most effective action we can take in promoting these same traits in our students, and modeling openness, agreeableness, and conscientiousness, for example, takes no extra time or effort. Since most people who go into teaching possess positive personality characteristics, modeling them will quickly become second nature. And we have nothing to lose in doing so. They will make a difference with at least some students, and even if they didn't, we would be happier people as a result of our own behavior.

Use Concrete Examples and Discussions to Teach Positive Personality Traits. We've emphasized the cognitive component of personality development, and the term *cognitive* refers to *thinking*. This means that with awareness and thought, students can work to develop these traits (McCoy, 2016; van der Linden et al., 2017). We emphasize thinking because students are often unaware of how they "come across." For instance, how many of us would describe ourselves as disagreeable? We all would like to believe that we are open, agreeable, conscientious, and emotionally stable.

Also, it's hard to tell students that they are, for instance, disagreeable. But we can illustrate and discuss desirable and undesirable personality characteristics, and this is what we mean by "Use concrete examples and discussions to teach positive personality traits."

Let's look at an illustration.

Ramon Jiménez, a middle school teacher, is making a formal effort to help his students develop positive personality traits. He displays a description of the traits on his document camera and then says, "These traits can influence our success in school and life outside of school. Let's look at a couple examples," and he then displays the following.

> Collin brings all his materials to school every day, and he always carefully does his homework. When he is involved in group work, he listens patiently when a group mate is talking and he will often make comments, such as "That's a good thought." Even when he disagrees, he'll say, "I don't quite agree with that, but it's an interesting point." Collin also eagerly dives into the study of new topics.

> Collin is learning a lot and he is well liked by the other students.

> Jonathan often gets into trouble with his teachers because he forgets to bring his book, notebook, or pencil to class, and he will periodically blow off his homework with comments like, "When will I ever need to understand this stuff?"

> When he works in groups, he'll sometimes make fun of his group mates and make comments such as, "That was a dumb idea."

> Jonathan's grades aren't very good, and his classmates sometimes say they don't want to be in the same group with him.

"What are some differences you notice between Collin and Jonathan?" Ramon asks after giving students a minute to read the vignettes.

The students make several comments, and in the process, Ronise concludes, "It's his own fault," in response to someone pointing out that Jonathan isn't learning very much and not getting along with the other students.

"Yes," Ramon nods, "if we aren't conscientious and don't take responsibility for ourselves, whose fault is it if we don't learn?"

"Our own," several students respond.

"Yes," Ramon emphasizes. "We're all responsible for ourselves."

With Ramon's guidance, the students also conclude that Collin is open and agreeable, which—in addition to his conscientiousness—helps explain why he is doing well in school and is well liked by his classmates.

Formally teaching personality traits such as conscientiousness and agreeableness, the way Ramon did, capitalizes on the cognitive component of personality development. For example, seeing illustrations of Collin's and Johnathan's behaviors, and hearing classmates discuss the consequences that follow, can be a powerful learning tool. And the fact that Ronise commented, "It's his own fault," in reference to Jonathan's problems, is likely to be more effective—because it comes from a peer—than hearing teachers lecture to them about being conscientious and agreeable. Further, they're less likely to be disagreeable when they understand that it can lead to negative outcomes, which is also reinforced by the realization that other students are aware of both the trait and its consequences. With this awareness, students can then practice displaying positive personality traits in the same way that they practice developing any other ability.

Classroom Connections

Promoting Personality Development in Classrooms

1. The development of positive personality traits is important for both success in school and success in life after the school years. Systematically promote these characteristics in students.

   - **Elementary:** In an effort to promote agreeableness and conscientiousness, a kindergarten teacher emphasizes and models being kind to classmates, sharing materials, and always doing assigned work. Knowing that young children bask in praise, she openly praises students when she sees them display these traits.

   - **Middle School:** Over the school year, a seventh-grade teacher discusses each of the "Big Five" personality traits with her students, and, knowing that peers and social acceptance are becoming increasingly important to them, emphasizes that some personality traits, such as agreeableness and emotional stability, are important for making and keeping friends. She conducts periodic classroom meetings to discuss what can be done to make their classroom a positive learning environment.

   - **High School:** An 11th-grade teacher presents information about personality traits and how they're related to success when her students go to college or enter the workplace. The information highlights the relationships between conscientiousness, emotional self-regulation, and success in the world of work. She also uses classroom incidents as opportunities to discuss personality traits and success in life after school.

APA Top 20 Principles

This discussion illustrates Principle 5: *Acquiring long-term knowledge and skill is largely dependent on practice*—from the *Top 20 Principles from Psychology for PreK–12 Teaching and Learning*.

Use an Authoritative Classroom Management Style.   Earlier in our discussion we saw that an authoritative parenting style is considered to be the most effective, and the description of authoritative parenting strongly parallels recommended classroom management practices for teachers (Emmer & Evertson, 2017; Evertson & Emmer, 2017). This suggests that we should set boundaries for our students, provide reasons for our rules, enforce them consistently, and explain how they help protect the rights and feelings of others. Over time, these practices contribute to positive personality traits, such as agreeableness and conscientiousness. (You will likely take a classroom management course as part of your teacher preparation program, and Chapter 12 of this text focuses on classroom management. In either case, you will study the topic in much more detail than in this short section.)

MyLab Education Self-Check 3.1

Development of Identity

3.2   Use descriptions of identity development to explain learner behavior.

There are no "right-wrong" or "good-bad" ratings for this exercise (although you probably wouldn't be terribly happy if you rated yourself low in each of the categories). Rather, the ratings are a measure of **identity**: our beliefs, assessments, and feelings about ourselves. It's who we are—our sense of self. It's important, because identity development is strongly linked to student motivation; students behave in ways that are consistent with their beliefs about themselves (Miller-Cotto & Byrnes, 2016). For example, if students

Ed Psych and You

On a scale from 0 to 5, rate yourself on each of the following. (For example, if you would give yourself a 0 for *athleticism*, you believe you're not athletic, whereas a 5 suggests you think you're very athletic.)

- Intelligence
- Athleticism
- Attractiveness
- Open-mindedness
- Friendliness

believe they're friendly, they're likely to seek the company of others; if they believe they're athletic, they engage in sports; and if they believe they're high achievers, they pay attention in class, work conscientiously, and persevere in the face of challenges.

The opposite is also true. For example, a negative identity with respect to achievement often results in lower effort and persistence, which makes success less likely, and a downward spiral of motivation, achievement, and identity is the result (Pajares, 2009; Pop, Negru-Subtirica, Crocetti, Opre, & Meeus, 2016). We discuss strategies for breaking this cycle in the section "Using Educational Psychology in Teaching: Promoting Identity Development" later in our discussion.

Influences on Identity Development

One of the principles of development, outlined in Chapter 2, states that our experiences have powerful influences on development, and this is particularly true for the development of identity. For instance, as we have academic successes, we come to believe that we're high achievers, and this belief becomes part of our identity. Similarly, if our participation in sporting activities suggests that we're fairly athletic, this also becomes part of our identity.

These influences have important social components. First, our conclusions about our academic ability or athleticism are typically based on how we compare to peers. If we usually achieve higher than our classmates, or if our athletic skills are advanced compared to our peers, we develop a more positive identity than if we are at the other end of the continuum (Miller-Cotto & Byrnes, 2016; Pop et al., 2016).

Second, the social component provides feedback from others, allowing us to determine how people react to us (Oyserman & Destin, 2010). For instance, if others seek our company, we develop a positive social identity; if we're picked first to be on a pickup soccer team, we develop a positive sense of our athleticism. The expectations adults have for children and the recognition the children receive for accomplishments also contribute to a positive identity (Pajares, 2009).

Third, group membership influences identity development, and loss of group membership can have a negative impact on a sense of self. "The relationships individuals find themselves in impact not only their well-being, but also their sense of who they are. . . . A strong group identity not only provides us with positive self-regard, but also reduces uncertainty about the self" (Slotter & Winger, 2015, p. 15). For example, when Paul's (one of your authors) daughter was in her high school band, she spoke with feigned disparagement—but actually barely concealed pride—about being a "band nerd." Don's (your other author) daughter had similar experiences with her membership on her high school volleyball team. And if students identify with a successful academic group, for example, their academic motivation is likely to increase (Cross, Bugaj, & Mammadov, 2016).

We turn now to a more detailed look at these social forces in identity development.

Erikson's Psychosocial View of Identity Development

Erik Erikson (1902–1994), a developmental psychologist and psychoanalyst, was interested in the relationships people have with their social and cultural environments, or what he termed *psychosocial identity* (Erikson, 1968; Roeser, Peck, & Nasir, 2006). The term *psychosocial* derives from his belief that the formation of identity (the psychological component of the term) stems largely from people's innate desire to connect with others (Erikson, 1968, 1980). More recent research corroborates the view that we, as people, are social animals, and social factors strongly influence who we are and how we behave (Lieberman, 2013; Turkle, 2015).

Erikson described this psychosocial identity development in a series of stages defined by "crises," life tasks and social contexts we encounter across the life span (Roeser et al., 2006). Each crisis is a psychosocial challenge that presents opportunities for development. For instance, for infants the challenge is to develop a sense of trust, and for toddlers and young children the challenge is to develop autonomy and initiative—Erikson's first three stages—as outlined in Table 3.1. Warm, predictable, and consistent caregiving with a moral compass that is neither too harsh nor to lenient helps children meet these challenges.

As children move through the school years, developing a sense of competence and identity—Erikson's 4th and 5th stages—become the challenges, and schools and teachers play a powerful role in helping students meet them. Teachers that maintain high expectations and help students meet the expectations promote a sense of competence, and a sense of positive academic identity helps resolves the challenges at these stages. In adulthood, developing intimacy, generativity, and integrity—Erikson's final stages—become the challenges, and the quality of social relationships contributes to positive resolutions of the challenges at these stages.

Although challenges are never permanently settled, a positive resolution of the challenge at one stage contributes to healthy identity formation at that stage and increases the likelihood of a positive resolution at the next. On the other hand, failure to meet the challenge leaves identity development at that stage incomplete. For instance, if you generally trust people, Erikson would say that you positively resolved the trust versus mistrust crisis, whereas failure to meet the challenge can leave one

TABLE 3.1 Erikson's eight life-span stages

Trust vs. Mistrust (Infancy)	Trust develops when infants receive consistently loving care. Mistrust results from unpredictable or harsh care.
Autonomy vs. Shame and Doubt (Toddler years)	Autonomy develops when children use their newly formed mental and psychomotor skills to explore their worlds. Parents support autonomy by encouraging exploration and completing tasks for themselves. Doubt results from highly restrictive parenting, doing for children what they should do for themselves, and criticism for the inevitable mistakes that children make.
Initiative vs. Guilt (Preschool years)	Initiative, a sense of ambition and responsibility, develops from encouragement of children's attempts to explore and take on new challenges. Overcontrol and criticism for accidents and other efforts that occur when children take initiatives can result in a sense of guilt and a reluctance to strike out and explore.
Industry vs. Inferiority (Elementary school)	School and home provide opportunities for students to develop a sense of competence through success on challenging tasks. A pattern of failure can lead to feelings of inferiority.
Identity vs. Confusion (Adolescence)	Adolescents experiment with various roles in an atmosphere of freedom with clearly established limits. Confusion results when the home environment fails to provide either the necessary structure or when it is overly controlling, failing to provide opportunities for individual exploration with different identity roles.
Intimacy vs. Isolation (Young adulthood)	Intimacy occurs when individuals establish close ties with others. Emotional isolation may result from earlier disappointments, rejection, or lack of a developing identity.
Generativity vs. Stagnation (Middle adulthood)	Generativity occurs when adults give to the next generation through activities such as child rearing, productive work, and contributions to other people or the larger society. Stagnation can result from apathy, self-absorption, or lack of ability to think about or contribute to the welfare of others.
Integrity vs. Despair (Old age)	Integrity occurs when people believe they've lived as well as possible and accept the inevitability of death. Remorse over things done or left undone can lead to despair.

wary of people—a sense of distrust. Similarly, meeting the challenge of industry versus inferiority results in a sense of competence and a positive identity with respect to your capabilities. Failure to meet the challenge can leave one with a sense of inadequacy and a negative identity at this stage.

Failure to resolve a crisis—by not meeting the psychosocial challenge—at one or more stages doesn't doom people to dysfunctional lives, and we all have personal "flaws." For example, we know people who seem to lack initiative, but function well in roles where initiative isn't a major requirement. Similarly, we know self-described "loners" who have satisfying careers and who seem perfectly happy with their lives.

Evaluating Erikson's Work

Erikson's work was popular and influential in the 1960s and 1970s, but since then theorists have taken issue with it on three major points. First, in spite of his reference to culture, they contend that his theory doesn't adequately address the role of culture in development. For instance, some cultures discourage autonomy, initiative, and self-assertiveness in children, instead emphasizing a collective sense of belonging and concern for others (Chen & Eisenberg, 2012). Research suggests that culture is indeed an important influence in all forms of development (Cole & Packer, 2011). Second, critics point out that Erikson based his theory primarily on his work with males, and research suggests that females may take different paths to identity development (DiDonato & Berenbaum, 2013; Gilligan, 1977, 1982, 1998). Third, Erikson based his theory on his personal notes and experiences dealing with clients, and his theory is difficult to validate empirically. Also, his work is grounded in the time in which he lived and practiced, and it may not accurately explain developmental changes influenced by our current society, which is quite different.

Erikson's work is intuitively sensible, however, and he was the first to recognize the role that identity formation plays in becoming a productive, happy adult. In addition, it helped focus attention on our need for relatedness, the innate need to feel loved, connected to, and respected by other people (Cerasoli, Nicklin, & Nassrelgrgawi, 2016; Deci & Ryan, 2008). It also helps us understand problems we encounter in classrooms. For example, we might explain Sean's contention—in our case study at the beginning of the chapter—that the other students are "out to get him" by saying that he hasn't positively resolved the trust–distrust crisis. This has left him less able to develop a sense of autonomy, initiative, or industry, which helps us understand why it's affecting his academic work. We've all met people we admire because of their positive outlook, openness, and commitment to making the world better. We've also encountered those who believe that others are trying to take advantage of them or are somehow inherently evil. We see good minds sliding into lethargy because of a lack of initiative or even substance abuse, and we're frustrated by people's apathy and lack of a zest for living. Erikson's work helps us understand these issues. His theory, including its contributions and criticisms, is outlined in Table 3.2.

Contemporary Views of Identity Development

As we saw in Table 3.1, Erikson identified identity versus confusion as the core developmental challenge of adolescence. However, he also acknowledged that identity formation is a lifelong process (Erikson, 1980). Throughout our lives we're faced with new experiences that may challenge our present sense of identity. "These new experiences may be approached by a search for information that is consistent with the current identity, or by changing the identity in response to the new experiences" (Carlsson, Wängqvist, & Frisén, 2015, p. 334). As an example, an employee holding a long-term position in her company was recently laid off. "I don't know who I am any more," she lamented. "That work has been my life." Erikson would describe this as an *identity crisis*, which can occur at any point in our lives.

TABLE 3.2 Analyzing theories: Erikson's theory of psychosocial development

Major question	How does psychosocial development occur throughout the life span?
Key concepts	Crisis (psychosocial challenge) Stages of development • Trust v. mistrust • Autonomy v. shame • Initiative v. guilt • Industry v. inferiority • Identity v. confusion • Intimacy v. isolation • Generativity v. stagnation • Integrity v. despair
Description of psychosocial development	Psychosocial development occurs when individuals accomplish positive resolutions of crises (psychosocial challenges) at a particular stage of development, which increases the likelihood of a positive resolution at the next stage.
Catalyst for development	• Meeting (or not meeting) life's challenges, which differ at various stages of our lives • Quality of support provided by the social environment, particularly parents and other caregivers
Contributions	• Reminds us that development is a process that continues throughout our life spans • Places the individual at the center of identity development and describes development as an active process • Helps explain a considerable amount of behavior we observe in others
Criticisms	• His theory fails to adequately account for the influence of culture (e.g., some cultures discourage rather than encourage autonomy and initiative). • Erikson based his theory primarily on his work with men, and for women the psychosocial challenge of intimacy often occurs before a focus on personal identity. • His theory is based on his notes and experiences rather than systematic research. • His theory may not reflect current societal conditions.

SOURCES: Berk, 2013; Erikson, 1963, 1968, 1972, 1980; Feldman, 2014.

Contemporary perspectives view identity development not so much as a crisis, but rather a gradual process of experimenting with different potential life directions and ultimately deciding on a course of action (Marcia, 1980, 1987, 2010). Let's look at an illustration.

Four high school seniors are talking about what they plan to do after they graduate.

"I'm not sure what I want to do," Sandy comments. "I've thought about veterinary medicine, and also about teaching. I've been working at the vet clinic, and I like it, but I'm not sure about doing it forever. Some of my parents' friends are teachers, so I hear what they say about it. I don't know."

"I'm off to the university in the fall," Nathan replies. "I'm going to be a lawyer. At least that's what my parents think. It's not a bad job, and lawyers make good money."

"How can you just do that?" Nancy wonders. "You said you don't want to be a lawyer. . . . I'm going to think about it for a while. . . . I'm only 17, and I'm not willing to decide yet."

"I'm going into nursing," Taylor comments. "I've been working part-time at the hospital, and it feels good to work with people and help them. I've talked with the counselors, and I think I can do the chemistry and other science courses."

The *identity status model* is commonly used to examine identity development. (Kroger & Marcia, 2011; Kroger, Martinussen, & Marcia, 2010; Schwartz, Luyckx, & Crocetti, 2015). According to this model, young people's decisions can be classified into one of four states, which vary in the extent to which they result in healthy identity development (Marcia, 1980, 1987, 1999, 2010). These states are outlined in Table 3.3.

As we see in Table 3.3, *identity diffusion*, common in younger adolescents and illustrated in our vignette above by Sandy's consideration of both veterinary medicine and teaching, reflects haphazard consideration of different career choices. If it persists,

TABLE 3.3 States in identity development

State	Description
Identity diffusion	A state of identity development that occurs when individuals fail to make clear choices. The state is characterized by haphazard experimentation with different career options. Individuals may not be developmentally ready to make decisions.
Identity foreclosure	A state of identity development that occurs when individuals prematurely adopt the positions of others, such as parents.
Identity moratorium	A state of identity development that occurs when individuals pause and remain in a "holding pattern." Long-range commitment is delayed.
Identity achievement	A state of identity development that occurs after individuals make decisions about goals and commitments.

it can result in apathy and confusion (Carlsson, Wängqvist, & Frisén, 2016). *Identity foreclosure* occurs when adolescents prematurely adopt the goals and values of others—usually their parents—without thoroughly examining the implications for their futures. Nathan's comment reflects this state. *Identity moratorium*—represented by Nancy's comment—involves active exploration without making a firm commitment. This is a positive state that can ultimately lead to *identity achievement*, the ideal identity development state (Carlsson et al., 2015). This is illustrated by Taylor's commitment to nursing.

The identity status model predicts that progress from identity diffusion to identity achievement typically exists on a continuum, which is outlined in Figure 3.1 (Carlsson et al., 2015; Carlsson et al., 2016).

More recent research suggests that healthy identity development also involves the process of connecting memories of past experiences to their imagined futures, described as a *narrative approach* to identity development (Carlsson et al., 2015; Carlsson et al., 2016). "The construction of a coherent life story begins in late adolescence and continues throughout the life course" (Carlsson et al., 2015, p. 335). Paul's and Don's—your authors—identities reflect this narrative approach. Both come from working class backgrounds, although Paul's is rural and Don's is urban, but our parents expected us to go to college, succeed, and ultimately make a contribution to the world. As university faculty members, our attempts to make this contribution are very much a part of our identities. This is part of our lives' narratives. Now our long history as authors is also a part of our life story and a major component of our identities, but at the same time we continue to value—and even make jokes about—our working class backgrounds. Fortunately, we have reached a solid and comfortable state of identity achievement, and our life stories have made a major contribution to reaching this state.

Sexual Identity

Sexual identity, people's definition of who they are with respect to gender orientation, is another important element of identity formation. Sexual identity influences student choices ranging from clothes and friends to the occupations they consider and ultimately pursue (Heck, Mirabito, LeMaire, Livingston, & Flentje, 2017).

Sexual orientation, the gender to which an individual is romantically and sexually attracted, is an important dimension of sexual identity. For most students, sexual

Figure 3.1 Progress through states of identity

Identity diffusion	Identity foreclosure	Identity moratorium	Identity achievement
Weak commitment Little exploration	Strong commitment Little exploration	Weak commitment Active exploration	Strong commitment Active exploration

orientation is not a major issue, but for an estimated 3% to 10% of the student population it is confusing and stressful (Macionis, 2015). Although some suggest that homosexuality is a choice, research overwhelmingly indicates that it is genetic in origin (Berk, 2019a; Gollnick & Chinn, 2017).

Identity Development and LGBTQ Youth

LGBTQ, an acronym that originated in the 1990s and replaced what was formerly known as "the gay community," refers to lesbian, gay, bisexual, transgender, and individuals who are exploring or questioning their identities. The acronym was created to be more inclusive of diverse groups (Human Rights Campaign, 2016).

Approximately 4.5% of American adults now identify as LGBTQ, up from 3.5% in 2012 when polls first began tracking the measure. This increase is largely a result of millennials—individuals born between the approximate years of 1980 and 2000—slightly more than 8% of whom identify as LGBTQ. Experts believe this number reflects millennials being more comfortable with acknowledging their orientation (Newport, 2018).

A survey of more than 10,000 young people who identified themselves as LGBTQ reveals some of the challenges they face. For example, a strikingly high number are homeless or in foster care, and many are profoundly disconnected from their communities and believe they must leave to make their hopes and dreams for the future come true. Compared to their non-LGBTQ peers, these young people report much lower levels of happiness, a higher incidence of alcohol and drug use, and less connection to adult support when they have personal problems (Human Rights Campaign, 2016).

LGBTQ students also face other problems (Human Rights Campaign, 2016):

- More than 4 of 10 say their community is not accepting of LGBTQ youth, and nearly 6 of 10 say that churches or places of worship in their community are not accepting of LGBTQ people.

- LGBTQ youth are twice as likely as their peers to say they have been physically assaulted, and more than half have been verbally harassed at school, compared to 25% for their non-LGBTQ peers.

- More than 1 in 4 say their biggest problem is not being accepted by their families.

- More than 90% say they hear negative messages about being LGBTQ, with primary sources being school, the Internet, and peers.

Research also indicates that LGBTQ students, and particularly girls, are subjected to discriminatory school discipline. "[T]he current study has provided new evidence that sexual minority students continue to face higher rates of exclusionary discipline than their peers" (Mittleman, 2018, p. 187).

In spite of these grim statistics, some positive factors exist. For example, 9 of 10 LGBTQ youth say they are out—acknowledging their sexual orientation or sexual identity—to their close friends, nearly 2 of 3 say they are out to their classmates, and 75% say their peers don't have a problem with their identity as LGBTQ. Further, nearly 8 of 10 say things will get better, although, as we saw above, many believe they must leave their communities to make this happen (Hodges, 2016).

Transgender Students.   **Transgender students** are those whose sense of personal identity does not correspond with the gender assigned to them at birth. Students born as one gender may discover at puberty that they identify instead as the opposite. Internally they're more comfortable with a different gender orientation than the one specified on their birth certificate (Kahn, 2016). About 0.6% of adults in the United States describe themselves as transgender, double a widely used previous estimate. Researchers say the new estimate reflects a growing awareness of transgender identity, people's increased willingness to identify as transgender, and improved survey techniques (Flores, Herman, Gates, & Brown, 2016). Estimates of the percentage of transgender students in the school population put the figure at between 0.5% and 1.5% percent for adolescent teenagers (Hoffman, 2016).

What is it like to be a transgender student? Responses range from personal, such as being uncomfortable in a body they feel doesn't fully belong to them, to social, dealing with people who think they are disgusting and sick and hate them as a result (Tritt, 2017).

Transgender youth experience many challenges. They face ongoing bias, discrimination, bullying, and harassment. Nearly half report being sexually assaulted at some point in their lifetime, 4 of 10 admit to attempting suicide—compared to less than 5% in the general population—and nearly 40% report serious psychological stress (Hodges, 2016). More than 1 of 10 report prostituting themselves—sex work in exchange for income—so the rate of HIV infection in the transgender community is high. In addition, their poverty rate is twice that of the general population (Centers for Disease Control and Prevention, 2016a).

Controversies surrounding transgender students were thrust into the national limelight in 2016 when North Carolina passed the highly controversial "bathroom bill," a bill requiring transgender students to use bathrooms matching the sex listed on their birth certificates instead of bathrooms consistent with their gender identity (Miller, 2016). The bill triggered a backlash that estimates indicated could have cost the state 5 billion dollars in lost federal funds, together with thousands of jobs and millions in tax revenue. It was also a likely factor in the governor losing a second term (Katz, 2016). The law was ultimately repealed in 2017, but criticism from LGBTQ groups, who argued that the bill still allowed for discrimination against transgender people, continued (Hanna & McLaughlin, 2017).

The legal status of transgender students is unclear. The Education Department in the Obama administration, citing Title IX, which prohibits discrimination on the basis of sex, instructed the nation's schools to let these students use bathrooms corresponding to their chosen genders (Wolf, 2017). Lawsuits challenging that directive were then filed in more than 20 states (Liptak, 2016). In 2017 these Obama-administration mandates were rolled back when he left office (U.S. Department of Education, 2017). Trump administration attorney general Jeff Sessions "ordered the Justice Department to take the position in court cases that transgender people are not protected by a civil rights law that bans workplace discrimination based on sex" (Savage, 2017, para. 1).

What can we do? All young people need accepting and supportive adults, and this is particularly true for LGBTQ youth. A positive school climate is associated with decreased depression, suicidal feelings, substance abuse, and unexcused school absences among these students (Saewcy, Konishi, Rose, & Homma, 2014).

Most important, we can attempt to create a safe and nurturing classroom environment. Some suggestions for meeting this goal include:

- Openly communicating that all students are welcome and valued in our classrooms, and demonstrating this assertion by treating all students equally.
- Establishing and enforcing rules that require all students to treat each other with respect. Harassment and ridicule, in any form, become unforgivable sins in all interactions.
- Conducting class meetings that include discussions of all forms of diversity and asking students from different backgrounds to describe their experiences and feelings.
- Encouraging students to join student-led and student-organized school clubs that promote a safe, welcoming, and accepting school environment (e.g., gay-straight alliances, which are school clubs open to youth of all sexual orientations).

These suggestions are particularly important for transgender students. Our use of respectful language and behavior with these young people will model the expectation of civil behavior for all students. If we hear others using derogatory or hurtful language, we should immediately stop it. Personal questions about a student's transition, anatomy, or any medical issues should be avoided. It is important to use the name and pronoun that matches the student's gender identity, even if the legal name on the school record is different, and to keep information about their prior name and pronoun confidential (Kahn, 2016).

Students often surprise us with their ability to "rise to the occasion." For example, as we saw earlier, LGBTQ youth report that 75% of their peers don't have a problem with their identity as LGBTQ. Open, honest, and supportive discussions can increase those percentages. When students learn that we are similar in more ways than we're different—we all want to be loved and respected; we all want to have friends; and we all want to lead happy and productive lives—whether we're LGBTQ or not becomes much less significant.

The Development of Self-Concept

Ed Psych and You

How smart are you? What subjects, such as math, English, or history, are you best at? How popular are you? Athletic?

Earlier we saw that identity reflects our beliefs, assessments, and feelings about ourselves, and **self-concept**, a component of identity, is a cognitive appraisal of our academic, physical, and social competencies. The term *assessment* in the definition of identity refers to this evaluative component, and your responses to our questions in *Ed Psych and You* reflect different dimensions of your self-concept (Schunk et al., 2014). If you believe you're good at math, for instance, you have a positive academic self-concept in math. Or, if you believe you're a good athlete, you have a positive physical self-concept, and if you think you get along well with people, you have a positive social self-concept.

Factors influencing identity development in general also apply to the development of self-concept (Pop et al., 2016). For example, if we have a history of success in math, our self-concept with respect to math will likely be positive; if we're successful in sports, we have a positive athletic self-concept; and if we get along well with others, our social self-concept will be positive.

These examples help us understand why self-concept is important for achievement. Let's look at this idea in more detail.

Self-Concept and Achievement

A strong and robust relationship exists between academic self-concept and achievement (Pop et al., 2016), and our examples in the last section help us understand why. If we're successful in math, for example, we have a positive math self-concept, and as a result, we're likely to work harder and persevere longer on challenging math activities. And the harder we work, the better we get at math, which confirms our belief about our math ability, and our self-concept becomes even more positive, creating a reinforcing cycle. The same applies in all areas. For example, we've heard about elite athletes who have unbounded work ethics. They're good at the sports they play, so they have positive athletic self-concepts; they work even harder to confirm their beliefs about their ability, so their skills improve, and the cycle is again reinforcing. Similarly, if we get along well with others, we likely seek out their company, which gives us additional opportunities to practice our social skills.

These examples help us understand why self-concept is domain specific, meaning that positive self-concepts of athletic ability, for example, have little impact on academic achievement (Wolff, Nagy, Helm, & Möller, 2018). We've all known highly skilled athletes who are modest achievers, and this makes sense. How we perform in athletics gives us no feedback about our academic performance, so it has little impact on our cognitive assessment of academic ability.

The relationship between social self-concept and achievement is more complex. For instance, believing that we're socially skilled doesn't necessarily relate to achievement, but a link between social competence and academic achievement has been found beginning with children in early elementary school (Walker & Henderson, 2012). We examine these ideas in more detail when we discuss social-emotional development later in the chapter.

Self-Concept and Self-Esteem

Self-esteem (*self-worth*) is an emotional reaction to, or an evaluation of, the self, and is an additional component of identity (Schunk et al., 2014). The term *feeling* in the definition of identity refers to this component. *Self-concept* and *self-esteem* are sometimes used interchangeably, but doing so reflects a misconception. Self-concept is *cognitive*, whereas self-esteem is *emotional* (Schunk et al., 2014). People who have high self-esteem believe that they are inherently worthy people and feel good about themselves. It's important, because low self-esteem during adolescence predicts poor health, criminal behavior, and limited economic prospects as adults (Danielsson & Bengtsson, 2016). Young children tend to have both high self-esteem and positive self-concepts—sometimes unrealistically so—probably because of a lack of social comparisons and the support they receive from parents. This optimism is desirable because it encourages young children to explore and take chances (Verschueren, Doumen, & Buyse, 2012). Self-esteem tends to drop during the transition from elementary to middle school, likely because of physical changes brought on by puberty and the less personal nature of middle schools. It then rises again during the high school years—to a greater extent for boys than girls (Matsumoto & Juang, 2012).

Although self-concept is cognitive and self-esteem is emotional, the two aren't totally unrelated. For example, people with positive self-concepts in a variety of areas also tend to have high self-esteem. This isn't always the case, however. We all know people who are high achievers, yet don't feel good about themselves, that is, they have low self-esteem.

The relationships between identity, self-concept, and self-esteem are illustrated in Figure 3.2.

Diversity: Ethnic Identity

"**Ethnic identity** [emphasis added] refers to an individual's sense of belonging to an ethnic group, which is defined by one's cultural heritage, and includes attributes such as values, traditions, and language" (Brittian, Umaña-Taylor, & Derlan, 2013, p. 178). Researchers suggest that ethnic identity is particularly important for members of cultural minorities living in a heterogeneous society, because it provides them with a sense of belonging and acceptance in societies where the majority group sometimes holds negative stereotypes about them (Miller-Cotto & Byrnes, 2016). This sense of belonging helps diffuse the negative effects of social devaluation that minorities sometimes feel (Brittian et al., 2013).

Positive ethnic identity is important. Students with positive ethnic identities are better adjusted, show higher achievements in school, and believe they are academically

Figure 3.2 The relationships between identity, self-concept, and self-esteem

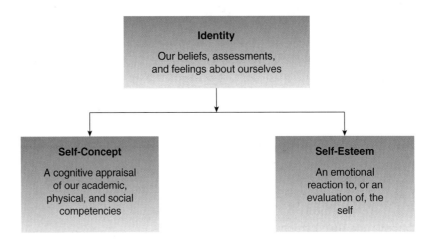

capable (Gollnick & Chinn, 2017; Miller-Cotto & Byrnes, 2016). In addition, they're less likely to use drugs or engage in risky behavior (Brook, Zhang, Finch, & Brook, 2010). This is particularly important in societies such as ours, where members of ethnic minorities often believe that majority groups have access to privileges that minority groups don't enjoy.

Self-esteem is an important part of positive ethnic identity. **Collective self-esteem** refers to individuals' perceptions of the relative worth of the groups to which they belong. When these groups are valued by society and perceived as having positive status, personal identities and individual self-esteem are enhanced (Jaspal & Cinnirella, 2012). The opposite is also true. Even very young children know they are members of an ethnic minority, and research dating back nearly 80 years indicates that children who are members of cultural minorities such as African Americans (Clark & Clark, 1939), Mexican Americans (Weiland & Coughlin, 1979), and Chinese Americans (Aboud & Skerry, 1984) evaluate their ethnic reference groups as less worthy than the White majority. As these children develop, they become increasingly aware of problems with inequality and discrimination (Brittian et al., 2013). The problems are especially acute for immigrants, who also face language barriers (Yoon et al., 2017). Many cultural minorities experience hardships linked to poverty, crime, and drug use, and schools that are unresponsive to their needs can retard their development (Jaspal & Cinnirella, 2012). Sensitive teachers are crucial in helping these students form healthy identities.

We examine ways you can contribute to positive ethnic identity formation in our next section.

Using Educational Psychology in Teaching: Suggestions for Supporting Your Students' Identity Development

As teachers we strongly influence our students' developing identities. The following suggestions can help us in our efforts.

1. Support autonomy and initiative in your students.
2. Maintain high expectations and provide students with evidence of increasing competence.
3. Create a safe and caring learning community in your classroom.
4. Communicate that students' ethnic backgrounds are valued and contribute to learning.

Let's see how John Adler, an eighth-grade English teacher, attempts to implement these guidelines with his students.

"Here are your papers," John announces on Friday as he hands back a set of quizzes from the day before. "You did a good job and I'm proud of you. Your writing is really improving. . . . I know I expect a lot, but you've always risen to the task.

"Put your scores in your logs, and add your improvement points."

"Who improved the most, Mr. Adler?" Jeremy asks.

"That's not important," John replies. "Remember, we're all in this together. You take responsibility for your learning, I help you as much as I can, and we all try to improve. . . . That's why I put your scores on the last page of the quizzes. They're your business, and no one else's.

"Now, I'd like to have a classroom meeting," he continues, changing the direction of the discussion. "One of you came to me after school yesterday, concerned about the way some of you are treating each other outside of class. . . . She didn't name names, and I really like it when someone takes the initiative to make our classroom better.

"I concur with her concern. . . . For instance, I saw one of you get tripped when you walked down the aisle, and another had water splashed on him at the water fountain. . . . I'm also seeing more litter on the floor.

"I'm disappointed with these behaviors. We're here to help one another. . . . So, I want to hear some ideas. What can we do to make our classroom better?"

The students offer comments, with suggestions ranging from kicking perpetrators out of class, to talking to them, to adding more rules. The students agree that John has been attempting to enforce the rules fairly, but because he expects everyone to be responsible, perhaps he has been too lenient in some cases. At the meeting's end, the students agree to be more responsible, and John agrees to renew his efforts to consistently enforce classroom rules.

Now, let's look at John's attempts to apply the guidelines.

Support Autonomy and Initiative in Your Students.   We can support autonomy and initiative in our students in a variety of ways. For example, if you're planning to teach in preschool or early elementary grades, you can encourage children to complete tasks for themselves and reward them for taking initiative. And, even though John is a middle school teacher, he realizes that no psychosocial crisis is ever permanently resolved, so he publicly reinforced one of his student's initiatives with his comment, "I really like it when someone takes the initiative to make our classroom better." Although the comment targeted one student, its positive tone communicated to all that personal initiative was valued in his classroom.

Maintain High Expectations and Provide Students with Evidence of Increasing Competence.   As we saw earlier, students' identity development depends largely on their experience with the world, and they develop self-concepts on the basis of feedback they receive about their competence. Efforts to improve self-concept (and self-esteem) directly through activities that focus explicitly on these constructs, such as having minority students study multicultural learning materials, sending children to summer camps, and implementing support groups, are largely unsuccessful and misguided (Schunk et al., 2014). The only way that students' self-concepts will improve is if they get evidence that their competence is increasing. Let's look again at the case study with John and his students.

John:	Here are your papers. You did a good job and I'm proud of you. Your writing is really improving. . . . I know I expect a lot, but you've always risen to the task. Put your scores in your logs, and add your improvement points.
Jeremy:	Who improved the most, Mr. Adler?
John:	That's not important. . . . Remember, we're all in this together. You take responsibility for your learning, I help you as much as I can, and we all try to improve. That's why I put your scores on the last page of the quizzes. They're your business, and no one else's.

Personal improvement is the key to perceptions of increasing competence, and it also helps students achieve a positive resolution of the industry–inferiority crisis. This is the reason John emphasized improvement versus actual scores, and it's also why, as a symbol of de-emphasizing competition, he put the students' scores on the last page of their quizzes. This makes sense. In competitive classrooms, only the highest achievers consistently receive top scores on assessments, which makes achieving a sense of competence—and with it, improved identities with respect to academic achievement—virtually impossible for many students. We realize that we can't stop students from comparing themselves to others, but we can de-emphasize competition, and we can model and focus on personal improvement. We have nothing to lose in doing so, and, in time, these efforts can make a difference.

Create a Safe and Caring Learning Community in Your Classroom. To understand how John attempted to make his classroom a safe and caring learning community, let's look again at some of his comments:

"Now, I'd like to have a classroom meeting. . . . One of you came to me after school yesterday, concerned about the way some of you are treating each other outside of class. . . . I concur with her concern. . . . For instance, I saw one of you get tripped when you walked down the aisle, and another had water splashed on him at the water fountain. . . . I'm also seeing more litter on the floor. I'm disappointed at these behaviors. We're here to help one another. . . . So, I want to hear some ideas. What can we do to make our classroom better?"

Creating a safe learning environment for all his students was John's goal in conducting the classroom meeting. A classroom structure that sets predictable limits for acceptable behavior, combined with the empathy that helps students negotiate the uncertainties of this period in their lives, is important. "[S]tudents . . . say that they want teachers to articulate and enforce clear standards of behavior. They view this not just as part of the teacher's job but as evidence that the teacher cares about them" (Brophy, 2010, p. 24). John teaches middle school students, but a safe and caring learning community is essential for students at all levels. This is particularly true for LGBTQ students who, as we saw earlier, are often mistreated and experience discrimination at the hands of other students (Hodges, 2016). Peer harassment is a major contributor to these problems, and we play an essential role in setting the tone for our classrooms, ensuring that they are a safe place for all students.

Communicate That Students' Ethnic Backgrounds Are Valued and Contribute to Learning. To begin this section, let's look at an example based on an actual incident between a teacher and one of his students.

Because Valdo Ayala, one of his Hispanic students, appears withdrawn and emotionally negative in class, David Haughy, an American history teacher, calls Valdo into his classroom early in the school year.

"Where are you from, Valdo?" David asks.

". . . Puerto Rico."

"Oh, wow!" David exclaims enthusiastically. "My wife and I were in San Juan during the summer, and we loved it. . . . We went down into old San Juan, ate in some of the local restaurants, and listened to some great music. . . . San Juan was great, and we're already talking about going back." (Excerpt based on a conversation Paul, one of your authors, had with a teacher and graduate student in one of his classes.)

As David described it in the conversation, this simple expression of enthusiasm about being in San Juan resulted in a complete turnaround in Valdo's attitude. We're all emotional beings, and David's affirmation communicated to Valdo that he was welcome and valued in David's classroom. Let's look at another teacher's efforts.

Maria Robles squeezes her mother's hand as they enter her new school. Her mother can tell she is nervous as she anxiously eyes the bigger boys and girls walking down the hallway.

As they enter a kindergarten classroom, Carmen Avilla, her teacher, comes to greet them. "Hola. ¿Cómo te llamas, niña?" (Hello. What is your name, little one?) Maria, hiding behind her mother, is still uneasy but feels some relief.

"Dile tu nombre" (Tell her your name), her mother prompts, squeezing her hand and smiling.

"Maria," she offers hesitantly. Her mother adds quickly, "Maria Robles. Yo soy su madre." (I am her mother.)

Carmen looks on her list, finds Maria's name, and checks it off. Then she invites them, in Spanish, to come into the room and meet the other boys and girls. Music is playing in the background. Maria recognizes some of her friends who are playing with toys in a corner of the room.

"Maria, ven aquí y juega con nosotros." (Maria, come here and play with us.)

Maria hesitates for a moment, looks up at her mother, and then runs over to join her friends.

You may not be able to greet students in Spanish, but you can make them feel welcome with simple gestures, such as those Carmen used. The way we react to students, as Carmen did with Maria, has a powerful impact on their developing identities and sense of cultural self-esteem (Gollnick & Chinn, 2017).

We can go farther by recognizing the achievements of ethnic minorities. For instance, providing a short biography of Julian Castro, a politician of Mexican descent who was elected and re-elected mayor of San Antonio, Texas, and led the Department of Housing and Urban Development in the Obama administration, communicates that the achievements of cultural minorities are recognized and respected.

As another example, if you have students with Middle Eastern backgrounds in your class, you could emphasize the contributions of Omar Khayyám, a Persian philosopher and mathematician, who in the 11th and 12th centuries laid down the principles

Classroom Connections

Promoting Identity Development

1. Erikson believed that social connections play a major role in promoting psychosocial development. Use social interactions as a vehicle to support identity development in your students.

- **Elementary**: A kindergarten student, while watering plants, knocks one over on the floor. Her teacher says evenly, "Sweep up the dirt, and wipe up the water with some paper towels." When the student is finished, the teacher hugs her and comments, "Everyone makes mistakes. The important thing is what we do about them."

- **Middle School**: A math teacher designs her instruction so that all students are successful enough to develop a sense of industry. She spends extra time with students after school, and she lets students redo some of their assignments if they make an honest effort the first time. She frequently comments, "Math is for everyone—if you try!"

- **High School**: A biology teacher pays little attention to the attire and slang of his students as long as offensive language isn't used, the rights of others are recognized, and learning occurs.

2. Success on challenging tasks is important for developing a sense of industry in students. Help students understand that effort leads to success and competence.

- **Elementary:** A second-grade teacher carefully teaches a topic and provides precise directions before making seatwork assignments. She conducts "monitored practice" with the first few items to be sure all students get started correctly. When students encounter difficulties, she meets with them separately to provide extra support.

- **Middle School:** A sixth-grade teacher develops a grading system based partially on improvement so that students can succeed by improving their performance. He regularly meets with them to help them monitor their learning progress.

- **High School:** An art teacher uses portfolios and individual conferences to help her students set goals and see their growth over the year. During conferences, she emphasizes improvement and the link between effort and accomplishments.

of algebra. Examples for members of all minorities can be found, and emphasizing them communicates that you value and respect the backgrounds of all students in your classes. Doing so can make an important contribution to their sense of identity and increase their motivation to learn.

MyLab Education Self-Check 3.2

Social-Emotional Development

3.3 Use an understanding of social-emotional development to explain behaviors of students and people beyond the school years.

Ed Psych and You

Think about some of your friends and acquaintances. Are those who seem happiest and have the greatest sense of well-being also the most intelligent or academically successful? If not, why do you think that's the case?

Most commonly, the answer to the first question in *Ed Psych and You* is: Not always. We all know people who are "smart" but still seem to struggle with life, and the opposite is also true; many people have modest ability, but seem happy, balanced, and well-adjusted.

This is where social-emotional learning comes into play. **Social-emotional learning (SEL)** is the ability to recognize and manage emotions, set and achieve positive goals, understand and establish positive relationships with others, and make responsible decisions (Collaborative for Academic, Social, and Emotional Learning [CASEL], 2013). Social-emotional *development* represents growth of these abilities. If, for example, life is a major challenge in spite of being highly intelligent, the ability to manage emotions or establish friendships may be underdeveloped—which helps answer our second question in *Ed Psych and You*. People who are intelligent as well as balanced and happy likely manage their emotions effectively and get along and work well with others.

The study of emotions and social skills has a long history, but the emphasis on SEL has rapidly increased in the last 25 years, and since Daniel Goleman's popular book *Emotional Intelligence* was published (Goleman, 1995). **Emotional intelligence** is the ability to perceive, understand, and manage emotions in ourselves and others, and to use emotional knowledge to enhance cognition (thought) (Goleman, 1995; van der Linden et al., 2017). Since Goleman's book was published, leaders in both the educational and business world have increasingly emphasized the importance of social-emotional development, including heavyweights such as Nobel laureate James Heckman, who has asserted that the greatest return on education investments are from nurturing these abilities (Heckman & Kautz, 2012).

This emphasis is well grounded in research that has identified strong relationships between SEL and outcomes ranging from increased school achievement, particularly with students at risk (Dougherty & Sharkey, 2017; McBride, Chung, & Robertson, 2016), to improved performance in the business world (NACE, 2016; Tran, 2017). And the importance of social-emotional skills has been identified as early as kindergarten (Jones, Greenberg, & Crowley, 2015).

Social-emotional learning programs have five goals (CASEL, 2013):

- **Self-awareness**—the ability of individuals to understand their own thoughts and emotions and how both influence their responses to their environments.
- **Self-management**—the ability of people to regulate their emotions, thoughts, and behaviors in a variety of contexts.
- **Social awareness**—an understanding of social and ethical norms for behavior as well as the ability to take others' perspectives and feel empathy for people from a variety of backgrounds and cultures.
- **Relationship skills**—the ability to establish and maintain healthy and rewarding relationships with diverse individuals and groups.
- **Responsible decision making**—the ability to make constructive choices about personal behavior and interactions with others, based on an understanding of the consequences of our actions.

Let's examine these goals in more detail.

Self-Awareness and Self-Management

Ed Psych and You

Have you ever had a person make a rude remark to you, felt yourself bristle, and thought, "I'd love to tell him [or her] where to go!"? But, realizing that you have a bit of a short fuse, you calmed down and held yourself back, thinking, "Maybe it wasn't meant the way it came across." How were you able to hold yourself back?

Your "bristling" is an *emotional* reaction, a form of anger. **Emotions** are feelings that are typically specific, short-lived, and intense (Schunk et al., 2014). Your anger was specific to the remark, it probably disappeared fairly quickly, but at the time it was quite intense.

Emotions range from positive, such as happiness, excitement, and hope, to negative, like boredom, anger, and stress, and the important role of emotions in our lives has been thoroughly researched. For instance, the well-established links between anxiety, stress, and cardiovascular disease (Chauvet-Geliniera & Bonina, 2017; Emdin et al., 2016), as well as the generally destructive effect of negative emotions on health, have been widely publicized (DeSteno, Gross, & Kubzansky, 2013). We also know that positive emotions are associated with improved resilience and mental health (Gloria & Steinhardt, 2016), as well as positive physical health outcomes, such as fewer chronic disease symptoms and ". . . better immune system and cardiovascular functioning" (Yoo, Miyamoto, & Ryff, 2016, p. 1137).

APA Top 20 Principles

This discussion illustrates Principle 15: *Emotional well-being influences educational performance, learning, and development*—from the *Top 20 Principles from Psychology for PreK–12 Teaching and Learning*.

Emotions involve "feelings," but they have cognitive, physiological, and behavioral components as well (Pekrun, Goetz, Frenzel, Barchfeld, & Perry, 2011). For instance, if confronted by an immediate threat, such as a car running a red light, fear is the emotion we experience, but we also perceive danger (a form of cognition), our muscles tense and our heart rates accelerate (physiological reactions), and we likely slam on our brakes to avoid a collision (a behavioral response).

Self-Awareness.   You realizing that you have a short fuse—in our example in *Ed Psych and You*—illustrates the cognitive component of emotions and relates to **self-awareness**—understanding our thoughts and emotions—the first of SEL programs' five goals. As with all forms of learning, understanding is a necessary first step. For example, before we can execute effective corner kicks in soccer, we must understand the fundamentals of the kick, and before we can write with accuracy and flair we must understand the mechanics of writing, such as grammar and punctuation and the use of metaphors and similes. This understanding leads to awareness.

Self-awareness increases with effort. As we think about and gradually come to understand our emotions, such as recognizing that we overreact or feel anxious for no apparent reason, we are then in a position to do something about it. This leads to self-management, the second SEL goal.

Self-Management.   As we saw above, **self-management** includes people's abilities to regulate their emotions, thoughts, and behaviors.

For instance, we saw in *Ed Psych and You* that you calmed down, which illustrates the concept of **emotional self-regulation** (sometimes called *emotional regulation* or simply *emotion regulation*), the processes we use to control and express our emotions (Graziano & Hart, 2016). Emotional self-regulation is a part of self-management. You also regulated your thoughts ("Maybe it wasn't meant the way it came across") and your behavior (you didn't lash back).

Self-management includes the following factors (Broekhuizen, Slot, van Aken, & Dubas, 2017):

- Controlling the impulse to behave in socially unacceptable ways, such as controlling the urge to tell the other person where to go in our example in *Ed Psych and You*.

- Managing negative emotions, such as calming down after initially feeling angry about the rude remark.

- Behaving in socially acceptable ways, such as deciding to talk calmly to the person about the remark, or simply letting it go.

- Managing stress, such as not letting the incident fester and cause long-term anxiety.

- Motivating oneself and setting and working toward personal and academic goals, such as setting the personal goal of always treating others with courtesy and respect.

Examples of the need for self-management are common. For example, we hear about incidents of road rage, where one driver cutting another off results in a shooting that destroys both lives—simply because one or both couldn't control an impulse. Friendships and marriages founder because, in a fit of fury, someone lashes out and says something that leaves permanent hurt.

On the other hand, we also see examples of people in the face of serious adversity who remain balanced and positive in their outlook and approach to life. This is the goal we strive for both in our students and in our own lives.

Diversity: Differences in Self-Management.   As we would expect, children differ considerably in self-management. And, as is intuitively sensible, older children are better able to control their emotions, thoughts, and behavior than are their younger counterparts (Loman & Gunnar, 2010).

Gender differences also exist. In general, girls are better at controlling both emotions and behaviors. Boys are more likely to display anger and aggression, whereas girls tend to report feeling sad, fearful, or guilty. In classrooms, girls are more compliant and less likely to act out (Emmer & Evertson, 2017; Evertson & Emmer, 2017). Explanations for these gender differences suggest that the part of the brain responsible for controlling emotions develops more quickly in girls (Rothbart, 2011), and they're socialized to behave in more acceptable ways (Kennedy Root, & Denham, 2010; Weisgram, Bigler, & Liben, 2010). These differences are reflected in the fact that boys are diagnosed as having emotional or behavioral problems much more often than girls (Hardman, Egan, & Drew, 2017).

Cultural differences also exist. Western cultures, such as ours, which tend to emphasize individualism, are more likely to teach and reinforce individuals' expressions of emotions (B. Miller, 2016). Collectivist cultures, such as those found in many Asian countries, are more likely to reward conformity, encourage individuals to think of the common good, and suppress individual emotions for the good of the group.

Poverty is an additional factor, and it influences emotional development in several ways. For example, the physical and psychological challenges that children experience growing up in poverty can inhibit healthy brain development (Miller et al., 2018; Phillips, 2016). Also, students worried about where their next meal will come from are more prone to depression, anxiety, and behavior problems (McCoy, 2016). And the challenges that many families in poverty face, such as paying bills and putting food on the table, can create home environments where the security needed for healthy emotional development is missing.

For all children, some emotional stress can be healthy because it provides challenges that can contribute to healthy development, but emotional challenges that are too great can have a negative impact on emotional self-regulation and overall social-emotional development (McCoy, 2016; B. Miller, 2016).

Social Awareness

Social awareness involves abilities that are important for establishing positive social relationships, both in school and the workplace. These abilities include:

- Social cognition
- Demonstrating empathy
- Perspective taking

Social Cognition.   **Social cognition** is the ability to understand social interactions. It's the way ". . . we make sense of and navigate our social worlds" (Müller, Cannon, Kornblum, Clark, & Powers, 2016, p. 192), and it's the foundation for relationship skills and social development (Absher, 2016). People who don't "get it," seem oblivious, or behave in inappropriate ways lack social cognition.

Social referencing, our ability to use vocal and nonverbal cues to evaluate ambiguous events and regulate our behaviors accordingly, is an important aspect of social cognition (Blair et al., 2016). For example, suppose we're in a social gathering with people we don't know well, and someone tells a story that has an unexpected ending. We don't know whether to laugh or express dismay, so we wait to see how others react in an effort to behave appropriately. Very young children and even dogs have this ability (Duranton, Bedossa, & Gaunet, 2016; Stenberg, 2017). People who lack social referencing skills struggle to develop positive social relationships.

Demonstrating Empathy.

As we know, for children, a simple stick, such as a small piece of tree branch, is one of their favorite playthings. Josh, a 6-year-old, finds a stick, but his friend, Matt, can't seem to find one of his own. Josh sees the look on Matt's face, and says, "Here Matt, you can have some of my stick," and he breaks the stick into two parts and gives one part to Matt.

We directly observed this incident, and it was enough to bring tears to our eyes. Josh was displaying **empathy**, ". . . the capacity to feel what you infer others are feeling" (Jordan, Amir, & Bloom, 2016, p. 1107). From the look on Matt's face, Josh inferred that he felt badly, felt badly himself, and resolved the issue by giving Matt some of his stick.

We see empathy displayed in a myriad of ways, and it warms the heart. If you find that a close friend has gotten an A on a test and you feel great about it yourself; you know another friend is struggling to lose weight, and comment, "I know it's frustrating to try and lose weight. I go through the same struggles myself"; or you see someone step on a piece of glass and wince, you're feeling empathy in each case. Empathy goes beyond caring and concern; it involves literally experiencing another's feelings.

Research indicates that empathy promotes cooperation and suggests that empathy lies at the root of compassion and morality (Jordan et al., 2016).

Perspective Taking.

Fifth-graders Mindy, Octavio, Sarah, and Bill are preparing a class presentation on westward expansion in our country, but they disagree about which topics each should present. Octavio, Sarah, and Bill all want to report on the Pony Express.

"I thought of it first," Octavio argues.

"But everyone knows I like horses," Sarah counters.

"Why don't we compromise?" Mindy suggests. "Octavio, you said you were interested in railroads because your grandfather worked for the railroad. Could you talk to him and get some information we could use? And Sarah, I know you like horses. Maybe you could report on how horses influenced the Plains Indians?. . . And Bill, I think you've been interested in the settlers as they moved west. How would that be?"

Mindy's realizing that Octavio was interested in railroads and understanding that Sarah liked horses demonstrates **perspective taking**, the ability to understand other people's thoughts, feelings, and actions—knowing where others are "coming from." It's a key to developing positive relationships (Todd, Simpson, & Tamir, 2016). Notice the term *understand* in the definition. Perspective taking is a cognitive process. For example, Mindy could understand Sarah liking horses without necessarily liking them herself, and this is how perspective taking differs from empathy. Empathy involves actually *feeling* what another feels.

Young children believe that everyone thinks and feels like they do, but over time they acquire a **theory of mind**, ". . . insight into other people's minds and reasoning about how mental states influence behavior" (Imuta, Henry, Slaughter, Selcuk, & Ruffman, 2016, p. 1192). We acquire a theory of mind when we realize that others have perceptions, feelings, desires, and beliefs that are different from our own. It's prerequisite to perspective taking.

As with social-emotional development in general, perspective taking develops slowly over time (Imuta et al., 2016). Young children typically don't understand events from others' perspectives, and it's often missing even in older students, as illustrated by Octavio's assertion, "I thought of it first." As they mature and acquire social experience it improves.

Perspective taking is a part of social cognition, and people who are empathetic and able to see events from others' perspectives are respected, well liked, and able to handle difficult social situations. Those less skilled and less empathetic are more likely to infer others as hostile, which can lead to conflict, and they don't feel guilty or remorseful when they hurt others' feelings (Imuta et al., 2016; Todd et al., 2016).

This section gives us some insight into Sean's reaction to his peers, in our chapter's opening case study. His belief that the other kids are "out to get him" suggests underdeveloped perspective taking.

MyLab Education Application Exercise 3.2: Perspective Taking in American Literature

In this exercise you will be asked to analyze a high school English teacher's attempts to help her students' develop their perspective taking abilities.

Relationship Skills

Relationship skills include the following abilities:

- *Communicating clearly*—using clear language, making assertions simply, and getting to the point without wandering off the subject.
- *Listening actively*—making eye contact with a speaker, leaning slightly forward, avoiding potential distractions, and asking clarifying questions.
- *Cooperating and being thoughtful*—displaying agreeableness (the personality trait—good-natured, tolerant, and compassionate), a willingness to compromise, and thoughtfulness, such as by sending an e-mail to give a person some information about a topic you've discussed.
- *Recognizing peer pressure*—Avoiding being pressured into inappropriate behaviors, such as drinking and driving or smoking, without appearing judgmental or sanctimonious.
- *Seeking and offering help*—Freely acknowledging that you lack some abilities and offering help to others without condescension or immodesty.

MyLab Education
Video Example 3.2

Understanding and establishing positive relations with others is an important part of social-emotional development. Here, a teenage boy describes the process of establishing positive social relationships.

APA Top 20 Principles

Relationship skills apply Principle 14: *Interpersonal relationships and communication are critical to both the teaching–learning process and the social-emotional development of students*—from the *Top 20 Principles from Psychology for PreK–12 Teaching and Learning*.

As with all skills, these abilities can improve with practice. For instance, we can all practice making eye contact with a speaker, asking clarifying questions, and offering help when it appears that someone needs it. We can also practice listening to another's point of view, even if we're likely to adamantly disagree with it. With young children we can see if they listen to their peers, share materials, are helpful, and solve problems with peers without conflict. Mindy, in our vignette at the beginning of our discussion of perspective taking, demonstrated advanced relationship skills when she suggested a compromise that was satisfying for each of her peers.

APA Top 20 Principles

This description illustrates Principle 5: *Acquiring long-term knowledge and skill is largely dependent on practice*—from the *Top 20 Principles from Psychology for PreK–12 Teaching and Learning*.

As is intuitively sensible, the better developed each of these skills are, the easier it will be to get along with others and make and keep friends.

Responsible Decision Making

Zoey, Corina, Madison, and Sage go out for a drink or two every couple weeks. Madison is visually impaired and can't drive at night, so one of the other girls picks her up, and they meet at their favorite hangout, which is centrally located. Zoey is the informal leader of the group, and she checks each time to see if everyone will be there and who will give Madison a ride. One problem periodically creeps up, however. Sage will commit to meeting and then cancel at the last minute, even when it's her turn to pick up Madison.

As we saw earlier, **responsible decision making** involves making constructive choices about personal behavior and interactions with others, based on our understanding of consequences for actions (CASEL, 2013).

Sage's behavior is a negative example of responsible decision making. Her periodic last-minute canceling is rude and self-absorbed, and it has negative consequences for the group. This type of behavior is common in our everyday world. For example, people say they'll call tomorrow with respect to some issue or topic, but they don't call. This is extremely irritating; it doesn't matter if the person isn't a close friend, it's a violation of social norms, and it's egocentric. We can do better.

Honoring commitments is one of the most important aspects of responsible decision making. So, if you say you'll e-mail an article to a friend, be sure you do it. If you say you'll call tomorrow, be sure you call. We can't control others' behaviors, but we can honor our own commitments, and people appreciate and respect us for doing so.

In addition to honoring commitments, the following are some questions that can help guide responsible decision making.

• Is it safe? For example, texting and driving is not safe, so deciding to text while driving is not responsible decision making.

- Is it legal? Drinking excessively and driving is irresponsible because it's illegal, and it's also obviously unsafe.

- Does it conflict with other responsibilities? Going out partying the night before an exam is not a responsible decision; you are responsible for staying home and studying.

- Will it harm or inconvenience others? Sage canceling at the last minute inconveniences her friends, and failing to honor commitments inconveniences others—or worse.

Keeping these simple guidelines in mind can help us with our own decisions, and we can also use them as a framework when we work with students.

Influences on Social-Emotional Development

Social-emotional development, as with all other forms of development, depends on experience, and the most important sources of these experiences for young people are parents, siblings, and peers. Initially, parents and siblings play the most important role, and as children mature and go to school, the importance of peers increases. Let's look at the influence of these groups.

Parents and Siblings

As we saw in our discussion of parenting styles earlier in the chapter, parents have a powerful influence on development. Parents who model healthy emotions and social skills, talk to their children, and provide loving, consistent, and predictable care create environments that promote healthy social-emotional development. In contrast, home environments that lack structure and predictability and are characterized by frenetic activity and high levels of ambient stimulation, such as a loud television on all day or too much time on electronic devices, detract from social-emotional development (Bobbitt & Gershoff, 2016).

Research has identified two aspects of parenting that are particularly important: maternal warmth and home learning stimulation. Maternal warmth includes expressions of affection, such as hugging, kissing, and praising children. It provides a foundation of caring that is essential for healthy social-emotional development. Home learning stimulation includes parent–child interactions, such as reading, visiting the library, telling stories, and providing reading materials (Baker & Rimm-Kaufman, 2014). "Maternal warmth" may actually be a misnomer, as research doesn't imply that fathers are not important. They are essential for providing the structure and modeling children need to develop positive identities and self-management skills (Bobbitt & Gershoff, 2016).

Siblings assist in the process. When we're young, we're in constant contact with our families and frequently interact with brothers and sisters. Competition, negotiation, and compromise are a part of family life, and these experiences also help promote social-emotional skills (Caspi, 2012).

Peers' Influence on Social-Emotional Development

Ed Psych and You

Think back to the friends you had in middle and high school. How did they influence you then, and how do your friends influence who you are today?

"A vast literature indicates that health-compromising risky behaviors increase when adolescents are with their peers. However, recent work finds that the influence of peers may be positive as well, for example in reinforcing prosocial development" (van Hoorn,

Fuligni, Crone, & Galván, 2016, p. 59). This quote captures the powerful influence peers have on social-emotional development—both negative and positive—and this is particularly true for adolescents. For example, if friends are involved in smoking or underage drinking, an individual is more likely to do the same. On the other hand, if peers display *prosocial behaviors*—voluntary actions intended to benefit others—such as helping and cooperating, and conforming to social norms, such as saying "Excuse me" when bumping someone, students are more likely to demonstrate these same behaviors.

Our choices of friends predict grades, involvement in school, and even behavior problems. For example, if peer groups are academically oriented, they promote effort and achievement, but if they reject school values, students are more likely to cut classes, skip school, cheat, and even use drugs. "One of the most consistent, robust findings in the youth development literature regards the similarity in attitudes and behaviors among adolescents and their friends" (Choukas-Bradley, Giletta, Cohen, & Prinstein, 2015, p. 2197).

Peers also provide students with opportunities to practice social skills, and students with well-developed relationship skills are accepted and liked by their peers, which gives them even more opportunities to practice. The opposite is also true; those lacking relationship skills are often rejected by peers, leading to fewer opportunities to practice and develop (Mayeux, Houser, & Dyches, 2011). Rejected students may become impulsive and aggressive, and over time they tend to withdraw and become social isolates, which can be particularly destructive. For example, research indicates that a relationship exists between social isolation in childhood and health problems, such as cardiovascular disease, in later life (Lacey, Kumari, & Bartley, 2014).

Peers are also a source of emotional support, and students fortunate enough to have emotionally supportive friends are more successful both academically and socially than those without it (Wentzel, Russell, & Baker, 2016). They tend to seek support from others similar in gender, ethnicity, socioeconomic status, academic orientation, and long-term goals (Kornienko, Santos, Martin, & Granger, 2016; MacPherson, Kerr, & Stirling, 2016). This makes sense, since we all gravitate toward others who are like us.

These influences address the questions we asked in *Ed Psych and You* in this section. As you think about what you've just read, you will realize that your friends' attitudes and values are likely to be similar to yours, you practiced social skills in interacting with them, and they provided you with emotional support.

Obstacles to Social-Emotional Development

Healthy social-emotional development is important not only for school success, but also for our quality of life later on. But our modern world includes challenges that can hamper this development. Four of the most important include:

- Alcohol and drugs
- Obesity
- Peer aggression
- School violence

Alcohol and Drugs

Consider these statistics gathered from national surveys (Johnston, O'Malley, Miech, Bachman, & Schulenberg, 2017):

- In 2016, nearly 1 of 5 8th-, 10th-, or 12th-graders have smoked cigarettes in the month prior to the administration of the survey.
- Also in 2016, a third of 12th-graders reported drinking alcohol in the 30-day period prior to the survey; 20% percent of 10th-graders and 7 percent of 8th-graders also reported drinking during the same period.
- Daily (not occasional) rates of marijuana use in 2016 were 0.7%, 2.5%, and 6.0%, for 8th-, 10th-, and 12th-graders, respectively.

- Percentages of students who say they've used cocaine at some point in their lives were 0.8%, 1.3%, and 2.3% for the three grades.

The opioid crisis is having a particularly devastating effect on our country. It has been described as "the deadliest drug crisis in American history" (Salam, 2017, para. 1). Overdoses fueled by opioids are the leading cause of death for Americans under age 50—more than either car accidents or guns. More than 64,000 people died from drug overdoses in 2016, with the sharpest increase occurring in deaths related to fentanyl and other opioids, such as hydrocodone and oxycodone (National Institute on Drug Abuse, 2017). And evidence suggests the problem continued to worsen in 2017. Over two million Americans depend on opioids, an additional 95 million use prescription painkillers—more than use tobacco—and the epidemic crosses age, ethnic, and socioeconomic boundaries. "Narcotics Anonymous meetings . . . are populated by lawyers, accountants, young adults and teenagers who described comfortable middle-class upbringings" (Katz, 2017, para. 18).

The rate of drug overdose deaths in teens aged 15 to 19 in the United States climbed 19% from 2014 to 2015, primarily from the same drugs (Kounang, 2017), and the opioid crisis is having additional impacts; many school districts are seeing increases in student absences, behavioral issues, and special education placements. School officials have even reported students witnessing their parents overdosing (Superville, 2017).

These statistics are particularly significant because student drug use, including smoking and the drugs described above, had been in decline, but attitudes are now wavering. For instance, cigarette smoking among 8th-graders decreased from a peak of nearly 50% in 1996 to 10% in 2016, but attitudes and beliefs about cigarette smoking are no longer moving in a positive direction. And, while 82%, 74%, and 69% of 8th-, 10th-, and 12th-graders, respectively, say they disapprove of marijuana use, between 80% and 90% of 12th graders say that it's easy to get, and nearly 1 of 3 say the same about cocaine (Johnston et al., 2017).

An increase in overdose deaths is obviously a matter of grave concern, and, in addition, the cognitive and social-emotional dangers of drug use are well known. For instance, research has identified a link between long-term marijuana use and lowered IQ (Khamsi, 2013; Rogeberg, 2013). Also, alcohol use in young people is associated with car accidents, delinquency, illicit drug use, long-term social-emotional problems, and criminal behavior (Donaldson, Handren, & Crano, 2016). Alcohol and drug users are less likely to exercise, and they're less likely to develop healthy mechanisms for coping with life's problems (Handren, Donaldson, & Crano, 2016).

School connectedness, the belief by students that adults and peers in the school care about both their learning and them as individuals, is an important protective factor against drug and alcohol abuse. Young people who feel connected to their school are less likely to smoke, use alcohol and drugs, or initiate sex. They also achieve higher performance, have better attendance, and are less likely to drop out of school (Handren et al., 2016).

We can help students develop connections to their school by getting to know them as individuals, addressing them by name, and pronouncing their names correctly (Rice, 2017). And creating classroom environments that are physically and emotionally safe is particularly important in this age of tumult, where classroom lockdown drills, in response to widely publicized school shootings, are commonplace. (We address the topic of school shootings later in this section.)

Obesity

We hear a great deal about the obesity "epidemic" in our country, and this concern is well justified. For instance, obesity rates for adults exceed 35% in 4 states, 30% in 25 others, and in no state is it less than 20% (State of Obesity, 2017).

In addition, more than 1 of 6 children in our country are obese, and experts estimate that that figure will be nearly 60% by the time they're 35. These trends are even more pronounced for members of cultural minorities, students from low SES backgrounds, and LBGTQ youth (Ward et al., 2017).

Long-term health risks, such as high cholesterol and blood pressure, heart disease, and diabetes are well known, but the social-emotional costs may be as, or more, significant. "Obese children face teasing, systematic discrimination, mistreatment, exclusion, and chronic victimization, and they experience more peer rejection, victimization, and teasing than children with other stigmatized attributes" (Jackson & Cunningham, 2015, p. 153).

The problems of obesity become even more pronounced as people get older. For instance, obese individuals are stereotyped as lazy, weak-willed, slovenly, and physically and sexually unattractive. This bias exists in the attitudes of health care professionals, hiring practices in the workforce, interpersonal relationships, and the media (Nutter et al., 2016).

Several factors contribute to the problem, with lack of exercise being one of the most important. Many children get little exercise outside of school, and the amount of exercise they get in school is inadequate (Ramsletter & Murray, 2017). Guidelines suggest that students should get a minimum of an hour of moderate to vigorous physical activity every day, but fewer than 40% of the states in our country require a specific amount of time be spent in gym class in elementary school, and it drops to less than 30% in middle and high schools (Society of Health and Physical Educators, 2016). Further, research indicates that regular exercise can help the brain build and retain durable memories and can even help mitigate the effects of stress and adversity (Miller et al., 2018). So, the benefits of exercise go beyond their impact on obesity and even physical health; they also support cognition.

In addition, the typical tween (ages 8–12) spends 4½ hours a day and teens (ages 13–18) spend 6½ hours a day on screen media (Rideout, 2015). Obviously, when they're sitting in front of their screens, they aren't exercising.

What can we as teachers do? Information and our own modeling are our best weapons. For example, research suggests that students have a limited understanding of the importance of exercise and healthy eating, so providing information about these topics can make a difference (Leatherdale, 2013). Modeling these habits, exercising, and making an effort to control our own weight (which is good for our health as well) can be even more important.

The Need for Recess in Elementary Schools. Only 16% of the states in our country require elementary schools to provide recess (Society of Health and Physical Educators, 2016). This is particularly problematic, because an expanding body of research suggests that recess makes an important contribution to children's total education—it increases learning, makes classroom management easier, contributes to physical well-being, and promotes social-emotional development (Chang & Coward, 2015). We have historically thought of recess as a time for children to simply play and burn off energy, but school leaders are now becoming aware of its wider contribution. "For most children, recess is a context and time when they can practice essential social skills with peers" (Locke, Shih, Kretzmann, & Kasari, 2016, p. 653).

Recess is so important that it is, in fact, described as ". . . a right of every child and by the American Academy of Pediatrics as an essential part of children's social, emotional, cognitive, and physical well-being" (London, Westrich, Stokes-Guinan, & McLaughlin, 2015, p. 53). This is particularly true for children who are economically disadvantaged, who have fewer opportunities for healthy physical activity outside of school (London et al., 2015).

Given its benefits, why are so many schools cutting back on recess? *Time* is the answer. Many schools are pressured to improve scores on high-stakes tests, so they allocate extra time to the areas—reading and math—that are covered on the tests. These decisions, however, are having adverse effects on children's development (Berk, 2019b).

Whether or not recess exists is a matter of school or district policy, so it appears that you—particularly as a beginning teacher—can do little if your school doesn't include it. However, you can share research confirming the importance of recess for elementary students, and in faculty meetings you can speak out, encouraging your school leaders to consider adding recess, or pressuring district leaders to add recess to children's total school experience. And, if nothing else, you can have periodic classroom breaks where you simply have students get out of their desks, move around, and do some exercises, such as jumping jacks. Even these minor breaks can help in multiple ways.

Peer Aggression

Peer aggression refers to words or physical actions that hurt, humiliate, or place other students at a disadvantage, and it exists in several forms. For example, instrumental aggression, the most common, is an action aimed at gaining an object or privilege, such as cutting in line, or a young child grabbing another's toy. Gaining an advantage, as opposed to hurting another child, is the goal, but being hurt may result. In contrast, physical and relational aggression are intended to hurt others, such as pushing another child down on the playground as in physical aggression, or spreading a rumor in an attempt to damage relationships or social status in the case of relational aggression. Stereotypes suggest that boys are more likely to be physical aggressors whereas girls more commonly use relational aggression, but evidence indicates that the different types of aggression are not gender specific (Mulvey & Killen, 2016). Aggression can be proactive, where students deliberately initiate aggressive acts, or reactive, an aggressive response to frustration or a perceived aggressive act (Donoghue & Raia-Hawrylak, 2016).

Highly aggressive students have difficulty relating to their peers, and they may seek out peer groups that can lead them to delinquency and—at an extreme—criminal behavior (Simons & Burt, 2011). Aggressive students often grow up to be aggressive adults who have trouble getting along with others in both the workplace and the world at large (Martocci, 2015; van Geel et al., 2017).

Genetics play a role, but home environments are primary causes of aggression (Wang, 2017). Parents of aggressive children tend to be authoritarian, punitive, and inconsistent, and they often use physical punishers such as slapping or spanking for unacceptable behavior. These environments can lead to hostile attribution bias, a tendency to interpret others' behaviors as antagonistic or belligerent (Hubbard, Morrow, Romano, & McAuliffe, 2010). Sean, in our chapter's opening case study, thinking that other students are "out to get him," appears to have this problem. Hostile attribution bias is also linked to deficits in perspective taking, empathy, and emotional self-regulation, as well as depression and impulsivity (Gagnon, McDuff, Daelman, & Fourmier, 2015; Smith, Summers, Dillon, Macatee, & Cougle, 2016).

Bullying. Bullying is a form of physical or relational aggression that involves a systematic or repetitive abuse of power between students (Barlett, Prot, Anderson, & Gentile, 2017). Bullying most often involves an imbalance of power, such as bullies being bigger, stronger, or having higher social status than bullying targets, who typically have characteristics that put them at risk for being bullied, such as being overweight, immature, anxious, physically underdeveloped, or having a disability. They are often socially isolated and lack self-confidence (Bartlett et al., 2017; Martocci, 2015).

Getting accurate information about the incidence of bullying is difficult because statistics vary. For example, one large study found that half of students said they were bullied (Josephson Institute Center for Youth Ethics, 2010), whereas another large study found that 35% of students reported being bullied (Modecki, Minchin, Harbaught, Guerra, & Runions, 2014). A more recent study put the figure at slightly more than 20% (National Center for Education Statistics, 2016). The pattern of decrease that we see in the three sets of statistics makes sense because additional research indicates that bullying in schools is generally decreasing (Lessne & Cidade, 2015; U.S. Department of Justice, 2016).

This decrease doesn't imply in any way that bullying is no longer a problem, because even if the figure is 20% it means that 1 of every 5 students in schools is the target of bullying. And the outcomes for both targets and those doing the bullying are destructive. For example, students who engage in bullying behavior are at increased risk for academic problems, substance abuse, and violent behavior later in adolescence and adulthood (Centers for Disease Control and Prevention, 2016b). Research also indicates that bullies lack positive personality traits, such as agreeableness (van Geel et al., 2017).

Targets of bullying are placed at particular risk. "Young people who are bullied report compromised well-being related to social relationships, mental health, and academic achievement" (Day, Snapp, & Russell, 2016, p. 416). And bullying that targets students because of race or ethnicity, gender, and perceived or actual sexual orientation is even more strongly linked to negative academic and social-emotional outcomes (Day et al., 2016). Further, targets of repeated bullying incidents begin to ask, "Why me?" and "Am I someone who deserves to be picked on?" which can lead to health problems, such as headaches, stomachaches, and destructive emotions such as depression and, in the extreme, suicide (Gini & Pozzoli, 2013; Martocci, 2015).

Because of the perceived seriousness of bullying, by 2015 all 50 states had passed anti-bullying laws (Temkin, 2015), and many districts have implemented zero-tolerance policies. These laws and policies have been largely ineffective for reducing incidents of bullying, however (Kull, Kosciw, & Greytak, 2015; Paluck, Shepherd, & Aronow, 2016). Students' comments give us some additional insights into what limits the effectiveness of anti-bullying programs. For example, they say that boring presentations, repetitive messages, negatively worded anti-bullying messages, presenters who lack credibility—such as people from outside the school—and consequences perceived as unfair or inconsistent all limit anti-bullying programs' effectiveness (Cunningham et al., 2016). Further, research indicates that anti-bullying interventions that focus on punishing perpetrators are also ineffective (Day et al., 2016; Kohn, 2016).

Peer juries and peer counselors are infrequently used, and their effectiveness is also uncertain, whereas school-wide efforts that include increasing adult supervision, talking with bullies after bullying incidents, and immediate, appropriate, and consistent consequences for bullying have been found to be more effective (Juvonen, Schacter, Sainio, & Salmivalli, 2016).

Awareness is the key factor in effective interventions. Making students aware of the negative personality characteristics often associated with students prone to bullying and what constitutes bullying behavior can often contribute more to reducing bullying than interventions focusing on punishment (Juvonen et al., 2016).

We examine bullying again in Chapter 12 when we discuss classroom management, and we offer specific suggestions for responding to bullying there.

Technology, Learning, and Development: Cyberbullying.   The Internet, whether accessed by smartphone or some other platform, is used by nearly 9 of 10 people in our country, and "[i]n 2014, approximately 70% of individuals between the ages of 18 and 24 years reported experiencing some form of online harassment, including being purposefully embarrassed, called offensive names, or repeatedly being physically threatened" (Gibb & Devereux, 2016, p. 313). This persecution illustrates **cyberbullying**, a form of bullying that occurs when students use electronic media to harass or intimidate other students, and it's an important problem. As an example, a girl breaks up with her boyfriend and he then spreads ugly rumors or private pictures of her on the Internet. Cyberbullying has received enormous attention after widely publicized incidents of suicide or other forms of violence that have resulted from being bullied in cyberspace. Both school officials and parents have become increasingly aware of this growing problem. Because of its anonymity, cyberbullying is also difficult to combat; consequences for perpetrators rarely exist.

Cyberbullying tends to follow the same patterns as traditional forms of bullying; students who are bullies and bullied on the playground play similar roles in cyberspace

(Lapidot-Lefler, & Dolev-Cohen, 2015). In fact, two-thirds of cyberbullies also exhibit aggressive behaviors in other contexts. The anonymity of the Internet is what distinguishes cyberbullying from other types, and it can make bullies even less sensitive to the hurtful nature of their actions (Whittaker & Kowalski, 2015).

You can take several steps to prevent being cyberbullied, and you can also share them with your students when you begin teaching. They include the following:

- *Protect passwords.* Create "strong" passwords, and don't share them with anyone, even your closest friends.

- *Watch what you post.* Remember that anything you post on social media or any other aspect of the Internet is out there for the world to see—even if you send it only to a trusted friend. For example, a cyberbully could use the suggestive picture you posted of yourself to make your life miserable. And a compromised post could damage your reputation and cost you a job, internship, or scholarship.

- *Use caution in what you open.* Never open a message—e-mail, text, social media message—or click on a link sent from someone you don't know or from known bullies. Delete them immediately without reading them.

- *Always log out.* Don't stay logged on when you walk away from your computer or smartphone. For example, if you don't log out of your Facebook account at the library, the next person who uses that computer can access your account.

- *"Google" yourself.* Search your name in major search engines (such as Google, Bing, or Yahoo, the three most popular, with 1.6 billion, 400 million, and 300 million estimated unique monthly visitors, respectively, in 2017 [eBiz, 2017]). If any personal information or photo comes up which cyberbullies could use to target you, immediately do what you can to have it removed.

- *Be a good citizen.* Treat others as you would want to be treated. If you misbehave online, you send the message that cyberbullying is acceptable.

If you're the target of cyberbullying, identify the source and print the message as evidence of harassment and share the information with school leaders or other officials.

These steps aren't guaranteed to stop all cyberbullying, but they can make a difference. And if bullies even think you can identify them, they're less likely to bully. When you teach, discussing the problem in class, emphasizing the hurt it causes to others, and promoting empathy, fair play, and appropriate treatment of others can make a long-term difference in cyberbullying.

MyLab Education Application Exercise 3.3: Preventing Bullying in Schools

In this exercise you will be asked to analyze strategies for preventing bullying.

School Violence

School violence is an extreme form of aggression that involves serious bodily injury or death. The following include some school violence statistics (Centers for Disease Control and Prevention, 2016b):

- Of all youth homicides, less than 2.6% occur at school, and this percentage has been relatively stable over the past decade. This figure appears small, but even 2 of 100 homicides occurring in schools is significant.

- Approximately 1 of 10 teachers report that they have been threatened with injury by a student from their school, and 5% say they have been physically attacked.

- Approximately 12% of students ages 12–18 report that gangs are present at their school during the school year.

- In grades 9–12, nearly 8% of students reported that they've been in a physical fight on school property in the 12 months before the survey was taken, and nearly 6% said they didn't go to school on one or more days because they didn't feel safe.

- Slightly more than 4% of students reported carrying a weapon—gun, knife, or club—on school property on one or more days in the 30 days before the survey, and 6% reported being threatened or injured with a weapon on school property.

All schools have policies designed to deal with issues such as these, and you will be provided with information about these policies when you take your first job.

School Shootings   School violence is increasingly in the public eye because of widely publicized school shootings that have occurred over the last two decades. The most prominent were the Columbine, Colorado, massacre in 1999, in which 12 students were killed; the Sandy Hook Elementary School shooting in Newtown, Connecticut, in 2012, where 20 students and 6 adults where shot and killed; and more recently at Marjory Stoneman Douglas High School in Parkland Florida, where 14 students, a teacher, a coach, and the school's athletic director were killed by a 19-year-old ex-student on Valentine's Day in 2018 (Gold, 2018). Then, only three months later, 8 students and 2 teachers were killed in a Santa Fe, Texas, shooting (Fernandez, Blinder, & Chokshi, 2018).

The Florida shooting became particularly noteworthy because it precipitated responses not seen in the aftermath of other school shootings. For instance, the massacre triggered student activism related to guns and gun control that hadn't occurred before. And, in response to customer outrage, a number of prominent businesses—such as First National Bank of Omaha; Hertz, Avis, and Budget car rental agencies; Allied and North American Van Lines; MetLife insurance company; the software company Symantec; Best Western Hotels; and Delta and United Airlines, among others—cut ties with the National Rifle Association (NRA). The NRA, however, continued its adamant support for gun rights despite the killing sprees, leaving the likelihood of significant political action on guns doubtful (The Associated Press, 2018).

The Florida shooting also resulted in suggestions that could, if implemented, have radical implications for teachers. For instance, in its aftermath the Trump administration suggested "arming some teachers" in our nation's schools (Klein, 2018). The reaction to this suggestion was swift and overwhelmingly negative. Teachers were uniformly opposed (Bosman, & Saulfeb, 2018; Gstalter, 2018; Palmer, 2018), the former head of the New York City police department described the idea as "the height of lunacy" (Devaney, 2018), and other experts argued that arming teachers is unethical (Yacek, 2018).

Deaths, and even non-fatal injuries, are only part of the problem; the emotional toll is also an important factor. For instance, a report by the Government Accountability Office (2016) found that nearly two-thirds of schools now conduct "active shooter" drills, and lockdown drills are implemented in nearly all schools (Will, 2018). These drills provide teachers and students with essential information but also incite fear, particularly in younger children. "[T]eachers say the lockdown drills never lose their impact. While some teachers say they're glad that their schools prepare for the worst-case scenario, many also say the drills have become increasingly surreal and unnerving" (Will, 2018, para. 5). Additional research indicates that exposure to youth violence can lead to a wide array of negative health problems, including alcohol and drug use, depression, anxiety, fear, and even suicide (Centers for Disease Control and Prevention, 2016b).

One of your most important roles as a teacher is to create a safe and orderly classroom environment for your students, and lockdown and "active shooter" drills admittedly make your job that much more challenging. You may take some solace, however, in the fact that in spite of the horrific acts that receive widespread publicity, school shootings—statistically—remain rare (Centers for Disease Control and Prevention, 2016b). For example, fewer than 240 schools—or one-fifth of 1 percent of more than 96,300 schools surveyed—reported at least one school-related shooting (Indicators of School Crime and Safety, 2018).

This comment isn't intended in the least to diminish the significance of these unspeakable events, but rather to remind you that the likelihood of your school being involved in a shooting is still small. Prepare yourself and your students—absolutely. Dwell on the possibility of being involved in a school shooting—no.

Using Educational Psychology in Teaching: Suggestions for Promoting Social-Emotional Development with Your Students

In our discussion of personality development, we suggested that you do the following to promote it in your students:

- Model positive personality traits.
- Use concrete examples and discussions to teach positive personality traits.
- Use an authoritative classroom management style.

Parallel suggestions exist for social-emotional development. As with all forms of development, it has a cognitive component, and it's on this factor—students' awareness and understanding—that we attempt to capitalize as we attempt to help our students develop socially and emotionally. In other words, we should model, explicitly teach and discuss social-emotional skills, and use a classroom management style that promotes social development.

Let's see how Teresa Manteras, a first-year teacher, attempts to promote social development in her students.

"How are you doing, Teresa?" Carla Ambergi, a veteran colleague, asks as Teresa enters the teachers' lounge.

"A little discouraged," Teresa sighs. "I learned about all those great cooperative learning activities in my university classes, but when I try them with my kids, all they do is snip at each other and argue about who is doing what. Maybe I should just lecture."

"They're not used to working in groups," Carla smiles, "and they haven't learned how to cooperate. They need practice."

"Yes, I know, . . . but I don't even know where to start."

"Would you like me to come in during my planning period? Maybe I can help."

"That would be great!" Teresa replies with a sense of relief.

Carla comes in the next day, and then she and Teresa sit down together after school. "First, I think you do an excellent job of modeling social skills," Carla comments. "You consider where the kids are coming from, you treat disagreements as an opportunity to solve problems, and you are supportive. . . . But, your modeling goes right over their heads. They don't notice what you're doing. So, I suggest that you be more specific; tell the kids what you're modeling and give them some examples. Then, add a few rules that will help guide their interactions with each other. It will take some time, but it will make a difference."

"Good points," Teresa nods. "I hadn't quite thought about it that way before."

Carla then helps Teresa develop several rules that address behavior in groups:

1. Listen politely until other people are finished before speaking.
2. Treat other people's ideas with courtesy and respect.
3. Paraphrase other people's ideas in your own words before disagreeing.
4. Encourage everyone to participate.

Teresa starts the next day. Before breaking students into groups, she tells them that they are going to work on their social skills, and she models several examples, such as making eye contact, checking perceptions, and listening attentively. Then, she presents and explains the new rules, has volunteers role play an example for each, and guides a discussion of the examples.

Students then begin their group work. Teresa monitors the groups, intervenes when they have difficulties, and reconvenes the class when she sees a similar problem in several groups. The students are far from perfect, but they are improving.

Now let's look at Teresa's attempts to apply the suggestions.

Model Social-Emotional Skills.   As with promoting all forms of development, modeling social-emotional skills is arguably the most effective action we can take in promoting these same skills in our students (and again we see the relevance of the quote,—"Be the change that you wish to see in the world," at the beginning of the chapter). For example, Teresa modeled making eye contact, checking perceptions, and listening attentively with her students. We can also model more advanced skills, such as perspective taking, self-management, and responsible decision making. And, as with all positive traits, attitudes, and behaviors, this modeling takes little extra time or effort. It's more a matter of being aware of the value of modeling these behaviors, and promoting your awareness is our goal in writing this section.

Explicitly Teach Social-Emotional Skills.   Earlier in the chapter we saw how Ramon Jiménez used vignettes to illustrate desirable and undesirable personality traits. Teresa used a similar approach in her attempts to teach social-emotional skills, but instead of using vignettes to illustrate the skills, she first modeled them and then had her students provide examples through role play. She used role play because it is concrete and actively involves students in the process.

Then, Teresa had her students practice the skills during group work, and she gave them feedback. Students won't become skilled after one or two activities, but with time, practice, and explicit instruction, these skills can be developed and refined.

Discussions are an important part of the process. Interestingly, students are often unaware of how they "come across," and they can't develop their social-emotional skills if they don't realize—in the first place—that these skills can be improved. So, our goal is to help students understand social-emotional development and its impact on success and satisfaction in school. And, in helping students reach this goal we're capitalizing on the cognitive component of social-emotional development. Specific examples, such as those provided by the students during role play, provide concrete reference points for discussions, and the discussions are the mechanisms that can lead to students' awareness and understanding. For example, when a discussion helps students realize that a lack of emotional control can lead to peer rejection, which then leads to fewer friends, the likelihood of them attempting to improve their skills increases.

Use Classroom Management to Promote Social-Emotional Development.   Finally, Teresa created a set of rules designed to support students as they worked together. She presented only four rules, first because they supplemented her general classroom rules, and because a small number makes them easier to remember. (We discuss rules and how to use them effectively in Chapter 12.)

Her combination of the rules, her students' role playing, discussions, and her own modeling all contributed to her students' awareness and understanding of social-emotional skills and their importance in their lives. In time, and with effort and practice, these efforts can make a difference in students' social development.

Classroom Connections

Promoting Social-Emotional Development in Classrooms

1. Self-awareness is individuals' ability to understand their own thoughts and emotions, and self-management is their ability to regulate their emotions, thoughts, and behaviors in a variety of contexts. Promote self-awareness and self-management in your students.

- **Elementary:** When one of her students displays inappropriate emotions, such as an emotional outburst, a second-grade teacher stops her learning activity and discusses the incident and what the child might have done differently. She then models an appropriate emotional response and openly praises students when she sees them demonstrate appropriate behaviors.

- **Middle School:** An eighth-grade teacher uses classroom incidents, such as a student behaving inappropriately, as concrete reference points for discussions of the importance of self-awareness and self-management. She then periodically has her students role play inappropriate and appropriate emotions and behaviors in different contexts, such as the classroom and also activities outside of school. Because social acceptance is becoming increasingly important to middle school students, she emphasizes the relationship between self-awareness and self-management and social success.

- **High School:** A 10th-grade teacher uses written case studies (similar to the case study with Ramon Jiménez earlier in the chapter) to illustrate the characteristics of self-awareness and self-management, and he revisits the discussions of the case studies throughout the school year to emphasize the relationships between self-awareness and self-management and success both in school and the world outside of school.

2. Social awareness is an understanding of social norms for behavior, the ability to take others' perspectives and feel empathy for people from a variety of backgrounds and cultures. Relationship skills are abilities needed to establish and maintain healthy and rewarding relationships with others. Promote social awareness and relationship skills in your students.

- **Elementary:** To teach perspective taking and promote empathy in her students, a fourth-grade teacher has them analyze different characters' motives and feelings when they discuss a story they've read. She asks, "What is each character thinking? Why do you believe they think that way? How would you feel if you were that person?" She then has the students discuss each of the characters, their perspectives, and their feelings, encouraging her students to "walk in the characters' shoes." As they discuss the characters, she has the students practice speaking clearly, making eye contact with each other, and asking clarifying questions.

- **Middle School:** A middle school science teacher stays after school to provide opportunities for small groups of students to talk both about class work and issues with parents and friends. When students bring up social conflicts, she listens patiently but encourages students to think about the motives and feelings of the other people involved. As the students discuss the issues, she reminds them to get to their points clearly and quickly, avoid interruptions, and offer supportive comments.

- **High School:** A history teacher encourages his students to consider points of view when they read reports of historical events. For example, when his students study the Civil War, he reminds them that both sides thought they were morally right and asks questions such as, "How did the different sides in the war interpret the Emancipation Proclamation? Why do you suppose they felt so differently? Why do you suppose each side thought they were morally right with respect to the issue?" As a framework for the discussions, he provides an outline of desirable relationship skills, and they use the framework throughout the school year.

3. Responsible decision making is the ability to make constructive choices about personal behavior and interactions with others, based on an understanding of consequences for actions. Promote responsible decision making in your students.

- **Elementary:** When her students "make irresponsible decisions"—the language she uses with her students—such as interrupting a classmate who is talking, she stops what she is doing and has a brief discussion about responsible decision making. She uses classroom incidents, such as this example, as concrete reference points to teach responsible decision making.

(continued)

- **Middle School:** An eighth-grade English teacher some-times purposefully leaves decisions about individual assign-ments up to the groups in cooperative learning activities, and then discusses the decisions in whole-class activities. During the discussions, she emphasizes consequences for irresponsible decisions, such as how learning is affected when students decide to avoid challenging tasks.
- **High School:** A history teacher strongly empha-sizes honoring commitments, and models honoring commitments in his teaching. For example, he makes it a point to tell his students that he will have their tests back at a designated time, he has them back then, and he reminds students that he made a commitment and is then obligated to honor it. He also formally teaches responsible decision making using the set of questions that appear in the section on responsible decision mak-ing as a framework for making decisions about appropri-ate behavior.

MyLab Education Self-Check 3.3

Development of Morality and Social Responsibility

3.4   Use theories of moral development to explain differences in people's responses to ethical issues.

Moral development involves advances in people's conceptions of right and wrong, the development of social responsibility, and acquiring prosocial traits such as honesty, cooperation, and supporting others. As we'll see in this section, moral development advances when children encounter moral issues, try to make sense of them, and in the process construct an individual sense of right and wrong (Jonas, 2016; Kretz, 2015).

Moral issues are common in schools. Let's look at a simple example.

MyLab Education
Video Example 3.3
Prosocial traits, such as cooperation and supporting others, are important components of moral development, and this process begins early in life. Here, kindergarten teacher Cecilia Fowler promotes an understanding of kindness and friendship in her young students.

Amanda Kellinger (our teacher in the case study at the beginning of the chapter) says to her students as they're working on a seatwork assignment, "I need to run to the main office for a moment. Work quietly until I get back. I'll only be gone a few minutes."

Amanda leaves, and amidst a shuffling of papers Gary whispers, "Psst, what math prob-lems are we supposed to do?"

"Shh! No talking," Talitha says, pointing to the rules on the bulletin board.

"But he needs to know so he can do his work," Krystal replies. "It's the evens on page 79."

"Who cares?" Jacob mumbles. "She's not here. She won't catch us."

How might we explain the differences between Talitha's, Krystal's and Jacob's reactions to the rule about no talking? More importantly, as students move through life, how do they think about and act upon their moral beliefs? These are all moral issues.

Society's Interest in Moral Development

Moral development has always been a priority in our society, and interest in it has increased in recent years, partially due to disturbing trends in our country. For example, as we saw earlier in the chapter, 1 of 5 students report being bullied in schools (National Center for Education Statistics, 2016). Also, cheating is common, and many students don't see a connection between cheating and morality (Tyler, 2015).

Outside of schools, political corruption and scandals that led to the "Great Recession" at the end of the first decade in this century sent shock waves through the financial com-munity and American society in general. Oxford Dictionaries dubbed "post-truth"—the idea that facts and evidence don't matter as much as emotion and personal belief in shaping public opinion—their international word of the year for 2016 (Wang, 2016).

Moral issues are also embedded in the curriculum. History, in addition to a chronology of events, is the study of people's responses to moral issues, such as human suffering, justice, and whether decisions to go to war are justified. And novels such as *To Kill a Mockingbird, The Scarlet Letter,* and *A Tale of Two Cities* have long been staples of the curriculum, not only because they are good literature but also because they examine moral issues.

Moral development is an integral part of development in general, and students' beliefs about right and wrong influence their behavior. For instance, research suggests that the extent to which adolescents believe the world is fair and just influences their attitudes toward the victims of bullying (Cunningham et al., 2016), and incidents of cheating and vandalism decrease if students believe they are morally wrong (Tyler, 2015). Also, the moral atmosphere of a school—for example, democratic and prosocial versus authoritarian—can influence not only moral development, but also student motivation and the value students place on their learning experiences (Paluck, Shepherd, & Aronow, 2016). Understanding moral development helps us better guide our students in this vital area.

Social Domain Theory of Moral Development

Ed Psych and You

Think about these questions:

Is it okay to pass a parked school bus with its stop sign out if no children are leaving the bus?

Is driving faster than the speed limit acceptable if everyone else is driving about the same speed?

Is it permissible to respond in class if your instructor hasn't called on you?

Is it okay to get a tattoo or pierce your nose or eyebrow?

To understand moral development we first need to make distinctions between *moral, conventional,* and *personal* domains. The **moral domain** deals with basic principles of right, wrong, and justice, whereas the **conventional domain** addresses societal norms and appropriate ways of behaving in specific situations. For instance, it's likely that your instructors allow students to respond in class without being called on, and it's okay to yell at an athletic event but not in a classroom. Social conventions also vary according to culture and setting. For example, young people addressing adults by their first names is acceptable in some cultures but not in others.

The **personal domain** refers to decisions that are not socially regulated and do not harm or violate others' rights. For instance, parents and other adults may think that tattoos and body piercing look awful, but they aren't morally wrong, and they aren't usually addressed by social conventions such as dress codes.

Children as young as 2 or 3 begin to make distinctions between moral, conventional, and personal domains (Josephs & Rakoczy, 2016). They understand, for example, that it's wrong to hit and hurt someone regardless of where you are and whether or not rules prohibiting it exist. Some researchers even suggest that we are born with a rudimentary sense of justice that can be observed in the first months of life (Bloom, 2010).

The lines between the moral, conventional, and personal domains are often blurred and depend on individuals' interpretations. Some teachers, for example, may view calling on all students in class as a matter of equal access and fairness, thereby making it a moral issue, whereas others are more likely to see it merely as a simple learning strategy and classify it in the conventional domain. Further, some researchers have historically viewed reasoning about social conventions and society's rules as an advance in moral development (Kohlberg, 1981, 1984).

Piaget's Theory of Moral Development

Although we think of cognitive development when examining Piaget's work, he also studied moral development, and he found that children's responses to moral problems can be divided into two broad stages. In the first, called **external morality**, children view rules as fixed, permanent, and enforced by authority figures. When Talitha said, "Shh! No talking," and pointed to the rules, she was thinking at this stage. It didn't matter that Gary was only asking about the assignment; rules are rules. In responding "Who cares? She's not here. She won't catch us," Jacob demonstrated a similar level of thinking; no authority figure was there to enforce the rule. External morality typically lasts to about age 10. Piaget believed that parents and teachers who stress unquestioned adherence to adult authority retard moral development and unintentionally encourage students to remain at this level.

When students advance to **autonomous morality**, Piaget's second stage, they begin to rely on themselves instead of others to regulate moral behavior, and their thinking (cognition) becomes more significant. For example, they begin to consider intention and view attempted help (a good intention) "more good" than help that occurs by accident (Margoni & Surian, 2017). Krystal's comment, "But he needs to know so he can do his work," demonstrates this emphasis on cognition; she reasoned that Gary's whispering was as an honest request for assistance rather than an infraction of rules.

Kohlberg's Theory of Moral Development

Lawrence Kohlberg, a Harvard educator and psychologist, built on and extended Piaget's work. He used **moral dilemmas**, ambiguous, conflicting situations that require a person to make a moral decision, as the basis for his research. Let's look at an example.

Steve, a high school senior, works at a night job to help support his mother, a single parent of three. Steve is conscientious and works hard in his classes, but he doesn't have enough time to study.

Because of his night work and lack of interest in history, he is barely passing. If he fails the final exam, he will fail the course and won't graduate. He isn't scheduled to work the night before the exam, so he has extra time to study. But early in the evening his boss calls, desperate to have Steve come in and replace another employee who called in sick at the last moment. His boss pressures him, so Steve goes to work at 8:00 p.m. and comes home exhausted at 2:00 a.m. He tries to study but falls asleep on the couch with his book in his lap. His mother wakes him for school at 6:30 a.m.

Steve goes to history, looks at the test, and goes blank. Everything seems like a jumble. Clarice, one of the best students in the class, happens to have her answer sheet positioned so that he can clearly see every answer by barely moving his eyes.

Is he justified in cheating?

This is a moral issue because it deals with matters of right and wrong, and it's a dilemma because any decision Steve makes has positive and negative consequences. If he cheats, he will pass the test, but cheating is wrong. On the other hand, if he doesn't cheat, he will likely fail the course and not graduate.

Kohlberg (1963, 1969, 1981, 1984) used children's responses to moral dilemmas as the basis for his research, which he later developed into his theory. Like Piaget, he concluded that moral reasoning exists in stages, and development occurs when people's reasoning advances to a higher stage. On the basis of research conducted in Great Britain, Malaysia, Mexico, Taiwan, and Turkey, Kohlberg concluded that the development of moral reasoning is similar across cultures.

Kohlberg originally described moral reasoning as occurring at three levels, consisting of two stages each. They're outlined in Table 3.4 and discussed in the sections that follow. As you read the descriptions, remember that the specific response to a moral dilemma isn't the primary issue; the level of moral development is determined by the reasons a person gives for making the decision.

Level I: Preconventional Ethics

Preconventional morality is an egocentric orientation that focuses on the consequences of actions for the self. In the **punishment–obedience** stage, people make moral decisions based on their chances of getting caught and being punished. If a person is caught and punished, an act is morally wrong; if not, the act is right. A person believing that Steve is justified in cheating because he's unlikely to get caught is reasoning at this stage. At Stage 2, **market exchange**, people reason that an act is morally justified if it results in reciprocity, such as "You do something for me, and I'll do something for you." Much of the politics in our country operates at this stage; the winner of an election then gives important jobs to his or her supporters.

Level II: Conventional Ethics

When development advances to **conventional morality**, reasoning no longer depends on the consequences for the individual but instead is linked to acceptance of society's conceptions of right and wrong and the creation of an orderly world. In Stage 3, **interpersonal harmony**, people make decisions based on loyalty, living up to the expectations of others, and social conventions. For example, a teenager on a date who believes she should meet a curfew because she doesn't want to worry her parents is reasoning at this stage. A person reasoning at Stage 3 might offer two different perspectives on Steve's dilemma. One could argue that he needs to work to help his family and therefore is justified in cheating. A contrasting view, but still at this stage, would suggest that he should not cheat because people would think badly of him if they found out.

At Stage 4, **law and order**, people follow laws and rules for their own sake. They don't make moral decisions to please other people or follow social norms as in Stage 3; rather, they believe that laws and rules exist to guide behavior and create an orderly

MyLab Education
Video Example 3.4
Young children's reasoning about moral issues tends to focus on consequences for actions, such as being caught and punished for a misdeed. Notice how this young student reasons about finding a lost wallet and what he should do in response to the find.

TABLE 3.4 Kohlberg's stages of moral reasoning

Level 1 Preconventional Ethics (*Typical of preschool and elementary students.*)	The ethics of egocentrism. Typical of children up to about age 10. Called preconventional because children typically don't fully understand rules set down by others.
Stage 1: Punishment–Obedience	Consequences of acts determine whether they're good or bad. Individuals make moral decisions without considering the needs or feelings of others.
Stage 2: Market Exchange	The ethics of "What's in it for me?" Obeying rules and exchanging favors are judged in terms of the benefit to the individual.
Level II Conventional Ethics (*Seen in older elementary and middle school students and many high school students.*)	The ethics of others. Typical of 10- to 20-year-olds. The name comes from conformity to the rules and conventions of society.
Stage 3: Interpersonal Harmony	Ethical decisions are based on concern for or the opinions of others. What pleases, helps, or is approved of by others characterizes this stage.
Stage 4: Law and Order	The ethics of laws, rules, and societal order. Rules and laws are inflexible and are obeyed for their own sake.
Level III Postconventional Ethics (*Rarely seen before college, and the universal principles stage is seldom seen even in adults.*)	The ethics of principle. Rarely reached before age 20 and only by a small portion of the population. The focus is on the principles underlying society's rules.
Stage 5: Social Contract	Rules and laws represent agreements among people about behavior that benefits society. Rules can be changed when they no longer meet society's needs.
Stage 6: Universal Principles	Rarely encountered in life. Ethics are determined by abstract and general principles that transcend societal rules.

world, and they should be followed uniformly. A person reasoning at Stage 4 would argue that Steve should not cheat because "It's against the rules to cheat," or "What kind of world would we live in if people thought cheating was okay?"

Stages 3 and 4 relate to the question, "Is it okay to drive faster than the speed limit if everyone else is driving about the same speed?" that we asked earlier in *Ed Psych and You*. People reasoning at Stage 3 would conclude that speeding is okay, since everyone else is doing it. On the other hand, still at Stage 3, they might conclude that it isn't okay, because it isn't safe, and it's wrong to put people in danger. People reasoning at Stage 4 would conclude that the speed limit is the law, and breaking the law is wrong.

Level III: Postconventional Ethics

Postconventional morality, also called *principled morality*, views moral issues in terms of abstract principles of right and wrong. People reasoning at Level III have transcended both the individual and societal levels. They don't follow rules for their own sake, as a person reasoning at Stage 4 would suggest; rather, they follow rules because the rules are principled agreements. Only a small portion of the population attains this level, and most of these don't reach it until their middle to late 20s.

In Stage 5, **social contract**, people make moral decisions based on socially agreed-upon principles. A person reasoning at Stage 5 would say that Steve's cheating is wrong because teachers and learners agree in principle that grades should reflect achievement, and cheating violates this agreement.

At the sixth and final stage, **universal principles**, the individual's moral reasoning is based on abstract, general principles that transcend society's laws. People at this stage define right and wrong in terms of internalized universal standards. "The Golden Rule" is a commonly cited example. Because very few people operate at this stage and questions have been raised about the existence of "universal" principles, Kohlberg de-emphasized this stage in his later writings (Kohlberg, 1984).

MyLab Education Application Exercise 3.4: Kohlberg's Theory of Moral Reasoning

In this exercise you will be asked to use concepts from Kohlberg's theory to analyze the moral reasoning of four different students, two in elementary school and two in middle school.

Evaluating Kohlberg's Theory of Moral Development

One of the most important issues related to Kohlberg's work is the extent to which moral *reasoning*—the focus of his theory—contributes to moral *behavior*. Some researchers suggest that virtually no relationship exists between the two (Kretz, 2015). They argue, for example, that an individual could suggest that failure to pay back a loan made by a friend is wrong, but have no compunctions about exceeding speed limits on heavily traveled city streets. Others cite research suggesting a robust link between moral reasoning and moral behavior (action). "Moral reasoning has a consistent effect on action. . . . This effect, . . . indicates that the strategy of promoting moral reasoning to enhance morality is a sound strategy and a way to overcome immorality and moral indifference" (de Posada, & Vargas-Trujillo, 2015, p. 418). Additional research supports this latter position (English, 2016; Segev, 2017). For instance, reasoning at the higher stages is associated with altruistic behaviors, such as defending victims of injustice, and adolescents reasoning at the lower stages are likely to be less honest and more likely to engage in antisocial behavior, such as delinquency and drug use (Brugman, 2010; Gibbs, 2014).

Other issues with respect to his theory exist. For example, research suggests that few people move beyond Stage 4 (Gibbs, 2014), so if postconventional reasoning is required

TABLE 3.5 Evaluating Kohlberg's theory of moral development

Key question	How do changes in moral reasoning occur?
Basic description of moral development	Moral development is a gradual, continuous cognitive process that occurs as a result of experience with moral issues and interactions with others.
Catalysts for change	• Encounters with moral dilemmas in everyday life • Social interactions with others
Key concepts	• Moral dilemma • Preconventional morality • Conventional morality • Postconventional morality • Punishment–obedience stage • Market exchange stage • Interpersonal harmony stage • Law and order stage • Social contract stage • Universal principles stage
Contributions	• Kohlberg's theory recognizes that moral development is a gradual, constructive process that depends on cognitive development. • People tend to move through the stages of moral reasoning in the order and rate predicted by his theory. • Evidence identifies links between moral reasoning and moral behavior. • Kohlberg's stages generally correspond to children's thinking about right and wrong. • Kohlberg's theory is consistent with Piaget's views of moral development.
Criticisms	• Many people never reach the postconventional level of moral reasoning, which raises questions about moral maturity. • Moral reasoning depends more on context than Kohlberg acknowledged. • Performance at a certain stage depends more on domain-specific knowledge than Kohlberg suggested. • The links between moral reasoning and moral behavior are relatively weak; people often reason at one stage but behave at another. • Kohlberg's theory doesn't adequately take cultural differences into account.

SOURCES: Berk, 2019a; Feldman, 2014; Kohlberg, 1963, 1981, 1984; Piaget, 1965

for people to be morally mature, few measure up. And moral reasoning depends on context to a greater extent than Kohlberg acknowledged (Kretz, 2015). For instance, in *Ed Psych and You* we asked if it was okay to exceed speed limits or pass a school bus with its sign out. Most people don't think passing a school bus is acceptable, even if no children are entering or leaving the bus, but many have no compunctions about exceeding speed limits. And some researchers—citing the widely publicized high-stakes testing cheating scandal in Atlanta as one example—believe that virtually all of us would cheat if the pressure is great enough (Catalano & Gatti, 2017).

Thinking about moral dilemmas also depends on domain-specific knowledge; knowledge about a topic influences moral decision making (Gibbs, 2014; Thornberg, 2010). For example, a medical doctor asked to deliberate about an educational dilemma or a teacher asked to resolve a medical issue would be hampered by their lack of professional knowledge.

Finally, because moral development, as with all forms of development, depends on experience, diversity is a factor (Rubin, Cheah, & Menzer, 2010). We examine this issue in our discussion of gender differences in morality in the next section. Table 3.5 outlines Kohlberg's theory, including its contributions and criticisms.

Gender Differences: The Morality of Caring

Some critics of Kohlberg's work also argue that it fails to adequately consider ways in which gender influences morality. Early research examining Kohlberg's theory identified differences in the ways men and women responded to moral dilemmas (Gilligan, 1982, 1998; Gilligan & Attanucci, 1988). Men were more likely to base their judgments on abstract concepts, such as justice, rules, and individual rights; women were more likely to base their moral decisions on interpersonal connections and attention to human needs. According to Kohlberg, these differences suggested a lower stage of development in women responding to moral dilemmas.

Carol Gilligan (1977, 1982), also a Harvard psychologist and Kohlberg's colleague, argued that the findings, instead, indicate an "ethic of care" in women that is not inferior; rather, Kohlberg's descriptions don't adequately represent the complexity of female thinking. Gilligan suggests that a morality of caring proceeds through three stages. In the first, children are concerned primarily with their own needs; in the second, they show concern for others who are unable to care for themselves, such as infants and the elderly; and in the third, they recognize the interdependent nature of personal relationships and extend compassion to all of humanity. To encourage this development, Gilligan recommends an engaging curriculum with opportunities for students to think and talk about moral issues involving caring.

Nell Noddings (2002, 2008) has also emphasized the importance of caring in schools, especially for teachers. Noddings argues that students should be taught the importance of caring through a curriculum that emphasizes caring for self, family and friends, and others throughout the world. Research corroborates this position; a just and compassionate school climate is more likely to promote students' moral development (Crystal, Killen, & Ruck, 2010).

Gilligan makes an important point about gender differences, but additional research is mixed; some studies have found gender differences, whereas others have not (Berk, 2019a; Kretz, 2015). Like cross-cultural studies, Gilligan's research reminds us of the complexity of the issues involved in moral development.

Emotional Factors in Moral Development

Ultimately, we want people to both reason and behave morally. Emotions provide a vital link between our moral reasoning and our actions. Let's see how.

"Are you okay?" her mother asks as Melissa walks in the house after school appearing dejected.

"I feel really bad, Mom," Melissa answers softly. "We were working in a group, and Jessica said something sort of odd, and I said, 'That's dumb. Where did that come from?' . . . She didn't say anything for the rest of our group time. She doesn't get really good grades, and I know saying something about her being dumb really hurt her feelings. I didn't intend to do it. It just sort of came out."

"I know you didn't intend to hurt her feelings, Sweetheart. Did you tell her you were sorry?"

"No, when I realized it, I just sat there like a lump. I know how I'd feel if someone said I was dumb."

"Tell you what," her mom suggests. "Tomorrow, you go directly to her, tell her you're sorry you hurt her feelings, and that it won't happen again."

"Thanks, Mom. I'll do it as soon as I see her. . . . I feel a lot better."

Piaget and Kohlberg emphasized cognition in moral development, and it's certainly important, but, as the exchange between Melissa and her mother illustrates, emotions are also an important part of morality (Kretz, 2015). For instance, Melissa felt both **shame**, the painful emotion aroused when people recognize that they have failed to act in ways they believe are good, and **guilt**, the uncomfortable feelings people get when they know they've caused someone else's distress. Although unpleasant, experiencing shame and guilt indicates that moral development is advancing and future behavior is likely to improve.

When Melissa said, "I know how I'd feel if someone said I was dumb," she was also describing feelings of *empathy*, which we defined earlier in the chapter as the capacity to feel what you infer others are feeling (Jordan et al., 2016). Empathy promotes moral and prosocial behavior, even in the absence of wrongdoing. In fact, some researchers argue that moral development largely depends on emotions, such as empathy (Kretz, 2015).

We turn now to what we, as teachers, can do to guide our students' moral development.

Using Educational Psychology in Teaching: Suggestions for Promoting Moral Development in Your Students

We have many opportunities to promote moral development in our students. The following suggestions provide a framework for us as we attempt to promote this essential form of development:

1. Model ethical thinking, behavior, and emotions in interactions with students.
2. Use moral dilemmas as concrete reference points for examining moral issues.
3. Use discussions to help students understand and respect the perspectives of others.
4. Use classroom management as a vehicle for promoting moral development.

Let's see how Rod Leist, a fifth-grade teacher, uses these suggestions as he works with his students.

Rod begins language arts by saying, "Let's look in the story we've been reading and talk about Chris, the boy who found the wallet. He was broke, so would it be wrong for him to keep it, . . . and the money in it? . . . Jolene?"

"No, because it didn't belong to him."

"Ray?"

"Why not keep it? He didn't steal it; and . . . "

"That's terrible," Helena interrupts. "How would you like it if you lost your wallet?"

"Helena," Rod admonishes. "Remember, we agreed that we would let everyone finish their point before we speak."

"Sorry for interrupting. . . . Please finish your point, Ray," Rod adds.

" . . . It wasn't his fault that the person lost it. . . . And he was broke."

"Okay, Helena, go ahead," Rod says.

"Just . . . how would you feel if you lost something and somebody else kept it? . . . . That's why I think he should give it back."

"That's an interesting point, Helena. When we think about these issues, it's good for us to try to put ourselves in someone else's shoes. . . . Of course, we would feel badly if we lost something and it wasn't returned.

"Go ahead, . . . Juan?"

"I agree. It was a lot of money, and Chris's parents would probably make him give it back anyway."

"And what if the person who lost the money really needs it?" Kristina adds.

After continuing the discussion for several more minutes, Rod says, "These are all good points. . . . Now, I want each of you to write a short paragraph that describes what you would do if you found the wallet and explain why you feel it would be right or wrong to keep it. Then, we'll discuss your reasons some more tomorrow."

Model Ethical Thinking, Behavior, and Emotions in Interactions with Students.   Again, we see why the quote "Be the change that you wish to see in the world" is a theme for this chapter. "Almost all approaches to moral education recognize the importance of modeling. If we would teach the young to be moral persons, we must demonstrate moral behavior for them" (Noddings, 2008, p. 168). Rod's actions were consistent with this quote and Gandhi's admonition to be the change we wish to see in the world. His simple and brief apology for interrupting the discussion communicated that he also obeyed their classroom rules. Also, he reinforced Helena for being empathic and modeled his own empathy by saying, "That's an interesting point, Helena. When we think about these issues, it's good for us to try to put ourselves in someone else's shoes." Efforts to be fair, responsible, and democratic in dealings with students speak volumes about teachers' values and views of morality, and research suggests that a warm, supportive classroom atmosphere supports their efforts (Bouchard & Smith, 2017; Noddings, 2008; Poulou, 2015).

We also see a strong link between moral development and social-emotional development. Moral development is problematic for people who struggle to regulate their emotions or behaviors, for example, or who consistently make irresponsible decisions.

Use Moral Dilemmas as Concrete Reference Points for Examining Moral Issues.   As research consistently indicates, most people's thinking is concrete operational, which means they need concrete examples if they are to develop a meaningful understanding of the topics they study. This is certainly true when dealing with abstract issues, such as morality, and it's particularly true of students in elementary schools, such as Rod's 5th-graders.

Rod recognized this factor and used the lost wallet as a concrete reference point to begin examining a moral issue. It was a moral dilemma because Chris—the boy in the example who found the wallet—was broke and needed the money, but, on the other hand, the wallet and money didn't belong to him.

Moral issues come up in classes more often than we realize. For instance, in elementary classrooms the question of whether or not it's okay to retaliate if someone on the playground pushes you down or butts in front of you in the lunch line can be raised. With older students, a friend, for example, asks if we think a new hairstyle looks good, and we think it is most unflattering. Do we respond truthfully, and likely hurt her feelings, or do we say it looks good, which is technically a lie? Alcohol use is another common example. Many teenagers use alcohol, and we know that drinking and driving is dangerous. However, if no one drives anywhere, is it immoral to drink before the legal age limit? Many other examples exist.

Use Discussions to Advance Moral Reasoning.   Moral development is largely a social process (Kretz, 2015; Sherblom, 2015). Moral dilemmas and issues provide concrete reference points, but discussions are the mechanisms that lead to higher levels of moral reasoning. To see an illustration, let's look again at some of the dialogue in Rod's lesson.

Rod:	Let's look in the story we've been reading and talk about Chris, the boy who found the wallet. He was broke, so would it be wrong for him to keep it, . . . and the money in it? . . . Jolene?"
Jolene:	No, because it didn't belong to him.
Rod:	Ray?
Ray:	Why not keep it? He didn't steal it; and . . .

Helena:	That's terrible. How would you like it if you lost your wallet?
Rod:	Helena. . . . Remember, we agreed that we would let everyone finish their point before we speak. . . . Sorry for interrupting. . . . Please finish your point, Ray.
Ray:	It wasn't his fault that the person lost it. . . . And he was broke.
Rod:	Okay, Helena, go ahead.
Helena:	Just . . . how would you feel if you lost something and somebody else kept it? . . . That's why I think he should give it back.
Rod:	That's an interesting point, Helena. When we think about these issues, it's good for us to try to put ourselves in someone else's shoes. . . . Of course, we would feel badly if we lost something and it wasn't returned. . . . Go ahead, . . . Juan?
Juan:	I agree. It was a lot of money, and Chris's parents would probably make him give it back anyway.
Kristina:	And what if the person who lost the money really needs it?

In this discussion the students each offered slightly different perspectives with respect to the issue. Discussing these differences can lead to advances in moral reasoning. And students generally enjoy the opportunity to express their opinions, particularly when they are not in danger of being judged right or wrong. So, discussions such as these are often motivating. Further, when Rod admonished Helena for interrupting Ray, he was promoting perspective taking and contributing to social-emotional development.

Rod then followed up on the discussion by having the students write a paragraph in which they were asked to justify their moral positions with respect to the issue. Research supports this approach. Discussions that encourage students to examine their own reasoning combined with exposure to more advanced thinking promotes moral development (Carlo, Mestre, Samper, Tur, & Armenta, 2011).

Use classroom management as a vehicle for promoting moral development. As we've seen throughout the chapter, classroom management can be used to promote much more than an orderly classroom, and Rod's management system is an illustration. For example, he stopped Helena's interruption and reminded the class that they agreed to let people finish a point before speaking. In doing so he was teaching fairness and tolerance for differing opinions. Understanding these values is an important part of self-regulation, which can only be developed if students understand rules and why they're important, and agree to follow them. This kind of learning environment, an environment in which students follow rules because the rules make sense, promotes *autonomous morality* (Rothbart, 2011).

As we've examined classroom applications designed to promote the different forms of development in this chapter, themes have emerged. For instance, a cognitive component exists for each, and it's on this component that we try to capitalize. In other words, we want our students to understand and think about the various aspects of personality, identity, social and emotional skills, and morality and how development in each of these areas can contribute to both success and satisfaction in school and quality of life after the school years.

In each case, modeling and explicitly teaching the skills using concrete examples are essential. Then, discussions of the examples combined with a classroom management style that promotes fairness, self-awareness, and self-management are the mechanisms we can use to promote each of the forms of development. We won't succeed with all students, but for the ones with whom we do, we will have made an immeasurable contribution to their total education.

Classroom Connections

Promoting Moral Development in Classrooms

1. Moral development is enhanced by opportunities to think about moral dilemmas and hear the positions of others. Openly discuss ethical issues when they arise.

- **Elementary:** The day before a new student with an exceptionality joins the class, a second-grade teacher has students discuss how they would feel if they were new, how new students should be treated, and how they should treat one another in general.

- **Middle School:** A seventh-grade teacher has a classroom rule that students may not laugh, snicker, or make remarks of any kind when a classmate is trying to answer a question. She has the students discuss reasons for the rule, emphasizing how people feel when others laugh at their efforts.

- **High School:** A teacher's students view cheating as a game, seeing what they can get away with. The teacher addresses the issue by saying, "Because you feel this way about cheating, I'm going to decide who gets what grade without a test. I'll grade you on how smart I think you are." This provocative statement precipitates a lively classroom discussion on fairness and cheating.

2. Moral development advances when students are exposed to moral reasoning and behavior at higher levels. Model moral and ethical behavior for students.

- **Elementary:** One election November, fifth-grade students jokingly ask if the teacher votes. The teacher uses this as an opportunity to discuss the importance of voting and each person's responsibilities in our democracy.

- **Middle School:** A science teacher makes a commitment to have students' tests and quizzes scored by the following day. One day, when asked if he has the tests ready, he replies, "Of course. . . . At the beginning of the year, I said I'd have them back the next day, and we can't go back on our agreements."

- **High School:** A group of students finishes a field trip sooner than expected. "If we just hang around a little longer, we don't have to go back to school," one student suggests. "Yes, but that would be a lie, wouldn't it?" their teacher counters. "We said we'd be back as soon as we finished, and we need to keep our word."

MyLab Education Self-Check 3.4

Developmentally Appropriate Practice

Promoting Personal, Social-Emotional, and Moral Development with Learners at Different Ages

Important differences exist in the personal, social-emotional, and moral development of elementary, middle, and high school students. Suggestions that can help you respond to these differences are outlined below.

Working with Students in Preschool Programs and Elementary Schools

As children enter preschool, they are developing autonomy and taking the initiative to seek out experiences and challenges. "Let me help!" and "I want to do it" are signs of this initiative. Criticism or overly restrictive directions detract from a sense of independence and, in extreme cases, lead to feelings of guilt and dependency. At the same time, children need the structure that helps them learn to take responsibility for their own behavior.

As children move through the elementary years, teachers attempt to help them succeed in learning activities challenging

enough to promote feelings of competence and industry. This is demanding. Activities that are so challenging that students frequently fail can leave them with a sense of inferiority, but success on trivial tasks does little to make students feel competent.

During the elementary years, students need opportunities to practice self-management and responsible decision making. Discussions and small-group work where students can interact with others and practice these skills are effective learning experiences.

The elementary grades also lay the foundation for students' moral growth and the development of social responsibility. Teachers who encourage students to understand the impact of their actions on others help them make the transition from preconventional morality, with its egocentric orientation, to conventional morality, at which stage students understand why rules are important for both classrooms and the world outside of school.

Working with Students in Middle Schools

Adolescence is a time of physical, emotional, and intellectual change, and adolescents are often uncertain about how to respond to new sexual feelings. They are concerned with what others think of them and are preoccupied with their looks. They want to assert their independence, yet long for the stability of structure and discipline. They want to rebel to assert their independence but need something solid to rebel against.

Most adolescents successfully negotiate this period, however, exploring different roles and maintaining positive relationships with their parents, teachers, and other adults. Students in middle and junior high schools need firm, caring teachers who empathize with them and their sometimes capricious actions while simultaneously providing the security of clear limits for acceptable behavior (Emmer & Evertson, 2017). Classroom management provides opportunities to advance moral reasoning from preconventional to conventional thinking. Effective teachers create clear classroom rules, discuss the reasons for them, and enforce them consistently.

Instruction in middle school classrooms should promote deep understanding of the topics being studied, while simultaneously providing students with opportunities to practice prosocial behaviors, such as tolerance for others' opinions, listening politely, and avoiding hurtful comments. Effective instruction in middle schools is highly interactive, and lecture is held to a minimum.

Working with Students in High Schools

High school students are continuing to wrestle with who they are and what they want to become. Peers become increasingly important to students and have an important influence on social, emotional, and moral development.

Linking content to students' lives is particularly valuable at this age. For example, examining ideas about gender and occupational trends in social studies and showing how math and science can influence their futures are important for these students.

Like younger learners, high school students need opportunities to try out new ideas and link them to their developing sense of self. Discussions, small-group work, and focused writing assignments provide valuable opportunities for students to integrate new ideas into their developing self-identities.

Chapter 3 Summary

1. Describe personality development and explain how it can influence academic success and success in life after the school years.
   - Personality is composed of five relatively independent traits that include openness, conscientiousness, extraversion, agreeableness, and neuroticism, and personality development describes improvements with respect to these traits.
   - Temperament, determined largely by genetics, describes relatively consistent inclinations to respond to events in the environment in particular ways.
   - Because of their early and extensive interactions with a child, parents have the largest influence on personality development, and some parenting styles are more effective than others.
   - Cultural differences exist with respect to parenting styles, with some cultures emphasizing characteristics such as individuality, and others focusing on a more collectivist orientation.
   - Child abuse is a major problem in our society and often involves neglect. Family members are most likely to engage in child abuse.
   - Personality development is strongly linked to both success in school and success in life after the school years.

2. Use descriptions of identity development to explain learner behavior.
   - Identity refers to our beliefs, assessments, and feelings about ourselves, and identity development is significantly influenced by social comparisons, feedback we receive from others, and group membership.
   - Erikson's psychosocial view of identity development is grounded in his belief that the formation of identity stems largely from people's innate desire to connect with others.
   - Contemporary views of identity development suggest that career identities usually occur during high school and beyond. Identity moratorium and identity achievement are healthy developmental states; identity diffusion and identity foreclosure are less healthy.
   - Sexual identity describes people's sense of self with respect to gender orientation, and sexual orientation refers to the gender to which an individual is sexually and romantically attracted. For a small portion of the school population gender orientation can be confusing and stressful.

   - LGBTQ youth face a number of challenges, such as homelessness, disconnection from their communities, lower levels of happiness, higher incidence of alcohol and drug use, and less connection to adult support when they have personal problems than their non-LGBTQ peers.
   - Self-concept, a component of identity, is a cognitive appraisal of our academic, physical, and social competencies, and it is developed largely through personal experiences. Academic self-concept, particularly in specific content areas, is strongly correlated with achievement.
   - Self-concept and self-esteem are often used interchangeably, but this is a misconception. Self-concept is a cognitive appraisal, whereas self-esteem is an emotional reaction to the self.

3. Use an understanding of social-emotional development to explain behaviors of students and people beyond the school years.
   - Social-emotional learning goals include self-awareness, self-management, social awareness, relationship skills, and responsible decision making.
   - Self-awareness describes people's ability to understand their thoughts and emotions and how both influence their responses to their environments, and self-management is their ability to regulate their emotions, thoughts, and behaviors in a variety of contexts.
   - Social awareness is an understanding of social and ethical norms for behavior as well as the ability to take others' perspectives and feel empathy for people from a variety of backgrounds and cultures.
   - Relationship skills are abilities to establish and maintain healthy and rewarding relationships with diverse individuals and groups.
   - Responsible decision making involves the ability to make constructive choices about personal behavior and interactions with others.
   - Parents, siblings, and peers all have strong influences on social-emotional development.
   - Students with well-developed social skills are generally more successful and satisfied with school than are their less skilled peers.
   - Obesity, alcohol and drug use, and peer aggression each detracts from healthy social-emotional development.
   - Teachers promote social-emotional development when they model effective social-emotional skills, use concrete examples and discussions to

promote social-emotional development, and use classroom management as a tool for promoting social-emotional development.

4. Use theories of moral development to explain differences in people's responses to ethical issues.
   - Moral development involves advances in people's conceptions of right and wrong, together with the development of prosocial traits such as honesty, cooperation, and supporting others.
   - Piaget suggested that moral development represents individuals' progress from external morality, the enforcement of rules by authority figures, to autonomous morality, the perception of morality as rational and reciprocal.

- Kohlberg's theory of moral development is based on people's responses to moral dilemmas. He developed a classification system for describing moral reasoning that occurs in three levels.
- At the preconventional level, people make egocentric moral decisions; at the conventional level, moral reasoning focuses on the consequences for our actions; and at the postconventional level, moral reasoning is based on principle.
- Feeling empathy and even unpleasant emotions such as shame and guilt mark advances in moral development.
- Teachers promote moral development by emphasizing personal responsibility and the functional nature of rules designed to protect the rights of others.

Preparing for Your Licensure Exam

Understanding Personal, Emotional, Social, and Moral Development

Your licensure exam will include items related to students' personal, emotional, social, and moral development, and we include the following exercises to help you practice for the exam in your state. This book will be a resource for you as you prepare for the exam.

Let's look now at a teacher working with a group of middle school students and how she contributes to these important aspects of development. Read the case study, and answer the questions that follow:

"This is frustrating," Helen Sharman, a seventh-grade teacher, mumbles as she scores a set of quizzes in the teachers' workroom after school.

"What's up?" her friend Mia asks.

"These students just don't want to think," Helen responds. "Three-quarters of them put an apostrophe between the *r* and the *s* in *theirs*. The quiz was on using apostrophes in possessives. I warned them I was going to put some questions on the quiz that would make them think. Not only that, but I had them practice on exercises just like those on the quiz. And I explained it so carefully," she sighs.

"What's discouraging is that some of the students won't even try. Look at this one. It's half blank. This isn't the first time Karl has done this, either. When I talked to him about it last time, he said, 'But I'm no good at English.' I replied, 'But you're doing fine in science and math.' He just shrugged and said, 'But that's different. I'm good at them.' I wish I knew how to motivate him. You should see him on the basketball floor—poetry in motion—but when he gets in here, nothing."

"I've got a few like that myself," Mia nods.

"What's worse, I'm almost sure some of the kids cheated. I left the room to go to the office, and when I returned, several of them were whispering and had guilt written all over their faces."

"Why do you suppose they did it?" Mia replies.

"I'm not sure; part of it might be grade pressure, but how else am I going to motivate them? Some just don't see any problem with cheating. If they don't get caught, fine."

"Well," Mia shrugs, "hang in there."

The next morning, as she returns the quizzes, Helen begins, "We need to review the rules again. You did so poorly on the quiz, and I explained everything so carefully. You must not have studied very hard.

"Let's take another look," she continues. "What's the rule for singular possessives?"

Helen explains the rules for forming possessives, and then asks, "Why didn't you do that on the quiz?"

Hearing no reply, she continues, "Okay, look at number 3 on the quiz."

It appears as follows:

The books belonging to the lady were lost.

"It should be written like this," Helen explains, writing, "The lady's books were lost" on the chalkboard.

"Ms. Sharman," Nathan calls from the back of the room. "Why is it apostrophe s?"

"Nathan," Helen says evenly. "What is our first rule?"

"Yes, Ma'am," Nathan says quietly.

"Good. If you want to ask a question, what else can you do other than shout it out?"

"Raise my hand."

"Good."

She then explains the item, also explains other items commonly missed on the quiz, and hands out a review sheet. "Now, these are just like the quiz," she says. "Practice hard on them, and we'll have another quiz on Thursday. Let's all do better. Please don't let me down again.

"One more thing. There was some cheating on this test. If I catch anyone cheating on Thursday, I'll tear up your paper and give you a zero. Now go to work."

Questions for Case Analysis

Use information from this chapter and the case study to answer the following questions.

Multiple-Choice Questions:

1. Based on Erikson's theory of psychosocial development, Karl's behavior could best be explained by failure to resolve which of the following stages?

    a. Trust v. mistrust

    b. Autonomy v. shame

    c. Initiative v. guilt

    d. Industry v. inferiority

2. Without raising his hand, which was against the classroom rules, Nathan called out from the back of the room, "Ms. Sharman, why is it apostrophe s?" With respect to the goals of social-emotional learning programs, Nathan's behavior best illustrates a need for more work on which of the following goals?

    a. Self-awareness

    b. Self-management

    c. Social awareness

    d. Relationship skills

Constructed-Response Question

1. Using concepts from Kohlberg's theory, analyze Helen's cheating problem. From Kohlberg's perspective, how well did she handle this problem?

MyLab Education Licensure Exam 3.1

Important Concepts

autonomous morality	emotions	interpersonal harmony	personal domain
bullying	empathy	law and order	personality
child abuse	ethnic identity	LGBTQ	perspective taking
collective self-esteem	external morality	market exchange	physical aggression
conventional domain	goodness of fit	moral development	postconventional morality
conventional morality	guilt	moral dilemma	preconventional morality
cyberbullying	hostile attribution bias	moral domain	proactive aggression
emotional intelligence	identity	parenting style	punishment–obedience
emotional self-regulation	instrumental aggression	peer aggression	reactive aggression

relational aggression
relationship skills
responsible decision
    making
school connectedness
self-awareness

self-concept
self-esteem (self-worth)
self-management
sexual identity
sexual orientation
shame

social awareness
social cognition
social contract
social referencing
social-emotional learning
temperament

theory of mind
transgender students
universal principles

Chapter 4
Learner Diversity

Andersen Ross/Getty Images

Learning Outcomes

After you have completed your study of this chapter, you should be able to:

4.1   Describe culture and explain how different aspects of culture influence learning.

4.2   Describe ways that teachers can accommodate linguistic diversity in their students.

4.3   Explain how gender can influence learning, and describe steps for eliminating gender bias in classrooms.

4.4   Define socioeconomic status, and explain how it can affect learning.

APA Top 20 Principles

Top 20 Principles from Psychology for PreK–12 Teaching and Learning explicitly addressed in this chapter.

Principle 1: Students' beliefs or perceptions about intelligence and ability affect their cognitive functioning and learning.

Principle 5: Acquiring long-term knowledge and skill is largely dependent on practice.

Principle 11: Teachers' expectations about their students affect students' opportunities to learn, their motivation, and their learning outcomes.

Principle 15: Emotional well-being influences educational performance, learning, and development.

National Council on Teacher Quality (NCTQ)

The NCTQ Essential Teaching Strategies that every new teacher needs to know specifically addressed in this chapter.

Strategy 2: Linking abstract concepts with concrete representations

Imagine that you're still in high school, your family is moving to Madrid, the capital of Spain, and you'll be attending school there. What barriers will you face? Will you succeed? How will you feel in your new school? Your questions are similar to those many students in our nation's schools face today.

Learner diversity refers to the group and individual differences in our students, it exists in every classroom, and it can strongly impact both your students' learning and your life as a teacher. As you read the following case study involving fifth-grade teacher Gary Nolan, think about the diversity in his class and how it influences his work with his students.

As we watch students come out of our country's schools today, we see that their backgrounds are more diverse than at any time in our nation's history. Gary's class is quickly becoming the norm, particularly in urban schools, and he took several steps to ensure that members of cultural minorities thrive and learn as much as possible. We will examine Gary's efforts in more detail as we move through the chapter.

MyLab Education
Video Example 4.1
The diversity in our schools is rapidly increasing. In this discussion, four educational leaders describe the growing diversity in their schools and the adaptations they're making to ensure that all students are provided with the services that will allow them to learn and develop as much as possible.

As part of his fifth-grade team, Gary teaches math, science, and social studies in a large, urban, elementary school and, as is the case with many urban classrooms, his students' backgrounds vary widely. Of his 28 students, 9 are Hispanic, 7 are African American, 3 are Asian, and 2, Baraz and Esta, are from Iran. Six are English language learners (ELLs), and most come from low socioeconomic backgrounds.

"You're improving all the time," Gary smiles at his ELL students as the rest of the class files into the room on a Friday morning. He spends a half hour with them each morning to help them work on their English.

"Good morning, Tu . . . Nice haircut, Baraz," Gary greets his students, as he does each morning when they come in the door.

After sitting down, the students immediately begin a "To Do" exercise that Gary has displayed on his document camera.

Today's "To Do" is:

Add the following:

$$\frac{1}{3} + \frac{1}{6} =$$

and

$$\frac{2}{3} + \frac{3}{4} =$$

They complete a "To Do" every morning, beginning without being reminded to do so.

After they finish, Gary has two students explain their thinking in solving the problems, they correct any mistakes they've made, and he then asks, "Who's up today?"

"Me," Anna says, raising her hand.

Every Friday Gary has one of his students make a presentation about their cultural backgrounds. They bring food, costumes, art, and music as illustrations; he encourages them to wear authentic dress from their heritage country, and they place their name with a push pin on a map at the front of the room.

"Go ahead, Anna."

Anna begins, "I was born in Mexico, but my father is from Guatemala, and my mother is from Columbia," she explains, pointing to the countries on the map.

"You know," Gary interjects, "All of Guatemala was once part of the Mayan civilization, and they were known for their art, architecture, and astronomy. Your father must be very proud of his heritage."

Gary frequently comments about how lucky they are to have classmates from so many parts of the world, making comments such as the one about the Mayans and "Remember when Baraz told us about Omar Khayyam, the famous Persian mathematician, astronomer, and poet . . . He solved math problems that people in Europe didn't solve until many years later. If Baraz wasn't in our class, we would never have learned that."

Differences in cultural and linguistic backgrounds, gender, and socioeconomic status—different dimensions of diversity—all exist in Gary's class. They're outlined in Figure 4.1.

As we examine this diversity, we will describe general patterns, but we should remember that it also includes individual differences. For instance, Katia and Angelo, two of his Hispanic students, come from Mexico, and both are native Spanish speakers, but Katia is thriving, whereas Angelo is struggling. This is true of all forms of diversity.

We begin our study by examining the concept of culture and how it can impact learning.

Figure 4.1 Types of Diversity in Today's Students

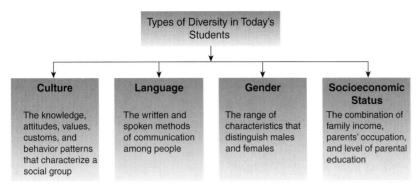

Culture

4.1   Describe culture and explain how different aspects of culture influence learning.

Ed Psych and You

Think about the clothes you wear, the music you like, and the activities you share with your friends. Or even think about food. What and when do you eat? Do you use a knife and fork, or chopsticks, or even your fingers?

The answers to our questions in *Ed Psych and You* all depend on our **culture**, which includes the knowledge, attitudes, values, and customs that characterize a social group (Banks, 2019; Bennett, 2019). Culture is one of the most important influences in our lives, and it exists in many forms, such as political culture, corporate culture, school culture, the culture of sports teams, and others. For instance, a school that adopts a vision of high expectations for academic achievement, an orderly environment, and respect and caring for everyone in the school is making this vision a part of the attitudes, values, and customs of the school; it represents the school's culture. The same applies in politics, corporations, and sports, and it strongly influences behavior in each case.

Ethnicity and Race

Ethnicity, individuals' ancestral heritage, language, value system, and customs, is an important part of culture (Banks, 2019). Immigration and other demographic shifts have resulted in dramatic changes in the ethnic makeup of our nation's population, and experts estimate that nearly 300 distinct ethnic groups now live in our country (Gollnick & Chinn, 2017).

    Race, shared biological traits, such as bone structure and skin, hair, and eye color, is another way of describing people. Our country tends to see three major racial categories, Black, White, and Asian, but considerable heterogeneity exists within each. For instance, *Asian* commonly refers not only to individuals from Japan, China, and Korea, but also those from Vietnam, the Philippines, and Thailand, all of whom have distinct customs and cultures. And South Asian ethnic groups, including people from India, Pakistan, Bangladesh, Nepal, and Sri Lanka, also display considerable variation.

    Historically, the concept of race was much more important than it is today. A number of states used it to limit access to institutions and services, such as schools and colleges, restaurants, public restrooms, drinking fountains, swimming pools, and even seats on buses. And prior to a Supreme Court decision in 1967, it was illegal in 16 states for mixed-race couples to marry, cohabit, or have sex (Macionis, 2017).

This has all changed, and more people are now describing themselves as multiracial or multiethnic. For instance, in 2013 more than 12% of all newlyweds married someone from a different race, and for African Americans and Asians, this figure was 19% and 28%, respectively (Wang, 2015). So, as we think about culture, ethnicity, and race it's important to remember that these are merely labels, they're constantly changing, and we teach people, not categories.

Immigrants and Immigration

Immigrants are people who migrate to another country, typically with the intent of living there permanently (Valenzuela, Shields, & Drolet, 2018). Historically, immigration in our country was largely restricted to people from Northern Europe, but the Immigration and Nationality Act of 1965 ended this restriction, and since then immigrants have come from all over the world, bringing a wide array of cultural attitudes and values with them. Our country has been the top immigration destination in the world since at least 1960, with about one fifth of the world's migrants living here as of 2016. During that year, nearly 44 million immigrants, slightly less than 14% of the population, were living in our country. India was the leading country of origin in 2016, followed by China/Hong Kong, Mexico, Cuba, and the Philippines. India and China surpassed Mexico in 2013 as the top countries of origin for recent arrivals (Zong, Batalova, & Hallock, 2018).

Refugees are a special group of immigrants who are fleeing unsafe conditions in their home countries. As of 1975, more than 3 million refugees have been resettled in our country, with children making up more than half of this number (Igielnik & Krogstad, 2017).

Despite its long history of immigration, our country has oscillated between perceiving immigration as a valuable resource and as a major challenge. And, since about 2016, immigration has become a hot button political issue, with some political factions suggesting that immigrants pose a threat to public safety. Evidence doesn't support this contention, however; research indicates that immigrants commit fewer crimes than do native-born citizens (Ewing, Martínez, & Rumbaut, 2015; Nowrasteh, 2015; Riley, 2015). "Several studies, over many years, have concluded that immigrants are less likely to commit crimes than people born in the United States" (Pérez-Peña, 2017, para. 2). Further, research indicates that "countries need immigrants, especially those with high human capital, as well as temporary migrants to do low paid work native-born populations are not willing to do" (Valenzuela et al., 2018, p. 67).

Immigration has strongly impacted our school population. For instance, in 2014, slightly fewer than 50% of our students were members of cultural minorities, and projections estimate that the figure will be 55% by 2026, with Hispanic students the largest minority at slightly less than 30% of the total school population (National Center for Education Statistics, 2017c). In addition, in 2016, more than 1 of 4 children under age 18 in our country lived with at least one immigrant parent, and this number is increasing rapidly (Zong et al., 2018). This helps us understand why the backgrounds of Gary's students are so diverse, and it's certain that in the future we'll have students from a variety of cultures in our classes.

Immigrant children, and children of immigrant parents, face challenges. For instance, they may feel discriminated against because of their status as immigrants or as members of ethnic minorities, and they may also feel discriminated against for their cultural backgrounds (Fleming, Villa-Torres, Taboada, Richards, & Barrington, 2017; Lo, Hopson, Simpson, & Cheng, 2017). Research, however, also identifies factors that contribute to their positive adjustment and increased self-esteem. For instance, their sense of well-being is strengthened as they develop facility with the English language, and self-esteem rises with each successive generation following immigration (Lo et al., 2017). We offer suggestions for contributing to this adjustment and sense of well-being later in this section.

Culture and Classrooms

Most of our nation's classrooms reflect mainstream, middle-class cultural attitudes, values, and customs. For instance, in typical classrooms students are expected to raise their hands in efforts to speak, answer questions when called on, use Standard English, and spend considerable time working independently (Banks, 2019; Gollnick & Chinn, 2017). If students' cultures don't emphasize these values and customs, **cultural mismatches**, clashes between a child's home culture and the culture of the school, can occur. These clashes can create conflicting expectations for students and their behavior.

Let's look at an example.

Cynthia Edwards, a second-grade teacher in an elementary school in the Southwest, is reading a story. "What do you think is going to happen next? . . . Tony?" Cynthia asks in response to his eagerly waving hand.

"I think the boy is going to meet his friend."

"How do you think the boy feels about meeting his friend?" she continues.

After Tony responds, Cynthia calls on Sharon Nighthawk, one of several Native Americans in her class. When Sharon doesn't answer, Cynthia prompts her by rephrasing the question, but Sharon continues to look at her in silence.

Cynthia is slightly confused because Sharon seems to both understand and enjoy the story. Why won't she answer?

Thinking about the lesson later, Cynthia realizes that this is a pattern; her Native American students rarely answer questions in class.

MyLab Education
Video Example 4.2

Students who are members of cultural minorities bring different experiences, attitudes, and emotions with them to our classrooms. Here three minority students describe their experiences in mainstream classrooms, and they offer suggestions to teachers that can help them work successfully with members of cultural minorities.

Cynthia's experience illustrates a cultural mismatch. Research indicates that Native American students, as a general pattern, are reluctant to speak in settings such as a classroom populated by 20 or more students (Gregg, 2018). Sharon's reserve wasn't a reflection on her, Cynthia, or the lesson; it was simply a mismatch.

Students from some cultures, such as Native American, Hispanic, and Asian, also tend to value cooperation and view competition as unnecessary or even distasteful. As a result, they may be uncomfortable in environments where students engage in a form of competition by raising their hands in attempts to answer questions. In addition, the typical teacher questions–student answers–teacher responds sequence found in many classrooms isn't consistent with the ways they interact at home (Aronson et al., 2016).

Cultural mismatch can even occur in the types of questions teachers ask. For instance, researchers have found that White children tend to respond comfortably to questions requiring specific answers, such as "Who is the main character in this story?" In contrast, African American children, accustomed to questions that are more open-ended, are sometimes confused by the specific questions because they aren't viewed as information givers in their homes. And they may be particularly bewildered when they're asked questions the answers to which adults already know (Paradise & Rogoff, 2009; Rogoff, 2003).

Cultural mismatches can also occur in interpretations of time, and different cultures view time differently. For instance, in many Mediterranean, predominantly Arab, and some Pacific Island countries, being late for an appointment, or taking several minutes to get a business meeting started is quite typical. By comparison, in Japan, much of Northern Europe and in our punctuality-conscious country, it's less acceptable (Pant, 2016). An "on time" train in Germany, for instance, means a delay of no more than a few seconds, whereas "on time" could mean a delay of several minutes in some other countries. As an example, a German business person watched partners from Brazil stare in amazement as a train scheduled to arrive at 8:52 a.m. screeched to a halt at 8:52 on the second. An entirely different meaning of time exists in South America, and views of punctuality are very different (Lamson, 2010).

Young people growing up in a culture that views time differently than it is typically viewed in our country might understandably behave in ways that we misinterpret. Almost certainly, they aren't intentionally behaving inappropriately; they are reacting in ways typical for their culture.

Becoming aware of the possibility of cultural mismatches can help us better understand some of the reactions we might have if we moved to another country, such as Spain, or even more so if we moved to a country where cultural differences are greater, like Bangladesh. It can also help us adapt our instruction so we avoid or accommodate potential cultural mismatches. We offer specific suggestions for doing so in the section "Using Educational Psychology in Teaching: Teaching Students Who Are Culturally and Linguistically Diverse" later in in our discussion.

The Cultural Achievement Gap

It makes sense that cultural attitudes, values, and customs will have an important influence on learning, and some cultural groups tend to excel. For instance, results from the Trends in International Mathematics and Science Study (TIMSS), an international comparative study designed to measure trends in mathematics and science achievement, indicate that students in Asian countries, such as Taiwan, Hong Kong, and Japan, typically score higher on math and science achievement tests than their counterparts in the United States (Provasnik et al., 2016). While structural factors probably account for some differences—the school year being longer than in the United States, for instance—cultural attitudes about the importance of study and hard work are also likely factors.

These values transfer to Asian American students, who also tend to score higher on achievement tests and have higher rates of college attendance and completion than do other groups, including European Americans (National Assessment of Educational Progress, 2015). Asian American parents often have high expectations for their children and encourage them to not only attend college but also earn graduate or professional degrees (Gollnick & Chinn, 2017). And they translate these aspirations into academic activities at home that augment school-assigned homework.

In contrast, members of some cultural minorities, such as Hispanic, African American, and Native American, consistently score lower on achievement tests (Dee & Penner, 2017; National Assessment of Educational Progress, 2015), although additional research indicates that Hispanic students actually equal or surpass the academic achievement of socioeconomically similar White students by middle school (Hull, 2017). Further, they appear to have bucked the trend of stagnant academic growth in U.S. history, civics, and geography (National Assessment of Educational Progress, 2014).

Two theories have historically been offered to explain achievement differences among groups of students. The first, a view from the 1960s which has since been largely discredited, suggested that achievement gaps persist because racial and ethnic minorities enter school lacking "cultural capital," the skills and dispositions that are important for success in school (Dee & Penner, 2017).

A second—and more persistent—view, largely grounded in the work of John Ogbu (1992, 2003, 2008), a prominent professor of anthropology at the University of California, Berkeley, suggests that members of cultural minorities form **oppositional peer cultures**. According to Ogbu, these cultures devalue academic efforts, such as doing homework, studying, and participating in class, as "acting White." This view suggests that maintaining their identity within their peer group requires members of oppositional peer cultures to reject attitudes and behaviors that lead to school success.

A great deal of research related to this issue has been conducted. And, although some supports the contention that oppositional cultures exist and impede the achievement of Black and Hispanic students (Egula, 2017), most does not (Dee & Penner, 2017; Harris, 2011). In fact, researchers have found, "in the aggregate U.S. school population there are few racial differences favoring Whites in students' attitudes toward school or their achievement-related behaviors" (Diamond & Huguley, 2014, p. 750). Further, the concept of oppositional peer cultures has been examined for immigrants in other countries around the world, with similar results (van Tubergen & van Gaans, 2016).

So, how can we explain the achievement gap between members of some minorities and their White and Asian peers? An important factor is defacto segregation, racial segregation in public schools that happens "by fact" rather than legal requirement, often resulting from the concentration of cultural minorities in certain neighborhoods served by these schools. For instance, in 2014, 57% of Black students and 60% of Hispanic students in our country attended schools that were at least 75% minority enrollment, whereas only 5% of Black and 6% of Hispanic students attended schools that were less than 25% minority enrollment. In contrast only 5% of White students attended schools that were more than 75% minority enrollment and more than half attended schools that were less than 25% minority enrollment (National Center for Education Statistics, 2017c).

This issue is complicated by the fact that many of the schools with high concentrations of minority students are urban and serve high poverty areas, so poverty is a major factor. "I find clear evidence that one aspect of segregation in particular—the disparity in average school poverty rates between White and Black students' schools—is consistently the single most powerful correlate of achievement gaps" (Reardon, 2016, p. 34). Because these schools are not viewed as desirable places to teach, they are often staffed by inexperienced teachers who lack the professional knowledge and skills needed to meet the unique needs of minority students (Goldhaber, Lavery, & Theobald, 2015); these teachers sometimes have low expectations for students of color (Gershenson, Holt, & Papageorge, 2016); the schools may lack adequate facilities; incidents of violence and disruption are more frequent; and parents of students in such schools may have fewer resources that can be used to benefit their children's education (García, 2015; Morsy & Rothstein, 2015). Our goal for this section of the chapter is to help you acquire the professional knowledge and skills that will help you work effectively with these students. (We examine the impact of poverty on achievement in detail later in the chapter.)

Stereotype Threat

As minority students struggle to adapt to and compete in schools, they sometimes experience **stereotype threat**, anxiety felt by members of a group resulting from concern that their behavior might confirm a stereotype (Aronson, Wilson, & Akert, 2016; Dee & Penner, 2017). In addition to high-achieving members of cultural minorities, stereotype threat is common for women in math and other content areas typecast as "male" (Luong & Knobloch-Westerwick, 2017). For stereotype threat to occur, some aspect of the situation must activate a negative stereotype about an individual's group. For instance, "African American students, who are stereotyped as poor academic performers, scored worse than Whites on a test when it was described as an assessment of intellectual ability" (Lewis & Sekaquaptewa, 2016; p. 40). Describing the test as a measure of "intellectual ability" activated the stereotype of low achievement for African American students. And its impact can be significant. For instance, when the same test was given but not described as a measure of academic ability, African American students performed as well as White students. The researchers explained the difference as resulting from no stereotype being activated (Lewis & Sekaquaptewa, 2016).

Stereotype threat has been most commonly researched in the context of academic testing, but it can affect other areas as well. For instance, it's been demonstrated to impact athletic performance (Krendle, Gainsburg, & Ambady, 2012), and it can influence the quality of intergroup relationships and particularly interracial interactions. For instance, when Blacks and Whites interact, members of each race become aware of stereotypes about their own race—Blacks concerned about being perceived as demonstrating a Black stereotype and Whites concerned about appearing racist—which can lead to uncomfortable and insincere social connections. As a result, communications aren't satisfying, motivations for more interactions in the future decrease, and opportunities for improving intergroup relations are diminished (Najdowski, Bottoms, & Goff, 2015).

The key to addressing stereotype threat is being sensitive to the possibility of triggering negative stereotypes, and the process can actually be quite simple. For example, emphasizing effort versus demonstrations of ability and improvement versus competition with others is wise practice for all teaching-learning situations, and it's effective for countering the negative effects of stereotype threat as well.

MyLab Education Self-Check 4.1

Linguistic Diversity

4.2 Describe ways that teachers can accommodate linguistic diversity in their students.

In the first section of the chapter we saw that immigration and cultural diversity are strongly impacting our school population. The impact on language is one of the most pronounced, and because of this diversity it's almost certain that you will have students in your classes who speak a native language other than English. For that matter, English may not be your first language. Let's see who these students are.

English Language Learners

English language learners (ELLs) are students who "participate in language assistance programs to help ensure that they attain English proficiency and meet the same academic content and achievement standards that all students are expected to meet" (National Center for Education Statistics, 2017b, para. 2). (*English language learners* are also called *English learners* [ELs], and you will see both ELL and EL used in research literature.)

Statistics describing the ELL population in our nation's schools in the school year 2014–2015 include the following (National Center for Education Statistics, 2017b):

- Nearly 10% of all students in our country were ELLs.
- Eight states—Alaska, California, Colorado, Illinois, Nevada, New Mexico, Texas, and Washington—plus the District of Columbia, had public school populations with 10% or more ELLs. In California this figure was more than 20%, with Texas second at more than 15%.
- The highest concentrations are in large cities, where nearly 17% of all students are ELLs. In rural areas the figure is less than 5%.
- They are most prominent in the lower elementary grades, where more than 1 of 6 students in kindergarten and first-grade are ELLs, followed by nearly 1 of 6 in second grade. This figure falls to fewer than 1 of 20 by the 11th grade.
- The vast majority of ELLs speak Spanish as a home language, followed in order by Arabic, Chinese, and Vietnamese.

The trend in our nation's schools is toward increasing language diversity. For instance, the ELL population increased 27% between 2001 and 2016, and projections suggest that 17% of all students will be ELLs by 2030 (Pope, 2016).

Being an ELL creates challenges and obstacles for students as they try to simultaneously learn English and classroom content. As a result, they typically lag behind in achievement and they're more likely to drop out of school (Turnbull, Turnbull, Wehmeyer, & Shogren, 2016; Vaughn, Bos, & Schumm, 2018). And they face additional obstacles. "[T]hey experience significant barriers to graduating from high school, stemming from high rates of poverty, higher mobility rates, segregation, underfunding, and unsafe schools, leading toward low K–12 academic performance" (Jiménez-Castellanos & García, 2017, p. 318). Schools have responded to these issues with a variety of programs. They're outlined in Table 4.1.

Evaluating ELL Programs

Research results examining ELL programs are mixed. For instance, some research indicates that maintenance and transitional programs in kindergarten and then transitioning to immersion programs as quickly as possible is most effective for English language development, particularly for boys (Pope, 2016). By comparison, other research found similar results for transition and immersion programs (Alvear, 2015), and a large review of research literature didn't find any differences in outcomes by the end of elementary school for children who were either taught in Spanish and transitioned to English or taught only in English (Cheung & Slavin, 2012).

However, additional research indicates that "two-way" dual language programs that include both native Spanish speakers and native English speakers in classrooms can lead to **bilingualism**, where students are fluent in both English and Spanish. In these programs, instruction occurs in both languages, and by the time they complete the program, native Spanish speakers and native English speakers are fluent in both languages (Holeywell, 2015). Bilingual students enjoy several advantages. For example, they better understand the sounds words make, how languages work, and the role language plays in communication (Mertz & Yovel, 2010). They also tend to perform better on tasks requiring advanced cognitive functions, such as intelligence tests and measures of creativity (Bialystok, 2011; Yow & Markman, 2011). Further, knowledge and skills acquired in a native language promote transfer to English (Bialystok, 2011; Ukrainetz,

TABLE 4.1 Types of ELL programs

Type of Program	Description	Advantages	Disadvantages
Immersion	Places students in classrooms where only English is spoken, with few or no linguistic aids.	Increased exposure to new language and multiple opportunities to use it.	Sink or swim approach may be overwhelming and leave students confused and discouraged.
Maintenance	Students maintain first language through reading and writing activities in first language while teachers introduce English.	Students become literate in two languages.	Requires teachers trained in first language. Acquisition of English may not be as fast.
Transitional	Students learn to read in first language, and teachers give supplementary instruction in English as a second language. After mastering English, students enroll in regular classrooms and discontinue learning in first language.	Maintains first language. Transition to English is eased by gradual approach.	Requires teachers trained in first language. Literacy skills in first language not maintained and may be lost.
ESL Pullout Programs	Pullout programs in which students are provided with supplementary English instruction along with regular instruction in content classes.	Easier to administer when dealing with diverse language backgrounds because it requires only the pullout teachers to have EL expertise.	Students may not be ready to benefit from content instruction in English. Pullout programs segregate students.
Sheltered English	Teachers adapt content instruction to meet the learning needs of EL students.	Easier for students to learn content.	Requires an intermediate level of English proficiency. Also requires teachers with EL expertise.

Nuspl, Wilkerson, & Beddes, 2011), and being able to speak two languages has obvious practical benefits in today's world (Adesope, Lavin, & Thompson, & Ungerleider, 2010).

Research has identified three additional, intuitively sensible outcomes, and they have important implications for us as teachers. First, effective programs do more than simply teach language; they also involve social-emotional learning and social integration into mainstream school culture (Przymus, 2016). Second, as with all forms of development, the more meaningful experiences students have, the greater their likelihood of success. High-quality PreK programs can provide these experiences (Ansari & Winsler, 2016), and where these programs don't exist, it's up to us to fill the gaps. Third, the quality of instruction is much more important than the specific program, whether it be transition, maintenance, or immersion (Cheung & Slavin, 2012).

As with students in general, significant differences exist in English language learners (Echevarria, Vogt, & Short, 2018a, 2018b). Some live in households where books and newspapers are readily accessible and parents talk and read to their children; others come from homes where both parents work and opportunities for language development are limited, making the transition to English challenging.

Developmental differences also exist. Learning to pronounce words in a second language such as English is easier for younger children than for those who are older, particularly if the second language is fundamentally different from the first (Petitto, 2009). For example, it is much easier for a native Spanish speaker to learn English than it is for someone whose first language is Chinese. On the other hand, older students have a greater knowledge of language and have mastered more learning strategies, making second-language learning more efficient (Diaz-Rico, 2014). Students of all ages can learn a new language, however, if they make the effort and are provided with adequate instruction.

English Dialects

If you've traveled around our country, you've likely noticed that people, although speaking English, talk differently, and sometimes the differences are enough to make communication a challenge. They're the result of **dialects**, variations of Standard English—distinct in vocabulary, grammar, or pronunciation—that are associated with a particular regional or social group. Everyone speaks a dialect; we merely react to those different from our own. They are such an integral part of our lives that researchers have found that they even appear on Twitter (Eisenstein, O'Connor, Smith, & Xing, 2011).

Many different dialects are spoken in our country; experts have identified at least 11 that are distinct (Owens, 2016). Some are more accepted than others, however, and research suggests that teachers tend to have lower expectations for students who use nonstandard English, and they assess the students' work accordingly (Thomas-Tate, Connor, & Johnson, 2013). These language patterns are often confused with mistakes during oral reading, and some believe that dialects, such as Black English, are substandard (Johnson, 2015). Linguists, however, assert that these variations are just as rich and semantically complex as Standard English (Pearson, Velleman, Bryant, & Charko, 2009).

Let's turn now to the implications that culture and linguistic diversity, including dialects, have for our teaching.

Using Educational Psychology in Teaching: Suggestions for Capitalizing on Culturally Responsive Teaching with Your Students

It's a virtual certainty that you will teach students who are members of cultural minorities, and it's highly likely that English will not be the first language for some. Their background knowledge will vary, as it does for all students, and, at a fundamental level, they learn in the same way (Otto, 2018; Schunk, 2016). For instance, regardless of cultural backgrounds, all students need to be cognitively active in learning activities—pay attention, think, and participate in class—and they need concrete experiences to understand abstract ideas, such as observing a live beetle and spider to help them understand the differences between insects and arachnids, or seeing that the shaded areas in the top and bottom sketches to the right are equal to help them understand the concept *equivalent fractions* (2/6 = 1/3).

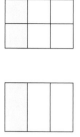

However, the attitudes, values, and customs that they bring with them to our classes can vary in ways that impact learning. For instance, research indicates that Black and Hispanic students sometimes don't feel as connected to school and their teachers as do White students. As a result, emotional climate gaps exist which contribute to differences in achievement (Voight, Adekanye, Hanson, & O'Malley, 2015).

Research indicates that **culturally responsive teaching** (also called "culturally relevant pedagogy"), instruction that reflects cultural knowledge and skills, communicates respect for all cultures, and attempts to instill a sense of school belonging in students, can address issues of school connectedness, improve the emotional climate in classrooms, and reduce achievement gaps (Banks, 2019; Gollnick & Chinn, 2017; Mahatmya, Lohman, Brown, & Conway-Turner, 2016).

Culturally responsive teaching is multidimensional. It attempts to create communities of learners, where teachers and all students work together to help everyone learn, and it focuses on the whole child by also emphasizing social and emotional development (Bennett, 2019).

Also, it's more than motivating disengaged students. It's about building trust with them and using that trust to get permission—emotionally—to push them into their zones of proximal development. High expectations for academic achievement and academic rigor are integral parts of culturally responsive teaching (Hammond, 2015).

APA Top 20 Principles

This discussion illustrates Principle 11: *Teachers' expectations about their students affect students' opportunities to learn, their motivation, and their learning outcomes*—from the *Top 20 Principles from Psychology for PreK–12 Teaching and Learning*.

Gary Nolan, our teacher in the case study at the beginning of the chapter, illustrated these dimensions in his work with his fifth-graders. Let's look at his efforts in more detail and see how he applied the following suggestions for culturally responsive teaching with his students.

1. Communicate respect for students and emphasize the contributions that cultural differences make to learning.
2. Involve all students in learning activities.
3. Use concrete experiences as reference points for language development.
4. Provide opportunities for students to practice language.
5. Help students adapt to the culture of school.

MyLab Education
Video Example 4.3
Cultural diversity can enrich learning for all students. Educational leader Else Hamayan explains how all students benefit from the diversity in their classrooms and why respecting and valuing all cultures is so important.

Communicate Respect for Students and Emphasize the Contributions Culture Makes to Learning. Feeling respect is emotional, and we're focusing on emotions when we attempt to make students feel welcome in our classrooms. Gary addressed this aspect of culturally responsive teaching with his students' Friday morning presentations, and we can see how their sense of pride and belonging would increase as a result. Imagine both Anna's and her parents' feelings on Thursday evening when Anna's mother helped her select an authentic form of dress for the next day, and they prepared a food item that Anna took to school Friday morning. They're certain to have positive emotional reactions to the entire process.

APA Top 20 Principles

This description illustrates Principle 15: *Emotional well-being influences educational performance, learning, and development*—from the *Top 20 Principles from Psychology for PreK–12 Teaching and Learning.*

Gary further capitalized on this sense of pride with his comments, "All of Guatemala was once part of the Mayan civilization, and they were known for their art, architecture, and astronomy. Your father must be very proud of his heritage," and "Remember when Baraz told us about Omar Khayyam, the famous Persian mathematician, astronomer, and poet . . . . If Baraz wasn't in our class, we would never have learned that." This is a win–win. First, for instance, many people in our country don't realize that advanced civilizations, such as the Mayans, Aztecs, and Incas, existed long before Europeans ever came to the Americas, and acquiring this kind of knowledge enriches us all. Gary's students are indeed fortunate to be in a classroom environment with such rich diversity. Second, we're all emotional beings, and being made to feel good about our cultural backgrounds is certain to have a positive impact on students.

Gary further communicated that he valued his students as both learners and people by spending additional time with his ELLs every morning and in the way he greeted his students as they came in the room. A simple greeting is a subtle gesture, but it takes no extra effort, and it's important when working with members of cultural minorities (Koppelman, 2017).

We can take three additional steps to demonstrate respect for our students as individuals. First, quickly learn students' names and always pronounce them correctly (Okonofua, Paunesku, & Walton, 2016; Rice, 2017). Correctly pronouncing a student's name may not seem like a big deal to us—teachers—but it is to them. "Mispronouncing a student's name fails to establish an environment of trust, sends the message that perseverance is not important, and communicates disrespect" (Rice, 2017, para. 4). And, when analyzed within a context of historical and current day racism, researchers argue that these incidents are **racial microaggressions**—subtle insults suggesting minority inferiority (Kohli & Solórzano, 2012). We all want our names pronounced correctly, and it takes little effort. Most significantly, we have nothing to lose in doing so.

Second, use positive body language, such as orienting ourselves directly toward students, leaning forward, and making eye contact when interacting with them. Up to 90% of the credibility of our communications with others is directed nonverbally (Kar & Kar, 2017), and dismissive body language, such as talking to someone over our shoulder, is a sign of disrespect. Members of cultural minorities are particularly sensitive to these gestures (Goman, 2017).

Third, we can promote cultural pride by emphasizing minority role models. NBC broadcaster Lester Holt and astrophysicist and author Neil deGrasse Tyson, among many others, provide models of success and influence for African American students; Julian Castro, three-sport athlete, Harvard Law School graduate, and former mayor of San Antonio, Texas, and Antonia Novello, physician, 14th Surgeon General of the United States and the first woman and first Hispanic to hold the position, do the same for Hispanic students. Similar examples can be found for all minority groups, such as Hindu congresswoman from Hawaii Tulsi Gabbard and Representative Keith Ellison from Minnesota, the first Muslim to serve in Congress. A simple Internet search provides pictures and biographical information for each.

MyLab Education Application Exercise 4.1: Demonstrating Respect for Culturally Diverse Learners

In this exercise you will be asked to analyze a teacher's attempts to demonstrate respect for her students.

Involve All Students in Learning Activities.   To illustrate this suggestion, let's return to Gary's work with his students. We join his class right after Anna has made her Friday morning presentation. In math, he is working with his class on the standard "Classify two-dimensional figures in a hierarchy based on properties" (Common Core State Standards Initiative, 2018e).

"Time for math," Gary announces after Anna has finished, and they've put everything away. "We're now going to practice classifying different figures," he says as he displays the following on his document camera:

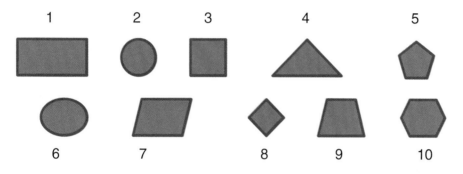

"Everyone look at the figures. . . . Now, I'm going to call on each of you to make some observations about them. . . . I want you to tell me anything you see. . . . Let's begin. Make an observation, . . . Felipe" (one of his ELL students who struggles with English).

"Straight lines," Felipe says hesitantly.

"Yes, good. Several of them have straight lines," Gary repeats, pointing to the figures composed of straight lines. "Another observation, . . . Baraz?"

"Some have 4 sides, but number 5 has 5 sides and number 10 has 6 sides," Baraz, whose English is quite well developed, responds.

Gary continues, and his students, who are used to this type of questioning, make a number of observations, such as:

- All sides are equal in #3.
- Opposite sides are equal in 1, 7, and 8—and Gary reminds them that is also true for #3.
- Two sides are equal in 4 and 9.
- Three different sets of sides are equal in #10.

After making observations for several minutes, Gary then directs, "We now want to identify the figures. So, let's practice. . . . Number 1 is a rectangle. Everyone say 'rectangle,'"

"Rectangle," the students respond in unison.

"Once more."

"Rectangle," the students respond again.

Gary continues identifying each of the figures, and then he says, "Okay, now we want to group the figures based on the way they look. . . . Think about it, and tell us which figures you think go together."

He pauses for a couple seconds, and then says, "Camila?"

"I think 2 and 6 go together, because they don't have straight lines, and the others do."

"Good thinking," and Gary then moves the figures around, so they now appear as follows:

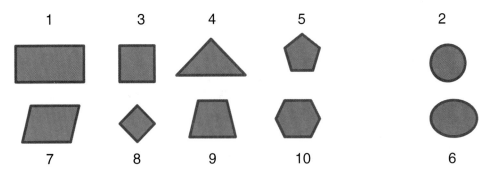

"Now, I want you to get with your partners and form subgroups of the figures with straight lines . . . . To help us get started, what might be one subgroup? . . . Anyone?"

After a few seconds, Tu volunteers, "Figures with 4 sides."

"Good thinking," Gary smiles. "Now go to work."

In addition to displaying the figures on his document camera, he has cardboard cutouts of each, a set of which he gives each group of three.

The students go to work, and Gary carefully monitors their efforts to ensure that all the students are actively involved.

Now, let's examine Gary's work more closely. He involved his students in two ways. First, he called on all of them as equally as possible. This simple—but admittedly demanding—strategy signaled that each one was expected to participate and learn, and it's particularly important for making minority students feel welcome and a part of the classroom learning community.

Gary facilitated the process by asking **open-ended questions**, questions for which a wide variety of answers are acceptable. For instance, he simply asked his students to make observations, so describing anything they could see in the figures was an acceptable answer. Using open-ended questions has several learning benefits, particularly when working with members of cultural minorities and ELLs:

- They take the pressure to answer off students. Earlier we said that some minority students are more comfortable when teachers ask questions that are more "open-ended, story-starter" types (Rogoff, 2003), and Gary capitalized on this factor.

- They're easy to ask, allowing us to call on a wide variety of students quickly, so promoting involvement becomes much easier. It's very difficult to call on a variety of students if each question requires a specific right-or-wrong answer.

- They increase student motivation. Students want to answer questions when they learn that their answers are acceptable and may result in praise from their teachers.

Some teachers believe that students don't want to answer questions. This isn't true. All students, including members of cultural minorities and ELLs, want to be called on if they believe they will be able to answer, and we can emphasize that answering incorrectly is an important part of learning. When learning a second language, listening and reading are easier than speaking, so they commonly develop first (Pinter, 2012). ELLs, reluctance to respond may not reflect their knowledge of, or interest in, the topic we're discussing. Instead it's more likely due to the difficulty they have using English to put their thoughts into words.

As the lesson developed, the "open-endedness" of Gary's questioning gradually narrowed. For instance, after asking for observations, he then had his students group the figures, which narrowed the possible responses. He then guided them to a hierarchical classification of the figures, which helped them meet the standard.

As the lesson progressed, Gary used group work as a second strategy for promoting involvement. Group work can be valuable for students who are shy and reluctant to speak in class, and it can also be valuable for breaking down interpersonal barriers between members of cultural minorities and their nonminority peers. We should decide the group composition, and groups should be composed of both minorities and non-minorities. Research indicates that the more contact different racial and ethnic groups have with each other, the more positive attitudes toward these different groups become (Bowman & Stewart, 2014). This is an additional reason for using group work as a strategy.

Involvement in learning activities is important for all students, and it's essential when working with cultural minorities and ELLs. Open-ended questioning and group work are effective strategies for meeting this goal.

Use Concrete Experiences as Reference Points for Language Development. With language development, we typically first learn terms that represent concrete concepts, such as *dog, car,* and *mom* and *dad.* When working with ELLs, the more concrete we can be the better. For instance, when using the term *force,* actually demonstrating the concept, such as pushing a book across a desk, makes the term meaningful (Otto, 2018; Peregoy & Boyle, 2017). And, just as when we learned our own language, the knowledge we accumulate about words and how language works helps us in learning a second language (Echevarria et al., 2018a, 2018b). Gary's figures were concrete reference points in his lesson.

Gary applied this suggestion in a second way. Let's take a look.

Gary also has a chart displaying common words and phrases, like "Hello," "Goodbye," and "How are you?" in English and students' native languages, with particular emphasis on Spanish, because so many of his students are native Spanish speakers. He does the same with objects around the room, such as the clock, windows, chairs, desks, tables, and other common objects.

Vocabulary development is a major part of instruction when working with minority students, and particularly ELLs.

Provide Opportunities for Students to Practice Language. Language development is obviously a demanding process. For instance, research indicates that it takes nearly 4 years for ELLs to achieve English proficiency (Motamedi, 2015), but they may need more time to reach a level that allows them to handle the demanding learning tasks found in classrooms. Vocabulary, and especially the technical vocabulary found in many content areas, is challenging for all students, and it's particularly challenging for ELLs who are simultaneously learning English and specific content (Echevarria et al., 2018a, 2018b). This suggests that we provide our students with as many opportunities to practice language as possible, and this process is even more important for ELLs (Otto, 2018).

Earlier we suggested using open-ended questions as a strategy for involving students, and these questions are also effective for promoting vocabulary development. For instance a question/directive, such as "Everyone look at the figures. . . . Now, I'm going to call on each of you to make some observations about them. . . . I want you to tell me anything you see. . . . Let's begin. Make an observation, . . . Felipe" allowed him to practice language without the pressure of having to provide a specific answer (Echevarria et al., 2018a). Gary also had his students practice by saying vocabulary words in unison—choral responding—and encouraging them to share personal experiences related to the concepts. (Notice also that choral responding is an additional strategy for promoting student involvement.)

APA Top 20 Principles

This description illustrates Principle 5: *Acquiring long-term knowledge and skill is largely dependent on practice*—from the *Top 20 Principles from Psychology for PreK–12 Teaching and Learning*.

Finally, patience is essential. If students perceive impatience in their teachers, or even worse, criticism or sarcasm, they're likely to emotionally withdraw, making them reluctant to participate in learning activities, so their opportunities to practice language are reduced.

Help Students Adapt to the Culture of School.   Earlier we saw the example with the school principal and students whose backgrounds were from the Pacific islands. To maximize student achievement, and particularly the achievement of cultural and linguistic minorities, our classroom environments must be orderly and learning focused (Emmer & Evertson, 2017; Evertson & Emmer, 2017). Our students must come to class on time and stay on task. And they can't disrupt learning activities and run around the room. To reach these goals Ogbu (2003) described a process called "accommodation without assimilation." It suggests that members of cultural minorities adapt to the school culture, including the use of language, without losing their cultural identities.

The process of accommodation without assimilation also applies to the use of dialects, and different dialects don't have to form barriers between home and school. **Bidialectalism**, the ability to switch back and forth between a dialect and Standard English, allows access to both (Gollnick & Chinn, 2017). For example, a high school teacher read a series of poems by Langston Hughes and focused on how Hughes used Black English to create vivid images. The class discussed contrasts with Standard English and ways in which differences between the two dialects could be used to accomplish different goals. As time went on, the students learned to use Standard English in school but understood that using different dialects in their home cultures was perfectly acceptable.

Minority role models are especially valuable in promoting the process of accommodation without assimilation. These models provide learners with evidence that they can succeed in mainstream classrooms and still retain their cultural identity (Tiedt & Tiedt, 2010).

As we see in Gary's efforts, working with students who come from diverse backgrounds is challenging. However, these students respond very positively to caring and genuine attempts to help them adapt to both school and mainstream American culture. It will take time, but for those with whom you succeed, the responses you get will be among the most rewarding you will have as a teacher.

Two aspects of these suggestions are significant. First, they take little extra effort. For instance, once we learn our students' names, calling on them by name will be automatic. And having his students make Friday presentations took class time, but Gary didn't have to do any extra preparation, and his personal life was enriched by hearing the presentations. Second, much of what we're suggesting is simply expert teaching. For instance, respect and caring for students, using concrete examples, and involving

MyLab Education Application Exercise 4.2: Culturally Responsive Teaching in Second Grade

In this exercise you will be asked to analyze a teacher's attempts to apply suggestions for culturally responsive teaching with her students.

students is part of expert teaching in any setting. And they're theoretically sound. Let's look at the theoretical framework in more detail.

Culturally Responsive Teaching: The Theoretical Framework

Culturally responsive teaching is thoroughly grounded in theory, with particular emphasis on theories of motivation, learning, and development. For instance, motivation theory indicates that we all have essential needs, with respect and a sense of belonging and connectedness being fundamental among them. This framework provides the foundation for our first suggestion—communicate respect for all cultures and the contribution culture makes to learning. We examine motivation theory in detail in Chapter 10. Learning theory suggests that students must be cognitively active—that is, consciously thinking—during learning activities, which is the basis for our second suggestion—involve all students in learning activities. If students know they're likely to be called on, they are more attentive and are more likely to be thinking than if they're passively listening to a teacher. Also, in Chapter 2 we saw that providing experiences, and particularly concrete experiences, is an essential component of Piaget's theory of development. This is the theoretical framework for suggesting that we provide concrete experiences as reference points for language development.

We also saw in Chapter 2 that Vygotsky strongly emphasizes language and language development in his theory of cognitive development. This is the foundation on which our suggestion for providing opportunities to practice language is based.

These orientations provide the theoretical framework for culturally responsive teaching.

Classroom Connections

Working with Students Who Are Culturally and Linguistically Diverse in Classrooms

1. Students' cultural attitudes and values can have a powerful effect on school learning. Communicate that you respect and value all cultures, and emphasize the contributions that cultural differences make to learning.

   - **Elementary:** A third-grade teacher designs classroom "festivals" that focus on different cultures and invites parents and other caregivers to help celebrate and contribute to enriching them. He also emphasizes values, such as courtesy and respect, which are common to all cultures.

   - **Middle School:** An art teacher in the Southwest decorates his room with pictures of Native American art and discusses how it contributes to art in general and how it communicates Native American values, such as a sense of harmony with nature and complex religious beliefs.

   - **High School:** An urban English teacher has students read works written by African American and Middle Eastern, South Asian, and far Eastern authors. They compare both the writing approach and the different points of view that the authors represent.

2. Language development is facilitated when teachers use concrete examples to refer to abstract concepts. Begin language development and concept learning activities with experiences that provide a concrete frame of reference.

   - **Elementary:** A fifth-grade teacher, in a unit on fractions, has students fold pieces of paper into halves, thirds, fourths, and eighths. At each point she has them state in words what the example represents, and she writes important terms on the board.

   - **Middle School:** A science teacher begins a unit on the skeletal and muscular systems by having students feel their own legs, arms, ribs, and heads. As they touch parts of their bodies, such as their Achilles tendon, she has them repeat the term tendon and has them state in words that tendons attach bones to muscles.

   - **High School:** An English teacher stops whenever an unfamiliar word occurs in a reading passage or discussion and asks for a definition and example of it. He keeps a list of these words on a bulletin board and encourages students to use them in class and in their writing.

3. Learning a second language requires that students use the language in speaking, writing, and reading. Provide students with multiple opportunities to practice language in your classroom.

(continued)

- **Elementary:** The fifth-grade teacher who had the students fold the papers has them describe each step they take when they add fractions with both like and unlike denominators. When they struggle to put their understanding into words, she prompts them, in some cases providing essential words and phrases for them.
- **Middle School:** A social studies teacher has students prepare oral reports in groups of four. Each student must make a 2-minute presentation to the other three members

of the group. After students practice their reports with each other in groups, each person presents a part of a group report to the whole class.

- **High School:** A history teacher calls on a variety of students to provide part of a summary of the previous day's work. As she presents new information, she frequently stops and has other students describe what has been discussed to that point and how it relates to topics discussed earlier.

MyLab Education Self-Check 4.2

Gender

4.3 Explain how gender can influence learning, and describe steps for eliminating gender bias in classrooms.

Ed Psych and You

Think about this class. What is the ratio of females to males? Is it similar to other classes you're taking? How would the ratio differ if it was a computer science or engineering class?

The fact that some of our students are boys and others are girls is so obvious that we tend to not notice it, but gender is another form of diversity, and, as with culture and language, it can influence learning, development, choice of professions, and other aspects of life. This is related to our questions in *Ed Psych and You*. If this class is typical, the ratio of females to males will be 2 to 1 or more, and it will be similar to other classes you're taking in your teacher-preparation program, because education is a female-dominated profession. For instance, in 2014, nearly 95% of early elementary teachers were women, and women made up more than two thirds of the teaching force in middle schools and more than 60% in secondary schools (UNESCO Institute for Statistics, 2017). Gender differences are equally, or more, pronounced in the field of nursing, where the ratio of women to men is nearly 10 to 1 (Rappleye, 2015).

On the other hand, Paul's two brothers are both on computer science faculties at their universities, and they report just the opposite. The vast majority of their students are male, and their experiences also represent a pattern. STEM content areas—science, technology, engineering, and math—are primarily male. For instance, women earn fewer than 1 of 5 bachelor's degrees in computer science and engineering (Neuhauser, 2015).

How might we explain these differences? We begin by examining differences between girls and boys, and women and men.

Differences Between Girls and Boys

Differences between girls and boys manifest themselves almost from birth; male infants tend to be more active and fussier, and they don't sleep as well as female babies (Brannon, 2017; Helgeson, 2017). Girls mature faster, master verbal and motor skills at an earlier age, prefer activities with a social component, and tend to be more cooperative. Boys are more oriented toward roughhouse play and tend to be more physically aggressive and competitive (Pellegrini, 2011; Wentzel, Battle, Russell, & Looney, 2010).

Girls also tend to be more extroverted and anxious, and they're more trusting, less assertive, and have slightly lower self-esteem than boys of the same age and background (Berk, 2019a).

Gender Identity and Gender Stereotypes

At birth, babies are labeled male or female based on their physical characteristics—sex organs, chromosomes, and hormones. This refers to the **sex** of the child, and at about age two, children become aware of physical differences between boys and girls. By age three, most children readily describe themselves as a girl or boy. By four they begin to establish a sense of **gender identity**, culturally and socially constructed conceptions of what it's like to be female or male and how each behaves, that is, things girls do and things boys do (Cassano & Zeman, 2010; Kennedy Root & Denham, 2010). By age three, children can differentiate between toys typically used by boys or girls, and they begin to play with children of their own gender in activities identified with that gender. For instance, girls tend to gravitate toward dolls and playing house, whereas boys are more likely to play with cars, trucks, and blocks (Martin & Ruble, 2010; Thommessen & Todd, 2010). Both prefer to play with members of the same sex (Parke & Clarke-Stewart, 2011).

Gender Identity, Stereotypes, and Women

What Marti Banes sees on the first day of her advanced-placement chemistry class is surprising and disconcerting. Of her 26 students, only 5 are girls, and they sit quietly, responding only when she asks them direct questions. Sharing her interest in science is one reason she has chosen teaching as a career, but this situation is giving her little opportunity to do so.

Gender identity is subtly influenced by cultural forces, including parents, teachers, and the society at large. And when certain factors become entrenched, they can lead to stereotypes. Research indicates, for instance, that by age 6, girls are less likely than boys to view their own gender as brilliant; they start to believe that certain activities are "not for them" simply because they think they aren't smart enough (Bian, Leslie, & Cimpian, 2017). Why? The researchers suggest that American children are internalizing cultural stereotypes about brilliance at an early age, and these stereotypes suggest that girls aren't as smart as boys. They cite examples such as intelligent and competent characters in books, movies, and television. In the majority of cases they're men. And the accomplishments of brilliant men, such as Abraham Lincoln, Albert Einstein, and Isaac Newton, have been widely publicized, but the same isn't true for women.

This stereotype also impacts teachers, who sometimes unwittingly communicate that courses, such as physics, are male domains, and when they do, girls are less likely to be motivated to take the courses (Thomas, 2017). They also tend to assume that boys have more "natural ability" for these courses than do girls (Cimpian, Lubienski, Timmer, Makowski, & Miller, 2016), in spite of the fact that girls' school achievement is generally higher (Voyer & Voyer, 2014). And this stereotype apparently even affects parents. For instance, a 2014 report found that parents are two and a half times more likely to ask "Is my son gifted?" than "Is my daughter gifted?" (Stephens-Davidowitz, 2014).

These stereotypes also impact students. For example:

- In math, girls are initially better at basic skills such as counting, arithmetic computation, and basic concepts, but fall behind boys later on.

- Girls consistently score lower on the mathematics portion of the SAT—widely used in college entrance—than do boys (College Board, 2017).

- In a survey of potential career choices, more than 6 of 10 boys said they could learn computer science if they wanted to, but fewer than half of girls said the same. And more than 40% percent of boys, but only a third of girls said they are likely to have a job in which they'd need computer science skills (OECD, 2015).

This research helps explain why women are underrepresented in fields perceived to require high ability, such as science and engineering (Storage, Horne, Cimpian, & Leslie, 2016).

Gender Identity, Stereotypes, and Men

Lori Anderson, the school counselor at an urban middle school, looks up from the desk where she is working on her annual report to the faculty. She knows that boys traditionally outnumber girls with respect to behavioral problems, but the numbers she is seeing are troubling. In every category—referrals by teachers, absenteeism, tardies, and fights—boys outnumber girls by more than 2 to 1. In addition, the number of boys that have been referred to her for special education testing far exceeds referrals for girls.

A long history of cultural stereotypes has also affected men. For instance, throughout history, the ideal man was portrayed as strong, silent, masculine, and wise. He was the family's breadwinner and source of support. This stereotype was reflected in TV programming, such as *Father Knows Best*, which ran from 1954–1960, and a host of Westerns, all of which fit the strong, silent, masculine stereotype. Even today, the vast majority of television shows and movies have a strong, male lead.

The school curriculum even contributes to the stereotype. For instance, male characters in stories are typically presented as strong and adventurous, but seldom warm and sensitive. Computer software programs and video games are heavily oriented toward boys, with male heroes as the main characters (Griffiths, 2010; Hamlen, 2011).

For scores of years, men could support their families with working-class jobs in mining and manufacturing, but economic and social conditions in our country have changed, and men have not fared well. For instance:

- In 2015 more than a fifth of American men—about 20 million—between ages 20 and 65 had no paid work, 7 million weren't even looking for work, and half of the men not in the labor force were in bad physical or mental health (Krueger, 2016).
- Men have been particularly hard hit by the opioid epidemic that has ravaged our country (Center for Behavioral Health Statistics and Quality, 2015).
- In 2015, 56% of total undergraduate enrollment was female; projections suggest that this trend is going to increase, and the graduation rate for women was higher (National Center for Education Statistics, 2017d, 2017e).
- Both men and women have been hit by the disappearance of middle-skill jobs. Women, however, have upgraded their skills and found better-paying jobs, whereas more than half of men had to settle for lower-paying occupations, and, as a result, wage inequality has grown more among men than women (Shierholz, 2014).
- High-paying, difficult-to-automate jobs increasingly require social skills, and research indicates that women consistently score higher on tests of emotional and social intelligence than do men (Deming, 2015).

These changes have put men in an uncertain state. For instance, undereducated men and men lacking in social skills are not viewed as desirable marriage partners. "Women have strong mate preferences such that they do not want to mate or marry men who are less educated, less intelligent, and less successful than they are" (Edsall, 2017, para. 23). As a result, fewer men at the lower end of the economic spectrum are getting married, so they lose the well-established benefits of marriage—greater longevity, better health, lower rates of alcohol and drug abuse, and less risky behavior. (Women also accrue benefits from healthy marriages.) (Strohschein, Ploubidis, Silverwood, DeStavola, & Grundy, 2016).

These societal factors have filtered down to schools. For instance, in the school year 2014–15, 16% of boys, but only 9% of girls received special education services (National Center for Education Statistics, 2017a). Girls get better grades than boys in all subjects, and they score higher than boys in both direct and indirect measures of reading and writing (Parker, Van Zanden, & Parker, 2017).

Family structure appears to be particularly significant. For instance, in two-parent households only modest school achievement differences between boys and girls exist, and men tend to earn more than women in early adulthood. However, in households headed by a single parent, boys' achievement is significantly lower than girls', they have higher rates of disciplinary problems, they're more likely to drop out of school, and their employment rate as young adults is lower (Autor, Figlio, Karbownik, Roth, & Wasserman, 2016).

Sexual Harassment and Sexual Assault

Ed Psych and You

Have you experienced one or more of the following?
Has someone:

- touched or rubbed up against you as they passed by?
- sent you an explicit sexual picture or drawing?
- made an offensive, sexual remark about your body?
- asked you to perform some sexual act?

These examples illustrate **sexual harassment**, "[i]n its simplest form . . . unwanted attention or conduct of a sexual nature, and can occur at institutional or personal levels" (Russ, Moffit, & Mansell, 2017, p. 391). It includes a variety of activities, such as touching of a sexual nature; making comments, jokes, or gestures that are directly sexual or have sexual overtones; displaying or distributing sexually explicit pictures, drawings, or written text; or spreading sexual rumors, such as suggesting that an individual had been involved in some sex act (Russ et al., 2017).

With respect to this issue, 2017 was unique in our nation's history. During this year, sexual harassment charges against powerful figures—almost exclusively male—in the entertainment, business, political, military, and mainstream press worlds seemed to be constantly in the news. Several were brought down from lofty positions, and many lost jobs. The charges, denials, and firings seemed to appear almost daily. Some commentators believe it represented a turning point. Sexual harassment has a long history, it has been widely recognized, but many women have been afraid to come forward for fear of personal reprisals or not being believed. Somehow, this all changed in 2017 (Garcia-Navarro, 2017; Ghitis, 2017). The issue remained prominent in 2018, and where it will go in the years to come remains uncertain (Frye, 2018).

Schools are not immune, and sexual harassment can affect both teachers and students. "[W]omen in fields like . . . education have raised a flag to say that their industries are not immune from such problems" (Blad, 2017, para. 6). For instance, the Albany, New York, school system completed a $400K settlement in a sexual harassment case against a male elementary school principal brought forward by four teachers (Bump, 2017).

Sexual harassment can interfere with students' learning and their social-emotional development, and schools have a legal responsibility to protect students under Title IX of the Education Amendments of 1972 (Doty, Gower, Rudi, McMorris, & Borowsky, 2017).

Sexual Assault

Sexual assault is a form of sexual violence involving non-consensual sexual touching or a forced sex act, such as rape, forced oral sex, or sodomy. Sexual assault was also in the news in 2017, with a widely publicized example being the former USA Gymnastics team doctor who pleaded guilty to a series of incidents under the guise of medical treatment (Hobson, 2017). In January of 2018, he received a 40–175 year sentence for his crimes (Hobson, 2018).

Sexual assault is a larger problem in our nation's schools than many educators realize. A large, yearlong investigation by the Associated Press using state education records identified roughly 17,000 cases—actual figures are likely much higher because these attacks are greatly underreported—of sexual assault in our nation's schools between the fall of 2011 and the spring of 2015, describing it as a "hidden horror." No type of school was immune, whether in upper-class suburbs, inner-city neighborhoods, or blue-collar farm towns, and assaults by peers was far more common than those by teachers (The Associated Press, 2017). "Ranging from rape and sodomy to forced oral sex and fondling, the sexual violence that AP tracked often was mischaracterized as bullying, hazing, or consensual behavior. It occurred anywhere students were left unsupervised: buses and bathrooms, hallways and locker rooms" (The Associated Press, 2017, para. 22). Even children as young as 5 or 6 are victimized, but the numbers increase significantly until about age 14, at which time they tend to decrease as students move through high school.

It's important to understand that sexual harassment, and particularly sexual assault, is an abuse of power. "Sexual predatory behavior is rooted in power and played out sexually with those who are vulnerable. Unless we understand it has less to do with sex and more to do with power, we will miss an important responsibility to our students" (Berkowicz & Myers, 2017, para. 3). This abuse of power is common in politics, where young interns' career starts depend in part on the recommendations of powerful politicians, leaving them vulnerable. In schools, it's more common among LGBTQ students or those who don't fit in socially (Doty et al. 2017).

So, what can we, as teachers, do? We address this question next.

Using Educational Psychology in Teaching: Suggestions for Responding to Gender Issues with Your Students

We can do a great deal to eliminate gender bias, stereotyping, and sexual harassment and assault in our teaching. The following suggestions can assist us in our efforts:

1. Discuss gender issues with students, including sexual harassment and sexual assault.
2. Eliminate gender bias in instructional activities.
3. Present students with non-stereotypical role models.

Discuss Gender Issues, Including Sexual Harassment and Sexual Assault. To begin this section, let's return to Marti Banes' work with her advanced-placement chemistry students.

Marti decides to directly address gender issues in her class, beginning with the fact that so few girls are in it. In a class discussion on the subject, Marti shares with her students, "I almost didn't major in chemistry. Some of my girlfriends scoffed, and others just rolled their eyes. 'You'll be in there with a bunch of geeks,' some of them said. 'Girls don't major in chemistry,' others added. They all thought science and math were only for guys."

"It is mostly for guys," Amy shrugs. "Look at us."

"It isn't our fault," Shane responds. "Guys didn't try to keep you out of the class."

After several other students add comments, Marti continues. "I'm not blaming either you guys, or you girls . . . And, there's no rule that says that girls can't be engineers or boys can't be nurses or special education teachers," she emphasizes. "In fact, there's a shortage of all of them."

As they continue, she discusses historical reasons for gender stereotypes and encourages both the boys and the girls to keep their career options open.

She has similar discussions in her other classes. During learning activities, she encourages girls and boys to participate equally, and she tells her students why she is doing so. For Career Week, she invites a female chemistry professor from a nearby university to come and talk about opportunities for women in chemistry, and she invites a male nurse from one of the local hospitals to talk about the role of science in his job and his experiences in a female-dominated profession.

Marti also asks her students how many of them have been subjected to unwanted sexual overtures or comments. She provides statistics about sexual harassment in schools, emphasizing, "No one, and I mean no one, should have to put up with that kind of behavior. . . . I realize that some of you might think it's no big deal, or maybe even funny, but it isn't. The world has changed, fortunately, and people are now speaking out about being harassed. You are the future leaders of our country, and it's your responsibility to ensure that this doesn't go on, in either schools or the workplace."

As with many aspects of teaching, and human relations in general, awareness that results from open communication can help eliminate stereotypes and perceptions. As an example, let's look again at some of the dialogue between Marti and her students.

Marti: I almost didn't major in chemistry. . . . Some of my girlfriends scoffed, and others just rolled their eyes. "You'll be in there with a bunch of geeks," some of them said. "Girls don't major in chemistry," others added. They all thought science and math were only for guys.

Amy: It is mostly for guys . . . Look at us.

Shane: It isn't our fault . . . Guys didn't try to keep you out of the class.

Marti: I'm not blaming either you guys, or you girls. . . . And, there's no rule that says that girls can't be engineers or boys can't be nurses or special education teachers . . . In fact, there's a shortage of all of them.

This type of discussion opens communication and can be important for changing perceptions about gender issues. For instance, the boys heard the girls' perspectives and vice versa. Students hearing Marti emphasize career choices, such as engineering for girls and nursing for boys, can make a difference in potential career choices (Cimpian et al., 2016).

Additional steps are possible. For instance, we can simultaneously de-emphasize the some-got-it-and-some-don't concept of intelligence, replacing it with the idea that ability can be increased with effort, commonly described as a "growth mindset" (Dweck, 2016). (We examine mindset in detail in Chapter 10.) Experts suggest that adopting a growth mindset might buffer girls against the stereotype that professions requiring smart people aren't for them. If innate ability is seen as secondary, then the power of these stereotypes is diminished (Bian et al., 2017).

APA Top 20 Principles

This description illustrates Principle 1: *Students' beliefs or perceptions about intelligence and ability affect their cognitive functioning and learning*—from the *Top 20 Principles from Psychology for PreK–12 Teaching and Learning.*

Some leaders have suggested that single-gender classrooms or schools might help eliminate gender stereotypes, but research examining the effectiveness of this organization is mixed (Tichenor, Welsh, Corcoran, Piechura, & Heins, 2016). Further, research indicates that boys' reading achievement is better in mixed gender classrooms (van Hek, Kraaykamp, & Pelzer, 2017). Also, in the "real world" men and women must work together, and single-gender schools don't prepare them for this reality (Zubrzycki, 2012).

This leads us to the problem of sexual harassment in schools. Researchers have found that while students generally don't see themselves as sexual harassers, 14% of girls and 18% of boys reported that they had harassed another student, either in person, online, or both. The researchers found that 44% of those who sexually harassed another student considered it "no big deal," and that another 39% said they were trying to be "funny" (Hill & Kearl, 2011). Marti directly addressed this issue in her discussion with her students.

Schools are where young people begin to learn about power, submission, fear, and shame. As students hear women and men speak out about the sexual abuse they have suffered at the hands of the more powerful, they begin to free themselves of the fear and shame associated with sexual harassment and assault. Part of our jobs is to help students in this process and return choice and power to them (Berkowicz & Myers, 2017).

Finally, as with culturally responsive teaching, teacher–student relationships and social connections are essential for preventing and ameliorating the impact of harassment and assault. Students with strong social connections to adults are much less likely to tolerate unwanted sexual advances, and if they do, the connections provide them with a source of strength that can help them better cope with the experience (Doty et al., 2017).

MyLab Education

Video Example 4.4

Eliminating gender bias in instructional activities can increase learning for both girls and boys. Notice how a middle school science teacher promotes gender equality in a learning activity by ensuring that girls and boys participate equally.

Eliminate Gender Bias in Instructional Activities. Throughout this text, we have consistently encouraged you to call on your students as equally as possible. This strategy is important for working with students from different cultural and linguistic backgrounds, and it's equally important for boys and girls. When girls see that they're being called on as often as boys in an algebra II class, for instance, or boys realize that they're being asked to participate in a unit on poetry in an English class, you communicate that math is as much for girls as it is for boys, and poetry is as much for boys as girls. These actions are both concrete and symbolic and probably do more to break down stereotypes than do any other strategies.

We want to emphasize that we're focusing here on academic behaviors. Boys and girls are indeed different, and no one is suggesting that they should be the same or always behave in the same way. Academically, however, boys and girls should be given the same opportunities and encouragement, just as students from different cultures and socioeconomic backgrounds should be.

Present Students with Non-Stereotypical Role Models. Modeling can be a most powerful influence on the ways people think and behave, and by inviting a female chemistry professor and a male nurse into her classes Marti made a powerful statement about potential career choices. Seeing that men and women can succeed and be happy in non-stereotypical fields can broaden the career horizons for both girls and boys (Bian et al., 2017; Cimpian et al., 2016; Storage, Horne, Cimpian, & Leslie, 2016).

MyLab Education Self-Check 4.3

Classroom Connections

Eliminating Gender Bias in Classrooms

1. Gender bias often results from a lack of awareness by both teachers and students. Actively attack gender bias in your teaching.

   - **Elementary:** A first-grade teacher consciously de-emphasizes sex roles and differences in his classroom. He has boys and girls share equally in chores, and he eliminates gender-related activities, such as competitions between boys and girls and forming lines by gender.

   - **Middle School:** A middle school language arts teacher selects stories and clippings from newspapers and magazines that portray men and women in nontraditional roles. She matter-of-factly talks about nontraditional careers during class discussions about becoming an adult.

   - **High School:** At the beginning of the school year, a social studies teacher explains how gender bias hurts both sexes, and he forbids sexist comments in his classes. He calls on boys and girls equally, and emphasizes equal participation in discussions.

Socioeconomic Status

4.4 Define socioeconomic status, and explain how it can affect learning.

Ed Psych and You

Were finances ever an important concern in your family? Did your parents go to college? What kinds of jobs do they have?

The questions in *Ed Psych and You* relate to your **socioeconomic status (SES)**, the combination of parents' income, level of education, and the kinds of jobs they have. Socioeconomic status describes people's relative standing in society and is a powerful factor influencing student achievement.

Definitions of different socioeconomic classes vary, but they are most commonly divided into upper, middle, working, and lower. Table 4.2 outlines characteristics of these classes.

Socioeconomic Status and Inequality

With respect to SES, educational inequality is a huge factor, and differences between college and high school graduates are increasing. For instance, for college graduates the divorce rate is less than 30%, but for those without college degrees it's more than 50%. Also, fewer than 10% of births to female college graduates are outside marriage, a figure barely higher than it was in the 1970s—the decade when inequality began to significantly increase—but for women with only a high school education, 65% of births are outside of marriage (Putnam, 2016).

And SES is more significant than race. For instance, the rate of out-of-wedlock births for college-educated African American women has fallen by a third since the 1970s, whereas the rate has quadrupled for high school–educated Whites. "Thus the class divide is growing even as the racial gap is shrinking" (Class and Family in America, 2015, para. 3).

Income inequality is also important. For instance, compared to other wealthy nations, the United States has the largest income gap between its wealthy and poor citizens, and academic achievement differences between disadvantaged American children and their more advantaged peers are far greater than in other wealthy

TABLE 4.2 Characteristics of different socioeconomic levels

	Upper Class	Middle Class	Working Class	Lower Class
Income	$160,000+	$80,000–$160,000 (½) $40,000–80,000 (½)	$25,000–$40,000	Below $25,000
Occupation	Corporate or professional (e.g., doctor, lawyer)	White collar, skilled blue collar	Blue collar	Minimum wage unskilled labor
Education	Attended college and professional schools and expect children to do the same	Attended high school and college or professional schools.	Attended high school; may or may not encourage college	Attended high school or less; cost is a major factor in education
Housing	Own home in prestigious neighborhood	Usually own home	About half own a home	Rent

SOURCE: Macionis, 2017

countries (Bradbury, Corak, Waldfogel, & Washbrook, 2016). High-SES students score higher than their low-SES counterparts on intelligence and achievement tests, they earn higher grades, they're suspended less often, and they're more likely to finish both high school and college (Bartik & Hershbein, 2018; Macionis, 2017). Low-income students are going to college in greater numbers than ever before, but few are leaving with degrees (The Pell Institute, 2018).

Lack of social mobility is an additional problem. Research indicates that Americans born poor or disadvantaged are less likely to succeed not only in college, but also in career and civic life. More than 4 of 10 students raised at the bottom of the income distribution are still there a generation later, and 70% never reach the middle class (The Pell Institute, 2018).

Socioeconomic Status and Home-School Support

Socioeconomic status strongly influences the school-related support students receive in their homes. Two factors, basic needs and parenting practices, have a powerful influence on student success in school.

Basic Needs.

Stephanie, a first-grader, was born premature to a single mother, who works two part-time jobs and has no health insurance. Stephanie often comes down with colds and ear infections, and if they're severe enough, her mother takes her to the emergency room because she has no other access to health care. These visits sometimes involve long waits, so Stephanie misses school, and her mom loses time at work. As a result, Stephanie is falling farther behind, and her mother's financial struggles are getting worse.

Stephanie's situation is unfortunately typical of many low-SES learners. Worldwide, more than 1 of 10 children are born premature—defined as born alive before 37 weeks of pregnancy are completed (World Health Organization, 2017). In our country the figure is slightly less than 1 of 10, an unimpressive—for an economically advanced country—C grade, according to the March of Dimes Foundation (2016), and this problem is most common in low-SES families. Premature birth is associated with learning disabilities and hearing and vision problems (Berk, 2019b). Low-SES parents are less likely to have personal physicians or nurse practitioners, so they don't have the luxury of calling a pediatrician if their child gets sick, and they also have less access to specialists in the case of chronic or unique health problems. Further, children from low-SES families are more likely to have high levels of lead in their blood—a prominent example being the widely publicized issue of lead-tainted water in Flint, Michigan. High lead levels in the blood are known to reduce cognitive ability and increase behavioral problems ranging from lack of impulse control to increased aggression and violence (Morsy & Rothstein, 2015). High levels of lead found in students in the Detroit Public Schools system have been linked to that city's low student test scores (Wilkinson, 2016). In addition, nearly 1 of 5 children in America experiences "food insecurity," which means they don't always know where they will find their next meal. And members of cultural minorities and single-parent families made up a disproportionate share of this figure (Feeding America, 2013). Poor nutrition can affect attention and memory and can lead to lower intelligence test scores (Berk, 2019b). Economic problems can also contribute to family and marital conflicts, which result in less stable and supportive homes. The majority of high-SES children grow up with two parents, whereas their lower-SES counterparts are increasingly, likely to live with one, most commonly a single mother. Children from low-SES families often come to school without the sense of security that equips them to tackle school-related tasks. As a result, they often have a greater incidence of depression, anxiety, and other emotional and behavioral problems than do their more advantaged peers (Morsy & Rothstein, 2015; Putnam, 2016). Low-SES families also relocate frequently; in some low-income schools, mobility rates are above 100% (Dalton, 2013). Nearly a third of the poorest students attend at least three different schools by third grade, compared to only 1 of 10 for middle-class students. These frequent moves are stressful for students and a challenge for teachers attempting to develop caring relationships with them (Phillips, 2016).

Parenting Practices that Prepare Students for Schooling.   The impact of SES is also transmitted through parenting practices that prepare children for success in school. For instance, prior to the 1970s few class differences existed in the amount of time parents spent reading and playing with their youngsters, but now the children of college-educated parents receive 50% more "nurturing time" (Putnam, 2016). Part of nurturing involves the amount of interaction between parents and their children (Putnam, 2016; Weisleder & Fernald, 2013). For instance, researchers have found that children from professional families hear more than 2,150 words an hour, compared to slightly more than half that many in working-class families, and little more than 600 words an hour for families on welfare. By age 3, children of professionals have vocabularies more than twice as large as peers in families receiving welfare (Zero to Three, 2015). And it goes beyond the simple number of words. Children of professionals hear twice as many unique words and have twice as many "encouraging" versus "discouraging" "conversations" such as "What did you think of that?" versus "Don't touch that." High-SES parents ask their children more questions, explain the causes of events, provide clearer directions and reasons for rules, and are more likely to encourage problem solving (Pace, Hirsh-Pasek, & Golinkoff, 2016). Higher SES parents are also more likely to attend school functions, help with projects, monitor homework, and talk to their children about school. Children see their parents reading and studying, so, through modeling, they learn that reading and study are important, making them more likely to become readers. Raising a child is demanding and time consuming, so it helps to have a supportive spouse to share the burden. Because lower-SES parents are often working two or more low-income jobs, they don't have this luxury of time, so they are more likely to simply demand obedience, which detracts from children learning to think for themselves and organize their lives, ever more important as the world grows more complex and the rewards for superior cognitive skills increase. The result is a decrease in social mobility (Putnam, 2016). High-SES families also have more resources that support their children. For instance, families from the top income quintile have twice as many books in the home as the lowest quintile (Morsy & Rothstein, 2015). Differences go much farther than books and language. By age 6, children from affluent families have spent 1,300 to 1,800 more hours in activities such as summer camps; travel; trips to libraries, zoos, and museums; and organized youth athletics, considerably more than their lower-SES counterparts. This gives children of high-income and highly educated families more background knowledge, the most important predictor of later academic achievement (Neuman & Celano, 2012).

Socioeconomic status also influences how children use technology. Research indicates that higher-SES parents are more likely to monitor computer use, which results in significantly less time spent on entertainment programs (Wood & Hawley, 2012). Lower-SES students spend more time with media such as video games and social networking and less on homework. Some experts call these differences the "new digital divide" (Richtel, 2012).

The summer months are also relevant. While their more affluent peers are reading books, playing educational games, and taking family trips during the summer, lower-SES students spend much less time in activities that support learning. The cumulative effects of these experiences result in summer learning loss for less advantaged students (Quinn & Polikoff, 2017). High-SES parents also have higher expectations for their children and encourage them to graduate from high school and attend college. Typically college graduates themselves, they understand the importance of education. They also know how to play the "schooling game," steering their sons and daughters into advanced high school courses and contacting schools for information about their children's learning progress. Low-SES parents, in contrast, tend to have lower aspirations for their children, allow them to "drift" into classes, and rely on the decisions of others. Students get lost in the shuffle, ending up in inappropriate or less challenging classes (Macionis, 2017).

Poverty

When Kirsten gets a spare moment, and there aren't many of these, she loves to draw fantasy creatures on her computer. (When it works. When it doesn't, she uses paper and pencil.) She likes to draw mermaids, fairies, and monsters—escapes from reality. But Kirsten's life is not a fairy tale. She hurries home from school with her brother, fixes them both a snack, and does her homework. Then she straightens up the small apartment, cleans up the room she shares with her brother, does the dishes left over from breakfast and last evening's meal, and cooks dinner. Quite an accomplishment for a fifth grader! She is sometimes hungry and she worries that she and her mother and brother won't have enough to eat. Kirsten has to work like this because her single mother works 10 hours a day on two jobs—one as a waitress and the other cleaning people's houses—to make ends meet. When her mother returns home from work, she collapses on the sofa, exhausted.

Kirsten has the misfortune to be a child of **poverty**, the lack of enough material possessions or money to maintain an adequate quality of life. Families in poverty are at the bottom rung of the socioeconomic ladder, and the differences between high and low-SES families that we described above are more extreme for students who live in poverty. For these students, access to food, clothing, and even shelter is severely limited (Marx, 2015). In 2017, the federal government defined the poverty level for a family of four in our country as $24,600. This definition is determined primarily by the cost of food, largely ignoring other factors such as housing, transportation, and energy (Obamacare. net, 2017). Statistics gathered from the United States Census Bureau indicate that the overall poverty rate in our country is slightly less than 13%, but is 18% for children (Federal Safety Net, 2017). Experts estimate that 40% of American children will live in poverty at some time in their lives (Koppelman, 2017). And, as with income inequality, the rate of poverty is much higher in the United States than in other wealthy nations (OECD, 2018). Further, our country devotes far fewer resources, as a percentage of gross domestic product, to welfare programs than other advanced nations (Rank, 2018). And, this doesn't appear to be wise economics. For instance, research indicates that for every dollar spent on reducing childhood poverty, the country would save at least seven dollars in the economic costs of poverty (McLaughlin & Rank, 2018).

Problems with poverty are increasing. A report released in 2018—a 50th anniversary follow-up to a report commissioned in 1968 that examined poverty and lack of economic opportunity—states that the percentage of people living in deep poverty—less than half the federal poverty level—has increased since 1975, and far more people are poor now than was true 45 years ago. Nearly half of all people in poverty in 2016 were classified as living in deep poverty, 16% higher than in 1975. Further, income inequality is increasing, and the result, the 2018 report asserts, means that people struggling with poverty are confined to poor areas with inadequate housing, underfunded schools, and law enforcement that views those residents with suspicion (Harris & Curtis, 2018).

Table 4.3 provides poverty statistics by race, educational attainment, and marital status.

Many students, such as you and your peers in teacher-preparation programs nationwide, may come from suburban middle-class backgrounds, so they often don't realize that poverty can be a potential issue in their classrooms. However, many changes have occurred over the years, and more than half of the poor populations in metropolitan areas now live in suburbs. This suggests that poverty may be a factor regardless of where you teach. Further, research consistently indicates that disadvantaged students are taught by fewer expert teachers than their more fortunate peers (Goldhaber et al., 2015). We're writing this section to help you become the kind of teacher that can provide your students with the expert instruction they need, should you begin your career in a school that serves large numbers of disadvantaged students. The federal government attempts to address some of the problems of poverty through the National School Lunch Program, a federally assisted meal program operating in public and nonprofit private schools and residential child care institutions. It provides nutritionally balanced, low-cost or no-cost lunches to children each school day. Children from families at or below 130% of the poverty level are eligible for free breakfasts and lunches; those with incomes between 130% and 185% of the poverty level are eligible for reduced-price

TABLE 4.3 Poverty statistics by race, educational attainment, and marital status

Poverty Statistics by Race

Race	Americans in the Category (millions)	Americans in Poverty (millions)	Poverty Rate
White, not Hispanic	195.2	17.3	8.8%
African American	42.0	9.2	22.0%
Asian	18.9	1.9	10.1%
Hispanic	57.6	11.1	19.4%

Poverty Statistics by Educational Attainment

Educational Attainment	Americans over 25 Years Old (millions)	Americans over 25 Years Old in Poverty (millions)	Poverty Rate
No High School Diploma	22.5	5.6	24.8%
High School Diploma	62.5	8.3	13.3%
Some College, No Degree	57.8	5.4	9.4%
College Degree or Higher	74.1	3.3	4.5%

Poverty Statistics by Marital Status

Marital Status	All Families (millions)	Families in Poverty (millions)	Poverty Rate
Married Couple	60.8	3.1	5.1%
Single Mother	15.6	4.1	26.6%
Single Father	6.5	.8	13.1%

SOURCE: Federal Safety Net, 2017; Semega, Fontenot, & Kollar, 2017.

meals, for which students can be charged no more than 40 cents. More than 30 million children participated in this program in 2016 (United States Department of Agriculture, 2017). Teachers worry about hungry students because they know hunger interferes with learning. In a survey of American public school teachers, 3 of 4 say they teach students who regularly come to school hungry. Nine of 10 say they are concerned about the long-term effects hunger has on children's education, and they respond in a variety of ways, such as keeping boxes of crackers, granola bars, and other snacks in their desks. They also help students sign up for free or reduced-priced meals at school (NoKid-Hungry, 2016).

The Impact of Poverty

The differences between high and low-SES families that we described earlier are exacerbated for children in poverty, and the impact begins in early childhood when the brain is developing most quickly. Research in neuroscience indicates that children growing up in poverty face high levels of the stress hormone cortisol, which changes the architecture of the brain and impairs brain circuits responsible for impulse control, working memory (we discuss working memory in detail in Chapter 7), emotional regulation, error processing, and healthy metabolic functioning (McCoy, 2016). These results are even more pronounced if children are coming to school hungry (NoKidHungry, 2016). As a result, children of poverty begin their schooling already at a significant disadvantage, and poverty related problems can have dramatic effects on learning. For instance, in addition to lower achievement, they are more likely to have emotional and behavioral problems in school, and they're twice as likely as their peers to be suspended and repeat a grade (Lesaux & Jones, 2016).

These problems are particularly pronounced for homeless children, who, as we would predict, don't attend school regularly, which exacerbates all of these problems. We examine homelessness in more detail next.

Homelessness

Emily sleeps on a mat on the floor of a city-managed shelter, with a tattered comforter as her only cover. "I'm cold," she murmurs through her half sleep. Her mom covers her with a worn winter coat while trying to not wake her younger brother and sister who are sleeping nearby.

Emily, her younger brother and sister, together with her mom and dad, have been living in one room in the shelter since her dad lost his job as a result of the downturn in the economy. He has been actively searching for a new job, but so far, no luck. They must go to a community wash area both to clean up and go to the bathroom. The only heat in their room is a space heater that they must share with the people in the next room. It isn't uncommon for Emily and her brother and sister to go to bed hungry, and their parents often skip meals so their children will have enough to eat. They continue to hope for a job, so they can get back to some semblance of a normal life again. (Adapted from Elliott, 2013)

This is what homelessness can feel like to a child. **Homeless students** are defined as those who lack a fixed, regular, and adequate nighttime residence, and this condition can have a powerful negative influence on learning and development (Hardin & Wille, 2017). Homelessness is a direct result of poverty, and the problems of poverty are particularly acute for these children. More than 1.3 million homeless students were enrolled in our nation's schools in the 2013–14 school year, an increase of more than 38% from 2009–10. High immigration states, such as California, Texas, and New York, have the largest numbers of homeless students, and the greatest increases have been in preschool-aged children and ninth graders (Jones, 2016). The federal government has acted. Under provisions of the Every Student Succeeds Act (ESSA), which we describe in Chapter 15, our nation's public school districts are required to (National Association for the Education of Homeless Children and Youth, 2016):

- Identify and prepare school personnel to locate, enroll, and support homeless students.
- Increase "school stability" for homeless children, that is, allow them to remain in the same school, even if they move, such as to a different shelter or motel.
- Ensure counseling for furthering their education and providing access to financial aid.
- Help young homeless children get into early childhood programs.
- Authorize more funding to support school districts' efforts to identify and serve homeless children.

If we have homeless children in our classes, we are professionally bound to do our best to help them learn and develop, so, ideally, they will be able to make their way out of their homelessness.

Students at Risk

Laurie Ramirez looks over the papers she has been grading and shakes her head. "Fourth grade, and some of these kids don't know what zero means or how place value affects a number. Some can't add or subtract, and most don't understand multiplication. How am I supposed to teach problem solving when they don't understand basic math facts?"

"Reading isn't much better," she thinks. "I have a few who read at a fourth-grade level, but others are still sounding out words like *dog* and *cat*. How can I teach them comprehension skills when they are struggling with ideas this basic?"

We find failing learners in every school. For some, a combination of obstacles makes them **students at risk** of failing to complete their education with the skills necessary to succeed in today's society. Historically these students were described as *underachievers*, but the term *at risk* more clearly reflects the long-term consequences of school failure.

Socioeconomic status is a primary factor in influencing students at risk. As we saw earlier, low socioeconomic status, and particularly poverty, creates a number of stress factors that detract from learning (American Psychological Association, 2018; Putnam, 2016). In addition, those students who are members of a cultural minority or non-native English speakers (who are also over-represented at lower income levels and often experience issues associated with poverty) are more likely to be students at risk (Diaz-Rico, 2013; Koppelman, 2017). The combination of these factors can result in a history of low achievement, which makes new learning even more challenging because students lack the background knowledge and skills on which new learning depends. A history of low achievement is compounded by lack of motivation, disengagement from school, and misbehavior (Schunk, Meece, & Pintrich, 2014). The problem can be exacerbated by the fact that students who need quality education the most are often provided with underqualified teachers (Goldhaber et al., 2015).

The Dropout Problem

Dropping out of school is one of the most pernicious outcomes of being at risk, with poverty being a major factor. Students from low-income families are five times more likely to drop out than their more fortunate peers (McCoy, 2016). Students who drop out of school decrease their chances of personal success and are more likely to have problems with transiency, crime, and drug abuse (Macionis, 2017). High school dropouts often end up in dead-end minimum wage jobs. As of January 1, 2017, the minimum wage in our country ranged from a low of $5.15 in Georgia to a high of $12.50 in Washington, DC, followed by $11.00 in Massachusetts and Washington.

Five states—Alabama, Louisiana, Mississippi, South Carolina, and Tennessee—have no minimum wage (National Conference of State Legislatures, 2017).

A wage of $5.15 an hour results in a yearly salary of $10,300 a year, based on a 40-hour work week for 50 weeks a year. Even the high of $12.50 results in only $25,000 a year. We can all imagine trying to live—let alone support a family—on that amount of money. In addition, dropping out of high school closes the door to college and well-paying jobs that require advanced training and expertise with technology. In the past, factory and farm jobs offered viable alternatives for dropouts; today, with employers outsourcing to other countries and smaller farms consolidating, these jobs no longer exist. Fortunately, the dropout statistics are moving in the right direction. For instance, between the years 2000 and 2015 the dropout rate declined from 6.9 to 4.6 percent for White youth; from 13.1 to 6.5 percent for Black youth; and from 27.8 to 9.2 percent for Hispanic youth. The gap between White and Black youth narrowed from 6.2 percentage points in 2000 to 1.9 percentage points in 2015, and the gap between White and Hispanic youth narrowed from 20.9 percentage points in 2000 to 4.6 percentage points in 2015 (U.S. Department of Education, National Center for Education Statistics, 2017). As teachers we obviously want to do everything we can to prevent students from dropping out. We address ways to accomplish this goal in the next section.

Students at Risk and Resilience

Attempts to help students at risk succeed now focus on developing **resilience**, a learner characteristic that, despite adversity, increases the likelihood of success in school and later life. Researchers, in studying young people who have survived and even prospered despite obstacles such as poverty and fragmented support services, have found that resilient children have well-developed self-systems, including high self-esteem, optimism, and feelings that they're in control of their destinies. Resilient children set personal goals, expect to succeed, and believe they're responsible for their success. They are motivated to learn and satisfied with school (Tichy, 2017).

How do these skills develop? Resilient children come from emotionally supportive environments, and one characteristic is striking. In virtually all cases, these children have one or more adults who have taken a special interest in them and hold them to high moral and academic standards, essentially refusing to let the young person fail. These adults are often parents, but they can also be older siblings or other adults, such as teachers, who take a young person under their wing (Edwards, Catling, & Parry, 2016). Schools can also make important contributions to resilience. Let's see how.

Schools That Promote Resilience

Research has identified four school practices that promote resilience:

- *Safety and structure.* The school and classes are orderly and highly structured. Teachers work with administrators to make the school safe and welcoming, and teachers consistently enforce rules and procedures (Emmer & Evertson, 2017; Evertson & Emmer, 2017).

- *Strong personal bonds between teachers and students.* Teachers become the adults who refuse to let students fail, and students feel connected to the schools (Castle Heatly & Votruba-Drzal, 2017; Kuhl, 2017).

- *High and uncompromising academic standards.* Teachers emphasize mastery of content and do not accept passive attendance and mere completion of assignments (Belfi, Gielen, De Fraine, Verschueren, & Meredith, 2015; Biag, 2016; Prelli, 2016).

- *Community outreach.* Schools reach out to invite parents and caregivers to participate in school activities (Bryk, Sebring, Allensworth, Luppescu, & Easton, 2010; Peters et al., 2010). These schools work closely with other community agencies to provide a web of services that support students and their families.

These schools are both demanding and supportive; in many instances, they serve as a refuge, essentially homes away from home. The emphasis on school–community links reduces alienation and increases academic engagement and achievement (Biag, 2016). School-sponsored activities also give teachers the chance to know students in contexts outside the classroom.

Teachers Who Promote Resilience

Schools are no more effective than the teachers who work in them. So, how do teachers promote resilience? As we would expect, easy answers don't exist, but research does provide some insights. The student–teacher relationship is the foundation on which resilience is developed. Supportive teachers create emotionally safe and low conflict learning environments, and positive relationships between teachers and students are associated with a host of learning benefits, including increased student engagement, even in students with negative attitudes (Archambault, Vandenbossche-Makombo, & Fraser, 2017), improved student self-regulation (Zee & de Bree, 2017), and increased achievement and higher levels of school satisfaction (Leff, Waasdorp, & Paskewich, 2016). The benefits of positive teacher–student relationships are thought to "trigger effort, persistence, and participation; to foster interest and enthusiasm; and to dampen negative emotions such as anger, frustration, anxiety, or boredom" (Castle Heatly & Votruba-Drzal, 2017, p. 1043).

To become resilient, students must believe beyond any doubt that their teachers are committed to their learning and their well-being as people, regardless of their attitude or how they behave. The relationship is analogous to children who come from stable, loving families; the children never consider the possibility that their parents have anything but their best interests at heart.

So, how is this relationship developed? Just as loving parents have high expectations for their children, set limits for acceptable behavior, and frequently interact with them, so do teachers who promote resilience. When students inevitably misbehave, don't care, or sometimes even resist learning, teachers don't give up on them; instead, they redouble their efforts and even display the "tough love" that students sometimes need in order to succeed (Archambault et al., 2017).

Recalling some of the anxieties and demands your parents experienced when you were growing up, it's easy to understand that promoting resilience in students can be stressful and challenging. Teachers who succeed have the high levels of social-emotional competence and the emotional sturdiness and sense of personal well-being that help them manage stress and avoid burnout (Jennings, Frank, Snowberg, Coccia, & Greenberg, 2013). Finally, and this is particularly important when working with members of cultural minorities, a sense of personal efficacy—the unrelenting belief that you can and will make a difference with these students—is essential (Belfi et al., 2015; Biag, 2016; Prelli, 2016). In addition to being emotionally demanding, promoting resilience is time consuming. It requires spending extra time before or after school both helping students with academic work and being a person students can talk to about personal issues, problems, and goals. Some who work with troubled students suggest that "empathetic listening" is one of the most important personal strategies we can use in building relationships with students who come from disadvantaged backgrounds (Warshof & Rappaport, 2013). What else do we know about teachers who promote resilience? They're expert teachers. They encourage their students to set personal and academic goals (Rowe, Mazzotti, Ingram, & Lee, 2017), interact frequently with students, maintain high expectations, use interactive teaching strategies, emphasize success and mastery of content, and look for opportunities to provide students with positive feedback (Sprouls, Mathur, & Upreti, 2015).

They provide both the personal and instructional support all students, and particularly students at risk, need to succeed in school.

SES: Cautions and Implications for Teachers

As with culture, language, and gender, it's important to remember that the patterns we're describing represent group differences, and individuals within groups will vary widely. For example, many low-SES parents read and talk to their children, encourage their involvement in extracurricular activities, and attend school events. We (Paul and Don, your authors) both come from low-SES families, but—fortunately for us—were given all the enriching experiences we've discussed in reference to high-SES parents. Conversely, belonging to a high-SES family doesn't guarantee a child enriching experiences and caring, involved parents. We know that certain home conditions can make it difficult for students to succeed in school, but we also know that schools and teachers can do much to overcome these problems. We turn now to specific suggestions for promoting resilience.

Using Educational Psychology in Teaching: Suggestions for Promoting Resilience in Your Students

We know that the teacher–student relationship is the foundation on which resilience is developed. So, what can we do that communicates to students that we're committed to them both as learners and as people? Teaching that insists—even demands—that they work hard and succeed communicates this process better than anything else. Students appreciate and respect teachers who help them meet high expectations. Here's what one student had to say: "She used to, like, pull me aside, and only me, and, like, make sure that I knew everything, . . . and she would do, like, . . . extra practice, like, to make sure that I got everything" (Jansen & Bartell, 2013, p. 40).

APA Top 20 Principles

This description illustrates Principle 11: *Teachers' expectations about their students affect students' opportunities to learn, their motivation, and their learning outcomes—*from the *Top 20 Principles from Psychology for PreK–12 Teaching and Learning.*

Research consistently indicates that the same strategies proven effective for all students, including members of cultural minorities and students with exceptionalities, promote resilience in students at risk (Good & Lavigne, 2018; Jennings et al., 2013). We don't need to teach in fundamentally different ways, but we do need to do it just that much better. The following suggestions can support these efforts.

1. Create and maintain a safe classroom environment with predictable routines.
2. Combine high expectations with frequent feedback about learning progress.
3. Use teaching strategies that involve all students and promote high levels of success.
4. Use high-quality examples that provide the background knowledge students need to learn new content.

Create a Safe Classroom Environment with Predictable Routines.   As we saw earlier, students at risk frequently come from backgrounds where a great deal of uncertainty exists, and school often becomes a haven of security for these students (Henderson, 2013). Creating a safe and predictable environment is important for all students, and for students at risk it's essential (Emmer & Evertson, 2017; Evertson & Emmer, 2017). We introduced the chapter with Gary Nolan, a fifth-grade teacher. Let's look again at his work with his students to see how he applies this suggestion.

"Good morning, Tu . . . Nice haircut, Baraz," Gary greets his students, as he does each morning when they come in the door.

After sitting down, the students immediately begin a "To Do" exercise that Gary has displayed on his document camera. Today's "To Do" is:

Add the following:

$$\frac{1}{3} + \frac{1}{6} =$$

and

$$\frac{2}{3} + \frac{3}{4} =$$

They complete a "To Do" every morning, beginning without being reminded to do so. After they finish, Gary has two students explain their thinking in solving the problems, they correct any mistakes they've made, and he then asks, "Who's up today?" "Me," Anna says, raising her hand.

Every Friday Gary has one of his students make a presentation about their cultural backgrounds. They bring food, costumes, art, and music as illustrations, he encourages them to wear authentic dress from their heritage country, and they place their name with a push pin on a map at the front of the room. "Go ahead, Anna."

Gary created a safe and predictable environment in two ways. First, he always greeted his students as they came in the door. This action is simple, and students might not even consciously react to it, but it's important for creating the perception of a warm and inviting classroom environment. Second, his students completed a "To Do" every morning, Gary provided them with feedback, and they were given time to correct any mistakes. This routine both added to a sense of predictability and provided his students with extra practice using the content they're studying. For students at risk, the routine of doing the problems itself can be more important than the exercises.

Gary also had one of his students make a presentation each Friday morning. In addition to enhancing the pride of his cultural minority students, his presentations were also predictable and added to the sense of organization and security important for students like his.

Combine High Expectations with Feedback About Learning Progress.   High expectations are important for all students, and they're particularly important for students at risk (Jansen & Bartell, 2013). And this process goes beyond the topic they're studying. Gary communicated high expectations by requiring students to explain their thinking in solving the problems, a requirement for all problems, and having students correct any mistakes they made. His actions are important for two reasons. First, because he always required his students to explain their thinking, this process became an additional routine, and second, they symbolized that he believes in his students and believes they're capable. Communicating this belief is crucial for members of cultural minorities and students at risk, who live with uncertainty more advantaged students don't experience.

Requiring students to explain their thinking is demanding and requires patience. Many students, and particularly those who aren't native English speakers, have trouble putting their understanding into words. The urge to give up—concluding "They can't do it"—can be great. Students struggle because they haven't had enough practice and support. The more they practice, the better they get at it, and practice is literally the only way they'll improve, so persevering, as Gary did, is essential.

APA Top 20 Principles

This description again illustrates Principle 5: *Acquiring long-term knowledge and skill is largely dependent on practice*—from the *Top 20 Principles from Psychology for PreK–12 Teaching and Learning*.

Use Teaching Strategies That Involve Students and Promote Success.   Because students at risk come from disadvantaged backgrounds, they often don't have a history of academic success. As a result, promoting success with them is even more important than it is with their more advantaged peers who are better equipped—academically and emotionally—to cope with occasional failure. Now, let's look again at Gary's efforts with his students as they work on the exercise involving the classification of two-dimensional geometric shapes.

Gary has displayed the figures on his document camera as we see here:

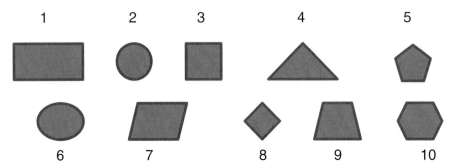

Now, let's look again at some of the dialogue.

Gary: Everyone look at the figures. . . . Now, I'm going to call on each of you to make some observations about them. . . . I want you to tell me anything you see. . . . Let's begin. Make an observation, . . . Felipe.

Felipe: Straight lines.

Gary: Yes, good. Several of them have straight lines. . . . Another observation, . . . Baraz?

Baraz: Some have 4 sides, but number 5 has 5 sides and number 10 has 6 sides.

As Gary continues, his students, who are used to this type of questioning, make a number of observations, such as:

- All sides are equal in #3.
- Opposite sides are equal in 1, 7, and 8—and Gary reminds them that is also true for #3.
- Two sides are equal in 4 and 9.

Gary then gradually narrowed his questioning, requiring more specific answers, ultimately leading to a classification of the figures.

MyLab Education
Video Example 4.5

Using high-quality examples is important for all students, and they're particularly important for promoting resilience in learners who may lack the background experiences that prepare them for success in school. Here, tenth-grade social studies teacher, Annie Rients, promotes the use of examples with her students in a lesson on ancient Rome.

We emphasized the effectiveness of using open-ended questions to promote involvement and success in our discussion of working with members of cultural minorities and ELLs, and, because they often lack a history of being academically successful, students at risk also benefit from the strategy. Because the students could respond with literally anything they observed, they were ensured of answering successfully. For students lacking a history of success, this experience can be very powerful, both emotionally and academically (Tichy, 2017). Admittedly, the strategy won't ensure that the students will be successful in all their academic experiences, but it's an important beginning. And, with additional support, students will gradually develop the perseverance that can dramatically increase the likelihood of more long-term success.

Promoting involvement and success is important for all students, and for students at risk it's imperative (Tichy, 2017; Vaughn et al., 2018).

Use High-Quality Examples That Provide Background Knowledge.   Students at risk often lack the school-related experiences that prepare them to succeed. This means that we must provide these experiences for them. Gary applied this suggestion with the figures he displayed on his document camera.

High-quality examples are important for all students, and for students at risk they're essential. For instance, using the students themselves or a pet hamster, snake, or lizard, are high-quality examples kindergarten teachers can use to teach the concept *living thing.* Objects around the classroom are high-quality examples of the concept *noun,* and using a pianica to demonstrate the concept *major chord* would provide a high-quality example in music.

We discuss high-quality examples, including the theoretical framework supporting them, in detail in Chapter 9.

National Council on Teacher Quality (NCTQ)

The National Council on Teacher Quality describes the use of examples as one of the six essential teaching strategies that all new teachers should know. "2. Linking abstract concepts with concrete representations. Teachers should present tangible examples that illuminate overarching ideas and also explain how the examples and big ideas connect" (Pomerance, Greenberg, & Walsh, 2016, p. vi).

The essence of using high-quality examples is simply that they provide the experiences—experiences more advantaged students often bring to school with them— that students at risk need to succeed academically. Helping students succeed while maintaining high expectations for students at risk isn't easy. Promoting resilience is not a task for the faint of heart, and it's also physically demanding. However, seeing these students meet challenges will be some of the most rewarding experiences you will ever have. As you've likely heard in other contexts, "It's the toughest job you'll ever love."

MyLab Education Application Exercise 4.3: Promoting Resilience in First Graders

In this exercise you will be asked to analyze a teacher's attempts to apply suggestions for promoting resilience with her students.

Classroom Connections

Promoting Resilience in Classrooms

1. Positive teacher expectations influence both motivation and achievement. Communicate positive expectations to students and their parents.

- **Elementary:** A fourth-grade teacher spends the first 2 weeks of school teaching students her classroom procedures and explaining how they promote learning. She makes short assignments, carefully monitors students to be certain the assignments are turned in, and immediately calls parents if an assignment is missing.

- **Middle School:** A math teacher carefully explains his course procedures. He emphasizes the importance of attendance and effort and communicates that he expects

all to do well. He also makes himself available before and after school for help sessions.

- **High School:** An urban English teacher sends home an upbeat letter at the beginning of the year describing her work requirements and grading practices. She has students help translate the letter for parents whose first language is not English and asks parents to sign the letter, indicating they have read it. She also invites questions and comments from parents or other caregivers.

2. Interactive teaching strategies are essential for students at risk. Use teaching strategies that elicit high levels of student involvement and success.

(continued)

- **Elementary:** A fifth-grade teacher arranges the seating in his classroom so that students who are and are not minorities are mixed. He combines small-group and whole-class instruction, and when he uses group work, he arranges the groups so they include students who are high and low achievers, students who are and are not minorities, and boys and girls.

- **Middle School:** An earth science teacher gives students a short quiz every day. He provides feedback the following day, and students frequently calculate their averages. The teacher closely monitors these scores and spends time before school to work with students who are falling behind.

- **High School:** An English teacher builds her teaching around questioning and examples. She comments, "My goal is to call on each student in the class at least twice during each lesson. I also use a lot of feedback and reinforcement as we cover the examples."

MyLab Education Self-Check 4.4

Developmentally Appropriate Practice

Learner Diversity at Different Ages

While many aspects of diversity are similar across grade levels, important developmental differences exist. The following paragraphs outline suggestions for responding to these differences.

Working with Students in Early Childhood Programs and Elementary Schools

The elementary grades pose developmental challenges for students learning a second language, as they face the dual tasks of learning to read and write while simultaneously learning English. While some research suggests that young language learners may be more adaptable than older ones, they still need special assistance to be successful (Echevarria et al., 2018a, 2018b). Instruction that maximizes opportunities for students to practice and use language is essential for these children. The strategies Gary Nolan used in *Educational Psychology and Teaching: Suggestions for Teaching Students in Your Classes Who Are Culturally and Linguistically Diverse* are effective for learners at all ages but are particularly important for elementary students. Writing assignments that encourage English learners to use their developing language skills are also important (Tompkins, 2018).

As we saw earlier, boys develop more slowly than girls, and girls have more-developed language abilities. Some experts suggest that developmental lags explain why boys outnumber girls in the number of special education placements. Giving children opportunities to get up and move around, providing concrete examples, and interactive instructional strategies proven effective with English learners are also effective with slower-developing boys.

Working with Students in Middle Schools

Developmental changes, such as going through puberty, and the transition to less personal middle schools where students often have five or six teachers, can be problematic for students who come from diverse backgrounds. Communicating that all students' backgrounds are respected and valued is even more important in diverse middle schools than it is in elementary schools. Safe and predictable classrooms provide both structure and security for middle school students (Emmer & Evertson, 2017). Well-established routines, consistent enforcement of rules, and emphasis on treating all students with courtesy and respect are essential. Establishing personal relationships with students, emphasizing that learning is the purpose of school, and de-emphasizing competition and differences among students are also important.

Working with Students in High Schools

High school is both the capstone of students' public school experience and an important transition period for both college and careers. Many students who come from low-SES backgrounds or are members of cultural minorities are unaware of the career and higher-education opportunities available to them, especially in rapidly developing fields like technology. Connecting content to students' future lives is particularly important for these students. For example, science teachers can discuss career options in related fields, and social studies and English teachers can examine the impact of technology on our lives.

High school is also an important time for both girls and boys who are trying to reconcile gender-role identities with societal expectations. For example, some high school girls are fearful that being intellectually assertive is not compatible with being feminine, whereas boys are struggling with decisions about whether to go to college or join the workforce. Open discussions with high school students can do a great deal to help them resolve these issues.

Chapter 4 Summary

1. Describe culture and explain how different aspects of culture influence learning.
   - *Culture* refers to the knowledge, attitudes, values, and customs that characterize a social group. The match between a child's culture and the school powerfully influences school success.
   - *Ethnicity* refers to a person's ancestry and the way individuals identify with their ancestors' nation of origin.
   - Culture and ethnicity can influence learning through the cultural attitudes and values that students bring to schools. Some values support learning, whereas others can detract from it.
   - Culture and ethnicity can also influence learning through the interaction patterns characteristic of the cultural group. If the interaction patterns are similar to those found in school, they enhance learning. If they are dissimilar, they can detract from learning.

2. Describe ways that teachers can accommodate linguistic diversity in their students.
   - Federal legislation, which ended quotas based on national origin, resulted in more immigrants coming to the United States from a wider variety of places. This has resulted in considerably more cultural, ethnic, and linguistic diversity in our classrooms.
   - Teachers can accommodate this diversity by first communicating that all cultures are valued and respected, involving all students in learning activities, and representing topics as concretely as possible.
   - Teachers also accommodate this diversity by providing students with opportunities to practice language and emphasizing important vocabulary.

3. Explain how gender can influence learning, and describe steps for eliminating gender bias in classrooms.
   - Gender can influence learning if either girls or boys adopt gender-stereotyped beliefs, such as believing that math or computer science are male domains, or believing that girls are inherently better at English and writing than boys.
   - Schools are important for helping students learn about power and vulnerability, providing a beginning point for the elimination of sexual harassment and sexual assault.
   - Teachers can attempt to eliminate gender bias by openly discussing gender issues, expecting the same academic behaviors from both boys and girls, and inviting non-stereotypical role models to their classes to discuss gender issues.

4. Define socioeconomic status (SES), and explain how it can affect learning.
   - Socioeconomic status describes the relative standing in society resulting from a combination of family income, parents' occupations, and the level of education parents attain.
   - SES can affect learning by influencing students' basic needs. Children of poverty often live in substandard housing and don't have access to medical care.
   - Low-SES children may also lack the school-related experiences they need to be successful, and lower SES parents may need to be encouraged and helped to be involved in their children's education.
   - SES can also influence learning through the attitudes and values of parents. Many high-SES parents encourage autonomy, individual responsibility, and self-control, whereas lower SES parents tend to value obedience and conformity. High-SES parents also tend to have higher expectations for their children than do their lower SES counterparts.
   - Resilient students succeed and even thrive in the face of adversity.
   - Having an adult who essentially refuses to allow a student to fail is a common denominator in students who develop resilience.
   - Schools promote resilience by creating safe and orderly learning environments, promoting strong personal bonds between teachers and students, and maintaining high and uncompromising academic standards.
   - Teachers further promote resilience by involving all students in learning activities and using high-quality examples that provide the background experiences students need to succeed.

Preparing for Your Licensure Exam

Understanding Learner Diversity

Because our students are becoming more diverse, your licensure exam will contain questions related to learner diversity. To help you practice for the exam in your state, we include the following exercises.

In this chapter, we've seen how culture, language diversity, gender, and SES can influence learning, and how certain combinations of these factors can place students at risk.

Let's look now at another teacher working with students from diverse backgrounds. Read the case study, and answer the questions that follow.

Teri Hall is an eighth-grade American history teacher in an urban middle school. Most of her students are from low-income families, many are members of cultural minorities, and some are ELLs. Today, her class is studying the colonization of North America. Teri takes roll as students enter the room, and she finishes entering the information into the computer on her desk just as the bell rings.

"What were we discussing yesterday?" Teri begins immediately after the bell stops ringing. "Ditan?"

" . . . The beginning of the American colonies." "Good. . . . Who can go up to the map, point out where we live, and show us the first British, French, and Spanish colonies. . . . Isabella?" After Isabella walks to the front of the room and points to four different locations on a large map of North America, Teri reviews important ideas from previous lessons for a few more minutes and then displays the following on the overhead:

> In the mid-1600s, the American colonists were encouraged to grow tobacco, because it wasn't grown in England. The colonists wanted to sell it to France and other countries, but were told no. In return for sending the tobacco to England, the colonists were allowed to buy textiles from England. They were forbidden, however, from making their own textiles. And all the materials were required to be carried on British ships.

> Early French colonists in the New World were avid fur trappers and traders. They got in trouble with the French monarchy, however, when they attempted to make fur garments and sell them to Spain, England, and others. They were told that they had to buy the manufactured garments from dealers in Paris instead. The monarchy also told them that traps and weapons would be made in France and sent to them as well. One of the colonists, Jean Forjea, complied with the monarchy's wishes but was fined when he hired a Dutch ship to carry some of the furs back to France.

"Take a few seconds to read the paragraphs you see on the screen," she begins. "Then, with your partner, write down three similarities between the French and English colonists. You have 5 minutes." Teri does a considerable amount of group work in her class. She sometimes has students work in pairs, and at other times in groups of four. The students are seated together, so they can move into and out of the groups quickly. Students initially protested the seating assignments, because they weren't sitting near their friends, but Teri emphasized that learning and getting to know and respect people different from ourselves were important goals for the class. Teri persisted, and the groups became quite effective.

Teri watches as students work, and at the end of the 5 minutes, she says, "Okay, you've done a good job. . . . Turn back up here, and let's think about this." As the class quickly turns their attention to the front of the room, Teri asks, "Serena, what did you and David come up with?" " . . . Both of the paragraphs deal with a colony from Europe." "Okay, Eric, how about you and Kyo?"

" . . . The colonies both produced something their countries, England and France, wanted—like tobacco or furs." "Excellent observation, you two," Teri smiles. "Go on Gustavo. How about you and Pam?" " . . . They sent the stuff to their country," Gustavo responds after looking at his notes. "And they couldn't send it anywhere else!" Tito adds, warming up to the idea. "That's very good, all of you. Where do you suppose Tito got that idea?. . . Connie?" "It says it right in the paragraphs," Connie responds. "Excellent, everyone! Connie, good use of information to support your ideas." Teri continues to guide students as they analyze the paragraphs. She guides the class to conclude that, in each instance, the colonies sent raw materials to the mother country, bought back finished products, and were required to use the mother country's ships to transport all materials. She then tells them that this policy, called mercantilism, was a strategy countries used to make money from their colonies. "Mercantilism helps us understand why Europe was so interested in imperialism and colonization," she adds. "It doesn't explain everything, but it was a major factor in the history of this period. Let's look at another paragraph. Does this description illustrate mercantilism? Be ready to explain why or why not when you've made your decision," she directs, displaying the following on the screen:

Canada is a member of the British Commonwealth. Canada is a large grain producer and exporter and derives considerable income from selling this grain to Great Britain, France, Russia, and other countries. This trade has also enhanced the shipping business for Greece, Norway, and Liberia, who carry most of the products. Canada, however, doesn't rely on grain alone. It is now a major producer of clothing, high-tech equipment, and heavy industrial equipment.

The class discusses the paragraph and, using evidence from the text, concludes that it does not illustrate mercantilism.

Questions for Case Analysis

Use information from this chapter and the case study to answer the following questions.

Multiple-Choice Questions

1. Which of the following strategies did Teri use to eliminate gender bias in her classroom?

   a. Strategically assigning girls to leadership roles in small-group work.

   b. Calling on both boys and girls equally.

   c. Openly taking about the problem of gender bias.

   d. Bringing female role models into her classroom.

2. Which two strategies did Teri use to actively involve her students in the lesson?

   a. Questioning

   b. Role-playing

   c. Small-group work

   d. Writing

Constructed-Response Question

1. Success and challenge are essential for effective instruction for students at risk. Evaluate Teri's attempts to provide these components.

MyLab Education Licensure Exam 4.1

Important Concepts

bidialectalism
bilingualism
cultural mismatch
culturally responsive
   teaching
culture
dialect

English language learners
   (ELLs)
ethnicity
gender identity
homeless students
immigrants
learner diversity

open-ended questions
oppositional peer cultures
poverty
race
racial macroaggressions
refugees
resilience

sex
sexual assault
sexual harassment
socioeconomic status
   (SES)
stereotype threat
students at risk

Chapter 5
Learners with Exceptionalities

FatCamera/Getty Images

Learning Outcomes

After you have completed your study of this chapter, you should be able to:

5.1 Describe different views of intelligence, and explain how ability grouping influences learning.

5.2 Describe the legal basis for working with students having exceptionalities, including the provisions of the Individuals with Disabilities Education Act (IDEA).

5.3 Describe the most common learning problems that classroom teachers are likely to encounter.

5.4 Identify characteristics of students who are gifted and talented, and explain how teachers identify and teach these students.

5.5 Describe regular education teachers' responsibilities in inclusive classrooms and explain how they relate to universal design for learning.

APA Top 20 Principles

Top 20 Principles from Psychology for PreK–12 Teaching and Learning explicitly addressed in this chapter.

Principle 5: Acquiring long-term knowledge and skill is largely dependent on practice.

Principle 7: Students' self-regulation assists learning, and self-regulatory skills can be taught.

When you begin teaching, you'll have students in your classes with learning or behavioral issues. Some may have trouble keeping up with their classmates academically, and others will struggle to stay mentally focused or sit still. And you may even have one or more with a visual or hearing impairment. They're like all students in many ways but will likely need extra help to succeed in our classrooms. Think about these issues as you read the following case study.

Celina Curtis, a beginning first-grade teacher in Grove Park Elementary, a large, urban elementary school, has survived her hectic first weeks. She is beginning to feel comfortable, but at the same time, she worries about some of her students.

"I hope I'm doing enough for Rodney and Amelia," she admits to Clarisse, a veteran who has become her friend and confidante. Rodney, diagnosed as ADHD, is a likable child whose engine is stuck on fast. He has trouble staying in his seat, let alone trying to do seatwork. The smallest distraction sets him off. His mother, part of the team whose mission it is to help him be successful, acknowledges that he's the same way at home.

Amelia has been diagnosed with an intellectual handicap. She is understandably easily frustrated because she struggles to keep up with her classmates. One-to-one work with her is a big help, but even then she struggles.

"This is part of reality," Clarisse responds sympathetically. "We all have, and will continue to have, students in our classes who need extra help and support. On the other hand, I've been around a long time, and I've seen some remarkable success stories with these kids. In fact, seeing them succeed are some of the most rewarding experiences I've had as a teacher."

In this chapter we'll learn about students like Rodney and Amelia, as well as others needing special help, and we'll also suggest what we, as regular education teachers, can do to help them grow and develop as much as possible. We all want to be able to enjoy the same rewards Clarisse describes as we work with students having special needs.

Learners with exceptionalities are students who need special help and resources to reach their full potential. They include students with **disabilities**; functional limitations, such as low cognitive ability or being unable to perform certain activities, like walk or listen; and **special education** services; which refers to instruction designed to meet the unique needs of these students. In the school year 2014–15, 13% of all public school students received special education services (National Center for Education Statistics, 2017a).

They also include students with **gifts and talents**, abilities at the upper end of the continuum that require additional support to reach full potential. Estimates indicate that slightly more than 6% of public school students in our country are enrolled in programs for the gifted and talented (National Center for Education Statistics, 2015).

Because it plays an important role in understanding and helping students with exceptionalities, we begin by examining the concept of *intelligence*.

Intelligence

5.1   Describe different views of intelligence, and explain how ability grouping influences learning.

We all know people we think are "sharp" because they're knowledgeable, perceptive, or learn new ideas quickly and easily. These are intuitive notions of **intelligence**, which experts define as the ability to acquire and use knowledge, solve problems, reason in the abstract, and adapt to new experiences (Gläscher et al., 2010; Kanazawa, 2010).

The ability to benefit from experience is a simple way to think about intelligence. For instance, if we could hypothetically give two people exactly the same set of experiences, the more intelligent of the two will derive more benefit from them.

Psychometric View of Intelligence

The **psychometric view of intelligence** describes it as a unitary trait which can be measured with a well-crafted instrument. The process of measuring mental capacities is the source of the term *psychometrics*.

The emphasis on measuring intelligence began in the early 1900s with the work of Alfred Binet, a French psychologist who invented the first practical intelligence test (Salvia, Ysseldyke, & Bolt, 2017). France had passed a law requiring all children to attend school, and Binet was commissioned to develop a test to help identify students who needed extra educational assistance. He developed a series of questions that correlated with school success, and he found that some younger students could answer questions typically answered by older learners, whereas some older students were only able to answer questions typically answered by younger learners. This led to the concept of *mental age* (MA).

Binet's work attracted attention in the United States, and the first Stanford-Binet intelligence test was introduced in 1916 (Bartholomew, 2004). It reported test performance as a single score, the famous Intelligence Quotient (IQ), with which we're all familiar. An IQ is determined by dividing mental age by chronological age (CA).

$$IQ = \frac{MA}{CA} \times 100$$

So, a ten-year-old who performed as well as a fifteen-year-old would have an IQ of 150 (15/10 × 100). Similarly a ten-year-old who scored as well as a nine-year-old would have an IQ of 90. But what does this number mean, and can a single number accurately reflect a person's intelligence? We address these questions next.

Cautions About Using and Interpreting IQ Scores

Ed Psych and You

Consider the following questions: If two buttons cost 15 cents, what would be the cost of a dozen buttons? In what way are a hammer and a saw alike? On what continent is Brazil? What do these questions have in common?

Think about the questions we asked in *Ed Psych and You*. Is the ability to answer them an indicator of intelligence? Experts think so; similar items appear on the Wechsler Intelligence Scale for Children—Fifth Edition (Wechsler, 2014), the most popular intelligence test in use today (Salvia, et al., 2017). These items are significant for two reasons. First, experts believe that everyday abilities, such as solving simple math problems; identifying relationships, such as the connection between a hammer and saw; and general knowledge—"On what continent is Brazil?" are indicators of intelligence.

Second, and perhaps more significant, experience influences our ability to answer the questions. Intelligence-test scores, while determined by psychometrically reliable instruments, don't provide a complete picture of students' learning potential. Instead, they reflect past exposure to the contents of a test, and they're influenced by facility with the English language and the unique experiences embedded within different cultures (Chen, Moran, & Gardner, 2009; Echevarria, Vogt, & Short, 2018a, 2018b; Sternberg, 2007). They can also be influenced by test-specific factors, such as fatigue, anxiety, or lack of familiarity with testing procedures (Popham, 2017).

This suggests that we should be cautious about using IQ scores alone in making decisions about our students. Other factors, such as conscientiousness, perseverance, access to school-related experiences, and past performance, all influence academic success (Grigorenko et al., 2009).

Intelligence: Nature and Nurture

The impact of experience on intelligence-test scores also relates to what is often called the *nature/nurture* issue. The extreme **nature view of intelligence** asserts that it is largely determined by genes; in essence, our intelligence is inherited from our parents and determined at birth (Horn, 2008; Toga & Thompson, 2005). The **nurture view of intelligence** emphasizes environmental influences and asserts that intelligence is malleable and can be changed by experience. As we've just seen, evidence supports the contention that past experiences strongly influence intelligence-test scores, and further, research in neuroscience suggests that learning potential is not fixed; that is, with the right kinds of experiences students can literally get "smarter" (Hohnen & Murphy, 2016; Van Dam, 2013). This evidence is important for us as teachers, because it means that we can actually increase our students' intelligence. This is indeed very good news.

Multi-Trait Views of Intelligence

Early researchers believed intelligence was essentially a single trait because scores on different measures of intelligence, such as verbal ability and abstract reasoning, are correlated (Johnson & Bouchard, 2005; Waterhouse, 2006). For example, Charles Spearman (1927) described it as "g," or general intelligence, a basic ability that affects performance on all cognitive tasks. This is consistent with the concept of IQ, a single score to describe intelligence.

Views of intelligence have changed, however, and many researchers now view it as composed of more than a single trait. For example, one perspective contrasts **fluid intelligence**, the flexible, culture-free ability to adapt to new situations and acquire knowledge easily, with **crystallized intelligence**, ability that's culture specific and depends on experience and schooling (Cattel, 1963, 1987). Fluid intelligence is closely related to underlying cognitive functions, such as working memory and executive functioning (Wang, Ren, & Schweizer, 2017). (We examine these cognitive functions in detail in Chapter 7.) Interventions designed to increase fluid intelligence through training in these cognitive functions have produced mixed results. For instance, research focusing on attention training resulted in improvements in attention but found no change in overall fluid intelligence (Sarzyńska, Żelechowska, Falkiewicz, & Nęcka, 2017). On the other hand, working memory training with young children resulted in increased fluid intelligence scores (Peng, Mo, Huang, & Zhou, 2017).

Fluid intelligence tends to be somewhat stable, whereas crystallized intelligence increases throughout our lives as we acquire new knowledge and skills. As we might expect, school learning is more closely related to crystallized than fluid intelligence (Zeller, Wang, Reiß, & Schweizer, 2017).

Another perspective views intelligence as hierarchical and multifaceted, with general ability at the top and those more specific, such as language and logical reasoning, at the bottom (Ackerman & Lohman, 2006). This view suggests that some cognitive abilities generalize to all situations, such as the inclination to search for evidence in making decisions, whereas others are content specific.

Other researchers have focused on different types of intelligence. For instance, considerable research has examined **social intelligence**, the ability to understand and work with people; **emotional intelligence**, the accurate perception, expression, and adaptation of emotions, and the ability to use emotional knowledge in thinking; and **cultural intelligence**, individuals' ability to effectively adapt to diverse cultural situations (Crowne, 2013; Khodadady & Hezareh, 2016). As we might expect, emotional intelligence is linked to success in romantic relationships (Malouff, Schutte, & Thorsteinsson, 2014), and, because the world is becoming ever more interconnected, cultural intelligence has received even more research emphasis, particularly in the business world (Magnusson, Westjohn, Semenov, Randrianasolo, & Zdravkovic, 2013).

We turn now to two of the more prominent multi-trait descriptions of intelligence: Gardner's theory of multiple intelligences, and Sternberg's triarchic theory of intelligence.

Gardner's Theory of Multiple Intelligences

Howard Gardner, a Harvard psychologist, analyzed people's performance in different domains and, dismissing the idea of "g," concluded that intelligence is composed of eight relatively independent dimensions (Cherry, 2017; Gardner, 1983; Gardner & Moran, 2006). Gardner's intelligences are outlined in Table 5.1.

Applications of Gardner's Theory. Gardner recommends that we present content in ways that capitalize on as many different intelligences as possible and help students understand their individual strengths and weaknesses in each (Denig, 2003; Kornhaber, Fierros, & Veenema, 2004). For example, to develop interpersonal intelligence (similar to social intelligence described above) we might use cooperative learning; we can encourage students to put their thoughts into words to develop linguistic intelligence; and we can have students practice defending their ideas with evidence to capitalize on logical-mathematical intelligence.

Gardner warns, however, that not all topics can be adapted for each intelligence: "There is no point in assuming that every topic can be effectively approached in [multiple] ways, and it is a waste of effort and time to attempt to do this" (Gardner, 1995, p. 206).

Evaluating Gardner's Theory. Gardner's theory is popular with teachers, and it makes sense intuitively (Cuban, 2004). We all know people who don't seem particularly

MyLab Education

Video Example 5.1

Howard Gardner views intelligence as existing in eight relatively independent dimensions. Here, a young student, in being able to group shells according to their common characteristics, demonstrates naturalistic intelligence, the ability to recognize patterns in the physical world.

TABLE 5.1 Gardner's theory of multiple intelligences

Dimension	Examples
Linguistic Intelligence Sensitivity to the meaning and order of words and the varied use of language	• Noticing differences in the meanings of words • Putting thoughts into language or writing creatively
Logical-Mathematical Intelligence The ability to reason logically, particularly in mathematics and quantitative sciences	• Making and defending conclusions based on evidence • Solving math problems and generating geometric proofs efficiently
Musical Intelligence Understanding and appreciating music	• Noticing differences in pitch, melody, and tone • Playing a musical instrument or singing
Spatial Intelligence The ability to perceive the visual world accurately	• Generating mental images of objects or creating drawings • Noticing subtle differences in similar objects
Bodily-Kinesthetic Intelligence The ability to skillfully use one's body	• Playing sports, such as basketball, soccer, or tennis, skillfully • Performing dances or gymnastic routines
Interpersonal Intelligence The ability to understand other person's behaviors	• Understanding others' needs, desires, and motives • Interacting with others in socially acceptable ways
Intrapersonal Intelligence Understanding one's own thoughts, moods, and needs	• Understanding what influences one's own motivations • Using knowledge of oneself to interact effectively with others
Naturalist Intelligence The ability to recognize patterns in the physical world	• Classifying natural objects, such as animals and plants • Working successfully in naturalistic settings, such as farming, ranching, forestry, or geology

SOURCE: Adapted from Gardner & Hatch, 1989; Checkley, 1997.

MyLab Education Application Exercise 5.1: Applying Multiple Intelligences in First Grade

In this exercise you will be asked to analyze a teacher's attempts to apply Gardner's theory of multiple intelligences with his students.

"sharp" analytically but who excel in getting along with others, for instance. This ability serves them well, and in some instances, they're more successful in life than their "brighter" counterparts. Others are extraordinary athletes or accomplished musicians. Gardner describes these people as high in interpersonal, bodily-kinesthetic, and musical intelligence, respectively.

Despite its popularity, research examining Gardner's theory is mixed. For instance, critics argue that the theory has not been validated by research, nor does it have support in cognitive neuroscience (Waterhouse, 2006). Critics also disagree with the assertion that abilities in specific domains, such as music, qualify as separate forms of intelligence (McMahon, Rose, & Parks, 2004). Some even argue that it isn't truly a theory (Chen, 2004).

Advocates counter these results, contending that attempts to apply Gardner's theory in classrooms increase achievement (Baş, 2016), and other advocates of the theory suggest that neuroscience does indeed support Gardner's contentions (Shearer, & Karanian, 2017).

Failure to account for the essential role that working memory plays in intelligent behavior is arguably the theory's most important weakness (Lohman, 2001). Research examining the way we process information suggests that a centralized working memory—the part of our memory system that consciously organizes and makes sense of our experiences—plays a special role in intelligence (Shelton, Elliott, Matthews, Hill, & Gouvier, 2010). For instance, when we solve word problems, working memory helps keep the problems' specifics in mind as we search our memories for similar problems, select strategies, and find solutions. This cognitive juggling act occurs in all types of intelligent behavior.

Working memory functioning is measured on both the Stanford-Binet and the Wechsler Intelligence Scale for Children (Wechsler, 2014), the two intelligence tests most widely used in our country. Gardner's work doesn't address this essential component of intelligence (Lohman, 2001).

Sternberg's Triarchic Theory of Intelligence

Robert Sternberg (Sternberg, 2017b), another multi-trait theorist, describes intelligence as existing in three dimensions:

- *Analytical*, similar to traditional definitions of intelligence and used in thinking and problem solving (Sternberg, 2003b).
- *Creative*, or experiential, the ability to deal effectively with novel situations and the ability to solve familiar problems efficiently (Sternberg, 1998a, 1998b).
- *Practical*, or contextual, the ability to effectively accommodate the task demands of the environment.

Intelligent behavior involves adapting to the environment, changing it if adaptation isn't effective, or selecting a better environment if necessary (Sternberg, 2007).

More recently, Sternberg has suggested that Active Concerned Citizenship and Ethical Leadership (ACCEL) is also an indicator of high ability (Sternberg, 2017a). Other authors have endorsed this view and suggest that this factor should be considered in criteria for giftedness (Ambrose, 2017).

Sternberg's emphasis on the creative and practical aspects of intelligence sets his theory apart from others. He sees functioning effectively in the real world as intelligent behavior, and because of this emphasis, he believes that individuals considered intelligent in one setting or culture may be viewed as unintelligent in another (Sternberg, 2004, 2006, 2007).

Influenced by Piaget's emphasis on the role of experience in development, and consistent with evidence documenting the influence of experience on intelligence, Sternberg believes that providing students with experiences in which they're expected to think analytically, creatively, and practically can increase intelligence. Some examples are outlined in Table 5.2.

What Does It Mean to Be Intelligent? Comparing Theories

The three perspectives we examined in this section provide us with different ways of thinking about what it means to be intelligent.

Psychometric views focus on intelligence as a single trait and assume that the trait can be measured—commonly on a paper-and-pencil test. In contrast, both Gardner and Sternberg view intelligence as composed of more than one trait, and people may be high in some but low in others. For instance, using Gardner's

TABLE 5.2 Applying analytic, creative, and practical thinking in different content areas

Content Area	Analytic	Creative	Practical
Math	Express the number 44 in base 2.	Write a test question that measures understanding of three different number bases.	How is base 2 used in our everyday lives?
Language Arts	Why is *Romeo and Juliet* considered a tragedy?	Write an alternative ending to *Romeo and Juliet* to make it a comedy.	Write a TV ad for the school's production of *Romeo and Juliet*.
Social Studies	In what ways were the American and the French revolutions similar and different?	What would our lives be like today if the American revolution had not succeeded?	What lessons can countries take away from the study of revolutions?
Science	If a balloon is filled with 1 liter of air at room temperature, and it is then placed in a freezer, what will happen to the balloon?	How would the balloon filled with air behave on the moon?	Describe two common examples where heating or cooling affects solids, liquids, or gases.
Art	Compare and contrast the artistic styles of Van Gogh and Picasso.	What would the Statue of Liberty look like if it were created by Picasso?	Create a poster for the student art show using the style of one of the artists we studied.

conception, an individual may be high in logical-mathematical intelligence, but low in bodily-kinesthetic intelligence.

Sternberg differs from other views with his emphasis on functioning in the real world as a measure of intelligence, a focus on citizenship and ethics, and attention to the role of experience and context—particularly cultural context—in thinking about intelligence.

Each perspective answers the question, "What does it mean to be intelligent?" a different way, and deciding which is more nearly correct is impossible. The three theoretical positions offer different, and valuable, perspectives on a complex concept central to learning and teaching. Our job is to equip students for success, both in school and in life after the school years. These views of intelligence remind us that children and young people can't be reduced to numbers, such as IQ, or even to a range of abilities. This understanding is liberating and puts us in a better position to make decisions about what is best for our students. This is why we study the work of researchers such as Gardner and Sternberg.

Table 5.3 summarizes the three theoretical positions, including the contributions and criticisms of each.

TABLE 5.3 Theoretical perspectives on intelligence

	Psychometric (Traditional) Theories of Intelligence	Gardner's Theory of Intelligence	Sternberg's Triarchic Theory of Intelligence
Major Question	How is intelligence reflected in learners' abilities to perform academic tasks, as measured by intelligence tests?	How are different dimensions of intelligence reflected in different tasks?	How is intelligent behavior reflected in the ability to think and solve problems, deal effectively with novel situations, and accommodate the daily task demands of our environments?
Key Concepts	Intelligence quotient (IQ) g—general intelligence	Linguistic intelligence Logical-mathematical intelligence Spatial intelligence Musical intelligence Body-kinesthetic intelligence Interpersonal intelligence Intrapersonal intelligence Naturalist intelligence	Analytic intelligence Creative intelligence Practical intelligence
Important Names	Charles Spearman Alfred Binet David Wechsler	Howard Gardner	Robert Sternberg
Basic View of Intelligence	• Intelligence is a trait that can be measured by performance on paper-and-pencil tests. • Performance on different subtests (e.g., verbal and quantitative) reflects different aspects of intelligence.	Intelligence is multi-faceted and composed of eight relatively independent "intelligences."	Intelligence is composed of analytic, creative, and practical abilities that people selectively employ in different contexts to achieve personal goals.
Contributions	• Pioneered efforts to define and measure intelligence • Led to the development of tests (e.g., Stanford-Binet and Wechsler Intelligence Scales) that are widely used to measure learner intelligence and diagnose learning issues	• Recognized that intelligence is multi-faceted and depends on contextual demands • Encouraged professionals to look beyond one or two scores when considering what it means to be intelligent	• Increased the focus of intelligence research on creative and practical dimensions of intelligence • Recognized that culture and context play a major role in what is considered to be intelligent behavior
Criticisms	• Relies too strongly on paper-and-pencil measures of intelligence measures • Doesn't adequately attend to cultural and contextual factors that influence intelligence	• Lacks empirical evidence supporting the existence of the various dimensions of intelligence • Agreement about the specific intelligences that Gardner has proposed is lacking	• Descriptions of how the three dimensions of intelligence interact to produce intelligent behavior are vague • Empirical evidence suggesting that the three dimensions of intelligence are distinct is lacking

SOURCES: Berk, 2019a; Gardner, 1983, 1995; Gardner & Hatch, 1989; Gardner & Moran, 2006; Garlick, 2010; Salvia, Ysseldyke, & Bolt, 2013; Siegler & Alibali, 2005; Spearman, 1904, 1927; Sternberg, 1998a, 1998b, 2003a, 2003b, 2004, 2006, 2007, 2009; Sternberg & Grigorenko, 2001.

Intelligence: Ability Grouping

Ability grouping, the process of placing students of similar abilities into groups and attempting to match instruction to the needs of each, is one of the most widely applied outcomes of thinking about the concept of intelligence (Chorzempa & Graham, 2006). In elementary schools, ability grouping typically exists in two forms. **Between-class grouping** divides students in a certain grade into levels, such as high, medium, and low. For example, an elementary school with 75 third graders might have one class of high achievers, one of average achievers, and one with low achievers. **Within-class grouping** divides students in a single class into groups, typically based on reading and math scores, such as a second-grade teacher having two or three different reading groups.

At the middle and high school levels, **tracking**, placing students in different curricula on the basis of aptitude and achievement, is common, and some form of tracking exists in most schools at these levels. For example, high-ability students in high schools study a curriculum intended to prepare them for college—and in some cases even earn college credit—and lower ability students receive vocational or work-related instruction (Oakes, 2005).

Ability Grouping: What Does Research Tell Us?

Ability grouping is controversial (Yee, 2013). Advocates argue that it allows teachers to keep instruction uniform for groups, helping them better meet learners' needs. Most teachers endorse it, particularly in reading and math. Approximately 7 of 10 elementary teachers report that they group in both reading and math, likely the result of accountability and high-stakes testing pressures (Yee, 2013).

Critics of ability grouping counter by citing several problems. They argue that within-class grouping creates logistical problems, because different lessons and assignments are required, and improper placements occur, which tend to become permanent (Good & Lavigne, 2018). And members of low-ability groups are often stigmatized by being labeled as low achievers (Oakes, 2005). Most significantly, research indicates that grouping students by ability makes them less successful. For instance, the 2012 Program for International Student Assessment (PISA) results found that the more schools group by ability, the lower the pupil performance overall (Program for International Student Assessment [PISA], 2012). Additional research indicates that homogeneously grouped low-ability students achieve less than heterogeneously grouped students of similar ability (Good & Lavigne, 2018). Further, critics argue, the assertion that low-ability students hinder the development of their higher ability peers isn't valid. For instance, if a high- and low-ability student are paired, the higher ability student often becomes an "explainer," an advanced cognitive process that deepens understanding for both students (DeWitt, 2016).

The negative effects of grouping are often related to the quality of instruction. As we would expect, the vast majority of teachers prefer working with high-ability students, and when assigned to low-ability groups, they sometimes lack enthusiasm and commitment and stress conformity instead of autonomy and the development of self-regulation (Chorzempa & Graham, 2006; Good & Lavigne, 2018). As a result, self-esteem and motivation to learn decrease and absenteeism increases. Tracking can also result in racial segregation of students, which has a negative influence on social development and opportunities to form friendships across cultural groups (Mandelman & Grigorenko, 2013; Oakes, 2005).

Heterogeneous grouping has the opposite effect. "Evidence gathered in more than 30 years of research indicates, if schools adopt mixed ability grouping, they are more likely to use inclusive teaching strategies and to promote higher aspirations for their pupils" (Higgins, Kokotsaki, & Coe, 2011, para. 33).

Ability Grouping: Implications for Teachers

Suggestions for dealing with the issues involved in ability grouping vary. At one extreme, critics argue that its effects are so negative that the practice should be abolished. A more moderate position suggests that grouping is appropriate in some areas, such as reading and math (Good & Lavigne, 2018).

When grouping is necessary, specific suggestions to reduce its negative effects include:

- Keeping group composition flexible, and reassigning students to other groups when their achievement warrants it.
- Keeping the quality of instruction high for low-ability groups.
- Teaching low-ability students learning strategies and self-regulation.
- Avoiding stigmatizing and stereotyping low-ability students.

These suggestions are demanding, and they have implications for us as we teach. Almost certainly, you will be assigned lower ability students at some point in your career, and likely in your first year, because teachers with seniority are often given higher ability groups. Lower ability students are indeed more difficult to teach, but making every effort to help them achieve as much as possible can be rewarding when you see the light bulb come on in a child who normally struggles.

Learning Styles

Historically, psychologists have used intelligence tests to measure mental abilities and have used concepts such as introvert and extrovert to describe different personality types. Researchers who study the interface between the two examine **learning styles**, students' personal approaches to thinking and problem solving (Denig, 2003). The terms *learning style, cognitive style, thinking style*, and *problem-solving style* are often used interchangeably, adding to confusion in this area.

One description of learning style distinguishes between deep and surface approaches to studying new content (Evans, Kirby, & Fabrigar, 2003). For instance, as you studied the Civil War, did you relate it to the geography, economies, and politics of the northern and southern states? If so, you were using a deep-processing approach. On the other hand, if you memorized important dates, locations, and prominent leaders, you were using a surface approach.

As we would expect, deep-processing approaches are vastly superior. Surface approaches can be successful only if tests emphasize facts and memorization. Further, students who use deep-processing approaches tend to be more intrinsically motivated and self-regulated, whereas those who use surface approaches tend to be extrinsically motivated and focus on grades and their performance compared to others (Schunk, Meece, & Pintrich, 2014).

Other perspectives contrast visual versus verbal approaches to learning. Visual learners prefer to see information, whereas verbal learners prefer hearing descriptions of ideas (Mayer & Massa, 2003). This shouldn't be a factor in our teaching because research indicates that, as a general pattern, we should be presenting information in both visual and verbal forms whenever possible (Pomerance, Greenberg, & Walsh, 2016).

Learning Styles and Learning Preferences

The concept of learning styles is popular in education, and many consultants use this label when they conduct staff development workshops for teachers. These workshops, however, typically focus on students' preferences for a particular learning environment, such as lighting and noise level, and consultants encourage teachers to match classroom environments to students' preferences.

MyLab Education
Video Example 5.2

Ability grouping is popular, but it has both advantages and disadvantages. Here, an elementary teacher describes the importance of grouping students appropriately to ensure that they are all successful. Notice the teacher's emphasis on changing the composition of the groups depending on the goals of the learning activity.

Research on these practices is controversial. Advocates claim the match results in increased achievement and improved attitudes (Farkas, 2003; Lovelace, 2005). Critics counter by questioning the validity of the tests used to measure learning styles or preferences (Coffield, Moseley, Hall, & Ecclestone, 2004; Krätzig & Arbuthnott, 2006). They also cite research indicating that attempts to match learning environments to learning preferences have failed to produce increases in achievement (Englander, Terregrossa, & Wang, 2017). "The contrast between the enormous popularity of the learning-styles approach within education and the lack of credible evidence for its utility is . . . striking and disturbing. If classification of students' learning styles has practical utility, it remains to be demonstrated" (Pashler, McDaniel, Rohrer, & Bjork, 2008, p. 117). Other researchers agree with this assessment (Brophy, 2010; Howard-Jones, 2014; Riener & Willingham, 2010). Riener and Willingham (2010) state simply "There is no credible evidence that learning styles exist" (p. 22), and Brophy (2010) goes on to say that the research supporting learning style assessments and the differentiated curriculum and instruction based on them is virtually nonexistent. He also points out that a teacher working with 20 or more students doesn't have the time planning and implementing such individualized instruction would take.

Others speak more strongly. "I think learning styles represents one of the more wasteful and misleading pervasive myths of the last 20 years" (Clark, 2010, p. 10).

Classroom Connections

Accommodating Ability Differences in Classrooms

1. Performance on intelligence tests is influenced by genetics, experience, language, and culture. Use intelligence-test scores cautiously when making educational decisions, keeping in mind that they are only one indicator of ability.

   - **Elementary:** An urban third-grade teacher consults with a school counselor in interpreting intelligence-test scores, and she remembers that language and experience influence test performance.

   - **Middle School:** When making placement decisions, a middle school team relies on past classroom performance and grades in addition to standardized test scores.

   - **High School:** An English teacher uses grades, assessments of motivation, and work samples in addition to aptitude test scores in making placement recommendations.

2. Intelligence is multifaceted and covers a wide spectrum of abilities. Use instructional strategies that maximize student background knowledge, interests, and abilities.

   - **Elementary:** In a unit on the Revolutionary War, a fifth-grade teacher assesses all students on basic information, but bases 25% of the unit grade on special projects, such as researching the music and art of the times.

   - **Middle School:** An eighth-grade English teacher has both required and optional assignments. Seventy percent of the assignments are required for everyone; the other 30% provide students with choices.

   - **High School:** A biology teacher provides students with choices in terms of the special topics they study in depth. In addition, he allows students to choose how they will report on their projects, allowing research papers, classroom presentations, or poster sessions.

3. Ability grouping has both advantages and disadvantages. Use ability grouping only when essential, view group composition as flexible, and reassign students when warranted by their performance. Attempt to provide the same quality of instruction for all group levels.

   - **Elementary:** A fourth-grade teacher uses ability groups only for reading. She uses whole-class instruction for other language arts topics such as poetry and American folktales.

   - **Middle School:** A seventh-grade team meets regularly to assess group placements and to reassign students to different groups based on their academic progress.

   - **High School:** A history teacher videotapes lessons to compare his teaching in high-ability compared to standard-ability groups. He continually challenges both types of classes with interesting and demanding questions and assignments.

Learning Styles: Implications for Teachers

While little evidence supports attempts to match instruction to students' learning styles, the concept does have implications for us as teachers. First, it reminds us that we should vary our instruction, because no instructional strategy works for all students, or even the same students all the time (Brophy, 2010). Second, we should help our students understand how they learn most effectively, something that they aren't initially good at (Krätzig & Arbuthnott, 2006). Third, our students differ in ability, motivation, background experiences, needs, and insecurities. The concept of learning style can sensitize us to these differences, encourage us to treat our students as individuals, and help us do everything we can to maximize learning for every student.

MyLab Education Self-Check 5.1

The Legal Basis for Working with Students with Exceptionalities

5.2   Describe the legal basis for working with students having exceptionalities, including the provisions of the Individuals with Disabilities Education Act (IDEA).

Ed Psych and You

You have three students in your class that you suspect have exceptionalities. Do you have professional obligations to them that go beyond those for all your students? If so, what are they?

In the past, students with disabilities were often placed in special classrooms or schools. Instruction in these placements was often inferior, achievement was no better than in general education classrooms, and students didn't learn the social and life skills needed in the real world (Smith, Polloway, Doughty, Patton, & Dowdy, 2016). In response to the problems, a series of federal laws redefined the way teachers assist and work with these students. We examine these laws next.

Individuals with Disabilities Education Act (IDEA)

In 1975 Congress passed Public Law 94-142, which made a free and appropriate public education a legal requirement in our country for all students with disabilities (Turnbull, Turnbull, Wehmeyer, & Shogren, 2016). This law, named the *Individuals with Disabilities Education Act* (IDEA), has several provisions, which are outlined in Table 5.4.

Amendments to IDEA

Since 1975, Congress has amended IDEA three times (Sack-Min, 2007). The first amendment, passed in 1986, held states accountable for locating young children who need special education. Amendment 1997—the second amendment—known as IDEA 97, attempted to clarify and extend the quality of services to students with disabilities. This amendment clarifies major provisions in the original IDEA, such as protection against discrimination in testing. It also ensures that districts protect the confidentiality of children's records and share them with parents on request.

The third amendment, IDEA 2004, includes mechanisms for reducing special education paperwork, creating discipline processes that allow districts to remove students

MyLab Education
Video Example 5.3

The Individuals with Disabilities Education Act (IDEA) is federal legislation making a free and appropriate public education for all students with disabilities a legal requirement in our country. Here two teachers describe the benefits of IDEA for working with their students who have exceptionalities.

TABLE 5.4 Provisions of IDEA

Provision	Description	Rationale
A Free and Appropriate Public education (FAPE)	A free and appropriate public education is one individually designed to provide educational benefits to a particular student.	Every student can learn. The 14th Amendment to the Constitution guarantees equal protection of all citizens under the law.
Least Restrictive Environment	A least restrictive environment (LRE), intended to ensure that students make progress in the general education curriculum, is a learning environment that places students with exceptionalities in as typical an educational setting as possible.	Separating students with exceptionalities from their peers doesn't meet these students' special needs.
Fair and Nondiscriminatory Evaluation	Any testing used for placement must be conducted in a student's native language by qualified personnel, and no single instrument, such as an intelligence test, can be used as the sole basis for placement.	Historically, students were often placed in special education programs based on invalid information.
Due Process and Parents' Rights	Parents have the right to be involved in their child's placement in special programs, to access school records, and to obtain an independent evaluation if desired. Protections also exist for parents who don't speak English.	Parents should have access to any and all information about their children.
Individualized Education Program	The IEP is a written statement that provides a framework for delivering a FAPE to every eligible student with an exceptionality.	Attempts to ensure that learners with exceptionalities don't get lost in the regular education classroom.

who "inflict serious bodily injury" from classrooms, and establishing methods to reduce the number of students from diverse backgrounds who are inappropriately placed in special education. It also makes meeting the "highly qualified teacher" requirements of federal legislation more flexible by allowing veteran teachers to demonstrate their qualifications by means other than a test (Council for Exceptional Children, 2014).

Most controversial is its provision that calls for including students with disabilities in accountability systems, with critics warning that testing students with exceptionalities in the standard ways harms more than helps them (Meek, 2006).

IDEA and its amendments have affected every school in the United States and have changed the roles of teachers in both general and special education. It also relates to the questions we asked in *Ed Psych and You* at the beginning of this section. The unequivocal answer to the question, "Do you have professional obligations to them [students with exceptionalities in your classroom] that go beyond those for all your students?" is yes. In the following sections we answer our second question: "If so, what are they?"

We turn now to inclusion and universal design for learning, important outcomes of IDEA.

Inclusion

Progress in the general education curriculum is one of the requirements of IDEA. "This is the principle of the **least restrictive environment (LRE)**, formerly known as mainstreaming or integration and now known as inclusion" (Turnbull et al., 2016, p. 19). **Inclusion** places students with exceptionalities in the school's academic curriculum, extracurricular activities, and other experiences alongside students not having exceptionalities (Justice, Logan, Lin, & Kaderavek, 2014; Pilon, 2013).

Inclusion has four components (Turnbull et al., 2016):

- Home-school placement
- The principle of natural proportions
- Age- and grade-appropriate placements
- Restructuring teaching and learning

Home-School Placement. When inclusion is in place, learners with exceptionalities attend the same school they would have attended if they didn't have an exceptionality (Munk & Dempsey, 2010). Rodney and Amelia, for instance, live in the geographical area served by Grove Park Elementary, so this is where they go; their exceptionalities don't impact where they attend school.

Principle of Natural Proportions. The principle of natural proportions states that students with exceptionalities should be placed in schools and classrooms in the same proportion as the existence of the exceptionality in the general population. For instance, as we saw at the beginning of the chapter, about 13% of all students in our nation's schools are served in special education programs (National Center for Education Statistics, 2017a). The principle of natural proportions would then suggest that no more than 4 students with a disability should be enrolled in a class of 30 students.

Age- and Grade-Appropriate Placements. Inclusion supports educating all students in the grade they would be in if they didn't have an exceptionality. For instance, Rodney just turned 7, and Amelia is age 6, so they're placed in the first grade with students of similar age, and they both spend all of their school time with students in this grade. IDEA favors inclusion, and research indicates that learners with exceptionalities can succeed in general education classrooms if they're provided adequate instruction and extra support (Turbull et al., 2016). This is accomplished by restructuring teaching and learning.

Restructuring Teaching and Learning. When inclusion is in place, general education teachers, special educators, outside services providers, and families work as a team. With the support of special educators, regular education teachers modify their instruction and the way they interact with their students to ensure that learners with exceptionalities have a chance to be successful. This leads us to the concept of *Universal Design for Learning.*

Universal Design for Learning

Ed Psych and You

As you approach a building with a short flight of steps, what else do you usually see adjacent to the steps, or nearby?

It's so commonplace that we essentially don't notice, but next to the steps we'll see a ramp. This ramp ensures that people restricted to wheelchairs have access to the building. This simple example illustrates the concept of **universal design**, the design of buildings, environments, and products to ensure that all people can access the building or environment, or use the product (Null, 2013). Paul, one of your authors, has historically joked with Don, your other author, about being subjected to discrimination, because, as a left-hander, he never had access to left-handed desks in university classrooms. More seriously, left-handed people with fine motor limitations often struggle with scissors, which are typically designed for right-handers. Universal design accommodates these differences.

Universal Design for Learning (UDL) takes this process a step farther and designs instructional materials and activities to make content accessible to all learners (Carnahan, Crowley, & Holness, 2016). UDL attempts to help learners with exceptionalities succeed in the regular education classroom by modifying curriculum and instruction and utilizing technology (Ok, Rao, Bryant, & McDougall, 2017). It is the process designed to ensure that inclusion is successful.

UDL is grounded in three principles (National Center on Universal Design for Learning, 2014a).

Principle I: Provide Multiple Means of Representation.   This principle, commonly referred to as the "what" of learning, suggests that, when appropriate, alternatives to printed text and verbal description be used to present content. For instance, text-to-speech (TTS) software allows struggling readers to have text read aloud to them, and it can convert ebooks to audiobooks. In other situations, graphics and videos can be utilized, and concrete examples are important in all content areas, such as using manipulatives to make mathematical symbols meaningful for learners who struggle with abstractions in math, showing students shrimp and crabs to illustrate the concept *crustacean,* or relating past events to their lives today to help them make sense of historical occurrences (Ok et al., 2017).

As alternatives to passive listening, this principle also calls for the active engagement of students and de-emphasizes seatwork and individual worksheets (Carnahan et al., 2016).

Principle II: Provide Multiple Means of Action and Expression.   Described as the "how" of learning, this principle provides for flexibility in helping learners express what they know. Typical modes of expression, such as handwriting, using a word processor, and responding orally, may not be feasible for learners whose motor skills are weak, have severe dyslexia, or are visually impaired. Audio recording and voice-recognition software provide alternative modes of expression, and adaptive keyboards that are contoured or allow learners to adjust the tilt, angle, height, and support of the keyboard can offer flexibility for performing computer-related tasks.

Principle III: Provide Multiple Means of Engagement.   The "why" of learning, multiple means of engagement calls for making content relevant to students' lives, emphasizing choice and autonomy, when possible, and creating a learning environment that's safe, orderly, and free of distractions. Emphasizing learning goals and self-regulation together with providing detailed feedback and ongoing support are essential for ensuring sustained student effort (National Center on Universal Design for Learning, 2014a).

Technology, Learning, and Development: Using Assistive Technology to Support Learners with Disabilities

Earlier we said that UDL's goal is to make content accessible to all learners (Carnahan et al., 2016). Technology support is an important tool in reaching this goal. Grounded in the principles of UDL, technology helps teachers tailor the curriculum to best meet the needs of individual students (National Center on Universal Design for Learning, 2014b). Let's see how this works in classrooms.

Julio is partially deaf, barely able to use a hearing aid to understand speech. Kerry Tanner, his seventh-grade science teacher, works closely with the special education instructor assigned to her classroom to help Julio. Seated near the front of the room to facilitate lipreading, he takes notes on a laptop during Kerry's presentations. Other students take turns sharing their notes with him so he can compare and fill in gaps. He likes to communicate with other students on the Internet, which helps level the communication playing field. When he views video clips on his computer, he uses a special device with earphones to increase the volume.

Jaleena is partially sighted, with a visual acuity of less than 20/80, even with corrective lenses. Despite this disability, she is doing well in fourth grade. Tera Banks, her teacher, has placed her in the front of the room so she can better see the board and displays on the document camera, and she's assigned students to work with Jaleena on projects. Using a magnifying device, she can read most written material, and she has access to a computer monitor that magnifies the display. Tara is confident these adaptations are working when she sees Jaleena working comfortably at her computer on a report due next Friday.

Julio and Jaleena are benefiting from **assistive technology**, a set of adaptive tools that support students with disabilities in learning activities and daily life tasks. These tools are required by federal law under IDEA and include motorized chairs, remote control devices that turn machines on and off with a head nod or other muscle movements, and machines that amplify sights and sounds (Heward, Alber-Morgan, & Konrad, 2017).

Originally, computer adaptations were the most widespread uses of assistive technology, but with mobile devices and apps, they've spread to other forms of support (Cook & Polgar, 2012; Lancioni, Sigafoos, & Nirbhay, 2013). For instance, a new device gives the visually impaired a way to read, and it can be worn like Google Glass and travel with the user to any learning situation (Markoff, 2013). It consists of a small camera that clips onto eyeglasses and a small computer that fits into a pocket. As it reads print information, it uses a bone conduction speaker to translate printed text into speech. In addition to being portable and easy to use, this device keeps track of frequently encountered words and phrases and stores them in the computer for quicker and more accurate word recognition.

Other applications of assistive technologies target students with learning problems. A number of software programs exist in reading and math to help students acquire essential facts and skills (Roblyer & Hughes, 2019). Many can also be combined with modified input and output devices to make them accessible to students with physical disabilities that make it difficult to use standard technologies. Let's take a closer look at some of these adaptations.

Adaptations to Output Devices.   Adaptations to output devices make it easier for students with sensory challenges to access and read information. For example, the size of the visual display can be increased by using a special magnifying monitor, such as the one Jaleena used. For students who are blind, portable speech synthesizers can read words and translate them into sounds, such as the one that clips to glasses. In addition, special printers can convert spoken words into Braille and vice versa (Roblyer & Hughes, 2019).

Adaptations to Input Devices.   To use technology effectively, students must also be able to input their ideas. This can be difficult for those with visual or other physical disabilities that don't allow standard keyboarding. Devices that enhance the keyboard, such as making it larger and easier to see, arranging the letters alphabetically to make them easier to find, or using pictures for nonreaders, are adaptations that accommodate these disabilities. For students with limited muscular control, specially adapted mouses and joysticks, as well as voice-recognition systems, can replace standard keyboards.

Assistive technology can also help struggling writers. A number of software programs help developing writers by providing spell-check and word-prediction scaffolding. When a student hesitates to finish a word, the computer, based on the first few letters, then either completes it or offers a menu of suggestions. Advocates claim it frees students to concentrate on ideas and text organization (Roblyer & Hughes, 2019).

Additional adaptations bypass the keyboard altogether. For instance, voice-recognition software can translate speech into text on the computer screen, which can be invaluable for students having disabilities that affect the use of their hands and fingers. Other adaptations use switches activated by a body movement, such as a head nod, to interact with the computer. Touch screens also allow students to go directly to the monitor to indicate their responses.

And students don't have to attend schools to benefit from these assistive technologies.

Lexie is a third-grader who was born with a heart disorder that weakened her immune system and increases health risks for her when she attends school. Tutoring at home works for her academically, but she misses interacting with her classmates. A four-foot-tall, 18-pound camera-and-Internet enabled robot, which Lexie named Princess, changed all that. The robot has a video camera and screen on its face, and Lexie controls it at home with a computer mouse. The robot can be moved around the room and flashes a light when Lexie needs her teacher's attention. Lexie's classmates look at the robot and say, "Hi, Lexie" when it rolls by (adapted from Brown, 2013).

It's no fun being forced to stay at home when other kids are at school enjoying each other's company. Robot technologies such as the example with Lexie and Princess can make their learning less lonely.

Assistive technologies are important because they reduce the extent to which disabilities become handicaps. As we saw above, technology is an important component of universal design for learning, and as it continues to increase in quality, it will become even more important for learners with exceptionalities.

The IEP

To ensure that inclusion works, UDL principles are applied, and learners with exceptionalities don't become lost in the general education classroom, educators prepare an **individualized education program (IEP)**, a written statement that provides a framework for delivering a FAPE—see Table 5.4—to every eligible student with a disability (Alarcon & Luckasson, 2017). The team responsible for developing the IEP includes (Turnbull et al., 2016):

- the student's parents
- the student's regular education teacher
- a special education teacher, who will likely be the team leader
- a school system representative who is qualified to supervise special education services and who is also knowledgeable about the general education curriculum and available resources
- a person qualified to interpret evaluation results, such as a school psychologist.

Parents may also bring along another family member or friend who is familiar with the special education process, and parental involvement and collaboration is particularly important when students are members of cultural or linguistic minorities (Rossetti, Sauer, Bui, & Ou, 2017). Also, when appropriate, the student may be included on the team.

The purpose of the IEP is to ensure that special education services are provided for the student on a regular basis, and it's also intended to promote effective communication between the school personnel and the child's family. IDEA 2004 requires that each child's IEP must include the following:

- A statement describing the child's achievement and functional performance, including a description of how the disability affects his or her progress in the general education curriculum.
- A statement of annual academic and functional goals designed to meet the child's special needs related to the disability.
- A description of how the child's progress toward meeting the goals will be measured and when reports on the child's progress will be provided.
- A statement of the special education and related services that will be provided for the child.

- An explanation of the extent, if any, to which the child will not participate with other children in the general education classroom.

- A statement of any individual accommodations, such as more time or an interpreter, that are needed to assess the academic achievement and functional performance of the child on state or district-wide assessments.

The IEP goals and descriptions of progress must be written clearly enough to provide observable evidence that goals are being met (Hauser, 2017), and the IEP goals must be aligned with states' content standards (Alarcon & Luckasson, 2017). The U.S. Department of Education issued a *Dear Colleague Letter* in 2015 to "clarify that an individualized education program (IEP) for an eligible child with a disability under the Individuals with Disabilities Education Act (IDEA) must be aligned with the State's academic content standards for the grade in which the child is enrolled" (Yudin & Musgrove, 2015, p. 1). The letter was grounded in the concern that low expectations for learners with exceptionalities can result in less challenging instruction, leading to students not learning what they need to succeed at their grade level (Yudin & Musgrove, 2015).

As we said earlier, you're virtually certain to have learners with exceptionalities in your classes, and IDEA, the concept of inclusion, universal design for learning, and the IEP ensure that you'll be directly involved in the education of these young people. It will be a daunting task, but it can also lead to some of the most rewarding experiences you'll have in your career.

Our responsibilities as regular education teachers go further. We examine them now.

Identifying Students with Exceptionalities

Current approaches to identifying students who may need special help are team based, and you, as a general education teacher, will be a key member of the team. Before referring a student for a special education evaluation, you will be asked to document the problem you believe exists and the strategies you're using in attempting to solve it (Hallahan, Kaufman, & Pullen, 2015). You will be expected to describe the following:

- The nature of the problem and how it affects classroom performance

- Dates, places, and times problems have occurred

- Strategies you've tried

- Assessment of the strategies' effectiveness

Assessment is an essential part of the identification process. In the past, special educators relied heavily on standardized intelligence tests, but as we saw earlier, the protection against discrimination in testing provision of IDEA prevents decisions based on an intelligence test alone. Teachers are now increasingly using **curriculum-based assessments**, which measure learners' performance in specific areas of the curriculum and link assessments directly to learning objectives (Vaughn, Bos, & Schumm, 2018).

Discrepancy Versus Response-to-Intervention Models of Identification

In the past, a **discrepancy model of identification** was used to identify students with learning problems. It looked for differences between (1) intelligence- and achievement-test performance, (2) intelligence-test scores and classroom achievement, or (3) subtests on either intelligence or achievement tests. Inconsistency between any of the two may suggest a learning problem.

Many experts are dissatisfied with the discrepancy model, arguing that it identifies an exceptionality only after—and sometimes long after—a problem surfaces (Brown-Chidsey, 2007). Instead, they argue, educators need early screening measures so that teachers can intervene before a major problem develops. Critics also contend that the

MyLab Education
Video Example 5.4
The discrepancy model and the response to intervention model are two different approaches to identifying students who may need additional help to succeed. Here school leader and author, Paige Pullen, describes the differences between the two models and explains the multi-tiered approach in the response to intervention model.

discrepancy model does not provide specific information about the nature of the learning problem and what should be done to correct it (Balu et al., 2015).

The **response-to-intervention model of identification** attempts to address both of these problems using a three-tiered approach. In the first tier, we use instruction documented as effective for all students. The second begins when a learning problem surfaces, and we provide extra support, such as small-group activities while the rest of the students do seatwork or help outside of school hours, in an attempt to meet the student's needs. The third tier includes intensive one-to-one help and perhaps a special needs assessment (Balu et al., 2015).

The model emphasizes developing skills and study strategies, such as highlighting important vocabulary, reading assignments aloud, or finding a place to study that's free of distractions. If the adaptations don't increase achievement, a learning problem that requires additional help may exist. As we adapt our instruction, we also document what is and is not working, which provides valuable information for later interventions.

Adaptive Behavior

In addition to academic performance, we will also assess students' **adaptive behavior**, their ability to perform the functions of everyday school life. The American Association on Intellectual and Developmental Disabilities (2017b) defines adaptive behavior as consisting of:

- *Conceptual skills:* The concepts of time and number, basic literacy, and self-direction
- *Social skills:* Fundamental interpersonal skills, social awareness and social problem solving, following rules, a sense of self-worth, and avoiding being victimized
- *Practical skills:* Personal and health care, the use of money, schedules and routines, basic safety, travel and transportation, and the use of the telephone

If you observe that students appear to have problems in these areas or are unable to perform routine school tasks, such as initiating and completing assignments, controlling their behavior, and interacting effectively with peers, a problem may exist, and you should report it to your school counselor or school psychologist. A number of validated instruments that formally assess the ability to adapt exist and can be used for a formal assessment (Heward et al., 2017).

Referral for Special Services

If you aren't able solve a student's learning problem by adapting instruction, you can then initiate a referral. When considering a referral, you should first check with an administrator or school psychologist to ensure that you understand your school's policies.

When data suggest that a student needs additional help, a pre-referral team is formed. The team usually consists of a school psychologist, a special educator, and you as the classroom teacher. The team further evaluates the problem, consults with parents, and begins the process of preparing the IEP.

Parents play an integral role in the process. They can provide valuable information about the student's educational and medical history, and notifying parents is simply the act of a professional, even if it wasn't required by law.

Diversity: Cautions in the Identification Process

The identification process designed to help students with exceptionalities can be problematic. Evidence gathered over a number of years reveals that certain subgroups of the school-age population are referred for special education services at higher rates than others. For instance, in the school year 2014–15, 13% of all students received special education services in our nation's schools, but that number was 15% for African American students and 17% for American Indian/Alaska Native students (National Center for Education Statistics, 2017c).

This information is important for us as teachers because we play a central role in identifying students who may need special help, and many of the categories we'll examine in the sections that follow are what experts call "high judgment" categories (Artiles, Kozleski, Trent, Osher, & Ortiz, 2010). For instance, teacher judgment is influential in determining whether a child has a learning, emotional, or behavioral disability. This makes sense, since regular education teachers work with children every day and are in the best position to notice potential problems. But it also places a heavy burden of responsibility on them and creates a bit of a dilemma. From teachers' perspectives, we don't want to refer students for special services if it's unwarranted, but, on the other hand, we don't want to deprive students of access to special education services if the students need them.

This suggests that sensitivity and caution are essential. For example, cultural and linguistic differences in students can influence classroom success, and we know these differences also influence their behavior and test performance. We also need to be cautious about letting our own cultural backgrounds and biases influence our educational decisions. Fortunately, when you begin teaching you'll receive assistance from special educators and other experts in your district when you wrestle with these problems. (We examine collaborative consultation and how it can help us in this process later in the chapter.)

MyLab Education Self-Check 5.2

Exceptionalities and Learning Problems

5.3 Describe the most common learning problems that classroom teachers are likely to encounter.

Ed Psych and You

Do you sometimes have trouble paying attention in class or are disorganized and distracted as you study? Do you feel as if particular areas of the curriculum are extra hard for you? Have you ever joked that you have some sort of learning problem?

We've seen that about 13% of all students enrolled in our nation's schools receive special education services, about two thirds for relatively minor learning problems (National Center for Education Statistics, 2017a).

Federal legislation has created categories to identify learning problems, and educators use the categories in developing special programs to meet the needs of students in each. We examine controversies surrounding this process and the specific categories in the sections that follow. We begin with the labeling controversy.

The Labeling Controversy

A number of categories and labels have been created to identify and accommodate learners with exceptionalities (Hardman, Egan, & Drew, 2017). *Disorders, disabilities,* and *handicaps* are terms commonly used to describe physical or behavioral differences. **Disorders**, the broadest of the three, refer to general malfunctions of mental, physical, or emotional processes. Disabilities are functional limitations, such as low cognitive ability, or being unable to perform certain activities, like walking or listening. **Handicaps** are conditions imposed on people's functioning that restrict their capabilities, such as being unable to enter a building in a wheelchair. Some, but not all, disabilities lead to handicaps. For example, a student with a visual disability may be able to wear glasses or sit in the front of the classroom; if these measures allow the student to function effectively, the disability isn't a handicap.

The use of categories and their labels is controversial (Friend, 2018). Advocates argue that categories provide a common language for professionals and encourage specialized instruction that meets students' needs (Heward et al., 2017). Opponents claim that categories are arbitrary, many differences exist within them, and categorizing encourages educators to treat students as labels instead of people (National Council on Disability, 2011). Despite the controversy, labels are widely used, so you'll need to be familiar with them.

Regardless of their position, special educators agree that labels shouldn't focus attention on students' weaknesses, so they endorse **people-first language**, which first identifies the student and then specifies the disability. For example, they use the description *students with a learning disability* instead of *learning-disabled students*. People-first language reminds us that all students are human beings who need to be treated with care and respect.

Categories of Exceptionalities

A range of categories for learners with exceptionalities exist. They include:

- Learning disabilities
- Communication disorders
- Autism spectrum disorders
- Intellectual disabilities
- Emotional and behavior disorders
- Visual disabilities
- Hearing disabilities

Over 90% of students with disabilities who receive special education services in our country are identified as having *learning disabilities, communication disorders, autism spectrum disorders, intellectual disabilities,* or *behavior disorders*. The vast majority of these students are in inclusive classrooms, so students with these disabilities are the ones we're most likely to encounter in our work (Hardman et al., 2017; National Center for Education Statistics, 2017a).

We turn to them now.

Learning Disabilities

Tammy Fuller, a middle school social studies teacher, is surprised when she scores Adam's first quiz. He seemed to be doing so well. He's rarely absent, pays attention, and participates in class. Why is his score so low? Tammy makes a mental note to watch him more closely.

In her second unit, she prepares study guide questions and has students discuss their answers in groups. As she moves around the room, she notices that Adam's sheet is empty, and when she asks him about it, he mumbles something about not having time the night before. Tammy asks Adam to come in after school to complete his work.

He arrives promptly and opens his book to the chapter. When Tammy checks his progress, his page is blank, and it's still empty 10 minutes later.

As she sits down to talk with him, he appears embarrassed and evasive. When they start to work on the questions together, she discovers that he can't read the text.

Some students, like Adam, are average or above in intelligence but have **learning disabilities** (also called *specific learning disabilities*), defined by the National Center for Learning Disabilities (NCLD) (2017) as "brain-based difficulties in reading, writing, math, organization, focus, listening comprehension, social skills, motor skills or a combination of these" (para. 5). Central nervous system dysfunction—resulting from genetics or adverse environmental conditions, such as malnutrition or alcohol or drug use during pregnancy—are believed to be the cause (Friend, 2018).

The term *learning disability* is broad and encompasses a number of specific problems—the source of the term "specific learning disability" (Gregg, 2009). For instance, the NCLD (2017) cites the following as examples that fit the category:

- *ADHD* (Attention-deficit/hyperactivity disorder), problems with inattention, hyperactivity, and impulsivity

- *Dyscalculia*, a specific disability identified by problems with math, such as number concepts, symbols, and functions

- *Dysgraphia*, a specific problem with writing legibly and putting thoughts down on paper

- *Dyspraxia*, problems with planning and completing tasks involving fine motor skills, such as using scissors, tying shoes, or using buttons and zippers

- *Dyslexia*, a specific disability related to reading, spelling, and other skills involving the use of printed language

- *Executive functioning deficits*, problems with planning, prioritizing, monitoring personal behavior, starting activities, and shifting from one task to another

- *Nonverbal disabilities*, difficulties with reading body language, recognizing sarcasm, and abstract reasoning

Learning disabilities illustrates the labeling controversy we discussed earlier. It is significant that the category was nonexistent in the early 1960s but now more than a third of all students served by special education programs are diagnosed with a learning disability (National Center on Education Statistics, 2017a). A third of classroom teachers and other educators believe that sometimes what people call a learning or attention issue is simply laziness. Stigma is also involved; more than 4 of 10 parents say they wouldn't want others to know that their child had a learning disability. And doctors who recommend having a child evaluated for learning or attention issues say that parents only follow their recommendation slightly more than half the time (NCLD, 2017).

Attention-Deficit/Hyperactivity Disorder (ADHD). As we saw in the previous section, the NCLD (2017) identifies **ADHD** as one specific type of learning disability, characterized by inattention, hyperactivity, and impulsiveness, and it isn't listed as a distinct category in IDEA. However, the American Psychiatric Association (2013), in its *Diagnostic and Statistical Manual of Mental Disorders (DSM 5)*, places it in its own category.

Estimates of the number of children with ADHD vary widely among the states in our country, ranging from a low of less than 6% in Nevada to nearly 20% in Kentucky. The Centers for Disease Control and Prevention (2017a) states that slightly more than 1 child in 10 in our country has been diagnosed with ADHD at some point in their lives, as indicated by parent reports from 2011–12. Research has also identified significant racial differences; for instance, African American and Hispanic students have been much less likely to be identified as having ADHD than their white counterparts (Morgan, Staff, Hillemeier, Farkas, & Maczuga, 2013). Lack of a clear definition of the disorder and the absence of ways to measure it help explain why so much difference exists in the statistics.

ADHD has received a great deal of media attention, and you will encounter many students who seem to fit the description. However, high activity levels and inability to focus attention are also characteristics of developmental lags, especially in young

MyLab Education
Video Example 5.5
Students with learning disabilities make up the largest category of learners with exceptionalities. Here a teacher describes the adaptations a high-school student with a learning disability in reading makes to succeed in school. Notice the teacher's emphasis on the student's motivation and ability to advocate for herself as she thrives in spite of her disability.

boys, so we should be cautious about drawing conclusions on the basis of these characteristics alone.

ADHD typically appears at age 2 or 3 and usually persists into adolescence or beyond (Hirvikoski et al., 2011). Some experts estimate that three to four times as many boys as girls are identified (Hallahan et al., 2015). As we might imagine, teens with ADHD face considerable obstacles when involved in tasks that include distractions and require concentration and quick decision making, such as learning to drive (O'Neil, 2012). ADHD can also be a debilitating adult problem, resulting in relationship and marital problems in adulthood (Parker-Pope, 2010).

Treatments range from medication to programs based on behaviorism. (We examine behaviorism in depth in Chapter 6.) Experts caution against the overuse of drug treatments, instead advocating early identification and structured learning environments that address behavioral problems (Clay, 2013). In addition, simple lifestyle changes, such as exercise and more sleep, sometimes work. Diagnosis and treatment of ADHD are usually conducted in consultation with medical and psychological experts.

Identifying and Working with Students Who Have Learning Disabilities.   As with all exceptionalities, early identification is important to prevent the accumulation of damaging effects. Identifying these students isn't easy, however, because students who may have learning problems but comply with rules and complete assignments on time are often passed over for referral. This is likely the reason Adam got to middle school before his difficulties with reading were discovered.

You are almost certain to have students with learning disabilities in your classes, and they will need extra structure and support to succeed. For example, you might present information both visually and verbally, eliminate distractions during seatwork, and provide additional study aids, such as content outlines and graphic organizers. Systematically teaching study strategies can also be effective (Mastoprieri & Scruggs, 2018).

This discussion addresses the questions we asked in *Ed Psych and You* at the beginning of this section. Most of us periodically display characteristics similar to those in students with learning disabilities; we aren't as efficient as we could be when studying and are often disorganized and distracted. However, unlike students who have a disability, our problems typically aren't chronic, and we make appropriate adaptations in our study.

This has implications for our teaching. If we provide sufficient emotional and instructional support, students with learning disabilities can indeed learn and succeed.

Communication Disorders

Communication disorders are the second most frequently occurring exceptionality in school-age children, making up nearly 20% of the school population served by IDEA (National Center for Education Statistics, 2017a). Two types exist. **Speech disorders** (sometimes called *expressive disorders*), which involve problems in forming and sequencing sounds, is the first. Stuttering and mispronouncing words, such as saying, "I taw it" for "I saw it," are examples. Specialists have identified three kinds of speech disorders (see Table 5.5).

TABLE 5.5 Types of speech disorders

Disorder	Description	Examples
Articulation Disorders	Difficulty in producing certain sounds, including substituting an incorrect pronunciation, and distorting or omitting sounds.	Saying "wabbit" for rabbit; "Thit" for sit; "Only" for lonely
Fluency Disorders	Repetition of the first sound of a word (stuttering) and other problems producing *smooth* speech.	"Y, Y, Y, Yes"
Voice Disorders	Problems with the larynx or air passageways in the nose or throat.	High-pitched, squeaky, or nasal voice

Language disorders, also called *receptive disorders*, is the second type, and they include problems with understanding language or, more commonly, using language to express ideas. Language disorders are often connected to other problems, such as a hearing impairment or learning disability (Turnbull et al., 2016). Because they more strongly detract from learning, language disorders are more serious than speech disorders. Seldom speaking, even during play, using few words or very short sentences, and over-relying on gestures to communicate are symptoms of language disorders.

The American Psychiatric Association (2013), in *DSM5*, has created a new category called *Social Communication Disorder*. This category is characterized by persistent difficulty in using verbal and nonverbal communication socially, such as being able to greet people, exchange information, and follow general rules of communication, like making eye contact and listening until another person has finished speaking. How this category will be applied in schools is uncertain at this point.

Keeping cultural diversity in mind if we suspect a student has a speech or language disorder is important. English is not the primary language for many learners, and the difficulties they encounter in attempting to learn both a second language and school content should not be confused with a communication disorder. Combined with patience and understanding, English learners will respond to an enriched language environment. Students with communication disorders require the help of a speech and language specialist.

Autism Spectrum Disorders

Originally thought of as a single issue, **autism spectrum disorder** describes a cluster of problems characterized by communication deficits and impaired social relationships and skills. Unusual sensitivity to sensory stimuli such as light and sound, perseveration, insistence on sameness, and highly ritualized and unusual behaviors, such as rocking or repeating words and phrases, are also associated with the disorder. It's thought to be caused by neurological abnormalities, and early identification is essential for effective treatment (Heward et al., 2017).

Statistics indicate that slightly less than 10% of youth ages 3–21 served under IDEA are diagnosed as being on the autism spectrum (National Center for Education Statistics, 2017a). The numbers are increasing rapidly, and rates are also higher for lower income and Hispanic and African American children (Baio et al., 2018). The term *autism spectrum disorder* is intended to reflect the wide range of disabilities it encompasses. They all involve problems with social relationships and range from conditions where language is severely impaired and social relations are virtually impossible to *Asperger's syndrome*, in which students have average to above-average intelligence and only moderately impaired language abilities and social relationships (American Psychiatric Association, 2013; Friend, 2018). Figure 5.1 illustrates the concept of the autism spectrum.

Most children with autism spectrum disorders are in general education classes for part or all of the school day, and two approaches for working with these students can be effective. One attempts to make the classroom environment as predictable as possible. Routines are helpful for all students, and they are essential for children on the autism spectrum. Also, clearly outlined rules and expectations that are consistently applied provide additional support.

A second approach focuses on social skills and attempts to help these students learn to interact with their peers and adjust to the social demands of classrooms. Students

MyLab Education
Video Example 5.6

Students with autism spectrum disorders often have underdeveloped social skills and sometimes demonstrate unusual and ritualized behaviors. Here a teacher describes working with a student who displays some of these behaviors. Notice in the teacher's description that the student successfully accommodated his disability, graduated from high school, and went on to college.

Figure 5.1 The autism spectrum

with autism spectrum disorders are often unaware of the effects of their behaviors on others, and behavioral approaches—using appropriate reinforcers and sanctions—that target specific behaviors can help improve both social and communication skills (Fein et al., 2013).

Because students on the autism spectrum have behavioral patterns that differ from their peers they are often bullied, and the problems are sometimes exacerbated in regular classrooms where their unusual behaviors set them apart (Sterzing, Shattuck, Narendorf, Wagner, & Cooper, 2012). As regular education teachers, we play an important role in both protecting these children and teaching their peers understanding and acceptance.

Intellectual Disabilities

To begin this section, let's return to Celina's work with her students.

She watches her children as they work on a reading assignment, and most of the class works quietly. Amelia, in contrast, is out of her seat for the third time, supposedly sharpening her pencil. Celina has reminded her once to get back to work and this time goes over to see what the problem is.

"I can't do this! I don't get it!" Amelia responds in frustration when Celina asks her why she hasn't started her work.

After helping her calm down, Celina works with her for a few moments, but she can tell by Amelia's responses and her facial expressions that she truly doesn't "get" the assignment.

Some students, like Amelia, struggle with learning and become frustrated when they can't keep up with their peers. Unfortunately, this problem often isn't identified until students are several years into school. Many have mild intellectual disabilities. (You may also encounter the terms *cognitive impairment*, *educationally* or *intellectually handicapped*, and *intellectual and developmental disabilities*, which some educators prefer.) *Mental retardation*, an antiquated term, has been rejected because it's considered offensive and stigmatizing. An intellectual disability is caused by genetic factors, such as Down syndrome, or brain damage to the fetus during pregnancy (Heward et al., 2017). Slightly more than 5% of students ages 3–21 served by IDEA are identified as having intellectual disabilities (National Center for Education Statistics, 2017a).

The American Association on Intellectual and Developmental Disabilities (AAIDD) defines **intellectual disability** as "[D]isability characterized by significant limitations in both **intellectual functioning** and in adaptive behavior, which covers many everyday social and practical skills" (AAIDD, 2017a, para. 1). *Intellectual functioning*, also simply called intelligence, refers to general mental capacity, such as learning, reasoning, and problem solving.

Earlier in the chapter we saw that adaptive behavior consists of (AAIDD, 2017b):

- *Conceptual skills:* The concepts of time and number, basic literacy, and self-direction
- *Social skills:* Fundamental interpersonal skills, social awareness and social problem solving, following rules, a sense of self-worth, and avoiding being victimized
- *Practical skills:* Personal and health care, the use of money, schedules and routines, basic safety, travel and transportation, and the use of the telephone

Students with intellectual disabilities lack general knowledge about the world, struggle with abstract ideas, and have underdeveloped motor and social skills. Some of these characteristics, such as struggles with abstract ideas, affect learning directly; others, like underdeveloped interpersonal skills, are less direct but still important, because they affect a student's ability to make friends and develop socially.

Before the 1960s, definitions of intellectual disability were based primarily on below-average scores on intelligence tests, but this approach had three problems. First, tests are imprecise, so misdiagnoses sometimes occurred. Second, disproportionate numbers of minorities and non-English-speaking students were identified as intellectually handicapped (Hallahan et al., 2015). Third, educators found that individuals with the same intelligence-test scores varied widely in their ability to cope with the real world. This is the reason *adaptive behavior* has become more important (American Psychiatric Association, 2013).

Emotional and Behavior Disorders

Kyle comes in from recess sweaty and disheveled, crosses his arms, and looks at his teacher defiantly. The playground monitor has reported another scuffle, and Kyle has a history of these disturbances. He struggles with his studies but can handle them if provided with enough structure. When he becomes frustrated, he sometimes acts out, often ignoring the rights and feelings of others.

Ben, who sits next to Kyle, is so quiet that his teacher almost forgets he is there. He never causes problems; in fact, he seldom participates in class. He has few friends and walks around at recess by himself, appearing to consciously avoid other children.

Although very different, Kyle and Ben both display symptoms of **emotional and behavior disorders**, serious and persistent age-inappropriate behaviors that result in social conflict and personal unhappiness. School failure is often an outcome. The terms *serious* and *persistent* are important. Many children occasionally fight with their peers, and we all want to be alone at times. However, if a pattern of these behaviors exists, and if the behaviors interfere with development and school success, the child may have an emotional or behavior disorder.

The term *emotional and behavior disorder* is often used interchangeably with *emotional disturbance, emotional disability,* or *emotional handicap,* and you may encounter any of these in your work. Researchers prefer the term emotional and behavior disorder because it focuses on overt behaviors that can be targeted and changed (Turnbull et al., 2016).

Students with this disorder often exhibit the following characteristics:

- Behaving impulsively and struggling to interact with others in socially acceptable ways
- Acting out and failing to follow school or classroom rules
- Displaying poor self-concepts
- Lacking awareness about the impact of their actions on others
- Frequently missing school (Turnbull et al., 2016)

Students with emotional and behavior disorders often have academic problems. "Their performance relative to other categories of students with disabilities consistently is the second lowest, with only the group of students with significant intellectual disorders achieving lower scores" (Ysseldyke et al., 2017, p. 792).

Approximately 5% of children ages 3–21 served under IDEA are diagnosed with this disorder (National Center for Education Statistics, 2017a), but it's difficult to identify, and identification is compounded by ethnic and cultural factors. For instance, American Indian/Alaska Native and African American students are more likely than their counterparts in the general population to be classified as having the disorder (Heward et al., 2017).

Emotional and behavior disorders are classified as either *externalizing* or *internalizing* (Hallahan et al., 2015). Students like Kyle fall into the first category, displaying characteristics such as hyperactivity, defiance, hostility, and even cruelty. *DSM5* from the American Psychiatric Association (2013) uses frequency of behaviors to differentiate this disorder from normal developmental issues in young children. For instance, many children will have a temper tantrum, but frequent tantrums may suggest a disorder. Boys are three times more likely to be labeled as having an externalizing emotional and behavior disorder than girls, and low SES children and members of cultural minorities are given this label more often than their mainstream peers (Turnbull et al., 2016).

Internalizing emotional and behavior disorders can be more destructive because they don't have the high profile of students who act out, and as a result, they may go unnoticed. They're characterized by social withdrawal, lack of friends, depression, and anxiety, problems more directed at the self than others. Like Ben, these children lack self-confidence and are often shy, timid, and depressed, sometimes even suicidal.

Suicide.   For young people ages 15–24, suicide is the second leading cause of death, exceeded only by accidents—with auto crashes making up more than half of all accidents. For those ages 10–14, it's the third leading cause, behind accidents and cancer (Centers for Disease Control and Prevention, 2017c). Not every student with a behavior disorder is at risk for suicide, of course, but a combination of factors often connected to behavior disorders, such as depression and substance abuse, stress, and family conflict and rejection, are directly linked to the problem. And, some experts believe that some of the negative effects of social media may also be contributing to the problem (Plemmons et al., 2018). Depression increases the risk of suicide because adolescents who experience this problem tend to be quiet and withdrawn and often go unnoticed by teachers. About a half million young people attempt suicide each year, and between 2,000 and 5,000 succeed, although accurate figures are hard to obtain because of the social stigma attached to suicide. The suicide rate among adolescents tripled in the time span from the mid-1960s to the mid-1990s, due perhaps to greater stressors and less family and social support. Girls are twice as likely as boys to attempt suicide, but boys are four times more likely to succeed. Boys tend to employ more lethal means, such as shooting themselves, whereas girls choose more survivable methods, such as overdosing on drugs (Berk, 2019a).

Potential suicide indicators include (American Psychological Association, 2014):

- An abrupt decline in the quality of schoolwork
- Withdrawal from friends or classroom and school activities
- Neglect of personal appearance or radical changes in personality
- Changes in eating or sleeping habits
- Lack of interest in school activities
- Comments about suicide as a solution to problems

If you observe any of these indicators in a student, contact a school counselor or psychologist immediately, because early intervention is essential.

Bipolar Disorder.   **Bipolar disorder** is a condition characterized by alternative episodes of depressive and manic states (Heward et al., 2017). Slightly fewer than 2% of children in our country have been diagnosed with the disorder, and its prevalence has been reported in about 3% of the adolescent population (Walker, Del Bellow, Landry, D'Souza, & Detke, 2017). The number diagnosed has dramatically increased, but experts believe the increase reflects a greater tendency to apply the diagnosis to children. The increase is also controversial, with critics claiming the label has become a catchall term applied to any child who is either depressed, the most common symptom, or explosively aggressive (Nierengarten, 2015). The American Psychiatric Association (2013) has created a category in *DSM5* called *Disruptive Mood Dysregulation Disorder* that attempts to identify children up to age 18 who exhibit persistent irritability and frequent, extreme temper tantrums. The category is intended to address concerns about the over-diagnosis of bipolar disorder in children. Since schools are primarily guided by IDEA, it's unclear how this new category will influence school practice (Heward et al., 2017).

The symptoms of bipolar disorder are similar to depression or anxiety and are often linked to other issues, particularly ADHD. Treatment typically includes powerful psychiatric drugs, which generally succeed in reducing or eliminating symptoms but may have negative side effects, such as weight gain. If you encounter students with this disorder, you can expect advice and assistance from special educators and school psychologists.

Teaching Students with Emotional and Behavior Disorders.   Students with emotional and behavior disorders require a classroom environment that invites participation and success while providing structure through clearly described and consistently enforced rules.

Behavior management strategies are often used with these students (Alberto & Troutman, 2017). They include rewarding desired behaviors, such as praising a student for behaving courteously; teaching replacement behaviors, like helping students learn to verbally express feelings instead of fighting; and time-out, isolating a child for brief periods of time.

Teaching self-management skills can also be effective (Heward et al., 2017). You will see an example when you analyze the case study at the end of the chapter.

Students with emotional and behavior disorders can be frustrating, and it's easy to forget that they have unique needs. This is where our sensitivity and acceptance are essential. Communicating to these students that their behaviors are unacceptable but that they are innately worthy as human beings, and we care about them and their learning, is essential. This acceptance and caring can do more for them than any other form of intervention.

Physical and Sensory Challenges

Students with physical and sensory challenges also attend our schools. IDEA uses the term *orthopedic impairments*, while educators prefer the term *physical disabilities* to refer to a large, diverse category of students who experience health or mobility problems that affect classroom performance (Turnbull et al., 2016). The National Center for Education Statistics (2017a) has a category described as "Other health impairments" and notes that slightly fewer than 15% of children ages 3–21 served by IDEA are diagnosed with these disorders. They range from mild to severe and vary greatly. Some examples include:

- Acquired immune deficiency syndrome (AIDS)
- Asthma
- Cancer
- Cerebral palsy
- Diabetes
- Epilepsy
- Seizure disorder
- Spina bifida
- Spinal cord or traumatic brain injury

You will have support from special education specialists and other health care professionals when working with any children who might have one or more of these challenges. Your caring and sensitivity will be paramount in helping these children.

Visual Disabilities.   About 1 in 5 of us has some type of vision loss. Fortunately, most problems can be corrected with glasses, surgery, or therapy. In some situations— approximately 1 child in 3,000—the impairment cannot be corrected (Hardman et al., 2017).

People with this condition have a **visual handicap**, an uncorrectable impairment that interferes with learning. Many of these students can read with the aid of a magnifying glass or large-print books, but others are entirely dependent on the spoken word or Braille.

Nearly two thirds of serious visual disabilities exist at birth, and most children are given visual screenings when they enter elementary school. Some vision problems appear during the school years as a result of growth spurts, however, so you should remain alert to the possibility of an undetected impairment in your students. Symptoms include:

- Holding the head in an awkward position or holding a book too close or too far away
- Squinting and frequently rubbing the eyes
- Tuning out or constantly asking about procedures, particularly when information is written on the board
- Using poor spacing in writing and having difficulty staying on the line

Students with visual disabilities differ from their peers with normal vision in areas ranging from understanding spatial concepts to general knowledge. Word meanings may not be as rich or elaborate because of students having fewer visual experiences. As a result, hands-on experiences are even more important for these students than they are for other learners.

If we have students with visual disabilities in our classes, we can make simple adaptations, such as seating them near writing boards and displays on screens, verbalizing while writing on the board, and ensuring that handouts are high contrast and clear (Heward et al., 2017). We can also supply large-print books and magnifying aids to adapt materials. Peer tutors can provide assistance in explaining and clarifying assignments and procedures.

Hearing Disabilities.   Students with a hearing loss have problems perceiving sounds within the normal frequency range of human speech. Two kinds of hearing disabilities exist. A **partial hearing impairment** allows students using hearing aids to hear well enough to be taught in typical school settings. For students who are **deaf**, hearing is impaired enough so they use other senses, usually sight, to communicate. Statistics indicate that nearly 15% of children ages 6–19 in our country have some degree of hearing loss (Centers for Disease Control and Prevention, 2017b), and about 1% of children ages 3–21 served under IDEA have this disability (National Center for Education Statistics, 2017a).

Hearing impairments are linked to genetics, infections—such as rubella—during pregnancy, low birth weight, visual impairments, intellectual disabilities, and autism spectrum disorders (Centers for Disease Control and Prevention, 2017b). However, in almost 40% of cases involving hearing loss, the cause is unknown, which makes prevention and remediation more difficult.

Testing by a trained audiologist is the best method of identifying students with hearing problems, but not all schools have these programs, and problems can be overlooked if students miss the screening. When such an omission occurs, teachers' sensitivity to possible hearing difficulties is essential. Some indicators of hearing impairment include (Hardman et al., 2017):

- Misunderstanding or not following directions and displaying nonverbal behaviors, such as frowns or puzzled looks, when directions are given
- Asking people to repeat what they've just said
- Articulating words, and especially consonants, poorly
- Turning up the volume when listening to audio recordings, radio, or TV
- Showing reluctance to participate in oral activities

Lack of proficiency in speech and language are learning problems that can result from hearing disabilities. These problems affect learning that relies on reading, writing, and listening. We should remember that these language deficits have little bearing on intelligence; these students can succeed if given appropriate help.

Effective programs for students with hearing disabilities combine general education classroom instruction with additional support. Programs for students who are deaf include lipreading, sign language, and finger spelling. Total communication is the simultaneous presentation of manual approaches, such as signing, and speech (through lipreading and residual hearing), and is increasing in popularity (Hardman et al., 2017).

We can also adapt our instruction by supplementing auditory presentations with visual information, speaking clearly and orienting ourselves so students can see our faces, eliminating distracting noise, and frequently checking for understanding.

Having peers without disabilities serve as tutors and work in cooperative groups with students who have hearing disabilities can also be helpful. Teaching students without disabilities the elements of American Sign Language and fingerspelling provides an added dimension to their education.

MyLab Education Application Exercise 5.2: Identifying Students with Exceptionalities

In this exercise you will be asked to analyze characteristics of students who may have exceptionalities and could benefit from special education services.

Diversity: Are Minorities Over- or Underrepresented in Special Education?

A major controversy has emerged with respect to members of cultural minorities and placement in special education programs. The controversy centers on whether members of cultural minorities are over- or underrepresented in these programs. Overrepresentation would mean that more of these students are placed in curricula for students with exceptionalities than would be expected by their numbers in the general population; underrepresentation would mean the opposite. For instance, data from the National Center for Education Statistics (2017b) indicate that in 2014, 16% of students enrolled in schools in our country were African American and 25% were Hispanic. So, if more than 16% of African American students or 25% of Hispanic students are enrolled in special education programs, they are over-represented, whereas if fewer than 16% or 25%, respectively, are enrolled, they're underrepresented.

Historically, the assumption has been that members of cultural minorities are overrepresented (Morgan, Farkas, Hillemeier, & Maczuga, 2017; Samuels, 2017). Further, it's been suggested that they are over-identified for specific learning problems, such as intellectual disabilities and emotional and behavior disorders, which can lead to stereotyping and stigmatizing these students (Office of Special Education and Rehabilitative Services, 2016). As a result, federal legislation, regulations, and policies increasingly seek to address concerns that members of cultural minorities are over-represented because of their race and ethnicity (U.S. Department of Education, 2016). This has led to some educational leaders and politicians believing that special education is a form of institutionalized racism that has legalized the segregation of minority students (Zhang, Katsiyannis, Ju, & Roberts, 2014).

But other researchers suggest that precisely the opposite is occurring. They argue that members of cultural minorities are underrepresented in special education programs, and, as a result, don't benefit from the services these programs can provide. "Recent work now reports that race and ethnic minority children may instead be under-identified as having disabilities and so be less likely to receive special education services as they attend U.S. schools" (Morgan et al., 2017, p. 306). This problem is particularly pronounced, the researchers contend, when these students are compared to white students displaying similar characteristics (Morgan et al., 2017).

The issue is complicated by the fact that members of cultural minorities typically struggle academically to a greater extent than white students. These struggles can be linked to prenatal issues leading to lower birth weights, greater exposure to toxic environmental conditions, such as lead exposure, and the devastating effects of poverty (García, 2015; Morsy & Rothstein, 2015). Children growing up in poverty face high levels of the stress hormone cortisol, which literally changes the architecture of the brain, impairing circuits responsible for impulse control, emotional regulation, and the ability to process and learn from errors (Lesaux & Jones, 2016; McCoy, 2016). Access to high-quality special education programs can help accommodate these disadvantages, making appropriate placement in them essential (Phillips, 2016).

Additional research indicates that schools are more likely to medicalize the struggles of white children while criminalizing those of minorities (Ramey, 2015). For instance, misbehaving white children are more likely to be diagnosed as having behavior disorders, with efforts then made to provide services designed to help them learn to cope with their disability. Minority children, in contrast, are more likely to be viewed as irresponsible or incorrigible, with some form of punishment, and even suspension or incarceration, the more likely response. Further, white children are more likely than similarly high achieving members of cultural minorities to be identified as gifted (Grissom & Redding, 2016).

This controversy has not been resolved. For instance, some researchers continue to contend that members of cultural minorities are over-represented in programs for learners with exceptionalities (Skiba, Aritles, Kozleski, Losen, & Harry, 2016), whereas others continue to assert precisely the opposite (Morgan et al., 2013; Morgan et al., 2017). The issue involves differences in the way different researchers interpret the existing data.

This controversy is a highly sensitive topic, and you may be understandably uncomfortable with it. It's impossible to view our students through a colorblind lens, and we want to be fair in our decisions about which students need additional help through special education services. Our goal should be to help ensure that all students get extra help if they need it. Our goal in providing this information is to increase your professional knowledge, so you will be in a better position to make reasoned judgments about your students. Also, close communication with your school's special education experts can help you in dealing with these highly sensitive issues.

MyLab Education Self-Check 5.3

Students Who Are Gifted and Talented

5.4 Identify characteristics of students who are gifted and talented, and explain how teachers identify and teach these students.

Although we don't typically think of students who are gifted and talented as having exceptionalities, they often don't reach their full potential in general education classrooms. At one time, *gifted* was the only term educators used, but now the enlarged category includes students who do well on IQ tests (typically 130 and above) as well as those who demonstrate talents in a range of areas, such as math, creative writing, or music (Rimm, Siegle, & Davis, 2018).

Characteristics of Students Who Are Gifted and Talented

Descriptions of gifted and talented students' characteristics vary, but they typically include the following (Colangelo & Wood, 2015; Rimm et al., 2018):

- Advanced language skills and the ability to learn abstract and difficult ideas quickly
- Divergent thinking, including original, innovative, and novel ideas
- Intense motivation, focus, and concentration, and high levels of energy on tasks to which they're committed
- Acute perception, being able to simultaneously consider multiple facets of a situation
- Superior memory and ability to retrieve information
- Abstract and flexible thinking
- Sensitivity, identification with others, and empathy

This last characteristic is receiving increased attention. For instance, we saw in our discussion of Sternberg's theory of intelligence that he views concerned citizenship and ethical leadership as indicators of high ability (Sternberg, 2017a). Other authors have endorsed this view and suggest that this factor should be considered in criteria for giftedness (Ambrose, 2017).

History of Gifted and Talented Education

The history of gifted and talented education in our country began with a longitudinal study conducted by Louis Terman and his colleagues (Terman, Baldwin, & Bronson, 1925; Terman & Oden, 1947, 1959). Using teacher recommendations and IQ scores (above 140 on the Stanford-Binet intelligence test), they identified 1,500 gifted individuals to be tracked over a lifetime (the study was projected to run until 2010). The researchers found that, in addition to being high academic achievers, these students were better adjusted as children and adults, had more hobbies, read more books, and were healthier than their peers. This study, combined with more current research, has done much to dispel the stereotype of gifted students as maladjusted and narrow "brains."

The definition used by the federal government describes gifted and talented students as "Children and youth with outstanding talent who perform or show the potential for performing at remarkably high levels of accomplishment when compared with others of their age, experience, or environment" (National Society for the Gifted and Talented, 2014, para. 1). Another historically popular definition of giftedness uses three criteria: (1) above-average ability; (2) high levels of motivation and task commitment; and (3) creativity (Renzulli & Reis, 2003). As we saw at the beginning of the chapter, estimates indicate that slightly more than 6% of public school students in our country are enrolled in programs for the gifted and talented (National Center for Education Statistics, 2015).

Social and Emotional Needs in the Gifted and Talented

Historically, the study of students with gifts and talents has focused on the cognitive domain, but more recent research is examining social and emotional factors in these students, arguing that emotional intelligence is important if they are to reach their full potential (Parker, Saklofske, & Keefer, 2017). And, as is the case with a great deal of research, results are mixed. For instance, some studies have found gifted and talented students more vulnerable to social and emotional problems like depression, shyness, and poor peer relationships than other groups (Wellisch & Brown, 2012). On the other hand, research indicating that gifted and talented students might indeed be better prepared to cope with emotional and social problems than their typically developed peers also exists (Eklund, Tanner, Stoll, & Anway, 2015).

Researchers have also identified myths surrounding gifted and talented students, one of which is high-ability students don't face problems and challenges. "There is a belief that the gifted individual's gift or talent (typically linked to high IQ) somehow inoculates the individual, making him or her immune to boredom, stress, depression, or confusion" (Colangelo & Wood, 2015, p. 135). Researchers note that gifted individuals are just as likely as others to have encountered anxiety, illness, separation, the impact of divorce, death or loss, peer conflicts, abuse and neglect, and substance abuse (Colangelo & Wood, 2015). According to these researchers, a second myth is that gifted and talented individuals don't have unique social and emotional needs, just as all people have issues with which they must cope (Peterson, 2009).

Most significant for us as teachers is to keep in mind that we're all fundamentally social and emotional beings, needs in these areas are more fundamental than cognitive and academic needs, and this applies as much to gifted and talented students as it does to any others. Just as all students need caring and committed teachers who invest in the well-being of their students, so do students with gifts and talents.

Identifying Students Who Are Gifted and Talented

Meeting the needs of students who are gifted and talented requires early identification and instructional modifications. Failure to do so can result in gifted underachievers with social and emotional problems linked to boredom and lack of motivation (Rimm et al., 2018). This is particularly true for students who come from disadvantaged backgrounds (Merrotsy, 2013). Conventional procedures often miss students who are gifted and talented because they rely heavily on standardized test scores and teacher nominations, and females and students from cultural minorities are typically underrepresented in these programs (Gootman & Gebelhof, 2008). When New York City, for instance, moved from a comprehensive approach to identifying kindergarten students who are gifted and talented to one based solely on tests, the number of Black and Hispanic students decreased from 46% to 27% (Winerip, 2010). To address this problem, experts recommend more flexible and less culturally dependent methods, such as creativity measures, tests of spatial ability, and peer and parent nominations in addition to teacher recommendations (Rimm et al., 2018).

As with all exceptionalities, we play an essential role in identifying learners who are gifted and talented because we work with these students every day and can identify strengths that tests may miss. However, research indicates that teachers often confuse conformity, neatness, and good behavior with being gifted or talented (Colangelo & Davis, 2003). As we work with our students we might think about the extent to which students demonstrate the characteristics of the gifted and talented that we outlined earlier.

Programs for Students Who Are Gifted and Talented

Programs for students who are gifted and talented are usually based on two processes: acceleration and ability grouping.

Acceleration

Acceleration keeps the curriculum the same but allows students to move through it more quickly, or at ages younger than conventional. Many different types of acceleration exist, including (Mandelman & Grigorenko, 2013):

- Early admission to kindergarten or first grade
- Skipping grades
- Continuous progress
- Self-paced instruction
- Correspondence courses and extracurricular programs

- Early graduation
- Dual enrollment in colleges and advanced placement
- Credit by examination
- Early entrance into middle school, high school, or college

As we see from these examples, some of what is described as acceleration, such as correspondence courses and extracurricular activities, might also be called forms of enrichment, described by some authors as programs for the gifted and talented (Rimm et al., 2018).

Ability Grouping

"The other most widely used educational accommodation is that of ability grouping, where students are grouped in various configurations by ability" (Mandelman & Grigorenko, 2013, p. 128). This practice places students in classes for advanced students, such as "gifted English" or "gifted math." Ability grouping, in general, is controversial, as we saw earlier in the chapter. Moreover, this instruction is essentially the same as instruction would be for any students, but because students are high ability, they move through the curriculum more rapidly, making it, in essence, a form of acceleration. And, because this is a class for the gifted, teachers feel they should be doing something different than they would with other students, but they're not sure what to do, so they simply pile on more work.

Research Examining Programs for the Gifted and Talented

Research examining the efficacy of programs for the gifted is limited (Mandelman & Grigorenko, 2013). However, some research has examined the impact of acceleration on achievement, and the results indicate that students in accelerated programs made significant gains compared to their peers not enrolled in these programs. Further, accelerated students were able to perform as well as their older peers in the accelerated subjects (Kulik & Kulik, 1984; Rogers, 1991; Steenbergen-Hu & Moon, 2011).

The same isn't true for research examining ability grouping as an accommodation for the gifted; it finds minimal support for the practice (Kulik & Kulik, 1992; Slavin, 1987, 1990).

The field of economics has also done research on programs for the gifted. For example, in one study researchers compared groups of students whose scores were right above the cut-off score for admission to gifted programming to those who were right below the cut-off score. They found no significant difference in achievement between the groups, despite the fact that one of the groups was enrolled in a gifted program for a year and a half. In a second study, students randomly assigned to attend a magnet school were compared to their equally able peers from the same lottery pool who were not selected, and again, researchers found no significant differences in achievement (Bui, Craig, & Imberman, 2011). Additional research examining programs for the gifted found similar results; students' achievement in these programs was minimally higher than students of similar ability not enrolled in the programs (Abdulkadiroglu, Angrist, & Pathak, 2011; Dobbie & Fryer 2011). "There was no evidence that these gifted programs had an impact on the students who attended them" (Mandelman & Grigorenko, 2013, p. 130).

We don't want to paint an inappropriately bleak picture of programs for students who are gifted and talented. However, the research reinforces two important factors. First, as we said earlier, students who are gifted and talented need the support of caring teachers, just as all students do. Second, no institution, school, or program is any better than the people in it. A program for the gifted that has the benefits of expert teachers will produce positive results. This is true for teaching in general. The quality of any students' education depends on the expertise of the teacher delivering it.

MyLab Education Self-Check 5.4

Teachers' Responsibilities in Inclusive Classrooms

5.5 Describe regular education teachers' responsibilities in inclusive classrooms and explain how they relate to universal design for learning.

Ed Psych and You

You're a regular education teacher. You were involved in helping identify students who may have exceptionalities, these students have now been identified, the nature of their exceptionalities has been described, and they've been placed in your regular education classes. What are your responsibilities now?

It's virtually certain that you'll have learners with exceptionalities in your classes, and earlier in the chapter we discussed the role of regular education teachers in identifying students who may have exceptionalities.

Now, we try to answer the question we asked in *Ed Psych and You* by examining our responsibilities as regular education teachers when working with these students in our classes. These responsibilities are outlined in Figure 5.2, and we discuss them in the sections that follow. In each area, we'll have assistance from special educators who have the expertise to help us.

MyLab Education

Video Example 5.7

Working with students having exceptionalities in their classrooms is one of teachers' most important roles. Here we see a regular education teacher modifying her instruction to ensure that her students with exceptionalities can be successful.

Modifying Instruction to Meet Students' Needs

Universal Design for Learning (UDL) provides the framework for modifying our instruction to help us best meet the needs of our students with exceptionalities. We want to emphasize an important point when using UDL as a guide: *The principles of UDL are valuable for not only students with exceptionalities, but for learners in general.* (You may want to review the principles before you continue your study here.) For instance, videos, graphics, manipulatives, and other concrete examples are essential for students with exceptionalities, but they're valuable for all other students as well. And fostering autonomy, promoting self-regulation, and creating a safe and supportive learning environment are also important for all students. The focus in UDL is on learners with exceptionalities, but its principles apply to every learner in our classrooms.

These assertions are supported by research. Instruction that's effective with students in general is also effective with learners having exceptionalities. "In general, the classroom management and instruction approaches that are effective with special education students tend to be the same ones that are effective with other students" (Good & Lavigne, 2018, p. 324). We will need to provide additional support, however, to help students overcome a history of failure and frustration and to convince them that increased effort will lead to success. For instance, while the majority of the class

Figure 5.2 Teachers' responsibilities in inclusive classrooms

is completing a seatwork assignment, we can work with individuals or small groups to provide additional support. Instruction effective for all students, and particularly important for students with exceptionalities, includes:

- Using concrete examples and carefully modeling solutions to problems and other assignments.
- Teaching in small steps, and providing students with detailed feedback about their learning progress.
- Developing lessons with questioning and calling on students with exceptionalities as often as we call on other students.
- Providing outlines, hierarchies, charts, and other forms of organization for the content you're teaching.
- Increasing the amount of time available for tests and quizzes.
- Organizing student groups to include both higher and lower achievers, and students with and without exceptionalities.
- Using available technology.
- Teaching learning and study strategies.

These instructional approaches are consistent with the principles of UDL, and the last item deserves special attention. Let's look at it in more detail.

MyLab Education Application Exercise 5.3: Working with Students Having Exceptionalities in the Regular Classroom

In this exercise you will be asked to analyze a geometry teacher's efforts to modify her instruction to accommodate students who may need extra support to succeed.

Strategy Instruction

Strategies are cognitive operations that exceed the normal activities required to meet a learning goal (Pressley & Harris, 2006). (We examine strategies in detail in Chapter 8.) Summarizing, for instance, is a strategy because it goes beyond the normal process of reading as we attempt to understand a written passage—the goal in using the strategy. Strategy instruction is one of the most promising approaches for helping students with exceptionalities (Hardman et al., 2017; Heward et al., 2017).

In working with Adam (the middle school student with a learning disability in reading that you encountered earlier in the chapter), Tammy Fuller, his teacher, helped him develop a strategy for understanding the content of a chapter in his history book. Tammy first had Adam study the chapter outline so he could see how the chapter was organized, and she had him keep the outline in front of him as he read the chapter. She then modeled reading sections of the chapter aloud, and stopped every 2–3 paragraphs and created a summary of the information she had just read. She then had him practice by doing the same. If he wasn't able to create a clear summary, she had him reread the section and again try to summarize it.

Learners with exceptionalities tend to approach tasks passively or use the same strategy for all types of content, so we must help them learn to use strategies and match the strategies to specific learning tasks (Vaughn et al., 2018). For instance, because Adam was trying to understand the content of the chapter, Tammy taught him a different strategy than he would have used if he was simply learning to spell a list of words. Students with learning problems can use strategies but they need specific instruction—including explanation and modeling—with the strategy, and they must also practice until they're comfortable with it (Coyne, Carnine, & Kame'emui, 2011). This is what Tammy did with Adam. This process is admittedly demanding, but students with exceptionalities require additional efforts to accommodate their learning issues. Our role is to help them learn the strategies needed to ensure their success. (The case study at the end of the chapter, involving Mike Sheppard's work with his students, illustrates another classroom application of these strategies.)

Developing Self-Regulation

Don (one of your authors) regularly tutors in a local elementary school in the city where he lives. The first-, second-, and third-grade students he works with all struggle academically and are behind in reading and math. When he works with these students and talks with their teachers, two patterns consistently emerge. First, the students are intelligent enough to succeed in school. The second is that they lack self-regulation.

Paul had a set of experiences that corroborated Don's observations. As part of a project, he was making a series of observations in first-grade classes, and he was struck by what he observed when the students were doing silent reading. Some of the students read intently for 45 minutes or more, whereas others spent little time reading, instead gazing around the room, or playing with pencils or other objects. In fact, in one observation he watched a boy work for 45 minutes to make his book stand up on the desk; he spent virtually no time actually reading. As students move through the grades, the gap between those who did and did not read conscientiously is likely to become wider and wider.

Many students with exceptionalities receive extra help in the form of tutoring but typically don't receive support that helps them develop **self-regulation**, the ability to direct and control our actions, thoughts, and emotions to reach goals. (We discuss self-regulation in detail in Chapter 6.) Self-regulation plays a powerful role in school success, and students who are self-regulated are happier in school, learn more, and make friends more easily (Berk, 2019a).

APA Top 20 Principles

The discussion in this section illustrates Principle 7: *Students' self-regulation assists learning, and self-regulatory skills can be taught*—from the *Top 20 Principles from Psychology for PreK–12 Teaching and Learning.*

Self-regulation is typically not well developed in students with exceptionalities (Hallahan et al., 2015; Heward et al., 2017). They struggle to stay on task, complete assignments, and use effective learning strategies, as both Paul and Don witnessed directly. They also have problems with controlling their impulses, such as shouting out in the middle of a teacher's explanation.

We can help these students in three ways. First, we can teach them learning strategies, as Tammy did with Adam (Mastropieri & Scruggs, 2018; Vaughn et al., 2018). Second, we can talk to them on-on-one in an effort to make them aware of their actions and how these actions affect learning and their ability to get along with their peers. As their self-awareness increases, they will gradually come to understand that they can control their own learning (Turnbull et al., 2016). And third, patience, support, and encouragement are essential as they gradually develop their self-regulatory abilities.

The Need for Practice

A few years back, a story circulated about a professional basketball superstar who, after returning home late at night from a road trip in which he felt he didn't play up to his usual standard, went to the gym at 2:00 a.m. and practiced for three hours before going home. And this was a person already viewed as one of the best ever to play the game!

APA Top 20 Principles

The discussion in this section illustrates Principle 5: *Acquiring long-term knowledge and skill is largely dependent on practice*—from the *Top 20 Principles from Psychology for PreK–12 Teaching and Learning*.

This brief anecdote helps us understand the importance of practice in learning. We bring it up here because it's particularly significant for learners with exceptionalities. For instance, many regular education students acquire learning strategies during the natural course of their development, and they use the strategies almost without thinking about it. This isn't the case for learners with exceptionalities; as we saw earlier, they can acquire strategies, but the strategies must be taught and practiced to the point that using them is essentially automatic. Without a great deal of practice they aren't likely to capitalize on the strategies.

Similarly, these students will need more practice than their regular education peers on skills ranging from multiplication of two-digit numbers and writing coherent sentences and paragraphs to learning to pay attention, keep track of assignments, and regulate their thoughts, actions, and emotions. These are all abilities that can be developed with practice. It won't happen overnight, but, with effort and perseverance, they can be acquired.

We all must practice to develop abilities to a high level. For learners with exceptionalities, practice is even more important. Overcoming disabilities cannot be achieved without a great deal of effort, but they can be overcome. The fact that it's possible is what's most important. Our job as teachers is to provide the caring, support, and opportunities to practice that will help them reach this goal.

Collaborating with Other Professionals

Collaborating with other professionals is our second responsibility in working with our students having exceptionalities. **Collaboration** is the process of working with other professionals to solve common problems. Initially, educators viewed inclusion as additive; students with exceptionalities received additional services to help them function in general education classrooms (Turnbull et al., 2016). Gradually, the idea of coordination replaced addition. Today, **collaborative consultation** combines general education teachers and special educators on teams to ensure that experiences for students with exceptionalities are integrated. On these teacher assistance teams you'll work with special educators, reading specialists, English language development teachers, school psychologists, and even school administrators to design and implement instructional programs.

Collaboration can take several forms:

- *Curriculum planning.* As we apply the principles of UDL in our work with students, adjusting the curriculum to ensure that it fits the abilities and needs of students with exceptionalities and that modifications meet standards is an essential task.

- *Co-teaching.* Often special educators will work alongside regular education teachers to assist with instruction.

- *Consultant teaching.* Sometimes a special educator will observe, assess, and help plan instruction for students in inclusive classrooms.

- *Coordination of paraprofessionals.* Some students with exceptionalities are assigned paraprofessionals to provide extra support. Their efforts need to be planned and coordinated with ongoing instruction.

- *Working with parents.* Parents are an integral part of every child's education and can provide valuable information and advice about their child's needs and strengths. Consulting with them helps bridge the gap between home and school. (Mastoprieri & Scruggs, 2018; Vaughn et al., 2018).

Collaboration takes time and effort, but it's essential for inclusion and application of the principles of UDL. By working together, professionals create a safety net for students who need extra help to ensure success.

Collaboration typically begins when a learning problem is identified (Mastoprieri & Scruggs, 2018; Vaughn et al., 2018). In the response-to-intervention model described earlier in the chapter, this occurs when the interventions we've tried don't result in success for a student. Once a learning problem that requires extra services is identified, a team of professionals meets to clarify the problem; design, implement, and evaluate more intense interventions; develop IEPs; and work with parents.

Promoting Social Integration and Development

Promoting the social integration and development of students with exceptionalities is our third important responsibility. These students often fall behind in their academic work, sometimes misbehave, and may lack social skills (Hallahan et al., 2015). As a result, other students develop negative attitudes toward them, which adversely affect their confidence and self-esteem. We need to make special efforts to promote the integration of these students into all aspects of our learning and teaching environments. We can do so first by helping classmates understand and accept them, and second by using strategies to promote social interaction among students.

Developing Classmates' Understanding and Acceptance

Students' negative attitudes toward their peers with exceptionalities often result from a lack of understanding, and open discussion and information about disabilities can help change these attitudes (Heward et al., 2017). Emphasizing that people with disabilities want to have friends, be happy, and succeed just as we all do can do much to change attitudes. These discussions can reduce stereotypes about learners with exceptionalities and break down the barriers between them and other students. Literature and videos that explore the struggles and triumphs of people with disabilities are also valuable sources of information.

We can also model patience as they try to express themselves, refrain from correcting their speech—which calls attention to the problem—and forbid any form of demeaning comments from peers. These actions are beneficial for both our learners with exceptionalities and their classmates. Modeling support and sensitivity to others less fortunate and making our regular education students aware of how important it is to treat our fellow human beings with dignity and respect can make a major contribution to their growth as people and citizens. Having learners with exceptionalities as classmates and working closely with them can be some of regular education students' most valuable learning experiences.

Strategies for Promoting Social Integration and Development

Students with disabilities often lack social skills and the ability to make friends, and they may avoid other students or unknowingly alienate them (Turnbull et al., 2016). Modeling, coaching, and involving students in learning activities can help them develop social skills. To teach a student how to initiate play, for example, we might say, "Barnell's over there on the playground. I think I'll say, 'Hi, Barnell! Want to play ball with me?' Now you try it, and I'll watch."

We can also model social problem solving. For instance we might ask, "Mary has a toy that I want to play with. What could I do to make her want to share that toy?" Direct approaches such as these have been successful in teaching social skills such as empathy, perspective taking, negotiation, and assertiveness (Vaughn et al., 2018).

Calling on students with exceptionalities as frequently as possible in learning activities and expecting them to be as involved as their classmates are two of the most effective ways to promote their integration and development. Doing so communicates that all students are valued and are expected to participate and succeed.

Cooperative learning can also help students learn social skills (Mastropieri & Scruggs, 2018). When students work in groups, emotional barriers often break down and students both with and without exceptionalities learn that they are more alike than they are different. In fact, developing this understanding may be one of the most important benefits of cooperative learning.

Most of us probably were aware that we had classmates with exceptionalities, but we didn't really get to know them. This was unfortunate for both them and us, because it didn't give us the chance to learn about—and possibly even become friends with—different kinds of students. As teachers we can do much to ensure that all students feel welcome in our classrooms and have opportunities to learn about and get to know each other.

Classroom Connections

Teaching Students with Exceptionalities in the General Education Classroom

1. Expert teachers adapt instruction to meet the needs and capabilities of students with exceptionalities. Provide additional instructional scaffolding to ensure success on instructional tasks.

   - **Elementary**: A third-grade teacher carefully monitors students during seatwork. She often gathers students with exceptionalities in a small group to provide additional assistance at the beginning of assignments.

   - **Middle School**: A sixth-grade math teacher organizes his students in groups of four for seatwork assignments. Each student completes a problem and confers with a partner. When two students disagree, they confer with the other pair in their group. The teacher carefully monitors the groups to be sure that all four are participating and contributing.

   - **High School**: A science teacher assesses frequently and provides detailed feedback on all assessment items. She spends time in one-on-one conferences with any students having difficulty.

2. Regular education students' lack of understanding is a major obstacle to social integration and growth. Discuss the subject of exceptionalities in an open and positive manner.

   - **Elementary**: A second-grade teacher uses role-playing and modeling to illustrate problems such as teasing and taunting others. She emphasizes treating students who look or act differently with the same respect that other students receive.

   - **Middle School**: An English teacher uses literature, such as *Summer of the Swans*, by Betsy Byars (1970), as a springboard for talking about individual differences. He encourages students to reflect on their own individuality and how important this is to them.

   - **High School**: An English teacher leads a discussion of students' favorite foods, activities, movies, and music, and also discusses topics and issues that concern them. She uses the discussions as a springboard for helping create a sense of community in the classroom.

3. Students with exceptionalities often pursue learning tasks passively. Use modeling and coaching to teach effective learning strategies.

   - **Elementary**: A fourth-grade math teacher emphasizes questions such as the following in checking answers to word problems: Does the solution answer the problem? Does it make sense? Are the units correct? He reinforces this process throughout the school year.

   - **Middle School**: A math teacher teaches problem-solving strategies by thinking aloud at the chalkboard while she's working through a problem. She breaks word problems into the following steps and place these on a poster at the front of the room: (1) *Read*: What is the question asking? (2) *Reread*: What information do I need? (3) *Stop and think*: What do I need to do—add, subtract, multiply, or divide? (4) *Compute*: Put the correct numbers in and solve. (5) *Label and check*: What answer did I get? Does it make sense?

   - **High School**: An English teacher teaches and models step-by-step strategies. A unit on writing one-paragraph

(continued)

essays teaches students to use four steps: (1) Write a topic sentence, (2) write three sentences that support the topic sentence, (3) write a summary sentence, and (4) reread and edit the paragraph. The teacher models the strategy and provides positive and negative examples before asking the students to write their own.

4. Students who are gifted and talented need challenging learning activities to motivate them. Provide supplementary enrichment activities to challenge students who are gifted and talented.

- **Elementary**: A fifth-grade teacher allows students who are gifted and talented to substitute projects of their choice for homework assignments once they have demonstrated that they have mastered the general education curriculum.

- **Middle School**: A pre-algebra teacher pretests students at the beginning of each unit. Whenever a student has mastered the concepts and skills, she receives an honor pass to work on an alternative activity in the school media center. The activities may be extensions or applications of the concepts taught in the unit, or they may involve learning about mathematical principles or math history not usually taught in the general education curriculum.

- **High School**: A social studies teacher caps off every unit with a hypothetical problem, such as "What would the United States be like today if Great Britain had won the Revolutionary War?" Students work in groups to address the question, and the teacher gives extra credit to those who want to pursue the topic further in a paper or project.

MyLab Education Self-Check 5.5

Developmentally Appropriate Practice

Teaching Students with Exceptionalities at Different Ages

Development plays an important role in understanding and dealing with student exceptionalities. Effective practices for students with exceptionalities are influenced by the age and developmental characteristics of students.

Working with Students in Early Childhood Programs and Elementary Schools

Early childhood and lower elementary teachers are in a unique position to help identify learning problems. Pretesting of all students at the beginning of the school year not only provides a baseline for future growth, but can also identify potential learning problems. When pretesting data alert teachers to a potential learning problem, detailed records that identify the nature of the problem and records of intervention attempts can provide special educators with the tools they need to create effective interventions.

Sensitivity to the possibility of developmental lags is particularly important with young children. Research on learner development indicates that considerable variation exists in students' rates of development, and developmental lags are often mistaken for more serious learning problems.

Similarly, being aware of the role of culture and language in early school success is important. Many students grow up in homes where English isn't the first language and where newspapers, magazines, and books are not readily available. Determining that problems cannot be traced to cultural or language differences is important before referring a child for special services.

Working with Students in Middle Schools

The middle school years present challenges to all students, but especially to those with exceptionalities. These challenges take the form of physical and emotional changes, as well as the move from self-contained elementary classrooms to the less personal environments in middle schools.

Adaptive behaviors, such as keeping track of assignments and taking notes, present special challenges for students with exceptionalities. Efforts to help these students acquire learning strategies can be particularly effective.

Peers become increasingly important to middle school students. Helping students with exceptionalities learn acceptable behaviors, together with strategies for promoting interaction and cooperation, are essential. Cooperative learning and peer tutoring can be effective, but students with exceptionalities need extra support to function effectively in these settings.

Working with Students in High Schools

High school—with large schools, less personal attention, and switching classes—can be particularly challenging for students with exceptionalities. Peer acceptance continues to be a priority for all high school students.

Special efforts to help students with exceptionalities—who are sometimes painfully aware of their differences—feel welcome in their classrooms are very important for high school students. Teachers set the tone by modeling courtesy and respect and requiring students to treat each other the same way. Cooperative learning and small-group work provide opportunities for students with exceptionalities to interact socially and learn from their peers.

With respect to acquiring a deep understanding of the topics they're studying, helping learners with exceptionalities acquire effective learning strategies is even more effective with high school students than with younger learners.

Chapter 5 Summary

1. Describe different views of intelligence, and explain how ability grouping influences learning.
   - Intelligence is the ability to profit from past experiences to solve future problems. It is also often defined as the ability to acquire and use knowledge, solve problems and reason in the abstract, and adapt to new situations in the environment.
   - Some theories suggest that intelligence is a single entity; others describe intelligence as existing in several dimensions.
   - Some experts believe that intelligence is largely genetically determined; others believe it is strongly influenced by experiences. Most suggest that it is determined by a combination of the two.
   - Gardner's theory of multiple intelligences describes intelligence as composed of eight relatively independent dimensions.
   - Sternberg describes intelligence as existing in three dimensions: Analytical, creative, and practical. Sternberg's emphasis on creative and practical aspects of intelligence sets his theory apart from other descriptions of intelligence.
   - Ability grouping can influence learning through the quality of instruction that learners are provided and through teachers' expectations for students.
   - Learning styles describe learners' personal approaches to thinking and problem solving. Little valid research supports making classroom adaptations to accommodate learning style differences.

2. Describe the legal basis for working with students having exceptionalities, including the provisions of the Individuals with Disabilities Education Act (IDEA).
   - The major provisions of the IDEA require instruction of students with exceptionalities in the least restrictive environment (LRE), parent involvement, protection of learners against discrimination in testing, and individualized education programs (IEPs) for each student with exceptionalities.
   - Amendments to IDEA made states responsible for locating children who need special services and strengthened requirements for nondiscriminatory assessment, due process, parental involvement in IEPs, and the confidentiality of student records.
   - Inclusion places students with exceptionalities in the school's academic curriculum, extracurricular activities, and other experiences alongside students not having exceptionalities.

   - Universal Design for Learning (UDL) attempts to help learners with exceptionalities succeed in the regular education classroom by modifying curriculum and instruction and utilizing technology. It is the process designed to ensure that inclusion is successful.
   - An individualized education program (IEP) is a written statement that provides a framework for delivering a free and appropriate education to every eligible student with a disability. The IEP is designed to ensure that inclusion works, UDL principles are applied, and learners with exceptionalities don't become lost in the general education classroom.

3. Describe the most common learning problems that classroom teachers are likely to encounter.
   - Categories and labels have been created to identify and accommodate learners with exceptionalities. Disorders refer to general malfunctions of mental, physical, or emotional processes. Disabilities are functional limitations, such as low cognitive ability, or being unable to perform certain activities, like walking or listening. Handicaps are conditions imposed on people's functioning that restrict their capabilities, such as being unable to enter a building in a wheelchair.
   - Labels are controversial but commonly used, so teachers are virtually certain to encounter them in their teaching.
   - Special educators agree that labels shouldn't focus attention on students' weaknesses, so they endorse people-first language, which first identifies the student and then specifies the disability.
   - The most common learning problems that classroom teachers encounter include learning disabilities, difficulties in reading, writing, reasoning, or mathematical abilities; communication disorders, which may include either speech or language disorders; autism spectrum disorders, disabilities that affect communication and social interaction; intellectual disabilities, limitations in both intellectual functioning and adaptive behavior; and behavior disorders, serious and persistent age-inappropriate behaviors.
   - Teachers may also encounter students with visual and hearing disabilities.

4. Identify characteristics of students who are gifted and talented, and explain how teachers identify and teach these students.
   - Students who are gifted and talented learn quickly and independently, possess advanced language and

metacognitive skills, and are often highly motivated and set high personal standards for achievement.

- Methods of identifying students who are gifted and talented include intelligence testing and teacher, parent, and peer reports of unique talents and abilities.
- The two most common methods of teaching students who are gifted and talented include acceleration, which moves students through the general education curriculum at a faster rate, and ability grouping, which groups students by various configurations based on ability.
- Research examining programs for gifted and talented students has produced mixed results; some have been demonstrated as effective, whereas students in others fare no better than students of similar ability not placed in the programs.

5. Describe regular education teachers' responsibilities in inclusive classrooms and explain how they relate to universal design for learning.
   - Teachers' roles in inclusive classrooms include adapting instruction to meet the needs of students with exceptionalities, working with other professionals on collaborative consultation teams, and promoting their social integration and growth.
   - Universal design for learning (UDL) is the framework for modifying instruction to meet the needs of students with exceptionalities.

- The principles of UDL, while focusing on students with exceptionalities, apply to students in general, and effective instruction for students with exceptionalities is similar to effective instruction in general. Providing additional scaffolding and helping students acquire learning strategies are also helpful.
- Strategy instruction and developing self-regulation are two of the most promising approaches for helping learners with exceptionalities succeed in inclusive classrooms.
- Collaboration is the process of working with other professionals to solve common problems, and collaborative consultation combines general education teachers and special educators on teams to ensure that experiences for students with exceptionalities are integrated.
- Developing regular education students' understanding of disabilities and helping them understand that learners with and without exceptionalities are much more alike than they are different can help promote the social integration and development of learners with exceptionalities.
- Helping learners with exceptionalities develop social skills, calling on them as often as regular education students, and cooperative learning can help ensure that they are fully integrated into inclusive classrooms.

Preparing for Your Licensure Exam

Understanding Learners with Exceptionalities

Because it's virtually certain that you will have students with exceptionalities in your classroom, your licensure exam will include items related to best practices for working with these students. We include the following exercises to help you practice for the exam in your state.

Let's look now at a junior high math teacher and his efforts to work with students in his class who have exceptionalities. Read the case study, and answer the questions that follow.

Mike Sheppard teaches sixth-grade math at Kennedy Middle School. He is working with his class on word problems involving rates to meet the following standard:

> CCSS.Math.Content.6.RP.A.3b Solve unit rate problems including those involving unit pricing and constant speed. *For example, if it took 7 hours to mow 4 lawns, then at that rate, how many lawns could be mowed in 35 hours? At what rate were lawns being mowed?* (Common Core State Standards Initiative, 2018f).

He has introduced his class to a procedure for solving word problems and has assigned five problems for homework.

Mike has 28 students in his second-period class, including five with exceptionalities: Ethan, Marcus, and Gwenn, who have learning disabilities, and Todd and Aiden, who have difficulty monitoring their own behavior. Ethan, Marcus, and Gwenn each have problems with decoding words, reading comprehension, and writing. Other teachers describe Todd as verbally abusive, aggressive, and lacking in self-discipline. He is extremely active and has a difficult time sitting through a class period. Aiden is just the opposite: a very shy, withdrawn boy.

At Mike's request, Ethan, Marcus, and Gwenn come to class a few minutes early each day so they have extra time to read the problems he has displayed on the document camera and get additional help. (As part of his daily routine, Mike displays two or three problems for students to complete while he takes roll and finishes other beginning-of-class tasks.)

Mike watches as Ethan, Marcus, and Gwenn take their seats, and then he slowly reads this displayed problem:

> On Saturday the Harris family drove 17 miles from Henderson to Newton, stopped for 10 minutes to get gas, and then drove 23 miles from Newton through Council Rock to Gildford. The trip took 1 hour and 10 minutes, including the stop. On the way back, they took the same route but stopped in Council Rock for lunch. Council Rock is 9.5 miles from Gildford. If they drive at the same rate, how long will it take them to get back to Henderson?

As Mike reads, he points to each displayed word. "Okay," he smiles after he finishes reading. "Do you know what the problem is asking you?"

"Could you read the last part again, Mr. Sheppard?" Gwenn asks.

"Sure, but make sure that you read along with me," Mike replies and repeats the part of the problem that describes the return trip, again pointing to the words as he reads.

"All right, jump on it. Be ready, because I'm calling on one of you first today," he directs with another smile.

The rest of the class comes in the room, and they're studying the screen as the bell rings. Mike quickly takes roll and then walks to Todd's desk.

"Let's take a look at your chart," he says. "You've improved a lot, haven't you?"

"Yeah, look," Todd responds, proudly displaying the following chart.

	2/9–2/13	2/16–2/20	2/23–2/27
Talking out	╫╫ ╫╫ ╫╫ ╫╫	╫╫ IIII ╫╫	╫╫ II
Swearing	╫╫ ╫╫	╫╫ II	IIII
Hitting/ touching	╫╫ III	╫╫ IIII	III
Out of seat	╫╫ ╫╫ ╫╫ III	╫╫ ╫╫ ╫╫ IIII	╫╫ ╫╫ ╫╫ III
Being friendly	II	IIII	╫╫ II

"That's terrific," Mike whispers as he leans over Todd's desk. "You're doing much better. We need some more work on 'out-of-seat,' don't we? I don't like getting after you about it, and I know you don't like it either. . . . Stop by at the end of class. I have an idea that I think will help. Don't forget to stop. . . . Okay. Get to work on the problem." Mike gives Todd a light thump on the back and returns to the front of the room.

"Okay, everyone. How did you do on the problem?"

Amid a mix of "Okay," "Terrible," "Fine," "Too hard," some nods, and a few nonresponses, Mike begins, "Let's review for a minute. . . . What's the first thing we do whenever we have a word problem like this?"

He looks knowingly at Marcus, remembering the pledge to call on one of the five students first today. "Marcus?"

"Read it over at least twice," Marcus replies.

"Good. . . . That's what our problem-solving plan says," Mike continues, pointing to the following chart hanging on the chalkboard:

PLAN FOR SOLVING WORD PROBLEMS
1. Read the problem at least twice.
2. Ask the following questions: What is asked for? What facts are given? What information is needed that we don't have? Are unnecessary facts given? What are they?
3. Make a drawing.
4. Solve the problem.
5. Check to see whether the answer makes sense.

"Then what do we do? . . . Melissa?"

"See what the problem asks for."

"Good. What is the problem asking for? . . . Rachel?"

" . . . How long it will take them to get back to Henderson?"

"Excellent. Now, think about this. Suppose I solved the problem and decided that it would take them an hour. Would that make sense? Why or why not? Everybody think about it for a moment."

"Okay. What do you think? . . . Ethan?" Mike asks after a moment.

" . . . I . . . I . . . don't know."

"Let's look," Mike encourages. "How long did the trip take from Henderson to Gildford altogether?"

" . . . An hour and 10 minutes . . . . Oh, I get it. It took an hour for the whole trip, so if they go at the same rate, it can't take them an hour for only part of the trip.

"Excellent thinking, Ethan. See, you could figure it out."

Mike continues to guide the students through the solution to the problem and then says enthusiastically, "Okay. Not too bad for the first time through . . . . Now, let's take a look at your homework."

Mike reviews each homework problem just as he did the first one, asking students to relate the parts to the steps in the problem-solving plan, drawing a sketch on the chalkboard, and calling on a variety of students to supply specific answers and describe their thinking.

With 20 minutes left in the period, he assigns five more problems for homework, and the students begin working. Once the class is working quietly, Mike gestures to Ethan, Marcus, and Gwenn to join him at a table at the back of the room.

"How'd you do on the homework?" Mike asks. "Do you think you get it?"

"Sort of," Gwenn responds, and the other two nod.

"Good," Mike smiles. "Now, let's see what we've got."

When about 5 minutes are left in the period, Mike tells the three students, "Run back to your desks now, and see whether you can get one or two more problems done before the bell rings."

The bell rings, and the students begin filing out of the room. Mike catches Todd's eye, Todd stops, and Mike leads him to a small area in the back of the room where a partition has been set up. The area is partially enclosed but facing the class.

"Here's what we'll do," Mike directs. "When you have the urge to get out of your seat, quietly get up and move back here for a few minutes. Stay as long as you want, but be sure you pay attention to what we're doing. When you think you're ready to move back to your seat, go ahead. All I'm asking is that you move back and forth quietly and not bother the class. . . . What do you think?"

Todd nods, and Mike puts a hand on his shoulder.

"You're doing so well on everything else; this will help, I think. You're a good student. You hang in there. . . . Now, here's a pass into Mrs. Miller's class."

In answering these questions, use information from the chapter, and link your responses to specific information in the case.

Questions for Case Analysis

Use information from this chapter and the case study to answer the following questions.

Multiple-Choice Questions

1. From the information in the case, it is most likely that Todd has which of the following exceptionalities?

   a. Learning disability

   b. Externalizing behavior disorder

   c. Intellectual disability

   d. Attention-deficit/hyperactivity disorder

2. From the information in the case, it is mostly likely that Aiden has which of the following exceptionalities?

   a. Attention-deficit/hyperactivity disorder

   b. Intellectual disability

   c. Internalizing behavior disorder

   d. Autism spectrum disorder

Constructed-Response Question

1. Success is important for all students, but is especially important for students with exceptionalities. Describe what Mike did to ensure that his students were successful.

MyLab Education Licensure Exam 5.1

Important Concepts

ability grouping
acceleration
adaptive behavior
assistive technology
attention-deficit/
    hyperactivity disorder
    (ADHD)
autism spectrum disorder
between-class grouping

bipolar disorder
collaboration
collaborative consultation
communication disorders
crystallized intelligence
cultural intelligence
curriculum-based
    assessment
deaf

disabilities
discrepancy model of
    identification
disorder
emotional and behavior
    disorder
emotional intelligence
fluid intelligence
gifts and talents

handicap
inclusion
individualized education
    program (IEP)
intellectual disability
intellectual functioning
intelligence
language disorders
    (receptive disorders)

learners with
  exceptionalities
learning disabilities
learning styles
least restrictive environment (LRE)
nature view of
  intelligence

nurture view of
  intelligence
partial hearing
  impairment
people-first
  language
psychometric view of
  intelligence

response-to-intervention
  model of identification
self-regulation
social intelligence
special education
speech disorders
  (expressive disorders)
strategies

tracking
universal design
universal design
  for learning
  (UDL)
visual handicap
within-class
  grouping

Chapter 6
Behaviorism and Social Cognitive Theory

Ariel Skelley/Blend Images/Getty Images

Learning Outcomes

After you have completed your study of this chapter, you should be able to:

6.1 Use classical conditioning to explain events in and outside of classrooms.

6.2 Identify examples of operant conditioning in and outside of classrooms.

6.3 Describe the influence of modeling and the outcomes of modeling on people's behaviors.

6.4 Use the concepts of vicarious learning, nonoccurrence of expected consequences, and self-regulation to explain people's behaviors.

APA Top 20 Principles

Top 20 Principles from Psychology for PreK–12 Teaching and Learning explicitly addressed in this chapter.

> Principle 7: Students' self-regulation assists learning, and self-regulatory skills can be taught.
> Principle 16: Expectations for classroom conduct and social interaction are learned and can be taught using proven principles of behavior and effective classroom instruction.

Have you ever tried harder at something after someone praised your efforts, or attempted some activity, such as a new dance step, after watching others do it? If you answer "yes" to either of these questions, studying this chapter will help you understand why. Our experience with the world and observations of others strongly influence the way we act, think, and feel. In the following case study, you will see their effects on Tim Spencer, a 10th-grader, as he struggles in one of his classes. As you read the case study, think about how an experience on a math quiz influences Tim and how his thinking and behavior change as a result of observing his friend, Susan.

Tim has been doing well in Algebra II—getting mostly B's on the weekly quizzes. On the last one, however, something inexplicably went wrong, and he became confused, panicked, and failed it. He was devastated.

Now, on the next quiz, he's so nervous that when he starts, the first few answers he circles have wiggly lines around them from his shaking hand. "I'm not sure I can do this," he thinks. "Maybe I should drop algebra."

His hand also shakes when he takes chemistry tests, but fortunately, he isn't nervous in world history, where he is doing fine.

Tim mentions his troubles to his friend Susan, who always does well on the quizzes.

"They're tough," she comments, "so I really study for them. . . . Maybe I can help you. Let's get together."

Tim is skeptical but agrees, and the night before the next quiz, he goes to Susan's home to study. He sees how she selects several problems from the book and solves them completely, rather than simply reading over the sample problems and explanations. As she begins working on her third problem, he asks her why she is doing another one.

"I try to do as many different kinds as I can to be sure I don't get fooled," she explains. "So, I'm more confident when I go into the quiz. . . . See, this one is different. . . . I even make a little chart. I do at least three problems of each type and then check them off, so I can see that I'm making progress. If I get them all right, I might treat myself to a dish of ice cream."

"Good idea," Tim nods. "I usually do a couple, and if I get them, I quit."

Tim adopts Susan's study habits and sets his own goal of doing three of each type of problem, selecting those with answers at the back of the book.

He does much better on the next quiz. "What a relief," he says to himself.

He's less anxious for the following week's quiz, and his efforts are paying off; he makes his highest score so far.

"Maybe I can do this after all," he says to himself.

Behaviorism and social cognitive theory can help us explain why Tim was nervous after his bad experience, why his nervousness later decreased, and why he changed his study habits and sustained his efforts. If you've taken a course in general psychology, these topics might already be somewhat familiar to you.

Behaviorist Views of Learning

Behaviorism is a theory that focuses on observable changes in behavior to explain learning. It defines **learning** as an enduring change in behavior that occurs as a result of experience (Schunk, 2016; Skinner, 1953). For example, Tim experienced failure on the quiz, which resulted in his hand shaking the next time he took a quiz; he learned to be nervous when he took quizzes. But additional experiences resulted in his nervousness later disappearing. We'll see how this happened as we move through the chapter.

As the term implies, behaviorism focuses on observable behavior and doesn't include any references to internal mental processes. "In behaviourism, there are no aspects of studying instruction related to internal states of mind like thinking . . . " (Stoilescu, 2016, p. 141). This narrow focus is controversial, but behaviorism continues to be widely applied in schools, especially in the area of classroom management (Jolstead et al., 2017) and in working with learners who have special needs (Perle, 2016). (We examine these controversies later in the chapter).

Behaviorism has two primary components: *classical conditioning*, which focuses on emotional and physiological responses to stimuli in the environment, and *operant conditioning*, which examines changes in behaviors that result from consequences, such as being praised or reprimanded. We begin with classical conditioning.

Classical Conditioning

6.1 Use classical conditioning to explain events in and outside of classrooms.

Ed Psych and You

Do you ever get nervous at the beginning of tests, particularly if you believe they're difficult? Are you fearful of spiders or snakes? On the other hand, have you ever felt romantic after listening to a song or had an emotional reaction to being in a particular location, such as a mountain lake or an ocean beach?

Think about the questions we asked in *Ed Psych and You*. If you answered yes to any of them, we can explain your reactions using classical conditioning, a component of behaviorism that explains how we learn involuntary emotional or physiological responses that are similar to instinctive or reflexive responses.

Your nervousness in tests, and Tim's similar experience on the quiz after his bad experience, illustrates what is commonly called *test anxiety*, and it's a common example of classical conditioning. As a result of his experience—failing the quiz—Tim was devastated. He didn't choose to feel this way; it was *involuntary*, that is, the feeling of devastation was out of his control. Tim *associated* his algebra quiz with his failure, and as a result, he was nervous when he took subsequent quizzes. His nervousness was similar to the devastation he felt in response to his original failure. He *learned* to be nervous when he took algebra quizzes; he learned an emotional response that was similar to his original response—his devastation.

We usually think of learning as acquiring knowledge, such as knowing the causes of the War of 1812, or skill, such as finding 42% of 65, but emotions can also be learned, and Tim's experience is an example.

Stimuli and Responses in Classical Conditioning

Russian scientist Ivan Pavlov originally discovered classical conditioning while investigating the process of salivation. As a part of his research, he had his assistants feed dogs meat powder so their rates of salivation could be measured. As the research progressed, however, the dogs began to salivate at the sight of the assistants, even when they weren't carrying the meat powder. This startling phenomenon caused a turn in Pavlov's work and opened the field of what is now known as classical conditioning.

Let's look at Pavlov's research in more detail and see how it applies to Tim. The meat powder for the dogs and the original failure Tim experienced were unconditioned stimuli (UCS), objects or events that cause unconditioned responses (UCR), instinctive or reflexive (unlearned) physiological or emotional responses caused by unconditioned stimuli. Salivation for Pavlov's dogs and the devastation Tim felt were unconditioned responses.

The dogs associated Pavlov's assistants with the meat powder, and Tim associated his algebra quiz with his failure, so the lab assistants for the dogs and quizzes for Tim became conditioned stimuli (CS), formerly neutral stimuli that become associated with the unconditioned stimulus (the meat powder and Tim's original failure). A neutral stimulus is an object or event that doesn't initially affect behavior one way or the other. The lab assistants originally had no impact on the dogs, nor did algebra quizzes impact Tim until the associations occurred—they were neutral.

As a result of associating lab assistants with meat powder and algebra quizzes with failure, the lab assistants and quizzes produced conditioned responses (CR)—salivation for the dogs and nervousness for Tim—physiological or emotional responses similar to the unconditioned responses.

Association is the key to learning in classical conditioning. To form an association, the unconditioned and conditioned stimuli must be *contiguous*, that is, they must occur together. Without this contiguity, an association can't be formed, and learning through classical conditioning won't take place.

Both real-world and classroom examples of classical conditioning are common (Schunk, Meece, & Pintrich, 2014), and the questions we asked in *Ed Psych and You* are examples. Let's consider the last question. You're on a date that turns out to be special, and you feel the attraction and sense of romance that can instinctively occur between two people. The encounter is an unconditioned stimulus, and the romantic feeling is the unconditioned response. Now, if a particular song is playing while you're on the date, the song can become associated with the encounter. So, because of the association, it becomes a conditioned stimulus that produces a romantic feeling—similar to the

TABLE 6.1 Classical conditioning in our lives

Example	Stimuli	Responses
Tim	US *Failure*	UR *Devastation* (involuntary and unlearned)
	CS *Quizzes* (associated with failure)	CR *Anxiety* (involuntary but learned; similar to the original devastation)
Us	US *Encounter with another person*	UR *Feeling of romance* (involuntary and unlearned)
	CS *Song* (associated with the encounter)	CR *Feeling of romance* (involuntary but learned; similar to the original romantic feeling)

Abbreviations: US, unconditioned stimulus; UR, unconditioned response; CS, conditioned stimulus; CR, conditioned response.

original feeling—as a conditioned response. The mechanisms involved in Tim's case and in the romantic encounter are outlined in Table 6.1.

As other examples, we probably react warmly when we smell Thanksgiving turkey; and we may be uneasy when we enter a dentist's office. And most of us have experienced test anxiety to some degree. In each of these examples we learned an emotional response through classical conditioning.

Even though Pavlov's original work was done at about the turn of the 20th century, the study of classical conditioning is alive and well, and it continues to be the theoretical framework for a great deal of contemporary research in areas ranging as widely as preschoolers' preferences for certain tastes (Lumeng & Cardinal, 2007), acquisition of different forms of fear and anxiety (Fanselow & Sterlace, 2014), reduction in sensitivity to cold (Vaksvik, Ruijs, Røkkum, & Holm, 2016), alcohol dependence (March, Abate, Spear, & Molina, 2013), and even memory (Garren, Sexauer, & Page, 2013).

Generalization and Discrimination

At the beginning of the chapter we saw that Tim was also anxious in chemistry tests. His anxiety had *generalized* to chemistry. **Generalization** occurs when stimuli similar—but not identical—to a conditioned stimulus elicit conditioned responses by themselves (Ahrens et al., 2016). Tim's chemistry tests were similar to his algebra quizzes, and they produced the conditioned response—anxiety—by themselves.

Generalization can also be positive. For example, if students associate their classroom with the warmth and respect of their teacher, their classroom becomes a conditioned stimulus, and they may generalize their responses to other classes and perhaps even the school in general. This is an ideal that schools with positive cultures are able to achieve.

Discrimination, the opposite of generalization, is the process of giving different responses to related but not identical stimuli (Schunk, 2016). For example, Tim wasn't nervous in world history tests. He *discriminated* between world history and algebra.

Extinction

After working with Susan and changing his study habits, Tim's performance began to improve on the quizzes. As a result, he was less nervous on each subsequent quiz. In time, if he continues to succeed, his nervousness will disappear; that is, the conditioned response will become extinct. **Extinction** in classical conditioning is the result of the conditioned stimulus occurring often enough in the absence of the unconditioned stimulus so that it no longer elicits the conditioned response (Harris & Andrew, 2017; Hall & Rodríguez, 2017). As Tim took additional quizzes (conditioned stimuli) without experiencing failure (the unconditioned stimulus), his anxiety (the conditioned response) gradually disappeared.

Using Educational Psychology in Teaching: Suggestions for Applying Classical Conditioning with Your Students

A great deal of research has been conducted on emotions, and their influence on learner motivation and achievement as well as our health and well-being is well established (DeSteno, Gross, & Kubzansky, 2013; Kok et al., 2013). For example, positive emotions, such as feelings of security, enjoyment, and hope, are associated with increased motivation and learning, whereas negative emotions have the opposite effect (Ganotice, Datu, & King, 2016). Classical conditioning provides us with a tool that we can use to promote positive emotions in our students. The following suggestions can help us in our efforts:

1. Consistently treat students with warmth and caring.
2. Personalize our classrooms to create an emotionally secure environment.
3. Require that students treat each other with courtesy and respect.

To see these suggestions in practice, let's look at the work of Sharon Van Horn, a second-grade teacher.

Sharon Van Horn greets each of her students with the same routine each morning: As they come in the classroom, they give her a handshake, hug, or high five. During the school day, Sharon simultaneously treats her students with a warm, caring manner, while requiring that they behave appropriately and work diligently. One of her rules forbids students from making demeaning or hurtful comments to their classmates, and they have a classroom meeting once a week, during which they discuss the importance of treating others as they would like to be treated.

Sharon takes digital pictures of her students and displays them on a large bulletin board. The students write short paragraphs about themselves, and Sharon displays them below the pictures.

Sharon also periodically displays posters and other artifacts from the heritage countries of her students who are not native English speakers. For example, colorful prints from Mexico are displayed on one wall, and vocabulary cards in both Spanish and English are hung around the room.

Alberto, who has emigrated from Mexico, comes in for extra help three mornings a week, and this morning Mariachi music is playing in the background.

"Buenos días, Alberto. How are you today?" Sharon asks before Alberto gives her a hug, which he prefers.

"Buenos días. I'm fine," Alberto responds, as he goes to his desk to take out his homework.

Now, let's look at Sharon's efforts to implement the suggestions with her students.

Treat Students with Warmth and Caring. A nearly 30-year history of research confirms that warm and caring teachers are essential for student motivation and achievement. "Caring is the very bedrock of all successful education" (Noddings, 1992, p. 27), and the importance of Noddings' assertion has been consistently confirmed since then (Broekhuizen, Slot, van Aken, & Dubas, 2017; Zhao, & Li, 2016).

We can use classical conditioning to explain this research and Sharon's work with her students to illustrate it. Here's how. To help her students learn to feel comfortable in her class—as we said earlier, emotions can be learned—Sharon is consistently warm and caring in her interactions with her students. People have instinctive positive responses to displays of warmth, so her manner is an unconditioned stimulus that triggers positive emotions, such as feelings of safety and security, in her students as unconditioned responses. In time, her students associate their classroom with Sharon's warmth and caring, so the classroom becomes a conditioned stimulus that triggers similar feelings of safety and security as conditioned responses. Over time the classroom can generalize to their school work, and perhaps even the rest of the school, producing the similar positive emotions that increase motivation and achievement (Ganotice et al., 2016). This is the ideal that we strive for in schools, and this is the reason a positive school climate is so important.

Personalize Your Classroom. When we personalize our classrooms we show our students that school is linked to their daily lives, and we capitalize on the positive emotional reactions that personalization provides (Narciss et al., 2014). Sharon capitalized on the emotional effects of personalization by taking pictures of her students, including descriptions they had written about themselves, and—particularly for Alberto—the music and pictures of his native Mexico. And she made similar efforts with all her students who weren't native English speakers. These efforts were further attempts, again using classical conditioning, to help her students learn to feel comfortable in her classroom.

Require That Students Treat Each Other with Courtesy and Respect. If students are going to experience the positive emotions associated with increased motivation and learning, they must feel safe and secure in our classrooms. And this requires more than teachers' displays of warmth and caring. Requiring that her students treat each other with courtesy and respect and holding periodic classroom meetings to discuss the ways students treat each other capitalize on this idea. Research indicates that rules consistently modeled and applied are essential for creating positive classroom environments (Emmer & Evertson, 2017; Evertson & Emmer, 2017), and Sharon applied this research with both her manner and the enforcement of her rules. (We discuss creating and implementing classroom rules in detail in Chapter 12.)

Our goal in all our decisions is to promote learning, and students learn more in classrooms that are emotionally safe and secure. Classical conditioning is a powerful tool we can use to promote these positive emotions.

MyLab Education Application Exercise 6.1: Classical Conditioning in the Classroom

In this exercise you will be asked to analyze a third-grade teacher's attempts to apply classical conditioning concepts with her students.

Classroom Connections

Developing a Positive Classroom Climate with Classical Conditioning

1. Classical conditioning explains how individuals learn emotional responses through the process of association. To elicit positive emotions as conditioned stimuli in your students, create a safe and welcoming classroom environment so your classroom elicits feelings of security.

   • **Elementary:** A first-grade teacher greets each of her students with a warm smile each morning when they come into the room. Her goal is to help her students—through classical conditioning—learn a positive emotional reaction to her classroom and their school work by associating them with her warmth and caring manner.

   • **Middle School:** A seventh-grade teacher enforces rules that forbid students from ridiculing each other in any way. His goal is to create a safe environment, so students will associate their classroom and school work with the safety of their school environment and, through classical conditioning, learn positive emotional reactions to school.

- **High School:** A geometry teacher clearly specifies what students will be held accountable for on her weekly quizzes. She also drops the students' lowest quiz score for grading purposes. Her goal is to use extinction to eliminate test anxiety in her students.

MyLab Education Self-Check 6.1

Operant Conditioning

6.2   Identify examples of operant conditioning in and outside of classrooms.

In the previous section we saw that classical conditioning can explain how people learn involuntary emotional and physiological responses to both classroom activities and events in their daily lives. People don't simply respond to stimuli, however; they often "operate" on their environments by initiating behaviors. This is the source of the term **operant conditioning**, which describes learning in terms of observable responses that change in frequency or duration as the result of **consequences**, events that occur following behaviors. B. F. Skinner (1953, 1954), historically the most influential figure in operant conditioning, suggested that our actions are controlled primarily by consequences. For example, being stopped by a highway patrol for speeding is a consequence, and it decreases the likelihood that we'll speed in the near future. A teacher's praise after a student's answer is also a consequence, and it increases the chance that the student will try to answer other questions. A myriad of consequences exist in classrooms, such as high test scores, attention from peers, and reprimands for inappropriate behavior. Each will influence students' subsequent behaviors.

Operant and classical conditioning are often confused. To help clarify important differences, we compare the two in Table 6.2. As you see in the table, a change in behavior

---

TABLE 6.2 A comparison of operant and classical conditioning

	Classical Conditioning		Operant Conditioning	
	Description	**Example**	**Description**	**Example**
Behavior	Involuntary (person does not have control of the behavior)	Tim could not control his test anxiety	Voluntary (person can control behavior)	Tim could control the way he studied
Order	Stimulus precedes behavior	The stimulus (the test) preceded and caused Tim's anxiety	Stimulus (consequence) follows behavior	Tim's improved test score (the consequence) came after (followed) Tim's changed study behavior
How learning occurs	Neutral stimulus becomes associated with an unconditioned stimulus	Tests (originally neutral stimuli) became associated with failure	Consequences of behaviors influence subsequent behaviors	Tim's improved test scores (consequences) influenced the way he studied (he continued to study diligently)
Can explain	How people learn involuntary emotional or physiological responses	How we learn to fear dogs if we're bitten by a dog. How a song elicits a romantic feeling if we have had a romantic encounter while the song is playing	How voluntary behaviors are strengthened or weakened	Why a student increases his efforts to answer questions if his teacher praises him for attempting to answer. Why a student sits quietly if she is admonished for speaking in class without permission

results from experience for both, but the type of behavior differs, and the behavior and stimulus occur in the opposite order for the two.

Now, let's see how different consequences affect behavior. They're outlined in Figure 6.1 and discussed in the following sections.

Reinforcement

Ed Psych and You

During a class discussion, you make a comment, and your instructor responds, "Very insightful idea. Good thinking." How are you likely to behave in later discussions? On the other hand, if you tend to be a little sloppy, your significant other or roommate may nag you to pick up after yourself. What will you probably do to get them to stop?

Consider the first question we asked in *Ed Psych and You*. If you're praised for your comments it's likely that you'll try to make similar comments in the future. Your instructor's comment is a **reinforcer**, a consequence that increases the likelihood of a behavior recurring, and **reinforcement** is the process of applying reinforcers to increase behavior.

Effective use of reinforcers requires good professional judgment. For instance, praising a student for answering a trivial question is not sound practice, because it can communicate to students that we believe they have low ability, which decreases motivation. Rather, we should reinforce students for insightful answers or diligent effort, which increases motivation (Panahon & Martens, 2013). And reinforcers should be given as soon as possible after the desired behavior is displayed; delaying a reinforcer reduces its impact (Melanko & Larkin, 2013).

Figure 6.1 Consequences of behavior

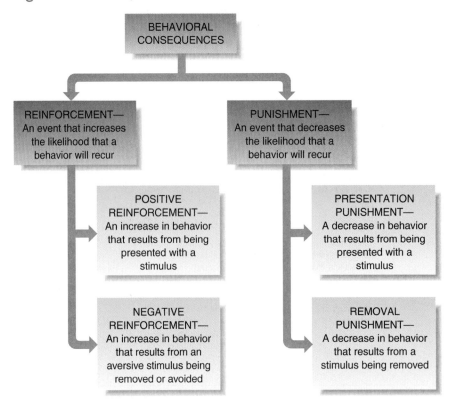

We sometimes attempt to reinforce too much, as in the case of praise for answering a trivial question, which can result in **satiation**, the process of using a reinforcer so frequently it loses its ability to strengthen behaviors. Just as we're "satiated" after eating a big meal, the overuse of praise, for instance, reduces its effectiveness.

On the other hand, if we don't reinforce behavior enough, **extinction**, the cessation of a behavior as a result of non-reinforcement, can occur. (Notice how extinction in operant conditioning differs from extinction in classical conditioning.) Let's look at an example.

Renita, a tenth-grader, enjoys school and likes to respond in her classes. She is attentive and eager to answer questions.

When Mr. Frank, her world history teacher, asks a question, Renita raises her hand, but someone usually blurts out the answer before she can respond. This happens repeatedly.

Now Renita rarely raises her hand and often catches herself daydreaming in class.

For Renita, being called on reinforced both her attention and attempts to respond. Because she wasn't called on, she wasn't reinforced, so her behaviors (paying attention and raising her hand) became extinct. So, we need to provide enough, but not too much, reinforcement when we work with our students.

With these ideas in mind, we turn now to three aspects of reinforcement:

- Primary and secondary reinforcers
- Positive reinforcement
- Negative reinforcement

Primary and Secondary Reinforcers.   Two basic types of reinforcers exist. **Primary reinforcers** are consequences that satisfy basic biological needs, such as food, water, air, sleep, and sex. Physical affection and touching, particularly for infants, are also primary reinforcers (Berk, 2019b), and alcohol and other drugs, including caffeine, can be primary reinforcers under certain conditions (Sheppard, Gross, Pavelka, Hall, & Palmatier, 2012).

Secondary reinforcers are consequences that reinforce behaviors through their association with other reinforcers. For instance, money—a common secondary reinforcer—allows people to get food, water, sleep, and under certain conditions, even sex. The role of secondary reinforcers has been confirmed with a variety of behaviors, such as addictions to the Internet and gambling (Alter 2017; Astur et al., 2016).

The vast majority of classroom reinforcers are secondary. For instance, teacher praise, attention, tokens, good grades, and free time are secondary reinforcers commonly used in classrooms.

Secondary reinforcers are learned, and they're socially dependent. For example, if praise, attention, or good grades aren't valued by students, they won't serve as secondary reinforcers. This reminds us that reinforcers we commonly consider to be effective, such as praise, may not be if they embarrass students or make them feel awkward (Bhutto, 2011). Again, sound professional judgment is required in using reinforcement.

Positive Reinforcement.   **Positive reinforcement** is the process of increasing the frequency or duration of a behavior as the result of *presenting* a reinforcer. Your instructor *presenting* you with the comment, "Very insightful idea. Good thinking" is an example; it increased the likelihood that you'd contribute again.

Positive reinforcers include:

- *Social reinforcers*: comments, signs, or gestures, such as your instructor's praise, high test scores, or a teacher's smile.

MyLab Education
Video Example 6.1
Primary reinforcers are consequences that satisfy basic biological needs, such as food, water, air, and sleep, whereas secondary reinforcers are consequences that reinforce behaviors through their association with primary reinforcers. Most reinforcers in classrooms, such as teacher praise and attention, are secondary. Here an elementary teacher uses extensive praise as a secondary reinforcer to encourage a student with his writing.

MyLab Education
Video Example 6.2

We all want to decrease inappropriate behaviors in our students, but we sometimes inadvertently reinforce the behaviors instead. In this animated description we see how this can occur in the regular classroom.

- *Concrete reinforcers*: objects that can be touched or held, such as "happy faces," tokens, candy, or stars on the bulletin board.
- *Activity reinforcers*: privileges or desired actions, such as free time or the opportunity to talk to peers.

In classrooms, we typically think of positive reinforcers as something *desired* or *valued*, such as the examples above, but we should remember that *any increase in behavior* as a result of being presented with a consequence is positive reinforcement, and we sometimes unintentionally reinforce inappropriate behavior. For instance, if a student is acting out, we reprimand him, and his misbehavior increases, the reprimand is a positive reinforcer. Our reprimand was intended to stop the behavior, but, instead, it *increased* as a result of being *presented* with the reprimand, so we inadvertently reinforced the behavior.

We also use positive reinforcement when we take advantage of the **Premack principle** (named after David Premack, who originally described it in 1965), which states that a more-desired activity can serve as a positive reinforcer for a less-desired activity. For example, we're using the Premack principle if we wait to watch a favorite movie until after we clean up our rooms; the movie reinforces us for cleaning up.

We can also use the Premack principle in our work with students. If you're a geography teacher, for instance, and you know your students like map work, you might say, "As soon as you've finished your summaries, you can start working on your maps." The map work serves as a positive reinforcer for completing the summaries.

Our students also reinforce us when we teach. Their attentive looks, nods, and raised hands are positive reinforcers, and they increase the chance that we'll call on them and keep doing what we're doing. High student test scores and compliments from students or their parents are also positive reinforcers for all of us.

Positive reinforcers are often used for **shaping**, the process of reinforcing successive approximations of a behavior. For example, you might have students who are so shy and reluctant to interact with their peers that they rarely speak. To "shape" their behavior you might first reinforce them for any interaction with others; later, you reinforce them for greeting other students as they enter the classroom; and finally you only reinforce more prolonged interactions. By reinforcing successive approximations of the desired behavior, you've *shaped* their behavior.

MyLab Education Application Exercise 6.2: Positive Reinforcement in Elementary School

In this exercise you will be asked to analyze an elementary teacher's use of positive reinforcement with her students.

MyLab Education
Video Example 6.3

Negative reinforcement is often confused with punishment. In this animated segment we see negative reinforcement explained and illustrated with different examples.

Negative Reinforcement.   Now, think about the second question we asked in *Ed Psych and You*: "On the other hand, if you tend to be a little sloppy, your significant other or roommate may nag you to pick up after yourself. What will you probably do to get them to stop?" We likely pick up our stuff to stop the nagging. We might even pick it up in advance to avoid the nagging in the first place. This is an example of **negative reinforcement**, the process of increasing behavior by removing or avoiding an aversive stimulus (Dishion, 2016; Skinner, 1953). Being nagged is aversive, so our *picking-up-our-stuff* behavior increases to eliminate or avoid the nagging.

Negative reinforcement is common in the real world, and many examples exist:

- You get into your car, and the seatbelt buzzer goes off, so you buckle the belt. You have been negatively reinforced for buckling the belt. The noise stopping is the negative reinforcer.

- You're sitting through a terrible movie. In fact, it's so bad that you get up and leave. You are being negatively reinforced for leaving the movie, and escaping the bad movie is the negative reinforcer.
- You are melting in the heat of an extraordinarily hot day. You're out, and you rush home to get into air conditioning. You are being negatively reinforced for rushing home, and escaping the heat is the negative reinforcer.

Negative reinforcement is offered as an explanation for problems people have with quitting smoking or stopping alcohol or drug abuse (Melanko & Larkin, 2013). For example, lighting up helps alleviate the aversive experience of craving the cigarette, and similar relief occurs when the addicted individual takes a drink or uses a drug.

Negative reinforcement is also common in classrooms. For example, you say to your students, "If you're all sitting quietly when the bell rings, we'll go to lunch. If not, we'll miss 5 minutes of our lunch period." In this case avoiding the aversive stimulus—missing some lunch time—acts as a negative reinforcer for the desired behavior—sitting quietly.

As with positive reinforcement, we sometimes negatively reinforce our students without realizing it.

Kathy Long is discussing the skeletal system with her science students.

"Why do you suppose the rib cage is shaped the way it is? . . . Jim?" she asks.

He sits quietly for a few seconds and then says, "I don't know."

"Can someone help Jim out?" Kathy continues.

"It protects our heart and other internal organs," Athenia volunteers.

"Good, Athenia," Kathy smiles.

Later, Kathy calls on Jim again, and he quickly says, "I don't know."

In this example, Kathy—unintentionally—negatively reinforced Jim for failing to respond. When she asked, "Can someone help Jim out?" she removed the potentially anxiety-provoking question. We know he was reinforced because his behavior increased; he said, "I don't know" more quickly the second time he was called on. If students struggle to answer questions, being called on can be aversive, so they may try and get off the hook as Jim did, or even avoid being called on by looking down or not making eye contact with us.

This example has implications for our teaching. We want to reinforce students *for* answering, as Kathy did with Athenia, instead of *for not* answering, as she did with Jim. Instead of turning the question to another student, prompting Jim to help him give an acceptable answer would have been more effective, and she could then have positively reinforced him for his answer.

Reinforcement Schedules   The process of using reinforcers to increase behavior isn't as simple as it appears on the surface, because the timing and spacing of reinforcers have different effects on the rate of increase and the durability of behavior. These effects are illustrated in **reinforcement schedules**, patterns in the frequency and predictability of reinforcers (Torelli, Lloyd, Diekman, & Wehby, 2017).

For example, suppose you initially praise a student for every attempt to answer a question, but later praise answers only some of the time. Your reinforcement schedule is initially **continuous**—every desired behavior is reinforced—but later you turn to an **intermittent schedule**, where some, but not all, of the desired behaviors are reinforced.

Two types of intermittent schedules exist, and they influence behavior differently. **Ratio schedules** depend on the number of individual behaviors, and **interval schedules** depend on time. Both can be either fixed or variable. In fixed schedules, the individual receives reinforcers predictably; in variable schedules the reinforcers are unpredictable. For instance, when playing slot machines, you insert a coin, hit a button, and other coins periodically drop into the tray. Receiving coins (reinforcers) depends on the number of times you hit the button—not on how long you play—and you can't predict when you'll receive coins, so it is a *variable-ratio schedule*.

Teacher praise and comments on papers are common classroom examples of variable-ratio schedules. The praise and comments depend on students' behaviors—not on time—and students usually cannot predict when they will receive either (Hulac, Benson, Nesmith, & Shervey, 2016).

Fixed-ratio schedules are uncommon in classrooms, except for some forms of drill-and-practice computer software. For instance, a student signs on to the program, receives a personalized greeting, and solves three problems. The program then replies, "Congratulations, Antonio, you have just correctly solved three problems." If the program then gives a similar response for every three problems answered correctly, it is using a fixed-ratio schedule.

Now, suppose you're in a class that meets Mondays, Wednesdays, and Fridays, you have a quiz each Friday, and your instructor returns the quiz on Monday. You study on Sunday, Tuesday, and particularly on Thursday evenings, but you aren't reinforced for studying until the following Monday when you receive your score. Reinforcement for your studying occurs at a predictable interval—every Monday—so it is a *fixed-interval schedule*. On the other hand, if instructors give pop quizzes, they are using *variable-interval schedules*, because you can't predict when you will be reinforced (Hulac et al., 2016).

Reinforcement schedules affect behavior differently, and each has advantages and disadvantages. For instance, a continuous schedule yields the fastest rates of initial learning (increase in behavior), so it is effective when students are acquiring new skills. However, when the reinforcers are eliminated, continually reinforced behaviors decrease more quickly than behaviors reinforced using intermittent schedules. "Behaviors reinforced by continuous reinforcement schedules are subject to high levels of extinction once the reinforcement is no longer available" (Hulac et al., 2016, p. 91).

Intermittent schedules promote more enduring behaviors but also have disadvantages. With fixed schedules, behavior increases rapidly just before the reinforcer is given and then decreases rapidly and remains low until just before the next reinforcer is given. Giving Friday quizzes is an example; students often study carefully just before the quiz and then don't study again until just before the next quiz (Campos, Leon, Sleiman, & Urcuyo, 2017).

The relationships among the different types of reinforcement schedules are illustrated in Figure 6.2, and additional classroom examples are outlined in Table 6.3.

Figure 6.2 Schedules of reinforcement

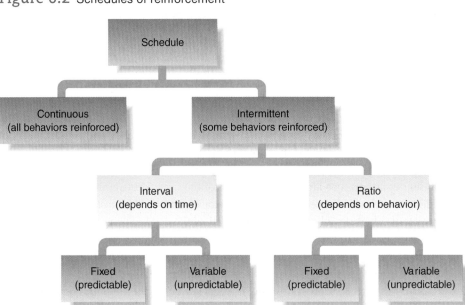

TABLE 6.3 Reinforcement schedules and examples

Schedule	Example
Continuous	A teacher "walks students through" the steps for solving simultaneous equations. Students are liberally praised at each step as they first learn the solution.
Fixed-ratio	The algebra teacher announces, "As soon as you've done two problems in a row correctly, you may start on your homework assignment so that you'll be able to finish by the end of class."
Variable-ratio	Students volunteer to answer questions by raising their hands and are called on at random.
Fixed-interval	Students are given a quiz every Friday.
Variable-interval	Students are given unannounced quizzes.

Punishment

Positive and negative reinforcers are consequences that increase behavior. Other consequences, called **punishers**, weaken behaviors—decrease the likelihood of the behaviors' recurring—and the process of using punishers to decrease behavior is called **punishment**.

Punishment and negative reinforcement are often confused, so keep the following two ideas in mind as you study this section.

- Punishment is a *decrease* in behavior, whereas *negative reinforcement*—as with all forms of reinforcement—is an *increase* in behavior.

- Think of the term "negative" in negative reinforcement as you might think of it in math. It involves avoiding or removing—subtracting—an aversive stimulus, such as the example of you increasing your picking-up-your-stuff behavior to remove or avoid your significant other's nagging.

Now, with these ideas in mind, let's examine the concept of punishment. Two types exist. As we saw in Figure 6.1, **presentation punishment** occurs when a learner's behavior decreases as a result of being presented with a punisher. For instance, when a teacher puts her fingers to her lips, signaling "Shh," and students stop whispering, the students are presented with the teacher's signal, and their behavior—whispering—decreases.

Removal punishment occurs when a behavior decreases as a result of removing a stimulus, or the inability to get positive reinforcement. For example, if students are noisy and their teacher keeps them in the room for 5 minutes of their lunch period, he is using removal punishment. Under normal conditions, they go to lunch at the scheduled time, and he takes away some of that free time.

MyLab Education Application Exercise 6.3: Reinforcement or Punishment?

In this exercise you will be asked to analyze differences between negative reinforcement and punishment.

Using Punishment Effectively.   Some critics suggest that punishment should never be used because of students' negative emotional reactions to being punished, which, the critics argue, can generalize to academic work, the classroom, and school in general. And, because punishment only decreases undesirable behaviors but doesn't teach desirable ones, systems based on reinforcement are superior to those using punishment (Alberto & Troutman, 2017). However, some students can become disruptive when all punishers are removed, and experts suggest that consequences for misbehavior are a necessary part of an effective classroom management system. So, punishment is sometimes necessary (Furukawa, Alsop, Sowerby, Jensen, & Tripp, 2017; Greenberg, Putman,

& Walsh, 2014). The most practical approach is to use punishment sparingly and judiciously, combined with appropriate reinforcement for good behavior.

Some punishers generally viewed as effective include:

- *Desists*. **Desists** are verbal or nonverbal communications that teachers use to stop a behavior (Kounin, 1970). A simple form of presentation punishment, such as the teacher signaling "Shh," is a desist. When administered immediately, briefly, and unemotionally, they can be effective for eliminating a variety of inappropriate behaviors (Emmer & Evertson, 2017; Evertson & Emmer, 2017).

- *Response cost*. **Response cost** involves the removal of reinforcers already given (Murphy & Lupfer, 2014). For example, some teachers design systems where students receive tokens or other reinforcers for desirable behavior, which they can then use to purchase items from a school store, or redeem for free time and other privileges. Taking some of them away because of inappropriate behavior is a form of response cost. Further, some research indicates that people in general are *loss averse*, meaning they react more strongly to loss, or the prospect of loss, such as the tokens, than they do to the possibility of gaining a reward (Kahneman, 2011). This research suggests that response cost can be an effective form of punishment.

- *Non-exclusion timeout*. **Non-exclusion timeout** involves seating a student near the teacher or on the edge of the classroom, with the goal of preventing the student from receiving reinforcers from other students (Ryan, Sanders, Katsiyannis, & Yell, 2007). Non-exclusion timeout is a variation of traditional timeout, which involves physically isolating students in an area away from classmates. Commonly used by parents to eliminate undesirable behaviors in their young children (Alberto & Troutman, 2017), traditional timeout is controversial. Questions about violating students' rights have been raised, and lawsuits have even been filed in some cases (Ryan, Peterson, & Rozalski, 2007). As a result non-exclusion timeout is viewed as more effective.

- *Detention*. Similar to timeout, and most commonly used with older students, detention involves taking away some of students' free time (typically a half hour or more) by keeping students in school either before or after school hours. While somewhat controversial (Johnson, 2004), it is generally viewed as effective (Cooper & Olsen, 2014). It is most effective when students are required to sit quietly and do nothing, because the possibility of positive reinforcement is eliminated (imagine sitting doing absolutely nothing for a half hour). When a parent "grounds" a teenager for inappropriate behavior, the parent is also using a form of detention.

  Logistical problems exist with detention because some students simply can't stay after school, transportation doesn't exist for getting them home, or they have other responsibilities, such as after-school jobs or taking care of younger siblings. If logistical problems can be solved, detention can be an effective form of punishment.

Ineffective Forms of Punishment. While judicious use of punishment can be effective, some forms are counter-productive, and should not be used. They include:

- *Corporal punishment*. **Corporal punishment** is commonly defined as "the use of physical force with the intention of causing a child to experience pain, but not injury, for the purpose of correcting or controlling a child's behavior (Mendez, Durtschi, Neppl, & Stith, 2016; p. 888). As of 2015, it remained legal in 19 states in our country, concentrated primarily in the south (Anderson, 2015). It has been widely researched, and evidence consistently indicates that is both ineffective and destructive. For example, it can negatively impact social-emotional and personality development (Holland & Holden, 2016; Mendez et al., 2016), and as we would intuitively expect, it detracts from student motivation and learning (Ahmad, Said, & Khan, 2013).

- *Embarrassment and humiliation.* Embarrassment and humiliation can lead to some of the same negative side effects as corporal punishment. It can also dampen students' interest in school and lower their expectations for success (Ellis, Fitzsimmons, & Small-McGinley, 2010).

- *Extra Class work.* Using class work as a form of punishment can teach students that the topic or subject is aversive and may, through classical conditioning, cause negative emotional reactions to it (Cooper & Olsen, 2014). Learners may generalize their aversion to other assignments, other teachers, and the school as well.

- *Out-of-school suspension.* For some students, and particularly underachievers, school is aversive, so being suspended can negatively reinforce their misbehavior by removing the aversive environment. Further, the suspension exacerbates their learning problems, detracts from their emotional attachment to school, and increases the likelihood that they will drop out before they graduate (Gregory, Skiba, & Noguera, 2010; Kennedy-Lewis & Murphy, 2016).

As with using reinforcers, the use of punishers requires sound judgment. For example, if you use desists with your students, but they're reinforced by your attention, the desists are ineffective, and you need a different strategy, such as non-exclusion timeout. On the other hand, if participating in class is aversive, timeout—instead of being an effective punisher—may be a negative reinforcer. In either case, we need to change the strategy.

The Influence of Antecedents on Behavior

So far, we've seen how consequences—reinforcers and punishers—can influence behavior. But we can also influence behavior through **antecedents**, stimuli that precede and induce behaviors. Environmental conditions and prompts and cues are the two most common types of antecedents. Let's look at them.

Ed Psych and You

You walk into a dark room. What is the first thing you do? Why do you do that?

Environmental Conditions. Almost certainly, the answer to our first question in *Ed Psych and You* is "turn on the light." The darkness is an environmental antecedent that causes us to flip the light switch. The light coming on reinforces us for flipping the switch, so we continue to do so, which answers our second question. Similarly, a traffic light turning red is an antecedent that causes us to stop, because running the light increases the likelihood of being punished by getting a ticket or being hit by another car.

Some teachers dim the lights when students come into the classroom or when the noise level becomes too great, using it as an environmental antecedent to remind them that they are inside and need to use inside voices and behaviors. We can use classroom environments as antecedents for desirable behaviors, which we can then reinforce.

Prompts and Cues. Prompts and cues are specific actions we can use to elicit desired behaviors, particularly in learning activities. For example:

Alicia Wendt wants her students to understand the concept *adverb*. She writes this sentence on the board:

John quickly jerked his head when he heard his name called.

She then asks, "What is the adverb in the sentence? . . . Jacob?"

"..."

"How did John jerk his head?"

"... Quickly."

"Okay, good .... So, what is the adverb in the sentence?"

"... Quickly."

"Yes, ... good, Jacob."

When Jacob didn't respond to Alicia's question, "What is the adverb in the sentence?" she prompted him by asking, "How did John jerk his head?" Jacob responded, "Quickly," which Alicia positively reinforced by saying, "Okay, good." She prompted him again when she asked, "So, what is the adverb in the sentence?" and after Jacob responded, she again reinforced him by saying, "Yes, good, Jacob."

A variety of cues exists. For instance, when you move to the front of the class or walk among students as they do seatwork, you are cuing them to turn their attention toward you or to remain on task. In each case, you can then reinforce the desired behaviors.

Using Educational Psychology in Teaching: Suggestions for Applying Operant Conditioning with Your Students

Although cognitive learning theory is the framework most commonly used to guide instruction, behaviorism can also be used as a tool to develop basic skills, and it is widely used in classroom management (Alberto & Troutman, 2017). The following suggestions can help us use operant conditioning as a tool in our work with students.

1. Use antecedents to elicit desired behaviors, which can then be reinforced.
2. Reinforce students for genuine accomplishments and good behavior.
3. Use reinforcers and punishers appropriately to help maintain an orderly classroom.
4. Employ drill-and-practice technologies to help students develop basic skills.

To see these guidelines in practice, let's look in on Danielle Stevens, a third-grade teacher, who is working with her students on rounding numbers.

Danielle introduces the topic of rounding numbers by having her students count to 100 by 10s, and then says, "Okay, keeping 10s in mind, let's think about the numbers 34 and 36. To which 10 are they the closest? . . . Juan?"

" . . . 34 is closest to 30, and 36 is closest to 40," Juan responds after thinking for a few seconds.

"Good," Danielle nods. "That's what we mean by *rounding*. Rounding helps us when we estimate answers, and we'll be using it throughout the year." After two more examples she then says, "Now, think about 128 . . . . Let's round it to the nearest 10," as she walks down the aisle, makes eye contact with Henry, and shakes her head, signaling "No," in response to his tapping Gretchen's desk with his foot.

Henry stops.

"A hundred," Andrea volunteers.

"Count from 100 to 200 by 10s," Danielle directs.

Andrea counts 100, 110, 120, and so on until she reaches 200.

"Good. So which 10 is 128 closest to?

" . . . One hundred . . . thirty," Andrea hesitantly responds.

"Very good," Danielle nods. "Yes, 128 is closer to 130 than it is to 120 . . . . Good thinking."

Danielle then continues the process by having her students count to 1,000 by hundreds, and gives them additional examples, such as 462, which they round to the nearest hundred.

"Now, let's be good thinkers," she continues. "Let's round 6,457 to the nearest 10. Everyone write your answer on your chalkboard and hold it up when you're finished." (Danielle's students have small individual chalkboards at their desks which they use to write and display answers to math problems.)

Seeing 6,460 on Michael's chalkboard, Danielle says, "Michael, explain to everyone how you arrived at your answer."

Michael explains that because they're thinking about 10s, 6,457 is closer to 6,460 than it is to 6,450.

"That's excellent thinking, Michael," Danielle smiles. "You showed a very good understanding of the problem."

Danielle continues the process with additional examples, and she then assigns 10 problems for homework.

As she checks on her students while they work, she sees that Andrea, David, Gus, and Suzanne are still struggling with the process. To provide them with additional practice, she sends them to four of the computers at the back of her room, has them log on to a "Rounding Numbers" program, and has them practice until the end of their allocated time for math.

As the students approach the end of their math time, Danielle kneels down by Jon's desk and quietly says, "Jon, I'm very proud of you today. You were paying attention, and I didn't have to remind you even once all period. How many checks did you give yourself?"

"Four," Jon responds.

"Very good, you earned them . . . . Keep it up," Danielle says, smiling warmly. Jon has ADHD and has trouble concentrating and controlling his behavior. Danielle has him keep a "behavior" chart, and for each 10 minutes that he is attentive, he gives himself a check. Danielle had to guide him carefully as they began the process, but he's now much improved.

Now, let's look at Danielle's efforts to apply the suggestions.

Use Antecedents to Elicit Desired Behaviors. Using antecedents in interactions with students can be effective for helping them generate desired responses. To illustrate, let's look again at some of the dialogue in Andrea's lesson.

Danielle: Now, think about 128 . . . . Let's round this to the nearest 10.

Andrea: A hundred.

Danielle: Count from 100 to 200 by 10s.

Andrea: [Counts 100, 110, 120, and so on until she reaches 200.]

Danielle: Good. So, to which 10 is 128 closest?

Andrea: . . . One hundred . . . thirty.

Danielle: Very good. Yes, 128 is closer to 130 than it is to 120. . . . Good thinking.

When Andrea incorrectly responded, "100" to the question about rounding 128 to the nearest 10, Danielle had her count from 100 to 200 by 10s and then asked, "So, to which 10 is 128 closest?" Her directive and question were antecedents (cues) that helped Andrea correctly answer, "One hundred thirty."

Strategically using antecedents to shape student behaviors can be applied with virtually any topic in any content area. For instance, a coach is working with her basketball team on fundamentals of the jump shot, and she displays a corresponding photo.

Coach:	Look at the player shooting the jump shot. What is important about the shooter's fundamentals? . . . Sonja?
Sonja:	. . .
Coach:	Look at the shooter's wrist. What do you notice about it?
Sonja:	It's bent . . . . And pointing to the basket.
Coach:	Yes, . . . good. It's important to follow through with your wrist when shooting a jump shot.

In this case, the coach's question, "What do you notice about it?" in reference to the shooter's wrist served as an antecedent that focused Sonja on an important aspect of jump shooting technique and allowed her to respond correctly.

Reinforce Students for Genuine Accomplishments. Being able to correctly respond to questions makes us feel good, and being reinforced for doing so is even better. Research corroborates this assertion and suggests that being reinforced for genuine accomplishment can increase both motivation and learning (Schunk et al., 2014).

Danielle's comment, "Very good. Yes, 128 is closer to 130 than it is to 120. Good thinking," and the coach's response, "Yes, good. It's important to follow through with your wrist when shooting a jump shot," are applications of this idea.

In these examples, Danielle's and the coach's reinforcers followed prompts (antecedents). Danielle further used appropriate reinforcement with Michael when she commented, "That's excellent thinking, Michael. You showed a very good understanding of the problem," after Michael explained how he arrived at 6,460 when the students had been directed to round 6,457 to the nearest 10.

Use Reinforcers and Punishers Appropriately to Maintain an Orderly Classroom. Research suggests that reinforcing students for good behavior is an important classroom management technique, and using punishment appropriately is sometimes necessary to maintain an orderly classroom (Furukawa et al., 2017; Greenberg et al., 2014). Danielle applied operant conditioning in this way as she worked with her students. Let's look again at some dialogue from her lesson.

APA Top 20 Principles

This description illustrates *Principle 16: Expectations for classroom conduct and social interaction are learned and can be taught using proven principles of behavior and effective classroom instruction*—from the *Top 20 Principles from Psychology for PreK–12 Teaching and Learning*.

Danielle:	[As she kneels down by Jon's desk] Jon, I'm very proud of you today. You were paying attention, and I didn't have to remind you even once all period. How many checks did you give yourself?
Jon:	Four.
Danielle:	Very good, you earned them. . . . Keep it up.

Because Jon is a student with ADHD and has trouble attending and controlling his behavior, he has likely been reprimanded more often for misbehavior than praised for good behavior. Demonstrating that he can control his behavior and then being reinforced for doing so can mean a great deal to a student like Jon. And it can make an important contribution to his long-term development.

Danielle also used punishment effectively when she walked down the aisle, made eye contact with Henry, and signaled "No" with a head shake in response to him tapping Gretchen's desk with his foot. Her signal was a simple and effective presentation punisher; it stopped his behavior and didn't disrupt the flow of her lesson.

Employ Drill-and-Practice Technologies to Develop Basic Skills. Behaviorism, and particularly operant conditioning, has historically had a strong influence on the use of technology in classrooms, and particularly on drill-and-practice software (Hritcu, 2016; Kanive, Nelson, Burns, & Ysseldyke, 2014). As an example, let's see how Danielle could use this technology to provide her students with additional practice in rounding numbers (adapted from IXL Learning, 2013).

You open the program, and the boxes at the bottom of the page appear.

You see the box on the left, then click on "New problem," and the problem in the middle box appears. You type in 675,000 as you see in the box on the right, click on "Check Your Answer," and "No, try again," pops up in a separate box. A bit uncertain about why your answer is incorrect, you click on "Hint," which tells you, "Look at the digit to the right of the rounding place. Is it 5 or greater?" Using the hint, you type in 676,000, and "Correct!" pops up. Had you answered incorrectly a second time, "Sorry, here is the answer" would have been displayed.

Let's see how this is an application of behaviorism. Your responses (behavior) changed from giving the incorrect answer, 675,000, to the correct answer, 676,000, as a result of: (1) being told your first answer was incorrect ("No, try again"); (2) the information you received in the hint; and (3) being told that your second answer was correct ("Correct!"). "No, try again," is a punisher, and "Correct!" is a reinforcer. The probability of you repeating the first answer decreases, and the chance of repeating the second answer increases. You can use software applications such as these with your students in a variety of areas, but the most common are in math and science.

Many programs provide more detailed feedback than simple hints, such as "Look at the digit to the right of the rounding place. Is it 5 or greater?", and some software asks students to enter personal information into the program, such as their names and friends, with the goal of increasing interest. For instance, consider this problem designed for elementary students in math:

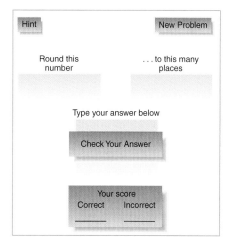 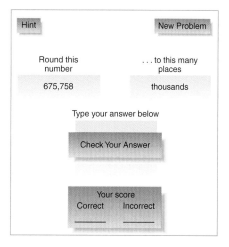 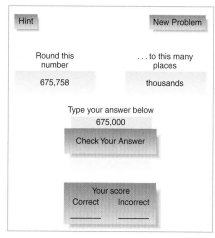

There are four objects, and each one is cut in half. In all, how many pieces will there then be?

Now, compare it to the one below, personalized for a student named Josh, whose teacher is Mrs. Gonzalez.

Mrs. Gonzalez surprised Josh with a treat for his good behavior by giving him four small candy bars. He wanted to share them with his friend, Zach, so he cut each one in half. How many pieces does Josh now have?

The program took the information Josh had entered and used it in the problem. Personalizing problems in this way can increase both learning and motivation (Schunk et al., 2014).

Drill-and-practice software based on operant conditioning principles is controversial, and some critics describe it as little more than "electronic flashcards" (Inan, Lowther, Ross, & Strahl, 2010). Used properly, however, evidence doesn't support this position. The benefits of drill-and-practice software have been well established by research (Roblyer & Hughes, 2019).

As you saw in the examples with rounding, this software provides students with individualized practice and increases student engagement, because the student must answer every question to proceed. Learners also report that they feel more comfortable because they can set their own pace, and their answers and the feedback they receive are private (Roblyer & Hughes, 2019). Finally, a computer, unlike a human, can be programmed to have unlimited patience.

Drill-and-practice software can supplement your teaching, but it isn't intended to replace you. For example, instead of having her students simply memorize a set of steps for rounding numbers, Danielle's goal was for rounding to make sense to them, and she, not the software, was instrumental in helping her students reach that goal. Then, she used the software to provide the students with extra practice. This is an effective application of technology grounded in behaviorism, and used this way, it can contribute to your students' learning.

Classroom Connections

Using Operant Conditioning Effectively in Classrooms

Reinforcers and Punishers

1. Reinforcers are consequences that increase behavior, and punishers are consequences that decrease behavior. Use positive reinforcement if possible, and removal punishment if necessary.

- **Elementary:** After assigning seatwork, a first-grade teacher gives tickets as positive reinforcers to students who are working quietly. If a student has to be reminded to stay on task, the teacher takes one of the students' tickets as an application of response cost—a type of removal punishment. Accumulated tickets can be exchanged for opportunities to play games and work at learning centers.

- **Middle School:** A seventh-grade teacher implements a system whereby all students in her class start off the week with three "behavior points." If they break a classroom rule, she applies removal punishment by removing one of their behavior points. For each day in which they break no rules they are awarded an additional behavior point as a positive reinforcer. If they earn an additional point every day of the week, they receive additional positive reinforcement by having their names displayed on a behavior honor roll in the class newsletter that goes home to parents at the end of each week.

- **High School:** A math teacher increases the effectiveness of grades as positive reinforcers by awarding bonus points for quiz scores that are higher than students' personal averages.

Shaping

2. Shaping is the process of reinforcing successive approximations of a desired behavior. Capitalize on the process to develop complex skills.

- **Elementary:** A preschool teacher is attempting to help one of her students learn to share toys. Initially, she praises any social behavior that the student demonstrates. As the student gradually progresses, she requires that he actually shares his toys during play to receive praise as positive reinforcers.

- **Middle School:** At the beginning of the year a language arts teacher is initially generous with positive comments as she scores students' paragraphs, but as students' writing develops they have to demonstrate higher levels of expertise to earn compliments as positive reinforcers.

- **High School:** An Algebra II teacher liberally praises students as they make the initial steps in solving equations. As they continue their work, they have to demonstrate higher levels of skill to receive compliments as reinforcers.

Reinforcement Schedules

3. Reinforcement schedules influence both the acquisition of responses and their extinction. Continuous schedules increase behavior most rapidly, but intermittent schedules result in the most enduring behavior. Select a schedule that is most effective for meeting your goals.

- **Elementary:** At the beginning of the school year, a first-grade teacher plans activities that all students can accomplish successfully. He uses a continuous reinforcement schedule by praising all desirable behaviors. As students' capabilities increase, he shifts to an intermittent schedule to increase the durability of the behaviors.

- **Middle School:** A sixth-grade teacher employs a variable-ratio reinforcement schedule by complimenting students only when they display conscientious effort and demonstrate thorough understanding. She also applies a variable-interval schedule by periodically sending emails home to parents when students demonstrate extra effort and insight in their class work.

- **High School:** A geometry teacher uses a fixed-interval schedule of reinforcement by giving frequent announced quizzes. He gives at least one quiz a week to help reduce the decline in effort that can occur when a fixed-interval schedule is used.

Antecedents

4. Antecedents are signals that induce desired behaviors, which can then be reinforced. Provide cues to elicit appropriate behaviors.

- **Elementary:** Before students line up for lunch, a first-grade teacher reminds them to stand quietly while waiting to be dismissed. The reminder serves as an antecedent for the desired behavior, and when they stand quietly, she positively reinforces them with compliments on their good behavior.

- **Middle School:** After assigning seatwork, a seventh-grade English teacher circulates around the room, reminding students to stay on task. Moving around the room serves as an antecedent for the conscientious work, for which she periodically compliments them, which is an application of a variable-interval schedule.

- **High School:** When a chemistry teacher's students don't respond, or respond incorrectly, he prompts them with additional questions that help them respond acceptably. The prompts serve as antecedents, and when they respond acceptably he positively reinforces them with a smile and nod or a compliment if they demonstrate a deeper level of understanding.

Applied Behavior Analysis

Applied behavior analysis (ABA) is the process of systematically implementing the principles of operant conditioning to increase desired behavior (Alberto & Troutman, 2017). (It has historically been called *behavior modification*, but this term has a negative connotation for some people, so experts prefer the term we use here.) Widely applied in schools with students having exceptionalities (Zoder-Martell & Dieringer, 2016), it has also been used to help people increase their physical fitness, overcome fears and panic attacks, learn social skills, and stop smoking (Ryan, Katsiyannis, & Peterson, 2007).

Nearly half of the research on ABA has focused on its use with students having autism or other developmental delays, another 20% on students with intellectual disabilities, and the remainder on an array of learning or behavioral issues (Shyman, 2016). ABA is also quite closely related to response to intervention (Zoder-Martell & Dieringer, 2016), which we examined in Chapter 5. Considerable employment opportunities exist for people with advanced degrees in ABA, so if you're a psychology or special education major, you may want to look into the possibility of further work in this area.

Steps in ABA

The application of operant conditioning principles in ABA typically involves the following steps (Alberto & Troutman, 2017).

1. Identify target behaviors.
2. Establish a baseline for the target behaviors.
3. Choose reinforcers and punishers (if necessary).
4. Measure changes in the target behaviors.
5. Gradually reduce the frequency of reinforcers as behavior improves.

To see how to implement these steps, let's look in on Mike Sheppard, a middle school math teacher, as he works with his students.

Mike has 28 students in his second-period class, including, as do most teachers, some with exceptionalities. Todd in particular has difficulty controlling his behavior, and other teachers describe him as verbally abusive, aggressive, and lacking in self-discipline. He is extremely active and he has trouble sitting through a class period.

As the bell rings, most students are studying the screen at the front of the room as they begin a warm-up problem that Mike displays as part of his beginning-of-class routine. He quickly takes roll and then walks to Todd's desk.

"Let's take a look at your chart," he says. "You've improved a lot, haven't you?"

"Yeah, look," Todd responds, proudly displaying the chart you see here.

	2/9–2/13	2/16–2/20	2/23–2/27
Talking out	‖‖ ‖‖ ‖‖ ‖‖	‖‖ ‖‖‖‖ ‖‖	‖‖ ‖‖
Swearing	‖‖ ‖‖	‖‖ ‖‖	‖‖‖‖
Hitting/ touching	‖‖ ‖‖‖	‖‖ ‖‖‖‖	‖‖‖
Out of seat	‖‖ ‖‖ ‖‖ ‖‖‖	‖‖ ‖‖ ‖‖ ‖‖‖‖	‖‖ ‖‖ ‖‖ ‖‖‖
Being friendly	‖‖	‖‖‖‖	‖‖ ‖‖

"That's terrific," Mike whispers as he leans over the boy's desk. "You're doing much better. We need some more work on 'out of seat,' don't we? I don't like getting after you about it, and I know you don't like it either. . . . Stop by at the end of class. I have an idea that I think will help. . . . Okay. Get to work on the problem." Mike taps Todd on the shoulder and then returns to the front of the room.

Mike goes over the warm-up exercise with the class, conducts the lesson, and gives the students five problems for homework. "Go ahead and get started now," he directs with 15 minutes left in the period.

The bell rings, and the students begin filing out of the room. Todd stops by Mike's desk, and Mike leads him to a small area in the back of the room where a partition has been set up. The area is partially enclosed but faces the class.

"Here's what we'll do," Mike directs. "When you have the urge to get out of your seat, quietly get up and move back here for a few minutes. Stay as long as you want, but be sure you pay attention to what we're doing. When you think you're ready to move back to your seat, go ahead. All I'm asking is that you move back and forth quietly. . . . What do you think?"

Todd nods, and Mike comments, "You're doing so well on everything else; this will help, I think. Remember to ask me for help with your seatwork if you need it. If you keep trying, this will work. . . . Now, here's a pass into Mrs. Miller's class."

Now, let's see how Mike implemented the steps in ABA.

Identify Target Behaviors. Identifying the specific behaviors we want to change is the first step in ABA. As we saw in Todd's chart, Mike identified five target behaviors: talking out, swearing, hitting/touching other students, being out of seat, and being friendly. Some experts might argue that Mike included too many target behaviors and might further suggest that "being friendly" isn't specific enough. As with most teaching–learning applications, these decisions are a matter of professional judgment.

Establish a Baseline. A baseline is established when we initially measure the target behaviors. For instance, during the baseline period (the week of 2/9 to 2/13), Todd talked out in class 20 times, swore 10 times, hit or touched another student 8 times, was out of his seat 18 times, and was friendly to other students twice. Mike measured Todd's behaviors to establish the baseline, which provides a concrete record of later progress.

Choose Reinforcers and Punishers. Before attempting to change behavior, we need to identify the reinforcers and punishers that are likely to work for an individual student. Ideally, an ABA system is based on reinforcers instead of punishers, and this is what Mike used with Todd. If punishers are necessary, they should also be established in advance.

Mike used personal attention and praise as his primary reinforcers, and they were effective, as indicated by the positive changes in Todd's behavior. And Todd could see evidence that his behavior was improving, which was, in itself, reinforcing. If the undesirable behaviors had not decreased, Mike would have needed to modify his system by trying different reinforcers and perhaps some punishers as well.

Measure Changes in Behavior. After establishing a baseline and identifying reinforcers and punishers, we then measure the target behaviors for specified periods to see if they change. For example, Todd talked out 20 times the first week, 14 times the second, and only 7 times the third. Except for "out of seat," improvement occurred for each of the other behaviors during the 3-week period.

Because Mike's first intervention didn't change Todd's out-of-seat behavior, he designed an alternative, the area at the back of the room where Todd could go when the urge to get out of his seat became overwhelming. He was free to move back and forth at his own discretion, which also reinforced him.

Reduce Frequency of Reinforcers. As Todd's behavior improved, Mike gradually reduced the frequency of reinforcers. Initially, you might use a continuous, or nearly continuous, schedule and then move to an intermittent one. Reducing the frequency of reinforcers helps maintain the desired behaviors and increases the likelihood that they will generalize to other classrooms and everyday activities.

Functional Analysis

In the preceding sections we focused on measuring changes in behavior based on using reinforcers and punishers. However, some experts recommend expanding the focus to include identifying both antecedents that trigger inappropriate behaviors and the consequences of those behaviors, a strategy called **functional analysis** (Larkin, Hawkins, & Collins, 2016; Miltenberger, 2012). For example, in a functional analysis of Todd's behavior, Mike found that Todd was most commonly abusive during class discussions, and Mike believed that the attention Todd received for the outbursts was reinforcing. Similarly, Mike found that Todd was out of his desk most often during seatwork and reasoned that leaving his seat allowed Todd to avoid tasks with which he struggled. Class discussions were antecedents for abusive behavior, and seatwork was an antecedent for leaving his seat. In further applying this analysis, Mike praised Todd for "being friendly." The praise was a form of attention, so it provided Todd with a reinforcer that served the same purpose that being abusive had previously served. As a result, Todd's tendency to be abusive decreased. Similarly, Mike provided Todd with a place he could go when the urge to leave his seat was overwhelming, and he reminded Todd to ask for help with his seatwork when he needed it. This process of using interventions that help replace problem behaviors with more appropriate behaviors that serve the same purpose for the student is called **positive behavior support**.

Like all interventions, ABA won't work magic, and it is labor intensive (Alberto & Troutman, 2017). For example, we can't assume that students will accurately measure target behaviors, so we will most likely have to monitor the behaviors ourselves. This makes managing an already busy classroom even more demanding.

Also, personal attention and praise were effective reinforcers for Todd, but if they hadn't been, Mike would have needed others. Finding reinforcers that are easy to administer yet consistent with school procedures can be challenging. However, ABA provides us with an additional tool if conventional classroom management methods, such as a basic system of rules and procedures, aren't working.

Diversity: Using Behaviorism in Working with Learners from Diverse Backgrounds

For some students, and particularly for members of cultural minorities, schools can seem cold and uninviting (Gollnick & Chinn, 2017). Let's see how behaviorism can be applied to help every student succeed and feel welcome in classrooms.

Julian, a fourth-grader, shuffles into class and hides behind the big girl in front of him. If he is lucky, his teacher won't discover that he hasn't done his homework—12 problems! How can he ever do that many? Besides, he isn't good at math. Julian hates school. It seems strange and foreign. His teacher sometimes frowns when he speaks because his English isn't as good as the other students'. And he often has trouble understanding what the teacher is saying.

Even lunch isn't much fun. If his friend Raul isn't there, he eats alone. One time when he sat with some other students, they started laughing at the way he talked and made fun of the tortillas he was eating. He can't wait to go home.

The way teachers and other students treat members of cultural minorities has a strong impact on their emotional reactions to school. For Julian, school wasn't associated with positive feelings, and he didn't feel comfortable, safe, or welcome.

It doesn't have to be this way. For example, if Julian's teacher learned to be warm and supportive, such as we saw in the example with Sharon Van Horn in our section "Using Educational Psychology in Teaching: Suggestions for Applying Classical Conditioning with Your Students," he may, through classical conditioning, gradually associate school and his academic work with his teacher's support. For instance, Alberto, in Sharon's class, had an instinctive positive reaction to Sharon's warmth, and, over time, her classroom became associated with her manner, which then produced positive emotions as conditioned responses. These responses were similar to the instinctive positive emotions—unconditioned responses—that were triggered by Sharon's warm and supportive manner. These experiences are particularly important for students who are members of cultural minorities, as are rules that forbid students from mistreating each other (Balagna, Young, & Smith, 2013).

We can also apply operant conditioning principles with members of cultural minorities. For instance, when students struggle, we can use prompts as antecedents to encourage them and then use praise as reinforcement when they give acceptable answers. These efforts, effective with all students, are particularly important for members of cultural minorities, because they communicate that we want these students in our classes and believe they are capable learners (Balagna et al., 2013).

Evaluating Behaviorism

As with any theory, behaviorism has both critics and proponents. Criticisms focus on the following areas:

- The ineffectiveness of behaviorism as a guide for instruction
- The inability of behaviorism to explain higher-order learning
- The impact of reinforcers on intrinsic motivation
- Philosophical positions on learning and teaching

Let's look at them.

First, critics charge that behaviorism distorts and oversimplifies the teaching–learning process. Instruction based on behaviorism requires that content is organized so that students can respond with observable behaviors—such as the examples with rounding that we saw earlier—which allows students to be reinforced for providing correct responses. Most of what we learn doesn't exist as specific, decontextualized items of information, however. For example, we learn to write by practicing writing, not by responding to isolated grammar or punctuation exercises often found in workbooks.

Also, learners hold misconceptions and sometimes generate "off-the-wall" ideas for which they haven't been reinforced. Because these ideas originate with the individual, behaviorism is unable to explain how students come up with them. Instead, cognitive theories that focus on learners' thought processes are required.

Also, behaviorism cannot adequately explain higher-order functions, such as language development. For instance, Noam Chomsky (1959) demonstrated that people with even very small vocabularies would have to learn sentences at a rate faster than one per second throughout their lifetimes if their learning was based on specific behaviors and reinforcers. Some psychologists have even argued that Chomsky's criticism " . . . hammered a nail in the lid of behaviorism's coffin" (Schlinger, 2008, p. 329).

Critics also argue that behaviorism's emphasis on rewards can have a negative impact on learner motivation. Research suggests that offering reinforcers for intrinsically motivating activities, such as solving puzzles or playing video games, can actually decrease interest in these activities (Ryan & Deci, 1996).

And some critics focus on larger, philosophical issues related to learning goals. Because behaviorism focuses on how the environment influences behavior, critics have historically argued that it fails to develop learners who take responsibility for their own achievement (Anderman & Maehr, 1994; Kohn, 1993). These critics believe that, instead of promoting meaningful learning, behaviorism is essentially a means of controlling people.

Despite these criticisms, behaviorism is alive and well; a survey of research publications suggests that behaviorism, now referred to by some as *behavior analysis*, has undergone slight but steady growth over the last several decades, and "[t]o borrow the words of Mark Twain, reports of the death of behaviorism were greatly exaggerated" (Schlinger, 2008, p. 329). Further, applied behavior analysis is a thriving area, particularly in working with students having exceptionalities, and many universities in our country offer masters and doctoral degrees in the area (Cihon, Cihon, & Bedient, 2016; Larkin et al., 2016).

Proponents of behaviorism respond to critics by simply pointing out that it works; reinforcers and punishers can and do impact the way we behave, and it also influences both motivation and achievement. For example, sincere compliments can increase both student motivation and the way students feel about themselves (Brophy, 2010; Schunk et al., 2014). Teachers' experiences corroborate these findings. Also, a large experimental study found that monetary incentives had a statistically significant positive effect on high school students' performance on a test modeled on the

TABLE 6.4 Analyzing theories: Behaviorism

Key question	What influences changes in observable behavior?
Definition of learning	Enduring change in observable behavior that occurs as a result of experience
Catalysts for learning	• Associations between stimuli • Reinforcement • Punishment
Key concepts	Unconditioned and conditioned stimuli Unconditioned and conditioned responses Reinforcement Punishment Generalization Discrimination Extinction Satiation Shaping
Contributions of theory	• Helps explain how the environment (in the form of associations, reinforcements, and punishments) influences a wide variety of behaviors • Is widely used as a conceptual framework for managing student behavior in classrooms • Is used as a conceptual framework for a range of drill-and-practice computer software
Criticisms of theory	• Is generally ineffective as a conceptual framework for guiding instruction • Cannot explain higher order functions, such as problem solving or language acquisition • Some evidence suggests that the use of behavioral techniques decreases intrinsic motivation in learners • Is viewed by some as mechanistic and even manipulative

National Assessment of Educational Progress (Braun, Kirsch, & Yamamoto, 2011). Supporters of behaviorism also ask how many of us would continue working if we stopped receiving paychecks, and do we lose interest in our work merely because we get paid for it (Gentile, 1996)?

Also, aspects of behaviorism provide us with tools we can use to create orderly classrooms. For instance, research suggests that praise for good behavior and consequences for misbehavior should be part of effective classroom management programs (Emmer & Evertson, 2017; Evertson & Emmer, 2017), and behaviorist strategies can be effective when others are not (Furukawa et al., 2017).

Further, as we saw in Danielle's use of technology, drill-and-practice software based on behaviorism can provide students with valuable practice in basic skills. And finally, because it focuses on observable—as opposed to inferential—evidence, supporters of behaviorism argue that it is the only truly scientific study of human behavior (Bar-Yam, 2016; Nahigian, 2017).

No learning theory is complete, and this is particularly true of behaviorism. However, if judiciously applied by knowledgeable professionals, it can be a useful tool for creating environments that optimize opportunity to learn for all students.

Table 6.4 summarizes the contributions and criticisms of behaviorism.

MyLab Education Self-Check 6.2

Social Cognitive Theory

To begin our discussion, let's look at three different learning experiences and see how they're similar.

"What are you doing?" Jason asks Kelly as he comes around the corner and sees her swinging her arms back and forth as if swinging a bat.

"I'm trying to swing at a ball like the softball players in college do, but I haven't been able to quite do it," Kelly responds. "I was watching a game on TV last night, and the way those girls swing looks so easy, but they hit it so hard. I think I can do that if I work at it."

Three-year-old Jimmy crawls up on his dad's lap with a book. "I read too, Dad," he says as his father puts down his own book to help Jimmy up.

"I really like the way Juanita has quickly put away her materials and is ready to listen," Karen Engle, a second-grade teacher, comments as the students are making the transition from one activity to another.

The other students quickly put away their materials and turn their attention to Karen.

These examples are similar in two ways. First, each involved learning by observing the behavior of others: Kelly tried to imitate the swing of college softball players she saw on TV, and Jimmy saw his dad reading and wanted to imitate him. The second-graders in Karen's class observed the consequence—Karen's praise—of Juanita's putting her materials away, so they did the same.

Second, behaviorism can't explain these examples. Behaviorism focuses on changes in behavior that have direct causes outside the learner. For instance, in our chapter-opening case study, taking algebra quizzes directly caused Tim's hand to shake. And in the third vignette at the beginning of this section, Karen's comment directly reinforced Juanita. But nothing directly happened to Kelly, Jimmy, or the other second-graders in Karen's class; it was observing others that caused them to change their behavior.

Social cognitive theory, a theory of learning that focuses on changes in behavior that result from observing others, emerged from the work of Albert Bandura (1925–) (Bandura, 1986, 1997, 2001). Because behaviorism and social cognitive theory both examine changes in behavior, let's compare the two.

Comparing Behaviorism and Social Cognitive Theory

As you begin this section, you might be asking yourself, "If behaviorists focus on observable behavior, and the term *cognitive* implies memory and thinking, why is a cognitive learning theory included in the same chapter with behaviorism?"

Here's why: social cognitive theory has its historical roots in behaviorism, but, as the name implies, it has evolved over the years into a more cognitive perspective (Schunk et al, 2014). And some authors have included aspects of social cognitive theory in books focusing on behavioral principles.

In addition, behaviorism and social cognitive theory are similar in three ways. They both:

- Focus on experience as an important cause of learning (as do other cognitive theories, which we'll see in later chapters).
- Include the concepts of reinforcement and punishment in their explanations of learning.
- Emphasize that feedback is an important aspect of the learning process.

Three important differences exist between the two, however.

First, they define learning differently; second, social cognitive theory emphasizes the role of cognitive processes—*beliefs, perceptions*, and *expectations*—in learning; and third, social cognitive theory emphasizes the concept *reciprocal causation*, which suggests that the environment, personal factors, and behavior are interdependent.

Definition of Learning.   Behaviorists define learning as a change in observable behavior, whereas social cognitive theorists view **learning** as a change in mental processes that creates the capacity to demonstrate different behaviors (Schunk, 2016). So, from a social cognitive perspective, learning may or may not result in immediate behavioral change. The role of mental activity (cognition/thinking) is illustrated in our examples. Kelly, for instance, didn't try to imitate the baseball swing until the next day, so her observations had to be stored in her memory or she wouldn't have been able to reproduce the behaviors. Also, nothing directly happened to Kelly, Jimmy, or Karen's second-graders—other than observing Juanita. They were reacting to mental processes instead of reinforcers and punishers that directly influenced them.

The Role of Expectations. Instead of viewing reinforcers and punishers as directly causing behavior, as behaviorists do, social cognitive theorists believe that reinforcers and punishers create *expectations and beliefs*, cognitive processes that then influence behavior. For instance, you study for an exam for several days, but you aren't reinforced until you receive your score. You sustain your efforts because you *expect* to be reinforced for studying. And Karen's second-graders believed they would be praised for following Juanita's example, so they all imitated her. Behaviorists don't consider the role of cognitive processes in learning, but they are central to social cognitive theory.

The fact that people respond to their expectations and beliefs means they are aware of which behaviors will be reinforced or punished. This is important because, according to social cognitive theory, reinforcement changes behavior only when learners know what behaviors are being reinforced (Bandura, 1986). Tim, for instance, expected his changed study habits to improve his math scores, so he maintained those habits. If he had expected some other strategy to be more effective, he would have used it.

Reciprocal Causation. Behaviorism suggests a one-way relationship between the environment and behavior; the environment—unconditioned or conditioned stimuli in the case of classical conditioning, and reinforcers and punishers in operant conditioning—influences behavior, but the opposite doesn't occur. Social cognitive theory's explanation is more complex, suggesting that behavior, the environment, and personal factors are interdependent, meaning each influences the other two. The term **reciprocal causation** describes this interdependence.

For instance, Tim's low score on his algebra quiz (an environmental factor) influenced both his expectations about future success on algebra quizzes (a personal factor) and his behavior (he changed his study habits). His behavior influenced the environment (he studied at Susan's home) and his later expectations (he became more confident about his capability in algebra). And the environment (his initial low score) influenced both his expectations and his behavior. Figure 6.3 outlines the process of reciprocal causation, illustrated with Tim's experience.

We turn now to the core concepts in social cognitive theory, beginning with modeling.

Figure 6.3 Reciprocal causation in Tim's behavior

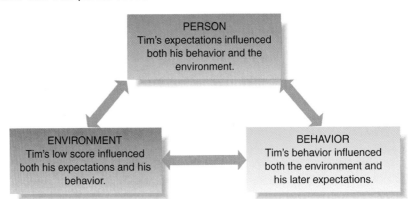

Modeling

6.3 **Describe the influence of modeling and the outcomes of modeling on people's behaviors.**

Modeling, a general term that refers to *behavioral, cognitive,* and *affective* changes deriving from observing the actions of others, is the central concept of social cognitive theory (Schunk, 2016). Tim, for example, observed that Susan was successful in her approach to studying for exams. As a result, he imitated her behavior; direct imitation is one form of modeling, and it was a behavioral change for Tim.

In other instances, cognitive changes can occur in individuals when they observe models articulate their thinking as they demonstrate skills, a process called **cognitive modeling** (Schunk, 2016). For instance:

MyLab Education
Video Example 6.4
Cognitive modeling involves individuals articulating their thinking at the same time they demonstrate skills. Here, fourth-grade teacher, Alicia Sanchez, uses cognitive modeling to help her students improve their reading comprehension.

"Wait," Jeanna Edwards says as she sees Nicole struggling with the microscope. "Let me show you. . . . Watch closely as I adjust it. The first thing I think about is getting the slide in place. Otherwise, I might not be able to find what I'm looking for. Then, I want to be sure I don't crack the slide while I lower the lens, so I watch from the side as I slowly lower the microscope. Finally, I slowly raise the lens until I have the object in focus. You were trying to focus as you lowered it. It's easier and safer if you try to focus as you raise it. Go ahead and try it."

By modeling her thinking as she demonstrated how to use the microscope, Jeanna created the potential for change in Nicole's thinking, that is, a change in her cognition.

Modeling can also result in affective (emotional) changes; when we see a person who is obviously uneasy or nervous in some situation, for example, we might also feel a bit uneasy. Or, when we watch a sitcom on TV and we see people laughing, we tend to spontaneously smile, or maybe even laugh out loud ourselves. The emotions we feel are the affective changes we experience as a result of seeing models display emotions.

Modeling can be *direct, symbolic,* or *synthesized.* For example, when teachers or coaches model intellectual or physical skills, they are *direct models.* Video recorded examples, as well as characters in movies, television, books, and plays, are *symbolic models,* and combining different portions of observed acts represents *synthesized modeling* (Bandura, 1986). Table 6.5 outlines these different forms of modeling.

TABLE 6.5 Different forms of modeling

Type of Modeling	Description	Examples
Direct modeling	An individual attempts to imitate the behavior or thinking of a live model.	Tim imitated Susan's study habits. A first-grader forms letters in the same way that the teacher forms them.
Symbolic modeling	People imitate behaviors and thinking displayed by characters in books, plays, movies, television, or the Internet.	People adopt fashion patterns displayed by influential people, such as movie stars or the First Lady of the United States. Teenagers adopt slang and slogans displayed by characters in a popular movie or television show oriented toward teens.
Synthesized modeling	People combine behaviors observed in different acts.	A child uses a chair to get up and open a cupboard door after seeing her brother use a chair to get a book from a shelf and seeing her mother open the cupboard door.

We find many applications of modeling in both our personal and professional lives. At a personal level, for instance, children learn acceptable ways of behaving by observing their parents and other adults. Teenagers' hair and dress are influenced by characters they see on television and in movies, and even as adults, we pick up cues from others in deciding how to dress and act.

In the professional world, businesses try to find leaders that can serve as models for both effective business practice and ethical behavior (Whitaker & Godwin, 2013; Wurthmann, 2013). In schools, teachers demonstrate a variety of skills, such as solutions to math problems, effective writing techniques, and critical thinking. When we teach, we also model positive personality traits, such as agreeableness and conscientiousness; social-emotional characteristics, such as self-management, empathy, and responsible decision making; tolerance for dissenting opinions; motivation to learn; and other positive attitudes and values in hopes that our students will develop these same characteristics. Coaches use modeling to demonstrate proper techniques for skills, such as hitting a serve in volleyball or making a corner kick in soccer, and they also model important ideas such as teamwork, a sense of fair play, humility in victory, and graciousness in defeat. And modeling is one of the most important mechanisms used to change learner behavior in applied behavior analysis (Daniel, Shabani, & Lam, 2013).

Modeling can also have unintended consequences, and we see examples in a range of areas. For instance, if a business culture focuses exclusively on profits or "the bottom line," and employees see their leaders modeling unethical behavior, they're more likely to behave in the same way (Whitaker & Godwin, 2013). In schools, modeling is suggested as a contributor to homophobic aggression in students; when students see others act negatively toward LGBTQ students, for instance, they conclude that these behaviors are acceptable (Prati, 2012). And professional athletes and other celebrities often unintentionally model inappropriate behaviors such as violence, aggression, and drug and alcohol abuse, inadvertently sending messages that these behaviors are acceptable or even valued.

As teachers we are models for our students, regardless of whether we choose to be or not. Our responsibility is to model the best that leaders and professionals have to offer.

We turn now to three important aspects of modeling:

- Outcomes of modeling
- Effectiveness of models
- Processes involved in learning from models

Outcomes of Modeling

So, what happens when we observe models? We call "what happens" the outcomes, or results, of modeling. These outcomes are the behavioral, cognitive, and affective changes that result from observing the actions of others. They can be classified into the categories we see in Figure 6.4. Let's look at them.

Learning New Behaviors.   Through imitation, we can acquire abilities we didn't have before observing a model. Solving an algebra problem after watching the teacher demonstrate a solution, making a new recipe after seeing it done on TV, or learning to write a clear paragraph after seeing an exemplary one are all examples. Kelly's comment, "I'm trying to swing at a ball like the softball players in college do, but I haven't been able to quite do it," indicates that she was attempting to learn a new behavior.

Facilitating Existing Behaviors.   You're attending a concert, and at the end of one of the numbers, someone stands and begins to applaud. You, and others, join in to create a standing ovation. Obviously, you already know how to stand and applaud, so you didn't learn something new. Instead, observing the model facilitated your behavior.

This outcome is also illustrated in Tim's case. He practiced solving problems before quizzes but admitted, "I usually do a couple, and if I get them, I quit." After observing

Figure 6.4 Outcomes of modeling

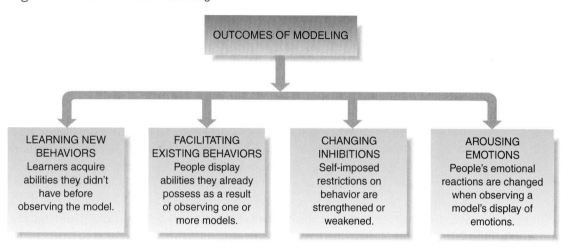

Susan, he changed the way he studied. Her approach to preparing for quizzes facilitated Tim's studying behavior.

Learning new behaviors and facilitating existing behaviors represent the "behavioral" changes we see in modeling.

Changing Inhibitions.   An **inhibition** is a self-imposed restriction on our behavior, and observing a model and the consequences of the model's behavior can either strengthen or weaken it. Unlike actions that facilitate existing behaviors, changing inhibitions focuses on socially unacceptable behaviors, such as breaking classroom rules (Schunk et al., 2014). For instance, students are less likely to break a rule if one of their peers is reprimanded; their inhibition about breaking the rule has been strengthened. Jacob Kounin (1970), a pioneer researcher in the area of classroom management, called this phenomenon the *ripple effect*. On the other hand, if a student speaks without permission and isn't reprimanded, other students are more likely to do the same. The inhibition is weakened.

Changed inhibitions represent some of the cognitive changes that can occur as a result of modeling. And, as we saw earlier, *cognitive modeling* can result in additional cognitive changes in learners.

Arousing Emotions.   Finally, a person's emotional reactions can be changed by observing a model's display of emotions, and these are the affective changes we see in modeling. For example, observing the uneasiness of a diver on a high board may cause an observer to become more fearful of the board. On the other hand, observing teachers genuinely enjoying themselves as they discuss a topic can generate similar enthusiasm in students.

An interesting aspect exists with respect to the affective changes that can result from modeling; the emotions we see modeled aren't necessarily the emotions that are aroused. For instance, suppose we observe two people involved in a heated argument in public. Anger is the emotion that is being modeled, but embarrassment or awkwardness is likely the emotion that we experience.

Effectiveness of Models

Ed Psych and You

We see a wide array of both direct models—people we encounter—and symbolic models, people we see in movies, on TV, and in written materials. We are more likely to model the behavior, thinking, or emotions of some than others. Why might this be the case?

The question we asked in *Ed Psych and You* relates to the "effectiveness" of a model—the likelihood that we will experience the behavioral, cognitive, or affective changes that can occur as a result of modeling. A model's effectiveness depends on three factors:

- Perceived similarity
- Perceived competence
- Perceived status

Perceived Similarity.   When we observe a model's behavior, we are more likely to imitate him or her if we perceive the model as similar to us. This helps us understand why presenting nontraditional career models and teaching students about the contributions of members of cultural minorities are important. Either gender can effectively demonstrate that engineering presents career opportunities, but girls are more likely to believe that it is a viable career if they observe a female instead of a male engineer, and research indicates that female college students are more likely to believe in their capabilities when taught by female faculty members (Johnson, 2017). Similarly, boys are more likely to consider nursing as a potential career if they observe male rather than female nurses, and members of cultural minorities are more likely to believe they can accomplish challenging goals if they see the accomplishments of successful members of their cultural group than one from another cultural group.

Perceived Competence.   Perception of a model's competence, the second factor influencing a model's effectiveness, interacts with perceived similarity. People are more likely to imitate models they perceive to be competent, regardless of similarity. Tim believed Susan was competent because she was a successful student. Although Tim and Susan are similar—they are classmates—he wouldn't have imitated her study habits if she hadn't been successful.

Perceived Status.   Perceived status is the third factor. Status is acquired when individuals distinguish themselves from others in their fields, and people tend to imitate models they perceive as having high status. Perceived status helps us understand why companies, such as Nike, will pay athletes millions of dollars to wear their clothing, and why entertainment stars are similarly rewarded for endorsing smartphones and other goods. At the school level, athletes, cheerleaders, and in some cases even gang members have high status.

High-status models enjoy an additional benefit. They are often tacitly credited for competence outside their own areas of expertise. This is why we see professional athletes (instead of nutritionists) endorsing breakfast cereal, and actors (instead of engineers) endorsing automobiles and other products.

Processes Involved in Learning from Models

How does modeling work? In other words, how do the behavioral, cognitive, or affective changes occur when we observe models? We address these questions in this section.

Four processes are involved in learning from models: *attention, retention, reproduction,* and *motivation* (Bandura, 1986). They're outlined in Figure 6.5 and described as follows:

- *Attention:* A learner's attention is drawn to the essential aspects of the modeled behavior.
- *Retention:* The modeled behaviors are transferred to memory and stored, which allows the learner to reproduce them later.
- *Reproduction:* Learners reproduce the behaviors that have been stored in memory.
- *Motivation:* Learners are motivated by the expectation of reinforcement for reproducing the modeled behaviors.

Figure 6.5 Processes involved in learning from models

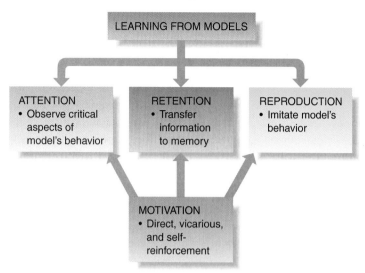

Three aspects of these processes are important. First, to learn from a model, our attention must be drawn to the essential features of the modeled behavior (Bandura, 1986). If we don't know what we're looking for, we don't know what behaviors we should attempt to retain and store. This is common in teacher education. For instance, preservice teachers often go into schools and observe expert veterans in action; the classroom is operating like a well-oiled machine, and the observer misses the actions the expert takes to make the class work this way. This suggests that we should specify the specific behaviors we attempt to model.

Second, attending to the modeled behaviors and recording them in memory doesn't ensure that observers will be able to reproduce them. Additional scaffolding and practice with feedback are often required. (We examine this issue in more detail in the section "Using Educational Psychology in Teaching: Suggestions for Applying Social Cognitive Theory to Increase Your Students' Learning," later in the chapter.)

Third, although motivation appears as a separate component in Figure 6.5, it is integral to each of the other processes. Motivated learners are more likely to attend to a model's behavior, to remember it, and to reproduce it. This is illustrated by the arrows from "motivation" pointing to each of the other processes.

Having examined modeling in detail, we turn now to other core concepts in social cognitive theory, beginning with vicarious learning.

MyLab Education Self-Check 6.3

Vicarious Learning

6.4 Use the concepts of vicarious learning, nonoccurrence of expected consequences, and self-regulation to explain people's behaviors.

Ed Psych and You

You're driving 75 miles an hour on the interstate, and you're passed by a sports car that appears to be going at least 80. The posted speed limit is 65. A moment later, you see the sports car pulled over by a highway patrol. You immediately slow down. Why do you slow down?

MyLab Education
Video Example 6.5

Vicarious learning occurs when people observe the consequences of others' actions and adjust their own behavior accordingly. Vicarious reinforcement is one type of vicarious learning, and here we see a teacher attempting to vicariously reinforce the students in her class by praising a particular student for being attentive and a good listener.

Think about the question we asked in *Ed Psych and You*. Nothing directly happened to you, and you didn't imitate anyone's behavior; you simply observed the consequence of the other driver's actions (he got pulled over), and you adjusted your behavior accordingly, a process called **vicarious learning** (Bandura, 1986; Myers, 2016). When you saw the sports car pulled over and you slowed down, you were *vicariously punished*—your speeding behavior decreased—and when a student is publicly reprimanded for leaving his seat without permission, other students in the class are also vicariously punished.

On the other hand, Tim saw how well Susan did on quizzes, so he was *vicariously reinforced* by her success, and his improved studying behavior increased. And, when Karen Engle—in one of the vignettes that introduced our discussion of social cognitive theory—said, "I really like the way Juanita has quickly put away her materials and is ready to listen," Juanita's classmates were also vicariously reinforced.

The influence of expectations helps us understand vicarious learning. Tim expected to be reinforced for imitating Susan's behavior, and the other students in Karen's class expected to be reinforced for putting their materials away. You expected to be ticketed (punished) if you continued speeding, so you slowed down.

Nonoccurrence of Expected Consequences

Earlier we saw that expectations are central to social cognitive theory, and they're also important because they influence behavior when they are not met. For instance, suppose you have instructors who give homework assignments, you work hard on the assignments, but the instructors don't collect them. The nonoccurrence of the expected reinforcers (credit for the assignments) can act as punishers; you are less likely to work as hard on subsequent assignments.

Just as the nonoccurrence of an expected reinforcer can act as a punisher, the nonoccurrence of an expected punisher can act as a reinforcer (Bandura, 1986). For instance, students expect to be reprimanded (punished) for breaking rules, so if they break rules and aren't reprimanded, they are more likely to break rules in the future (Skatova & Ferguson, 2013). The nonoccurrence of the expected punisher (the reprimand) acts as a reinforcer for the misbehavior.

The nonoccurrence of expected consequences is common in our everyday world. If you send an email to an acquaintance, you expect a reply, and receiving the reply is reinforcing. If the person doesn't reply, you're less likely to send her emails in the future. Sports fans buy season tickets to see their local team play, but if the team consistently loses, they're less likely to buy tickets in the future. Seeing the team win is reinforcing, and its nonoccurrence decreases fans' season-ticket-buying behavior.

Self-Regulation

Ed Psych and You

How well do you control your emotions? Are you impulsive? Do you set goals? How important is it to you to believe that you control the events that influence your life?

The answers to the questions in *Ed Psych and You* are related to the concept of **self-regulation (SR)**, "the ability to control thoughts and actions to achieve personal goals and respond to environmental demands. One key within this definition is that self-regulating individuals take deliberate control over their engagement in daily activities" (Butler, Schnellert, & Perry, 2017, p. 2). Self-regulation is an integral component of social cognitive theory, which assumes that people want to control the events that affect their lives (Bandura, 1997).

Self-regulation is essential, both in classrooms and in life outside of school. "[D]eficits in self-regulation are found in a large number of psychological disorders including attention-deficit/hyperactivity disorder [ADHD], antisocial personality disorder, . . . addiction, eating disorders, and impulse control disorders" (Legault & Inzlicht, 2013, p. 123). In contrast, well-developed self-regulation has benefits ranging from improved social relationships, to the tendency to exercise, to the treatment of chronic diseases, such as diabetes, and the ability to eliminate bad habits (Fiala, Rhodes, Blanchard, & Anderson, 2013; Plotnikoff, Costigan, Karunamuni, & Lubans, 2013).

APA Top 20 Principles

This description illustrates Principle 7: *Students self-regulation assists learning, and self-regulatory skills can be taught*—from the *Top 20 Principles from Psychology for PreK–12 Teaching and Learning*.

Self-regulation is particularly important to you as a college or university student because of the many demands on your time, thinking, and emotions. Let's look at a possible case.

You're tired from a long day at school, perhaps combined with work, and some friends suggest that you go out for a while. You have a homework assignment for one of your classes, but it's about the last thing you want to do. Your first thought is to simply bag it and go out with your friends, since the assignment probably won't have a major impact on your grade in the class.

You know that completing the assignment is important, however, so you set the goal of finishing at least half of it before you go to bed. You get a cup of coffee, sit down, and before too long, you see that you've reached your goal. Rejuvenated, you redouble your efforts and finish the entire assignment.

Some research suggests that self-regulation is the primary factor influencing the success or failure of university students, and our example helps us understand why (Cohen, 2012).

Self-regulation is complex, and in the case you exhibited several of its dimensions (outlined in Figure 6.6). First you displayed impulse control by resisting the temptation to go out instead of working on your homework, you showed self-motivation by deciding to stay in and complete the assignment, and because you received little immediate reward for completing it, you also demonstrated **delay of gratification**, the ability to forgo an immediate pleasure or reward in order to gain a more substantial one later—the more substantial being the knowledge and skills you acquire from doing your homework and perhaps the higher grade you earn in your class.

Now, let's look at *self-regulated learning* in more detail.

Self-Regulated Learning

In Figure 6.6 we see that *self-regulated learning* is one of the components of the SR model. **Self-regulated learning** is the process of setting personal goals, combined with the motivation, thinking, strategies, and behaviors that lead to reaching the goals (Zimmerman & Schunk, 2013). It was the process Tim, in our chapter-opening case study, used to change his study strategies and improve his performance on algebra quizzes. He knew that Susan was a successful student, so he went to her home, observed her in action, and, as a result of her modeling, adopted study strategies similar to hers. Self-regulated learning is the mechanism that allows students like Tim to capitalize on what they learn from observing models (Hessels-Schlatter, Hessels, Godin, & Spillmann-Rojas, 2017).

Figure 6.6 A model of self-regulation

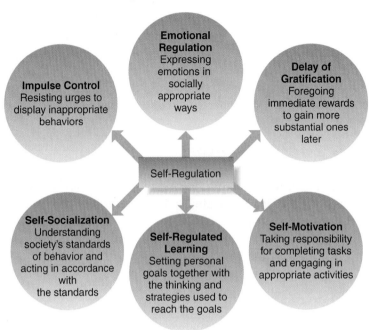

Choice is an essential element of self-regulated learning (Schunk, 2016). When learners have choices, they can decide who to observe and how they will integrate the modeled behaviors into their own actions. Tim, for example, chose to go to Susan's house and work with her and, based on the behaviors she modeled, he chose his own goals. The development of self-regulated learning is difficult, if not impossible, when all aspects of a task are controlled. For example, if a teacher requires that students write 5 typewritten pages on an assigned topic, in a given format, that includes a minimum of 10 references, opportunities to develop self-regulated learning are reduced.

Self-regulated learning includes the following components (Hessels-Schlatter et al., 2017; Zimmerman & Schunk, 2013):

- Goal setting
- Self-monitoring
- Self-assessment
- Strategy use

Goal Setting.   Goals provide direction for our actions and benchmarks for measuring progress. The goals and actions we select are often outcomes of behaviors we see modeled by others. For instance, Susan set the goal of working at least three of each type of algebra problem, and Tim imitated her behavior by setting a similar goal of his own. As a result of seeing other people exercise or succeed in losing weight, we might set the goal of jogging 25 miles a week, or limiting our food intake to 1,800 calories per day, for instance.

Goal setting is at the heart of self-regulated learning, and it is one of the most difficult aspects of the process to implement with students. For it to work, students must be committed to challenging but realistic goals, and they are more likely to commit to goals they set for themselves than to goals set by others (Schunk et al., 2014). This is often problematic, because many students aren't motivated to set goals in the first place, and when they do, the goals are often simple and easy to attain.

Self-Monitoring. Once we've set goals, as self-regulated learners we continually monitor our actions. For instance, we can keep track of the number of miles we've jogged during a week, or monitor the number of calories we consume each day. Susan said, "I sometimes even make a little chart. I try to do at least three problems of each type we study, and then I check them off as I do them."

Students can be taught to monitor a variety of behaviors. For example, they can keep a chart and make a check every time they catch themselves "drifting off" during an hour of study, whenever they blurt out an answer in class, or when they compliment a classmate. Self-monitoring combined with appropriate goals can improve concentration, study habits, and even social skills (Alberto & Troutman, 2017).

Self-Assessment. Self-assessment helps us determine the extent to which our goals are being met. For instance, if we jog 5 miles on Sunday, 3 on Monday, 5 on Tuesday, and 5 more on Thursday, we know that we'll need to get in 7 more miles by Saturday to reach our goal of 25 miles for the week. Similarly, if we've consumed 1,200 calories but still haven't had our evening meal, we might forgo dessert.

Students can also learn to assess their own work (Chappuis & Stiggins, 2017). For example, they can determine the quality of their solutions to word problems by comparing their answers with estimates and asking themselves if the answers make sense. Tim's comparing his answers to those in the back of the book is a form of self-assessment.

Self-assessment can also contribute to motivation and personal satisfaction. For instance, when we realize that we need seven more miles to reach our goal for the week, we will be motivated to go out for a run. The satisfaction associated with reaching goals often leads to a form of self-reward (Schunk, 2016). For instance, if we've reached our weekly calorie goals for a month straight, we may reward ourselves with a nice dinner out with friends, a new outfit, or a couple days off from dieting. Susan, for example, commented, "If I get them [the problems] all right, I might treat myself with a dish of ice cream." Reaching the goal is satisfying, and the more challenging—within reason—the goal, the more satisfying reaching it will be. In fact, the more times we reach our weekly goal, the more motivated we'll be to attain it in the future.

Self-assessment can also help solve the problem of students' not wanting to set goals or wanting to set trivial and easily-attainable goals. As they see progress toward reaching their goals, their motivation will increase, and they'll be more likely to commit to other goals in the future.

Strategy Use. Strategy use connects actions to our goals. To be self-regulated, learners must be able to match effective strategies to their goals. For example, Tim initially worked a few practice problems, and if he was able to do them, he quit. But, because of Susan's modeling, he selected a wider variety of problems. This simple change was a more effective strategy.

Even young children can use strategies. For example, if a first-grader practices more on spelling words he doesn't know than on those he can already spell, he is being strategic.

Helping students become self-regulated learners is powerful but demanding. For example, students need a great deal of help in setting challenging but realistic goals, and students won't initially be good at monitoring their own progress, conducting self-assessments, and selecting appropriate strategies (Dalland & Klette, 2016). **Cognitive behavior modification**, a procedure that promotes behavioral change and self-regulation through self-talk and self-instruction, is a tool that we can use to help our students develop these abilities (Meichenbaum, 2000). The procedure begins with cognitive modeling. If a student is disorganized and scattered, for example, we model both the actions and the thinking involved in setting an appropriate goal, such as bringing a pencil, notebook paper, textbook, and completed homework assignment to class each day. We can also model the process of monitoring progress and assessing the extent to which our student is meeting the goal. The student can use a simple checklist that includes each of the items, and we can demonstrate how the items are checked off each day, for instance.

After observing cognitive modeling, our students practice the skill with our support and then use self-talk as a guide when performing the skills without supervision. Cognitive behavior modification strategies are particularly effective with students having exceptionalities (Turnbull, Turnbull, Wehmeyer, & Shogren, 2016).

In spite of our best efforts, not all of our students will become self-regulated learners, but for those with whom we succeed, we will have made a lifelong contribution to their success as a student and to their lives in general.

Diversity: Learner Differences in Self-Regulation

As with all aspects of learning and development, students differ with respect to self-regulation. It develops over time, and older students are better at it than their younger counterparts. But even students of the same age will differ considerably in their ability to regulate their cognition, behavior, and emotions, and these differences are a function of both genetics and the environment (Berk, 2019a). For instance, when self-regulation breaks down, as it inevitably will, learners who have developed a greater sense of autonomy tend to adapt their goals and approaches to both social and cognitive problem solving (Legault & Inzlicht, 2013). This suggests that we should be doing whatever we can to help learners acquire a sense of autonomy and independence when we work with young people; it can make a significant difference in their development of self-regulation. Providing students with choices in their learning and communicating that they are personally responsible for their own behavior can help promote a sense of autonomy.

Gender differences in self-regulation also exist, particularly in the ability to resist destructive impulses and substitute behaviors that are more productive. For example, girls are more likely to discuss a disagreement and seek a cognitive resolution than boys, who are more inclined to behave aggressively in a similar circumstance (Walker, Shapiro, Esterberg, & Trotman, 2010). Brain development tends to progress more quickly in girls than in boys, and differences in self-regulation can be found as early as kindergarten (Berk, 2019b).

Cultural differences exist as well. For instance, as a general pattern, students from East Asian cultures, such as Chinese, Japanese, and Korean, place a great deal of emphasis on self-discipline and emotional control. They also strongly emphasize the role of hard work and sustained effort in academic success, and they develop self-regulated learning processes, such as goal setting, monitoring, and strategy use, at an early age (Chen & Wang, 2010).

As with all aspects of diversity, we're describing general patterns here, and many exceptions exist. The patterns contribute to our professional knowledge, but ultimately we are working with individuals and we must make decisions that we believe are in those individuals' best interests, even if they don't fit a pattern.

Using Educational Psychology in Teaching: Suggestions for Applying Social Cognitive Theory to Increase Your Students' Learning

Social cognitive theory has a wide range of classroom applications, and these applications can make a significant difference in student learning. Suggestions for applying the theory with your students include:

- Capitalize on modeling.
- Use vicarious reinforcement and punishment as learning and management tools.
- Follow through on all aspects of instruction and classroom management.
- Promote self-regulation.

Let's examine these suggestions in more detail.

Capitalize on Modeling.   Modeling is one of the most powerful influences on learning, and it is at the heart of social cognitive theory. We can capitalize on it in several ways:

- Putting students in modeling roles and emphasizing cognitive modeling.
- Using guest role models.
- Carefully modeling skills, solutions to problems, and other desirable behaviors and emotions.

Let's see how Sally Campese, an eighth-grade algebra teacher, capitalizes on modeling with her students. Sally is working with her students on simultaneous equations, she has modeled the process for solving them, and she has assigned homework in which her students are required to reproduce the modeled behaviors, that is, solve systems of equations on their own. We join her class now.

"We'd better get going," Logan says to Tameka as they approach Sally's room. "You know how she is. She thinks algebra is sooo important."

"Yes, and I hope you did your homework. She makes such a big deal about being responsible for doing it every night," Tameka comments in return.

As Sally begins her class, she comments, "Just a reminder. I've invited a man named Javier Sanchez to speak on Friday. He is an engineer who works at a local factory, and he's going to tell you how he uses math in his job.

"Okay, look here," Sally says, turning to the day's topic. "We had a little difficulty with our homework, so let's go over a few more problems.

"Try this one," she says, writing the following on the board:

$$4a + 6b = 24$$

$$5a - 6b = 3$$

Sally watches, and seeing that Gabriela has solved the problem successfully, says, "Gabriela, come up to the board and describe your thinking for us as you solved the problem."

Gabriela explains that she added the two equations to get $9a + 0b = 27$, and as she writes the new equation on the board, Sally then asks, "So what do we get for the value of a? . . . Chris?"

" . . . Three."

"And how did you get that?"

"Zero b is zero, and I divided both sides by 9, so I have 1a equals 3."

"Good! . . . Now, let's find the value of b. What should we do first? . . . Mitchell?"

Now, let's look at Sally's attempts to use modeling to promote learning in her students. First, she used Gabriela as a model, and by asking Gabriela to explain her thinking, she also took advantage of cognitive modeling. A classmate can often be a more effective model than a teacher because of perceived similarity.

Sally also utilized modeling by inviting Mr. Sanchez to her class. Because he was Hispanic, he would, also through perceived similarity, be an effective model for her students who are members of cultural minorities. Inviting someone like Mr. Sanchez even once or twice a year can do much to capitalize on the influence of minority role models.

Finally, and perhaps most important, Sally—herself—was a positive model in two important ways. First, she carefully modeled solutions to simultaneous equations, and when students struggled to reproduce solutions on their own, she didn't simply re-explain the topic. Instead, she interacted with them, addressed them by name, and guided their developing understanding with her questioning. This illustrates expert instruction.

Second, at a personal level, Logan's comment, "She thinks algebra is sooo important," almost certainly resulted from Sally's modeling her own genuine interest in the topic. Modeling won't make all students enthusiastic learners, but it can make a difference in student motivation, as we saw in Logan's remark (Brophy, 2010). Tameka's reply, "Yes, and I hope you did your homework. She makes such a big deal about being responsible for it every night," provides more evidence of modeling. Sally modeled elements of self-regulation that we hope to see our students develop. She is working with students early in their teen years, and teens learn what's effective and appropriate by observing their parents, teachers, and other adults. When we communicate by our words and actions that learning is not only important, but also requires hard work and self-discipline, over time students will get the message. Sally's modeling probably did as much to promote self-regulation in her students as any formal strategy would have done.

Use Vicarious Reinforcement and Punishment as Learning and Management Tools. Vicarious learning can be an effective tool, particularly when working with younger children. Comments, such as "Stephanie is doing a very good job of staying on task" and "I really like the way Fernando is standing so quietly in line," have a positive impact on both the behavior and achievement of your students.

With older students, comments that suggest progress toward goals can be helpful. For instance, saying "Good job of identifying evidence to support your conclusion, Natalie. That's one of our goals" helps keep the focus on achievement rather than personal behavior or characteristics, and reduces issues that sometimes exist when publically praising older students.

Follow-Through on All Aspects of Classroom Management and Instruction. "Never establish a rule or procedure you aren't committed to enforcing" is a principle that applies in classroom management, and expectations are important cognitive processes that apply to the principle. We know that the nonoccurrence of expected punishers can act as reinforcers, so if you establish a rule, students *expect* to be admonished—or punished in some other way—for breaking the rule. If they aren't, its nonoccurrence can act as a reinforcer, making it more likely that they'll break the rule in the future. If we aren't committed to consistently enforcing rules, we're better off without the rules in the first place.

APA Top 20 Principles

This description illustrates *Principle 16: Expectations for classroom conduct and social interaction are learned and can be taught using proven principles of behavior and effective classroom instruction*— from the *Top 20 Principles from Psychology for PreK–12 Teaching and Learning.*

Expectations are also important with respect to academic work. For instance, if we give assignments, students expect some recognition, such as credit on their final grades and feedback for what they've done, which are reinforcers. If the reinforcers aren't received, their nonoccurrence can act as punishers, making it less likely that they will exert the same amount of effort on subsequent assignments. This is why follow-through is so important, both in classroom management and in instruction.

Promote Self-Regulation. As we saw earlier, "good self-regulators—those who can aptly manage the circumstances and impulses that obstruct goal attainment—are happier, healthier, and more productive" (Legault & Inzlicht, 2013, p. 123). Developing our students' self-regulation is one of the most worthwhile goals we can strive for in our teaching.

We can promote self-regulation in a number of ways. With young students it can be as simple as establishing rules, such as listening quietly while classmates are talking and raising hands for permission to speak; routines, such as turning in papers and lining up for breaks; and discussions about how to treat others, combined with practicing appropriate social responses. Because cognition (thinking) is an important component of self-regulation, it's important to discuss reasons for each of these processes.

The importance of the cognitive component of self-regulation is even more important with older students, who are still learning how to control their actions and emotions. Several suggestions to help them in the process include (Miller, 2013):

- Discuss the importance of different aspects of self-regulation, such as impulse control and the consequences of not controlling impulses. The adolescent years are filled with temptations for instant gratification and the disregard of control. Helping students understand consequences can make a difference.

- Explain expectations for appropriate behavior. Adolescents sometimes display inappropriate behaviors simply because they're not clear about what is expected of them. Clear expectations also communicate that you care and help them acquire a sense of equilibrium in their lives.

- Teach students positive self-talk and stress management techniques to help them stay cool in stressful or anxiety-provoking circumstances. This can help when they feel anxious or experience the impulse to behave aggressively.

- Encourage physical activity or participation in sports. Physical activity has a calming effect by helping students blow off steam and release stress. And it has general health benefits and can teach the importance of setting and monitoring goals.

MyLab Education Application Exercise 6.4: Learning through Modeling in Second Grade

In this exercise you will be asked to analyze a second-grade grade teacher's applications of modeling to promote learning in her students.

Evaluating Social Cognitive Theory

Like all theories, social cognitive theory has both limitations and strengths. The following are some criticisms:

- Social cognitive theory can't explain why learners attend to some modeled behaviors but not others, and it can't explain why learners can reproduce some behaviors they observe but can't reproduce others.

- It doesn't account for the acquisition of complex abilities—beyond mere mechanics—such as learning to write.

- It can't explain the role of context and social interaction in complex learning environments. For example, research indicates that student interaction in small groups facilitates learning (Schunk, 2016). The processes involved in these settings extend beyond simple modeling and imitation.

On the other hand, social cognitive theory has important strengths. For example, modeling is one of the most powerful factors influencing both our behavior and classroom learning, and social cognitive theory provides us with suggestions about how to use modeling effectively in our teaching. Social cognitive theory also overcomes many of the limitations of behaviorism by helping us understand the importance of learner cognitions, and particularly expectations, on our actions (Schunk et al., 2014). It provides us with additional tools that we can use to maximize learning for all our students.

Table 6.6 outlines the contributions and criticisms of social cognitive theory.

TABLE 6.6 Analyzing theories: Social cognitive theory

Key question	How does observing others influence cognition and behavior?
Definition of learning	Change in mental processes that creates the capacity to demonstrate a change in behavior
Catalysts for learning	• Observations of others' behaviors • Observations of the consequences of others' behaviors • Expectations
Key concepts	Modeling Reciprocal causation Vicarious learning • Vicarious reinforcement • Vicarious punishment Nonoccurrence of expected consequences Self-regulation
Contributions of theory	• Explains how observations of others' behaviors (modeling and the consequences of modeled behavior) influence our behavior, and modeling is one of the most powerful influences on people's behavior • Is able to explain changes in behavior that behaviorism cannot explain • Provides an effective framework for working with students in general and teaching practice in particular
Criticisms of theory	• Cannot explain why people attend to and reproduce some modeled behaviors, but not others • Has difficulty explaining the acquisition of complex cognitive abilities • Doesn't account for the role of context and social interaction in learning

---

MyLab Education Self-Check 6.4

Classroom Connections

Capitalizing on Social Cognitive Theory in Classrooms

1. Cognitive modeling involves verbalizing your thinking as you demonstrate a skill. Use cognitive modeling in your instruction, and act as a role model for your students.

   • **Elementary:** A kindergarten teacher helps her children form letters by saying as she writes on the board, "I start with my pencil here and make a straight line down," as she begins to form a *b*.

   • **Middle School:** A seventh-grade teacher has a large poster at the front of his room that says, "I will always treat you with courtesy and respect, you will treat me with courtesy and respect, and you will treat each other with courtesy and respect." When a problem surfaces in his classroom he talks about it, discussing possible causes and alternate solutions. He hopes that by modeling this strategy his students will learn to problem solve interpersonal problems themselves.

   • **High School:** A physics teacher solving acceleration problems writes F = ma on the board and says, "First, I know I want to find the force on the object. Then, I think about what the problem tells me. Tell us one thing we know about the problem, . . . Lisa."

2. Effective modeling requires that students attend to a behavior, retain it in memory, and then reproduce it. To capitalize on these processes, provide group practice by walking students through examples before having them practice on their own.

   • **Elementary:** A fourth-grade class is adding fractions with unlike denominators. The teacher displays the problem 1/4 + 2/3 = ? and then asks, "What do we need to do first? . . . Karen?" She continues guiding the students with questioning as they solve the problem.

   • **Middle School:** After showing students how to find exact locations using longitude and latitude, a seventh-grade geography teacher says to his students, "We want to find the city closest to 85° west and 37° north. What do these numbers tell us? . . . Josh?" He continues to guide students through the example until they locate Chicago as the closest city.

   • **High School:** After demonstrating several proofs, a geometry teacher wants her students to prove that angle 1 is greater than angle 2 in the accompanying drawing.

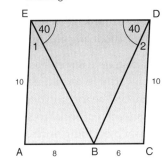

She begins by asking, "What are we given?" After students identify the givens in the problem, she asks, "What can we conclude about segments BE and BD?" and continues to guide students to a completion of the proof with her questions.

3. When learners observe a classmate being reinforced, they are vicariously reinforced. Use vicarious reinforcement to improve behavior and increase learning.

- **Elementary:** As students in a reading group move back to their desks, a first-grade teacher comments, "I like the way this group is quietly returning to their desks. Karen, Vicki, Ali, and David each get a star."

- **Middle School:** An eighth-grade English teacher displays (anonymous) examples of well-written paragraphs on the overhead and comments, "Each of these has excellent paragraph structure, and each shows some imagination. Let's look at them more closely."

- **High School:** An art teacher displays several well-done pottery pieces and comments, "Look at these, everyone. These are excellent. Let's see why . . . . "

The English and art teachers accomplished three things. First, the students whose paragraphs or pottery were displayed were directly reinforced, but they weren't put on the spot, because the teachers didn't identify them. Second, the rest of the students in the classes were vicariously reinforced. Third, the teachers gave their classes feedback and provided concrete models for future imitation.

4. Self-regulated learning is the process of students taking responsibility for their own understanding. Teach students to be self-regulated learners by providing opportunities for them to set goals, use strategies, and monitor progress toward those goals.

- **Elementary:** A third-grade teacher helps his students, who are having problems staying in their seats, design a checklist that they can use to monitor their own behavior. The teacher initially reminds them to make a check when they are out of their seats, and later he monitors the students to see if they've given themselves checks when appropriate.

- **Middle School:** A pre-algebra teacher helps her students create a rating scale to assess their progress on homework. For each assignment, they circle a 3 if they complete the assignment and believe they understand it, a 2 if they complete it but are uncertain about their understanding, and a 1 if they do not complete it. The teacher asks for feedback on these ratings and discusses common problems the students encountered.

- **High School:** An English teacher helps his students set individual goals by asking each to write a study plan. He returns to the plan at the end of the unit and has each student assess his or her progress.

Developmentally Appropriate Practice

Applying Behaviorism and Social Cognitive Theory with Learners at Different Ages

While many applications of behaviorism and social cognitive theory apply at all grade levels, some important developmental differences exist. The following paragraphs outline some of these differences.

Working with Students in Early Childhood Programs and Elementary Schools

The emotional environment we create for our students is important at all levels but is crucial when we work with young children. This explains why preschool, kindergarten, and first-grade teachers make a special effort to connect with students by, for example, giving hugs or "high fives" when children come into their classrooms.

Young children bask openly in positive reinforcement, and it is virtually impossible to satiate them with praise. On the other hand, they respond to punishment quite differently. Because their moral reasoning tends to be external, they conclude that they must be "bad" if they're punished, so punishment should be used sparingly and judiciously (Berk, 2019b). Physical

punishment and humiliation should never be used in classrooms, and they are particularly destructive with young children.

When using modeling, attention is important. Because young children's attention wanders, modeling can be problematic; children often don't attend to the modeled behavior and may not focus on important aspects of the modeled behavior. This means that modeling must be very explicit and concrete.

Working with Students in Middle Schools

A warm and supportive classroom environment continues to be important with middle school students, and, because they are going through many physical, intellectual, and emotional changes, consistent enforcement of rules and procedures is essential to help them maintain their sense of equilibrium. Middle school students become increasingly sensitive to inconsistent treatment by their teachers, and fairness is very important to them.

Middle school students evaluate the praise they receive and may even react negatively to praise they view as insincere or unwarranted.

(continued)

Because of improved language skills, cognitive modeling becomes a valuable instructional tool. They are capable of developing self-regulation but are unlikely to do so without extensive guidance and support.

Working with Students in High Schools

Classroom climate remains important with high school students, but the focus turns more to treating students with respect and communicating that you're genuinely committed to their learning. These students continue to be sensitive to perceptions of fairness and teachers' favoring some students over others (Emmer & Evertson, 2017).

Praise that communicates that their understanding is increasing is very effective and can increase these students' intrinsic motivation (Deci & Ryan, 2002).

High school students are increasingly self-regulated, and they're capable of setting and monitoring goals and using sophisticated learning strategies. However, they—and particularly lower achievers—are unlikely to use strategies effectively without extensive monitoring and support (Pressley & Hilden, 2006). Modeling effective strategy use becomes particularly important, and cognitive modeling can be a very effective tool for promoting self-regulation.

Chapter 6 Summary

1. Use classical conditioning to explain events in and outside of classrooms.
   - Classical conditioning occurs when a formerly neutral stimulus, such as a teacher's room, becomes associated with a naturally occurring (unconditioned) stimulus, such as the teacher's warm and inviting manner, to produce a response similar to an instinctive or reflexive response, such as feelings of safety.
   - Generalization occurs when a stimulus similar to a conditioned stimulus triggers the conditioned response, and discrimination occurs when a stimulus fails to trigger the conditioned response.
   - Extinction occurs when the conditioned stimulus occurs often enough in the absence of the unconditioned stimulus that the conditioned response disappears.

2. Identify examples of operant conditioning in and outside of classrooms.
   - Operant conditioning focuses on voluntary responses that are influenced by consequences. Consequences that increase behavior are reinforcers. Teacher praise, high test scores, and good grades are common reinforcers.
   - Schedules of reinforcement influence both the rate of initial learning and the persistence of the behavior.
   - Shaping is the process of reinforcing successive approximations of a behavior.
   - Antecedents precede and induce behaviors that can then be reinforced. They exist in the form of environmental stimuli, prompts and cues, and past experiences.
   - Consequences that decrease behavior are punishers. Teacher reprimands and removing students' free time are common punishers.

3. Describe the influence of modeling and the outcomes of modeling on people's behaviors
   - Modeling is the core concept of social cognitive theory. Modeling can be direct (from live models), symbolic (from books, movies, and television), or synthesized (combining the acts of different models).
   - Cognitive modeling occurs when models describe their thinking as they demonstrate skills.
   - The outcomes of modeling include learning new behaviors, facilitating existing behaviors, changing inhibitions, and arousing emotions.
   - The effectiveness of models describes the likelihood of an observer imitating a model's behavior, and it depends on the perceived similarity, perceived status, and perceived competence of the model.
   - When modeling occurs, observers first attend to the model, retain the modeled behaviors in memory, and reproduce the modeled behavior. Motivation supports each of the other modeling processes.

4. Use the concepts of vicarious learning, the nonoccurrence of expected consequences, and self-regulation to explain people's behaviors.
   - Vicarious learning occurs when people observe the consequences of others' behaviors and adjust their own behavior accordingly, such as students increasing their attempts to answer teachers' questions after seeing a classmate attempt to answer, or students stopping talking after seeing a classmate reprimanded for talking without permission.
   - The nonoccurrence of expected reinforcers can act as punishers, and the nonoccurrence of expected punishers can act as reinforcers. As an example, students expect to be reprimanded if they break a rule, and if they aren't, the nonoccurrence of the expected reprimand can become a reinforcer for talking without permission, thereby increasing the likelihood of speaking without permission.
   - Social cognitive theory assumes that people want to control events that affect their lives, and they exercise this control by directing and controlling their actions, thoughts, and emotions toward meeting goals, a process called *self-regulation*. People who are self-regulated are more successful in both school and life after the school years than are their less well-regulated peers.
   - Self-regulation includes factors such as impulse control, delay of gratification, self-motivation, and self-regulated learning.
   - Self-regulated learning, one aspect of self-regulation, includes setting goals, monitoring and assessing goal attainment, and strategy use.

Preparing for Your Licensure Exam

Understanding Behaviorism and Social Cognitive Theory

You will be required to take a licensure exam before you go into your own classroom. This exam will include information related to behaviorism and social cognitive theory, and it will include both multiple-choice and constructed-response questions. We include the following exercises to help you practice for the exam in your state. This book and these exercises will be a resource for you as you prepare for the exam.

You've seen how you can use behaviorism and social cognitive theory to explain and influence student learning. Let's look now at a lesson to see how effectively the teacher applied these theories in his work with his students.

Warren Rose's fifth-graders are working on a unit on decimals and percentages. He begins class on Thursday by saying, "Let's look at this problem."

Hearing some mumbles, he notes wryly, "I realize that percentages and decimals aren't your favorite topic, and I'm not wild about them either, but we have to learn them, so we might as well get started."

> You are at the mall, shopping for a jacket. You see one that looks great, originally priced at $84, marked 25% off. You recently got a check for $65 from the fast-food restaurant where you work. Can you afford the jacket?

"Now, . . . when I see a problem like this, I think, 'What does the jacket cost now?' I have to figure out the price, and to do that I will take 25% of the $84. . . . That means I first convert the 25% to a decimal. I know when I see 25% that the decimal is understood to be just to the right of the 5, so I move it two places to the left. Then I can multiply 0.25 times 84."

Warren demonstrates the process as he talks, working the problem to completion. He has his students work several additional examples at their desks and discusses their solutions. He then continues, "Okay, for homework, do the odd problems on page 113."

"Do we have to do all eight of them?" Robbie asks.

Several other students chime in, arguing that eight word problems are too many. "Wait, people, please," Warren holds up his hands. "All right. You only have to do 1, 3, 5, 7, and 9."

"Yeah!" the class shouts, and they then go to work on the problems.

Questions for Case Analysis

Use information from this chapter and the case study to answer the following questions.

Multiple-Choice Questions:

1. Which of the following best illustrates a case of negative reinforcement in Warren's interaction with his students?

   a. Warren commenting, "I realize that percentages and decimals aren't your favorite topic, and I'm not wild about them either, but we have to learn them, so we might as well get started."

   b. Warren saying, "Now, . . . when I see a problem like this, I think, 'What does the jacket cost now?' I have to figure out the price . . . "

   c. The students working several examples at their desks and discussing the solutions.

   d. The students complaining and Warren decreasing the length of the homework assignment in response to their complaints.

2. Which of the following best illustrates a case of punishment in Warren's interaction with his students?

   a. Warren reducing the length of the homework assignment in response to the students' complaints.

   b. Warren originally assigning eight problems for homework.

   c. Warren commenting, "I'm not wild about them either," as he talked about decimals and percentages.

   d. Warren having his students solve several problems at their desks and discussing their solutions.

Constructed-Response Question

1. Assess Warren's application of modeling in his work with his students. Include both effective and ineffective applications if they exist.

Important Concepts

antecedents

applied behavior analysis
   (ABA)

behaviorism

classical conditioning

cognitive behavior
   modification

cognitive modeling

conditioned response
   (CR)

conditioned stimuli (CS)

consequences

continuous reinforcement
   schedule

corporal punishment

delay of gratification

desist

discrimination

extinction (classical
   conditioning)

extinction (operant
   conditioning)

functional analysis

generalization

inhibition

intermittent reinforce-
   ment schedule

interval schedule of
   reinforcement

learning (behaviorism)

learning (cognitive)

modeling

negative reinforcement

neutral stimulus

non-exclusion timeout

operant conditioning

positive behavior support

positive reinforcement

Premack principle

presentation punishment

primary reinforcers

punishers

punishment

ratio schedule of
   reinforcement

reciprocal causation

reinforcement

reinforcement schedules

reinforcer

removal punishment

response cost

satiation

secondary
   reinforcers

self-regulated
   learning

self-regulation (SR)

shaping

social cognitive theory

unconditioned response
   (UR)

unconditioned stimulus
   (US)

vicarious learning

Chapter 7
Cognitive Views of Learning

Maskot/Getty Images

Learning Outcomes

After you have completed your study of this chapter, you should be able to:

7.1 Describe principles of cognitive learning theory, and identify applications of the principles in classrooms and life outside of school.

7.2 Use the memory stores in the human memory model to explain events in classrooms and in our daily lives.

7.3 Describe the cognitive processes in the human memory model, and identify applications in classrooms and everyday events.

7.4 Define metacognition and identify examples of metacognitive monitoring in classroom activities and experiences outside of school.

7.5 Analyze classroom applications of information processing and the model of human memory.

APA Top 20 Principles

Top 20 Principles from Psychology for PreK–12 Teaching and Learning explicitly addressed in this chapter.

Principle 2: What students already know affects their learning.
Principle 4: Learning is based on context, so generalizing learning to new contexts is not spontaneous but instead needs to be facilitated.
Principle 5: Acquiring long-term knowledge and skill is largely dependent on practice.

National Council on Teacher Quality (NCTQ)

The NCTQ Essential Teaching Strategies that every new teacher needs to know specifically addressed in this chapter.

Strategy 2: Linking abstract concepts with concrete representations
Strategy 3: Posing probing questions

Cognitive is in the title of this chapter, and the terms *cognitive* and *cognition* imply "thinking." Because cognitive learning theory has become the predominant framework for understanding learning and guiding teaching, we begin this chapter by presenting a classroom application of it.

Mike Davis, a ninth-grade English teacher, wants his students to understand figurative language concepts, such as *metaphor, simile,* and *personification,* and he wants his students to see how Harper Lee (1960) used figurative language to make her classic of modern American literature, *To Kill a Mockingbird,* vivid and interesting. His efforts are designed to help his students meet the following standard:

CCSS.ELA-Literacy.RL.9-10.4 Determine the meaning of words and phrases as they are used in the text, including figurative and connotative meanings . . . (Common Core State Standards Initiative, 2018g).

Mike begins on a Monday morning by writing the following on the board:

You people are a breath of fresh air.

This class is like the sugar in my morning coffee.

"What do you think about that?" he asks as he sees his students look quizzically at the sentences. "Go ahead. . . . Tell me what these statements mean to you."

The students offer comments, such as, "That's nice," "Do you really mean it?" and "What are you talking about?"

Mike continues, "When you look at the statements, do you think I mean you are really, . . . or *literally*, a breath of fresh air, or are you *literally* like the sugar in my coffee?"

Several of them shake their heads and some comment, "Not really."

"True," Mike smiles. "I do enjoy all of you, but no, I don't *literally* mean you're a breath of fresh air. . . . However, isn't it more interesting to read, 'You're a breath of fresh air,' than, 'You're good young people,' or something like that?"

He then continues, "That's what *figurative language* is about, and that's what we're going to examine today. Then, we'll see how authors use it to make their writing more interesting.

"To start, we're going to focus on three types of figurative language: *metaphor, simile,* and *personification*."

He then displays the following on his document camera.

A metaphor is figurative language that directly equates two items for literary effect, such as equating our class and fresh air.

A simile is figurative language that does not equate two items, but rather makes a comparison using the words 'like' or 'as,' such as "This class is *like* the sugar in my morning coffee."

Personification is figurative language that attributes human characteristics to something nonhuman, such as "Thunder grumbled in the distance, signaling an approaching storm."

"Oh, I get it," Troy blurts out after looking at the definitions for a few seconds. "My Mom always says, 'You are what you eat' when she gets after me to have a good breakfast before I come to school. . . . That's a metaphor."

"Good example, Troy. . . . Now, explain why. . . . Jeanette?" seeing her raised hand.

" . . . It equates us with food."

"Yes, good thinking, Jeanette," Mike nods.

He offers additional examples of *simile* and *personification*, asks the class to explain each, and then says, "Now, I want you to turn to your partners and come up with at least two more examples of each of the types of figurative language you see here. You have five minutes." (Mike frequently has students work in teams of three on short activities such as we see here.)

We'll return to Mike and his class later, but for now, let's think about his actions—why he began his lesson with the sentences on the board, asked his students what the sentences meant to them, displayed the definitions on his document camera, and interacted with the students the way he did. Each was a conscious decision, and they were all applications of cognitive learning theory. We'll see how as the chapter unfolds.

Cognitive Learning Theory

7.1   Describe principles of cognitive learning theory, and identify applications of the principles in classrooms and life outside of school.

According to behaviorism, learning is an observable change in behavior that occurs as a result of experience, such as you picking up your dishes in the living room after your significant other has complimented you for previously doing so, or students attempting to answer questions after their teacher has praised them for earlier attempts to answer.

Social cognitive theory focuses on the effects of observing others, such as the tendency in all of us to imitate other people's behaviors. However, think about times you've gotten completely original ideas. They weren't the result of reinforcement, and they haven't been modeled for you, so neither behaviorism nor social cognitive theory can explain how you came up with them. We need a different explanation.

Similarly, neither behaviorism nor social cognitive theory can explain why Troy was able to identify his mother's comment as an example of a metaphor.

Research examining the development of complex skills, such as problem solving, behaviorism's inability to explain how we learn language (Chomsky, 2006), and the development of computers all led to a shift toward **cognitive learning theories**, theories that focus on the thinking involved in acquiring, organizing, storing, and using knowledge to explain learning (Schunk, 2016). Cognitive learning theories help us explain tasks from as simple as remembering a phone number to those as complex as solving problems, using figurative language to make writing more interesting, or applying sophisticated computer algorithms. A "cognitive revolution"—the increased emphasis on using cognitive theory to explain learning and development—occurred between the mid-1950s and early 1970s, and its influence on education has steadily increased since that time (Berliner, 2006). For example, as we just saw, Mike directly applied cognitive learning theory in a number of ways in his teaching.

Principles of Cognitive Learning Theory

Principles, or **laws**, are statements in a field of study that are generally accepted as true. For example, one of Newton's laws of motion in science states, "A moving object will keep moving in a straight line unless a force acts on it." We accept this statement as true, and it helps us understand everyday events, such as why we wear seatbelts while driving, or why we're "thrown" against a car door when we round a curve too rapidly.

Principles of learning serve the same purpose; they help us understand the way people learn and develop, and they provide guidance for us when we teach. The principles of learning in which cognitive learning theory is grounded are outlined in Figure 7.1 and discussed in the sections that follow.

Learning and Development Depend on Experience

Ed Psych and You

If you're typical for students taking this class, you likely own a smartphone or tablet computer, such as Apple's iPad or Google's Android. Are you skilled with its functions? If so, why? If not, why not?

Our experiences, both in and out of classrooms, provide the raw material for learning and development, and this principle helps answer the questions we asked in *Ed Psych and You*. If you're skilled with your smartphone or tablet, you've read directions, talked with other people, and experimented with your new tech toy. In short, your experiences helped you develop the skills needed to use the technology efficiently. The same is true for all learning and development; we use experiences to help us acquire the background knowledge we need to understand how our world works. Mike's definitions and examples provided experiences with figurative language for his students. Similarly, to learn how to write effectively, we need a great deal of experience with writing, and to get good at problem solving, we must solve

Figure 7.1 Principles of cognitive learning theory

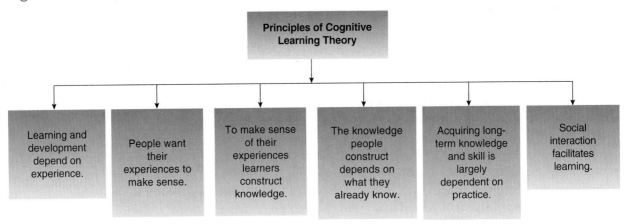

a lot of problems. Athletes acquire experience as they practice and compete in their sports, and your work in classrooms will provide teaching experiences that will help you develop expertise as a teacher.

This principle has important implications for our teaching. Providing students with the experiences they need to grow and develop is the essence of what we do as teachers.

People Want Their Experiences to Make Sense

Think about the number of times we've all said or heard statements such as "That makes sense" or its opposite, "I don't get it; it doesn't make any sense." They are so common in our day-to-day world that we usually don't react when we hear them.

The need to make sense of our experiences is arguably the most basic cognitive principle. "The view that perception and cognition seeks to make sense of the world has a long and varied history" (Chatera & Loewenstein, 2016, p. 138). All societies and cultures, from the ancient Egyptians, Greeks, and Romans to Native Americans and our own, have constructed systems of beliefs about life, what it means, and what happens when we die. These systems are mechanisms societies have used to make sense of experiences they couldn't make sense of in any other way.

This need also exists in classrooms. Cognitive learning theorists describe students as cognitively active beings who continually strive to make sense of their learning experiences (Bransford, Brown, & Cocking, 2000). Information that makes sense is easier to learn and remember than isolated facts, and this helps us understand why students often recall so little of what we've taught. Too much of what they study doesn't fully make sense to them, so they memorize enough to pass tests and then promptly forget the information. Helping our students make sense of the experiences we provide is one of our most important goals. This book is designed to help you reach that goal.

To Make Sense of Their Experiences Learners Construct Knowledge

Ed Psych and You

Look at the sketch that follows. Think about the baseball in flight *after it leaves the thrower's hand but before that receiver catches it*. Draw an arrow at each point—1 through 5—that represents the forces on the ball. (A force is simply a push or a pull, such as pushing a coffee cup across a table, or pulling a chair across the floor. So, you are drawing an arrow that shows one or more pushes or pulls on the ball at each point.) (Ignore air resistance, which is minimal.)

Now, if you're typical, your arrows look like this:

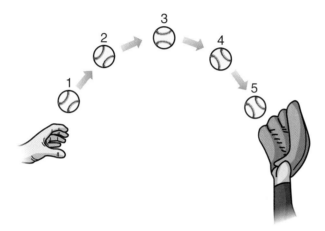

As it turns out, this is a very common misconception. The only force—pull—on the ball at each point is the pull of gravity as shown in the third sketch, below.

Why did you draw the forces—arrows—as we see them in the second sketch? Simply, you "constructed" the ideas on your own because they made sense to you. Cognitive learning theory suggests that as thinking human beings we don't passively receive knowledge and store it in the form in which it is presented—such as a conversation, lecture, or reading. Rather, we mentally (cognitively) reorganize the information so it makes sense to us. Knowledge is "constructed by learners as they attempt to make sense of their experiences" (Hattie & Gan, 2011, p. 256).

As another example, young children were asked to define "love." Here are a few of their comments. (They have been widely circulated on the Internet.)

"Love is when a girl puts on perfume and a boy puts on shaving cologne and they go out and smell each other." Karl - age 5

"Love is when you go out to eat and give somebody most of your French fries without making them give you any of theirs." Chrissy – age 6

"Love is when you tell a guy you like his shirt, then he wears it every day." Noelle - age 7

Where did the children get these notions? As in our case with the thrown ball, they constructed the ideas because, to them, the ideas made sense. This is the case with our knowledge in general.

The process of knowledge construction helps us understand why two people can have identical experiences but interpret them very differently. It also helps us understand why we get ideas essentially "out of the blue" and why we develop misconceptions.

The fact that we construct, rather than record, knowledge has important implications for our teaching. If we present information to our students, but the information doesn't make sense to them, they will (mentally) reorganize it so that it does, and they will then store the misinterpretation in their memories. Or they will memorize as much of the information as they can and then quickly forget it.

Knowledge That Learners Construct Depends on What They Already Know

Ed Psych and You

Think again about the example with the thrown baseball. If you were typical and represented the forces—arrows—as we see them in the second sketch, why—beyond your need to make sense of your experiences—did you represent them this way? On the other hand, if you represented the forces accurately, as we see them in the third sketch, why did you represent them correctly?

MyLab Education
Video Example 7.1
The knowledge learners construct depends on what they already know is a principle of cognitive learning theory. Here, fourth-grade teacher, Debra Jongebloed, helps her students capitalize on what they already know about animals that live in the sea to help them construct knowledge about barnacles.

Our experience and what we already know helps us answer both questions. Virtually all of our experiences suggest that to make an object move in a certain direction, we must exert a force (a push or pull) in that direction, such as simply sliding a book across a table, lifting a bag of groceries onto a counter, or moving our car down the street.

On the other hand, if you represented the forces correctly, you likely had background knowledge/experience, such as a physics course, that helped you understand why gravity is the only force operating on the ball.

We all construct new knowledge based on what we already know. For instance, knowledge of addition and subtraction help us understand multiplication and division, and our understanding of simple, descriptive prose provides a framework for more sophisticated writing, such as the use of figurative language.

APA Top 20 Principles

This discussion illustrates Principle 2: *What students already know affects their learning*—from the *Top 20 Principles from Psychology for PreK–12 Teaching and Learning*.

Background knowledge can be a double-edged sword, however. For instance, consider this problem:

$$\frac{1}{3} + \frac{1}{4}$$

Which answer, 7/12 or 2/7, makes more sense? For some students, the answer is initially 2/7. Based on their understanding of addition, simply adding the numerators and then the denominators is very sensible. And, when multiplying fractions, we do indeed multiply the numerators and denominators, so if we were multiplying instead of adding the fractions above, we would get an answer of 1/12.

Similarly, because we've had experiences such as feeling warmer when we move closer to a burning fireplace or hot stove, many people believe that our summers are warmer than our winters because we're closer to the sun in the summer.

This helps us understand why good teaching is so sophisticated. We don't simply provide experiences when we teach; we need to provide the kinds of experiences that help our students construct valid knowledge.

Acquiring Long-Term Knowledge and Skill Is Largely Dependent on Practice

APA Top 20 Principles

This is Principle 5: *Acquiring long-term knowledge and skill is largely dependent on practice*—from the *Top 20 Principles from Psychology for PreK–12 Teaching and Learning.*

If we want to get good at anything, we must practice. There are no shortcuts to good writing or skilled problem solving, for example, and we all know about the enormous amounts of time world-class athletes or musicians spend honing their skills.

The importance of practice is intuitively sensible, and it received attention in academic circles as a result of research examining its role in the development of expertise (Ericsson, Krampe, & Tesch-Romer, 1993). Then it was popularized by journalist Malcolm Gladwell (2008), who frequently referred to the "10,000 hour rule" in his best-selling book *Outliers.* The rule, first offered by Ericsson et al. (1993), simply states that 10,000 hours of practice are required to develop a high level of expertise in any field. Additional research suggests that the 10,000 hour rule is an overgeneralization; that is, some people need more than 10,000 hours for some skills, whereas others need less (Ericsson & Pool, 2016; Macnamara, Hambrick, & Oswald, 2014). However, the importance of practice in promoting learning is unquestioned.

Social Interaction Facilitates Learning

Ed Psych and You

You're trying to download pictures from your smartphone to your desktop computer, but when you connect your phone to your computer, it won't recognize your phone. You go to Google, but what you find isn't helpful.

A friend comes over, and she isn't sure either, but you begin working on the problem, and finally, together, you resolve the issue, and you now have all your phone pictures downloaded.

We've all heard "Two heads are better than one," and we've all had experiences similar to the one in *Ed Psych and You* above. We work with someone on a problem neither fully understands nor can solve alone, but collaboratively we figure it out. These examples illustrate the importance of social interaction, and it has three learning benefits:

- Providing information
- Building on others' ideas
- Putting thoughts into words

To illustrate these benefits, let's look again at some dialogue from Mike's lesson.

Mike: What do you think about that? Go ahead. . . . Tell me what these statements mean to you. (pointing to the board)

You people are a breath of fresh air.

You're like the sugar in my morning coffee.

Students: That's nice.

Do you really mean it?

What are you talking about?

Mike: When you look at the statements, do you think I mean you are really, . . . or *literally*, a breath of fresh air, or are you *literally* like the sugar in my coffee?

Students: Not really.

Then, after Mike displays his definitions:

Troy: Oh, I get it. My Mom always says, 'You are what you eat' when she gets after me to have a good breakfast before I come to school. . . . That's a metaphor."

Mike: Good example, Troy. Now, explain why. . . . Jeanette.

Jeanette: It equates us with food.

Mike: Good thinking, Jeanette.

In this simple exchange, Troy saying, "Oh, I get it. . . . That's a metaphor," provided his classmates with information. Then, in saying, "It equates us with food," Jeanette built on Troy's ideas and put her own thoughts into words. Troy providing an example and having Jeanette explain it was more effective than it would have been if Mike had provided and explained an example himself, because the students were more cognitively active—doing more thinking—than they would have been if they had simply been listening to Mike. Interacting with students in this way is an essential aspect of all effective instruction (Eggen & Kauchak, 2013; Hattie, 2012; Lemov, 2015). (We discuss the need for cognitive activity in more detail later in the chapter.)

MyLab Education Application Exercise 7.1: Identifying Principles of Cognitive Learning Theory

In this exercise you will be asked to analyze a second-grade teacher's application of principles of cognitive learning theory with her students.

A Model of Human Memory

Ed Psych and You

We've all had the experience of knowing some fact or person's name, but can't think of it right then, only to have it pop into our minds sometime later. And we've made comments, such as, "I'm suffering from memory overload," or "It's on the tip of my tongue, but I can't quite dredge it up." Why do our minds work like this?

Because it's such an integral part of our daily living, we rarely think about "memory." We rack our brains to recall isolated facts, such as the capital of Columbia (Bogotá), and we use our memories to solve problems, identify relationships, and make decisions. And we've almost certainly encountered the issues we asked about in *Ed Psych and You* above. In this section, we introduce a widely accepted model of human memory, and we examine this model in detail throughout the rest of the chapter.

Cognitive learning theorists don't totally agree on the exact structure of human memory, but most use a model similar to what you see in Figure 7.2. It was initially proposed by Atkinson and Shiffrin (1968), and it's become a central component of **information processing theory**, a cognitive learning theory that helps explain "the process of acquiring, processing, storing, and retrieving information from memory and provides guidance on how memory can be enhanced" (Tangen & Borders, 2017, p. 100). Since originally proposed, information processing theory and this model have generated a great deal of research and have undergone considerable refinement (Schunk, 2016). (We also examine criticisms of information processing and the model later in the chapter.)

In this context, a **model** is a representation that helps us visualize what we can't observe directly. It's used in the same way the model of the atom is used in science courses we've taken.

For example, just as we can't directly observe the nucleus or electrons in an atom, we can't look inside our heads to see the components of our memory systems. So we create a model to help us visualize and understand them.

The human memory model is composed of three major components:

- *Memory stores*—Sensory memory, working memory, and long-term memory. These are repositories that hold information, in some cases very briefly and in others almost permanently.

- *Cognitive processes*—Attention, perception, rehearsal, encoding, and retrieval. These processes move information from one memory store to another.

- *Metacognition*—The supervisory system we have for monitoring and regulating both the storage of information and how it's moved from one store to another.

Although this model is only a representation, it provides us with valuable information about how our minds work. As one simple example, in the model we see that working memory is smaller than either sensory memory or long-term memory. This reminds us that its capacity is smaller than the other two stores. We will refer to the model and why it's constructed the way we see it as we examine each of its components. As we also see in the model, the memory stores, cognitive processes, and metacognition are interconnected, but we examine them separately for the sake of clarity, beginning in the next section with the memory stores.

Figure 7.2 A model of human memory

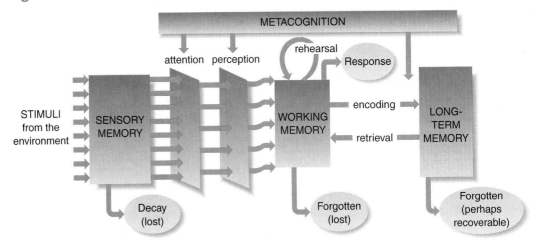

Memory Stores

7.2 Use the memory stores in the human memory model to explain events in classrooms and in our daily lives.

The **memory stores**—sensory memory, working memory, and long-term memory—are repositories that hold information as we organize it in ways that make sense to us and store it for further use. We examine them in this section.

Sensory Memory

Ed Psych and You

Hold your finger in front of you and rapidly wiggle it. What do you notice? Now, press firmly on your arm with your finger, and then release it. What do you feel?

Think about the questions we just asked. In the first case, did you see a faint "shadow" that trailed behind your finger as it moved? And did the sensation of pressure remain for an instant after you stopped pressing on your arm? We can explain these events with the concept of **sensory memory**, the information store that briefly holds incoming stimuli from the environment in a raw, unprocessed form until they can be meaningfully organized (Neisser, 1967; Vlassova & Pearson, 2013). For example, the shadow is the image of your finger that has been briefly stored in your visual sensory memory, and the sensation of pressure that remains has been briefly stored in your tactile sensory memory.

Our sensory memories are essential for both learning and functioning in our everyday lives. For instance, if a friend says something as simple as, "I have a dentist appointment at two o'clock on Thursday," we must briefly retain the first part of the sentence in our auditory sensory memories until we hear the complete sentence, or we won't be able to make sense of the statement. Sensory memory is nearly unlimited in capacity, but if processing doesn't begin almost immediately, the memory trace quickly fades away (Öğmen & Herzog, 2016; Pashler & Carrier, 1996). Sensory memory holds information until we attach meaning to it and then transfer it to working memory, the next store.

Working Memory

To make sense of their experiences, people construct knowledge is a principle of cognitive learning theory, and this is where working memory comes into play. **Working memory** is the conscious component of our memory system, often called a "workbench" because it's where our thinking occurs, and it's where we construct our knowledge (Paas, Renkl, & Sweller, 2004). We aren't aware of the contents of either sensory memory or long-term memory until they're pulled into working memory for processing.

A Model of Working Memory

Figure 7.2 represents working memory as a single unit, and this is how it was initially described (Atkinson & Shiffrin, 1968). However, additional research suggests that working memory has three components that work together to process information (Baddeley, 1986, 2001). They're outlined in Figure 7.3.

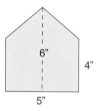

To introduce you to the components of working memory, try to calculate the area of the sketch you see here.

In thinking about the problem, you probably did something like the following. You subtracted the 4 from the 6 to determine that the height of the triangular portion of the sketch is 2 inches. You recalled that the formula for the area of a triangle is $\frac{1}{2}(b)(h)$ ($\frac{1}{2}$ times base times height) and for a rectangle it's (l)(w) (length times width). You then calculated the areas to be $(\frac{1}{2})(5)(2) = 5$ sq. in. for the triangular portion and $(5)(4) = 20$ sq. in. for the rectangular part, making the total area of the figure 25 square inches.

Now, let's see how the different components of your working memory helped you execute the task. The **phonological loop**, a short-term storage component for words and sounds (Papagno et al., 2017), temporarily held formulas for finding areas and the dimensions of the figure while you made calculations. Impairment in the phonological loop is often associated with reading difficulties because of the role it plays in processing verbal information (Kibby, Marks, & Morgan, 2004).

The **visual-spatial sketchpad**, a short-term storage system for visual and spatial information, allowed you to visualize the figure as you made decisions about how to

Figure 7.3 A model of working memory

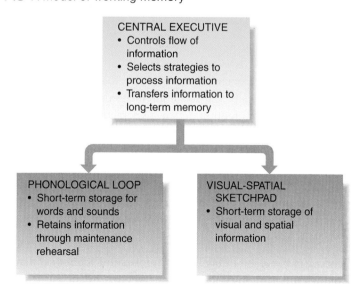

solve the problem. The visual-spatial sketchpad and the phonological loop are independent, so each can perform mental work without taxing the resources of the other (Baddeley, 1986, 2001).

Both of these storage systems are limited in capacity and duration, able to hold about as much information as we can say to ourselves in $1\frac{1}{2}$ to 2 seconds (Baddeley, 1986, 2001). They serve the functions that historically have attributed to **short-term memory**. So, for example, when we hear or read information about "short-term memory loss," it refers to decrements in these components of working memory.

As you held information in your phonological loop and visual-spatial sketchpad, your **central executive**, a supervisory system that controls and directs the flow of information to and from the other components, guided your problem-solving efforts. For instance, your central executive guided your decision to break the figure into a triangle and rectangle, then find the area of each, and finally add the two.

Executive Functioning. The central executive plays a broader role in school and life than solving a simple problem like the one above. It governs **executive functioning**, "an umbrella term used to describe the cognitive processes responsible for purposeful, goal-directed behavior" (Cantin, Gnaedinger, Gallaway, Hesson-McInnis, & Hund, 2016, p. 66). To see how it affects our lives, let's look at an exchange between two young adults.

As Jack, Olivia's significant other, walks in the door, she excitedly tells him, "Dana called to invite us to a big party later this month. I told her we wouldn't miss it."

"Sounds great," Jack responds. "But, you know I'm going to be out of town the last week of the month, so you probably should have checked with me before committing. . . . When is the party?"

"I'm not quite sure. I was going to write it down as soon as I hung up with Dana, but then my phone rang again, and it slipped my mind."

"Well, I have to know to be sure we can make it," Jack responds. "Please call Dana back and find out the particulars."

"I'll call her tomorrow," Olivia promises.

"We'll see," Jack thinks to himself, knowing Olivia's tendencies.

Sound like anyone you know? Olivia's behavior illustrates what we sometimes think of as "flakey," but in fact it's an issue with her executive functioning. Executive functioning is linked to both academic and social success in school and success and satisfaction in life after the school years. For example, well-developed executive functioning predicts higher reading and math achievement in school (Blair & McKinnona, 2016; Cantin et al., 2016), and it's also associated with social-emotional competence, such as behaving appropriately in social interactions and detecting subtleties like irony and sarcasm in conversations (Cantin et al., 2016; Devine & Hughes, 2013). In adults, executive functioning deficits are associated with anxiety and social interaction problems (Jarrett, 2016), and both students and adults with attention-deficit/hyperactivity disorder (ADHD) often struggle with it (Karatekin, 2004). While Olivia's behavior in this instance probably isn't serious, we can see how it could lead to problems in the workplace.

On the other hand, well-developed executive functioning is associated with job success and satisfaction, and older adults with effective executive functioning report higher levels of health and well-being (McHugh & Lawlor, 2016).

Effective executive functioning includes three subskills (Cantin et al., 2016; Fuhs, Hornburg, & McNeil, 2016):

- *Effective working memory*, the ability to hold information in mind and manipulate it. The date of the party slipping Olivia's mind suggests a deficit in this area.

- *Inhibitory control*—sometimes called *self-control*—the ability to attend to relevant and avoid being distracted by irrelevant information, as well as inhibiting inappropriate behaviors. Olivia impulsively responded to the invitation without thinking about checking with Jack before making a commitment.
- *Cognitive flexibility*, the ability to mentally shift when a task demands change. Olivia was unable to switch from her phone call to getting the information on her calendar.

We saw that executive functioning is associated with academic success, and underdeveloped executive functioning in students is a source of frustration for teachers. Let's see how Mike Davis, our teacher at the beginning of the chapter, accommodates executive functioning issues in his work with his students, and particularly with Owen, who has executive functioning problems.

Owen has a history of failing to bring his homework to school, and he forgets even short sets of directions, a working memory issue. He tends to blurt out comments and answers in class in spite of rules requiring students to raise their hands before speaking, which suggests he lacks inhibitory control, and he frequently asks for help when completing even simple tasks that require more than one step, a problem with cognitive flexibility.

Anticipating the possibility of these issues with his students, a few days before the beginning of the school year Mike has written an e-mail to his students' parents or other caregivers, telling them to be sure their child brings a three-ring binder to school with them the first day. He then hands out the checklist we see below and tells his students to put it at the front of the binder. (Inevitably, some students fail to bring the binder, so he sends a reminder e-mail, and he calls parents if the second e-mail doesn't work.)

He reminds his students to complete the checklist each morning before they leave home, as we see with the Monday column. Students pick up a checklist for the following week from a pile sitting on a desk by the door just before they leave school each Friday afternoon.

	Monday	Tuesday	Wednesday	Thursday	Friday
Homework	✓				
Textbook	✓				
Two sharp pencils	✓				
Eraser	✓				
Three-hole paper	✓				
Personal items	✓				

Mike writes every homework assignment on the board, directs students to copy it into their binders, and watches to be sure that they do. He also explains and role plays the use of the checklist.

He also strongly emphasizes personal responsibility, and he models it by describing and illustrating his own responsibilities as he teaches. And his classroom management system provides rewards for students who comply with rules, such as avoiding calling out comments and answers without being recognized, as well as sanctions for students who chronically break rules.

Mike also attempts to promote executive functioning in the way he interacts with his students. To see how, let's return to his lesson on figurative language, which we first saw at the beginning of the chapter. He has just assigned his teams of three the task of generating two additional examples of each of the types of figurative language.

We rejoin his lesson now.

"Now, I want you to turn to your partners and come up with at least two more examples of metaphors, similes, and personification. You have five minutes."

Mike waits a few seconds as the students turn their desks to face their teammates, and then asks, "So, just a reminder, . . . what's the first thing you're going to do? . . . Amy?"

"Come up with an example of a metaphor."

"Okay, good. . . . After you've found one, what do you always do? . . . Monica?"

"Write it down."

"Then what? . . . Owen?"

" . . . Find another one."

"Or?"

" . . . Find an example of a simile."

"Yes, good, Owen. . . . Now, get started everyone."

We expect our students to behave in class, and we also hope they'll accept personal responsibility and follow our directions the first time they're given. Many do, and they're a source of satisfaction when we teach.

Others, however, struggle, so we must intervene, and this is what Mike did with his students. We know that practice is essential for all forms of learning, and even simple abilities, such as retaining information in working memory, inhibiting inappropriate behaviors, and moving flexibly from one task to another, may—for some students, such as Owen—need to be practiced. Mike's checklist and his asking students to describe their task provide practice with working memory function, his classroom management system helps students learn to inhibit inappropriate behaviors, and his questioning related to the group task provide his students with practice in cognitive flexibility. Mike's efforts won't work all the time or with all students, and we can't be sure that Owen's issues will vanish as a result of Mike's efforts. It will make a difference with many, however, and making a difference with as many students as possible is what we're always trying to do when we teach.

From our discussion to this point, we see that working memory plays a huge role in both learning and functioning effectively in our daily lives. It seems almost ironic that a component so important is also limited.

Limitations of Working Memory

At the beginning of our discussion of human memory, we suggested that you may have made a comment, such as "I'm suffering from memory overload," at one time or another. If you have, working memory is the culprit, because its capacity is severely limited, and it's directly related to the limitations in the phonological loop and visual-spatial sketchpad that we described in the last section (Sweller, van Merrienboer, & Paas, 1998). Early research suggested that adult working memories can hold about seven items of information at a time and can hold the items for only about 10 to 20 seconds (Miller, 1956). (Children's working memories are more limited.) Selecting and organizing information also uses working memory space, so we "are probably only able to deal with two or three items of information simultaneously when required to process rather than merely hold information" (Sweller et al., 1998, p. 252). As we saw in Figure 7.2, working memory is represented as smaller than either sensory memory or long-term memory, which is designed to remind us that its capacity is limited. This limited capacity is arguably its most important feature, because working memory is not only responsible for executive functioning, but it's also where we make sense of our experiences and construct our knowledge (Clark & Mayer, 2003). Think about it: The most important processes in learning—functioning effectively and constructing meaningful knowledge—take place in the component of our memory system that is the most limited! Little wonder that students miss important information, construct misconceptions, and are sometimes confused. It also helps us understand why people don't remember, or misinterpret, what we say in simple day-to-day conversations.

The limitations of working memory help us understand research results that have important implications for learning and teaching:

- Students write better essays using computers if their keyboarding skills are well developed. If not, handwritten essays are superior (Roblyer & Hughes, 2019).

- Students' writing often improves more rapidly if they are initially allowed to ignore grammar, punctuation, and spelling (McCutchen, 2000).

- In spite of research about its ineffectiveness, and staff-development efforts to promote more sophisticated and effective forms of instruction, lecturing persists as the most common teaching strategy (Brophy, 2006b; Cuban, 1993; Lemov, 2015).

We can explain these examples using the concept of **cognitive load**, which is the amount of mental activity imposed on working memory. It's what you referred to when you said, "I'm suffering from memory overload."

Cognitive load depends on two factors. The number of elements we must attend to is the first (Paas et al., 2004), such as remembering this sequence of digits—7 9 5 3—versus this one—3 9 2 4 6 7 8. The second imposes a heavier cognitive load than the first simply because there are more numbers in it.

The complexity of the elements is the second factor (Paas et al., 2004). For example, attempting to create a well-organized essay is a complex cognitive task (requires a great deal of thought), and if learners must also spend working memory space thinking about where to place their fingers on a keyboard, the cognitive load becomes too great, and they write better essays by hand. Similarly, thinking about grammar, punctuation, and spelling while simultaneously trying to compose an essay also imposes a heavy cognitive load on students, so initially being allowed to ignore these rules reduces the load.

And cognitive load also helps us understand why so many teachers lecture instead of interacting with their students. Sophisticated teaching strategies, such as guiding students with questioning, requires us to keep our learning goals in mind while simultaneously thinking of the best questions to ask, deciding who to call on, knowing how to respond when students are unable to answer, and monitoring the rest of the class for inattention or misbehavior. All this imposes a very heavy cognitive load on teachers, so they often reduce the load by simply lecturing. This helps us understand why expert teaching is so difficult, and, even with practice, not all teachers become experts.

Lecturing also imposes a heavy cognitive load on students. When lecturing, it's easy to fall into the trap of presenting too much information too quickly, so the cognitive load on students' working memories results in them misinterpreting information and missing some altogether. We're then surprised at their lack of understanding, reasoning, "I explained it so carefully." We can now see why this problem is so common.

So what can we—as learners and teachers—do about the limitations of working memory? We address this question next.

Reducing Cognitive Load

To accommodate the limitations of working memory, our goal is to reduce cognitive load. Three strategies can help us reach this goal:

- Chunking
- Automaticity
- Distributed processing

Chunking. **Chunking** is the process of mentally combining separate items into larger, more meaningful units (Miller, 1956). For example, 9 0 4 7 5 0 5 8 0 7 is a phone number, and it is 10 digits long, so it exceeds the capacity of working memory. Now, as normally written, 904-750-5807, these numbers have been "chunked" into three larger units, so it reduces cognitive load by taking up less working memory space. This is the reason phone numbers are chunked; they're easier to read and remember.

Chunking is common in our daily lives. For instance, American Express credit cards are 15 digits long chunked into 3 units; Visa cards are 16 digits chunked into 4 units. Drivers' license numbers, memberships in organizations, such as the American Automobile Association, and the long license numbers on computer software are all presented as chunks instead of a continuous string of numbers and letters. Later in our discussion we'll see how we can capitalize on our memory's capacity for chunking to dramatically reduce cognitive load.

Ed Psych and You

If you have an electric garage door opener, have you ever left your house or apartment wondering if you've put the garage door down? You may have even driven around the block so you can check, and you likely find that you didn't forget. Or do you ever wonder if you've shut off your coffee pot (manufacturers understand this, and most coffee pots shut themselves off after a period of time). If so, why?

Automaticity. **Automaticity** is the ability to perform mental operations with little awareness or conscious effort (Feldon, 2007), and it's enormously important for both learning and everyday living. For instance, once keyboarding and grammar skills become automatic, that is, once we can type and use correct grammar, punctuation, and spelling "without thinking about it," we can then devote all of our limited working memory space to composing quality written work. This helps us understand why students write better essays using computers if their keyboarding skills are well developed; they use the keyboard automatically.

Similarly, if our learning objectives are clear and we develop important teaching skills, such as questioning, to a high level, thinking of questions, deciding who to call on, and how to respond to students who don't answer correctly become essentially automatic. This leaves working memory space to guide discussions and monitor student behavior.

Automaticity is essential for reducing cognitive load, and research indicates that **experts**, people who are highly skilled or knowledgeable in a domain, such as math, computer science, basketball, or teaching, have as many of their skills developed to automaticity as possible. And in our daily lives we all develop simple routines that reduce cognitive load. For instance, Paul (one of your authors) automatically puts his keys and wallet in a cabinet drawer the moment he walks into his house, so he has one less thing to think about.

Automaticity is a double-edged sword, however, and it helps answer the questions we asked in *Ed Psych and You* at the beginning of this section. If you answered yes to either, it was because you put the garage door down or completed the other routine task "automatically"— you did it without thinking about it. As another example, because driving is nearly automatic, many people believe they can simultaneously talk on their cell phones or text while driving, both of which are very dangerous (Cismaru, 2014).

Distributed Processing. Earlier we saw that the phonological loop and the visual-spatial sketchpad operate independently in working memory, so each can perform mental work without taxing the resources of the other. The visual processor supplements the verbal processor and vice versa, which "distributes" the processing task across the two components, reduces cognitive load, and helps accommodate working memory's limitations. This suggests that we should combine our verbal explanations with visual representations when we teach. "The integration of words and pictures is made easier by lessons that present the verbal and visual information together rather than separated" (Clark & Mayer, 2003, p. 38). For instance, in math, diagrams are helpful in problem solving; pictures of cells with their components are used in biology; videos illustrating the correct technique for shooting a jump shot are used in coaching basketball; and replicas of masterpieces are used in art classes. Each capitalizes on the capacity of working memory to distribute cognitive load.

Long-Term Memory

The knowledge people construct depends on what they already know is a cognitive learning principle, and this is where **long-term memory**, our permanent information store, comes into play. What we know is stored in long-term memory, and being able to access this knowledge plays an essential role in later learning. Long-term memory's capacity is vast and durable, and some experts believe that information in it remains for a lifetime (Schacter, 2001; Sweller, 2003). Two important types of knowledge, *declarative knowledge* and *procedural knowledge*, are stored in long-term memory. We examine them next.

Declarative Knowledge in Long-Term Memory

To this point in the chapter, we hope you've acquired a considerable amount of knowledge, such as the principles of cognitive learning theory; concepts, such as *working memory* and *automaticity*; and facts, such as the adult capacity of working memory is approximately seven bits of information. In addition, we all have stored a great many personal experiences. This information exists as **declarative knowledge**, often described as knowing "what."

Acquiring declarative knowledge involves integrating different items of information. To illustrate, think about how we can integrate principles of cognitive learning theory and the model of human memory. We want to make sense of our experiences (a learning principle), so we construct knowledge (a learning principle). This knowledge is constructed in working memory (a human memory component), and it depends on prior knowledge (a learning principle), which is stored in long-term memory (a human memory component). This integrated information exists in the form of **schemas** (also called schemata), cognitive structures that represent the way information is organized in long-term memory (Schunk, 2016; Willingham, 2007). Figure 7.4 represents a schema that might help us visualize this integration.

We construct our own individual schemas, so they make sense to us. However, this doesn't mean they will necessarily make sense to someone else. For example, the schema in Figure 7.4 makes sense to us—Paul and Don, your authors—since we constructed it. So, if it doesn't make complete sense to you, it's because you didn't construct it. The same thing occurs in classrooms when our students construct schemas that make sense to them, but not to us or to each other.

Meaningfulness.   We just saw how principles of cognitive learning theory and components of human memory are integrated, as illustrated in Figure 7.4. This integration results from the connections between the individual items, and it illustrates the concept of **meaningfulness**, the extent to which items of information are linked and related to each other.

Meaningfulness is a very powerful factor in learning, for two reasons. First, research indicates that although the number of "chunks" working memory can hold is limited, the size and complexity of the chunks are not (Sweller et al., 1998). Because the individual items in our schema are interconnected, it behaves like a single chunk, so it uses only one working memory slot and significantly reduces cognitive load (Bransford et al., 2000). Second, the more meaningful (interconnected) a schema is, the more places exist to which we can connect new information. This helps us understand a statement by Bill Gates, co-founder of Microsoft, "The more you learn, the more you have a framework that knowledge fits into" (Sakr, 2013).

MyLab Education
Video Example 7.2

Meaningfulness describes the extent to which items of information are linked and related to each other. Here a high school student describes strategies she uses to make connections in the topics she's studying and how doing so increases the meaningfulness of the content for her.

Figure 7.4 A schema for integrating learning principles and the model of human memory

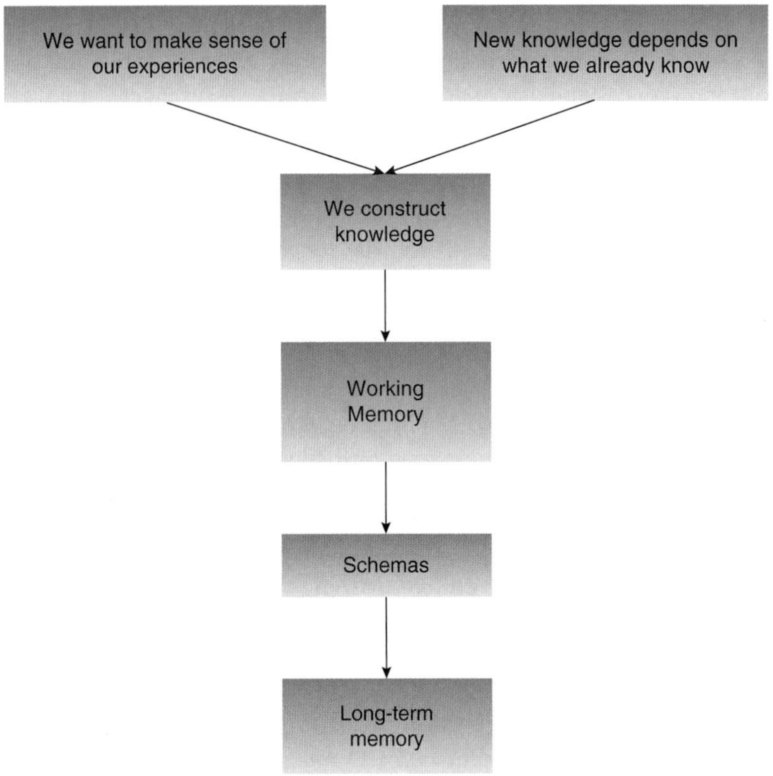

Meaningfulness: Implications for Learning and Teaching.   Let's think about three American History topics that we've all studied: (1) the French and Indian War, (2) the Boston Tea Party, and (3) the American Revolutionary War. We know that the French and Indian War was fought between the French and British, colonists dumped tea in Boston harbor, and the Revolutionary War led to our country's independence. They are important separate ideas, but not particularly meaningful.

The three events are, in fact, closely related. The French and Indian War, fought between 1754 and 1763, was very costly for the British, so to raise revenue they imposed onerous taxes on the colonists for goods such as tea. This led to rebellion, one important example of which was dumping tea into Boston harbor in 1773, ultimately leading to the Revolutionary War, fought between 1775 and 1783. Now the three events make a lot more sense; they are more meaningful.

This suggests that as learners, we should always be looking for relationships in the topics we study, and as teachers, we should emphasize connections among the ideas we're teaching instead of presenting information in isolated pieces and asking factual questions on quizzes. For instance, the question, "How did the French and Indian War contribute to the Boston Tea Party?" is a much better way to promote meaningful learning than questions, such as "Which two countries fought in the French and Indian War?" or "The Boston Tea Party occurred in what year?"

Isolated information also imposes a heavy cognitive load on students' working memories, which helps explain why they seem to retain so little of what they're taught. Connecting ideas helps integrated information behave as chunks, which reduces cognitive load and makes the information more interesting and easier to remember.

Emotions and Meaningfulness.   In addition to increasing meaningfulness by identifying relationships among different items of information, emotional connections to information also increase meaningfulness. "Research on emotion–memory interactions has suggested that emotional information may be more likely to be remembered and persist longer in memory than neutral material" (Mizrak & Öztekin, 2016, p. 33). For example, those of us who are older remember exactly where we were and what we were doing when we received word of the infamous terrorist attacks of September 11, 2001 (9/11). You likely recall the events surrounding your first date or kiss. These events were highlighted by emotions, which made them more meaningful (Sutherland, McQuiggan, Ryan, & Mather, 2017).

Mike, in our case study at the beginning of the chapter, attempted to capitalize on the influence of emotions for promoting meaningfulness by introducing figurative language with:

You people are a breath of fresh air.

and

This class is like the sugar in my morning coffee.

These examples of *metaphor* and *simile* personalized the concepts, which created an emotional link to them and made them more meaningful than "neutral" examples, such as *stars are the windows of heaven* and *she sleeps like a baby* would have been.

We should attempt to capitalize on the influence of emotions whenever opportunities exist. It often takes little extra effort, such as we saw in Mike's case, and the result can be more meaningful learning.

Procedural Knowledge in Long-Term Memory

Procedural knowledge, knowledge of how to perform tasks, such as solving problems, composing essays, performing pieces of music, executing physical skills (such as a back flip in gymnastics), and teaching, is the second type of knowledge stored in long-term memory. Procedural knowledge depends on declarative knowledge. For instance, consider this problem:

$$\frac{1}{4} + \frac{2}{3}$$

Knowing that we must find a common denominator before we can add the fractions is a form of declarative knowledge. Then, finding the common denominator and adding the fractions require procedural knowledge. To compose an essay—which requires procedural knowledge—we must understand grammar, punctuation, and spelling rules, all types of declarative knowledge. To serve effectively in tennis, we must understand the fundamentals of the stroke before we're able to practice it effectively. The same is true for all forms of procedural knowledge.

Our goal in developing procedural knowledge is to reach automaticity, which requires a great deal of time, effort, and practice (Colvin, 2010; Taraban et al., 2007). It's the source of the old joke in which a tourist asks, "How do you get to Carnegie Hall?" The native New Yorker replies, "Practice, practice, practice." Becoming a good writer requires practice; playing a musical instrument well demands a great deal of practice; and to become an expert teacher, we must practice. The same is true for all forms of procedural knowledge, and unfortunately, no shortcuts exist. So, we, as teachers, must provide our students with ample opportunities to practice.

APA Top 20 Principles

This discussion again applies Principle 5: *Acquiring long-term knowledge and skill is largely dependent on practice*—from the *Top 20 Principles from Psychology for PreK–12 Teaching and Learning*.

Context is important for optimal practice (Star, 2004). For example, to become skilled writers students practicing grammar, spelling, and punctuation in the context of their writing is more effective than working on isolated sentences, and math students developing their skills in the context of word problems instead of simple operations is much more desirable (Bransford et al., 2000). Similarly, to become good drivers, we need to drive a car in different conditions, and athletes must perform their skills in the context of competition.

APA Top 20 Principles

This description illustrates Principle 4: *Learning is based on context, so generalizing learning to new contexts is not spontaneous but instead needs to be facilitated*—from the *Top 20 Principles from Psychology for PreK–12 Teaching and Learning*.

The characteristics of the different memory stores are summarized in Table 7.1.

Developmental Differences in the Memory Stores

Because it doesn't address developmental differences, the model of human memory tacitly implies that people of all ages process information in essentially the same way, and to a certain extent this is true. For example, both small children and adults briefly store stimuli from the environment in their sensory memories, make sense of it in their working memories, and store it in their long-term memories.

Important developmental differences exist, however. For instance, older children retain sensory memory traces longer than their younger counterparts (Nelson, Thomas, & De Haan, 2006). This means that if you're planning to teach first-graders, for example, your directions should be simple and concrete. Also, both the capacity and efficiency of working memory increase as children get older (Berk, 2019a). For example, more of their procedural knowledge becomes automatic, so they process information more quickly and handle complex tasks more efficiently (Feldman, 2014; Luna, Garver, Urban, Lazar, & Sweeney, 2004). Also, because they've had more experiences, older children bring more prior knowledge to learning activities, which better helps them make new learning meaningful.

Experience can also result in differences between learners the same age. For instance, one third-grader may excel in reading comprehension, whereas another derives little meaning from what he's read.

The Cognitive Neuroscience of Memory

Cognitive neuroscientists consider memory as the retention, reactivation, and reconstruction—when necessary—of internal representations in our brains (Oudiette, Antony, Creery, & Paller, 2013). For instance, Troy, in identifying his mother's you-are-what-you-eat comment as a *metaphor*, created an internal (mental) representation of the concept, which includes its characteristics, such as equating two items for literary effect, and how it relates to other concepts, such as *simile*. This representation was then stored—retained—in his memory to be reactivated and reconstructed when necessary. To the cognitive neuroscientist, this process of retaining, reactivating, and reconstructing these internal representations is *neural*, that is, it depends on neurons.

TABLE 7.1 Characteristics of the memory stores

	Capacity	Duration	Form of Information	Awareness
Sensory memory	Virtually unlimited	Very short	Raw, unprocessed	Unaware
Working memory	Severely limited	Relatively short unless rehearsed	In the process of being organized	Aware (the conscious part of our memory system)
Long-term memory	Virtually unlimited	Durable (some researchers believe permanent)	Schemas organized in ways that make sense to individuals	Unaware

As we saw in Chapter 2, neurons are nerve cells composed of cell bodies together with *dendrites*—short, branchlike structures that extend from the cell body and receive messages from other neurons—and *axons*—longer branches that also extend from the cell body and transmit messages. Messages are transmitted across *synapses*, tiny spaces between neurons that allow signals to be sent from axons to dendrites. The learning capability of our brains depends on the strength and permanence of these neural connections (Feldman, 2014).

As with all other aspects of learning and development, forging neural connections depends on our experiences (DiSalvo, 2011; Seung, 2012). For instance, a classic study of taxi drivers in London found that navigating its labyrinth-like streets resulted in increased growth of the visual-spatial part of their brains, and the longer they drove these streets, the greater the increase (Maguire et al., 2000). Another study found differences in the brain functions of Chinese and English speakers during problem-solving activities in math (Tang et al., 2006). Chinese speakers' brains showed increased activity in the motor or movement area as they thought about math problems, whereas the English speakers showed increases in the language areas of the brain. The researchers concluded that the differences were linked to Chinese speakers' use of the *abacus*, a calculating tool historically used by Chinese students that requires physical movement and spatial positioning.

These findings confirm other research identifying relationships between different kinds of mental activity and brain growth and development (Kurzweil, 2012; Seung, 2012). Additional research demonstrates the benefits of physical exercise, and particularly continuous aerobic exercise such as running, cycling, and swimming, on the neural activity of our brains (Alkadhi, 2018; Slusher, Patterson, Schwartz, & Acevedo, 2018). Exercise improves oxygen and nutrient delivery to our brains, and increased neural activity—connections between neurons—are some of its benefits (Erickson et al., 2011; Ruscheweyh et al., 2009). For schools, this research suggests that activities such as recess and P.E. have more benefits for students than simply helping them blow off steam or control their weight. It can literally improve academic performance, and its benefits are particularly pronounced for the executive functioning of working memory (van der Niet et al., 2016). And hope exists for us all as we get older; research indicates a positive link between exercise and general cognitive function in older individuals (Bootsman et al., 2018; Karssemeijer et al., 2017).

Researchers have also found links between neural activity and students' approaches to learning (Delazer et al., 2005). For instance, students who memorized problem solutions had more neural activity in parts of the brain involved in retrieval of verbal information, whereas students who implemented cognitive strategies had more activity in visual and spatial parts of the brain.

So, what does this information suggest to us as teachers? A lot. First, we must provide students with high-quality experiences, experiences that can increase the number of neural connections in our students' brains, which ultimately lead to the formation of permanent links, such as the brain growth in the London taxi drivers (Dubinsky, Roehrig, & Varma, 2013). For example, emphasizing the relationships between the French and Indian War, the Boston Tea Party, and the Revolutionary War is a higher-quality experience than simply describing the events and the dates on which they occurred. And it helps us understand why *meaningfulness* is such an important concept. When our students study relationships among different ideas, they form neural connections that wouldn't be created otherwise. These connections result in more efficient storage of information in long-term memory and also aid transfer of understanding to new contexts (Mayer, 2008).

Similarly, if you're a science teacher, and you want your students to understand the concept *crustacean*, having students see and touch a real crab and a real shrimp is a much higher-quality experience than merely describing the animals, or even showing pictures of them, would be. (Showing a picture is, of course, preferable to merely describing the animals.)

Then, linking the actual animals to their descriptions creates neural links that make the entire learning experience meaningful.

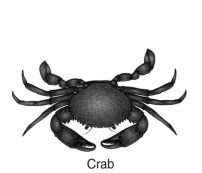

Crab

Shrimp

Second, this information helps us better understand why well-designed practice is so important. Practice requires that certain synapses are used over and over, which results in "neural commitments" that streamline and speed the transmission of neural messages that ultimately result in automaticity, such as being able to state that $7 \times 8 = 56$ without thinking about it, or using a keyboard without thinking about where we put our fingers when we type (Kuhl, 2004). Practice over time facilitates this streamlining.

As with many aspects of teaching and learning, this streamlining is another double-edged sword, and it's why we used the term "well-designed" practice. For example, practicing a corner kick in soccer with poor fundamentals is counterproductive, because undesirable neural connections will be formed. This helps us understand why bad habits, such as making the same error while keyboarding, are so hard to break.

As some neural connections are streamlined, others atrophy from lack of use. Experts suggest that this is one reason learning to speak a second language is difficult for adult learners; the neural pathways for the first language dominate the new ones (Kuhl, 2004). Overly tuned neural connections can also impede transfer. This suggests that we should present new content in a variety of contexts, so that new information will be connected in a variety of ways. For instance, presenting a range of word problems that require different operations, and wording problems differently when the same operation is required, help create different neural pathways and increase the odds that the new skill will transfer to new situations in the future. The same processes apply in all content areas.

Neuroscience research reinforces much of what we already know about teaching and learning. For instance, it reinforces the importance of high-quality experiences for learners and the need for meaningful learning. It also reinforces the importance of applying content in real-world contexts and confirms the need for practice. It also validates the applications we suggest in this chapter.

Classroom Connections

Capitalizing on the Characteristics of the Memory Stores to Promote Learning in Your Students

Sensory Memory

1. Sensory memory briefly holds incoming stimuli from the environment until the information can be processed. To keep students from losing important information, allow them to attend to one message before presenting a second one.

- **Elementary:** A second-grade teacher asks one question at a time and gets an answer before asking a second question.

- **Middle School:** A pre-algebra teacher displays two similar problems on the document camera and waits until students have copied them before she starts discussing them.

- **High School:** A geography teacher places a map on the document camera and says, "I'll give you a minute to examine the geography of the countries on this map in the front of the room. Then we'll discuss what you're noticing."

Working Memory

2. Working memory is where learners consciously process information, and its capacity is limited. To avoid overloading learners' working memories, develop lessons with questioning and avoid extended periods of lecturing.

- **Elementary:** A third-grade teacher writes directions for seatwork on the board. He asks different students to explain the directions before they begin.

- **Middle School:** A teacher in a woodworking class begins by saying, "The density of wood from the same kind of tree varies, depending on the amount of rainfall." He waits a moment, holds up two pieces of wood, and says, "What do you notice about the rings on these pieces?"

- **High School:** An Algebra II teacher "walks" students through the solutions to problems by having a different student describe each step in the solution.

3. Automaticity is the ability to perform tasks with little conscious effort. To develop automaticity in your students, provide frequent practice and present information in both verbal and visual forms.

- **Elementary:** A first-grade teacher has his students practice their writing by composing two sentences each day about an event of the previous evening. As they practice their letters, he demonstrates how they should look and describes correct procedures verbally.

- **Middle School:** To capitalize on the distributed processing capability of working memory, an eighth-grade history teacher prepares a flowchart of the events leading to the Civil War. As she questions students, she refers to the chart for each point and shows students how to use the chart to organize their notes.

- **High School:** A physics teacher drops a tennis ball and a softball together from the same height. Then, to provide the students practice with putting their thoughts into words, she has them describe what they see in writing and make conclusions about the acceleration of gravity (the balls hit the floor at the same time, so the acceleration of gravity is independent of weight).

Long-Term Memory

4. Information is organized into schemas in learners' long-term memories. To help your students make these schemas meaningful, encourage them to look for relationships among the ideas they study.

- **Elementary:** During story time, a second-grade teacher uses "how," "when," and "why" questions to encourage students to explain how the events in a story are related and contribute to the conclusion.

- **Middle School:** A middle school social studies teacher provides his students with examples of primary and secondary sources and has them examine and identify the similarities and differences between the two.

- **High School:** To help his students understand cause-and-effect relationships, a world history teacher asks questions such as "Why was shipping so important in ancient Greece?", "Why was Troy's location so important?", and "How do these questions relate to the location of today's big cities?"

MyLab Education Self-Check 7.2

Cognitive Processes

7.3 **Describe the cognitive processes in the human memory model, and identify applications in classrooms and everyday events.**

How does information move from sensory memory to working memory and from working memory to long-term memory? More importantly, how can we help our students store the information we want them to learn most efficiently? To answer these questions, let's look at Figure 7.5, which is similar to the model you first saw in Figure 7.2 but this time with cognitive processes—*attention, perception, encoding,* and *retrieval*—highlighted. As you compare Figure 7.5 to Figure 7.2, focus on these processes, and as you study the following sections, remember that they are responsible for moving information from one store to another.

Attention

Ed Psych and You

Think about a quarter (the coin). What is on one face of the coin? What's on the opposite face for your state?

Figure 7.5 Cognitive processes in the model of human memory

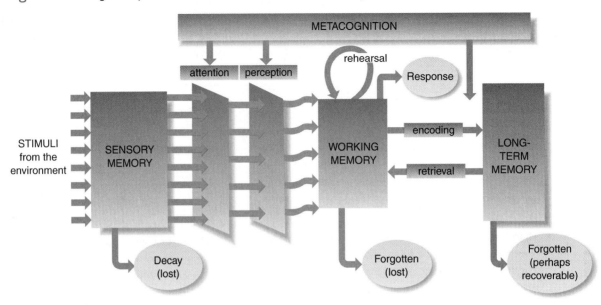

Think about our questions in *Ed Psych and You*. We routinely handle quarters, but most of us don't know what's on either side, and we may not know that each state has developed its own unique face; we don't pay attention to this information. **Attention** is the process of selectively focusing on one stimulus in the environment while ignoring other stimuli, everything we experience through our five senses (Radvansky & Ashcraft, 2014). It's impossible to attend to all the stimuli—represented in Figure 7.5 as arrows to the left of the model—we encounter, and the screening function of attention is represented by fewer arrows to its right than to its left. Without this screening function, we would be overwhelmed by an endless stream of stimuli (Davidson, 2012).

Attention has several important characteristics that can influence learning. First, it's emotion laden; we're more likely to attend to stimuli that arouse our emotions than those lacking an emotional component (Sutherland et al., 2017). Second, although individual differences exist, attention for all of us is limited (Jiang, Swallow, & Rosenbaum, 2013; Sutherland et al., 2017). For instance, we miss parts of conversations, even when we're directly involved, and, regardless of how clear, students miss parts of our explanations. Third, we're easily distracted; our attention wanders from one stimulus to another, and we often drift off without realizing it. "Unfortunately, we are not always aware when our thoughts drift off, since the propensity to do so is spontaneous and often occurs without awareness" (Xu & Metcalfe, 2016, p. 681). Research suggests that we're inattentive up to 50% of the time, and preventing the drifting off is difficult (Xu & Metcalfe, 2016).

Fourth, attention is a social process. People display a strong sensitivity to others' eye gaze, tending to follow the gaze of others (Gregory & Jackson, 2017). So, for instance, if even a small number of students in a class drift off, others are more likely to do the same.

These factors help us understand why students learn less than they should. A myriad of distractions exist—other students (especially those of the opposite sex for adolescents), noises both inside and outside the room, and people in the hallway, among many others. Any of these can distract students' attention and cause them to miss parts of our lessons. (In the last section of the chapter, "Using Educational Psychology in Teaching," we provide suggestions for attracting and maintaining students' attention.)

Technology, Learning and Development: The Impact of Technology on Attention

The impact of technology on attention is the subject of a great deal of research, with much of it focusing on the dangers of distracted attention while driving. For example,

MyLab Education
Video Example 7.3

Capturing students' attention need not be difficult or time consuming. See how middle school teacher, Richard Nelms, uses one of his students as a means of attracting the attention of his class. Notice that using the student as an attention getter required no additional planning time for Richard.

statistics from the Centers for Disease Control and Prevention (2016) and the National Highway Traffic Safety Administration (2017) indicate that:

- In 2015, more than 4 of 10 high school students who drove in the past 30 days reported sending a text or e-mail while driving. Those who reported frequent texting were also less likely to wear a seatbelt and more likely to drink and drive.

- One of 10 fatal crashes and 15% of injury crashes are reported as distraction-related.

- Drivers under the age of 20 have the highest proportion of distraction-related fatal crashes.

- Nearly 15% of all fatal distraction-affected crashes involved talking on, or otherwise manipulating, cell phones.

People texting or talking on their cell phones obviously aren't paying adequate attention to their driving, and in response, as of June 2017, 14 states and the District of Columbia had banned drivers from hand-held phone use, and 46 states and the District of Columbia banned texting while driving (Insurance Institutes for Highway Safety, 2017). The impact of these laws has yet to be determined.

And the impact of technology on attention goes beyond distracted driving. For example, Maggie Jackson (2009), in her book *Distracted: The Erosion of Attention and the Coming Dark Age*, contends we have developed a form of attention-deficit disorder, which limits our ability to remain focused. Immersed in an important writing project, for instance, we can't resist checking when we hear the familiar "ping" telling us we have a new e-mail. We then spend time reading and responding to the notes, maybe even making a little sojourn to the Internet, and before we realize it, we've spent an hour away from our writing project. Some researchers argue that this constant stimulation provokes an excitement that can be addictive, and in its absence, people feel bored (Alter, 2017).

Multitasking.   **Multitasking**, the process of engaging in two or more activities at the same time, is a technologically related factor influencing attention. Although not new, media saturation and the wide variety of available technologies have made multitasking increasingly prominent, particularly among young technology users (Magen, 2017). Some evidence suggests that teenagers use as many as six different kinds of media simultaneously during out-of-school time. As a result, they pay "continuous partial attention" to everything but have a difficult time attending carefully to any one thing (Rosen, 2012).

Multitasking is a paradox. Even as it continues to increase in popularity, an expanding body of evidence indicates that it detracts from learning and performance (Chen & Yan, 2016; Magen, 2017). Most significant for our discussion in this chapter, it negatively impacts executive functioning by limiting attention, planning, self-monitoring, and emotional control. Researchers suggest that it is associated with deficits in many aspects of everyday goal-directed behavior (Magen, 2017).

Why is multitasking so popular? Researchers believe three factors are important. First, it appears easy. For instance, with today's smartphones, we can simultaneously talk to a friend, look up information related to the conversation, and watch TV, all without getting up from a chair.

Second, the experience is emotionally satisfying. For example, we enjoy the conversation and learn something new in the process. For students studying while watching TV, watching the TV made the studying more pleasant. And the emotional satisfaction leads to the misperception that multitasking is efficient and productive. For instance, discussing work-related topics while driving may seem like an efficient way to take care of some business, but distracted driving is a serious safety issue, as mentioned earlier.

Third, technology fosters a desire to be continually connected. Because of technology, we're socially connected to a greater degree than we've ever been, and for many people this connection can result in a fear of missing out on something important (Zagorski, 2017).

So, what should we, as both learners and teachers, do? We can't simply remove technology and other distractions; they're woven into our lives, and particularly the lives of middle and high school students. And some forms of multitasking are positive, such as learning something new while in a conversation with a friend. We must try to acquire and teach our students the skills that will allow us to appropriately switch our attention from one task to another and from one technology to another. Suggestions for promoting these skills include:

- While studying, mute your computer speakers and shut off your cell phones, or at least put the phone on vibrate.

- Require students to turn off cell phones and other electronic gadgets as they enter your classroom.

- Encourage parents to eliminate distractions when their children study and do homework.

- Create a to-do work or study list, prioritizing the items on it. Beginning with the first one, move through the list. Crossing items off as you complete them increases the satisfaction of finishing each task. If you have tasks that you can't complete in one work session, do as much as you can before turning to another activity.

- Set time aside—perhaps near the end of your workday—to respond to e-mails, text messages, and phone calls. Avoid allowing them to interrupt your work or study.

- Avoid multitasking. Research consistently indicates that it detracts from learning (Chen & Yan, 2016; Magen, 2017).

Further, some researchers suggest that multitasking technically doesn't exist (Chen & Yan, 2016; Visser, 2017). Rather, what we commonly call multitasking is " . . . rapid attention switching in which individuals only process one stimulus at a time but rapidly shift back and forth between the stimuli" (Chen & Yan, 2016, p. 35). Switching back and forth both takes more processing time and results in missing some of the information (Chen & Yan, 2016; Visser, 2017).

Technology is now an integral part of our lives, and it has revolutionized the way we live. In adapting to its impact, we want to be sure it's working for us instead of the other way around.

Perception

Ed Psych and You

Look at the picture.
    Do you see a vase, or do you see two faces looking at each other?

This classic example illustrates the nature of **perception**, the process people use to find meaning in stimuli (Feldman, 2014). For those of you who "saw" a vase, for instance, this is the meaning you attached to the picture, and the same is true for those of you who "saw" two faces. Technically, we were asking, "Do you 'perceive' a vase or two faces?" In our everyday world, the term perception is commonly used to describe the way we interpret objects and events (Way, Reddy, & Rhodes, 2007). For instance, some of us "interpreted" the picture as a vase, whereas others "interpreted" it as two faces.

Perception is influenced by our past experiences and expectations (Cole, Balcetis, & Zhang, 2013; Huan, Yeo, & Ang, 2006). To illustrate these influences, let's look at a conversation between two young women interviewing for teaching positions at the same school.

"How was your interview?" Emma asks her friend, Kelly.

"Terrible," Kelly responds. "He grilled me, asking me specifically how I would teach a certain topic and what I would do in the case of two students disrupting my class. He treated me like I didn't know anything. Madison, a friend of mine who teaches there, told me about him. . . . How was yours?"

"Gosh, I thought mine was good," Emma replies. "He asked me the same questions, but I thought he was just trying to find out how we would think about teaching if he hired us. I had an interview at another school, and the principal there asked almost the same questions."

Kelly's and Emma's perceptions—the way they interpreted their interviews—were very different, Kelly viewing hers as being "grilled," but Emma feeling good about hers. Kelly anticipated the interview with negative expectations, influenced by her friend, Madison. On the other hand, Emma's expectations were influenced by her experience at another school. Perceptions are personally constructed, so they differ among people. The arrows to the right of "perception" in Figure 7.5 are curved to remind us that our students' perceptions will vary.

Accurate perceptions in learning activities are essential, because students' perceptions of what they see and hear enter working memory. If these perceptions are inaccurate, the information ultimately stored in long-term memory will also be inaccurate. The primary way to determine if our students accurately perceive the information we're presenting is to ask them. For instance, if we're teaching geography and are discussing the economies of different countries, we can check students' perceptions by simply asking, "What do we mean by the term *economy*?"

Mike did a simple perception check with his students in his lesson at the beginning of the chapter. Let's look again.

Mike has written

> **You people are a breath of fresh air.**
>
> **This class is like the sugar in my morning coffee.**

on the board.

Mike:	What do you think about that? . . . Go ahead. . . . Tell me what these statements mean to you.
Students:	That's nice.
	Do you really mean it?
	What are you talking about?
Mike:	When you look at the statements, do you think I mean you are really, . . . or *literally*, a breath of fresh air, or are you *literally* like the sugar in my coffee?
Students:	Not really (shaking their heads).

By having his students tell him what the statements meant to them, Mike was checking their perceptions. And he continued with the process when he asked, " . . . do you think I mean you are really . . . or *literally*, a breath of fresh air . . . ?" Getting in a habit of checking perceptions simply takes a bit of practice. It's easy to do, so it will quickly become automatic, and it will make a significant difference in the amount your students learn.

Perception also influences student performance on quizzes and tests. Students commonly misperceive—misinterpret—questions on quizzes, tests, and homework, which is why discussing frequently missed items on each and providing feedback for all student work is so important (Hattie, 2012).

Encoding and Encoding Strategies

After we attend to and perceive information and organize it in working memory so that it makes sense to us, we next **encode** the information, which means we represent it in long-term memory (McCrudden & McNamara, 2018; Radvansky & Ashcraft, 2014).

As an example of encoding, let's think about Mike's lesson at the beginning of the chapter once more. He had displayed the definition of the concept *metaphor* as:

Figurative language that directly equates two items for literary effect, such as equating our class and fresh air.

This was followed by Troy saying, "Oh, I get it. My Mom always says, 'You are what you eat' when she gets after me to have a good breakfast before I come to school. . . . That's a metaphor."

Troy made the connection between Mike's definition and his mother's comment in his working memory, and he then represented the connection in his long-term memory. This illustrates the process of encoding.

The three most common strategies designed to promote meaningful encoding are outlined in Figure 7.6 and discussed in this section:

- Rehearsal
- Elaboration
- Organization

Figure 7.6 Strategies for promoting meaningful encoding

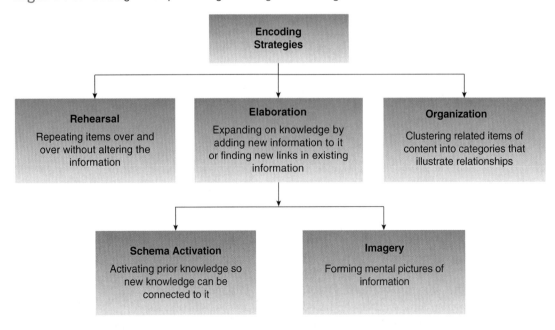

To see how Mike applies these strategies, we continue to examine his work with his class. As we saw at the beginning of the chapter, he taught his lesson on figurative language on Monday. Then, on Tuesday and Wednesday the class discussed *To Kill a Mockingbird*. We now revisit his class on Thursday.

"Okay everyone," Mike smiles. "Today, we're going to pull together some of the ideas we've been working on. Remember, on Monday we discussed the concepts *metaphor*, *simile*, and *personification* and identified examples of each. . . . Today we're going to look for examples of each of these concepts in our discussions of *To Kill a Mockingbird* to see how they make the novel more interesting.

"Let's review for a minute. Tell us what a metaphor is, and give us an example, . . . Everett?"

Everett provides a definition and example, and Mike continues his review by doing the same with *simile* and *personification*.

He then displays the following on his document camera, and comments, "We'll use this as a guide for our work today."

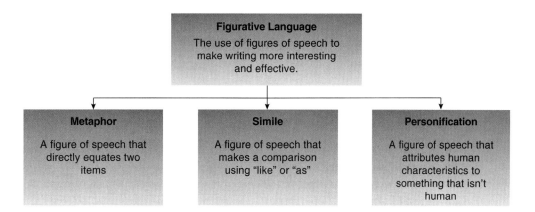

Figurative Language
The use of figures of speech to make writing more interesting and effective.

| **Metaphor** | **Simile** | **Personification** |
| A figure of speech that directly equates two items | A figure of speech that makes a comparison using "like" or "as" | A figure of speech that attributes human characteristics to something that isn't human |

"Now," Mike continues, "turn to your partners and identify at least two examples of each of the figures of speech in *To Kill a Mockingbird*. You have 20 minutes." (To help narrow the task, Mike provides page numbers in the novel as places to look for examples.)

"Now, when I face a task like this," he continues, "I try to listen carefully when my partners are talking, so I'm sure I'm paying attention to what they say. And then I write down the information we find. That way I'll be sure I don't forget. . . . Now, go ahead."

We will rejoin Mike's lesson as our discussion unfolds, but now let's see how he applied the encoding strategies in his teaching.

Rehearsal

Rehearsal is the process of repeating information over and over without altering it, such as repeating $7 \times 9 = 63$, and it serves two important functions. First, it can be used to retain information in working memory until the information is used or forgotten, such as repeating a phone number over and over until we dial it. Usually, once dialed, we forget the number. (This process is represented by the "loop" above working memory in Figures 7.2 and 7.5.)

If rehearsed long enough, however, information can be transferred into long-term memory through "brute force," making it a primitive, but widely used, encoding strategy. For example, we've all used rehearsal to remember definitions, such as a verb is a part of speech that shows action or a state of being, and other factual information, like $8 \times 9 = 72$, or Abraham Lincoln was our country's president during the Civil War. In

Mike's lesson, Everett's ability to provide a definition of the concept *metaphor* was likely the result of rehearsal; he rehearsed the definition enough times so that it was encoded in his long-term memory.

Knowing some factual information, like important events or math facts, is important, and using flash cards to remember definitions and other factual information is a common form of rehearsal. It's an inefficient encoding strategy, however, because it can result in **rote learning**, learning that involves storing information in isolated pieces, most commonly through memorization (Lin, 2007; Mayer, 2002). This is why we call it a primitive strategy.

Rehearsal can be made more meaningful, however, by connecting the to-be-remembered factual information to other facts (Bruning, Schraw, & Norby, 2011). As an example, we can help students remember the location of the Atlantic Ocean—factual information—by reminding them that it's between Africa and the Americas, and all three—Atlantic Ocean, Africa, Americas—begin with "a." And we can do something similar when we remember that the sum of the digits in the product of any number times 9 is always equal to 9 (e.g., $6 \times 9 = 54$ [$5 + 4 = 9$]; $8 \times 9 = 72$ [$7 + 2 = 9$]). Research confirms the advantage of making information meaningful in this way compared to simple "brute force" rehearsal for long-term retention (Schunk, 2016).

Mnemonics. **Mnemonics** are strategies that can be used to remember factual information by creating associations—links—between knowledge to be acquired and familiar information (Schunk, 2016). Because they create associations, mnemonics are more effective than "brute force" for remembering factual information, such as vocabulary, names, rules, and lists. Mnemonics have been proven effective in a variety of content areas and with a wide range of learners (Brehmer & Li, 2007; Bruning et al., 2011). For example, they've been used to increase cognitive performance of aging adults (Willis et al., 2006), and one study was so successful that it was picked up and discussed in the popular press (Begley, 2010).

Mnemonics can take several forms. We can use acronyms, such as HOMES to remember the names of the Great Lakes (Huron, Ontario, Michigan, Erie, and Superior), and phrases, such as "Every good boy does fine" to remember the names of the notes in the treble clef (E, G, B, D, and F). Some additional mnemonics are outlined and illustrated in Table 7.2.

Because of rehearsal's limitations, Mike placed limited emphasis on it. We turn now to more effective strategies.

Elaboration

You're at a noisy party, and when you miss some of a conversation, you fill in details, trying to make sense of an incomplete message. You do the same when you read a text or listen to a lecture. You expand on—and sometimes distort—information to make it

---

TABLE 7.2 Types and examples of mnemonic devices

Mnemonic	Description	Example
Method of loci	Learner combines imagery with specific locations in a familiar environment, such as the chair, sofa, lamp, and end table in a living room.	Student wanting to remember the first seven elements in order visualizes hydrogen at the chair, helium at the sofa, lithium at the lamp, and so on.
Peg-word method	Learner memorizes a series of "pegs"—such as a simple rhyme like "one is bun" and "two is shoe"—on which to-be-remembered information is hung.	A learner wanting to remember to get pickles and carrots at the grocery visualizes a pickle in a bun and carrot stuck in a shoe.
Link method	Learner visually links items to be remembered.	A learner visualizes *homework* stuck in a *notebook*, which is bound to her *textbook*, *pencil*, and *pen* with a rubber band to remember to take the (italicized) items to class.
Key-word method	Learner uses imagery and rhyming words to remember unfamiliar words.	A learner remembers that *trigo* (which rhymes with *tree*) is the Spanish word for *wheat* by visualizing a sheaf of wheat sticking out of a tree.
First-letter method	Learner creates a word from the first letter of items to be remembered.	A student creates the word *Wajmma* to remember the first six presidents in order: Washington, Adams, Jefferson, Madison, Monroe, and Adams.

fit your expectations and current understanding. In each case, you are elaborating on the message or what you already know.

Elaboration is an encoding strategy that involves adding new information to our existing knowledge, or creating new connections (links) in existing information (Schunk, 2016). Elaboration is a powerful encoding strategy, and Mike used it extensively in his teaching. For instance, on Monday he provided his students with the definitions of *metaphor, simile,* and *personification* and then had them identify examples of each. The examples made their schemas for each concept more meaningful because links between the examples and definitions were created. Then, he had the students further elaborate on their understanding. To see how, we rejoin his lesson on Thursday after the class has attempted to identify examples of *metaphor, simile,* and *personification* in *To Kill a Mockingbird*.

At the end of the 20 minutes, Mike reassembles the class and says, "Okay, let's see what you found. . . . Let's start with your group, Emma, Isabella, and Miguel."

"We think an example of a metaphor is on page 48," Emma offers. "It says, 'Summer was our best season . . . it was a thousand colors in a parched landscape.'"

"Okay," Mike nods. "Let's see what we think. Do you agree or not? . . . Everyone think about this example for a few seconds."

After a short pause, he continues, "Go ahead, Ethan."

"We agree. . . . Summer is being equated to a thousand colors, but it isn't really a thousand colors. . . . So, so it's a metaphor."

"Okay, good," Mike smiles. "And, just imagine, you can close your eyes and essentially picture the colors of summer. By using this metaphor the writer invites us to think about summer in a different way. . . . This is why authors use figurative language."

Mike continues with the discussion and his students identify and explain other examples. In each case, he has the students explain why they agree or disagree with the suggestions as he did with the example of metaphor.

In this discussion, Mike had his students identify examples of the concepts in *To Kill a Mockingbird*. Now, examples the students identified in the novel were linked to both the definitions and the examples they provided on Monday, making their schemas for the concepts even more complex and more meaningful. This is the essence of elaboration.

Finding or creating examples is one of the most powerful and meaningful forms of elaboration, and for students who lack experience with a topic, examples also provide them with the background knowledge they need to construct new knowledge. This is why we so strongly emphasize the use of examples in this text and why we try to provide you with examples of each of the ideas we present. In this chapter our case studies with Mike and his students are our attempts to capitalize on this encoding strategy.

When examples aren't available, using **analogies**, descriptions of relationships that are similar in some but not all respects, can be an effective elaboration strategy (Radvansky & Ashcraft, 2014). As an example, consider the following analogy from science:

Our circulatory system is like a pumping system that carries the blood around our bodies. The veins and arteries are the pipes, and the heart is the pump.

The veins and arteries are similar—but not identical—to pipes, and the heart is a type of pump. The analogy is an effective form of elaboration because it links new information to a pumping station, an idea learners presumably understand.

Schema Activation.   **Schema activation** is a form of elaboration that involves activating relevant prior knowledge so that new information can be connected to it (Mayer & Wittrock, 2006).

For example, when Mike introduced his lesson he said,

"Let's review for a minute. Tell us what a metaphor is, and give us an example, . . . Everett."

MyLab Education
Video Example 7.4

Schema activation is an encoding strategy that helps students retrieve information from their long-term memories so new information can be connected to it. Here, middle school science teacher, Scott Sowell, uses a review to help his students activate their existing schemas.

By asking his students to provide a definition and example of each of the concepts, *metaphor, simile,* and *personification,* Mike's review "activated" the concepts, definitions, and earlier examples so the students could attach additional examples from the novel to them.

As you think back to your best teachers, in most cases they probably began their classes with a review, and a long history of research supports the effectiveness of well-structured reviews in promoting learning (Good & Lavigne, 2018; Hattie, 2012; Rutter, Maughan, Mortimore, Ouston, & Smith, 1979).

The most effective way of activating students' prior knowledge is to ask them what they already know about a topic, or ask them to provide some personal experiences related to the topic. Any teaching strategy that helps students form conceptual bridges between what they already know and what they are to learn is a form of schema activation.

Ed Psych and You

Look at the two excerpts below.

1. Traveling by rail from the Midwest to California is a pleasant experience. As you sit in the dining car, you might meet interesting people, it's relaxing, and you hear the sound of the train rolling over the rails.
2. At the next table a woman stuck her nose in a novel; a college kid pecked at a laptop. Overlaying all this, a soundtrack: choo-k-chook, choo-k-chook, choo-k-chook, the metronomic rhythm of an Amtrak train rolling down the line to California (Isaacson, 2009).

How are these two excerpts different?

Imagery.   Now, let's think about our question in *Ed Psych and You*. The first is rather bland, whereas in the second we can virtually "see" in our mind's eye the woman reading her novel and the student at his computer, and we can almost hear the clicking of rails. It capitalizes on **imagery,** a form of elaboration that capitalizes on the process of forming mental pictures of an idea (Schunk, 2016; Schwartz & Heiser, 2006). It's a common strategy novelists and other writers use to make their stories vivid and interesting.

Mike capitalized on imagery when he said,

"And, just imagine, you can close your eyes and essentially picture the colors of summer. By using this metaphor the writer invites us to think about summer in a different way. . . . This is why authors use figurative language."

He was encouraging his students to use imagery to make the information more meaningful.

Imagery is also widely used by coaches to help their athletes develop skills ranging from corner kicks in soccer and jump shots in basketball to performance in Olympic events (Clarey, 2014; Glover & Dixon, 2013; Guillot, Moschberger, & Collet, 2013). Through imagery, coaches encourage their athletes to visualize successfully executing the skill they're trying to develop.

Imagery is an effective encoding strategy because our long-term memories have one system for verbal information and a separate system for images (Paivio, 1991; Sadoski & Paivio, 2001). Ideas that can be represented both visually and verbally, such as *ball, house,* or *dog,* are easier to remember than concepts more difficult to visualize, such as *honesty* or *truth* (Paivio, 1986). The fact that we can both read about the components of our memory systems and visualize the models in Figures 7.2 and 7.5 helps us capitalize on these two systems in long-term memory. Information in the models is more meaningfully encoded than if we had only described it verbally (Clark & Paivio, 1991). The dual storage systems in our long-term memories again remind us of the importance of supplementing verbal information with visual representations and vice versa (Igo, Kiewra, & Bruning, 2004).

We can take advantage of imagery in several ways when we teach (Schwartz & Heiser, 2006). For instance, we can use pictures and diagrams, we can ask students to form mental pictures of the ideas they study, and we can ask students to draw their own diagrams about ideas they are learning. Imagery is particularly helpful in problem solving (Bruning et al., 2011; Schunk, 2016). It would have been harder to solve the area-of-the-pentagon problem that we presented in our discussion of working memory, for example, without the drawing. Seeing the sketch is more effective than simply being asked to find the area of a pentagon that is 5 inches at the base, 4 inches at the side, and 6 inches at the peak. This also helps us understand why imagery is a form of elaboration; the drawing elaborates the original problem.

Organization

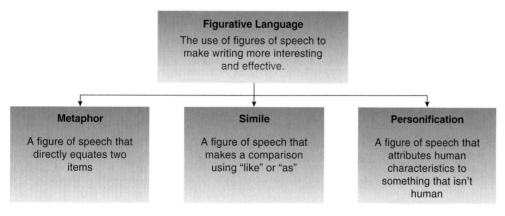

Now, let's look at Mike's work again. After he asked his students to provide a definition and example of each concept, he displayed his hierarchy, and commented, "We'll use this as a guide for our work today." He realized that some students being able to provide a definition and example—such as Everett in the case of *metaphor*—didn't imply that all students would be able to do so. His hierarchy was designed to help bridge the gap.

Mike's hierarchy is a form of **organization**, an encoding strategy that clusters related items of content into categories that illustrate relationships. His hierarchy indicated that each—*metaphor, simile,* and *personification*—are forms of figurative language, and each is designed to make writing more interesting, but they have their own sets of characteristics.

Because well-organized content contains connections among its elements, cognitive load is decreased, and encoding (and later retrieval) is more efficient.

Research in reading, memory, and classroom instruction confirms the value of organization in promoting learning (Mayer, 2008). Research also suggests that experts learn more efficiently than novices because their knowledge in long-term memory is better organized, allowing them to better access and connect new information to it (Radvansky & Ashcraft, 2014; McCrudden & McNamara, 2018).

We can help our students organize information in several ways:

- *Hierarchies:* Effective when new information can be subsumed under existing ideas. Mike's hierarchy is an example, and in Figure 7.6 we used a hierarchy to organize the encoding strategies we're discussing in this section.
- *Charts and matrices:* Useful for organizing large amounts of information into categories. For instance, Table 7.1 is our attempt to organize information about the memory stores so it's meaningful to you.
- *Models:* Helpful for representing relationships that cannot be observed directly. The models of human memory in Figures 7.2 and 7.5 in this chapter are examples.
- *Outlines:* Useful for representing the organizational structure in a body of written material. The detailed table of contents for this book is an example.

Other ways to organize content include graphs, tables, flowcharts, and maps. As a student, you can also use these organizers as aids in your attempts to make the information you're studying meaningful.

Now, a word of caution. We know that people construct knowledge in ways that make sense to them, so if the organizational structure we offer doesn't make sense to our students, they will cope in one of three ways: (1) they will (mentally) reorganize and encode the information in a way that does, whether it's correct or not; (2) they'll memorize as much of it as they can and promptly forget it later; or (3) they will ignore it altogether. The only way to avoid these possibilities is to check our students' perceptions of the forms of organization that we present. This means we must interact with them, because the only way to find out if they perceive the information accurately is to ask them.

Cognitive Activity: The Essence of Encoding

Ed Psych and You

You and a friend are studying this book. You click on the link at the end of each major section to access the *MyLab Self-Check* questions, you respond to the questions, and you then click on the feedback to see how you've done. Your friend also clicks on the links, reads each question, and then clicks on the feedback. Which of you is likely to learn more?

You will learn more, because you are more cognitively active than your friend. **Cognitive activity** is the process of thinking carefully about, and engaging in, the learning task at hand. For instance, writing an answer encourages you to search your long-term memory for connections and construct a response. It requires you to think carefully about an answer, and focused thinking is the essence of cognitive activity. No matter how hard we try, when we simply read the question and the feedback, we aren't likely to think as deeply about our answer. It is less cognitively active, resulting in fewer connections to information in long-term memory and less meaningful learning. Similarly, asking students to provide additional examples of a concept places them in more cognitively active roles than they would be if we provide the example for them (Bransford et al., 2000). Regardless of the encoding strategy we use, putting ourselves in cognitively active roles is essential.

Forgetting

Forgetting is the loss of, or inability to retrieve, information from memory, and it is a real part of both classroom learning and our everyday lives. To understand *forgetting*, look again at the model first presented in Figure 7.2. There we see that information lost from both sensory memory and working memory is permanent. It is literally gone because we never transferred it to long-term memory. However, information in long-term memory has been encoded. Why can't we remember it?

Forgetting as Interference

One way to explain forgetting uses the concept of **interference**, the loss of information because something learned either before or after detracts from understanding (Howe, 2004). For example, students learn that singular possessives are formed by adding an apostrophe s to the singular noun, as in "One of the car's fenders was bent," and later learn rules for forming plural possessives, such as, "The boys' lockers were all in a mess" or "The children's clothes have been washed and folded." If their understanding of the rule for forming singular possessives later confuses their understanding of rules for forming plural possessives (or contractions), or if the rules for forming plural possessives confuse their prior understanding, interference has occurred.

We can reduce the possibilities of interference by teaching closely related ideas together, such as the rules for forming possessives, adjectives and adverbs, longitude and latitude, and adding fractions with similar and different denominators. The goal in each case is to help students recognize similarities and differences, such as how apostrophes are used differently when forming singular and plural possessives. We can also reduce interference by using reviews to capitalize on schema activation, such as doing some practice problems with fractions where the denominators are the same and then moving to fractions with unlike denominators. Studying easily confused items of information together helps students identify easily confused similarities and promotes elaboration.

Forgetting as Retrieval Failure

Retrieval is the process of pulling information from long-term memory back into working memory, and it's represented in Figures 7.2 and 7.5 by the arrow pointing from long-term memory back to working memory. We've all had the experience of knowing a name or fact, but we simply can't dredge it up; we can't retrieve the information. Many researchers believe that "forgetting" is actually our inability to retrieve information from long-term memory (Williams & Zacks, 2001). Retrieval failure is a second explanation for forgetting.

Ed Psych and You

Quickly name the months of the year. Now, do the same, but this time list them alphabetically. Why were you so much slower the second time?

The Role of Context in Retrieval. Retrieval depends on context and the way we originally encode information, which helps answer the question we asked in *Ed Psych and You* (Williams & Zacks, 2001). We encode the months of the year chronologically, since that's the way we've learned and experienced them, and remembering them this way is automatic. Attempting to state them alphabetically is a different context and different retrieval challenge. We can do it, but we must laboriously go through the process. Similarly, you know a person at school, but you can't remember his name when you see him at a party; his name was encoded in the school context, and you're trying to retrieve it in the context of the party.

APA Top 20 Principles

This description illustrates Principle 4: *Learning is based on context, so generalizing learning to new contexts is not spontaneous but instead needs to be facilitated*—from the *Top 20 Principles from Psychology for PreK–12 Teaching and Learning*.

Meaningfulness is the key to retrieval. The more meaningful—interconnected— our knowledge is in long-term memory, the easier it is to retrieve. Mike attempted to make information about figurative language meaningful by first providing definitions of *metaphor, simile,* and *personification*, then having his students generate examples they could link to the definitions, and finally identifying examples in the context of *To Kill a Mockingbird* to create additional links. In doing so, he strongly emphasized elaboration as an encoding strategy.

Practice to the point of automaticity, such as we've done with the months of the year, also facilitates retrieval (Chaffen & Imreh, 2002). When math facts are automatic, for example, students easily retrieve them for use in problem solving, leaving more working memory space to focus on solutions to problems.

Developmental Differences in Cognitive Processes

As with the memory stores, developmental differences exist in our cognitive processes (Feldman 2014; Nelson et al., 2006). One of the most important involves attention, because it's essential for dealing with the demands of everyday life (Atkinson & Braddock, 2012). Developmental differences can appear by age two, with those better able to focus their attention later developing superior language skills (Beuker, Rommelse, Donders, & Buitelaar, 2013). Over time, children gradually learn to focus their attention and avoid distractions, but students with learning disabilities, such as ADHD, tend to be developmentally delayed in this area (Bental & Tirosh, 2007; Davidson, 2012).

Developmental differences also exist in perception. Because older students have more background experiences than their younger counterparts, their perceptions are more likely to be accurate. And differences also exist in encoding. For instance, students typically don't use rehearsal until about the second or third grade (Jarrold & Citroën, 2013), and as they further develop, they learn to use more advanced (and effective) encoding strategies, such as organization, elaboration, and imagery (Pressley & Hilden, 2006). If you're planning to teach young children, you can promote their development by modeling cognitive processes, such as attention and perception checks, encouraging their use with reminders and reinforcement, and praising particularly good examples, such as a classmate demonstrating an awareness of differences in perception.

These developmental changes in processing efficiency will take time and effort, but over the course of a year, you will see significant growth in your students.

Diversity: The Impact of Diversity on Cognition

Our students' diversity has a powerful effect on their cognition, with their prior knowledge and experiences being two of the most important factors. As a simple example, because Troy had experience with his mother saying "You are what you eat," he was able to identify it as an example of a metaphor. He had a personal experience his classmates lacked. As another example, Paul (one of your authors) grew up in a rural, relatively low socioeconomic environment in Montana and attended a very small high school. As a result, access to a rich menu of educational experience, such as advanced math and science courses, foreign languages, and technology, was limited. When he went to college, he competed with students from larger schools and had to work extra hard to overcome these deficiencies. Don (your other author), who taught in a low socioeconomic status neighborhood outside of Chicago, found that many of his urban students, because of parental work pressures, family issues, and other factors, never had the chance to capitalize on the educational opportunities available in the city. Although less than an hour away from world-class museums, a planetarium, and an aquarium, for example, many students didn't even know they existed. More advantaged students frequently visited these sites, and their performance in class reflected their educational benefits.

In spite of these differences, however, we can do a great deal to accommodate the diversity in our students' background knowledge (Huan et al., 2006):

- Assess students' prior knowledge and perceptions by asking them what they know about a topic. For example, because he has several recent-immigrant children in his class, a third-grade teacher begins a unit on communities by saying, "Tell us about the communities where you lived before coming to this country." He then uses the information as a framework for the study of their current community.

- Supplement students' prior experiences with high-quality examples that promote meaningful encoding through elaboration. For instance, a kindergarten teacher helps her students understand *living things* by bringing a plant, pet hamster, and rock to class, and—including themselves—observe and compare the examples.

- Use students' experiences to augment the background knowledge of their class-mates. For instance, a teacher whose class is studying modern Europe says, "Celeena, you lived in Europe. Tell us about the thinking of people in countries that were part of the former Eastern Bloc."

In each case, the teacher then uses students' existing background knowledge as a launching point for the lesson. Evidence suggests that sharing information in this way leads to collaborative encoding, encoding information in a group setting that wouldn't be possible alone (Harris, Barnier, & Sutton, 2013). This ability is particularly valuable when working with students from diverse backgrounds, because they bring a rich array of prior experiences to learning activities. The ability to adapt lessons in this way is an important component of teaching expertise.

Classroom Connections

Helping Your Students Capitalize on Cognitive Processes to Increase Their Learning

Attention

1. Attention is the beginning point for learning. Begin and conduct lessons to attract and maintain attention.

- **Elementary:** To be sure that all students are attending to the lesson, a third-grade teacher calls on all his students whether they have their hands up or not.

- **Middle School:** A science teacher introducing the concept *pressure* has students stand by their desks, first on both feet and then on one foot. They then discuss the force and pressure on the floor in each case.

- **High School:** To be sure that her students attend to important points, a world history teacher uses emphasis: "Everyone, listen carefully now, because we're going to look at three important reasons that World War I broke out in Europe."

Perception

2. Perception is the process of attaching meaning to the information we attend to, so accurate perceptions are essential

for understanding. Check frequently to be certain that students perceive your examples and other representations accurately.

- **Elementary:** In a lesson on living things, a kindergarten teacher holds up a large potted plant, asks, "What do you notice about the plant?" and calls on several children for their observations.

- **Middle School:** A geography teacher downloads colored pictures of different landforms from the Internet and asks students to describe different features in each.

- **High School:** Students are reading an essay and encounter the line, "The revolution often bordered on anarchy; the citizens were out of control." Their teacher stops and asks, "What does the author mean by 'anarchy'?"

Meaningful Encoding

3. Meaningful encoding is the process of connecting new information to information already in long-term memory. To aid encoding, carefully organize the information you present, and

(continued)

promote cognitive activity by interacting with your students.

- **Elementary:** A fourth-grade teacher illustrates that heat causes expansion by placing a balloon-covered soft drink bottle in a pot of hot water and by presenting a drawing that shows the spacing and motion of the air molecules before and after the bottle is heated. She then guides the students with questioning to understand the relationship between heat, molecular activity, and expansion.

- **Middle School:** A math teacher presents a flowchart with a series of questions students should ask themselves as they solve word problems (e.g., What do I know? What am I trying to find out?). As the class works on problems, he asks them to describe their thinking and tell where they are on the flowchart.

- **High School:** A history teacher presents a matrix comparing different immigrant groups, their reasons for relocating to the United States, the difficulties they encountered, and their rates of assimilation. The students then search for patterns in the information in the chart.

4. Learners elaborate their understanding when they make new connections between the items of information they're studying. Encourage students to relate items of information to each other and form mental images as often as possible.

- **Elementary:** A first-grade teacher, after displaying charts showing different kinds of dress and activities during the seasons, says, "Let's see what we can learn about the seasons. Look at the charts. Tell us something you see that is similar in the different seasons and something that is different."

- **Middle School:** A geography teacher encourages her students to visualize parallel lines on the globe as they think about latitude, and vertical lines coming together at the North and South Poles as they think about longitude. She then asks her students to compare them.

- **High School:** An English teacher asks students to imagine the appearance of the characters in a novel by pretending they are casting them for a movie version. He then asks them to suggest a current actor or actress to play each role.

Retrieval

5. Retrieval occurs when learners pull information from long-term memory back into working memory, and interference can inhibit this process. To prevent interference and aid retrieval, teach closely related ideas together.

- **Elementary:** To teach area and perimeter, a fifth-grade teacher has her students lay squares side by side to illustrate area, and she has them measure the distance around the pieces to illustrate perimeter.

- **Middle School:** An English teacher displays a passage on the document camera that includes gerunds and participles. He then asks the students to compare the way the words are used in the passage to demonstrate that gerunds are nouns and participles are adjectives.

- **High School:** A biology teacher begins a unit on arteries and veins by saying, "We've all heard of hardening of the arteries, but we haven't heard of 'hardening of the veins.' Why not?"

MyLab Education **Self-Check 7.3**
MyLab Education **Application Exercise 7.2:** Cognitive Processes in Young Children

In this exercise you will be asked to analyze a kindergarten teacher's application of cognitive processes with her students.

Metacognition: Knowledge and Regulation of Cognition

7.4 Define metacognition and identify examples of metacognitive monitoring in classroom activities and experiences outside of school.

Ed Psych and You

Have you ever said to yourself something like, "I'm beat today. I better drink a cup of coffee before I go to class," or "I better sit near the front of the class so I won't fall asleep." What do these comments suggest about your approach to learning?

If you answered yes to the first question above, or have had similar thoughts about your learning, you were being metacognitive. **Metacognition**, commonly described as "thinking about thinking," is knowledge and regulation of our cognition (Medina, Castleberry, & Persky, 2017). **Meta-attention**, such as you knowing that your drowsiness might affect your ability to attend, is one type of metacognition. You knew about the importance of attention for learning, and you regulated it by drinking coffee or sitting near the front of the class. **Metamemory**, knowledge and regulation of memory strategies, is another form of metacognition.

In addition to the examples we saw in *Ed Psych and You*, many others exist in our everyday lives. Paul, for instance, knows that he is likely to misplace his keys (knowledge of cognition), so he immediately puts them in a desk drawer when he comes in from the garage (regulates his cognition). Don, a self-described absent-minded professor, realizes that he sometimes forgets important dates like his wedding anniversary and kids' birthdays, so he's put them on his computer with a reminder. And virtually everyone prepares lists when grocery shopping. In all cases, we're aware of our cognition (thinking), and we regulate it with our lists and other strategies.

Research on Metacognition

Intensive research on metacognition has been conducted for nearly half a century, and it has found a variety of applications. For instance, it's been emphasized as a tool for dealing with emotional issues, such as stress, negative thinking, and worry, in both adults and children (Kertz & Woodruff-Borden, 2013; McEvoy, Moulds, & Mahoney, 2013). It has also been identified as a positive influence on decision making, cooperation, and social interaction (Pescetelli, Rees, & Bahrami, 2016).

Most important for our discussion, metacognition plays an essential role in classroom learning. "It has been well established that metacognition plays a central role in learning and academic achievement" (Hessels-Schlatter, Hessels, Godin, Spillmann-Rojas, 2017, p. 110). It performs this crucial role by controlling and guiding our thinking (Medina et al., 2017), and, in fact, it's so important that it can overcome many of the disadvantages associated with low socioeconomic status and poverty (Callan, Marchant, Finch, & German, 2016).

Metacognition can also improve achievement without significant increases in work or effort (Tullis, Finley, & Benjamin, 2013). When we teach our students to be metacognitive, we're asking them to work "smarter," not harder. And metacognition is relatively independent of general academic ability. "Evidence suggests that metacognitive awareness can compensate for low ability and insufficient knowledge" (Bruning et el., 2011; p. 82). For instance, realizing that attention to a task is essential doesn't depend on ability. And this realization can lead students to create personal learning environments free of distractions, such as simply moving to the front of a class or turning off a cell phone and TV while studying at home.

Metacognition is complex. For instance, research indicates that it's influenced by emotion, with hope and optimism having a positive effect and anxiety having a negative impact (González, Fernández, & Paoloni, 2017). And it has been positively linked to personality characteristics, particularly conscientiousness (Kelly & Donaldson, 2016).

As we would expect, metacognition is influenced by task difficulty. When tasks are challenging, the cognitive load on working memory may be too great to allow effective metacognitive monitoring. This suggests that we should have students divide difficult tasks into smaller, more manageable parts (Kalyuga, 2010).

Finally, as we would also predict, neither students—including college students—nor adults are particularly good at metacognitive monitoring (Medina et al., 2017), but it can be significantly improved with instruction and effort (Bruning et al., 2011). This suggests that teaching all students to be metacognitive is important, and it's even more important with low-ability learners, because they're less likely to develop metacognitive abilities on their own.

Modeling metacognition is the most effective way to promote it in our students. As a simple example, Mike was modeling when he said,

---

"Now, when I face a task like this, I try to listen carefully when my partners are talking, so I'm sure I'm paying attention to what they say. And then I write down the information we find. That way I'll be sure I don't forget."

Mike's actions were simple and took little additional effort. They won't result in all students becoming immediately metacognitive, but over time they will make a difference with many. This is what we're trying to do when we teach.

The metacognitive component of the memory model is illustrated in Figure 7.7.

Developmental Differences in Metacognition

As we would expect, young learners' metacognitive abilities are limited. Young children often show little evidence of either metacognitive monitoring or control (O'Leary & Sloutsky, 2017). For instance, they are often unaware of the need to pay attention in learning activities, whereas their older counterparts are more likely to realize that attention is important. With teacher support, however, even young children quickly become more strategic about their learning. For example, students as early as the third grade can be taught metacognitive strategies, such as stopping after reading a few paragraphs and asking themselves what they've just read. But they sometimes tend to overestimate their abilities, particularly when tasks are challenging (Metcalfe & Finn, 2013).

More sophisticated metacognition, such as consciously using advanced encoding strategies like organization, elaboration, and imagery, begin to appear in early adolescence, advance with age, and then level off in adulthood (Weil et al., 2013). As we noted earlier, in spite of these developmental differences, older learners and even college students are not as metacognitive about their learning as they could or should be (Medina et al., 2017; O'Leary & Sloutsky, 2017). So, if you're planning to teach in middle or high schools, your students will still need a great deal of guidance

MyLab Education

Video Example 7.5

Developmental differences exist in learners' metacognitive abilities. Notice in this segment that the older student is better able to predict how many items he will remember from a list than is the younger student. We see that the younger student overestimates the number he will remember, which is typical of younger learners.

Figure 7.7 Metacognition in the model of human memory

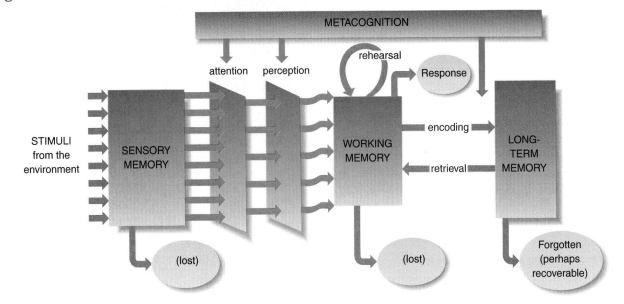

and support to develop their metacognitive abilities. Finally, as with learning and development in general, the development of metacognition has an important social component. So, the more you interact with your students, and the more you emphasize and model metacognition, the more advanced their development will become (Brinck & Liljenfors, 2013).

Diversity: Metacognitive Differences in Gender, Culture, and Learners with Exceptionalities

As with all aspects of learning and development, differences exist in our students with respect to metacognition. As one example, some evidence indicates that girls tend to be more metacognitive than boys in their approaches to learning (Weil et al., 2013). And, as we would expect, students' cultural beliefs also influence their metacognition. Asian students, for example, tend to believe that learning is a demanding process that requires a great deal of perseverance. They also believe that ability can be improved with effort, so they are likely to use metacognitive strategies. Students from mainstream American culture are more likely to believe that ability is essentially fixed, so they are less likely to search for and use these strategies (Chen & Trommsdorff, 2012; Li, 2005).

Issues also exist for second language learners. For instance, the cognitive load on their working memories is high because, in addition to the topic they're studying, they are also learning English. As a result, metacognitive monitoring can be pushed off the workbench, taking a backseat to the immediate task at hand (Wright, 2012).

Learners with exceptionalities represent another aspect of diversity. For instance, students with learning disabilities and behavior disorders are often "cognitively inert," that is, they don't acquire metacognitive strategies through the normal course of development in the same way as their peers. However, with effort and practice they can be taught to be metacognitive, and promoting the development of these abilities represents one of the most promising educational trends in working with students having exceptionalities (Hardman, Egan, & Drew, 2017).

In summarizing this section, we want to emphasize that these are general patterns. For instance, not all Asian students, and not all mainstream American students, fit the patterns we identified earlier. And all students can benefit from our efforts to teach metacognitive awareness in our classrooms. As with all aspects of learning and teaching, we need to be cautious about overgeneralizing and stereotyping.

Classroom Connections

Promoting Metacognition in Your Students

1. Metacognition is knowledge of and control over the way we study and learn, and learners who are metacognitive learn more and retain information longer. To capitalize on metacognition, integrate metacognitive strategies into your instruction and model your own metacognition.

- **Elementary:** During a lesson, a fourth-grade teacher holds up a card with the sentence, "If you're paying attention, raise your hand." He acknowledges those who are, and encourages them to share their strategies for maintaining attention during class.

- **Middle School:** A social studies teacher emphasizes metamemory by saying, "Suppose you're reading, and the book states that there are three important differences between capitalism and socialism. What should you do?"

- **High School:** An economics teacher models metacognitive strategies by making statements like, "Whenever I read something new, I always ask myself, 'How does this relate to what I've been studying?' For example, how is the liberal economic agenda different from the conservative agenda?"

Evaluating Information Processing and the Model of Human Memory

Information processing and the model of human memory make important contributions to our understanding of the way we learn and develop. However, as with all theories, they have both strengths and weaknesses. We examine them in the following section, beginning with some of the prominent criticisms.

Criticisms of Information Processing and the Human Memory Model

Critics suggest that the model, as initially presented in Figure 7.2, is an oversimplification of the complexities involved in processing and learning new information. For example, the model presents attention as a filter between sensory memory and working memory, but some evidence suggests that the central executive in working memory influences both our attention and how we perceive information. So, attending and attaching meaning to incoming stimuli are not as simple as the one-way flow of information suggested by the model (Kiyonaga & Egner, 2013; Shipstead & Engle, 2013). "Put simply, we argue that WM and attention should no longer be considered as separate systems or concepts, but as competing and influencing one another because they rely on the same limited resource (Kiyonaga & Egner, 2013, p. 228). Further, some researchers question whether working memory and long-term memory are as distinct as the model suggests, and some argue that they simply represent different activation states, that is, differences in the extent to which individuals are actively processing information in a single memory. According to this view, when people are processing information, it's in an active state, which is information we typically describe as being in working memory. As attention shifts, other information becomes active, and the previous information becomes inactive. Most of the information in our memories is inactive, information we typically describe as being in long-term memory (Baddeley, 2001; Radvansky & Ashcraft, 2014).

The memory model has also been criticized for failing to adequately consider the social context in which learning occurs, as well as cultural and personal factors that influence learning, such as students' emotions (Nasir, Rosebery, Warren, & Lee, 2006). Critics also argue that it doesn't adequately account for the extent to which learners construct their own knowledge, a basic principle of cognitive learning theory (Kafai, 2006).

Finally, the model of human memory is assumed to be a logical, sequential information processing system that is governed by metacognition. It assumes that information is consciously processed, that is, we attend to the information, attach meaning to it through perception, consciously organize and make sense of it in working memory, and then encode and store it in long-term memory. However, an expanding body of evidence indicates that we make many conclusions and decisions without thinking about them (Kahneman, 2011; Thaler & Sunstein, 2008; Vedantam, 2010). Others go further and argue that much of what we do happens below our level of awareness (Aronson, Wilson, & Akert, 2016). Examples, both in our everyday lives and in classrooms, corroborate this view. Retailers, for example, pay big bucks to supermarkets to have their products displayed at eye level, because marketing research indicates that we—subconsciously—are more likely to buy goods placed this way. Dairy items are usually in the back so we have to weave our way through the store to get a carton of milk, and the more time we spend in the supermarket, the more likely we'll spend extra money (Urban, 2014).

Subconscious processing also exists in classrooms. For instance, a long history of research indicates that teachers assess physically attractive students as more intelligent and socially skilled than their less attractive peers. And they have different expectations for attractive students, which can result in differences in achievement for the two groups

(Ritts, Patterson, & Tubbs, 1992; Talamas, Mayor, & Perrett, 2016; Tartaglia & Rollero, 2015). These subconscious evaluations also influence teachers' perceptions of ethnic and cultural groups. For example, one study found that teachers rated unattractive black males lower in perceived ability and social skills than any other group (Parks & Kennedy, 2007). They obviously aren't making these assessments consciously, and information processing and the model of human memory cannot account for these findings.

Strengths of Information Processing and the Model of Human Memory

Despite criticisms, virtually all cognitive descriptions of learning accept the basic structure of human memory, including a limited-capacity working memory, a long-term memory that stores information in organized form, cognitive processes that move the information from one store to another, and the regulatory mechanisms of metacognition (Bransford et al., 2000; Schunk, 2016). These components help explain aspects of learning that other theories can't.

Perhaps most important for our work as teachers, this theory of learning arguably offers more guidance for instruction than any other. For example, it helps us understand why:

- getting and maintaining students' attention is essential.
- checking students' perceptions is necessary.
- reviews are valuable.
- examples are crucial for learning.
- interacting with our students instead of simply lecturing to them is important.

And it provides, through metacognition, a mechanism for dealing with processing that occurs below the level of consciousness. For example, simply being aware of teachers' tendencies to treat attractive students better than their less attractive peers increases the likelihood that we will be more equitable in the treatment of all our students. (We offer specific suggestions for applying the theory in your teaching in the next section of the chapter.) Table 7.3 summarizes this information.

MyLab Education Self-Check 7.4

Using Educational Psychology in Teaching: Suggestions for Applying Information Processing and the Model of Human Memory with Students

7.5   Analyze classroom applications of information processing and the model of human memory.

Throughout the chapter we have seen how Mike Davis applied information processing and human memory with his students. In this section, we provide the following specific suggestions for using this theory in your teaching:

- Conduct reviews to activate schemas and check perceptions.
- Attract and maintain students' attention.
- Develop students' background knowledge with high-quality examples and other representations of content.
- Interact with students to promote cognitive activity and reduce cognitive load.

TABLE 7.3 Analyzing theories: Information processing and the model of human memory

Key question	How do people gather, organize, and store information in memory?
Information stores Sensory memory (SM) Working memory (WM) Long-term memory (LTM)	Repositories that hold information: • Vary from large capacity but short duration (SM) to small capacity and relatively short duration (WM) to large capacity and long duration (LTM) • Vary in function from initial input (SM) to the conscious organizer of information (WM) to the permanent information store (LTM)
Cognitive processes Attention Perception Rehearsal Encoding Retrieval	Processes that move information from one information store to another by: • Initially focusing on a stimulus (attention) • Finding meaning in the stimulus (perception) • Repeating information to keep it in WM or move it to LTM (rehearsal) • Representing organized information in LTM (encoding) • Pulling information from LTM back to WM for further processing (retrieval)
Metacognition	Executive mechanism that: • Controls cognitive processes • Regulates the flow and storage of information through the memory system
Catalysts for effective processing	• Reducing cognitive load—decreasing the amount of mental activity imposed on working memory • Developing automaticity—overlearning cognitive operations to where they can be performed without thinking about them • Using encoding strategies—finding relationships in separate items of information which make information meaningful and reduce cognitive load
Key concepts	• Sensory memory • Working memory • Long-term memory • Cognitive load • Automaticity • Chunking • Attention • Perception • Rehearsal • Encoding • Retrieval • Meta-attention • Metamemory
Criticisms of information processing theory	• Doesn't adequately explain important influences on learning, such as social context, culture, and emotion • Oversimplifies the processes involved in gathering, organizing, and storing information by implying a one-way transfer of information through the memory stores • Doesn't adequately explain the constructive processes in knowledge acquisition • Considers all information processing as a conscious, deliberate process, but some evidence indicates that a considerable amount of processing is below the conscious level
Contributions of information processing theory	• Explains how we gather information through our senses, organize it, and store it in memory • Most descriptions of learning accept this basic structure of our memory system, including a limited-capacity WM and an LTM that stores organized information, cognitive processes that move information from one store to another, and the regulatory mechanisms of metacognition • Provides important implications for designing and implementing instruction

• Capitalize on encoding strategies to promote meaningful learning.

• Model and encourage metacognition.

These suggestions overlap and interact with each other, and we'll see how as we discuss each.

Conduct Reviews to Activate Schemas and Check Perceptions

New learning depends on what students already know, and reviews capitalize on schema activation as an encoding strategy; they help students pull knowledge from long-term memory back into working memory so new knowledge can be connected to it. For example, Mike conducted a review of figurative language before he had his students look for examples in *To Kill a Mockingbird*.

Let's look again.

"Let's review for a minute. Tell us what a metaphor is, and give us an example, . . . Everett?"

Everett provides a definition and example, and Mike continues his review by doing the same with *simile* and *personification*.

He then displays the following on his document camera, and comments, "We'll use this as a guide for our work today."

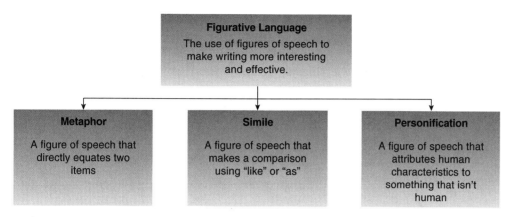

Surprisingly, teachers often fail to conduct reviews when beginning lessons. This is more likely due to simply not thinking about it rather than conscious neglect.

We can review in a number of ways, ranging from simply saying something as simple as "Let's review" to more elaborate activities. Four of the most direct involve:

- Asking for a definition of a previously taught concept. This is what Mike did; he asked his students to provide definitions of *metaphor, simile*, and *personification*.

- Asking students for examples. Mike also had his students provide examples of figures of speech. Providing examples is particularly effective because, in addition to schema activation, it capitalizes on elaboration, which makes both the definition and examples more meaningful.

- Having students solve problems or provide applications. For example, if we want to introduce adding fractions with unlike denominators, we can review by having our students solve one or more problems with like denominators. Or, if we're working on punctuation with our students, we might present the following sentence, "The womans purse had a broken strap so she went into a womens store and found three purses that she liked on sale," and then ask, "Is this sentence punctuated correctly? How do you know?"

National Council on Teacher Quality (NCTQ)

The National Council on Teacher Quality describes posing probing questions as one of the 6 essential teaching strategies that all new teachers should know. Asking students questions such as "why," "how do you know," and "what if" encourages them to link ideas to each other, which makes the topics they study more meaningful (Pomerance et al., 2016).

- Asking for a recap of the previous day's lesson. For instance, a teacher discussing the novel *The Scarlet Letter*, says, "We talked about the characters in the novel yesterday. What were some of the most important features of each?"

These are merely examples, and any form of review that activates students' prior understanding can be effective. Conducting reviews in this way also checks students' perceptions, because the way they answer our review questions gives us insight into their existing understanding.

Attract and Maintain Students' Attention

We know our students' attention is limited, and they're easily distracted. And because attention is where information processing begins, attracting attention is essential for learning at any level (Sutherland et al., 2017). So when we prepare our **learning activities**—the new learning experiences that follow our reviews—we should consciously plan to begin these activities in ways that attract students' attention. Then, we try to maintain their attention throughout the lesson.

We can't always begin our lessons with unexpected events, but we can still take steps to attract our students' attention, and these steps don't take a great deal of effort. For example, Mike, in our chapter opening case study, attempted to attract his students' attention by personalizing his examples when he wrote

You people are a breath of fresh air.

and

This class is like the sugar in my morning coffee.

on the board. Research indicates that personalizing examples in this way is effective for attracting students' attention (Walkington & Bernacki, 2015).

Then, Mike attempted to maintain his students' attention in the way he interacted with them. Let's look again at some of the dialogue after he assigned his students the task of finding examples of figurative language.

Mike: So, just a reminder, . . . what's the first thing you're going to do? . . . Amy? (After waiting a few seconds for the students to turn their desks to face their teammates)

Amy: Come up with an example of a metaphor.

Mike: Okay, good. . . . After you've found one, what do you always do? . . . Monica?

Monica: Write it down.

Mike: Then what? . . . Owen?

Owen: . . . Find another one.

Mike: Or?

Owen: . . . Find an example of a simile.

Mike: Yes, good, Owen. . . . Now, get started everyone.

In this interchange, which took only a matter of seconds, Mike called on three students, each by name. Also, in each case he asked the question first, paused briefly to give all students time to think about an answer, and then successively called on Amy, Monica, and Owen. When students know they're likely to be called on, they are much more likely to pay attention. This strategy is confirmed by a long and consistent history of research (Good & Lavigne, 2018; Kerman, 1979; Lemov, 2015; McDougall & Granby, 1996). Additional strategies for attracting attention are outlined in Table 7.4.

TABLE 7.4 Strategies for attracting attention

Type	Example
Discrepant events	• A world history teacher who normally dresses conservatively comes to class in a sheet, makeshift sandals, and a crown to begin a discussion of ancient Greece. • A science teacher blows between two sheets of paper, but instead of the papers flying apart, they come together.
Pictures	• An English teacher shows a picture of a bearded Ernest Hemingway as she introduces 20th-century American novels. • An art teacher displays Pablo Picasso's *Les Demoiselles d'Avignon* as an introduction to *Cubism*, the avant-garde art movement.
Problems	• A math teacher says, "We want to go to the concert on Saturday night, but we're broke. The tickets are $80 and we need another $25 for something to eat. We make $7.50 an hour in our part-time jobs. How many hours will we have to work to be able to pay for the concert? • An economics teacher says, "Sally is having a drink with her friend Kristen, who encourages her to have a Coke, but she responds, 'I would love one, but I think I'd better stick with water today. So I'll pass.' . . . What is the opportunity cost of drinking the water?"
Thought-provoking questions	• A history teacher begins a discussion of World War II with the question, "Suppose Germany had won the war. How would the world be different now?" • A fourth-grade teacher says, "When we add two fractions, we get a larger fraction, but when we multiply fractions, we get a smaller number. How can this be?"
Emphasis	• A physical education teacher says, "Pay careful attention to the way the person rolls in the video," as she prepares to show a video clip demonstrating a move in gymnastics. • A music teacher says, "Listen carefully now to the blend of the two instruments," just before she plays a musical excerpt.

Develop Students' Background Knowledge with High-Quality Examples and Other Representations of Content

As we've said several times in the chapter, all new learning depends on what students already know. So, what do we do when they lack background knowledge? Simply, we provide it for them, and examples are the most effective way to provide this knowledge. As we plan, a guiding question might be, "What can I show the students," or "What can I have students do that will illustrate this idea?" Mike answered the question with his sentences on the board—his examples of *metaphor* and *simile*—and he elaborated on these sentences with examples the students provided as well as examples from *To Kill a Mockingbird*. Providing these examples didn't require a lot of effort, and they're enormously important for promoting learning.

National Council on Teacher Quality (NCTQ)

The National Council on Teacher Quality describes the use of examples as one of the 6 essential teaching strategies that all new teachers should know. "2. Linking abstract concepts with concrete representations. Teachers should present tangible examples that illuminate overarching ideas and also explain how the examples and big ideas connect" (Pomerance, Greenberg, & Walsh, 2016, p. vi).

For some topics, specific examples don't exist, which is why we say, " . . . and other representations of content" in the heading of this section. For example, suppose you're a history teacher with the goal of having your students understand factors leading to the Civil War. You might present them with the chart and map that follows.

The chart and map that follow provide students with information about the people, land and climate, economy, and geography of the two sections of the country. This

	People	Land and Climate	Economy
Northern states	Small towns Religious Valued education Cooperative	Timber covered Glacial remains Poor soil Short growing season Cold winters	Syrup Rum Lumber Shipbuilding Fishing Small farms
Southern states	Aristocratic Isolated Social class distinction	Fertile soil Hot weather Long growing season	Large farms Tobacco Cotton Unskilled workers Servants and slaves

information can help them identify relationships between, for example, the geography and the economy, and the economy and the land and climate. These representations help students understand why slavery initially occurred in the South instead of the North, and without them you would have to provide this information in a lecture, which would be less meaningful. Table 7.5 provides additional examples of different ways teachers attempt to develop students' background knowledge.

Interact with Students to Promote Cognitive Activity and Reduce Cognitive Load

A long history of research confirms that lecture has been, and remains, the most commonly used teaching strategy (Cuban, 1982; Goldsmith, 2013; Kaddoura, 2011). "This traditional approach has its place, but we rely on it all too often" (Goldsmith, 2013, p. 49).

With respect to information processing and human memory, lecture has two problems. First, we often provide too much information too quickly, so we overload students' limited working memories, and information is lost (Marois & Ivanoff, 2005). Second, lectures place students in cognitively passive roles, which means they typically

TABLE 7.5 Developing students' background knowledge

Content Area and Goal	Example/Representation
Music: For students to understand major and minor chords	Examples of major and minor chords played on a pianica (powered by blowing through a tube).
Health: For students to be able to identify healthy and unhealthy foods	A matrix showing a number of popular foods, such as soft drinks, potato chips, vegetables, fruits, and meats in the left column and the amount of fat, protein, fiber, sugar, and salt in the other columns.
Science: For students to understand the concepts *force* and *work*	A demonstration where the teacher has students push down on their desks and blow on their hands to show that *force* is a push combined with having them pull up on their chairs to illustrate that *force* is also a pull. A demonstration where the teacher has her students slide a book across a desk to show that *work* is a combination of force and movement.
Physical education: For students to understand the mechanics of an effective serve in tennis	Video clips of different tennis players demonstrating correct service motions.
Math: For students to understand how to solve simultaneous equations	Sets of simultaneous equations together with worked examples demonstrating step-by-step solutions to the equations.
Language arts: For students to understand folk tales	Folk tales about different teachers in the school written to include the characteristics of folk tales.

aren't carefully thinking about the content as they listen, or they even drift off and don't link new information to what they already know. The result is less meaningful learning (Latif & Miles, 2013).

Research confirms the importance of interacting with students (Vandenbroucke, Split, Verschueren, Piccinin, & Baeyens, 2018), and questioning is the most widely applicable strategy we can use to promote this interaction. Questioning has two strengths. First, it reduces cognitive load, because we can move through a learning activity only as rapidly as students can answer our questions. If they're able to correctly answer our questions, they're processing the information, so their working memories aren't overloaded. Second, to successfully answer questions, students must be "thinking," which is the essence of cognitive activity. As we saw in the descriptions of Mike's work with his students, he developed each of his learning activities with questioning, and he did very little lecturing. (We discuss questioning in detail in Chapter 13.)

Group work is a second strategy that can be effective for promoting cognitive activity. For example, when Mike had his students work in teams of three to first identify their own examples of *metaphors, similes*, and *personification*, and later identify examples of each concept in *To Kill a Mockingbird*, he capitalized on group work.

Simply putting students into groups doesn't ensure that they will be cognitively active, however, so we must carefully monitor their group work. They may be talking to each other during the activity but may not be "thinking about" what they're doing. Group work is popular in schools, but if these activities aren't carefully structured and monitored, they may be no more effective than a dry lecture (Brophy, 2006a; Mayer, 2004).

MyLab Education
Video Example 7.6

Develop students' background knowledge with high-quality examples and interact with students to promote cognitive activity and reduce cognitive load, are two suggestions for applying information processing and the model of human memory with students. See how sixth-grade teacher, Dani Ramsey, applies these suggestions in her work with her students.

Capitalize on Meaningful Encoding Strategies

Schema activation, organization, elaboration, and *imagery* are all effective for promoting meaningful encoding. (Rehearsal is an encoding strategy, but it may or may not result in meaningful learning.) We capitalize on schema activation when we begin lessons with reviews, and we promote the other encoding strategies in the way we conduct our lessons. For instance, Mike's simple hierarchy describing figures of speech was a form of organization.

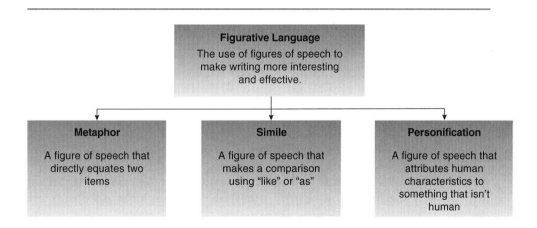

Then he capitalized on elaboration when he had his students first identify their own examples of figurative language and then find examples in *To Kill a Mockingbird*. As we saw earlier, linking examples to each other and to definitions is a powerful form of elaboration.

We also saw how a history teacher used a matrix and map to organize information about the Northern and Southern states before the Civil War. And representing content in this way also helped capitalize on imagery. For example, from the map the students could visualize the differences in geography between the two regions. As they continue their study of the chart and map, students could see how the land and climate influenced the economies of the two regions, and making these connections promotes elaboration.

This discussion illustrates how the suggestions we outlined at the beginning of this section overlap and reinforce each other.

Model and Encourage Metacognition

As we saw earlier, modeling is the most effective way of promoting metacognition in our students (Bruning et al., 2011), and we saw how Mike modeled metacognition in saying

---

"Now, when I face a task like this, I try to listen carefully when my partners are talking, so I'm sure I'm paying attention to what they say. And then I write down the information we find. That way I'll be sure I don't forget."

We can also directly teach metacognition by illustrating and discussing it as we would any other topic. Let's look at an example.

Norma Layton, a language arts teacher, is attempting to help her students develop their study skills, and she displays the following vignette on her document camera.

> Danielle is reading a difficult chapter in her science text. She first looks at the organization of the chapter so she can identify the main topics and the subtopics that fit under each main heading. Then, she reads the section under the first main heading, stops, and asks herself, "Okay, what was this section about?" She repeats the process for each of the sections of the chapter.
>
> "I need to study this way," she comments to Ginger, her friend. "If I don't, I don't remember anything I've read."
>
> "Really?" Ginger replies. "I mostly just read and try to remember as much as I can."

"Now, let's look at the vignette," Norma directs. "What are some differences in the way Danielle approaches her study compared to the way Ginger approaches hers?"

As students discuss the vignette, they gradually arrive at the conclusion that Danielle is more aware of the way she studies and learns, and she takes steps to regulate her study. Norma then emphasizes that this is the way that everyone should approach their study, and most important, to think about the ways that work best for them.

Attempting to develop metacognition in this way—teaching it directly as we would teach any other topic—is more effective than simply encouraging students to "think about what you're doing." Students hear many suggestions from their teachers, and, as a result, they sometimes tune out. Using a conceptual approach, as Norma did, is more effective (Bruning et al., 2011).

Developmentally Appropriate Practice

The Human Memory Model with Students at Different Ages

While the implications of cognitive learning theory and the model of human memory apply at all grade levels, important developmental differences exist. The following guidelines outline ways to respond to these differences.

Working with Students in Early Childhood Programs and Elementary Schools

Our attention is limited, and this limitation is even more pronounced in young children. Young children haven't learned to activate and maintain their attention during lessons (Berk, 2019b). If you plan to teach young children, it will be doubly important to start lessons with an activity that attracts their attention, and you'll need to continually monitor attention during lessons. To maintain the attention of young children, learning activities must be short and frequently changed.

You'll also need to make directions for every task simple and precise and continually check children's perceptions of the task requirements to make sure they understand what you want them to do. Complex tasks should be broken into shorter and simpler ones, and each should be completed before moving to the next one (Trawick-Smith, 2014).

Young children's thinking tends to be concrete, so abstract ideas need to be illustrated with concrete and personalized examples. Because their language is developing, young children benefit from opportunities to practice putting their developing understanding into words.

Modeling metacognition and helping children develop an awareness of factors that influence their learning is particularly helpful with young students. Children who become aware of how attention influences learning acquire a learning skill that they can use throughout their lifetimes.

Working with Students in Middle Schools

Middle school students are beginning to understand how their metacognitive capabilities influence learning. To capitalize on their increased ability to monitor their own learning, effective middle school teachers help their students develop learning strategies that emphasize metacognition. For example, encouraging students to ask themselves questions, such as "How is this idea similar to and different from the previous idea?" and "What would be a real-world example of this idea?", models effective learning strategies that can significantly increase learning.

Much of middle school students' thinking still remains concrete, however, especially when the topic is new or abstract, so you'll need to continue to use concrete examples and analyze them using questioning. And because so much of learning is verbal, guiding students as they put their understanding into words not only increases learning but also promotes language development.

Working with Students in High Schools

High school students can use sophisticated learning strategies, but they are unlikely to use them unless the strategies are modeled and encouraged (Pressley & Hilden, 2006). If you're a high school teacher, modeling the use of encoding strategies, such as organization, elaboration, and imagery, is an effective way to promote their use in classrooms. Even high school students are likely to use rehearsal as a strategy when material is difficult for them, however, so practice with other strategies is important.

Teaching strategies like questioning and small-group work that place students in cognitively active roles are important. Unfortunately, many high school teachers tend to rely on lecture in the mistaken belief that "telling" is teaching. High school students are social beings and love nothing more than to sit around and talk about who is dating whom and what's happening that weekend. Carefully structuring and monitoring group work to ensure that students who are socially active are also cognitively active is important.

High school students are capable of abstract thinking and problem solving but may need prompting to do so. They should be encouraged to examine questions in depth, and consider cause-and-effect relationships.

MyLab Education Self-Check 7.5
MyLab Education Application Exercise 7.3: Applying Information Processing Theory to the Study of the Solar System

In this exercise you will be asked to analyze a case study in which a science teacher applies information processing and the model of human memory in his work with his students.

Chapter 7 Summary

1. Describe principles of cognitive learning theory, and identify applications of the principles in classrooms and life outside of school.
   - *Learning and development depend on experience.* Teachers apply this principle when they provide quality experiences for their students.
   - *People want their experiences to make sense.* This principle is illustrated in how commonly statements such as "That makes sense" or "That doesn't make any sense" are used both in and outside of school.
   - *To make sense of their experiences, people construct knowledge.* This helps us understand how people create original ideas, ideas that they haven't gotten from any outside source.
   - *The knowledge people construct depends on what they already know.* Knowledge isn't constructed in a vacuum. Expert teachers link new knowledge to information learners already possess.
   - *Acquiring long-term knowledge and skill is largely dependent on practice.* To become knowledgeable or skilled in any area requires a great deal of deliberate practice.
   - *Social interaction facilitates learning.* Social interaction contributes to learning by encouraging students to put their ideas into words and allowing them to access others' perspectives. Expert teachers use a variety of strategies to involve students in their learning activities.

2. Use the memory stores in the human memory model to explain events in classrooms and in our daily lives.
   - Sensory memory is the store that briefly holds stimuli from the environment until these stimuli can be processed.
   - Working memory is the conscious part of our information processing system, and its capacity is limited. The limitations of working memory help us understand why learners miss information in lectures and why we all periodically experience "memory overload."
   - We accommodate the limitations of working memory by developing skills to automaticity, organizing and interconnecting information so that it behaves as larger chunks, and combining visual and verbal displays of information to distribute processing.
   - Long-term memory is our permanent information store, and it is where knowledge is stored until it is needed for further processing.
   - Information in long-term memory makes more sense to people and is more easily retrieved and used when it is meaningfully organized.

3. Describe the cognitive processes in the human memory model, and identify applications in classrooms and everyday events.
   - Attention and perception move information from sensory memory to working memory. Attention is the process of consciously focusing on a stimulus, and perception attaches meaning to a stimulus.
   - People use rehearsal to retain information in the phonological loop of working memory, and intensive rehearsal can move information into long-term memory.
   - Encoding represents information in long-term memory. Learners encode information more effectively if it is represented both visually and verbally.
   - Retrieval is the process of pulling information from long-term memory back into working memory for problem solving or further processing.
   - Students' use of the cognitive processes improve as they develop, with older learners better focusing their attention and more effectively using strategies to promote meaningful encoding.

4. Define metacognition and identify examples of metacognitive monitoring in classroom activities and experiences outside of school.
   - Metacognition is individuals' knowledge of, and regulation of, their cognition.
   - Metacognition influences learning by making learners aware of the way they study and learn and providing strategies to increase learning.
   - Metacognition is developmental, with young children being less aware of their cognitive activities than their older counterparts.

5. Analyze classroom applications of information processing and the model of human memory.
   - Beginning lessons with reviews of previously learned content activates prior knowledge and helps students connect new information to existing understanding.
   - Beginning learning activities with events that attract student attention helps students focus on appropriate stimuli and ignore irrelevant information.
   - Using examples and other representations of content to be taught during learning activities helps students

acquire the background knowledge they need to construct meaningful knowledge.
   - Interacting with students during learning activities puts them in cognitively active roles and reduces cognitive load.
   - Schema activation, organization, elaboration, and imagery can help students meaningfully encode information.
   - Modeling and encouraging metacognition can help learners become aware of the ways they best study and learn.

Preparing for Your Licensure Exam

Understanding Information Processing and Human Memory

You will be required to take a licensure exam before you go into your own classroom. This exam will include information related to information processing and human memory, and it will include both multiple-choice and constructed-response questions. We include the following exercises to help you practice for the exam in your state. This book and these exercises will be a resource for you as you prepare for the exam.

Sue Southam, a high school English teacher, wants her students to understand different characters in *The Scarlet Letter*, a novel set in Boston in the 1600s, which describes a tragic and illicit love affair between the heroine (Hester Prynne) and a minister (Arthur Dimmesdale). The novel's title refers to the letter A, meaning "adulterer," which the Puritan community makes Hester wear as punishment for her adultery. Sue is using the novel to help her students meet the following standard:

> CCSS.ELA-Literacy.RL.11-12.3 Analyze the impact of the author's choices regarding how to develop and relate elements of a story or drama (e.g., where a story is set, how the action is ordered, how the characters are introduced and developed) (Common Core State Standards Initiative, 2018h).

The class has been discussing the book for several days and is now examining Reverend Dimmesdale's character. Sue begins by reading a passage from the novel describing Dimmesdale, has the students write down what they believe are the most important aspects of the description in their logs, and then reads a speech he gives in front of the congregation, in which he confronts Hester and exhorts her to identify her secret lover and partner in sin (while all the time hoping and believing that she will not confess and name him as her lover).

Sue then divides the class into "Dimmesdales" and "Hesters," directs the "Dimmesdales" to write in their logs what they believe Dimmesdale is thinking during his speech, and tells the "Hesters" to write what they believe Hester is thinking as she listens. After the students write in their logs, she organizes them into groups, each composed of two Hesters and two Dimmesdales, and says, "In each group, I want you to start off by having Dimmesdale tell what he is thinking during the first part of the speech. Then I'd like a Hester to respond. Then continue with Dimmesdale's next part, then Hester's reaction, and so on. . . . Go ahead and share your thoughts in your groups."

She gives the students 5 minutes to share their perspectives, calls the class back together, and then says, "Okay, let's hear it. A Dimmesdale first. What was he thinking during his speech? . . . Mike?"

"The only thing I could think of was, 'Oh God, help me. I hope she doesn't say anything. If they find out it's me, I'll be ruined.' And then here comes Hester with her powerful speech," Mike concludes, turning to Nicole, his partner in the group.

"I wrote, 'Good man, huh. So why don't you confess then? You know you're guilty. I've admitted my love, but you haven't. Why don't you just come out and say it?'" Nicole comments.

"Interesting. . . . What else? How about another Hester? . . . Sarah?"

"I just put, 'No, I'll never tell. I still love you, and I'll keep your secret forever,'" Sarah offers.

Sue pauses for a moment, looks around the room, and comments, "Notice how different the two views of Hester are. . . . Nicole paints her as very angry, whereas Sarah views her as still loving him."

Sue again pauses, Karen raises her hand, and Sue nods to her. "I think the reason Hester doesn't say anything is that people won't believe her, because he's a minister," Karen suggests. "She's getting her revenge just by being there, reminding him of his guilt."

"But if she accuses him, won't people expect him to deny it?" Brad adds.

"Maybe he knows she won't accuse him because she still loves him," Julie offers.

"Wait a minute," Jeff counters. "I don't think he's such a bad guy. I think he feels guilty about it all, but he just doesn't have the courage to admit it in front of all of those people."

The students continue their analysis of Dimmesdale's character, including a debate about whether he is a villain or a tragic figure.

"Interesting ideas," Sue says as she closes the discussion for the day. "Be sure to keep them in mind, and for tomorrow, I'd like you to read Chapter 4, in which we begin our analysis of Hester's husband."

Questions for Case Analysis

In answering these questions, use information from the chapter, and link your responses to specific information in the case study.

Multiple-Choice Questions

1. As she conducted the lesson, Sue most nearly applied which of the following encoding strategies in her attempt to make the content meaningful for her students?

   a. Rehearsal

   b. Schema activation

   c. Organization

   d. Elaboration

2. Of the following, which suggestion for applying information processing theory and the model of human memory did Sue most nearly apply in her work with her students?

   a. Conduct reviews to activate schemas and check perceptions.

   b. Begin learning activities with attention-getting experiences.

   c. Interact with students to promote cognitive activity and reduce cognitive load.

   d. Model and encourage metacognition.

Constructed-Response Question

3. Assess the extent to which Sue applied information processing theory and the model of human memory model in her lesson. Include both strengths and weaknesses in your assessment.

Important Concepts

analogies	cognitive activity	elaboration	imagery
attention	cognitive learning	encoding	information processing
automaticity	theories	executive functioning	theory
central executive	cognitive load	expert	interference
chunking	declarative knowledge	forgetting	learning activities

long-term memory

meaningfulness

memory stores

meta-attention

metacognition

metamemory

mnemonics

model

multitasking

organization

perception

phonological loop

principles (laws)

procedural knowledge

rehearsal

retrieval

rote learning

schema activation

schemas (schemata)

sensory memory

short-term memory

visual-spatial
    sketchpad

working memory

Chapter 8
Complex Cognitive Processes

Antenna/Getty Images

Learning Outcomes

After you have completed your study of this chapter, you should be able to:

8.1 Define concepts and describe strategies for helping students learn concepts.

8.2 Recognize examples of ill-defined and well-defined problems, and describe strategies for teaching problem solving in classrooms.

8.3 Identify applications of study strategies and critical thinking.

8.4 Analyze factors that influence the transfer of learning.

APA Top 20 Principles

Top 20 Principles from Psychology for PreK–12 Teaching and Learning explicitly addressed in this chapter.

Principle 2: What students already know affects their learning
Principle 4: Learning is based on context, so generalizing learning to new contexts is not spontaneous but instead needs to be facilitated.
Principle 5: Acquiring long-term knowledge and skill is largely dependent on practice.
Principle 6: Clear, explanatory, and timely feedback to students is important for learning.
Principle 8: Student creativity can be fostered.

National Council on Teacher Quality (NCTQ)

The NCTQ Essential Teaching Strategies that every new teacher needs to know specifically addressed in this chapter.

Strategy 1: Pairing graphics with words
Strategy 2: Linking abstract concepts with concrete representations
Strategy 3: Posing probing questions
Strategy 4: Providing students with worked examples
Strategy 5: Distributing practice
Strategy 6: Assessing learning

"Complex Cognitive Processes" is the title of this chapter, and *cognitive* implies "thinking." So, the chapter focuses on complex forms of thinking, which typically include concept learning, solving problems, and reading and understanding conceptually demanding material. We begin with Laura Hunter, a fourth-grade teacher, who has her students involved in a problem-solving activity with *area*.

Laura begins by reviewing the concepts *area* and *perimeter*, including practice problems such as the following:

Find the area and the perimeter of the following figure:

10 ft.

7 ft.

With Laura's guidance, the students recognize that the figure is a rectangle, so opposite sides are equal, and they find the perimeter of 34 feet by adding the lengths of the sides and the area of 70 square feet by multiplying the length times the width.

After a few additional practice problems, the students appear comfortable with the concepts, so Laura moves into her lesson by saying, "We're trying to update our classroom, so we're thinking about replacing the carpet, but we need to figure out how much to order. Here's a diagram of our classroom," and she displays the following on her document camera.

She explains that the parts of the diagram marked L are covered with linoleum, and she walks around the classroom and points those areas out.

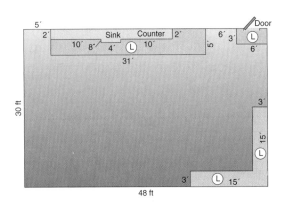

"So, what, exactly, is our problem? . . . What are we trying to find out?"

The students study the diagram, and after a pause, Yashoda offers, "We have to find out how much carpet we need."

"Good," Laura smiles, "and what makes our problem a little more challenging?"

After some discussion, the students conclude that they don't need carpet for the areas marked L on the diagram, and Laura asks, "So, how can we figure out how much we actually need?"

After some additional discussion, her students decide that they should find the area of the whole classroom and then subtract the areas covered with linoleum.

She then has her students work in groups of three to try to find the respective areas. She gives them 15 minutes to complete the task. As she monitors the groups, she sees that they are getting widely varying answers. For instance, one group gets an answer of 1,600 square feet for the carpeted portion of the classroom—more than the area of the entire classroom. She reminds the group that the classroom's dimensions are 48 by 30, and asks them to rethink their answer. She does the same with other groups, encouraging them to think about the answers they're getting.

At the end of the 15 minutes, she calls the groups together, and they begin discussing their results.

"So, what did we need to find out first?" she begins.

They agree that they needed to find the area of the entire room, so she sends Avery to the board to show how he found the area. He goes and demonstrates 30 times 48 to get an area of 1,440 square feet.

"Now what?" Laura asks. "What did we do next?"

The students agree that they needed to subtract the parts marked "L," and most say they started at the top of the diagram.

"How will we find the area of this part? . . . Fred?" Laura asks, pointing to the top of the diagram.

" . . . Multiply 31 times 5."

"Why? . . . Tu?" Laura probes.

" . . . That part is a rectangle, and it's 31 feet long and 5 feet wide, . . . so we multiply them," Tu responds.

"What about the 2?" Zoey asks, pointing at the 2—for the sink and counter—in the diagram.

"What about it? Laura asks.

" . . . That's just a part," Audrey explains. "Linoleum is under all of it, so that's why it's 31 times 5 . . . . The 2 doesn't matter."

"So, what did we get? . . . Aiden?" Laura asks, recalling that he was one of the students who was a bit uncertain during the group work.

" . . . A hundred fifty-five," Aiden responds after taking a few seconds to multiply 31 times 5.

Laura then has them repeat the process with the portion by the door, where they get 18 square feet, and the portion at the lower right, where they get 81 square feet.

"Now what? . . . Nephi?" Laura asks.

"We need to add the 155, 18, and 81, and then subtract them from 1,440."

Laura has Nephi explain her thinking, and the students add the 155, 18, and 81 to get a total of 254 square feet, which they subtract from 1,440 to get an area of 1,186 square feet for the carpeted portion of the classroom.

Laura then assigns three additional problems for seatwork and carefully monitors their progress as they work.

This case study illustrates three important aspects of Laura's teaching. First, she attempted to make the activity meaningful for her students by presenting them with a real-world problem—the carpeted area of their classroom. Second, she took steps to ensure that they were successful; and third, she applied principles of cognitive learning theory in her lesson. We'll see how as the chapter unfolds.

The cognitive learning principles, which we first examined in Chapter 7, are:

- Learning and development depend on experience.
- People want their experiences to make sense.
- To make sense of their experiences, people construct knowledge.
- The knowledge that people construct depends on what they already know.
- Acquiring long-term knowledge and skill is largely dependent on practice.
- Social interaction facilitates learning.

We begin our discussion with concept learning, which also applies these principles.

Concept Learning

8.1   **Define concepts and describe strategies for helping students learn concepts.**

Ed Psych and You

Look at the first list of 16 words below for 10 seconds. Cover up the list, and try to write down as many as you can remember in any order.

Then, do the same with the second list of 16 words. Which list is easier to remember? Why do you think so?

Here is the first list.

broom	work	salary	some
sooner	plug	jaw	fastener
jug	president	friend	evening
planet	else	salmon	destroy

Now, here's the second list:

north	blue	cucumber	quarter
celery	west	nickel	purple
red	penny	brown	east
dime	carrot	south	cauliflower

If you're like most people, you were able to recall more items from the second list than the first, because the items could be classified into four categories—*directions, colors, vegetables*, and *coins*. The first list is difficult to categorize, so it is harder to remember.

Now, let's see how your experience relates to principles of cognitive learning theory. *Learning and development depend on experience* is a cognitive learning principle. We all have experiences, and we want to make sense of them—a second principle—so we construct knowledge, a third principle, and **concepts**, mental representations of categories, are among the most basic forms of the knowledge we construct (Schunk, 2016). "Humans are faced with the task of making sense of a world that contains a seemingly endless array of unique objects and living things. To reduce this endless uniqueness to something that is mentally manageable, people form concepts" (McDonald, 2016, para. 1).

Each category—*directions, colors, vegetables*, and *coins*—is a concept. Just as forming the categories simplified the list of items, constructing concepts helps us simplify the world, which then reduces the cognitive load on our working memories. Remembering the concept *coin*, for instance, is much easier than trying to remember *penny, nickel, dime*, and *quarter* separately, so it imposes a lower cognitive load.

Concepts are the fundamental building blocks of our thinking, and they provide a foundation for more complex cognitive processes, such as problem solving (Schunk, 2016). Before they could find the area of the carpeted portion of their classroom, for example, Laura's students needed to understand that the concept *area* is a physical quantity describing the size of surfaces, such as those in Figure 8.1. The concept *area* allows us to think about and compare the surfaces of figures regardless of dimension or orientation.

Concepts are an important part of the school curriculum, and Table 8.1 includes examples in language arts, social studies, science, and math. Many others exist, such as *rhythm* and *tempo* in music, *perspective* and *balance* in art, and *aerobic* and *isotonic exercises* in PE. And concepts such as *honesty, bias, love*, and *internal conflict* appear across the curriculum.

Theories of Concept Learning

Theorists offer different explanations for how people construct concepts. In this section, we examine *rule-driven* and *exemplar* theories, each explaining concept learning differently.

Rule-Driven Theory of Concept Learning

Rule-driven theory suggests that we construct concepts based on their attributes or **characteristics**—concepts' essential elements. For some, such as *square, longitude*, or

Figure 8.1 Areas of different polygons

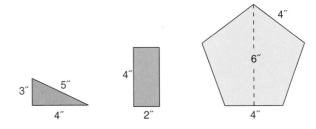

TABLE 8.1 Concepts in different content areas

Language Arts	Social Studies	Science	Math
Adjective	Culture	Acid	Prime number
Verb	Longitude	Conifer	Equivalent fraction
Plot	Federalist	Element	Set
Simile	Democracy	Force	Addition
Infinitive	Immigrant	Inertia	Parabola

adverb, these elements are well-defined. For instance, *closed, four equal sides*, and *equal angles* are the characteristics of the concept *square*. When we see plane figures with these characteristics, we classify them as squares based on the rule stating that squares must have these attributes. Other characteristics, such as size or color, aren't essential, so we don't consider them when classifying the figures. This rule-driven theory was investigated by early researchers (e.g., Bruner, Goodenow, & Austin, 1956), who found that people identify concepts based on their defining attributes. Remembering a rule, such as an *adverb* must modify a verb, adjective, or other adverb, allows us to identify and accurately use a huge number of adverbs, so it doesn't impose a heavy load on working memory. This makes concept learning based on rules easier than those based on exemplars.

Exemplar Theory of Concept Learning

Many concepts don't have well-defined characteristics, so creating rules to help identify them is difficult. For instance, what are the characteristics of the concepts *Democrat* or *Republican*? They're familiar, but most people can't define them with precision. Even common concepts, such as *car*, don't have precise attributes. For instance, some people describe sport utility vehicles as cars, but others don't. And how about minivans, crossovers, or railroad "cars"?

A second theory of concept learning suggests that people construct concepts based on **exemplars**, the most highly typical examples of a concept (Radvansky & Aschcraft, 2014). For instance, prominent politicians may be exemplars for *Democrat* or *Republican*; popular autos, such as a Toyota Camry or Ford Mustang, could be stored as exemplars for the concept *car*; and a child may construct the concept *dog* using exemplars such as a golden retriever, cocker spaniel, collie, and German shepherd.

Although exemplar theory helps explain how we construct concepts that don't have well-defined characteristics, it has two disadvantages (Schunk, 2016). First, we may store a large number of exemplars in long-term memory, so when retrieved, they impose a heavy cognitive load on working memory. This makes elaborating on the concept more difficult than simply retrieving a rule, such as the rule for squares or adverbs. Second, learners may store an incomplete set of exemplars, or exemplars that are incorrect. For instance, if a child stored *eagle, hawk, robin*, and *cardinal*, but didn't store *penguin* or *ostrich* (flightless birds) for the concept *bird*, she would have an incomplete set of exemplars. On the other hand, if a child stored *dolphin* as an exemplar for the concept *fish*, he would be constructing a misconception, because dolphins are mammals, not fish.

Each theory explains different aspects of concept learning. For instance, concepts such as *square* or *odd number* are likely constructed based on their characteristics, whereas others, such as *car* or *dog*, are probably represented with exemplars.

Concept Learning: A Complex Cognitive Process

As you read this section, you may be saying to yourself, "Concept learning seems simple enough. Why is it described as a *complex cognitive process*?" In fact, the thinking involved in constructing concepts is often more demanding than it appears on the surface. For instance, Paul—one of your authors—taught a group of fourth-graders the concept *arthropod*, animals such as beetles (insects), spiders (arachnids), and crabs and lobsters (crustaceans) that have an *exoskeleton, three body parts*, and *jointed legs* as characteristics. After showing the students a crab, beetle, and spider, and helping them identify arthropods' characteristics, he showed them a clam and asked them if it was an arthropod. Several of the students said yes, reasoning that its hard shell was an exoskeleton. They didn't realize that to be an arthropod an animal must have all the essential characteristics. He then asked them if their teacher was an arthropod, and again, some said yes, centering on the fact that she had jointed legs.

Now, consider concepts such as *above, large, far*, and *right*. These concepts are "relational," meaning they make sense only in relation to other concepts (Schunk, 2016). For instance, *above* exists only in relation to *below*, and *large* exists only when compared to *small*. In spite of the complexity of these concepts, we expect young children to learn them, as anyone who has watched *Sesame Street* knows. For example, Bert—the Muppet—sits next to a flowerpot and says, "Now, I'm *near*," then runs off in the distance and says, "Now, I'm *far*."

These concepts are important for future learning. For example, consider these problems:

$$\begin{array}{c} 76 \\ -24 \end{array} \quad \text{and} \quad \begin{array}{c} 74 \\ -26 \end{array}$$

If children don't understand relational ideas, they may get 52 for both answers by ignoring their location and simply subtracting the 4 from the 6 in each case.

Other concepts are also complex. For instance, the concept *integer* can be a negative number, or a positive number, or zero. A polynomial can be either a single number, such as 4, or a number and variable, such as $4x$, or a more complex expression, such as $4x^2 + 2x + 3$. This either–or nature can be confusing, and these examples help us understand why concept learning is indeed a complex cognitive process.

Using Educational Psychology in Teaching: Suggestions for Helping Your Students Learn Concepts

Because concepts are an important part of the school curriculum, effective concept learning is essential for students.

The following suggestions can help us in our classrooms.

1. Promote meaningful learning by defining the concept and linking it to related concepts.
2. Provide a variety of examples and non-examples of the concept.
3. Sequence the examples beginning with the most typical and ending with the least familiar.
4. Present the examples in a real-world context.
5. Interact with students to promote cognitive activity.

Let's see how Maria Lopez, a sixth-grade teacher, applies these suggestions as she attempts to help her students understand the concepts *fact, opinion*, and *reasoned judgment*, part of the middle school curriculum that focuses on the following standard:

CCSS.ELA-Literacy.RH.6-8.8 Distinguish among fact, opinion, and reasoned judgment in a text (Common Core State Standards Initiative, 2018i).

The class has been studying events leading to the Civil War, so Maria uses this topic as the context for studying the concepts.

She begins, "The ability to distinguish between fact, opinion, and reasoned judgment is important in both school and in our lives outside of school, and it's also one that appears in the standards for this grade. . . . So, that's what we're focusing on today," and she then displays the following on her document camera:

> Fact: A statement that is based on observation or directly proven.
>
> Example: Diet soda contains less sugar than regular soda.
>
> Opinion: A statement that describes a belief that depends on a person's personal perspective, feelings, or desires.
>
> Example: Diet soda tastes bland compared to regular soda.
>
> Reasoned judgment: An assertion or conclusion that is supported by objective information.
>
> Example: Diet soda is preferable to regular soda because it contains fewer calories.

After giving the students a couple minutes to study the definitions and examples, she has them explain differences among the three concepts. After some discussion she displays the following:

> Eli Whitney invented the cotton gin in 1793. This reduced the amount of time it took to separate the cotton seeds from the cotton fibers. As a result, raising cotton became very profitable, so the South became a one-crop economy that depended on cotton. As it turns out, the lack of variety in the Southern economy was a big mistake.
>
> Abraham Lincoln was the best president in our country's history. He was president from 1861 until his assassination in 1865. One of Lincoln's primary accomplishments was getting the 13th amendment to the Constitution passed, because it permanently outlawed slavery.

"Look at the information we see here . . . . Think about it and identify an example of a fact . . . . Juanita?

" . . . Eli Whitney invented the cotton gin in 1793," Juanita responds.

Maria has the students identify other facts in the text, and then does the same with opinions and reasoned judgments.

After Jeremy identifies the statement 'One of Lincoln's primary accomplishments was passing the 13th amendment to the Constitution' as a reasoned judgment, Maria asks, "What makes this a reasoned judgment? . . . Kristie?"

" . . . It says, 'because it permanently outlawed slavery,' so that's information that supports the conclusion about Lincoln's accomplishments."

Maria then has the students provide rationales for the other examples they identify as reasoned judgments, they summarize what they've done, and she closes the lesson by assigning for homework the task of creating two additional examples of each concept.

Now, let's see how Maria applied the suggestions.

Define the Concept and Link It to Related Concepts.   Maria began her lesson by noting that the ability to distinguish between fact, opinion, and reasoned judgment is important, both in and out of school, and she displayed definitions of the three concepts together with an example of each. Each definition contained the essential characteristics of the concepts, and by presenting the three definitions together, she linked fact, opinion, and reasoned judgment—concepts that are closely related and sometimes confused—to each other.

MyLab Education

Video Example 8.1

High-quality examples are essential for helping students construct their knowledge of concepts. Here, an elementary teacher uses concrete fraction parts to illustrate the concept *equivalent fractions*.

Provide a Variety of High-Quality Examples Together with Non-Examples of the Concept. **High-quality examples** are examples that contain all the information students need to construct their knowledge of a concept. Regardless of a concept's complexity or the theory that explains concept learning, students will construct their understanding based on the examples we present, combined with non-examples that help them differentiate the concept from closely related others (Rawson, Thomas, & Jacoby, 2015). For instance, if we're teaching the concept *reptile*, ideal high-quality examples would be a real *alligator, turtle* (both sea and land, so they don't conclude that all reptiles live on land), *lizard*, and *snake*. Since we can't bring an actual alligator or sea turtle into a classroom, detailed color pictures are a reasonable compromise. Our goal in all cases is to provide examples that are as realistic as possible.

National Council on Teacher Quality (NCTQ)

The National Council on Teacher Quality describes the use of examples as one of the 6 essential teaching strategies that all new teachers should know. "2. Linking abstract concepts with concrete representations. Teachers should present tangible examples that illuminate overarching ideas and also explain how the examples and big ideas connect" (Pomerance, Greenberg, & Walsh, 2016, p. vi).

We would also include a *frog* as a non-example, because many people believe frogs are reptiles. Similarly, if we're teaching the concept *metaphor*, we would include a variety of metaphors, combined with *similes* as non-examples, because *metaphors* and *similes* are closely related and often confused.

Examples provide the experiences learners need to construct their knowledge, and they help develop the background knowledge students need to expand and deepen their understanding. Many teachers, however, attempt to help their students learn concepts with definitions alone (İlhan, 2017). Definitions, regardless of how clearly they're stated, are abstract, so students don't get the concrete representations they need to construct the concepts.

Maria avoided this trap by combining the definitions of *fact, opinion*, and *reasoned judgment* with her examples. In doing so, examples of opinions and reasoned judgments served as non-examples of facts, and the same applied for the other two concepts. Teaching the concepts together in this way is more effective than teaching them separately (Sana, Yan, & Kim, 2017). It also made her instruction efficient and made the concepts more meaningful for her students.

Maria also provided at least two examples of each. For instance, the following are facts she used:

- Eli Whitney invented the cotton gin in 1993.
- This reduced the amount of time it took to separate the cotton seeds from the cotton fibers.
- He [Lincoln] was president from 1861 until his assassination in 1865.

  Opinions included:

- The lack of variety in the Southern economy was a big mistake.
- Abraham Lincoln was the best president in our country's history.

  And the following were examples of reasoned judgments.

- The South became a one-crop economy that depended on cotton.
- One of Lincoln's primary accomplishments was getting the 13th Amendment to the Constitution passed.

In teaching concepts, some experts have historically suggested that we should present a sequence of examples and guide students' constructions of the concept, and this is the approach advocated by Jerome Bruner (1966). Others have suggested that presenting a definition and then illustrating it with examples is more effective, an approach preferred by David Ausubel (1977). Maria chose the strategy advocated by Ausubel, but, if high-quality examples are used, either can be effective (Rawson et al., 2015).

Sequence the Examples Beginning with the Most Typical and Ending with the Least Familiar. Maria also sequenced the examples so an obvious fact, such as "Eli Whitney invented the cotton gin in 1793," appeared first in the passage, and more nuanced examples, such as "One of Lincoln's primary accomplishments was getting the 13th amendment to the Constitution passed, because it permanently outlawed slavery"—which included both a reasoned judgment and a fact—were displayed at the end of the text. Sequencing examples this way capitalizes on elaboration as an encoding strategy by helping students link less-obvious examples to those that are clear and concrete (Sana et al., 2017).

Present Examples in Real-World Contexts. By embedding the examples and non-examples in the context of the historical passage, Maria helped her students see how fact, opinion, and reasoned judgment apply in the world outside of school. It also helped her focus on the standard, which emphasized that learners should distinguish among the concepts *in a text*.

APA Top 20 Principles

This description applies Principle 4: *Learning is based on context, so generalizing learning to new contexts is not spontaneous but instead needs to be facilitated—* from the *Top 20 Principles from Psychology for PreK–12 Teaching and Learning*.

Maria grounded her lesson in the principles of cognitive learning theory and our understanding of human memory. Her examples provided the experiences the students needed to construct their knowledge of the concepts, the examples made sense to the students, and they provided the background knowledge students needed to construct their understanding of the concepts.

Interact with Students to Promote Active Cognitive Processing. Finally, Maria applied the cognitive learning principle *social interaction facilitates learning* by using questioning to put her students in cognitively active roles—to think about what they were doing. Involving her students also reduced the cognitive load on their working memories, because she couldn't move through the learning activity any faster than the students could correctly answer her questions. And her examples combined with the social interaction made the information meaningful, and helped the students encode the concepts in their long-term memories.

MyLab Education Self-Check 8.1
MyLab Education Application Exercise 8.1: Concept Learning in Middle School English

In this exercise you will be asked to analyze a middle school English teacher's application of suggestions for helping students learn concepts.

Classroom Connections

Promoting Concept Learning in Schools

1. Examples provide learners with the experiences they need to construct concepts. To connect concepts to the real world, use realistic examples that include all the information learners need to understand the concept.

   - **Elementary:** To illustrate the concept *mammal*, a second-grade teacher brings a hamster to class, and has the students feel and pet it. He also has the students think about themselves, and he shows pictures of a horse, dog, bat, dolphin, and seal. He also includes pictures of an eagle, lizard, and salmon as non-examples.

   - **Middle School:** An eighth-grade English teacher provides his students with examples of verbals—gerunds, participles, and infinitives—to help them understand their function in general, as well as how they work in particular sentences.

   - **High School:** A tennis coach is helping his students learn how to serve. He videotapes several people, some with good serves and others less skilled. He shows students the videotapes and asks them to identify the differences in the serves.

2. To help make concepts meaningful, link new concepts to related concepts.

   - **Elementary:** A kindergarten teacher wants her class to understand that living things exist in many different forms. She tells her children that they themselves, as well as pets and plants in their classroom, are living things. In a discussion they identify "the ability to grow and change" and "the need for food and water" as two characteristics the examples have in common.

   - **Middle School:** To help his students understand the relationships between descriptive and persuasive writing, an English teacher displays paragraphs illustrating each and asks the class to identify their similarities and differences.

   - **High School:** A social studies teacher instructs her students to compare cultural revolutions to other revolutions, such as the Industrial Revolution, the American Revolution, and the technological revolution, pointing out similarities and differences in each case.

Problem Solving

8.2 Recognize examples of ill-defined and well-defined problems, and describe strategies for teaching problem solving in classrooms.

Ed Psych and You

What do the following have in common?

- You want to send a birthday card to a friend who has moved to New York, but you don't know her address.
- You're in a romantic relationship with another person, but it isn't satisfying.
- You're taking classes, but also have a job, and you always seem to be short of time.

Let's look at the examples in *Ed Psych and You*. They each illustrate a **problem**, which exists when people have a goal but don't have an obvious—or automatic—way to reach it (Schunk, 2016). For instance, the goals are accessing your friend's address, making your relationship more satisfying, and finding more time in your life. Laura's students, in the lesson at the beginning of the chapter, also faced a problem, the goal for which was finding the area of the carpeted portion of their classroom. Problems are a part of our daily lives, and this broad view of problem solving helps us apply effective strategies to solve them.

Well-Defined and Ill-Defined Problems

Experts distinguish between **well-defined problems**, problems with clear goals, one correct solution, and a certain method for solving them, and **ill-defined problems**, those with ambiguous goals, a variety of acceptable solutions, and no established strategy for solving them (Mayer & Wittrock, 2006; Radvansky & Aschcraft, 2014). Our first example in *Ed Psych and You* is well-defined; your friend has only one address, and a straightforward strategy for finding it exists. Many problems in math, physics, and chemistry are well-defined.

On the other hand, your unsatisfactory relationship and lack of time are ill-defined problems, because your goals aren't clear. For instance, you want your relationship to be more satisfying, but what does that mean? Perhaps you want to communicate more openly, spend more time together, or feel better emotionally when you're together. In our third example, lack of time is also vague. Do you want more time to study? To exercise? To simply kick back and relax?

Because the goals in ill-defined problems are ambiguous, no obvious solutions exist for them. In the case of your relationship, for instance, you might try talking to your partner about your feelings, consider couples' counseling, or even end the relationship. For your lack of time, you might cut back on your work hours if possible, drop a class, or even take a semester off from school.

A paradox with problem solving also exists. Our formal training with problem solving largely occurs in schools, but most of our experiences there involve well-defined problems. For instance, students in elementary schools are asked to solve problems like the following:

Jeremy and Melinda are saving up so they can go to iTunes to buy some of their favorite songs. They need 15 dollars. Jeremy has saved 5 dollars, and Melinda has saved 7. How much more money do they have to save to get their 15 dollars?

In high school students solve problems such as this one:

Kelsey and Mitch are dating but live in different cities, and they adopt the same cell phone plan. Over one billing period, Kelsey used 45 peak minutes and 50 nonpeak minutes, and her bill was $27.75. Mitch used 70 peak minutes and 30 nonpeak minutes at a charge of $36. What is the peak and the nonpeak rate in their cell phone plan?

Even though the second is more complex, both are well-defined.

In life we face problems related to money, careers, social relationships, or personal happiness, and they are usually ill-defined. Our lack of experience in solving problems such as these helps us understand why so many people struggle with these issues (Ansari, Fathi, & Seidenberg, 2016; Cheek, Piercy, & Kohlenberg, 2015).

The Problem-Solving Process

Some experts believe that most human learning involves problem solving (Radvansky & Aschcraft, 2014), and it is one of the most thoroughly researched areas in the study of learning and teaching. And, as we might expect, a great deal of emphasis is now being placed on the ability to solve problems in technology-rich environments (Hämäläinen, De Wever, Malin, & Cincinnato, 2015).

A number of approaches to solving problems exist, including, among others, mathematician George Pólya's historically famous *How to Solve It* (1957) as well as more recent efforts by other well-known researchers (e.g., Bransford & Stein, 1993; Mayer & Wittrock, 2006). Slightly different language may be used, but the approaches are similar and they typically include the steps outlined in Figure 8.2.

Figure 8.2 Steps in solving problems

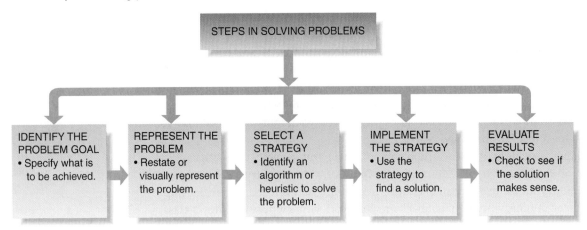

Experts have applied these steps to problems varying as widely as well-defined problems in math and science (Wong & Ho, 2017) to ill-defined problems with school leadership (Canter, 2004), cost management in business (Ansari et al., 2016), and even family therapy (Williamson, Hanna, Lavner, Bradbury, & Karney, 2013). We turn to these steps next.

Identify the Problem Goal

Problem solving begins when a problem solver has a goal but lacks an obvious way of reaching the goal. Understanding the problem so the goal can be identified is the first step. The *central executive*—the supervisory system in working memory that controls the flow of information to and from long-term memory—is crucial in this process. For instance, appropriate information must be retrieved from long-term memory, and the meaning of the problem must be encoded. The central executive controls this process, but it sometimes goes awry. For instance, consider the following problem, which was presented to a group of second-graders.

There are 26 sheep and 10 goats on a ship. How old is the captain?

In one study, 75% of the children answered 36 (cited in Prawat, 1989)! Obviously, the students didn't understand the problem.

In some cases, identifying the problem goal is straightforward, such as it was in Laura's lesson. In other cases, particularly when working with ill-defined problems, it can be one of the most difficult aspects of problem solving, and even advanced university students (Naci, 2013) and highly-experienced people in the business world (Wedell-Wedellsborg, 2017) have trouble with this step.

When attempting to solve ill-defined problems, identifying subgoals is a helpful beginning. Then, as we reach each subgoal, we eventually solve our problem. For instance, in the case of your unsatisfying relationship, suppose you identify spending more time together, improving communication, and feeling better emotionally as your subgoals. In doing so you've better defined your problem. In general, solving problems that are ill-defined involves converting them to well-defined sub-problems with clear goals.

Represent the Problem

If a problem is complex, it can be helpful to represent it in ways that make it more meaningful, such as stating it in more familiar terms, relating it to problems previously solved, or, if possible, representing it visually. This is what Laura did. She began her lesson by displaying the diagram of their classroom and using it as a visual framework for solving the problem.

Representing a problem visually capitalizes on the fact that working memory has both a visual and a verbal processor that "distribute" the task across the two components and reduce cognitive load (Clark & Mayer, 2003; Moreno & Duran, 2004). For instance, consider the following problem:

Find the area of a pentagon with a base of 3 inches, a vertical height of 2 inches, and a total height of 4 inches.

Without the sketch we see here, this might be difficult for some students, but with the sketch, the problem is straightforward and much easier to solve.

Select a Strategy

After identifying and representing the problem, we need a strategy to solve it. In Laura's lesson, the students—with her guidance—decided to find the total area of their classroom and then subtract the areas covered by linoleum. This was a straightforward strategy.

If a problem is well-defined, an **algorithm**, a specific step or set of steps for solving it, can be used. For instance, to find the area of a rectangle, we use a simple algorithm—multiply the length times the width—and we use other simple algorithms when we solve problems such as adding fractions with unlike denominators or finding the percent decrease of a marked-down retail item. Similarly, computer experts use complex algorithms to solve sophisticated, but well-defined, programming problems.

Because algorithms don't exist for ill-defined problems, or even for some that are well-defined, problem solvers use **heuristics**, general, widely applicable problem-solving strategies (Chow, 2015). The more complex and unfamiliar the task, the greater the need for heuristics (Youssef-Shalala, Ayres, Schubert, & Sweller, 2014).

Several widely applicable heuristics exist. Trial and error, although primitive and inefficient, is one, and many people use it as a first step in trying to solve unfamiliar problems (Davidson & Sternberg, 2003).

Drawing analogies, comparing new problems to those already solved, is a second heuristic. It can be difficult to implement, however, because learners are often unable to identify problems similar to the one they want to solve, or they make invalid connections between the two problems (Langley, Pearce, Barley, & Emery, 2014).

Means–ends analysis, a strategy that breaks the problem into subgoals and works successively on each, is an effective heuristic for solving ill-defined problems, and you might use it in attempting to solve your dissatisfying-romantic-relationship problem. Even this can be difficult, however. For instance, you identified spending more time together, improving communication, and feeling better emotionally as your subgoals. So, for instance, what strategy will you use to feel better emotionally? An easy answer to this question doesn't exist, but you must identify clear and workable strategies, or reaching the subgoal will be impossible. This is the case for many ill-defined problems.

Teaching heuristics can improve your students' problem-solving abilities (Langley et al., 2014), but ultimately, prior knowledge and practice with problem solving are essential for successfully selecting a strategy, and no heuristic can replace them (Lester, 2013).

Implement the Strategy

Having selected a strategy, problem solvers are now ready to implement it. If the goal is clear, the problem is represented effectively, and a strategy for reaching it is specified, implementing the strategy is straightforward.

This was the case for Laura's students, but even then challenges may occur. To illustrate, let's look again at some dialogue from her lesson.

The students have agreed that they needed to subtract the parts marked "L," and most say they should start at the top of the diagram.

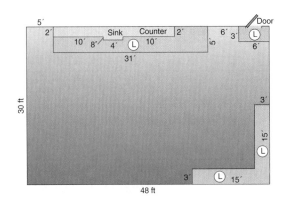

Laura: How will we find the area of this part? . . . Fred? (pointing to the top of the diagram).

Fred: . . . Multiply 31 times 5.

Laura: Why? . . . Tu?

Tu: . . . That part is a rectangle, and it's 31 feet long and 5 feet wide, . . . so we multiply them.

Zoey: What about the 2? (pointing at the 2—for the sink and counter—in the diagram)

Laura: What about it? . . . Audrey?

Audrey: . . . That's just a part. Linoleum is under all of it, so that's why it's 31 times 5 . . . . The 2 doesn't matter.

Laura: So, what did we get? . . . Aiden?

Aiden: . . . A hundred fifty-five. (after taking a few seconds to multiply 31 times 5)

For most problems that students encounter, using all the information in the problem is required when implementing a strategy. So, students are inclined to try to use information, even if it's irrelevant. This helps us understand Zoey's reaction, and it suggests that we should provide students with experiences in identifying relevant and irrelevant information in problems—a very real aspect of problem solving in life outside of school.

Evaluate the Results

Evaluating results is the final problem-solving step, and it requires students to think (Lester, 2013; Mayer & Wittrock, 2006)! Often, they simply don't, as we saw in the example with second-graders adding the number of sheep and goats on a ship to get the age of the captain. And we saw that one group in Laura's lesson initially got an answer of 1,600 square feet for *the carpeted portion of the classroom*—160 square feet more than the area of the entire room. This tendency is understandably maddening for teachers, but it's part of reality in classrooms. Also, students tend to accept answers they see on calculators whether or not the answers make sense, an issue that is becoming more prominent as students increasingly rely on technology for basic math operations (Lester, 2013). (We offer suggestions for dealing with these issues in the section "Using Educational Psychology in Teaching: Suggestions for Helping Your Students Become Better Problem Solvers" later in the chapter.)

Creativity

As we said earlier, most of the problems we face in life are ill-defined, and solving them often requires original thinking and solutions. This leads to the concept of **creativity**, the ability to produce original works, or solutions to problems, that are productive and task appropriate (Malycha & Maier, 2017). *Original* implies that the action is not learned from someone else, *productive* suggests that the product or solution is useful in our culture, and *task appropriate* means that the solution, product, document, or new idea meets a set of task requirements.

Here is a teaching example.

Dan Stevens, a physics teacher, attempts to promote creativity in his students with lab work. After completing the lab's required portion, he tells them to design and complete an extension of the experiment that hasn't been described as an original part of the lab. The students perform well on this requirement, and they also report that designing and conducting these extensions are the most fun and interesting aspects of their experience.

(Based on a conversation Paul, one of your authors, had with a teacher in one of his classes.)

This simple example meets the criteria for creativity. Dan's students had to create original investigations—they didn't get the ideas from someone else; the investigations were productive; and they were conducted within the framework of their labs, so they were task appropriate.

Creativity has been widely researched, and some evidence links it to personality traits—particularly extraversion and openness (Puryear, Kettler, & Rinn, 2017). Additional research suggests that it's largely a social process; because people can feed off the ideas of others, groups are more likely to be creative than people working alone (Binyamin & Carmeli, 2017). And, contrary to historical beliefs, if handled judiciously, rewarding creativity enhances rather than stifles the creative process (Gong, Wu, Song, & Zhang, 2017). As we would expect, creativity doesn't exist in a vacuum. Rather, it requires a great deal of prior knowledge and motivation (Gong et al., 2017; Malycha & Maier, 2017).

Creativity exists on a continuum. At one end, for instance, it might result in a time-honored symphony, great work of art, Pulitzer Prize–winning piece of literature, or contribution to science, such as Einstein's theory of relativity. At the other, it can involve a simple, personal interpretation, such as a student's unique solution to a problem or an employee designing a new marketing strategy for a company. Both ends and everything in between are important, and most of the creativity that exists in schools and our daily lives involves relatively simple, personal interpretations (Beghetto & Kaufman, 2013). For instance, in our discussion of concept learning, we saw how important examples are, and the ability to generate unique and clever examples is one of the best ways to personally demonstrate creativity in our teaching.

Environments that Nurture Creativity

Research indicates that creativity can be nurtured, both in our students and in our own teaching (Binyamin & Carmeli, 2017; Malycha & Maier, 2017; Yadav & Cooper, 2017). And, instead of competing, creativity and the regular curriculum can exist in a hand-in-glove relationship. "Teachers who understand that creativity combines both originality and task appropriateness are in a better position to integrate student creativity into the everyday curriculum in ways that complement, rather than compete with, academic learning" (Beghetto & Kaufman, 2013, p. 12). Dan Stevens' work with his physics students illustrates this idea.

APA Top 20 Principles

This discussion illustrates Principle 8: *Student creativity can be fostered*—from the *Top 20 Principles from Psychology for PreK–12 Teaching and Learning*.

So, how can we promote creativity? Some suggestions include:

- *Creating a safe emotional environment.* Attempts at creativity involve risk. For instance, when a student shares a unique solution to a problem, she risks having her thinking laughed at by peers or dismissed by her teacher. Students quickly learn that sharing personal ideas isn't worth the risk. Students must feel emotionally safe to make attempts at creativity (Kuhl, 2017; Zee & de Bree, 2017).

- *Developing students' background knowledge.* We saw earlier that creativity requires a great deal of background knowledge; creativity without knowledge is impossible (Gong et al., 2017; Malycha & Maier, 2017). For instance, Dan's physics students wouldn't have been able to extend their lab activities if they didn't thoroughly understand the labs in the first place.

- *Encouraging and rewarding creativity but avoiding competition and social comparisons.* For instance, Dan encouraged creativity in his students, but avoided any comparisons among his lab groups. Creativity can be discreetly rewarded while at the same time competition is discouraged and social comparisons are avoided, and expressing enthusiasm in response to unusual ideas communicates that creativity is valued (Gong et al., 2017).

- *Capitalizing on the social nature of creativity.* Having students work together to generate unique examples or alternative solutions to problems can promote creativity (Binyamin & Carmeli, 2017). For instance, Laura's students decided to find the total area of their classroom and then subtract the areas covered with linoleum. An alternative solution, offered by some in the class, suggested finding the area of an inside rectangle and then adding the additional carpeted areas.

- *Present constraints.* This counterintuitive suggestion, which focuses students' creative efforts, has been documented as effective. For instance, in an experiment, individuals were asked to generate creative rhymes that conveyed messages for the following: *Happy birthday, Thank you, Good luck, I am sorry, Happy New Year, Congratulations, Feel better,* and *I love you.* When they were required to limit their rhymes to two lines for each, the messages were more creative than when the constraints didn't exist (Haught-Tromp, 2017).

Teachers sometimes complain that the emphasis on standards and high-stakes testing reduces opportunities to be creative or encourage creativity in students. This doesn't have to be the case, as we saw in the example with Dan and his physics students. Further, his efforts took little or no extra preparation time or effort on his part. Fostering creativity in students depends primarily on the kind of learning environments that we create.

Problem-Based Learning

Problem-based learning is a teaching strategy that uses problems as the focus for developing content, skills, and self-regulation (Akcay, 2017; Servant, & Schmidt, 2016). It's widely used in a variety of areas ranging from medical education and public health (de Jong, Verstegen, & Tan, 2013; Wardley, Applegate, & Van Rhee, 2013) to computer programming (Tiantong & Teemuangsai, 2013) and business (Smart, Hicks, & Melton, 2013), among others.

Problem-based learning activities have the following characteristics (Horak & Galluzzo, 2017; Sipes, 2016).

- Lessons begin with a problem, and solving it is the lesson's focus.
- Students are responsible for designing strategies and finding solutions to the problem.
- Learners work in groups small enough—typically 3 or 4—so that all students are involved in the process.
- The teacher guides students' efforts with questioning and other forms of scaffolding.

Some evidence indicates that problem-based learning activities result in content retained longer and transferred better than with direct instruction (Horak & Galluzzo, 2017; Mayer & Wittrock, 2006). Additional evidence indicates that learners are more motivated in problem-based lessons (Fukuzawa, Boyd, & Cahn, 2017). However, most of the research has been conducted with older or advanced students, and additional evidence indicates that lack of guidance from teachers in problem-based learning lessons results in misconceptions and superficial learning (Kirschner, Sweller, & Clark, 2006). Further, some research indicates that students, including those in universities, often use the most superficial strategies possible to solve problems, particularly if they aren't carefully monitored by their instructors (Loyens, Gijbels, Coertjens, & Côté, 2013).

Prior knowledge is an additional issue with problem-based learning, and lack of adequate background knowledge is the primary issue with problem-based learning activities that aren't successful. Unless learners' have extensive background knowledge, they're likely to flounder and waste time.

Using Technology to Promote Problem Solving

A number of technological supports exist for developing students' problem solving, and you'll likely encounter some of them when you begin teaching. For instance, **virtual manipulatives**, operated with a keyboard or mouse, now commonly replace the physical manipulatives, such as Cuisenaire rods and blocks, that have been historical mainstays in elementary classrooms (Roblyer & Hughes, 2019; Shin et al., 2017), and evidence indicates that these virtual tools are as effective as their concrete counterparts (Satsangi, Bouck, Taber-Doughty, Bofferding, & Roberts, 2016).

Simulations, such as the *Geometer's Sketchpad* (Informer Technologies, Inc., 2017), allow students to manipulate fractions, number lines, and geometric patterns and observe the outcomes. Middle and high school students can explore ratio and proportion, graphical representations of physical events, such as a dropped ball, and linear and trigonometric functions. The software is quite engaging, which can contribute to students' involvement and motivation (Roblyer & Hughes, 2019). *Sketchpad* and other simulations are compatible with **interactive whiteboards**, large displays that connect to computers. A projector displays information from the computer's desktop onto the board's surface, while the teacher or a student controls the information.

Teaching Students to Code

More recently, a major problem-solving initiative—teaching middle and high school students to *code*—is finding its way into our nation's schools. **Coding** is using the languages programmers use to design apps, websites, and software. The initiative is designed, as Timothy Cook, chief executive of Apple, has stated, to help solve a "huge deficit in the skills that we need today" (cited in Singer, 2017, para. 1). This emphasis has been triggered in part by American technology companies' heavy reliance on foreign engineers, which became even more urgent because of the Trump administration's antipathy toward immigration (Wingfield & Wakabayashijan, 2017). Technology experts, such as Cook, argue that coding should be a requirement in all schools and that the government should do its part to ensure that students learn computer programming. Others have stated the case even more strongly, arguing that our country is failing its students by not teaching coding in every high school (Kohli, 2015).

A major push to advance the coding agenda has come from Silicon Valley through Code.org, an industry-backed nonprofit group founded in 2012. Code.org describes itself as dedicated to expanding access to computer science and increasing participation by women and underrepresented minorities. Its goal is to give every student in every school the opportunity to learn computer science, just as they would learn algebra, biology, or chemistry. Encryption is as foundational as photosynthesis, it argues (Code.org, 2017).

Since its founding, Code.org has become a major force economically, pedagogically, and politically. For instance, it has raised more than $60 million from companies, such as Microsoft, Facebook, and Google, to support its initiatives, and it's created free online coding lessons, developed curricula, and offered training for teachers. Politically, these efforts appear to have paid off. For instance, Code.org has helped persuade more than 20 states to change education policies (Singer, 2017), and coding competitions for public school students are now becoming more common (D'Amico, 2017).

As is virtually always the case, Code.org's initiatives have stirred some controversy, with critics suggesting that their motives—developing software engineers to help power their companies—are self-serving (Singer, 2017). Obviously, their initiatives are designed to support their industry, and educators will have to decide whether or not a negative element exists in these initiatives.

Regardless of controversy, other companies are getting involved. For instance, in 2016 Apple offered a free app, called *Swift Playgrounds*, designed to teach basic coding in Swift, a programming language the company unveiled in 2014. And in 2017 Apple introduced a year-long curriculum for high schools and community colleges to teach app design in Swift (Apple Inc., 2017). Another example, *EdSurge*, an educational technology company founded in 2011, describes itself as providing the most up-to-date resources for people who want to implement or build educational technology. It publishes newsletters and operates databases that can be accessed by teachers, school administrators, and others (EdSurge, 2017).

These are only a few examples, and given the rate at which technology advances, several other initiatives will likely exist by the time you read this. Most significantly, problem solving in our nation's schools is likely to take a new turn, with technological literacy and abilities such as coding likely becoming basic skills in the same way that reading, writing, and math are now. These changes likely will impact both what and how you teach.

An important reminder as we close this section, however. Without question, technology is changing our lives, both in classrooms and in the outside world. However, no matter how sophisticated, technology will not automatically increase learning; its effectiveness will always depend on the professional ability of the teacher using it. Implemented with professional skill, it can be a major contributor to learning; used improperly, it's largely a waste of valuable learning time. You, not technology, remain the most important influence on your students' learning.

Using Educational Psychology in Teaching: Suggestions for Helping Your Students Become Better Problem Solvers

We now have an ill-defined problem of our own. We want our students to develop their problem-solving abilities, but often they aren't very good at it. In fact, teaching problem solving is one of the most challenging aspects of our work (Lester, 2013). The following suggestions can help us meet this challenge.

1. Present problems in real-world contexts, and provide practice in identifying problem goals.
2. Use worked examples to expand students' background knowledge.
3. Develop students' expertise with deliberate practice.
4. Capitalize on social interaction to engage students and assess understanding.
5. Encourage sense making as students solve problems.

Let's see what these suggestions look like in classrooms.

Present Problems in Real-World Contexts and Provide Practice in Identifying Problem Goals. *Learning and development depend on experience* is a principle of cognitive learning theory, and development in problem solving requires two types of experiences. First, students must solve problems in real-world contexts (Budwig, 2015; Jurow, 2016). Problems such as the one Laura posed will result in deeper and more useful understanding than solving a series of abstract addition, subtraction, multiplication, and division problems.

APA Top 20 Principles

As with concept learning, this description applies Principle 4: *Learning is based on context, so generalizing learning to new contexts is not spontaneous but instead needs to be facilitated*—from the *Top 20 Principles from Psychology for PreK–12 Teaching and Learning*.

Second, people, including even well-educated adults, are not good at identifying problem goals (Wedell-Wedellsborg, 2017), so Laura also attempted to provide her students with experiences in this area. To see how, let's look again at some dialogue from her lesson.

Laura: We're trying to update our classroom, so we're thinking about replacing the carpet, but we need to figure out how much to order. . . . So, what, exactly, is our problem? . . . What are we trying to find out? (after displaying the diagram of the classroom and explaining that the parts marked L are covered with linoleum)

Yashoda: We have to find out how much carpet we need.

Laura: Good°. . . And what makes our problem a little more challenging?

Natalie: We don't need carpet for the areas marked L on the diagram.

Laura: So, how can we figure out how much we actually need?

By presenting her problem with this slight twist, Laura provided her students with valuable experience in identifying problem goals.

Mixing the types of problems we're asking students to solve can also be helpful (Taylor & Rohrer, 2010). For instance, when elementary students learn to add fractions, they typically first practice with problems with like denominators and then move to problems with unlike denominators. This is followed by practice with subtraction, multiplication, and division. Simply mixing these problems provides students with beginning experiences in identifying problem goals. For example, the goals in the following problems are, respectively, to subtract, add, divide, and multiply the fractions, and the second problem also requires finding a common denominator.

$$\frac{3}{5} - \frac{2}{5} = \qquad \frac{2}{3} + \frac{3}{4} = \qquad \frac{4}{7} \div \frac{3}{4} = \qquad \frac{5}{6} \times \frac{2}{3} =$$

Students can then be given real-world problems requiring the same operations. This strategy won't immediately result in students being good at identifying problem goals, but it's a first step.

We can also present students with problems outside the context of math, and the fact that they're often ill-defined is one of the benefits of these types of problems. For instance, you might have your students work on a problem such as the following:

A new girl, named Rosalina, has recently joined our class. She is a native Spanish speaker, and she struggles with English. She is quite shy, and appears to be uneasy in our class. So, what might we do about it?

This is an ill-defined, real-world problem, and practicing solving problems such as this one provides students with valuable experience in both identifying problem goals and social problem solving. Problem solving need not be restricted to math in elementary schools and math, chemistry, and physics in high schools.

Use Worked Examples to Develop Students' Background Knowledge.   We've strongly emphasized the need for background knowledge throughout this text, and students' lack of prior knowledge is one of the most vexing problems teachers face. Regardless of whether our problems are well- or ill-defined, background knowledge is essential for solving them, and lack of this knowledge is almost always an issue in teaching problem solving (Lester, 2013). The steps outlined in Figure 8.2 provide a conceptual framework for problem solving, but these steps will be largely meaningless if students lack the background knowledge needed to solve specific problems.

APA Top 20 Principles

This discussion illustrates Principle 2: *What learners already know affects their learning*—from the *Top 20 Principles from Psychology for PreK–12 Teaching and Learning*.

Worked examples, problems with completed solutions, provide us with a tool for helping students acquire the background knowledge they need to become skilled problem solvers. Let's look at an example with David Chin, a fifth-grade teacher, who is working with his students on adding and subtracting fractions with unlike denominators in order to meet the following standard:

National Council on Teacher Quality (NCTQ)

The National Council on Teacher Quality describes using worked examples as one of the 6 essential teaching strategies that all new teachers need to know. "4. Repeatedly alternating problems with their solutions provided and problems that students must solve. Explanations accompanying solved problems help students comprehend underlying principles, taking them beyond the mechanics of problem solving" (Pomerance et al., 2016, p. vi).

CCSS.Math.Content.5.NF.A.1 Add and subtract fractions with unlike denominators (including mixed numbers) by replacing given fractions with equivalent fractions in such a way as to produce an equivalent sum or difference of fractions with like denominators. (Common Core State Standards Initiative, 2018k).

He begins by displaying the following on his document camera.

We're at a party, and our host serves pizza. She orders several pizzas, all of which are the same size, but some are cut into six pieces and others cut into 8 pieces. You eat 2 pieces from a pizza cut into six pieces, and 1 piece from a pizza cut into 8 pieces. How much pizza did you eat?

Step 1:

$$\frac{2}{6} + \frac{1}{8} =$$

Step 2:

$$\frac{2}{6} = \frac{8}{24}$$

Step 3:

$$\frac{1}{8} = \frac{3}{24}$$

Step 4:

$$\frac{8}{24} + \frac{3}{24} = \frac{11}{24}$$

"Now, let's look at our problem," David begins. "Read the problem and then look at step 1."

He waits a few seconds and then asks, "Where did we get the 2/6 and the 1/8 in step 1? . . . Lenore?"

" . . . It's the amount of pizza we ate. We ate two sixths of one pizza and one eighth of another."

"Now look at steps 2 and 3. Why did we do these steps? Why were they necessary? . . . Take a few minutes to check with your partner and see if you know. Derek, what did you and your partner conclude?"

" . . . We need to have the same denominator," Derek responds hesitantly after peering at the steps for several seconds.

David continues guiding the students, asking them to explain each step as they go, and ends the activity by asking, "So, what did we find out? . . . Juanita?

"We ate 11/24ths of a pizza altogether."

David then assigns a problem for students to work on their own, monitors their progress, and provides feedback.

After they've worked and discussed the problem, he presents another worked example, and they repeat the process.

Worked examples are most common in math, physics, and chemistry, but they can be used in other curriculum areas as well. For instance, students faced with the problem of writing a short passage that includes at least three different kinds of figurative language could be presented with the following:

Adrian, as lithe as a gazelle, sprinted around the track, a virtual vortex of vibrant velocity in motion. "She's the greatest athlete in the world!" her coach exudes, "a Phoenix rising from the starting blocks and soaring like the winged bird of mythology."

In this short passage students see simile, *as lithe as a gazelle* and *like the winged bird of mythology*; alliteration, *a virtual vortex of vibrant velocity*; hyperbole, *"She's the greatest athlete in the world!"*; and metaphor, *"a Phoenix rising from the starting blocks,"* so they can actually see four examples embedded in a text. Using this as a model can help students get started with their task.

Using worked examples applies cognitive learning theory. David, for instance, provided his students with the experience they needed to help them construct their understanding of the procedure; each step made sense; and he guided their understanding with questioning, which capitalized on social interaction.

Research provides additional support. Learners from elementary schools through universities find using worked examples both more meaningful and more motivating than traditional instruction for developing problem-solving abilities (Lee & Chen, 2016; ter Vrugte et al., 2017).

Worked examples are particularly important when students are first learning a procedure or when content is difficult (Ngu & Yeung, 2013). Earlier we examined the initiative to teach coding in schools, and, because of its sophistication and demands, worked examples would be particularly effective in teaching students coding skills. "Especially for difficult content, giving several written-out solutions for each unsolved problem is helpful. As students become more skilled, teachers can increase the number of problems that students solve on their own following each solved example" (Pomerance et al., 2016, p. 23).

Develop Students' Expertise with Deliberate Practice. Increasing learners' expertise is the goal of all schooling. **Experts** are individuals who are highly knowledgeable or skilled in a specific domain, such as math, history, chess, or teaching. The term *specific domain* is important. An expert in math, for instance, may be a novice in teaching or history, because a great deal of time and effort are required to develop expertise. "Experts are made, not born. This is not to say that intellectual ability and talent do not exist, or are unimportant, but that effort, deliberate practice, and feedback from experts are essential to the development of high-level expertise" (Schraw, 2006, p. 255).

The previous quote refers to **deliberate practice**, a systematic approach to the development of a wide range of abilities including athletics, music, art, and academic skills, such as writing or problem solving. "Deliberate practice—a challenging yet highly effective form of practice—leads to world-class eminence across domains . . . . Even critics, who point to other relevant determinants of skill improvement, including talent, acknowledge deliberate practice is an 'unquestionably important' predictor of success" (Eskreis-Winkler et al., 2016, p. 728).

APA Top 20 Principles

This description applies Principle 5: *Acquiring long-term knowledge and skill is largely dependent on practice*—from the *Top 20 Principles from Psychology for PreK–12 Teaching and Learning.*

Deliberate practice has the following components (Eskreis-Winkler et al., 2016; Panero, 2016):

- The individual has a well-defined goal for improving a specific aspect of performance. For instance, being able to add and subtract fractions with unlike denominators was the specific goal for David's students.

- The degree of challenge is just beyond learners' present skill level. His students were not yet skilled at adding and subtracting fractions with unlike denominators.

- Learners receive detailed feedback about how to improve the skill. When his students solved fraction problems on their own, David carefully monitored their progress and provided feedback.

- Learners repetitively focus on correcting errors and advancing their skills. David gradually increased the level of difficulty in the problems the students were expected to solve on their own.

Two additional aspects of practice are important. First, **distributed practice**, the process of spacing practice over time, is more effective than clustering it in a short period (McCrudden & McNamara, 2018). For example, a half hour each day for 4 days is more effective than 2 hours all at once. When we practice, information is activated in memory, it is deactivated after we stop, and it's then reactivated when we begin the next practice period. "This cycle of activation-deactivation-reactivation is beneficial for memory because it strengthens neural pathways in our brains, which increase our access to the information at later times" (McCrudden & McNamara, 2018, p. 46).

Second, **interspersed practice**, the process of mixing the practice of different skills, is more effective than practicing one skill extensively and then moving to a different one. For instance, if elementary students are practicing subtraction problems that require regrouping, such as 45 − 27, their learning will be enhanced if they are also given subtraction problems that don't require regrouping, such as 74 − 43, as well as addition problems that do and do not require regrouping. This applies in all domains. For example, soccer practice is more effective if players practice dribbling for a few minutes, passing for a few more, goal scoring for an additional time, and then return to each skill instead of massing practice on a particular skill and then turning to a different one. "Students will improve as problem solvers only if they are given opportunities to solve a variety of types of problematic tasks" (Lester, 2013, p. 272).

There is no substitute for practice, and this applies in all domains. Accomplished musicians practice for hours every day, and great athletes do the same. If our students are to develop problem-solving expertise, we must provide them with the opportunities to practice, practice, and practice some more. And this includes practice in solving a variety of problems over an extended period of time.

National Council on Teacher Quality (NCTQ)

The National Council on Teacher Quality describes distributing practice as one of the 6 essential teaching strategies that all new teachers should know. Students need a great deal of practice to develop knowledge and skills, and distributing this practice over time makes storage in memory more efficient and boosts retention (McCrudden & McNamara, 2018).

Capitalize on Social Interaction to Engage Students and Assess Learning. In our discussion of the steps involved in problem solving, we looked at some dialogue from Laura's lesson. Let's look at it again.

Laura has reassembled the class after they've worked in groups to find the area of the carpeted portion of their classroom, and she has just sent Avery to the board to demonstrate how he multiplied 30 times 48 to get 1,440 square feet as the total area of the classroom.

> Laura: Now what? . . . What did we do next?

The students have agreed that they needed to subtract the parts marked "L," and most say they should start at the top of the diagram.

> Laura: How will we find the area of this part? . . . Fred? (pointing to the top of the diagram).

> Fred: . . . Multiply 31 times 5.

> Laura: Why? . . . Tu?

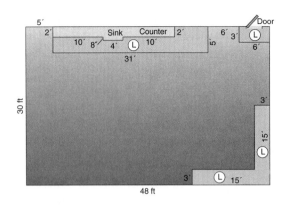

Tu: . . . That part is a rectangle, and it's 31 feet long and 5 feet wide, . . . so we multiply them.

Zoey: What about the 2? (pointing at the 2—for the sink and counter—in the diagram)

Laura: What about it? . . . Audrey?

Audrey: . . . That's just a part. Linoleum is under all of it, so that's why it's 31 times 5 . . . . The 2 doesn't matter.

Laura: So, what did we get? . . . Aiden?

Aiden: . . . A hundred fifty-five. (after taking a few seconds to multiply 31 times 5)

Social interaction facilitates learning is a cognitive principle, and Laura applied it with her students. She didn't simply explain how they should find the areas of each piece covered by linoleum; instead she guided her students through the process with questioning. The importance of interacting with students is particularly illustrated by Zoey's uncertainty about why they didn't consider the dimensions of the sink and counter in their calculations. If Laura had simply explained the solutions, her question likely wouldn't have come up.

Regardless of the content area or topic, interacting with students is essential. For instance, we saw how Maria Lopez in her concept learning lesson interacted with her students, and we also saw that David Chin didn't simply present and explain his worked example; he also guided his students through social interaction.

Encourage Sense Making as Students Solve Problems.   Students' tendencies to accept answers whether or not the answers make sense is one of the most frustrating aspects of teaching problem solving. The second-graders who added the number of sheep and goats to get the age of the captain illustrates this tendency, as does the thinking of Laura's students who initially got an answer for the carpeted area of the classroom that was greater than the classroom's total area. It's an ongoing issue in attempts to help students become better problem solvers.

Students' tendencies to solve problems with superficial strategies is an additional challenge (Gamo, Sander, & Richard, 2010). For instance, they'll use key words, such as *altogether*, which suggests addition, or *how many more*, which implies subtraction, as a strategy. Other superficial strategies include using the operation most recently taught or looking at cues in the chapter headings of the text. These strategies can bypass understanding completely, yet are often quite successful (Hunt & Empson, 2015). And students' increasing dependency on technology, such as calculators, can exacerbate the problem. Whatever appears on the calculator screen must be the right answer.

A simple solution to this problem doesn't exist, but two strategies can help. First, we can emphasize and model sense making in our teaching. Simple questions, such as, "Now, does this make sense?" and then discussing why it does or doesn't can, over time, make a

MyLab Education
Video Example 8.2

We know that students are inclined to accept answers to problems whether or not the answers make sense. As a result, "sense making" is strongly emphasized when teaching problem solving. Here seventh-grade teacher, Kim Crosby, emphasizes sense making as she works with her students on a problem involving the height of a stack of books.

Classroom Connections

Developing Learners' Problem-Solving Abilities

1. The learning sciences suggest that real-world applications are important, and principles of cognitive learning theory suggest that social interaction facilitates learning. Embed problems in real-world contexts and use high levels of interaction to improve your students' problem-solving abilities.

- **Elementary:** A fourth-grade teacher breaks her students into pairs and gives each pair a chocolate bar composed of 12 square pieces. She gives them problems involving 1/4 and 1/3 and has students break off certain numbers of pieces to represent the numbers as fractions of the whole bar. She has them explain their thinking in each case.

- **Middle School:** A middle school teacher has a "problem of the week." Each student is required to bring in one real-world problem each week that relates to the topics they are studying. The teacher selects from among them, and the class solves them.

- **High School:** A physics teacher gives students problems such as, "If you're shooting a free throw and launch it at a 45-degree angle, what velocity will you need to put on the ball in order for it to go through the hoop?" After students

attempt the problem, she uses questioning to guide them to a solution.

2. Learners require extensive practice and instructional support to develop their problem-solving abilities. As students practice solving problems, provide students with scaffolding and encourage them to put their understanding into words.

- **Elementary:** A second-grade teacher begins a lesson on graphing by telling them she's planning for a party and asking students how they might determine their classmates' favorite jelly bean flavor. She guides them as they identify the problem and how they might represent and solve it.

- **Middle School:** A pre-algebra teacher uses categories such as "We Know" and "We Need to Know" as scaffolds for analyzing word problems. His students then use the scaffolds to solve at least two word problems each day.

- **High School:** In a unit on statistics and probability, a teacher requires her students to make estimates before solving problems. They then compare the solutions to their estimates.

difference. Second, having students estimate answers can be very effective. For instance, a sensible estimate of the carpeted area of Laura's classroom would be something less than 1,440 square feet—the total area of the classroom. This estimate might have caused the students who got 1,600 for the carpeted area to say, "Wait a minute. This can't be right." With time and practice, they'll get better at it. Then, combining estimating with deliberate practice can be a powerful tool for promoting sense making.

MyLab Education Self-Check 8.2
MyLab Education Application Exercise 8.2: Problem Solving in Third Grade

In this exercise you will be asked to analyze a third-grade teacher's application of the suggestions for helping students become better problem solvers.

The Strategic Learner

8.3   Identify applications of study strategies and critical thinking.

Ed Psych and You

As you sit in your university classes, what do you typically do to learn from your instructors' presentations?

You're studying this textbook. What do you commonly do to better understand the content?

MyLab Education
Video Example 8.3

Strategies are cognitive operations that go beyond the normal activities, such as reading or listening, required to understand a topic. Here we see Dan Shafer, a middle school social studies teacher, work with his students on strategies designed to help them remember the primary causes of World War One.

If you answered the first question in *Ed Psych and You* by saying, "Take notes," you're typical. Lecture is the most common teaching method in universities, and virtually all students take notes (Bui, Myerson, & Hale, 2013). And "highlight," underline, or something similar is your likely answer to the second question. Taking notes and highlighting are **strategies**, cognitive operations that exceed the normal activities required to meet a learning goal (Pressley & Harris, 2006). Note taking is a strategy because it goes beyond merely listening to your instructor as you attempt to remember what he or she is saying, as is highlighting, because it does more than simply reading, the normal activity involved in trying to meet the goal of understanding a written passage. Many learning strategies, such as note taking, highlighting, summarizing, self-questioning, and concept mapping, exist, and each can increase learning (Alexander, 2006).

Metacognition: The Foundation of Strategic Learning

Think again about the questions we asked in *Ed Psych and You*. You most likely take notes because you believe that doing so will help you better remember the information your instructor is presenting. In doing so you're being *metacognitive*. **Metacognition**, often described as "thinking about thinking" (Medina, Castleberry, & Persky, 2017), is knowledge and regulation of our cognition. You believe you'll remember more of the lecture if you take notes (knowledge of cognition), and you regulate it with the note-taking process. Metacognition is the mechanism we use to match a strategy to a goal, and students who are metacognitive perform learning tasks better than their peers who are less aware (Callan, Marchant, Finch, & German, 2016).

When taking notes, for example, metacognitive learners ask questions such as:

- Am I writing down important ideas or trivial details?
- Am I taking enough notes, or too many?
- When I study, am I simply reading my notes, or do I elaborate on them by searching for examples or asking myself questions?

Without metacognitive monitoring, strategies are ineffective. "The issue of selecting study strategies is complicated because a requirement for selecting a learning strategy is metacognitive knowledge about which learning strategies are beneficial for long-term memory" (Medina et al., 2017, p. 2).

We have repeatedly emphasized the importance of background knowledge, and it's also essential for strategy use (Pomerance et al., 2016). This knowledge allows learners to make better decisions about what's important to study and how to meet their learning goals (O'Leary & Sloutsky, 2017).

And, just as expert problem solvers draw on a wealth of experiences with problems, effective strategy users access a variety of strategies (Su, Ricci, & Mnatsakanian, 2016). For instance, they take notes, skim, use bold and italicized print, capitalize on examples, and create concept maps. Without this repertoire, matching strategies to specific tasks is difficult.

Becoming a strategic learner takes time and effort, and even after instruction, many learners use strategies only when prompted by their teachers (Pressley & Harris, 2006). Also, most students, including those in college, tend to use primitive strategies, regardless of the difficulty of the material. "Several studies show students using low-impact study strategies, such as rereading or highlighting notes" (Medina et al., 2017, p. 2).

Study Strategies

Study strategies are specific techniques students use to increase their understanding of written materials and teacher presentations. Some of the most widely used include:

- Note taking
- Using text signals

- Summarizing
- Elaborative questioning
- Concept mapping

Taking Notes

Note taking is probably the most common study strategy, it's the most widely researched, and, when well done, it increases achievement. However, most students are not good at it (Bui et al., 2013; Peverly et al., 2013). Effective notes include both the main ideas presented in lectures or texts, combined with supporting details, but students, including those in college, often fail at one or both (Kiewra, 2016). Note taking can be made more efficient with simple aids, such as bulleted items for lists of information (Olive & Barbier, 2017), and some evidence indicates that collaborative note taking, that is, students comparing and revising notes in groups, can enhance their quality (Ahn, Ingham, & Mendez, 2016).

Our information processing system helps explain the positive effects of note taking. First, taking notes helps maintain attention and encourages active cognitive processing, and second, the notes provide a form of external storage so the cognitive load on working memory is reduced (Bui & Myerson, 2014). Because of working memory's limited capacity, we often lose information before it's encoded, or we may reconstruct our understanding in a way that makes sense to us but isn't valid. Notes provide a form of external storage, against which we can check our understanding.

We can help our students improve their note taking with **guided notes**, teacher-prepared handouts that "guide" students with cues, combined with space available for writing key ideas and relationships. Using guided notes increases achievement in students ranging from low achievers to those in college (Boyle, 2013). Figure 8.3 illustrates a guided-notes form in geography used for different climate regions of the United States.

Figure 8.3 A guide for note taking in U.S. geography

1. Give an example of how each of the following influences climate:

Latitude _____

Wind direction _____

Ocean currents _____

Land forms _____

2. Describe each climate, and identify at least one state that has this climate. Then identify one type of plant that lives in this climate and two different animals that are typically found in the climate.

The Mediterranean Climate _____

_____ State _____

Plant _____ Animals _____

The Marine West Coast Climate _____

_____ State _____

Plant _____ Animals _____

The Humid Subtropical Climate _____

_____ State _____

Plant _____ Animals _____

The Humid Continental Climate _____

_____ State _____

Guided notes also model the organization and key points of a topic. As students use the notes in their study, they gradually develop organizational skills they can apply on their own.

Using Text Signals

Text signals are elements in written materials that highlight important concepts or communicate the organization of the content (Clariana, Rysavy, & Taricani, 2015). Common text signals include:

- *Headings.* For example, in this chapter, *taking notes, using text signals,* and *summarizing* are subheadings under the heading *study strategies,* so this organization signals that each is a study strategy.
- *Numbered and bulleted lists.* For instance, the bulleted list you're reading now identifies different text signals.
- *Underlined, bold, or italicized text.* Each of the important concepts in this text, for example, is emphasized in bold print.

Strategic learners use these signals to help them understand the topic they're studying (Vacca, Vacca, & Mraz, 2014). We can encourage this strategy with our students by discussing the organization of a topic and reminding them of other text signals that help make information meaningful.

Summarizing

Summarizing is the process of preparing a concise description of verbal or written passages (Saddler, Asaro-Saddler, Moeyaert, & Ellis-Robinson, 2017). It's effective for **comprehension monitoring**—checking to see if we understand what we've read or heard. As we would expect, learning to summarize takes training, time, and effort (Alexander, 2006). Training usually involves walking students through a passage and helping them generate statements that relate ideas to each other, identify important information, and construct general descriptions (Pressley & Harris, 2006).

For instance, we might summarize the problem-solving section of this chapter as follows:

To solve problems, we identify the problem goal, represent the problem, select and implement a strategy to solve it, and check to see if the solution makes sense. We can help our students become better problem solvers by using worked examples, providing them with a great deal of spaced deliberate practice and focusing on sense making in the problem-solving process.

Research suggests that summarizing increases both students' understanding of the topics they study and their metacognitive skills. Having students generate key terms that capture the essence of a text passage is a modified form of summarizing that can also increase comprehension (Saddler et al., 2017).

Asking Elaborative Questions

Elaborative questioning is the process of drawing inferences, identifying examples, and forming relationships in the material they're studying. Often described as *elaborative interrogation,* it is an effective strategy for increasing comprehension of written information in both traditional and online text (Chen, Teng, Lee, & Kinshuk, 2011). It's effective for comprehension monitoring because it encourages students to create connections in the material they're studying. Three elaborative questions are particularly effective:

- What is another example of this idea?

- How is this topic similar to or different from the one in the previous section?
- How does this idea relate to other ideas I've been studying?

For example, as you were studying the section on problem solving, the following questions might have been helpful:

What is another example of a well-defined problem in this class?
What is an example of an ill-defined problem?
What makes the first well-defined and the second ill-defined?
How are problem-solving and learning strategies similar? How are they different?

Questions such as these create links between new information and knowledge in long-term memory, making both more meaningful.

Forming Concept Maps

A **concept map** is a visual representation of the relationships among concepts. It includes the concepts themselves, sometimes enclosed in circles or boxes, together with relationships among concepts indicated by lines linking them to each other (Harris & Shenghua, 2017). Words on the line, referred to as *linking words*, specify the relationship between the concepts. A concept map is analogous to the way a road map represents locations of highways and towns, or a circuit diagram represents the workings of an electrical appliance. Figure 8.4 is a concept map for the complex cognitive processes that we've discussed in the chapter.

Concept mapping is an effective strategy because, first, a concept map presents information both visually and verbally, and second, concept mapping capitalizes on effective encoding strategies (Rye, Landenberger, & Warner, 2013). The visual representation promotes *imagery*, and preparing the map itself requires *organization*. As learners' understanding increases, maps are modified and expanded, which utilizes *elaboration*. Research indicates that the strategy makes initial learning more effective and conceptual change more durable (Harris & Shenghua, 2017).

National Council on Teacher Quality (NCTQ)

The National Council on Teacher Quality describes presenting information both visually and verbally as one of the 6 essential teaching strategies that all new teachers should know. "1. Pairing graphics with words. Young or old, all of us receive information through two primary pathways—auditory (for the spoken word) and visual (for the written word and graphic or pictorial representation). Student learning increases when teachers convey new material through both" (Pomerance et al., 2016, p. vi).

Conceptual hierarchies are concept maps that visually illustrate superordinate, subordinate, and coordinate relationships among concepts. Because each subordinate concept is a subset of the one above it, the relationships among the concepts in a hierarchy are clear, so linking words aren't needed. Many concepts, such as our number system, the animal and plant kingdoms, parts of speech, and figurative language, can be organized hierarchically.

A conceptual hierarchy for the concept *closed-plane figures* is illustrated in Figure 8.5. *Closed-plane figures* is superordinate to the other figures in the hierarchy; *four-sided figures, three-sided figures,* and *curved figures* are subordinate to *closed-plane figures* (they're all subsets); and *four-sided figures, three-sided figures,* and *curved figures* are coordinate to each other. Similar relationships exist among the other concepts in the hierarchy.

Figure 8.4 Concept map for complex cognitive processes

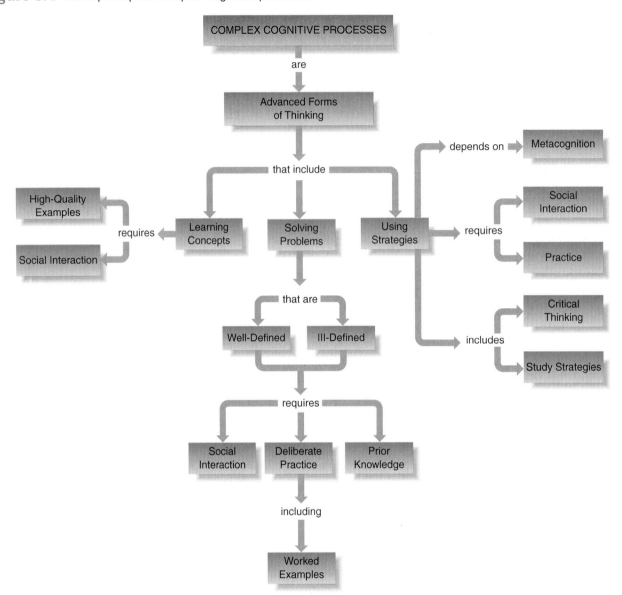

Concept mapping can also be an effective assessment tool (Dougherty, Custer, & Dixon, 2012). For example, the student who created the conceptual hierarchy in Figure 8.5 didn't include figures with more than four sides or curved shapes other than circles. If a concept map indicates that students' understanding is incomplete, we can then provide additional examples, such as pentagons and ellipses in the case of closed-plane figures.

The type of concept map students use should be the one that best illustrates relationships among the concepts. Hierarchies often work best in math and science; in other areas, such as reading or social studies, a traditional concept map is often more effective.

Most students can learn study strategies, and strategy instruction is especially valuable for younger students and low achievers, because they have a smaller repertoire of strategies and are less likely to use them spontaneously (Bruning, Schraw, & Norby, 2011). However, the effectiveness of any strategy depends on learners' motivation, their ability to activate relevant prior knowledge, and their metacognition. If one or more of these factors is missing, no strategy is effective.

Figure 8.5 Conceptual hierarchy for the concept *closed-plane* figures

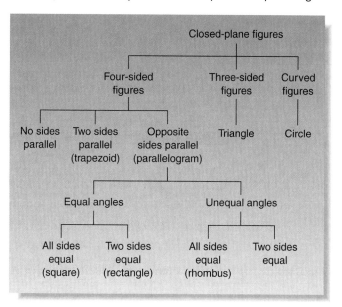

Research on Study Strategies

Ed Psych and You

How do you study? Do you study one topic thoroughly and then move on to the next? Do you have a designated place in your home where you usually do your studying? Do you study in large chunks of time, or shorter ones? In your estimation, how effective are your study strategies?

Conventional wisdom suggests that we should study a topic until we thoroughly understand it and then move to a second topic. It also suggests that we should have a designated place to study that's free of distractions. However, some of this conventional wisdom is invalid. For example, in a classic study conducted more than four decades ago, researchers found that simply varying the environment in which students studied resulted in better recall than studying the same information in a single environment (Smith, Glenberg, & Borg, 1978). This suggests that studying at home some of the time, in the library at other times, and even in a coffee shop is more effective than always studying in the same place. Research also indicates that studying different but related topics in one sitting is more effective than focusing intensely on a single topic (Taylor & Rohrer, 2010). For example, our study of human memory is likely to be more effective if we also study cognitive learning principles and the relationships between the two in a single study session, rather than studying human memory in one session and cognitive learning principles in another. "Forcing the brain to make multiple associations with the same material may, in effect, give the information more neural scaffolding" (Carey, 2010, para. 11).

Also, as we said in our discussion of deliberate practice earlier in the chapter, spacing study is vastly superior to intense periods of cramming. So, an hour of study tonight, another hour tomorrow, and a third hour over the weekend will result in more learning than cramming three hours in one session right before a test. Cognitive scientists also suggest that seeming to forget some information and struggling to remember it later benefits learning. We don't literally forget it, and the relearning results in deeper and more thorough understanding (McCrudden & McNamara, 2018). This research gives us all something to think about as we study.

Critical Thinking

Critical thinking has been described in various ways, but most definitions center on individuals' inclination and ability to make and assess conclusions based on evidence. This means that critical thinkers are able to justify their conclusions with factual information—" . . . justification as being the most important element in terms of our being able to say that we 'know' something" (Lack & Rousseau, 2016, p. 15).

Critical thinking is clearly a complex cognitive process, and its need in both our schools and in the larger society has never been greater. Further, 82% of parents say it's extremely or very important for the public schools to teach critical thinking. Only 29% think schools are doing extremely or very well in this area (Langer Research Associates, 2016). Let's see why.

Critical Thinking: Conspiracy Theories, Post-Truth, Fake News, and Sound Bites

Ed Psych and You

The Sandy Hook Elementary School Shooting that was described as occurring in December of 2012 never really occurred. It was a vast hoax perpetrated by the Federal Government in order to promote stricter gun control laws.

The attack on the twin towers in New York City on September 11, 2001 (9/11), was actually committed by our country's government to justify attacking Afghanistan and Iraq to further America's geopolitical interests.

How do you react to these assertions?

Our descriptions in *Ed Psych and You* illustrate **conspiracy theories**, explanations for events that invoke plots or schemes by governments or other powerful actors for nefarious motives (Hagen, 2018). Conspiracy theories' explanations contradict basic facts or accepted explanations, and their harm goes well beyond their simple lack of truth. For instance, a number of Sandy Hook parents, who lost their children in the shooting, have been harassed by conspiracy theorists (Wiedeman, 2016). This unspeakable cruelty is incomprehensible. Not only did the parents lose their young children, but they also had to endure the brutality and vindictiveness of the people questioning their loss. The prevalence of conspiracy theories, while not new, represents an increasing trend in our world that goes beyond simple falsity to potentially seriously destructive outcomes.

Post-truth, another trend in today's world, describes "circumstances in which objective facts are less influential in shaping public opinion than appeals to emotion and personal belief" (Peters, 2017, p. 563). Post-truth was Oxford Dictionaries' "Word of the Year" for 2016, but experts argue that the tendency to make facts subservient to emotion and beliefs began long before then (Bowell, 2017; Lack & Rousseau, 2016).

Fake news, a third trend, is deliberate misinformation that uses exaggerated and attention grabbing headlines for political, economic, or social gain. "The cornerstone of a fake news publication is its falsity. . . . Further, fake news publications are intentionally or knowingly false. Fake news publishers do not reasonably believe that the stated facts are true" (Klein & Wueller, 2017, p. 6).

Sound bites are sentences or short phrases intended to attract the attention of readers or viewers and capture the essence of what a speaker or writer is trying to say. Coined by the American media in the 1970s, they have been increasingly used as tools by politicians and people in sales to drive home points of emphasis. Because they're intentionally designed to be brief, simple, and easy to remember, sound bites often overshadow the larger context in which they exist, so they can be misleading or inaccurate (Rinke, 2016). For instance, a campaigning politician might say, "You want your property taxes to go down, elect me." He uses it repeatedly, so his name becomes associated with lower property taxes, thereby increasing his likelihood of election. However, its oversimplification doesn't consider possible economic, population, or needed infrastructure changes, so it's likely to be misleading.

How do we respond when confronted with this misinformation? A large body of research and commentary indicates that we are not good at identifying conspiracy theories, recognizing post-truth reactions, ferreting out fake news, or looking beneath the surface of sound bites (Fernbach & Sloman, 2017; Lack & Rousseau, 2016; Lynch, 2016; Sloman & Rabb, 2016). Some critics state the case more strongly, arguing, "[R]eluctance to change our minds in light of evidence has been described as so pervasive as to suggest that we're living in an 'age of willful ignorance'" (McIntyre, 2015, p. 8). In other words we're not good at thinking critically. We attempt to explain why in the next section.

Why Don't We Think Critically?

So, why are we so poor at critical thinking? Many causes exist, but research has identified three important factors that contribute to the problem:

- The Internet
- The power of emotion
- Our cognitive architecture

The Internet. Ease of access to information has revolutionized today's world. For instance, we're in a conversation with friends, a question about an obscure piece of information comes up, we pull out our smartphone and find the answer so quickly that it doesn't interrupt the flow of conversation. We don't even use our fingers. We simply ask the question and voice recognition does the rest. Never before has this been possible.

This is a double-edged sword, however, because any information—valid or invalid—can be posted on social media and the Internet at large. We can find any information we desire, regardless of how bizarre or far-fetched, that will confirm an existing belief. For instance, if we were inclined to believe the conspiracy theories about Sandy Hook or 9/11, we can find information on the Internet that will support this belief. This leaves us with the possibility of "social media and its propensity to disseminate fake news through Facebook, Google and Twitter, and thereby to create a 'bubble world' where . . . selected news sources simply reinforce existing prejudices" (Peters, 2017, p. 564). This tendency helps us understand the results of a widely publicized study published in 2016 that found, "[o]verall, young people's ability to reason about the information on the Internet can be summed up in one word: *bleak*" (Stanford History Education Group, 2016, p. 4). The Internet is both a wonderful source of information and a major source of misinformation. The key is knowing the difference.

Ed Psych and You

Which do you fear more: Terrorism or gunshot deaths? Sharks or dogs? Flying or driving? How do you think your feelings compare to people in general?

The Power of Emotion. Fear is one of our most powerful emotions; it strongly influences perception (Guess, McCardell, & Stefanucci, 2016), and it's the focus of our questions in *Ed Psych and You*. For most people, the answer is the first in each pair—terrorism, sharks, and flying. Statistics, however, tell a completely different story. For instance, "For every one American killed by an act of terror in the United States or abroad in 2014, more than a thousand died because of guns" (Bower, 2016, para. 6). In 2015, worldwide, 471 people died in plane crashes (Pemberton, 2017), whereas in the same year more than 35,000 Americans died in auto accidents (Insurance Institute for Highway Safety, 2017). And the odds of being killed in a shark attack are less than 1 in 3.7 million, whereas it's 1 in about 110 thousand for dogs—very favorable odds, but still a more than 33 times greater likelihood than a shark attack.

How can we explain these fears, when reason is supposed to be the highest achievement of the human mind, and the facts so strongly counter them? The answer: as human beings, we are capable of rational thought, but we are not innately rational beings. We are, instead, fundamentally emotional animals, and our tendency to first react emotionally to people and events helps us understand, first, why "post-truth" is now a factor in our lives, and second, why critical thinking is such a challenge (Lack & Rousseau, 2016). For instance, research suggests that people feeling powerless and experiencing high levels of personal and social stress—both strongly emotion laden—are more likely to believe conspiracy theories and fake news (Prooijen, 2017; Radnitz & Underwood, 2017; Swami, Funham, Smyth, Weis, Lay, & Clow, 2016). As another example, in a widely publicized encounter, a high school science student burst out of a teacher's class, never to return, because she had such a strong negative emotional reaction to the information he was presenting about climate change (Harmon, 2017).

Our Cognitive Architecture. We just saw that people's emotions help us understand why they tend to believe in conspiracy theories. Research indicates that our search for simplistic solutions to complex problems also contributes to this tendency (Prooijen, 2017).

Our information processing system and the concept of cognitive load helps us understand why. In Chapter 7 we saw that this system, our cognitive architecture, is composed of memory stores—sensory memory, a limited-capacity working memory, and long-term memory—and cognitive processes that move information from store to store.

Understanding complex problems and solutions imposes a heavy cognitive load on our limited-capacity working memory, and accepting a simplistic solution reduces the load. Our cognitive architecture also helps us understand our vulnerability to sound bites. They're simple, easy to understand, and easy to remember. As a result they impose a low cognitive load on our working memories.

Confirmation bias, the tendency of individuals to focus on information that confirms their beliefs and ignore evidence that disputes these beliefs, is another barrier to critical thinking (Lack & Rousseau, 2016). Many examples exist, but climate change is one of the most prominent and controversial. The overwhelming majority of scientific evidence supports the notion of human-caused climate change (National Aeronautics and Space Administration, 2017). However, some studies do not. "Nearly 4,000 studies . . . suggest humans are culpable, compared to . . . about 80 that say we have nothing to do with the problem" (Dickerson, 2015, para. 2). Climate change deniers—and some of you reading this material may be among them—focus on the results of the 80 studies and tend to ignore the 4,000. (In presenting this example, we're not trying to foment controversy or denigrate or disrespect anyone's beliefs. Rather, we're simply trying to model critical thinking by presenting available evidence. We'll comment further on this idea in the next section.)

Confirmation bias is an issue in many fields, such as forensics, health, and even "pure" research (Hernandez & Preston, 2013; Kassin, Dror, & Kukucka, 2013), and our cognitive architecture helps us understand why. Retaining an existing belief imposes a much lower cognitive load than changing our thinking. Also, retaining an existing belief allows us to remain at equilibrium, a concept we examined in detail in Chapter 2.

Some researchers argue that we're simply not wired for thinking. "Humans don't think very often because our brains are designed not for thought, but for the avoidance of thought" (Willingham, 2009, p. 4). We function more effectively when cognitive load is low and we perform tasks automatically, essentially without conscious thought (Willingham, 2009).

So, what can we do about both our own and our students' lack of critical thinking abilities? We attempt to answer this question in the next section.

Using Educational Psychology in Teaching: Suggestions for Helping our Students Become Strategic Learners and Critical Thinkers

Cognitive learning theory offers suggestions for helping our students become better strategy users and critical thinkers. The following suggestions can help us in our efforts (Prooijen, 2017):

1. Explicitly teach and have students practice study strategies.
2. Model critical thinking and use questioning and discussion to promote critical thinking in our students.
3. Use assessment with feedback as learning tools.

We discuss these suggestions in the following sections.

Explicitly Teach Study Strategies.   Regardless of what we're attempting to learn—physical skills, such as dribbling a basketball, art or music performance, critical thinking, or academic skills, such as concept learning or problem solving—explicit instruction combined with modeling and the regulation of our thinking (metacognition) are essential to maximize the amount learned (Peverly et al., 2013; Prooijen, 2017). This also applies to study strategies.

Let's look at an example.

Donna Evans, a middle school social studies teacher, is attempting to help her students learn to summarize and meet the following standard:

> CCSS.ELA-Literacy.RI.7.2 Determine two or more central ideas in a text and analyze their development over the course of the text; provide an objective summary of the text (Common Core State Standards Initiative, 2018l).

Donna begins her geography class by directing her students to a section of the text that describes the low-, middle-, and high-latitude climates, and says, "One way to become more effective readers is to summarize the information we read in a few short statements."

She then displays the following on her document camera, "Summarizing is the process of preparing a short, concise description of a passage," and says, "This makes it easier to remember, and it will help us understand how one climate region compares with another. You can do the same thing in all of your classes. . . . Now read the section on page 237 and see if you can identify the features of a low-latitude climate."

After the class reads the section, Donna continues, "As I was reading, here's how I thought about it." She then displays the following information on the document camera and describes her thinking as she writes it.

> Low latitudes can be hot and wet or hot and dry. Close to the equator, the humid tropical climate is hot and wet all year. Farther away, it has wet summers and dry winters. In the dry tropical climate, high-pressure zones cause deserts, like the Sahara.

She then says, "Now, let's all give it a try with the section on the middle-latitude climates. Go ahead and read the section and try to summarize it the way I did. . . . Write your summaries, and we'll share what you've written."

After they finish, Donna asks a student to volunteer a summary.

Kari volunteers, displays her summary on the document camera, and Donna and other students add information and comments to what Kari has written. Donna then has two other students display their summaries, and then the class practices again with the section on the high-latitude climates.

Throughout the school year, Donna continues to have her students practice summarizing as they encounter new information in their texts.

Now let's look at Donna's efforts. She explicitly taught the process of summarizing by describing it and explaining why it's useful. For instance, she said, "One way to become more effective readers is to summarize the information we read in a few short statements. This makes information easier to remember . . . "

She also modeled both the skill and her thinking when she commented, "As I was reading, here's how I thought about it. . . ." Research indicates that students' metacognitive awareness can be increased with this kind of explicit instruction (Alexander, Johnson, & Leibham, 2005).

Donna then had her students practice preparing their own summaries; she displayed students' examples on the document camera, so everyone would be responding to the same information; and the class discussed the summaries and provided feedback. Discussion and interaction at this point in the process is essential for helping students develop their skills with the strategy. And she continued the process throughout the school year.

Donna taught summarizing, but her approach—explicitly teaching the strategy—applies equally well to all study strategies. For instance, if we want students to use concept maps, we explain and model the use of concept maps, and we do the same for taking notes, using text signals, or asking elaborative questions. And, no substitute exists for practice. The more students practice with the strategy, the more skilled they become in using it. Donna continuing with the process throughout the school year provided her students with the deliberate practice they needed to develop their ability as strategic learners.

Model and Promote Critical Thinking.   Earlier we painted a fairly bleak picture of the state of critical thinking in both our students and our population at large. Not all news is bad, however, because research indicates that formally teaching critical thinking can make a significant difference in our students' abilities to recognize conspiracy theories and fake news, as well as our tendencies to react emotionally and cling to existing beliefs (Prooijen, 2017). Further evidence suggests that directly confronting confirmation bias can help dispel the tendency (Miller, 2016), and providing practice and feedback within the context of the regular curriculum can improve students' critical thinking abilities (Niu, Behar-Horenstein, & Garvan, 2013).

The process begins with awareness. For instance, becoming aware of our tendencies to cling to a belief in spite of strong evidence to the contrary increases the likelihood that we'll change our thinking (Prooijen, 2017).

Second, we can model thinking dispositions, such as a sense of curiosity, a desire to be informed, a willingness to respect opinions different from our own, and most important in our teaching, to provide evidence for our conclusions. Statements such as, "The first thing I ask myself when I read an opinion piece in the newspaper is, 'what evidence does the writer provide . . . ?'" can, over time, make an important difference in our students' inclination to look for evidence when they hear opinions or conclusions.

Third, asking our students questions, such as "why" and "how do you know," requires that they provide evidence for their conclusions, and, in many cases, the questions follow naturally from others. For instance:

Lisa Adams is working with her middle schoolers on verbals, verb forms that behave as other parts of speech in sentences, and she displays the following for her students:

Swimming and running are great forms of exercise. And, if we like to run, it's simple. All we have to do is jump into our running gear, and off we go.

She then directs, "Identify a participle in our example," and Ramone responds, "Running in the third sentence."

"How do you know it's a participle? . . . Nicole?" Lisa probes.

" . . . Running is a verb form, but it modifies 'gear,' which is a noun, so it's an adjective. And verb forms that act as adjectives are participles."

Your students won't initially be able to make statements as complete as Nicole's, but with your questioning as guidance, they will improve. As they practice putting their evidence into words, they will simultaneously deepen their understanding and develop their critical thinking abilities.

National Council on Teacher Quality (NCTQ)

The National Council on Teacher Quality describes asking probing questions as one of the 6 essential teaching strategies that all new teachers should know. "3. Posing probing questions. Asking students "why," "how," "what if," and "how do you know" requires them to clarify and link their knowledge of key ideas" (Pomerance et al., 2016, p. vi).

In addition to questioning, if students have adequate background knowledge, class discussions can help illuminate different points of view, and these discussions can be powerful and influential in promoting critical thinking (Resnick, Asterhan, & Clarke, 2015). It's harder for a student to believe in a conspiracy theory, for instance, if the majority of his or her classmates strongly debunk it. And we can contribute to the discussion by keeping students focused on the topic and asking them to provide evidence to support their beliefs.

Finally, in the unlikely event that you encounter students who simply refuse to accept evidence, such as the example with the high school student who had the strong emotional reaction to her science teacher's instruction on climate change, you can emphasize that all your students have a right to their own beliefs, but they remain accountable for understanding the content you're teaching, that is, the evidence and factual information that exists. If a student refuses to learn the content, you've done all you can do, you've behaved professionally, and your conscience is clear.

Use Assessment and Feedback as Learning Tools. Research suggests that as teachers we have a powerful learning tool at our immediate disposal: assessment. Assessment not only measures knowledge but changes it, and, if the assessments require more than fact learning, deeper understanding is the result (Chappuis & Stiggins, 2017). Assessment is relevant to study skills and critical thinking, because students tend to study and learn based on the way they're assessed (Gonzalez & Eggen, 2017). More than 30 years of research supports this contention. "Here is something approaching a law of learning behavior for students: Namely that the quickest way to change student learning is to change the assessment system" (Crooks, 1988, p. 445). Additional research

MyLab Education
Video Example 8.4
Critical thinking is the process of making and assessing conclusions based on evidence. In classrooms we can promote students' critical thinking by asking questions, such as "Why?" and "How do you know?" which requires that they provide evidence for their conclusions. Here, middle school teacher, Scott Sowell, encourages his students to think critically by asking them how they know a conclusion they made is valid.

has found that study combined with assessments, such as quizzes, results in more learning than simply reviewing or rereading the content (Rohr & Paschler, 2010).

This research suggests that we should frequently and thoroughly assess student learning, and these assessments should do more than measure recall of factual information. If, for instance, our assessments require students to identify relationships and evidence to support conclusions, they will use deep study strategies, such as concept mapping and elaborative questioning. In other words, our assessments can be tools that encourage our students to develop their critical thinking and use effective study strategies (Chappuis & Stiggins, 2017).

National Council on Teacher Quality (NCTQ)

The *National Council on Teacher Quality* describes the use of the assessment processes to increase student learning as one of the six essential strategies that all new teachers need to know. "6. Assessing to boost retention . . . . [A]ssessments that require students to recall material helps information 'stick'" (Pomerance et al., 2016, p. vi).

In all cases, assessments should be accompanied by feedback. "There is a preponderance of evidence that feedback is a powerful influence in the development of learning outcomes. . . . The average effects of feedback are among the highest we know in education . . . " (Hattie & Gan, 2011, p. 249). Common forms of feedback include discussing frequently missed items on quizzes and tests, providing written comments or model answers for students' written work, and comments, checklists, or rating scales for student presentations. Because student interest is high when discussing quiz items, for instance, feedback often results in more learning than the original instruction (Hattie & Gan, 2011).

APA Top 20 Principles

This description illustrates Principle 6: *Clear, explanatory, and timely feedback to students is important for learning*—from the *Top 20 Principles from Psychology for PreK–12 Teaching and Learning*.

Classroom Connections

Promoting Strategic Learning in Classrooms

Study Strategies

1. Students use study strategies to increase their understanding of written materials and teacher presentations. Teach study strategies across the curriculum and throughout the school year to make them most effective.

- **Elementary:** A second-grade teacher models elaborative questioning and encourages her children to ask themselves what each lesson was about and what they learned from it.

- **Middle School:** A sixth-grade teacher introduces note taking as a study skill. He then provides note-taking practice in his social studies class by using skeletal outlines to organize his presentations and by having his students use them as a guide for their note taking.

- **High School:** A biology teacher closes each lesson by having her students provide summaries of the most important parts of the lesson. She adds material to summaries that are incomplete.

Critical Thinking

2. Helping students learn to make and assess conclusions based on evidence promotes critical thinking. Integrate critical thinking into the regular curriculum.

- **Elementary:** A fourth-grade teacher makes it a point to ask questions, such as (1) What do you observe? (2) How are these alike or different? (3) Why is A different from B? (4) What would happen if . . . ? (5) How do you know?

- **Middle School:** A seventh-grade geography teacher develops her topics with examples, charts, graphs, and tables. She develops lessons around students' observations, comparisons, and conclusions related to the information they see, and she requires students to provide evidence for their conclusions.

- **High School:** An English teacher helps his students analyze literature by asking questions such as, "How do you know that?" and "What in the story supports your idea?"

MyLab Education Self-Check 8.3
MyLab Education Application Exercise 8.3: Developing Study Skills in Middle School

In this exercise you will be asked to analyze a middle school social studies teacher's application of suggestions for helping students become strategic learners and critical thinkers.

Transfer of Learning

8.4   Analyze factors that influence the transfer of learning.

Ed Psych and You

You're studying for a quiz in one of your classes with a friend, and after a considerable amount of discussion, you comment, "Talking it over this way sure helps. I get it better than when I study by myself."

What idea from your study of Ed Psych does your comment best illustrate?

How did you answer the question in *Ed Psych and You*? If you concluded that your comment illustrates an application of the cognitive learning principle *social interaction facilitates learning*, you have demonstrated **transfer**, the ability to take understanding acquired in one context and apply it to a different context (Mayer & Wittrock, 2006). "A primary goal of education is transfer of knowledge from the learning context to future novel situations" (Kaminski, Sloutsky, & Heckler, 2013, p. 14). Recognizing or providing a new example of a concept, solving a unique problem, or applying a learning strategy to a new situation are all examples of transfer.

Simply retrieving information from memory doesn't involve transfer. If, for instance, your instructor had previously discussed the example in *Ed Psych and You*, you merely remembered the information.

Transfer can be either positive or negative. Positive transfer occurs when learning in one context facilitates learning in another, whereas negative transfer occurs if prior learning inhibits future performance (Mayer & Wittrock, 2006). For instance, positive transfer results if students know that a mammal breathes through lungs and nurses its young, and they then conclude that a whale is a mammal. On the other hand, if they believe that a fish is an animal that lives in the sea and conclude that a whale is a fish, negative transfer has occurred.

General and Specific Transfer

At one time, educators advocated taking courses such as Latin to "discipline" the mind. If they had accomplished this goal, **general transfer**, the ability to apply knowledge or skills learned in one context to a variety of different contexts, would have occurred. For example, if playing chess would help a person learn math because both require logic, general transfer would occur. **Specific transfer** is the ability to apply information in a context similar to the one in which it was originally learned. For example, when students know that the Greek prefix *photos* means "light" and it helps them better understand the concept *photosynthesis*, specific transfer has occurred.

Research over many years has consistently confirmed that general transfer is essentially non-existent (Barnett & Ceci, 2002; Thorndike, 1924). Studying Latin, for example, results in specific transfer to the Latin roots of English words, but it does little to improve thinking in general. Similarly, learning to play chess does little to improve students' math abilities.

Factors Affecting the Transfer of Learning

Several factors affect students' ability to transfer:

- *Depth of understanding.* The more thoroughly and meaningfully information is encoded, the greater the likelihood it will transfer to new contexts. This also applies to skills. Procedural knowledge developed to automaticity is more likely to transfer than skills less thoroughly learned.
- *Similarity.* Transfer is more likely when the new context is similar to the context in which the information is learned.
- *Type of knowledge.* Conceptual knowledge—concepts, principles, and theories—is more likely to transfer than isolated facts.
- *Real-World Applications.* Knowledge and skills are more likely to transfer when they are learned and applied to real-world contexts.

Depth of Understanding. Successful transfer requires a high level of original understanding, and students often fail to transfer because the topic wasn't meaningful—they didn't fully understand it—in the first place (Honke et al., 2015; Kulasegaram et al., 2017). The more practice and feedback learners have with the topics they study, the greater the likelihood that transfer will occur (Moreno & Mayer, 2005).

Similarity. The more closely two learning situations are related, the more likely transfer will occur (Kaminski et al., 2013). For instance, when first-graders are given this problem to solve first,

---

Angi has two pieces of candy. Kim gives her three more pieces of candy. How many pieces does Angi have now?

---

they do well on this one:

Bruce had three pencils. His friend Orlando gave him two more. How many pencils does Bruce have now?

However, when they're given the first problem followed by this problem,

---

Sophie has three cookies. Flavio has four cookies. How many do they have together?

---

they perform less well. The first two are more closely related than the first and third, and transfer is more likely to occur between them.

Similarly, if children understand that a dog, horse, mouse, and deer are mammals, they're more likely to conclude that a cow is a mammal than to conclude that a seal is one, because a cow is more similar to the other examples than is a seal. These results further demonstrate the specificity of transfer.

Type of Knowledge.   Facts, such as the chemical symbol for gold is Au, Abraham Lincoln was our president during the Civil War, and Leo Tolstoy wrote *War and Peace*, are important parts of learning, but alone, they contribute little to transfer. In contrast, conceptual knowledge, such as understanding the characteristics of *longitude* and *latitude*, or the principle *moving objects continue moving in a straight line unless a force acts on them*, is more likely to transfer (Bransford & Schwartz, 1999). For instance, when we understand longitude and latitude, we can identify any location on the globe, and understanding that moving objects continue to move unless a force acts on them helps us understand why we should maintain a safe driving distance between ourselves and the car in front of us. This suggests that we should emphasize concepts and principles in our instruction more strongly than isolated facts.

Real-World Applications.   Content applied to our everyday lives is more likely to transfer than abstract and distant ideas (Botma, Van Rensburg, Coetzee, Heyns, 2015). For instance, the principle *moving objects continue to move in a straight line* helps us understand why we have seatbelts in our cars and why speeding can result in "missing" a curve.

Similarly, students' grammar skills are more likely to transfer when they're developed in the context of written passages than in isolated sentences, and math skills better transfer if they're practiced with realistic word problems. The same applies in all content areas.

Diversity: Learner Differences That Influence Transfer of Complex Cognitive Processes

The basic cognitive processes involved in concept learning, problem solving, and strategic learning are essentially the same for all students. However, their cultural knowledge, approaches to problem solving, and attitudes and beliefs will vary, and each can influence transfer. For example, the Yu'pik people living in the Bering Sea just west of Alaska have 99 different concepts for ice (Block, 2007). This is knowledge important to their culture, but it's alien to most of us. So, when they think about weather and travel, the ideas they transfer differ from ours.

Cultural differences also exist in the way people approach concept learning. For example, adults in western cultures tend to classify items taxonomically, such as putting animals in one group, food items in another, and tools in a third. However, adults in some other cultures classify items into functional categories, such as putting a shovel and potato together, because a shovel is used to dig up a potato (Luria, 1976).

Attitudes and beliefs are also influenced by cultural differences. For instance, learning-related attitudes are offered as an explanation for the impressive problem-solving achievements of Japanese students, who consistently score high on international comparisons. "Attitudes toward achievement emphasize that success comes from hard work (not from innate ability). . . . Teachers examined a few problems in depth rather than covering many problems superficially; children's errors were used as learning tools for the group" (Rogoff, 2003, pp. 264–265). Students exposed to this type of instruction learn different perspectives about math than a more fact-based, memory-oriented approach.

In view of their impressive academic achievements, the fact that early childhood education in Japan focuses on social development instead of academics may be surprising (Abe & Izzard, 1999). Some experts believe this emphasis helps children feel part of a group and responsible to it, which results in greater attention to the topics being taught and fewer classroom-management problems (Rogoff, 2003).

Culture also influences strategic learning. For instance, students use more effective comprehension-monitoring strategies when exposed to written materials consistent with their cultural experiences (Pritchard, 1990). Once again we see how important background knowledge is to thinking.

Interestingly, fewer cultural differences are found when tasks are embedded in real-world contexts. For example, when people such as vendors, carpenters, or dieters use math for practical purposes, they rarely get answers that don't make sense. "However, calculations in the context of schooling regularly produce some absurd errors, with results that are impossible if the meaning of the problem is being considered" (Rogoff, 2003, p. 262). This was illustrated in Laura's lesson. Even though finding the carpeted area of the classroom was a real-world task for her students, some were willing to accept an answer that didn't make sense. This demonstrates the need to promote metacognition and provide a great deal of scaffolding for all learners, regardless of their cultural backgrounds.

Experiences and cultural and religious beliefs can also influence critical thinking. Learners whose early school experiences focus on memorization are more likely to use primitive study strategies, such as rehearsal, and they are less equipped to be critical thinkers than peers with opportunities to practice higher-order thinking. Memory-level tasks are common in urban schools, and these schools typically have large numbers of minorities. This results in fewer opportunities to practice complex mental processes for members of cultural minorities (Kozol, 2005). Also, members of cultures who have been taught to respect elders and learners with authoritarian religious beliefs may be less disposed to critical thinking (Kuhn & Park, 2005; Richey, 2017).

Despite these differences, the need to embed learning experiences in real-world contexts, promote high levels of interaction, and provide the scaffolding that helps learners make sense of those experiences is essential for all students, regardless of their cultural backgrounds.

Using Educational Psychology in Teaching: Suggestions for Promoting Transfer with Your Students

To promote transfer, our goal is to make the topics we teach as meaningful for students as possible. The following suggestions are intended to help us reach this goal.

1. Provide students with a variety of high-quality examples and other experiences.
2. Apply content to real-world contexts.
3. Use high levels of interaction to promote learning and to provide different perspectives on the topics students are learning.

Now, let's analyze the extent to which the teachers you've studied in this chapter—Maria Lopez in her lesson on the concepts *fact, opinion*, and *reasoned judgment*, Laura Hunter in her problem-solving lesson, and Donna Evans in her attempts to help her students develop their study skills—applied these suggestions in their instruction.

Provide Students with a Variety of High-Quality Examples and Other Experiences.   To begin, let's look again at the passages Maria used to illustrate the concepts *fact, opinion*, and *reasoned judgment* with her students.

> Eli Whitney invented the cotton gin in 1793. This reduced the amount of time it took to separate the cotton seeds from the cotton fibers. As a result, raising cotton became very profitable, so the South became a one-crop economy that depended on cotton. As it turns out, the lack of variety in the Southern economy was a big mistake.

Abraham Lincoln was the best president in our country's history. He was president from 1861 until his assassination in 1865. One of Lincoln's primary accomplishments was getting the 13th amendment to the Constitution passed, because it permanently outlawed slavery.

The students could see, for example, that "Eli Whitney invented the cotton gin in 1793" is a fact, whereas "Abraham Lincoln was the best president in our country's history" is an opinion, and the same was true for the examples of reasoned judgment. These examples provided the experiences her students needed to construct their knowledge of the concepts, and using the examples in this way also applied the cognitive learning principles "Learning and development depend on experience," "People want their experiences to make sense," and "To make sense of their experiences, learners construct knowledge."

The passage also provided an adequate variety of examples, which is essential for promoting transfer (Renkl, 2011; Schwartz, Bransford, & Sears, 2005). For instance, "He [Lincoln] was president from 1861 until his assassination in 1865" is another example of a fact, and "As it turns out, the lack of variety in the Southern economy was a big mistake" is a second example of an opinion. Each example adds information, which increases the likelihood of experiencing examples that are meaningful and capitalizes on elaboration as an encoding strategy.

Transfer in problem solving is similar. To become good problem solvers students need to solve a wide variety of problems, and worked examples are particularly valuable in this process. "Proponents of teaching and learning by examples propose that after the explicit introduction of one or more domain principles (e.g., mathematical theorem . . .), learners should be presented with several examples . . . " (Renkl, 2011, p. 273). Laura could apply this suggestion by having her students find the area of the school parking lot, another area of the classroom, the area of an irregularly shaped desk, or a variety of others that are part of her school's environment.

The same applies with strategic learning. As we saw earlier, Donna had her students practice creating summaries throughout the year. She also needs to model these strategies and have students practice with other study strategies in the same way she did with summarizing.

Apply Content to Real-World Contexts.   Maria's vignette also applied this suggestion. Her examples of *fact, opinion,* and *reasoned judgment* were embedded in the context of paragraphs, which is more "real world" than a series of isolated sentences would have been. Similarly, Laura having her students find the area of a school parking lot or other parts of the school environment is more real world than solving written problems on a worksheet would be, and Donna having her students practice their study skills in a variety of content areas would meet the same goal.

MyLab Education
Video Example 8.5

We can promote transfer in our students by providing them with a variety of high-quality examples and other experiences. Here, fifth-grade teacher, DeVonne Lampkin, promotes transfer of the concept *arthropod* by showing them examples such as a lobster, cockroach, and shrimp.

APA Top 20 Principles

This description again illustrates Principle 4: Learning is based on context, so generalizing learning to new contexts is not spontaneous but instead needs to be facilitated—from the *Top 20 Principles from Psychology for PreK–12 Teaching and Learning*.

Use High Levels of Interaction.   Learning is largely a social process (Aronson, Wilson, & Akert, 2016), and "Social interaction facilitates learning" is a cognitive learning principle. This makes sense. We've all struggled to learn ideas on our own but later understood them as a result of a discussion with another person. Each of the teachers applied this principle by interacting with their students during their lessons. And using examples, connecting them to the real world, and promoting interaction are synergistic.

Classroom Connections

Promoting Transfer of Learning in Schools

1. Transfer occurs when knowledge learned in one context is applied in a different context. To promote transfer, apply the content you teach in a variety of different contexts.

- **Elementary:** A fourth-grade teacher selects samples of student writing to teach grammar and punctuation rules. She displays samples on the document camera and uses the samples as the basis for her instruction.

- **Middle School:** A science teacher begins a discussion of light refraction by asking students why they can see better with their glasses on than they can without them. He then illustrates refraction by putting a pencil in a glass of water, so the pencil appears differently above and below the water line, and asks the students to look at objects through magnifying lenses.

- **High School:** A geometry teacher uses examples from architecture to illustrate how geometry applies to structural design. She also uses photographs from magazines and slides to illustrate how math concepts relate to the real world.

2. Involve students in activities that allow them to construct knowledge and understand the topics you are teaching. Use high-quality examples and representations to promote transfer by applying content to diverse settings.

- **Elementary:** A fifth-grade teacher illustrates the concept *volume* by putting 1 cm cubes in a box 4 cm long, 3 cm wide, and 2 cm high. He instructs the students to count the cubes until the box is filled with 24 cubes. Then he relates the activity to the formula for finding volume.

- **Middle School:** A history teacher writes short cases to illustrate hard-to-understand concepts, such as *mercantilism*. She guides students' analyses of the cases, helping them identify the essential characteristics of the concepts.

- **High School:** An English teacher prepares a matrix illustrating the characters, setting, and themes for several of Shakespeare's plays. Students use the information to summarize and draw conclusions about Shakespeare's works.

"To fully exploit the potential of example-based instruction, it is necessary to elicit explanations from the learners" (Renkl, 2011, p. 273). The combination of the three suggestions is greater than the sum of their individual parts.

Promoting transfer is the ultimate goal of schooling. It takes time, but with effort it can be accomplished. Our job as teachers is to make this effort.

MyLab Education Self-Check 8.4

Developmentally Appropriate Practice

Complex Cognitive Skills with Learners at Different Ages

Although learners of all ages can develop higher-level cognitive skills, important developmental differences exist. The following paragraphs outline these and offer suggestions on how to adapt your instruction to the developmental needs of your students.

Working with Students in Early Childhood Programs and Elementary Schools

The concepts that we teach young children are generally concrete and best explained by rule-driven theories of concept learning. This explains why we see concepts such as *triangle, circle, pets,* and *farm animals* taught to kindergarten children. Young learners often overgeneralize, classifying spiders as insects, for example, or they undergeneralize, such as limiting adverbs to words that end in *ly*. Because of this tendency, providing a variety of high-quality examples and discussing them thoroughly are important with young learners.

Their tendencies to center on prominent information also impact their problem solving. For example, young children tend to use superficial strategies in solving word problems, such as looking for key words like *altogether*, which suggests addition, *or how many more*, which suggests subtraction. These strategies can bypass understanding completely but are often quite successful. To accommodate these developmental patterns, ask young students to put their thinking into words, explaining how they solved a problem. They need a great deal of scaffolding, so patience and effort are required.

Young children also tend to be "strategically inert," either not using learning strategies at all or employing primitive strategies such as rehearsal. While their lack of prior knowledge is often a factor, with effort and patience, they can learn to use strategies quite effectively.

Working with Students in Middle Schools

Middle school students' maturation makes them capable of constructing abstract concepts, such as *culture* and *justice*, which are often learned through prototypes and exemplars. However, many older students lack the experiences needed to make abstract concepts meaningful, so they are best represented as concretely as possible. For instance, a middle school social studies teacher illustrates the concept culture with the following vignette:

> **Pedro is a boy living in a small Mexican village. Every day he rises early, as he must walk the two kilometers to his school. He has breakfast of beans and bread made from ground corn, leaves the house, and begins his trek.**
>
> **He likes the walk, because he can wave to Papa toiling daily in the cornfields that provide the food and income for the family.**
>
> **When Pedro comes home from school, he often plays soccer with his friends in the village, then does his homework, and after dinner his mother usually plays songs on a guitar while Papa sings.**

Concrete representations of topics such as these are much more meaningful for middle school students than simply describing them.

Middle school students also tend to lack the metacognition needed to monitor their problem solving. For example, 13-year-olds were given the following problem:

> **An army bus holds 36 soldiers. If 1,128 soldiers are being bused to their training site, how many buses are needed?**

Fewer than one fourth of the 13-year-olds answered it correctly; most of the other students either dropped the remainder or reported 31 1/3 buses, ignoring the fact that a third of a bus is meaningless (O'Brien, 1999). With middle school students, teachers need to emphasize evaluating the results of problem solving to ensure that the results make sense.

Middle school students can use sophisticated learning strategies but rarely do so unless their teachers model and encourage these strategies. Efforts such as Donna Evans made can be very effective (see "Using Educational Psychology in Teaching: Suggestions for Helping our Students Become Strategic Learners and Critical Thinkers".

Working with Students in High Schools

Although Piaget described high school-aged students as formal operational, many are not, especially when the content is new to them. This suggests that using analogies, role playing, simulations, and vignettes, such as the ones illustrating anaphylactic shock, continues to be important for making abstract concepts meaningful to these students.

With respect to problem solving, authentic activities and real-world applications are particularly important for older students who want to see the utility of their learning activities.

Many older students use strategies such as highlighting passively instead of making decisions about what is most important to highlight. Often, they fail to monitor their comprehension as well as they should, which leads them to overestimate how well they understand the topics they study. This is why it's important for you to encourage study strategies across the curriculum and to emphasize metacognition when working with high school students.

Chapter 8 Summary

1. Define *concepts* and describe strategies for helping students learn concepts.
    *   A *concept* is a mental construct or representation of a category that allows us to identify examples and non-examples of the category.
    *   Rule-driven theories of concept learning explain how people can learn well-defined concepts such as perimeter, adjective, and latitude with definitions and examples.
    *   Exemplar theories explain how learners construct concepts on the basis of the most highly typical examples of a class or category.
    *   Theories of concept learning can be applied in classrooms by embedding examples and non-examples of concepts in real-world contexts, sequencing the examples from most typical to least familiar, and linking the concept to related concepts.

2. Recognize examples of ill-defined and well-defined problems, and describe strategies to teach problem solving in classrooms.
    *   A problem exists when a person has a goal but lacks an obvious way of achieving the goal.
    *   A well-defined problem, such as finding the solution for $3x + 4 = 13$, has only one correct solution and a certain method for finding it.
    *   An ill-defined problem, such as students' failing to accept personal responsibility for their own learning, has an ambiguous goal, more than one acceptable solution, and no generally agreed-upon strategy for reaching a solution.
    *   Identifying the problem goal, representing the problem, selecting a strategy, implementing the strategy, and evaluating the results are stages in the problem-solving process.
    *   Worked examples, examples that include problem solutions, can help develop students' background knowledge.
    *   Deliberate practice is important for developing expertise in problem solving, particularly for novice problem solvers.
    *   Social interaction and an emphasis on sense making are important for helping students develop their problem-solving abilities.

3. Identify applications of study strategies and critical thinking.
    *   Strategies are cognitive operations that exceed the normal activities required to carry out a task. Taking notes is a strategy, for example, because it is a cognitive operation used to help learners remember more of what they hear or read.
    *   Learners who use strategies effectively are metacognitive about their approaches to learning. They also possess a repertoire of strategies and prior knowledge about the topics they're studying. Ineffective strategy users are less metacognitive, and they lack prior knowledge and possess fewer strategies.
    *   Critical thinking is the process of making and assessing conclusions based on evidence.
    *   The influence of the Internet, people's tendency to first react emotionally to events and other people, and our cognitive architecture make critical thinking a problematic process.
    *   Teachers promote critical thinking in their students when they have students justify their thinking and provide evidence for their conclusions.

4. Analyze factors that influence the transfer of learning.
    *   Transfer occurs when learners can apply previously learned information in a new context. Specific transfer involves an application in a situation closely related to the original; general transfer occurs when two learning situations are quite different.
    *   Teachers promote transfer when they provide students with a variety of high-quality examples embedded in a real-world context. These examples provide the experiences learners need to construct their knowledge and apply it in new settings.

Preparing for Your Licensure Exam

Understanding Complex Cognitive Processes

You will be required to take a licensure exam before you go into your own classroom. This exam will include information related to concept learning, problem solving, learning strategies, and transfer, and it will include both multiple-choice and constructed-response questions. We include the following exercises to help you practice for the exam in your state. This book and these exercises will be a resource for you as you prepare for the exam.

In the following case study, Sue Brush is working with her second-graders in a lesson on graphing to meet the following standard:

CCSS.Math.Content.2.MD.D.10 Draw a picture graph and a bar graph (with single-unit scale) to represent a data set with up to four categories. Solve simple put-together, take-apart, and compare problems using information presented in a bar graph. (Common Core State Standards Initiative, 2018j).

After reading the case study, answer the questions that follow.

Sue introduces the lesson by saying that she is planning a party for the class but has a problem because she wants to share jelly beans with the class but doesn't know the class's favorite flavor of jelly bean.

Students offer suggestions for solving the problem, and they finally settle on having students taste a variety of jelly beans and indicate their favorite.

Having anticipated the idea of tasting the jelly beans, Sue has prepared plastic bags, each with seven different-flavored jelly beans. She gives each student a bag, and after students taste each one, she says, "Okay, I need your help. . . . How can we organize our information so that we can look at it as a whole group?"

Students offer several suggestions, and Sue then says, "Here's what we're going to do. Stacey mentioned earlier that we could graph the information, and we have an empty graph up in the front of the room." She moves to the front of the room and displays the outline of a graph:

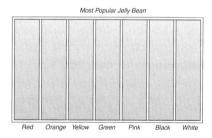

Most Popular Jelly Bean

Red   Orange   Yellow   Green   Pink   Black   White

She then asks students to come to the front of the room and paste colored pieces that represent their favorite jelly beans on the graph, and the results are what we see here.

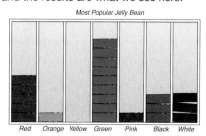

Most Popular Jelly Bean

Red   Orange   Yellow   Green   Pink   Black   White

"Now, look up here," she smiles. "We collected and organized the information, so now we need to analyze it. I want you to tell me what we know by looking at the graph. . . . Candice?"

"People like green," Candice answers.

"How many people like green?"

" . . . Nine."

"Nine people like green. . . . And how did you find that out? Come up here and show us how you read the graph."

Candice goes up to the graph and moves her hand up from the bottom, counting the nine green squares as she goes.

Sue continues asking students to interpret the graph, and then changes the direction of the lesson by saying, "Okay, here we go. . . . How many more people liked green than red? . . . Look up at the graph, and set up the problem on your paper."

She watches as students look at the graph and set up the problem, and when they're finished, she says, "I'm looking for a volunteer to share an answer with us. . . . Dominique?"

"Nine plus 5 is 14," Dominique answers.

"Dominique says 9 plus 5 is 14. Let's test it out," Sue responds, asking Dominique to go up to the graph and show the class how she arrived at her answer.

As Dominique walks to the front of the room, Sue says, "We want to know the difference. . . . How many more people liked green than red, and you say 14 people, . . . 14 more people liked green. Does that work?"

Dominique looks at the graph for a moment and then says, "I mean 9 take away 5."

"She got up here and she changed her mind," Sue says with a smile to the rest of the class. "Tell them."

"Nine take away 5 is 4," Dominique says.

"Nine take away 5 is 4," Sue continues, "so how many more people liked green than red? . . . Carlos?"

"Four," Carlos responds.

"Four, good, four," she smiles at him warmly. "The key was, you had to find the difference between the two numbers."

Sue has students offer additional problems, they solve and explain them, and she then continues, "I have one more question, and then we'll switch gears. How many people took part in this voting?"

Sue watches as students consider the problem for a few minutes, and then says, "Matt? . . . How many people?"

"Twenty-four."

"Matt said 24. Did anyone get a different answer? So we'll compare. . . . Robert?"

"Twenty-two."

"How did you solve the problem?" she asks Robert.

"Nine plus 5 plus 3 plus 3 plus 1 plus 1 equals 22," he answers, adding up all the squares on the graph.

"Where'd you get all those numbers?"

"There," he says, pointing to the graph. "I went from the highest to the lowest, added them, and the answer was 22."

Sue then breaks the children into groups and has them work at centers where they gather and summarize information in bar graphs. They tally and graph the number of students who have birthdays each month, interview classmates about their favorite soft drinks, and call pizza delivery places to compare the cost of comparable pizzas.

As time for lunch nears, Sue calls the groups back together, and after they're settled, says, "Raise your hand if you can tell me what you learned this morning in math."

"How to bar graph," Jenny responds.

"So, a graph is a way of organizing information so we can look at it and talk about it. Later we'll look at some additional ways of organizing information," and she ends the lesson.

Questions for Case Analysis

Use information from this chapter and the case study to answer the following questions.

Multiple-Choice Questions:

1. Of the following, which suggestion for developing students' problem solving did Sue *most prominently* illustrate in her lesson?

   a. Present problems in real-world contexts and provide practice in identifying problem goals.

   b. Develop students' expertise with deliberate practice and worked examples.

   c. Capitalize on social interaction to engage students and monitor their learner progress.

   d. Encourage sense making in the problem-solving process.

2. Of the following, which aspect of Sue's lesson was most effective for promoting transfer?

   a. Sue initially using the jelly bean activity to illustrate bar graphs, because the activity provided students with a real-world experience

   b. Sue asking the students how many people took part in the voting

   c. Sue having Dominique correct herself when she initially suggested adding 9 and 5 to find out how many more children liked green than red jelly beans.

   d. Combining her group work at centers with her learning activity using the jelly beans, because each center activity added variety to the students' experiences

Constructed-Response Question:

1. To what extent did Sue promote critical thinking in her lesson? What could she have done to give her students more practice with critical thinking? Offer specific suggestions in your response.

MyLab Education Licensure Exam 8.1

Important Concepts

algorithm
characteristics
coding
comprehension
  monitoring
concept map
concepts
conceptual hierarchies
confirmation bias
conspiracy theory
creativity

critical thinking
deliberate practice
distributed practice
drawing analogies
elaborative questioning
exemplars
experts
fake news
general transfer
guided notes
heuristics

high-quality examples
ill-defined problem
interactive whiteboards
interspersed practice
means–ends analysis
metacognition
post-truth
problem
problem-based learning
sound bite
specific transfer

strategies
study strategies
summarizing
text signals
transfer
virtual manipulatives
well-defined problem
worked examples

Chapter 9
Knowledge Construction and the Learning Sciences

Steve Debenport/Getty Images

Learning Outcomes

After you've completed your study of this chapter, you should be able to:

9.1 Describe the processes involved in knowledge construction and analyze examples that illustrate these processes.

9.2 Explain misconceptions, how they occur, and how they can be eliminated.

9.3 Describe suggestions for using knowledge construction in teaching, and explain how they are grounded in the learning sciences.

APA Top 20 Principles

Top 20 Principles from Psychology for PreK–12 Teaching and Learning explicitly addressed in this chapter.

> Principle 2: What students already know affects their learning
> Principle 4: Learning is based on context, so generalizing learning to new contexts is not spontaneous but instead needs to be facilitated.
> Principle 6: Clear, explanatory, and timely feedback to students is important for learning.

National Council on Teacher Quality (NCTQ)

The NCTQ Essential Teaching Strategies that every new teacher needs to know specifically addressed in this chapter.

> Strategy 2: Linking abstract concepts with concrete representations
> Strategy 6: Assessing to boost retention

We began Chapter 7 with a discussion of the following principles of cognitive learning theory:

- Learning and development depend on experience.
- People want their experiences to make sense.
- To make sense of their experiences, learners construct knowledge.
- Knowledge that learners construct depends on what they already know.
- Acquiring long-term knowledge and skill is largely dependent upon practice.
- Social interaction facilitates learning.

We revisit the principles in this chapter with a special focus on the third: *To make sense of their experiences, learners construct knowledge.* The construction of knowledge has enormous implications for the way we teach, as we'll see.

We begin by examining the thinking of fourth-graders as they work on the problem of making a beam balance. The goal in the lesson is for students to understand that a beam will balance if the weight times the distance on one side of the fulcrum (the beam's balance point) equals the weight times the distance on the other side of the fulcrum ($w_1 \times d_1 = w_2 \times d_2$).

Keep the principles of cognitive learning theory and the thinking of the students in mind as you read the case study.

Jenny Newhall, their teacher, begins by dividing the class into groups of four and giving each group a balance with tiles on it that appears as follows (all the tiles have the same weight):

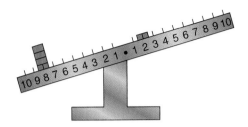

Jenny tells the students that they need to figure out how to balance the beam, but before experimenting by adding tiles to the balances, they need to write down possible solutions and explain to their group mates why they think their solutions will work.

As the students work, Jenny circulates around the room and then joins one of the groups—Suzanne, Molly, Tad, and Drexel—as they attempt to solve the problem.

During the discussion Suzanne offers the following solution: "There are 4 on the 8 and 1 on the 2. I want to put 3 on the 10 so there will be 4 on each side."

Here's the solution she proposes:

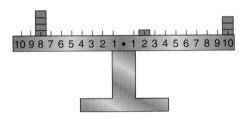

Molly agrees that Suzanne's arrangement of tiles will make the beam balance but offers a different explanation. "I think we should put 3 on 10, because 4 on the 8 is 32 on one side. And since we only have 2 on the other side, we need to make them equal. So 3 on 10 would equal 30, plus 2, and we'd have 32 on both sides."

We'll return to the lesson later in the chapter, but for now, think about these questions.

1. Where did Suzanne get the idea that the beam would balance if the numbers of tiles on each side of the fulcrum were equal?
2. How might we explain the differences in Molly's and Suzanne's thinking?

We answer these questions and consider the implications they have for our teaching as we examine the process of constructing knowledge.

Knowledge Construction

9.1 **Describe the processes involved in knowledge construction and analyze examples that illustrate these processes.**

Constructivism is a view of learning that says learners don't acquire knowledge directly from others; rather they construct it for themselves. " . . . [C]onstructivism considers knowledge as constructed by learners as they attempt to make sense of their experiences" (Hattie & Gan, 2011, p. 256). This fundamental idea was illustrated in Suzanne's thinking in Jenny's lesson, and it helps us answer our first question above: "Where did Suzanne get the idea that the beam would balance if the numbers of tiles on each side of the fulcrum were equal?" Simply, she *constructed* the incorrect idea on her own, because it made sense to her.

The Transition from Cognitive to Social Constructivism

Historically, theorists haven't completely agreed on the process of knowledge construction. Initially, based on Piaget's work, theorists and researchers focused on what is commonly called *cognitive constructivism*.

Cognitive Constructivism

Cognitive constructivism is a view of knowledge construction that describes the process of constructing knowledge as an individual, internal process (Bozkurt, 2017). It's grounded in the work of Jean Piaget, whose work we studied in Chapter 2. It emphasizes individuals' efforts to make sense of their experiences as they interact with the environment and continually test and modify their existing understanding.

Cognitive constructivism helps us understand Suzanne's thinking in Jenny's lesson. She constructed the idea that a beam will balance if the numbers of tiles on each side of the fulcrum are equal, and she didn't get the idea from Jenny, or her group mates; she did it on her own. This is the essence of cognitive constructivism.

Cognitive constructivists describe a role for social interaction, but this role is to provide a catalyst for individual cognitive conflict. To see this role in practice, let's look at the thinking of students in another classroom.

Alicia Evans is working with her third-graders on pronoun-antecedent agreement. She presents them with the following sentence, and asks them to decide which of each pair of words in the parentheses is correct.

Each of the boys has (his, their) own lunch box with pictures of cars on (it, them).

Alicia:	What do you think, and why do you think so . . . Brittany?
Brittany:	I think it should be "their" because it says *boys* and boys is more than one. "His" is only one, so that doesn't fit.

Alicia gives the students a few seconds to think about Brittany's answer and then recognizes Carlos's raised hand.

Carlos:	I think it should be "his," . . . because it says *each*, and each is "one" [singular], so it should be "his" because "his" is also "one."

After some additional discussion, the class agrees that it should be "his."

Alicia:	What about this one? (pointing to the parentheses [it, them] at the end of the sentence)
Brittany:	I know. "It" is correct.
Alicia:	Tell us why.
Brittany:	They're talking about one lunch box, and "it" is one, so it can't be "them."

Cognitive constructivists would interpret this exchange by saying that Carlos's comment and the discussion that followed disrupted Brittany's equilibrium, and she individually resolved the problem by changing her thinking—reconstructing her knowledge—to accommodate the new evidence Carlos and other classmates offered.

A literal interpretation of the cognitive constructivist position emphasizes learning activities that are experience-based and discovery oriented. This view would suggest, for example, that children learn math most effectively if they discover math concepts while manipulating concrete objects, such as blocks and sticks, rather than having them presented by a teacher or other expert.

One interpretation of this perspective suggests that we should avoid directly teaching or imposing our thinking on our students, but many others question this view of teaching and learning (Bozkurt, 2017; Clark, Kirschner, & Sweller, 2012; McWilliams, 2016). As a result, cognitive constructivism as a framework for guiding instruction has been largely replaced by an alternate view that focuses more strongly on social processes in knowledge construction.

Social Constructivism

Ed Psych and You

You and a friend are working on a problem, but neither understands it completely nor can solve it alone. As you continue to struggle and discuss the problem, however, gradually you arrive at a solution. Why were you were able to solve the problem together when neither could solve it alone?

We've all had experiences similar to our example in *Ed Psych and You*. And the answer to our question is: Outside of classrooms learning is largely social in nature. Research has ". . . revealed that outside of formal schooling, almost all learning occurs in a complex social environment, and learning is hard to understand if one thinks of it as a mental process occurring within the head of an isolated learner" (Sawyer, 2006, p. 9).

This illustrates the basic premise of **social constructivism**, which suggests that learners first construct knowledge in a social context and then individually internalize it (Barak, 2017). Lev Vygotsky, whose work we also studied in Chapter 2, is viewed as the inspiration for social constructivism. He observed, "Every function in the child's cultural development appears twice: first, on the social level, and later on the individual level. . . . All the higher functions originate as actual relationships between individuals" (Vygotsky, 1978, p. 57).

To illustrate, think again about the exchange between Brittany and Carlos in Alicia's lesson. In contrast with cognitive constructivists, who would interpret the episode as Brittany individually resolving the problem, social constructivists would suggest Brittany's thinking changed as a direct outcome of the discussion itself. The dialogue—directly—helped Brittany more clearly understand pronoun-antecedent agreement, and, following the discussion, she then individually internalized it, a process called **appropriating understanding** (Li et al., 2007).

Social constructivism has become the primary framework for designing and delivering instruction in schools (Martin, 2006). It doesn't imply that learners should discover everything on their own, nor does it suggest that teachers shouldn't share their thinking with students. Rather, it suggests that teachers consider all the traditional questions related to instruction: planning, conducting learning activities, and assessing learning. The focus, however, is on facilitating students' constructions of knowledge using social interaction as a catalyst, instead of simply explaining ideas while they listen passively. From a social constructivist perspective, creating learning environments in which learners are cognitively active in the process of constructing and internalizing valid ideas is an essential role for us as teachers.

We turn now to the processes involved in creating these environments as we examine:

- Sociocultural learning theory
- The classroom as a community of learners
- Cognitive apprenticeships

Sociocultural Learning Theory.   **Sociocultural theory**, while continuing to emphasize the social dimensions of learning, places greater emphasis on the larger cultural contexts in which learning occurs (Beck, 2017; Ramos, 2017). Patterns of interaction in homes illustrate this emphasis. In some cultures, for instance, children are not viewed as legitimate partners in conversation, and as a result, they may be reluctant to raise their hands to volunteer answers to our questions. And they may even be hesitant to respond when we call on them directly. Differences also exist in the cultural experiences, attitudes, and values that students bring to school, all of which influence learning (Rogoff, 2003). As teachers, we need to be sensitive to these differences and help our students understand and adapt to the culture of our classrooms.

The Classroom as a Community of Learners.   A sociocultural view of learning shifts the emphasis from the individual to the group and from acquiring knowledge, per se, to belonging, participating, and communicating within a community of learners. A **community of learners** is a learning environment in which the teacher and students all work together to help everyone learn (Moser, Berlie, Salinitri, McCuistion, & Slaughter, 2015; Sewell, St. George, & Cullen, 2013). This perspective reminds us that our management, rules and procedures, and the way we interact with students create microcultures in our classrooms, making them cooperative and inviting or competitive and even frightening.

In a learning community:

MyLab Education
Video Example 9.1

A community of learners is a learning environment in which the teacher and students work together to help everyone learn. Here we see a teacher explain why promoting this type of environment is so important in classrooms

- All students participate in learning activities. To promote involvement, Jenny had her students work in groups, and all students in her class were involved.

- Teachers and students work together to help one another learn; promoting learning isn't the teacher's responsibility alone. As we'll see later in the chapter, Suzanne changes her thinking largely as a result of interacting with her group mates.

- Student–student interaction is an important part of the learning process. Jenny promoted this interaction by requiring the students to explain to their group mates why they thought their solutions would work.

- Teachers and students respect differences in interests, thinking, and progress. Molly, even though she disagreed with Suzanne's thinking, didn't offer her solution to the problem until Suzanne had finished her explanation.

- The thinking involved in learning activities is as important as the answers themselves. Jenny emphasized the explanations for solutions, not just finding the solution itself.

Each of these characteristics is grounded in the idea that knowledge is first socially constructed and then appropriated and internalized by individuals.

In attempting to create a community of learners, we are trying to develop a classroom culture in which students feel as if "We're all in this together." We do our best to support their learning, and students help each other whenever they can. Test and quiz scores and grades reflect the extent to which they've mastered the content instead of how well they compete with each other.

Cognitive Apprenticeship.   Historically, apprenticeships have helped novices—as they worked with experts—acquire skills they couldn't learn on their own (Lerman, 2016). Apprenticeships are common in vocational trades such as plumbing, weaving, or cooking, but they're also used in areas such as learning to play musical instruments or creating pieces of art. **Cognitive apprenticeships** are social learning processes that occur when less-skilled learners work alongside experts in developing cognitive skills, such as reading comprehension, writing, or problem solving (Essary, 2012; Peters-Burton, Merz, Ramirez, & Saroughi, 2015).

Cognitive apprenticeships focus on developing thinking, and include the following components:

- *Modeling*: Teachers, or other, more knowledgeable students, demonstrate skills, such as solutions to problems, and simultaneously model their thinking by describing it out loud.
- *Scaffolding*: As students perform tasks, teachers ask questions and provide support, decreasing the amount of support as students' proficiency increases.
- *Verbalization*: Students are encouraged to express their developing understanding in words, which allows teachers to assess their developing thinking.
- *Increasing complexity*: As students' proficiency increases, teachers present them with more challenging tasks and problems.

We know that social interaction is essential; it's a principle of cognitive learning theory. Unfortunately, in classrooms it's quite rare; teachers spend much of their instructional time lecturing and explaining or having students do seatwork (Pianta, Belsky, Houts, & Morrison, 2007). Scaffolding and verbalization, two essential components of cognitive apprenticeships, aren't possible if we simply explain the topics we teach. A rule of thumb for all of us is: *If we explain an idea, our students may or may not "get" it; if they explain it to us, we know they have it.*

The Learning Sciences

Ed Psych and You

1. For which of the following problems will the answer be greater:
   392 ÷ 14 = or 360 ÷ 12 =
2. Now, consider this problem:
   Jennifer makes a trip to see a college friend in a town 392 miles from her home town. Her car uses 14 gallons of gas to make the trip. Christina is going home for spring break from college, 360 miles from her home town. Her car uses 12 gallons of gas on the trip. Whose car, Jennifer's or Christina's, is more fuel efficient?
   Which set of problems is more meaningful? Why do you think so?

MyLab Education
Video Example 9.2

The learning sciences focus on learning as it exists in real-world setting. Here we see high school teacher, Rachael Klick, applying this emphasis as she has her students analyze the nutritional value of commonly consumed foods and how healthy or unhealthy they are.

Let's look now at the problems in *Ed Psych and You*. In both sets we simply divide 392 by 14 and 360 by 12 to answer the questions. However, most people find the second set more meaningful, because they focus on common, real-world problems. We all spend money on gas, so we want to know how fuel efficient our cars are.

Studying learning in real-world contexts, such as our second problem above, is the focus of the **learning sciences**, a field of study that focuses on ". . . learning as it exists in real-world settings and how learning may be facilitated both with and without technology" (International Society of the Learning Sciences, 2017, para. 1).

Leaders in the field suggest that schools in our country have traditionally been designed to help students acquire facts, such as "Lincoln was president during our Civil War," and procedures, such as the method for solving the first set of problems in *Ed Psych and You* above. These leaders assert that historically, "The goal of schooling is to get these facts and procedures into the student's head. People are considered to be educated when they possess a large collection of these facts and procedures"

(Sawyer, 2006, p. 1). Schooling is then evaluated by seeing how many of these facts and procedures students can identify or produce on a standardized test (Sawyer, 2006). This approach may have prepared students for our country's industrialized economy of the past, but as we've moved into the 21st century with its technological- and knowledge-based orientation, researchers and educational leaders find this approach inadequate.

Knowing that learning is largely a social process, and that learners construct rather than receive knowledge, learning scientists came to several conclusions about learning and teaching (Yoon & Hmelo-Silver, 2017). We outline them Figure 9.1 and discuss them in the sections that follow.

Useful Learning Requires Deep Conceptual Understanding

The two sets of problems in *Ed Psych and You* illustrate this idea; the first set merely requires a memorized procedure, whereas the second leads to learning that's connected to other important ideas. And this emphasis applies in all content areas. For instance, as students we all learned about Marco Polo's visit to the Far East, the names of Portuguese explorers, such as Prince Henry the Navigator and Vasco DaGama, and Columbus's trip to the New World in 1492. We usually learned this information as isolated facts and dates, consistent with the historical emphasis on teaching and learning that we described earlier. They're conceptually connected, however. Because of Marco Polo's travels and the influential book he wrote afterward, many merchants and traders, including the Portuguese explorers, wanted to go to the Far East. The passage around the tip of Africa and through the Indian Ocean was dangerous, however, so Columbus seized on the idea of getting to the Far East by traveling west (not realizing, of course, that he would run into the Americas instead). Understanding the connections between Marco Polo's travels, the Portuguese navigators, and Columbus's voyage to the New World at this deeper conceptual level makes all the information much more connected and meaningful. The learning sciences assert that all schooling should focus on this type of understanding instead of facts and memorized procedures (Penuel, Bell, Bevan, Buffington, & Falk, 2016).

Deep Conceptual Understanding Requires Personal Reflection

"Students learn better when they express their developing knowledge—either through conversation or by creating papers, reports, or other artifacts—and then are provided the opportunities to reflectively analyze their state of knowledge" (Sawyer, 2006, pp. 2–3). This suggests that students must "do something" with their developing understanding—connect

Figure 9.1 Learning sciences conclusions about learning and teaching

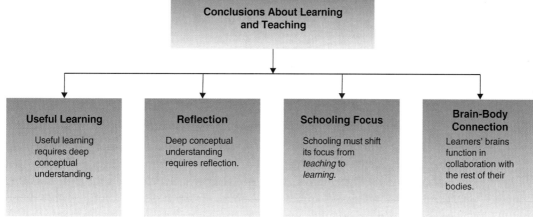

it to other information, solve real-world problems, or apply it in their daily lives. As a simple example, Jenny had her students apply their developing understanding to teeter totters and other levers.

Schooling Must Shift Its Focus from *Teaching* to *Learning*

This statement may appear paradoxical, that is, haven't schools always focused on learning? On the surface, yes, but, as we saw in the example with Columbus's voyage, when probed a bit deeper, not quite. "The notion is that the teacher needs to construct environments and activities that optimize making the learning of the student visible to the teacher (and preferably also to the student)" (Hattie & Gan, 2011, p. 257).

We saw this idea illustrated in Jenny's lesson. Both Suzanne's and Molly's thinking were visible to the group. (Later in the chapter we'll see a change in Suzanne's thinking and what caused the change.)

Learners' Brains Function in Collaboration with the Rest of Their Bodies

Our brains are obviously part of our bodies, and almost as obviously, we don't think well if we're overtired or undernourished. Less obvious, however, is the concept of embodied cognition, the idea that cognition (our thinking) depends on characteristics of our physical bodies, and our bodies significantly influence the way we process information (McMorris, 2016; Skulmowski & Günter, 2017).

Many examples exist. For instance, researchers have found that sitting upright in the face of stress can maintain self-esteem, reduce negative mood, and increase positive mood compared to a slumped posture. Also, sitting upright increases rate of speech and reduces focus on the self (Nair, Sagar, Sollers, Consedine, & Broadbent, 2015). The researchers believe that sitting upright may be a simple behavioral strategy to help build resilience to stress (Nair et al., 2015). As another example, people perceive distances they've walked as longer and hills as steeper if they're carrying a heavy backpack (Profitt, 2006). Also, people are able to detect the emotion expressed on another's face more quickly if they mimic the facial expression being evaluated (Balcetis & Dunning, 2007).

This all suggests that, when appropriate, encouraging students to use their bodies when responding to tasks may enhance their thinking. For instance, simply forming the shape of a parallelogram with our fingers or moving our hands over a map can help us think about problems and visualize distances more effectively than we would without using these gestures (Alibali, Spencer, Knox, & Kita, 2011).

Situated Cognition

As we've seen above, the learning sciences focus on the study of learning as it occurs in real-world settings. Situated cognition (or situated learning) goes further to suggest that learning depends on, and cannot be separated from, the context in which it occurs (Morgan, 2017; Robbins & Aydede, 2009). So, for instance, not only is it important to apply knowledge and understanding to real-world situations, as the learning sciences suggest, but, in fact, situated cognition researchers suggest that literally a different kind of learning occurs in real-world contexts.

APA Top 20 Principles

This discussion illustrates Principle 4: *Learning is based on context, so generalizing learning to new contexts is not spontaneous but instead needs to be facilitated*—from the *Top 20 Principles from Psychology for PreK–12 Teaching and Learning*.

For example, proponents of situated cognition would argue that a different kind of learning occurs when we solve the second set of problems compared to the first set in *Ed Psych and You* (Williamson, 2016). Similarly, when you apply your understanding of learning theories to case studies and examples from classrooms, you acquire a different level of understanding than you would if you studied them in the abstract.

Situated cognition, when taken to the extreme, suggests that **transfer**, the ability to apply understanding acquired in one context to a different context, is difficult, if not impossible. It would suggest, for example, that people who learn to drive in rural areas would be unable to drive in big cities with their heavy traffic, because their driving expertise is situated (located) in the rural setting. Transfer does exist, however, or we would be faced with learning everything anew (Mayer & Wittrock, 2006). For example, the ability to drive in a myriad of contexts occurs, and with practice people can become comfortable driving in rural areas, large cities, and even other countries.

Similarly, we can promote transfer in schools by consciously varying the contexts in which learning occurs (Vosniadou, 2007). Math students, for example, should practice solving a variety of real-world problems, and language arts students should practice writing in each of their content areas (Mayer & Wittrock, 2006). Situated cognition reminds us that context is crucial, and we can accommodate it by asking our students to apply their developing knowledge in a number of different contexts. All this is consistent with the learning sciences.

Diversity: Its Influence on Knowledge Construction

Our students' diversity strongly impacts the beliefs they bring to school, which can influence the way they respond to our instruction and construct knowledge. For example, because of their different beliefs, Muslim and Jewish students are likely to construct very different understandings about issues in the Middle East, such as the historical Arab–Israeli conflict, the American interventions in Iraq and Afghanistan, and the Iran Nuclear Agreement. Also, students whose religious beliefs conflict with scientists' description of the earth being four and a half billion years old, or the idea that humans evolved from more primitive species, may construct ideas that reject the tenets of evolution (Tracy, Hart, & Martens, 2011).

Diversity, and particularly students' cultures, also influences the way they use feedback to modify their knowledge constructions. "[S]tudents from collectivist cultures (e.g., Confucian-based Asia, South Pacific nations) preferred indirect and implicit feedback, more group-focused feedback and no self-level feedback. Students from individualistic/Socratic cultures (e.g., the USA) preferred more . . . individual focused self-related feedback" (Hattie & Gan, 2011, p. 262).

So, realizing that our students bring different beliefs to our learning activities and have different feedback preferences, what should we do? We know they're unlikely to change their thinking unless compelling evidence indicates that a belief is invalid, and even with this evidence, students will sometimes retain the original belief (Harmon, 2017). And completely compelling evidence often doesn't exist, as we see with differing political views.

The most effective approach to this cognitive conflict is to clearly communicate to students that they are accountable for understanding an idea, theory, or interpretation whether or not they believe it (Southerland & Sinatra, 2003). For instance, the theory of evolution being controversial for some students doesn't mean that they shouldn't understand its principles. Whether they choose to accept the principles is up to them.

With respect to feedback, we can provide both indirect—feedback given to the whole class—and direct feedback whenever appropriate. If we create a classroom climate in which we're all in this together, our students who prefer indirect and implicit feedback will realize that we're on their side and will accept our direct feedback in the spirit we intend—to produce as much learning as possible.

The idea of classrooms as learning communities is important when dealing with all forms of diversity. All students should be given the opportunity to share their beliefs, and diversity in thinking should be respected. Recognizing that classmates have beliefs different from their own and have different preferences with respect to interaction and feedback, and learning to acknowledge and respect those differences, are worthwhile learning experiences in themselves.

MyLab Education **Self-Check 9.1**

MyLab Education **Application Exercise 9.1:** Knowledge Construction in Fifth Grade

In this exercise you will be asked to analyze a fifth-grade teacher's attempts to help her students construct their knowledge of advanced vocabulary.

Misconceptions: When Learners Construct Invalid Knowledge

9.2 Explain misconceptions, how they occur, and how they can be eliminated.

Ed Psych and You

Are you right brained or left brained? If you think you're right brained, do you believe you're more intuitive and subjective than logical and objective (which are considered to be left-brain orientations)? How does your left-brain or right-brain orientation influence the way you operate in the world?

MyLab Education

Video Example 9.3

Students commonly construct misconceptions, ideas they hold that make sense to them but are inconsistent with accepted explanations. Here we see a student construct the idea that the improper fraction 13/6 can be converted to the mixed number 1 3/6 (one and three sixths).

Think about the questions in *Ed Psych and You* here. The idea that we tend to be right brained or left brained grew out of research conducted in the 1970s that has been popularized since that time. It is, however, a myth, or misconception (Boehm, 2012; Tatera, 2015). The misconception suggests that right-brained people are spontaneous and creative, whereas left-brained people are logical and analytical. This, however, is a myth, and if people struggle with a content area, such as math, because of it's logical and analytical orientation, it isn't because they're right-brained (Tatera, 2015).

Misconceptions are understandings that are inconsistent with evidence or commonly accepted explanations. They are most common in science, but they exist in other content areas as well. Examples in science, math, history, and language arts are outlined in Table 9.1.

Misconceptions in Teaching and Learning

A number of misconceptions also exist in teaching and learning, and two are particularly significant. *The most effective way to help students understand a topic is to explain it to them* is the first and most pernicious. Even though research consistently indicates that interacting with students results in more learning than simply lecturing and explaining, many teachers continue to hold—and practice—this misconception (Kunter et al., 2013; Mosher, Gjerde, Wilhelm, Srinivasan, & Hagen, 2017).

Knowledge of content, such as math, English, or history, is all that's necessary to be an effective teacher is the second. Many people, including educational leaders and politicians, have this misconception, and it's significant because these are the people largely responsible for setting educational policy. Knowledge of content is important, of course, but teaching expertise requires much more, such as understanding how students learn and develop, how to represent content in ways that are understandable, and how to organize and manage classrooms (Hattie, 2012; Kunter et al., 2013; Sadler, Sonnert, Coyle, Smith, & Miller, 2013).

TABLE 9.1 Misconceptions in science, math, history, and language arts

Science	Math	History	Language Arts
• *It's warmer in summer, because we're closer to the sun.* (The seasons are caused by the earth's tilt, and we're tilted toward the sun in summer.) • *We "feed" plants in much the same way as we feed animals.* (Plants manufacture their own food.) • *Phases of the moon are caused by the earth casting a shadow over part of the moon.* (The moon's phases are caused by the moon's location in relation to the earth and sun.) • *The force pushing forward on an object moving at constant speed, such as a car traveling a steady 70 mph, is greater than the force pushing backward.* (The forces are equal.)	• *.1 × .1 = .1* (.1 × .1 = .01.) • *Multiplication results in a larger number and division results in a smaller number.* (.01 in the first example is smaller than .1, and .1 ÷ .1 = 1.) • *Fractions are a part of 1, not bigger than 1.* (The fraction 3/2 is larger than 1.) • A number of misconceptions exist with respect to fractions. When students were asked to order the following fractions, 4/5, 1/3, 5/4, 4/9, and 1/2, from smallest to largest, only 2% ordered them correctly: 1/3, 4/9, 1/2, 4/5, and 5/4 (Alghazo & Alghazo, 2017).	• *Columbus discovered America.* (The continent was populated by Native Americans, and the Vikings were the first Europeans to visit the continent.) • *People were burned at the stake during the Salem witch trials.* (Some were hanged, but no one was burned, and obviously there were no witches.) • *Benjamin Franklin discovered electricity.* (Many people knew about electricity before Franklin conducted his experiments. He did, however, significantly expand understanding of electricity.) • *Paul Revere rode through the Massachusetts countryside shouting, "The British are coming! The British are coming!"* (He and others went quietly from door to door to warn about the British.)	• *Adverbs are words that end in 'ly.'* (Many adverbs do end in 'ly,' but many others do not. For instance, in the sentence, "They soon left for the game," *soon* is an adverb modifying the verb *left.*) • *Adjectives precede the noun they modify.* (They often follow the noun. For instance, in the sentence, "The game was incredibly exciting," *exciting* is an adjective describing the noun *game.*) • *A sentence must not end in a preposition.* ("Nearly all grammarians agree that it's fine to end sentences with prepositions, at least in some cases") (Fogarty, 2011, p. 45). • *Contractions are not appropriate in proper English.* (This is one of the "big myths of English usage") (Walsh, 2004, p. 61).

Many other misconceptions about teaching and learning exist:

• Teachers' work days end at 3 o' clock. Virtually all teachers work nights and weekends.

• Teachers have their summers off. Teachers are often involved in professional development during summers, and many take second jobs to supplement their salaries.

• Teachers are solely responsible for student learning. Student motivation and parental support are essential.

Misconceptions about learner development also exist. For example, because middle and high school students' chronological ages suggest that they are formal operational in their thinking, some teachers believe they can be taught in the abstract—using words alone to help students understand the ideas they're teaching (İlhan, 2017). This is a common misconception about Piaget's (1970, 1977) developmental theory. If they lack experience related to a topic, learners of all ages need concrete experiences to help them understand the topic.

The Origin of Misconceptions

We can explain the origin of misconceptions with principles of cognitive learning theory. Simply, we construct misconceptions because they make sense to us. And the misconceptions we construct largely depend on our prior knowledge and experiences. For instance, in looking at the first science example in Table 9.1, we've all had the experience of feeling the increasing heat as we move our hand closer to a hot stove burner, so it being warmer in the summer because we're closer to the sun makes complete sense. Also, with the first math example, our prior knowledge tells us that $1 \times 1 = 1$, so $.1 \times .1 = .1$ also makes sense. And, in history, we celebrate Columbus Day as the day he arrived in the Americas, so it isn't much of a leap to "discovering America," and our experience indicates that many adverbs do indeed end in *ly*. Each of these misconceptions is grounded in prior knowledge that is misapplied.

Experience also influences our misconceptions about teaching and learning. For instance, lecture is the most common teaching method, particularly in high schools and universities (Andrew, 2007; Mosher et al., 2017), so it's the method with which we've had the most experience, causing us to equate lecturing with effective instruction.

APA Top 20 Principles

This discussion illustrates Principle 2: *What students already know affects their learning*—from the *Top 20 Principles from Psychology for PreK–12 Teaching and Learning*.

Language, appearances, and "intuitive appeal" also contribute to misconceptions. For instance, with respect to language, we refer to lead and mercury as "heavy" metals, which can lead to misconceptions about relationships between the concepts *weight, mass,* and *density.* And we describe the sun and moon as "rising" and "setting." Further, they both *appear* to rise and set as they move across the sky, which can lead children to believe that they revolve around the earth.

As an example of "intuitive appeal," think again about our example in *Ed Psych and You.* The idea of right-brain–left-brain dominance is intuitively appealing, and some clever people have capitalized on it. "[T]he seductive idea of the right brain and its untapped creative potential also has a long history of being targeted by self-help gurus peddling pseudo-psychology" (Jarett, 2012, para. 2). And makers of self-improvement video games and smartphone apps perpetuate the misconception. "Did you know that the different sides of the brain control different human traits? Scientific studies have shown that the right brain and the left brain have different effects on the way we think and act" (Mirpuri, 2014, para. 1). A statement such as this, although lacking valid research evidence, can be compelling.

Learning styles, students' personal approaches to thinking and problem solving, is another misconception with intuitive appeal. It's sensible, for instance, to believe that people learn differently, so the idea of "learning styles" is intuitively appealing. However, research has been unable to identify links between the amount students learn and teachers' attempts to accommodate students' learning styles. Also, expert teachers present information in both visual and verbal forms—and tactile when appropriate—as a matter of general practice. The idea of learning styles has largely been discredited by research (Howard-Jones, 2014). And some critics go farther. "I think learning styles represents one of the more wasteful and misleading pervasive myths of the last 20 years" (Clark, 2010, p. 10).

Misconceptions' Resistance to Change

As teachers we typically try to correct students' misconceptions by providing evidence that contradicts the misconception (Rich, Van Loon, Dunlosky, & Zaragoza, 2017). This often doesn't work, however, because the misconception they've constructed makes sense to them, perhaps more sense than our explanations, so they retain the misconception.

To see an illustration of students' reluctance to give up their misconceptions, let's return to Suzanne, Molly, Tad, and Drexel, the group of four students at the beginning of the chapter. Recall that Jenny, their teacher, had assigned them the task of placing tiles on the balance and explaining why this placement would make the beam balance.

She had given each group a balance with tiles on it as it appears here.

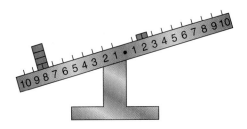

Suzanne had offered the following solution: "There are 4 on the 8 and 1 on the 2. I want to put 3 on the 10 so there will be 4 on each side."

Here's the solution she proposed:

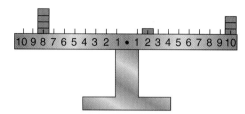

Molly agreed that Suzanne's arrangement of tiles would make the beam balance but offered a different explanation. "I think we should put 3 on 10, because 4 on the 8 is 32 on one side. And since we only have 2 on the other side, we need to make them equal. So 3 on 10 would equal 30, plus 2, and we'd have 32 on both sides."

We rejoin the lesson now.

After Suzanne and Molly offer their solutions and explanations, the group discusses them, and Jenny has the students test their ideas on the balances. She then reassembles the class and has Mavrin, who has solved the problem correctly, go to the board and explain it, using the sketch you see here, which Jenny has drawn on the board.

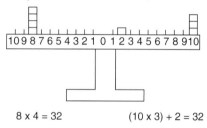

$$8 \times 4 = 32 \qquad (10 \times 3) + 2 = 32$$

Mavrin explains that $8 \times 4 = 32$ on the left side of the fulcrum equals $(10 \times 3) + 2 = 32$ on the right side, referring to the sketch in his explanation. Jenny reviews it, describes Mavrin's thinking, and says, "He has an excellent number sentence here."

An interviewer from a nearby university is observing the class, and following the lesson, he talks with Suzanne, Molly, Tad, and Drexel about their understanding of beam balances. He gives them the following problem, gives them a few seconds to think about it, and then says, "Suzanne, tell us where you would put tiles to make the beam balance."

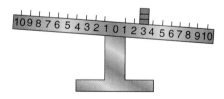

Suzanne offers the following solution:

She reasons, "I put 2 here (indicating that she had added 2 tiles to the right side of the fulcrum) so that 2 plus 3 equals 5 . . . and 2 plus 1 plus 2 here, so it will be 5" (indicating that she had put 5 tiles on the left side of the fulcrum).

MyLab Education
Video Example 9.4

Learners are often reluctant to change their thinking and give up their misconceptions. Here we see that Suzanne, in spite of hearing three valid explanations for making a beam balance, retains her original misconception when given an additional problem.

This explanation tells us a great deal about students' thinking, and we were struck by Suzanne's reasoning when we conducted the interview. (Paul, one of your authors, was the interviewer from the nearby university.)

This is what was striking. Suzanne heard three correct explanations for making a beam balance—Molly's in their group work, Mavrin's at the board, and Jenny's review. Yet her thinking didn't change a whit. She retained the belief that a beam would balance if the numbers of tiles on each side of the fulcrum were equal.

Principles of cognitive learning theory and Piaget's concept of equilibrium help us understand why misconceptions are so resistant to change. As we said earlier, we construct misconceptions because they make sense to us. And, when the misconception makes sense, we're at cognitive equilibrium (Sinatra & Pintrich, 2003). Changing thinking—accommodation—requires us to reconstruct our understanding, which is disequilibrating. Assimilating an experience into an existing understanding is simpler and imposes a lower cognitive load, so we're inclined to retain the misconception. When Suzanne believed that the numbers of tiles on both sides of the fulcrum being equal will make a beam balance, she was at equilibrium with this belief, so she retained it.

The intractability of misconceptions illustrates another essential idea about learning: *Wisdom can't be told.* It was originally proposed by Charles Gragg (1940) more than three quarters of a century ago, and it has been emphasized repeatedly by researchers since then (Loveland, 2014; Mosher et al., 2017). This simple but powerful idea helps us understand why lecturing and explaining, as strategies for promoting learning in general and for changing students' thinking in particular, are often ineffective.

Knowing that students bring misconceptions to learning experiences and realizing that these misconceptions are resistant to change, what can we do in response? We address this question in the next section.

MyLab Education Self-Check 9.2

Using Educational Psychology in Teaching: Suggestions for Helping Students Construct Valid Knowledge

9.3 Describe suggestions for using knowledge construction in teaching, and explain how they are grounded in the learning sciences.

We discussed misconceptions, including those prominent in teaching and learning, in the previous section. However, an additional one, specifically related to constructivism, exists: *Because learners' construct their own knowledge, teachers have reduced roles in promoting learning.* Little could be further from the truth. In fact, the traditional teaching roles—planning instruction, conducting learning activities, and assessing student understanding—are even more important when we ground our instruction in constructivism than they would be with "traditional" instruction (Donovan & Bransford, 2005; Sawyer, 2006). Our roles as teachers are more complex and demanding, because we realize, as we saw in the example with Suzanne's thinking, that simply explaining content—the most common teaching method—often doesn't work very well.

We know our students construct their own knowledge, and we know that they often form misconceptions. Keeping these ideas in mind, we now examine the following suggestions for helping students construct valid knowledge.

- Provide students with experiences that promote deep understanding
- Make interaction an integral part of instruction

- Connect content to the real world
- Promote learning with assessment

Let's look at these suggestions in more detail.

Provide Students with Experiences That Promote Deep Understanding

Learning and development depend on experience, and prior experiences contribute to the knowledge students bring to our classrooms. So, what do we do when students lack experiences and have insufficient or even inaccurate prior knowledge? The answer is simple (but admittedly, often not easy): *We provide the necessary experiences.*

Most commonly, these experiences exist in the form of **high-quality examples**, examples that—ideally—include all the information our students need to understand the topic. The balance, as you see here, contains all the information the students need to help them understand what makes beams balance.

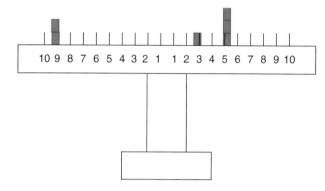

National Council on Teacher Quality (NCTQ)

The *National Council on Teacher Quality* describes the use of examples as one of the 6 essential teaching strategies that all new teachers need to know. "2. Linking abstract concepts with concrete representations. Teachers should present tangible examples that illuminate overarching ideas and also explain how the examples and big ideas connect" (Pomerance, Greenberg, & Walsh, 2016, p. vi).

To understand the theoretical framework for using high-quality examples, think about our experiences in the world outside of school. In the natural world, for instance, as small children see, pet, and play with friendly pooches they gradually construct the concept *dog*. The dogs they encounter are examples, and the wider the variety they encounter, the more fully their concept of *dog* is developed. The same is true for the myriad of other concepts we all acquire from our natural experiences. As another illustration, watch *Sesame Street* with a child some time. Elmo, for instance, jumps above a group of flowers, and says, "I'm above the flowers." Then, he pops up below the flowers, and says, "Now, I'm below the flowers." Elmo is simply providing examples of the concepts *above* and *below*. Everything children's educational programming teaches is through the clever and attractive use of examples.

When we use examples with our students we use the same processes that children use in the natural world (Rawson, Thomas, & Jacoby, 2015). We, however, create specific examples to help our students reach specified learning objectives and standards. Literally, our examples provide the experiences our students use to construct their knowledge. High-quality examples lead to the deep conceptual understanding the learning sciences describe as essential, they're important for all topics at all grade levels, particularly when learners first encounter a new idea, and they are especially important

TABLE 9.2 Teachers' use of examples in different content areas

Content Area	Learning Objective	Example and Topic
Language arts: Parts of speech	For students to understand comparative and superlative adjectives	Students' pencils of different lengths to show that one is "longer" and another is "longest" Students' hair color to show that one is "darker" and another is "darkest"
Social studies: Longitude and latitude	For students to understand longitude and latitude	A beach ball with lines of longitude and lines of latitude drawn on it (as you see here)
Math: Decimals and percents	For students to understand decimals and percents by calculating cost per ounce to determine which product is the best buy	12-ounce soft drink and its cost 16-ounce soft drink and its cost 6-pack of soft drinks and its cost
Science: Properties of matter	For students to understand the concept *density*	Cotton balls pressed into a drink cup Wooden cubes of different sizes to show that the ratio of weight to volume remains the same Equal volumes of water and vegetable oil on a balance

for limited-English-proficiency-learners who may lack the school-related experiences of their peers (Echevarria & Graves, 2015).

Table 9.2 provides addition illustrations of teachers' use of examples in different content areas.

Make Interaction an Integral Part of Instruction

Although essential, high-quality examples won't—by themselves—necessarily produce learning. Our students sometimes misinterpret the examples or center on aspects of them that lead to misconceptions, as we saw in Suzanne's thinking related to the balance beam.

To see how important interaction is, we return to the interview with Suzanne, Molly, Tad, and Drexel.

Suzanne has offered the solution we saw earlier, indicating that her thinking hadn't changed, which appeared as we see below.

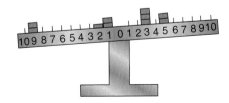

After Suzanne offers her solution, the interviewer asks, "Molly, what do you think of that solution?"

"It won't work," she responds. "It doesn't matter how many blocks there are. It's where they're put."

The interviewer asks Drexel and Tad what they think. Drexel corroborates Molly's answer by saying, "Because of Molly's reasoning. It isn't just the blocks. It's also where you put them."

Tad shrugs with uncertainty.

The students try Suzanne's solution, and the beam tips to the left.

Suzanne suggests taking a block off the 9, reasoning that the blocks near the end of the beam bring it down more, indicating that her thinking is starting to change as a result of seeing the example and interacting with her group mates.

The interviewer nods but doesn't affirm any explanation, instead giving the students the following problem and asking for solutions:

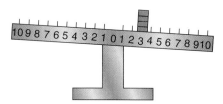

Molly offers, "Put 1 on the 8 and 4 on the 1."

"What do you think? . . . Tad?" the interviewer asks.

Tad stares at the beam for several seconds, concludes that the solution is correct, and when asked to explain his thinking, says, "Oh, okay, . . . 3 times 4 is 12, . . . and 4 times 1 is 4, . . . and 8 times 1 is 8, and 8 plus 4 is 12."

They try the solution, see that the beam is balanced, the interviewer asks for another solution, and Drexel offers, "1 on the 2 and 1 on the 10."

"Okay, I want you to tell us whether or not that'll work, Suzanne."

" . . . I think it will."

"Okay, explain why you think it will."

"Because, 10 times 1 equals 10, . . . and 2 times 1 equals 2, and 10 plus 2 equals 12. . . . So it'll be even."

Molly, Tad, and Drexel confirm the solution, and they try the solution, as we see here.

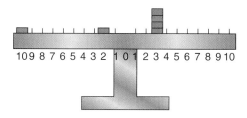

The interview is then ended.

MyLab Education
Video Example 9.5

Provide students with experiences that promote deep understanding, and make interaction an integral part of instruction, are two suggestions for helping students construct valid knowledge. Here we see how Suzanne's thinking has changed as a result of the examples she experiences and the interaction that takes place in her group.

In spite of experiencing the same examples as her classmates, Suzanne retained her misconception, which helps us understand why examples, alone, are not enough. Without interaction students may misinterpret the examples or fail to recognize the features of the examples that are essential for constructing a valid understanding of the topic.

Making interaction an integral part of our instruction serves three important learning purposes. First, it puts students in cognitively active roles—they must think about what they're studying. As we saw earlier, Suzanne heard three clear and valid explanations, but her thinking didn't change in the least; she continued to center on the numbers of tiles and ignore the distance from the fulcrum. She remained cognitively passive, as many students do during teacher explanations. (We want to emphasize here that we aren't suggesting that you shouldn't explain topics to students. Rather, we're saying *don't conclude that your students understand an idea because you've explained it to them.* Interacting with them is essential. Combining your explanations with questions that probe their thinking will help ensure that their knowledge constructions are valid.)

Second, interaction makes students' thinking visible, which allows us to informally assess their learning progress and address misconceptions. (We discuss assessment in more detail later in our discussion.) For instance, if Suzanne hadn't been asked to offer an explanation, the interviewer would likely have remained unaware of her misconception. And, the only way learners' misconceptions can be eliminated is to address them in such a way that they no longer make sense to the individual (Rich et al., 2017). This requires a combination of high-quality examples and interaction that ultimately results in a new conception making more sense than the original misconception.

Third, interaction makes feedback—both from peers and the teacher—effective (Hattie, 2012). For instance, because the students were interacting, Molly and Drexel were both able to offer their explanations, which provided Suzanne with the feedback she needed to change her thinking.

APA Top 20 Principles

This description illustrates Principle 6: *Clear, explanatory, and timely feedback to students is important for learning*—from the *Top 20 Principles from Psychology for PreK–12 Teaching and Learning*.

A positive and supportive classroom climate is essential to maximize the benefits of interaction and feedback. Students must feel emotionally safe and believe that periodic wrong answers are a normal and positive part of learning. Then, feedback can help them clear up incomplete or inaccurate understanding (Hattie & Gan, 2011).

Using Group Work to Promote Interaction
Questioning is the primary tool we use to promote interaction in our teaching (we examine questioning in detail in Chapter 13). It's effective and widely used in whole-class instruction, but if we have 20 or more students in our classes, the sheer number makes it difficult to involve all of them. Less confident or less assertive students may get few chances to participate, so they drift off.

Group work, as we saw implemented in Jenny's class, offers an alternative that we can use to increase the level of interaction among our students in learning activities. Group work is popular for involving learners in activities ranging as widely as having kindergarteners identify materials that will sink or float to solving word problems in math and critiquing products peers have written at a range of grade levels. We saw how Jenny organized the group work in her lesson to maximize the involvement of her students. In addition to promoting the social interaction so important for learning, group work adds variety to our instructional methods, and periodic change is more effective than teaching the same way all or most of the time (Good & Lavigne, 2018).

Using Open-Ended Discussions to Support Interaction
Jenny's students were involved in a form of discussion when they made conclusions about what's necessary to make a beam balance, but the discussion focused on specific right-or-wrong answers. Ultimately the students had to conclude that the weight times the distance on one side of the fulcrum must equal the weight times the distance on the other side if the beam is to balance.

In contrast, open-ended discussions involve topics that aren't cut and dried and where differences of opinion can and do appear. Examples might include analysis of a novel's characters and plot in English, issues in American government, and controversial topics, such as stem-cell research, climate change, or even evolution.

Properly conducted, many of the benefits of group work apply to open-ended discussions. In addition to promoting interaction, they help students learn courtesy, tolerance for differing opinions, and respect for evidence, social-emotional outcomes that may be as important as the topic being discussed.

Discussions are most commonly used with older students, and background knowledge is essential if the discussions are to be meaningful. It's impossible to conduct a successful discussion if students lack background knowledge, and attempting to do so is a waste of time.

Emphasis on social interaction is the common thread in both group work and open-ended discussions, and they both capitalize on the fact that learning is primarily a social process.

Developing Interactive Teaching Abilities

Learning to interact with students is one of the most challenging aspects of our development as teachers, for two reasons. First, most of the instruction we experience as learners involves lecture or "teaching as telling." Rarely do we take classes, particularly at the university level, where instructors make interaction an integral part of their instruction. So, we don't have many models to emulate. And, consequently, many teachers continue to believe that lecturing and explaining are the best ways to help students learn.

Second, until we acquire high levels of expertise—expertise developed to the point where interacting with students is essentially automatic—the process is demanding. It's much harder to guide students with questioning than it is to simply tell them what we want them to know. This helps explain why so few teachers become truly competent and proficient with it.

We strongly encourage you to persevere, literally practice questioning and other interaction skills until you can involve your students with a minimum of effort. When your expertise is developed to this point, you will find that your students will be more attentive and motivated, they will learn more, and your teaching will be more satisfying. Most people can learn to deliver acceptable lectures, but developing the skills needed to interact effectively with students requires a true professional.

Connect Content to the Real World

To motivate students and promote transfer, we want to connect the topics we teach to the real world whenever possible. This suggestion is supported by social constructivist learning theory, the learning sciences, and particularly situated cognition (Morgan, 2017; Robbins & Aydede, 2009).

In many cases, making real-world connections need not be difficult. Jenny's students, for instance, can connect their study of balance beams to levers and teeter totters. In the example we saw earlier with subject-verb and pronoun-antecedent agreement, simply embedding the correct usage in a paragraph is more realistic than using isolated sentences.

In other content areas, when geography students, for instance, connect longitude and latitude to the location of a favorite hangout, science students relate *inertia* to seatbelts in their cars, art students create a portrait of a family member, or math students solve making-change problems for items purchased at the school store, their learning is more meaningful than it would be if they studied the topics in the abstract. And experiences such as these are supported by the learning sciences (Penuel et al., 2016). The same is true for each of the teachers in Table 9.2. Building the content of chapters around classroom case studies is our effort to apply this suggestion as we write this book.

Promote Learning with Formative Assessment

If our students behaved like recording devices, teaching and learning would be simple. We could merely explain a topic accurately, and our students would record the information in the same form. Straightforward, uncomplicated. This isn't how the learning and teaching world works, however; we know they don't. Instead, they construct their knowledge and store it in memory in a form that makes sense to them, and because they do, individuals' understanding of the topics they study will vary. We saw, for instance, that Suzanne constructed a misconception about making beams balance, and she retained it in spite of three clear explanations.

However, when we teach, we have classes of 20 or more, so it's impossible to know how all of our students are thinking. Jenny didn't have the interviewer's luxury of working with only four students—Suzanne, Molly, Tad, and Drexel—so it's unlikely that she was aware of Suzanne's misconception. Even when our lessons are highly interactive, we can't involve all students all the time, so we need a mechanism to determine the extent to which their knowledge constructions are valid. This leads us to the role of **assessment**, the process of gathering information and making decisions about students' learning progress. We tend to think of assessment as giving tests and assigning grades, but it's much more than that. It is an essential part of the entire teaching–learning process (Chappuis & Stiggens, 2017).

When using assessment as a guide for making decisions designed to increase learning, formative assessment is the process we use. **Formative assessment** "is the collection of formal and informal processes teachers and students use to gather evidence for the purpose of informing next steps in learning. Formative assessment practices occur during the learning, while students are practicing and improving" (Chappuis & Stiggens, 2017, pp. 20–21). (Formative assessment differs from **summative assessment**, the process of gathering information used to make conclusions about the level of learner achievement and typically used as a basis for assigning grades. We examine formative and summative assessment in detail in Chapter 14.) When Jenny watched Mavrin at the board, for example, and when she listened to students' discussions as she circulated around the room, she was involved in formative assessment.

National Council on Teacher Quality (NCTQ)

The *National Council on Teacher Quality* describes the use of the assessment processes to increase student learning as one of the six essential strategies that all new teachers need to know. "6. Assessing to boost retention. . . . [A]ssessments that require students to recall material help information 'stick'" (Pomerance et al., 2016, p. vi).

Formative assessment goes further than simply watching or listening to students. Mavrin's solution at the board only told Jenny that *he* understood the principle for making beams balance; it didn't tell her anything about the rest of her students. And she didn't have access to the students' responses during the interview. Realizing that she didn't have information from all her students, Jenny gave them two additional problems to assess their understanding. The problems together with Tad's responses are in Figure 9.2.

Tad's answers suggest that his understanding of the topic is "a work in progress." He was able to determine that the beam would balance in the first problem, but was unable to draw or write a solution to the second. His experience is not unique; Jenny's assessment revealed that several other students were also still uncertain about solving similar problems.

Based on her assessment information, Jenny's next steps are quite simple. She can first provide the students with feedback by discussing the two problems and having students who answered correctly explain their thinking to serve as cognitive

Figure 9.2 Balance beam problems for assessment

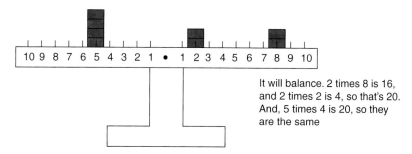

It will balance. 2 times 8 is 16, and 2 times 2 is 4, so that's 20. And, 5 times 4 is 20, so they are the same

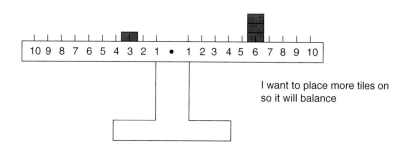

I want to place more tiles on so it will balance

models for their classmates, a process consistent with *cognitive apprenticeships*, which we examined earlier in the chapter. She can then give her students additional problems for practice, for which she will also provide feedback. While this process doesn't ensure that all students will totally understand beam balances, it's certain that their understanding will have advanced. This is the essential role that assessment plays in promoting valid knowledge constructions.

APA Top 20 Principles

This description again illustrates Principle 6: *Clear, explanatory, and timely feedback to students is important for learning*—from the *Top 20 Principles from Psychology for PreK–12 Teaching and Learning*.

MyLab Education Application Exercise 9.2: Applying Suggestions for Helping Students Construct Knowledge in Fourth Grade

In this exercise you will be asked to analyze the application of suggestions for helping students construct valid knowledge.

Technology, Learning, and Development: Capitalizing on Technology to Provide Meaningful Experiences

Providing the experiences our students need to construct their knowledge is demanding, and the difficulty in finding or creating high-quality examples for many of the topics we teach is a primary reason. The lack of readily available examples is precisely the reason the topics are hard for students to learn (Rawson et al., 2015). In these cases, technology can be a valuable tool (Roblyer & Hughes, 2019). We might simply

Developmentally Appropriate Practice

Guiding Knowledge Construction with Students at Different Ages

Although students at all ages construct knowledge, and learning theories apply to learners of all ages, a number of developmental differences exist. The following sections outline suggestions for responding to these differences.

Working with Students in Early Childhood Programs and Elementary Schools

To make sense of the world they live in, young children construct knowledge as do learners of all ages. However, they often lack many of the experiences that older students have acquired, so providing *concrete examples* is crucial in working with early childhood and elementary students.

Young children tend to center on the most perceptually obvious aspects of objects and events, such as Brittany centering on the word "boys" in the sentence "Each of the boys has (his, their) own lunch box with pictures of cars on (it, them)" and as a result, they commonly form misconceptions or incomplete understanding. They also tend to be quite literal in their thinking, which can also lead to the construction of misconceptions. For instance, they tend to equate size with age, believing someone who is bigger is older, and in social studies they may think that lines of latitude and longitude actually exist on the earth.

As a result, explanations presented in the abstract are often ineffective with elementary students. When working with young children, concrete, high-quality examples are even more important than with older learners. In addition, interactive instruction allows teachers both to investigate the ideas students currently hold and to assist them as they construct new ones.

Using language to describe their world and communicate with each other not only develops language skills but also promotes meaningful learning. Language is crucial for later learning, and the more opportunities young children have to practice and use language, the better.

Young children also need to learn to accept responsibility for their learning and how to interact positively with their peers. This suggests learning tasks in which young students can interact with their peers in challenging activities. These opportunities to interact with peers provide a foundation for later learning.

Working with Students in Middle Schools

Middle school students overcome much of the tendency to interpret events literally, but often, in the process of knowledge construction, they fail to recognize relationships among objects and events. For instance, instead of recognizing that rectangles and squares are subsets of parallelograms, they often classify the figures into different categories.

Middle school students are also developing social interaction skills, such as perspective taking and social problem solving. This allows you to use cooperative learning and other small-group strategies to integrate social interaction into your instruction. Cognitive apprenticeships, in which students work with other students in small groups, can provide opportunities for students to think and talk about new ideas. Encouraging students to verbalize their developing understanding during learning activities is important for promoting learning. Experts caution, however, that we should carefully structure and monitor small-group activities to ensure that students are cognitively active and remain on task.

Working with Students in High Schools

High school students' experiences provide them with a rich store of prior knowledge that increases the validity of their knowledge constructions. However, they continue to construct a variety of misconceptions, particularly when working with symbols and abstract ideas. For instance, in simplifying the expression $2 + 5 \times 3 - 6$, they often get $15 (2 + 5 = 7; 7 \times 3 = 21; 21 - 6 = 15)$ instead of the correct answer: $11 (5 \times 3 = 15; 15 + 2 = 17; 17 - 6 = 11)$.

As students move to more advanced classes in high school, such as physics, chemistry, and calculus, making interaction an integral part of instruction is even more important. And it is in these classes that teachers tend to act more like college instructors, where lecture is the most common instructional strategy. High school teachers sometimes even resist the idea of interaction, believing that lectures are efficient and that students will be subject to lectures in college, so they might as well "get used to it." This is neither valid nor wise. The most effective way to prepare students for advanced studies is to help them acquire the background knowledge needed to understand more abstract and sophisticated topics. And using high-quality examples, connecting content to the real world, making interaction an integral part of instruction, and using assessment as a learning tool are as important with high school students as they are with students at other developmental levels for helping them acquire this background knowledge.

High school students can also participate in and benefit from classroom discussions, which provide opportunities to refine their thinking based on the ideas of others. As with all forms of instruction, high school teachers need to structure and monitor discussions closely to ensure that they are aligned with learning goals.

drop a baseball and a golf ball, for instance, to demonstrate that all objects, regardless of weight, fall at the same rate, but it's virtually impossible to illustrate their actual acceleration.

Here, technology can be effective (Roblyer & Hughes, 2019). For instance, Figure 9.3 illustrates the position of a falling ball at uniform time intervals. We see that the distance between the images becomes greater and greater, indicating that the ball is accelerating—falling faster and faster. This simulation provides an example of acceleration that's impossible to represent without the use of technology.

An expanding variety of technology simulations exist that we can use to illustrate ideas that are difficult to represent directly. For instance, if you're a biology teacher, you might use software to simulate a frog dissection rather than using an actual frog. Although the simulation doesn't allow students the hands-on experience of working with a real frog, it's less expensive because it can be used over and over; it's more flexible because the frog can be "reassembled"; and it avoids sacrificing an animal for science (Roblyer & Hughes, 2019).

Simulations that can be used to illustrate topics exist in all the content areas. In language arts, for instance, simulations illustrate letters and their matching sounds, words and their meanings, and vocabulary development. In math, software such as *The Geometer's Sketchpad* (Informer Technologies, 2017) provides visual representations of abstract math concepts; in social studies, software allows students to take **virtual field trips**, visits to Internet sites that allow them to experience locations that they are unlikely to see in real life, such as the ancient Egyptian pyramids; and in art, Internet and CD collections allow access to a variety of different art forms. These are merely examples; simulations exist in content areas ranging from the samples seen here to special education, foreign language, music, and PE (Roblyer & Hughes, 2019). When you begin teaching and have your own classroom, you will be able to explore the resources available for your content area. And as the quality of software improves, representations are becoming more sophisticated and the simulations are more interactive, further increasing student motivation and understanding.

Figure 9.3 Simulation of a falling object

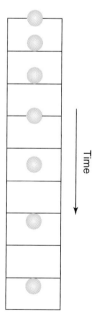

Time

Your classroom computer can also be an efficient tool for storing the examples you create. Then, all you have to do is pull up the examples the next time you want to use them. Once created to your satisfaction, no additional preparation beyond simply accessing the file is necessary. You can also easily modify your examples if you believe they need to be improved. This efficiency in terms of teacher time and effort is essential. When you begin teaching, your workload will be enormous, so anything you can do to reduce it—without sacrificing learning—is invaluable. Being able to efficiently store and retrieve your examples is an important part of this process.

Technology will never replace you and your teaching expertise, but it can be a valuable tool to help you provide your students with the experiences they need to construct valid knowledge and develop the deep conceptual understanding called for by the learning sciences.

Evaluating Constructivism

Cognitive learning theories suggest that people construct knowledge in attempts to make sense of their experiences. Constructivism makes an important contribution to our understanding of learning because it reminds us that people don't behave like recording devices, and it helps us understand the origin of misconceptions. Constructivism is the only view of learning that is able to explain why misconceptions exist and why we construct them. Constructivism also helps us understand why background knowledge, social interaction, and making students' thinking visible are so important in the learning process. Because we know that students want their experiences to make sense and they construct their own knowledge, we better understand why they don't grasp an idea that's been discussed several times, why they seem to ignore a point that's been emphasized, and why they retain misconceptions that have been directly refuted.

However, misconceptions about constructivism, itself, also exist. One of the most pervasive is confusing constructivism as a theory of learning with constructivism as an approach to teaching. " . . . [M]any educators confuse 'constructivism,' which is a theory of how one learns and sees the world, with a prescription for how to teach" (Clark et al., 2012, p. 8). And, as we suggested earlier, another misconception about constructivism suggests that teachers shouldn't actively guide student learning, but rather have students discover concepts and principles for themselves. This misconception is widely held (Clark et al., 2012). It also implies that teaching methods, such as small-group work, cooperative learning, discovery, and hands-on activities, are "constructivist," whereas other methods, such as whole-class discussions, are not. This is also a misconception. Large-group instruction, effectively done, can promote knowledge construction, and cooperative learning, improperly done, may not.

Hands-on activities are particularly problematic. It's easy to assume that if students are behaviorally active as they work in groups they are also cognitively active. This may or may not be the case. "Simply put, cognitive activity can happen with or without behavioral activity, and behavioral activity does not in any way guarantee cognitive activity" (Clark et al., 2012, p. 8). We saw this illustrated in Jenny's lesson. Suzanne remained cognitively passive until she was directly involved during the interview that followed the lesson.

Constructivism, as a description of learning, is also incomplete. It doesn't, for instance, take into account the way our human memory systems work, the important role of practice in developing skills, and the influence of emotions on motivation and learning. These are topics better explained with other theories.

The idea that learners construct their own knowledge instead of passively recording it marks an important advance in our understanding of learning, however, and it has important implications for our teaching.

Table 9.3 summarizes constructivism and outlines its contributions and criticisms.

TABLE 9.3 Analyzing theories: Evaluating constructivism

Basic question	What are the processes involved in people's attempts to make sense of their experiences?
Catalysts for learning	• Experiences with the physical and social world • Background knowledge • Social interaction and language
Key concepts	• Communities of learners • Cognitive apprenticeship • Appropriating understanding • Situated cognition • Misconceptions
Primary theorist	• Vygotsky • Piaget (historically)
Suggestions for teaching	• Provide students with the experiences they need to construct valid knowledge • Connect content to real-world applications • Make interaction an integral part of instruction • Use assessment as a tool to increase learning
Contributions	• Explains how learners develop original ideas and form misconceptions • Helps us understand why prior (background) knowledge is crucial for learning • Demonstrates the essential role that social interaction plays in promoting learning • Helps us understand why assessment is an essential part of the teaching–learning process
Criticisms	• Is sometimes misinterpreted as a theory of teaching instead of a theory of learning • Fails to consider the influence of our memory systems and particularly the limitations of working memory • Doesn't account for the role of practice in developing skills • Doesn't explain how emotional responses are developed or how emotions influence learning • Doesn't account for the role of praise and other reinforcers in learning

Classroom Connections

Helping Students Construct Valid Knowledge

1. Students construct their own knowledge, and the knowledge they construct depends on what they already know. To accommodate differences in prior knowledge, provide a variety of examples and other representations of the content you want students to understand.

   • **Elementary:** A fifth-grade teacher in a unit on chemical and physical change has students melt ice, crumple paper, dissolve sugar, and break toothpicks to illustrate physical change. She then has them burn paper, pour vinegar into baking soda, and chew soda crackers to illustrate chemical change.

   • **Middle School:** An English teacher presents the following excerpts to illustrate internal conflict:
   Kelly didn't know what to do. She was looking forward to the class trip, but if she went, she wouldn't be able to take the scholarship-qualifying test.
   Calvin was caught in a dilemma. He saw Jason take Olonzo's calculator but knew that if he told Mrs. Stevens what he saw, Jason would realize that it was he who reported the theft.

   • **High School:** While teaching about the Great Depression, a social studies teacher has students read excerpts from *The Grapes of Wrath*, shows a video of people standing in bread lines, shares statistics on the rash of suicides after the stock market crash, and discusses how a current recession is similar to and different from the Great Depression.

2. Knowledge construction is most effective when learners have real-world experiences. Develop learning activities around realistic problems.

   • **Elementary:** In a lesson relating geography and the way we live, a fourth-grade teacher has students describe the way they dress for their favorite forms of recreation. She also asks students who have moved from other parts of the country to do the same for their previous locations. She then guides them as they construct an understanding of the effect of geography on culture and lifestyle.

   • **Middle School:** In a unit on percent increase and decrease, a math teacher has students look for examples of marked-down clothes while shopping. He also brings in newspaper ads. The class discusses the examples and calculates the amount saved in each case.

   • **High School:** To help her students understand the importance of persuasive writing, an English teacher brings in three examples of "Letters to the Editor" on the same topic. Students discuss the letters, determine which is most effective, and with the teacher's guidance, identify the characteristics of effective persuasive writing.

(continued)

3. Social constructivist views of learning emphasize the role of social interaction in the process of knowledge construction. Make social interaction an integral part of your instruction, and avoid relying too heavily on explanations to promote learning.

- **Elementary:** A fourth-grade teacher wants his students to understand the concept of scale on a map. He places them in groups and has them create a map of their desktops. Then he has them draw a map of their room, and finally, they go outside and draw a map of their playground. When finished, he guides a class discussion to help them understand how the maps are similar and different.

- **Middle School:** A sixth-grade science teacher has his students take eight identical wooden cubes and make one stack of five and another stack of three. He has them discuss the mass, volume, and densities of the two stacks. Then, with questioning, he guides them to conclude that the mass and volume of the stack of five are greater than the mass and volume of the stack of three but that the densities of the two stacks are equal.

- **High School:** An algebra teacher "walks" students through the solutions to problems by calling on individuals to provide specific information about each step and explain why the step is necessary. When students encounter difficulties, the teacher asks additional questions to help them understand the step.

MyLab Education Self-Check 9.3

Chapter 9 Summary

1. Describe the processes involved in knowledge construction and analyze examples that illustrate these processes.
   - Learning and development depend on experience, people want their experiences to make sense, and they construct knowledge in attempts to make sense of their experiences.
   - Cognitive constructivism focuses on individual construction of knowledge. Cognitive constructivists believe that when an experience disrupts individuals' equilibrium, they reconstruct understanding to reestablish equilibrium.
   - Social constructivism emphasizes that individuals first construct knowledge in a social environment and then appropriate it. Knowledge grows directly out of the social interaction. Social constructivism has become the primary framework for guiding instruction in our nation's schools.
   - Emphasis on sociocultural theory, communities of learners, cognitive apprenticeships, and situated cognition are all applications of social constructivism to instruction.

2. Explain misconceptions, how they occur, and how they can be eliminated.
   - Misconceptions are beliefs that are inconsistent with evidence or commonly accepted explanations.
   - Prior experiences, superficial appearances, misuse of language, and "intuitive appeal" can all contribute to misconceptions.

   - Changing misconceptions is difficult because the change disrupts individuals' equilibrium, the misconceptions are often consistent with everyday experiences, and individuals often don't recognize inconsistencies between new information and their existing beliefs.

3. Describe suggestions for using knowledge construction in teaching, and explain how they are grounded in the learning sciences.
   - High-quality experiences include examples and other representations learners use to construct knowledge that makes sense to them.
   - Connecting content to the real world applies the primary emphasis of the learning sciences, which focuses on learning as it exists in real-world settings.
   - Making interaction an integral part of instruction capitalizes on the premise that learning is primarily a social process.
   - Using assessment to promote learning recognizes that learners' knowledge constructions will vary and these constructions will sometimes be invalid. Assessment can then be used to help learners reconstruct their knowledge and increase their understanding.
   - Technology can be an effective tool for representing topics that are hard to represent in any other way.

Preparing for Your Licensure Exam

Understanding the Process of Knowledge Construction

You will be required to take a licensure exam before you go into your own classroom. This exam will include information related to the processes involved in knowledge construction, and it will include both multiple-choice and constructed-response questions. We include the following exercises to help you practice for the exam in your state. This book and these exercises will be a resource for you as you prepare for the exam.

Throughout the chapter, we examined students' thinking, saw the process of knowledge construction illustrated, and studied suggestions for facilitating these processes.

In the following case, Scott Sowell, a middle school science teacher, wants his students to understand how to design experiments and control variables. To do so, he wants his students to design and conduct a study to examine factors that influence the frequency of a simple pendulum. Read the case study, and answer the questions that follow.

To help his students meet his goal Scott carefully explains the process for controlling variables, and explains and demonstrates how they would control variables with an experiment using plants, explaining that plant growth is essential for maintaining the world's food supply. He then decides to give them additional experience with controlling variables with simple pendulums in small groups.

Scott begins by demonstrating a simple pendulum with paper clips attached to a piece of string. He explains that frequency means the number of swings in a certain time period and asks students what factors they think will influence the frequency. After some discussion they suggest length, weight, and angle of release as possible hypotheses. (In reality, only the length of the pendulum determines its frequency.)

"Okay, your job as a group is to design your own experiments," Scott continues. "Think of a way to test how each affects the frequency. Use the equipment at your desk to design and carry out the experiment."

One group of four (Marina, Paige, Wensley, and Jonathan) ties a string to a ring stand and measures its length, as shown here:

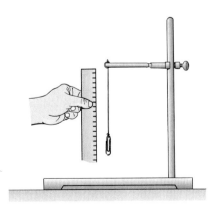

They measure the length of the string to be 49 centimeters, select 15 seconds as the amount of time to let the pendulum swing, using one paper clip as weight. Maria counts 21 swings.

A few minutes later, Scott again walks by the group, examines their results, and says, "So you've done one test so far. . . . What are you going to do next? . . . I'm going to come back after your next test and look at it," and he moves to another group.

The group conducts their second test by shortening the string and adding a second paper clip (which violates the principle of altering only one variable at a time).

"Mr. Sowell, we found out that the shorter it is and the heavier it is, the faster it goes," Marina reports to Scott when he returns to the group.

Scott then asks which of the two variables—length or weight—was responsible for the change in the frequency, and Wensley and Jonathan say simultaneously, "They both changed."

"Think about that. You need to come up with a conclusion about length, about weight, and about angle—how each of them influences the frequency of your pendulum," Scott reminds them as he moves from group to group.

As the group investigates the three variables—length, weight, and height (angle of release)—they continue to change two of these at the same time, confounding their results. And as Scott moves from group to group, he finds that most of the groups are doing the same thing. As a result the groups, in general, conclude that each of the three variables—length, weight, and height (angle of release)—influence a pendulum's frequency.

In response to this misconception, Scott reassembles the class and conducts a whole-class demonstration. "Let's take a look at something here," Scott says, placing a ring stand on his demonstration table. He attaches a paper clip to the pendulum, puts it in motion, and asks a student to count the swings. He adds a second paper clip and again has the students count. They find that the number of swings is the same with one, two, three and four paper clips, which demonstrates that weight doesn't affect the frequency. He has a student state this conclusion and he writes it on the board. Then he does a second demonstration with different angles of release to show that angle also has no effect on the frequency and again asks a student to make a conclusion so he can write it on the board.

After the demonstrations, he says, "Now I want someone to make a conclusion about what we learned about designing experiments and how we use our variables when we design experiments. . . . Who wants to talk about that? . . . Wensley? Tell me what we learned about how to set up an experiment. What did we learn from this?"

"Each time you do a different part of the experiment, only change one of the variables," Wensley explains.

"Why is that?"

"You're only checking one thing at a time. If you do two, you can't tell which one caused the change," Wensley continues.

"Right, you couldn't tell which one was causing it, could you? . . . It might go faster, but you would wonder, is it the weight or is it the length?"

Seeing that it is near the end of the class period, Scott asks if there are any questions, and hearing none, he has Marina summarize what they learned about designing experiments, hears the bell ring, and dismisses the students.

Questions for Case Analysis

Use information from this chapter and the case study to answer the following questions.

Multiple-Choice Questions

1. Scott's students changed more than one variable at a time—such as changing both the length and the weight—when they designed their experiments. Of the following, which statement *best explains* why they changed more than one variable, even though Scott had explained the process for controlling variables?

   a. The students were cognitively passive during the group work.

   b. The students constructed the idea of changing more than one variable at a time, because doing so made sense to them.

   c. The students failed to reflect on the processes involved, so they used an inappropriate technique.

   d. Scott grounded his learning activity in cognitive constructivism rather than social constructivism, so the learning activity was ineffective.

2. Scott explained the process of controlling variables, and did a demonstration with plants to illustrate the process.

However, the groups in his class failed to control variables when they did their activities with the pendulum. Of the following, which statement is the *best explanation* for the students' continued inability to control variables?

   a. Scott failed to provide a high-quality example that illustrated how to control variables.

   b. Scott didn't connect his topic with plants to the real world, so he didn't adequately apply the suggestions of the learning sciences to his lesson with simple pendulums.

   c. Scott failed to adequately make social interaction an integral part of his instruction.

   d. As Scott explained the process of controlling variables the students remained cognitively passive, so the information wasn't meaningful to them.

Constructed-Response Question

3. Scott's students had some misconceptions about controlling variables. They failed to keep length constant, for example, as they changed the weight. How effectively did Scott address their misconception in his instruction? Use information from the case study to support your explanation.

MyLab Education Licensure Exam 9.1

Important Concepts

appropriating understanding	community of learners	learning sciences	sociocultural theory
assessment	constructivism	learning styles	transfer
cognitive apprenticeships	embodied cognition	misconceptions	virtual field trips
cognitive constructivism	formative assessment	situated cognition	
	high-quality examples	social constructivism	

Chapter 10
Motivation and Learning

Learning Outcomes

After you have completed your study of this chapter, you should be able to:

10.1 Define motivation and describe different theoretical explanations for learner motivation.

10.2 Describe learners' needs and how they influence motivation to learn.

10.3 Explain how learners' beliefs impact their motivation to learn.

10.4 Describe how learners' goals affect their motivation to learn.

10.5 Explain how interest and emotion influence learner motivation.

APA Top 20 Principles

APA Top 20 Principles

Top 20 Principles from Psychology for PreK–12 Teaching and Learning explicitly addressed in this chapter.

Principle 1: Students' beliefs or perceptions about intelligence and ability affect their cognitive functioning and learning.

Principle 5: Acquiring long-term knowledge and skill is largely dependent on practice.

Principle 9: Students tend to enjoy learning and perform better when they are more intrinsically than extrinsically motivated to achieve.

Principle 10: Students persist in the face of challenging tasks and process information more deeply when they adopt mastery goals rather than performance goals.

Principle 12: Setting goals that are short term (proximal), specific, and moderately challenging enhances motivation more than establishing goals that are long term (distal), general, and overly challenging.

Principle 15: Emotional well-being influences educational performance, learning, and development.

National Council on Teacher Quality (NCTQ)

The NCTQ Essential Teaching Strategies that every new teacher needs to know specifically addressed in this chapter.

Strategy 6: Assessing learning

If you're a typical student, you like some of your classes more than others. Why? And why do you enjoy certain activities, such as talking to friends, reading, sports, and others? *Motivation*, arguably the greatest influence on learning that exists, is the answer. The *Top 20 Principles from Psychology for PreK–12 Teaching and Learning* underscore motivation. As you see here, 6 of the 20 are emphasized in this chapter.

Understanding student motivation is an essential part of your professional knowledge, and it can make the difference between a successful year of teaching and one you'd rather forget.

As you read the following case study—involving a world history class—think about the students' motivation and how Kathy Brewster, their teacher, influences it.

Kathy is working with her students on the historical period spanning the 11th through the 16th centuries, which encompasses part of the Middle Ages, the Renaissance, and the Crusades.

"We'd better get moving," Susan urges Jim as they approach the door of Kathy's classroom. "The bell's going to ring, and you know how Brewster is about this class. She thinks it's sooo important."

"Did you finish your homework?" Jim asks and then stops himself. "What am I talking about? You always do your homework."

"Actually, I've always liked history and knowing about the past, . . . and I'm pretty good at it. . . . My dad sometimes helps me. He says he wants to keep up with the world," Susan laughs.

"In some classes, I just do enough to get a decent grade, but not in here," Jim responds. "I used to hate history, but I sometimes even read ahead a little, because Brewster makes you think. She's so gung ho, and it's kind of interesting the way she's always telling us about the way we are because of something that happened a zillion years ago—I never thought about this stuff in that way before."

"Sheesh, Mrs. Brewster, that assignment was impossible," Mason grumbles as he comes into the classroom. "You're working us to death."

"That's good for you," Kathy smiles. "I know you're working hard, but it's paying off. Look at how much both your writing and your thinking have improved as a result of your effort. . . . Hard work is the key to everything, and you know how important being a good writer is."

We will refer to Kathy's lesson throughout the chapter, and as you study it, think about these questions.

1. How is Susan's motivation different from Jim's?
2. How does Jim's motivation in Kathy's class differ from his other classes?
3. How has Kathy influenced her students' motivation?

Let's begin.

What Is Motivation?

10.1 Define motivation and describe different theoretical explanations for learner motivation.

"**Motivation** is the process whereby goal-directed activity is instigated and sustained" (Schunk, Meece, & Pintrich, 2014, p. 5). If we work hard to solve a math problem or attempt to perfect a tennis serve, for instance, we're motivated in each case. Solving the problem and perfecting the serve are the goals, and motivation helps us sustain our efforts to reach each one.

As we would expect, motivated students have more positive attitudes toward their schoolwork, persist longer on difficult tasks, and process information in greater depth (Schunk et al., 2014). Simply, motivated students learn more than their less motivated peers, and this is the reason we title the chapter *Motivation and Learning*.

Extrinsic and Intrinsic Motivation

Ed Psych and You

Think about your classes. Do you study primarily to get good grades, or is understanding the course content more important to you? Do you believe understanding the content is important, even if you're not terribly interested in it?

Motivation is classified into two broad categories. **Extrinsic motivation** is motivation to involve ourselves in a task as a means to an end, and **intrinsic motivation** is motivation to engage in an activity for its own sake (Schunk et al., 2014). If you answered the questions in *Ed Psych and You* by saying that you study primarily to get good grades, you are extrinsically motivated, whereas if you said understanding the course content is more important, you're intrinsically motivated. This helps us understand the difference between Susan's and Jim's motivation and answers our first question above: "How is Susan's motivation different from Jim's?" His comment, "In some classes, I just do enough to get a decent grade," reflects extrinsic motivation; Susan's comment, "I've always liked history and knowing about the past" suggests intrinsic motivation. As we would expect, intrinsic motivation is preferable because of its focus on learning and understanding, and it has implications for you as you go through your program. Research on students like you suggests that "the single most influential learning and study skill promoting positive academic performance was level of intrinsic motivation" (Griffin, MacKewn, Moser, & VanVuren, 2013, p. 53).

MyLab Education
Video Example 10.1
Intrinsic motivation is motivation to engage in an activity for its own sake. Here a student describes her intrinsic motivation related to math and science in general and project work in particular.

APA Top 20 Principles

This discussion illustrates Principle 9: *Students tend to enjoy learning and perform better when they are more intrinsically than extrinsically motivated to achieve*—from the *Top 20 Principles from Psychology for PreK–12 Teaching and Learning*.

Motivation is also contextual and can change over time (Cleary & Kitsantas, 2017). For instance, we saw that Jim is extrinsically motivated in his other classes, but saying "I sometimes even read ahead a little" and "it's kind of interesting . . . " suggests that he is intrinsically motivated in Kathy's. This answers our second question above: "How does Jim's motivation in Kathy's class differ from his other classes?"

Experiences that include one or more of the following tend to promote intrinsic motivation (Schunk et al., 2014):

- *A challenge.* Meeting challenges is emotionally satisfying, and challenge exists when goals are moderately difficult and success isn't guaranteed.

- *Autonomy.* People in general, and students in particular, are more motivated when they feel they have influence over, and can control, their own fate.

- *Arouse curiosity.* Personalized experiences and novel, surprising, or discrepant events arouse curiosity.

- *Involve fantasy.* All we have to do is watch a small child mesmerized by *Sesame Street,* or other children's programming, or notice the success of books such as the *Harry Potter* stories or science fiction, to see that people are motivated by fantasy.

These factors help us understand the context of Kathy's class. Both Jim's—"Brewster really makes you think"—and Mason's—"Sheesh, Mrs. Brewster, that assignment was impossible"—comments suggest that they were reacting to challenges in her class, and

Jim saying, "It's kind of interesting the way she's always telling us about the way we are . . . " suggests her teaching aroused his curiosity. Both impacted their intrinsic motivation.

People tend to think of extrinsic and intrinsic motivation as two ends of a single continuum, meaning the higher the extrinsic motivation, the lower the intrinsic motivation and vice versa, but they are actually on separate continua (Schunk et al., 2014). For example, we asked if you study to understand the content or primarily to get good grades. You most likely want good grades but you may also want to understand the content, as many students do. This suggests that you're high in both intrinsic and extrinsic motivation. People may be high in both, low in both, or high in one and low in the other.

The relationships between extrinsic and intrinsic motivation are outlined in Figure 10.1.

Flow

Have you ever been so immersed in an activity that you've literally lost track of time? This experience is described as **flow**, an intense form of intrinsic motivation in which an individual is completely absorbed, focused, and concentrating on a challenging activity (Csikszentmihalyi, 1990, 1996, 1999). *Flow* carries people away in a combination of pleasure, satisfaction, and engagement (Chen & Sun, 2016). It's the experience musicians feel when they're "in the groove," or athletes have "in the zone." And, because intrinsic motivation is linked to high performance, the concept of flow has even sparked interest in the business world as leaders attempt to increase their employees' productivity (Cranston, & Keller, 2013).

We—your authors—periodically enjoy *flow* as we work on this book. We do indeed lose track of time, and when we're most immersed in study and writing, we don't even want to stop to eat. It's not easily captured, but little like it exists when we have the good fortune to experience it.

As would be expected, flow is rare, and it has the following prerequisites:

- *Autonomy:* We are more likely to be strongly intrinsically motivated in activities we choose for ourselves than in those required by others (Chang, Chen, & Chi, 2016).
- *Expertise:* The motivation associated with flow can only result when our understanding and skills have been developed to a high level (Csikszentmihalyi, 1999).
- *Optimal Challenge:* It is impossible to experience flow when working on trivial tasks (Schunk et al., 2014).

Figure 10.1 Extrinsic and intrinsic motivation

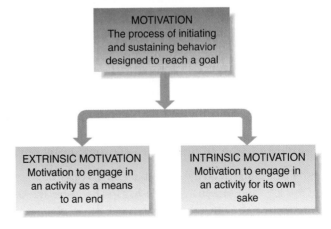

Some research has also linked *flow* to personality traits and has found that agreeable and conscientious people are more likely to experience it, whereas people who have a "glass half empty" outlook on life are less likely to do so (Ullén et al., 2012). *Flow* is not the same as "going with the flow," which suggests that the activity is simply spontaneous and feels good. We offer suggestions that can help contribute to *flow* in classrooms in the section "Using Educational Psychology in Teaching: Suggestions for Capitalizing on Needs to Increase Your Students' Motivation to Learn" later in the chapter.

Motivation to Learn

It would be great if our students were always intrinsically motivated, and we're sometimes led to believe that if our instruction is stimulating enough, they will be. This is a nice ideal, but it isn't realistic for all, or even most, learning activities. Here's why (Brophy, 2010):

- School attendance is compulsory, and content reflects what society believes students should learn, not what students may choose for themselves.

- Teachers work with large numbers of students and can't always meet individual needs.

- Students' performances are evaluated and reported to parents and other caregivers, so students focus on meeting external demands instead of the personal satisfaction they might derive from the experiences.

Jere Brophy (2010) offers an alternative. "I believe that it is realistic for you to seek to develop and sustain your students' **motivation to learn**: their tendencies to find academic activities meaningful and worthwhile and to try to get the intended learning benefits from them" (Brophy, 2010, p. 11).

Motivation to learn is related to the second question we asked in *Ed Psych and You* earlier: "Do you believe understanding the content is important, even if you're not terribly interested in it?" If you answered yes, your *motivation to learn* is high. Motivation to learn will be our focus in this chapter, and if students' intrinsic motivation increases in the process, so much the better.

Theoretical Views of Motivation

As with learning, different theoretical orientations help us understand students' motivation to learn (Schunk et al., 2014). We outline them in Figure 10.2 and discuss them in the sections that follow.

Figure 10.2 Theoretical views of motivation

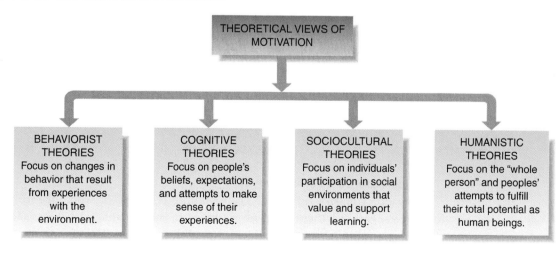

THEORETICAL VIEWS OF MOTIVATION

BEHAVIORIST THEORIES
Focus on changes in behavior that result from experiences with the environment.

COGNITIVE THEORIES
Focus on people's beliefs, expectations, and attempts to make sense of their experiences.

SOCIOCULTURAL THEORIES
Focus on individuals' participation in social environments that value and support learning.

HUMANISTIC THEORIES
Focus on the "whole person" and peoples' attempts to fulfill their total potential as human beings.

Behaviorist Views of Motivation

Behaviorism views learning as a change in observable behavior that results from experience, and it treats motivation the same way. An increase in the amount of time spent studying, for example, is viewed as evidence of motivation, so reinforcers such as praise, comments on homework, and good grades are motivators.

Critics argue that using rewards sends the wrong message about motivation and learning, and some research suggests that rewards actually decrease interest when tasks are already intrinsically motivating (Ryan & Deci, 1996).

Critics also suggest that behaviorism cannot adequately explain motivation (Perry, Turner, & Meyer, 2006). For instance, if we believe we can't complete a difficult task, we're unlikely to work hard on it. Our motivation is influenced by our beliefs, a cognitive factor not considered by behaviorists.

In spite of these criticisms, rewards are commonly used as motivators in classrooms. For example, teachers in elementary schools use praise, candy, and entertainment, such as computer games, as rewards, and middle and secondary teachers use high test scores, comments on written work, free time, and quiet compliments in attempts to motivate students.

Also, research suggests that judicious use of rewards can be motivating. For instance, praise for genuine achievement and rewards that recognize increasing competence can increase intrinsic motivation (Cameron, Pierce, & Banko, 2005). We revisit this issue later in the chapter.

Cognitive Views of Motivation

"C'mon, let's go," Melanie urges her friend Yelena as they're finishing a series of homework problems.

"Just a sec," Yelena mutters. "I'm not quite getting this one."

"Let's work on it tonight. Everybody's leaving," Melanie urges.

"Go ahead, I'll catch up to you in a minute. I know that I can figure this out. . . . I just don't get it right now."

How might we explain Yelena's behavior? She's struggling with the problem but persists anyway, and she isn't being reinforced, so behaviorism can't explain her efforts. She also commented, "I know that I can figure this out," which indicates that she believes she can resolve the discrepancy. Our beliefs are cognitive factors that behaviorism doesn't consider in either learning or motivation.

People's desire to make sense of their experiences is at the heart of both cognitive learning theory and cognitive motivation theory. "Individuals are motivated to make sense of events" (Hillebrandt & Barclay, 2017, p. 747), and "[t]he view that perception and cognition seeks to make sense of the world has a long and varied history" (Chatera & Loewenstein, 2016, p. 138). The desire to make sense of experiences is reflected in Yelena's comment, "I just don't get it right now," and it explains why she perseveres.

Social cognitive theory elaborates on these views by emphasizing the influence of modeling and learners' expectations on motivation (Schunk & Pajares, 2004). They help explain Jim's comment about Kathy, "She's so gung ho, and it's kind of interesting the way she's always telling us about the way we are . . . " His motivation increased as a result of observing her model enthusiasm and interest in the topic she was teaching.

Sociocultural Views of Motivation

Sociocultural theory focuses on "communities of learning" where the teacher and students work together to help everyone learn, and it emphasizes the importance of social interaction in motivation (McInerney, Walker, & Liem, 2011). Sociocultural theory suggests that students will be more motivated in classrooms that are supportive and cooperative than in competitive environments, and it helps us understand why people are more motivated to engage in an activity if others in their social group are doing the same.

Some experts suggest that a **motivational zone of proximal development** exists (Brophy, 2010). It describes the match between a learning activity and learners' prior knowledge that's close enough to stimulate interest but not so familiar that it's boring or insignificant. For example, multiplying 243×694 would not be motivating for us, nor would calculating the effects of the moon's perigee and apogee on the earth's tides. The first is trivial, and the second is too difficult for most of us to understand or appreciate. Neither falls within our motivational zone of proximal development.

From a sociocultural perspective, our task as teachers is to design learning experiences that are familiar enough to help students see their potential value, but not so familiar that they aren't challenging.

Humanistic Views of Motivation

Behaviorism focuses on rewards (reinforcers), and cognitive theories focus on thinking—making sense of our experiences—in their explanations for motivation. Humanistic views of motivation, which became popular in the mid-20th century, suggest that both of these approaches are too narrow. These theories assert that it's impossible to fully understand motivation without taking people's needs, emotions, attitudes, and even their physical state—in addition to their thoughts and behaviors—into account (Whitehead, 2017). This represents an emphasis on the "whole person" and views motivation as people's attempts to fulfill their total potential as human beings and become "self-actualized" (Schunk et al., 2014).

Humanistic psychology is experiencing a resurgence. "[O]ne of the greatest rebirths of the humanistic movement in the last 50 years . . . comes in the form of a global movement of humanistic skills, termed "soft skills" by business and industry, and "social-emotional learning" in education (Starcher & Allen, 2016, p. 227). (You might want to review your study of social-emotional learning in Chapter 3.)

Carl Rogers, a psychologist who founded "person-centered" therapy, and Abraham Maslow, famous for his hierarchy of needs (we discuss his hierarchy in the next section of the chapter), were the two most prominent leaders in the humanistic movement, and both emphasized people's attempts to become self-actualized (Maslow, 1968, 1970; Rogers, 1963). Rogers introduced the concept of **unconditional positive regard (UPR)**, treating people in general, and students in particular, as if they are innately worthy, regardless of their behavior, and he argued that UPR is essential if people are going to reach their maximum potential (Rogers & Freiberg, 1994).

Unconditional positive regard isn't as simple as it appears. Parents usually feel it for their small children, but as they get older, their regard often becomes "conditional" and depends on factors such as high grades or choosing the right partner or career (Kohn, 2005a). Outside the home, regard is almost always conditional, and in schools, high achievers are regarded more positively than their lower-achieving peers, as are students who are well behaved or excel in extracurricular activities such as music or sports.

On the other hand, when people are afforded UPR, powerful results can occur. Research indicates that children who are afforded UPR in the home develop a greater sense of autonomy (Roth, Kanat-Maymon, & Assor, 2016), and they develop more positive personality traits, such as conscientiousness and agreeableness (Rocha Lopes, van Putten, & Moormann, 2015). In schools, "Students who felt unconditionally accepted by their teachers were more likely to be interested in learning and to enjoy challenging academic tasks, instead of just doing schoolwork because they had to" (Kohn, 2005b, p. 21). And others state the case even more strongly. "Being recognized and affirmed by a powerful adult can be life-changing for a young person" (Benson, 2016, p. 23). UPR doesn't suggest that teachers lower expectations for students or allow them to behave as they please. Rather, it can mean, for instance, that a middle school teacher takes a misbehaving student out in the hall, reminds the student in no uncertain terms that his behavior is unacceptable and won't be tolerated. (Notice that the focus here is on the misbehavior, and not the person.) Then, when the student returns to the classroom, they're back to square one. The misbehavior is no commentary on the student's intrinsic worth as a human being, and the teacher's behavior toward the student is as it was before the incident.

The theoretical views you've seen here provide the conceptual framework for studying motivation in more detail. Using this framework, we examine the topics outlined in Figure 10.3.

Each influences motivation to learn, and each is grounded in the theoretical views we've just discussed. We begin by examining needs.

MyLab Education Self-Check 10.1

The Influence of Needs on Motivation to Learn

10.2 Describe learners' needs and how they influence motivation to learn.

Ed Psych and You

Think about the number of times you've said something like, "I need to get organized," "I need to lose weight," or simply, "I need to pick up some milk at the store." How do these statements influence your motivation?

As we see in *Ed Psych and You*, the notion of *needs* is pervasive in our lives and we use the term so often that we rarely think about it. In motivation theory, a **need** is an internal force or drive to attain or to avoid a certain state or object (Schunk et al., 2014). We can see how needs influence motivation. For instance, when we say, "I need to get organized," the need pushes (motivates) us to reach the desired state—being organized.

Food, water, and sex are considered to be the most basic needs in all species, because they're necessary for survival. Getting them is the force, and survival is the desired

Figure 10.3 A conceptual framework for motivation

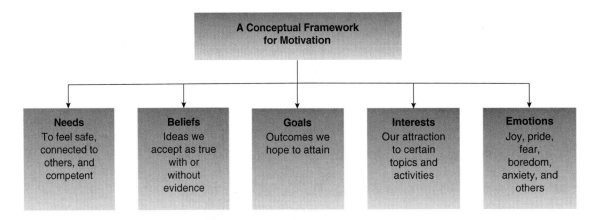

state. Human needs are more complex, however, and in this section, we examine the influence of three sets of needs on motivation to learn:

- Maslow's hierarchy of needs
- The need for self-determination
- The need to preserve self-worth

Maslow's Hierarchy of Needs

Earlier we said that humanistic views of motivation emphasize the *whole person—* physical, social, emotional, intellectual, and aesthetic. Maslow's (1968, 1987) hierarchy of needs is grounded in this holistic view. As we look at Maslow's hierarchy, outlined in Figure 10.4, we see the whole person reflected in it. For instance, we see the *physical* person in survival and safety needs, the *social* person in belonging needs, the *emotional* person in self-esteem needs, and the intellectual and aesthetic person in the need for self-actualization.

Maslow (1968, 1970) described human needs as existing in two groups: *deficiency needs* and *growth needs*.

Deficiency Needs

Deficiency needs are those that energize people to meet them when unfulfilled. *Survival, safety, belonging,* and *self-esteem* are the deficiency needs in the hierarchy, and, according to Maslow, people won't move to a higher need unless the one below it is met. So, for example, if people's safety needs are not being met, they won't move to the need for belonging or any above it. Representing the deficiency needs as a series of steps in Figure 10.4 reminds us of this idea.

Growth Needs

After all deficiency needs are met, people can move to growth needs, needs in intellectual achievement and aesthetic appreciation that increase as people have experiences with them. Ultimately, growth can lead to self-actualization, reaching our full potential and becoming all we're capable of being. In contrast with deficiency needs, the needs for intellectual achievement and aesthetic appreciation are never "met." For instance, as we develop a greater understanding of a certain area, such as literature, our interest in it increases rather than decreases. Using Maslow's work, we

Figure 10.4 Maslow's hierarchy of needs

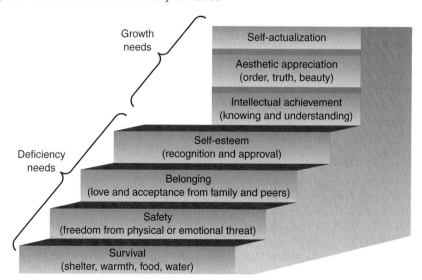

SOURCE: Maslow, Abraham H., Frager, Robert D. (Editor), Fadiman, James (Editor), *Motivation and Personality*, 3rd ed., © 1987. Printed and electronically reproduced by permission of Pearson Education, Inc., Upper Saddle River, New Jersey.

can explain this by saying we are responding to our need for intellectual achievement. Similarly, we can explain some people's continuing desire to experience fine art or music by saying they're responding to their need for aesthetic appreciation. Engaging in these activities also gives them pleasure and can lead to *peak experiences*, a concept that originated with Maslow.

Evaluating Maslow's Work

Maslow's work has been criticized on three grounds. First, it's unable to consistently predict people's behavior. For instance, we've all known of individuals—such as Stephen Hawking, the late world renowned, but paralyzed, theoretical physicist—who make dramatic achievements in spite of illness or disabling conditions. Maslow's work would predict that this could not happen, because, according to his description, people will not move to growth needs unless deficiency needs are met.

Second, it's difficult to validate his hierarchy with traditional research methods. "The hierarchy of needs has been heavily criticized on the grounds that it is unamenable to scientific validation" (Winston, 2016, p. 143).

Third, more recent critics suggest that Maslow's emphasis on self-actualization implies an approach to personal fulfillment and happiness that comes from within, instead of connecting with others. In contrast, these critics assert, "Study after study shows that good social relationships are the strongest, most consistent predictor there is of a happy life" (Whippman, 2017, para. 13). They also note that this inward orientation has resulted in Americans spending less and less time actually connecting with other people. For instance, more of us now eat meals alone than with others, and teens and young millennials aren't just "hanging out" with friends as they have in the past, instead replacing real-world interactions with tablets and smartphones (Whippman, 2016). This represents a chilly, impersonal, and unsatisfying version of self-fulfillment, critics argue. Ultimately, they assert, "Maslow's hierarchy of needs too easily devolves into self-absorption. It's time to put it away" (Brooks, 2017b, para. 16).

On the other hand, his work is intuitively sensible and appealing, and it helps explain many events in our lives. For instance, after we first meet someone, we're likely to say, "He seemed really nice" (hopefully not, "Wow, what a jerk"), rather than "He sure seemed smart." We first react to how friendly, outgoing, and "human" people are, not how bright or successful they seem to be. The same likely applies to your instructors; you first react to their personality, support, and helpfulness, not their intellect or achievements. Maslow's hierarchy suggests that personal, social, and emotional needs precede intellectual ones, our day-to-day experiences corroborate this suggestion, and research supports the idea that emotions are important in both motivation and learning (Dougherty & Sharkey, 2017; McBride, Chung, & Robertson, 2016). (We examine the influence of emotions on motivation in detail later in the chapter.)

Perhaps most important, it makes sense that students will learn less if they're hungry, tired, or don't feel physically or emotionally safe in school. Schools respond by providing free or reduced-cost breakfasts and lunches, and school safety is a high priority throughout our country. Maslow's work reminds us that the human side of teaching is essential, and ignoring it will have a negative impact on both motivation and learning.

The Need for Self-Determination

Self-determination is the need to act on and control one's environment, and having choices and making decisions are intrinsically motivating (Ryan & Deci, 2000). According to self-determination theory, people have three innate psychological needs: *competence, autonomy,* and *relatedness* (Levesque, Stanek, Zuehlke, & Ryan, 2004; Ryan & Deci, 2000). Let's see how they influence motivation.

MyLab Education

Video Example 10.2

Maslow's work helps us understand why students will learn less if they come to school hungry. Here, sixth-grade teacher Dani Ramsay, describes a program called "Breakfast in the Classroom" to help accommodate some of Maslow's deficiency needs.

The Need for Competence

> # Ed Psych and You
>
> Think about your interactions with people or peers in your classes. How often do they attempt to demonstrate how much they know about a topic, how good they are at some skill, or simply how "smart" they are? Why do you think this is the case?

Self-determination theory would answer our question in *Ed Psych and You* by saying that people are attempting to meet their need for **competence**, the ability to function effectively in the environment. This need was originally described by Robert White (1959) in a paper that's become a classic. He suggested that people acquire proficiency and skill "because it satisfies an intrinsic need to deal with the environment" (p. 318).

Our need for competence can be explained at several levels. At its most basic, if an organism can't function effectively in its environment, it isn't likely to survive. Competent people succeed and grow in their careers, whereas those less competent languish and stagnate, and competent students succeed and find school satisfying and rewarding (Schunk et al., 2014).

Evidence that knowledge and skills are increasing is the most important factor influencing students' perceptions of competence, and this helps explain why high teacher expectations, challenging activities, experiences that evoke curiosity, and praise for genuine accomplishment are motivating. Meeting expectations and challenges, understanding novel or puzzling experiences, and the praise provide evidence that our competence is increasing. In contrast, completing trivial tasks, solving predictable problems, and receiving grades that haven't been earned provide little evidence about developing competence, so they don't increase motivation.

The Need for Autonomy

Do you prefer to study at home, in the library, or perhaps in a coffee shop? Would you rebel if someone dictated how and where you had to study? These questions relate to **autonomy**, independence, and the ability to alter the environment when necessary. It's the second innate need described by self-determination theory, and lack of autonomy causes stress and reduces intrinsic motivation. For instance, it has historically been believed that the stress of assembly line work results from workers having little control over their environments (Park & Jang, 2017). And extreme stress can become toxic and destructive. "So, the stress that kills . . . is characterized by a lack of a sense of control over one's fate" (Velasquez-Manoff, 2013; para. 7). We want to feel that we are in control of our lives, and when we don't, motivation decreases.

Autonomy and competence are strongly related. As learners' competence increases, their perceptions of autonomy also increase (Bruning, Shraw, & Norby, 2011). So if we can help students feel competent, we also help them feel autonomous, and motivation and learning both increase. (We offer some suggestions for increasing our students' perceptions of autonomy later in this section.)

The Need for Relatedness

Relatedness, the feeling of being connected to others in one's social environment and feeling worthy of love and respect, is the third innate need described by self-determination theory. Relatedness and Maslow's concept of *belonging* are often treated synonymously, and the need for relatedness is also similar to the need for *affiliation* as described by early motivational researchers (e.g., Exline, 1962; Terhune, 1968).

We can help meet our students' needs for relatedness by communicating unconditional positive regard and a genuine commitment to their learning. Students are more

MyLab Education
Video Example 10.3
Because genuine accomplishment indicates that competence is increasing, praising students for effort and evidence of accomplishment is one of the suggestions for capitalizing on needs to increase students' motivation to learn. Here, social studies teacher, Annie Rients, praises her students' descriptions and the quality of the examples they provide in their study of ancient Rome.

engaged—behaviorally, cognitively, and emotionally—in classroom activities when they believe their teachers understand, like, and empathize with them. They also report more interest in their class work, behave in more socially responsible ways, and are more likely to seek help when they need it (Cornelius-White, 2007).

Consistent with sociocultural theory, we also help students meet their needs for relatedness by involving them in learning activities, ensuring that no one is left out, and creating a classroom environment where students treat each other with courtesy and respect.

Self-determination theory is powerful, vibrant, and widely applied, and it's been used as a theoretical framework for topics ranging as widely as people's emotional well-being (Emery, Heath, & Mills, 2016) to new teacher satisfaction (Green & Muñoz, 2016), students' tendency to be physically fit (Cuevas, García-López, & Serra-Olivares, 2016), and even environmental activism (Cook, Fielding, & Louis, 2016). It has important implications for our teaching, which we examine later in the chapter.

Diversity: Learner Differences in the Need for Self-Determination

Self-determination theory describes general patterns in people's needs for competence, autonomy, and relatedness, and virtually everyone, regardless of culture, gender, or socioeconomic status, has these needs. Their influence on motivation can vary among groups and individuals, however (Rogoff, 2003). For instance, with respect to competence, *demonstrating* that we're knowledgeable and skilled in school or the workplace tends to be more important in mainstream American culture than in East Asian cultures, where self-improvement is more strongly valued (Li, 2005; Sedikides & Gregg, 2008).

Gender differences also exist. For instance, girls tend to be more easily discouraged by failure than are boys (Bian, Leslie, & Cimpian, 2017), and boys' perceptions of their competence tend to be higher than girls' in spite of the fact that girls earn higher grades (Voyer & Voyer, 2014).

With respect to autonomy, research indicates that some Native American groups give young children more autonomy in decision making than do other parents in our country (Ayers, Kulis, & Tsethlikai, 2017), whereas African American parents tend to give their children less autonomy (Smetana & Cottman, 2006). Also, while being allowed to make choices increases learner autonomy, Asian students may prefer letting people they trust, such as parents or teachers, make choices for them (Vansteenkiste, Zhou, Lens, & Soenens, 2005).

Differences in learners' need for relatedness also exist. Some Asian students, for example, meet this need by excelling in school and gaining the approval of their parents and teachers (Li, 2005). And, while the need for parental and teacher approval may be higher in some cultural groups than others, achievement and parental approval is important to virtually all students (Wang, Hill, & Hofkens, 2014).

Technology, Learning, and Development: The Influence of Technology on Self-Determination

Paul, one of your authors, was at dinner with his wife recently, and we were both struck by the fact that two pairs of young couples at each of two other tables in the same area of the restaurant were doing no talking; all eight people were intently studying their smartphones. This behavior illustrates a pervasive pattern; wherever we go, individuals are hunched over their phones, tablets, and laptops, and they drive with phones glued to their ears, in some cases violating state or city laws. Even people in fitness clubs will—usually slowly—do exercises on one of the machines while simultaneously studying their phones.

Some researchers suggest that technology is literally addictive and cite Instagram as an example. "[S]ome photos attract many likes, while others fall short. Users chase the next big hit of likes by posting one photo after another and return to the site regularly to support their friends" (Alter, 2017, p. 9). Others suggest that many people experience "Facebook addiction syndrome" (Rosen, Whaling, Rab, Carrier, & Cheever, 2013).

Additional concerns have been raised. When people spend a great deal of time on social networking sites, the anonymous intimacy can give them the feeling that their social media "friends" are true friends when they likely are not (Zagorski, 2017). Further, an expanding body of research indicates that social media may be having an adverse effect on marriages and other interpersonal relationships (McDaniel, Drouin, & Cravens, 2017). And the mental health of young people is being affected as well. For instance, a widely publicized study of young adults found that increased use of multiple social media platforms is strongly associated with both depression and anxiety (Primak et al., 2017). Additional research indicates that since smartphone use has become widespread, teens are less likely to date or work and are much less likely to hang out with friends, instead spending time in their rooms on social media (Twenge, 2017).

Even the mainstream press has sounded the alarm, suggesting that technology is having a negative impact on our lives, echoing the association with depression and anxiety, and asking—barely tongue in cheek—if technology is evil (Brooks, 2017a; Douthat, 2017). "[T]here are also excellent reasons to think that online life breeds narcissism, alienation and depression, . . . and that it takes more than it gives from creativity and deep thought" (Douthat, 2017, para. 8).

Without question, however, people are motivated to spend time on the Internet and particularly on social media. The question is, "Why?" What is it about technology that is motivating to the point of addiction? Self-determination theory provides some possible answers. First, strong social connection is one aspect of behavioral addiction (Alter, 2017). Connecting with others through technology is rewarding; it makes us feel as if we're not alone in the world. Self-determination theory can explain this by saying it meets our need for relatedness. And talking about ourselves, giving advice, and sharing information that makes us look good can increase our sense of self-worth. (We examine the need for self-worth in the next section.)

Meeting the need for competence also helps explain technology's impact on motivation. The ability to manipulate devices to carry out once-laborious tasks, such as finding an obscure location in an unfamiliar city without struggling with a map, quickly and conveniently accessing information about virtually any topic from the convenience of an easy chair or coffee shop, or downloading and using a new app, makes us feel "smart" and contributes to our perceptions of competence (Nikou & Economides, 2017). These devices' ease of use may also increase people's motivation to work with them (Jeno, Grytnes, & Vandvik, 2017). We like technology because it makes our lives easier and becoming skilled with it makes us feel competent.

And certain forms of educational technology can also contribute to feelings of competence. For instance, drill-and-practice software allows learners to proceed at their own rate, provides corrective feedback, and reinforces learning progress, all of which contributes to perceptions of competence.

Autonomy is also a factor. People using their smartphones and tablets have complete autonomy—they can choose when, where, and how long they use their devices, and *they* choose the topics of discussion or inquiry (Bakke & Henry, 2015).

Technology in general and social media, in particular present challenges for us, first as people, and second as teachers. Addictions aren't healthy, and, as the experience in the restaurant illustrates, we don't want to lose face-to-face communication (Whippman, 2016, 2017). It is "the most human—and humanizing—thing we do. It's where we learn to listen. It's where we develop the capacity for empathy. . . . But these days, we find ways around conversation" (Turkle, 2015, p. 3). We semi-hide from each other even as we're constantly connected through social media. We simply must put down our devices and talk to each other (Turkle, 2015; Whippman, 2017).

Technology also presents challenges for us as teachers. For instance, the autonomy we enjoy with our devices in the outside world doesn't exist in school. Learners rarely get to choose the topics they study, and times and locations for technology use are specified for students. This helps us understand why technology use in classrooms is neither as motivating nor as widely used as many people believe it to be (Stanhope & Rectanus, 2015). "A mountain of evidence indicates that teachers have been painfully slow to transform the ways they teach, despite that massive influx of new technology into their classrooms. The student-centered, hands-on, personalized instruction envisioned by ed-tech proponents remains the exception" (Herold, 2015, para. 2).

Our goal here is not to paint a bleak picture of technology. We know it's motivating, in some cases to the point of addiction, and self-determination theory helps us understand why. We also know that it is a virtually unlimited source of information and has the potential to make our lives and our teaching easier and more efficient. We examine these issues in each of the chapters of this text.

The Need to Preserve Self-Worth

"I'm a genius; I'm a genius," Andrew, an eighth-grader, enthusiastically shouts to his mom as he bounces into the house after school. "I got a 97 on my history test, and I didn't study a lick. I'm a genius; I'm a genius."

We can explain Andrew's behavior using the concept of **self-worth** (or self-esteem, as it is also commonly called), which is an emotional reaction to or an evaluation of the self (Schunk et al., 2014). Self-worth theory suggests that people have an innate need to protect their sense of self-worth and accept themselves as they are. According to self-determination theory, as we saw earlier, we all have a basic need for competence, which is often reflected in our efforts to "look smart."

Self-worth theorists would explain Andrew's behavior by suggesting that we appear to have higher ability—look smarter—if we're able to accomplish tasks without having to work hard (Covington, 1992). So, by emphasizing that he got his high score without studying, Andrew was implying that he had high ability, which enhanced his feelings of self-worth.

Some interesting developmental patterns in learners' perceptions of effort and ability exist. For instance, when asked, most kindergarteners say they're smart. Young children assume that people who try hard are smart, and people who are smart try hard. However, as students move through school, they begin to equate effort with low ability, and simultaneously their need to *appear* smart increases (Bishop & Johnson, 2011). For instance, we've all heard statements such as, "He isn't all that sharp, but he really works hard."

Because of their need to be perceived as having high ability, older students may hide the fact that they've studied hard for a test, for instance, so if they do well, they can, at least in the eyes of their peers, attribute their success to being smart. Others engage in "self-handicapping" strategies to protect their self-worth, such as procrastinating ("I could have done a lot better, but I didn't start studying until after midnight"), making excuses ("This test was so tricky"), anxiety ("I understand the stuff, but I get nervous in tests"), or making a point of not trying. If they didn't try, failure isn't evidence of low ability (Covington, 1998; Seli, Dembo, & Crocker, 2009). Self-handicapping behaviors have been found in a range of academic areas, including even physical education (Standage, Treasure, Hooper, & Kuczka, 2007). They are most common in low achievers, who may choose to not seek help when it's needed (Marchand & Skinner, 2007).

We examine ways that you can respond to these tendencies in the next section.

Using Educational Psychology in Teaching: Suggestions for Capitalizing on Needs to Increase Your Students' Motivation to Learn

Understanding learners' needs has important implications for us as we attempt to increase our students' motivation to learn. The following suggestions can help in our efforts to apply this understanding with our students.

- Treat students as people first.
- Involve students in decision making.
- Praise students for effort and evidence of accomplishment.
- Avoid social comparisons among students.

Treat Students as People First. "Treat students as people first" means that our foremost commitment is to students as human beings who are worthy of the respect that all people deserve, regardless of their behavior. Treating students as human beings helps meet their needs for belonging/relatedness (Cornelius-White, 2007), and it also applies the concept of unconditional positive regard. To see an example, let's look at a conversation Kathy has with Mason after school.

As she is working in her room after school, Mason pokes his head into the room.

"Come in," she says with a smile. "How's our developing writer?"

"I just came by to say I hope you're not upset with me, complaining so much about all the work."

"Not at all. . . . I haven't given it a second thought."

"You already know how much you've done for me. . . . You believed in me when the rest of the world wrote me off. . . . My drug conviction is off my record now, and I'm okay. I couldn't have made it without you. You made me work, and you put in all kinds of extra time with me. You wouldn't let me give up on myself. I was headed for trouble, and now . . . I'm going to college."

"We all need a nudge now and then." Kathy smiles. "That's what I'm here for. I appreciate your kind words, but I didn't do it; you did. . . . Now, scoot. I'm working on a rough assignment for you tomorrow."

"Mrs. Brewster, you're relentless." Mason waves as he heads out the door.

Students know when their teachers are committed to them as people. Asking a student to stop by after class because she doesn't seem to be herself is an example, as was separating Mason's drug conviction from his innate worth as a person. And research suggests that this commitment may be particularly important for boys; " . . . boys need to *feel* their teachers—their warmth, their mastery, their inspiration—before opening up to invest themselves in learning" (Reichert, 2010, p. 27). Kathy demonstrated the unconditional positive regard with Mason and the rest of her students that's rare in the everyday world, but important to us all.

Treating students "as people first" in no way implies that we lower our learning or behavioral expectations for them, as suggested by Mason's grumbling about how hard Kathy makes her students work. She demonstrated commitment to her students by maintaining high standards, helping them meet the standards, and emphasizing the value of what they were learning. She also expected her students to treat her and each other with the same respect she demonstrated with them.

Involve Students in Decision Making. Involving our students in decision making can help meet students' need for autonomy and can also contribute to a positive classroom climate. Allowing students to makes choices is one of the most effective ways to do this, and it can involve simple actions. Let's look in Kathy's class again.

"Just a reminder," Kathy says to her students near the end of the class period, "group presentations on the Renaissance are on Thursday and Friday. You decide what groups will present on each day. Remember, we're all doing our best; we're not competing with each other. . . . Also, for those who chose to write the paper on the Renaissance instead of making a group presentation, we agreed that they're due on Friday."

Kathy involved her students in decision making in two simple ways. First, she gave them the choice of either making a group presentation or writing a paper, and second, she had the students decide the order of the group presentations. These simple moves can increase students' motivation. And, significantly, letting the students make these decisions required no extra effort on her part—important because teaching is very demanding in terms of time and energy.

Additional suggestions for promoting feelings of autonomy by involving students in decision making include:

- Soliciting student input in creating classroom rules and procedures.
- Encouraging students to set and monitor their own learning goals.
- Asking for and accepting different opinions during class discussions.
- Conducting classroom meetings to discuss issues, such as student behavior and treatment of others. Even young children are capable of providing this type of input.
- Modeling and emphasizing the influence of effort and strategy use on achievement.

Modeling is one of the most powerful strategies we have for dealing with students' tendencies to equate effort with lack of ability. Let's look at another brief comment Kathy makes during a class discussion.

She has just finished providing her students with a number of facts about the Crusades and the Renaissance, and Jeremy pipes up, "Man, Mrs. Brewster, how do you know all this stuff?"

"I study," Kathy says simply. " . . . I study every night to keep up with you people, and the harder I study, the smarter I get. . . . If I struggle, I redouble my efforts and maybe change the way I'm attacking the problem. . . . And it really feels good when I get it."

In spite of suggestions to the contrary, if the classroom climate is positive and students respect a teacher, the teacher enjoys high status with his or her students. This is obviously the case with Kathy. When a respected teacher models the relationship between effort and increased ability, exerting effort becomes emotionally acceptable to students, and their need to communicate accomplishment without effort—as Andrew did at the beginning of our discussion of self-worth—decreases. It's the most powerful tool we have, and, as with the decisions Kathy allowed her students to make, it requires no extra effort on our part.

Praise Students for Effort and Evidence of Accomplishment.   Let's look again at the short conversation between Kathy and Mason as he walked into her room after school.

"Sheesh, Mrs. Brewster, that assignment was impossible," Mason grumbles as he comes into the classroom. "You're working us to death."

"That's good for you," Kathy smiles. "I know you're working hard, but it's paying off. Look at how much both your writing and your thinking have improved as a result of your effort . . . . Hard work is the key to everything."

In saying to Mason, "Look at how much both your writing and your thinking have improved as a result of your effort," Kathy praised him for his accomplishments while simultaneously linking increased ability to effort.

Praise for genuine accomplishment can increase motivation to learn because the praise provides students with evidence that their competence is increasing (Cameron et al., 2005). Developing perceptions of competence is one of the most powerful motivating factors that exists, and, in fact, if we could make all our students feel competent, motivation and learning issues would disappear.

Notice also that Kathy said, "Look at how much both your writing and your thinking have improved as a result of your effort" but didn't say, "Look at how good a writer you are" or "Look at how good a thinker you are." This is a subtle but important difference. Research suggests that praise worded in "person" terms, such as "You are a smart girl," can decrease motivation, particularly if learners later experience failure, whereas praise worded in "process" terms, such as "you tried hard" or "you found a good way to do it," can increase motivation (Zentall & Morris, 2012). For those of you who have children, this pattern also exists with mothers as they interact with their sons and daughters (Pomerantz & Kempner, 2013).

Self-worth theory helps us understand these findings. For instance, if children are told they're "smart" and they later fail, the failure suggests that they might not be so smart after all, which can detract from their sense of self-worth, and subsequently, their motivation. On the other hand, if they're praised for working hard, and they later fail, the failure suggests that effort, not intelligence, is the cause and by redoubling their effort or changing their strategies, they can succeed. In either case, motivation increases.

Avoid Social Comparisons Among Students.   Social comparisons among students are destructive because they emphasize competition instead of content mastery. Practices such as writing distributions of scores on the board or announcing the number of people who got A's on a test divide classes into winners and losers, and for students who are consistently at the bottom end of the distribution, motivation decreases (Shin, Lee, & Seo, 2017). Few people continue to play games in which they consistently lose. To preserve their sense of self-worth, students conclude that what they're studying isn't important and give up.

In contrast, comments such as Kathy saying "Remember, we're all doing our best; we're not competing with each other" remind students that effort and increasing competence are more important than "winning." Consistently emphasized over time, they can make a difference in both motivation and learning.

As with all suggestions, the ones we offer here won't work all the time or with all students. And, in the real world, you won't turn every student into a motivated learner. You can make a difference with many, however, and for them, you will have made an immeasurable contribution to their lives.

MyLab Education Application Exercise 10.1: Applying Theories of Motivation in Fifth Grade

In this exercise, you will be asked to analyze a fifth-grade teacher's attempts to capitalize on learner needs to increase motivation to learn.

Classroom Connections

Capitalizing on Students' Needs to Increase Motivation to Learn in Classrooms

Maslow's Hierarchy of Needs

1. Maslow described people's needs in a hierarchy with deficiency needs—survival, safety, belonging, and self-esteem—preceding the growth needs. Address students' deficiency and growth needs both in instruction and in the way you interact with students.

   - **Elementary:** A fourth-grade teacher calls on all students to involve everyone and promote a sense of belonging in his classroom. He makes them feel safe by helping them respond correctly when they are unable to answer.

   - **Middle School:** To help meet learners' belonging needs, a seventh-grade teacher asks two of the more popular girls in her class to introduce a new girl to other students and to take her under their wings until she gets acquainted.

   - **High School:** To address learners' growth needs, an American government teacher brings in a newspaper columnist's political opinion piece, comments that it was interesting to her, and asks students for their opinions on the issue.

Learners' Needs for Self-Determination

2. Self-determination theory suggests that people have innate needs for competence, autonomy, and relatedness. Design challenging learning tasks that, when completed, can provide evidence for increasing competence, and emphasize these accomplishments when students succeed.

   - **Elementary:** A fifth-grade teacher drops an ice cube into a cup of water and a second cube into a cup of alcohol and asks them why it floats in one and sinks in the other. He guides students' efforts until they solve the problem and then praises them for their thinking.

   - **Middle School:** A math teacher has students bring in a challenging "problem of the week." He helps them solve each problem and comments on how much their problem solving is improving.

   - **High School:** A biology teacher guides a discussion of our skeletal system until students understand the function of the skull, rib cage, and other bones, and then comments on how good the students are getting at analyzing our body systems.

3. Learners' perceptions of autonomy increase when teachers ask them for input into classroom procedures, involve them in learning activities, and give them feedback on assessments. Create a classroom environment that helps meet learners' needs for autonomy.

   - **Elementary:** A fourth-grade teacher holds periodic class meetings in which she encourages students to offer suggestions for improving the classroom environment.

   - **Middle School:** A pre-algebra teacher returns all tests and quizzes the following day and discusses frequently missed problems in detail. He comments frequently on students' continually improving skills.

   - **High School:** In a simulation, a world history teacher asks students to identify specific archeological evidence for sites that represent different civilizations. When successful, she comments that the students' ability to link evidence to conclusions has improved significantly.

4. Learners' needs for relatedness are met when teachers communicate a commitment to students both as people and as learners.

   - **Elementary:** A first-grade teacher greets her students each morning at the door with a hug, "high five," or handshake. She tells them what a good day they're going to have.

   - **Middle School:** A seventh-grade teacher calls a parent to express concern about a student whose behavior and attitude seem to have changed.

   - **High School:** A geometry teacher in an urban school conducts help sessions after school on Mondays through Thursdays. When they come in for extra help, she also encourages students to talk about their personal lives and their hopes for the future.

Learners' Needs to Preserve Self-Worth

5. Self-worth theory suggests that people link self-worth to high ability. Emphasize that ability can be increased with effort.

   - **Elementary:** When her second-graders succeed with word problems during their seatwork, a teacher comments, "You're really understanding what we're doing. The harder we work, the smarter we get."

   - **Middle School:** A life-science teacher comments, "You're really seeing the connections between animals' body structures and their ability to adapt. This is not an easy idea to grasp and you should feel good about figuring this out."

   - **High School:** As students' understanding of balancing equations increases, a chemistry teacher comments, "Balancing equations is important in chemistry and I know it isn't easy, but you people are really improving with this stuff."

MyLab Education Self-Check 10.2

The Influence of Beliefs on Motivation to Learn

10.3 Explain how learners' beliefs impact their motivation to learn.

What do the following statements have in common?

- "If I study hard for the next test, I'll do well."
- "Learning a foreign language doesn't come naturally for me, but with some more work, I'm going to be good at it by the end of the year."
- "I'm not that crazy about algebra, but I need to understand it. I want to major in engineering in college, and I know I'll need it."

Each describes a **belief**, an idea we accept as true without necessarily having evidence to support it. As with needs, people's beliefs strongly influence their motivation to learn (Brady et al., 2016), and in this section we'll see how as we examine:

- Expectations: Beliefs about future outcomes
- Mindset: Beliefs about intelligence
- Self-efficacy: Beliefs about capability
- Attainment, utility, and cost: Beliefs about value
- Attributions: Beliefs about causes of performance

Expectations: Beliefs About Outcomes

Ed Psych and You

Do you like to play games? Do you like playing all games or only certain ones? Why do you enjoy some and not others? Is succeeding in some games more important to you than succeeding in others?

Look again at the statement, "If I study hard for the next test, I'll do well." It describes an **expectation**, a belief about a future outcome—in this case a high score on the next test (Schunk & Zimmerman, 2006). The motivating influence of expectations can be described using **expectancy × value theory**, which says that people are motivated to engage in a task to the extent that they *expect* to succeed on the task *times* the *value* they place on the success (Wigfield & Eccles, 1992, 2000). (We examine the influence of task value on motivation later in this section.) The "×" implies multiplication, and it's important because anything times zero is zero. So, if we don't expect to succeed on a task, we won't be motivated, regardless of how much we value success on it. Similarly, if we don't value success on a task, our motivation will also be low, even if success is assured. This relates to the questions in *Ed Psych and You*. For most people, the games they most enjoy are those in which they generally succeed, winning more often than not. Their expectations for success are quite high, or they quit playing. Only rarely do people continue to play if they usually lose.

Students who expect to succeed persist longer on tasks, choose more challenging activities, and achieve higher than those whose expectations are lower (Eccles, Wigfield, & Schiefele, 1998; Wigfield, 1994).

Past experience is the primary factor influencing expectations. Students who usually succeed expect to do so in the future, and the opposite is true for their less successful peers. This helps us understand why promoting motivation to learn is such a challenge when working with low achievers. Because they have a history of failure, their motivation to learn is low as a result of low expectations for success. This, combined with their need to preserve their sense of self-worth, creates a problem that is doubly difficult for all of us who teach.

Designing learning experiences that ensure some degree of success is the only way we can increase motivation to learn in students whose success expectations are low. This is, of course, an enormous challenge, but in time, and with effort, it can be done. (We discuss ways of doing so later in the chapter.)

Mindset: Beliefs About Intelligence

Our beliefs about intelligence also affect our motivation. To see how, let's look at the words of Sarah, an eighth-grader, as she comments on her math ability: "My brother, I, and my mom aren't good at math at all, we inherited the 'not good at math gene' from my mom and I am good at English, but I am not good at math" (Ryan, Ryan, Arbuthnot, & Samuels, 2007, p. 5).

APA Top 20 Principles

This section focuses on Principle 1: *Students' beliefs or perceptions about intelligence and ability affect their cognitive functioning and learning*—from the *Top 20 Principles from Psychology for PreK–12 Teaching and Learning*.

Sarah is describing a **fixed mindset**, a belief that intelligence or ability is stable (fixed) and can't be changed over time or for different task conditions (Dweck, 2008, 2016). (An *entity view of intelligence* is also commonly used to describe a fixed mindset.) According to Sarah, "some have it and some don't," and there is little she can do about it.

Compare this view with our second statement at the beginning of this section: "Learning a foreign language doesn't come naturally for me, but with some more work, I'm going to be good at it by the end of the year." This statement reflects a **growth mindset** (also called an *incremental view of intelligence*), the belief that intelligence, or ability, can be increased with effort. People with a growth mindset essentially equate ability with learning (Schunk et al., 2014).

The concept of *mindset* was originated by Carol Dweck, whose book, *Mindset: The New Psychology of Success* (2016), has received a great deal of attention both in academic circles and in the popular media. Dweck's research suggests that mindset is a powerful factor in motivation, it begins to appear in childhood, and it impacts aspects of our lives ranging from work, sports, parenting, and personal relationships to academic success. For instance, people with a growth mindset are more successful in the workplace. "We found that employees' mindset had a direct relationship with job performance—employees with a more incremental mindset had higher job performance" (Zingoni & Corey, 2017, p. 42). Additional research suggests that mindset is even more important than skills because skills can be acquired, whereas mindset impacts people's entire approach to their work (Kennedy, Carroll, & Francoeur, 2013). Mindset even influences consumer behavior, suggesting that people with growth mindsets seek products that help them reach personal goals, improve, and learn (Murphy & Dweck, 2016).

Mindset also has important implications for parents and the way they praise their children. Dweck's (2008, 2016) research suggests that children who are repeatedly told how smart they are become sensitive to failure, shy away from new challenges, and acquire the belief that effort indicates low ability (our earlier example, "He's not that smart, but he really works hard"). As a result, their performance declines. Instead, she stresses, parents should praise their children for qualities they can control, such as concentration, effort, and the strategies they use.

In school settings, students with growth mindsets more conscientiously attend to—and try to correct—mistakes than do students with fixed mindsets (Schroder et al., 2017). Mindset also helps us understand why learners engage in self-handicapping behaviors. Failure suggests a lack of ability, so if students have fixed mindsets, they protect their self-worth by avoiding situations that reflect negatively on their ability, and motivation and learning decrease. On the other hand, if learners believe that ability can be increased with effort—growth mindsets—challenge and failure merely suggest that more effort or better strategies are needed. As a result, their motivation and learning increase, and successes provide evidence that their ability is increasing (Schunk & Zimmerman, 2006).

Creating awareness is our primary goal in writing this section. For instance, we know that our brains are plastic, and high-quality, concrete, meaningful experiences can rewire our brains—literally make us smarter. Understanding this fact increases the likelihood of adopting a growth mindset. In fact, we, your authors, regularly comment to each other, "Well, as we study, we get smarter." If we weren't aware of brain plasticity and the power of a growth mindset, we probably wouldn't feel this way. Hopefully, passing this kind of information along to your students can make a difference with them as well.

Self-Efficacy: Beliefs About Capability

To begin this section, let's look again at the conversation between Melanie and Yelena, which introduced our discussion of cognitive theories of motivation.

"C'mon, let's go," Melanie urges her friend Yelena as they're finishing a series of homework problems in math.

"Just a sec," Yelena mutters. "I'm not quite getting this one."

"Let's work on it tonight. Everybody's leaving," Melanie urges.

"Go ahead, I'll catch up to you in a minute. I know that I can figure this out. . . . I just don't get it right now."

Yelena's statement suggests that she believes she is capable of solving this problem if she perseveres. It illustrates the concept of self-efficacy, the belief that we are capable of accomplishing a specific task (Bandura, 1997, 2004). *Self-efficacy, self-concept,* and *expectation for success* are closely related, but they aren't synonymous (Schunk, 2016). For example, if Yelena believes she is generally competent in math, we would say that she has a positive self-concept in math. **Self-efficacy** is more specific. She believes she can solve this problem and those similar to it, but it doesn't mean that she believes she will succeed in all forms of math or in other domains, such as writing essays. Also, believing she can solve this problem doesn't suggest that she will expect to succeed on her next math quiz if she doesn't study and do her homework.

The concept of self-efficacy has wide-ranging applications, and it's particularly important in the areas of health and well-being. For instance, research indicates that patients who believe they will recover fully—high self-efficacy—after total joint replacement are much more conscientious about their rehab than patients with lower self-efficacy, and, as a result, do indeed recover more completely and quickly (Fiala, Rhodes, Blanchard, & Anderson, 2013). Additional research suggests that self-efficacy, which leads to self-regulation, is the primary factor influencing whether or not young people will exercise on a regular basis (Dewar, Lubans, Morgan, & Plotnikoff, 2013).

Self-efficacy depends on four factors (see Figure 10.5). As with expectation for success, past performance on similar tasks is the most important. If you have a history of success giving oral reports in your classes, for example, your self-efficacy in this area will be high. Modeling, such as seeing others deliver excellent reports, can also increase your self-efficacy by raising expectations and providing information about the way a skill should be performed (Bandura, 1997; Kitsantas, Zimmerman, & Cleary, 2000).

Although limited in effectiveness, verbal persuasion, such as a teacher's comment, "I know you will give a fine report," can also increase self-efficacy by encouraging students to attempt challenging tasks, which increases efficacy if they succeed.

Finally, students' emotional state as well as physiological factors, such as fatigue or hunger, can influence self-efficacy. If they're anxious, for example, their working memories might be filled with thoughts of failure, so they're less likely to succeed, and self-efficacy then decreases (Linnenbrink-Garcia & Pekrun, 2011). Or, if they're too tired to study, their self-efficacy is likely to be temporarily reduced.

Self-efficacy is a component of social cognitive theory. "Self-efficacy is a central motivational variable in social cognitive theory and can affect choice of activities, effort, and persistence" (Schunk et al., 2014, p. 145). For instance, compared to low-efficacy students, high-efficacy learners attempt more challenging tasks, exert more effort, persist longer, use more effective strategies, and generally perform better (Bandura, 1997; Schunk & Ertmer, 2000).

Attainment, Utility, and Cost: Beliefs About Value

Value refers to the benefits and advantages individuals believe can result from participating in an activity. It is the second component of expectancy × value theory.

Three types of values influence motivation (Wigfield & Eccles, 2000, 2002):

- Attainment value
- Utility value
- Cost

Attainment Value. **Attainment value** describes the importance individuals attach to doing well on a task (Wigfield & Eccles, 2000, 2002), and we attach more importance—attainment value—to the task if we believe we're good at it or want to be good at it.

Figure 10.5 Factors influencing self-efficacy

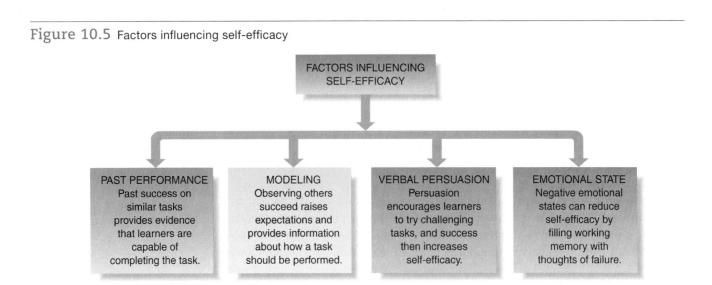

For instance, it's important to Don (one of your authors) that he swims his laps in a certain amount of time, because he believes he's a good swimmer, and winning in tennis is important to Paul (your other author) because he—perhaps naively—believes he plays tennis well. Succeeding validates their beliefs about their ability (Anderman & Wolters, 2006). On the other hand, winning at chess isn't important to either one, since neither believes he's a good chess player, nor cares about being good at it.

Attainment value helps us understand the last question we asked in *Ed Psych and You* earlier: "Is succeeding in some games more important to you than succeeding in others?" The answer almost certainly is "yes," and success is more important to you if you believe you're good at the game or want to be good at it.

Utility Value.   Now, think about your study of educational psychology and this book. We hope you view it as interesting for its own sake, but perhaps more importantly, we want you to believe that understanding its content will make you a better teacher. If you do, it has high **utility value**, the belief that an activity or course of study will be useful for meeting future goals, including career goals (Wigfield & Eccles, 1992). Believing that studying educational psychology will make you a better professional increases its utility value and your motivation to study educational psychology.

Cost.   Have you ever dropped a class because your workload was too heavy? Many of us have, and we can explain why using the concept of **cost**, the consideration of what we must give up to engage in an activity (Wigfield & Eccles, 2002). In the case of an impossible workload, for instance, the cost is too high, so you're not motivated to continue in the class.

Beliefs about outcomes (expectations), intelligence (mindset), capability (self-efficacy), and value help us understand why our students are likely to engage in and persevere on tasks. Their beliefs about the reasons they perform the way they do can also influence their motivation. This leads us to a discussion of attributions.

Attributions: Beliefs About Causes of Performance

When you succeed on a task, why are you successful? If you don't succeed, why not? The explanations we offer for our successes and failures influence our motivation, and to see how, let's look at four students' reactions to the results of a test.

"How'd you do, Bob?" Anne asks.

"Terrible," Bob answers sheepishly. "I just can't do this stuff. I'll never get it."

"I didn't do so good either," Anne replies, "but I knew I wouldn't. I just didn't study hard enough. I won't let that happen again."

"Unbelievable!" Armondo adds. "I didn't know what the heck was going on, and I got a B. I really lucked out."

"I think the test was too tough," Ashley says, shaking her head. "I looked at it and just went blank. All I could think was, 'I've never seen this stuff before. Where did it come from?' If tests are going to be like this, I'm sunk."

The students are offering **attributions**, beliefs explaining the causes of their performance. Bob, for example, believed it was low ability—"I just can't do this stuff," whereas Anne believed it was lack of effort. Armondo thought he was lucky, and Ashley suggested that the test was too hard. **Attribution theory** attempts to systematically describe learners' beliefs about the causes of their successes and failures and how these beliefs influence motivation to learn. It's a cognitive theory of motivation, because it's based on the assumption that people want to make sense of their experiences (Weiner, 1992).

"Students engage in the attribution process to make sense of the world and regain control over their environment" (Fishman & Husman, 2017, p. 560). Understanding why they perform the way they do helps them meet this goal, and it helps explain why they seek information about their performance (Savolainen, 2013).

Historically, research on attributions for academic achievement focused on four primary causes for success or failure—*ability, effort, task difficulty,* and *luck*—but more recent research has expanded this list of causes (Schunk et al., 2014). Some examples of attributions in different domains are outlined in Table 10.1. Regardless of the variety we see in the table, attribution theory categorizes them along three causal dimensions (Weiner, 1992, 2000).

- *Stability:* Whether the attribution—perceived cause—is likely or not likely to change. For instance, in the physical skills domain in Table 10.1, natural ability would be considered stable, because it isn't going to change.

- *Locus:* Whether the attribution is within or outside the individual. As an example, in the academic achievement domain, ability and effort are *internal*—within the learner—whereas task difficulty and quality of instruction are *external*.

- *Control:* Whether or not we can change the factor. In the respective domains, we can control effort (academic achievement), amount of practice (physical skills), personal hygiene (interpersonal relationships), and personal habits (health and well-being). On the other hand, in these same domains we can't, for the most part, control fairness of teachers, quality of coaching, social status, or heredity.

In general, people tend to attribute successes to internal causes, such as high ability or effort in the case of academic achievement, and failures to external causes, such as quality of coaching in the case of physical skills, or character of others in the case of interpersonal relationships (Rhodewalt & Vohs, 2005). This makes sense. In the academic domain, attributing success to internal causes, such as ability, and failures to external causes, such as poor teaching, allows us to maintain our sense of self-worth.

Attributions are also related to mindset. For example, individuals with a growth mindset are more likely than those whose mindset is fixed to attribute academic failure to lack of effort, because they believe, with effort, ability can be increased.

In this section, we focus on academic achievement, but attribution theory is much broader. For instance, people form attributions for a range of experiences, including the degree to which they're successful in their work, their health and well-being, and even social relationships (Hillebrandt & Barclay, 2017).

The Impact of Attributions on Emotions, Cognition, and Motivation
Attributions impact motivation in three ways (Weiner, 2000, 2001):

- *Emotions:* Emotional reactions to success and failure
- *Motivation:* Future effort
- *Cognition:* Expectations for future success

TABLE 10.1 Attributions in different domains

Academic Achievement	Physical Skills	Interpersonal Relationships	Health and Well-Being
Ability	Natural ability	Personality	Heredity
Effort	Amount of practice	Physical attractiveness	Exercise
Task difficulty	Quality of coaching	Social status	Luck
Luck	General health	Money	Working conditions
Interest	Diet	Personal hygiene	Personal habits
Quality of instruction	Body structure	Availability	Attitude
Fairness of teachers	Emotional makeup	Character of others	
Fatigue			
Help from others			

SOURCE: Adapted from Weiner (2000).

To see how these influences work, let's look at Anne's and Bob's attributions again. Anne attributed her poor score to lack of effort, for which she was responsible, so guilt was her most likely emotional reaction. Her comment, "I won't let that happen again," suggests that she is motivated to increase her effort, which will also increase her expectations for success. As a result, her achievement is likely to improve.

Bob attributed his failure to lack of ability, and he has a *fixed mindset*, as indicated by his comment, "I'll never get it." So, instead of guilt, his emotional reaction is embarrassment and shame since he views himself as having low ability. His comment also suggests that he doesn't expect future success, so both his effort and achievement are likely to decrease. Motivation tends to increase when students attribute failure to ineffective strategies or lack of effort, as Anne did, because strategy use and effort can be controlled, whereas it tends to decrease when they attribute failure to bad luck or lack of ability, which—particularly if they have a fixed mindset—they can't control (Weinstock, 2007). (We ask you to analyze Armondo's and Ashley's reactions in Application Exercise 10.2 at the end of this section.)

Learned Helplessness

If attributing failure to lack of ability becomes a pattern, **learned helplessness**, the debilitating belief that one has little control over the environment and is incapable of accomplishing specified tasks, can result. Bob's comment, "I'll never get it," indicates that he's a candidate for learned helplessness, which can lead to overwhelming feelings of shame and self-doubt and devastating effects on motivation.

Learned helplessness has both an affective and a cognitive component. Affectively, students in this state often have low self-esteem and suffer from anxiety and depression (Graham & Weiner, 1996). Cognitively, students "begin to attribute their failures to personal inadequacy, spontaneously citing deficient intelligence, memory, or problem-solving ability as the reasons for their failure" (Sorrenti, Filippello, Costa, & Buzzai, 2015, p. 923). They expect to fail, so they exert little effort and use ineffective strategies, which result in less success and an even greater expectation for failure (Sorrenti et al., 2015).

Fortunately, efforts to intervene through attribution training have been successful.

Attribution Training

Learners can improve their attributions with training, and teachers are central to the process (Robertson, 2000). In a pioneering study, Dweck (1975) provided students who demonstrated learned helplessness with both successful and unsuccessful experiences. When the students were unsuccessful, the experimenter specifically stated that the failure was caused by lack of effort or ineffective strategies. Comparable students were given similar experiences but no training. After the training, learners responded more positively to failure by persisting longer and adapting their strategies more effectively. More recent research has corroborated Dweck's findings (Schunk et al., 2014).

Using Educational Psychology in Teaching: Suggestions for Applying an Understanding of Beliefs to Increase Your Students' Motivation to Learn

So, now we have an understanding of how students' beliefs can influence their motivation. But what can we do about it? We try to answer that question in this section, with the following suggestions for applying an understanding of students' beliefs to increase their motivation.

- Model a growth mindset, internal attributions for successes, and control attributions for failures.
- Promote expectations for success and self-efficacy with effective teaching.
- Emphasize the utility value of what we're teaching.

Model a Growth Mindset, Internal Attributions for Successes, and Control Attributions for Failures.   To begin this section, let's look again at the comment Kathy made in a learning activity earlier in the chapter.

She has just finished providing her students with a number of facts about the Crusades and the Renaissance.

Jeremy: Man, Mrs. Brewster, how do you know all this stuff?

Kathy: I study . . . I study every night to keep up with you people, and the harder I study, the smarter I get. . . . If I struggle, I redouble my efforts and maybe change the way I'm attacking the problem. . . . And it really feels good when I get it."

In saying, " . . . the harder I study, the smarter I get," Kathy modeled a growth mindset, and she also modeled an internal attribution for success by suggesting that her "getting smarter" was a result of her effort. Then, in saying "If I struggle, I redouble my efforts and maybe change the way I'm attacking the problem," she suggested that she was still in control, that is, she modeled a control attribution for failure.

This modeling, combined with encouraging our students to believe the same way, is the most effective strategy we have for promoting a positive mindset and healthy attributions. Also, encouraging students to attribute failure to ineffective strategies is particularly effective for those who believe they are already trying hard. And as students see their competence increase, their motivation to learn also increases.

MyLab Education
Video Example 10.4

Promote expectations for success and self-efficacy with effective teaching, is one of the suggestions for applying an understanding of beliefs to increase students' motivation to learn. Here, sixth-grade teacher, Dani Ramsay, teaches effectively by providing her students with clear examples and scaffolding to ensure that they're successful when they write personal biopoems.

Promote Expectations for Success and Self-Efficacy with Effective Teaching.   Success on similar tasks is the most important factor influencing both self-efficacy and expectations for success, because students high in either choose more challenging tasks, persist longer on them, and generally learn more than their peers lower in either.

Promoting these beliefs is obviously a challenge, particularly for students with a history of underachievement. The situation is not hopeless, however. The following suggestions, all components of effective teaching, can make a difference.

- Establish clear goals and create learning activities, homework assignments, and assessments directly linked to the goals. When students know exactly what they're supposed to learn, the likelihood of their success increases, and with it, both their expectations and their self-efficacy.

- Provide students with practice in developing their abilities. For instance, Kathy's comment to Mason, "Look at how much both your writing and your thinking have improved as a result of your effort," suggests that she has her students do a lot of writing. No substitute exists for practice in developing skills and abilities, and some experts believe that deliberate practice is even more important than natural ability (Eskreis-Winkler et al., 2016).

APA Top 20 Principles

This discussion applies Principle 5: *Acquiring long-term knowledge and skill is largely dependent on practice*—from the *Top 20 Principles from Psychology for PreK–12 Teaching and Learning*.

- Thoroughly discuss assignments and assessments after they're given and provide students with the information—feedback—they need to improve their abilities.

- Make statements such as "If you study hard, I know you can do well on the quiz," "Yes, this assignment will be a challenge, but I know you can do it," or even, "I know we struggled a little on the last quiz, but if we work a little harder, we'll improve on the next one." Statements such as these have a much more positive effect on motivation than saying something like "I'm not sure what you were thinking about on the last quiz," "You'd better get going or you'll be back in this class next year," or "I'm not sure what your problem is." Our use of language has an important impact on our students' motivation to learn.

Because of its influence on motivation, increasing our students' self-efficacy is one of our most important goals, and effective instruction is our best tool. We discuss effective instruction in detail in Chapter 13.

Emphasize the Utility Value of What We're Teaching.   Earlier in our discussion we saw that *utility value* is the belief that a topic, activity, or course of study will be useful for meeting future goals. Kathy's emphasis on utility value was indicated by Susan's comment in the case study at the beginning of the chapter when she said, "We'd better get moving. The bell's gonna ring, and you know how Brewster is about this class. She thinks it's sooo important." Believing what we teach is important and valuable won't automatically cause our students to believe the same way, but even subtly suggesting that a topic isn't important will surely detract from their motivation. So, we have nothing to lose by communicating that we believe what we're teaching is valuable, and it takes little additional time or energy to do so.

Kathy's comment, "You know how important being a good writer is," in her encounter with Mason at the beginning of her class captures the essence of utility value. Let's look at this exchange once more.

Mason: Sheesh, Mrs. Brewster, that assignment was impossible (grumbling as he comes into the classroom). You're working us to death.

Kathy: That's good for you. . . . I know you're working hard, but it's paying off. Look at how much both your writing and your thinking have improved as a result of your effort. . . . Hard work is the key to everything, and you know how important being a good writer is.

"Why do we have to learn this?" is a common student question. Communicating the utility value of what we're teaching can help address this issue.

As with applying an understanding of needs, the suggestions for applying an understanding of beliefs are synergistic—the effect of their combination and interaction is greater than the sum of the individual elements. For instance, if our students believe we're committed to them both as people and as learners, the likelihood of them taking us seriously when we model a growth mindset increases. Similarly, if we involve our students in decision making, they are more likely to believe we respect them as people, and the likelihood of them believing us when we emphasize the utility value of what we're teaching also increases. This synergy is true for all the suggestions we offer.

MyLab Education Application Exercise 10.2: The Impact of Attributions on Emotions, Cognition, and Motivation

In this exercise, you will be asked to analyze the impact of Armondo's and Ashley's attributions on their emotions, cognition, and motivation to learn.

Classroom Connections

Using Students' Beliefs to Increase Their Motivation to Learn

1. Expectations are beliefs about future outcomes, and self-efficacy describes beliefs about our capability to accomplish specific tasks. Develop expectations for success and self-efficacy by providing enough scaffolding to ensure that students make progress on challenging tasks.

   - **Elementary:** A fourth-grade teacher presents students with a word problem, has them try it, and then provides enough guidance so they are successful in solving it.

   - **Middle School:** A seventh-grade English teacher has his students write paragraphs, and he then anonymously displays some of them on the document camera and makes suggestions for improvement.

   - **High School:** An art teacher has students keep a portfolio of their work. She periodically asks them to review their products to see evidence of their learning progress.

2. Learners with a growth mindset believe that ability can increase with effort. Emphasize a growth mindset with your students.

   - **Elementary:** After her students have solved a series of word problems, a second-grade teacher comments, "See how our work is paying off. When we work hard, we get better and better."

   - **Middle School:** A seventh-grade geography history teacher says, "Your efforts to understand how geography influences countries' economies and politics are really helping. I tell the other teachers what geography experts I have in my class."

   - **High School:** A chemistry teacher emphasizes that he studies every night. "The harder I work, the more capable I become." He smiles. "And you can do the same thing."

3. Utility value is the belief that a topic or activity will be useful for meeting future goals. Emphasize the utility value of the topics students study.

   - **Elementary:** A fifth-grade teacher emphasizes the importance of understanding our bodies so we can make good decisions about keeping our bodies healthy.

   - **Middle School:** A seventh-grade math teacher working on percentage problems brings in newspaper advertisements for marked-down products. The class determines the actual reduction in cost, and the teacher then emphasizes the value of percentages in understanding how much people save in promotions.

   - **High School:** An English teacher displays examples of well-written (and not so well-written) attempts to make and defend an argument. She uses the examples to emphasize the value of being able to express oneself clearly.

4. Attributions describe beliefs about causes of performance. Model and encourage students to attribute success to increasing competence and failure to lack of effort or ineffective strategies.

   - **Elementary:** As his students initially work on word problems, a third-grade teacher carefully monitors student effort during seatwork. When he sees assignments that indicate effort, he makes comments to individual students, such as "Your work is improving all the time."

   - **Middle School:** A sixth-grade English teacher comments, "I wasn't good at grammar for a long time. But I kept trying, and I found that I could do it. You can become good too, but you have to work at it."

   - **High School:** A chemistry teacher comments, "The way we're attacking balancing equations is working much better, isn't it? You tried to memorize the steps before, and now you're understanding what you're doing."

MyLab Education Self-Check 10.3

The Influence of Goal Orientation on Motivation to Learn

10.4 Describe how learners' goals affect their motivation to learn.

To begin this section, let's examine the thinking of six of Kathy's students as they prepare their group presentation on the Renaissance.

Susan: This should be interesting. I don't know much about the Renaissance, and it began a whole new emphasis on learning all over the world. Mrs. Brewster has given us a lot of responsibility, so we need to come through. We need to make a presentation she'll like.

Damien: I'll get my Dad to help us. He's really up on history. Our presentation will be the best one of the bunch, and the class will be impressed.

Sylvia: Yikes! Everyone in my group is so smart. What can I do? They'll think I'm the dumbest one. I'm going to just stay quiet when we're working together.

Charlotte: This should be fun. We can get together to work on this at one of our houses. If we can get the project out of the way quickly, I might have time to get to know Damien better.

Antonio: I don't know anything about this. I'd better do some studying so my group will think I'm pulling my weight.

Patrick: I like group activities. They're usually easy. Somebody is always gung ho and does most of the work.

Each of the students' thinking reflects a **goal**, an outcome an individual hopes to attain (Anderman & Wolters, 2006). Susan's was to understand the Renaissance and please Mrs. Brewster, Charlotte wanted to socialize, and Patrick simply wanted to do as little work as possible. These different goal orientations influence both motivation and learning, as we'll see in this section.

Mastery and Performance Goals

Ed Psych and You

When you take tests or quizzes in your classes, do you want to know how you do compared to others in the course? Why do you think this is the case?

Research examining goals focuses primarily on differences between **mastery goals** (also called *learning goals*)—goals that focus on accomplishing tasks and increasing understanding—and **performance goals**—goals that focus on ability and comparisons to others (Chatzisarantis et al., 2016; Shin & Seo, 2017). For instance, Susan's desire to understand the Renaissance is a mastery goal.

Performance goals exist in two forms (Sommet, Darnon, & Butera, 2015). **Performance-approach goals** emphasize looking competent and receiving favorable judgments from others. Damien's wanting to make the best presentation and impress the class is an example. Sylvia's thinking, "They'll think I'm the dumbest one. I'm going to just stay quiet when we're working together," reflects a **performance-avoidance goal**, an attempt to avoid looking incompetent and being judged unfavorably. Students with this orientation often have low self-efficacy, experience anxiety about tests and other assessments, and try to avoid challenging tasks (Sommet et al, 2015). They're also the ones who scooch down in their seats and try to hide so their teacher won't call on them. Teachers contribute to a performance orientation if they post distributions of scores on tests or use course management systems that display class averages. Our questions in *Ed Psych and You* relate to performance goals, and if you answered yes to the first one, you're typical (Sommet, Pillaud, Meuleman, & Butera, 2017); because ability becomes increasingly important to students as they get older, they want to know how they perform compared to others.

While some performance orientation in students is inevitable, performance goals are less effective than mastery goals. Here's why. Students with a mastery orientation persist in the face of challenge and difficulty, attribute success to effort, use effective strategies (such as self-questioning), and maintain their interest and effort after formal instruction is finished (Sommet et al., 2017). Students with performance-approach goals tend to be confident and have high self-efficacy, but they often use superficial strategies, such as memorization, to reach them. When goals become challenging, they may engage in self-handicapping behaviors, such as reducing their effort if they're not sure they can meet the goals, or even cheat (Brophy, 2010). A performance-avoidance orientation is the most destructive for motivation and learning (Ryan et al., 2007). For example, learning was essentially irrelevant to Sylvia; she simply wanted to avoid looking "dumb."

APA Top 20 Principles

This discussion illustrates Principle 10: *Students persist in the face of challenging tasks and process information more deeply when they adopt mastery goals rather than performance goals*—from the *Top 20 Principles from Psychology for PreK–12 Teaching and Learning*.

Students with fixed mindsets tend to adopt performance goals, whereas a mastery orientation is more common for those with growth mindsets (Dweck, 2016). This makes sense. For instance, wanting to make the best presentation in the class, Damien's performance-approach goal, could be an indicator of high ability, which is important for individuals who view ability as fixed. This is problematic, however, because we all periodically fail. In contrast, individuals with growth mindsets are more likely to seek challenges and persevere, because failure merely indicates that more work is required, and with more work competence and ability increase.

Social Goals

Now, let's look at the students' thinking again. Charlotte thought, "If we can get the project out of the way quickly, I might have time to get to know Damien better," and Antonio decided, "I don't know anything about this. I'd better do some studying so my group will think I'm pulling my weight." Both are **social goals**, goals to achieve particular social outcomes (Wentzel, 2005). More specifically, Antonio's was a *social-responsibility* goal.

Social goals can both increase and decrease motivation (Horst, Finney, & Barron, 2007). For instance, Charlotte's wanting to "get the project out of the way quickly" detracts from her motivation. As we would expect, low achievers report this orientation more often than do their higher-achieving peers (Wentzel, 2005). On the other hand, social-responsibility goals, such as Antonio's, are associated with both high motivation and achievement (Goncalves, Niemivirta, & Semos, 2017).

Motivation is highest when mastery and social-responsibility goals are combined (Goncalves et al., 2017; Wentzel, 2005). This is illustrated in Susan's thinking, "This should be interesting. I don't know much about the Renaissance" (a mastery goal) and "Mrs. Brewster has given us a lot of responsibility, so we need to come through. We need to make a presentation she'll like" (a social-responsibility goal).

Work-Avoidance Goals

Patrick's comment, "I like group activities. They're usually easy. Somebody is always gung ho and does most of the work," indicates a **work-avoidance goal**. A work-avoidance orientation is different from mastery and performance goals, ". . . because it represents the absence of an achievement goal. For students who endorse a work-avoidance goal, 'success' is defined in terms of minimal work expenditure and not on any measure of competence" (King & McInerney, 2014, p. 43). Disengagement from learning activities is common for students with this orientation. As a result, they tend to make minimal contributions to group activities, ask for help even when they don't need it, complain about challenging tasks, and avoid involvement in whole-group instruction (King, 2014). Not surprisingly, students like Patrick are a source of frustration for teachers.

Table 10.2 summarizes the different types of goals and their influence on motivation and achievement.

Diversity: Learner Differences in Goal Orientation

As with many aspects of learning and motivation, differences with respect to goal orientation exist. For instance, research indicates that Asian American students are more likely than their mainstream American peers to have growth mindsets, and both Asian American and African American students tend to focus on mastery goals, whereas their mainstream counterparts are more performance oriented (Qian & Pan, 2002). However, independent of culture, a mastery orientation has a positive impact on motivation and achievement (King, McInerney, & Nasser, 2017).

Results of studies examining gender differences in goal orientation are mixed; differences have been found in some areas but not others. For instance, some research indicates that girls tend to have a stronger mastery orientation than do boys, and this orientation increases the likelihood that they will engage in academic self-assessment, a part of self-regulation strongly associated with achievement (Yan, 2018).

Additional research has found that social goal orientation dramatically increases for both girls and boys as they move into middle school (Dawes & Xie, 2017). However, this orientation differs slightly. Girls' social goals are more likely to focus on the formation of close friendships and acceptable social behavior, whereas boys are more likely to concentrate on social acceptance and avoiding appearing socially awkward or undesirable (Ben-Eliyahu, Linnenbrink-Garcia, & Putallaz, 2017).

On the other hand, for both girls and boys, adopting mastery goals as a primary orientation—versus performance goals or social goals—has a positive impact on both achievement and the perception that learning is the primary purpose of school (Jones, 2017).

As you apply this information in your teaching, please remember that these are general patterns, and individuals within groups vary significantly. We want to avoid thinking that stereotypes members of any group.

TABLE 10.2 Goals, motivation, and achievement

Type of Goal	Example	Influence on Motivation and Achievement
Mastery goals	Understand the influence of the Renaissance on American history.	Leads to sustained effort, high self-efficacy, willingness to accept challenges, and high achievement.
Performance-approach goals	Produce one of the best presentations on the Renaissance in the class.	Can lead to sustained effort and high self-efficacy for confident learners. Can increase achievement. Can detract from willingness to accept challenging tasks, which decreases achievement.
Performance-avoidance goals	Avoid the appearance of low ability in front of peers and teachers.	Detracts from motivation and achievement, particularly for learners lacking confidence.
Social goals	Be perceived as reliable and responsible. Make friends and socialize.	Can increase motivation and achievement. *Social-responsibility goals* enhance motivation and achievement, particularly when combined with mastery goals. Can detract from motivation and achievement if social goals compete for time with mastery goals.
Work-avoidance goals	Complete assignments with as little effort as possible.	Detracts from effort and self-efficacy. Strongly detracts from achievement.

Grit: Commitment to Achieving Long-Term Goals

To begin this section, let's look again at Kathy's response to Jeremy when he asked, "Man, Mrs. Brewster, how do you know all this stuff?"

"I study," Kathy says simply. " . . . I study every night to keep up with you people, and the harder I study, the smarter I get. . . . If I struggle, I redouble my efforts and maybe change the way I'm attacking the problem. . . . I feel like if I hang in long enough I'll eventually get it. And it really feels good when I do."

In responding, "I feel like if I hang in long enough, I'll eventually get it," Kathy was demonstrating **grit**, the ability to develop and sustain passion and commitment to achieving long-term goals. The concept of grit, conceived by former public school math and science teacher and University of Pennsylvania psychologist Angela Duckworth (Duckworth, Peterson, Matthews, & Kelly, 2007), is associated with growth mindsets, mastery goals, high levels of perseverance, delay of gratification, and an absence of pleasure seeking (Von Culin, Tsukayama, & Duckworth, 2014). It has, since its inception, been widely researched (e.g., Aelenei, Lewis, & Oyserman, 2017; Fisher & Oyserman, 2017; West et al., 2016). And it's now even more popular as the result of Duckworth's book *Grit: The Power of Passion and Perseverance* (2016), in which she explores and explains her research on the concept. Her work and book have even been featured in the popular press, such as the *The Washington Post* (McGregor, 2016) and the *New York Times* (Shulevitz, 2016).

Grit has become familiar to teachers and policy makers as emphasis on self-regulation and social-emotional skills have received increased attention in education. (You may want to review your study of social-emotional learning in Chapter 3.) It's even found its way onto report cards (Blad, 2017), with teachers being asked to evaluate students on factors such as (Character Growth Card, 2017):

- Finished whatever activity was begun
- Stuck with a project or activity for more than a few weeks
- Tried very hard even after experiencing failure
- Stayed committed to goals
- Kept working hard even when the student felt like quitting

Duckworth's work is controversial, with some critics arguing that it is essentially another term for the personality trait conscientiousness, so it is little more than "old wine in new bottles" (Credé, Tynan, & Harms, 2016; Ion, Mindu, & Gorbănescu, 2017; Ivcevic & Brackett, 2014). Duckworth counters that conscientiousness is a trait that is within an individual, whereas grit is a skill that can be learned (Engber, 2016). Regardless, the inclination and ability to "hang in," as Kathy put it, for the long term, even in the face of extreme challenge and difficulty, is valuable, more valuable than native ability, Duckworth (2016) argues.

So, if grit is indeed a skill, what can we—teachers—do to promote it, and to promote broader mastery goal orientations in our students? We address this question in the next section.

Using Educational Psychology in Teaching: Suggestions for Capitalizing on Goals to Increase Your Students' Motivation to Learn

As we saw earlier, students' performance orientation tends to increase while their mastery orientation decreases as they move through school. Further, suggesting to students that grades aren't important is unrealistic. Parents focus on grades, grade-point averages are included in college applications, and you want a good grade in this class. However, we can take steps to avoid an unhealthy emphasis on performance goals. The following suggestions can help.

- Promote a mastery and social-responsibility orientation by emphasizing that learning is the goal of schooling.
- Model a growth mindset and provide students with deliberate practice.
- Create assessments that measure deep understanding of content and avoid over-emphasizing factual information.
- Encourage students to set and monitor measurable, near-term, moderately challenging goals.

Promote a Mastery and Social-Responsibility Orientation. Inevitably, students will make social comparisons, and at least to a certain extent, compete with their classmates (Chatzisarantis et al., 2016). We can't eliminate this tendency completely, but we can contribute to a mastery orientation with statements like Kathy's comment, "Remember, we're all doing our best; we're not competing with each other," and by avoiding comments such as "Only four people got A's on the last test" or "Karen and Liam got the highest grades on this quiz," which promote performance orientation in students.

We can take additional steps by writing students' scores on the last page of their tests and telling them that they are not to share their scores with each other. We won't be able to enforce this "don't share" policy, but it symbolizes a focus on learning instead of performance. We can also combine small-group work, which helps meet students' social goals, with whole-class instruction, which is often preferred by students with a performance-approach orientation (Goncalves et al., 2017). And we can help develop social responsibility by creating learning communities that communicate a we're-all-in-this-together emotional climate. Further, emphasizing deep understanding of the topics we teach will help students eventually realize that grades take care of themselves if they understand the content. This is the ideal we strive for.

Model a Growth Mindset and Provide Students with Deliberate Practice. Earlier we saw that people with growth mindsets tend to adopt mastery goals. A growth mindset is essential if learners are to maintain the commitment to long-term goals, even in the face of extreme challenge and adversity, which we associate with *grit*. If we didn't believe that we are "getting smarter"—or more skilled, such as in the case of athletic or musical ability—as a result of all this effort, remaining committed to a goal over the long term would be unlikely (Duckworth, White, Matteucci, Shearer, & Gross, 2016). Kathy modeled a growth mindset with her comment, "I study, . . . I study every night to keep up with you people, and the harder I study, the smarter I get." This is the orientation we want to present to our students.

Simply encouraging students to maintain their effort, and even modeling, isn't enough, however. They need the support required to provide them with evidence that their efforts are paying off. This is why deliberate practice is so important. As you saw in Chapter 8, deliberate practice includes the following features (Eskreis-Winkler et al., 2016):

- A clear and precise goal
- A focus on understanding and sense making (not rote drill)
- Frequent, spaced practice in real-world settings
- Extensive and detailed feedback

We know this for sure: If we practice enough, we'll improve, and this applies to all forms of learning. And as learners see their understanding and skills improving, their perceptions of competence increase, which, in turn, can dramatically increase motivation (Schunk et al., 2014).

APA Top 20 Principles

This discussion applies Principle 5: *Acquiring long-term knowledge and skill is largely dependent on practice*—from the *Top 20 Principles from Psychology for PreK–12 Teaching and Learning*.

Create Effective Assessments. How do you feel after you've solved a challenging problem, generated a new idea, or found a relationship in information that you hadn't thought of before? For virtually everyone, the feeling is "good"! We aren't thinking about anyone else or how we compare to them. It simply feels good to figure something out after we've worked hard at it. In fact, research in neuroscience indicates that the pleasure centers in our brains are activated when we accomplish something challenging, particularly as a result of hard work (Zink, Pagnoni, Martin-Skurski, Chappelow, & Berns, 2004).

This relates to the importance of assessment in our classrooms. The most effective mechanism we have for contributing to a mastery orientation in our students is to give them evidence that their understanding is increasing, and assessment is the most powerful tool we have for providing this evidence (Rohrer & Pashler, 2010). Suggestions for using assessment effectively include (Schunk et al., 2014):

- Presenting clear expectations for students and ensuring that assessments are consistent with the expectations.
- Assessing at levels beyond knowledge and recall.
- Assessing frequently, emphasizing the assessments' learning benefits, and avoiding comments that make assessments appear punitive or controlling.
- Discussing frequently missed items and emphasizing the reasons for answers as much as the answers themselves.
- Dropping one or two of students' lowest test or quiz scores for grading purposes.

Clear expectations and assessments that are aligned with them increase the likelihood that students will be successful, and succeeding on assessments that measure higher-level learning is one of the most effective tools we have for making students feel competent. And the more competent they feel, the less concerned they are about their performance compared to others.

Clear expectations also contribute to students' perceptions of autonomy. If they know what is expected of them, they can either choose to study or not study, and they will understand the consequences of not studying. Either way, they're in control.

Assessing frequently removes pressure, because no single quiz carries an inordinate amount of weight. Discussing frequently missed items provides students with the information—feedback—they need to increase their understanding, which further contributes to perceptions of both competence and autonomy (El, Tillema, & van Koppen, 2012). And dropping one or two quizzes in calculating grades communicates that increasing learning is the purpose of assessment (Chappuis & Stiggins, 2017). Each of these factors contributes to a mastery orientation.

National Council on Teacher Quality (NCTQ)

The National Council on Teacher Quality describes assessing learning as one of the six essential teaching strategies that every new teacher should know. Assessment is a learning tool, and assessment and feedback help students effectively store and retain information (Chappuis & Stiggins, 2017).

Encourage Students to Set and Monitor Goals. Goal setting has been widely used to increase motivation and performance in a variety of areas. For instance, it's the foundation of the weight loss program *Weight Watchers*, and research indicates that the program can be highly effective (Graham et al., 2017). Goal setting and monitoring has also been used in other health-related areas (Mann, de Ridder, & Fujita, 2013), the business world (Crossley, Cooper, & Wernsing, 2013), athletics (Guan, Xiang, McBride, & Keating, 2013), and academic settings (Schunk et al., 2014).

Effective goals have three characteristics:

- Specific (versus broad and general).
- Immediate or close at hand (versus distant).
- Moderately challenging.

APA Top 20 Principles

This description applies Principle 12: *Setting goals that are short term (proximal), specific, and moderately challenging enhances motivation more than establishing goals that are long term (distal), general, and overly challenging*—from the *Top 20 Principles from Psychology for PreK–12 Teaching and Learning*.

As an example, the goal of jogging 20 miles a week is effective, because it's specific, immediate, and easy to monitor. So, suppose you jog 4 miles each on Sunday and Monday, rest Tuesday, go 5 on Wednesday, rest again Thursday, and do 4 on Friday. You don't feel like running Saturday, but you need 3 more miles to reach your goal, so you go for a run anyway. This is how goal setting can increase motivation.

Some additional examples of effective goals include the following:

- To answer and understand all of the Self-Check questions in each chapter of this book.
- To Google each new vocabulary term we encounter and write down the definition.
- To solve a minimum of five practice exercises before each quiz.
- To write a brief summary at the end of each class period that outlines the important ideas discussed in class.

As with our jogging example, they're effective because they're specific, immediate, and easy to monitor. On the other hand, goals such as "to lose weight," "to get in better shape," or "to learn more in this class" are ineffective because they're general and distant.

As students monitor progress toward their goals, their level of commitment is likely to increase, because their self-efficacy and perceptions of competence grow. And you can support their efforts with some concrete tools. For instance, you can have your students create personal charts that allow them to monitor the number of homework problems they've solved. You can also ask them to share new vocabulary they've learned, and you can spend a few minutes near the end of each class having students write and discuss their summaries. You can also enlist the support of parents in encouraging their sons and daughters to set and monitor goals.

The appropriate degree of challenge is a matter of judgment. For instance, 20 miles a week wouldn't be challenging enough for a serious runner, whereas it might be too challenging for someone just beginning an exercise regimen.

Speaking from personal experience, setting and monitoring goals can be highly motivating if—and this is sometimes a big if—we're committed to the goals (Schunk et al, 2014). For example, Paul and Don, your authors, have both used goals to increase their level of exercise and lose weight.

> **MyLab Education** Application Exercise 10.3: Analyzing Goals
> In this exercise, you will be asked to make suggestions for improving stated goals.

Classroom Connections

Capitalizing on Goals to Increase Student Motivation to Learn

1. Goals are outcomes learners hope to achieve. Emphasize mastery goals in your work with your students.

- **Elementary:** As a fifth-grade teacher begins a writing project, he comments, "Our goal is to improve our writing. When it improves, the grade you get will take care of itself."

- **Middle School:** An eighth-grade history teacher puts her students' test scores on the last page of their tests and says, "Our scores are our own business. We're here to learn, not compete with each other."

- **High School:** In response to students asking how many A's were on the last test, a biology teacher says, "We don't care about that. Instead, ask yourself if your understanding is increasing."

2. A combination of mastery goals and social-responsibility goals can lead to the highest levels of motivation to learn. Emphasize social responsibility with your students.

- **Elementary:** A third-grade teacher instructs her students to work in pairs to solve a series of math problems. "Work hard," she emphasizes, "so you can help out your partner if he or she needs it."

- **Middle School:** An eighth-grade English teacher is discussing *To Kill a Mockingbird* with her students. "In order for us to get the most out of the book, we're all responsible for making a contribution to the class discussions," she emphasizes.

- **High School:** An American history teacher asks her students to work in groups of four to prepare a project comparing the American, French, and Russian revolutions. "Remember, the quality of your project depends on all of you doing your parts to contribute to the final product," she emphasizes.

3. Grit involves sustaining commitment to achieving long-term goals. Promote the development of grit in your students by emphasizing growth mindsets and providing your students with deliberate practice.

- **Elementary:** A kindergarten teacher has a routine called beginning-sound-of-the-day. Each day students are asked to offer examples of words that begin with a certain sound, such as *cat, cow, crumb, coin, cup,* and *card,* for the "c" sound. She also has them practice on worksheets by having them circle all the words that begin with the sound-of-the-day.

- **Middle School:** At the beginning of each class period a seventh-grade math teacher gives her students a problem, such as, for ratio and proportion problems, "If a person walks 1/2 mile in each 1/4 hour, what is her walking rate in miles per hour?" After the students are finished, they discuss the problem in detail, and the teacher has them solve an additional problem on the same topic. She emphasizes, "We can all be good math students. All we have to do is practice."

- **High School:** During the last 10 minutes of each class period, a social studies teacher has his students write a brief summary of the topic discussed that day, including the essential facts and details involved. He collects and reviews the summaries and the next day displays (with students' names covered) summaries that are well done, explains why they're well done, and uses them as segues into the day's lesson. As time goes on he emphasizes how much their writing has improved and that effort and practice are the keys to becoming good writers.

In spite of your best efforts, not all of your students will set or remain committed to learning goals. However, for the ones who do, you will have implemented one of the most powerful motivators that exist. And they will make your efforts well worth it (Kanfer, Frese, & Johnson, 2017).

MyLab Education Self-Check 10.4

The Influence of Interest and Emotion on Motivation to Learn

10.5 Explain how interest and emotion influence learner motivation.

"Because it's interesting" is an intuitively sensible answer to why learners are motivated to engage in an activity, and as teachers the most common way we attempt to motivate students is by increasing their interest in what we're teaching (Carmichael, Callingham, & Watt, 2017; Yang, 2016). We look at the idea of interest in more detail now.

Personal and Situational Interest

Let's briefly go back to the conversation between Susan and Jim in the case study at the beginning of the chapter as they entered Kathy's classroom. Susan commented, "I've always liked history and knowing about the past . . . and I'm pretty good at it," to which Jim replied, "In some classes I just do enough to get a decent grade, but not in here. . . . It's kind of interesting the way she's always telling us about the way we are because of something that happened a zillion years ago."

Susan's and Jim's comments suggest that they're both interested in Kathy's class but in different ways. Susan expressed **personal interest**, "a person's ongoing affinity, attraction, or liking for a domain, subject area, topic, or activity" (Anderman & Wolters, 2006, p. 374), whereas Jim demonstrated **situational interest**, a person's current enjoyment or satisfaction generated by the immediate context (Flowerday & Shell, 2015).

Personal interest is relatively stable, and it depends heavily on prior knowledge (Renninger, 2000). This stability and background are illustrated in Susan's comment, "I've always liked history . . . and I'm pretty good at it." Situational interest, in contrast, depends on the current situation and can change quickly.

Some topics, such as death, danger, power, money, romance, and sex, seem to be universal in their ability to create situational interest (Hidi, 2001), and this helps answer the questions we asked in *Ed Psych and You*. For younger students, fantasy, humor, and animals also seem to generate situational interest.

Because we have more control over it, the vast majority of research in this area focuses on situational interest instead of personal interest (Carmichael et al., 2017; Patall, Vasquez, Steingut, Trimble, & Pituch, 2016; Yang, 2016). Also, regardless of the utility value learners believe a topic has, without at least some situational interest, they are not likely to persist on challenging tasks (Tullis, & Fulmer, 2013). However, as individuals' expertise develops, situational interest often leads to personal interest, so we can develop personal interest in our students by helping them acquire as much expertise as possible with respect to the topics we teach.

We examine strategies for increasing student interest in more detail in the section "Using Educational Psychology in Teaching: Applying an Understanding of Interest and Emotion to Increase Your Students' Motivation to Learn" later in this discussion.

MyLab Education
Video Example 10.5

Personal interest describes a person's attraction, or liking for a subject area or topic, and situational interest represents a person's enjoyment or satisfaction generated by the immediate context. Here a student describes his personal interest in history, and situational interest generated by challenging classes.

Emotion and Motivation

In our first example in *Ed Psych and You*, you probably felt a sense of accomplishment and pride; the second may have caused feelings of outrage, and the third likely left you feeling discouraged and frustrated. Each involves an **emotion**, a feeling that is often short-lived, intense, and specific (Schunk et al., 2014). Emotions strongly influence our motivation to learn.

We typically think of emotions as "feelings," but they also have cognitive, physiological, and behavioral components as well (Pekrun, Goetz, Frenzel, Barchfeld, & Perry 2011). For instance, suppose we're confronted by an immediate threat, such as a large, snarling dog. Fear is the emotion we experience, but we also perceive danger (a form of cognition), our muscles tense and our heart rates accelerate (physiological reactions), and we likely run—a behavioral response.

Because of their potential to influence student motivation, interest in the study of emotions in academic settings has grown (Linnenbrink-Garcia & Pekrun, 2011). For instance, positive emotions, such as enjoyment, hope, and pride, increase motivation and achievement (Graziano & Hart, 2016; Pekrun et al., 2011).

They do so in the following ways (Broekhuizen, Slot, van Aken, & Dubas, 2017):

- *Mindset:* Learners with positive emotions are more likely to adopt a growth mindset.
- *Goal orientation:* Positive emotions are associated with a mastery goal orientation.
- *Self-regulation:* Learners with positive emotions are more likely to be metacognitive when they study, prepare more strategically for tests, and exert more effort and persistence on homework.
- *Information processing:* Emotions are encoded with information, so positive emotions also result when information is retrieved.

APA Top 20 Principles

This discussion illustrates Principle 15: *Emotional well-being influences educational performance, learning, and development*—from the *Top 20 Principles from Psychology for PreK–12 Teaching and Learning.*

The influence of negative emotions is more complex. For instance, boredom, a sense of hopelessness, and shame—particularly if shame is associated with beliefs about lack of ability—are destructive for motivation and achievement (Broekhuizen et al., 2017; Pekrun et al., 2011). On the other hand, guilt—particularly if the guilt results from students' believing they didn't try hard enough—can increase persistence on challenging tasks (Tullis & Fulmer, 2013). To illustrate, let's look again at Anne's and Bob's comments at the beginning of our discussion of attribution theory earlier in the chapter.

Anne: How'd you do, Bob?

Bob: Terrible . . . I just can't do this stuff. I'm no good at essay tests. . . . I'll never get it.

Anne: I didn't do so good either . . . but I knew I wouldn't. I just didn't study hard enough. I won't let that happen again.

Both Anne and Bob experienced negative emotions, but their motivational impacts are likely very different. Bob expressed hopelessness, which is linked to decreased motivation and achievement, whereas Anne felt guilty about her lack of effort, which is associated with increased motivation and achievement.

As we would expect, classroom climate and perceptions of teachers' support have an important influence on students' emotions. For example, high-quality instruction, teacher enthusiasm, and achievement-contingent feedback, such as praise for achievement and support after failure, are positively linked to enjoyment, whereas perceptions of teacher punishment and ineffective instruction are linked to boredom (Yang, 2016).

Motivation and Anxiety

Now, let's look at Ashley's comment again in the same conversation with Anne and Bob.

"I looked at the test, and just went blank. All I could think of was, 'I've never seen this stuff before. Where did it come from?' I thought I was going to throw up."

Ashley was describing **anxiety**, a general uneasiness and feeling of tension related to a situation with an uncertain outcome. We've all experienced anxiety—particularly test anxiety—and it's one of the most studied emotions in motivation and learning.

The relationship between anxiety, motivation, and achievement is curvilinear; some is good, but too much can be damaging (Strack, Lopes, Esteves, & Fernandez-Berrocal, 2017; Tullis & Fulmer, 2013). For instance, some anxiety makes us study harder, and relatively high anxiety improves performance on tasks where our expertise is well developed, such as in the case of highly-trained athletes (Schaefer, Velly, Allen, & Magee, 2016). Too much, however, can decrease motivation and achievement, and classrooms where the evaluation threat is high are particularly anxiety inducing (Durmaz & Akkus, 2016). The characteristics of human memory help explain its debilitating effects. First, anxious students have difficulty concentrating, and because they worry about—and even expect—failure, they often misperceive the information they see and hear. Also, test-anxious students often use superficial strategies, such as memorizing definitions, instead of approaches that are more productive, like self-questioning (Ryan et al., 2007). In essence, highly test-anxious students often don't learn the content very well in the first place, which increases their anxiety when they take tests. Then, during tests they often waste working memory space on thoughts similar to Ashley's, "I've never seen this stuff before. Where did it come from?" leaving less cognitive energy and space available for focusing on the task.

Some interesting and highly applicable research addresses the issue of anxiety. Researchers found that simply writing about test-related worries for 10 minutes immediately before taking an exam improved test scores in a classroom setting, and particularly when high-stakes tests were involved (Ramirez & Beilock, 2011). These researchers concluded that writing about their worries unloaded the thoughts that were occupying students' working memories, thereby making more working memory space available to devote to the assessment task.

The solution to anxiety is simple—but not necessarily easy. Study the content so thoroughly that you perform well in spite of anxiety. Paul, one of your authors, was a test-anxious student throughout his schooling. A comment to his wife during graduate school illustrates his approach: "There isn't anything they can ask me that I don't know." While the comment wasn't totally true, he studied extremely hard, and he succeeded in spite of his anxiety.

Using Educational Psychology in Teaching: Suggestions for Capitalizing on Interest and Emotion to Increase Students' Motivation to Learn

An understanding of learners' interests and emotions has important implications for the way we work with our students.

As we saw earlier, situational interest is essential if students are going to persist in their efforts (Tullis, & Fulmer, 2013). We also saw that topics such as death, danger, power, money, romance, and sex seem to be universally interesting (Hidi, 2001). We can't develop much of our instruction around these topics, but we can increase situational interest in other ways (Carmichael et al., 2017; Kiemer, Gröschner, Pehmer, & Seidel, 2015; Yang, 2016):

- Personalize content by linking topics to students' lives.
- Focus on real-world applications.
- Promote high levels of student involvement.
- Model our own interest in the topics we teach.

Personalizing content and connecting topics to the real world can also capitalize on students' emotions by increasing their enjoyment. And involving students essentially eliminates the chances of boredom, one of the most destructive emotions for motivation (Pekrun et al., 2011). It's harder for students to be bored when they're involved and know they're likely to be called on, even if they don't have high personal interest in the topics.

To see these suggestions applied, let's return to Kathy's work with her students in a later learning activity.

"We've been discussing the Crusades for several days now. . . . How did we start?" she asks.

"We imagined that Lincoln High School was taken over by people who believed that extracurricular activities should be eliminated," Carnisha volunteers. (Lincoln is the students' school.)

"Good. . . . Then what?"

"We decided we'd talk to them. . . . We'd be on a 'crusade' to change their minds and save our school."

"Very good. . . . Now, what were the actual Crusades all about? . . . Selena?"

"Well, the Christians wanted to get the Holy Land back from the Muslims, but according to the first book we studied [Armstrong, 2001], there were a bunch of bad wars conducted in the name of religion . . . that has contributed to the problems between Christians, Jews, and Muslims that we still see in the Middle East today.

"Excellent analysis. . . . Think about that. The Crusades nearly 1000 years ago have had an influence on us here today," she continues energetically. "Now, how about a different perspective? . . . What did our other author [Asbridge, 2012] have to say? . . . Becky?"

"His book almost read more like an adventure novel. He focused more on the role of leaders like Richard the Lionheart and Saladin.

"And, who were they? . . . Miguel?"

"Richard the Lionheart was king of England, and Saladin was the great Muslim leader who fought against the Crusaders."

"What else did our author, Asbridge, offer? . . . Anyone?"

After pausing several seconds, Josh volunteers, "He talked about how the religious aspects of the Crusades were also tied up in secular politics, like hanging on to power and that kind of thing."

"And he also talked a lot about the way they fought high-risk wars in medieval times, where one battle could turn the tide of a war," Ashley adds.

"Can you think of any other historical examples of battles that have turned the tides of wars?"

The students discuss some possibilities, such as the battle of Gettysburg in our Civil War, and Zach even offers the Battle of the Bulge in World War II as a possibility.

"Outstanding, everyone," Kathy says, smiling. She then continues, "Now, for today's assignment, you were asked to write an analysis comparing our two sources.

"So, let's see how we did. Go ahead. . . . Nikki?"

Kathy asks three students to present their positions and then closes the discussion by saying, "See how interesting this is? Here we see ourselves influenced by people who lived hundreds of years ago. . . . This is what history is all about."

"Brewster loves this stuff," David whispers to Kelly.

"Now, we heard from Nikki, Steve, and Mike," Kathy continues, "but the rest of you haven't had your analyses critiqued. So, exchange your work with your partner, and give each other some feedback based on our discussion of Nikki's, Steve's, and Mike's papers."

Now, let's see how Kathy applied the suggestions.

Personalize Content by Linking Topics to Students' Lives.   A large body of research confirms that personalizing topics increases student motivation (Narciss et al., 2014; Høgheim & Reber, 2015). Kathy capitalized on this factor by using the students' "crusade" to prevent having extracurricular activities eliminated from the school as a metaphor for the real Crusades. Personalizing topics isn't as hard as it might appear. For instance, simply putting students' names in examples, applications, and even quizzes and tests is a simple and positive first step. Being aware of the need to do so, you'll think of additional ways to personalize your topics when you plan.

Connect Topics to the Real World.   When students see how the topics they study link to the real world, their motivation also increases. The class's "crusade" to prevent extracurricular activities from being eliminated also capitalized on this suggestion. Word problems in math can easily be applied to the real world, writing can focus on real-world topics, and with some thought, most topics can be connected to the way we live today. As with personalization, with your awareness you'll quickly develop ideas for connecting topics to the real world.

Promote High Levels of Student Involvement.   Kathy involved her students in two ways. First, during their discussion she directly called on them by name and asked for their points of view. When students expect to be called on, they become more attentive and interested, and boredom decreases (Lemov, 2015). She further involved her students by having them work in pairs to critique each other's analyses. Combining whole-group instruction with small-group work adds variety to learning activities and also helps reduce the likelihood of boredom. ←

Model Our Own Interest in the Topics We Teach.   Finally, Kathy modeled her own interest in the topic by saying,

MyLab Education
Video Example 10.6

Personalize content by linking topics to students' lives, connect topics to the real world, and promote high levels of student involvement, are three suggestions for capitalizing on interest and emotion to increase students' motivation to learn. Here second-grade teacher, Sue Brush, applies these suggestion with her students in a problem-solving activity, where they graph the class's favorite flavor of jelly bean.

"Think about that. The Crusades nearly 1000 years ago have had an influence on us here today" and "See how interesting this is? Here we see ourselves influenced by people who lived hundreds of years ago. . . . This is what history is all about."

David's comment, "Brewster loves this stuff," is a testimony to the influence teachers' modeling of their own interest can have on students, and research confirms this influence (Kim & Schallert, 2014).

We can also take steps to reduce our students' anxiety by making expectations clear, assessing frequently and thoroughly, and providing specific and detailed feedback on the assessments (Rohrer & Pashler, 2010). And particularly if you teach older students, you might simply offer them the opportunity to write about their worries for a few minutes before they take a test. As we saw earlier, this process can help reduce the debilitating effects of anxiety (Ramirez & Beilock, 2011).

The suggestions we've outlined in this chapter won't increase motivation to learn in all situations or for all students, but they can increase motivation and learning for many. This is the essence of professionalism. We do our best to maximize motivation and learning for as many of our students as possible.

MyLab Education Application Exercise 10.4: Promoting Interest in Second Grade

In this exercise, you will be asked to analyze a second-grade teacher's attempts to apply suggestions for capitalizing on interest and emotion to increase motivation to learn.

Summarizing and Evaluating Theories of Motivation

Studying motivation is challenging. The topic is complex and includes a number of individual theories. A unified theory such as behaviorism, social cognitive theory, or information processing doesn't exist for theories of motivation. Further, concepts from different theories overlap. For instance, *self-worth* and *self-esteem* are used interchangeably, and the concept of *belonging* from Maslow's hierarchy and *relatedness* from self-determination theory are essentially the same. Also, *competence* from self-determination theory and *self-efficacy* are sometimes equated (Schunk et al., 2014). Further, concepts, such as *expectancy for success*, *self-efficacy*, and *self-concept* are so closely related that distinguishing among them is challenging for most people.

Inconsistencies also exist. For example, the concept of needs has been criticized by some of the most prominent leaders in the field. "Given these problems, needs are not investigated often in current research. However, reconceptualizing needs as goals, contemporary cognitive theories represent an improvement on traditional needs theories" (Schunk et al., 2014, p. 174). On the other hand, self-determination theory, one of the most prominent and powerful theories of motivation, is based on the premise that we

Classroom Connections
Using Students' Interests and Emotions to Promote Motivation to Learn in Classrooms

1. Promote interest in your learning activities by using personalized, concrete examples and promoting high levels of student involvement.

   - **Elementary:** A fourth-grade teacher puts his students' names into word problems. He is careful to be sure that all students' names are used by jotting down the names he uses and keeping track over time.

   - **Middle School:** A geography teacher begins the study of longitude and latitude by asking the students how they would tell a friend the exact location of one of their favorite hangouts.

   - **High School:** A physics teacher creates problems using the velocity and momentum of soccer balls after they've been kicked, and she asks students to determine the acceleration and speed players must run to intercept the kicks.

2. To reduce anxiety, emphasize understanding the content of tests instead of grades, provide opportunities for practice, and give students ample time to finish assessments.

   - **Elementary:** A second-grade teacher monitors his students as they work on a quiz. When he sees their attention wander, he reminds them of the work they have done on the topic and to concentrate on their work.

   - **Middle School:** An eighth-grade algebra teacher gives her students extensive practice with the types of problems they'll be expected to solve on their tests.

   - **High School:** An AP American history teacher knows that her students are nervous about passing the end-of-year exam. She frequently reminds them, "If you thoroughly understand the content, you'll be fine on the test. So, as you study, try to connect the ideas, and don't just memorize information."

MyLab Education Self-Check 10.5

Developmentally Appropriate Practice
Motivation to Learn in Students at Different Ages

Many applications of motivation theory apply to learners at all grade levels, such as using high-quality and personalized examples, involving students, and creating safe and orderly learning environments. Developmental differences exist, however. The following paragraphs outline suggestions for responding to these differences.

Working with Students in Early Childhood Programs and Elementary Schools

In contrast with older students, young children bask openly in praise and they rarely evaluate whether the praise is justified. They also tend to have incremental views of intelligence and set mastery goals. Because of these factors, emphasizing that all students can learn, avoiding social comparisons, praising students for their effort, and reminding them that hard work "makes us smart" can increase motivation to learn.

Working with Students in Middle Schools

As learners grow older, their mastery orientation tends to decrease, while their performance orientation increases. Modeling the belief that intelligence is incremental and emphasizing the relationship between effort and increased competence and ability are important. Middle school students increasingly meet their needs for belonging and relatedness with peer relationships, so social goals tend to increase in importance. Combining whole-group with small-group activities can help students meet these needs and goals.

Middle school students' need for autonomy also increases, so involving them in activities that increase their sense of autonomy, such as asking them to provide input into classroom rules, can be effective.

Working with Students in High Schools

High school students are beginning to think about their futures, so emphasizing the utility value of the topics they study and the skills they develop can increase their motivation to learn.

Because of the many experiences that high school students can access, such as video games and the Internet, generating interest in school topics can be a challenge. However, using concrete and personalized examples and promoting high levels of interaction remain effective.

Evidence that their competence is increasing is important to high school students, so sincere praise and other indicators of genuine accomplishment can increase motivation to learn.

all have *needs* for competence, autonomy, and relatedness, Maslow's hierarchy of needs remains prominent in the field, and "Covington (1992) proposed that the need for self-worth is a basic need of all individuals" (Schunk, et al., 2014, p. 224). So, needs remain prominent in theories of motivation.

Despite their complexity, overlap, and inconsistency, theories of motivation help explain a great deal about the way we act and feel, and some examples are outlined in Table 10.3. Further, the theories have many implications for both the way we live and the way we teach. For instance, we commonly see cases of people attempting to demonstrate how smart they are or how good they are at some activity. And everyone appreciates being asked how we're doing after being ill, and we're all annoyed when someone says they'll call us back, but they don't. The concepts of competence and relatedness from self-determination theory help us understand why.

As another simple example, it makes sense that we will be motivated to engage in an activity if we've previously been successful in similar activities, and we all want to understand why we succeed or fail on different tasks. Self-efficacy and attribution theory help us understand these tendencies. And setting and monitoring goals can be highly motivating if we are committed to reaching the goals. It also makes sense that we will persist longer and more diligently in activities that we enjoy and give up more quickly when we're bored. Many other examples exist.

We, Paul and Don, your authors, have spent major portions of our careers studying motivation. The topic is a challenge, but it is always stimulating, and seeing motivation theory illustrated both in everyday living and in classrooms is enormously rewarding.

Table 10.3 outlines variables involved in motivation, the basic premise involved in each, examples that can be explained using the variables, and the theoretical framework that supports the variables.

TABLE 10.3 Variables that influence motivation

Variable Influencing Motivation	Basic Premise	Examples the Variables Can Explain	Theoretical Framework
Needs			
Needs for • Survival • Safety • Belonging • Self-esteem • Intellectual achievement • Aesthetic appreciation • Self-actualization	People are motivated to satisfy deficiency needs and have continuing experiences with growth needs	• Why we first react to how "nice" people are rather than how "smart" they are (need for belonging) • Why some people have an insatiable thirst for learning (continuing experiences with intellectual achievement)	Maslow's hierarchy of needs
Needs for • Competence • Autonomy • Relatedness	People are motivated to meet needs for competence, autonomy, and relatedness	• Why praise for genuine accomplishment increases motivation but accomplishment of trivial tasks does not (perceptions of competence) • Why leaders in large corporations experience less stress than those who work for them (higher levels of autonomy) • Why we first react to people at a human level (need for relatedness)	Self-determination theory
Need to • Preserve self-worth	People are motivated to preserve their sense of self-worth and perceptions of high ability	• Why students value being able to succeed without studying (evidence of high ability) • Why students sometimes engage in self-handicapping behaviors (preserve perceptions of high ability in case of failure)	Self-worth theory
Beliefs			
• Future outcomes (expectations)	Motivation to engage in an activity increases when people expect to succeed in the activity	• Why we persist longer and choose more challenging tasks if we expect to succeed on them	Expectancy x value theory
• Intelligence/ability (mindset)	Motivation tends to increase if people believe that intelligence can be increased with effort	• Why people who believe "some got it and some don't" attempt to communicate perceptions of high ability by avoiding challenging tasks (preserve perceptions of high intelligence) • Why people who believe "the harder we work, the smarter we get" choose challenging tasks and persevere (failure simply indicating more effort or better strategies needed)	Self-worth theory Attribution theory
• Capability (self-efficacy)	Motivation increases if people believe they're capable of accomplishing specific tasks	• Why a person who has been scoring consistently in the high 80s believes that he will have a good day on the golf course (past success being the source of beliefs about capability) • Why a teacher's students work harder when she models effort and perseverance for them (modeling influencing self-efficacy)	Self-efficacy theory (social cognitive theory)
• Attainment value • Utility value • Cost	Motivation increases if an activity is important to them, will have some future benefit, and they don't have to give up too much to engage in the activity	• Why a person who plays tennis is motivated to win if she believes she is a good player but less so if she believes she isn't a good player (high attainment value) • Why a student takes an extra course in math if she wants to major in engineering in college (high utility value) • Why a student drops a course if he has to care for an ailing parent (too high a cost)	Expectancy x value theory
• Causes of performance	People are motivated to understand the causes of their performance	• Why students get upset when they don't get feedback on tests, quizzes, and other assignments (the desire to understand reasons for performance) • Why doing poorly because of too little effort is motivating (internal and controllable attribution)	Attribution theory
Goals			
• Mastery goals • Performance goals • Social goals • Work-avoidance goals	Specific, moderately challenging, and near-term goals that focus on understanding and improvement increase motivation to learn	• Why a person who has resolved to consume no more than 1,500 calories a day avoids eating a cookie because it is a measurable, short-term goal (near-term and specific goal) • Why a person who resolves to lose weight fails to do so (distant and general goal)	Goal theory
Interest (particularly situational interest)			
• Sex and violence • Power and money • Involvement • Personalization	People are motivated to participate in activities they find interesting	• Why there are so many "cop" shows on TV, and why "sex sells" (intrinsically interesting) • Why being able to apply understanding to a personal, real-world application is satisfying (increases intrinsic interest) • Why people enjoy conversations when they're directly involved but drift off when they are not (increases intrinsic interest)	Expectancy x value theory
Emotions			
• Enjoyment • Hope • Pride • Anger • Boredom	Positive emotions contribute to motivation and learning and negative emotions generally detract from motivation and learning	• Why we persist longer in activities we enjoy • Why we set mastery goals and regulate our learning when we take pride in our learning progress • Why we pay attention and process information less effectively when we're bored	Information processing theory Social cognitive theory

Chapter 10 Summary

1. Define motivation and describe different theoretical explanations for learner motivation.
   - Motivation is a process by which goal-directed activity is instigated and sustained.
   - Extrinsic motivation is motivation to engage in an activity as a means to an end; intrinsic motivation is motivation to be involved in an activity for its own sake.
   - Behaviorism describes motivation and learning in the same way; an increase in behavior is evidence of both learning and motivation.
   - Cognitive theories of motivation focus on learners' beliefs, expectations, and the desire to make sense of their experiences.
   - Sociocultural views of motivation focus on individuals' participating in learning communities.
   - Humanistic views of motivation are grounded in the premise that people are motivated to fulfill their total potential as human beings.

2. Describe learners' needs and how they influence motivation to learn.
   - A need is an internal force or drive to attain or avoid certain states or objects.
   - According to Maslow, all people have needs for survival, safety, belonging, and self-esteem. Once these needs are met, people are motivated to fulfill their potential as human beings.
   - According to self-determination theory, all people have needs for competence, autonomy, and relatedness. Helping students meet these needs increases motivation.
   - Self-worth theory suggests that all people have the need to protect their sense of self-worth, which depends on maintaining the perception that they have high ability.

3. Explain how learners' beliefs can impact their motivation to learn.
   - A belief is an idea we accept as true without necessarily having definitive evidence to support it.
   - Learners' motivation increases when they expect to succeed.
   - Learners with a growth mindset—those who believe that ability can be improved with effort—tend to have higher motivation to learn than learners with a fixed mindset—those who believe that ability is fixed.
   - Students who believe they are capable of accomplishing specific tasks have high self-efficacy and are more motivated to learn than students whose self-efficacy is lower.
   - Believing that increased understanding will help them meet future goals increases students' motivation to learn.
   - Students who believe that effort and ability are the causes of their success, or that lack of effort is the cause of failure, are likely to be more motivated to learn.

4. Describe how learners' goals affect their motivation to learn.
   - A goal is an outcome an individual hopes to attain.
   - Learners whose goals focus on mastery of tasks, improvement, and increased understanding have higher motivation to learn than do learners whose goals focus on social comparisons.
   - Social goals can decrease motivation to learn if they focus exclusively on social factors. Social-responsibility goals, however, and particularly social-responsibility goals combined with mastery goals, can lead to sustained motivation and achievement.
   - Grit involves individuals' commitment to achieving long-term goals, even in the face of extreme challenge and adversity.
   - We can develop grit in students by emphasizing growth mindsets and providing them with extensive opportunities for deliberate practice.

5. Explain how interest and emotion influence learner motivation.
   - As would be expected, learners are more motivated to study topics in which they're interested.
   - Students who have high personal interest in a topic or course of study generally have extensive background knowledge related to the topic, and their interest is usually quite stable.
   - Situational interest depends on the immediate context and can change quickly.
   - Personalized topics, real-world applications, involvement, and seeing interest modeled all contribute to situational interest.
   - Positive emotions, such as enjoyment, hope, and pride, generally increase both motivation to learn and achievement, whereas negative emotions, such as anger, frustration, and particularly boredom, generally decrease motivation to learn.
   - Learners with positive emotions are more likely to adopt mastery goals, self-regulate their learning, and have a growth mindset than are students with negative emotions.

Preparing for Your Licensure Exam

Understanding the Relationship Between Motivation and Learning

You will be required to take a licensure exam before you go into your own classroom. This exam will include information related to learner motivation, and it will include both multiple-choice and constructed-response questions. We include the following exercises to help you practice for the exam in your state. This book and these exercises will be a resource for you as you prepare for these tests.

You saw in this chapter how Kathy Brewster applied an understanding of the relationship between motivation and learning in her teaching. We look in now at another world history teacher who is also teaching about the Crusades. Read the case study, and then answer the questions that follow.

Michael Jensen watches as his students take their seats, and then announces, "Listen, everyone, I have your tests here from last Friday. Liora, Ivan, Lynn, and Segundo, super job on the test. They were the only A's in the class."

After handing back the tests Michael comments, "There were 7 D's or F's on this test. It wasn't that hard. . . . We have another one in two weeks. Let's give these sharp ones with the A's a run for their money. . . . Maybe this will motivate you."

"Now let's get going. We have a lot to cover today. . . . As you'll recall from yesterday, the Crusades were an attempt by the Christian powers of Western Europe to wrestle control of what is now the Middle East away from the Muslims. Pope Urban II proclaimed the first crusade in 1095 with the goal of restoring Christian access to the holy places around Jerusalem, and the Crusades went on for another 200 years, but finally ended in failure, because, as we know today, the Middle East remains largely Muslim with respect to religion."

Michael continues presenting information about the Crusades until he sees that 20 minutes are left in the period.

"I know that has been a lot to write down," he continues, "and I realize that learning dates and places isn't the most pleasant stuff, but you might as well get used to it, because that's what you'll have to do when you go to college. Plus, they'll be on the next test.

"Now, in the time we have left in the period, I want you to write a summary of the Crusades that outlines the major people and events and tells why they were important. You should be able to finish by the end of the period, but if you don't, turn your papers in at the beginning of class tomorrow. You may use your notes. Go ahead and get started."

As he monitors students, he sees that Jeremy has written only a few words on his paper. "Are you having trouble getting started?" Michael asks quietly.

"Yeah, . . . I don't quite know how to get started," Jeremy mumbles.

"I know written assignments are hard for you . . . . Let me help you," Michael says.

He takes a blank piece of paper and starts writing as Jeremy watches. He writes several sentences on the paper and then says, "See how easy that was? That's the kind of thing I want you to do. Go ahead—that's a start. Keep that so you can see what I'm looking for. Go back to your desk and give it another try."

Questions for Case Analysis

Use information from this chapter and the case study to answer the following questions.

Multiple-Choice Questions

1. In an attempt to motivate his students, Michael listed the names of the students who earned A's on the test and encouraged the rest of the students to " . . . give these sharp ones with the A's a run for their money." Of the following, which choice describes the best assessment of the effectiveness of Michael's strategy for motivating his students?

   a. It was an effective strategy, because it encouraged his students to increase their effort.

   b. It was an effective strategy, because it provided students with feedback about their performance.

   c. It was an effective strategy, because it encouraged the students who did well to attribute their success to high ability and those who did poorly to lack of effort.

d. It was an ineffective strategy, because it encouraged social comparisons, which detract from motivation.

2. Michael spent most of the class period lecturing to his students about the Crusades, and lectures have consistently been identified as ineffective teaching strategies. With respect to motivation, which of the following best explains why his lecture might have a negative impact on his students' motivation to learn?

a. Lectures are inconsistent with self-determination theory, because lectures cannot provide students with information that helps increase their perceptions of competence.

b. Lectures are commonly boring, and boredom is a negative emotion shown to detract from motivation to learn.

c. Lectures are inconsistent with expectancy × value theory because they cannot provide students with information that students believe has utility value.

d. Lectures detract from motivation to learn because it isn't possible for students to establish mastery goals when their teachers lecture.

Constructed-Response Question

1. Assess the extent to which Michael promoted situational interest in his topic (the Crusades). Provide evidence from the case study and the chapter in making your assessment.

Important Concepts

anxiety
attainment value
attribution theory
attributions
autonomy
belief
competence
cost
deficiency needs
emotion
expectancy × value theory
expectation

extrinsic motivation
fixed mindset
flow
goal
grit
growth mindset
growth needs
intrinsic motivation
learned helplessness
mastery goals
motivation
motivation to learn

motivational zone of
    proximal development
need
performance goals
performance-approach
    goals
performance-avoidance
    goals
personal interest
relatedness
self-actualization
self-determination

self-efficacy
self-worth
situational interest
social goals
unconditional positive
    regard
utility value
value
work-avoidance goal

Chapter 11
A Classroom Model for Promoting Student Motivation

Ariel Skelley/Getty Images

∨ Learning Outcomes

After you have completed your study of this chapter, you should be able to:

11.1 Describe the difference between a mastery-focused and a performance-focused classroom.

11.2 Describe the personal characteristics of teachers who increase students' motivation to learn.

11.3 Identify the learning climate variables that increase students' motivation to learn.

11.4 Explain how different instructional variables increase students' motivation to learn.

APA Top 20 Principles

Top 20 Principles from Psychology for PreK–12 Teaching and Learning explicitly addressed in this chapter.

Principle 6: Clear, explanatory, and timely feedback to students is important for learning.

Principle 11: Teachers' expectations about their students affect students' opportunities to learn, their motivation, and their learning outcomes.

Principle 14: Interpersonal relationships and communication are critical to both the teaching–learning process and the social-emotional development of students.

National Council on Teacher Quality (NCTQ)

The NCTQ Essential Teaching Strategies that every new teacher needs to know specifically addressed in this chapter.

Strategy 2: Linking abstract concepts with concrete representations
Strategy 3: Posing probing questions
Strategy 6: Assessing learning

In Chapter 10, we examined theories of motivation and suggestions for applying these theories with your students. In this chapter, as we extend this emphasis as building on our knowledge of theories of motivation, as we present "A Classroom model for Promoting Student Motivation," which describes specific motivational concepts that can be applied in our work with students to increase their motivation to learn. Although some students may seem intractable in their lack of motivation, we can make a difference with many, if not most of them. This model is designed to help us reach this goal.

We begin with a lesson conducted by DeVonne Lampkin, a fifth-grade teacher. As you read the case study, think about her students' motivation and how DeVonne influences it.

Because they are so prominent in our lives, DeVonne wants her students to understand the concept *arthropod*—animals such as beetles (insects), spiders (arachnids), and crabs, lobsters, and shrimp (crustaceans). She decides she'll use examples and nonexamples of arthropods to help her students understand the concept and then compare arthropods to our own body structures.

She begins the lesson by reaching into a cooler and taking out a live lobster.

The students "ooh" and "aah" at the wriggling animal, and DeVonne asks Stephanie to carry it around the room so her classmates can see and touch it.

As she does, DeVonne says, "Look carefully, because I'm going to ask you to tell us what you see."

When everyone has had a chance to observe the lobster, DeVonne asks, "Okay, what did you notice?"

"Hard," Tu observes.

"Pink and green," Saleina comments.

"Wet," Kevin adds.

DeVonne lists the students' observations on the board, and based on these observations, guides them to conclude that the lobster has a hard outer covering (exoskeleton), three body parts, and segmented legs. "These are the essential characteristics of arthropods," she notes, as she writes them on the board.

DeVonne then pulls a cockroach from a jar, and amid more squeals, walks around the class holding it with tweezers. She asks the students if it's an arthropod.

After discussion to resolve uncertainty about whether the cockroach has an exoskeleton, the class decides that it does, and concludes that it is indeed an arthropod.

DeVonne next takes a clam out of her cooler, and asks, "Is this an arthropod?"

Some students conclude that it is, reasoning that it has a hard shell.

"But," A. J. comments, "it doesn't have any legs," and, following additional discussion, the class decides that it isn't an arthropod.

"Now," DeVonne asks, "Do you think Mrs. Sapp [the school principal] is an arthropod? . . . Tell us why or why not."

Amid giggles, some students conclude that she is, because she has segmented legs. Others disagree because she doesn't look like a lobster or a roach. After some discussion, Tu observes, "She doesn't have an exoskeleton," and the class finally agrees that she isn't an arthropod.

DeVonne then has the students form pairs, passes out shrimp, calms the excited students, and asks them to carefully observe the shrimp and decide if they're arthropods.

During the whole-group discussion that follows, she finds that some of the students are still uncertain about the idea of an exoskeleton, so she has them peel the shrimp and feel the head and outer covering. After seeing the peeled covering, they conclude that the shrimp does have an exoskeleton, and with additional discussion conclude that shrimp are indeed arthropods.

We'll revisit DeVonne's lesson throughout the chapter, but we can see, even from the written case study, that her students were highly involved and motivated, and their reactions are even more obvious in the video episode. Using the *Classroom Model for Promoting Student Motivation* as a conceptual framework, we'll see how DeVonne applied it in her teaching. Before we do, however, we want to revisit a topic we introduced in Chapter 10.

Creating a Mastery-Focused Classroom

11.1 Describe the difference between a mastery-focused and a performance-focused classroom.

We'll base our discussion on students' mastery-goal orientations, which emphasize improvement and increasing understanding, as compared to performance-goal orientations, where students focus on ability and comparisons to others. Here, we extend these ideas to classrooms by examining mastery-focused classrooms, classroom environments that emphasize effort, making and correcting mistakes, continuous improvement, and developing understanding, compared to performance-focused classrooms, environments that stress high grades, public displays of ability, correct answers, and performance compared to others (Chatzisarantis et al., 2016; Sommet, Pillaud, Meuleman, & Butera, 2017). High levels of teacher-student and student-student interaction occur in mastery-focused classrooms, students accept responsibility for their learning, and the teacher and students are "in this together" to promote as much learning as possible for everyone.

DeVonne attempted to create a mastery-focused classroom in three ways: (1) She demonstrated personal qualities which contribute to the positive teacher–student relationships necessary for all motivation and learning; (2) she helped her students succeed on challenging tasks within the context of a safe and orderly classroom environment; and (3) she generated situational interest with the lobster, cockroach, and shrimp, she involved her students in the learning activity, and she promoted deep understanding of her topic. Differences in mastery-focused compared to performance-focused classrooms are summarized in Table 11.1.

MyLab Education
Video Example 11.1

Mastery-focused classroom environments emphasize effort, continuous improvement, and understanding. In this environment, mistakes are viewed as a normal and important part of the learning process. Notice in this segment how science teacher Matt Swope describes the way he handles student mistakes in an effort to promote a mastery-focused classroom.

A Classroom Model for Promoting Student Motivation

The *Classroom Model for Promoting Student Motivation* is grounded in this mastery-focused framework and combines learning and motivation theory and research. The model is outlined in Figure 11.1 and has three major components:

1. *Teacher*: Demonstrating personal qualities that increase student motivation to learn.
2. *Learning climate*: Creating a motivating environment for learning.
3. *Instruction*: Developing interest in learning activities.

Four variables exist within each component, and the components and variables in the model are synergistic, that is, the effect of their combination and interaction is greater than the sum of the individual variables; a single variable cannot be effectively applied if others are missing.

TABLE 11.1 Mastery-focused and performance-focused classrooms

	Mastery Focused	Performance Focused
Success defined as . . .	Mastery, improvement	High grades, doing better than others
Value placed on . . .	Effort, improvement	High grades, demonstration of high ability
Reasons for satisfaction . . .	Meeting challenges, hard work	Doing better than others, success with minimum effort
Teacher oriented toward . . .	Student learning	Student performance
View of errors . . .	A normal part of learning	A basis for concern and anxiety
Reasons for effort . . .	Increased understanding	High grades, doing better than others
Ability viewed as . . .	Incremental, alterable	An entity, fixed
Reasons for assessment . . .	Measure progress toward preset criteria, provide feedback	Determine grades, compare students to one another

Figure 11.1 A classroom model for promoting student motivation

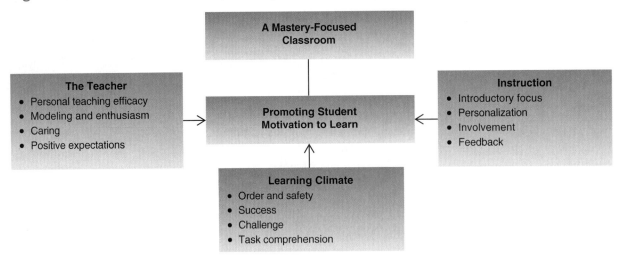

SOURCE: Based on Andeman, E. M., & Wolters, C. A. (2006). Goals, values, and affect: Influences on motivation. In P. A. Alexander & P. H. Winne (Eds.), *Handbook of education psychology* (2nd ed., pp. 369–389). Mahwah, NJ: Erlbaum.

The Teacher–Student Relationship

A positive teacher–student relationship is the foundation for all motivation, and it is one of the essential characteristics of a motivating classroom and school (Kuhl, 2017). Supportive teachers create emotionally safe and low-conflict learning environments, and positive relationships between teachers and students are associated with a host of learning benefits, including increased student engagement in school, even in students with negative attitudes (Archambault, Vandenbossche-Makombo, & Fraser, 2017); improved student self-regulation (Zee & de Bree, 2017); and increased achievement and higher levels of school satisfaction (Leff, Waasdorp, & Paskewich, 2016). The benefits of positive teacher–student relationships are thought to "trigger effort, persistence, and participation; to foster interest and enthusiasm; and to dampen negative emotions such as anger, frustration, anxiety, or boredom" (Castle Heatly & Votruba-Drzal, 2017, p. 1043).

APA Top 20 Principles

The discussion in this section illustrates Principle 14: *Interpersonal relationships and communication are critical to both the teaching–learning process and the social-emotional development of students*— from the *Top 20 Principles from Psychology for PreK–12 Teaching and Learning*.

Positive teacher–student relationships both support learner motivation in the immediate context and also provide a foundation for future motivation and achievement. Further, teachers' social and emotional support is particularly important for children who are academically at-risk and/or who come from predominantly low-income and ethnic minority backgrounds (Liew, Chen, & Hughes, 2010). This benefit is grounded in theory. "Consistent with attachment and self-determination theories, our findings suggest that academically at-risk learners' perceptions of teachers as supportive have a beneficial effect on their academic effort in the classroom and confidence in their academic abilities" (Hughes, Wu, Kwok, Villarreal, & Johnson, 2012, p. 362).

Teachers who create positive relationships with students realize that teaching— instead of being a *personal* endeavor—is an *interpersonal* venture, and they consciously set "relational goals," goals to create close and caring relationships with students. Teachers with this goal orientation also use mastery rather than performance approaches in their instruction, that is, they focus on increasing understanding, emphasize that grades take care of themselves if students understand content, avoid social comparisons among students, and use assessments as tools for increasing learning (Chatzisarantis et al., 2016; Sommet et al., 2017).

Creating positive teacher–student relationships in no way implies that we lower either achievement or behavioral standards for our students. Classrooms are for conscientious work and rigorous learning, not horseplay and off-task behaviors. Nor does a positive teacher–student relationship suggest that we are our students' "buddies." Rather, we are adults who are committed to our students both as people and as learners, and we're there to guide and support their learning and development.

As we turn to the variables in the *Classroom Model for Promoting Student Motivation*, remember that the teacher–student relationship is the emotional architecture that provides a foundation for each variable and the interdependence among them.

We turn now to the personal characteristics of teachers who promote student motivation to learn.

MyLab Education Self-Check 11.1
MyLab Education Application Exercise 11.1: Creating a Mastery-Focused Classroom

In this exercise, you will be asked to analyze a high school teacher's efforts to create a mastery-focused environment in his classroom.

The Teacher: Personal Qualities that Increase Motivation to Learn

11.2 **Describe the personal characteristics of teachers who increase students' motivation to learn.**

Ed Psych and You

Think about some of your best teachers. What were they like? What kind of learning environment did they create? What did they do that made their classes interesting and worthwhile?

Other than parents, you—their teachers—are the most important influences on students' learning and motivation. And this influence strongly depends on your own personal qualities. You are responsible for creating a mastery-focused learning environment and positive emotional climate, implementing effective instruction, and establishing supportive teacher–student relationships that are the foundation for all motivation and learning. None of the other components of the model are effective if the teacher qualities highlighted in Figure 11.2 are lacking. We examine these qualities now.

Personal Teaching Efficacy: Beliefs About Teaching and Learning

Self-efficacy describes individuals' beliefs about their capability of accomplishing specific tasks. **Personal teaching efficacy**—teachers believing that they're capable of promoting learning for all students, regardless of prior knowledge, ability, or personal backgrounds—is an extension of the concept of self-efficacy (Summers, Davis, & Woolfolk Hoy, 2017).

Figure 11.2 The teacher: Personal qualities that increase motivation to learn

```
          ┌─────────────────────────────────┐
          │         The Teacher:            │
          │    Personal Qualities that      │
          │    Increase Motivation to Learn │
          └─────────────────────────────────┘
```

Personal Teaching Efficacy	Modeling and Enthusiasm	Caring	Teacher Expectations
• Beliefs about teaching and learning	• Communicating genuine interest	• Meeting needs for belonging and relatedness	• Holding students to high standards

Significant differences exist between high- and low-efficacy teachers. High-efficacy teachers take personal responsibility for student learning; they are demanding but fair, maximize time available for instruction, praise students for increasing competence, and persevere with low achievers. Low-efficacy teachers are more likely to blame low achievement on students' lack of intelligence, poor home environments, or other causes outside the classroom. They have lower expectations, spend less time on learning activities, give up on low achievers, and are more critical when students fail. They are more controlling and value student autonomy less than do high-efficacy teachers (Ware & Kitsantas, 2007).

Differences in goal orientations also exist between the two groups. High-efficacy teachers are more likely to have a mastery-goal orientation, and they maintain it even if their schools emphasize performance goals, such as high-stakes test results. Low-efficacy teachers are more likely to adopt the performance goals of their schools (Yoon & Sungok, 2013). These results make sense. If we believe we can influence learning for all students we are more likely to maximize our instructional time, demand more of our students, and spend more time with those who struggle. And students tend to adopt goals consistent with the goal orientations of their schools and teachers; that is, students are more likely to adopt mastery goals if they believe their schools and teachers have this orientation (Sommet et al., 2017).

"Teachers with higher self-efficacy beliefs showed higher instructional quality, as indicated by the three dimensions of cognitive activation, classroom management, and individual learning support, whether instruction was rated by the teachers themselves or by their students" (Holzberger, Philipp, & Kunter, 2013, p. 782). These high-efficacy beliefs influence not only motivation, but also learning. "In classrooms where teachers have high levels of teaching efficacy, high levels of learning occur" (Tanel, 2013, p. 7).

Efficacy can also affect the learning climate of an entire school. Students benefit from **collective efficacy**, beliefs that the faculty as a whole can have a positive effect on student learning, and it is particularly important for students who come from diverse backgrounds (Belfi, Gielen, De Fraine, Verschueren, & Meredith, 2015; Prelli, 2016). In schools where collective efficacy is high, low-socioeconomic status (SES) students have achievement gains almost as high as those of high-SES students from schools with low collective efficacy (Lee, 2000). Teachers in high-collective-efficacy schools reduce the achievement gap between advantaged and disadvantaged students.

As with self-efficacy, personal teaching efficacy depends on background, experience, and the culture and leadership of the school (Pierce, 2014). Teachers with extensive professional knowledge are higher in personal teaching efficacy than their less knowledgeable colleagues (Tanel, 2013), which suggests that we should continually strive to increase our professional knowledge and demonstrate the desire for lifelong learning that we hope to inspire in our students.

Modeling and Enthusiasm: Communicating Genuine Interest

Social cognitive theory explains why teacher modeling is one of the most powerful influences on student interest. Expert teachers model several aspects of learning and teaching that influence student motivation (Kim & Schallert, 2014; Schunk, Meece, & Pintrich, 2014). They include:

- *A growth mindset*, the belief that our intelligence or ability can be increased with hard work.
- *A mastery and social-responsibility goal orientation*, a focus on learning and improvement and meeting our commitments to others.
- *Internal attributions*, the belief that we control both our successes and our failures.
- *A link between hard work and self-worth*, the view that our self-worth is determined by our work ethic and not the appearance of high ability.

Expert teachers also model enthusiasm, and teacher enthusiasm is linked to both motivation and learning. "[T]eacher enthusiasm first and foremost is associated with students' motivational and affective outcomes (e.g., enjoyment, interest), whereas achievement is indirectly related to enthusiasm, mediated by students' motivation or attention during class" (Keller, Goetz, Becker, Morger, & Hensley, 2014, p. 29). In other words, teacher enthusiasm directly impacts student motivation, and, as a result of their increased motivation, students pay better attention and learn more.

We can demonstrate enthusiasm in a variety of ways, such as using humor, describing our own personal experiences, and demonstrating excitement and energy. However, we won't always have a relevant personal experience to describe, and we won't always feel humorous or energetic. So, the way we can most consistently demonstrate enthusiasm is *to communicate our own genuine interest in the topics we're teaching* (Keller et al., 2014). We all have different personalities, and some are naturally more energetic and outgoing than others. However, we can all make statements such as the following to increase student motivation: "Geography strongly influences our lives. For example, most of our major cities, such as New York, Chicago, and San Francisco, became important because of their geography," or "Think about the needles on a cactus compared to the leaves on an oak tree; they're actually related and are adaptations to their environments. Now, that's interesting." Regardless of our personalities, statements like these increase the likelihood that our students will also be interested in the topic and believe the content is valuable and worth learning (Keller, Hoy, Goetz, & Frensel, 2016). And it takes no extra preparation or energy on our part. Better yet, with a bit of awareness and practice, it will become essentially automatic. It won't work for every student or for every learning activity, but it will for many, and we have nothing to lose in doing so.

MyLab Education
Video Example 11.2

Teachers communicate their enthusiasm by demonstrating their own interest in the topics they teach. Notice here how middle school teacher, Scott Sowell, demonstrates his interest in the topic with his excitement and energy when he interacts with his students.

Caring: Meeting Needs for Belonging and Relatedness

A first-grade teacher greets each of her children every morning with a hug, handshake, or "high five."

A fifth-grade teacher immediately calls parents if one of his students fails to turn in a homework assignment or misses more than two days of school in a row.

An algebra teacher learns the name of each student in all five of her classes by the end of the first week of school, and she stays in her room during her lunch hour to help students who are struggling.

Each of these teachers is demonstrating **caring**, a teacher's empathy and investment in the protection and development of young people (Noddings, 2013; Roeser, Peck, & Nasir, 2006).

The importance of "caring" as a personal characteristic is grounded in both philosophy and theory. "The ethics of care," part of a philosophical movement which emphasizes that all people are vulnerable and interdependent, suggests that we should treat all students as worthy human beings (Gilligan, 2008; Noddings, 2013). With respect to theory, caring people help meet others' needs for belonging, which is preceded only by safety and survival in Maslow's (1970) hierarchy of needs, and caring helps meet people's needs for relatedness, emphasized by self-determination theory (Deci & Ryan, 2008).

Caring is essential in schools. All parents want teachers who care about their children, and caring is one of the characteristics principals first look for when they recruit new teachers (Engel, 2013). Evidence also suggests that caring teachers strongly affect students' motivation and learning. "Students who perceived that teachers cared about them reported positive motivational outcomes such as more prosocial and social-responsibility goals, academic effort, and greater internal control beliefs" (Perry, Turner, & Meyer, 2006, p. 341). Students want teachers to care for them both as learners and as people.

Caring is particularly important for boys (Kimmel, 2018) and new immigrant youth (Suarez-Orozco, Pimentel, & Martin, 2009). This might be surprising, because on the surface boys want to appear tough, resilient, and unemotional. Research suggests that exactly the opposite is true; all students, and especially boys, need to feel wanted and cared about (Chu & Gilligan, 2015).

The concept of caring can be misinterpreted as "touchy-feely" and flaky education that emphasizes feelings and self-esteem above academic learning. Quite the opposite is the case; requiring appropriate behavior from students and holding them to high academic standards is fundamental to caring. Teachers who do this are sometimes described as "warm demanders" (Poole & Evertson, 2013). Further, "Holding students accountable to high academic standards strengthens their sense of connection to school" (Biag, 2016, p. 36). And, some evidence indicates that high academic standards even lead to a reduction in risky health behaviors, such as binge drinking, smoking, and marijuana use (Hao & Cowan, 2017).

Respect is an important aspect of caring; we model it for our students, we expect students to respect us, and we require them to respect each other. Further, respect and appropriate standards of behavior are interrelated. "Treat everyone with respect" is a rule that should be universally enforced. An occasional minor incident of rudeness can be overlooked, but chronic disrespect, either for us or other students, should not be tolerated; it has no place in a caring classroom environment.

Teacher Expectations: Promoting Competence and Positive Attributions

Communicating high expectations is the final teacher quality in our Model for Promoting Student Motivation (Figure 11.1), and research confirms the link between high teacher expectations and increased student achievement. "Evidence indicates that when there is strong academic press, students on average spend more time on learning tasks, exert greater effort on their schoolwork, and demonstrate higher performance" (Biag, 2016, p. 36).

APA Top 20 Principles

This description illustrates Principle 11: *Teachers' expectations about their students affect students' opportunities to learn, their motivation, and their learning outcome*—from the *Top 20 Principles from Psychology for PreK–12 Teaching and Learning*.

These effects can be profound. "High school students whose first-grade teachers underestimated their abilities performed significantly worse on standardized tests. . . . Conversely, when early abilities were overestimated, high school students performed better than expected" (Sorhagen, 2013, p. 472). Teachers' beliefs about students are so important that expectations in first-grade continue to have an effect on students' achievement as much as 10 years later!

Self-determination theory helps us understand these results. As students meet teachers' expectations, perceptions of their competence—one of three innate psychological needs according to the theory—increase, and as perceptions of competence increase, so does motivation to learn.

Teachers' expectations influence the way they interact with students, and they often treat students they perceive to be high achievers differently from those they believe are low achievers. This differential treatment occurs in four ways (Good & Lavigne, 2018):

- *Emotional support*: Teachers interact more with perceived high achievers; their interactions and nonverbal behaviors are more positive; and they seat these students closer to the front of the class.

- *Effort*: Teachers are more enthusiastic when working with high achievers, their instruction is more thorough, and they require more complete and accurate student answers.

- *Questioning*: Teachers call on perceived high achievers more often, they allow these students more time to answer, and they provide high achievers with more prompts and cues when they're unable to answer.

- *Feedback and assessment*: Teachers praise perceived high achievers more, criticize them less, and offer perceived high achievers more complete feedback on assessments.

At an extreme, teachers' expectations for students can become **self-fulfilling prophecies**, outcomes that occur when people's performance results from and confirms beliefs about their capabilities (Lòpez, 2017). The powerful influence of self-fulfilling prophecies has been widely researched, particularly in the business world (Russo, Islam, & Koyuncu, 2017).

Let's see how it works with teacher expectations. Communicating positive expectations suggests to students that they will be successful, and when they're successful, their perceptions of competence increase, their motivation increases, and, as a result, achievement increases. The opposite is also true. "Underestimated students have a lower expectancy of success, have a lower self-concept, and report more test anxiety than overestimated students" (Zhou & Urhahne, 2013, p. 283). Communicating low expectations can result in students exerting less effort, so they perform less well, which confirms perceptions about their capabilities. And these experiences influence their attributions. Students who believe their teachers have low expectations for them tend to attribute success to external factors, such as luck, and attribute failure to internal factors, such as lack of ability (Zhou & Urhahne, 2013). Either has a negative impact on motivation. Instead, we want them to attribute their success to effort, and high expectations contribute to that effort.

Children of all ages are aware of teachers' expectations. In a study conducted nearly 30 years ago, researchers concluded, "After ten seconds of seeing and/or hearing a teacher, even very young students could detect whether the teacher talked about or to an excellent or a weak student" (Babad, Bernieri, & Rosenthal, 1991, p. 230). More recently, researchers concluded, "Although teachers in general seem to be fair and objective . . . differential teacher treatments, even sometimes implicit or unintentional, will be sensitively perceived by students and impact their self-concept" (Zhou & Urhahne, 2013, p. 276).

Our expectations for our students are often out of our conscious control. For instance, because they're more likely to be able to answer, we—without thinking about it—fall into a pattern of calling on mostly higher achievers during a learning activity. We're a bit surprised when they're unable to answer, so we prompt them. On the other hand, if we call on a lower achiever, and he isn't able to answer, we're not surprised, so we don't try as hard, instead turning the question to another student, with a "Can someone help out?"

As we saw earlier, students are aware of these differences, which have a negative impact on their perceptions of competence, and, in turn, their motivation and achievement.

Our goal in this section is first to remind us of the powerful influence expectations have on student motivation and learning, and second, to make us aware of the fact that our expectations are often below the level of consciousness. With awareness, we are more likely to maintain appropriately high expectations, such as calling on all our students as equally as possible.

This discussion helps answer the first question we asked in *Ed Psych and You* at the beginning of the section, "What were your best teachers like?" Most likely they cared about you both as a person and as a student, they communicated their beliefs in your ability to learn, they were enthusiastic, and they had high expectations for all your work. These are the qualities we want to display in our work with our students.

Using Educational Psychology in Teaching: Suggestions for Demonstrating Personal Qualities That Increase Students' Motivation to Learn

Personal qualities that promote motivation to learn can be applied in a number of ways. The following suggestions can help you in your efforts to demonstrate these qualities with your students.

- Maintain high personal teaching efficacy.
- Establish appropriately high expectations for all students.
- Model responsibility, effort, and interest in the topics you're teaching.
- Demonstrate caring and commitment to your students' learning.

To see these suggestions in action, let's look again at DeVonne's work with her students.

"Wow, you're here early," Karla Utley, one of DeVonne's colleagues, comments to her early one morning.

"I've got kids coming in," DeVonne replies. "I did a writing lesson yesterday, and the class evaluated some of their paragraphs." (DeVonne's writing lesson is the case study at the end of this chapter.) "Several of the kids, like Tu and Saleina, did really well . . . but some are behind. So, Justin, Picey, and Rosa are coming in before school this morning, and we're going to work on it. They aren't my highest achievers, but I know I can get more out of them than I am right now. They're good kids; they're just a little behind."

A half hour before school, DeVonne is working at her desk as the three students come in the door. She smiles and says, "We're going to practice a little more on our writing. I know that you can all be good writers, and it's the same thing for me. I've practiced and practiced, and now my effort is paying off. . . . And the more we improve, the more fun writing becomes. I enjoy it more now than I ever have. You can do the same thing. . . . Let's look at your paragraphs again."

She displays Justin's paragraph on the document camera and asks, "What did we suggest that you might do to improve this?" (The lesson in which Justin's paragraph was initially evaluated is the case study at the end of the chapter in the section "Preparing for Your Licensure Exam." You will see his paragraph again there.)

"He needs to stay on either the boy or the house," Rosa offers.

"Good," DeVonne says with a nod. "Staying focused on your topic sentence is important."

> *There was a boy named Josh. He lives in a house with the roof falling in and the windows were broke. He had holes in the wall and the ceiling leaked when it rained. But then again it always rained and thunder over his house. Noone ever goes to his gate because he was so weird. They say he is a vampire.*

Together, the group examines each student's original paragraph and makes specific suggestions for improvement.

DeVonne then says, "Okay, now each of you rewrite your paragraphs based on our suggestions. When you're finished, we'll look at them again."

The students rewrite their paragraphs, and they again discuss the products.

"Much improvement," DeVonne says after they've finished. "If we keep at it, we're going to get there. . . . I'll see you again tomorrow at 7:30."

Now, let's see how DeVonne applies the suggestions.

Maintain High Personal Teaching Efficacy.   As we saw earlier, teachers with high personal teaching efficacy believe they are capable of promoting learning in their students regardless of personal or academic conditions. DeVonne's comment, "I know I can get more out of them than I am right now. They're good kids; they're just a little behind," reflects this belief. And her belief was reflected in her efforts. This applied the first suggestion.

Maintaining high personal teaching efficacy can be a challenge. You will work with students who don't seem to care, virtually refuse to do homework, and, in spite of your best efforts to involve them, won't pay attention in class. This will be understandably discouraging. However, if we maintain the belief that we can and do make a difference with our students, we will. We will admittedly be more successful with some than others. However, if we do our very best with every student, we will have done our jobs, and that's all we can be expected to do.

Establish High Expectations for Students.   In having Justin, Picey, and Rosa come to school a half hour early to get extra practice with their writing, and saying to them, "I know that you can all be good writers," she communicated positive expectation for her students.

In some cases, students may essentially refuse to come in for extra help. In situations such as these, you've still done your best, and this is all you can do. You can sleep at night knowing that you've made all the efforts that can be expected of a professional.

Model Responsibility, Effort, and Interest in the Topics You're Teaching.   As she worked with Justin, Picey, and Rosa, DeVonne said, "It's the same thing for me. I've practiced and practiced, and now my effort is paying off. . . . And, the more we improve, the more fun writing becomes. I enjoy it more now than I ever have." This comment modeled responsibility, effort, and interest in writing. It won't work all the time or with every student, but it will make a difference with many, and moreover, modeling these characteristics takes little extra effort, so we have nothing to lose in doing so.

Demonstrate Caring and Commitment to Your Students' Learning.   Finally, and perhaps most significantly, DeVonne demonstrated caring and commitment by arriving at school an hour early and devoting her personal time to helping students who needed additional support. She kept the study session upbeat and displayed the respect for her students that's essential for promoting motivation to learn.

We can also demonstrate that we care about our students in other ways. Some examples include (Aaron, Auger, & Pepperell, 2013):

- Learning students' names quickly, and calling on them by their first names, or nicknames if preferred.
- Getting to know students as individuals by asking about, or commenting on, personal items, such as a family member, friend, or activity.
- Making eye contact, smiling, demonstrating relaxed body language, and leaning toward them when talking.
- Using the terms "we" and "our" rather than "you" and "your" in reference to class activities and assignments.
- Spending time with students.

We want to especially emphasize the last item. We all have exactly 24 hours in our days, and the way we choose to allocate our time is the truest measure of our priorities. Deciding to spend some of this time with an individual student, or a small group, as DeVonne did, communicates caring better than any other single factor. Helping students who have problems with an assignment or calling a parent after school hours communicates that you care about students as learners. Spending your personal time to ask a question about a baby brother or compliment a new hairstyle communicates caring about students as people.

As with the other personal qualities, caring won't turn all our students into motivated learners, but caring about them sends a powerful message that we respect them as human beings and want the best for them. And, for those we do impact, we will have made an invaluable contribution to their lives.

Classroom Connections

Demonstrating Personal Characteristics in the Model for Promoting Student Motivation

Caring

1. Caring teachers promote a sense of belonging and relatedness in their classrooms and commit to the development of students both as people and as learners. Demonstrate caring by respecting students and giving them your personal time.

- **Elementary:** A second-grade teacher stands at the door of her classroom and greets each of her students by name every morning as they come into the classroom and makes it a point to talk to each student about something personal as often as possible.

- **Middle School:** A geography teacher calls parents as soon as he sees a student having academic or personal problems. He solicits parents' help and offers his assistance in solving problems. He also makes periodic "positive" calls

to tell parents about noteworthy examples of academic improvement or good behavior.

- **High School:** An Algebra II teacher conducts help sessions after school three afternoons a week. Students are invited to attend to get help with homework or to discuss any other concerns about the class or school.

Modeling and Enthusiasm

2. Teachers demonstrate enthusiasm by modeling their own interest in the content of their classes. Communicate interest in the topics you're teaching.

- **Elementary:** During individual reading time, a fourth-grade teacher comments on a book she's interested in, and she reads while the students are reading.

- **Middle School:** A life science teacher brings science-related clippings from the local newspaper to class and asks students to do the same. He guides class discussions of the clippings and pins them on a bulletin board for students to read.

- **High School:** A world history teacher frequently describes connections between classroom topics and their impact on today's world.

Positive Expectations

3. Teacher expectations strongly influence motivation and learning. Maintain appropriately high expectations for all students.

- **Elementary:** During learning activities a third-grade teacher calls on all her students as equally as possible. She provides prompts and cues when students are unable to answer.

- **Middle School:** When his students complain about word problems, a pre-algebra teacher reminds them of how important problem solving is for their lives. Each day, he guides a discussion of at least two challenging word problems.

- **High School:** When her American history students turn in sloppily written essays, the teacher displays a well-written example on the document camera, discusses it, and requires her students to revise their original products.

MyLab Education Self-Check 11.2

Learning Climate: Creating a Motivating Classroom Environment

11.3 Identify the learning climate variables that increase students' motivation to learn.

Students quickly sense if their classrooms are safe and positive places to learn, and in a **positive learning climate**, the teacher and students work together as a community of learners to help everyone achieve (Boersma, Dam, Wardekker, & Volman, 2016). Our goal in creating this kind of classroom is to promote students' feelings of safety and security, together with beliefs about success, challenge, and understanding (see Figure 11.3).

We examine the components of this type of learning environment next.

Order and Safety: Classrooms as Secure Places to Learn

The classroom climate variable, **order and safety**, creates a predictable learning environment and promotes feelings of physical and emotional security. The importance of safe and orderly classrooms is well established by a long history of research (Korpershoek, Harms, de Boer, van Kuijk, & Doolaard, 2016), and additional work suggests that a safe environment is particularly important for members of cultural minorities (Cooper, 2013). Our ability to create this type of environment is a high priority for principals; it's one of the first characteristics they look for as they recruit new teachers (Engel, 2013).

Figure 11.3 Learning climate variables in the Model for Promoting Student Motivation

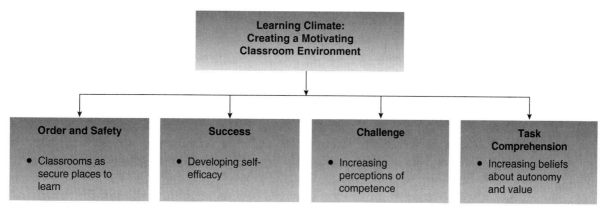

Four different theoretical perspectives help us understand why order and safety are so important for promoting motivation:

- *Piaget's concept of equilibrium.* The need for equilibrium—when experiences make sense to students—is the foundation of Piaget's theory of cognitive development, and a safe, orderly, and predictable classroom helps students meet this need (Piaget, 1977).
- *Maslow's Work.* According to Maslow's (1970) hierarchy, safety is an essential deficiency need, preceded only by survival.
- *Self-Determination Theory.* Learners feel more autonomous—an innate need according to self-determination theory—in a safe environment (Deci & Ryan, 2008).
- *Human memory.* A safe environment allows learners to focus their limited working memory space on learning. In chaotic environments, students waste some of this crucial mental capacity thinking about ways to avoid threat, criticism, or ridicule (Schunk et al., 2014).

We set the tone for this essential variable by creating positive teacher–student relationships, modeling and requiring mutual respect, establishing predictable routines, and consistently enforcing rules and standards for appropriate behavior (Jones, Jones, & Vermete, 2013).

Success: Developing Student Self-Efficacy

Students believing they are capable of accomplishing specific tasks—their self-efficacy—is one of the most powerful motivators that exist. Success is the most significant factor contributing to these beliefs, so, once we've established a safe and orderly learning environment, helping our students succeed is our most important goal. And this is true for learners ranging from elementary school to those in colleges and universities (Fong et al., 2017; Scogin, 2016). To feel a sense of self-efficacy, students must believe their learning is progressing. Scoring higher than classmates on a quiz might temporarily increase these beliefs, but success of this sort is fleeting, and students aren't always able to score higher than classmates regardless of how hard they try. They can make personal learning progress, however, and this is the form of success that most contributes to self-efficacy.

Attempting to inoculate our students against failure is an integral part of this process. We all fail periodically, and we should try to help students understand that failures are inevitable and even valuable. Mistakes and failure are normal parts of learning, and students who understand this and persevere are those that succeed over the long term (Zhou & Urhahne, 2013).

Challenge: Increasing Perceptions of Competence

Ed Psych and You

Think about how you feel when you solve a difficult problem, make a computer application work, or figure out a puzzling event. Why do you feel this way?

According to self-determination theory, developing a sense of competence is an innate need in all of us, and seeing our competence increase is intrinsically motivating (Deci & Ryan, 2008). "All students, even the seemingly unmotivated, care about being seen as competent and able in the eyes of others" (De Castella, Byrne, & Covington, 2013, p. 861).

This helps answer the question we asked in *Ed Psych and You.* Solving difficult problems or figuring out a computer application or puzzling event increases our perception of competence. "Attainment of challenging goals conveys to learners that they are becoming more competent, which raises self-efficacy and perceived control over outcomes. In turn, learners are apt to set new, challenging goals, which serve to maintain intrinsic motivation" (Schunk et al., 2014, p. 268). Research in neuroscience indicates that successfully responding to challenges can provide a dopamine-reward rush in the pleasure sensors of our brains (Zink, Pagnoni, Martin-Skurski, Chappelow, & Berns, 2004). It's personally rewarding to attempt and succeed on challenging tasks.

This helps us understand why success, alone, is not necessarily motivating. We can all successfully memorize lists of facts and rules or solve routine problems, but this success does little to increase our perceptions of competence, and it isn't emotionally satisfying. We need to experience success in activities we perceive as challenging (Hung, Sun, & Yu, 2015). In addition, students' beliefs about utility value—believing that studying a topic will be useful for meeting future goals—are increased when they succeed on challenging tasks (Akers, 2017).

We can capitalize on the motivating characteristics of challenge by asking our students to identify relationships in the topics they study and identify the implications of these relationships for new learning (Brophy, 2010). For example, DeVonne didn't immediately tell her students that arthropods had an exoskeleton, three body parts, and segmented legs. Instead, with her guidance, they identified these characteristics for themselves. Then, she had them observe and decide if a cockroach, clam, and even Mrs. Sapp (the school principal) were arthropods. Her approach challenged her students, as indicated by some of them initially concluding that both the clam and Mrs. Sapp were indeed arthropods.

We can readily see how this approach is richer and more motivating than memorizing a set of characteristics for these animals would have been. When tasks are challenging, students might initially complain, but when they do succeed, their sense of accomplishment is much greater, which contributes to their perceptions of competence and increases motivation (Hung et al., 2015).

Task Comprehension: Increasing Beliefs About Autonomy and Value

Students' understanding of what they are expected to learn and why it's important also increase motivation. To see how, we return to DeVonne's class the day after her lesson on arthropods.

MyLab Education
Video Example 11.3
Task comprehension, which describes learners' awareness of what they are supposed to be learning, can help meet students' needs for autonomy and their beliefs about the value of what they're learning. Here an educational leader describes why these factors are so important for learning and motivation.

"Now, let's review for a few minutes," she begins. "What were the characteristics of arthropods that we identified yesterday?"

"Exoskeleton," Seleina volunteers.

"Three body parts," Tu adds.

"Jointed legs," Kevin offers.

"Good. . . . And what are some examples of arthropods?"

The students offer crabs, lobsters, roaches, beetles, spiders, and others as examples, and DeVonne then asks, "Why is it important to study these animals?"

After hesitating for a moment, Stephanie says, "We eat them, like shrimp and stuff."

"Good," DeVonne smiles. "Indeed, they're an important food source. In fact, did you know that insects are as nutritious as meat, and they're eaten both cooked and raw in many cultures?"

Amid reactions such as "eeww," "yuck," and "gross" from students, DeVonne adds, "More than 80% of all animal species are arthropods, and there are more than a million different species. . . . Think about that. More than 8 out of 10 animals on this earth are arthropods. . . . And they're essential for pollinating our plants. Without them, we wouldn't have enough food. We really do need to understand our most abundant, and one of our most important, neighbors."

This discussion reflects DeVonne's emphasis on **task comprehension**, learners' aware-ness of what they are supposed to be learning and an understanding of why the task is important and worthwhile.

As with success, a challenging task won't increase motivation if students don't believe it's meaningful and worth understanding (Akers, 2017). For example, DeVonne could have simply said, "Be sure you know the characteristics of arthropods and some examples of them, because they will be on our next test." Statements like this are com-mon in classrooms. Instead, she suggested they were studying arthropods because these animals have a major impact on our daily lives. Task comprehension increases when learners see that what they're studying has practical applications.

Expectancy × value theory helps us understand why task comprehension is impor-tant. If we understand why we study a topic, we will certainly value it more than we would if we studied it for no apparent reason.

We can increase task comprehension in a number of ways. For instance, DeVonne emphasized the contributions of arthropods to our food supply. In other cases, courses of study are prerequisite for more advanced work, such as studying algebra because we need it for trigonometry and calculus. Topics can also contribute to our work and careers (utility value). We, Paul and Don, your authors, hope you believe that studying educational psychology will help you become a better teacher.

We also study some topics simply because they're intrinsically interesting. Any and all of these reasons are worthwhile, and it's important that we communicate the reasons to our students. This is the essence of task comprehension.

As with teacher qualities, climate variables are synergistic. For instance, if students feel safe enough to share their thinking without fear of criticism or ridicule, the moti-vating effects of challenge will be increased. Similarly, if students know why they're studying a topic, experiencing success as they study will be more enjoyable than if they don't understand why they're studying it.

Using Educational Psychology in Teaching: Suggestions for Applying an Understanding of Climate Variables in Your Classroom

As with all aspects of learning and teaching, creating a classroom climate that promotes students' motivation to learn is a challenge, particularly with learners who have a history of low achievement. The following suggestions can help us meet the challenge.

- Create a safe and orderly classroom environment
- Use teaching strategies that promote student success
- Capitalize on challenge
- Help students understand the *why* of studying certain topics

Create a Safe and Orderly Classroom Environment.   Creating a safe and orderly learning environment is a classroom management issue, and it's understandably one of begin-ning teachers' primary concerns (Emmer & Evertson, 2017; Evertson & Emmer, 2017). If you haven't already done so, you will likely take an entire course in your teacher preparation program devoted to this important topic. At the very least one or more of your other courses will have components that focus on classroom management. (In fact, courses in educational psychology, such as the one you're now taking, often include classroom management as one of its topics, and Chapter 12 of this text is devoted to it.) As you study this topic, remember that a strong relationship exists between student motivation and safe and orderly classrooms.

Use Teaching Strategies that Promote Student Success.   Promoting student success can be an enormous challenge, certainly one of our most demanding tasks. If it were easy, we wouldn't see mainstream media lament school dropout rates, teachers complaining about students who don't seem to care about learning—or their own futures—and a myriad of other motivation-related issues.

We can, however, use teaching strategies that increase the likelihood of our students succeeding. Two of the most important include: 1) using open-ended questions, and 2) using high-quality examples.

Open-ended questions are questions for which a variety of answers are acceptable. To illustrate, let's look again at some dialogue from DeVonne's lesson as she had Stephanie carry the lobster around the room.

DeVonne:	Look carefully, because I'm going to ask you to tell us what you see. . . . Okay, what did you notice?
Tu:	Hard.
Saliena:	Pink and green.
Kevin:	Wet.

DeVonne asked a simple, straightforward question: "What do you notice?" and Tu, Saliena, and Kevin each responded with a different answer. This question, or others, such as "What do you observe?" or "What do you see?", can be very effective for helping students—and particularly those who are often unable to answer—experience success, because virtually anything they say is acceptable.

Using open-ended questioning may take a little "getting used to." Students are so commonly asked questions requiring a specific answer that they may initially be reluctant to try and respond. In our own teaching we've had students say, "I'm not sure what you're looking for," to which we reply, "I'm looking for whatever you notice."

Our experience suggests that open-ended questioning works. As one example, Paul was recently teaching a lesson with a group of fifth-graders, and within a matter of minutes, students who were initially reluctant to respond were raising their hands attempting to volunteer answers. Open-ended questions aren't a panacea for success, but using them can be an effective strategy for helping students who rarely experience the pleasure of being able to answer and participate. Then, as their confidence increases, we can gradually raise the cognitive level of our questions, and the result is increased learning.

High-quality examples are examples for which all the information students need to understand a topic is observable in them. DeVonne's lobster was a high-quality example. For instance, she wanted her students to understand that arthropods have an *exoskeleton, three body parts,* and *segmented legs.* Her students could see these characteristics in the lobster, so they essentially couldn't miss, and success was ensured.

National Council on Teacher Quality (NCTQ)

High-quality examples are so important that the National Council on Teacher Quality describes using them as one of the six essential teaching strategies that all new teachers should know. "2. Linking abstract concepts with concrete representations. Teachers should present tangible examples that illuminate overarching ideas and also explain how the examples and big ideas connect" (Pomerance, Greenberg, & Walsh, 2016, p. vi).

Combining open-ended questions with high-quality examples also makes it easier to prompt students when they are initially unable to answer. To illustrate, let's look again at some dialogue.

DeVonne:	[holding up the lobster] What do you notice about the lobster's legs? . . . Damien?
Damien:	They're long.
DeVonne:	[wiggling the legs] Are they all in one part or more than one part?
Damien:	More than one.
DeVonne:	Yes, good. When we see legs like this, we say they're segmented.

Damien was able to answer successfully, to which DeVonne responded, "Yes, good." This is admittedly a small success, but if he has enough experiences like this one, his motivation will gradually increase.

In other content areas, such as math or language arts, where students must develop problem-solving or grammar and punctuation skills, providing scaffolded practice before expecting students to work successfully also contributes to their success.

Here's what we mean by scaffolded practice. Suppose you're teaching percent increase and percent decrease, and you've presented your students with the following problem:

You see a sharp looking shirt at one of the stores in the mall that was originally priced at $70, and it's now marked down to $50. What is the percent decrease in the price?

You have the students all work the problem while you monitor their efforts. When they've finished, you discuss the solution, give them another problem, and continue until you believe most understand the process. Then, you give them a homework assignment, and while the majority of the students work on the assignment, you provide extra support for those who need it in a small group format. (If more than five or six students need extra support, your whole-group instruction has probably been inadequate, and you should reteach the topic to the whole class.) This scaffolding is one of the most effective strategies we have for maximizing our students' success.

The importance of promoting success also illustrates the synergy among the variables in the *Model for Promoting Student Motivation*. For instance, open-ended questions and scaffolded practice are only effective if the classroom environment is safe and orderly. Students won't answer if they're afraid others will ridicule or laugh at them. And if students are involved in horseplay instead of doing homework, it will be impossible for you to provide extra help for the students who need it. Similarly, students will make more of an effort to answer if they believe that you're truly committed to their learning and care about them as people. This again illustrates the interdependence of the variables in the model.

Capitalize on Challenge.   As we saw earlier, success—alone—won't necessarily increase students' motivation; they need to believe that they're succeeding on tasks that are meaningful and worthwhile.

Before we continue, we want to remind you of what *challenge is not*. All teachers want to believe they're challenging their students, but some aren't sure how. So, in misguided efforts, they simply increase students' workload, such as, instead of assigning 10 problems for homework, they assign 15, or instead of assigning 20 pages to be read, they assign 40. The effect is precisely the opposite of what we intend. Instead of increasing motivation, students interpret these practices as meaningless busy work, or even a form of punishment, and decreased motivation is often the result (Geraci, Palmerini, Cirillo, & McDougald, 2017).

Instead of piling on more work, we should instead ask our students to examine the topics they're studying in more depth, to link ideas to each other, and to find different ways to solve problems. In essence, challenge requires students to "think."

And doing so need not be difficult; it's more a matter of "getting used to." For instance, DeVonne's asking her students if the clam, and even Mrs. Sapp—the school principal—were arthropods was a simple form of challenge. Notice that some of her students thought they were; they centered on the hard shell of the clam in concluding that it was an arthropod and on Mrs. Sapp's jointed legs in concluding that she was. This form of challenge provides additional benefits; DeVonne's students developed a deeper understanding of arthropods, and they learned that concepts must include all the essential characteristics rather than only one, such as the clam's hard shell.

Probing questions, such as those that ask students to explain or offer conjectures, are excellent for challenging students. For instance, again suppose you're teaching percent increase and percent decrease and you pose this problem:

An item marked down from $40 to $30 is a 25% decrease, but an item whose value increases from $30 to $40 is a 33% increase. How can that be?

Students often struggle with this type of problem, but when they eventually meet the challenge, their sense of competence will markedly increase, as will their motivation.

Similarly, probing questions, such as "We know the clam shell has two parts. What if it had three parts instead? Would it then be an arthropod?", challenges students by asking them to think hypothetically. And, in addition to challenging students, it promotes deeper understanding of the topic.

National Council on Teacher Quality (NCTQ)

The National Council on Teacher Quality describes asking probing questions as another of the 6 essential teaching strategies that every new teacher should know. "Asking students 'why,' 'how,' 'what if,' and 'how do you know' requires them to clarify and link their knowledge of key ideas" (Pomerance et al. 2016, p. vi).

Challenging students has an additional benefit. It makes teaching more fun, and we may be surprised by the results. Students who are traditionally low achievers sometimes generate ideas we didn't believe they were capable of. The result is a win-win. The students win because their understanding and motivation increase; we win because it's more fun, and our personal teaching efficacy also gets a boost.

Help Students Understand the *Why* of Studying Certain Topics.   When you begin teaching, a question you'll commonly hear is "Why do we have to learn this?" The single most effective way to ensure that students understand why they're studying a topic is to apply it to their daily lives. For instance, after asking her students why it's important to study arthropods, DeVonne noted that they are an important food source and they're essential for pollinating plants.

Valid reasons exist for studying virtually all the topics we teach, and we merely need to communicate these reasons to our students. We know why the topics are important, and we need to ensure that our students have the same understanding. They won't all be convinced, but as we've repeatedly said in our discussion of motivation, we have nothing to lose by doing so, and the effort it takes is minimal.

MyLab Education Application Exercise 11.2: Capitalizing on Climate Variables to Promote Learner Motivation

In this exercise, you will be asked to analyze an elementary teacher's efforts to capitalize on the climate variables with his students.

Classroom Connections

Promoting a Positive Learning Climate in Classrooms

Order and Safety

1. Order and safety create a predictable learning environment and support learner autonomy and security. Create a safe and secure learning environment.

- **Elementary:** A first-grade teacher establishes and practices daily routines until they're predictable and automatic for students.

- **Middle School:** An eighth-grade American history teacher leads a discussion focusing on the kind of environment the students want to work in. They conclude that all "digs" and discourteous remarks should be forbidden. The teacher consistently enforces the agreement.

- **High School:** An English teacher reminds her students that all relevant comments about a topic are welcome, and she models acceptance of every idea. She requires students to listen courteously when a classmate is talking.

Success and Challenge

2. Succeeding on challenging tasks promotes self-efficacy and helps students develop a sense of competence. Structure instruction so students succeed on challenging tasks.

- **Elementary:** A fourth-grade teacher comments, "We're really getting good at fractions. Now I have a problem that is going to make us all think. It will be a little tough, but I know that we'll be able to do it." After students attempt the solution, he guides a discussion of the problem and different ways to solve it.

- **Middle School:** A sixth-grade English teacher has the class practice two or three homework exercises as a whole

group each day and discusses them before students begin to work independently.

- **High School:** As she returns their homework, a physics teacher gives her students worked solutions to the most frequently missed problems. She has students put solutions in their portfolios to study for the weekly quizzes.

Task Comprehension

3. Task comprehension reflects students' awareness of what they are supposed to be learning and an understanding of why the task is important and worthwhile. Promote task comprehension by describing rationales for your learning activities and assignments.

- **Elementary:** As he gives students their daily math homework, a third-grade teacher says, "We know that understanding how math applies to our lives is really important, so that's why we practice word problems every day."

- **Middle School:** A seventh-grade English teacher carefully describes her assignments and due dates and writes them on the board. Each time, she explains why the assignment is important and how it links to other things they've learned.

- **High School:** A biology teacher displays the following on the document camera:

  We don't just study flatworms because we're interested in flatworms. As we look at how they've adapted to their environments, we'll gain additional insights into ourselves.

  He then says, "We'll return to this idea again and again to remind ourselves why we study each organism."

MyLab Education Self-Check 11.3

Instructional Variables: Developing Interest in Learning Activities

11.4 Explain how different instructional variables increase students' motivation to learn.

Teacher qualities and climate variables form a general framework for motivation. Within this context, we can do much to ensure that students' learning experiences enhance their motivation to learn. From an instructional perspective, a motivated student is someone who is actively engaged in a learning activity (Brophy, 2010). To promote motivation and learning, we need to initially capture—and then maintain—students' attention and engagement throughout a learning activity. Figure 11.4 outlines ways of meeting this goal.

Introductory Focus: Attracting Students' Attention

Attention is the beginning point of all learning, so attracting our students' attention is the essential first step for all learning activities. **Introductory focus** is a lesson beginning that attracts student attention and provides a conceptual framework for the learning activity (Lemov, 2015). It also attempts to capitalize on the effects of curiosity and novelty, which are characteristics of intrinsically motivating activities (Adams & Willis, 2015; Goodwin, 2014). DeVonne, for instance, began her lesson on arthropods by bringing a live lobster to class. The "oohs" and "aahs" from her students suggested that she had indeed attracted their attention. Let's look at another example.

As an introduction to studying cities and their locations, Marissa Allen, a social studies teacher, hands out a map of a fictitious island. On it are physical features such as lakes, rivers, and mountains. Information about altitude, rainfall, and average seasonal temperature is also included.

Marissa begins, "The name of this activity is *Survival*. Our class has just been sent to this island to settle it. We have information about its climate and physical features. Where should we make our first settlement?"

We can attract our students' attention with unique problems, such as Marissa's survival task; by asking paradoxical questions ("If Rome was such a powerful and advanced civilization, why did it collapse?"); offering demonstrations with seemingly contradictory results (e.g., dropping two balls of different weights and seeing that they hit the floor at the same time); using eye-catching examples, such as DeVonne's lobster (Goodwin, 2014), or asking emotion-laden questions, such as, "Why do you think Kim is so happy in the story?" (Sutherland, McQuiggan, Ryan, & Mather, 2017).

Teachers tend to not use effective lesson introductions (Brophy, 2010), but it need not be as difficult as it initially appears. All that's required is an effort to connect the content of each lesson to students' prior knowledge and interests. We offer several additional examples for providing introductory focus in the section "Using Educational Psychology in Teaching: Suggestions for Applying the Instructional Variables with Your Students" later in the chapter.

Once our students are attending and a conceptual framework for the lesson exists, we have to maintain their attention and provide information about learning progress. *Personalization, involvement,* and *feedback* can help meet these goals.

Figure 11.4 Instructional variables in the Model for Promoting Student Motivation

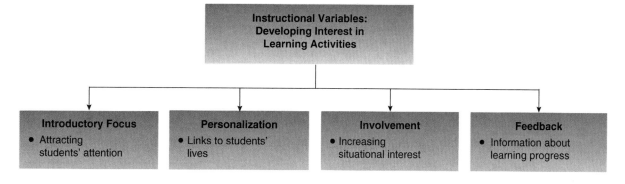

Personalization: Links to Students' Lives

Sue Crompton, a second-grade math teacher, introduces the topic of graphing by measuring her students' heights. She continues by giving them a length of construction paper and has them place their strip of paper on the spot on a graph that corresponds to their height. After discussing the results, she does a similar activity with hair color to reinforce the idea of graphing. Chris Emery, a science teacher, begins a unit on genetics by saying, "Reanne, what color are your eyes?"

"Blue," Reanne responds.

"And how about yours, Eddie?"

"Green."

"Interesting," Chris smiles. "When we're done with this unit on genetics, we'll be able to figure out why Reanne's eyes are blue and Eddie's are green, and a whole bunch of other things related to the way we look."

Sue and Chris both attempted to increase their students' interest through **personalization**, the process of using intellectually and/or emotionally relevant examples to illustrate a topic. DeVonne also capitalized on personalization when she helped her students understand why they were studying arthropods, how these animals affect their lives, and by asking them if Mrs. Sapp, their school principal, was an arthropod.

The value of personalization as a motivational strategy can be explained with practical experience, theory, and research (Ertem, 2013; Narciss et al., 2014). First, it's intuitively sensible (we all like to learn things that relate to us) and widely applicable. Experienced teachers describe it as one of the most important ways they have of promoting their students' interest in learning activities (Schraw & Lehman, 2001).

Information processing and self-determination theory also help us understand its importance. For example, personalized content is meaningful because it encourages students to connect new information to structures already in long-term memory (Moreno & Mayer, 2000). Ultimately, all learning is personal, and students' ability to link new information to what they already know is essential. Also, students feel an increased sense of autonomy—a basic need according to self-determination theory—when they study topics to which they personally relate.

As with introductory focus, we offer additional examples for personalizing content in the section "Using Educational Psychology in Teaching: Suggestions for Applying the Instructional Variables with Your Students" later in the chapter.

Diversity: Personalizing Content to Increase Motivation in Students Having Diverse Backgrounds

Jack Seltzer, a high school biology teacher on the Navajo Nation reservation, uses his students' background experiences to illustrate hard-to-understand science concepts. He uses Churro sheep, a local breed that Navajos use for food and wool, to illustrate genetic principles. When they study plants, he focuses on local varieties of squash and corn that have been grown by students' ancestors for centuries. Geologic formations in nearby Monument Valley are used to illustrate igneous, sedimentary, and metamorphic rocks (Baker, 2006).

We know that belonging (from Maslow's work) and relatedness (from self-determination theory) are needs that strongly influence students' motivation to learn, and students who don't develop a sense of belonging or identify with their schools have higher dropout rates (Geraci et al., 2017). This problem is particularly acute among members of cultural minorities and students who are disadvantaged (Wentzel & Wigfield, 2007). Further, minority students' disengagement is often exacerbated by the school curriculum, much of which is oriented toward mainstream, middle-class, nonminority students (Anderson & Summerfield, 2004).

Now, let's look back to Jack Seltzer and his work with his Navajo students. He attempted to create a sense of belonging and interest in his class by capitalizing on the motivating effects of personalization. This variable is important for all students, but it can be particularly effective with members of cultural minorities, who often say they don't belong or don't feel welcome in school (Geraci et al., 2017). When we present these students with examples and experiences that directly relate to their lives, as Jack did, their interest and sense of belonging can significantly increase.

Involvement: Increasing Situational Interest

Ed Psych and You

Think about your experiences at lunch with friends or at a party. How do you feel when you're engaged in conversations compared to when you're on the fringes?

The question in *Ed Psych and You* addresses the topic of **involvement**, the extent to which people are directly participating in an activity. For instance, when we're talking and actively listening (involved), we pay more attention to the conversation and our interest in it is higher than when we are on its fringes. The same applies in classrooms. Involvement increases situational interest, and it encourages students to become cognitively active. And we know from our study of human memory that cognitive activity is essential for meaningful learning (Vandenbroucke, Split, Verschueren, Piccinin, & Baeyens, 2018).

Expectancy × value theory helps us understand the importance of involvement. This theory suggests that intrinsic interest is one of the factors that increases task value in learning activities, and involvement increases intrinsic interest. This makes sense. When we're involved in a conversation, such as we suggested in *Ed Psych and You*, we almost can't help being interested in the topic of discussion.

Questioning is our most generally applicable tool for increasing involvement; students' attention is high when they're thinking about and answering questions, but it drops during teacher monologues. In our discussion of strategies for promoting student success earlier in the chapter, we talked about open-ended questioning, and in addition to promoting success, these questions can also be effective for involving students. Questions, such as "What do you see?", are easy to ask, and once students get used to them, they're easy to answer, so we can call on several different students very quickly.

In addition to questioning in general, and open-ended questioning in particular, providing hands-on activities is a second strategy that can be effective for promoting involvement. For instance, when students work with manipulatives in math, concrete materials in science, maps and globes in geography, or computers in language arts, their level of interest often increases significantly. In DeVonne's lesson, her students' involvement was highest when they actually worked with the shrimp. Periodically using hands-on activities adds variety to learning activities, and variety also increases learner interest (Perry et al., 2006).

Group work, in which students work together toward common learning goals, is a third common strategy for increasing involvement (Slavin, 2011; Wentzel & Watkins, 2011). Group work provides opportunities for students to interact and compare their ideas with others, both of which increase interest. (We examine group work and cooperative learning in detail in Chapter 13.)

Feedback: Information About Learning Progress

We all want to know how we're doing when we learn something new, and information about our current understanding helps us make sense of our efforts. Feedback contributes to motivation by providing this information (El, Tillema, & van Koppen, 2012). In fact, feedback is one of the most powerful factors that exist for increasing motivation and learning (Hattie, 2012; Hattie and Timperley, 2007). Its value can be explained in several ways:

- *Self-determination theory.* Feedback indicating that competence is increasing contributes to self-determination.
- *Attribution theory.* Feedback helps us understand why we perform the way we do, which in turn helps us make sense of our experiences.
- *Knowledge construction.* Feedback gives us information about the validity of our knowledge constructions, which allows us to change our thinking and reconstruct our understanding if necessary.
- *Self-regulated learning.* Feedback gives us information about progress toward goals, and when they're met, our self-efficacy increases. If they're not met, we can increase our effort or change strategies.

The type of feedback is important. When it provides information about learning progress, motivation increases, but if it has a performance orientation, such as emphasizing high grades and social comparisons, it can detract from motivation (Brophy, 2010; Schunk et al., 2014). Performance-oriented feedback has a particularly detrimental effect on lower ability students and detracts from intrinsic motivation for both low and high achievers.

APA Top 20 Principles

This discussion illustrates Principle 6: *Clear, explanatory, and timely feedback to students is important for learning—* from the *Top 20 Principles from Psychology for PreK–12 Teaching and Learning.*

Using Educational Psychology in Teaching: Suggestions for Applying the Instructional Variables with Your Students

In this section, we've focused on the instructional variables in the Model for Promoting Student Motivation, but throughout the chapter we've emphasized that the variables in each component are interdependent. The instructional variables, without teachers' personal qualities and the climate variables, won't—alone—increase students' motivation.

With that thought in mind, the following suggestions can help us apply the instructional variables in the Model for Promoting Student Motivation in our teaching.

- Attract students' attention with provocative examples, questions or activities.
- Link topics to students' lives.
- Maintain high levels of student involvement in learning activities.
- Promote learning with assessment.

To see how a teacher applies the suggestions, let's look at a lesson taught by David Crawford, a world history teacher.

David is working with his students to develop their skills with examining evidence.

His students are in their seats and have their notebooks on their desks as the bell rings. David moves to the front of the room and begins, "I'm going to show you some objects on the table here, and as you look at them, think about this question: What do the items have to do with technology?"

David reaches into a box, pulls out two animal skulls, a piece of woven fabric, and a stone spear point ground to a fine edge. He puts them on the table at the front of the room. Then, he puts another stone spear point that is also sharp but chipped, two small animal bones, and a fragment from an animal skin next to the first group.

As students look at the objects, they offer a few uncertain ideas, and then David begins directing the lesson with the question, "What are some common forms of technology in our world today? Go ahead. . . . Brenda?"

The students offer examples such as computers, smartphones, and tablets, and then David continues, "Good examples. . . . Now, we tend to think of technology as something recent, but it's existed throughout history, and we can tell a great deal about a civilization by looking at its artifacts."

He defines the term *artifact* and then says, "Today we're going to examine some artifacts to see what they might tell us about the technologies people used who left them behind. This will give us the thinking tools to understand the civilizations we study as we look at the history of the world."

"We'll call this Civilization A, and this one Civilization B," he says, pointing to the sets of materials.

"What do you notice about the artifacts?" David directs. "Go ahead and start. . . Kelly?" As he calls on them, a number of students make observations, and then with David's guidance they conclude that the skulls are from a cow and a sheep and the bones are leg and rib bones from an antelope or deer.

"Now," David smiles, "we're archeological teams, and we found these sites. . . . I want you to work with your partners and write down as many conclusions as you can about the people associated with each group of objects, and any comparisons between the two, such as which one you believe was more advanced. In each case, provide evidence for your conclusions."

At the end of their allotted time, David says, "Okay, what did you come up with?"

"We think those are newer," Lori says, pointing at the chipped spear points. "The points are sharp, and they're sort of like art."

"Rod?" David acknowledges, seeing his raised hand.

"I sort of disagree," Rodney responds, referring to the points with fine edges. "These look like they're ground, and grinding would be more advanced technology than chipping."

The class continues discussing the artifacts, and from the cow and sheep skulls and the cloth, the students conclude that Civilization A had domesticated animals and the ability to weave. And they decide that the antelope bones and skin indicate that Civilization B probably consisted of hunter-gatherers.

After completing the discussion, David says, "Okay, for tonight, I want you to read about the Old, Middle, and New Stone Ages on pages 35 to 44 of your books and decide what ages these artifacts probably belonged to. . . . You did a great job today. You made some excellent conclusions and supported them in each case."

Now, let's see how David applies the suggestions.

Attract Students' Attention with Provocative Examples, Questions, or Activities.   David began his lesson with a conscious effort to attract his students' attention by displaying artifacts—examples—and asking, "What do the items have to do with technology?" The combination of the examples and questions was a good form of introductory focus because we don't typically think of skulls, bones, and spear points as indicators of technology.

Creating motivating lesson beginnings need not take a great deal of extra work and preparation. Initially, it will require a bit of extra thought, but once we get used to this type of thinking, the process will become nearly automatic.

Some additional examples for providing introductory focus are outlined in Table 11.2.

Link Topics to Students' Lives. David personalized his learning activity by beginning the lesson with examples of today's technology and by placing his students in the role of archeologists. As with introductory focus, personalizing content merely requires a bit of thought; it need not require a great deal of extra planning and effort.

Expectancy × value theory helps us understand the motivating influence of personalizing topics. Students value success on topics that affect them personally, or to which they can personally relate, more than remote and disconnected topics.

Table 11.3 outlines additional examples of teachers' attempts to personalize the topics they teach.

Maintain High Levels of Student Involvement. Now, let's think again about the way David conducted his lesson. Three aspects are significant.

- He began by saying, "I'm going to display some objects on the table here, and as you look at them, think about this question: What do the items have to do with technology?"

- He then asked, "What are some common forms of technology in our world today?"

- As he directed the students to the items on the table he asked, "What do you notice about the artifacts?"

MyLab Education
Video Example 11.5

Attract students' attention with provocative examples, questions, or activities, and *maintain high levels of student involvement* are two suggestions for applying the instructional variables in the model for promoting student motivation with your students. Here we see how DeVonne implements these suggestions with her fifth-graders.

TABLE 11.2 Tools and techniques for providing introductory focus

Tool/Technique	Example
Problems and questions	• A literature teacher shows a picture of Ernest Hemingway and says, "Here we see 'Papa' in all his splendor. He seemed to have everything—fame, adventure, romance. Yet he took his own life. Why would this happen?" • A science teacher asks the students to explain why two pieces of paper come together at the bottom (rather than move apart) when students blow between them. • An educational psychology instructor introducing social cognitive theory displays the following vignette: *You're driving 75 mph on the interstate—with a posted speed limit of 65—when another car blazes past you. A minute later, you see the car stopped by the highway patrol. You immediately slow down. How would behaviorism explain your slowing down?*
Inductive sequences	• An English teacher displays the following: *I had a ton of homework last night! I was upset because I had a date with the most gorgeous girl in the world! I guess it was okay, because she had on the ugliest outfit ever!* The students find a pattern in the examples and develop the concept hyperbole. • An educational psychology instructor begins a discussion of development with these questions: Are you bothered when something doesn't make sense? Do you want the world to be predictable? Are you more comfortable in classes when the instructor specifies the requirements, schedules the classes, and outlines the grading practices? Does your life in general follow patterns more than random experiences? The class looks at the pattern and arrives at the concept of *equilibrium*.
Concrete examples	• An elementary teacher begins a unit on amphibians by bringing in a live frog. • A geography teacher draws lines on a beach ball to demonstrate that longitude lines intersect at the poles and latitude lines are parallel to each other. • An educational psychology instructor introduces the concept *negative reinforcement* by describing his inclination to take a pain killer to reduce his discomfort after a demanding workout.
Objectives and rationales	• A math teacher begins, "Today we want to learn about unit pricing. This will help us decide which product is a better buy. It will help us all save money and be better consumers." • A world history teacher says, "Today we're going to look at the concept of *mercantilism*. It will help us understand why, throughout history, Europe came to the New World and went into South Asia and Africa." • An educational psychology instructor says, "We know that learners construct, rather than record, understanding. Today we want to see what that principle suggests about the way we should teach most effectively."

TABLE 11.3 Teachers' efforts to personalize topics

Topic	Example
Creating bar graphs	A second-grade teacher uses her students' favorite flavor of jelly beans to create a large bar graph at the front of her classroom.
The concept *population density*	A teacher uses masking tape to create two identical areas on the classroom floor. She then has three students stand in one area and five students stand in the other to demonstrate that the population density of the second is greater. The class then looks up the population density of their city and other cities in their state.
Comparative and superlative adjectives	A language arts teacher has students hold up different length pencils and writes on the board: Devon has a long pencil. Andrea has a longer pencil. Steve has the longest pencil. She then has students identify the characteristics of comparative and superlative adjectives.
Finding equivalent fractions	A math teacher arranges the 24 desks in his classroom into 4 rows of 6 desks each with two rows close together and the other two rows close together. He then guides the students to conclude that two rows are 12/24ths of the desks. He next guides students to conclude that the two rows together are also 1/2 of the desks, so 12/24ths is equivalent to 1/2.
The Crusades	A World History teacher uses the class's "crusade" to prevent extracurricular activities from being eliminated at the school as an analogy for the actual Crusades in history.
Shakespeare	A literature teacher introduces the study of *Hamlet* by saying, "Suppose you've been away from home for several years. When you return, you learn that your father has died and your mother has married your uncle— your father's brother. Then, you begin to find clues suggesting that your uncle might be responsible for your father's death" (Brophy, 2010).

Each question was open-ended, which allowed him to call on several different students easily and quickly. Using questions such as these is the most widely applicable strategy we have for involving students. As you attempt to use open-ended questioning in your teaching, remember that any question you ask that has a variety of acceptable answers can be effective for involving students. For instance, a teacher in a lesson on Shakespeare's *Julius Caesar* might ask questions such as:

"What has happened so far in the play?"
"What are some of the major events?"
"How are Brutus and Marc Antony similar? How are they different?"
"How does the setting for Act I compare with that for Act II?"

As another example, a teacher in a lesson on amphibians and reptiles might ask questions such as:

"How is a frog similar to a lizard?"
"How are the frog and a toad similar to or different from each other?"

Open-ended questions also provide us with insights into our students' thinking and allow us to build on their prior knowledge. For instance, if we ask them to make observations, and the observations have little or nothing to do with the characteristics we want to identify, we know our students lack relevant background knowledge, and we can then try to provide it.

In addition to his use of open-ended questions, David had his students work with partners to make conclusions about the civilizations. This simple form of group work and the whole-class discussion that followed also promoted involvement—perhaps at an even higher level—because the students had a personal investment in their conclusions. So, they were keenly interested in their classmates' reactions to their ideas.

Some additional strategies for promoting involvement are outlined in Table 11.4, and each promotes cognitive engagement. Improvement drills add an element of game-like novelty to otherwise routine activities, and personal improvement increases self-efficacy. Having students use chalkboards at their desks is similar to having them solve

TABLE 11.4 Strategies for involving students

Technique	Example
Improvement drills	Students are given a list of 10 multiplication facts on a sheet. Students are scored on speed and accuracy, and points are given for individual improvement.
Games	The class is divided equally according to ability, and the two groups respond in a game format to teacher questions.
Individual work spaces	Students are given their own chalkboards on which they solve math problems and identify examples of concepts. They hold the chalkboards up when they've solved the problem or when they think an example illustrates a concept. They also write or draw their own examples on the chalkboards.
Student group work	Student pairs observe a science demonstration and write down as many observations of it as they can.

problems on paper at their desks, but the chalkboards allow sharing and discussion, and students often will use them to attempt problems they wouldn't try on paper.

Promote Learning with Assessment.   Feedback is the final variable in the Model for Promoting Student Motivation. We combine the discussion of feedback with assessment, because assessment is one of the most powerful influences on learning and motivation (Gonzalez & Eggen, 2017; Rohrer & Pashler, 2010).

To examine this influence, let's return to David's work with his students.

The next day, David begins by saying, "One of our goals for yesterday and throughout the year is to be able to examine evidence and conclusions. . . . You did a good job, but we need a little more practice. . . . I'm going to display the conclusions and evidence that some of you offered. . . . Now, remember the spirit we're doing this in. It's strictly for the sake of learning and improvement. It's not intended to criticize any of you. . . . I've covered up your names, so everyone remains anonymous. . . . Let's take a look at what two groups wrote," as he displays the following on the document camera:

    Conclusion: The people had cloth.

    Evidence: There is cloth from Civilization A.

    Conclusion: The people in Civilization A were more likely to survive.

    Evidence: They had cows and sheep, so they didn't have to find wild animals. The cloth piece suggests that they wove cloth, so they didn't have to depend upon animal skins.

"What comments can you make about the two sets of conclusions?"

"The first one isn't really a conclusion," Shantae offers. "You can see the cloth, so it really doesn't say anything."

"Good observation, Shantae. . . . Yes, a conclusion is a statement based on a fact; it isn't the fact itself."

The class then discusses the second example and agrees that the conclusion is based on evidence.

"This is the kind of thing we're looking for," David comments. "I know that you're all capable of this kind of thinking, so let's see it in your next writing sample."

He then brings out several cans of soup and asks students to make conclusions about the civilization that might have produced such an artifact and to give evidence that supports each conclusion.

The class, beginning to understand the process, makes a number of comments, and David writes the students' conclusions and supporting evidence on the board.

Assessment with detailed feedback is essential for learning, and collecting and reading the students' papers was a form of assessment. Because they had limited experience with forming conclusions based on evidence, without the assessment and accompanying feedback, David's students were unlikely to understand the difference between good and poor conclusions. The same is true for all forms of learning beyond simple memory tasks.

National Council on Teacher Quality (NCTQ)

The National Council on Teacher Quality describes assessing learning as another of the six essential teaching strategies that every new teacher should know. Assessment is a learning tool, and assessment and feedback help students effectively store and retain information (Chappuis & Stiggins, 2017).

Detailed feedback on traditional assessments such as tests and quizzes is equally important. Frequently missed test and quiz items should be discussed in enough detail so students know why they missed the item. This may seem time consuming, but it's time well spent. If questions persist, students should be offered the opportunity to come in and discuss their tests and quizzes one-on-one.

Feedback is important for motivation because it helps students improve the quality of their work. And as they see their quality increasing, their perceptions of competence, self-determination, and intrinsic motivation also increase. None of this is possible without ongoing assessment and feedback.

MyLab Education Application Exercise 11.3: Capitalizing on Instructional Variables to Promote Student Motivation

In this exercise, you will be asked to analyze a fifth-grade teacher's effort to apply the instructional variables with her students.

Classroom Connections

Using Instructional Variables to Promote Motivation to Learn

Introductory Focus

1. Introductory focus attracts students' attention and provides a conceptual umbrella for the lesson. Plan lesson introductions to capitalize on this variable.

- **Elementary:** A fifth-grade teacher introduces a lesson on measuring by bringing in a cake recipe and ingredients that have to be modified if everyone in the class is going to get a piece of cake. He says, "We want to make enough cake so we can all get a piece. This is what we're going to figure out today."

- **Middle School:** A physical science teacher begins her lessons with a simple demonstration, such as whirling a cup of water suspended on the end of a string around her head. "Why doesn't the water fly out of the cup? . . . Let's try to figure this out," she says in beginning the lesson.

- **High School:** An English teacher introduces *A Raisin in the Sun* (Hansberry, 1959) by saying, "Think about a Muslim family in Detroit. How do you think they felt after the events of 9/11? Keep those questions in mind as we read *A Raisin in the Sun.*"

Personalization

2. Personalization uses intellectually or emotionally relevant examples to illustrate a topic. Personalize content to create links between content and students' lives.

- **Elementary:** A fourth-grade teacher begins a lesson comparing animals with exoskeletons and those with endoskeletons by having students squeeze their legs to demonstrate that

their bones are inside. He then passes out a number of crayfish and has the students compare the crayfish to themselves.

- **Middle School:** A seventh-grade teacher begins a lesson on percentages by bringing in an ad for computer games and products from a local newspaper. The ad says "10% to 25% off marked prices." The class works problems to see how much they might save on popular computer games.

- **High School:** As her class studies the Vietnam War, a history teacher asks students to interview someone who served in the military at the time. The class uses the results of the interviews to remind themselves of the "human" dimension of the war.

Involvement

3. Involvement describes the extent to which students are actively participating in a lesson. Promote high levels of involvement in all learning activities.

- **Elementary:** Each day, a second-grade teacher passes out a sheet with 20 math facts on it. The students quickly write the answers and then score the sheets. Students who improve their scores from the previous day or get all 20 facts correct receive a bonus point on their math averages.

- **Middle School:** A seventh-grade pre-algebra teacher assigns students to work in pairs to complete seatwork assignments. He requires them to work each problem individually, then check with each other, and ask for help if they can't agree on the solution.

- **High School:** An English teacher randomly calls on all students as equally as possible, whether or not they raise their hands. At the beginning of the year, he explains that his intent is to encourage participation, and that students will soon get over any uneasiness about being "put on the spot." He prompts students who are unable to answer until they give an acceptable response.

Feedback

4. Feedback provides students with information about their learning progress. Provide prompt and informative feedback about learning progress.

- **Elementary:** A fourth-grade teacher discusses the most frequently missed items on each of her homework assignments and quizzes, providing detailed information about each of the items.
- **Middle School:** A seventh-grade teacher writes on a student paper, "You have some very good ideas. Now you need to rework your essay so that it is grammatically correct. Look at the notes I've made on your paper."
- **High School:** A world history teacher displays an "ideal answer" on the document camera for each of the items on his homework assignments and essay items on his tests. Students compare their answers to the ideal and take notes with suggestions for improving their responses.

MyLab Education **Self-Check 11.4**

Developmentally Appropriate Practice

Applying the Model for Promoting Student Motivation with Learners at Different Ages

The components of the Model for Promoting Student Motivation apply to learners at all grade levels. For example, caring teachers, a safe and orderly environment, success, and high levels of student involvement are essential for all students. Developmental differences exist, however. We outline these differences in this section.

Working with Students in Early Childhood Programs and Elementary Schools

Elementary students enter school wide-eyed and optimistic, with only vague ideas about what they will do or learn. However, school is often the first time they are separated from their homes and parents, and anxiety about the unfamiliar may result. Taking extra time to make classrooms inviting places to learn is important with these children.

Interest can be a powerful motivating factor for elementary students. Topics such as animals, cartoon characters, sports, dinosaurs, and fantasy are interesting for most children. Incorporating these topics into reading, writing, and math assignments can be effective.

Elementary students' ability to set goals and use learning strategies are largely undeveloped, but the beginnings of self-regulation can be established with conscious efforts to model and teach metacognition.

Working with Students in Middle Schools

Middle school students have become savvy about rules and procedures and the schooling "game." However, the transition to middle school can be challenging for adolescents, and both motivation and learning often suffer. Classes are usually larger and less personal, and students leave the security of one teacher

for a schedule that sends them to different classrooms and teachers. Caring teachers who take the time to form personal relationships with their students are essential at this age.

Peers become increasingly important during the middle school years, and cooperative learning and group work become effective vehicles for increasing involvement and motivation. However, the growing influence of peers can result in off-task behaviors during group work, so structuring it carefully, monitoring students during activities, and holding students accountable for a product are important.

Variables such as challenge and task comprehension become more important than they were with elementary students. Middle schoolers also begin to assess the relevance and value of what they're studying, so personalization also becomes an increasingly important variable.

Working with Students in High Schools

While more mature, many high school students still have not reached a high level of self-regulation. Modeling self-regulation and conscious efforts to teach more sophisticated and effective learning strategies can help these students meet their needs for self-determination.

High school students are also self-aware and are thinking about their futures after high school, so they frequently assess the value of the topics they study. In addition, high school students' needs for competence and autonomy are prominent. As a result, climate variables, such as challenge and task comprehension, and instructional variables, such as personalization and feedback, become increasingly important.

Chapter 11 Summary

1. Describe the differences between a mastery-focused and a performance-focused classroom.
   - Mastery-focused classrooms emphasize effort and increased understanding. Performance-focused classrooms emphasize demonstrating high ability and comparisons among students.
   - Mastery-focused environments increase student motivation to learn, whereas performance-focused environments can detract from motivation to learn for all but the highest achievers.

2. Describe the personal qualities of teachers who increase students' motivation to learn.
   - Teachers who are high in personal teaching efficacy believe they can help students learn, regardless of students' prior knowledge or other factors.
   - Modeling courtesy and respect is essential for motivation, and communicating genuine interest in the topics they teach demonstrates teacher enthusiasm.
   - Teachers demonstrate that they care about their students by spending personal time with them and showing respect for each individual. Holding students to high standards is one of the most effective ways to simultaneously show respect and communicate that teachers expect all students to succeed.

3. Identify the learning climate variables that increase students' motivation to learn.
   - Motivating environments are safe, secure, and orderly places that focus on learning.
   - Success on tasks students perceive as challenging increases motivation to learn. Meeting challenges provides evidence that competence is increasing and leads to feelings of autonomy.
   - In motivating environments, students understand what they're expected to learn. Understanding what they're learning and why increases perceptions of autonomy and contributes to task value.

4. Explain how different instructional variables increase students' motivation to learn.
   - Teachers can increase motivation to learn by beginning lessons with examples, activities, or questions that attract students' attention and providing framework for information that follows.
   - Students maintain their attention and interest when teachers make content personally relevant to them and keep them involved in learning activities.
   - Teachers increase student motivation to learn by providing feedback about learning progress. When feedback indicates that competence is increasing, self-efficacy and self-determination both improve, and intrinsic motivation increases.

Preparing for Your Licensure Exam

Understanding Student Motivation

You will be required to take a licensure exam before you go into your own classroom. This exam will include information related to students' motivation, and it will include both multiple-choice and constructed-response questions. We include the following exercises to help you practice for the exam in your state. This book and these exercises will be a resource for you as you as you prepare for the exam.

We saw at the beginning of the chapter how DeVonne Lampkin taught the concept *arthropod*. Now read about a language arts lesson on the construction of paragraphs that DeVonne taught later that same day. After reading the case study, answer the questions that follow.

DeVonne is working with her fifth-graders on their writing skills. She plans to have them practice writing paragraphs and conduct self-assessments using criteria in a three-point rubric.

She begins, "Today, we're going to practice some more on composing good paragraphs. . . . Now, we know the characteristics of a good paragraph, but let's review for a moment. . . . What do we look for in a well-composed paragraph?"

"Topic sentence," several students say immediately.

"Okay, what else?"

"Sentences that go with the topic," others add.

"Yes, 'go with the topic' means that the sentences support your topic sentence. You need to have at least four supporting sentences."

DeVonne reminds students that they also need to use correct grammar and spelling, and then displays the following paragraphs:

Computers come in all shapes and sizes. One of the first computers, named UNIVAC, filled a room. Today, some large computers are as big as refrigerators. Others are as small as books. A few are even tiny enough to fit in a person's pocket.

Ann's family bought a new color television. It had a 54-inch screen. There were controls for color and brightness. Ann likes police stories. There were also controls for sound and tone.

After some discussion, the class concludes that the first example meets the criteria for an acceptable paragraph, but the second one does not, because the topic sentence doesn't have four supporting sentences and the information "Ann likes police stories" doesn't pertain to the topic.

She then says, "Now, you're going to write a paragraph on any topic that you choose, and then the class is going to grade your paper." DeVonne smiles as she hears several calls of "Woo, hoo" from the students.

The students go to work, and when they've finished, DeVonne says, "Okay, now we're going to grade the paragraphs." She reviews the criteria from the 3-point rubric, and then says, "Okay, who wants to go first?"

"Me!" several of the students shout.

"I should have known that," DeVonne says, smiling. "Okay, Tu, come on up."

Tu displays his paragraph on the document camera and reads it aloud:

The class discusses his paragraph, agrees that it deserves a 3, and then several students call out, "I want to go next! I want to go next!"

DeVonne asks Justin to display his paragraph:

> There was a boy named Josh. He lives in a house with the roof falling in and the windows were broke. He had holes in the wall and the ceiling leaked when it rained. But then again it always rained and thunder over his house. Noone every goes to his gate because he was so weird. They say he is a vampire.

She asks students to raise their hands to vote on the score for this paragraph. The students give it a mix of 2's and 1's.

"Samantha, why did you give it a 2?" DeVonne asks, beginning the discussion.

"He didn't stay on his topic. . . . He needs to stay on either the boy or the house," Samantha notes.

"Haajar?. . . You gave him a 1. . . . Go ahead."

"There was a boy named Josh, and then he started talking about the house. And then the weather and then the boy again," Haajar responds.

A few more students offered comments, and the class agrees that Justin's paragraph deserves a 1.5. DeVonne then asks for another volunteer.

"Me, me! I want to do mine!" several students exclaim with their hands raised. DeVonne calls on Saleina to display her paragraph, the students agree that it deserves a 3, and DeVonne then says, "I am so impressed with you guys. . . . Your work is excellent."

"Okay, let's do one more," DeVonne continues. "Joshua."

"No! No!" the students protest, wanting to continue the activity and have theirs read.

"Okay, one more after Joshua," DeVonne relents with a smile. The class assesses Joshua's paragraph and one more, and just before the end of the lesson, several students ask, "Are we going to get to do ours tomorrow?"

DeVonne smiles and assures them that they will get to look at the rest of the paragraphs the next day.

Questions for Case Analysis

Use information from this chapter and the case study to answer the following questions.

Multiple-Choice Questions

1. The students were very eager to display their paragraphs. Of the following, which variable in the Model for Promoting Student Motivation likely best explains why the students were so eager to display their paragraphs?

   a. Teacher modeling and enthusiasm

   b. Personalization

c. Introductory focus

d. Task comprehension

2. After each student displayed his or her paragraph, the class discussed the paragraph and then gave it a score of 3, 2, or 1. The variable in the Model for Promoting Student Motivation that is best illustrated by this process is

   a. positive expectations.

   b. order and safety.

c. task comprehension.

d. feedback.

Constructed-Response Question

1. In spite of the fact that they were having their paragraphs publicly evaluated, DeVonne's students were very enthusiastic about displaying their work. Offer an explanation for their enthusiasm, including as many of the variables in the Model for Promoting Student Motivation as apply.

MyLab Education Licensure Exam 11.1

Important Concepts

caring	involvement	order and safety	personalization
collective efficacy	mastery-focused	performance-focused	positive learning climate
high-quality examples	classroom	classroom	self-fulfilling prophecy
introductory focus	open-ended questions	personal teaching efficacy	task comprehension

Chapter 12
Classroom Management: Developing Self-Regulated Learners

Robert Daly/Getty Images

Learning Outcomes

After you have completed your study of this chapter, you should be able to:

12.1 Define the goals of classroom management, and identify applications of the goals in classrooms.

12.2 Describe the processes involved in planning for classroom management.

12.3 Describe effective communication strategies for involving parents.

12.4 Use cognitive and behavioral learning theories to explain effective interventions.

12.5 Describe your legal and professional responsibilities in cases of aggressive acts and steps you can take in response to defiance and aggression.

APA Top 20 Principles

Top 20 Principles from Psychology for PreK–12 Teaching and Learning explicitly addressed in this chapter.

> Principle 16: Expectations for classroom conduct and social interaction are learned and can be taught using proven principles of behavior and effective classroom instruction.
> Principle 17: Effective classroom management is based on (a) setting and communicating high expectations, (b) consistently nurturing positive relationships, and (c) providing a high level of student support.

Classroom management includes all the actions teachers take to establish an environment that supports academic learning, self-regulation, and social and emotional development. As we see in the definition, it's much more than maintaining an orderly classroom, and perhaps most significant, a long history of research suggests that students are more motivated to learn and learn more in orderly classrooms (Back, Polk, Keys, & McMahon, 2016). This research is consistent for different age groups (Morris et al., 2013), content areas (Adeyemo, 2013), and cultural groups (Adeyemo, 2013; Balagna, Young, & Smith, 2013). Keep these ideas in mind as you read the following case study and see how Judy Harris, a middle school teacher, handles classroom management incidents in her classroom.

Judy's seventh-grade geography class is involved in a cultural unit on the Middle East.

As the students enter the room, they see a large map, together with the following directions displayed on the document camera.

Identify the longitude and latitude of Damascus and Cairo.

Judy's students begin each class by completing a review exercise while she takes roll and returns papers. They also pass their day's homework forward, each putting his or her paper on top of the stack.

Judy waits for the students to finish, and then begins, "About what latitude is Damascus. . . . Bernice?" as she walks down one of the rows.

" . . . About 34 degrees north, I think," Bernice replies.

Judy's 30 students are in a room designed for 24, so the aisles are narrow, and as she walks past, Darren reaches across the aisle and pokes Kendra with a pencil.

"Stop it, Darren," Kendra mutters loudly.

Judy turns, comes back up the aisle, stands near Darren, and continues, "Good, Bernice. It is close to 34 degrees.

"So, would it be warmer or colder than here in the summer? . . . Darren?" she asks, looking directly at him.

" . . . Warmer, I think," Darren responds after Judy repeats the question, because he didn't initially hear it.

"Okay. Good. And why might that be the case? . . . Jim?"

As she waits for Jim's answer, Judy moves over to Rachel, who has been whispering to Deborah and playing with her cell phone. She kneels down so they're at eye level, points to the rules displayed on a poster, makes eye contact with Rachel, and says quietly but firmly, "We agreed that it's important to listen when other people are talking, and we know we must honor our agreements. . . . We can't learn when people aren't paying attention," and she stands back up after Rachel puts her cell phone in her purse.

"It's warmer because Damascus is south of us and also in a desert," Jim responds.

"Good, Jim. Now let's look at Cairo," she says as she waits to be sure that Rachel is looking at the map.

As she worked with her students, Judy made several moves that created an orderly environment and simultaneously promoted student learning and development. As we go through the chapter, we'll specifically examine these moves and also see how we can promote a similar environment in virtually all classrooms.

We begin by examining the goals of classroom management.

Goals of Classroom Management

12.1 Define the goals of classroom management, and identify applications of the goals in classrooms.

Ed Psych and You

As you anticipate your first teaching position, what is your greatest concern? Why do you feel that way?

If you're typical, *classroom management* is the answer to our first question in *Ed Psych and You*. It was for us (Paul and Don, your authors) when we taught in the P–12 world, and most beginning teachers perceive it as their most serious challenge "New teachers report that challenging behavior/classroom management is their top professional development need" (Rispoli et al., 2017, p. 58). It's also a major cause of teacher burnout and job dissatisfaction for veteran teachers (Aloe, Amo, & Shanahan, 2014).

Administrators understand these concerns, and the ability to create and maintain orderly and learning-focused classrooms is one of the characteristics they most look for in teachers, a capability they rank above knowledge of content and teaching skills (Engel, 2013). And, as has historically been the case, public opinion polls continue to identify it as one of schools' most challenging problems (Langer Research Associates, 2017).

The complexities of working with students help us understand why classroom management is challenging, and it answers our second question in *Ed Psych and You* (why classroom management is likely your greatest concern). For instance, Judy had to deal with Darren's and Rachel's misbehavior while simultaneously maintaining the flow of her lesson. And, to prevent the incident between Darren and Kendra from escalating, she needed to immediately react to Darren while also deciding if she should intervene in the case of Rachel's off-task behavior. Also, had she reprimanded Kendra instead of Darren—the perpetrator—it would have suggested that she didn't know what was going on in her class.

To accommodate this complexity and to create a classroom that facilitates "academic learning, self-regulation, and social and emotional development," the major goals of classroom management include:

- Developing learner self-regulation
- Creating a positive classroom climate
- Maximizing time for teaching and learning

We discuss them next.

Developing Learner Self-Regulation

Teachers frequently lament students' lack of effort and willingness to take responsibility for their own learning—their lack of self-regulation.

"My kids are so irresponsible," Kathy Hughes grumbles to her friend and colleague, Mercedes Blount, in a conversation at lunch. "They don't bring their books, they forget their notebooks in their lockers, and they come without pencils. . . . I can't get them to come to class prepared, let alone get them to read their assignments."

"I know." Mercedes smiles wryly. "Some are totally spacey, and others just don't seem to give a rip."

The solution to this problem, while not simple or easy, is the development of student **self-regulation**, which is the ability to direct and control our actions, thoughts, and emotions to reach academic and personal goals (Berk, 2019a; Schunk, 2016). We first encountered self-regulation in Chapter 6, where we found it has the following components:

- *Self-motivation*—taking responsibility for completing tasks and engaging in appropriate activities
- *Delay of gratification*—forgoing immediate rewards to gain more substantial ones later
- *Impulse control*—resisting urges to display inappropriate behaviors
- *Emotional regulation*—expressing emotions in socially appropriate ways

Figure 12.1 Developing learner self-regulation

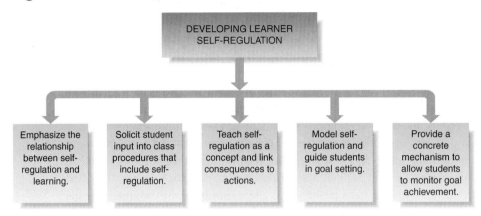

- *Self-socialization*—understanding society's standards of behavior and acting in accordance with those standards
- *Self-regulated learning*—setting personal learning goals together with the thinking and strategies used to reach these goals

Developing self-regulation takes a great deal of time, effort, and teacher support (Hessels-Schlatter, Hessels, Godin, & Spillmann-Rojas, 2017). Suggestions for providing your students with this support are outlined in Figure 12.1 and illustrated in the case study that follows.

Sam Cook, a middle school math teacher, begins the first day of school by welcoming his students, having them introduce themselves, and then saying, "To learn as much as possible, we need to work together and support each other. For instance, I need to bring the examples and materials that will help you understand our topics. . . . That's my part. . . . So, what is your part?"

With some guidance from Sam, the students conclude that they should bring their books and other materials to class each day. They also realize that they need to be in their seats when the bell rings, listen until others finish talking, support their classmates' efforts, and attempt to understand their homework instead of merely finishing it.

"Now, who is responsible for all this?" Sam asks.

"We are," several students respond.

"Yes. . . . I'm responsible for my part, and you're responsible for your parts."

"Now, let's see what happens when people aren't responsible," Sam says, displaying the following on the document camera:

Josh brings all his materials to school every day, and he carefully does his homework. He has a list that he checks off to be sure that he has each of the items and understands his homework. If he's uncertain about any part, he asks the next day. He participates in class discussions and is supportive when his classmates talk.

Josh is learning a lot, and he says his classes are interesting. His teachers respect his effort.

Andy gets in trouble with his teachers because he often forgets to bring his book, notebook, or pencil to class. He sometimes forgets his homework, so he doesn't get credit for the assignment, and he isn't learning very much. Andy also snaps at classmates in discussions, and sometimes hurts their feelings. Now, some of the other students don't want to be in groups with him.

Figure 12.2 Monitoring sheet

Week of _____ Name _____					
Self-Regulation Goals	Monday	Tuesday	Wednesday	Thursday	Friday
Bring sharpened pencil					
Bring notebook					
Bring textbook					
In seat when bell rings					
Listen while a classmate is speaking					
Extend courtesy and respect					
Learning Goals	Monday	Tuesday	Wednesday	Thursday	Friday
Finish homework					
Understand homework					

Andy's teacher called his mom to discuss his behavior and lack of responsibility, and now Andy can't watch TV for a week.

"What are some differences you notice between Josh and Andy?" Sam asks after giving his students a minute to read the vignettes.

The students make several comments, and in the process, Ronise concludes, "It's his own fault," in response to someone pointing out that Andy isn't learning very much and not getting along with the other students.

"Yes," Sam nods, "if we don't take responsibility for ourselves and control our own actions and emotions, whose fault is it if we don't learn?"

"Our own," several students respond.

"Yes," Sam emphasizes. "We're all responsible for ourselves."

With Sam's guidance, the students set goals that will help them take responsibility and control themselves, and the next day, he distributes a monitoring sheet (see Figure 12.2), which he's prepared based on the discussion. He has them put the sheet in the front of their notebooks and check off the items the first thing each morning. As the sheets accumulate, the students have a "self-regulation portfolio" that gives them a record of their progress.

Sam then asks the students how they will determine if they understand their homework, and they agree that they could either explain it in class or to their parents. Finally, they decide that each week the students who get 18 or more checks for the self-regulation goals and 8 or more for the learning goals will have free time on Fridays. Those with fewer than 15 checks on the self-regulation goals will spend "quiet time" alone during that period, and those with fewer than 8 checks for the learning goals will work with Sam on areas that need improvement.

Now, let's see how Sam applied the suggestions in Figure 12.1. First, he emphasized from the beginning of the year that they were in school to learn and that self-regulation was necessary if they were to learn as much as possible. Second, he asked for students' input into class procedures, which increases the likelihood that students will be conscientious about following them. Being asked to provide input also promotes students' feelings of autonomy, which is, according to self-determination theory, a basic psychological need for us all (Deci & Ryan, 2008).

Third, Sam treated self-regulation as a concept, and he illustrated it with an example (Josh) and non-example (Andy). Students often lack self-regulation simply because they don't realize they are, for instance, behaving irresponsibly or failing to control their impulses and emotions. Also, they sometimes don't recognize the relationship between actions and consequences. By illustrating the consequences of being—or not being—self-regulated, Sam helped promote this awareness and understanding (Korpershoek, Harms, de Boer, van Kuijk, & Doolaard, 2016).

Then, in saying "I need to plan for what we're trying to accomplish, and I need to bring the examples and materials that will help you understand our topics. . . . ," he personally modeled responsibility, and he also guided his students as they set goals. And finally, he prepared a concrete mechanism (the monitoring sheet) to help his students track their progress. We want our students to gradually accept responsibility for following these procedures and also learn to make decisions that will increase their own learning. Doing so marks progress on the path to self-regulation.

APA Top 20 Principles

This discussion illustrates Principle 16: *Expectations for classroom conduct and social interaction are learned and can be taught using proven principles of behavior and effective classroom instruction*—from the *Top 20 Principles from Psychology for PreK–12 Teaching and Learning*.

Sam's students initially met goals to receive rewards (free time) and avoid punishers (quiet time alone during the free period). As self-regulation develops, his students hopefully will begin setting their own goals because they see that setting and monitoring goals increase learning.

Regardless of how hard we try, some of our students will periodically misbehave and fail to accept responsibility, as we saw with Darren and Rachel in Judy's class. However, for students who do become self-regulated, we'll have made a lifelong contribution to their learning and overall well-being.

Creating a Positive Classroom Climate

As we saw earlier, classroom management is intended to support both academic and social-emotional learning. **Classroom climate**, the shared beliefs, values, and attitudes that set the parameters for acceptable behavior and shape interactions between students and teachers, and students with each other, will have an important influence on the extent to which these goals are met (Gage, Larson, Sugai, & Chafouleas, 2016; Joe, Hiver, & Al-Hoorie, 2017).

Classroom climate has been widely researched, and in environments where the climate is positive, students are more motivated, their interactions with their teachers and peers are more positive, they are less likely to be disruptive, and they learn more (Back, Polk, Keys, & McMahon, 2016; Çengel & Türkoğlu, 2016). Positive classroom climate is also linked to decreases in bullying and use of drugs (Gage et al., 2016). Feeling physically and emotionally safe is a key feature of a positive classroom climate. "This requires a school and classroom climate in which students can afford to be emotionally vulnerable, and in which that vulnerability extends to the student's willingness to risk engagement in acts of kindness and concern for others" (Nucci, 2006, p. 716). In addition, in a positive emotional climate, students feel respected and emotionally connected to their classmates and teachers (O'Connor, Dearing, & Collins, 2011).

When classroom climate is positive, students are involved, social interaction is prominent, and students perceive their teachers as supportive (Kearney, Smith, & Maika, 2016). Let's examine this idea of supportive teachers in more detail.

The Teacher–Student Relationship

The teacher–student relationship is the foundation of a positive classroom climate (Kuhl, 2017). Positive teacher–student relationships ". . . trigger effort, persistence, and participation; . . . foster interest and enthusiasm; and . . . dampen negative emotions such as anger, frustration, anxiety, or boredom" (Castle Heatly & Votruba-Drzal, 2017, p. 1043). So how do we promote positive relationships with our students and communicate to them that we're supportive?

We offer four suggestions. First, quickly learn their names or preferred nicknames, call them by name, and pronounce their names correctly. It communicates that we care about our students as people (Okonofua, Paunesku, & Walton, 2016). Here's a brief example reported by a teacher in one of our graduate classes, who described her efforts with her students.

MyLab Education
Video Example 12.1

A teacher-student relationship based on mutual respect is essential for the type of classroom climate that leads to orderly learning environments. Notice in this segment how the teacher describes his efforts to promote this kind of relationship with his students.

Kelsey Adams [not her real name] has a total of 150 students in her 5 classes. She has made a commitment to know all her students' names by the end of the first week of school.

"Okay, a test," she comments on Friday of that week. "I'm going to go down the rows and identify each of you by name. If I mispronounce a name, please let me know."

She then goes down the rows lightly tapping each student on the shoulder and stating his or her name.

Kelsey told us with justifiable pride that for the last 6 years she's known every student's name and pronounced each one correctly by the end of the first week of school. She also lamented that she had colleagues who went through the entire school year without learning all their students' names. Our names are part of who we are, and we want to be recognized as unique individuals. This simple, but powerful, strategy communicates that we believe all our students are important, valued, and welcome; it sets the tone for interactions throughout the year.

Second, interact with students on a personal level. For instance, noticing a student limping and checking to see if he's okay, asking about a parent or sibling, inquiring about a recent trip, commenting on a new hairdo or item of clothing, or simply bantering about a recent event communicates a level of caring, sensitivity, and simple "humanness" that promotes positive emotional reactions. As Maslow's work indicates, personal and social needs precede more academic ones, and, according to self-determination theory, we all have a need to relate to others. Simple gestures such as these help meet those needs and contribute to a positive emotional climate.

Third, model respect by using a positive—or at least neutral—tone of voice when communicating with students, and avoid sarcastic, demeaning, or condescending statements. "Much research shows that feeling respect for and being respected by authority figures can motivate people to follow rules enforced by those figures, especially in conflicts" (Okonofua et al., 2016, p. 5221). By treating students with respect, your expectation that they respect you and each other will have more heft or gravitas and will increase the likelihood of compliance when student disruptions inevitably occur (Kearney et al., 2016).

Fourth, hold students to high academic standards. Doing so communicates that we view them as capable learners and respect both them and their capabilities. These beliefs, values, and attitudes that we communicate to students are an essential part of classroom climate. But we don't simply have high standards for our students; we also provide the support that helps them meet those standards. "A convincing accumulation of research has shown that students who feel supported by their teachers tend to be more engaged in academic work and have fewer disciplinary interactions with adults in school, relative to their peers who experience less support" (Gregory, Skiba, & Mediratta, 2017, p. 261).

We can provide this support in a number of ways:

- Making learning objectives clear and keeping instruction aligned with the objectives.
- Using high-quality examples and other representations of content to make topics meaningful.
- Interacting with students to promote their involvement in learning activities.
- Using formative assessments to assess learning progress and provide feedback.

APA Top 20 Principles

This discussion illustrates Principle 17: *Effective classroom management is based on (a) setting and communicating high expectations, (b) consistently nurturing positive relationships, and (c) providing a high level of student support*—from the *Top 20 Principles from Psychology for PreK–12 Teaching and Learning*.

We discuss each of these forms of support in detail in Chapters 13 and 14.

Maximizing Time for Teaching and Learning

When students' self-regulation develops and a positive classroom climate is created, misbehavior decreases, so we have more time to devote to teaching and learning, the third goal of classroom management.

But "time" isn't as simple as it appears on the surface, and different types exist:

- **Allocated time**—the amount of time a teacher or school designates for a content area or topic, such as elementary schools allocating an hour a day to math or middle and secondary schools having 55-minute periods.
- **Instructional time**—the amount of time left for teaching after routine management and administrative tasks are completed.
- **Engaged time**—the amount of time students are paying attention and involved in learning activities.
- **Academic learning time**—the amounts of time students are successful while engaged in learning activities.

When reformers suggest lengthening the school day or year, they're suggesting an increase in allocated time. Its value, however, depends on how efficiently it's used. For instance, the benefits of increased allocated time are reduced if instructional time is lost because we have to deal with misbehavior; engaged time is lost if students aren't paying attention; and academic learning time is decreased if students are confused and unsuccessful.

The ideal we strive for is to maximize instructional, engaged, and academic learning time so as much of our allocated time as possible is devoted to teaching and learning. Although we must spend some time on routine activities, such as taking roll and collecting homework, we try to come as close as possible to this ideal. For instance, each day Judy's students complete a review exercise while she takes roll and collects and hands back papers. The exercise activates students' prior knowledge, focuses their attention on the day's topic, and eliminates non-instructional time when disruptions are most common. She also maintained the flow of her lesson—so she didn't lose instructional time—while simultaneously dealing with Darren's and Rachel's misbehavior. These are the actions we referred to at the beginning of the chapter when we said, "As she worked with her students, Judy made several moves that created an orderly environment and simultaneously promoted student learning and development."

The different types of time help us understand why classroom management is so essential for motivation and learning. In classrooms where students are engaged and successful, achievement is high, learners feel a sense of competence and self-efficacy, and interest in the topics increases (Korpershoek et al., 2016).

MyLab Education Self-Check 12.1

Planning for Classroom Management

12.2 Describe the processes involved in planning for classroom management.

Some of the earliest research examining classroom management was conducted by Jacob Kounin (1970), who found that the key to an orderly classroom is a teacher's ability to prevent management problems instead of focusing on **discipline**, which is the response to misbehaviors after they occur. "Effective teachers manage their classrooms. Ineffective teachers discipline their classrooms" (Lester, Allanson, & Notar, 2017, p. 410). This assertion and Kounin's findings have been consistently corroborated over the years (Hochweber, Hosenfeld, & Klieme, 2013).

Our goal is to prevent as many management problems as possible, leaving us with fewer incidents of misbehavior to deal with later. This requires planning, and beginning teachers tend to underestimate the amount of time and energy it takes. Because they sometimes don't plan carefully enough, they find themselves continually responding to misbehavior, which increases their uncertainty and stress (Dicke, Elling, Schmeck, & Leutner, 2015).

Before examining the process of planning for classroom management, we first consider the role of effective instruction in classroom management.

Planning for Instruction

Ed Psych and You

As you reflect on your experiences as a student, in which classes are you most likely to pay attention? In which are you most likely to drift off, perhaps text a friend, or even chat with the person next to you?

Think about the questions we asked in *Ed Psych and You*. Typically, we're most likely to drift off, or worse, if the instruction isn't motivating. "Dry lessons with limited opportunities for students to participate are boring and erode students' motivation; this is when management problems begin" (Evertson & Emmer, 2017, p. 131). This was certainly true when we were students, and you've likely had similar experiences. In Judy's case, it would have been virtually impossible to maintain an orderly classroom if her instruction had been ineffective. "Walk the halls of any school, and you'll find that it's not the strictest teacher with the most rules, but the personable teacher with the most interesting and challenging lesson plan that has the best behaved students" (Kraft, 2010, p. 45).

MyLab Education
Video Example 12.2

The close link between orderly classrooms and effective instruction has been consistently corroborated by research, and it's true whether we plan to teach in elementary, middle, or high schools. Notice in this segment that both school leaders emphasize the importance of effective instruction in creating positive and orderly learning environments.

The close link between management and instruction has been consistently corroborated by research, and it is true whether we plan to teach in elementary, middle, or high schools (Korpershoek et al., 2016). This suggests that as we plan for classroom management, we must simultaneously plan for instruction (Greenberg, Putman, & Walsh, 2014). These plans include:

- Being clear about learning goals, preparing examples of the topics we plan to teach, and having materials ready so instruction can begin immediately. Judy's map, for instance, was displayed when her students walked into her classroom, and Sam had his vignettes prepared and waiting when he began his lesson.

- Starting classes and activities on time. Judy had a warm-up activity waiting for the students when they walked in the room. The activity eliminated "dead time," when disruptions are most likely.

- Creating well-established routines. Judy's students complete a warm-up activity every day, and they begin without being told to do so. Routines keep students at equilibrium, reduce the cognitive load on both teachers' and students' working memories, and help them focus on learning. Some experts suggest that effective routines are the foundation of classroom management (Lester et al., 2017).

- Making transitions quickly and smoothly. This includes seating members of groups near each other, so they simply turn in their seats to move from whole-group to small-group activities and back again. If students have to get up to move back and forth from group work, time is wasted, and disruptions are more likely.

- Planning to involve students, which makes them more likely to pay attention. As soon as her students finished their warm-up activity, Judy immediately began her lesson with questioning.

Having carefully planned for instruction, we're now ready to consider the specific planning challenges for classroom management at different grade levels.

Planning for Classroom Management in Elementary Schools

Regardless of whether you're preparing to teach in elementary, middle, or high schools, a clear system of **rules**, standards for acceptable behavior, and **procedures**, guidelines for accomplishing recurring tasks, such as turning in papers and making transitions from one activity to another, will be essential elements of your classroom management system (Emmer & Evertson, 2017; Evertson & Emmer, 2017). However, if you're preparing to teach in an elementary school, rules and procedures will be different than if you're working with older students. To understand why, let's look at one intern's experience with first-graders.

Jim Cramer, an elementary education major, is beginning his internship in a first-grade classroom. It's a disaster. Students get up from their seats and wander around the room. They begin playing with materials at their desks while he is trying to explain a topic. They argue about their roles in cooperative learning activities. Reminders to pay attention have no effect. They're not destructive or intentionally misbehaving; they're little kids. His directing teacher has a rather laissez faire approach to classroom management, and the lack of focus in her classroom doesn't seem to bother her.

The developmental characteristics of young children help us understand why Jim's experience didn't go well.

Developmental Characteristics of Elementary Students

As we know, young children's thinking tends to focus on the concrete and tangible, and their attention spans are limited (Jiang, Swallow, & Rosenbaum, 2013; Piaget, 1970). Socially and emotionally, they're eager to please their teachers and are vulnerable to criticism and harsh treatment (Carter & Doyle, 2006).

Developing a sense of personal autonomy as they move from their family to the school setting is one of their most important tasks. A predictable classroom environment is important, because it mirrors the stability they—hopefully—experience at home. For children who don't have this stability, an orderly classroom can be a positive force that helps build a sense of trust and security (Watson & Ecken, 2003).

Young children need enough freedom to develop initiative but sufficient structure to maintain their sense of equilibrium. As they progress through the elementary grades, they continue to need acceptance and the recognition that helps them develop a sense of industry and self-assurance. This can be a challenge. "It is difficult to meet the misbehaving child's needs for autonomy, belonging, and competence, and also maintain a safe and productive classroom" (Watson & Ecken, 2003, p. 3).

Our rules and procedures help us meet this challenge. We turn to them next.

Rules and Procedures in Elementary Classrooms: The Theoretical Framework

As with most aspects of learning and teaching, rules and procedures in elementary classrooms are grounded in cognitive learning theory. *People want their experiences to make sense* is basic, so, to be effective, our rules and procedures must make sense to our students. One elementary teacher had the following rules:

- We raise our hands before speaking.
- We listen when someone else is talking.
- We leave our seats only when given permission by the teacher.
- We stand politely in line at all times.
- We keep our hands to ourselves.

These rules make sense. For instance, waiting to speak, listening while a classmate is talking, and remaining in seats until given permission help maximize time for learning and contribute to self-regulation, two goals of classroom management. Standing politely and keeping hands to themselves contributes to social and emotional development, a third classroom management goal. The opposite is also true. Blurting out answers or comments, failing to listen, and poking or hitting while standing in line indicate both a lack of self-regulation and underdeveloped social-emotional learning.

Research provides further evidence for the importance of rules in promoting social and emotional development. For example, researchers have found that implementing a rule preventing the exclusion of classmates promotes social acceptance to a greater extent than do individual efforts to help excluded children (Schwab & Elias, 2015).

The rules above are merely examples, and you will make your own decisions about rules when you begin teaching. We offer specific suggestions for creating rules and procedures in the section "Using Educational Psychology and Teaching: Creating and Teaching Your Classroom Rules" later in our discussion.

Arranging the Physical Environment in Elementary Classrooms

Because it's the space in which a variety of activities take place, the physical environment in elementary classrooms is also important. "You will facilitate these activities if you arrange your room to permit orderly movement, keep distractions to a minimum, and make efficient use of available space" (Evertson & Emmer, 2017, p. 32). Tables, chairs, cubbies, carpeted areas, plants, easels, building blocks, and shelves should physically accommodate whole-group, small-group, and individual study and should be flexible and adaptable.

While everyone's classroom will look different, some suggestions can help as we think about our room arrangement:

- Be sure all students can see the board, document camera, and other displays. If students have to move or crane their necks to see, disruptions are more likely.
- Design the room so we can see all our students. Monitoring their behaviors is important for both learning and classroom management.
- Be sure students can easily access commonly used materials without disrupting their classmates.
- Keep high-traffic areas free from obstructions, and provide ample space for student movement.

Figure 12.3 illustrates the physical arrangement of one elementary classroom. Note how it is designed to maximize these suggestions. It's merely an example, and you may choose to arrange your classroom differently.

Planning for Classroom Management in Middle and Secondary Schools

Middle and secondary classes are populated by adolescents, and they're more developmentally advanced than elementary students. So, we must also consider these developmental changes if we plan to teach in middle or secondary schools. Let's take a look.

Developmental Characteristics of Middle and Secondary Students

As students move through school, several developmental trends become significant:

- The influence of peers increases.
- Needs for belonging and social acceptance increase.
- The search for a sense of identity begins.
- The desire for autonomy and independence increases.

Figure 12.3 The physical arrangement of an elementary classroom

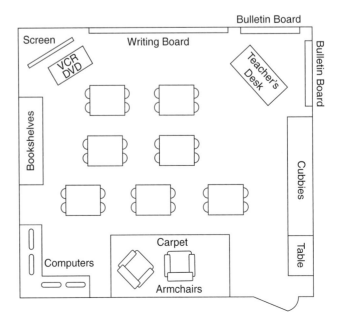

Learning and motivation theories help us understand the implications of these trends for classroom management. First, for instance, social cognitive theory explains why students tend to imitate peers who are accomplished in academics, athletics, or even delinquency (Kidron & Fleischman, 2006). Vicarious reinforcers and punishers can be effective if peers believe they're administered consistently, that is, they make sense to the students. Judy's interventions with Darren and Rachel are examples. Their classmates could see they were breaking agreed upon rules and that Judy was enforcing the rules fairly.

Second, Maslow's work and self-determination theory remind us that belonging and relatedness are important to all students, and the need to be accepted by peers increases as they move into adolescence. This helps us understand why they're conforming in their speech, dress, and behavior even if seemingly bizarre by adult standards.

Third, adolescents are beginning their search for identity, and their needs for autonomy and independence increase. This can result in the sometimes frustrating capricious and even rebellious behavior typical of this age group. Understanding these tendencies reminds us that adolescents need the stability and support that result from the firm hand of caring teachers who set clear limits for acceptable behavior.

Rules and Procedures in Middle and Secondary Classrooms: The Theoretical Framework

Although much of the theoretical framework guiding rules and procedures for middle and secondary students is the same as for those in elementary schools, some differences exist. For instance, the need for everything to make sense to students is even more important as they mature, and perceptions of fairness, inequitable treatment, and teachers having "favorites" or "pets" increase. Because students are increasingly sensitive to these issues, understanding why rules exist and consistent enforcement of them become increasingly important.

Self-determination theory also identifies autonomy as a need for all of us, and soliciting students' input into the formation of rules and procedures helps meet this need.

The following are rules from one seventh-grade class:

- Be in your seat and quiet when the bell rings.
- Follow directions the first time they're given.
- Bring covered textbooks, notebook, pen, pencils, and planner to class every day.
- Raise your hand for permission to speak or leave your seat.
- Keep hands, feet, and objects to yourself.
- Leave class only when dismissed by the teacher.

As with the examples of rules for elementary classrooms, they make sense, accommodate the developmental characteristics of middle school students, and help meet the goals of classroom management. For instance, students in middle schools tend to be "social," so the first rule addresses a potential problem than can result from this tendency. And as students gradually learn to socialize appropriately, follow directions, and bring necessary materials to class, their self-regulation develops. And keeping hands, feet, and objects to themselves contributes to both self-regulation and social-emotional learning.

As in elementary classrooms, the specific rules you create will depend on your professional judgment. For example, the third rule above might appear to be too specific, but the teacher who created these rules noted that the specifics were needed to be sure her students actually brought the materials to class.

As students move into high school, their behavior tends to stabilize, they communicate more effectively at an adult level, and they respond generally well to clear rationales.

Figure 12.4 Classroom arrangement in traditional rows

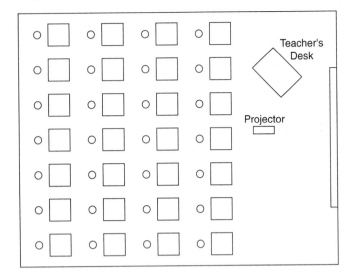

The following are rules taken from a tenth-grade class:

- Do all grooming outside of class.
- Be in your seat before the bell rings.
- Stay in your seat at all times.
- Bring all materials daily. This includes your book, note-book, pen/pencil, and paper.
- Give your full attention to others in discussions, and wait your turn to speak.
- Leave when I dismiss you, not when the bell rings.

Again, these rules are designed to accommodate the characteristics of more mature students. For example, older students sometimes obsess about their looks and decide, for example, to brush their hair in the middle of a class discussion, which explains "Do all grooming outside of class." Rules requiring students to be in their seats when the bell rings, and stay in their seats, promote self-regulation. And listening attentively to classmates contributes to social and emotional learning.

MyLab Education

Video Example 12.3

The way students' desks in a room are arranged depends on teachers' goals. Here a high school social studies teacher describes his rationale for arranging his classroom in a somewhat non-traditional way.

Arranging the Physical Environment in Middle and Secondary Classrooms

The physical environment in middle and secondary classrooms tends to be the more nearly traditional arrangement of desks in rows or in a semicircle facing the front of the room. Figures 12.4 and 12.5 illustrate these arrangements.

If you use a combination of whole-group and small-group instruction, you may want to arrange the room as you see in Figure 12.6. Students are seated with their group mates so they don't have to move. Then, when the learning activity moves from small to whole group, students merely turn their heads to see you, the board, and the document camera.

No single arrangement works for all situations, and you will experiment to find what works the best for you. Suggestions for room arrangements in secondary schools include (Emmer & Evertson, 2017):

- Being sure the layout is consistent with instructional goals.

Figure 12.6 Sample seating arrangement for group work

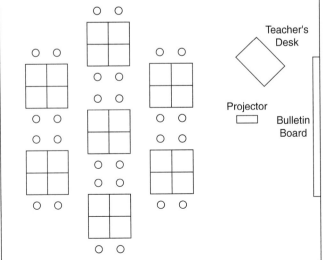

Figure 12.5 Classroom arrangement in a semicircle

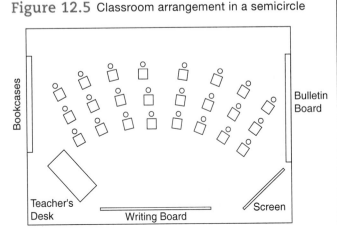

- Keeping high-traffic areas free of congestion.
- Ensuring that you can easily see all your students and they can easily see instructional displays.
- Keeping frequently used materials and supplies readily accessible.

Personalizing Your Classroom

Many classrooms, and particularly those in middle and secondary schools, are quite impersonal, and they reveal little about the people who spend time in them (Emmer & Evertson, 2017).

We can make our classrooms more inviting by displaying personal items such as individual or class pictures, artwork, poetry, and other products prepared by students on bulletin boards or posters. One section of a bulletin board might display names of students who improved from one test to another or some other form of recognition that allows all students an equal chance of being honored.

We can also personalize our classrooms by involving students in decisions about its arrangement. If they know the goal is promoting learning, and if self-regulation is stressed, their input provides a sense of ownership that increases their security, sense of belonging, and perceptions of autonomy.

Planning for the First Days of School

Research consistently indicates that the patterns of behavior for the entire year are established in the first few days of school (Jones & Jones, 2016). In elementary schools "the beginning of school is a critical time for classroom management because your students will learn attitudes, behavior, and work habits that will affect the tone of your class for the rest of the year" (Evertson & Emmer, 2017, p. 95). This is also the time when students learn what is expected of them and what is required to successfully accomplish school tasks. The beginning of the year is similar for middle and secondary students, and in addition we want to "strengthen each student's belief that school tasks are worth doing and that he or she can be successful" (Emmer & Evertson, 2017, p. 90). Positive teacher–student relationships—which we discussed earlier—contribute to this belief.

Let's look at differences between two middle school teachers in how they begin their school year.

Donnell Alexander is waiting at the door for her eighth-graders with prepared handouts as students come in the room. As she distributes them, she says, "Take your seats quickly, please. You'll find your name on a desk. The bell is going to ring in less than a minute, and everyone needs to be at his or her desk and quiet when it does. Please read the handout while you're waiting."

She is standing at the front of the room, surveying the class as the bell rings. When it stops, she begins, "Good morning, everyone."

Vicki Williams, who also teaches eighth-graders across the hall from Donnell, is organizing her handouts as the students come in the room. Some take their seats while others mill around, talking in small groups. As the bell rings, she looks up and says over the hum of the students, "Everyone take your seats, please. We'll begin in a couple minutes," and she turns back to organizing her materials.

In these first few minutes, Donnell's students learned that they were expected to be in their seats and ready to start at the beginning of class, whereas Vicki's learned just the opposite. Students quickly understand these differences, and unless Vicki changes this pattern, she will soon have problems, perhaps not dramatic, but chronic and low grade, like nagging sniffles that won't go away. Problems such as these cause more teacher stress and fatigue than any other (Jones & Jones, 2016). Specific suggestions for the first few days include the following:

- *Establish expectations.* Hand out a description of the class requirements and your grading system the first day. Emphasize that all the decisions you make are intended to promote learning.

- *Teach rules and procedures.* Teaching your rules and procedures the first day of class is part of establishing expectations; discuss and practice the rules with extra frequency the first few days.

- *Plan structured instruction.* Begin your instruction on the first day with an eye-catching and motivating learning activity, and avoid group work for the first few days.

- *Begin communication with parents.* Write a letter to parents, which includes a description of your class requirements together with rules and procedures, display it for your students, email it to parents, and request that they reply back to you. (If parents don't have access to email, give students a hard copy, and have them return the letter with parents' signatures the following day.)

Establishing expectations and communicating with parents immediately demonstrates that you're in charge of your classroom and that you have your act together. Combined with effective instruction, nothing does more to prevent classroom management problems.

MyLab Education Application Exercise 12.1: Introducing the School Year

In this exercise, you will be asked to analyze a seventh-grade English teacher's application of suggestions for getting the school year off to a good start.

Using Educational Psychology in Teaching: Suggestions for Creating and Teaching Your Classroom Rules

As we've seen in the preceding sections, clear and specific rules and procedures help promote academic learning, self-regulation, and social and emotional development. Combined with effective instruction, they are the cornerstone of an effective classroom management system. The following suggestions can help in our efforts to create and teach rules effectively:

- Create a small number of positively stated rules.
- Solicit student input in the rule-setting process.
- Emphasize rationales for rules.
- Use concrete examples to illustrate rules and procedures.
- Monitor and practice rules and procedures until they become automatic.

(We focus mostly on rules in this section, but each suggestion applies equally well to procedures.)

Let's do a flashback to the beginning of the school year to see how Judy Harris created and taught her rules:

Judy begins by having students introduce themselves, including any personal information they would like to share, and she does the same.

When they're finished, she says, "Our goal for this class is to learn about the geography of our world and how it impacts the way we live. In order to learn as much as possible, we need some rules that will guide the way we operate. So, think about some rules that make sense and are fair to all of us. . . . Go ahead, Jonique."

" . . . We should listen," Jonique offers after pausing a few seconds.

The class agrees that the rule makes sense, Judy writes it on the board, and then asks, "Why is this rule so important?"

" . . . It's rude if we don't listen to each other or if we interrupt when someone is talking," Enita offers.

"Of course." Judy smiles. "What's the very most important reason?"

"To learn," Antonio responds, remembering what Judy said at the beginning of the discussion.

"Absolutely, that's what school is all about. We learn less if we don't listen. . . . And we're all responsible for our own behavior, so this will help us meet that goal. . . . And listening attentively is a part of treating everyone with courtesy and respect."

The students agree that they all want to be treated courteously, Judy writes it on the board, and she continues to lead the discussion until the rules you see here appear on the list.

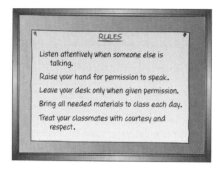

In each case she emphasizes why the rule is important, how it will increase learning, and why it will help them take responsibility for their behavior.

Particularly during the first few weeks of school, and then throughout the year, when an incident occurs, such as one student interrupting another, Judy stops what they're doing, reminds the class of the rule, and again asks the students why it's important. The students gradually adapt to the rules and become acclimated to the classroom environment.

Immediately after school, Judy includes the rules in a letter, which she emails to the parents of all the students in her class.

Now, let's see how Judy applied the suggestions.

Create a Small Number of Positively Stated Rules.   The first suggestion is illustrated in the rules themselves: She created only five and she stated them positively. A small number decreases the cognitive load on students' working memories and increases the likelihood that they will remember the rules. Students commonly break rules—particularly in elementary schools—because they simply forget.

Stating rules positively is grounded in cognitive learning theory: the rules establish expectations for students, which they can encode in their long-term memories as schemas. Negatively stated rules merely identify what students are "not to do" and don't contribute to schema construction. Also, stating rules positively helps promote a classroom environment that supports self-regulation and social and emotional development.

Solicit Student Input.   Judy applied the second suggestion—solicit student input in the rule-setting process—when she said, "In order to learn as much as possible, we need some rules that will guide the way we operate. So, think about some rules that make sense and are fair to all of us. . . . Go ahead, Jonique." Being asked for input creates social contracts that can increase moral development, students' feelings of autonomy, and motivation to learn (Brophy, 2010; Deci & Ryan, 2008). This suggestion is more important at the middle and secondary level than in elementary schools, and we endorse doing so because it reinforces the idea that students are responsible for their actions. However, some teachers choose to create rules and procedures without student input, and this process can also be effective (Emmer & Evertson, 2017; Evertson & Emmer, 2017).

Emphasize Rationales for Rules. As we have repeatedly emphasized throughout this text, the need to make sense of our experiences is basic, and providing rationales for rules helps students make sense of them. If, for example, we emphasize that *learning* in all its forms is the reason we're in school, and students understand that blurting out answers and comments detracts from learning, they are less likely to speak without permission because the rule makes sense. If the rule makes sense, they're more likely to obey it, and holding themselves in check represents an advance in both self-regulation and social-emotional development.

Let's look again at how Judy applied this suggestion.

Judy: Why is this rule [to listen] so important?

Enita: It's rude if we don't listen to each other or if we interrupt when someone is talking.

Judy: Of course. . . . What's the very most important reason?

Antonio: To learn.

As we can see from this brief dialogue, providing rationales is easy; we merely discuss why the rule is important. It doesn't take much time, and the benefits are often greater than we anticipate.

Whether or not you solicit student input into the rule-making process, providing reasons (rationales) for rules is essential. Without reasons, students might view rules as arbitrary, or even punitive, which increases the likelihood that they will disregard or disobey the rules.

Use Concrete Examples to Illustrate Rules and Procedures. Judy applied the fourth suggestion by using classroom incidents that occurred during the normal course of learning activities to illustrate rules. As an example, let's review a brief excerpt from the case study at the beginning of the chapter.

As she waits for Jim's answer, Judy moves over to Rachel, who has been whispering to Deborah and playing with her cell phone. She kneels down so they're at eye level, points to the rules displayed on a poster, makes eye contact with Rachel, and says quietly but firmly, "We agreed that it's important to listen when other people are talking, and we know we must honor our agreements. . . . We can't learn when people aren't paying attention."

Here, Judy used Rachel's off-task behavior as an opportunity to reinforce the rule "Listen attentively when someone else is talking." Using examples in this way can be effective because they're immediate, concrete, and personal. In time, students will come to understand why the rules are important and disruptions will gradually decrease.

Practice Rules and Procedures Until They're Automatic. We know that automaticity—the ability to perform an action without thinking about it—is important for reducing cognitive load. This means that procedures, such as turning in papers and lining up for lunch, must be practiced to the point that students perform them without thinking about it. For instance, because Judy's students complete a warm-up activity every day when they begin class, they immediately began the activity in the case study at the beginning of the chapter without being reminded to do so—it was automatic.

Judy teaches in a middle school. Let's look at an elementary teacher's efforts.

MyLab Education
Video Example 12.4

Practice rules and procedures until they're automatic is a suggestion for creating and teaching classroom rules. Notice here that the students come into the classroom, gather their materials and begin work immediately without a word of direction spoken by the teacher.

Martha Oakes, a first-grade teacher, is helping her students understand the procedure for putting away worksheets.

"I put each of their names, and my own, on cubby holes on the wall of my room. Then, while they were watching, I did a short worksheet myself and walked over and put it in my storage spot, while saying out loud, 'I'm finished with my worksheet. . . . What do I do now? . . . I need to put it in my cubby hole. If I don't put it there, my teacher can't check it, so it's very important. . . . Now, I start on the next assignment.'

"Then I gave my students the same worksheet, directing them to take it to their cubbies, quietly and individually, as soon as they were finished. After everyone was done, we spent a few minutes discussing the reasons for immediately taking the finished work to the cubbies, not touching or talking to anyone as they move back and forth to their desks, and starting right back to work. Then I gave them another worksheet, asked them what they were going to do and why, and had them do it. We then spent a few more minutes talking about what might happen if we didn't put papers where they belong.

"We have a class meeting nearly every day just before we leave for the day. We discuss classroom life and offer suggestions for improvement. Some people might be skeptical about whether first-graders can handle meetings like this, but they can. This is also one way I help them keep our rules and procedures fresh in their minds."

We can see how Martha's approach both applied the suggestion and is grounded in cognitive learning theory. First, she modeled the process for taking worksheets to the cubbies, used cognitive modeling in verbalizing what she was doing, and had her students practice doing the same. Being specific and concrete was essential for Martha's students because they're first-graders, and these actions provided the concrete examples they needed to construct their understanding of the process and to promote self-regulation. With enough practice, the procedure will become automatic, which will reduce the cognitive load on both Martha and the children.

MyLab Education Self-Check 12.2
MyLab Education Application Exercise 12.2: Constructing Rules in Second Grade

In this exercise, you will be asked to analyze a second-grade teacher's application of suggestions for creating and teaching classroom rules.

Communicating with Parents

12.3 Describe effective communication strategies for involving parents.

"Students typically spend only 25% of their waking hours in school. Accordingly, out-of-school factors account for the vast majority of differences in educational

Classroom Connections

Planning and Teaching Rules and Procedures in Classrooms

Planning Rules and Procedures

1. Effective classroom management begins with planning. Carefully plan your rules and procedures before you meet your first class.

- **Elementary:** A third-grade teacher prepares a handout for his students and their parents and gives it to his students the first day of school. The students take the handout home, have their parents sign it, and return it the next day.

- **Middle School:** A pre-algebra teacher prepares a short written list of rules before she starts class on the first day. She plans to ask her students to suggest additional rules that will increase everyone's opportunity to learn.

- **High School:** An English teacher prepares a description of his procedures for the way writing drafts will be handled and how his class will use peer comments to improve essays. He displays and discusses the procedure the first day of class.

Teaching Rules and Procedures

2. The developmental characteristics of students influence teachers' management strategies. Consider the developmental level of your students when teaching rules and procedures.

- **Elementary:** At the beginning of the school year, a first-grade teacher takes a few minutes each day to have her students practice procedures such as turning in materials and lining up for lunch. She continues having them practice until students follow the procedures without being reminded.

- **Middle School:** A sixth-grade teacher has a rule that says "Treat everyone with respect." She offers specific examples, and asks students to discuss whether the example illustrates treating everyone with respect.

- **High School:** A chemistry teacher takes a full class period to teach safe lab procedures. She models correct procedures, explains the reasons for them, and carefully monitors students as they work in the lab.

achievement in the United States" (Kraft & Rogers, 2015, p. 49). In other words, parents are crucial for student achievement, and research consistently confirms a positive relationship between students' success in school and their parents' involvement. Children whose parents are involved have more positive attitudes and higher long-term achievement, better attendance, and greater self-regulation (Kraft, 2016). They are also more likely to enroll in postsecondary education (Page & Scott-Clayton, 2016).

These outcomes result from a variety of influences. For instance, children are more motivated when parents are involved, and increased motivation contributes to higher achievement. And parents' participation in school activities, higher expectations for their children, and teachers' increased understanding of learners' home environments also contribute to higher achievement (Adamski, Fraser, & Peiro, 2013). And some research suggests that parental involvement can even increase students' cognitive ability (Phillipson & Phillipson, 2012).

Parental involvement is particularly important in classrooms with large numbers of students from diverse backgrounds. Because of factors such as language barriers and questions about whether or not their involvement will be welcomed, parents who are members of cultural minorities may be reluctant to become involved in their children's education. We need to make special efforts to initiate and maintain home–school communication with these parents (Walker & Hoover-Dempsey, 2015).

Parent–teacher collaboration also has benefits for us as teachers. For instance, teachers who encourage parental involvement report more positive feelings about teaching and their school, and rate parents higher in helpfulness and follow-through (Weinstein & Romano, 2015).

Parents are often underutilized (Kraft, 2016; Kraft & Rogers, 2015), but capitalizing on them as an educational resource can be a challenge. For instance, some research indicates that only 10% of teachers report that parents of their students are actively involved. A number of factors, such as parents' inflexible work schedules, contribute to this lack of involvement (Smith, 2015).

So, what can we do to increase parental involvement? We address this question next.

Strategies for Involving Parents

All schools have formal communication channels, such as open houses—usually within the first 2 weeks of the school year—when teachers introduce themselves and describe their policies; interim progress reports, which tell parents about their youngsters' achievements at the midpoint of each grading period; parent–teacher conferences; and, of course, report cards. These processes are school-wide and valuable, but you can go well beyond them. Let's see how Jacinta Escobar, a fifth-grade teacher, attempts to increase communication with her students' parents.

Every year, as soon as she's able to access the email addresses of her students' parents, Jacinta creates an email group (sometimes called a *listserve*) and prepares a letter which states that she expects to have a productive and exciting year, outlines her expectations and classroom procedures, and solicits parents' support. She shares and discusses it with her students the first day of class, and explains why having their parents involved is so important. She also asks for their suggestions for rules and procedures to include in the letter. She then takes the letter home, revises it, and emails a copy to parents, and requests that parents reply to the email as a form of contract indicating their support. She follows up on those that aren't returned with additional emails and even phone calls in some cases.

Her letter appears in Figure 12.7.

Every other week throughout the year, Jacinta sends assignments, including worksheets and graded work, home to be signed by parents—indicating that they have looked at the student products. Jacinta also encourages parents to contact her by phone, text, or email if they have any questions about the packets or any other aspect of their children's work.

Jacinta also frequently texts or emails parents to let them know about their children's progress. If students miss more than one assignment, she sends a note expressing her concern. She also emails parents to report positive news, such as a student exceeding requirements, overcoming an obstacle, or showing kindness to a classmate.

Jacinta promoted communication with parents in three ways. The first was her letter. It began the communication process, expressed positive expectations, specified class rules (described as "guidelines"), and outlined procedures for homework, absences, and extra credit.

The letter also asked for parents' replies, which makes it a contract soliciting their support. Replies aren't guarantees, but they symbolize a commitment and increase the likelihood that parents and students will attempt to honor it. Also, because students have input into the content of the letter, they feel greater ownership of the process.

Notice also that the letter is free from grammar, punctuation, and spelling errors. Teachers sometimes send communications home with errors in them. Don't. First impressions are important and lasting. Your first letter creates a perception of your competence, and errors detract from your credibility.

As a second attempt to promote communication, Jacinta sent packets of students' work home every other week and asked parents to sign and return them. In addition to creating a link between home and school, the packets give parents an ongoing record of their child's progress.

Third, she periodically emailed parents, which effectively maintains communication and enlists their cooperation (Thompson, Mazer, & Flood, 2015). Allocating some of your personal time to text or email parents communicates caring better than any other way.

Figure 12.7 Letter to parents

August 27, 2018

Dear Parents,

I am looking forward to a productive and exciting year, and I am writing this letter to encourage your involvement and support. You always have been and always will be the most important people in your youngster's education. We cannot do the job without you.

For us to work together most effectively, some guidelines are necessary. With the students' help, we prepared the ones listed here. Please read this information carefully, and reply to this email with a simple statement saying, "I have read and support these guidelines."

If you have any questions, please feel free to call me at Southside Middle School (441-5935) or personally (221-8403) in the evenings.

Sincerely,

Jacinta Escobar

AS A PARENT, I WILL TRY MY BEST TO DO THE FOLLOWING:
1. I will ask my youngsters about school every day (evening meal is a good time). I will ask them about what they're studying and try to learn about it.
2. I will provide a quiet time and place each evening for homework, and I will set an example by also working, studying, or reading while my youngsters are working.
3. I will ask to see my youngsters' homework after they've finished it, and I will have them explain some of the information to see if they understand it.

STUDENT GUIDELINES FOR SUCCESS:

Self-regulation guidelines:
1. I will be in class and seated when the bell rings.
2. I will follow directions the first time they are given.
3. I will bring a covered textbook, notebook, paper, and two sharpened pencils to class each day.
4. I will raise my hand for permission to speak or leave my seat.
5. I will keep my hands, feet, and objects to myself.

Homework guidelines:
1. Our class motto is "I will always try and I will never give up."
2. I will complete all assignments. I understand that I will not receive credit for homework turned in late.
3. If I am absent, I am responsible for coming in before school to get makeup work as soon as I return to school.
4. I know that I have one day for each day I'm absent to make up missed work.
5. I understand that extra credit work is not given. If I do the required work, extra credit isn't necessary.

Student Signature _____

Notice that we're emphasizing texting and emailing here more than calling. We're not suggesting that you don't call parents, but calling can be problematic, because—for a variety of reasons—parents often don't answer their phones. Teacher surveys indicate that attempts to call are often ineffective (Smith, 2015). If you can reach parents by phone, by all means do so, and calling has some distinct advantages. For example, talking to a parent allows you to be specific in describing a student's needs and gives you a chance to again solicit support. If a student is missing assignments, for instance, you can find out why and can encourage parents to more closely monitor their child's study habits.

When we talk to parents, we want to establish a positive, cooperative tone that lays the foundation for joint efforts. Consider the following:

"Hello, Mrs. Hansen? This is Jacinta Escobar, Jared's teacher."

"Oh, uh, is something wrong?"

"Not really. I just wanted to call to share with you some information. He's a bright, energetic boy, and I enjoy seeing him in class every day. But he's missing some homework assignments."

"I didn't know he had homework. He never brings any home."

"That might be part of the problem. He just might forget that he has any to do. . . . I have a suggestion. I have the students write their homework assignments in their folders each day. Please ask Jared to share his folder with you in the evening, and make sure that his homework is done. Then, please initial it so I know you and he have talked. I think that will help. How does that sound?"

"Sure. I'll try that."

"Good. We don't want him to fall behind. If he has problems with the homework, have him come to my room before or after school, and I'll help him. Is there anything else I can do? . . . If not, I look forward to meeting you soon."

This conversation was positive, created a partnership between home and school, and offered a specific plan of action.

Decisions about when to call, text, or email parents about a management issue depend on your professional judgment. The question "To what extent does the issue influence learning?" is a good guideline. For instance, you should probably handle an incident where a student slips and uses a cuss word in class. On the other hand, if the student's language or behaviors are detracting from other students' learning, you should probably contact the parents.

Finally, emphasizing accomplishments should be a part of all types of communication with parents. When you call about a problem, first try to describe accomplishments and progress if possible. You can also initiate communication for the sole purpose of reporting good news, as Jacinta did in her emails. All parents want to feel proud of their children, and sharing accomplishments can further improve the home–school partnership.

As it continues to expand, technology will increasingly provide an important channel for improving home–school communication. For instance, most schools now have websites that provide information, and you can create your own email list that allows you to keep parents informed. You can also create an electronic template and involve your students in inserting information into it, which can then be used as a class newsletter. When it becomes a routine you can maintain communication with parents efficiently and with a minimum of time and effort.

A final note with respect to communication. Earlier we emphasized that you should carefully proof all forms of written communication to ensure that they are free of grammar, punctuation, and spelling errors. We also want to strongly emphasize that you quickly respond to any queries by parents. Parents react very well when they send a text or email and they receive a timely response. It communicates your commitment to their children and signals a desire to maintain communication. In fact, parents' perceptions of your competence and professionalism will be more strongly affected by your responsiveness than by your actual instruction. You can deliver the most creative lessons possible, but if they text or email you and you don't respond, they'll conclude that you're not a good teacher. Rarely will parents send so many communications as to become "pests." Your responsiveness is essential.

Parent–Teacher Conferences

Parent–teacher conferences are a unique and important form of communication with parents, they can be initiated by either teachers or parents, and they can be stressful, particularly for young, beginning teachers (Khasnabis, Goldin, & Ronfeldt, 2018; Walker & Legg, 2018). Because an element of uncertainty exists—we're not quite sure why parents have requested a conference—those initiated by parents are potentially more stressful than those we request.

Regardless of who initiates the conference, we can take steps that help reduce potential stress in anticipating and conducting the conference (Ediger, 2016).

Preparing for a Conference. The best preparation for a parent–teacher conference is ongoing communication. For instance, if we apply the suggestions we discussed earlier, such as sending packets of work home, emailing parents, or sending a class newsletter, parents will feel informed, and a possible contentious conference will be less likely.

Second, keep detailed records. For instance, if you've initiated a conference to solicit parents' help with a chronically misbehaving student, documenting the misbehaviors, including factual information, such as specific descriptions of the behaviors and dates of occurrence, is important. If the issue is academic, such as missing assignments, having copies of the assignments that you can show parents is also important.

Nothing is more compelling and disarming than evidence. If you can provide parents with facts, detailed records, and other information, such as standardized test results, and what those results mean, the likelihood of a successful conference is high, and your level of stress in anticipating the conference will be reduced. (We discuss standardized testing and interpreting standardized test scores in Chapter 15.)

Conducting the Conference. How you handle yourself during the actual conference will go a long way toward it being a success. Some veteran teachers we've talked to also suggest including the student in the conference, or at least part of it, whereas others believe the student should not be included. Whether or not you include the student is a matter of school policy and your own professional judgment. The following are some suggestions for ensuring a successful conference:

- First, attempt to make the parent feel comfortable by displaying a warm and inviting manner and seating parents without a barrier, such as your desk, between them and you. This makes the conference seem less formal and more inviting.
- Thank the parents for coming and note that research confirms how important parental involvement is in the education of their children. Remind them that you feel that they and you are in a partnership designed to help their child develop to his or her full potential.
- Begin the conference by saying something positive about the student—if it can be done sincerely—and include a concrete example. A comment, such as "I enjoy having Colin in class. The other day, I saw him stop what he was doing and help one of his classmates clean up a spill after she dropped some materials on the floor," documents the comment and makes it more believable than "I enjoy having Colin in class."

- Be sensitive to your use of language. For instance, the question "What would you specifically like to discuss?" is more inviting than "Why did you want this conference?" Or, if the conference focuses on behavioral issues, a statement such as "Nathan has been leaving his seat and moving around the room without permission" (combined with documentation) is more effective than "Nathan has a tendency to misbehave." The first focuses on a behavior, whereas the second might be interpreted as an indictment of his character.

- Let parents talk, essentially for as long as they want. Doing so makes you seem sympathetic and supportive and helps reduce defensiveness that parents might feel in anticipating the conference. It's also important to maintain a calm, even-tempered manner, even if parents become critical or hostile.

- If the conference focuses on a behavioral or academic problem, propose an action plan for resolving the issue or problem, and discuss it until you and the parents agree about its implementation.

- Offer examples of simple activities that parents might conduct with their children to supplement their academic work.

- Take notes during the conference, include the action plan and suggested supplemental activities, and email a copy to the parents to provide a record of the discussion and suggestions.

- If you believe the conference could become contentious, ask a colleague or administrator to attend. Some schools have policies requiring more than a single teacher in a conference. You will learn about your school's policy with respect to conferences during pre-planning for the school year.

Parent–teacher conferences are emotional times for parents, because conferences are commonly scheduled to try to resolve a problem or issue, and they may feel defensive or ill at ease either in anticipating the meeting or in the conference itself. The way you handle yourself will go a long way toward ensuring that the parents leave believing you're positive, supportive, and committed to the well-being of their child (Pillet-Shore, 2016).

Classroom Connections

Communicating Effectively with Parents

1. Communication with parents is an essential part of effective classroom management. Establish communication links during the first few days of school, and maintain them throughout the year.

   - **Elementary:** A kindergarten teacher emails each of her students' parents during the first week of school, tells them how happy she is to have their children in her class, learns as much as she can about them, and encourages them to contact her at any time.

   - **Middle School:** Each week, a sixth-grade social studies teacher sends home a "class communicator" describing the topics his students will be studying and giving suggestions parents can follow in helping their children. Students write notes to their parents on the communicator, describing their personal efforts and progress.

   - **High School:** A geometry teacher sends a letter home at the beginning of the school year, describing his homework and assessment policies. He calls parents when more than one homework assignment is missing.

2. Effective communication with parents is positive, clear, and concise. Communicate in nontechnical language, and make specific suggestions to parents for working with their children.

   - **Elementary:** A third-grade teacher asks all her parents to sign a contract agreeing that they will (a) designate an hour each evening when the television is turned off and children do homework; (b) ask their children to show them their homework assignments each day; and (c) look at, ask their children about, and sign the packet of papers that is sent home every other week.

(continued)

- **Middle School:** A sixth-grade teacher discusses a letter to parents with his students. He has them explain what each part of the letter says and then asks the students to read and explain the letter to their parents.

- **High School:** A ninth-grade basic math teacher makes a special effort at the beginning of the school year to explain to parents of students with exceptionalities how she'll modify her class to meet their children's needs. She strongly encourages parents to monitor homework and assist if they can.

3. Take extra steps to communicate with the parents of children who are members of minorities.

- **Elementary:** A second-grade teacher in an urban school enlists the aid of teachers who are bilingual. When he sends messages home, he asks them for help in translating notes for parents.

- **Middle School:** At the beginning of each grading period, a sixth-grade teacher sends a letter home, in each student's native language, describing the topics that will be covered, the tests and the approximate times they will be given, and any special projects that are required.

- **High School:** A biology teacher, who has many students with parents who speak little English, holds student-led conferences in which the students report on their progress. As she participates in each conference she has students serve as translators.

MyLab Education Self-Check 12.3

MyLab Education Application Exercise 12.3: Conducting Parent-Teacher Conferences

In this exercise, you will be asked to analyze a third-grade teacher's attempts to apply suggestions for conducting a successful parent-teacher conference.

Intervening When Misbehavior Occurs

12.4 Use cognitive and behavioral learning theories to explain effective interventions.

Our focus to this point has been on efforts to *prevent* management problems. Despite our best efforts, however, some students will periodically misbehave or fail to pay attention. In our opening case study, for instance, Judy had carefully planned her rules and procedures, she was well organized, she promoted student involvement in her learning activity, but she still had to intervene with Darren and Rachel. This is common in classrooms.

In the following sections, we discuss interventions from emotional, cognitive, and behaviorist perspectives. Each contributes to our understanding and provides guidance as we make decisions about how to intervene most effectively.

Emotional Factors in Interventions

MyLab Education

Video Example 12.5

When intervening, expert teachers protect students' emotional safety and only move along the intervention continuum as far as necessary to eliminate the misbehavior. Notice here that the teacher meets a student at eye level and quietly uses a desist to stop a misbehavior.

Ed Psych and You

Have you ever been criticized or chewed out in front of other people or have been in a public argument? How did it make you feel? How did you feel afterward?

From our study of humanistic views of motivation, and particularly Maslow's work, we understand that safety—including emotional safety—is an important need for all of us. This need relates to the questions we ask in *Ed Psych and You*. We all want to avoid being humiliated in front of our peers, and the same applies in classrooms. The emotional tone of our interventions influences both the likelihood of students complying with them and their attitudes toward us and the class afterward (Goodboy, Bolkan, & Baker,

2018). Loud public reprimands, criticism, and sarcasm reduce students' sense of safety and are particularly destructive in elementary schools, where children are vulnerable and seek the approval of their teachers. In middle and secondary schools, they create resentment, detract from classroom climate, and lead to students finding creative ways to be disruptive without getting caught (Kearney et al., 2016; Okonofua et al., 2016).

Similarly, arguing with students about the interpretation of a rule or compliance with it also detracts from the emotional climate of classrooms. We never "win" arguments with students. We can exert our authority, but doing so isn't sustainable throughout a school year, resentment is often a side effect, and the encounter may expand into major conflict (Pellegrino, 2010).

Consider the following incident that occurred after a teacher directed a chronically misbehaving student to move:

Student: I wasn't doing anything.

Teacher: You were whispering, and the rule says listen when someone else is talking.

Student: It doesn't say no whispering.

Teacher: You know what the rule means. We've been over it again and again.

Student: Well, it's not fair. You don't make other students move when they whisper.

Teacher: You weren't listening when someone else was talking, so move.

The student knew what the rule meant and was simply playing a game with the teacher, who allowed herself to be drawn into an argument. In contrast, consider the following.

Teacher: Please move up here (pointing to an empty desk in the first row).

Student: I wasn't doing anything.

Teacher: One of our rules says that we listen when someone else is talking. If you would like to discuss this, come in and see me after school. Please move now (turning back to the lesson as soon as the student moves).

This teacher maintained an even demeanor and didn't allow herself to be pulled into an argument or even a brief discussion. She handled the event quickly and efficiently, offered to discuss it with the student later, and immediately turned back to the lesson.

Students' inclination to argue often depends on the emotional climate of the classroom. If rules and procedures make sense to students, and if they're enforced consistently, students are less likely to argue. When students break rules, simply reminding them of the rule and why it's important, and requiring compliance, as Judy did with Rachel, are as far as minor incidents should go. (We discuss serious management issues, such as defiance and aggression, later in the chapter.)

Cognitive Interventions

We said earlier that rules and procedures should make sense to students, and we want our interventions to make sense as well. If they do, the likelihood of serious management problems is sharply reduced. Interventions that make sense also contribute to self-regulation. When students understand the impact of their behavior on learning and others, they're more likely to regulate their actions and emotions. Keep these ideas in mind as we examine the following interventions.

Demonstrate Withitness

"Withitness," a teacher's awareness of what's going on in all parts of the classroom at all times, and communicating this awareness to students, is an essential component of successful interventions (Emmer & Evertson, 2017; Evertson & Emmer, 2017; Kounin, 1970). Withitness is often described as "having eyes in the back of your head." To understand this powerful idea, let's compare two teachers.

Ron Ziers is explaining the process for finding percentages to his seventh-graders. While Ron illustrates the procedure, Steve, in the second desk from the front of the room, is periodically poking Katilya, who sits across from him. She retaliates by kicking him in the leg. Bill, sitting behind Katilya, pokes her in the arm with his pencil. Ron doesn't respond to the students' actions. After a second poke, Katilya swings her arm back and catches Bill on the shoulder. "Katilya!" Ron says sternly. "We keep our hands to ourselves! . . . Now, where were we?"

Karl Wickes has the same group of students in life science. He puts a drawing displaying a flowering plant on the document camera. As the class discusses the information, he notices Barry whispering something to Julie, and he sees Steve poke Katilya, who kicks him and loudly whispers, "Stop it." As Karl asks, "What is the part of the plant that produces fruit?" he moves to Steve's desk, leans over, and says quietly but firmly, "We keep our hands to ourselves in here." He then moves to the front of the room, watches Steve out of the corner of his eye, and says, "Barry, what other plant part do you see in the diagram?"

We can see why demonstrating withitness is a cognitive intervention. In Ron's class, being reprimanded when she was innocent didn't make sense to Katilya, whereas seeing Karl immediately respond to Steve's misbehavior did. This is why withitness is important.

Karl demonstrated withitness in three ways:

- He identified the misbehavior immediately, and quickly responded by moving near Steve. Ron did nothing until the problem had spread to other students.

- He correctly identified Steve as the cause of the incident. In contrast, Ron reprimanded Katilya, leaving students with a sense that he didn't know what was going on in his classroom.

- He responded to the more serious infraction first. Steve's poking was more disruptive than Barry's whispering, so Karl first responded to Steve and then called on Barry, which drew him back into the activity and made further intervention unnecessary.

Withitness goes further (Hogan, Rabinowitz, & Craven, 2003). It also involves watching for evidence of inattention or confusion and responding with questions, such as "Some of you look puzzled. Do you want me to rephrase the question?" And it includes approaching or calling on inattentive students to bring them back into lessons.

Lack of withitness is often a problem for beginning teachers because the complexities of teaching add to the heavy cognitive load on their working memories, making the process of continually monitoring student behavior difficult (Wubbels et al., 2015). You can best address this issue by creating well-established routines and carefully planning your instruction, which reduce your cognitive load during teaching and contribute to your own self-confidence (Greenberg et al., 2014). As you acquire experience, you'll learn to be sensitive to students and make adjustments to ensure that they are as involved and successful as possible.

Be Consistent

"Be consistent" is recommended so often that it is nearly a cliché, but it's essential nevertheless. If one student is reprimanded for breaking a rule and another is not, for instance, students can't make sense of the inconsistency. They are likely to conclude that the teacher doesn't know what's going on or has "pets," either of which detracts from classroom climate.

Although consistency is important, achieving complete consistency in the real world is virtually impossible, and we should adapt our interventions to both the student and context. For example, most classrooms have a rule about speaking only when recognized by the teacher. So, as you're monitoring seatwork, suppose one student asks another a question about the assignment and then immediately goes back to work. Failing to remind the student that talking is not allowed during seatwork is technically inconsistent, but an intervention in this case isn't needed. On the other hand, a student who is repeatedly whispering becomes a disruption, and intervention is necessary. Students understand the difference, and the "inconsistency" is appropriate and effective.

Follow-Through

Following through means that we ensure compliance with rules. Without follow-through, our management systems break down because students learn that we aren't fully committed to creating an orderly environment. This is confusing and leaves them with a sense of uncertainty.

In fact, failing to follow through can—by decreasing students' inhibitions—actually increase misbehavior (Skatova & Ferguson, 2013). The concept of expectations in social cognitive theory helps us understand why. When students break a rule, they expect to be reprimanded. The nonoccurrence of the expected punisher—the reprimand—acts as a reinforcer, making it more likely that students will continue to misbehave.

Once again, the first few days of the school year are important. If you follow through consistently during this period, enforcing rules and procedures will be much easier during the rest of the year.

Keep Verbal and Nonverbal Behaviors Congruent

For interventions to make sense to students, our verbal and nonverbal behaviors must be congruent (Doyle, 2006). Compare the following interventions:

Karen Wilson's eighth-graders are working on their homework as she circulates among them. She is helping Jasmine when Jeff and Mike begin whispering loudly behind her.

"Jeff. Mike. Stop talking, and get started on your homework," she says, glancing over her shoulder.

The two slow their whispering, and Karen turns back to Jasmine. Soon, the boys are whispering as loudly as ever.

"I thought I told you to stop talking," Karen says over her shoulder again, this time with irritation in her voice.

The boys glance at her and quickly resume whispering.

Isabel Rodriguez is in a similar situation with her pre-algebra students. As she is helping Vicki, Ken and Lance begin horseplay at the back of the room.

Isabel excuses herself, turns, and walks directly to the boys. Looking Lance in the eye, she says evenly and firmly, "Lance, we have plenty to do before lunch, and noise during seatwork detracts from learning. Begin your work now." Then, looking directly at Ken, she continues, "Ken, you, too. Quickly now. We have only so much time, and we don't want to waste it." She waits briefly until they are working quietly and then returns to Vicki.

The teachers had similar intents, but the impact of their actions was very different. When Karen glanced over her shoulder as she reprimanded the boys, and then failed to follow through, her communication was confusing. Her words said one thing, but her body language said another. When messages are inconsistent, people attribute more credibility to tone of voice and body language than to spoken words (Aronson, Wilson, Akert, & Sommers, 2016).

In contrast, Isabel's communication was clear and consistent. She responded immediately, faced her students directly, explained how their behavior detracted from learning, and made sure her students were on task before she went back to Vicki. Her verbal and nonverbal behaviors were congruent, so her message made sense.

Making eye contact with students is an important aspect of this process. Research indicates that the most effective teachers make more eye contact with their students than their less effective peers (McIntyre, Mainhard, & Klassen, 2017). Eye contact increases learner attention and communicates respect for students (Jarick, Laidlaw, Nasiopoulos, & Kingstone, 2016).

Characteristics of effective nonverbal communication are outlined in Table 12.1.

Maintain Constructive Assertiveness

Assertiveness is commonly described as being self-assured and confident without being aggressive. Even if we're not naturally inclined in this direction, most experts suggest that assertiveness is a skill that can be learned (Pfafman & McEwan, 2014). In the context of classroom management, **constructive assertiveness** involves "communicating your concerns clearly, insisting that misbehavior be corrected, and resisting being coerced or manipulated" (Emmer & Evertson, 2017, p. 188). The "constructive" component emphasizes that we avoid attacking, demeaning, or personally criticizing students in any interactions. We focus on the behavior, we clearly communicate why it's unacceptable, we don't argue with students, and we follow through to ensure that they comply.

To illustrate, let's look again at Judy's encounter with Rachel in the case study at the beginning of the chapter.

She moves over to Rachel, who has been whispering to Deborah and playing with her cell phone, and kneels down so they are at eye level. She points to the rules displayed on a poster, makes eye contact with Rachel, and says quietly but firmly, "We agreed that it was important to listen when other people are talking, and we know that we must honor our agreements. . . . We can't learn when people aren't paying attention," and she stands back up after Rachel puts her cell phone in her purse.

Judy demonstrated constructive assertiveness in this encounter. She communicated clearly, maintained congruent verbal and nonverbal behavior, and waited until Rachel complied—put her cell phone away. Judy's communication reminded Rachel that her behavior was unacceptable while simultaneously avoiding any personal criticism. She also reminded Rachel of the rule and why it was important—"We can't learn when people aren't paying attention." Her communication was designed to make sense, as is

TABLE 12.1 Characteristics of effective nonverbal communication

Nonverbal Behavior	Example
Proximity	A teacher moves close to an inattentive student.
Eye contact	A teacher looks an off-task student directly in the eye when issuing a directive.
Body orientation	A teacher directs himself squarely to the learner, rather than over the shoulder or sideways.
Facial expression	A teacher frowns slightly at a disruption, brightens her face at a humorous incident, and smiles approvingly at a student's effort to help a classmate.
Gestures	A teacher puts her palm out (Stop!) to a student who interjects as another student is talking.
Vocal variation	A teacher varies the tone, pitch, and loudness of his voice for emphasis and displays energy and enthusiasm.

the case with all effective cognitive interventions. And, over time, it will contribute to Rachel's self-regulation. Perhaps most significant, Judy communicated that she was in charge of her class and that learning was paramount. Teacher assertiveness, combined with perseverance and consistency, is part of expert classroom management (Jones & Jones, 2016). Further, some research indicates that teacher assertiveness contributes to students' social development by providing models for students who tend to be shy and withdrawn, while simultaneously reducing aggressive behaviors in students who tend to dominate their peers (Martínez, Justicia, & Fernández, 2016).

Apply Logical Consequences

Logical consequences are outcomes that are conceptually related to misbehavior; they help learners make sense of an intervention by creating a link between their actions and the consequences that follow. For example:

Allen, a rambunctious sixth-grader, is running down the hall toward the lunchroom. As he rounds the corner, he bumps Alyssia, causing her to drop her books.

"Oops," he replies, continuing his race to the lunchroom.

"Hold it, Allen," Doug Ramsay, who is monitoring the hall, says. "Go back and help her pick up her books and apologize."

Allen walks back to Alyssia, helps her pick up her books, and mumbles an apology. As he turns toward the lunchroom, Doug again stops him.

"Now, why did I make you do that?" Doug asks.

"Cuz we're not supposed to run."

"Sure," Doug says evenly, "but more important, if people run in the halls, they might crash into someone, and somebody might get hurt. . . . Remember that you're responsible for your actions. Think about not wanting to hurt yourself or anybody else, and the next time you'll walk whether a teacher is here or not. . . . Now, go on to lunch."

Doug applied a logical consequence in this incident, and we can see why it's important. Having to pick up Alyssia's books after bumping her made sense to Allen, and this is our goal in applying logical consequences. They help students understand the effects of their actions on others and promote self-regulation (Watson & Battistich, 2006).

Behavioral Interventions

While interventions that make sense and contribute to self-regulation are the ideals we strive for, in the real world, some students seem either unable or unwilling to control their actions and emotions. In these cases behaviorism, with its applications of reinforcement and appropriate punishment, may be necessary (Rispoli et al., 2017). Further, in the real world actions have consequences, and learning that consequences exist for misbehavior is part of students' total education (Greenberg et al., 2014). Experts recommend using behavioral interventions as short-term solutions to specific problems, with development of self-regulation remaining the long-term goal (Emmer & Evertson, 2017; Evertson & Emmer, 2017).

Let's see how Cindy Daines, a first-grade teacher, uses a behavioral intervention with her students:

Cindy has a problem with her students' making smooth and orderly transitions from one activity to another.

In an attempt to improve the situation, she makes "tickets" from construction paper, gets local businesses to donate small items to be used as prizes, and displays the items in a fishbowl on her desk. She then explains, "We're going to play a little game to see how quiet we can be when we change lessons. . . . Whenever we change, I'm going to give you 1 minute, and then I'm going to ring this bell," and she rings the bell to demonstrate. "Students who have their books out and are waiting quietly when I ring the bell will get one of these tickets. On Friday afternoon, you can turn them in for prizes we see in this fishbowl. The more tickets you have, the better the prize will be."

During the next few days, Cindy moves around the room, handing out tickets and making comments such as "I really like the way Merry is ready to work," "Ted already has his books out and is quiet," and "Thank you for moving to math so quickly."

She realizes her strategy is starting to work when she hears "Shh" and "Be quiet!" from the students, so she is gradually able to space out the rewards as the students become more responsible.

Cindy used concepts from both behaviorism and social cognitive theory in her system. Her tickets and prizes were positive reinforcers for making quick and quiet transitions, and her comments, such as "I really like the way Merry is ready to work" and "Ted already has his books out," were vicarious reinforcers for the other children.

Reinforcers are more effective than punishers for changing behavior, so we want to use positive reinforcers if possible (Alberto & Troutman, 2017). However, some students can become disruptive when all punishers are removed, so they are sometimes necessary (Furukawa, Alsop, Sowerby, Jensen, & Tripp, 2017; Greenberg et al., 2014). In these cases, effective punishers include **desists**, verbal or nonverbal communications teachers use to stop a behavior, such as putting a finger to the lips signaling "Shh"; **detention**, taking away students' free time (typically a half hour or more) by keeping them in school either before or after hours; or **non-exclusionary timeout**, seating a student near the teacher or on the edge of the classroom to prevent him or her from receiving reinforcers. The following are guidelines for using punishment in management interventions:

- Use punishment as infrequently as possible.
- Apply punishers immediately and directly to the behavior.
- Use punishers only severe enough to eliminate the misbehavior.
- Administer punishers dispassionately, and avoid displays of anger.
- Explain and model alternative desirable behaviors.

The goal of these guidelines is to maximize the effectiveness of punishments in our classrooms, while minimizing their negative effects on students.

Corporal Punishment

Corporal punishment is a form of physical punishment that involves deliberately inflicting pain on a child in response to misbehavior. It's common in our culture, with more than 90% of parents reporting that they spank their toddlers (Simons, Simons, & Su, 2013).

However, the worldwide trend is away from corporal punishment, and as of 2016, it was outlawed in 50 countries (Lansford et al., 2016). Although its use is declining in our schools, it remains legal in 21 states, primarily in the south, with Mississippi being the national leader in number of schools that permit paddling or other forms of physical punishment (Sparks & Harwin, 2016).

Corporal punishment is highly controversial, and professional organizations and educational leaders are uniformly opposed to hitting children for any reason (American Academy of Pediatrics, 2011; Simons et al., 2013). Some argue that the practice is immoral and should be totally banned (Lenta, 2012).

Research documents the devastating effects of corporal punishment. For instance, a 2016 study analyzing 50 years of research on 160,000 children found that the more children are spanked, even with an open hand, the lower they achieve in school, and the more likely they are to later defy adults, demonstrate mental-health disorders, and display aggressive and anti-social behaviors. When implements such as paddles or belts are used, the effects are even worse (Gershoff & Grogan-Kaylor, 2016). Further, evidence indicates that children subjected to corporal punishment in the home are more likely to become abusers as adults (Afifi, Mota, Sareen, & MacMillan, 2017).

Earlier research has also found that adolescents who had been paddled regularly over a three-year period showed less gray matter in the area of the brain associated with self-control and problem solving (Tomodo et al., 2010), and students who display conduct problems in schools tend to have smaller gray matter volume in these areas (Rogers & DeBrito, 2016).

Arguments against corporal punishment can also be made on theoretical grounds. For instance, through modeling, corporal punishment suggests that hitting people is an appropriate response to unacceptable behavior. This doesn't make any sense when we're trying to develop self-regulation in students, aspects of which are impulse control, resisting urges to display inappropriate behaviors, and expressing emotions in socially appropriate ways. We certainly don't teach these characteristics by hitting students.

We endorse all of these arguments and suggest to you, our readers, that corporal punishment is never an acceptable behavioral intervention under any circumstance. There are better ways to manage behavior and teach self-control.

Removing Students from Classrooms

Unfortunately, in the real world, a few students will be incorrigible and disruptive enough that they must be removed. This practice isn't as simple as it appears on the surface, however, because students who can't or won't accept responsibility for their behavior often blame their teachers for the exclusion (being removed from the classroom).

This has implications for us if we feel we must ultimately have a student taken out of our classroom. We should, before deciding to have students removed, first remind them that their behaviors are unacceptable, and if the reminder doesn't work, punish them using acceptable forms of punishment, such as non-exclusionary time out. If neither works, and the student is removed, we should have a follow-up conversation with the student, explaining why the exclusion was necessary. In the process, we should highlight the impact of the misbehavior on classmates and how it detracts from learning and the emotional atmosphere in our classroom (Lewis, Romi, & Roache, 2012).

Ideally, we should try to avoid removing students from classrooms if possible. Research indicates that frequent use of exclusionary discipline strategies (removing students from classrooms) is associated with higher frequencies of discipline problems and less positive classroom climates and teacher–student relationships (Mitchell & Bradshaw, 2013). Except in extreme circumstances, removing students from our classrooms should be an intervention of last resort (Skiba & Raush, 2015).

Designing and Maintaining a Behavioral Management System

Clear rules and expectations followed by consistently applied consequences (reinforcers and punishers) are the foundation of a behavioral management system. Designing a management system based on behaviorism involves the following steps:

- Prepare a list of specific rules that clearly define acceptable behavior.
- Specify reinforcers for obeying each rule and punishers for breaking the rules, such as the consequences in Table 12.2.
- Display the rules and explain the consequences.
- Consistently apply consequences.

TABLE 12.2 Sample consequences for breaking or following rules

Consequences for Breaking Rules	
First infraction	Name on list
Second infraction	Check by name
Third infraction	Second check by name
Fourth infraction	Half-hour detention
Fifth infraction	Email parents

Consequences for Following Rules
A check is removed for each day that no infractions occur. If only a name remains, and no infractions occur, the name is removed.
All students without names on the list are given 45 minutes of free time Friday afternoon to do as they choose. The only restrictions are that they must stay in the classroom, and they must not disrupt the students who didn't earn the free time.

A behavioral system doesn't preclude providing rationales or creating the rules with learner input. However, in contrast with a cognitive approach, which emphasizes understanding and self-regulation, the primary focus is on clearly specifying behavioral guidelines and applying consequences.

In designing a comprehensive management system, teachers probably combine elements of both cognitive and behavioral approaches. Behavioral systems have the advantage of being immediately applicable; they're effective for initiating desired behaviors, particularly with young students, and they're useful for reducing chronic misbehavior. They also help students understand that actions have consequences, and we're all accountable for our behaviors (Greenberg et al., 2014). Cognitive systems take longer to produce results but are more likely to develop learner self-regulation.

Positive Behavior Support

When you begin teaching, you will almost certainly have students in your classes who have exceptionalities, such as specific learning disabilities or behavior disorders. You will be expected to create a classroom environment that meets the needs of all of your students, including those with exceptionalities. Let's see what this looks like in the classroom.

You have a student named Tanya who has been diagnosed with a mild form of autism. She displays behaviors typical of the disorder, such as underdeveloped social skills, highly ritualistic behavior, and a strong emotional attachment to a particular adult. For example, she is sometimes abusive to other students when you do group work, so you remove her from the group. And she frequently becomes upset and will even periodically shout and try to leave the room when you have your students begin their homework for the next day.

With the help of your school's special education specialist, you analyze Tanya's behavior and conclude that her behavior toward other children and running out of the room serve two purposes: (1) they allow her to escape social situations in which she is uncomfortable, and (2) they get your attention.

Based on the analysis, you both work with Tanya to help her learn to make appropriate comments and ask questions during group work, and you design a system so she earns points that she can trade for treats of her choosing when she behaves appropriately. You also spend extra time helping her with her seatwork, and you create a private area in the back of the room where she can go whenever she feels she needs a break from academic tasks.

Your interventions are examples of **positive behavior support**, interventions that replace problem behaviors with alternative, appropriate actions that serve the same purpose for the student (Scheuermann & Hall, 2016). For example, Tanya was negatively reinforced for behaving abusively (she was allowed to escape the uncomfortable situation), and when she was taught some specific interaction skills, the negative reinforcer was replaced with a positive reinforcer (the points). Similarly, the attention she received when she shouted and tried to leave the room was replaced with your attention when you worked with her one-on-one.

Positive behavior support is widely used and is commonly implemented on a school-wide basis (Allen & Steed, 2016). Research indicates that it is generally effective for dealing with problems that traditional classroom management systems can't solve (Lewis, Mitchell, Trussell, & Newcomer, 2015). You are likely to be involved in positive behavior support when you begin teaching, and special educators and staff development experiences will provide you with the extra help you need to implement it effectively.

An Intervention Continuum

Despite your best efforts to plan for both classroom management and instruction, students will misbehave, so you will periodically have to intervene, as Judy did in the case study at the beginning of the chapter.

Disruptions vary from isolated incidents, such as a student briefly whispering to a neighbor, to chronic infractions, such as a student repeatedly poking a classmate, or even fighting. Because the severity of infractions vary, your interventions should also vary, and they will include both cognitive and behavioral elements.

To maximize instructional time, intervening should be as unobtrusive as possible. A continuum of interventions is outlined in Figure 12.8 and discussed in the following sections.

Praising Desired Behavior. Because promoting positive behaviors is an important goal, praising students for displaying them is a sensible first intervention, and experts suggest that praise for desirable behavior should be a part of all effective classroom management systems (Greenberg et al., 2014). Praise occurs less often in classrooms than we might expect, so efforts to "catch 'em being good" are worthwhile, especially as a method of prevention. Elementary teachers praise openly and freely, and middle and secondary teachers often make private comments such as "I'm extremely pleased with your work this week. . . . Keep it up," or write private notes to students praising them for their work and behavior. Some research suggests that praising middle school students in notes significantly reduces discipline referrals (Greenberg et al., 2014).

Reinforcing behaviors that are incompatible with misbehavior is an extension of this idea (Alberto & Troutman, 2017). For instance, participating in a learning activity is incompatible with daydreaming, so calling on a student and reinforcing any attempt to respond are more effective than reprimanding a student for not paying attention.

Ignoring Inappropriate Behavior. Behaviors that aren't reinforced become extinct. The attention students receive when they're admonished for minor misbehaviors is

Figure 12.8 An intervention continuum

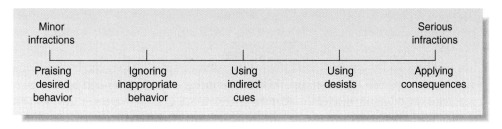

often reinforcing, so ignoring the behavior can eliminate the reinforcers you might inadvertently provide. This is effective, for example, when two students briefly whisper but soon stop. A combination of praising desired behaviors, reinforcing incompatible behaviors, and ignoring misbehavior can all be effective in responding to minor disruptions.

Using Indirect Cues.   You can also use indirect cues—such as proximity, methods of redirecting attention, and vicarious reinforcers—when misbehaviors can't be ignored but can be stopped or diverted without addressing them directly (Jones & Jones, 2016). For example, Judy moved near Darren and called on him after she heard Kendra mutter. Her proximity stopped his misbehavior, and calling on him directed his attention back to the lesson.

Some educators disagree with calling on a student who isn't paying attention, as Judy did in calling on Darren. However, her move was not punitive, her tone was matter-of-fact, and her goal was simply to re-engage him. A long history of research confirms the efficacy of calling on students and establishing in them the expectation that they are likely to be called on during learning activities. The research indicates that when this expectation is established, students pay better attention and achieve higher (Good & Lavigne, 2018; Kerman, 1979; McDougall & Granby, 1996).

Vicarious reinforcement can also be effective. Elementary teachers often use students as models and vicariously reinforce the rest of the class with statements such as "I really like the way Row 1 is working quietly" or "Elisa has already started the assignment." If you plan to teach in middle or secondary schools, you can also use vicarious reinforcers, but you need to be sensitive to possible student reactions, because older students are sometimes uncomfortable being singled out in front of peers.

Using Desists.   As we said earlier, a *desist* is a verbal or nonverbal communication a teacher uses to stop a behavior (Dhaem, 2012; Kounin, 1970). "Glenys, we leave our seats only when given permission," "Glenys!" and a finger to the lips, or a stern facial expression are all desists. They are the most common teacher reactions to misbehavior.

Clarity and tone are important when using desists. For example, "Randy, what is the rule about touching other students?" or "Randy, how do you think that makes Willy feel?" are more effective than "Randy, stop that," because they link the behavior to a rule or to the behavior's effects. Students react to these subtle differences and prefer rule and consequence reminders to teacher commands (Alberto & Troutman, 2017).

The tone of desists should be firm but not angry—consistent with the concept of *constructive assertiveness*. Kounin (1970) found that kindergarten students managed with rough desists actually became more disruptive, and older students are uncomfortable in classes where harsh desists are used. In contrast, firm, even reprimands, the suggestion of alternative behaviors, and questioning that maintains student involvement in learning activities can reduce off-task time in most classrooms.

Clear communication, including congruence between verbal and nonverbal behavior, an awareness of what is happening in the classroom (withitness), and effective instruction are essential in using desists. However, even when these elements exist, simple desists may not be enough.

Applying Consequences.   If you've tried all other options on the intervention continuum, and they simply aren't working, you'll then need to apply consequences. Logical consequences are most desirable and should be tried first, but classrooms are complex and busy, so it isn't always possible to solve management problems with them. In these cases behavioral consequences—simply intended to change a behavior quickly and efficiently—can be effective (Alberto & Troutman, 2017). Let's look at an example.

Jason is an intelligent and active fifth-grader. He loves to talk and seems to know just how far he can go before Mrs. Aguilar becomes exasperated with him. He understands the rules and the reasons for them, but his interest in talking seems to take precedence. Ignoring him isn't working. A call to his parents helped for a while, but soon he's back to his usual behavior—never quite enough to require a drastic response, but always a thorn in Mrs. Aguilar's side.

Finally, she decides to give him only one warning. At a second disruption, he's placed in timeout from regular instructional activities. She meets with him and explains the rules. The next day, he begins to misbehave almost immediately.

"Jason," she warns, "you can't work while you're talking, and you're keeping others from finishing their work. Please get busy."

He stops, but a few minutes later, he's at it again.

"Jason," Mrs. Aguilar says quietly as she moves back to his desk, "Please go back to the timeout area."

Now, a week later, Jason is working quietly with the rest of the class.

Behavior such as Jason's is common, particularly in elementary and middle schools, and it causes more teacher stress than do highly publicized threats of violence and bodily harm (Friedman, 2006). The behavior is disruptive, so it can't be ignored; praise for good work helps to a certain extent, but students get much of their reinforcement from friends; using desists works briefly, but the constant monitoring is tiring. Mrs. Aguilar had little choice but to apply behavioral consequences with Jason.

Consistency is the key to promoting change in students like Jason. He understood what he was doing, and he was capable of controlling himself. When he could predict the consequences of his behavior, he quit. He knew that his second infraction would result in a timeout, and when it did, he quickly changed his behavior. There was no argument, little time was used, and the class wasn't disrupted.

Diversity: Classroom Management with Members of Cultural Minorities

Working with learners who are members of cultural minorities presents a unique set of challenges. A long history of research suggests that discrepancies exist in disciplinary referrals and punishment for these students. "Academic studies produced over the past 30 years have consistently found racial disparities in the administration of discipline. Discipline is imposed more frequently and with heavier penalties on African American students than White students who engage in the same conduct" (Ware, 2017, p. 39). Also, White students are often disciplined for observable infractions, such as smoking, leaving school without permission, or profanity, whereas African American students are more often disciplined for infractions that require a teacher's interpretation, such as disrespect, defiance, or class disruptions. Further, research indicates that these disparities are increasing instead of decreasing (Office for Civil Rights, 2018).

The issue involves more than African Americans. "Disproportionate discipline has also been documented for . . . Latinos, American Indians, and students in special education" (Gregory et al., 2017, p. 253), and additional evidence indicates that lesbian, bisexual, gay, and transgender students are at heightened risk of disproportionate sanctions (Mittleman, 2018).

Research also suggests that communication breakdowns between teachers and students who are English language learners (ELLs) sometimes result in students being punished for what teachers thought they heard and not for what children actually said. Some researchers believe this miscommunication occurs because most teachers are women who are white and in the middle class, whereas students who are ELLs are cultural minorities and are often from families with lower socioeconomic status (Kirylo, Thirumurthy, & Spezzini, 2010).

Culturally responsive classroom management, which combines cultural knowledge with teachers' awareness of possible personal biases, can help overcome some of these problems. A culturally responsive classroom management model designed to address this problem has four essential elements:

- Becoming personally aware of possible cultural biases.
- Learning about students' cultural heritage, neighborhoods, and home environments.
- Creating an inclusive learning environment.
- Maintaining consistency.

Becoming Aware of Possible Bias.   Awareness is an important first step. "Emerging findings raise the possibility that educators' disciplinary decision making may be influenced by implicit racial bias—unconsciously held negative associations linked to racial stereotypes" (Gregory et al., 2017, pp. 261–262). As we become aware of our own possible unconscious biases and come to understand our students' interaction patterns, we may realize that student responses that appear threatening or disrespectful aren't intended that way (Okonofua & Eberhardt, 2015).

Learning About Students' Backgrounds.   Earlier in the chapter, we emphasized the importance of the teacher–student relationship for classroom management, as well as motivation and learning. Attempting to learn about students' cultural heritage and their neighborhood and home environments can do a great deal to promote positive relationships with students. And it can do much to dispel the idea that they aren't welcome in school, a perception that members of cultural minorities often have (Voight, Hanson, O'Malley, & Adekanyel, 2015).

Sometimes teacher–student interactions, even those that are brief and simple, can be powerful in reducing student uneasiness.

Claribel Torres, one of Owen Jackson's 10th-graders, frequently displays negative nonverbal behaviors in class. She is sometimes borderline defiant, and at other times, unresponsive. The quality of her work is mixed.

One day Claribel comes into Owen's room after school, looking for a misplaced personal item. Owen, having waited for an opportunity such as this, asks, "How are you doing, Claribel?"

"Fine," she mumbles, head down.

"I can't quite detect your accent," Owen continues. "Where is your family from?"

"Puerto Rico," Claribel again mumbles.

"Oh, wow!" Owen gushes. "My wife and I were in San Juan last year. We loved it. We went into some of the local places in Old San Juan, talked to the people, and had an absolute ball. The people were great, very friendly, and very warm. . . . Where is your family from?"

"They are from near Ponce, on the other side of the island," Claribel responds, notably brightening.

Owen then asks a number of questions about Claribel's background.

Owen, a teacher in one of our graduate classes, reported that Claribel did a 180, simply—he believed—as a result of this conversation. We're all emotional beings, and we all want others to care for and respect us. Owen's simple actions demonstrated this care and respect, they took virtually no energy, and they made a huge difference in his relationship with Claribel; they made her feel welcome in his class. This may not work with every student, but we have nothing to lose in making the effort.

Creating Inclusive Environments.   We create inclusive learning environments in the way we arrange our rooms and how we engage students. And one simple, but significant, factor is assigning seats. Some teachers allow students to select their own seats, believing it affords them a measure of freedom, "[b]ut most students experience open seating not as freedom but as a form of abandonment. To youth dealing with rigid social hierarchies and peer rivalries, a classroom with no set seating arrangement offers only the illusion of choice" (Toshalis, 2015, p. 39). By seating members of minorities next to non-minorities and using the seating arrangement to form groups, we encourage students to mix with others who aren't part of their social group or clique.

We can then further efforts to be inclusive in the way we interact with our students. Another simple, but important, step is making an effort to call on all students— members of both minorities and non-minorities—as equally as possible. This process signals that we expect all students to be involved and learn and that we believe they're all capable learners. Calling on and in other ways involving students as equally as possible is an important step toward eliminating any disparities among cultural groups (Lawyer, 2018).

Maintaining Consistency.   Finally, consistency in dealing with incidents of misbehavior is paramount. Earlier in our discussion we emphasized consistency in cognitive interventions, and it's even more important when working with students who are members of cultural minorities. Particularly as they get older, they are increasingly sensitive to perceptions of inequitable treatment, and if they believe we're more strict or harsh in dealing with them, both the teacher–student relationship and classroom climate will suffer. In cases where they claim we've been unfair, frank and open discussions where we allow them to express their feelings and even "vent" can help alleviate potentially troublesome incidents and events.

The classroom management strategies we've discussed in this chapter are effective with all students, and they're particularly important for members of cultural minorities. As with all strategies, they won't solve every problem, but they will contribute to your students' academic and social-emotional learning.

Using Educational Psychology in Teaching: Suggestions for Responding Effectively to Misbehavior

Incidents of misbehavior will inevitably occur in your classroom. The following suggestions can help you intervene effectively.

- Maintain the flow of instruction while intervening in cases of misbehavior.
- Protect students' emotional safety when intervening.
- Use cognitive interventions when possible; revert to behavioral interventions when necessary.
- Move along the intervention continuum only as far as necessary.

Maintain the Flow of Instruction While Intervening.   If possible, we should intervene without disrupting the flow of our instruction. To illustrate, let's look again at Judy's work with her students in the case study at the beginning of the chapter.

Judy: About what latitude is Damascus, . . . Bernice?

Bernice: About 34 degrees north latitude, I think.

Judy: Good, Bernice. It's close to 34 degrees. . . . So, would it be warmer or colder than here in the summer? . . . Darren? (walking toward Darren after seeing that he has poked Kendra with his pencil)

Judy: And why might that be the case? . . . Jim? (as she moves over to Rachel)

In this brief episode, Judy intervened with both Darren and Rachel without disrupting the flow of her lesson, an ability called **overlapping** (Kounin, 1970). This amounts to doing two things at once, which imposes a heavy cognitive load on teachers, so you might not be good at it immediately. However, with careful planning—both for instruction and for classroom management—and with practice, the process can gradually become much easier. Judy's work is an example. Because her expertise was highly developed, her questioning was essentially automatic, so she was able to devote most of her working memory space to monitoring her students' behavior.

Protect Students' Emotional Safety.   As we said earlier, our interventions should take students' emotional reactions into account. We're all human, we can't help becoming angry with students at times, and it's even appropriate to acknowledge that we're angry. However, harsh, critical, and sarcastic interventions do little to eliminate problem behaviors, and they severely detract from classroom climate. Research indicates that even slight antagonism can decrease student motivation and engagement, even if instruction is otherwise effective (Goodboy et al., 2018). If you feel angry, give yourself a few seconds to calm down before you do something you might be sorry for later. Judy maintained an even demeanor in her interventions, which helped her students feel emotionally safe, and she intervened with virtually no interruption in the flow of her lesson.

Use Cognitive Interventions when Possible.   In all cases, we should do our best to ensure that our interventions make sense to learners. If they do, all but the most incorrigible of students are likely to comply because they understand why we're intervening.

Judy's interventions were primarily cognitive. For example, she was "with it" in recognizing that Darren was the perpetrator of the incident with Kendra; she was consistent and followed through to be sure Rachel complied; she kept her verbal and nonverbal behavior consistent, such as looking directly at Darren when she called on him and making eye contact with Rachel when talking to her; and she responded to Rachel with constructive assertiveness. Further, she knelt down to eye level when talking to Rachel. This move tacitly communicates to students that a problem exists, and they and their teacher are working on it together (Dhaem, 2012).

Move Along the Intervention Continuum Only as Far as Necessary.   When we intervene, we should only go as far as necessary. For instance, if a simple desist stops a misbehavior, this is as far as we should go. Elaborating on the intervention gives the incident more significance than it deserves. Judy only had to go as far as using indirect cues with both Darren and Rachel. She simply moved near Darren and called on him, she referred Rachel to the class rule and ensured that she complied, and neither action disrupted the flow of her lesson.

MyLab Education Application Exercise 12.4: Addressing Off-Task Behavior

In this exercise, you will be asked to analyze a third-grade teacher's interventions in instances of off-task behavior.

Careful planning for classroom management combined with efforts to promote self-regulation can prevent many management problems from occurring in the first place, and applying the suggestions we've discussed here can quickly eliminate most others. Unfortunately, however, serious problems can sometimes occur. We discuss them in the next section of the chapter.

Classroom Connections

Intervening Successfully in Classrooms

1. Cognitive interventions target learners' need to make sense of their experiences. Use logical consequences to help students develop responsibility. Hold discussions regarding fairness or equity after class and in private.

   - **Elementary:** During daily classroom chores, two first-graders begin a tug-of-war over a cleaning rag and knock over a potted plant. Their teacher talks to them, they agree to clean up the mess, and they write a note to their parents explaining that they will be working in the classroom before school the next week to pay for a new pot.

   - **Middle School:** A social studies teacher makes her interventions learning experiences by identifying rules that were broken and explaining why the rules exist. In cases of uncertainty, she talks privately to students.

   - **High School:** After having been asked to stop whispering for the second time in 10 minutes, a ninth-grader protests that he was asking about the assigned seatwork. His teacher reminds him of the incidents, points out that his behavior is disruptive, and reprimands him without further discussion. His teacher talks to him after class, explaining why rules exist, and reminding him that he is expected to accept responsibility for his behavior.

2. Positive reinforcement can be used to increase appropriate behavior. Use positive reinforcers to initiate and teach desirable behaviors.

   - **Elementary:** A first-grade teacher, knowing that the time after lunch is difficult for many students, gives students 1 minute after a timer rings to settle down and get out their materials. When the class meets the requirement, they earn points toward free time.

   - **Middle School:** To encourage students to clean up quickly after labs, a science teacher offers 5 minutes of free time to talk in their seats if the lab is cleaned up in time. Students who don't clean up in time are required to finish in silence.

   - **High School:** A ninth-grade basic math teacher is encountering problems getting his students to work quietly in small groups. He discusses the problem with the class and then closely monitors the groups, circulating and offering praise and reinforcement when they are working smoothly.

3. Linking consequences to behaviors helps students see the connection between their actions and their effects on others. To help students see the logical connection between behaviors and consequences, follow through consistently in cases of disruptive behavior, and explain your actions.

   - **Elementary:** A second-grade teacher finds that transitions to and from lunch and bathroom breaks are sometimes disruptive. She talks with the class about the problem, initiates a "no-talking" rule during these transitions, and carefully enforces the rule.

   - **Middle School:** A teacher separates two seventh-graders who disrupt lessons with their talking, telling them the new seat assignments are theirs until further notice. The next day, they sit in their old seats as the bell is about to ring. "Do you know why I moved you two yesterday?" the teacher says immediately. After a momentary pause, both students nod. "Then move quickly now, and be certain you're in your new seats tomorrow. You can come and talk with me when you believe you're ready to accept responsibility for your talking."

   - **High School:** An 11th-grade history teacher reminds students about being seated when the bell rings. As it rings the next day, two girls remain standing and talking. The teacher turns to them and says, "I'm sorry, but you must not have understood me yesterday. To be counted on time, you need to be in your seats when the bell rings. Please go to the office and get a late-admit pass."

MyLab Education Self-Check 12.4

Serious Management Problems: Defiance and Aggression

12.5 Describe our legal and professional responsibilities in cases of aggressive acts and steps you can take in response to defiance and aggression.

Ed Psych and You

We've all heard about highly publicized incidents of school shootings and other stories about teachers being assaulted by students. Do you worry about these possibilities as you anticipate your first teaching job?

If you answered yes to our question in *Ed Psych and You*, you're like many other beginning teachers. We discussed school shootings and the impact they've had on teachers' and students' emotions and feelings of vulnerability in Chapter 3. Here we examine defiance and aggression, another topic about which beginning teachers are often concerned.

Fortunately, incidents of defiance and aggression toward teachers are rare in schools, with statistics indicating that in the school year 2011–12 school year, 10% of elementary teachers and 9% of secondary teachers were threatened with a physical attack by a student, and 8% and 3%, respectively, were actually attacked (Musu-Gillette, Zhang, Wang, Zhang, & Oudekerk, 2017). However, as the statistics indicate, these incidents can happen, so you should be aware of the possibility and prepared to deal with an incident in the unlikely event that it occurs.

Responding to Defiant Students

Zach, one of your students, has difficulty maintaining attention and staying on task. He frequently makes loud and inappropriate comments in class and disrupts learning activities. You warn him, reminding him that being disruptive is unacceptable, and blurting out another comment will result in timeout.

Within a minute, Zach blurts out again.

"Please go to the timeout area," you say evenly.

"I'm not going, and you can't make me," he says defiantly. He crosses his arms and remains seated at his desk.

What do we do when a student like Zach says, "I'm not going, and you can't make me?" Experts offer two suggestions (Skvorak, 2013; Wilson, 2014). First, remain calm to avoid a power struggle. Our natural tendencies are to become angry and display a show of force to demonstrate to students that they "can't get away with it." Remaining calm gives us time to control our tempers, and the student's mood when facing a calm teacher is likely to change from anger and bravado to fear and contrition (Skvorak, 2013).

Second, if possible, give the rest of the class a brief assignment, and then tell the student calmly but assertively to please step outside the classroom so you can talk. Communicate with an assertive, but not threatening, tone.

Defiance is often the result of negative student–teacher relationships (Archambault, Vandenbossche-Makombo, & Fraser, 2017), and they occur most commonly with students who display externalizing behavior problems, such as aggression, temper tantrums, or impulsiveness and hyperactivity (Alberto & Troutman, 2017). When a problem occurs with such students, it's important to let them say everything that's on their minds in private conferences, such as outside the classroom, before responding. Finally, arrange to meet with the student before or after school, focus on the defiance as a problem, and attempt to generate solutions that are acceptable to both of you.

If the student refuses to leave your classroom, or becomes physically threatening, immediately send someone to the front office for help. Most schools now have security personnel who can be summoned immediately through the communication system from the classroom. In this case, immediately contact security. Defiance at this level likely requires help from a mental-health professional.

Responding to Fighting

As you work with a small group of your fourth-graders, a fight suddenly breaks out between Trey and Neil, who are supposed to be working on a group project together. You hear sounds of shouting and see Trey flailing at Neil, who is attempting to fend off Trey's blows. Trey is often verbally aggressive and sometimes threatens other students.

What do you do?

Incidents of student aggression toward each other are much more common than threats to teachers, but statistics indicate that these incidents are decreasing. For instance, the percentage of students in grades 9–12 who reported being in a physical fight anywhere decreased from 42% in 1993 to 23% in 2015, and fights on school property decreased from 16% to 8% during this same time period (Musu-Gillette et al., 2017).

In a situation such as the one between Trey and Neil, you are required by law to intervene. If you don't, you and the school can be sued for **negligence**, the failure to exercise sufficient care in protecting students from injury (Schimmel, Stellman, Conlon, & Fischer, 2015). However, the law doesn't require you to physically break up the fight; immediately reporting it to administrators is acceptable.

An effective response to fighting involves three steps: (1) stop the incident (if possible), (2) protect the victim, and (3) get help. For instance, in the case of the classroom scuffle, a loud noise, such as shouting, clapping, or slamming a chair against the floor, will often surprise the students enough so they'll stop (Evertson & Emmer, 2017). At that point, you can begin to talk to them, check to see if the victim is all right, and then take the students to the main office, where you can get help. If your interventions don't stop the fight, you should immediately send an uninvolved student for help. Don't attempt to separate the students unless you're sure you can do so without danger to yourself or them. You are responsible first for the safety of the other students and yourself, second for the involved students, and finally for property.

Responding to Bullying

Matt, one of your seventh-graders, is shy and a bit small for his age. As he comes into your class this morning, he appears disheveled and depressed. Concerned, you take him aside and ask if anything is wrong. With some prodding he tells you that he repeatedly gets shoved around on the school grounds before school, and two boys have been taunting him and calling him gay. "I hate school," he comments.

How do you respond?

MyLab Education
Video Example 12.6

Bullying is increasingly recognized as a problem in today's schools. Here a school leader describes strategies that teachers might employ to address the problem. Notice her emphasis on the need to be aware of minor bullying incidents in order to prevent them from escalating into full-blown bullying episodes that can lead to serious problems.

Bullying, a form of peer aggression that involves a systematic or repetitious abuse of power between students, is a serious management problem in our schools. In 2015, nearly 20% of students reported that they had been bullied on school property during the previous 12 months, with a much higher percentage for self-identified gay, lesbian, or bisexual students—more than a third. Further, in this same year about 15% of fourth-graders and 7% of eighth-graders in our nation's schools reported experiencing bullying at least once a month (Musu-Gillette et al., 2017).

Dramatically increased attention has been directed at bullying in recent years, partially because of more frequent incidents of **cyberbullying**, a form of bullying that occurs when students use electronic media to harass or intimidate other students. Statistics indicate that more than 15% of high school students and close to 1 of 4 middle school students are cyberbullied (Center for Disease Control, 2015).

Attention has also increased because of some widely publicized cases of students committing suicide after being bullied, particularly after being cyberbullied (Almasy, Segal, & Couwels, 2013; Low & Espelage, 2013).

Our society in general and school officials in particular are now recognizing that bullying is a serious problem. "The courts are very clear that all facets of the school community must police and report any bullying behavior that is observed. . . . It is no longer OK . . . to call bullying 'horse play'" (Padgett & Notar 2013, p. 88). Bullying obviously detracts from students' feelings of safety, and it can carry serious problems for both perpetrators and victims. And research indicates that many adults vividly remember incidents of being bullied many years after they've completed their schooling (Cooper, & Nickerson, 2013), and the long-term effects of being bullied can be as damaging as maltreatment in childhood (Lereya, Copeland, Costello, & Wolke, 2015).

Forty-nine states have passed anti-bullying laws, and many districts have implemented zero-tolerance policies. However, the impacts of these laws and policies have been mixed (Cosgrove & Nickerson, 2017; Cunningham et al, 2016). Further, seeing that zero-tolerance policies are leading to increased arrest records, low academic achievement, and high dropout rates that particularly affect minority students, many school districts around the country are moving away from these policies, particularly for minor offenses (Alvarez, 2013).

Teachers are central to schools' efforts to eliminate bullying, so you will play an important role in the process (Perron, 2013). Because you will be on the front line with students, you will be in a better position than other school authorities to observe incidents of bullying, and you must be prepared to deal with this serious problem. Three levels of intervention exist.

At the first level, you should intervene immediately and apply appropriate consequences for the perpetrators. Trey, for example, must understand that his aggressive actions won't be tolerated. Because immediately stopping the practice is imperative, behavioral interventions will likely be needed, particularly in the near term (Kuppens, Laurent, Heyvaert, & Onghena, 2013). Most important, bullies must learn that their actions are unacceptable.

At the second level, open and frank discussions about bullying that include information about the maladaptive personal and social characteristics of bullies can reduce their social status among other students. For instance, research indicates that, as general patterns, bullies tend to have the following characteristics.

- They lack empathy and don't understand the negative impact their behaviors are having on others (Craig & Pepler, 2007).
- Academically, they tend to perform poorly and don't adjust well to school (Dake, Price, & Telljohn, 2003).
- They are more likely than other students to have problems with substance abuse, criminal activity, delinquency, and school misconduct (Merrell, Gueldner, Ross, & Isava, 2008).

Our goal in these discussions is to make bullying a socially unacceptable practice. We're all human, we all have feelings, and it will be harder for students to behave as bullies when they realize that other students may see them as unintelligent delinquents who don't care about anyone else. These discussions can also address topics such as ideas about right and wrong, appropriate treatment of others, tolerance for differences, and abuse of power. They can also focus on aspects of self-regulation, such as impulse control, emotional regulation, and self-socialization (Graham, 2010).

We can also talk to bullies in private, ask them if they want to be seen in this way by their peers, and discuss more socially acceptable ways to express themselves. Because bullies tend to also come from homes with poor parental role models who fail to set limits on their children's behavior and who tend to use physical discipline to control their children (Merrell et al., 2008; Veenstra et al., 2005), you may be the only adult they can turn to for guidance and emotional support (Kuppens et al., 2013).

Openly discussing the maladaptive characteristics of bullies may seem extreme, but it's heartbreaking, for example, to see a student small for his age being pushed around every day by bigger boys who think the abuse is funny or even cool, or to see a girl socially ostracized for some capricious reason. Bullying is a serious problem and we must do what it takes to stop it. As you can see, bullying is an issue about which we feel strongly. We've witnessed it first hand, and the destruction is palpable. It must be stopped, and you will be on the first line of intervention.

At the third level, and long term, the most effective responses to bullying are school-wide and include all members of the school community—administrators, teachers, students, support staff, custodians, parent–teacher organizations, bus drivers, cafeteria personnel, and parents. These programs are time and energy intensive and demanding but they are effective (Padgett & Notar, 2013). If students know, for example, that their bus driver will report an incident of bullying on the ride home from school, and consequences exist, they are less likely to bully. The same is true for incidents in the cafeteria, on the school grounds, and activities outside of school.

Both intermediate and long-term interventions will take time, and they won't reach every student. But they can make a difference, and for the students you, and your school, reach, the results can be increased self-regulation, healthier social development for individuals, and a safer and more positive school environment for all students.

MyLab Education Self-Check 12.5

Developmentally Appropriate Practice

Classroom Management with Learners at Different Ages

While many aspects of classroom management, such as creating a caring classroom community, developing learner responsibility, and careful planning, apply across the K–12 continuum, developmental differences exist. The following paragraphs outline suggestions for responding to these differences.

Working with Children in Early Childhood Programs and Elementary Schools

Earlier in the chapter, we discussed the importance of teaching rules and procedures to elementary students. Young children are often unaware of rules and procedures and may not understand how they contribute to learning. Because their cognitive development is likely to be preoperational, special efforts to explain the importance of rules and their connection to personal responsibility and learning are helpful, if not essential.

Young children are trusting and vulnerable, so criticism and harsh reprimands and desists are particularly harmful. They respond well to praise, but ignoring inappropriate behavior and using indirect cues are less likely to be effective with them than with older students. Behavioral interventions, such as timeout for chronic interruptions, can be effective if they are not

(continued)

overdone. Developing personal responsibility for behavior should be an important long-term goal and will assist learners as they progress through school.

Working with Students in Middle Schools

As students develop, they become more cognitively, personally, and socially aware. As a result, consistency and logical consequences become increasingly important and effective. Middle school students continue to need a caring teacher; clear boundaries for acceptable behavior and consistently enforced boundaries are indicators of caring for these students. Timely and judicious praise continues to be important, but ignoring inappropriate behavior and using indirect cues can also be effective for minor rule infractions.

The increasing importance of peers presents both challenges and opportunities in middle schools. Whispering, note passing, and general attempts to socialize become problems, and clear, consistently applied rules are essential. Middle school students appreciate being involved in rule setting, and periodic class meetings are effective in enlisting student commitment to and cooperation with classroom rules and procedures.

Working with Students in High Schools

High school students react well to being treated as adults. Developing personal responsibility is important, and private conferences that appeal to their sense of responsibility can be effective. Peers continue to exert a powerful influence on behavior, so avoiding embarrassing students in front of their peers is important. Often, a simple request to turn around or get busy is all the intervention needed.

High school students are also becoming increasingly skilled at reading social and nonverbal cues, so congruence between verbal and nonverbal channels is important. Honest interventions that directly address the problem and leave students' dignity intact, but still communicate commitment and resolve, are very effective.

A positive teacher–student relationship remains the foundation of an effective management system, and high school students react well to personal comments, such as a compliment about a new outfit or hairstyle, or questions, such as asking about an ill parent's progress or how a new brother or sister is doing.

Chapter 12 Summary

1. Define the goals of classroom management, and identify applications of the goals in classrooms.
   - Promoting student self-regulation, the ability to control one's actions and emotions, is a primary goal of classroom management.
   - When students learn to behave in acceptable ways and control their impulses, a positive classroom climate, an emotional environment in which students feel safe to share their thinking without fear of humiliation or ridicule, is developed.
   - In classrooms where learners are self-regulated and the emotional climate is positive, time available for learning is maximized.

2. Describe the processes involved in planning for classroom management.
   - The processes involved in planning for classroom management include taking developmental characteristics of students into account.
   - Young children's thinking is perceptual and concrete; they are eager to please their teachers and are vulnerable to criticism and harsh treatment.
   - Effective teachers in elementary schools teach rules and procedures and provide concrete opportunities to practice them, which create orderly and predictable environments that build trust and develop autonomy.
   - Middle school students are increasingly influenced by peers, and needs for social acceptance and independence increase.
   - Effective teachers in middle schools treat students with unconditional positive regard and provide the firm hand of a caring teacher who sets clear limits for acceptable behavior.
   - As students move into high school, they communicate more effectively at an adult level, and they respond well to clear rationales for rules and procedures that make sense to them.

3. Describe effective communication strategies for involving parents.
   - Effective communication with parents begins with early communication and maintains links throughout the school year.
   - Home–school cooperation increases students' achievement, increases willingness to do homework, improves attitudes and behaviors, and increases attendance and graduation rates.
   - Parent–teacher conferences are unique forms of communication. Maintaining ongoing communication and keeping detailed records that can be used in conferences are key to successful meetings between teachers and parents.

4. Use cognitive and behavioral learning theories to explain effective interventions.
   - Cognitive learning theory is grounded in the premise that people want their experiences to make sense.
   - Cognitive interventions include demonstrating withitness, being consistent, keeping verbal and nonverbal messages congruent, and applying logical consequences.
   - Praising desired behavior, ignoring inappropriate behavior, using desists, and applying consequences all capitalize on behavioral concepts, such as reinforcement, extinction, and punishment, to maintain an orderly classroom.

5. Describe your legal and professional responsibilities in cases of aggressive acts and steps you can take in response to defiance and aggression.
   - Teachers are required by law to intervene in cases of violence or aggression.
   - Stopping the incident, protecting the victim, and seeking assistance are the first steps involved in responding to fighting.
   - Responding immediately and applying appropriate consequences are the most effective responses to incidents of bullying.

Preparing for Your Licensure Exam

Understanding Classroom Management

You will be required to take a licensure exam before you go into your own classroom. This exam will include information related to classroom management, and it will include both multiple-choice and constructed-response questions. We include the following exercises to help you practice for the exam in your state. This book and these exercises will be a resource for you as you prepare for the exam in your state.

In the opening case study, you saw how Judy Harris maintained an orderly and learning-focused classroom. In the following case study, Janelle Powers, another seventh-grade geography teacher, also has her students working on a lesson about the Middle East. Analyze Janelle's approach to classroom management, and answer the questions that follow.

In homeroom this morning, Shiana comes through the classroom doorway just as the tardy bell rings.

"Please quickly take your seat, Shiana," Janelle directs. "We need to get started. . . . All right. Listen up, everyone," she continues. "Ali?"

"Here."

"Gaelen?"

"Here."

"Chu?"

"Here."

When Janelle finishes taking the roll, she walks around the room, handing back a set of papers.

"You did quite well on the assignment," she comments. "Let's keep up the good work. . . . Howard and Manny, please stop talking while I'm returning papers. Can't you sit quietly for 1 minute?"

The boys, who were whispering, turn back to the front of the room.

"Now," Janelle continues, returning to the front of the room, "we've been studying the Middle East, so let's review for a moment. . . . Look at the map, and identify the longitude and latitude of Cairo. Take a minute, and jot these down right now. I'll be collecting these in a few minutes."

The students begin as Janelle goes to her file cabinet to get out some materials to display on the document camera.

"Stop it, Damon," she hears Leila blurt out behind her.

"Leila," Janelle responds sternly, "we don't talk out like that in class."

"He's poking me, Mrs. Powers."

"Are you poking her, Damon?"

" . . . "

"Well?"

"Not really."

"You did, too," Leila complains.

"Both of you stop it," Janelle warns. "Another outburst like that, Leila, and your name goes on the board."

As the students are finishing their work, Janelle looks up from the materials on her desk to check an example on the overhead. She hears Howard and Manny talking and laughing at the back of the room.

"Are you boys finished?"

"Yes," Manny answers.

"Well, be quiet then until everyone is done," Janelle directs and goes back to rearranging her materials.

"Quiet, everyone," she again directs, looking up in response to a hum of voices around the room. "Is everyone finished? . . . Good. Pass your papers forward. . . . Remember, put your paper on the top of the stack. . . . Roberto, wait until the papers come from behind you before you pass yours forward."

Janelle collects the papers, puts them on her desk, and then begins, "We've talked about the geography of the Middle East, and now we want to look at the climate a bit more. It varies somewhat. For example, Syria is extremely hot in the summer but is actually quite cool in the winter. In fact, it snows in some parts."

Janelle then continues presenting information about the Middle East for the remainder of the period, stopping twice to remind Manny and Howard to stop talking and pay attention.

Questions for Case Analysis

Use information from this chapter and the case study to answer the following questions.

Multiple-Choice Questions

1. Think about the way Janelle began her class—by first taking roll and then handing back a set of papers. With respect to classroom management, which of the following is the best assessment of Janelle's class beginning?

   a. It was effective because she began taking roll just as the tardy finished ringing.

   b. It was effective, because she immediately began handing the papers back as soon as she had finished taking roll.

   c. It was ineffective, because she told Shiana to quickly take her seat as the bell was ringing.

   d. It was ineffective, because the time spent taking roll and handing back papers allowed off-task behaviors, such as Manny and Howard talking.

2. Look at the encounter between Damon and Leila that began with Leila saying, "Stop it, Damon," and ending with Janelle saying, "Another outburst like that, Leila, and your name goes on the board." Of the following, which is the best assessment of Janelle's handling of this incident?

   a. It was effective because she intervened immediately to stop the disruption.

   b. It was ineffective because Janelle's reprimand of Leila indicated a lack of withitness.

   c. It was effective because Janelle responded assertively instead of aggressively or passively in responding to Leila.

   d. It was ineffective because Janelle didn't use an "I"-message in responding to Leila.

Constructed-Response Question

1. With respect to classroom management and the synergy between classroom management and instruction, assess Janelle's overall effectiveness. Provide evidence from the case study to support your assessment.

MyLab Education Licensure Exam 12.1

Important Concepts

academic learning time	corporal punishment	discipline	overlapping
allocated time	culturally responsive	engaged time	positive behavior support
bullying	classroom management	instructional time	procedures
classroom climate	cyberbullying	logical consequences	rules
classroom management	desist	negligence	self-regulation
constructive assertiveness	detention	non-exclusionary timeout	withitness

Chapter 13
Learning and Effective Teaching

Learning Outcomes

After you have completed your study of this chapter, you should be able to:

13.1 Describe the steps in planning for instruction, including planning in a standards-based environment.

13.2 Describe the process of implementing instruction and explain how it incorporates personal qualities of effective teachers and essential teaching skills.

13.3 Describe models of instruction and explain the relationships between models of instruction and essential teaching skills.

13.4 Identify the essential characteristics of effective assessments.

APA Top 20 Principles

Top 20 Principles from Psychology for PreK–12 Teaching and Learning explicitly addressed in this chapter.

Principle 2: What students already know affects their learning.
Principle 5: Acquiring long-term knowledge and skill is largely dependent on practice.
Principle 6: Clear, explanatory, and timely feedback to students is important for learning.
Principle 11: Teachers' expectations about their students affect students' opportunities to learn, their motivation, and their learning outcomes.

National Council on Teacher Quality (NCTQ)

The NCTQ Essential Teaching Strategies that every new teacher needs to know specifically addressed in this chapter.

Strategy 2: Linking abstract concepts with concrete representations
Strategy 3: Posing probing questions

Imagine you're sitting in the back of a classroom observing a teacher working with students. How would you know if his or her instruction is "good" or "effective"? What would you look for? What would you expect to see? Keep these questions in mind as we follow the work of Scott Sowell, a middle school science teacher, throughout this chapter.

As Scott is working on a Saturday afternoon to plan his next week, he looks in his textbook, examines the professional standards for his grade level, and thinks about his past experience with the topic. Based on this information, he decides he will focus on two topics: 1) The concept of *force,* and 2) Bernoulli's Principle, the principle that helps us understand how airplanes are able to fly. (If you don't fully understand Bernoulli's Principle, please use the link below for a detailed explanation. You will also have some simple activities that you can use to entertain your friends.)

MyLab Education Content Extension 13.1

He identifies four learning objectives. They are for students:

- To know that a force is a *push* or a *pull*—the definition of the concept *force*
- To be able to identify examples of forces
- To understand that when two forces operate on an object, the object will move in the direction of the greater force
- To explain examples of Bernoulli's Principle

He types the information into his lesson plan (which appears in Figure 13.3).

"Now," Scott continues thinking to himself, "I'll have them give me some examples of forces, I'll ask them which direction an object will move when more than one force acts on it, and I'll show them some drawings and have them sketch and explain the forces in each case. That will let me know if they've gotten to the objectives."

Scott then identifies a series of examples he'll use to illustrate the concept *force*, the direction an object moves when more than one force operates on it, and Bernoulli's Principle. "This lesson will be perfect for guided discovery, and it will give me a chance to promote a lot of interaction with the kids," Scott thinks.

We'll revisit Scott's work throughout the chapter, but now we want to introduce the idea of **effective teaching**, teaching that promotes as much learning as possible in all students. Our goal for the chapter is to help you understand what effective teachers do to maximize their students' learning, how their actions relate to cognitive learning theory, and how you can become this kind of teacher. We'll use Scott's work with his students to illustrate our discussion.

Effective teaching can be summarized in three interdependent phases, which are outlined in Figure 13.1. The process begins with planning, and we turn to it next.

Planning for Instruction: Backward Design

13.1 Describe the steps in planning for instruction, including planning in a standards-based environment.

Ed Psych and You

You have a personal project that you want to complete, such as redecorating the living room in your apartment or house. What is the first thing you think about? What else do you consider?

Think about the questions we ask in *Ed Psych and You*. After identifying the project, you'll likely ask yourself three questions, the first being, "What is my purpose, or objective, in doing it?" Maybe you want to use the space more efficiently, or you want it to be more comfortable and inviting for both yourself and guests. Perhaps both.

Second, you'll think about what evidence you will use to determine if you've reached your objective, that is, how will you know if you're using the space more efficiently or the room is more inviting? For instance, you might decide that less clutter will indicate that you're using the space better, or perhaps you'll see if guests comment that they like the way you've arranged your room.

Finally, you'll make decisions about what you will specifically do to reach your objective, such as moving furniture around, or perhaps adding an item, such as a small love seat or easy chair.

Figure 13.1 Phases of effective teaching

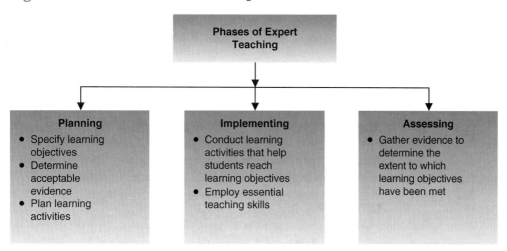

The thinking you've done parallels the way we think about instruction, and it illustrates the concept of **backward design**, a systematic approach to instructional planning that identifies learning objectives, assessments, and learning experiences during the planning process (Wiggins & McTighe, 2006). It's most popular at the P–12 level, but it's becoming increasingly common in colleges and universities (Michael & Libarkin, 2016; Reynolds & Kearns, 2017).

Backward design has three elements, illustrated by both your personal project in *Ed Psych and You* and by Scott's thinking as he planned (Wiggins & Mc Tighe, 2006):

1. *Identify desired results*—the purpose of the redecorating project in your case, and Scott's learning objectives above.
2. *Determine acceptable evidence*—lack of clutter or guests' comments for you, and his students' ability to identify and explain examples and applications of forces for Scott.
3. *Plan learning activities*—the experiences designed to reach the objectives. The examples Scott selected and his decision to use guided discovery and emphasize interaction were the learning activities he designed. In your case, technically you weren't devising "learning" activities, but you were making decisions about how to reach your objectives.

Scott's thinking about high levels of interaction in his planning is testimony to his teaching expertise. Research indicates that the amount of interaction between teachers and students is one important indicator of expert instruction (Stringfield, Teddlie, & Suarez, 2017). This is the reason we emphasize interaction so strongly.

How Is Backward Design Different from Traditional Planning?

Backward design differs from traditional planning in how we think as we plan. When using this approach, our thinking focuses on objectives, acceptable evidence, and learning activities, in that order. In traditional planning, the focus of our thinking is typically on either *activities* or *coverage of content,* without clear thinking about what students are expected to know, understand, or be able to do—the knowledge or skills they're supposed to acquire—as a result of participating in the activity or studying the content.

With the *activity* orientation, teachers often have "nifty" or attractive activities that both they and students enjoy, students engage in the activities, but what they're supposed to learn from their participation is uncertain. Let's look at an example:

A kindergarten teacher has her children plant grass seeds in cups with faces drawn on the cups. The seeds sprout, so they look somewhat like growing hair, and the children give their "cup people" haircuts by trimming the grass as it grows.

This is a perfectly good activity, but its purpose isn't clear. Are the children supposed to understand germination? Conditions plants need to grow? Learn responsibility by maintaining their cups? (Scott, by the way, used some attractive activities in his lesson, but his purpose in using them was very clear.)

With a *content coverage* orientation, content is presented in a textbook, so teachers feel it must be "covered," commonly in a lecture. Let's look at an example in this case.

An American history teacher is working with his students on the Civil War. He presents information about factors leading up to the war, the respective advantages held by the North and the South, significant battles, dates, and leaders, and Lincoln's assassination.

As with the kindergarten activity, the knowledge or skills the students are supposed to acquire aren't specified, so what learning occurs is uncertain.

The *activity* orientation is more common in elementary and lower middle schools, whereas the *coverage* orientation is more prevalent in secondary schools and universities. "In neither case can students see and answer such questions as these: What's the point? . . . What does this help us understand or be able to do? To what does this relate? Why should we learn this?" (Wiggins & McTighe, 2006, p. 16).

Backward design attempts to remedy these issues by specifying learning objectives, identifying evidence to determine the extent to which the objectives are met, and designing learning experiences to help students reach the objectives. Backward design in no way eliminates or precludes engaging activities or clear lectures; rather, it focuses on what the students are supposed to learn from them.

We turn now to a more detailed discussion of each of the backward design elements.

MyLab Education Application Exercise 13.1: Implementing Backward Design

In this exercise you will be asked to analyze a teacher's thinking during an interview as he discusses planning and conducting lessons.

MyLab Education
Video Example 13.1

Clear goals are essential for promoting students' learning. Here an educational leader explains why clear goals are so important and also explains how they're related to the concept of backward design.

Identify Desired Results: Specifying Learning Objectives

When we plan, we use our textbooks, curriculum guides, standards, and past experiences to make decisions about the topics we teach. This makes sense. Our textbooks, however, commonly include more topics than we can reasonably expect to cover in a school year, so we must identify those most important to teach. Curriculum guides and standards help us with this decision, and then we rely on our professional judgment.

After identifying a topic, specifying **learning objectives**, what we want students to know or be able to do with respect to the topic, is our first design decision. Clear learning objectives are essential because they guide the rest of our planning decisions. It's impossible to identify evidence of learning or design learning experiences if we're not clear about what we're trying to accomplish (our objectives) in the first place. Unsuccessful lessons are often the result of teachers not being clear about their objectives.

Objectives in the Cognitive Domain

Scott identified four objectives in his planning. He wanted his students to: (1) know the definition of the concept *force,* (2) identify examples of forces, (3) understand that when two forces operate on an object, the object will move in the direction of the greater force, and (4) explain examples of Bernoulli's Principle.

These are objectives in the **cognitive domain**, the area of learning that focuses on students' thinking and the processes involved in acquiring, applying, and analyzing knowledge. Objectives can also be written for the **affective domain**, which centers on people's attitudes, values, and emotions, and the **psychomotor domain**, the learning domain that concentrates on physical skills. Because the majority of formal instruction in our country's schools focuses on the cognitive domain, and because a cognitive component is involved in attitudes, emotions, and physical skills, we will focus our discussion on this area of learning.

Taxonomies for Cognitive Objectives

Let's think about Scott's objectives again. Each involves thinking, so they are all in the cognitive domain, but the specific cognitive (thought) processes required of learners are quite different. To respond to these differences, experts developed a system to classify objectives, questions, and assessment items. The result was the famous "Bloom's Taxonomy," which has been a cornerstone of education for more than a half century (Bloom, Englehart, Furst, Hill, & Krathwohl, 1956). The categories in the system include:

- *Knowledge:* Knowing facts, definitions, and other forms of memorized information, such as knowing the definition of the concept *force:* force is a push or a pull (Scott's first objective).

- *Comprehension:* Understanding information, such as the ability to state a problem in one's own words or identify an original example of a concept. (Scott's second objective).

- *Application:* Using what one knows to solve an original problem, such as determining what will happen when different forces act on an object (Scott's third objective).

- *Analysis:* The ability to break information into component parts and provide evidence to support conclusions, such as explaining examples of Bernoulli's Principle (Scott's fourth objective).

- *Synthesis:* Combining information to create an original process or product, such as constructing a unique process for finding a solution to a problem.

- *Evaluation:* Making judgments about the validity or quality of work based on a set of criteria, such as determining which of two approaches to solving a problem is more efficient.

To reflect our increased understanding of teaching and learning since the middle of the 20th century, when the original taxonomy was published, it has been revised and now more nearly reflects the influence of cognitive learning theory on teaching and learning (Anderson & Krathwohl, 2001). This newer taxonomy describes objectives in terms of students' cognitive processes and uses the term *knowledge* to reflect what students should know or acquire (Anderson & Krathwohl, 2001). For example, in Scott's first objective, "Know that force is a push or a pull," *force* is the knowledge, and *know* is the cognitive process.

The result is a matrix with 24 cells that represent the intersection of four types of knowledge with six cognitive processes (Anderson & Krathwohl, 2001). This taxonomy appears in Figure 13.2.

To understand this matrix, let's look at Scott's objectives again:

- Know the definition of the concept *force*—that *force* is a push or a pull

- Identify examples of the concept force

Figure 13.2 A taxonomy for learning, teaching, and assessing

The Knowledge Dimension	The Cognitive Process Dimension					
	1. Remember	2. Understand	3. Apply	4. Analyze	5. Evaluate	6. Create
A. Factual knowledge						
B. Conceptual knowledge						
C. Procedural knowledge						
D. Metacognitive knowledge						

Source: Based on "A Taxonomy for Learning, Teaching, and Assessing" from *A Taxonomy for Learning, Teaching, and Assessing: A Revision of Bloom's Taxonomy of Educational Objectives, Abridged Edition*, 1st Edition by Anderson et al. Copyright © 2001 by Anderson/Krathwohl/Cruikshank/Mayer/Pintrich/Raths/Wittrock. Printed and electronically reproduced by permission of Pearson Education, Inc., Upper Saddle River, New Jersey.

- Understand that when two forces act on an object, the object will move in the direction of the greater force
- Explain examples of Bernoulli's Principle

The first focuses on the concept *force* and involves memory, so it would be classified into the cell where *conceptual knowledge* intersects with *remember*. Because being able to identify examples of the concept *force* requires understanding, the second objective would be classified into the cell where *conceptual knowledge* intersects with *understand*. The third objective, "When two forces act on an object, the object will move in the direction of greater force," belongs in the cell where *procedural knowledge* intersects with *apply*, because making this determination requires the application of procedural knowledge. His fourth objective, "Explain examples of Bernoulli's Principle," requires learners to analyze the influence of air flowing over a surface, so it would be classified into the cell where *procedural knowledge* intersects with *analyze*.

The taxonomy helps us understand the complexities of learning, and it reminds us that we want our students to do more than remember factual knowledge. Schooling often focuses more on this most basic type of learning than it does on the other 23 cells combined. These other forms of knowledge and more advanced cognitive processes are even more important now in the 21st century, as student thinking, decision making, and problem solving are increasingly emphasized.

Determine Acceptable Evidence: Assessment

Once we identify learning objectives for a lesson, we next need to decide how we'll determine if students have reached them. To see how this works, let's look at Scott's thinking again. He had specified the following objectives:

- To know the definition of the concept *force*—that *force* is a push or a pull
- To identify examples of forces
- To understand that when two forces act on an object, the object will move in the direction of the greater force
- To explain examples of Bernoulli's Principle

He then thought to himself:

"I'll review and ask them for the definition of a force. Then, I'll have them give me some examples of forces, I'll give them a couple examples where two forces act on an object, such as one of the students and I holding a stapler and pulling in opposite directions, and ask them which direction the object will move, and why, and I'll show them some drawings and have them sketch and explain the forces in each case. That will let me know if they've gotten to the objectives."

Scott's thinking identified the evidence he would use to determine if his students had reached his learning objectives, and it illustrates the role of **assessment**, the process of gathering information—evidence—and making decisions about students' learning progress in teaching and learning. Evidence for the first two is straightforward; the students would merely have to state the definition and provide examples. For the third objective, their ability to identify the direction an object would move, and explain why, would be adequate, and for the fourth objective, being able to sketch and explain the forces in drawings would be acceptable evidence. (We examine the process of assessment in detail in Chapter 14.)

Here is why these forms of assessment are so important. If Scott's students could provide examples of forces, for instance, he would move forward with the lesson. If they couldn't, he would back up and provide some additional examples of his own to ensure that they understood the concept *force.* This is how to use assessment when "making decisions about students' learning progress."

Scott's thinking as he planned is the most important aspect of this process. Instead of first teaching the topics and then—sometime *after* instruction has been completed—thinking about assessment, such as a quiz or test, which is typical of traditional planning and instruction, Scott thought about evidence—assessment—*during* planning. This made assessment an integral part of the teaching–learning process, and this is an essential element of backward design.

Plan Learning Activities

Learning activities are all the experiences we provide and actions we take to help our students reach our learning objectives. In all cases, what we want our students to know, understand, or be able to do—our objectives—guide our thinking as we plan these activities.

The planning process involves three steps:

1. *Identify the components of the topic*—the concepts, principles, and relationships among them—that the students should understand. Scott wanted his students to understand the concept *force,* that an object will move in the direction of the greater force when two forces act on it, and Bernoulli's Principle.
2. *Sequence the components.* Scott knew that his students needed to understand the concept *force* and the effect of different forces on an object in order to understand Bernoulli's Principle. So, he first planned to teach *force,* then the relationships among forces, and finally the principle itself.
3. *Prepare and sequence examples with the most concrete and obvious first.* We saw the examples Scott planned to use in our explanation of Bernoulli's Principle earlier. He planned to first demonstrate the concept *force,* then illustrate how an object will move if two forces act on it, and finally present examples of Bernoulli's Principle.

Examples are essential in this process. They're the experiences learners use to construct their knowledge, and they provide the information students unfamiliar with the topic need to make the content meaningful.

National Council on Teacher Quality (NCTQ)

The National Council on Teacher Quality describes the use of examples as one of the six essential teaching strategies that all new teachers should know. "2. Linking abstract concepts with concrete representations. Teachers should present tangible examples that illuminate overarching ideas and also explain how the examples and big ideas connect" (Pomerance, Greenberg, & Walsh, 2016, p. vi).

These steps and Scott's thinking as he planned his learning activity illustrate a **task analysis**, the process of breaking content into component parts and sequencing the parts. While different forms of task analyses exist, a subject matter analysis, such as Scott used, is most common in classrooms (Alberto & Troutman, 2017).

Instructional Alignment

Ed Psych and You

Have you ever been studying for a test with a friend, and one of you asked the other, "Do you think this will be on the test?" as you think about a topic covered in class.

We're confident in believing that the answer to our question in *Ed Psych and You* is *yes*. It was when we were students, and it most likely still is.

The issue involved is lack of **instructional alignment**, the congruence between learning objectives, learning activities, and assessments. For instance, you attend class, your instructor lectures, and then you have a test, but you're not sure what aspects of the content are going to be covered on the test. This uncertainty is most likely because your instructor doesn't think about the test until sometime after, and perhaps well after, the lecture. As a result, topics emphasized in the lecture may be only minimally covered on the test, whereas the test extensively covers topics only superficially covered in the lecture. This is common in classrooms, particularly at the high school and university levels (Abrams, Varier, & Jackson, 2016).

If instruction isn't aligned, it's hard to know what is being learned. For instance, if poor test results come back, "We can't tell if (a) students were taught what they needed to know, but they didn't learn it, or (b) students weren't taught what they needed to know" (Hess & McShane, 2013, p. 63).

Backward design—identifying clear learning objectives, determining evidence that the objectives have been met, and then designing learning activities to help students reach the objectives—helps ensure instructional alignment. It's crucial for promoting learning, and research suggests that it's an essential element of high-quality instruction (Early, Rogge, & Deci, 2014).

The lesson plan that guided Scott's instruction is outlined in Figure 13.3.

MyLab Education Application Exercise 13.2: Planning for Effective Teaching

In this exercise you will be asked to analyze Scott's use of examples and instructional alignment to promote learning.

Planning in a Standards-Based Environment

Look at the following short statements:

CCSS.Math.Content.1.OA.B.3 Apply properties of operations as strategies to add and subtract. *Examples: If* 8 + 3 = 11 *is known, then* 3 + 8 = 11 *is also known.*

Figure 13.3 Scott's lesson plan in middle school science

Topic:
Force and Bernoulli's Principle

Learning Objective(s):
Students will:

1. Know the definition of the concept *force*.
2. Identify examples of the concept force.
3. Understand that when two forces act on an object, the object will move in the direction of the greater force
4. Explain examples of Bernoulli's Principle

Learning Activity:

1. Show examples of forces to illustrate the concept *force*.
2. Tug objects back and forth to demonstrate that objects move in the direction of the greater force.
3. Have students blow over a piece of paper, ask for observations, and use questioning to lead them to observe that the paper rises.
4. Have students blow between two pieces of paper and observe that the papers come together.
5. Have students blow through the neck of a funnel with a ping-pong ball in the mouth and observe that the ball stays in the mouth of the funnel.
6. Sketch the examples on the board and have them identify where the force was greater in each case. Guide them to conclude that the force under the paper, on the outside of the two papers, and in front of the ball was greater than the force on top of the paper, between the papers, and behind the ball.
7. Have students identify where the speed of the air was greater in each case.
8. Guide students to conclude that where the speed of the air was greater, the force was less (the force is greater on the opposite side). Label this relationship "Bernoulli's Principle."

Assessment:

1. Have students sketch the flow of air over the surface for each of the examples and prepare a written description of the relationship between the speed and force.
2. Have students use Bernoulli's principle to explain how airplanes are able to fly.

(Commutative property of addition.) To add 2 + 6 + 4, *the second two numbers can be added to make a ten, so* 2 + 6 + 4 = 2 + 10 = 12. *(Associative property of addition.)* (Common Core State Standards Initiative, 2018p).

CCSS.ELA-Literacy.L.3.1f Ensure subject–verb and pronoun–antecedent agreement. (Common Core State Standards Initiative, 2018o).

CCSS.ELA-Literacy.RH.9-10.8 Assess the extent to which the reasoning and evidence in a text support the author's claims. (Common Core State Standards Initiative, 2018q).

These statements are **standards**, descriptions of what students should know or be able to do at the end of a prescribed period of study. The first is in first-grade math, the second is in third-grade language arts, and the third is a literacy standard in history/social studies for grades 9–10.

The examples we see here were established by the **Common Core State Standards Initiative (CCSSI)**, which we first examined in Chapter 1. As of 2015, 42 states had adopted the common core standards (Common Core State Standards Initiative, 2018u), so you are likely to encounter them when you begin teaching. However, the states that haven't adopted Common Core have developed their own standards, so standards will be a part of your teaching life regardless of the state in which you teach. This means you must be able to incorporate standards into your planning.

Standards are essentially statements of objectives. (As we see, the definition of standards is virtually synonymous with the definition of objectives.) However, standards vary in specificity, so we may or may not need to first interpret the meaning of the standard and then construct our own specific learning objectives based on the interpretation. To illustrate, let's look again at the standards above. Here is the first one.

CCSS.Math.Content.1.OA.B.3 Apply properties of operations as strategies to add and subtract. *Examples: If 8 + 3 = 11 is known, then 3 + 8 = 11 is also known. (Commutative property of addition.) To add 2 + 6 + 4, the second two numbers can be added to make a ten, so 2 + 6 + 4 = 2 + 10 = 12. (Associative property of addition.)* (Common Core State Standards Initiative, 2018p).

In this case, the standard is specific and concrete, so interpreting it is quite easy, and the two objectives below follow logically from it:

1. For students to understand that addition is commutative.
2. For students to understand that addition is associative.

A lesson plan based on this standard appears in Figure 13.4.

Now, let's look at the second standard again:

CCSS.ELA-Literacy.L.3.1f Ensure subject–verb and pronoun–antecedent agreement. (Common Core State Standards Initiative, 2018o).

This standard requires a bit more interpretation and thought about objectives, acceptable evidence, and learning activities. For instance, what does "Ensure subject–verb and pronoun–antecedent agreement" mean? One interpretation would suggest that students should be able to identify examples of correct and incorrect subject–verb and pronoun–antecedent agreement, and a second might be the ability to correctly demonstrate the two forms of agreement in their writing.

Objectives that would logically follow from these interpretations would be for:

1. Students to select correct verbs for singular and plural subjects.
2. Students to select correct pronouns for their antecedents.
3. Students to use correct subject–verb and pronoun–antecedent agreement in their writing.

Acceptable evidence for the first objective might be the following exercise, which could be presented to the students as an assessment during the lesson.

Bill (brings, bring) his lunch to the cafeteria when it's time to eat. His friend, Leroy, and his other friend, Antonio, (takes, take) theirs to the cafeteria too. The boys (eats, eat) their lunch together, but each of the boys (leaves, leave) the table clean and clear of clutter. Bill doesn't like apples, so he will give his to anyone else who (wants, want) it.

A similar exercise could be designed for the second objective, and for the third objective acceptable evidence could be a student-composed short paragraph that illustrates correct subject–verb and pronoun–antecedent agreement. Figure 13.5 includes a lesson plan for the subject–verb component of this standard.

Finally, let's look at the third standard above.

CCSS.ELA-Literacy.RH.9-10.8 Assess the extent to which the reasoning and evidence in a text support the author's claims. (Common Core State Standards Initiative, 2018q).

Objectives based on this standard might be:

1. For students to determine the extent to which authors provide evidence to support the claims presented in their writing.
2. For students to determine the extent to which authors' reasoning supports the claims presented in their writing.

Figure 13.4 Lesson plan for Common Core State Standard in first-grade math

Topic:
Commutative and associative properties of addition

Standard:
CCSS.Math.Content.1.0A.B.3 Apply properties of operations as strategies to add and subtract. *Examples: If* $8 + 3 = 11$ *is known, then* $3 + 8 = 11$ *is also known. (Commutative property of addition.) To add* $2 + 6 + 4$, *the second two numbers can be added to make a ten, so* $2 + 6 + 4 = 2 + 10 = 12$. *(Associative property of addition.)*

Learning Objectives:
1. For students to understand that addition is commutative.
2. For students to understand that addition is associative.

Learning Activity:
Commutative Property:

1. Give each student 12 plastic circular discs.
2. Have them count out 8 discs and put them in a group. Then, have them count out three more discs and put them in a separate group.
3. Ask them how many discs they have altogether.
4. Ask them to explain in words what they did, and guide them to say, "We first counted 8 discs and then we counted 3 more discs, and we got 11 discs altogether."
5. Write $8 + 3 = 11$ on the board.
6. Now have them count 3 discs and put them in a group; then count 8 discs and put them in a group, and count how many they have altogether. Again, have them explain in words what they did, guiding them to say, "We first counted 3 discs and then we counted 8 discs, and we got 11 discs altogether."
7. Write $3 + 8 = 11$ directly below where you've written $8 + 3 = 11$.
8. Ask them what they notice about the two problems, and guide them to conclude that they both equal 11. Then, guide them to conclude that the order of the numbers doesn't matter when we add, and write $8 + 3 = 3 + 8$. Tell them that this works for all numbers when we add and tell them this is called the commutative property of numbers. Do some additional examples similar to this one.

Associative Property:

1. Have the students count 2 discs and put them in a group; count 6 discs and put them in a second group; count 4 discs and put them in a third group.
2. Ask them how many discs they have altogether, ask them to explain in words what they did, and guide them to conclude that they added 2 plus 6 plus 4, and they got 12 altogether.
3. Write $2 + 6 + 4 = 12$ on the board.
4. Have them count 2 discs and put them in a group; count six discs and put them in a group, and ask them how many they have altogether. Write $2 + 6 = 8$ on the board.
5. Then, have them count 4 more discs and ask them how many they have altogether. Write $8 + 4 = 12$ directly below $2 + 6 + 4 = 12$.
6. Ask them to explain what they did and guide them to say that they first grouped the 2 and the 6 to get 8 and then grouped the 8 and the 4 to get 12.
7. Repeat the process by first grouping the 6 and the 4 to get 10 and then adding the 10 and the 2.
8. Tell them this works for all numbers and tell them this is called the associative property of numbers.
9. Do some additional examples.

Assessment:
1. Give them a worksheet with the following problems on it: $5 + 2 =$ $7 + 1 =$ $3 + 8 =$
Tell them to demonstrate the commutative property on their worksheets.
2. On the same worksheet give them the following problems: $5 + 2 + 4 =$ $3 + 1 + 6 =$
Tell them to demonstrate the associative property on their worksheets.
3. Have students who demonstrate the properties correctly go to the front of the room and explain what they did in each case.

A lesson plan based on this standard appears in Figure 13.6.

When first faced with the task of interpreting standards and creating objectives based on them, you might feel a bit overwhelmed. As you acquire experience interpreting standards and creating learning activities, however, the task will become much easier. We hope this section helps you get started with this process.

Figure 13.5 Lesson plan for Common Core State Standard in third-grade language arts

Topic:
Subject–verb agreement

Standard:
CCSS.ELA-Literacy.L.3.1f Ensure subject–verb and pronoun–antecedent agreement.

Learning Objective(s):
Students will:

1. Select correct verbs for singular and plural subjects.

2. Use correct subject–verb in their writing.

Learning Activity:

1. Explain that singular subjects take singular verbs and plural subjects take plural verbs. Display the following sentences:

Susan runs to the store. Susan and Kelly run to the store.

He plays soccer. They play soccer.

This shirt is too small for me. These clothes are too big for me.

2. Have the students identify the subjects and verbs in each sentence.

3. Guide them to conclude that "Susan" is singular, and "runs" is also singular.

4. Repeat with the other sentences.

Assessment

1. Display the following:

Bill (brings, bring) his lunch to the cafeteria when it's time to eat. His friend, Leroy, and his other friend, Antonio, (takes, take) theirs to the cafeteria too. The boys (eats, eat) their lunch together, but each of the boys (leaves, leave) the table clean and clear of clutter. Bill doesn't like apples, so he will give his to anyone else who (wants, want) it.

2. Have the students identify the correct verb in each pair enclosed by parentheses.

3. Survey the results, and discuss the exercise.

4. Depending on the results, provide more examples, or have the students write a short paragraph that includes at least three examples of subject–verb agreement.

Classroom Connections

Planning Effectively in Classrooms

1. Backward design ensures that assessments and learning activities are aligned with objectives. Specify learning objectives, identify acceptable evidence, and prepare learning experiences as you plan.

- **Elementary:** A fourth-grade teacher wants her students to understand the functions of the different parts of the skeletal system, such as why the skull is solid, why ribs are curved around the trunk, and why the femur is such a large bone. As acceptable evidence, she plans to have the students respond to the following directive: "Suppose humans walked on all fours, as chimpanzees and gorillas do. Describe how our skeletons would be different from our skeletons now." She then plans to display a model skeleton, have students make observations, and then guide them to conclusions about different parts of the skeleton.

- **Middle School:** A geography teacher wants his students to understand how geography influences the location of cities. As acceptable evidence, he plans to give them a map of a fictitious island with different mountain ranges, wind directions, ocean currents, and latitude and longitude, and have them identify and explain where the largest city on the island would most likely be. He then plans to show maps and pictures of major cities in our country, such as New York, Chicago, San Francisco, and Miami, and discuss the geographical features of each of the cities.

- **High School:** A biology teacher wants her students to understand the relationships between an organism's body

(continued)

structure and its adaptation to its environment. As acceptable evidence, she plans to present her students with two organisms, one with radial symmetry and the other with bilateral symmetry, and ask them to identify the one that is most advanced with respect to evolution and to explain their choices. For her learning activity, she plans to present her students with examples of different kinds of worms and discuss their characteristics.

2. Knowledge can vary from factual to metacognitive, and cognitive processes range from remembering to creating. Prepare objectives that require students to do more than remember factual knowledge.

- **Elementary:** The fourth-grade teacher focuses on the function of different parts of the skeletal system instead of simply identifying its different parts and identifying the

names of specific bones. In the process, the students acquire basic information.

- **Middle School:** The geography teacher focuses on the influence of geography on locations of cities as opposed to identifying the names and locations of different geographical features, such as the names of the states and the locations and features of the Rocky Mountains and Great Plains. Students are held accountable for names and locations as prerequisite knowledge.

- **High School:** The biology teacher focuses on organisms' adaptations to their environments instead of the names and structures of the organisms. The names and structures become a part of the incidental knowledge that students acquire. Students are also required to know this incidental information.

Figure 13.6 Lesson plan for Common Core State Standard in middle school literacy for social studies

Topic:
Evidence and reasoning

Standard:
CCSS.ELA-Literacy.RH.9-10.8 Assess the extent to which the reasoning and evidence in a text support the author's claims.

Learning Objective(s):
Students will:
1. Determine the extent to which authors provide evidence to support the claims presented in their writing.
2. Determine the extent to which authors' reasoning supports the claims presented in their writing.

Learning Activity:
1. Define the concept *evidence* as facts or observations related to a claim or conclusion.
2. Provide examples of evidence supporting a claim or conclusion and provide additional examples where evidence refutes a claim or conclusion.
3. Ask students if they're familiar with the controversy over the name of the Washington Redskins professional football team. If not, explain that some people claim that the name "Redskin" is inherently racist, whereas others claim it is not.
4. Display two columns, one by Rick Reilly, a sports writer for ESPN.com (Reilly, 2013), and the other by Kathleen Parker, a *Washington Post* columnist (Parker, 2013), both of which discuss the controversy related to the name "Washington Redskins" and offer assertions as to whether or not the name "Redskin" should be changed.
5. Have students read the two columns and then work in pairs to assess the extent to which the two authors support their claims related to the need to change the name.
6. Have the groups report to the whole class.
7. As the groups report, write items they consider to be evidence supporting each author's claim on the board.
8. Discuss the items as a whole group.

Assessment:
1. Give students a column related to the issue of immigration and immigration reform in our country (Bandow, 2013).
2. Have them write a paragraph that assesses the extent to which the author supports his claims with evidence and sound reasoning.

MyLab Education Self-Check 13.1

Implementing Instruction

13.2 Describe the process of implementing instruction and explain how it incorporates personal qualities of effective teachers and essential teaching skills.

Ed Psych and You

You've thought about and made the necessary decisions about redecorating your living room. In other words, you've identified your objectives and planned the redecorating process. Now, what do you do?

The answer to the question in *Ed Psych and You* is simply *implement your plans*. For example, after planning, you actually will do the painting, rearrange the furniture, or add some artwork.

Teaching is similar. **Implementing instruction** is the process of putting the decisions made during planning into action. Planning is a series of sequential thought processes combined with gathering necessary materials, whereas implementation focuses on action. A great deal of thinking is involved during implementation as well, but if we plan carefully, the load on our working memories will be significantly reduced when we actually conduct our learning activities.

Conducting Learning Activities

Earlier, we said that learning activities involve all the experiences we provide and actions we take to help our students reach our objectives. These actions can range from a simple lecture to a complex simulation and everything in between. They include presenting examples, questioning students, guiding group work, completing and providing feedback for assessments, and anything else we do that is designed to help our students reach our learning objectives.

We saw how Scott planned his instruction. We turn now to the way he conducted his learning activity. On Monday, he had taught the concept of *force* and the idea that an object will move in the direction of the greater force when two forces are operating on it. We join him as he begins class Tuesday with a review.

"Let's go over what we did yesterday," he begins immediately after the bell stops ringing. "What is a force? . . . Shantae?"

" . . . A push or a pull," she responds, after thinking for a second.

"Good," Scott smiles and then reviews the concept of force by pushing on the board, blowing on an object sitting on his desk, and asking students to explain why they are forces.

He continues by holding a stapler and having Damien try to pull it away from him to review the idea that objects move in the direction of the greater force.

Reminding students to "keep these ideas in mind" and raising his voice to emphasize his points, he gives each student two pieces of paper, telling them to pick up one of the pieces and blow over it as you see here. He demonstrates with a similar piece of paper.

He then asks, "What did you notice when we blew over the top? . . . David?"

"The paper moved."

"How did the paper move? Let's do it again."

David again blows over the surface of the paper, and Scott repeats, "What did the paper do?"

" . . . It came up."

"Yes," Scott says, waving energetically. "When you blow over it, it comes up."

He then has students pick up both pieces of paper and demonstrates how to blow between them, as shown here.

"What did you notice here? . . . Sharon?" Scott asks after they've done the same.

" . . . The papers came together."

"Okay, good. Remember that, and we'll talk about it in a minute," Scott says, smiling. "Now, let's look at one more example. . . . I have a funnel and a ping-pong ball. . . . I'm going to shoot Tristan in the head when I blow," he jokes, pointing to one of the students.

He blows through the funnel's stem, and to the students' surprise, the ball stays in the funnel.

Scott has students repeat the demonstration and make observations, and he then draws sketches of the three examples on the board and says, "Let's look at these."

Referring to the first sketch, Scott asks, "Was I blowing on the top or the bottom? . . . Rachel?"

"The top."

"And what happened there? . . . Heather?"

"The paper rose up."

Referring to the second sketch, he asks, "What did we do here? . . . Shantae?"

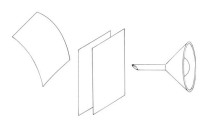

"We blew in between them."

"And what happened there? . . . Ricky?"

"They came together."

Scott does a similar analysis with the ball and funnel and then says, "Let's think about the forces here. What forces are acting on the paper? . . . Colin?"

"Gravity."

"And which direction is gravity pulling?"

"Down."

Scott draws an arrow pointing downward, indicating the force of gravity, and labels it "A."

"What other force is acting on the paper? . . . William?" he continues.

"Air," William says, pointing up.

"How do you know it's pushing up?"

"The paper moved up."

"Exactly. You know there's a force pushing up, because objects move in the direction of the greater force, and the paper moved up." Scott then draws an arrow pointing up and labels it "B."

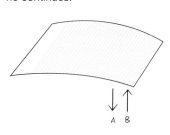

Scott guides the students through a similar analysis of the second and third examples, leading them to conclude that the forces pushing the two papers together were greater than the forces pushing them apart, and the force pushing the ball into the funnel was greater than the force pushing the ball out.

"Now let's look again at the forces and where we blew," Scott continues, as he moves back to the first sketch. "Study the drawings carefully, and see what kind of relationship exists between the two."

After several seconds, Heather concludes, "It seems like wherever you blew, the force was stronger on the opposite side."

Seeing that the bell is going to ring in a minute, Scott continues, "Yes, excellent, Heather. . . . A person named Bernoulli discovered that every time you increase the speed of the air over a surface, the force goes down. . . . So, when I speed up the air over the top of the paper (holding up the single sheet of paper), the force goes down and this force takes over (motioning underneath the paper to illustrate a force pushing up)."

He summarizes the other two examples in the same way, finishing just as the bell ending the period begins to ring.

As Scott implemented his plans and conducted his learning activity, he demonstrated a number of personal qualities and essential teaching skills, basic qualities and abilities that all teachers, including those in their first year, should possess to maximize student learning. They are equally important for working with members of cultural minorities, those in urban, suburban, and rural environments, and learners who have exceptionalities. In short, the personal qualities of teachers and essential teaching skills apply to all students and all teaching situations.

We begin with the personal qualities of effective teachers.

Personal Qualities of Effective Teachers

Research has identified several personal qualities of teachers who maximize learning in their students. They include what researchers call *prerequisites* of effective teachers (Lavy, 2016; Meng, Muñoz, King, & Liu, 2016):

- *Verbal ability*. Effective teachers are articulate and use language succinctly and accurately.
- *Content knowledge*. They understand the content they're teaching, such as math, science, history, or literature.
- *Professional knowledge and dedication*. Effective teachers understand the way people learn and develop, and are dedicated to students and teaching as a profession. Developing professional knowledge is the reason you're taking this course.

In addition to these prerequisites, effective teachers possess the personal qualities we discussed in Chapter 11, which include:

- *High personal teaching efficacy*—believing that they're capable of getting all students to learn, regardless of prior knowledge, ability, or personal background.
- *Modeling and enthusiasm*—demonstrating their own interest in the topics they're teaching, and communicating a desire for knowledge and understanding.
- *High expectations*—maintaining high academic standards and treating students with respect and requiring the same in return.

APA Top 20 Principles

This description illustrates Principle 11: *Teachers' expectations about their students affect students' opportunities to learn, their motivation, and their learning outcomes*—from the *Top 20 Principles from Psychology for PreK–12 Teaching and Learning*.

- *Caring*—investing in the protection and development of young people.

These personal qualities increase motivation and learning and decrease the likelihood of classroom management problems. They contribute to positive teacher–student relationships and a warm and secure classroom climate. They provide the foundation on which all teaching and learning is grounded.

Scott's interactions with his students suggest that he possesses both the prerequisites of effective teaching and the personal qualities of effective teachers. He was articulate, he obviously understood the topic he was teaching, and the examples he provided and the way he interacted with his students suggest that he understands the way students learn. He was energetic and enthusiastic, he demonstrated the respect for students that indicates caring, and his questioning suggested that he expected all students to participate and learn. These are the personal qualities we hope to see in all teachers.

Essential Teaching Skills

Essential teaching skills are the professional skills that all teachers, including those in their first year, should possess to maximize student learning. Essential teaching skills are analogous to what we commonly describe as *basic skills,* the skills in reading, writing, math, and technology that all people need in order to function effectively in today's world. You will be expected to understand and demonstrate these skills regardless of the content area or grade level that you're planning to teach.

Derived from nearly 40 years of research (Duke, Cervetti, & Wise, 2016; Fisher et al., 1980; Good & Lavigne, 2018), these skills are outlined in Table 13.1 and discussed in the sections that follow.

Organization

To teach effectively, we must first be well organized. This means that we (1) prepare the materials we need in advance, (2) start our instruction on time, (3) make transitions from one activity to another quickly and smoothly, and (4) develop well-established classroom routines. These aspects of organization increase achievement by maximizing instructional time and helping prevent classroom management problems (Lester, Allanson, & Notar, 2017).

Scott began his lesson immediately after the bell stopped ringing, he had the sheets of paper, balls, and funnels ready to distribute, and he made the transition from his review to the learning activity quickly and smoothly. This organization was the result of careful planning.

TABLE 13.1 Essential teaching skills, components, and cognitive learning theory applications

Essential Teaching Skill	Essential Teaching Skill Components	Application of Cognitive Learning Theory
Organization	• Starting instruction on time • Having materials ready • Creating well-established routines	Reduces the cognitive load on teachers' and students' working memories and helps establish and maintain students' equilibrium.
Review	• Beginning-of-lesson review • Interim reviews	Activates prior knowledge retrieved from long-term memory, to which new knowledge is attached.
Focus	• Capture attention • Maintain attention	Attracts learners' attention and provides a conceptual umbrella for the lesson.
Questioning	• Questioning frequency • Equitable distribution • Prompting • Wait-time	Encourages learners to become cognitively active. Provides scaffolding.
Feedback	• Immediate • Specific • Corrective information • Positive emotional tone	Provides students with information they use to determine whether the knowledge they've constructed is valid.
Closure and Application	• End-of-lesson summary • Use acquired information in a new context	Contributes to schema construction and meaningful encoding.
Communication	• Precise terms • Connected discourse • Transition signals • Emphasis	Makes information understandable and meaningful. Maintains learner attention.

Review

Implementing instruction is a systematic process, and it begins with a **review**, a summary that helps students link what they've already learned to new information you're planning to teach. It can occur at any point in a lesson, although it is most common at the beginning and end. Let's look at Scott's review again.

"Let's go over what we did yesterday," he begins immediately after the bell stops ringing. "What is a force? . . . Shantae?"

" . . . A push or a pull," she responds, after thinking for a second.

"Good," Scott smiles and then reviews the concept of force by pushing on the board, blowing on an object sitting on his desk, and asking students to explain why they are forces.

He continues by holding a stapler and having Damien try to pull it away from him to review the idea that objects move in the direction of the greater force.

The knowledge learners construct depends on what they already know is a cognitive learning principle, and beginning reviews help students activate what they know to help them as they construct new knowledge (McCrudden & McNamara, 2018).

APA Top 20 Principles

This description also illustrates Principle 2: *What students already know affects their learning*—from the *Top 20 Principles from Psychology for PreK–12 Teaching and Learning*.

Scott's beginning review on Tuesday was one of the most effective aspects of his lesson. He didn't just ask his students to recall the definition of *force* and the influence of different forces on an object; he illustrated the ideas with examples, such as pushing on the board and blowing on an object. Because he had shown examples on Monday, showing additional ones during his review may have seemed unnecessary, but this isn't true. Using concrete examples during the review increased its effectiveness by providing additional links between new information and information already in students' long-term memories. And Scott's review was essential because his students had to understand force and the influence of different forces on an object in order to understand Bernoulli's Principle.

Focus

We know from our understanding of human memory that all learning begins with attention, so we need a mechanism to capture and maintain students' attention throughout the lesson. **Focus** provides this mechanism (Lemov, 2015; McCrudden & McNamara, 2018).

Scott's demonstrations—blowing over the piece of paper, between the papers, and through the neck of the funnel—provided focus in his lesson. They were eye catching, so they attracted his students' attention, and his sketches on the board helped maintain their attention throughout the learning activity. Concrete objects, pictures, models, materials displayed on the document camera, or even information written on the board can all act as focus during a lesson.

Questioning

We've conducted a review and used a form of focus to attract and maintain our students' attention. Our next challenge is to involve them in the lesson and encourage cognitive activity, that is, encourage them to *think* about what they're studying instead of passively receiving information. Research indicates that teachers who promote the highest achievement involve their students by spending more time in active instruction and less time having students do independent seatwork than their less effective colleagues (Good & Lavigne, 2018; Stringfield et al., 2017). Further, teachers who are the most effective spend a minimum amount of time simply lecturing (Lemov, 2015).

Questioning is the most widely applicable tool we have for promoting this involvement and thinking. "The use of good questioning, by teachers, may mean the difference between constraining thinking and encouraging new ideas, and between recalling trivial facts and constructing meaning" (McCarthy, Sithole, McCarthy, Cho, & Gyan, 2016, p. 80). Further, some researchers suggest that teacher questioning is one of the most important indicators of teaching expertise (Wang & Wang, 2013).

Skilled questioning is sophisticated, but in our work with teachers we've seen that with practice and experience they can become expert at it, and you can, too (Eggen & Kauchak, 2012; Kauchak & Eggen, 2012). To avoid overloading your working memory, you need to practice questioning strategies until they're essentially automatic, which leaves working memory space available to monitor students' thinking and assess learning progress. Once you develop this ability, you'll find that using questioning to guide your students' increasing understanding will be some of your most rewarding professional experiences.

The components of effective questioning are outlined in Figure 13.7.

Questioning Frequency. **Questioning frequency** refers to the number of questions we ask during a learning activity, and expert teachers ask many more questions than teachers with less expertise (Good & Lavigne, 2018). Scott demonstrated his expertise by developing his entire lesson with questioning, and, as with many aspects of teaching, it isn't as simple as it appears on the surface. To maximize learning, questions must remain focused on the learning objectives, which is why careful planning is so important. If you're clear about your objectives, guiding your students' learning with questioning will be much easier.

Equitable Distribution. **Equitable distribution** is the process of calling on all students in a class as equally as possible (Kauchak & Eggen, 2012; Kerman, 1979; McDougall & Granby, 1996), and it accommodates teachers' tendencies to call on high achieving or more outgoing students more often than their peers (Good & Lavigne, 2018). To emphasize that we should call on students whether or not they have their hands raised, some experts use the term "cold call" when describing equitable distribution (Lemov, 2015).

MyLab Education
Video Example 13.2
Equitable distribution, the process of calling on all students in a class as equally as possible, is an important questioning skill. Notice here that Scott first asks the question and then identifies the student he expects to answer. This process communicates that the teacher believes students are capable learners and expects all students to participate in learning activities.

Figure 13.7 Elements of effective questioning

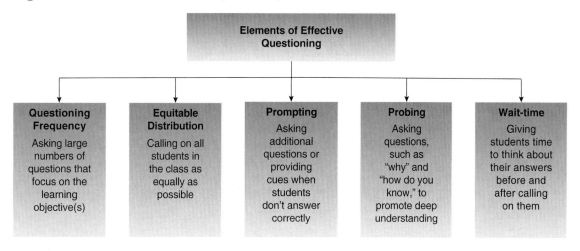

To illustrate this idea, let's return to Scott's lesson:

Scott:	(Referring to the sketch of the single piece of paper.) Was I blowing on the top or the bottom? . . . Rachel?
Rachel:	The top.
Scott:	And what happened there? . . . Heather?
Heather:	The paper rose up.
Scott:	(Referring to the sketch of the two pieces of paper.) What did we do here . . . Shantae?
Shantae:	We blew in between them.
Scott:	And what happened there . . . Ricky?
Ricky:	They came together.

In this short episode, Scott called on four different students, and he first asked the question and then identified who he wanted to respond. Equitable distribution makes everyone responsible for generating an answer and creates the expectation that all learners are capable of responding and should be paying attention (Lemov, 2015). "All students benefit from opportunities to practice oral communication skills, and distributing response opportunities helps keep them attentive and accountable" (Good & Lavigne, 2018, p. 443).

Equitable distribution is a simple but demanding idea because it requires that we carefully monitor our students to keep track of who we have and haven't called on, and who might be drifting off. Our experience suggests that students can and will help us in this process. First, when they get used to the idea that everyone in the class will be called on and being unable to answer is simply one aspect of learning, classroom climate improves. Then, we can simply ask, "Whom haven't I called on?" Students will often quickly answer, "You haven't called on . . . " This helps promote the idea that "We're all in this together."

Prompting. In attempting to call on all our students, you might wonder, "What do I do when the student I call on doesn't answer or answers incorrectly?" **Prompting**—an additional question or statement used to elicit an appropriate response after a student fails to answer correctly—is the answer. Its value to both learning and motivation is well documented (Brophy, 2006).

To illustrate, let's look again at Scott's work with his students.

Scott:	What did you notice when we blew over the top? . . . David?
David:	The paper moved.
Scott:	How did the paper move? Do it again. (David again blew over the surface of the paper.)
Scott:	What did the paper do?
David:	It came up.

David didn't initially give the answer necessary to help him understand the relationship between force and the movement of the paper, so having him recall the previous demonstration was a form of prompting.

As another example, Ken Duran, in a language arts lesson on adjectives, displays the following on his document camera:

The girl was very athletic.

Let's look at some brief dialogue:

Ken:	Identify an adjective in the sentence . . . Chandra?
Chandra:	. . .
Ken:	What do we know about the girl?
Chandra:	She was athletic.

Ken's prompt, which elicited an acceptable response, kept Chandra involved in the activity and helped her be successful. She hadn't quite arrived at the answer Ken wanted, but the question kept her active and in her zone of proximal development, which helped her make learning progress.

We need to be strategic when we prompt. For instance, if a question calls for factual knowledge, such as "What is 7 times 8?" or "Who was our president during the Civil War?" and a student doesn't answer, prompting isn't useful; students either know the fact or they don't. It's important, however, when studying conceptual, procedural, and metacognitive knowledge, and when using cognitive processes beyond remembering (Anderson & Krathwohl, 2001).

Probing. Prompting is important for involving students. However, when questioning, our goal is to promote deep understanding of the topics we teach, and **probing questions**, questions that require students to explain or provide evidence, help us meet this goal. "Asking students 'why,' 'how,' 'what if,' and 'how do you know' requires them to clarify and link their knowledge of key ideas" (Pomerance et al., 2016, p. vi). To illustrate, let's look again at some brief dialogue from Scott's lesson. He is working with the sketch of the single piece of paper.

MyLab Education
Video Example 13.3

The ability to ask probing questions, such as "Why?" and "How do you know?" has been identified as an essential teaching strategy that all teachers need to know. Notice here how seventh-grade math teacher, Kadean Maddix, uses probing questions to help his students develop a deep understanding of the topic he is teaching.

Scott draws an arrow pointing downward, indicating the force of gravity, and labels it "A."

Scott:	What other force is acting on the paper? . . . William?
William:	Air (as he points up)
Scott:	How do you know it's pushing up?
William:	The paper moved up.
Scott:	Exactly. You know there's a force pushing up, because objects move in the direction of the greater force, and the paper moved up. (He then draws an arrow pointing up and labels it "B.")

Scott's question, "How do you know it's pushing up?", followed naturally from the interaction in the lesson. Once you become aware of the opportunity to ask questions such as these, they will take little extra effort, and they help students develop a deeper understanding of the topics they study.

National Council on Teacher Quality (NCTQ)

The National Council on Teacher Quality describes posing probing questions as one of the six essential teaching strategies that all new teachers should know (Pomerance et al., 2016).

Wait-Time.   For questions to be effective, we need to give our students time to think. And if we wait a second and survey the room after asking a question, we alert all students that they may be called on. Then, after identifying a student, we wait a few more seconds to give the student some "think" time. This period of silence, both before and after calling on a student, is called **wait-time**, and in most classrooms, it is very short, often less than 1 second (Kastens & Liben, 2007; Rowe, 1986).

Increased learning is linked to longer wait times (Kastens & Liben, 2007; Rowe, 1986). "Longer wait times consistently resulted in longer student responses, an increase in the number of students volunteering to respond, and an increase in the number of follow-up questions posed by students" (Tofade, Elsner, & Haines, 2013, p. 7). In addition, the number of times students responded "I don't know" decreased, and test scores increased (Tofade et al., 2013). Some research also suggests that increasing wait times results in instruction becoming more learner centered (Smith & King, 2017), and it's even more effective when working with students having disabilities (Johnson & Parker, 2013).

As with prompting and probing, we should use wait-time strategically. For example, if students are practicing basic skills, such as multiplication facts, quick answers are desirable, and wait times should be short (Good & Lavigne, 2018). Also, if a student appears uneasy, we may choose to intervene earlier. However, if we expect students to think—using cognitive processes such as apply, analyze, or evaluate—wait times should be longer, sometimes exceeding the 3- to 5-second rule of thumb.

Feedback

Feedback is information we provide learners that helps them determine the extent to which their knowledge constructions are accurate and complete, and its impact on learning is well documented (Hattie, 2012; Hattie & Gan, 2011). In fact, a meta-analysis of more than 800 studies identified feedback as one of the most powerful influences on learning (Hattie, 2012). It also contributes to motivation because it provides learners with information about their increasing competence, an important psychological need according to self-determination theory (Brophy, 2010; Schunk, Meece, & Pintrich, 2014).

APA Top 20 Principles

This discussion illustrates Principle 6: *Clear, explanatory, and timely feedback to students is important for learning*—from the *Top 20 Principles from Psychology for PreK–12 Teaching and Learning*.

Effective feedback has four characteristics:

- It is immediate or given soon after a learner response.
- It is specific.
- It provides corrective information for the learner.
- It has a positive emotional tone (Hattie & Gan, 2011).

To illustrate these characteristics, let's compare three illustrations of feedback after the following sentences have been displayed on the document camera.

Our team's running game was in high gear last night.

Running is one of the best forms of exercise that exists.

Mr. Dole:	What does the word *running* illustrate in the first sentence . . . Jo?
Jo:	A verb.
Mr. Dole:	Not quite. Help her out . . . Steve?
Ms. West:	What does the word *running* illustrate in the first sentence . . . Jason?
Jason:	A verb.
Ms. West:	No, it's a participle. How is *running* used in the second sentence? . . . Albert?
Ms. Baker:	What does the word *running* illustrate in the first sentence? . . . Donna?
Donna:	A verb.
Ms. Baker:	Not quite . . . . How is the word *running* used in the sentence?
Donna:	It tells us about the game.
Ms. Baker:	Good. So, it behaves as an adjective. Verb forms that behave as adjectives are called participles. Now, let's look at the second sentence.

The feedback was immediate for each teacher, but neither Mr. Dole nor Ms. West gave the students any corrective information. Ms. Baker, in contrast, provided Donna with specific information that helped her understand the concept, which is the most important feature of effective feedback (Hattie, 2012).

Although these examples don't illustrate the emotional tone of the teachers' responses, it's important. Harsh, critical, or sarcastic feedback detracts from students' feelings of safety and relatedness, which decreases both motivation and learning (Schunk et al., 2014).

Praise.   Praise is the most common form of positive feedback, and a study examining college students' reactions to praise is revealing. The researchers found that the desire for praise, and the boost to self-esteem that comes with it, trumped other desires and needs, including alcohol, money, or even sex (Bushman, Moeller, & Crocker, 2010).

Other research examining the use of praise in P–12 classrooms has identified the following general patterns:

- It's used less often than most teachers believe—less than five times per class.

- Praise for good behavior is rare; it occurs once every 2 or more hours in the elementary grades and even less as students get older.

- It depends as much on the type of student (e.g., high achieving, well behaved, and attentive) as on the quality of the student's response.

- Teachers praise students based on the answers they expect to receive as much as on those they actually hear (Good & Lavigne, 2018).

Using praise effectively is complex. For instance, young children accept it at face value even when overdone, whereas older students assess the validity of the praise and what they believe it communicates about their ability. Young children bask in praise given openly in front of a class, whereas adolescents often react better if it's given quietly and individually. However, with students of all ages, *process praise*, praise for hard work and perseverance, such as "You're trying hard," is more effective than *person praise*, praise for personal qualities, such as "You're a good student," because person praise can detract from students' motivation when they fail (Droe, 2013). This is particularly true for students who have a low sense of academic self-worth (Brummelman et al., 2013).

Further, overpraising students for correct answers to easy questions can create the perception in students that their teachers believe they have low ability (Kaspar & Stelz, 2013). This research suggests that—for all students—we should praise them for their effort or for what they are accomplishing, instead of who they are, and we should praise in a simple, natural, and genuine manner.

Written Feedback. Much of the feedback we provide occurs as we interact with students, but they also need information about the quality of their written work. Because writing detailed comments is enormously time-consuming, providing each student with individual, written feedback is difficult.

Providing model responses to written assignments is one solution to this problem. For instance, to help students evaluate their responses to essay items, we can write ideal answers, display them, and have students compare their responses to the model. Combined with discussion and time available for individual help, the model provides feedback that's manageable in terms of time and effort.

Closure and Application

Closure is a summary that occurs at the end of lessons. It pulls different aspects of the topic together, helps students construct meaningful schemas, and signals the end of the lesson. When students are involved in higher-level learning, a summary statement, such as defining a concept, stating a principle, or summarizing the thinking involved in solving a problem, is an effective form of closure.

Application is the process of having students use the information they've acquired in the lesson in a new context. Asking them to identify additional examples of a concept, use a principle to explain a previously unexplained event, or solve additional problems are effective applications. Applications help students form new connections in the information, which makes the content they've studied more meaningful. Scott having his students use Bernoulli's Principle to help explain how airplanes are able to fly is an example of application.

Communication

Earlier, we saw that verbal ability is a prerequisite of effective teachers. In all aspects of our lessons—reviews, focus, questioning, the feedback we provide, and the way we bring lessons to closure—clear and concise communication is important. It increases student achievement, and students are more satisfied with instruction when their teachers communicate clearly (Good & Lavigne, 2018). In a sense, it's an umbrella under which the other essential teaching skills fall.

Effective communication has three characteristics:

- Precise language
- Transition signals
- Emphasis

Precise language omits vague terms—such as *perhaps, and so on, maybe, might,* and *usually*—from explanations and responses to students' questions. For example, if you ask, "What do high-efficacy teachers do that promotes learning?" and your instructor responds, "Usually, they use their time somewhat better and so on," you're left with a sense of uncertainty about the idea. In contrast, if the instructor says, "They believe they can increase learning, and one way they do this is by using their time efficiently," you're given a clear picture, which makes the idea more understandable.

Transition signals are verbal statements indicating that one idea is ending and another is beginning. For example, an American government teacher might signal a transition by saying, "We've been talking about the Senate, which is one house of Congress, and now we'll turn to the House of Representatives." Not all students are cognitively at the same place, and a transition signal alerts them that the lesson is making a conceptual shift—moving to a new topic—and allows them to prepare for it.

Emphasis consists of verbal and vocal cues that alert students to important information in a lesson. For example, Scott used a form of vocal emphasis—raising his voice—when he said, "Keep these ideas in mind" as he moved from his review to the lesson itself. Whenever you say something such as "Now remember, everyone, this is very important" or "Listen carefully now," you're using verbal emphasis.

MyLab Education
Video Example 13.4

Closure is a summary that helps learners pull different aspects of a topic together at the end of a lesson. Notice here how fifth-grade teacher, Myrlene Schenck, who has a number of ELL students in her class, helps them arrive at closure in a lesson emphasizing vocabulary development.

Repeating a point is another form of emphasis. Asking students, "What did we say these problems have in common?" stresses an important feature in the problems and helps them link new information to knowledge stored in their long-term memories. Redundancy is particularly important when reviewing abstract concepts, principles, and rules (Good & Lavigne, 2018).

Effective teachers also stay focused on their learning goals. If goals aren't clear, or if incidental information is interjected without indicating how it relates to the topic, students will struggle to follow the theme of the lesson, and learning will be reduced (Good & Lavigne, 2018).

Clear communication depends on knowledge of content. If we clearly understand the topics we teach, we'll use clearer language, our lessons will be more thematic, and we'll remain focused on our learning objectives to a greater extent than we would if we don't fully understand the topic (Staples, 2007). This suggests that, as we plan, we should carefully study any topics about which we're uncertain.

A final note with respect to our discussion of essential teaching skills. A large review of educational research indicates that effective teachers are adaptable. For instance, they adapt the way they ask questions, provide feedback, challenge and encourage students, and help them make connections. They " . . . adjust their teaching according to the social, linguistic, cultural, and instructional needs of their students" (Parsons et al., 2018, p. 205). The ability to adapt when necessary is an important aspect of expert teaching.

Classroom Connections

Implementing Instruction Effectively

Personal Qualities of Effective Teachers

1. Personal teaching efficacy, high expectations, modeling and enthusiasm, and caring are personal qualities of teachers that increase student motivation and achievement. Try to demonstrate these qualities in your work with students.

   - **Elementary:** A third-grade teacher communicates her personal efficacy and caring by calling a student's parents and soliciting their help as soon as the student fails to turn in an assignment or receives an unsatisfactory grade on a quiz or test.

   - **Middle School:** A seventh-grade teacher commits himself to being a role model by displaying the statement "I will always behave in the way I expect you to behave in this class" on the bulletin board. He uses the statement as a guiding principle in his class.

   - **High School:** A geometry teacher, knowing that her students initially have problems with proofs, conducts help sessions twice a week after school. "I would much rather help them than lower my expectations," she comments.

Organization and Communication

2. Effective organization helps teachers begin classes on time, have materials prepared, and maintain well-established routines. Carefully plan and organize materials and communicate clearly to maximize instructional time.

   - **Elementary:** A first-grade teacher has several boxes filled with frequently used science materials, such as soft drink bottles, balloons, matches, baking soda, vinegar, funnels, and a hot plate. The day before a science demonstration, he spends a few minutes selecting his materials from the boxes and sets them on a shelf near his desk so that he'll have everything ready at the beginning of the lesson.

   - **Middle School:** An eighth-grade American history teacher asks a member of her team to visit her class to provide feedback about her instruction. She also asks her colleague to check if she clearly emphasizes the important points in the lesson, sequences the presentation logically, and communicates changes in topics.

   - **High School:** A biology teacher begins each class with an outline of the day's topics and activities on the board. As she makes transitions from one activity to the other, she calls students' attention to the outline so students can understand where they've been and where they're going.

Focus and Feedback

3. Lesson focus helps attract and maintain student attention, and feedback provides students with information about their learning progress. Use problems, demonstrations, and displays to provide focus during lessons. Provide feedback throughout all learning experiences.

(continued)

- **Elementary:** A fourth-grade teacher beginning a study of different groups of animals brings a live lobster, a spider, and a grasshopper to class and builds a lesson on arthropods around these animals. After making a list of arthropods' characteristics on the board, she asks students if a clam is an arthropod. When some say it is, she provides feedback by referring them to the list and asking them to identify each characteristic in the clam. After a short discussion, they conclude that the clam isn't an arthropod.

- **Middle School:** A science teacher dealing with the concept of kindling temperature soaks a cloth in a water–alcohol mix, ignites it, and asks, "Why isn't the cloth burning?" He provides feedback during the class discussion by asking guiding questions to help students develop their understanding.

- **High School:** A physical education teacher shows students a video of a professional tennis player executing a nearly perfect backhand. She then records the students as they practice backhands, and they attempt to modify their technique to more nearly imitate the pro's swing.

Questioning and Review

4. Reviews help activate and consolidate students' prior knowledge, and questioning puts them in cognitively active roles. Begin and end each class with a short review and guide the review with questioning.

   - **Elementary:** A fifth-grade teacher whose class is studying different types of boundaries says, "We've looked at three kinds of boundaries between the states so far today. What are these three, and where do they occur?"

- **Middle School:** An English teacher begins, "We studied pronoun–antecedent agreement yesterday. Give me an example that illustrates this idea and explain why your example is correct."

- **High School:** An art teacher says, "Today we've found that many artists use color to create different moods. Let's summarize some of the ideas that we've learned about. Go ahead, offer one, someone."

Closure and Application

5. Closure and application are the processes of summarizing the topic and using the information in a different context. Bring lessons to closure and help students apply their understanding in new situations.

   - **Elementary:** A first-grade teacher has her students summarize the essential characteristics of basic shapes, such as a triangle has three sides and is a closed figure, versus non-essential characteristics, such as overall size, color, or orientation. She then has the students draw and label each of the basic shapes—square, circle, rectangle, triangle, parallelogram, and trapezoid.

   - **Middle School:** An eighth-grade English teacher has her students describe the difference between active and passive voice in writing. He then has his students write a short paragraph in which two examples of active voice and two examples of passive voice are embedded.

   - **High School:** An American history teacher has his students explain how we evaluate authors' premises and conclusions. She then presents her students with a political essay and two additional commentaries and has them use the commentaries to either corroborate or challenge the conclusions the author makes in the political essay.

MyLab Education Self-Check 13.2
MyLab Education Application Exercise 13.3: Implementing Instruction

In this exercise you will be asked to analyze a middle school geography teacher's demonstration of the personal qualities of effective teachers and application of essential teaching skills.

Models of Instruction

13.3 Describe models of instruction and explain the relationships between models of instruction and essential teaching skills.

As we saw in the previous section, displaying the personal qualities of effective teachers and demonstrating essential teaching skills increases students' learning regardless of content area or grade level. By comparison, **models of instruction** are prescriptive approaches to teaching designed to help students acquire deep understanding of specific forms of knowledge. Each is grounded in cognitive learning theory and supported by research.

Just as students use reading in all their content areas, essential teaching skills are used with all these models, and promoting student involvement is an integral and essential component of each. "Psychologists and educational scientists seem to converge on the notion that student involvement is key to successful learning" (Lazonder & Harmsen, 2016, p. 681).

Research also suggests that no single model is most effective for all students or all learning objectives (Knight, 2002; Marzano, 2003). In this section we examine four of the more widely used models:

- Direct instruction
- Lecture–discussion
- Guided discovery
- Cooperative learning

Direct Instruction

Direct instruction is a teaching model designed to help students acquire well-defined knowledge and skills needed for later learning. Young students using basic operations in math, students applying correct grammar and punctuation in writing, and chemistry students balancing equations are examples of these skills. Direct instruction is widely used, particularly in reading (Carnine, Silbert, Kame'enui, Slocum, & Travers, 2017) and math (Stein, Kinder, Rolf, Silbert, & Carnine, 2018).

The model has been thoroughly researched, and, when used by expert teachers, it's highly effective (Clark, Kirschner, & Sweller, 2012; Matlen & Klahr, 2013). And it's particularly effective in working with low achievers and students with exceptionalities (Turnbull, Turnbull, Wehmeyer, & Shogren, 2016).

Direct instruction occurs in four phases:

- Introduction and review
- Developing understanding
- Guided practice
- Independent practice

Table 13.2 outlines the phases and the cognitive learning component that provides the framework for each phase.

Now, let's look at the use of direct instruction in two different content areas.

Sam Barnett, a second-grade teacher, is working with his students on addition and subtraction of whole numbers to meet the standard:

> CCSS.Math.Content.2.OA.A.1 Use addition and subtraction within 100 to solve one- and two-step word problems involving situations of adding to, taking from, putting together, taking apart, and comparing, with unknowns in all positions, e.g., by using

TABLE 13.2 Phases in direct instruction

Phase	Cognitive Learning Component
Introduction and Review: Teachers begin with a form of introductory focus and review previous work.	- Attract attention. - Access prior knowledge from long-term memory.
Developing Understanding: Teachers describe and model the skill or explain and present examples of the concept. Teachers emphasize understanding.	- Acquire declarative knowledge about the skill or concept. - Encode declarative knowledge into long-term memory.
Guided Practice: Students practice the skill or identify additional examples of the concept, and the teacher provides scaffolding.	- Move through the associative stage of developing procedural knowledge.
Independent Practice: Students practice on their own.	- Develop automaticity with the skill or concept.

drawings and equations with a symbol for the unknown number to represent the problem. (Common Core State Standards Initiative, 2018n).

He begins by displaying the following problem on his document camera:

> Jana and Patti are saving special soda cans to get a free CD. They can get the CD if they save 35 cans. Jana has 15 cans and Patti has 12. How many do they have together?

[Jana and Patti are two students in Sam's class.]

He reviews adding single digit numbers, such as 8 + 7, and has his students represent the numbers as 1 group of 10 interlocking cubes and 5 single cubes at their desks as we see here.

He also writes

$$\begin{array}{r} 7 \\ +8 \\ \hline 15 \end{array}$$

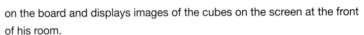

on the board and displays images of the cubes on the screen at the front of his room.

He refers the class back to the word problem he displayed, discusses the information in it, and then writes the following on the board

$$\begin{array}{r} 15 \\ +12 \\ \hline \end{array}$$

He demonstrates the solution with both the cubes and the numbers on the board and describes his thinking during the process.

He repeats each step with a second example and then gives the students a problem of their own to solve and demonstrate with their cubes as he watches their work. They discuss the solution and describe their thinking during the discussion. He repeats the process with two more examples, and then assigns five problems as seatwork. While most of the class works on the problems, he calls Cathy, Josh, and Jeremy to the back of the room, where he provides them with extra instructional support.

Now, let's look at another example.

Vanesa Rodriguez, an eighth-grade English teacher, is working with her students on the following standard:

> CCSS.ELA-Literacy.L.8.1a Explain the function of verbals (gerunds, participles, infinitives) in general and their function in particular sentences. (Common Core State Standards Initiative, 2018r).

She is focusing on gerunds and participles in today's lesson, and she begins by writing the words *jumping, running, talking,* and *sleeping* on the board and asking students what part of speech they represent, to which they respond, "Verbs." She continues by reviewing other parts of speech, such as nouns, pronouns, adjectives, and adverbs.

She then explains that context can determine the way verb forms are used, and she displays the following on her document camera.

> Running is a very good form of exercise, and athletes, such as running backs in football, have to be in very good physical shape. I'm going to go running this afternoon.

She notes that *running* is used in three different ways in the two sentences and explains that it is first used as a noun (Running is the subject in "Running is a very good form of exercise"). Then "running" (in "running backs") is used as an adjective, and in the second sentence it's used as a verb. She explains that verb forms used as nouns are called gerunds, and used as adjectives, they're called participles. She then has the students explain how they will know if a verb form is a verb or if it is a different part of speech, and she asks them to explain how this relates to context.

Vanesa then displays the following:

I'm not going to be jumping up to do any work anytime soon. In the first place, I don't want to feel like a jumping bean in my own house, and in the second, I don't think that jumping is all that good for you.

She gives the students a few seconds to identify the way *jumping* is used in the two sentences, and then asks them to discuss what they've found. They conclude that it's a verb in the first sentence, a gerund in the first clause of the second sentence, and a participle in the second clause of the second sentence.

She gives the students an additional example and has them discuss it as they did with the first, and finally she has them write a paragraph in which they must embed and label at least two examples each of verb forms used as verbs, gerunds, and participles.

Now, let's look at Sam's and Vanesa's use of direct instruction.

Introduction and Review. Sam began his lesson with the problem involving Jana and Patti, which provided focus for the lesson, and he then reviewed addition of single digit numbers. Vanesa began hers by writing examples of verb forms on the board and reviewing other parts of speech.

Both lessons were grounded in cognitive learning theory. We know that learning begins with attention, and Sam used his problem—and personalized it by embedding two of his students' names in it—to attract their attention, and Vanesa provided focus with her words on the board and asking her students what part of speech they represented. They both then activated their students' background knowledge with their reviews. These actions make sense and are supported by research (Kirschner, Sweller, & Clark, 2006). However, many lessons begin with little or no attempt to attract attention or activate relevant prior knowledge (Brophy, 2010).

Developing Understanding. After a review, the next phase in direct instruction is designed to provide students with new information they can connect to their existing understanding. Once this connection is made and organized in working memory, they will encode their new knowledge—represent it in long-term memory, ready to be retrieved and connected to the next set of new information.

Sam completed this phase when he modeled the process—including cognitive modeling as he described his thinking—for adding two-digit numbers. Vanesa used her example displayed on the document camera for the same purpose. She also used cognitive modeling by explaining that *running* was used as a noun in the first part of her example, as an adjective in the second, and as a verb in the third.

Sam and Vanesa both emphasized understanding in this phase. When solving problems, students often follow procedures mechanically or use superficial strategies, such as adding when they see the words "how many altogether" or subtracting when they see "how many more" in math problems (Jitendra et al., 2007; Mayer, 2008). Instead, Sam had his students demonstrate the solution with their cubes and use them to explain what they had done.

Vanesa emphasized understanding with her simple—but clever—example combined with her explanation and students verbalizing their understanding. Her example provided the context her students needed to see that *running* was first used as a noun, then an adjective, and finally a verb.

It is important to have students verbalize their understanding, as both Sam and Vanesa did. Vygotsky's work reminds us that language is an essential part of learning and development, and the more opportunities students have to put their understanding into words, the deeper that understanding becomes.

Not spending the time needed to develop adequate levels of understanding is the most common mistake teachers make when using direct instruction. Students won't develop deep understanding if we emphasize memorization, don't ask enough questions, or move too quickly to practice. Or we may involve learners in hands-on activities but fail to establish the connection between the materials, such as the cubes, and the abstractions they represent (the numbers in the problem) (Ball, 1992). For instance, asking students to explain and demonstrate the difference between 2 in 12 and 2 in 21 helps them understand place value, but teachers often fail to emphasize this connection.

Guided Practice.   Once students have developed an understanding of the procedure, they begin practicing as we monitor their progress. Initially, we use questioning to provide enough scaffolding to ensure success, but not so much that challenge is eliminated. As students practice, they gradually develop automaticity and become confident with the new content (Péladeau, Forget, & Gagné, 2003). Sam had his students work a problem, and they discussed it afterward so he could be sure that they understood the process. He continued with guided practice until he believed that most students were ready to work on their own.

APA Top 20 Principles

This description illustrates Principle 5: *Acquiring long-term knowledge and skill is largely dependent on practice*—from the *Top 20 Principles from Psychology for PreK–12 Teaching and Learning*.

During her guided practice, Vanesa provided another example, in which the verb form *jumping* was used first as a verb, then as a participle, and finally as a gerund. She did this on purpose. In her first example *running* was initially used as a gerund, then a participle, and finally a verb. Vanesa purposely changed the sequence so her students would need to make their conclusions based on context instead of the same order as the original example. This simple but thoughtful move on her part is a mark of teaching expertise.

Independent Practice.   In this final phase of direct instruction, we reduce scaffolding and shift responsibility to students. Our goal is for them to be able to perform the skill automatically, so working memory space can later be devoted to higher-level applications. This is the phase in which students apply their understanding in new contexts and employs the essential teaching skill *closure and application* (Feldon, 2007).

Monitoring students' progress continues to be important. Expert teachers move around the room to ensure that students are on task and working successfully; their less effective counterparts are more likely to work at their desks or merely check to see that students are on task (Brophy, 2006; Safer & Fleischman, 2005).

Homework.   Homework is a common form of independent practice, and, perhaps surprisingly, it's somewhat controversial. Some authors have argued that it's ineffective and even destructive (Bennett & Kalish, 2006; Kohn, 2007).

Research, however, consistently indicates that homework, properly designed and implemented, increases achievement. For instance, in a review examining 16 years of research, Cooper, Robinson, and Patall (2006) found " . . . generally consistent evidence for a positive influence of homework on achievement" (p. 1). More recent research confirms these findings (Baş, 2017; Williams, Swift, Williams, & Van Daal, 2017). Further, because students must take responsibility for doing the homework, some research suggests that it increases conscientiousness and self-regulation (Göllner et al., 2017; Xu & Wu, 2013).

Properly designed and implemented is the key to homework's effectiveness. Simply assigning homework doesn't increase achievement, and more isn't necessarily better. Increasing the amount of homework in the name of academic rigor is ineffective at best and, at worst, can decrease both motivation and achievement (Carr, 2013; Vatterott, 2014).

The amount of cognitive effort—thinking—students apply in completing homework is the primary factor influencing its effectiveness, and cognitive motivation theory helps us understand how to increase effort (Trautwein, Ludtke, & Schnyder, 2006). Three factors are involved. The first is perceived value. If students believe that homework will increase their understanding, they're likely to conscientiously work on it (Carr, 2013). Homework perceived as busywork, particularly for older students, detracts from motivation and does little to promote learning. Assigning more exercises than necessary can be counterproductive, and older students are unlikely to complete homework assignments for which they receive no credit (Marzano & Pickering, 2007).

Second, students must be generally successful, so their perceptions of competence and self-efficacy are increased (Carr, 2013). Third, students are much more likely to do homework if their parents expect it and monitor the extent to which it is done (Williams et al., 2017).

The characteristics of effective homework are summarized in Table 13.3, together with developmental differences between elementary and middle/secondary students (Carr, 2013; Marzano & Pickering, 2007).

Lecture–Discussion

Lecture–discussion is an instructional model designed to help students acquire **organized bodies of knowledge**, topics that connect facts, concepts, and generalizations, and make the relationships among them explicit (Eggen & Kauchak, 2012; Rosenshine, 1987). For example, students acquire organized bodies of knowledge when they examine the relationships among plot, character, and symbolism in a novel such as *To Kill a Mockingbird* in literature; study landforms, climate, and economy in different countries in geography; or compare parasitic and nonparasitic worms and how differences between them are reflected in their body structures in biology.

Because lecture–discussions are modifications of traditional lectures, and because lecturing is so common in classrooms, we briefly examine them before turning to lecture–discussions.

Lectures

The prevalence of lecturing in our nation's schools is paradoxical. Although the most criticized of all teaching methods, it is the most widely used (Cuban, 1993; Friesen, 2011). Some reasons for its popularity include:

- *Efficiency*. Planning time for lectures is limited to organizing content.
- *Flexibility*. Lectures can be applied to most content areas and topics.
- *Simplicity*. When lecturing, cognitive load is low, so teachers' working memory space can be devoted exclusively to presenting content. Sophisticated teaching skills, such as questioning, prompting, and providing feedback, aren't used, so even novice teachers can learn to deliver acceptable lectures.

Lectures also have some strengths. For instance, they can help students acquire information not readily accessible in other ways, and they can be effective if the goal

TABLE 13.3 Characteristics of effective homework at different developmental levels

Level	Characteristic
All Levels	• Aligned with learning objectives and learning activities • Clear directions • High success rates • Feedback provided • Parental involvement
Elementary	• A quiet place, free from distractions, to do homework • Part of the regular class routine
Middle and Secondary	• Clear reasons for the importance of the homework • Credit, such as points toward an overall grade

is to provide students with information that would be time-consuming to find on their own (Friesen, 2011). They can also help students integrate information from a variety of sources, and they can expose students to different points of view. If we're trying to accomplish one or more of these goals, lecturing can be effective.

Despite their strengths and popularity, lectures have important weaknesses:

- They often fail to maintain students' attention. We've all sat through mind-numbing lectures, hoping to simply pass the time as quickly as possible.
- They don't allow teachers to gauge students' understanding.
- While lowering cognitive load for teachers, they impose a heavy cognitive load on learners, so information is frequently lost from working memory before it can be transferred to long-term memory.
- They put learners in cognitively passive roles. This is inconsistent with cognitive views of learning and is arguably their primary disadvantage.

Lectures are especially problematic for young students because of their short attention spans and limited vocabularies, and they're ineffective if higher-order thinking is a goal. In a historical analysis of seven studies comparing lecturing to discussion, discussion was superior in all seven on measures of retention and higher-order thinking. In addition, discussion was superior on measures of student attitude and motivation (McKeachie & Kulik, 1975). Because lectures have a long history of criticism, considerable emphasis—including emphasis at the college and university level—is being placed on teaching methods that put students in more cognitively active roles (Poirier, 2017; Riley & Ward, 2017).

Overcoming the Weaknesses of Lectures: Lecture–Discussions

Lecture–discussions help overcome the weaknesses of lectures by combining teacher questioning with the presentation of information.

Lecture–discussions exist in four phases:

- Introduction and review
- Presenting information
- Comprehension monitoring
- Integration

Table 13.4 outlines these phases and the cognitive learning theory components that support each phase.

Now, let's look at a lesson in which Diane Anderson, a 10th-grade American history teacher, is working with her students on events leading up to the American Revolutionary War. Look for the phases of lecture–discussion as you read the case study.

TABLE 13.4 Phases of lecture–discussion and cognitive learning components

Phase	Cognitive Learning Component
Introduction and Review: The teacher begins with a form of introductory focus and reviews previous work.	• Attract attention. • Access prior knowledge from long-term memory.
Presenting Information: The teacher presents information. The teacher keeps presentations short to prevent overloading learners' working memories.	• Acquire declarative knowledge about the topic.
Comprehension Monitoring: The teacher asks a series of questions to check learners' understanding.	• Check students' perceptions. • Put students in cognitively active roles. • Begin schema construction.
Integration: The teacher asks additional questions to help learners integrate new and prior knowledge.	• Construct integrated schemas that organize information and reduce cognitive load.

Diane's students have been reading about American history prior to the Revolutionary War in their textbooks, and she wants them to meet the following standard.

> CCSS.ELA-Literacy.RH.9-10.3 Analyze in detail a series of events described in a text; determine whether earlier events caused later ones or simply preceded them (Common Core State Standards Initiative, 2018s).

She asks her students how historical events, such as the French and Indian War and the Boston Tea Party, relate to the Revolutionary War, and after they offer some ideas, she notes that their objective for the day is to understand these relationships. She then reviews a timeline starting with Jamestown in 1607 and leading to the middle 1700s.

She continues by describing French efforts to settle in North America, notes that at least 35 of our present 50 states were originally mapped by the French, and points out that they founded some of our major cities, such as St. Louis, Detroit, and New Orleans.

She has her students summarize what she's said, uses a map at the front of the room to identify the geography of the French and British settlements, and presents information about French relationships with Native Americans and French policies of giving land to settlers if they would serve in the military.

She then notes that the British wanted to expand across the Appalachian Mountains, has the students discuss the conflict that was inevitable—the French and Indian War—and explains why it was costly for the British, and what the British did to raise revenue—impose heavy taxes on the colonists. She has them link these events to the colonists' rebellion, such as the Boston Tea Party, and finally, she has her students link the entire discussion to the standard.

Now, let's look at another example.

Dan Roundfield, a seventh-grade life science teacher, is working with his students on the classification of living things, and he wants them to meet the following standard:

> CCSS.ELA-Literacy.RST.6-8.4 Determine the meaning of symbols, key terms, and other domain-specific words and phrases as they are used in a specific scientific or technical context relevant to grades 6–8 texts and topics. (Common Core State Standards Initiative, 2018t).

He begins by displaying a rock, paper clip, potted plant, clam shell, lobster, and a picture of the class (which he had taken the first day of the school year) on a desk at the front of the room. He then asks his students how the rock and paper clip are different from the other items and prompts them to say "living things."

He then notes that scientists wanted a system to organize and classify these living things and says that developing an understanding of this classification system is their objective for the next several days.

He then takes the rock and paper clip off the desk, points to the rest of the items, and notes that most macroscopic creatures are either plants or animals, so they belong to either the plant kingdom or animal kingdom, as he points to the plant and then to the other items. He points out that the distinction is primarily based on sources of nutrition and the capability of locomotion, with plants producing their own food through photosynthesis, but unable to move on their own. Animals, in contrast, are able to move on their own, but must eat other organisms to obtain food.

He then stops and asks the students to describe the following terms: classification, kingdom, locomotion, and photosynthesis. When they struggle with a term, such as locomotion, he writes the following on the board:

> Because plants can't move on their own, we say they aren't capable of locomotion.

He does the same with the other terms, reminding the students that they should use the context in which words are used to help them understand the meaning of technical terms.

He then continues by noting that the next level of classification is the phylum; holds up the lobster, noting its external skeleton, three body parts and jointed limbs; and says it belongs to the phylum Arthropoda, commonly called arthropods. He then holds up the clam and notes that it belongs to the phylum Mollusca (mollusks) and explains that mollusks are usually enclosed in hard shells and have soft, unsegmented bodies. He notes that classification into a phylum depends largely on body structure and organization.

He stops providing information again; shows them pictures of insects, spiders, oysters, and snails; and asks them to what kingdom and phylum they belong. He also asks the students if they (the students) are either arthropods or mollusks, and after they conclude they aren't, he asks them why not.

Dan then continues the process by introducing the phylum Chordata (chordates) and asking them to identify a number of examples that would fit this phylum, such as themselves and other animals with backbones, such as fish, birds, reptiles, and other mammals. He then asks them to try and identify examples that don't fit any of the three phyla, and with some prompting, the students identify different types of worms as examples.

Now, let's look at Diane's and Dan's applications of the lecture–discussion model.

Introduction and Review.   As with direct instruction, lecture–discussion is grounded in cognitive learning theory, and, as we've emphasized repeatedly, all learning begins with attention. Diane attempted to attract her students' attention by asking them how events such as the French and Indian War and the Boston Tea Party relate to the Revolutionary War. Then, to activate her students' background knowledge, she had them review a historical timeline.

Dan attempted to attract his students' attention by referring them to the items displayed on the desk at the front of the room and asking how the rock and paper clip were different from the other items. He then reviewed the concept of classification.

Presenting Information.   Diane began this phase by presenting information about Jamestown, Quebec, French settlements in the present-day United States, and cities in our country that were originally founded by the French.

Dan presented information about the animal and plant kingdoms and the characteristics of each, such as plants lacking locomotion but making their own food, and animals being able to move on their own but needing to acquire food from others.

The *presenting information* phase capitalizes on the advantages of lectures, that is, it provides students with information they would have trouble acquiring on their own and integrates information from a variety of sources.

Both Diane and Dan kept this phase very short. We know that attention spans, for all people, are short, and we're easily distracted, so to maximize the likelihood of maintaining students' attention, both Diane and Dan quickly turned to *comprehension monitoring*, the next phase.

Comprehension Monitoring.   After her brief presentation, Diane used questioning to involve her students in the comprehension-monitoring phase. To check their perceptions, she had them summarize the information she presented, and she also referred them to a map so they could see how the geography of the area related to the English and French settlements.

Dan's efforts in this phase were more complex and demanding. To meet his standard, he wanted his students to understand technical terms, such as *classification, kingdom, locomotion,* and *photosynthesis.* Understandably, they struggled with some of the terms, and so he elaborated by writing statements on the board that would help them use context (and meet the standard) to aid in making the terms meaningful. (He would also spend a great deal more time helping them understand photosynthesis, but for today's lesson, he merely wanted them to understand that it's the process by which plants make their own food.)

The comprehension-monitoring phase is designed to cognitively engage students, check their perceptions, make sure they understand the new information, and begin the process of schema construction, ultimately leading to encoding.

Integration.   After interacting with their students to check their perceptions and understanding of the topics to this point in their lessons, both teachers then presented additional information designed to be integrated with the students' existing knowledge. Diane, for example, presented information about the French policy of giving land to settlers if they served in the military, the French relationship with Native Americans, British desires to move west across the Appalachian Mountains, and the inevitable conflict it caused with the French. All this led to war, which was costly, leading to onerous tax demands on the colonists, and ultimately to the colonists' revolt.

After ensuring that his students understood key concepts and how they could use context to help them with their understanding, Dan presented information about phyla, provided examples of arthropods, mollusks, and chordates, and asked his students for examples of each.

Integration exists in a series of cycles, with each cycle adding more related information to the preceding cycle. As the information is integrated, learners' schemas become more complex and interconnected, with the goal of well-organized understanding ultimately being encoded in students' long-term memories.

Because students construct their own knowledge, their schemas won't necessarily mirror the way we organize the body of knowledge. The discussion components of lecture–discussions allow us to assess the validity of students' schema constructions and help them reconstruct their understanding when necessary. This is a primary reason lecture–discussion is more effective than traditional lecture.

Lecture–Discussions Versus "Pure" Student-Led Discussion

The quality of lecture–discussion lessons largely depends on how effectively we guide the discussions. One of the problems with discussions that are student led is their tendency to meander and drift off the point (Will, 2016). Students resent both this loss of focus and classrooms that become controlled by students instead of teachers. "Repeatedly, students told me they could learn twice as much in half the time if teachers rein in their rambling peers" (Downey, 2016, para. 3).

Student-led discussions can be effective learning tools, but two conditions are essential. First, the students must have enough background knowledge to make the discussion meaningful. Often, they do not, so the discussion disintegrates into rambling, uninformed opinions that are dominated by the most extroverted and socially aggressive students.

Second, teachers must carefully monitor the progress of the discussion to ensure that it stays focused on the learning objectives. Failure to do so can lead to the issues we mentioned above. For these reasons, we prefer lecture–discussions to pure student-led discussions. The lecture component helps develop students' background knowledge, and teachers carefully monitor the progress of the discussion component.

Guided Discovery

Guided discovery is an instructional model that involves teachers' scaffolding students' constructions of concepts and the relationships among them (Eggen & Kauchak, 2012; Mayer, 2008). When using the model, we identify learning objectives, arrange information so that patterns can be found, and guide students to the objectives.

When using "discovery" models, teachers sometimes believe that students should be left essentially on their own to *discover* the ideas being taught (Kirschner et al., 2006). Teachers correctly believe that learners construct their own knowledge, but sometimes assume " . . . that the best way to promote such construction is to have students try to discover new knowledge or solve new problems without explicit guidance from the teacher. Unfortunately, this assumption is both widespread and incorrect" (Clark et al., 2012, p. 8).

Doing so allows misconceptions to form, wastes time, and often leaves students frustrated (Purpura, Baroody, Eiland, & Reid, 2016).

In contrast, "guided" discovery—and other forms of learner-centered instruction, such as inquiry and problem-based learning—is highly scaffolded, and teachers play an essential role in guiding students' learning progress (Lazonder & Harmsen, 2016; Purpura, et al., 2016).

When done well, guided discovery is highly effective (Mardanparvar, Sabohi, & Rezaei, 2016; Yuliana, Tasari, & Wijayanti, 2017). "Guided discovery may take more or less time than expository instruction, depending on the task, but tends to result in better long-term retention and transfer than expository instruction" (Mayer, 2002, p. 68).

When using guided discovery we spend less time explaining and more time asking questions, so students have more opportunities to share their thinking and put their developing understanding into words. Also, because of the high levels of student involvement, guided discovery tends to increase students' intrinsic interest in the topic being studied (Yuliana et al., 2017).

Guided discovery occurs in four phases:

- Introduction and review
- The open-ended phase
- The convergent phase
- Closure and application

Table 13.5 outlines these phases and the cognitive learning components that provide the theoretical framework for them.

Scott's lesson on Bernoulli's Principle is an application of guided discovery. Let's look at another example. We saw how Vanesa Rodriguez used direct instruction to help her students understand verbals. Steve Kapner, another teacher in the same school, is working with his students on the same topic and standard, but he decides to use guided discovery instead of direct instruction.

Steve begins, as Vanesa did, by reviewing parts of speech and having his students provide examples of each. He then displays the following.

> I'm running three miles on Mondays, Wednesdays, and Fridays now. I'm walking four miles a day on Tuesdays and Thursdays. And, I'm relaxing on Saturdays and Sundays.

> Running is the best form of exercise that exists, I think. But, walking is also good, and it's easier on my knees. Relaxing a couple days a week also helps my body recover.

TABLE 13.5 The phases of guided discovery and cognitive learning components

Phase	Cognitive Learning Component
Introduction and Review: The teacher begins with a form of introductory focus and reviews previous work.	• Attract attention. • Activate prior knowledge.
The Open-Ended Phase: The teacher provides examples and asks for observations and comparisons.	• Provide experiences from which learners will construct knowledge. • Promote social interaction.
The Convergent Phase: The teacher guides students as they search for patterns in the examples.	• Begin schema production. • Promote social interaction.
Closure: With the teacher's guidance, students state a definition of the concept or a description of the relationship among concepts.	• Complete schema production.
Application: The teacher has students use the concept or principle to explain another (ideally) real-world example.	• Promote transfer.

My running times have gone down since I've lost some weight. I have some new walking gear, so I look decent out on the road. Both make my relaxing environment just that much more pleasant.

"Now, look at the three short paragraphs, and tell me what you notice," Steve begins.

He calls on several individual students to make observations about the paragraphs, which range from "Each paragraph has three sentences in it" to "Each is about exercise" and "The words *running, walking,* and *relaxing* are in all three," among a number of others.

After the students have made their observations, Steve directs them to the first paragraph and has them identify the subject and verb in each sentence, to which they respond "I" for the subject in each case, and *running, walking,* and *relaxing* as the verbs.

He does the same with the second paragraph, and the students conclude that *running, walking,* and *relaxing* are the subjects of these sentences.

Steve notes that the words are used differently in the first two paragraphs and asks the students to decide how they're used in the third. After some discussion, they conclude that *running, walking,* and *relaxing* are used as adjectives.

He tells the students that the words are *gerunds* in the second paragraph and *participles* in the third, and he then helps the students verbalize a definition of each, which he writes on the board.

He then has them write a paragraph in which they must embed and label at least two examples of verb forms used as verbs, two examples of verb forms used as gerunds, and two examples used as participles.

Now, let's look at both Steve's and Scott's use of guided discovery to help students reach their standards. (You might want to review Scott's lesson again before studying the following sections.)

Introduction and Review.   Scott began his lesson by reviewing the concept of *force* and the influence of different forces on an object (objects move in the direction of a greater force). Steve began by reviewing parts of speech. The reviews activated students' prior knowledge, and both teachers used examples to attract their students' attention, such as Scott pushing on the board and tugging on the stapler, and Steve having his students offer examples of each part of speech.

The Open-Ended Phase.   Scott implemented the open-ended phase when he had students blow over the pieces of paper, between the papers, and through the necks of the funnels. Each example illustrated Bernoulli's Principle. After his students worked with the examples, Scott asked for observations, such as "What did you notice when we blew over the top? . . . David?" and "What did you notice here? . . . Sharon?"

Steve displayed his three paragraphs and began by saying "Now, look at the three short paragraphs, and tell me what you notice."

The open-ended phase has several benefits for both the teacher and students. First, open-ended questions are easy to ask, so we can call on a wide variety of students—practice equitable distribution—very quickly. Second, questions in this phase are easy to answer—students literally describe what they're observing—so we can involve students who typically don't try to answer or are often unable to answer correctly. Third, when students understand that we really do want them to tell us what they observe—as opposed to typical questions requiring a specific answer—their efforts to respond increase, sometimes dramatically; student involvement is easier to achieve; and motivation often increases. And, finally, students respond according to what they perceive in the examples, so the questions give us some insight into their thinking.

The Convergent Phase.   During the convergent phase, the teacher helps students find patterns in the data they are analyzing. The convergent phase continues to capitalize on social interaction to promote schema construction and encourage active involvement of all students. Scott began the transition to the convergent phase when he drew the sketches on the board and had students restate the observations and conclusions. Let's look again at some dialogue.

Scott:	Was I blowing on the top or the bottom? . . . Rachel? (Referring to the first sketch)
Rachel:	The top.
Scott:	And what happened there? . . . Heather?
Heather:	The paper rose up.

Scott then guided the students to conclude that still (not moving) air pushed the paper up because the paper rose up, and in the second example conclude that the still air pushed the papers together, and held the ping-pong ball in the mouth of the funnel in the third.

Steve's process was similar. He began moving to the convergent phase when he had his students identify the subject and verb in the first paragraph and conclude that *running, walking,* and *relaxing* were the verbs in each case. He continued by guiding the students to conclude that *running, walking,* and *relaxing* were the subjects of the sentences in the second paragraph, and he did the same with the third paragraph, guiding them to conclude that the verb forms were used as adjectives in this case.

Neither Scott nor Steve simply "told" their students what they were supposed to understand, as might occur in a more teacher-centered lesson, but they both strongly guided their students' developing understanding. As we saw earlier, this guidance is essential.

Closure and Application.   Closure completes the process of schema construction. Scott's lesson came to closure when he said, "Now let's look at the forces and where we blew. Study the drawings carefully and see what kind of relationship exists between the two." Steve brought his lesson to closure when he had his students verbalize a definition of *gerunds* and *participles.*

When we move lessons to closure, our questioning provides scaffolding for students as they attempt to put their understanding into words.

Closure is particularly important when using guided discovery because the direction of the lesson may be less obvious than it is with either direct instruction or lecture–discussion. Putting the definition of a concept into words, as was the case in Steve's lesson, or stating the principle, in Scott's, helps eliminate uncertainty that may remain in students' thinking.

Scott had his students apply their understanding by having them use Bernoulli's Principle to help explain how airplanes are able to fly, and Steve had his students apply their understanding by writing a paragraph in which verb forms were used as verbs, gerunds, and participles.

Notice also that Steve's and Vanesa's lessons (even though Steve used guided discovery and Vanesa used direct instruction) were similar in several ways. For instance, their reviews were similar, as were the ways in which they had their students apply their understanding. They both used examples to illustrate *gerunds* and *participles,* and they embedded their examples in the context of short paragraphs. And they both strongly guided their students' developing understanding.

The primary difference between the two was in the amount and kind of interaction between the teacher and students. As we saw earlier, when using guided discovery, we spend less time explaining and more time asking questions, so student involvement is higher than with direct instruction. This was illustrated in Steve's lesson compared to Vanesa's.

Because of this involvement and because students have more opportunities to put their understanding into words, guided discovery tends to increase students' intrinsic interest in the topic being studied, which can also lead to deeper understanding (Baeten, Struyven, & Dochy, 2013; Yuliana et al., 2017).

Guided discovery is a sophisticated strategy, and you might initially be a bit intimidated by it. However, research indicates that, with practice and effort, it can be mastered (Janssen, Westbroek, & Driel, 2014). And, when you do master it, you will have a powerful learning tool at your disposal. Further, seeing the light go on over students' heads after you've guided their knowledge constructions can be both fun and rewarding.

MyLab Education Application Exercise 13.4: Using Models of Instruction

In this exercise you will be asked to explain how you would teach a topic using two of the models of instruction described in this section.

Cooperative Learning

Cooperative learning is a set of instructional strategies in which students work in mixed-ability groups to reach specific cognitive and social development objectives. Cooperative learning strongly emphasizes social interaction, and research suggests that groups of learners co-construct more powerful understanding than individuals do alone (Slavin, 2015). This co-constructed knowledge can then be internalized by individuals.

Although a single view doesn't exist, most researchers agree that cooperative learning consists of students working together in groups small enough so that everyone can participate in a clearly assigned task. Groups can range from two to five, but four is an ideal number, because it allows the flexibility of students working in pairs in addition to working as a whole team (Slavin, 2014). Cooperative learning also shares four other features (Cohen & Lotan, 2014; Johnson & Johnson, 2017; Slavin, 2014):

- Learning objectives direct the groups' activities.

- Discussions in small groups require explanation and argumentation, not merely social interaction. Groups must be carefully monitored to ensure that the activity doesn't become simply a social encounter.

- Teachers hold students individually accountable for their understanding. The effort and performance of each group member is assessed, and the results are given back to the group and the individual to ensure that each group member contributes to the group effort.

- Learners depend on one another to reach objectives.

The last characteristic, called *positive interdependence,* exists when individuals believe they can reach their goals only if others in their group also reach *their* goals (Johnson & Johnson, 2017). It's important because it emphasizes the role of peer cooperation in learning.

Unlike direct instruction, lecture–discussion, and guided discovery, cooperative learning activities don't follow a specific set of steps, which is why we describe them as "strategies" instead of "models." However, successful implementation of cooperative learning requires as much thought and planning as does using any model.

Forming Cooperative Groups

Although some teachers allow students to form their own groups, experts believe this is unwise (Johnson & Johnson, 2017; Slavin, 2014). Groups should be as heterogeneous as possible, which means they should be composed of higher and lower achievers, boys and girls, members of cultural minorities and mainstream students, and students with and without exceptionalities. Cognitive objectives guide the group activities, but social-emotional development is an important reason for using cooperative groups, and the heterogeneous makeup is important for promoting this development.

MyLab Education
Video Example 13.5

Cooperative learning, instructional strategies that involve students working in groups to reach both cognitive and social-emotional learning objectives, strongly emphasizes social interaction. Notice here that the teacher, when satisfied that the students are interacting effectively, leaves the group to help them acquire the independence that can lead to productive learning on their own.

Introducing Cooperative Learning

Students aren't automatically good at cooperative learning, and some—particularly in middle schools—may view cooperative activities more as opportunities to socialize than to meet learning objectives (Wentzel, 2009). The following suggestions can help get the process started with students.

- Seat group members together so they can move back and forth from group work to whole-class activities with little disruption.
- Have materials ready for easy distribution to each group.
- Introduce students to cooperative learning with short, simple tasks, and make objectives and directions very specific.
- Specify the amount of time available to accomplish the task and keep it relatively short.
- Monitor groups while they work.
- Require that students produce a product, such as written answers to specific questions, as an outcome of the activity.

These suggestions are designed to minimize disruptions and maximize the likelihood of students remaining on task, particularly when we first introduce them to cooperative learning activities.

Cooperative Learning Strategies

Social constructivism provides the framework for all cooperative learning strategies, and those most widely used are outlined in Table 13.6. Other forms of cooperative learning exist, and although they differ in format, all incorporate the suggestions described earlier. As with all forms of instruction, no single cooperative learning strategy can reach all learning objectives, and cooperative learning should not be overused.

Evaluating Cooperative Learning

As an instructional strategy cooperative learning is very popular worldwide, and a great deal of research examining the strategies has been conducted in countries ranging as widely as Iran (Ghahraman & Tamimy, 2017), Turkey (Kirbas, 2017), Switzerland (Buchs, Filippou, Volpé, & Pulfrey, 2017), and Canada (Gagné & Parks, 2013). It's also been used at all levels of instruction, including doctoral programs (Roseth, Akcaoglu, & Zellner, 2013).

TABLE 13.6 Cooperative learning strategies

Strategy	Description	Example
Think–Pair–Share	Individuals in a pair answer a teacher question and then share it with their partner. The teacher calls on pairs to respond to the original question.	A world history teacher says, "Identify two factors or events that the Russian Revolution, which began in 1917, had in common with the French Revolution that began in 1789. . . . Turn to your partner, see what both of you think, and we'll discuss your answers in a minute."
Reciprocal Questioning	Pairs work together to ask and answer questions about a lesson or text.	A teacher provides question stems, such as "Summarize . . ." or "Why was . . . important?", and students use the stems to create specific questions about the topic.
Scripted Cooperation	Pairs work together to elaborate on each other's thinking.	Math: First member of a pair offers a problem solution. The second member then checks the answer, asks clarifying questions, and the process is repeated. Reading: Pairs read a passage, and the first member offers a summary. The second edits and adds to it, and the process continues.
Jigsaw II	Individuals become expert on subsections of a topic and teach it to others in their group.	One student studies the geography of a region, another the economy, a third the climate. Each attends "expert" meetings, and the "experts" then teach the content to others in their group.
Student Teams Achievement Divisions (STAD)	Social interaction helps students learn facts, concepts, and skills.	The independent practice phase of direct instruction is replaced with team study, during which team members check and compare their answers. Team study is followed by quizzes, and individual improvement points lead to team awards.

Research conducted more than 20 years ago found that even then it was one of the most widely used approaches to instruction in our country's schools, with more than 90% of elementary teachers using some form of cooperative learning in their classrooms (Antil, Jenkins, Wayne, & Vadasy, 1998). This figure is misleading, however, because teachers commonly describe any form of student group work as cooperative learning. But, as we saw earlier, it involves much more than simply having students work in groups (Cohen & Lotan, 2014).

Reactions to cooperative learning are mixed. For instance, some advocates suggest that it can increase student achievement and improve problem-solving abilities and interpersonal skills (Gillies, 2014; Slavin, 2014). And it can also increase motivation. When implemented effectively, it involves all students, which can be difficult in whole-class activities where less confident learners have fewer chances to participate. Cooperative learning advocates go further and suggest that research results are generally positive (Tsay & Brady, 2010) or even "overwhelmingly positive" (Brown & Ciuffetelli, 2009).

On the other hand, simply putting students into groups doesn't ensure either increased achievement or motivation (Baloche & Brody, 2017). And, in fact, teachers are much more likely to involve students in simple group work than in the structured cooperative learning strategies we've described here (Buchs, Filippou, Volpé, & Pulfrey, 2017). One factor detracting from the effectiveness of groups is status. Cohen (1994) observed that pupils implicitly rated themselves along a status continuum, and these ratings impacted their interactions in groups, with high-status students dominating discussions and lower-status students emotionally withdrawing. The result was inequitable interaction in the groups, which detracted from the social-emotional development considered an important outcome of working in cooperative groups.

The problem of status and ability goes farther. For instance, when students are organized into mixed-ability groups, those with higher ability often feel they are being exploited by slackers and, in fact, frequently prefer to work alone (Cohen & Lotan, 2014; Will, 2016). "Speaking of group projects, most students hate them and wonder why schools revere them" (Downey, 2016, para. 8). While cooperative learning and group projects aren't the same thing, some of the issues involved in group projects also apply to cooperative learning.

Also, the methods used to assess the effectiveness of cooperative learning can be problematic (Tsay & Brady, 2010), so the suggestion that research uniformly supports the effectiveness of cooperative learning needs to be viewed with caution.

These results have several implications for us when we plan cooperative activities. For instance, simply telling students that we expect them to collaborate improves interaction (Saleh, Lazonder, & de Jong, 2007). Second, carefully monitoring groups to ensure that they're meeting our expectations is important. And third, individual accountability is essential. Students know that not all group members make equal contributions to tasks, so group grading—grading in which all students in groups receive the same grade—causes resentment in students who make greater contributions (Slavin, 2014).

Finally, cooperative learning is a set of strategies, and only strategies, which means we use them to help reach different learning objectives, such as learning to work together, developing communication skills, or content objectives. They are never objectives in themselves. If we believe we can best reach learning objectives with a cooperative strategy, using it is appropriate; putting students into groups for its own sake, however, is not.

Like all strategies and models, cooperative learning has both strengths and weaknesses, and overusing any one is not effective. Used judiciously and thoughtfully, however, cooperative learning can be effective for adding variety to your instruction, increasing student interest, and improving the social skills important for students' overall education. We examine this idea in more detail next.

Diversity: Using Cooperative Learning to Capitalize on Differences in Students

Although important for constructing knowledge, meaningful social interaction doesn't always occur, especially in classrooms with diverse student populations. People tend to be wary of those different from themselves, and this tendency also exists in classrooms. Members of specific ethnic groups tend to spend most of their time together, so they don't learn that all of us are much more alike than we are different (Juvonen, 2006; Okagaki, 2006).

We can't mandate tolerance, trust, and friendship among our students, but classroom activities that encourage mixed-group cooperation can make a difference, and evidence suggests that they're effective. For example, students working in cooperative groups often improve their social skills; they develop friendships and positive attitudes toward others who differ in achievement, ethnicity, and gender; and they increase their acceptance of students with exceptionalities (Juvonen, 2006; Okagaki, 2006).

Let's see how Olivia Costa, a middle school math teacher, attempts to promote these elements of development in her classroom.

As Olivia watches her students work, she is both pleased and uneasy. They've improved in their academics, but little mixing occurs between her minority and nonminority students. She worries about six children from Central America who are struggling with English and three students with exceptionalities who leave her class every day for extra help.

In an attempt to promote a more cohesive atmosphere, Olivia spends time over the weekend organizing students into groups of four, with equal numbers of high- and low-ability students in each group. She also mixes students by ethnicity and gender, and she makes sure that no group has more than one non-native English speaker or more than one student with an exceptionality.

On Monday, she explains how they are to work together and changes the seating arrangement of the room, so group members are seated together. To introduce the process, she sits with one group and models cooperation and support for the others. After she finishes a short lesson on problem solving, she has the students turn to their groups to work on practice problems. All students in each group solve a problem and then share answers with their partner. Then, they share with the other pair in the group. If they can't solve the problem, or resolve differences about the correct answer, Olivia intervenes. She carefully monitors the groups to be sure that each student first attempts the problems before conferring with partners or the whole team.

Monitoring the groups is demanding, but her first session is fairly successful. "Phew," she thinks to herself at the end of the day. "This isn't any easier, but it's clearly better."

Now, let's look at Olivia's efforts in more detail. First, because her objective was to promote interpersonal relationships, she organized the groups to be as diverse as possible. Second, knowing that meaningful interaction must be planned and taught, she modeled desired behaviors, such as being supportive, listening, asking questions, and staying on task. We can directly teach interaction strategies or use role-plays and video recordings of effective groups to help students learn cooperation skills (Vaughn, Bos, & Schumm, 2018). These skills are especially important for students who are members of cultural minorities because they sometimes hesitate to seek and give help.

Third, she carefully monitored her students while they worked. Initial training, alone, won't ensure cooperation. Groups need constant monitoring and support, particularly with young children and when cooperative learning is first introduced (Vaughn et al., 2018). If problems persist, we may need to reconvene the class for additional training.

The benefits of student cooperation primarily result from students with different backgrounds working together and learning about each other as individuals (Slavin, 2015). As they work together, they often find they have more in common than they

Developmentally Appropriate Practice
Using Models of Instruction with Learners at Different Ages

Essential teaching skills are important at all developmental levels, and the models of instruction discussed in this section can be used at all levels as well. But when using the models, some adaptations are necessary to accommodate developmental differences in students. The following paragraphs outline suggestions for responding to these developmental differences.

Working with Students in Early Childhood Programs and Elementary Schools

Because it is effective for teaching basic skills, direct instruction is probably the most widely used instructional model in the lower elementary grades. When using direct instruction with young children, the developing understanding and guided practice phases are crucial because they lay a foundation for independent practice. Monitoring learner progress during guided practice and spending extra time with lower achievers while the majority of the students are practicing independently is an effective adaptation with young children.

Lecture–discussions should be used sparingly with young children because of their short attention spans and lack of prior knowledge. Verbal explanations must be kept short and combined with frequent episodes of comprehension monitoring for young children. Models other than lecture–discussion are often more effective with young students.

Guided discovery can be particularly effective with young children if the goal is for them to understand topics that you can illustrate with concrete examples, such as crustaceans, fractions, or parts of speech. When using guided discovery with young children, you should verbally link examples to the concept being taught and emphasize and clarify new terms.

Young children need a great deal of scaffolding and practice to work effectively in groups. Clearly describing procedures for turning in materials and participating in the activities is also crucial.

Working with Students in Middle Schools

In middle schools, direct instruction is an effective model for learning procedural skills that require practice, such as in pre-algebra, algebra, and language arts. As with younger students, the developing understanding and guided practice phases are essential for the success of the activity.

Guided discovery is one of the most effective models with middle school students, but establishing rules about treating each other with courtesy and respect during the activities is important with these students. If you use high-quality examples, middle school students are capable of learning more abstract concepts such as symmetric and asymmetric body structures in life science or culture in social studies. Guided discovery continues to be an effective model for teaching concepts that can be represented with concrete examples.

Cooperative learning can be effectively used to complement direct instruction, as Olivia Costa did with her eighth-graders. Cooperative learning can also help middle school students develop social and communication skills, perspective taking, and collaboration.

Lecture–discussion can be effective for teaching organized bodies of knowledge in science, literature, and social studies, but should be used strategically, with short lectures and frequent comprehension-monitoring questions.

Working with Students in High Schools

High school students typically pose fewer management challenges than younger students, but their greater willingness to sit passively can be a problem. Using lecture–discussions as an alternative to pure lectures is desirable.

Each of the other models can also be effective as instructional alternatives, depending on your goals. High school students are often familiar with the other models, as they've encountered them in earlier grades. Frequent monitoring is still needed to keep lessons on track and aligned with learning objectives.

---

would expect. They all want to be accepted and respected, get along with their peers, and succeed academically. One of the most effective tools we have for helping students achieve common goals is to have them learn to work together.

Flipped Instruction

Flipped instruction (commonly called the "flipped classroom") is an approach to teaching that has students study new content online by watching video lectures, usually on home computers, but also on other devices, such as smartphones or tablets (Coyne, Lee, & Petrova, 2017). Then, they apply the content in class by solving problems and doing exercises where teachers, instead of lecturing, can interact with students and offer personalized guidance. This is the source of the term "flipped." Instead of listening to a teacher presentation in class and doing homework later, they watch the lecture outside of class and do the "homework" during class time.

As an example, consider Diane Anderson's lesson on the events leading up to the Revolutionary War. If she wanted to "flip" her instruction, she would create a video lecture in which she would provide all the information she presented in class and then make the video available to students through a delivery system such as YouTube. The students' assignment would be to view the video and be prepared to discuss the information in it the next day. Class time would then be spent in a detailed discussion of topics, such as the relative advantages of the French and the English during the French and Indian War, the links between that war and the Revolutionary War, why part of Canada is French speaking, and a number of others.

Similarly, if Scott wanted to flip his instruction, he would create a video lecture during which he would provide examples of Bernoulli's Principle using the demonstrations he used in class. Class time would then be spent analyzing applications of Bernoulli's Principle, such as explaining how it helps airplanes fly, why a shower curtain moves in and wraps around our legs when we're taking a shower, atomizers on perfume bottles, and many others.

Although precursors to the flipped classroom go back to about the turn of the 21st century, major impetus for the idea was created by the *Khan Academy*, a nonprofit educational website created in 2006 by Salman Khan, an MIT and Harvard Business School graduate. The website features hundreds of short video lectures stored on YouTube that teach subjects ranging from math and science to economics and art history and more (Sparks, 2011). Since its inception, the Khan Academy videos have been viewed by literally millions of people.

Flipped instruction has garnered a great deal of interest, and some educators even describe it as revolutionary. For instance, in 2011 a school in Michigan completely converted its entire instructional delivery system to this approach (Rosenberg, 2013). And an increasing number of articles focusing on flipped instruction in classrooms ranging from elementary schools to colleges and universities have been appearing in a variety of professional journals (e.g., Casasola, Tutrang, Warschauer, & Schenke, 2017; Chiang & Chen, 2017; He, Holton, Farkas, & Warschauer, 2016; Olakanmi, 2017). The results reported in these articles are generally positive (Casasola et al., 2017; Olakanmi, 2017).

Issues Involved with Flipped Instruction

As with any educational innovation, some issues exist with respect to flipped instruction. For instance, what if students don't have available technology, so they're unable to view the videos? Also, what if students choose not to view the video lectures (He et al., 2016)?

And considerable logistics are required (Ford, 2015; Palmer, 2015). For example, if you decide to use flipped instruction in your classroom—and no school policies in our country prevent you from doing so—you will have to prepare the video lectures, and the presentation and technical quality must be good enough to be meaningful to students. Then, you must prepare the exercises and applications to be used in class. Flipped instruction requires a great deal of time and effort.

On the other hand, flipped instruction makes sense from a learning perspective. Unlike a classroom lecture, students can rewind the video and watch it as many times as they would like. Second, flipped instruction is consistent with essential teaching skills, models of instruction, and traditional modes of presentation. For instance, teacher enthusiasm, focus, review, clear communication, and closure are as important in a video lecture as they are in one delivered live to students in class. Also, the video lectures essentially apply the *developing understanding* phase of direct instruction and the *presenting information* phase of lecture–discussions. If presentation software, such as Microsoft PowerPoint, Apple Keynote, Prezi, or Google Slides, is used in a traditional lecture, it can also be used in a video lecture. And video lectures can even incorporate aspects of guided discovery. For instance, Scott could present his demonstrations in a video and then go back and identify the patterns in them, just as he did in class. The difference, of course, is that he would be presenting all the information without interacting with students. And, finally, students can work in groups, if appropriate, as they apply the content presented in the video lectures in class.

With respect to students not watching the videos, if they aren't inclined to watch videos at home, they're probably even less inclined to do traditional homework (Casasola et al., 2017; He et al., 2016). Also, most schools now have facilities that allow students without access to technology at home to watch videos after school.

And, finally, with respect to logistics, once the video lectures and application materials have been prepared and you're satisfied with their quality, they can be used over and over.

Whether or not flipped instruction is the revolutionary innovation that proponents say it is remains to be seen. The idea appears to have potential, however, and it is, and will be, applicable for you when you begin teaching.

Differentiating Instruction

Our students are more diverse than at any time in our nation's history. **Differentiating instruction**, the process of adapting learning experiences to meet the needs of students who vary in background knowledge, skills, needs, and motivations, is a response to this diversity.

MyLab Education
Video Example 13.6

Differentiating instruction, the process of adapting learning experiences to meet the needs of all students, is a response to the fact that our country's schools have an increasing number of students whose backgrounds are very diverse. Here, third-grade teacher, Sheila Brown, describes the diversity in her school and explains how she differentiates her instruction to accommodate this diversity.

Two factors related to differentiated instruction are important. First, it's not individualized learning (Tomlinson & McTighe, 2006). Tutoring is the only true form of individualization, and it's impossible for us to tutor each of our students.

Second, much of what we do when we carefully plan and implement instruction will include forms of differentiation. For example, differentiation advocates suggest the following (Parsons, Dodman, & Burrowbridge, 2013; Tomlinson, 2015):

- Plan thoroughly, and carefully teach the essential knowledge and skills needed for further learning. This is part of all forms of effective instruction.

- Use assessment as a tool to extend rather than simply measure learning. Emphasize critical thinking by requiring students to provide evidence for their conclusions. This goal is often neglected in instruction with students who are lower achievers or members of cultural minorities.

- Actively engage all learners. Equitable distribution and cooperative learning can help us reach this goal.

- Vary instruction. For example, using direct instruction in one lesson, guided discovery in another, and cooperative learning in combination with the other models helps meet students' varying needs and interests.

In addition to these suggestions, two specific differentiation strategies can be effective. They are:

- Small-group support
- Personalizing content

Small-Group Support.   Providing extra instructional support for small groups is one of the most applicable and practical forms of differentiation. For instance, when Sam's students began independent practice in his lesson on adding whole numbers, he called Cathy, Josh, and Jeremy to the back of the room, where he provided additional assistance to help them keep up with their classmates. Because he was working with only three students, his instruction could provide the support called for by differentiation experts.

Effectively implementing the *developing understanding* and *guided practice* phases of direct instruction are crucial for making small-group support work. The rest of the class must be working quietly and successfully. If we have to repeatedly get up to help other students or deal with off-task behavior, our small-group support will be less effective.

Connecting Content to Students' Lives.   Connecting content to students' lives is another way to differentiate instruction. For example, Sam implemented a simple form of connecting content to students' lives by putting two of his students' names in his original problem. Doing so took no additional effort, and it can significantly increase student interest and motivation (Schraw & Lehman, 2001).

Connecting content to students' lives simply requires awareness and some imagination. If we're aware of the need, and make attempts to do so, we'll find that the process gets easier and easier. Improved interest and motivation will often result.

Other ways of differentiating instruction exist, such as varying learning objectives, learning materials, and assessments, but they are extremely demanding and difficult to implement (O'Meara, 2011).

Evaluating Differentiating Instruction

Reactions to differentiating instruction are mixed. When properly implemented, advocates argue, it can capture student interest, increase motivation, clarify teachers' understanding of important goals, and help them better understand their students as individuals (Tomlinson, 2014; Tomlinson & Moon, 2013).

Critics counter that differentiating instruction is another educational fad and argue that empirical evidence supporting its efficacy is lacking. "Several recent reviews of research by prominent scholars in the field demonstrate that the concept has been running largely on enthusiasm and a certain superficial logic" (Schmoker, 2010, para. 6). Some critics go farther, arguing simply that differentiating instruction doesn't work in classrooms (Delisle, 2015).

Advocates, critics, and those who have tried to implement it agree on one aspect of the process: differentiating instruction is extremely demanding (Petrilli, 2011; Turner, Solis, & Kincade, 2017). Even Carol Ann Tomlinson, one of its most prominent advocates, acknowledges, "For the record, I've never felt differentiation was a panacea. . . . I absolutely understand that differentiating instruction well is not easy. But then, I've never felt that teaching should be easy" (Tomlinson, 2015, para. 18).

Differentiating instruction may or may not be another educational fad, but one thing is certain; the idea is popular with educational leaders. So, you take your first job, and your principal or other school leader communicates that you're expected to differentiate instruction in your classes. Where does this leave you? Here's our suggestion. Assert that you are indeed differentiating instruction, and then offer the following examples to support your assertion. First, you suggest, you involve all your students in your instruction, and you differentiate by varying the level of questions for individual students. Second, you provide additional support for students who need it, as we suggested in our discussion of small-group support above. Third, you note, you personalize the content you teach and connect it to your students' lives. These efforts can be reflected in your lesson plans, they are indeed forms of differentiating instruction, and they're manageable. As a first-year teacher, expecting more is unrealistic.

Personalized Learning

Personalized learning refers to " . . . instruction in which the pace of learning and the instructional approach are optimized for the needs of each learner. Learning objectives, instructional approaches, and instructional content (and its sequencing) may all vary based on learner needs" (Office of Educational Technology, 2017, p. 9). In optimal personalized learning environments learning activities are often self-initiated, driven by student interests, with the goal of making the activities meaningful and relevant to learners (Netcoh, 2017).

In spite of the specific definition above, teachers and schools vary widely in their conceptions and applications of personalized learning. Some rely on technology and use computer software to tailor curriculum, pacing, and modes of presentation to specific students' needs, interests, and abilities (Lin, Yeh, Hung, & Chang, 2013). Other approaches rely more heavily on teachers for accomplishing these same tasks. Teachers remain largely in control and use their knowledge of students' capabilities and interests to determine the pace, style, and content of curriculum for each student (Bray & McClaskey, 2015).

Personalized learning and differentiated instruction are similar, but they have an important distinction. With differentiated instruction learning goals remain the same for all students but instructional methods vary. For instance, in our discussion of differentiating instruction, we described *small-group support* as a form of differentiation. Students in the small group are expected to meet the same objectives as the rest of the students in the class, but they get additional explanations and practice that their classmates don't receive.

By comparison, *choice* is a major provision in a personalized learning environment; students have considerable choice in content, goals, and the means of reaching the goals (Bray & McClaskey, 2015; Williams, Wallace, & Sung, 2016).

As is the case with most educational innovations, personalized learning has its ardent supporters and equally ardent critics. For instance, proponents argue that student learning is increased if students have more power over what they learn, and they further argue that students are given little choice about what they learn in today's schools (Netcoh, 2017; Williams et al., 2016). Critics counter that teachers are in a better position to make decisions about what is important for students to learn (Riley & Hernandez, 2015). "Nothing replaces the teacher, and [a] teacher's ability to know a student and what they need" (Cavanaugh, 2014, para. 37). This argument makes sense. For instance, how many middle schoolers would choose algebra or pre-algebra as content they want to study, and how many would choose writing persuasive essays as desirable content? Both are viewed as essential by educational leaders.

Further, in today's world of standards and accountability, allowing student choice about content and objectives raises a number of issues. Students are expected to meet specific standards, and teachers are being held accountable for ensuring that students do so. Standards and accountability are part of reality in today's schools, and they aren't going away. This limits the amount of choice that students and teachers have (Pane, Steiner, Baird, Hamilton, & Pane, 2017). And, finally, critics argue that research doesn't support "the most enthusiastic claims being made by personalized-learning supporters" (Herrold, 2017, para. 2).

Personalized learning is a nice ideal, but its widespread application is laden with enormous challenges. It probably won't be a major part of your teaching life anytime soon.

Technology, Learning, and Development: Presentation Software in Classrooms

Presentation software is computer software designed to display text, images, audio, and video information in a slideshow format (Roblyer & Hughes, 2019). It has replaced the photo slides that were historically presented with slide projectors. Originally designed to support presentations in the business world, it has, like spreadsheets and word processing programs, quickly made the transition to education.

Many types of presentation software are available for teachers. The following is just a small sample (Daugherty, 2015):

- *Google Slides*. Now popular in classrooms, Google Slides is free presentation software that can be accessed from any device with an Internet connection. It can be used to create, present, and edit anywhere at any time. It has an auto save feature to reduce the likelihood of losing work.

- *Keynote*. Introduced in 2003, Keynote is considered by many to be the flagship presentation software for Mac. Because it allows photo and video integration with other Mac programs and is simple and user friendly, it's an industry leader.

- *Prezi.* This software has become popular because it allows "non-linear presentations," meaning presenters can easily skip to any part of a presentation, unlike other programs that require users to move back and forth one slide at a time.
- *PowerPoint.* PowerPoint has been in use for more than 30 years and is commonly considered to be the industry standard. Some estimates suggest that 30 million presentations using PowerPoint are given somewhere around the world every day. Because of its widespread use, the name *PowerPoint* is often used interchangeably with *presentation software,* much as the brand name *Kleenex* is used instead of *facial tissue,* or *Xerox* is used instead of *copier.*

Because presentation software helps organize thinking about a topic and provides visual supplements to verbal presentations, it's very popular in classrooms, in which it sometimes leads to instructional issues.

Let's look at an example of potential problems with presentation software. Earlier in the chapter, we saw how Diane Anderson used the lecture–discussion model to help her students understand events leading up to the American Revolution. Let's look now at Jack Wilson, another American history teacher, and how he teaches similar information.

Jack introduces the topic and then comments, "We need to know why the colonists in our country originally fought the war," he says. ". . . There were several causes, and we're going to look at them today."

He then brings PowerPoint up on his computer, and displays the following information:

- The French and Indian War (1754–1763)
    The war was costly for the British, who looked to the colonies to help pay some
    of the costs.

"This is where it all started," he comments, pointing to the display on the screen. "The French and Indian War was incredibly costly for the British, so they needed to figure out a way to make additional money to pay for the debt that resulted from the war."

As Jack watches, his students quickly write down the information they see, and he then displays the following slides, making brief comments after each one, and allowing students time to copy the information on them.

- The British impose new taxes (1764)
    The British felt they were spending a great deal of money to protect the colonists, so
    they imposed new taxes to cover the costs of stationing British troops in North America.

- Boston Massacre (1770)
    In response to taunts by colonists, British soldiers killed five colonists. The event
    turned colonists' opinions against the British.

- Boston Tea Party (1773)
    In response to an act granting a monopoly on tea trade, colonists dumped tons of
    tea into Boston harbor, one of the most famous events leading up to the Revolutionary War.

After Jack displays his slides, makes comments, and allows his students time to copy the information, he summarizes the lesson by saying, "Keep these events in mind as we begin our discussion of the Revolutionary War. . . . We'll start our discussion of the war itself tomorrow."

Look familiar? We've all had experiences where a presenter or instructor displayed information with presentation software, read it to us, and gave us time to copy it. Jack fell into this pattern. Instead of involving his students in a discussion of the events leading up to the American Revolution and how they contributed to it, he reduced the causes to a series of bullet points, and his students simply copied the information, a cognitively passive process. This isn't an effective use of presentation software.

Teachers are using more technology in their work with students, and presentations such as Jack's are one of the most popular uses, particularly at the secondary school and college level (Hill, Arford, Lubitow, & Smollin, 2012; Lawson, 2013). However, some experts, school administrators, and even teachers have begun to question the effectiveness of these presentations, suggesting that they are inconsistent with efforts to involve students and teach higher-order thinking (Roblyer & Hughes, 2019). Others go further and suggest that the technologies are an impediment to using student-centered forms of instruction, such as guided discovery (Hill et al., 2012). Because of its widespread use, PowerPoint has been subjected to particularly harsh criticism. "Every day, on every campus, in every town across the United States, due specifically to PowerPoint, there are lackluster students not paying attention and often sleeping in class. In these classes, the professors are reading PowerPoint slides word-for-word" (Lawson, 2013, p. 2). Although this quote is probably a bit overstated, most of us have had experiences similar to this one.

Presentation software itself is not the issue. Rather, it's the way it's often used. The presenter does everything—gathers the information, summarizes it, and determines the direction and duration of the presentation (Isseks, 2011).

From a learning perspective, presentation software—the way it's commonly used—tends to put learners in cognitively passive roles, similar to their experiences with lectures. Students can ask questions, but usually only to clarify information on a slide.

The allure of presentation software is understandable. Information can be easily copied onto slides, and the slides organize the lecture, which dramatically reduces the cognitive load on teachers. Further, in an era of high-stakes testing, the presentations are effective for "covering" content and creating the illusion that doing so equals teaching (Isseks, 2011).

Using Presentation Software Effectively.

None of the criticisms we've outlined above suggest that presentation software shouldn't be used in teaching. The issue is *how* we use it. Combined with information available on the Internet, it can be a powerful learning tool. Two suggestions can be helpful.

First, reduce the number of bullet points, and include pictures, videos, diagrams, and maps that stimulate student interest and thought. For example, Jim Norton, an earth science teacher, simply Googled the Rocky and Appalachian Mountains and downloaded detailed, colored pictures onto Google Slides, which he used to illustrate the characteristics of young and mature mountains. He did the same with other landforms, such as young and old rivers, and used them to provide detailed, concrete examples of each of the concepts.

Second, make presentations interactive. Jim, for instance, displayed the slides of the Rockies and Appalachians, and had his students make observations to identify differences between them and then suggest possible reasons for the differences. Instead of passively looking at a series of bullet points and attempting to remember the information displayed in them, his students were involved in a form of inquiry. Other suggestions include inserting questions in the slides that encourage students to think about the content and link ideas (Valdez, 2013).

Used effectively, presentation software has the potential to enhance learning, as you saw in the example with Jim Norton and his students. He was also able to store everything on a thumb drive, making it easy for him to retrieve, revise, and improve the presentation for the next time he teaches the topic.

In a large review of research examining the effectiveness of PowerPoint, researchers found that the software had little impact one way or the other on learning; it was almost exclusively the way it was used (Jordan & Papp, 2013). How effective any model, strategy, or tool is in promoting student learning depends on us—our professional judgment and expertise as teachers.

The Neuroscience of Effective Teaching

Earlier, we said that both essential teaching skills and models of instruction were supported by research. In addition, they're grounded in neuroscience. Let's see how.

The brain is instinctively a pattern-seeking organ. "The brain is constantly forming links and connections. Ultimately, by consolidating and integrating ideas, we create a synthesis of knowledge for 'life readiness' that serves us well" (Scalise & Felde, 2017, p. 121). So, our instruction should be geared toward helping students find patterns and make connections in everything we teach, and this is where essential teaching skills apply. In this discussion, we'll examine the neuroscience that supports the essential teaching skills—*review, focus, questioning, feedback,* and *closure and application*. Each is grounded in the idea that the brain instinctively searches for links and connections.

When we *review*, for instance, we help students connect new knowledge to what they already know. As the new and prior ideas are integrated, neural pathways that consolidate learning become more firmly established. So reviewing supports the way the brain instinctively functions.

Capitalizing on *focus* is also consistent with brain functioning. Our senses are constantly inundated with huge numbers of stimuli, but learning requires that we connect only to the stimuli relevant to the knowledge or skills we're trying to acquire. For example, executing an accurate corner kick in soccer means the brain must send the signal to the foot at precisely the right instant, and opposing players, noise, field position, wind, and sun must be ignored. The same is true for all learning. Vanesa Rodriguez's and Steve Kapner's students, for instance, needed to focus on the verb forms in the passages they were studying and ignore the irrelevant information in order to make their understanding of gerunds and participles meaningful. Then, they connected the verb forms to the parts of speech they represented—nouns and adjectives. Without this focus, it would have been impossible to make the connections their brains instinctively sought.

Questioning is the tool we use to help students link and connect the separate items of information, and realizing that forming connections is our goal helps guide the kinds of questions we ask. For instance, Steve presented these three short passages:

> I'm running three miles on Mondays, Wednesdays, and Fridays now. I'm walking four miles a day on Tuesdays and Thursdays. And I'm relaxing on Saturdays and Sundays.

> Running is the best form of exercise that exists, I think. But, walking is also good, and it's easier on my knees. Relaxing a couple days a week also helps my body recover.

> My running times have gone down since I've lost some weight. I have some new walking gear, so I look decent out on the road. Both make my relaxing environment just that much more pleasant.

When he had his students make observations, they ultimately arrived at three patterns. In the first paragraph, the verb forms were used as verbs; in the second, as nouns; and in the third, as adjectives. Finding patterns is precisely what the brain instinctively tries to do. This also helps us understand research suggesting that guided discovery, done properly, leads to deeper understanding than more expository approaches to instruction; its procedure is consistent with the way our brains instinctively work.

Feedback provides information that lets our brains know whether or not the neural connections they're making are valid. For instance, in Chapter 9, we saw that learners commonly think that adverbs are words that end in *ly*. If they have experiences that support this misconception, a neural connection is formed. Feedback, hopefully before the connection is too firmly established, helps eliminate this neural connection and instead create one that's valid. (These connections also help us understand why bad habits are so hard to break. Once a neural connection is formed, it takes a great deal of effort to eliminate the link and form a new one.)

Closure and application form additional links in the content, which further reinforce neural connections that support what our brains do instinctively. "For effective learning, knowledge must be 'conditionalized' in the brain; in other words, what is learned must be clearly associated with situations for which the new knowledge is useful" (Scalise & Felde, 2017, p. 28). So, for instance, when Diane Anderson helped her students identify relationships between the French and Indian War and the American Revolution, or Vanesa Rodriguez and Steve Kapner had their students write paragraphs in which verbals were used properly, students formed links in the content they were studying. The process in each case is precisely what the brain instinctively tries to do. This is the essence of "brain-based" education.

Classroom Connections

Using Models of Instruction Effectively in Classrooms

Direct Instruction

1. Direct instruction includes an introduction and review, a phase for developing understanding, and guided and independent practice. Emphasize understanding, and provide sufficient practice to develop automaticity.

- **Elementary:** A fourth-grade teacher, in a lesson on possessives, first explains the difference between singular and plural possessives and then asks students to punctuate the following sentences.

  The students books were lost when he forgot them on the bus.
  The students books were lost when they left them on the playground.
  Who can describe the boys adventure when he went to the zoo?
  Who can describe the boys adventure when they swam in the river?

  He then has students write paragraphs that incorporate both singular and plural possessives.

- **Middle School:** In a unit on percentages and decimals, a math teacher comments that the star quarterback for the state university completed 14 of 21 passes in last Saturday's game. "What does that mean? Is that good or bad? Was it better than the 12 of 17 passes completed by the opposing quarterback?" she asks. She then explains how to calculate the percentages with the class and then has the students practice finding percentages in other real-world problems.

- **High School:** A ninth-grade geography teacher helps his students locate the longitude and latitude of their city by "walking them through" the process, using a map and a series of specific questions. He then has them practice finding the longitude and latitude of other cities, as well as finding the major city nearest sets of longitude and latitude locations.

Lecture–Discussion

2. Lecture–discussions include an introduction and review, a phase where information is presented, and questions that check comprehension and help students integrate ideas. Keep presentations short, and use high levels of interaction to maintain students' attention and promote schema production.

- **Elementary:** A first-grade teacher wants her students to know similarities and differences between farm animals and pets. To do this, she constructs a large chart with pictures of both. As they discuss the two groups of animals, she continually asks students to identify similarities and differences between the two groups.

- **Middle School:** An American history teacher discussing immigration in the 19th and early 20th centuries compares immigrant groups of the past with today's Cuban population in Miami, Florida, and Mexican immigrants in San Antonio, Texas. He asks students to summarize similarities and differences between the two groups with respect to the difficulties they encounter and the rates of assimilation into the American way of life.

- **High School:** A biology teacher is presenting information related to transport of liquids in and out of cells, identifying and illustrating several of the concepts in the process. After about 3 minutes, she stops presenting information and asks, "Suppose a cell is in a hypotonic solution in one case and a hypertonic solution in another. What's the difference between the two? What would happen to the cell in each case?"

Guided Discovery

3. When teachers use guided discovery, they present students with examples and guide students' knowledge construction. Provide examples that include all the information students need to understand the topic, and guide student interaction.

- **Elementary:** A fifth-grade teacher begins a unit on reptiles by bringing a snake and turtle to class. He also includes color

(continued)

pictures of lizards, alligators, and sea turtles. He has students describe the animals and pictures and then guides them to an understanding of the essential characteristics of reptiles.

- **Middle School:** A seventh-grade English teacher embeds examples of singular and plural possessive nouns in the context of a paragraph. She then guides the discussion as students develop explanations for why particular sentences are punctuated the way they are. For example, "The girls' and boys' accomplishments in the middle school were noteworthy, as were the children's efforts in the elementary school."

- **High School:** A world history teacher presents students with vignettes, such as this one:

  You're part of an archeological team, and at one site you've found some spear points. In spite of their ages, the points are still quite sharp, having been chipped precisely from hard stone. You also see several cattle and sheep skulls and some threads that appear to be the remains of coarsely woven fabric.

  He then guides the students to conclude that the artifacts best represent a New Stone Age society.

Cooperative Learning

4. Cooperative learning requires that students work together to reach learning objectives. Provide clear directions for groups, and carefully monitor students as they work.

- **Elementary:** A second-grade teacher begins the school year by having groups work together on short word problems in math. When students fail to cooperate, she stops the groups and immediately discusses the issues with the class.

- **Middle School:** A life science teacher has students create and answer questions about the characteristics, organelles, and environments of one-celled animals. He periodically offers suggestions to the pairs to help them ask more meaningful questions.

- **High School:** A geometry teacher has pairs use scripted cooperation to solve proofs. When they struggle, she offers hints to help them continue to make progress.

5. Because of its emphasis on group interdependence, cooperative learning can promote healthy interactions between students from different backgrounds. Use cooperative learning groups to capitalize on the richness that learner diversity brings to classrooms, and design tasks that require group cooperation.

- **Elementary:** A second-grade teacher waits until the third week of the school year to form cooperative learning groups. During that time, she observes her students and gathers information about their interests, talents, and friendships. She then uses the information in making decisions about group membership.

- **Middle School:** A sixth-grade math teacher uses cooperative learning groups to practice word problems. He organizes the class into pairs, forming, whenever possible, pairs that are composed of a minority and nonminority student, a student with and a student without an exceptionality, and a boy and a girl.

- **High School:** An English teacher has students work in groups of four to provide feedback on one another's writing. The teacher organizes all groups so that they're composed of equal numbers of boys, girls, minorities and nonminorities, and students who do and do not have exceptionalities.

MyLab Education Self-Check 13.3

Assessment and Learning: Using Assessment as a Learning Tool

13.4 Identify the essential characteristics of effective assessments.

In our discussion of planning, we saw that identifying acceptable evidence—assessment— during the planning process is an essential element of backward design. This is essential for determining whether or not our students have reached our learning objectives.

To illustrate these ideas, let's look a bit further at an assessment Scott used with his students.

Look at the drawing that represents the two pieces of paper that we used in the lesson. Explain what made the papers move together. Make a sketch that shows how the air flowed as you blew between the papers. Label the forces in your sketch as we did during the lesson.

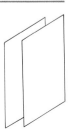

Review these two students' sketches of the flow of air between the papers.

The students' responses illustrate an essential characteristic of effective assessments: *Assessments should provide information about students' thinking* (Chappuis & Stiggins, 2017). For instance, the sketches show that students correctly concluded that the force (pressure) on the outside of the papers pushing in was greater than the force (pressure) between the papers pushing out. This doesn't provide a great deal of evidence about their understanding, however, because the lesson emphasized this conclusion.

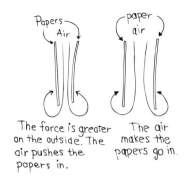

The force is greater on the outside. The air pushes the papers in.   The air makes the papers go in.

The students' explanations of their sketches of the air flow are more revealing. They concluded that the moving air curled around the bottoms of the papers and pushed the papers together, which is a misconception. (The papers moved together because increasing the speed of the air over a surface [in this case over the surface of the papers] decreases the pressure the air exerts on the surface [the papers], and the still air on the outside of the papers pushes them together, as illustrated in the sketch here. This is an application of Bernoulli's Principle.)

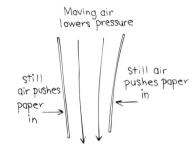

If Scott's assessment hadn't asked for both an explanation and a drawing, he might not have learned that his students constructed misconceptions during the lesson. Effective assessment provides opportunities to directly address misconceptions, such as these, which we can then attempt to correct to increase our students' understanding. A detailed discussion of these responses together with additional examples (such as demonstrating that air exerts pressure in all directions and that all objects, including air particles, move in a straight line unless a force acts on them) would greatly expand the students' understanding of basic principles in science. In fact, teaching these principles after the assessment likely produces more learning than trying to teach them beforehand, because the students' responses to the assessment provide both motivation and context for learning. Ideally, all assessments provide similar opportunities to extend learning.

Scott's lesson was in science, so let's look at another example in a different content area. In our discussion of misconceptions in Chapter 9, we saw that learners commonly believe that adjectives always precede the noun they modify and adverbs are words that end in *ly*. Aware of this possibility, we might design the following as an assessment to see if students have eliminated these misconceptions.

Underline each adjective in the paragraph and circle each adverb.

Madison and Sloan prepared to meet their friends, Bradley and Noah. "We'll go quite soon," Madison comments, "because Noah is somewhat busy, and we'll quickly run into heavy traffic. Driving will become hazardous, so we might have a full experience that's exciting."

In this exercise, for instance, students should recognize that *busy, heavy, hazardous, full,* and *exciting* are adjectives, and *quite, soon, somewhat,* and *quickly* are adverbs. For the adjectives, *busy, hazardous,* and *exciting* follow the noun they modify, and *quite, soon,* and *somewhat* are adverbs that don't end in *ly*. The assessment will determine the extent to which students recognize these parts of speech in the paragraph. If they don't, we can then provide additional examples, which will help eliminate the misconceptions.

Exercises such as this one—and those that Scott used—both assess students' current understanding and contribute to further learning through what researchers call the *testing effect*. "There is growing evidence that teachers using low-stakes testing and intermittent quizzing as students are acquiring new information can enhance learning" (Scalise & Felde, 2017, p. 223).

The same is true for all classroom learning. We tend to think of assessment as giving tests and assigning grades, but it's much more than that; it's an essential part of the entire teaching–learning process, and it's one of the most powerful tools we have for promoting learning (Chappuis & Stiggins, 2017).

MyLab Education **Self-Check 13.4**

Chapter 13 Summary

1. Describe the steps in planning for instruction, including planning in a standards-based environment.
   - Backward design is a systematic approach to instructional planning that identifies learning objectives, evidence used to determine the extent to which learning objectives have been met—assessment—and learning experiences during the planning process.
   - When using backward design, planning focuses on objectives, acceptable evidence, and learning activities, in that order, whereas with traditional planning, thinking tends to focus on *activities* or *coverage of content*, without clear thinking about learning objectives and assessment evidence.
   - Backward design helps ensure that instruction is aligned, which means that learning objectives, learning activities, and assessments are congruent.
   - Learning objectives in the cognitive domain should focus on more than simple memorized information.
   - When using standards to plan for instruction, teachers first need to interpret the standard and then design learning activities to help students meet the standard and assessments to determine whether the standard has been met.

2. Describe the process of implementing instruction and explain how it incorporates personal qualities of effective teachers and essential teaching skills.
   - Implementing instruction is the process of putting the decisions made during planning into action.
   - Learning activities involve all the experiences we provide and actions we take to help our students reach our objectives. They include presenting examples, questioning students, guiding group work, completing and providing feedback for assessments, and anything else we do to help our students reach our learning objectives.
   - Personal qualities of effective teachers include high personal teaching efficacy, the belief that they are responsible for student learning and can increase it, modeling and enthusiasm, high expectations for student achievement and behavior, and caring—investment in the protection and development of young people.
   - Essential teaching skills include the professional abilities that all teachers, including those in their first year of teaching, should possess to maximize student learning. These skills include the ability to organize efficiently, communicate clearly, attract and maintain student attention, provide informative feedback, and deliver succinct reviews.
   - Effective questioning is an important essential teaching skill and should include high frequency and equitable distribution, prompts when students can't answer, and sufficient wait-time for students to think about their answers.

3. Describe models of instruction and explain the relationships between models of instruction and essential teaching skills.
   - Essential teaching skills support and are incorporated in all models of instruction.
   - Direct instruction is an instructional model designed to teach knowledge and essential skills that students need for later learning. Teachers conduct direct instruction in four phases: (a) introduction and review, to attract students' attention and activate prior knowledge; (b) developing understanding, to acquire declarative knowledge about the skill; (c) guided practice, to begin the development of procedural knowledge; and (d) independent practice, to further develop the skill to automaticity.
   - Lecture–discussion is an instructional model designed to help students acquire organized bodies of knowledge. It consists of (a) an introduction and review, to attract attention and activate prior knowledge; (b) presenting information, to provide knowledge; (c) comprehension monitoring, to check students' perceptions; and (d) integration, to promote schema production.
   - Guided discovery is an instructional model that helps students learn concepts and the relationships among them. It consists of (a) an introduction and review, to attract students' attention and activate prior knowledge; (b) an open-ended phase in which students make observations of examples; (c) a convergent phase in which teachers help students identify patterns and begin schema production; (d) closure, when students, assisted by teachers, complete schema production and clarify the learning objective; and (e) application, which helps promote transfer.
   - Cooperative learning is a set of instructional models that uses group interaction to reach specified learning objectives. Teachers hold learners individually accountable for understanding, and learners must depend on each other to reach the objectives.
   - Differentiating instruction is the process of adapting instruction to meet the needs of students who vary in background knowledge, skills, needs, and motivations.

4. Identify the essential characteristics of effective assessments.
   - Productive learning environments are assessment centered. This means that assessment is an integral part of the learning–teaching process and that assessments are aligned with objectives and learning activities.
   - Effective assessments provide teachers with information about students' thinking, which both teachers and students can use as feedback about learning progress.
   - Effective assessments provide opportunities for increasing students' understanding through detailed feedback and discussion. Discussion following assessments often increases understanding as much as or more than the learning activity itself.

Preparing for Your Licensure Exam

Understanding Effective Teaching

You will be required to take a licensure exam before you go into your own classroom. This exam will include information related to effective teaching, and it will include both multiple-choice and constructed-response questions. We include the following exercises to help you practice for the exam in your state. This book and these exercises will be a resource for you as you prepare for the exam in your state.

In this chapter, you saw how Scott planned his lesson, demonstrated essential teaching skills, and assessed his students' learning. Let's look now at a teacher working with a class of ninth-grade geography students. As you read the case study, consider the extent to which the teacher applied the information you've studied in this chapter in her lesson. Read the case study and answer the questions that follow.

Judy Holmquist, a ninth-grade geography teacher, has her students involved in a unit on climate regions of the United States and is working on the following standard:

> CCSS.ELA-Literacy.RH.9-10.7 Integrate quantitative or technical analysis (e.g., charts, research data) with qualitative analysis in print or digital text. (Common Core State Standards Initiative, 2018v).

To meet the standard, she had her students work in groups to gather information about the geography, economy, ethnic groups, and future issues in Florida, California, New York, and Alaska from a variety of sources. Then, she and the students worked together to enter the information they've gathered on a matrix. The first two columns of the matrix are shown on the next page.

In today's lesson, Judy wants her students to integrate the information in the chart and to determine how the geography of each region influences its economy.

As the bell signaling the beginning of the class stops ringing, Judy refers students to the matrix, hung at the front of the classroom. She reminds them they will be looking for similarities and differences in the information about the states, organizes students into pairs, and begins, "I want you to get with your partner and write down three differences and three similarities that you see in the geography portion of the chart."

As groups begin their work, Judy moves around the classroom, answering questions and making brief suggestions.

A few minutes later, she calls the class back together. "You look like you're doing a good job. . . . Okay, I think we're ready."

"Okay, go ahead, Jackie," Judy begins, pointing to the chart.

"Mmm, they all have mountains, except for Florida."

"Okay, they all have mountains, except for Florida," Judy repeats and writes the information under "Similarities" on the chalkboard.

"Something else? . . . Jeff?"

"They all touch the oceans in places."

"What else? . . . Missy?"

"New York and Florida both have coastal plains."

The class continues identifying similarities for a few more minutes, and Judy then says, "How about some differences? . . . Chris?"

"The temperature varies a lot."

"All right. . . . John?"

"Different climate zones."

"Alaska is the only one that has an average low temperature below zero," Kiki puts in.

"Carnisha, do you have anything to add?"

"All except Alaska have less than 4 inches of moisture in the winter," Carnisha adds.

After students offer several more differences, Judy asks, "Okay, have we exhausted your lists? Anyone else have anything more to add?"

Judy waits several seconds and then says, "Okay, now I want you to look at the economy, and I want you to do the same thing; write down three similarities and three differences in the economies of the different states. Use the economy

	Geography	Economy
	Coastal plain	Citrus industry
F	Florida uplands	Tourism
L	Hurricane season	Fishing
O	Warm ocean currents	Forestry
R		Cattle

		Temp.	Moisture
I	Dec.	69	1.8
D	March	72	2.4
A	June	81	9.3
	Sept.	82	7.6

	Geography	Economy
C	Coastal ranges	Citrus industry
A	Cascades	Wine/vineyards
L	Sierra Nevadas	Fishing
I	Central Valley	Lumber
F	Desert	Television/Hollywood
O		Tourism
R		Computers

		Temp.	Moisture
N	Dec.	54	2.5
I	March	57	2.8
A	June	66	T
	Sept.	69	.3

	Geography	Economy
N	Atlantic Coastal Plain	Vegetables
E	New England uplands	Fishing
W	Appalachian Plateau	Apples
	Adirondack Mountains	Forestry
Y		Light manufacturing
O		Entertainment/TV

		Temp.	Moisture
R	Dec.	37	3.9
K	March	42	4.1
	June	72	3.7
	Sept.	68	3.9

	Geography	Economy
	Rocky Mountains	Mining
	Brooks Range	Fishing
A	Panhandle area	Trapping
L	Plateaus between mountains	Lumbering/forestry
A	Islands/treeless	Oil/pipeline
S	Warm ocean currents	Tourism
K		

		Temp.	Moisture
A	Dec.	−7	.9
	March	11	.4
	June	60	1.4
	Sept.	46	1.0

column of our matrix like you did with geography. You have 3 minutes."

The students again return to their groups, and Judy monitors them as she had earlier.

After they finish, she again calls for and receives a number of similarities and differences based on the information in the matrix.

She then shifts the direction of the lesson, saying, "Okay, great. . . . Now, let's see if we can link geography and economics. For example, why do they all have fishing?" she asks, waving her hand across the class as she walks toward the back of the room. "John?"

"They're all near the coast."

"And, why do they all have forestry? . . . Okay, Jeremy?"

"They all have lots of trees," Jeremy replies as the rest of the class smiles at this obvious conclusion.

"So, what does this tell you about their climate?"

"They all have the right temperature . . . and soil . . . and enough rain for trees."

"Good, Jeremy," Judy responds, smiling. "Now, let's look again at our chart. We have the citrus industry in California and Florida. Why do these states have a citrus industry?"

"It's the climate," Jackie answers hesitantly.

"All right, what kind of climate allows the citrus industry? . . . Tim?"

"Humid subtropical."

"Humid subtropical means that we have what? . . . Go ahead."

"Long, humid summers. . . . Short, mild winters," he replies after thinking for a few seconds.

"Now let's look at tourism. Why is tourism a major factor in each state's economy?" Judy continues. "Okay, Lance?"

"Because they're all spread out. They're each at four corners, and they have different seasons that they're popular in."

"Good, Lance," Judy says with a nod. She notices that they are near the end of the period. "Okay, I want you to describe in a short summary statement what effect climate has on the economy of those regions."

She gives the class a couple minutes to work again in their pairs, and then says, "Let's see what you've come up with. Braden, go ahead."

"If you have mountains in the area, you can't have farmland," he responds.

"Okay, what else? . . . Becky?"

"The climate affects what's grown and what's done in that area."

"Okay, great. Climate affects what's grown, and what was the last part of that?"

With Judy's guidance, the class makes a summarizing statement indicating that the climate of a region is a major influence determining the economy of the region, and she then dismisses the class.

Questions for Case Analysis

In answering these questions, use information from the chapter, and link your responses to specific information in the case.

Multiple-Choice Questions

1. Look at the interaction in the case study beginning with, "A few minutes later, she calls the class back together, and says, 'You look like you're doing a good job. . . . Okay, I think we're ready,'" and ending with, "Carnisha, do you have anything to add?" Of the following, this segment of the interaction between Judy and her students best illustrates which of the following?

   a. Review

   b. Closure

   c. Direct instruction

   d. Equitable distribution

2. Of the models of instruction discussed in the chapter, which model, or models, most closely resemble the ones Judy used in her lesson?

   a. Direct instruction, because she directed the progress of her lesson with her questioning.

   b. Lecture–discussion, because the students discussed the information on the chart.

   c. Guided discovery, because, with Judy's guidance, the students searched for patterns in the information on the matrix.

   d. A combination of cooperative learning and direct instruction, because the students worked in groups to gather information, and Judy directed the analysis of the information.

Constructed-Response Question

1. Describe three planning decisions that Judy made as she planned her lesson, and then analyze the extent to which Judy's instruction was aligned. Use information from the case study to document your analysis.

MyLab Education Licensure Exam 13.1

Important Concepts

affective domain
application
assessment
backward design
closure
cognitive domain
Common Core State Standards Initiative (CCSSI)
cooperative learning
differentiating instruction

direct instruction
effective teaching
emphasis
equitable distribution
essential teaching skills
feedback
flipped instruction
focus
guided discovery
implementing instruction

instructional alignment
learning activities
learning objectives
lecture–discussion
models of instruction
organized bodies of knowledge
personalized learning
precise language
presentation software

probing questions
prompting
psychomotor domain
questioning
    frequency
review
standards
task analysis
transition signals
wait-time

Chapter 14
Increasing Learning with Assessment

Ariel Skelley/Getty Images

Learning Outcomes

After you have completed your study of this chapter, you should be able to:

14.1 Describe assessment *for* student learning and explain how formative and summative assessments contribute to it.

14.2 Identify the characteristics of selected-response items, and evaluate specific selected-response items.

14.3 Describe written-response formats, and explain how to increase the validity and reliability of written-response items.

14.4 Describe different performance assessments, and explain how they contribute to the total assessment process.

14.5 Identify the elements of an effective summative assessment system.

APA Top 20 Principles

Top 20 Principles from Psychology for PreK–12 Teaching and Learning explicitly addressed in this chapter.

Principle 5: Acquiring long-term knowledge and skill is largely dependent on practice.
Principle 6: Clear, explanatory, and timely feedback to students is important for learning.
Principle 18: Formative and summative assessments are both important and useful but require different approaches and interpretations.
Principle 19: Students' skills, knowledge, and abilities are best measured with assessment processes grounded in psychological science with well-defined standards for quality and fairness.
Principle 20: Making sense of assessment data depends on clear, appropriate, and fair interpretation.

National Council on Teacher Quality (NCTQ)

The NCTQ Essential Teaching Strategies that every new teacher needs to know specifically addressed in this chapter.

Strategy 6: Assessing learning: Using assessment is a learning tool.

"Assessments of any nature—a low-stakes quiz or high-stakes test, final exam, medical board, bar exam, or driver's test—are all useful not only to determine if someone knows or has learned material but also to boost learning and retention" (Pomerance, Greenberg, & Walsh, 2016, p. 25).

The quote above captures the essence of this chapter. Assessment, used effectively, is one of the most powerful tools we have to increase our students' learning. In the following case study, DeVonne Lampkin, a fifth-grade teacher, attempts to use this tool to increase her students' understanding of equivalent fractions and the process of adding and subtracting fractions.

DeVonne is beginning a unit on fractions as she is working with her students to reach the following standard.

> CCSS.Math.Content.5.NF.A.1. Add and subtract fractions with unlike denominators (including mixed numbers) by replacing given fractions with equivalent fractions in such a way as to produce an equivalent sum or difference of fractions with like denominators. *For example,* 2/3 + 5/4 = 8/12 + 15/12 = 23/12. (*In general, a/b + c/d = (ad + bc)/bd.*) (Common Core State Standards Initiative, 2018w).

She knows that fractions were introduced in the fourth grade, but she isn't sure how much her students remember, so she first plans to give them a pretest. She plans to use the pretest results to make decisions about her learning activities, and she also constructs the test she plans to give at the end of the unit.

When DeVonne gives her pretest, this is what she finds.

Draw a figure that will illustrate each of the fractions.

3/4   3/8   1/3

You need 3 pieces of ribbon for a project. The pieces should measure 2 5/16, 4 2/16, and 1 3/16 inches. How much ribbon do you need in all?

$$7 \frac{10}{16}$$

Her students seem to understand the basic idea of a fraction, and how to add fractions with like denominators. But the following answers suggest they struggle with adding fractions when the denominators are different.

Latoya made a punch recipe for a party.

Punch Recipe
3/4 gallon ginger ale   1/2 gallon grapefruit juice
1 2/3 gallon orange juice   2/3 gallon pineapple juice

a. Will the punch she made fit into one 3-gallon punch bowl? Explain why or why not.

No because when added correctly it is more.

b. How much punch, if any, is left over?

None

On Saturday, Justin rode his bicycle 12 ½ miles.

On Sunday, he rode 8 3/5 miles.

  a. How many miles did he ride altogether?

  21

  b. How many more miles did Justin ride on Saturday
     than on Sunday?

  4 miles more.

Based on these results, DeVonne plans to focus on *equivalent fractions* in her first lesson, because her students need to understand this concept to be able to add fractions with unlike denominators.

She begins the lesson by passing out chocolate bars divided into 12 equal pieces, and with her guidance, the students show how 3/12 is the same as 1/4, 6/12 is equal to 1/2, and 8/12 equals 2/3. In each case she has them explain their answers.

DeVonne then goes to the board and demonstrates how to create equivalent fractions using numbers. At the end of the lesson, she gives a homework assignment that includes the following problems:

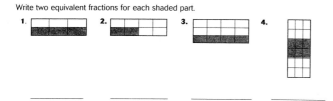

When she examines students' homework, she sees that some students are still having difficulties.

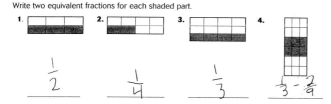

She designs another activity for the next day to further illustrate equivalent fractions. She begins the activity by having students construct a model fraction city with equivalent-length streets divided into different parts:

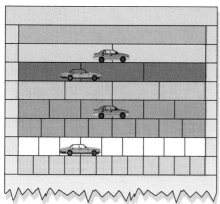

When the students are finished making their strips, she has them move cars along the different streets to illustrate equivalent fractions such as 1/2 = 3/6 and 1/3 = 3/9. Then, she illustrates adding fractions with like denominators, using the cars and strips as concrete examples. Next, she uses the same cars and strips to illustrate adding fractions with unlike denominators.

Finally, DeVonne goes to the board and demonstrates how to perform the same operations using numbers, and gives her students a homework assignment on adding fractions with unlike denominators.

At the end of the week, she gives a cumulative test on fractions. Her students' answers suggest that they understand equivalent fractions and how to add fractions with unlike denominators, and she records the scores of the test in her grade book.

DeVonne made several decisions designed to increase her students' understanding of fractions, and each was grounded in assessment. For instance, she first decided to give a pretest, and based on the results, she designed a lesson on equivalent fractions and gave a homework assignment. Students' responses to the homework suggested that they still struggled with the concept of *equivalent fractions*, so she designed another learning activity focusing on equivalent fractions. Devonne's goal in all her decisions was to increase her students' learning—this is what we mean by "Assessment *for* student learning."

Assessment *for* Student Learning

14.1 Describe assessment *for* student learning and explain how formative and summative assessments contribute to it.

Classroom assessment includes all the processes involved in making decisions about our students' learning progress (Chappuis & Stiggens, 2017). Our observations of their written work, answers to our questions in learning activities, responses on teacher-made and standardized tests, and performance assessments, such as watching first-graders print, are all forms of assessment. It also involves decisions about assigning grades, such as DeVonne deciding to give a test at the end of the unit and using the results as one basis for assigning grades in math.

Why Do We Assess?

We use assessment for three reasons:

- To increase student learning
- To enhance student motivation
- To develop learner self-regulation

Increasing Student Learning

Research dating back more than 30 years documents the powerful impact assessment has on student learning. In fact, it may be the most powerful effect on learning that exists. In a comprehensive review of research, Crooks (1988) concluded, "Here is something approaching a law of learning behavior for students: Namely that the quickest way to change student learning is to change the assessment system" (p. 445). More recent research corroborates these findings, and they hold true at the elementary school level (Rohrer, Taylor, & Sholar, 2010), in middle and high schools (Carpenter, Pashler, & Cepeda, 2009; McDaniel, Agarwal, Huelser, McDermott, & Roediger, 2011; Rohrer & Pashler, 2010), and at the university level (Crooks, 1988; Gonzalez & Eggen, 2017).

MyLab Education
Video Example 14.1

Assessment is one of the most powerful learning tools that we have. Here educational leader and author, James Popham, explains the difference between assessment *of* student learning and assessment *for* student learning and why assessment *for* learning is so important.

Research also indicates that expert teachers capitalize on assessment as an important learning tool (Parsons et al., 2018). So, from a student's perspective, instead of lamenting the number of quizzes and tests your instructors give—assuming they give frequent assessments—be grateful; you'll learn more. It might seem a bit stressful at the time, but in the long run, you're far better off.

Increasing Student Motivation

Ed Psych and You

Think about the classes you're now in. In which do you study the hardest? Why do you think so?

Think about the questions we asked in *Ed Psych and You*. If you're typical, you study hardest in classes in which you're frequently and thoroughly assessed. Students sometimes protest that they would study just as hard if they weren't tested so much, but research suggests that quite the opposite is true (Pennebaker, Gosling, & Ferrell, 2013; Rohrer & Pashler, 2010). We're all human, and we study the hardest when we know we're being held accountable for our understanding. This was true for us—Paul and Don—your authors, when we were students, and we believe it's true for students in general.

Motivation theory supports this contention. The harder we study, the more we learn. And, the more we learn, the more competent we feel. As our perceptions of our competence increase, so does our intrinsic motivation (Deci & Ryan, 2008; Ryan & Deci, 2000; Schunk, Meece, & Pintrich, 2014).

Developing Self-Regulated Learning

Self-regulated learning occurs when we set personal learning goals and monitor progress toward those goals. High-quality assessments contribute to this process by providing us with information that helps focus our efforts. For instance, if assessments require more than memorized information, we quickly adapt our study habits and focus on deeper understanding. As we saw earlier, research suggests that assessment has more influence on the way students study than any other aspect of the teaching–learning process (Crooks, 1988; Pennebaker et al., 2013). We can contribute to learner self-regulation by making our expectations clear and emphasizing that assessments are designed to increase learning (Schunk et al., 2014; Chappuis & Stiggens, 2017).

Planning for Assessment: Backward Design

In Chapter 13, we saw that **backward design** is a systematic approach to instructional planning that identifies learning objectives, assessments, and learning experiences during the planning process (Reynolds & Kearns, 2017; Wiggins & McTighe, 2006). For instance, DeVonne made the decision to give her students a pretest as she planned her unit on addition and subtracting fractions. Perhaps more significantly, she also constructed her unit test at the same time. Doing so helped ensure that her learning objectives, assessments, and learning activities were aligned, and that she placed appropriate emphasis on different aspects of her instruction.

Now, let's examine DeVonne's planning and work with her students in more detail. She began with her pretest, designed and conducted two different learning activities, and gave a cumulative test at the end of the unit. Her actions illustrate the processes of formative and summative assessment. We look at them now in more detail.

MyLab Education

Video Example 14.2

The key to effective assessment is being very clear about learning objectives. Here high school social studies teacher, Annie Rients, explains how her learning objectives guide and dictate her assessments.

Formative Assessment

The results of DeVonne's pretest indicated that her students understood the concept *fraction* and could add fractions with like denominators, but they had misconceptions about adding fractions when the denominators were different. So, she designed her first lesson on equivalent fractions and gave a homework assignment. Students' responses to the homework, however, indicated that their understanding of *equivalent fractions* was still incomplete. For instance, they wrote only one fraction for the first three problems and answered the fourth problem incorrectly.

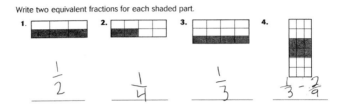

MyLab Education

Video Example 14.3

Formative assessment involves formal and informal processes teachers and students use to gather evidence for the purpose of informing next steps in learning. Here we see that DeVonne uses a pretest as a form of formative assessment. The pretest results indicate that her students don't have a clear understanding of equivalent fractions, so, based on this information, she designs a learning activity to help them understand this important concept.

So, she designed a second learning activity on *equivalent fractions.*

DeVonne's decisions illustrate **formative assessment**, "the collection of formal and informal processes teachers and students use to gather evidence for the purpose of informing next steps in learning. Formative assessment practices occur during the learning, while students are practicing and improving" (Chappuis & Stiggens, 2017, pp. 20–21). For instance, DeVonne's pretest results *informed* her decision to design a lesson on equivalent fractions, and her students' responses to their homework *informed* her decision to conduct a second lesson on equivalent fractions. Her pretest and homework assignment were formative assessments.

Formative assessment involves more than giving pretests and assigning homework. To see how, let's look at DeVonne's work with her students again. The class has added fractions with unlike denominators using their cars, and she now wants them to be able to add fractions having unlike denominators without the support of the concrete examples.

"Let's review what we've done," she begins. "Look at your cars again, and move one of your cars to First Street and Fourth Avenue and your other car to First Street and Eighth Avenue. . . . How far have your two cars moved altogether? . . . Write the problem on your paper using fractions."

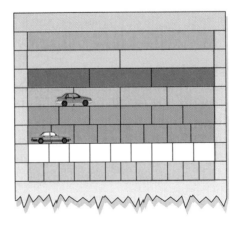

She sees that Jeremy has written the following on his paper:

$$\frac{1}{4} + \frac{1}{8} = \frac{2}{8}$$

She also sees that Juanita, Michael, and Cassie have written 1/4 + 1/8 = 2/12 on their papers.

$$\frac{1}{4} + \frac{1}{8} = \frac{2}{12} \qquad \frac{1}{4} + \frac{1}{8} = \frac{2}{12} \qquad \frac{1}{4} + \frac{1}{8} = \frac{2}{12}$$

I'll work with them when I assign seatwork, she thinks to herself.

She waits for the students to finish and then, seeing that Nikki has a clear solution, she says, "Nikki, please come up and show us how you solved the problem."

Nikki goes to the board and writes:

$$\frac{2}{2} \times \frac{1}{4} = \frac{2}{8}$$

"Explain why Nikki could write 2/2 times 1/4 to get 2/8. Amir."

" . . . "

"What does 2/2 equal?"

"One," Amir responds.

"Good, and whenever we multiply something by one, we don't change the value. So, now what can Nikki do? . . . Thelicia?"

"Add the 2/8 and 1/8 to get 3/8."

"Good, Thelicia," DeVonne says with a smile. "Now, let's try this one." She gives the students another problem, watches again as they attempt to solve it, and discusses it as they discussed the first one. After two more problems, she gives a seatwork assignment and then calls Jeremy, Juanita, Michael, and Cassie to a table at the back of the room to provide additional help.

In this episode, DeVonne used formative assessment in three ways:

- She observed that Jeremy, Juanita, Michael, and Cassie didn't understand how to add fractions with unlike denominators and decided to give them extra help while the rest of the class worked on their seatwork.

- She decided to use Nikki as a peer model instead of demonstrating the correct solution to the problem herself, which gave her the opportunity to hear Nikki articulate her understanding.

- She decided to call on Amir to see if he understood the process—instead of having Nikki explain—and she also decided to prompt him when he was unable to answer, instead of turning the question to another student.

Devonne's observations and her decisions were all part of formative assessment, each was designed to promote learning, and each was based on information she gathered during the learning activity.

Formative assessment is an integral part of instruction. For instance, we see some of our students drifting off during a lesson, so we stop and ask a series of questions to review what we've covered. Or, we're monitoring students as they work on a seatwork assignment, we see that several have made the same mistake on one of the problems, so we reassemble the class and provide more information about the problem.

Our observations in both cases are formative assessments. As a result in the first case, we stop and review, and in the second, we spend additional time on a particular problem. Both observations occurred during learning, and both decisions were designed to increase our understanding.

Students' responses to our questions during learning activities are important forms of formative assessment. If our students are responding quickly and correctly, for instance, we move forward with the lesson. If they struggle, we slow down, provide more examples, and ask more prompting questions. Our students' responses provide us with information that we use to make decisions designed to increase their learning (Clinchot et al., 2017).

MyLab Education Application Exercise 14.1: Formative Assessment in the Fifth Grade

In this exercise you will be asked to analyze the way DeVonne Lampkin, the teacher in the case study at the beginning of the chapter, uses formative assessment and backward design to promote her students' learning.

MyLab Education

Video Example 14.4

Summative assessment is the process of gathering information used to make conclusions about the level of learner achievement. Here we see that DeVonne gives her students a summative assessment to determine the extent to which they understand equivalent fractions and are able to add fractions with unlike denominators.

Summative Assessment

Summative assessment is the process of gathering information used to make conclusions about the level of learner achievement. In contrast with formative assessment, which is designed to increase learning, summative assessments evaluate how much learning has occurred, and summative information is typically reflected in a grade and communicated with others using a mechanism such as a report card (Popham, 2017). DeVonne's unit test was intended as a summative assessment because she was going to use it as a basis for determining her students' grades in math.

Tables of Specifications: Improving Summative Assessments Through Planning. A **table of specifications** is a matrix that helps us organize our learning objectives by topic and cognitive level and helps us link our instruction and assessment to objectives and standards. Preparing a table of specifications is one way to ensure that learning objectives and assessments are aligned. For example, DeVonne based her unit test on the following objectives:

1. Understands fractions
2. Understands equivalent fractions
   a. Identifies equivalent fractions
   b. Constructs equivalent fractions
3. Adds and subtracts fractions
   a. Adds fractions with like denominators
   b. Adds fractions with unlike denominators
   c. Subtracts fractions with like denominators
   d. Subtracts fractions with unlike denominators

TABLE 14.1 Table of specifications for unit test in math

	Outcomes	
Content	Comprehension Items	Application items
Fractions	2	
Equivalent fractions	2	3
Adding fractions with like denominators		2
Adding fractions with unlike denominators		2
Subtracting fractions with like denominators		2
Subtracting fractions with unlike denominators		2

A table of specifications based on these objectives is outlined in Table 14.1.

The table of specifications helps ensure that we place appropriate emphasis, during both instruction and assessment, on each of our objectives.

As another example, a geography teacher based her assessment of a unit on the Middle East on the following objectives:

1. Understands location of cities

   a. Identifies locations of major cities
   b. Explains historical factors in settlements

2. Understands climate

   a. Identifies major climate regions
   b. Explains factors that influence existing climates

3. Understands influence of physical features

   a. Describes topography
   b. Relates physical features to climate
   c. Explains impact of physical features on location of cities
   d. Analyzes impact of physical features on economy

4. Understands factors influencing economy

   a. Describes economies of countries in the region
   b. Identifies major characteristics of each economy
   c. Explains how economies relate to climate and physical features

Table 14.2 outlines a table of specifications based on these objectives. Unlike DeVonne's table, which focused on comprehension and application, this teacher had levels ranging from knowledge to "higher order thinking and application," which included both application and analysis. She also included a mix of items, with greater emphasis on physical features than other topics. This emphasis reflects her objectives, which stressed the influence of physical features and climate on the economy and location of cities in the region. It also reflects the time and effort spent on each area. Again, a table of specifications helps ensure that planning, assessments, and learning activities are aligned.

We realize that when you begin teaching you'll be very busy, so you may not construct formal tables of specifications as you see here. However, the concept of *table of specifications* is important, because it reminds us to think about the emphasis we place on different knowledge and skills when we plan our summative assessments.

Formative and summative assessments aren't characteristic of the assessments themselves; rather, they depend on the way the assessments are used. For instance, if a series of multiple-choice items are used to decide the next step in a learning activity,

TABLE 14.2 Table of specifications for unit test in geography

Content	Outcomes			
	Knowledge	Comprehension	Higher Order Thinking and Problem Solving	Total Items in Each Content Area
Cities	4	2	2	8
Climate	4	2	2	8
Economy	2	2	—	4
Physical features	4	9	7	20
Total items	14	15	11	—

the items would be formative assessments; if used as a measure of how much learning has occurred, they would be summative assessments. DeVonne used the results of her homework assignment as a basis for her decision to design another learning activity on equivalent fractions, so it was a formative assessment. On the other hand, if she had used the assignment as one basis for determining her students' grades, it would have been a summative assessment.

APA Top 20 Principles

This discussion of formative and summative assessment illustrates Principle 18: *Formative and summative assessments are both important and useful but require different approaches and interpretations*—from the *Top 20 Principles from Psychology for PreK–12 Teaching and Learning*.

Figure 14.1 outlines the characteristics of formative and summative assessment.

Data-Driven Instruction

To begin this section, let's consider DeVonne's work with her students once more. Her standard indicated that her students should know how to add fractions with unlike denominators, which required that they understood the concept *equivalent fractions*. To guide her instruction, she gave a pretest, and because the results indicated that their understanding of the concept was incomplete, she designed and conducted a lesson on equivalent fractions and then gave a homework assignment.

Figure 14.1 Characteristics of formative and summative assessment

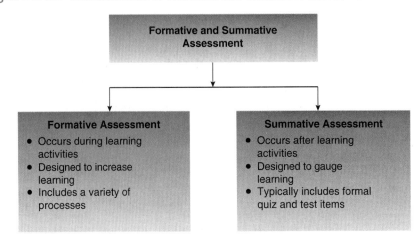

However, the students' responses to the homework indicated that they still lacked a complete understanding of equivalent fractions, so she did a second lesson on the topic. DeVonne's actions illustrate the essence of **data-driven instruction**, an approach to teaching that relies on information about student performance to inform teaching and learning (Lewis, Madison-Harris, Muoneke, & Times, 2017). Data-driven instruction includes four components (Park & Datnow, 2017):

- *Clear learning objectives.* DeVonne's objective, dictated by the standard, was for her students to be able to add fractions with unlike denominators. When implementing data-driven instruction, goals are sometimes broader, such as raising the percentage of students who score proficient or higher on a standardized assessment.

- *Baseline data.* Baseline data provide teachers with information about students' present level of understanding. DeVonne's pretest indicated that her students understood adding fractions with like denominators but lacked understand of adding fractions when denominators are different. Baseline data can also come from other sources, such as a prior year's state test.

- *Frequent assessments throughout the school year.* Frequent assessments provide ongoing sources of information that are used to guide instruction and mark student progress throughout the school year.

- *Expert instruction based on assessment evidence.* DeVonne designed her first lesson on equivalent fractions based on the pretest results—one data source—and she designed a second lesson based on her students' responses to her homework assignment—a second source of data.

As we see from DeVonne's work, formative assessment is an integral part of data-driven instruction. And it obviously makes sense to base instructional decisions on information about student understanding. This is data-driven instruction at its best, and research confirms its effectiveness. "Research has shown that using data in instructional decisions can lead to improved student performance" (Lewis et al., 2017, para. 2).

As we can see in DeVonne's work, expert teachers have always used information about their students for making decisions about instruction, so data-driven instruction, in essence, isn't new. However, critics argue that schools' attempts to implement data-driven instruction, grounded in the accountability and high-stakes testing movement (we examine accountability and high-stakes testing in detail in Chapter 15), sometimes lead to ineffective teaching practices, such as inappropriate ability grouping and overreliance on seatwork and worksheets to improve skills identified as lacking on standardized assessments (Neuman, Pinkham, & Kaefer, 2016; Park & Datnow, 2017). Instead, critics assert, students need more expert instruction that will help them "acquire the background knowledge essential to comprehending complex materials—but that doesn't mean more time spent doing mindless worksheets focused on basic skills. . . . Instead of worksheets, these students need content-rich instruction that provides skill-building opportunities" (Neuman, 2016, p. 26).

This is the kind of instruction DeVonne provided. When the data indicated that her students lacked understanding of equivalent fractions, she didn't quickly explain how to find equivalent fractions and then assign seatwork. Instead, she conducted two highly interactive lessons designed to help them develop a deep understanding of the concept. Long-term, this is the kind of instruction that leads to student success and high achievement.

To be effective, the assessments on which data-driven instruction is based must be valid and reliable. We examine these concepts next.

Designing Quality Assessments

We obviously want our assessments to be as high quality as possible. To reach this goal, assessment information must be valid and reliable.

Validity

Validity involves making accurate inferences from assessment information and using the inferred information appropriately (Chappuis & Stiggens, 2017). For instance, based on her pretest, DeVonne inferred that her students didn't have a clear understanding of equivalent fractions. Then, based on her inference, she designed her first learning activity. She made an accurate inference and an appropriate decision based on the inference, so her pretest was a valid assessment.

Ed Psych and You

How many classes have you been in where your instructor determined your course grade on the basis of a final exam? Or a midterm and final? Or a project?

On the other hand, think about the questions we asked in *Ed Psych and You*. Most of us have been in classes where our course grade has been determined by a final exam. It's difficult to make accurate inferences on this amount of information, so a grade based on these inferences is not likely to be appropriate; its validity is questionable at best. Even a midterm and final provide limited information, and a project is even worse, because assessing it can be quite subjective.

As another example, if we decide that our students understand a topic based on the answers of a few high achievers in a learning activity, we're inferring that all our students understand the topic, and if we move forward with the activity without gathering more formative data, we're also using the information inappropriately. Again, the validity of our assessment is uncertain.

APA Top 20 Principles

This discussion of validity illustrates Principle 20: *Making sense of assessment data depends on clear, appropriate, and fair interpretation*—from the *Top 20 Principles from Psychology for PreK–12 Teaching and Learning*.

Reliability

Reliability describes the extent to which assessments are able to provide consistent results. For instance, if our bathroom scale is reliable, and our weight doesn't change from one day to the next, the readings will be the same. Hypothetically, if we could repeatedly give students the same reliable test, and if no additional learning or forgetting occurred, the scores would remain the same. Unreliable assessments cannot be valid, even if they are aligned with learning objectives, because they provide inconsistent information.

Reliability is an intuitively sensible and commonly used concept in our day-to-day lives. For instance, we may have described acquaintances, or even friends, as unreliable. They sometimes follow through on what they say they'll do, but fail to do so at other times, or they show up at agreed-upon times, and at other times, they don't. Their behavior is inconsistent, which is why we describe them as unreliable.

We will revisit both validity and reliability as we discuss specific assessment formats and effective assessment practices later in the chapter.

Commercially Prepared Test Items

Because you will be very busy when you teach, you are likely to use test items included in the ancillary materials for your textbooks. Although using these items saves time, you should be careful, for three reasons (Brookhart & Nitko, 2019; Popham, 2017):

1. *Compatibility of learning objectives.* The textbook authors' learning objectives may not be the same as yours. If items don't reflect the objectives in your lesson or unit, they aren't valid.
2. *Uneven quality.* Textbook authors often don't prepare the test items included with ancillary materials; the items are often prepared by a graduate student or some other person not intimately familiar with the textbook's content. As a result, many commercially prepared test items are of poor quality.
3. *Emphasis on lower level items.* Commercially prepared items typically measure at a knowledge/recall level. This is particularly true in content areas other than math and quantitative sciences, such as chemistry and physics.

The time and energy you save in using commercially prepared items are important advantages, however. If you decide to use them, the following guidelines can help you capitalize on these benefits:

- Select items that are consistent with your learning objectives and put them in a computer file.
- Use feedback from students and analysis of test results to revise ineffective items.
- Create additional items that help you accurately assess your students' understanding.

In the sections that follow, we discuss different assessment formats in detail. As you study these sections, keep in mind that specific items in these formats can be used as either formative and summative assessments.

Classroom Connections

Using Formative and Summative Assessment Effectively

1. The process of backward design suggests that assessments should be prepared during planning. This helps ensure that assessments are aligned with learning objectives, saves time, and increases validity. Prepare both formative and summative assessments during planning.

   - **Elementary:** A fourth-grade teacher, as part of an extended unit on reading comprehension, is planning lessons focusing on cause-and-effect relationships. As he plans, he identifies passages he will use for practice and others he'll use on summative assessments.

   - **Middle School:** A middle school social studies teacher is planning a unit focusing on the relationships between technological events, such as the Industrial Revolution, and changes in societies. As she plans, she writes a series of short essay questions that she will use as summative assessments for the unit.

   - **High School:** A geometry teacher is planning a unit on the construction of segments and angles, angle bisectors, and parallel and perpendicular lines. As he plans, he creates problems that he will use to assess his students' understanding of these processes.

2. Formative assessment is used primarily to promote learning; summative assessments are used for grading. Use both to promote learning in your assessment system.

   - **Elementary:** A second-grade teacher discusses math problems that several students missed on their homework and then asks them to rework the problems. If students are still having problems with the content, he reviews the material with the students before he gives them a summative assessment.

   - **Middle School:** A sixth-grade science teacher has created and filed an item pool on her computer. She uses some of the items to create a "practice test," which the class discusses immediately after they've taken it. She then uses additional items on a summative assessment.

   - **High School:** A 10th-grade English teacher provides extensive individual comments on students' papers. In addition, he identifies problem areas common to the whole class and uses anonymous selections from students' papers to discuss and provide feedback to the whole class.

3. Validity is the process of making accurate inferences from assessment information and using the information appropriately. Reliability is the extent to which assessments provide consistent information. Increase validity and reliability by carefully planning assessments.

(continued)

- **Elementary**: A third-grade teacher compares items on her quizzes, tests, and graded homework to the standards in the curriculum guide and the objectives in her unit plan to be sure all the important objectives are covered. To increase reliability, she frequently and thoroughly assesses her students.

- **Middle School**: A social studies teacher writes a draft of a test item at the end of each day to be certain the emphasis

on his summative assessments is consistent with his instruction. When he puts the test together, he checks to be sure that all content areas and difficulty levels are covered.

- **High School**: After composing a test, a biology teacher rereads the items to eliminate wording that might be confusing or too advanced for her students. This increases both validity and reliability.

MyLab Education Self-Check 14.1

Selected-Response Items

14.2 Identify the characteristics of selected-response items, and evaluate specific selected-response items.

Selected-response items are assessment items that require learners to *select* the correct answer from a list of alternatives. The three selected-response formats are:

- Multiple choice
- Matching
- True–false

We examine them in this section.

Multiple-Choice Items

Multiple choice is an assessment format that consists of a stem and a series of answer choices called distractors. The **stem** is the beginning part of the item, and it presents a problem to be solved, a question to be answered, or an incomplete statement. Multiple-choice items also include options—typically four or five. One option is the correct or best choice, and the rest are **distractors**, designed to identify students who don't understand the content the item is measuring. The distractors should address students' likely misconceptions, which we can then discuss when providing our students with feedback about their test performance.

Guidelines to help us prepare effective multiple-choice items include the following (Gieri, Bulut, Guo, & Zhang, 2017):

1. Present one clear problem or question in the stem. A clear, unambiguous stem tells students what we're looking for and how to answer the question.
2. Make distractors plausible to students who lack deep understanding of the content. If students can eliminate distractors based on superficial knowledge or wording, we will get unreliable information, and the item will be invalid.
3. Vary the position of the correct choice, and avoid overusing choice *c* (teachers tend to overuse choice c). After constructing a quiz or test, take a few minutes to ensure that the correct responses are randomly assigned.
4. Avoid using similar wording in the stem and the correct choice. For example, in the following item, forms of the term *circulate* appear in both the stem and the correct answer—choice *b*.

1. Which of the following is a function of the circulatory system?

    a. To support the vital organs of the body

    b. To circulate the blood throughout the body

    c. To transfer nerve impulses from the brain to the muscles

    d. To provide for the movement of the body's large muscles

5. Avoid using more technical wording in the correct choice than in distractors. For example, in the following item, the correct choice—*c*—is written in more technical terms than the distractors.

1. Of the following, the definition of *population density* is:

    a. the number of people that live in your city or town.

    b. the number of people that voted in the last presidential election.

    c. the number of people per square mile in a country.

    d. the number of people in cities compared to small towns.

We might fall into this trap if we take the correct choice directly from the text and then make up the distractors. Our informal language appears in the distractors, whereas text language appears in the correct answer.

6. Keep the correct choice and the distractors similar in length. If one choice is significantly longer or shorter than others, it should be a distractor. For example, in the following item, the correct choice—*d*—is significantly longer than the incorrect choices. (We give a similar clue if the correct choice is shorter than the distractors.)

1. Of the following, the most significant cause of World War II was:

    a. American aid to Great Britain

    b. Italy's conquering of Ethiopia

    c. Japan's war on China

    d. The devastation of the German economy as a result of the Treaty of Versailles.

7. Avoid using absolute terms, such as *always* or *never*, in incorrect choices. Absolute terms, such as *all, always, none,* and *never,* are usually found in incorrect answers. If used, they should be in the correct answer, such as "All algae contain chlorophyll." For example, in the following item, distractors *a* and *c* are stated in absolute terms, so test-wise students only have to choose between the correct choice—*b*—and distractor *d*.

1. Which of the following is the best description of an insect?

    a. It always has one pair of antennae on its head.

    b. It has three body parts.

    c. It does not live in water.

    d. It has eight legs.

8. Keep the stem and distractors grammatically consistent. Again, our goal is to determine what students know or understand, not their ability to use grammatical cues to eliminate incorrect answers.

9. Avoid including two distractors with the same meaning. For example, in the following item, choices *a* and *c* are automatically eliminated, because both are gerunds, and only one answer can be correct. Also, the item uses "All of the above" as a choice; it can't be correct if *a* and *c* are eliminated. That makes the correct choice—*b*—the only one possible. A student could answer correctly and have no idea what a participle is.

---

1. Which of the following illustrates a verb form used as a participle?
   a. Running is good exercise.
   b. I saw a jumping frog contest on TV yesterday.
   c. Thinking is hard for many of us.
   d. All of the above.

---

10. Use negative wording infrequently, and emphasize it when used. In the following item, for example, the stem is stated in negative terms without emphasizing it; the word *not* should be underlined, set in bold print, or italicized. Also, choice *a* is grammatically inconsistent with the stem. One solution to this issue is to end the stem with "a(n)," so grammatical consistency is preserved. (Also *c* is the correct choice, which can be a problem if it's overused.)

---

1. The one of the following that is not a reptile is a(n):
   a. alligator
   b. lizard
   c. frog
   d. turtle

---

11. Avoid using "all of the above" as a choice, and use "none of the above" infrequently. It's difficult to write valid and reliable items using these alternatives, and gaps in student knowledge are harder to interpret.

Items may be written so that only one choice is correct, or they may be in a *best-answer* form, in which two or more choices are partially correct but one is clearly better than the others. The best-answer form promotes higher level thinking and measures more complex understanding. Many of the multiple-choice questions that assess your understanding of the content in this text use the best-answer form.

Assessing Higher Level Learning

Multiple choice can be an effective format for assessing higher order thinking, and *interpretive exercises* are useful for meeting this goal. These exercises present information covered in class in a different context, and the distractors represent different "interpretations" of it (Waugh & Gronlund, 2013). The material that students are asked to interpret may be a graph, chart, table, map, picture, or written vignette. This type of exercise promotes critical thinking and transfer, and because they're challenging, they can increase learner motivation. Most of the higher order multiple-choice items that you will respond to as you take this class are interpretive exercises. The following is an example that uses a vignette as a stem.

Ms. Ramsay is discussing the Civil War with her students. She poses the question, "What would life have been like as a child during this time?" Her students are able to generate some plausible explanations. Using Piaget's theory as a basis, which stage of cognitive development does her students' thinking most nearly demonstrate?

   a. Sensorimotor
   b. Preoperational
   c. Concrete operational
   d. Formal operational

In this item, we see that Ms. Ramsay has asked her students a hypothetical question, and we know that the ability to think hypothetically is characteristic of formal operations, a topic we examined in Chapter 2, so we *interpret* the information to conclude that her students are formal operational in their thinking and correctly select *d* as our choice.

Writing interpretive exercises is demanding, but once we've constructed the items and revised them to ensure that they're worded clearly and unambiguously, we can reuse them, which dramatically decreases our workload. We address this idea in more detail later in the chapter.

MyLab Education Application Exercise 14.2: Analyzing Selected Response Items

In this exercise you will be asked to analyze a series of multiple-choice items based on the criteria outlined in this section.

Matching Items

The multiple-choice format can be inefficient if all of the items require the same set of answer choices, as in the following (asterisk indicates correct answer):

1. The statement "Understanding is like a light bulb coming on in your head" is an example of the concept:

   *a. simile
   b. metaphor
   c. hyperbole
   d. personification

2. The statement "That's the most brilliant comment ever made" is an example of the concept:

   a. simile
   b. metaphor
   *c. hyperbole
   d. personification

These assessments can be made more efficient by using a **matching format**, which requires learners to classify a series of statements using the same alternatives. The following is an example based on the multiple-choice items above.

Match the following statements with the figures of speech by writing the letter of the appropriate figure of speech in the blank next to each statement. You may use each figure of speech once, more than once, or not at all.

_____ 1. Understanding is like a light bulb coming on in your head.
_____ 2. That's the most brilliant comment ever made.
_____ 3. His oratory was a bellow from the bowels of his soul.
_____ 4. Appropriate attitudes are always advantageous.
_____ 5. Kisses are the flowers of love in bloom.
_____ 6. He stood as straight as a rod.
_____ 7. I'll never get this stuff, no matter what I do.
_____ 8. The colors of his shirt described the complex world in which he lived.

a. alliteration
b. hyperbole
c. metaphor
d. personification
e. simile

As we see from the example, the matching format is essentially a series of multiple-choice items, so the guidelines for preparing multiple-choice questions should also be used for matching items. The following additional guidelines also apply (Chappuis & Stiggins, 2017):

1. Provide clear and concise directions for matching the alternatives to the statements. For instance, the directions for using the figures of speech (the alternatives) in the example above state, "You may use each figure of speech once, more than once, or not at all."
2. Keep content homogeneous. For instance, all the statements in the example are figures of speech, and only figures of speech appear as alternatives. Other topics for which the matching format is effective include people and their achievements, historical events and dates, terms and definitions, and authors and their works.
3. To prevent getting the right answer through the process of elimination, include more statements than possible alternatives. The example includes eight statements and five alternatives.
4. Keep the list of statements relatively short. For instance, the item includes eight statements. As a rule of thumb, if a matching item involves more than 10 statements, we should create two separate items to prevent confusion.

True–False Items

True–false is an assessment format that includes statements learners judge as being correct or incorrect. The following guidelines can improve the effectiveness of this format.

1. Write more false than true items. Teachers tend to do the reverse, and students tend to mark items they're unsure of as "true."
2. Make each item one clear statement. For instance, look at the following.

T F 1. Mammals are animals with four-chambered hearts that bear live young.

The item contains two ideas: (a) mammals have four-chambered hearts, and (b) they bear live young. The first is true, but the second is not true in all cases; some mammals, such as the duck-billed platypus, are egg layers. So, the item is false and likely confusing for students. If both ideas are important, they should be written as separate items.

3. Avoid clues that allow students to answer correctly without fully understanding the content. For instance, look at the following items.

T F 2. Most adverbs end in the letters *ly*.

T F 3. Negative wording should never be used when writing multiple-choice items.

The first includes the qualifying term *most*, which usually indicates a true statement; although not all adverbs end in *ly*, adverbs most commonly do indeed end in these two letters.

The second item uses *never*, which suggests a false statement. (As we said in our discussion of multiple-choice items, negative wording should be used with care, but saying we should "never" use negative wording is false.)

This guideline doesn't imply that qualifying terms, such as *most, never,* or *all,* should always be avoided. For instance, look at the following item.

T F 4. All spiders have exoskeletons.

The item uses the term *all*, which usually indicates a false statement, but the item is true.

Interpretive Exercises with the True–False Format

The true–false format can also be used with interpretive exercises, and they can sometimes be more efficient than multiple-choice items. The following is an interpretive exercise in science where our goal is to assess students' understanding of *mass, volume, density, heat,* and *expansion.*

Look at the drawings above. They represent two identical soft drink bottles covered with two identical balloons, sitting side-by-side on a table. No air can enter or escape from the systems—the bottles, balloons, and enclosed air. After the balloons were attached to the bottles, system A was heated.

Identify each of the following statements as true or false by circling the correct choice.

1. T F The mass of the air in system A is greater than the mass of the air in system B.
2. T F The volume of the air in system A is greater than the volume of the air in system B.
3. T F The density of the air in system A is greater than the density of the air in system B.
4. T F The molecules of air in system A are moving faster than the molecules of air in system B.
5. T F There are more molecules of air in system A than there are in system B.

Each of these items could be written in a multiple-choice format, but in this case the true–false format measures students' understanding more efficiently.

Using the format in this way helps overcome some of its disadvantages. If you plan to use the true–false format, we encourage you to create interpretive exercises whenever the content allows. Now, let's look at the advantages and disadvantages of these formats.

Evaluating Selected-Response Items

The selected-response formats have advantages and disadvantages. Their advantages include:

- *Ease of scoring.* They're easy to score and are amenable to machine scoring.
- *Efficiency.* They can be used to efficiently assess a large amount of content.
- *Reliability.* Because scorers don't have to interpret learners' answers, they can be scored consistently.

Their primary disadvantages include:

- *The "guess" factor.* Assuming four choices are offered, learners have a 1 in 4 chance of guessing the right answer with multiple choice, and a 50-50 chance with true–false. The process of elimination can sometimes impact the validity of matching items.
- *Limitations.* The outcomes they can measure are limited. For instance, because learners' are *selecting*, as opposed to constructing responses, it's impossible to assess learners' ability to organize and express their thinking in writing.

With respect to multiple-choice items, people often think that they only measure factual information that focuses on memorization, but this is a misconception. Most aptitude and achievement tests, such as the SAT, ACT, Graduate Record Exam, and many others, use this format. If it only measured low-level outcomes, it wouldn't be so widely used. Earlier, we saw how *interpretive exercises* can be used to measure higher level learning and thinking. If well-designed interpretive exercises are used, the multiple choice is a valid and highly effective format for assessing a range of thinking levels in Bloom's taxonomy or the Anderson-Krathwohl taxonomy table, which we examined in Chapter 13.

In fact, "multiple-choice testing is considered one of the most effective and enduring forms of educational assessment that remains in practice today" (Gieri et al., 2017, p. 1082). This helps us understand why, in an era of educational accountability, multiple choice is by far the most common format used on high-stakes tests by states around our country. This practice has implications for you as you prepare your students for these assessments. Because your students will likely encounter this format, you should provide them with practice in responding to multiple-choice items as you help them prepare for these tests.

Here is a simple example of what we mean. When we have our students work on spelling, for instance, we typically give them lists of words that they should be able to spell, and then we assess this ability by saying words out loud and having students spell them in writing. On a standardized test, however, they will encounter items such as the following:

Which of the following words is spelled correctly?

    a. perserve

    b. preserve

    c. pesrerve

    d. persreve

If our students have no experience in responding to items such as these, they're unlikely to perform as well. Therefore, we must help them practice.

The matching format is more limited than multiple choice. For instance, the format doesn't allow for the construction of interpretive exercises. However, it can be an effective and efficient format for measuring learners' ability to identify examples of concepts, as we saw in our illustration with figures of speech.

Because true–false items usually measure lower level outcomes, and because students have a 50-50 chance of guessing the correct answer, it is considered to be a weak format. This doesn't have to be the case, however, as we saw in the interpretive exercise earlier. On the other hand, because of its limitations, we don't include true–false items in the test bank that accompanies this text.

Classroom Connections

Using Selected-Response Items Effectively

1. Multiple-choice items can be used to measure higher level outcomes. Use interpretive exercises whenever possible to capitalize on this capacity.

- **Elementary:** A second-grade teacher constructs the following item, which he uses on an assessment.

  Cindy has a pet. Her pet is warm and has hair. Her pet is a:

  a. lizard

  b. bird

  c. butterfly

  d. mammal

- **Middle School:** A middle school earth science teacher wants to assess her students' understanding of the moon's phases. She includes the following item on an assessment.

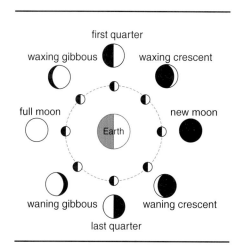

Look at the drawing above. We see each phase of the moon labeled. Based on this drawing, the

(continued)

sun's rays are coming from:

a. the right side of the drawing

b. the left side of the drawing

c. above the drawing

d. below the drawing

- **High School:** A math teacher working on percent increase and percent decrease with his students gives them the following assessment item:

  You see a sweater originally priced for $60 marked down to $45. Which of the following is the percent decrease in price of the sweater?

  a. 15%

  b. 25%

  c. 33%

  d. 45%

2. Matching items can be used for material that is homogeneous, such as authors and their works, dates and events, and people and their accomplishments. If this is an assessment goal, matching can be a viable alternative to multiple choice.

- **Elementary:** A fourth-grade teacher uses the matching format to assess her students' understanding of

declarative, interrogative, exclamatory, and imperative sentences. She includes 10 examples of the different types of sentence as statements, and *declarative, interrogative, exclamatory,* and *imperative* as alternatives.

- **Middle School:** A history teacher wants his students to know dates of important events in the Civil War. He constructs a matching item that includes the events as statements, and dates as alternatives.

- **High School:** A chemistry teacher wants his students to be able to match ions with their valences. He constructs a matching item that includes descriptions of ions as statements, and valences as alternatives.

3. The true–false format is limited. Use the format sparingly and for measuring knowledge of specific content.

- **Elementary:** A fifth-grade teacher uses true–false items to measure her students' knowledge of different animal classifications.

- **Middle School:** A middle school English teacher uses true–false items to assess her students' knowledge of grammar rules before he begins a unit on writing.

- **High School:** A biology teacher uses true–false items to measure her students' knowledge of different systems in the human body.

In spite of their disadvantages, selected-response items, and particularly multiple choice, can be highly effective for assessing a range of outcomes, and we encourage you to make them a major component of your summative assessment system.

> **MyLab Education** Self-Check 14.2

Written-Response Items

14.3 Describe written-response formats, and explain how to increase the validity and reliability of written-response items.

Written-response items are assessment items that require learners to produce, instead of select, a response. The response can be as short as one word or as long as several paragraphs. *Completion* and *essay* are the two written-response formats. We examine them now.

Completion Items

Completion (also called short answer) is an assessment format that includes a question or incomplete statement requiring learners to write a short—often one word—answer.

This format is popular with teachers, probably because the questions seem easy to construct. However, writing completion items so that only one possible answer is correct is a challenge, so using this format isn't as easy as it appears. For instance, consider the following:

What is an opinion? _____ .

The novel *For Whom the Bell Tolls* was set where? _____

More than one defensible response could be given in each case. For instance, "A point of view, not necessarily based on fact" would be an acceptable answer for the first item, as would "The estimation of the quality of someone or something," such as people having a high opinion of themselves, or "The advice of a professional," as in seeking a second medical opinion. For the second, "Spain," "The Spanish Civil War," or "Europe" would all be technically correct answers. Overuse of completion items can put students in the unenviable position of trying to guess the answer we want instead of writing the one they think is correct.

Also, completion items are usually written at low cognitive levels, as in the items below. They are clearly written but only measure recall of information.

Name the capital of Brazil. _____

Who is the author of the book *I Know Why the Caged Bird Sings*? _____

This doesn't have to be the case, however. For instance, let's look again at the interpretive exercise we saw in our discussion of multiple-choice items.

Ms. Ramsay is discussing the Civil War with her students. She poses the question, "What would life have been like as a child during this time?" Her students are able to generate some plausible explanations. Using Piaget's theory as a basis, which stage of cognitive development does her students' thinking most nearly demonstrate?

    a. Sensorimotor
    b. Preoperational
    c. Concrete operational
    d. Formal operational

Instead of using multiple choice, the item could be written in a completion format.

Ms. Ramsay is discussing the Civil War with her students. She poses the question, "What would life have been like as a child during this time?" Her students are able to generate some plausible explanations. Using Piaget's theory as a basis, which stage of cognitive development does her students' thinking most nearly demonstrate?

When the response can be written in one or two words, a completion item can be used as an alternative to multiple choice. Doing so has the disadvantage of making the item harder to score but the advantage of requiring learners to produce, instead of merely recognize, the correct choice.

The completion format is also useful for problems such as the following.

A light jacket originally priced at $95 has been marked down to $75. What is the percent decrease in the price of the jacket? _____

Guidelines for preparing completion items include the following:

1. Ask one clear question. We saw above that writing a clear question can be challenging.
2. Use only one blank, and relate it to the main point of the statement. Several blanks are confusing, and one answer may depend on another. Consider the following item.

The _____ system is composed of the heart, _____, and _____.

In this item, we're required to name the system, as well as two of its components. A better item would be:

What is the name of the body system that is composed of the heart, blood, and blood vessels?

_____

If we want students to be able to name the parts of the system, we should write separate items.

3. Keep blanks the same length. Different length blanks may provide a clue to the correct answer.
4. For numerical answers, indicate the degree of precision and the units desired. This clarifies the task and helps students avoid spending more time than necessary on the item.

Because of its weaknesses—the difficulty in writing clear statements and its tendency to focus on low-level cognitive outcomes—some experts recommend not using the completion format (Waugh & Gronlund, 2013). However, as we saw above, if statements are carefully written and interpretive exercises are constructed, it can be used effectively.

Essay Items: Measuring Complex Outcomes

Essay is an assessment format that requires students to make extended written responses to questions or problems. Responses to essay items can range from one or two sentences, sometimes called *short-answer* items, to several paragraphs. Essay items make three valuable contributions to our assessment efforts:

- They can assess dimensions of learning, such as the ability to make and defend an argument, that can't be measured with other formats.
- The ability to organize thinking and describe ideas in writing is an important goal across the curriculum and in life, and the essay format is an effective way to measure progress toward these goals.
- Essay items can improve the way students study. If they know an essay will be required, for instance, they are more likely to look for relationships in what they study and to construct more meaningful schemas.

But essay items also have three important disadvantages. Content coverage is the first. Because essay tests require extensive writing time, it isn't possible to assess learning across as broad a spectrum as can be covered with selected-response items. The amount of time it takes to score essay items is a second disadvantage. You will be extremely busy when you begin teaching, and having to carefully read each student's response increases the demands on your time.

Third, and perhaps most significantly, reliability is a continuing challenge with this format. Essay items appear easy to write, but they're often ambiguous, so students' ability to interpret the question more than their understanding of the topic is sometimes the outcome measured.

Reliability of essay items has had important implications for college admissions exams. For instance, in 2014 the decision was made to make the essay portion—which had been implemented in 2005—of the SAT optional, and this decision was put into practice in 2016. The inability to reliably score the essay portion of the test was a significant factor in this decision (Lewin, 2014). Reliability is also influenced by writing skill, including grammar, spelling, and handwriting (Brookhart & Nitko, 2019).

Let's look at the issue of reliability in more depth.

Increasing the Reliability of Essay Items

National and state standards now include more demanding writing requirements, making assessment formats that require students to write essential. As a result, essay items will be an even more important component of assessment systems, so our efforts should be directed at making them as reliable as possible. Suggestions for increasing the reliability of essay items include the following:

1. Be specific when writing essay items. Generally stated items leave students, and particularly elementary students, with a sense of uncertainty.
2. Require students to answer all items. Allowing students to select particular items prevents comparisons and detracts from reliability.
3. Limit the amount of space students have to write their answers. Test-wise students tend to write down everything they know about the topic and then hope the right answer is in it somewhere. This makes scoring an item problematic. Correct information may be in the response, but so is irrelevant information, which indicates that the student's understanding is uncertain.
4. Score all students' answers to a single item before moving on to the next one, and attempt to score all students' responses to the item in one sitting. Doing so increases the likelihood that scoring will be consistent.
5. Score answers without knowing students' identity. We have a tendency to award higher scores to students who are generally high achievers. Not knowing students' identities helps reduce this influence.
6. Write a model answer for each item. Doing so serves three purposes. First, it helps ensure that we've written the item clearly. Second, because we can compare students' answers to the model, it helps with scoring. Third, the answer will provide students with feedback because they can compare their answers to the model. Writing a model answer takes time, but, once written, it can be utilized whenever you use the item.
7. Prepare scoring criteria in advance and use the model answer as the basis for the criteria.

Let's look at scoring criteria in more detail.

Scoring Criteria: Using Rubrics

A **rubric** is a scoring scale that explicitly describes criteria for grading (Brookhart, 2013). For example, suppose we have worked with our students on constructing paragraphs, and we've emphasized that a high-quality paragraph includes a topic sentence, one or more supporting sentences, and a summarizing sentence. We've provided our students with examples of well-constructed paragraphs and other examples of paragraphs that are not well designed. We then give our students the following essay item:

Select a topic of your choice, write it down, and then write a paragraph about it. Include a minimum of five sentences in the paragraph.

The item is clear and specific, which is essential. If the item isn't clearly written, the effectiveness of the rubric as a scoring guide is sharply reduced, as is the reliability. A rubric that might be used for scoring this item appears in Figure 14.2. Notice how the following features are contained in the rubric.

- *Criteria.* It includes criteria based on the elements that must exist in students' answers. For instance, in our instruction we've emphasized that a high-quality paragraph must include a topic sentence, supporting sentences, and a summarizing sentence. These elements are specified in the left column of the rubric.
- *Levels of achievement.* The rubric includes three levels of achievement for each of the criteria, outlined in the rubric's rows.
- *Descriptors.* Each level of achievement is described. For instance, for the topic-sentence criterion, level-of-achievement 3 is described as, "Provides a clearly stated overview of the paragraph."
- *Rating scale.* The rubric specifies that nine points are possible for the paragraph.

As a final planning step, we make decisions about grading criteria. For instance, we might decide that 9 points would be an A, 7–8 points a B, and 5–6 points would be a C. So a student would be required to be at achievement level 3 on all three criteria to earn an A, at level 2 on two of the three elements and at level 3 on the third to earn a B, and so on.

Rubrics can be important tools to help us increase reliability when we score essays. They can also be used with performance assessments, which we examine later in the chapter.

Figure 14.2 Rubric used as a guide for assessing paragraph structure

| Criteria | Levels of Achievement | | |
	1	2	3
Topic Sentence	Not present; reader has no idea what paragraph is about	Present but does not give the reader a clear idea what the paragraph is about	Provides a clearly stated overview of the paragraph
Supporting Sentences	Rambling and unrelated to topic sentence	Provides additional information but not all focused on topic sentence	Provides supporting detail relating to the topic sentence
Summarizing Sentence	Nonexistent or unrelated to preceding sentences	Relates to topic sentence but doesn't summarize information in paragraph	Accurately summarizes information in paragraph and is related to topic sentence
Overall Score (9 Possible)			

Evaluating Written-Response Formats

The two written-response formats aid in the assessment process by providing us with additional tools. They have the advantage of being more cognitively demanding than the selected-response formats, but they have the disadvantage of being harder to score.

The primary challenge in using either completion or essay items is in writing questions clearly enough so students don't struggle with interpreting the items. And, when using the completion format, preparing items that require more than knowledge and recall is an additional challenge. As we saw earlier, however, we can use interpretive exercises with the completion format, so it can be an effective alternative to multiple choice. We include additional classroom examples in *Classroom Connections* at the end of this section.

When we assess our students, we are measuring two outcomes: 1) their understanding of the topics on the assessment, and 2) their skills in responding to particular items, such as multiple choice, completion, or essay. So, when considering your total assessment strategy, our recommendation is the following: Use different assessment formats to accommodate differences in students' ability to respond to a particular format, and to provide students with practice using the formats. Because of its prominence on standardized tests, make multiple choice your primary assessment format. Then, when learning goals require students to write responses, such as assessing their ability to make and defend an argument, use the essay format and capitalize on model answers to improve reliability and create a tool we can use to provide students with feedback.

Classroom Connections

Using Written-Response Items Effectively

1. Completion items require students to write a short answer— usually one or two words—in response to a specific question. Be careful to ensure that questions are clearly written, and avoid over-emphasizing low levels of thinking by using interpretive exercises when possible.

   - **Elementary:** A fifth-grade teacher wants to assess his students' understanding of longitude and latitude. He includes the following item on his assessment:

     Look at the map. Which major American city is closest to longitude 88 degrees west and 42 degrees north? _____

     The students are expected to answer "Chicago."

   - **Middle School:** An eighth-grade American history teacher wants to assess her students' understanding of the different branches of our country's government. She includes the following item on her assessment.

     Our country's leaders have decided that texting while driving is dangerous, so they pass a law which states that any person caught texting while driving will be ticketed by police and fined. Which of the three branches of our federal government is responsible for initiating this law? _____

     The students are expected to write "Legislative," or "The legislative branch."

   - **High School:** A high school biology teacher is working with her students on the three major classifications of worms. She includes the following item on a quiz:

     You have a friend who has largely lost his appetite, is losing weight, feels weak, and is complaining that he is experiencing stomach pains. He comments that he had been hiking and drank water from a stream that didn't look completely clean. You suspect he is suffering from a worm infection. Of the three major classifications of worms, which class of worms has he most likely ingested? _____

     The person's symptoms suggest a tapeworm infection, so the students are expected to answer "Flatworm."

2. Essay items require students to write an extended response to a question or problem. To increase the reliability of essay items and create a tool for providing feedback, write model answers for items. Include scoring criteria.

   - **Elementary:** A fourth-grade teacher wants to assess his students' understanding of quadrilaterals. He writes the following item to be included on an assessment.

     Describe four ways in which rectangles, squares, and rhombuses are alike.

     He then prepares the following model response.

(continued)

Rectangles, squares, and rhombuses are alike in the following ways. They are all closed figures. They have four sides. They have four angles. They are composed of straight lines. Opposite angles in each are equal.

Criteria: 1 point for each comparison, for a total of 4 points.

After returning the students' papers, he displays a rectangle, square, and rhombus on his document camera, identifies their common characteristics, and refers to the model answer.

- **Middle School:** A seventh-grade life science teacher is working with his students on the concept of adaptation. He writes the following item to be included on an assessment.

Describe the most important advantage of an animal being warm blooded compared to it being cold blooded. Explain how the advantage relates to the concept of adaptation and provide an example as evidence for your description.

She then prepares the following model response.

The ability to live in a wide variety of places is the primary advantage of warm-blooded animals compared to cold-blooded animals. As a result, warm-blooded animals are more capable of adapting to their environments. For example, we see penguins in Antarctica. They are able to live in this cold climate because they are warm blooded.

Criteria: 2 points each for describing the advantage and how it relates to adaptation, and 2 points for the example, for a total of 6 points. A number of different examples would be appropriate.

After returning the students' papers, the teacher displays and discusses the model answer.

- **High School:** A world history teacher has been working with his students on factors leading up to World War I. He writes the following item to be included on an assessment.

Describe three important causes of World War I. Include a specific example to provide evidence for your description of each cause.

He then prepares the following model response.

Treaties and alliances were one cause. In the years preceding WWI several European nations formed alliances that could send a nation into war if another nation in the alliance was attacked. For instance, one alliance was composed of France, Britain, and Russia—called the Triple Entente—and another was composed of Germany, Austria-Hungary, and Italy—called the Triple Alliance.

Imperialism, the desire for larger empires which could provide nations with raw materials, such as minerals, timber, and agricultural products, was a second cause. The competition led to an increase in hostilities among European nations. For instance, Great Britain was the largest empire in the world—"the sun never sets on the British empire"—but Germany had control of several territories in Africa, as well as Pacific islands.

Militarism was a third cause. An arms race existed among several European nations. For instance, Germany had a major military buildup in the early 1900s, and both Germany and Great Britain greatly increased the size of their navies.

Criteria: 1 point for each comparison, 1 point for each supporting example, for a total of 6 points.

After returning the students' papers he displays the model on his document camera and discusses each of the causes, such as noting that identifying the names of the two alliances was not required to receive full credit.

MyLab Education Self-Check 14.3

Performance Assessments

14.4 Describe different performance assessments, and explain how they contribute to the total assessment process.

Some critics argue that paper-and-pencil assessments, most commonly in the form of multiple-choice tests, lack validity and fail to assess higher level outcomes (Brookhart & Nitko, 2019). In response to these criticisms, the use of **performance assessments**, direct examinations of student performance on tasks relevant to life outside of school, have been emphasized (Popham, 2017). The term *performance assessment* originated in content areas like science and the performing arts, where students were required to demonstrate ability in a real-world situation, such as a laboratory demonstration or recital.

Here are two examples.

A high school auto mechanics teacher wants his students to be able to troubleshoot and diagnose what is wrong with a car engine that won't start. He provides an overview of common starting problems along with actual examples of auto engine malfunctioning. Students discuss the problems in each example; with the assistance of the teacher, they arrive at steps and criteria for troubleshooting unresponsive engines and then use these to guide their work on other engines.

A health teacher reads in a professional journal that the biggest problem people have in applying first aid is not the mechanics per se, but knowing what to do and when. In an attempt to address this problem, the teacher periodically plans "catastrophe" days. Students entering the classroom encounter a catastrophe victim with an unspecified injury. In each case, they must first diagnose the problem and then apply first aid. The teacher observes them as they work and uses the information she gathers in discussions and assessments.

Designing Performance Assessments

Designing performance assessments involves three steps, each designed to make them more valid and reliable (Miller, Linn, & Gronlund, 2013).

1. Specify the performance components we're trying to assess.
2. Structure the setting, balancing realism with safety and logistics.
3. Design assessment procedures with clearly identified criteria.

Specifying Performance Components

The first step in designing any performance assessment is specifying the components you're attempting to measure. A clear description of the performance helps students understand what's required and assists in planning instruction. An example of component specification in the area of persuasive writing is outlined in Figure 14.3.

In some cases, the performance components will be processes—what students actually do—and in others they will be final products. Typically, the focus is initially on processes, with the emphasis shifting to products after procedures are mastered (Waugh & Gronlund, 2013). Examples of processes and products as components of performance are outlined in Table 14.3.

Structuring the Evaluation Setting

For many performance assessments, the evaluation setting already exists. For instance, if we want to assess our students' ability to design and conduct a lab experience in

---

Figure 14.3 Performance outcomes in persuasive writing

Persuasive essay
1. Specifies purpose of the essay
2. Provides evidence supporting the purpose
3. Identifies audience
4. Specifies likely counterarguments
5. Presents evidence dispelling counterarguments

TABLE 14.3 Processes and products as components of performance

Content Area	Product	Process
Math	Correct answer	Problem-solving steps leading to the correct solution
Music	Performance of a work on an instrument	Correct fingering and breathing that produce the performance
English Composition	Essay, term paper, or composition	Preparation of drafts and thought processes that produce the product
Word Processing	Letter or copy of final draft	Proper stroking and techniques for presenting the paper
Science	Explanation for the outcomes of a demonstration	Thought processes involved in preparing the explanation

chemistry, our chemistry classroom is an acceptable evaluation setting, because these classrooms typically contain the infrastructure needed to conduct lab activities. A similar situation exists in our earlier example with auto mechanics.

In cases where time, expense, or safety prevent a real-world setting, intermediate steps can be used. For instance, in driver education, we can't initially put beginning drivers in heavy traffic, so we might begin by having students respond to written case studies, progress to using a simulator, then drive on roads with little traffic, and finally drive in a variety of conditions. As students' driving skills develop, they progress to higher degrees of realism.

When simulations aren't possible, we can design interpretive exercises, similar to those we discussed earlier in the chapter. For instance, a geography teacher wanting to measure students' understanding of the impact of climate and geography on the location of cities might construct the following item.

Look at the following map of a fictitious island and pay particular attention to the latitude, prevailing winds, and ocean currents. Based on this information, identify the best location on the island for a city, and provide a rationale for the location, taking all the available information on the map into account.

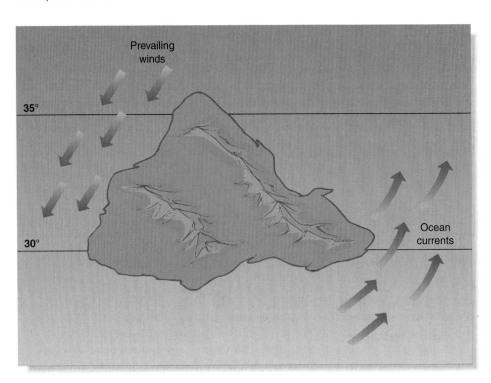

The students' rationales provide insights into their thinking, and their responses could then be compared to the locations of actual cities, such as Hilo on Hawaii or Honolulu on Oahu, in the Hawaiian Island archipelago, so the exercise captures an acceptable level of realism when locating an actual city is obviously impossible.

Designing Evaluation Procedures

Designing evaluation procedures is the final step in using (or implementing) performance assessments. Scoring rubrics, similar to those used with essay items, increase both reliability and validity (Chappuis & Stiggins, 2017). For instance, the rubric in Figure 14.4 could be used to assess geography students' thinking about the location of their cities on the island in our exercise above.

In addition to rubrics, such as those in Figures 14.3 and 14.4, additional tools exist for assessing learner performance. We examine them next.

Tools for Assessing Learner Performance: Systematic Observation, Checklists, and Rating Scales

Systematic observations, checklists, and rating scales can each serve different functions in our assessment systems. Let's examine them in detail.

Systematic Observation

Teachers routinely observe students in classroom settings, but these observations are typically informal, and records are rarely kept. **Systematic observation**, the process of specifying criteria for acceptable performance and taking notes based on the criteria, makes these processes more systematic and thorough. For example, if you're a science teacher assessing your students' ability to use the scientific method in a lab experiment, you might establish the following criteria:

1. States problem or question
2. States hypotheses
3. Specifies independent, dependent, and controlled variables
4. Gathers and displays data
5. Evaluates hypotheses based on data

Your notes then refer directly to the criteria, making them consistent for all groups. You can also use these notes to give students feedback and provide information for use in future planning.

Figure 14.4 Rubric for assessing geography students' thinking

Levels of Achievement

Criteria	1	2	3
Geography	Doesn't include geography in rationale for location of city	Includes geography in rationale, but the link to city location isn't clear	Clearly describes the impact of geography on city's location
Prevailing winds	Doesn't include prevailing winds in rationale for location	Includes prevailing winds, but doesn't explain how the winds impact factors that influence the location of cities	Clearly explains how prevailing winds influence factors such as climate, and how climate impacts the location of cities
Ocean currents	Doesn't include ocean currents in rationale for location of city	Includes ocean currents but doesn't clearly explain how they influence factors that impact the location of cities	Clearly explains how ocean currents will influence livability of cities and how this factor influences the choice of location
Latitude	Doesn't include latitude in rationale for location of city	Includes latitude in discussion of rationale, but doesn't clearly describe how it would impact the location of a city	Clearly explains how latitude would influence the location of a city

Overall Score (9 possible)

Checklists

Checklists, written descriptions of dimensions that must be present in an acceptable performance, extend systematic observation by specifying important aspects of performance, which we can then share with our students. During the assessment, we simply check off the dimensions instead of describing them in notes. Figure 14.5 includes a checklist that could be used to assess students' ability to use the scientific method.

For instance, when using the checklist in Figure 14.5 we would check off each of the five criteria as they appear in students' reports.

Involving students in the process can be an effective for encouraging students' self-assessment when using checklists. For instance, as students are working on a lab project, they could use the checklist in Figure 14.5 as a guide to help them determine whether or not they're meeting the criteria for using the scientific method, and they, rather than we, check off each criterion.

As another example, students could use a checklist to monitor their writing, and criteria such as the following might be included:

1. All sentences begin with a capital letter.
2. Each sentence ends with a period, question mark, or exclamation point.
3. All words are spelled correctly.
4. Each sentence is a complete statement.

Checklists are useful when a component either is or is not present, such as "All sentences begin with a capital letter." The sentences either do or do not begin with capital letters.

However, in the case of the scientific method, for instance "Evaluates hypotheses based on data," some items don't fit the simple present/not present description; some evaluations will be more thorough and precise than others. The same is true in the case of writing with the criterion "Provides evidence to support a conclusion." Some evidence is better than others. Rating scales address this issue.

Rating Scales

Rating scales are written descriptions of the dimensions of an acceptable performance along with scales of values on which each dimension is rated. They can be constructed in numerical, graphic, or descriptive formats. An example of a rating scale that expands the checklist in the previous section appears in Figure 14.6.

As another example, a rating scale similar to one you might encounter when you begin teaching is outlined in Figure 14.7.

Unlike the rating scale in Figure 14.6, the one in Figure 14.7 includes descriptions only for "Levels of effectiveness" 1, 3, and 5. In making an assessment, the observer would infer levels 2 and 4 based on the existing descriptions.

Rating scales are similar to the scoring rubrics we described and illustrated earlier. The primary difference is that a rubric is typically used to assess a written product, such as an essay, whereas a rating scale is used to assess a performance, such as students' ability to use the scientific method, or a teacher's questioning when a supervisor observes a lesson.

Figure 14.5 Checklist for assessing students' use of the scientific method

Criteria	Present	Not Present
1. States problem or question		
2. States hypotheses		
3. Specifies independent, dependent, and controlled variables		
4. Gathers and displays data		
5. Evaluates hypotheses based on data		

Figure 14.6 Rating scale for assessing students' use of the scientific method

Criteria	1	2	3	4	5
1. Problem or question	No problem or question stated	Problem vaguely stated. Uncertain what the problem means	Problem stated but unclear and imprecise	Problem clearly stated but could be more precise	Clearly and precisely stated problem or question
2. Hypotheses related to the question	No hypotheses stated	Hypotheses vaguely stated but not relevant to the problem	Hypotheses vaguely stated but indirectly related to the problem	Hypotheses directly related to the problem but could be stated more clearly	Hypotheses clearly stated and directly related to the problem
3. Independent, dependent, and controlled variables	Variables not specified	Some variables incompletely and vaguely described	Incomplete description of independent, dependent, and controlled variables	Variables specified but could be described more clearly	Variables clearly specified and related to the problem
4. Data gathering	Data not specified	Data gathered but unrelated to the hypotheses	Data gathered but inadequate to assess hypotheses	Data gathered essentially, but not totally complete	Thorough and complete data gathered to allow evaluation of hypotheses
5. Evaluation of hypotheses	No evaluation of hypotheses	Evaluation statements made, but unrelated to hypotheses	Hypotheses evaluated but vague and unclear	Hypotheses evaluated but could be more thorough	Hypotheses thoroughly evaluated

Detailed rating scales also create concrete mechanisms for delivering feedback. In a conference with a student, or teacher in the case of Figure 14.7, the observer can refer directly to the dimensions in the scale to provide specific information about the performance. Rating scales can be valuable tools in our assessment of learner performance.

MyLab Education Application Exercise 14.3: Performance Assessments: Checklists and Rating Scales

In this exercise you will be asked to analyze the way a first-grade teacher and a fifth-grade teacher use checklists to assess their students' learning progress, together with conditions where rating scales would be more appropriate.

Portfolio Assessment: Developing Self-Regulation

Portfolio assessment is the process of selecting collections of student work that both you and your students evaluate using preset criteria (Chappuis & Stiggens, 2017; Popham, 2017). The portfolio is the actual collection of works, and it might include essays written over the school year, projects, samples of poetry, lab reports, video recorded performances, and quizzes and tests. The use of portfolios is common in a wide variety of areas including measuring school readiness for preschool children or assessing art students' developing skills in drawing. As the use of technology advances, electronic portfolios are becoming increasingly popular. Table 14.4 contains examples of portfolio assessments in different content areas.

A major goal of using portfolios is to develop student self-regulation. In the context of assessment, self-regulation means that students take responsibility for their own learning and they use assessments to gather information about their learning progress (Hofer, 2010; Schneider, 2010). For instance, a student writes an essay, and his teacher's written feedback indicates that he didn't provide adequate evidence to support his conclusions. He includes the essay with feedback in his portfolio, and in his next essay, he more carefully documents his conclusions. He rereads his work and concludes that his second essay is better than his first. In her feedback, his teacher corroborates his conclusion. This example illustrates learning progress as a result of his increased self-regulation.

When students are directly involved in the assessment process, they become more metacognitive about their approaches to studying and more reflective about what

MyLab Education
Video Example 14.5

Portfolio assessment involves selecting collections of student work that both teachers and students evaluate using preset criteria. Here we see a teacher and student working together to evaluate the content of the student's portfolio.

Figure 14.7 Rating scale for teaching effectiveness

Levels of Effectiveness

Criteria	1	3	5
Lesson scope	No learning objective is apparent. The focus and scope of the lesson are uncertain.	Learning objective is unclear. The lesson covers too much or too little content.	A clear learning objective is apparent. The scope of the lesson is effective for reaching the objective.
Organization	Materials are not prepared and ready prior to the lesson. Routines are not apparent. Instructional time is wasted.	Some materials are prepared in advance, and some routines are apparent. Instructional time used reasonably well.	Instructional time is maximized with materials prepared in advance and well-established routines apparent.
Quality of examples/ nonexamples	Examples/nonexamples are not used.	Examples/nonexamples are used but are inadequate to accurately represent the topic.	A variety of high-quality examples in context are used to represent the topic.
Review	No review of previous work is conducted.	A brief and superficial review of previous work is present.	A thorough review of ideas necessary to understand the present topic is conducted.
Questioning frequency	Teacher lectured. Few questions were asked.	Some questions were asked. Much of the content was delivered through lecture.	The lesson was developed with questioning throughout.
Equitable distribution of questions	Questions were not directed to specific students.	Some questions were directed to individual students. Volunteers were called on most frequently.	All students in the class were called on as equally as possible, and questions were directed to students by name.
Wait-time and prompting	Little wait-time was given. Unanswered questions were directed to other students.	Intermittent assistance was provided as well as adequate wait-time in some cases.	Students were consistently given wait-time and were prompted when they were unable to answer correctly.
Closure	Lesson lacked closure.	The teacher offered a summary and closure of the lesson.	The teacher guided students as they stated the main ideas of the lesson.
Instructional alignment	Learning objectives, learning activities, and assessment are out of alignment.	Objectives, learning activities, and assessment are partially aligned.	Learning objectives, the learning activity, and assessment are clearly aligned.

Source: Based on *An Examination of the Relationships Between Elementary Teachers' Understanding of Education Psychology and Their Pedagogical Practice,* paper presented at the annual meeting of the American Education Research Association, Chicago, April 2007.

TABLE 14.4 Portfolio examples in different content areas

Content Area	Example
Elementary Math	Homework, quizzes, tests, and projects completed over time.
Writing	Drafts of narrative, descriptive, and persuasive essays in various stages of development. Samples of poetry.
Art	Projects over the course of the year collected to show growth in an area perspective or in a medium painting.
Science	Lab reports, projects, classroom notes, quizzes, and tests compiled to provide an overview of learning progress.

works for them. Portfolios also help develop a sense of ownership and autonomy, both of which increase learner motivation (Schunk et al., 2014).

The following guidelines can increase the effectiveness of portfolios as learning tools:

- Integrate portfolios into our instruction, and refer to them as we teach.
- Provide sample portfolios when introducing students to portfolio assessment.
- Involve students in the selection and evaluation of their work.
- Require students to provide an overview of each portfolio, a rationale for the inclusion of individual works, criteria used to evaluate individual pieces, and a summary of progress.
- Provide students with frequent and detailed feedback about their decisions.

Portfolio assessment is demanding. Also, in the real world, not all students will be responsible for trying to improve, and their seeming lack of effort will be frustrating. For those we reach, however, we make an invaluable contribution to their development—both in school and in life after the school years.

Evaluating Performance Assessments

As with paper-and-pencil formats, such as multiple choice or essay, performance assessments have strengths and weaknesses. For instance, advocates of performance and portfolio assessment contend that these formats tap higher level thinking and problem-solving skills, emphasize real-world applications, and focus on the processes learners use to produce their products (DiMartino & Castaneda, 2007).

Issues exist with these alternatives, however. First, they are time and labor intensive. Examining individual students' portfolios, for example, is very time consuming and demanding. Second, reliability is an issue, and obtaining acceptable levels of reliability has historically been a problem (Barnes, Torrens, & George, 2007; Tillema & Smith, 2007).

At the classroom level, allowing students to determine portfolio content creates additional problems. For example, when students choose different items to place in their portfolios, cross-student comparisons are difficult, which decreases reliability. To address this issue, experts recommend supplementing portfolios with traditional measures to obtain the best of both processes (Chappuis & Stiggens, 2017).

As with all aspects of learning and teaching, assessment is complex, and your knowledge, skill, and professional judgment will be crucial in designing assessments that maximize learning for all your students. Our recommendation is that you make selected-response and written-response items the core of your assessment system and you supplement them with performance assessments where appropriate. This is efficient and accommodates the reliability issues that exist with performance assessments, while at the same time capturing an acceptable level of realism.

Classroom Connections

Using Performance Assessments Effectively

1. Performance assessments directly examine students' ability to perform tasks similar to those they will be expected to perform in life outside of school. Increase the validity of your assessments by using performance assessment when appropriate.

- **Elementary:** A first-grade teacher uses a rating scale to assess his students' oral reading ability. While he listens to each student read, he uses additional notes to help him remember each student's strengths and weaknesses. He uses these

at parent–teacher conferences to provide caregivers with an accurate picture of each student's reading progress.

- **Middle School:** A math teacher working on decimals and percentages brings in store ads from three local supermarkets and asks students to compare prices on five household items. Students must determine which store provided the best bargains and the percentage difference between the stores on each item.

(continued)

- **High School:** A teacher in business technology has students write letters in response to job notices in the newspaper. The class then critiques the letters in terms of format, grammar, punctuation, and clarity, using a rubric the class had developed previously.

2. Portfolio assessments involve students in the assessment process. Use portfolios to develop learner self-regulation.

- **Elementary:** A fourth-grade teacher uses portfolios as an organizing theme for his language arts curriculum. Students collect pieces of work during the year and evaluate and share them with other members of their writing teams.

- **Middle School:** A math teacher asks each student to compile a portfolio of work and present it at parent–teacher conferences. Before the conference, the teacher meets with students and helps them identify their strengths and weaknesses.

- **High School:** An auto mechanics teacher makes each student responsible for keeping track of the competencies and skills each has mastered. Each student is given a folder and must document the completion of different shop assignments.

MyLab Education Self-Check 14.4

Effective Summative Assessments

14.5 Identify the elements of an effective summative assessment system.

High-quality formative assessment is essential for making decisions designed to increase our students' learning. A second essential process involves determining how much students have learned and assigning grades that reflect their achievement. This process allows us to communicate how much learning has occurred to students, their parents, and others, such as school and district administrators.

APA Top 20 Principles

The discussion in this section of the chapter illustrates Principle 19: *Students' skills, knowledge, and abilities are best measured with assessment processes grounded in psychological science with well-defined standards for quality and fairness*—from the *Top 20 Principles from Psychology for PreK–12 Teaching and Learning*.

This is the essence of summative assessment, the topic of this portion of the chapter. Here, we focus primarily on quizzes and tests and how we use them in making decisions about learning progress and grades. (The concepts *quiz* and *test* are not precisely defined. In essence, a quiz is a short test, so the two terms can be used interchangeably.)

As you study this section, keep one important idea in mind. Just because the function of summative assessment is to help us determine how much our students have learned, and reflect that learning in a grade, this does not imply in any way that these assessments are not learning tools. Exactly the opposite is true. For instance, if we give our students a quiz and record their scores in our gradebook, we should also discuss the quiz with them and provide detailed feedback. As we said at the beginning of the chapter, a long history of research suggests that combining assessments with feedback is one of the most powerful learning tools we have (Crooks, 1988; Hattie, 2012; Pomerance et al., 2016; Rohrer et al., 2010).

We have four suggestions designed to make summative assessments effective learning tools. First, emphasize that promoting learning is the primary purpose of all tests and quizzes and that we and our students are "in this together." They're responsible for studying diligently, and we're responsible for helping them as much as we can. This suggestion can help change the perception that quizzes and tests are somehow punitive.

Second, assess thoroughly and often. Give more rather than fewer quizzes and tests. Research indicates that the more times learners revisit a topic, the deeper their understanding becomes (Rohrer et al., 2010; Rohrer & Pashler, 2010). So, for instance, if they practice with homework, then respond to a quiz that covers that same content, and finally respond a third time on a 9-week test, they will first work with the topic and then revisit it two more times. It makes sense that their understanding will deepen with each encounter. Research confirms this contention both at the P–12 level (McDaniel et al., 2011) and for students at universities (Crooks, 1988; Gonzalez & Eggen, 2017).

Third, provide students with detailed feedback for all assessments—homework, tests, quizzes, and performance assessments. We address this idea in detail later in this section.

Finally, provide students with ample practice in preparing for assessments. We turn to this suggestion now.

Preparing Students

Preparing students for assessments is important, because we want our assessments to reflect our students' understanding and not their ability to interpret what we're asking. To illustrate this idea, let's look at DeVonne's work with her students the day before she gives her unit test.

"Get out your chalkboards," DeVonne directs, referring to individual chalkboards each student has to show his or her work on math problems.

"We're having a test tomorrow on finding equivalent fractions and adding fractions, and the test will go in your math portfolios. . . . I have some problems on the test that are going to make you think. . . . But you've all been working hard, and your hard work is paying off, so you'll be able to do it. You're my team, and I know you'll come through," she says, smiling.

"To be sure we're okay, I have a few problems that are just like ones on the test, so let's see how we do. Write these on your chalkboards."

$$\frac{1}{3} + \frac{1}{4} = ? \qquad \frac{2}{7} + \frac{4}{7} = ?$$

DeVonne watches as they work on the problems and hold up their chalkboards when they finish. Seeing that three students miss the first problem, she reviews it with the class, and then displays the following three:

$$\frac{2}{3} + \frac{1}{6} = ? \qquad \frac{4}{9} + \frac{1}{6} = ? \qquad \frac{2}{9} + \frac{4}{9} = ?$$

Two students miss the second one, so again she reviews it carefully.

"Now, let's try one more," she continues, displaying the following problem on the document camera:

> You are at a pizza party with 5 other people, and you order 2 pizzas. The 2 pizzas are the same size, but one is cut into 4 pieces and the other is cut into 8 pieces. You eat 1 piece from each pizza. How much pizza did you eat in all?

Again, she watches the students work and reviews the solution with them when they finish, asking questions such as:

- "What information in the problem is important?"
- "What do we see in the problem that's irrelevant?"
- "What should we do first in solving it?"

After discussing two more word problems, she tells students, "The problems on the test tomorrow are like the ones we practiced here today," asks if they have any additional questions, and finishes her review by saying, "All right, when we take a test, what do we always do?"

"We read the directions carefully!" they shout in unison.

"Okay, good," DeVonne says, smiling. "Now, remember, what will you do if you get stuck on a problem?"

"Go on to the next one so we don't run out of time."

"And what will we be sure not to do?"

"We won't forget to go back to the one we skipped."

DeVonne prepared her students for her test in four ways. She:

- Specified what would be on the test.
- Gave students a chance to practice under test-like conditions.
- Established positive expectations and encouraged students to link effort and success.
- Encouraged her students to use specific test-taking strategies.

By specifying what will be on a test and identifying the test format, the teacher provides structure for students, leading to higher achievement, which is particularly important for those who struggle with the content.

Specifying test content often isn't enough, however, particularly with young learners, so giving students practice exercises and presenting them in a format that parallels their appearance on the test is important (Geno, 2014). In learning math skills, for instance, DeVonne's students first practiced adding fractions with like denominators, then learned to find equivalent fractions, and finally added fractions with unlike denominators, each in separate lessons. On the test, however, the problems were mixed, so DeVonne gave students a chance to practice integrating these skills before they took the actual test.

APA Top 20 Principles

This entire discussion illustrates Principle 5: *Acquiring long-term knowledge and skill is largely dependent on practice*—from the *Top 20 Principles from Psychology for PreK–12 Teaching and Learning*.

DeVonne also communicated that she expected her students to do well on the test, and the motivational benefits of establishing positive expectations on our assessments is confirmed by research (Schunk et al., 2014). She also emphasized effort and the influence of hard work on success by saying, "But you've all been working hard, and your hard work is paying off, so you'll be able to do it." Encouraging students to believe that ability can be improved with effort benefits both immediate performance and long-term motivation.

Finally, DeVonne encouraged her students to employ specific test-taking strategies. Let's look at this idea in more detail.

Teaching Test-Taking Strategies

We can help our students improve their performance by teaching them strategies such as the following:

- Read directions carefully.
- Identify important information in questions.
- Use time efficiently and pace themselves.

DeVonne encouraged the use of these strategies. To illustrate, let's look again at some of the dialogue in her lesson.

DeVonne:	All right, when we take a test, what do we always do?
Students:	We read the directions carefully!
DeVonne:	Okay, good. . . . Now, remember, what will you do if you get stuck on a problem?
Students:	Go on to the next one so we don't run out of time.
DeVonne:	And what will we be sure not to do?
Students:	We won't forget to go back to the one we skipped.

With older students, explaining how questions will be scored and describing the nuances of different testing formats is also helpful. Strategy instruction improves performance and especially benefits young and low-ability students and those who have limited test-taking experience (Geno, 2014).

Reducing Test Anxiety

Ed Psych and You

Have you ever felt that you were prepared for a big test and "blanked" when you turned it over? Have you ever felt like you knew the content but didn't do well on the test because of being nervous? What can you do about it?

Think about the first two questions we asked in *Ed Psych and You*. If you answered yes—and most of us have had this experience—you experienced classic **test anxiety**, an unpleasant emotional reaction to testing situations that can lower performance. Usually, it is momentary and minor, but for a portion of the school population (estimates run as high as 10%), it can be a serious problem (Schunk et al., 2014; Wood, Hart, Little, & Phillips, 2016).

Test anxiety is triggered by testing situations that: (1) involve pressure to succeed, (2) are perceived as difficult, (3) impose time limits, and (4) contain unfamiliar items or formats (Schunk et al., 2014). Research suggests that test anxiety has both an emotional and a cognitive component (Cassady, 2010; Englert & Bertrams, 2013). Its emotional component can lead to physiological symptoms, such as increased pulse rate, dry mouth, upset stomach, and headache, as well as feelings of dread and helplessness. Its cognitive—or worry—component involves preoccupation with test difficulty, thoughts of failure, and other concerns, such as parents being upset by a low score. Thoughts such as "I've never seen this stuff before," "This stuff is hard," and "I'm going to flunk" occupy working memory, which leaves less of its limited capacity to focus on the test itself.

As teachers, we can help reduce test anxiety in our students, and the most successful efforts focus on the worry component (Schunk et al., 2014). Suggestions include:

- Discussing test content and procedures before testing, as DeVonne did, and giving clear directions for responding to test items.
- Giving more—rather than fewer—quizzes and tests to lower the significance of any one assessment.
- Minimizing the competitive aspects of tests by focusing on criterion measures (e.g., 90 and above is an A, 80 is a B, and so on) and avoiding social comparisons, such as public displays of test scores. (We discuss criterion referencing later in this section.)
- Teach test-taking skills, and give students ample time to take tests.
- Use a variety of assessment formats to allow students to demonstrate their understanding and skills in different ways.

Now, let's look again at the third question we asked in *Ed Psych and You*: "What can you do about it?" (being nervous when beginning a test). The first thing is to realize that a certain amount of anxiety is normal, and if you're well prepared, it can even increase test performance (Cassady, 2010). Then, the most effective way to deal with test anxiety is to study and prepare to the point that your understanding is so thorough that you succeed in spite of your nervousness. From a student's perspective, this is the best strategy for coping with text anxiety.

We offer this advice from personal experience. We were both highly test-anxious as students, so we would study to the point where we'd say to ourselves, "There isn't anything they can ask me that I don't know." Students, including those in college, often fail to study as thoroughly as necessary, and they tend to believe they understand a topic better than they do (Bembenutty, 2009). As a result, their anxiety can spike when they're faced with a test, particularly if the test measures understanding beyond recall of factual information.

Pop Quizzes.   We recommend that you don't give unannounced quizzes—**pop quizzes**—for two reasons. First, they're one of the most powerful triggers for test anxiety, so they exacerbate the negative feelings that test-anxious students experience. Second, research suggests that they don't increase learning (Alizadeh, KarimiMoonaghi, Haghir, JafaeiDalooei, & Saadatyar, 2014). When pop quizzes are part of an instructor's policy, anxiety spikes, but students don't necessarily study more. Instead, they simply hope their instructor doesn't give a quiz that day. On the other hand, when quizzes are announced, students know they're going to be assessed, and they can then decide how much, or how little, they're going to study. If they choose to not study, and then do poorly, they realize it was their choice. Pop quizzes are not a part of an effective assessment system.

The Summative Assessment Process

The summative assessment process includes three components:

- Giving quizzes and tests
- Analyzing results
- Providing feedback

Giving Quizzes and Tests

When we give a quiz or test, we want to ensure that results accurately reflect what students know and can do. Let's return to DeVonne's work with her students to see how she increased her assessments' validity.

Just before she gives her test, DeVonne shuts a classroom window because of noise from delivery trucks outside. She considers rearranging the desks in the room but decides to wait until after the test.

"Okay, everyone, let's get ready for our math test," she directs, as students put their books under their desks.

She waits a moment, sees that everyone's desk is clear, and says, "When you're finished, turn the test over, and I'll come and get it. Now look up at the board. After you're done, work on the assignment listed there until everyone is finished. Then we'll start reading." As she hands out the tests, she says, "If you get too warm, raise your hand, and I'll turn on the air conditioner. I shut the window because of the noise outside."

"Work carefully," she says after everyone has a copy. "You've all been working hard, and I know you will do well. You have as much time as you need."

As students begin working, DeVonne stands at the side of the room, watching them.

After several minutes, she notices Anthony doodling at the top of his paper and glancing around the room. She goes over and says, "It looks like you're doing fine on these problems," pointing to some near the top of the paper. "Now concentrate a little harder. I'll bet you can do most of the others." She smiles reassuringly and again moves to the side of the room.

DeVonne goes over to Hajar in response to her raised hand. "The lead on my pencil broke, Mrs. Lampkin," she whispers.

"Take this one," DeVonne responds, handing her another pencil. "Come and get yours after the test."

As students finish, DeVonne picks up their papers, and they begin the assignment on the board.

Now let's consider DeVonne's efforts. First, she arranged her classroom to be comfortable and free from distractions. Distractions can depress test performance, particularly in young or struggling students (Vaughn, Bos, & Schumm, 2018). Second, she gave specific directions for taking the test, turning in the papers, and spending time afterward. These directions helped maintain order and prevented further distractions for late-finishing students. Finally, she carefully monitored students as they worked. This both allowed her to encourage those who were distracted and also discouraged cheating. In the real world, some—and particularly older—students will cheat if given the opportunity. However, an emphasis on learning versus performance and efforts to create a safe and emotionally supportive classroom environment decrease the likelihood of cheating (O'Connor, 2011; Pulfrey, Buchs, & Butera, 2011). In addition, external factors, such as leaving the room, influence the likelihood of cheating more than students going into testing situations inclined to do so.

In DeVonne's case, monitoring was more a form of support than of being a watchdog. For example, when she saw that Anthony was distracted, she quickly intervened, encouraged him, and urged him to increase his efforts. This encouragement is particularly important for students who are underachieving or test-anxious.

Analyzing Results

Both the overall difficulty of the test and the difficulty of individual items are important factors to consider when analyzing our assessment results. Difficulty levels are especially important in this era of accountability and criterion-referenced assessment. We need to know how many students master essential content and whether or not we can go on to the next topic. We can get a measure of the test's overall difficulty by simply calculating the average score. Then, if we choose to do so, we can compute difficulty levels for individual items with the following simple formula (Miller et al., 2013):

$$D = \frac{\text{Number of students answering correctly}}{\text{Number of students taking the assessment}}$$

Teachers typically use more informal methods, such as scanning the results and looking for frequently missed items and items that most students answer correctly.

We can get valuable information by analyzing individual items, and we urge you to do so. For example, look at the results for the following multiple-choice item. (The numbers in parentheses indicate the number of students who selected each option.)

The Vietnam War primarily occurred during which time period?

    a. 1930–1940 (0)
    b. 1940–1950 (3)
    c. 1950–1960 (4)
    d. 1960–1970 (18)
    e. 1970–1980 (4)

This suggests that most of the class (60%) understood the relative time frame for the Vietnam War.

Now, consider this item.

Which of the following is a reptile?

    a. Frog (7)
    b. Shrimp (5)
    c. Trout (6)
    d. Turtle (8)

Responses to the item suggest that students have misconceptions about the topic—8 students answered correctly, but 18 didn't. So, we will need to take steps to deal with these misconceptions. This leads us to the process of providing feedback.

Providing Feedback
Before revisiting the items above, let's see how DeVonne provided her students with feedback on her tests.

As DeVonne returns their papers, she comments, "Overall, you did well, and I'm proud of you. I knew all that hard work would pay off. . . . There are a few items I want to go over, though. We had a little trouble with number 13, and you all made nearly the same mistake, so let's take a look at it."

She waits a moment while students read the problem and then asks, "Now, what are we given in the problem? . . . Saleina?"

"Mr. El had two dozen candy bars."

"Okay. Good. And how many is that? . . . Kevin?"

"Umm . . . two dozen is 24."

"Fine. And what else do we know? . . . Hanna?"

DeVonne continues the discussion of the problem and then goes over two others that were frequently missed. In the process, she makes notes at the top of her copy, identifying the problems that were difficult. She writes "Ambiguous" by one and underlines some of the wording in it. By another, she writes, "Teach them how to draw diagrams of the problem." She then puts her copy of the test in a folder, lays it on her desk to be filed, and turns back to the class.

Here, we see that DeVonne discussed frequently missed items, and perhaps more importantly, she didn't simply explain how to solve the problem. Rather, she interacted with her students as she did during her learning activity. Providing feedback in this way is much more effective than simply explaining the problem, for one important reason. If her students didn't understand the problem, a simple verbal explanation is unlikely to clear up the misunderstanding.

Now, let's look at the two multiple-choice items again.

The Vietnam War primarily occurred during which time period?

a. 1930–1940 (0)
b. 1940–1950 (3)
c. 1950–1960 (4)
d. 1960–1970 (18)
e. 1970–1980 (4)

Although the majority of students answered correctly, 11 did not. As a form of feedback that would increase learning for the whole class, we could display a timeline on which important historical periods, such as the Great Depression, World War II, the Korean War, and the Vietnam War, are displayed. The timeline would provide a visual representation of these time periods and would be informative feedback.

Now, let's look at the second item.

Which of the following is a reptile?

a. Frog (7)
b. Shrimp (5)
c. Trout (6)
d. Turtle (8)

Responses to this item suggest that students have misconceptions about the topic—8 students answered correctly, but 18 didn't. This is the kind of information we want when we assess, and armed with this information, we can provide students with additional examples of amphibians, crustaceans, fish, and reptiles. Doing so would increase students' understanding of each type of animal.

In many cases, more learning occurs as a result of feedback on quizzes and tests than in original instruction, because student motivation is high. For instance, students who selected choice *a*—frog—in the second item will want to know why their answer was incorrect. As the item is discussed, their understanding of amphibians and reptiles, and why they're often confused, will be advanced. This example helps us understand why assessment is such a powerful learning tool, and why feedback is so important. "There is a preponderance of evidence that feedback is a powerful influence in the development of learning outcomes. . . . The average effects of feedback are among the highest we know in education. . . ." (Hattie & Gan, 2011, p. 249).

Informative feedback is particularly important for items written at levels above knowledge and recall. Students typically struggle with these items because they don't have a great deal of experience with these cognitive levels, and informative feedback helps advance students' thinking.

APA Top 20 Principles

The discussion in this section illustrates Principle 6: *Clear, timely, and explanatory feedback to students is important for learning*—from the *Top 20 Principles from Psychology for PreK–12 Teaching and Learning*.

Finally, clearly writing essay items and interpretive exercises using the multiple-choice items is a challenge, and inevitably some students will misinterpret the items. Feedback and discussion help us identify wording in items that are misinterpreted; we can then revise the items and reuse them. DeVonne's notes at the top of her test will help her in this process. This leads us to suggestions for reducing our assessment workload.

Increasing the Efficiency of Assessment Practices

Throughout this chapter we've emphasized that assessing more than knowledge and recall of information is important. We can reach this goal with selected-response items, and particularly multiple choice, but the items must be largely interpretive exercises, as we saw earlier in our discussion. Constructing these items is extremely challenging. For instance, we—your authors—have spent literally hundreds of hours constructing the test bank that accompanies this text.

So, to meet this challenge, we have two suggestions.

Create an Item File

Creating an item file of paper-and-pencil items, both selected response and written response, is one of the most important actions you can take for improving both the quality and the efficiency of your summative assessment practices. Use the best items from tests that are included with your textbook, and supplement them with those you construct yourself. Store the information in your computer, so that next time you can create tests and quizzes from the file.

As your item file expands, assessing your students will become more and more efficient. During planning, you merely select items from the file that best help you determine if your students are meeting your learning objectives and create your tests and quizzes from them.

You will be very busy when you teach, and it's literally impossible to create high-quality interpretive exercises for every summative assessment. You simply cannot continually create new items at levels above recall of factual information from scratch. You won't have the time. This helps us understand why the overwhelming majority of teacher-made test items measure knowledge and recall instead of higher level thinking.

In addition, it's challenging to create items that are clear and unambiguous. So, for instance, we administer an item, realize students misinterpret it, revise it, and store it back in the item file. Then, as we use the items over and over, we have high-quality assessments, and our workload is dramatically reduced.

Collect and File Students' Quizzes and Tests

After giving a quiz or test, returning it, and providing students with detailed feedback, collect the tests and store them in a file for your students. (We use this practice with our students.)

This suggestion may seem counterintuitive, and might even be controversial, but, again, it's impossible to continually create high-quality test items that measure more than knowledge and recall. So, you need to reuse your items. By collecting quizzes and tests, and storing them for students, you're able to reuse your items, which increases your efficiency.

This suggestion doesn't detract from providing feedback, because you have thoroughly discussed frequently missed items before collecting the quizzes or tests. You can invite students to come in to review a quiz or test anytime after it's given. You only need to get it from the student's file and discuss it in as much detail as necessary. You can also provide students with extra help before or after school—or during other free times—by simply pulling their quiz from the file and going over it in detail. You can do the same with parents who might want detailed information about their child's performance.

These suggestions will help you increase the quality of your assessments, because they will improve over time. It will also dramatically increase the efficiency of the assessment process because you won't be spending time trying to create new, high-quality items. This process takes time and effort, but once you have created a file of high-quality items, you can use your test and quizzes as "assessment *for* learning."

Designing a Grading System

Creating high-quality assessment items and effective test administration procedures increase the likelihood that your assessments will be valid and reliable. But individual tests, quizzes, and assignments must be integrated into a comprehensive grading system. Designing a grading system raises several questions:

- How many tests and quizzes should I give?
- How will I count homework?
- How will I use performance assessments?
- How will I assess and report affective dimensions, such as cooperation and effort?

The answers to these questions will be your responsibility, a prospect that may seem daunting, because you have little experience to fall back on. However, knowing that the decisions are yours removes some of this uncertainty. We discuss these issues in this section.

An effective grading system provides feedback to students, helps them develop self-regulation, and increases motivation. It also aids communication with our students' parents. The following suggestions can help you design an effective grading system:

- Create a system that is clear, understandable, and consistent with school and district policies.
- Design the system to support learning by gathering frequent and systematic information from each student.
- Base grades on observable data.
- Assign grades consistently regardless of gender, class, race, or socioeconomic status.

MyLab Education
Video Example 14.6

In designing assessment systems, expert teachers combine results from paper-and-pencil items with performance measures in their grading practices. Here we see third-grade teacher, Brooke Bigsby, describe the components she includes in her overall assessment system.

These suggestions are important because we must be able to confidently defend our system to a parent or administrator if necessary (Miller et al., 2013).

Norm-Referenced and Criterion-Referenced Grading Systems

Ed Psych and You

After taking a test, do you want to know how you performed compared to the other students in your class? Or do you want to know what your grade is? How do these two kinds of information differ?

Grading is an integral part of summative assessment, and norm-referenced and criterion-referenced systems are two ways of assigning grades. When **norm-referenced grading** is used, assessment decisions are based on an individual's performance compared to the performance of peers. The following is an example:

A Top 15% of students
B Next 20% of students
C Next 30% of students
D Next 20% of students
F Last 15% of students

When using **criterion-referenced grading**, we make decisions according to a predetermined standard, such as 90–100 for an A, 80–89 for a B, and so on. The specific standards vary among school districts, schools, and teachers. These standards are usually established by the district or school, but in some cases, the decision will be yours.

Criterion-referenced systems have two important advantages over those that are norm-referenced (Chappuis & Stiggens, 2017). First, because they reflect the extent to which learning objectives are met, they more accurately describe content mastery, which is important in this era of accountability. Second, they de-emphasize competition. Competitive grading systems discourage students from helping each other, threaten peer relationships, and decrease motivation, especially for students with a history of low achievement. While norm-referencing is important in standardized testing, it is rarely used in classrooms, and it's highly unlikely that you'll encounter it when you begin teaching.

This discussion addresses the questions we asked in *Ed Psych and You*. If you're like most students, you will want to know the criteria for earning grades at the beginning of the semester. In addition, while we don't want to openly compete with our classmates, most of us want to know how we've done on a quiz or test compared to others.

We encourage you to minimize these comparisons in your work with students. Statements such as "Our goal is to learn as much as possible, not compete with our classmates, so don't think about how you did compared to others" can help. They won't completely eliminate students' tendencies to compare themselves to others, but they can make a difference in promoting a learning-focused instead of a performance-focused learning environment.

Combining Paper-and-Pencil and Performance Assessments

For those of you who will teach in upper elementary, middle, and high schools, paper-and-pencil assessments—the selected-response and written-response formats we discussed earlier—will be the cornerstones of your grading system. Some teachers add tests and quizzes together and count them as a certain percentage of the total grade; others weigh them differently in assigning grades.

If performance assessments or portfolios are part of an assessment system, they should be included in determining grades. Not including them communicates that they're less important than the paper-and-pencil measures, and students won't take them seriously. If we use well-defined criteria in rating student performance, we can achieve acceptable reliability.

Homework

Properly designed homework contributes to learning, but to be most effective, it should be included in grading systems. Students—particularly those who are older—exert little effort on homework when credit isn't given (Lee & Shute, 2010; Marzano, 2007). Beyond this point, research provides little guidance for managing homework. Accountability, feedback, and your own workload will all influence this decision. Table 14.5 outlines some homework-assessment options.

As we see in Table 14.5, each option has advantages and disadvantages. The best strategy is one that encourages students to do their homework conscientiously without requiring an inordinate amount of time and effort from you.

Assigning Grades

Having made decisions about paper-and-pencil and performance assessments, portfolios, and homework, you're now ready to design your grading system. At this point, you'll need to make two decisions: (1) what to include, and (2) the weight to assign each element.

In addition, some teachers include affective factors, such as effort, class participation, and attitude. Assessment experts discourage this practice, although it's common in classrooms (Miller et al., 2013). Gathering systematic information about affective variables is difficult, and assessing them is highly subjective. In addition, including affective factors in determining grades can be misleading—suggesting that important content has been learned when it may not have been. Factors such as effort, cooperation, and class attendance should be reflected in a separate section of the report card.

Let's look at two teachers' systems for assigning grades:

Kim Sook (Middle school science)		Lea DeLong (High school algebra)	
Tests and quizzes	50%	Tests	45%
Homework	20%	Quizzes	45%
Performance assessments	20%	Homework	10%
Projects	10%		

TABLE 14.5 Homework-assessment options

Option	Advantages	Disadvantages
Grade it yourself	Promotes learning. Allows diagnosis of students. Increases student effort.	Is very demanding for the teacher.
Grade samples	Reduces teacher work, as compared with first option.	Doesn't give the teacher a total picture of student performance.
Collect at random intervals	Reduces teacher workload.	Reduces student effort unless homework is frequently collected.
Change papers, students grade	Provides feedback with minimal teacher effort.	Consumes class time. Doesn't give students feedback on their own work.
Students score own papers	Also provides feedback with minimum teacher effort. Lets students see their own mistakes.	Is inaccurate for purposes of evaluation. Lets students not do the work and copy in class as it's being discussed.
Students get credit for completing assignment	Gives students feedback on their work when it's discussed in class.	Reduces effort of unmotivated students.
No graded homework, frequent short quizzes	Is effective with older and motivated students.	Reduces effort of unmotivated students.

We see that these two grading systems are quite different. Kim, an eighth-grade physical science teacher, emphasizes both homework and **alternative assessments**, which include projects and performance assessments. Traditional tests and quizzes count only 50% in his system. Lea emphasizes tests and quizzes more heavily; they count 90% in her system. The rationale in each case is simple. Kim believes that homework is important for learning and has found that students won't do it unless it's graded. He also includes projects as part of his system, believing they involve his students in the study of science. He uses performance assessments to chart students' progress as they work on experiments and other lab activities. Lea, a secondary Algebra II teacher, believes that students understand the need to do their homework in order to succeed on tests and quizzes, so she de-emphasizes this component in her grading system. Instead, she gives a weekly quiz and three tests during a nine-week grading period.

Standards-based grading, a practice that has become more popular with the emphasis on standards and accountability, targets specific standards and the extent to which students have met them (Deddeh, Main, & Fulkerson, 2010). By focusing on mastery of content, standards-based grading eliminates factors such as effort or credit for homework. Teachers who implement this system claim that it simplifies communication with students and parents because it specifically identifies content and skills that students have learned and provides them with information about knowledge and skills that need additional work.

To maximize learning, students need to understand our grading systems. Even young students can understand the relationship between effort and grades if they are assessed frequently and if their homework is scored and returned promptly. On the other hand, even high school students will have trouble understanding a grading system if it's too complex.

Parents also need to understand our grading systems (Chappuis & Stiggins, 2017). Report cards and graded examples of their child's work are sources of information parents use to gauge their children's learning progress, and this information can be the framework for parent–teacher conferences. An understandable grading system is essential in this process.

Points or Percentages?   In assigning scores to quizzes and tests, we have two options. In a percentage system, we convert each score to a percentage and then average the percentages at the end of the marking period. In a point-based system, students accumulate raw points, and we convert them to a percentage only at the end of the marking period.

A percentage-based system has one important weakness. If a student misses one item on a 10-item quiz, for example, the student's score is 90%. If you give another short quiz, and the student gets three of five items correct, the student's score on the second quiz is 60%, and the average of the two quizzes is 75%. This process gives the two quizzes equal weight, even though the first had twice as many items. The student got 12 of 15 items correct, which is 80%, so a point system more accurately reflects the student's performance.

If averaging percentages is flawed, why is it so common? Simplicity is the primary reason. It is both simpler for teachers to manage and easier to communicate to students and parents. Many teachers, and particularly those in elementary and middle schools, have attempted point systems and later returned to percentages because of pressure from students.

As with most aspects of teaching, the design of a grading system is a matter of your professional judgment. A percentage system is fair if assignments are similar in length, tests are also similar in length, and tests receive more weight than quizzes and assignments. On the other hand, a point system can work if students keep a running total of their points and we tell them the number required for an A, a B, and so on at frequent points in the marking period.

Technology, Learning, and Development: Using Technology to Improve Your Assessment System

Because of its ability to store large amounts of information and process it quickly, technology is a valuable tool for reducing our workload. Technology, and particularly computers, serve three important and time-saving assessment functions (Roblyer & Hughes, 2019):

- Planning and constructing tests
- Analyzing test data, and particularly data gathered from tests using selected-response formats
- Maintaining student records

Planning and Constructing Tests

As we saw earlier, we strongly advocate creating an item file, constructing tests with items from the file, collecting quizzes and tests after you've given them, and revising and storing individual items to be reused in the future. Doing so will both increase the quality of your assessments and save you time and energy.

A number of commercial software programs can assist in this process. These programs have the following capabilities:

- Develop a test file for a variety of formats that can be stored in the system. Within a file, items can be organized by topic, chapter, objective, or difficulty.
- Revise items to eliminate misleading wording and ineffective distractors.
- Select items from the file to generate tests.
- Produce an answer key and student-ready test copies.

You can also store model answers to essay items on your computer, which allow them to be reused. So, once you've written a model answer, you need only revise it to make it clearer; you don't need to re-create the answer every time you use the item.

Analyzing Test Data

Once administered, tests need to be scored and analyzed. If you're a middle or high school teacher with five sections of 30 students and you've given a 40-item test, for example, you face the task of scoring $5 \times 30 \times 40 = 6000$ individual items!

Most schools now have technology that can machine score or scan tests if they're in multiple-choice, true–false, or matching formats, and a number of software programs exist that can machine-score tests. These programs can:

- Score objective tests and provide statistics such as the test average and range of scores.
- Identify the number of students who select each choice in multiple-choice items, the percentage of students who didn't respond to an item, and the correlation of each item with the total test.
- Sort student responses by score, grade/age, or gender.

Your school will most likely also have a technology expert who can help you with each of these tasks.

Maintaining Student Records

We've advocated testing thoroughly and often, because evidence indicates that it increases learning. To take advantage of this capability, you need to be able to store and readily access the information you gather about each student. In addition, your students need to know where they stand in the course to make the best use of their study time. Computer software provides an efficient way of storing, analyzing, and reporting student assessments.

Let's see how one teacher uses them.

I use an electronic gradebook in my teaching, and the program allows me to set it up either by total points or percentages. It also allows me to decide the amount of weight I want to assign to tests, quizzes, homework, and anything else, such as projects, for students' final averages. The program is very user friendly, and it's an enormous time saver. (Nicole Yudin, personal communication, January 2018. Used with permission.)

Your school will have access to one or more electronic gradebook programs, and you will be provided with technical support in setting up and using this software. And, as it continues to improve, technology will become an even more useful tool to make your teaching more efficient.

Diversity: Effective Assessment Practices with Students from Diverse Backgrounds

The current reform movement, with its emphasis on standards, has heightened awareness of the need to increase achievement in all students, and particularly those from diverse backgrounds. The issue is particularly pronounced in urban settings, where diversity is the greatest (Macionis & Parrillo, 2017).

Student diversity influences classroom assessment in three ways. First, learners from diverse backgrounds may lack experience with general testing procedures, different assessment formats, and test-taking strategies. Second, language may be an obstacle, particularly for non-native English speakers, because most assessments are strongly language based (Forte, 2010; Kieffer, Lesaux, Rivera, & Francis, 2009). Third, some learners may not fully understand that assessments promote learning and instead view them as punitive. The following suggestions respond to these issues:

- Attempt to create a learning environment where all actions, and particularly assessments, are designed to promote learning.

- Increase the number of assessments, and provide detailed feedback for all items. Have students explain their thinking when they answer incorrectly. Their explanations can reveal misconceptions or possible ambiguity in individual items, which we can address in our instruction and when we revise our test items.

- Be aware of possible content bias. For example, some students may have limited experiences with household items, such as an iron or vacuum cleaner, activities like camping and hiking, or musical instruments, such as a banjo. If answering a test item correctly requires experience with these ideas, we're measuring both the intended topic and students' general knowledge. Feedback and discussion helps us identify these issues, which we can address when we revise our items.

- Emphasize that mistakes are a normal and valuable part of learning, and present students with ongoing evidence of learning progress.

- De-emphasize grades, and keep all assessment results private. Establish a rule stating that students may not share their scores and grades with each other. (We can't enforce this rule, but it's a symbolic gesture intended to protect students.) This suggestion is also helpful for students with exceptionalities.

- Allow students to drop one or two quizzes a marking period for purposes of grading. This practice reduces test anxiety and communicates that we're "on their side" and want them to succeed. It also contributes to a positive classroom climate.

- Allow non-native English speakers to use a translation dictionary when taking tests, and give them extra time. Read directions to them aloud if necessary, and provide extra help with interpreting language. You may even consider allowing them to take a test at a different time.

- Provide students with extra support outside of regular class time, such as before or after school hours. No substitute exists for the one-to-one help that we can provide during these times.

These suggestions are valuable for all students, and they're particularly important for students who are members of cultural minorities, non-native English speakers, and learners with exceptionalities (Banks, 2015; Turnbull, Turnbull, Wehmeyer, & Shogren, 2016). They characterize the theme of this chapter—assessment *for* student learning.

Classroom Connections

Designing Effective Summative Assessments

1. Frequent and thorough assessments, combined with feedback, promote learning. Design your summative assessment system so that gathering systematic information from each student is a regular part of your class routines.

   - **Elementary:** A second-grade teacher has his students solve two problems each morning that focus on the previous day's math topic. He scores the items, records the scores, and discusses each in detail before moving to the topic for the day.

   - **Middle School:** A geography teacher gives a weekly quiz and three tests during each nine-week grading period, with the majority of the items written a level above the recall of factual information. She provides detailed feedback on each of the items and then collects the quizzes and tests, so she can reuse the items.

   - **High School:** A history teacher gives at least one quiz a week in which students must respond to items such as "Before the Civil War, the South was primarily agricultural rather than industrial. Explain how this might have influenced the outcome of the Civil War." The day after each quiz, she displays an ideal answer to the item and a second, lower-quality response, and the class discusses differences between the two.

2. Preparing students for quizzes and tests is an important part of the summative assessment process. Prepare students by providing them with practice on items similar to those that will appear on the quiz or test, and express positive expectations about their performance.

   - **Elementary:** In anticipation of a quiz on cause and effect, a third-grade teacher gives his students reading passages and has them identify cause-and-effect relationships in the passages.

   - **Middle School:** A middle school social studies teacher presents example items and responses to essay questions similar to those she plans to use on unit tests. With her guidance, students identify both well-written and poorly written responses and explain differences between the two.

   - **High School:** A geometry teacher has his students practice creating constructions similar to those that will appear on an end-of-chapter test.

3. Feedback and discussion of assessment items increases students' understanding of the topics they are studying. Provide detailed feedback on frequently missed items.

   - **Elementary:** The third-grade teacher returns students' papers and discusses each of the items in detail.

   - **Middle School:** The social studies teacher creates ideal responses to the essay items and helps her students identify the components that made those responses ideal.

   - **High School:** The geometry teacher demonstrates how each of the constructions of the items on the test could be created. He guides a discussion of alternate ways the constructions could be accomplished.

4. Effective grading systems are understandable to both students and their parents. Create a grading system that is understandable and consistent with school policies.

   - **Elementary:** A fourth-grade teacher's school uses a 70–79, 80–89, and 90–100 grading system for a C, B, and A, respectively. She explains the system in a letter to her students' parents, and routinely sends home packets of student papers that indicate the students' learning progress.

   - **Middle School:** A math teacher displays his grading system on a wall chart. He explains the system and what it requires of students. He emphasizes that it is designed to promote learning and returns to the chart periodically to remind students of their learning progress.

   - **High School:** A history teacher in a school with high percentages of minority students takes extra time and effort during parent–teacher conferences to explain how she arrives at grades for her students. She saves students' work samples and shares them with parents during conferences.

Developmentally Appropriate Practice
Assessment of Learning with Students at Different Ages

While many aspects of assessment, such as using backward design to align assessments with learning objectives, ensuring that assessments are valid and reliable, and using them to promote learning, apply at all developmental levels, important differences exist. The following paragraphs outline suggestions for responding to these differences.

Working with Students in Early Childhood Programs and Elementary Schools

Young children are just learning to play the school game, and assessment is often one of its more puzzling aspects. They come from environments where play and informal social interaction are parts of their daily lives, and sit-down, paper-and-pencil assessments, such as multiple choice, are often strange and confusing to them.

To accommodate these developmental factors, performance assessments, such as checklists and rating scales, can be used to provide information about achievement. Performance tasks, such as identifying vowel and consonant sounds, decoding words, printing letters, writing and ordering numbers, and representing numbers on a number line, all provide valuable assessment information. When paper-and-pencil assessments are used, support in the form of detailed directions and ample opportunities to practice is helpful.

In addition to gathering accurate information about learning progress, helping students begin to understand how assessment influences learning is an important goal. Positive experiences with assessment tasks can lay a firm foundation for future classroom learning and motivation.

Affective outcomes, such as "Gets along well with others," are also more prominent on elementary report cards than with older students. Because of these emphases, being aware of the possibility that our casual observations may be unreliable is important. Attempting to gather the same information from all students and increasing the frequency of assessments are essential when assessing young children's knowledge and skills.

Working with Students in Middle Schools

The cognitive demands on middle school students increase significantly, and teachers use paper-and-pencil assessments to a much greater degree than do elementary teachers. For example, in social studies, eighth-graders are expected to understand ideas such as the ways in which architecture, language, and beliefs have been transmitted from one culture to another; in science they are expected to understand the difference between weight and mass, and the relationships between the temperature and the motion of particles; in math they are expected to solve systems of linear equations; and in language arts they are expected to understand literary devices, such as meter and figurative language.

These are all abstract ideas, and instructional alignment is the key to effective assessment of these topics. If topics are taught in the abstract, they won't be meaningful to students, and students will memorize what they can in order to perform acceptably on the assessments. Instruction that includes high-quality examples and a great deal of discussion is necessary to make the topics meaningful. Then, assessments that also employ examples, such as the interpretive exercises, are effective for promoting learning.

Working with Students in High Schools

Standards for high school students typically require a great deal of abstract thinking. For instance, in language arts they are expected to understand how strategies such as hyperbole, rhetorical questioning, and glittering generalities are used as persuasive techniques; in science they are required to understand atomic theory, and in social studies they are asked to understand why ancient civilizations such as those in Mesopotamia, Egypt, and the Indus Valley evolved and were successful. As with middle school students, unless these topics are meaningfully taught, students will try memorizing enough information to survive assessments, and then information will be promptly forgotten. To make the information meaningful, teachers need to use a variety of ways to represent topics, such as vignettes, timelines, and artifacts in history, and well-designed models and simulations in science. If the topics are meaningfully taught, and assessments are aligned with the instruction, assessment for learning can be accomplished.

Chapter 14 Summary

1. Describe assessment *for* student learning and explain how formative and summative assessments contribute to it.
   - Assessment *for* learning makes assessment an integral part of the teaching–learning process, designed to support and increase learning, enhance learner motivation, and develop self-regulation.
   - Backward design is a systematic approach to planning that emphasizes making assessment decisions during the planning process.
   - Formative assessment involves processes teachers use to gather information that helps them make decisions about the next steps in learning activities. Summative assessments provide information that is used as a basis for making conclusions about how much learning has occurred.
   - Both formative and summative assessments are designed to increase student learning.
   - High-quality assessments are valid and reliable. Validity involves making accurate inferences from assessment information and using the inferred information appropriately; reliability describes the extent to which assessments provide consistent results.

2. Identify the characteristics of selected-response items, and evaluate specific selected-response items.
   - The multiple-choice format consists of a description or question called a stem and answer choices, one of which is correct, with the others called distractors.
   - The multiple-choice format can be a highly effective format for assessing a range of cognitive levels and critical thinking.
   - Interpretive exercises are used when higher order thinking is being assessed.
   - The matching format requires learners to classify a series of statements using the same alternatives. It can be an effective format for assessing homogeneous topics, such as authors and their works, historical events and dates, and terms and definitions.
   - True–false is an assessment format that includes statements learners judge as being correct or incorrect. True–false typically measures lower level cognitive outcomes, but with some topics interpretive exercises can be used to measure higher order thinking.
   - Selected-response formats have the advantages of being easy to score, efficient (because they can assess a large amount of content), and reliable. They have the disadvantages of being limited in the outcomes they can measure, such as the ability to make and defend an argument in writing, and the "guess" factor.

3. Describe written-response formats, and explain how to increase the validity and reliability of written-response items.
   - Written-response items are assessment items that require learners to produce, instead of select, a response.
   - Completion is an assessment format that includes a question or incomplete statement requiring learners to write a short—often one word—answer.
   - The completion format is popular with teachers, because completion items seem easy to construct. This can be misleading, because writing clear items that students are unlikely to misinterpret is challenging.
   - Essay is an assessment format that requires students to make extended written responses to questions or problems. Responses can range from one or two sentences, sometimes called *short-answer* items, to several paragraphs.
   - Reliability of scoring is an ongoing issue with the essay format. Reliability can be increased by using rubrics—scoring scales that explicitly describe criteria for grading—and constructing model answers to essay items. The model answers can also be used to provide students with feedback.
   - Written-response items, and particularly the essay format, have the advantage of being able to measure high-level cognitive outcomes but the disadvantage of being time consuming and challenging to score reliably.

4. Describe different types of performance assessments, and explain how they contribute to the total assessment process.
   - Performance assessments involve direct examination of student performance on tasks relevant to life outside of school.
   - Systematic observation, checklists, and rating scales are tools we can use to assess learner performance. Rubrics similar to those used with essay items can help increase the reliability of performance assessments.
   - Portfolio assessment is the process of selecting collections of student work that both teachers and students evaluate using preset criteria. Developing student self-regulation is an important goal when using portfolio assessment.
   - Performance assessments contribute to the total assessment process by being able to measure outcomes that paper-and-pencil formats—both selected-response and written-response—can't measure. Achieving acceptable levels of reliability is a challenge with all forms of performance assessment.

5. Identify the elements of an effective summative assessment system.

- An effective summative assessment system includes emphasizing that increasing learning is the primary function of assessment, assessing thoroughly and often, and providing detailed feedback on all assessments.
- We can prepare students for assessments by having them practice on items similar to those that will be in the quiz or test, teaching test-taking strategies, and taking steps to decrease test anxiety. We recommend avoiding "pop" quizzes.
- Technology can be a valuable tool for constructing test item files, gathering information about specific test items, and storing results.

- Decisions involved in designing a grading system include the number of tests and quizzes, the use of performance assessments, homework, and the assessment and reporting of affective dimensions such as cooperation and effort.
- When working with learners from diverse backgrounds, emphasizing that assessments are designed to increase learning, increasing the number of assessments, dropping one or two quizzes for purposes of grading, looking for signs of content bias, de-emphasizing grades, allowing non-native English speakers and learners with exceptionalities more time, and providing extra support outside of class can increase both achievement and learner motivation.

Preparing for Your Licensure Exam

Understanding Effective Assessment Practices

Your licensure exam will include information related to classroom assessment. We include the following exercises to help you practice for the exam in your state. This book and these exercises will be a resource for you as you prepare for the exam.

At the beginning of the chapter, you saw how DeVonne Lampkin used assessment to help increase her students' achievement.

Let's look now at Ron Hawkins, an urban middle school English teacher, who is involved in assessing his students' understanding of pronoun cases. Read the case study, and answer the questions that follow.

"Today, we're going to begin studying pronoun cases," Ron announces as he starts the lesson. "Everybody turn to page 484 in your text. . . . This is important in our writing because we want to be able to write and use standard English correctly, and this is one of the places where people get mixed up. So, when we're finished, you'll all be able to use pronouns correctly in your writing."

He then writes the following on the board:

Pronouns use the nominative case when they're subjects and predicate nominatives. Pronouns use the objective case when they're direct objects, indirect objects, or objects of prepositions.

"Let's review," Ron continues, briefly discussing direct and indirect objects, predicate nominatives, and objects of prepositions.

"Now let's look at some additional examples," he continues, as he displays the following sentences on the document camera:

1. Did you get the card from Esteban and (I, me)?
2. Will Meg and (she, her) run the concession stand?

3. They treat (whoever, whomever) they hire very well.
4. I looked for someone (who, whom) could give me directions to the theater.

"Okay, look at the first one. Which is correct? . . . Omar?"
"*Me*."
"Good, Omar. How about the second one? . . . Lonnie?"
"*Her*."
"Not quite, Lonnie. . . . Suppose I turn the sentence around and say, 'Meg and her will run the concession stand.' That doesn't sound right, does it? 'Meg and she' is a compound subject, and when we have a subject, we use the nominative case. . . . Okay?"

Lonnie nods and Ron continues, "Look at the third one. . . . Chloe?"

"I'm not sure . . . *whoever*, I guess."

"This one is a little tricky," Ron says with a nod. "When we use *whoever* and *whomever*, *whoever* is the nominative case and *whomever* is the objective case. In this sentence, *whomever* is a direct object, so it is the correct form."

After he finishes, Ron gives students another list of sentences to practice on for homework in which they are to select the correct form of the pronoun.

On Tuesday, Ron reviews these exercises and discusses several additional examples that use *who, whom, whoever,* and *whomever.* He then discusses the rules for pronoun–antecedent agreement (pronouns must agree with their antecedents in gender and number). He again has students analyze examples as he did with pronoun cases.

He continues with pronouns and their antecedents on Wednesday and begins a discussion of indefinite pronouns as antecedents for personal pronouns—*anybody, either, each, one, someone*—and has students analyze examples as before.

Near the end of class on Thursday, Ron announces, "Tomorrow, we're going to have a test on this material: pronoun cases, pronouns and their antecedents, and indefinite pronouns. You have your notes, so study hard. . . . Are there any questions? . . . Good. I expect you all to do well. I'll see you tomorrow."

On Friday morning, as students file into class and the bell rings, Ron picks up a stack of tests from his desk. The test consists of 30 sentences, 10 of which deal with case, 10 with antecedents, and 10 with indefinite pronouns. The final part of the test directs students to write a paragraph. The following are sample items from the test:

Part I. For each of the items below, mark A on your answer sheet if the pronoun case is correct in the sentence, and mark B if it is incorrect. If it is incorrect, supply the correct pronoun.

1. Be careful who you tell.
2. Will Renee and I be in the outfield?
3. My brother and me like water skiing.

Part II. Write the pronoun that correctly completes the sentence.

1. Arlene told us about ____visit to the dentist to have braces put on.
2. The Wilsons planted a garden in ____backyard.
3. Cal read the recipe and put ____ in the file.
4. Each of the girls on the team wore ____school sweater to the game.
5. None of the brass has lost ____shine yet.
6. Few of the boys on the team have taken ____physicals yet.

Part III. Write a short paragraph that contains at least two examples of pronouns in the nominative case and two examples of pronouns in the objective case. (Circle and label these.) Include also at least two examples of pronouns that agree with their antecedents.

Remember! The paragraph must make sense. It cannot be just a series of sentences.

Ron watches as his students work, and seeing that 15 minutes remain in the period and that some students are only starting on their paragraphs, he announces, "You only have 15 minutes left. Watch your time and work quickly. You need to be finished by the end of the period."

He continues monitoring students, again reminding them to work quickly when 10 minutes are left and again when 5 minutes are left.

Luis, Simao, Moy, and Rudy are hastily finishing the last few words of their tests as the bell rings. Luis finally turns in his paper as Ron's fourth-period students are filing into the room.

"Here," Ron says. "This pass will get you into Mrs. Washington's class if you're late. . . . How did you do?"

"Okay, I think," Luis says over his shoulder as he scurries out of the room, "except for the last part. It was hard. I couldn't get started."

"I'll look at it," Ron says. "Scoot now."

On Monday, Ron returns the tests, saying, "Here are your papers. You did fine on the sentences, but your paragraphs need a lot of work. Why did you have so much trouble with them, when we had so much practice?"

"It was hard, Mr. Hawkins."

"Not enough time."

"I hate to write."

Ron listens patiently and then says, "Be sure you write your scores in your notebooks. . . Okay, does everyone have them written down? . . . Are there any questions?"

"Number 3," Enrique requests.

"Okay, let's look at 3. It says, 'My brother and me like waterskiing.' There, the pronoun is part of the subject, so it should be *I* and not *me.*"

"Any others?"

A sprinkling of questions comes from around the room, and Ron responds, "We don't have time to go over all of them. I'll discuss three more."

He responds to the three students who seem to be most urgent in waving their hands. He then collects the tests and begins a discussion of adjective and adverb clauses.

Questions for Case Analysis

Use information from this chapter and the case study to answer the following questions.

Multiple-Choice Questions

1. During his lessons preparing for the test on Friday, Ron gave his students sample sentences similar to the ones that would appear on the test and provided them with feedback. Doing this best described:

   a. alternative assessment

   b. formative assessment

   c. performance assessment

   d. standards-based assessment

2. As Ron gave his students the sample exercise, he watched his students' nonverbal cues for confidence or confusion. This would be an example of:

   a. systematic observation

   b. performance assessment

   c. informal assessment

   d. standards-based assessment

Constructed Response Question

1. In the section on effective assessment practices, suggestions for preparing students for assessments, administering them, and analyzing results were offered. How effectively did Ron perform each task? Describe specifically what he might have done to be more effective in these areas.

MyLab Education Licensure Exam 14.1

Important Concepts

alternative assessments	distractors	portfolio assessment	systematic observation
backward design	essay	rating scales	table of specifications
checklists	formative assessment	reliability	test anxiety
classroom assessment	matching format	rubric	true–false
completion	multiple choice	selected-response items	validity
criterion-referenced grading	norm-referenced grading	standards-based grading	written-response items
data-driven instruction	performance assessments	stem	
	pop quizzes	summative assessment	

Chapter 15
Standardized Testing and Learning

Caiaimage/Chris Ryan/Getty Images

Learning Outcomes

After you have completed your study of this chapter, you should be able to:

15.1 Describe the relationships between standards, accountability, and standardized testing.

15.2 Understand standardized tests and describe their role in the total assessment process.

15.3 Interpret standardized test results for students, parents, and other caregivers.

15.4 Explain how learner diversity can influence the validity of standardized test results.

15.5 Describe your roles in standardized testing processes.

APA Top 20 Principles

Top 20 Principles from Psychology for PreK–12 Teaching and Learning explicitly addressed in this chapter.

> Principle 19: Students' skills, knowledge, and abilities are best measured with assessment processes grounded in psychological science with well-defined standards for quality and fairness.
> Principle 20: Making sense of assessment data depends on clear, appropriate, and fair interpretation.

We've all had experiences with standardized tests and standardized testing. For instance, you likely took the SAT or ACT as part of your college application, and we all took other standardized tests, such as the Stanford Achievement Test, when we were in school.

To introduce this topic, read the following case study and consider how standardized testing influences the work of Mike Chavez, a fourth-grade teacher.

"Hello, Mrs. Palmer," Mike says, offering his hand in greeting. "I'm glad you could come in."

"Thank you," Doris Palmer responds. "I'm a little confused by a report that was sent home with David after he took the Stanford Achievement Test."

"Well, let's take a look," Mike replies as he offers Mrs. Palmer a seat next to his desk.

"Here's what we received," Mrs. Palmer offers, showing Mike the information on the next page.

"I'm not sure what this information means," she continues. "For instance, it says 'Reading' and then this number 65 under 'National PR.' And then there's this information in the box."

"I understand completely," Mike says, smiling. "Let me try to clarify the information. . . . First, the PR stands for percentile rank. That means he scored as well as or better than 65 percent of the students who took this test around the country."

"And what about these 'percentile bands' that we see here?" she continues, pointing to the information in the box.

"A percentile band shows a range in which a student's true score is likely to fall. For instance, see the 30 and the 70 in the box?" Mike says, pointing to the numbers and sliding his finger up the lines. "This represents the range into which scores considered to be average fall. David's percentile rank of 65 is at the high end of this range . . . it's close to 70. However, because

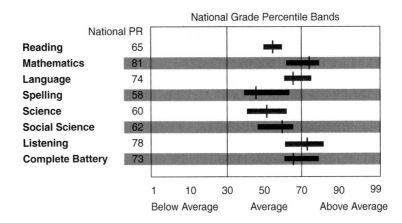

National Grade Percentile Bands

National PR	
Reading	65
Mathematics	81
Language	74
Spelling	58
Science	60
Social Science	62
Listening	78
Complete Battery	73

1 10 30 50 70 90 99
Below Average   Average   Above Average

Home Report | David Palmer

Teacher: Chavez
School: Jennings Elementary
District: Liberty
Grade: 04   **Age:** 10 Yrs. 03 Mos.
Test Date: 04/19   **Student No.** 2971463652

About This Student's Performance Report David recently took the *Stanford Achievement Test Series*, Tenth Edition (Stanford 10). This test is one measure of the student's achievement. This report compares the student's performance to students in the same grade across the nation. Percentile bands show ranges within which this student's true scores likely fall. For example, a student whose percentile band spans the 70th percentile performed as well or better than 70% of the students nationally on that subject—but not as well as 30% of students. The chart below shows this student's performance on each subject area tested.

Reading	Mathematics
The reading subsets measure reading skills, such as relating word sounds and spelling, determining word meanings and synonyms, as well as the understanding, interpretation, and analysis of literary, informational, and functional reading selections.	The mathematics subtests measure problem-solving skills involving number sense, operations, patterns and algebra, data and probability, geometry, and measurement concepts. Also measured is the student's fluency with arithmetic operations involving whole numbers, decimals and fractions.
David's score is in the average range for the grade. Ask your student to help with a grocery list. Go to the store together and read the labels from favorite foods. Read about and talk about community and school events.	David's score is in the Above Average range for the grade. Use library resources to explore Internet sites related to mathematics. Explore mathematics activities in everyday life. Ask if your school offers enriched mathematics studies. Use home projects to investigate relationships between units used to measure length, area, and volume.

[Similar descriptions for *language, spelling, science, social studies,* and *listening* are included on the "Home Report."]

a possibility of some measurement error always exists in a test, the manufacturers use the percentile band to accommodate this possibility. This means his number could be a little higher or a little lower than the 65 we see here," he says, pointing again to the 65 next to the box.

"The description in the chart below also points this out," Mike continues, pointing to the reading section of the chart. "Each of the descriptions in the chart outline what is measured on that section of the test, describes David's score, and offers suggestions for activities you might do with him at home."

"Is all this testing really necessary?" Mrs. Palmer queries. "Every time we turn around, David seems to be taking another test."

"That's a good question, and a lot of other people also wonder about it. They do give us some valuable information, however. For example, they give us an objective, outside measure that helps us understand how David and the rest of our students are doing compared to others around the country. And, we, the teachers, receive some additional and more detailed information about our students' performance, so the tests give us information that can help us provide them with extra support when necessary. . . . Here, let me share some of this information about David with you."

We'll examine this and other information related to David's test results in more depth as we go through the chapter. Now, we want to begin our discussion by examining the relationship between standardized testing and accountability, an issue prominent in today's schools.

Standardized Testing and Accountability

15.1 Describe the relationships between standards, accountability, and standardized testing.

Ed Psych and You

How good were the schools you attended through your elementary, middle, and high school years? How do you know?

A great deal has been written over the last several years about American's—both students' and adults'—lack of knowledge. For instance, the National Assessment of Educational Progress, commonly described as "The nation's report card," found, in 2015, only 37% of fourth-graders and 36% of eighth-graders were "at or above proficient" in reading, and in math the figures were 40% for fourth-graders and 34% for eighth-graders (National Center for Education Statistics, 2018). Adults perform no better, if as well. For instance, a 2016 survey found that only a quarter of American adults can name all three branches of government, and nearly a third couldn't name even one branch (Annenberg Public Policy Center, 2016). This is a decline from earlier surveys, so if this represents a trend, the number is even lower today.

The results are no better in science; a 2014 survey, for instance, found that 1 of 4 American adults believe that the Sun orbits the Earth (Neuman, 2014). Experts suggest that this lack of knowledge imperils our country's future, because it makes us less able to make informed political, economic, and environmental decisions (Romano, 2011).

Similar concerns have been raised at the school level. Evidence indicates that students are sometimes promoted from one grade to the next without mastering essential content and graduate from high school without the skills needed to function effectively in life after school (Tucker, 2015; West, 2012).

In response to these concerns, educators have established academic standards, statements that describe what students should know or be able to do at the end of a period of study. The Common Core State Standards Initiative, which we first examined in Chapter 1, is part of this process (Common Core State Standards Initiative, 2018u).

Accountability is the process of requiring students to demonstrate that they've met specified standards and making teachers responsible for students' performance. This information addresses the questions we asked in *Ed Psych and You*. In this era of standards and accountability, the "quality" of a school is being operationally defined as how well students score on standardized tests. If students score well, it's a good

MyLab Education
Video Example 15.1

Standards and accountability are part of reality in education today. Here we see school leaders discuss the role of standards and accountability in promoting student learning.

school; if they don't, it isn't. But not all people agree with this definition of excellence (Popham, 2017).

We turn now to the role of our federal government in accountability and standardized testing.

The Federal Role in Accountability Systems

Historically, the federal government viewed its role as limited to providing aid to states. However, from about 1980 onward, Congress substantially increased funding designed to support low-income and minority school children, with disappointing results; achievement didn't significantly increase. So, the federal government designed policies to hold public schools accountable for doing whatever it took to improve the achievement of students, and particularly those who were disadvantaged (Tucker, 2014). These efforts resulted in three pieces of legislation:

- The No Child Left Behind Act of 2001
- Race to the Top
- The Every Student Succeeds Act (ESSA)

No Child Left Behind

The current standards-based reform movement began in 2001, with the passage of the **No Child Left Behind (NCLB) Act**, a far-reaching federal government attempt to identify and serve all students in every segment of our society. The impetus behind this legislation was a growing realization that many children in our least affluent schools were indeed being left behind, as indicated by achievement gaps between low-income and more affluent students, and members of cultural minorities and their White counterparts. Leaders concluded that requiring states to create standards and measure students' attainment of them was the most effective way to address these disparities.

NCLB expanded the federal role in public education with emphasis on measurable academic progress, teacher qualifications, and annual testing—using standardized tests. The emphasis on testing is how the legislation is relevant to this chapter.

Advocates of NCLB believed the act focused our nation's attention on the importance of education and especially on the basic skills essential for success in school and later life. Also, by requiring states to report the academic progress of specific subgroups, such as members of cultural minorities, it highlighted the problem of unequal achievement (Miller, 2012).

Problems arose, however. For instance, NCLB allowed each state to design its own standards and assessments, which resulted in accountability systems that varied from state to state and were sometimes inaccurate and misleading (Alexander, 2012). For instance, faced with possible federal sanctions for not meeting their benchmarks, some states "gamed the system" by lowering standards and creating accountability systems that rewarded mediocre, or even poor, performance (Ravitch, 2010).

Race to the Top

Race to the Top is a multibillion dollar U. S. Department of Education competitive grant program implemented in 2009 and designed to spur and reward innovation and reforms in state and local district P–12 education (U.S. Department of Education, 2009). Race to the Top encouraged individual states and districts to design comprehensive accountability systems that included common learning standards for students, data systems to track student performance, feedback to teachers, and even merit pay plans based on students' standardized test performance (Howell, 2015; Weiss & Hess, 2015).

Every Student Succeeds Act

The most recent federal effort to improve education in our country, the **Every Student Succeeds Act (ESSA)**, was passed in 2015 and replaced its predecessor, No Child Left

Behind. Accountability remains a central component of the ESSA legislation, but the federal government has handed responsibility for defining accountability to the states (Weiss & McGuinn, 2016). Under ESSA, each state must set achievement goals for students, and the definition of student achievement was broadened to include measures of school quality that go beyond standardized test results to include other measures of student learning, such as student motivation and self-regulation (Batel, 2017; Ujifusa, 2018). States are also required to provide information on graduation rates for members of cultural minorities, English learners, and students with exceptionalities. The goal is to ensure that all students have good teachers (Will, 2018).

But standardized testing remains a central component of ESSA. To receive federal funds, states must test all students every year in grades three through eight and once in high school on statewide assessments in math and reading/language arts. In addition, students must be tested in science once between grades three and five, once again between grades six and nine, and once again in high school. States are also required to provide information on the learning progress of English learners, and exemption rates for students with exceptionalities is strictly limited. ESSA sends the clear message that states and districts must gather information about and report on the educational progress of all students.

High-Stakes Tests

Standardized testing is central to the current accountability movement originally spawned by NCLB. It is the mechanism used to determine if students have met standards, and its influence on schools and classrooms is enormous. The fact that students in other industrialized countries score higher than American students on these tests has alarmed leaders in our country, and current reform movements are largely due to concerns about low scores on standardized tests.

High-stakes tests are standardized tests used to make important decisions that affect students, teachers, and schools (Popham, 2017). High-stakes tests usually occur at the state level and are used to measure the extent to which students have met standards. The term "high stakes" refers to the practice of making decisions about student promotion, and even high school graduation, based on test results. When students can't move to the next grade level or graduate from high school because they don't perform well enough on a standardized test, for instance, the "stakes" are very high.

Advocates of this process claim the tests help clarify the goals of school systems, send clear messages to students about what they should be learning, and provide the public with hard evidence about school effectiveness (Hirsch, 2006; Phelps, 2005). They also assert that the tests highlight good schools and predict success; students who do well on the tests are the same students who do well throughout school (DeWitt, 2015). A number of states around our country give schools grades ranging from A to F on the basis of standardized test performance, and state leaders defend the practice, suggesting " . . . it does a good job of driving student improvement" (Smiley, 2014, para. 8).

MyLab Education Application Exercise 15.1: High-Stakes Testing and Teaching

In this exercise you will be asked to analyze the implications of high-stakes testing for teachers.

Teacher Evaluation and the Accountability Movement

The accountability movement has also changed the way you'll be evaluated when you begin teaching. You may have encountered aspects of this process in your program already, and if you haven't, you will. For instance, the vast majority of states use national tests, such as Praxis, which we first examined in Chapter 1, or state tests to ensure that teacher candidates possess essential knowledge and skills before they're licensed.

More significantly, how your students perform on standardized tests can impact the evaluation of your teaching, through a process called *value-added modeling.*

Value-Added Modeling

Value-added modeling is a method of teacher evaluation that measures a teacher's contribution to student learning in a given year by comparing students' current test scores to the same students' scores in previous school years and to scores of other students in the same grade. When using value-added models, researchers use statistical methods to accommodate factors such as student background, ability, and socioeconomic status in an attempt to determine how much a teacher contributes to students' learning. This contribution is considered the "value" the teacher added. For example, if a second-grader scores at the 50th percentile on a reading test, but at the 60th percentile in the third grade, researchers conclude that the gain is a result of the teacher's expertise and the "value" that had been added. This approach seeks to isolate the contribution that the individual teacher makes (the value added) during the year, which can then be compared to the performance of other teachers (Bausell, 2013; Darling-Hammond, Amrein-Beardsley, Haertel, & Rothstein, 2012).

Value-added modeling can have important implications for you. If used in your state and district, for instance, it will become part of your evaluation. And it could influence factors such as your salary and even tenure and retention as a new teacher.

edTPA

edTPA (Educational Teacher Performance Assessment) is a high-stakes preservice assessment process designed to answer the question, "Is a new teacher ready for the job?" If you're evaluated with edTPA, it will occur during your internship, and it's high stakes, because, if fully implemented, it can determine whether or not you become a licensed teacher.

edTPA was developed by the Stanford Center for Assessment, Learning and Equity; it become fully operational in 2013; and it's been endorsed by professional organizations such as the American Association of Colleges for Teacher Education (AACTE), as well as the National Education Association, the nation's largest labor union (Layton, 2015). Candidates evaluated with the edTPA prepare a portfolio of lesson plans, video-recorded instruction, samples of student work, and their own written narrative that describes reflections on evidence for how well their students learn and what they would do next to improve their performance. The portfolio is then submitted and assessed by an independent, external team of evaluators hired by Operational Systems of Pearson, partners in the process (Adkins, Spesia, & Snakenborg, 2015).

The developers of edTPA contend that it's research-based, and because it has been developed at the national level, it gives states, districts, and teacher preparation programs an assessment and support system independent of local influence. Further, they assert, this is in stark contrast with existing assessment systems where leaders from different teacher preparation routes and programs lack a shared understanding of effective practice (Adkins, Haynes, Pringle, Renner, & Robinson, 2013; Adkins, et al. 2015). New teachers, while acknowledging that the assessment is demanding, also conclude "it was an invaluable step in my preparation as a teacher. . . . Most importantly, I practiced analyzing and thinking critically about my instruction" (Jette, 2014; para. 3).

As of the fall of 2016, 16 states had either adopted statewide policies requiring a performance assessment for aspiring teachers or were actively considering such a step.

The long-term expectation of edTPA's developers is that teacher preparation programs, states, and professional-standards boards will adopt edTPA as a standard requirement for a degree in education and/or for teacher licensure (American Association of Colleges of Teacher Education [AACTE], 2017).

High-stakes evaluations, both for students and for teachers, has resulted in a backlash, however (Popham, 2017). We examine this backlash next.

The Backlash Against High-Stakes Evaluations

Advocates of high-stakes evaluations believe they improve both student and teacher performance. But a strong and ongoing backlash has occurred, and it focuses on three areas:

- High-stakes testing of students
- Value-added models of teacher evaluation
- Criticisms of edTPA

High-Stakes Testing of Students

Critics of high-stakes tests for students assert that the process has both narrowed the curriculum—teachers focus their instruction on content covered on the tests—and lowered the level of instruction (Morgan, 2016). They also contend that the tests provide misleading information about what students actually know and emphasize that evidence supporting the argument that these tests increase student achievement doesn't exist (Lavigne, 2014). Critics also argue that the tests further racial inequality (Au, 2016).

Critics also describe intervening variables that can skew test results. For instance, research suggests that differences in student test-taking strategies and motivation can influence validity (Stenlund, Eklöf, & Lyrén, 2017), and additional evidence indicates that test anxiety can be a factor (Wood, Hart, Little, & Phillips, 2016).

And because pressure to perform well on the tests is enormous, cheating is also a problem. For instance, one report indicated that teachers in 18 schools in Washington, D.C., cheated on students, high-stakes tests in 2012 (Brown, 2013), and in 2013, the former superintendent of schools in Atlanta was indicted for racketeering related to a cheating scandal in the district's schools (Winerip, 2013). These are only two examples, and many others exist. Some argue that the pressures involved in high-stakes testing make cheating inevitable (Morgan, 2016).

The backlash also contends that students are overtested. For instance, a survey of 66 school districts around the country found that students typically take eight standardized tests in a given year, at an annual cost of billions of dollars. High-stakes testing has become a lucrative business for companies that construct and sell the tests (Hart et al., 2015). Many educators and parents—as you saw illustrated in Mrs. Palmer's question to Mike—feel that standardized testing is overemphasized in our nation's schools (Langer Research Associates, 2017).

Value-Added Models of Teacher Evaluation

The backlash against value-added models of teacher evaluation has been particularly acute. "The use of standardized tests . . . to evaluate schools and teachers in the United States has contributed to severe dilemmas, including misleading information on what students know, lower-level instruction, cheating, less collaboration, unfair treatment of teachers, and biased teaching" (Morgan, 2016, p. 67).

Critics question the assumption that tests can accurately measure what teachers are accomplishing in their classes, arguing that invalid tests necessarily produce invalid value-added measures (Berliner, 2014; Holloway-Libell, 2015). They further contend that grade level and subject-matter bias exist in these measures. For instance, because of the emphasis on reading/language arts and math, teachers who teach those subjects have an advantage in achieving "added value," which leads to more positive evaluations (Holloway-Libell, 2015).

In addition, test results may not capture important learning outcomes that aren't immediately apparent. We've all had teachers, for instance, who presented intriguing ideas and asked thought-provoking questions that only made sense to us later, perhaps even years later. And we've also had teachers whose inspiration had a long-term impact on our motivation and even career choice. Value-added models can't capture these long-term outcomes, critics assert.

The move to publish the results of teacher evaluations based on students' test scores and make these evaluations open to the public—with listings of names of individual teachers in newspaper articles—have added to the backlash (Sawchuk, 2012). (How would you like to have your evaluations made public during your first year of teaching?)

Critics caution that data gathered over several years are often necessary to make valid conclusions about a teacher's performance, and publishing these data indiscriminately could damage individual teachers as well as schools (Darling-Hammond, 2012).

These evaluations have taken an emotional toll on teachers. For instance, evidence suggests that the pressure detracts from the development of a positive school climate and leads to more negative teacher–student interactions (von der Embse, Pendergast, Segool, Saeki, & Ryan, 2016). They're also a source of stress and have been linked to an increase in the number of teachers leaving the profession (Ryan et al., 2017; Thibodeaux, Labat, Lee, & Labat, 2015).

Most importantly, critics assert that evidence indicating that value-added models are making teachers more effective and increasing student learning simply doesn't exist (Amrein-Beardsley, Pivovarova, & Geiger, 2016). "There is no evidence that high-stakes teacher evaluation can produce a more effective teacher workforce and improve student achievement" (Lavigne, 2014, para. 4).

Criticisms of edTPA

Developers of edTPA acknowledge that the process has been controversial. For example, the operational partner, Evaluation Systems of Pearson, is a for-profit entity with a great deal of influence on the accountability and testing movement throughout education. Concerns about the cost of the assessment—$300 in 2015 and almost certain to increase—in a profession widely acknowledged as underpaid also exist (Adkins, Spesia, & Snakenborg, 2015). Critics strongly question the relationship between profit, educational policy, and academic scholarship (Dover, Shultz, Smith, & Duggan, 2015b).

Critics also question the validity of a process in which external scorers make high-stakes evaluations on the basis of "their review of 3–5 written lesson plans, 20 minutes of video, samples of student work, and candidates' written narratives" (Dover, Shultz, Smith, & Duggan, 2015a, para. 2).

Critics also contend that, as with all high-stakes assessments, the process is reductionist. Just as teachers' instruction is reduced to content that is covered on the high-stakes standardized tests students take, teacher candidates' efforts are reduced to a focus on the abilities they know will be assessed with edTPA, in essence, "if edTPA doesn't assess it, I don't have to do it" (Conley & Garner, 2015; Soslau, Kotch-Jester, & Jornlin, 2015).

In spite of this backlash against high-stakes evaluations, you'll likely encounter them, particularly high-stakes testing of students and value-added models of teacher evaluation. In other words, the way your students perform on standardized tests will be a part of your teaching evaluations. The specific tests that are used will vary from state to state, and you should learn about the tests that are used in your state when you begin teaching (Mandinach & Gummer, 2016). Standardized testing will be a part of reality when you begin teaching. So, you need to know as much about it as possible. Helping you acquire this knowledge is our goal in the sections that follow.

MyLab Education Self-Check 15.1

Standardized Tests

15.2 Understand standardized tests and describe their role in the total assessment process.

Ed Psych and You

What standardized tests did you take as you went through grades P–12? How did you do on these tests? Did they influence your academic career, and if so, how?

Standardized tests are assessments given to large samples of students—nationwide in many cases—under uniform conditions and scored and reported according to uniform procedures, which is the source of the term *standardized*.

In the previous section, we saw how standardized testing is related to the accountability movement, but it goes well beyond accountability. For instance, these tests are designed to answer questions that teacher-made assessments alone can't, such as:

- How do the students in my class compare with others across the country?
- How well is our curriculum preparing students for college or future training?
- How does a particular student compare to those of similar ability?
- Are students learning essential knowledge and skills that will prepare them for later learning and life after the school years? (Brookhart & Nitko, 2019; Miller, Linn, & Gronlund, 2013).

To answer these questions, an individual's test scores are compared to the scores of a **norming group**, a representative sample whose scores are compiled for the purpose of national comparisons. The norming group includes students from different geographical regions, private and public schools, boys and girls, and different ethnic and cultural groups (Miller et al., 2013). **National norms** are scores on standardized tests earned by representative groups from around the nation. Individuals' scores are then compared to the national norms.

Now, let's see how standardized tests are used.

Functions of Standardized Tests

Standardized tests serve three primary functions:

- Assessment and diagnosis of learning
- Selection and placement
- Accountability and program evaluation

Diagnosis and Assessment of Learning

From a teacher's perspective, providing an external objective measure of our students' progress is an important function of standardized testing. In Mike's class, for instance, David consistently receives B's in reading, but this doesn't show his parents, Mike and other teachers, or school administrators how he compares to other children at his grade level across the nation. Were his grades due to above-average achievement, generous grading, or some other factor? Standardized tests help answer this question, and, together with teacher-made assessments, they provide a more complete picture of student progress.

Selection and Placement

Selecting and placing students in specialized or limited enrollment programs is a second function of standardized tests. For instance, students entering a high school may come from "feeder" middle schools, private schools, and schools outside the district, many with different academic programs. Scores from the math section of a standardized test, for example, can help the math faculty place students in classes that will best meet their needs. Similarly, teachers often use standardized test results, together with their own assessments, to place students in different ability reading and math groups.

Standardized test results are also used to make decisions about admission to college or placement in advanced programs, such as programs for the gifted. As we already know, SAT and ACT scores are important in determining whether students are accepted by the college of their choice.

Accountability and Program Evaluation

In the first section of the chapter, we saw how standardized tests are used for holding students, teachers, and schools accountable. In addition to this controversial process, however, they can provide helpful information about program effectiveness. For instance, if an elementary school moves from a reading program based on writing and children's literature to one that emphasizes phonics and basic skills, standardized test results can provide teachers with information about the efficacy of this change.

Norm- Versus Criterion-Referenced Standardized Tests

Norm-referenced grading—sometimes called "grading on the curve"—compares a student's performance to that of others in a class, while criterion-referenced systems assign grades based on predetermined standards, such as 90+ = A, 80–90 = B, and so on. Similarly, **norm-referenced standardized tests** compare (reference) a student's performance to the performance of others, while **criterion-referenced standardized tests**, sometimes called standards-referenced, content-referenced, or domain-referenced tests, compare performance against a set standard. They may even be called objectives-based tests when the standards are in the form of learning objectives (Miller, et al., 2013).

These two types of tests differ in the way scores are reported. Norm-referenced scores describe a student's performance compared to peers, so they don't specifically describe what students know. In Mike's class, for instance, David's percentile rank in reading was 65, which only indicates that he scored as well as, or better than, 65% of the students who took the test. In contrast, criterion-referenced scores compare students' performance to a standard, so they provide information about mastery of specific skills, such as the ability to identify the main idea in a paragraph or add two-digit numbers.

With the current focus on standards and accountability, increased emphasis is being placed on criterion-referenced tests, especially at the state and district levels. However, nationally, norm-referenced tests, such as the Stanford Achievement Test that David took, are still much more widely used, because they allow location-to-location comparisons, and the general nature of test content allows them to be used in a wide variety of situations. Both are useful and depend on our assessment goals.

Types of Standardized Tests

Five types of standardized tests are commonly used in education.

- Achievement tests
- Diagnostic tests

- Intelligence tests
- Aptitude tests
- Readiness tests

Achievement Tests

Achievement tests, the most widely used type of standardized test, are designed to assess how much students have learned in specific content areas, such as those we saw on David's home report. These areas are then broken down into descriptions of more specific skills. For example, David's student report in Total Reading includes scores for *word study skills, reading vocabulary,* and *reading comprehension,* and his Total Math report includes scores for *mathematics problem solving* and *mathematics procedures.* In addition to the Stanford Achievement Test, other popular achievement tests include the Iowa Test of Basic Skills, the California Achievement Test, and the Metropolitan Achievement Test, as well as statewide assessments developed by different states (Brookhart & Nitko, 2019). Simply Google any of these tests if you want to find out more information about them.

Standardized achievement tests typically include batteries of subtests administered over several days. They reflect a curriculum common to most schools, which means they will assess some, but not all, of the goals of a particular school. This is both a strength and a weakness. Because they are designed for a range of schools, they can be used in a variety of locations, but this "one size fits all" approach may not accurately measure achievement for a specific school or classroom.

The **National Assessment of Educational Progress (NAEP)** is a battery of achievement tests administered periodically to carefully selected samples of students. Called the "Nation's Report Card," the NAEP is designed to provide a comprehensive picture of achievement in students across our country. NAEP assessments exist for mathematics, reading, science, writing, the arts, civics, economics, geography, U.S. history, and technology and engineering literacy. The NAEP began administering digitally based assessments in reading, writing, and math in 2017, with plans to add additional subjects in 2018 and 2019. Each subject is assessed at grades 4, 8, and 12, although not all grades are assessed each time (National Center for Education Statistics, 2017b).

Because of increased interest in the global economy and how our students are doing compared to students in other countries, NAEP has coordinated its testing efforts with the **Trends in International Mathematics and Science Study (TIMSS).** Using comparable standardized test score data from other industrialized countries, TIMSS data have revealed that students in our country lag behind many other countries in math and science. For instance, in 2015, American fourth-graders ranked 11th in math and 8th in science compared to other advanced countries, such as Singapore, Hong Kong, Japan, South Korea, and Chinese Taipei, and eighth-graders ranked ninth in math and eighth in science compared to these same countries (Provasnik et al., 2016). These standardized-based international comparisons have resulted in increased scrutiny of our own educational system, as well as questions about how to import the best educational practices from other countries (Sparks, 2016).

Diagnostic Tests

Achievement tests measure students' progress in a range of curriculum areas; **diagnostic tests** are designed to provide a detailed description of learners' strengths and weaknesses in specific skill areas. They're most commonly used in the primary grades, where instruction is designed to match the developmental levels of children.

Diagnostic tests are usually administered individually, and, compared to achievement tests, they include a larger number of items, use more subtests, and provide scores in more specific areas. A diagnostic test in reading, for instance, might measure letter recognition, word analysis skills, sight vocabulary, vocabulary in context, and reading comprehension. The Detroit Test of Learning Aptitude, the Durrell Analysis of Reading Difficulty, and the Stanford Diagnostic Reading Test are popular diagnostic tests.

MyLab Education
Video Example 15.2

Diagnostic tests provide detailed information about learner's strengths and weaknesses in specific skill areas. Here we see a teacher administer a diagnostic test in reading with an English language learner.

Intelligence Tests

Intelligence tests, also called school ability tests or cognitive ability tests, are standardized tests designed to measure an individual's capacity to acquire and use knowledge, solve problems, and think in the abstract. A trend away from using "intelligence tests" as a label is occurring, because the term is often misinterpreted to suggest an innate, fixed ability and because disagreement exists about the meaning of *intelligence*. The Stanford-Binet and the Wechsler Scales are the two most widely used intelligence tests in the United States (Salvia, Ysseldyke, & Bolt, 2017). We turn now to a more detailed look at them.

The Stanford-Binet. The **Stanford-Binet**, currently called the Stanford-Binet Intelligence Scales, Fifth Edition, or SB5 (Roid, 2003), is an individually administered test composed of several subtests. The subtests include:

- *Knowledge*: vocabulary, procedural knowledge, and picture absurdities, such as explaining a person in a bathing suit sitting in snow.
- *Working memory*: such as asking a student to reproduce a display of blocks after a short delay or remembering a sentence.
- *Fluid reasoning:* being able to identify the next object in a series or recognize verbal analogies and verbal absurdities.
- *Quantitative reasoning:* such as recognizing the next number in a sequence, or solving a word problem.
- *Visual–spatial processing*: such as identifying and forming patterns, or identifying position and direction (Roid, 2003).

The Stanford-Binet is a technically sound instrument that is second in popularity only to the Wechsler Scales (described in the next section). It has been revised and re-normed a number of times, most recently in 2003, using 4800 schoolchildren, stratified by economic status, geographic region, and community size. The U.S. Census was used to ensure proportional representation of White, African American, Hispanic, Asian, and Asian/Pacific Islander subcultures (Bain & Allin, 2005).

The Wechsler Scales. The **Wechsler Intelligence Scale for Children (WISC)** is an individually administered intelligence test for children between the ages of 6 and 16. The fifth edition is the most current version (Wechsler, 2014). Developed by David Wechsler over a period of 40 years, the Wechsler Scales are the most popular intelligence tests in use today (Salvia et al., 2017).

The WISC produces five index scores (Wechsler, 2014):

- *Verbal comprehension index:* A child's ability to verbally reason, such as identifying how two words are alike, defining words, general knowledge, and understanding of social situations.
- *Visual–spatial index:* Visual–spatial processing, such as putting together red and white blocks in a pattern according to a displayed model, and viewing a puzzle in a book and choosing three pieces from an array that could construct the puzzle.
- *Fluid-reasoning index:* Inductive and quantitative reasoning, such as seeing an array of pictures with a missing square and selecting the picture that fits the array from a series of options, identifying which pictures go together from a series of pictures, and solving arithmetic problems.
- *Working memory index*: Working memory ability, such as hearing a sequence of numbers and repeating the sequence as heard and in reverse, viewing pictures and selecting the pictures they saw in order, and providing the examiner with a series of numbers and letters in a predetermined order.
- *Processing speed index:* Processing speed, such as marking rows of shapes with different lines according to a code, identifying symbols in a row after being given

symbols and rows, and marking specific targets in a series of pictures within a limited amount of time.

Like the Stanford-Binet, the Wechsler Scales are considered technically sound by testing experts (Kaplan & Saccuzzo, 2018).

Aptitude Tests

Although *aptitude* and *intelligence* are often used synonymously, **aptitude**—the ability to acquire knowledge—is only one characteristic of intelligence. *Intelligence* includes a wider range of cognitive abilities, such as problem solving and thinking in the abstract.

As opposed to measuring the general construct of intelligence, **aptitude tests** are standardized tests designed to predict the potential for future learning and measure general abilities developed over long periods of time. The concept of aptitude is intuitively sensible; for example, people will say, "I just don't have any aptitude for foreign language," implying that their potential for learning a foreign language is limited. Aptitude tests are commonly used in selection and placement decisions, and they correlate highly with achievement tests (Popham, 2017).

The SAT and ACT, both designed to measure students' potential for success in college, are the two most common aptitude tests in use today. This potential is heavily influenced by experience, however, and classroom-related knowledge, particularly in language and mathematics, is essential for success on the tests.

The SAT was revised in 2005 when a writing component was added and the point scale was increased to 2400 from the original 1600. However, the SAT came under increasing scrutiny after the revision, and even David Coleman, president of the College Board (developers of the SAT), criticized his own test and its main rival, the ACT, saying that both had become disconnected from the work of high schools in our country (Lewin, 2014). Other critics argued that high school grades better predict college success and further asserted that the SAT discriminates against low-income students whose families can't afford the expensive test preparation more advantaged students use to score well on the exam. In addition, both the predictive power and the reliability of the writing component have been questioned (Balf, 2014; FairTest, 2014).

In response to these criticisms, the College Board announced additional revisions of the exam in 2014 (Jaschik, 2014). These revisions included the following:

- The writing component was made optional.
- The point scale returned to 1600.
- Points were no longer deducted for incorrect answers on the multiple-choice portion of the test.
- The vocabulary portion was revised to include terms believed to be more widely used in college and the workplace.

These revisions took effect in 2016 (College Board, 2017).

In spite of criticisms, aptitude tests such as the SAT and ACT will likely remain a rite of passage for many students in the foreseeable future, although an increasing number of colleges and universities around our country no longer require either as part of the admission process (Fairtest, 2017).

Readiness Tests

Readiness tests are standardized tests designed to assess the degree to which children are prepared for an academic or pre-academic program (Salvia et al., 2017). They are most often used to assess children's readiness for academic work in kindergarten or first grade. In this regard, they have qualities of both aptitude and achievement tests. They're similar to aptitude tests in that they are designed to assess a student's potential for future learning. However, most readiness tests are narrower, measuring the extent to which students have mastered basic concepts in a particular domain. For instance, a preschool readiness test might measure students' understanding of basic concepts such as *up* and *down*, *left* and *right*, or *big* and *small*, which are part of the foundation for reading and math. In this regard, they're similar to achievement tests.

Readiness tests, like other standardized tests, can provide valuable information for decision-making, but scores should not be the only criterion used for assessing a child's school readiness. Virtually every 5- or 6-year-old can benefit from school experiences, and observations of a child's ability to function in a school setting should also be a part of the assessment process.

Now, think again about the questions we asked in *Ed Psych and You* at the beginning of this section—"What standardized tests did you take as you went through grades P–12? How did you do on these tests? Did they influence your academic career, and if so, how?" Almost certainly, you took a number of standardized achievement tests, such as the Stanford Achievement Test David Palmer took. It's also likely you took several state-sponsored achievement tests, designed to measure the extent to which you mastered state standards. These tests may have influenced the reading and math groups to which you were assigned in elementary school, and perhaps the track in which you were placed in high school. You probably also took either the SAT or ACT as part of your college application process. The fact that you're in college and taking this course suggests that you performed well on these tests, but this isn't the case for all students. As educators, we must be careful about the decisions we make on the basis of standardized test scores.

Evaluating Standardized Tests: Validity Revisited

Test validity is important to us as teachers because we're the primary consumers of standardized test results. Let's look at how validity can influence classroom decisions, using Mike Chavez, our teacher in the case study at the beginning of the chapter.

Mike has been asked to serve on a districtwide committee to consider a new standardized achievement battery for the elementary grades. His job is to get feedback from the faculty at his school about the California Achievement Test as an alternative to the Stanford Achievement Test, which they're now using.

After providing an overview of the tests during a faculty meeting, Mike asks if people have questions.

"How much problem solving does the California Achievement Test cover?" a fifth-grade teacher asks.

"We're moving our language arts curriculum more in the direction of writing. Does the new test emphasize writing?" a second-grade colleague asks.

As the discussion continues, another colleague asks, "Which is better? That's really what we're here for. How about a simple answer?"

MyLab Education
Video Example 15.3

Validity involves the process of making accurate inferences from assessment information, and using the inferred information appropriately. Here, James Popham, author and educational leader, explains the concept of *validity* and offers his perspective on the role of testing in promoting learning.

Mike couldn't offer a simple answer, not because he was unprepared, but instead because he was asked to make judgments about validity, the process of making accurate inferences from assessment information and using the inferred information appropriately (Chappuis & Stiggens, 2017). When we create our own tests, we try to ensure validity by aligning the test with our learning objectives. Standardized tests are already constructed, so we must judge the suitability of a test for a specific purpose. (A complete review of more than 1000 standardized tests can be found in *The Twentieth Mental Measurements Yearbook* [Carlson, Geisinger, & Jonson, 2017]). As we use these tests we need to remember that validity involves the appropriate use of a test, not the design of the test itself.

Experts describe three kinds of standardized test validity—*content*, *predictive*, and *construct*—and each provides a different perspective on the issue of appropriate use.

Content Validity

Content validity refers to a test's ability to accurately sample the content taught and measure learners' understanding of it. It's determined by comparing test content with curriculum objectives, and it's a primary concern when considering standardized achievement tests (Miller et al., 2013). The question Mike was asked about which test was "better" addresses content validity. The "better" test is the one with the closer match between your school's curriculum and the content of the test.

Predictive Validity

Predictive validity is the measure of a test's ability to gauge future performance (Miller et al., 2013). It's central to the SAT and ACT, which are designed to measure a student's potential for doing college work, and it's also the focus of tests that gauge students' readiness for academic tasks in the early elementary grades.

Predictive validity is usually quantified by correlating two variables, such as a standardized test score and student grades. For example, a correlation of .47 exists between the SAT and freshman college grades (FairTest, 2008). High school grades are the only predictor that is better (a correlation of .54).

Why isn't the correlation between standardized tests and college performance higher? The primary reason is that the SAT and ACT are designed to predict "general readiness," but other factors such as motivation, study habits, and prior knowledge also affect performance (Popham, 2017).

Construct Validity

Construct validity is an indicator of the logical connection between a test and what it is designed to measure. The concept of construct validity is somewhat abstract but is important in understanding the total concept of validity. It answers the question, "Do these items actually assess the ideas the test is designed to measure?" For instance, many of the items on the SAT are designed to measure the ability to think abstractly about words and numbers, tasks that students are likely to face in their college experience. Because of this, the test has construct validity.

APA Top 20 Principles

This discussion illustrates Principle 19: *Students' skills, knowledge, and abilities are best measured with assessment processes grounded in psychological science with well-defined standards for quality and fairness* — from the *Top 20 Principles from Psychology for PreK–12 Teaching and Learning*.

MyLab Education Self-Check 15.2

Understanding and Interpreting Standardized Test Scores

15.3 Interpret standardized test results for students, parents, and other caregivers.

APA Top 20 Principles

This section of the chapter illustrates Principle 20: *Making sense of assessment data depends on clear, appropriate, and fair interpretation*— from the *Top 20 Principles from Psychology for PreK–12 Teaching and Learning*.

In our case study at the beginning of the chapter, we saw David Palmer's Stanford Achievement Test Home Report, a one-page description intended for students' parents or other caregivers. It offers a brief snapshot of the student's performance in the box at the upper right and additional information and suggestions for parents in the chart on the bottom half of the page. It's intended to be easily understood, but as we found in the conversation between Mrs. Palmer and Mike, parents are often uncertain about test results and what they actually mean. For this reason, it's important that we as teachers thoroughly understand the information on these reports so we can communicate clearly with parents. Our credibility is also involved. If we're able to clearly explain test results to parents, we appear credible and professional; if not, the opposite is true.

Test results include much more than the home report. For example, a *Student Report* provides more detailed information about students' performance on all subtests and specific information about the skills tested. This information is intended for teachers and counselors, but it can also be shared with parents who want more detailed information about their child's performance.

Table 15.1 shows the subtests and totals in David's Student Report for reading and math. Similar information is provided for each of the other areas tested—language, spelling, science, social science, and listening (Stanford Achievement Test, Tenth Edition, 2009).

The subtests are broken down farther in what the test describes as "clusters." For instance, the *word study skills* subtest under Total Reading is broken down into *structural analysis, phonetic analysis—consonants,* and *phonetic analysis—vowels.* Each of the other subtests is broken down into similar clusters.

Now, let's see what the numbers in David's student report mean. The number possible and number correct are self-explanatory. For instance, 114 items were possible for the Total Reading subtest, 30 of which were *word study skills*, 30 more were *reading vocabulary,* and 54 were *reading comprehension.*

Of these, David correctly answered 17 of the 30-word study skills items, 22 of the 30 reading vocabulary items, and 42 of the 54 reading comprehension items, for a total of 81 items answered correctly of the 114 total possible. We can identify his math results the same way. Numbers correct are sometimes described as **raw scores**, so David's Total Reading raw score would be 81.

The other headings on David's student report require deeper understanding. We look at them now.

Scaled Scores

When we take a standardized test, a label, such as "Form A," will be on it somewhere. Because these tests are repeatedly given to large numbers of people, the content of the test, over time, becomes "exposed"—that is, test takers remember some of the questions and pass the information along to people who will take the test in the future (Tan & Michel, 2011). This sharing of information reduces validity, so developers create different "forms" of the test to deal with the issue. As a result, people taking the test at

TABLE 15.1 Student report for David Palmer in reading and math

Subtests and Totals	Number Possible	Number Correct	Scaled Score	National PR-S	National NCE	AAC	National Grade Percentile Bands Range 1 10 30 50 70 90 99
Total Reading	114	81	613	65-6	58.1	MIDDLE	
Word Study Skills	30	17	604	55-5	52.6	MIDDLE	
Reading Vocabulary	30	22	603	54-5	52.1	MIDDLE	
Reading Comprehension	54	42	622	73-6	62.9	HIGH	
Total Mathematics	80	64	631	81-7	68.5	HIGH	
Math Problem Solving	48	39	633	82-7	69.3	HIGH	
Math Procedures	32	25	624	75-6	63.2	HIGH	

different times may take different forms of the test, or people taking the test at the same time may be given different forms to address concerns about security.

Even though developers adhere to strict test specifications, it's virtually impossible to create different forms of standardized tests that are exactly equal in difficulty (Tan & Michel, 2011). So, percent-correct scores or raw scores might not provide accurate comparisons of different test takers' performance. For instance, a student getting 70% correct on an easier form may actually have less knowledge or skill than a student getting 60% correct on a harder form. Similarly, if two students get the same raw score on two different forms, the one taking the harder form is demonstrating greater knowledge and skills.

In an effort to ensure that results reported from different forms represent the same level of performance, standardized testing programs report **scaled scores**. These scores are obtained by statistically adjusting and converting raw scores to a common scale in an effort to accommodate differences in difficulty among different forms of the test. For instance, a student taking an easier form of the test would need to get a slightly higher raw score to achieve the same scaled score as a student who took a harder form of the test. This effort to ensure that scores accurately represent test takers' performance is the reason standardized test results are commonly reported as scaled scores.

David's scaled score of 613 for Total Reading is only meaningful in comparison to the scaled scores of other students who take the test. So, this is how you should explain the number to parents. The next column in Table 15.1, National PR-S, which refers to *percentile rank-stanine*, is easier to explain. However, to do so, we need to understand what the concept *normal distribution* means.

The Normal Distribution

A **normal distribution** is a set of measures that distribute themselves symmetrically in a bell-shaped curve. Figure 15.1 is a visual representation of a normal distribution.

Many large samples of human characteristics, such as height and weight, tend to distribute themselves this way. For instance, the average height for women in our country is just under 5'4" (Fryar, Gu, Ogden, & Flegal, 2016), and for men it's approximately 5'10" (Arbuckle, 2017). Now imagine that the vertical axis of the distribution in Figure 15.1 represents numbers of women, and the horizontal axis represents height. We see that the peak of the figure is at zero on the horizontal axis because this represents the average height—5'4". However, a great many women range in height from

Figure 15.1 Normal distribution

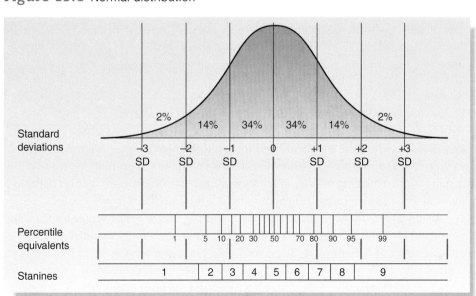

approximately 5′2″ to 5′6″, which is represented by the clustering near the middle of the figure, but not nearly as many are either 4′6″, which is at the left side of the figure, or 6′0″, on the right side of the figure. A similar distribution exists for men. Statistical analysis indicates that approximately 68% of subjects in a normal distribution are between −1 and +1 SD. SD refers to **standard deviation**, which is a statistical measure of the way scores spread out in a distribution.

Standardized tests are administered to large—in the hundreds of thousands—samples of students, and the scores approximate a normal distribution. So, for instance, if a 100-item test were given to a large sample of students, the results would fit a normal distribution, and if the average score on the test were 50, we would see many scores between approximately 40 and 60, but few scores of between 0 and 5 or between 95 and 100.

This helps us understand percentiles and stanines, the next heading in David's student report.

Percentile Rank and Stanine

The PR-S in the heading of David's student report refers to *percentile rank-stanine,* which is a reporting description designed to be simple and easy for teachers, students, and parents to understand. This may or may not be the case.

Percentile Rank

Percentile rank (PR) represents the percentage of students in the norming sample that scored at or below a particular raw score. For instance, David's raw score (number correct) of 81 for Total Reading placed him at the 65th percentile nationally. That means his score was as high as or higher than 65% of the scores of students who took the test across the nation.

Parents and students often confuse *percentiles* with *percentages.* Percentages reflect the number of correct items compared to the total number possible. Percentile rank, in contrast, is a description that indicates how a student did compared to other students taking the test. So David's percentage correct score was 71% (81/114), but his percentile rank was 65. The two measures provide us with different types of information, and, as we see in Table 15.1, percentages are not reported.

Percentiles are used because they are simple and straightforward. However, they are *rankings,* and the differences between the ranks are not equal. For instance, look at the National Grade Percentile Bands section of Table 15.1. There we see that the distance between the 30th, 50th, and 70th percentiles is smaller than the distance between the percentiles at either end of the range.

The normal distribution helps us understand why. Many more scores are clustered near the center of the distribution than at the ends, just as many more women are between 5′2 and 5′6″ than between 4′6″ and 4′8 or between 5′11″ and 6′1″. This clustering is illustrated by the percentile equivalents scale in Figure 15.1.

Stanine

The stanine is another commonly used way to describe standardized test scores, and it's represented by the "S" in David's *National PR-S* score. A **stanine**, or "standard nine," describes an individual's standardized test performance using a scale ranging from 1 to 9, and we see in Figure 15.1 how the stanines relate to the normal distribution. For instance, approximately 68% of all scores will fall between the third and seventh stanine, and this will also range from about the 15th through the 80th percentiles.

Stanines are widely used because they're simple, and they encourage teachers and parents to interpret scores based on a possible range, instead of fine distinctions that may be artificial (Chappuis & Stiggens, 2017). For instance, a score in the 57th percentile may be the result of 1 or 2 extra points on a subtest compared to a score in the 52nd percentile, and the student may have guessed the answer correctly, so the difference between the two wouldn't be meaningful. Both scores fall in stanine 5, however.

Because it describes performance as a range of possible scores, the stanine is probably a more realistic indicator of performance. Reducing the scores to a 9-point band sacrifices information, however, so it's important to keep the advantages and disadvantages of stanines in mind as we help parents and students understand the meaning of standardized test scores.

Normal Curve Equivalent

The next column in David's student report is labeled *National NCE*, which refers to the national **normal curve equivalent (NCE)**, a measure resulting from a statistical process that standardizes scores on a test into a 0–100 scale similar to a percentile rank, but preserves equal interval properties that don't exist with percentiles. The fact that NCEs can be averaged is their major advantage over percentile rankings. To illustrate the difference, let's consider David's percentile rank of 65 for his Total Reading score. Now, imagine two of David's classmates, Lisa and Grayson, and suppose that Lisa's percentile rank is 75, and Grayson's is 55. Because percentile intervals are not equal, the difference in raw score between Lisa's 75 and David's 65 is greater than the difference in raw score between David's 65 and Grayson's 55.

Now, consider David's National NCE of 58 (we'll ignore the 0.1 for sake of illustration), and consider two other classmates, Owen and Kelsey. Now, suppose Owen's NCE is 64 and Kelsey's is 52. In this case, because the intervals for NCEs are equal, the differences in raw score are also equal.

NCEs don't have a great deal of meaning for typical standardized test users. They're included in test results typically because of school system reporting requirements by federal agencies, and their equal interval property makes reporting comparisons easier (Willson, 2013).

And, finally, David's report shows a column for *AAC Range*, which refers to **achievement/ability comparison (AAC)**, which represents his average performance compared to the total norm group. The AAC range is described as low, middle, or high when compared to students of similar measured ability, and this is what we see in David's student report.

Grade Equivalents

The **grade equivalent** is a score determined by comparing an individual's score to the scores of students in a particular age group, and it is another common way test results are described. This score doesn't appear on David's Student Report, but grade equivalents are commonly reported, so we're including a description here (Stanford Achievement Test Series, 2009). For instance, suppose David's grade equivalent for Total Math was 5.2. That means that he scored as well on the test as the average score for those students taking the test who are in the second month of the fifth grade.

This does not imply that David, a fourth-grader, should be in the fifth grade. Grade equivalents can be misleading because they oversimplify results and suggest comparisons that aren't necessarily valid. A grade equivalent of 5.2 tells us that David is somewhat advanced in math, and this is confirmed by the "high" in the AAC Range for Total Math. It doesn't suggest that he should be promoted to fifth grade, and it doesn't suggest that he should be working with fifth-graders. Because of the possibility of misinterpretation, some standardized tests no longer use grade equivalents (Salvia et al., 2017).

Standard Error of Measurement

Although standardized tests are technically sophisticated, like all tests they contain measurement error; scores represent only an approximation of a student's "true" score. If, hypothetically, we could give a student the same test over and over, for instance, and the student neither gained nor lost any knowledge, we would find that the scores would vary. If we averaged those scores, we would have an estimate of the student's "true" score. A true score is the hypothetical average of an individual's scores if repeated testing under ideal conditions were possible. An estimate of the true score is obtained using the **standard error of measurement**, the range of scores within which an individual's true score is likely to fall. Standard error of measurement is similar to what we commonly read as "margin of error" in surveys in our everyday world.

The range in standard error of measurement is sometimes termed the confidence interval, score band, or profile band. For example, suppose Ben has a raw score of 46 and Kim has a raw score of 52 on a test with a standard error of 4. This means that Ben's true score is between 42 and 50, and Kim's is between 48 and 56. At first glance, Kim appears to have scored significantly higher than Ben, but considering the standard error, their scores may be equal, or Ben's true score may even be higher than Kim's. Understanding standard error is important when we make decisions based on standardized tests. For instance, it would be unwise to place Ben and Kim in different ability groups based solely on the results illustrated here.

In this section, we described the different ways that standardized tests are reported, using David Palmer's Stanford Achievement Test results as a concrete example. The total report will include much more information, such as local comparisons and rankings. In all cases, however, the headings we see in Table 15.1 are used, that is, the larger report will include scaled scores, percentile rankings, stanines, and normal curve equivalents.

As you examine your students' test results and explain them to parents, please remember that a single score—or even a cluster of scores—only captures one aspect of our students' abilities and characteristics. And be particularly wary of lowering expectations for students who, at this point in their schooling, don't score high on an achievement test, such as the one David took. We can cite examples of students who have overcome long odds, such as dyslexia or other disabilities, and have gone on to be high achievers in college and the world outside of schooling. These tests don't measure essential characteristics, such as motivation, perseverance, and conscientiousness. They are but one measure that we can use in making educational decisions.

Classroom Connections

Using Standardized Tests Effectively in Classrooms

1. The validity of a standardized achievement test depends on the match between learning objectives and test content. Carefully analyze results to increase instructional alignment.

   - **Elementary:** A fourth-grade team goes over the previous year's test scores to identify areas in the curriculum that need greater attention.

   - **Middle School:** The math teachers in a middle school go over standardized results item by item. Seeing that a large number of students missed a particular item, the teachers plan to place more emphasis on this topic in their instruction.

   - **High School:** English teachers in an urban high school use a scoring rubric to analyze student scores on a statewide writing assessment. They share the rubric with their students and use it to help them improve their writing skills.

2. The value of standardized test scores to consumers depends, in large part, on the extent to which they understand the results. Communicate test results clearly to both students and their caregivers.

   - **Elementary:** Third-grade teachers in an urban elementary school prepare a handout that explains standardized test scores, including examples and answers to frequently asked questions. They use the handout in parent–teacher conferences.

   - **Middle School:** A middle school team integrates standardized test scores into a comprehensive packet of assessment materials. When they meet with students and their caregivers, they use the information to identify individual student's areas of strength and those that need improvement.

   - **High School:** During an orientation meeting with parents, members of an English Department first give an overview of tests that students will encounter in high school and describe how scores are reported. During individual meetings with parents, teachers provide specific information about individuals' scores.

MyLab Education Self-Check 15.3

Diversity and Standardized Testing

15.4 Explain how learner diversity can influence the validity of standardized test results.

Ed Psych and You

Did you ever take a standardized test where certain parts of the content were unfamiliar to you? Did you ever encounter items on a standardized test that contained vocabulary that you didn't understand? What did these mismatches between test content and you say about you, and what did these mismatches say about the test?

One of the most volatile controversies in standardized testing involves critics' claims that the tests are biased against members of cultural minorities (Balkin, Heard, ShinHwa, & Wines, 2014; Toldson, 2012). This is particularly true for Hispanic and African American students, who, on average, consistently score lower on standardized tests than do White and Asian students (National Center for Education Statistics 2017a). And because scoring below established minimums on high-stakes standardized tests can result in grade retention or failure to graduate from high school, the controversy has increased (Popham, 2017). Some cases have gone to court, and the validity of tests for cultural minorities and the extent to which students have had the opportunity to learn test content have been key issues (Schimmel, Stellman, Conlon, & Fischer, 2015). The question of whether or not members of cultural minorities will be treated fairly becomes essential as standardized tests are increasingly used to make important decisions about students.

Two important issues related to standardized testing with minority students remain unresolved (Salvia et al., 2017). The first is whether the tests are valid and reliable enough to justify using results to make decisions about students' academic careers and lives. The second relates to technical problems involved in testing members of minorities and particularly students who speak English as a second language. Significantly, in 2000, the American Educational Research Association (AERA), the nation's largest professional organization devoted to the scientific study of education, in a position also endorsed by the American Psychological Association and the National Council on Measurement in Education, stated the following as part of a formal position: "Decisions that affect individual students' life chances or educational opportunities should not be made on the basis of test scores alone" (American Educational Research Association [AERA], 2017, para. 6).

Student Diversity and Assessment Bias

Because of controversies surrounding standardized testing, increased attention is being focused on the issue of assessment bias. **Assessment bias** is a form of discrimination that occurs when a test or other assessment instrument unfairly penalizes a group of students because of their gender, ethnicity, race, or socioeconomic status (SES).

Measurement experts identify three types of assessment bias that detract from validity (Miller et al., 2013):

- Bias in content
- Bias in testing procedures
- Bias in test interpretation and use

As you study these topics, remember that average differences between groups do not necessarily indicate bias. Underlying causes, such as poverty or inadequate educational opportunities, may account for these differences (Brookhart & Nitko, 2019).

Bias in Content

Critics contend that the content of standardized tests is geared to White, middle-class American students, and members of cultural minorities are disadvantaged by this content. For example, the following item is similar to a standardized science test item used to measure the knowledge of sixth-graders:

If you wanted to find out if a distant planet had mountains or rivers on it, which of the following tools should you use?

    a. binoculars

    b. microscope

    c. telescope

    d. camera

Performance on this item is likely to be influenced by SES and a student's exposure to high-cost items like microscopes and telescopes.

Bias can also occur in word problems (Miller et al., 2013). For example:

Jose Altuve, of the Houston Astros, at one point in the 2017 post season was batting .579 on 19 trips to the plate. In his next three times at bat, he gets a single, double, and home run. What is his batting average now?

This item requires that students know how batting averages are computed and whether doubles and home runs count more than singles. Also, phrases such as "trips to the plate" may not be meaningful to students unfamiliar with baseball, and efforts to interpret the phrase can detract from success on solving the problem. This is particularly acute for students with limited skills in English.

Mismatches between test content and the cultural backgrounds of students can also result in content bias. For example, students from a remote Inuit community were asked the following question on a standardized vocabulary test: "Which of the following would most likely take you to the hospital if you got hurt?" The "correct" answer was *ambulance*, but Inuit students replied airplane because that is how people in their village receive emergency medical aid (Platt, 2004).

Bias in Testing Procedures

Because students from different cultures respond differently to testing situations, bias can also occur in testing procedures. For example, in one historical study researchers found that Navajo students were unaware of the consequences of poor test performance, instead treating tests as game-like events (Deyhle, 1987). Other research has found that some minority students believe tests will be biased, and as a result, they don't try to do well on them (Morgan & Mehta, 2004; Ryan & Ryan, 2005). And, if students are unfamiliar with a particular format, such as multiple-choice, bias in testing procedures can exist.

Bias in Test Interpretation and Use

Bias can also occur in the ways test results are interpreted and used. Experts are concerned about the adverse effects of testing on minority students' progress through public schools and entrance into college. Evidence suggests that test results are sometimes used in ways that discriminate against members of cultural minorities and those who do not speak English as a first language. For example, a historic study of 812 students classified as reportedly having mental disabilities found 300% more Mexican Americans and 50% more African Americans than would be expected from their numbers in the general population, and the study population had 40% fewer Anglo Americans than would be expected. Further, people in lower-income brackets were overrepresented, whereas people in the upper brackets were underrepresented (Mercer, 1973). More recent research suggests this problem still exists (Turnbull, Turnbull, Wehmeyer, & Shogren, 2016).

Standardized Testing and English Language Learners

Standardized testing poses special challenges for students who are English Language Learners (ELLs). Research indicates that students whose first language isn't English consistently score lower than other students on both standardized achievement and intelligence tests (Robinson, 2010). This isn't surprising, because the tests are developed for native English speakers and depend heavily on English language skills. This also presents a problem for teachers who are required to use standardized test scores in their work with ELLs—students must be able to read and understand English if a test written in English is to measure performance accurately. The problem of standardized testing with limited-English speakers is not new, but its importance has increased with the current emphasis on accountability (Echevarria, Vogt, & Short, 2018a, 2018b).

MyLab Education
Video Example 15.4

Critics of standardized testing argue that the process is biased against members of cultural minorities and particularly against students who speak English as a second language. Here we see an educational leader describe the impact of language on people's thinking and ultimately how we learn.

Language is not the only reason ELLs underperform on standardized tests. These students tend to come from lower-SES families, and research consistently demonstrates the adverse effects of poverty on achievement (Macionis, 2017). In addition, ELLs often attend schools with fewer resources and greater numbers of unqualified or inexperienced teachers (Brimley, Verstegen, & Garfield, 2012; Kozol, 2005).

The linguistic complexity of the tests is an additional factor. The tests are administered in English, and they often contain technical terms such as *ion*, *colonization*, and *simile* that aren't commonly used in conversation (Echevarria et al., 2018b). This puts ELLs at a disadvantage, because everyday conversation is the primary way they acquire language proficiency. And, finally, standardized tests are timed, placing an additional cognitive burden on ELL test takers.

Testing Accommodations for English Language Learners

Accommodations to address these problems focus on either the test itself or testing procedures. For instance, modifications include attempts to translate the test into students' first language or simplify vocabulary or sentence structure, such as shortening sentences or converting them from passive to active voice (Maxwell, 2013). Technical and logistical problems exist with these efforts, however. For instance, experts are skeptical about whether or not the modified and original forms of the test are comparable, which raises questions of validity (Maxwell, 2013), and it isn't possible to translate tests into all the native languages that exist in some urban districts. Even when students speak a common language, cultural differences, such as variations in Spanish dialects spoken in Spain, Mexico, Cuba, and Puerto Rico, make it difficult to construct a test that is culturally and linguistically meaningful (Echevarria et al., 2018b; Popham, 2017).

Attempts to increase validity through modifications of testing procedures, such as providing regular and bilingual dictionaries and allowing more time for ELLs, appear more promising (Abedi & Gandara, 2006). Providing more time, especially when combined with test-specific glossaries, appears to be the most feasible accommodation.

Accommodating Students with Disabilities

In the United States, the Individuals with Disabilities Education Act (IDEA) requires appropriate accommodations for students with disabilities. Many of these accommodations are similar to those for ELLs, and include:

- Modifying the presentation format, such as reading questions out loud if reading is an issue.
- Modifying the response format (e.g., allowing students to dictate their answers when writing is a problem).
- Providing extra time for tests.
- Administering tests in smaller time increments to prevent fatigue or frustration.
- Administering tests individually or in separate, quieter settings, free from distractions (Samuels, 2013; Turnbull et al., 2016).

Modifying standardized assessment procedures can alter the validity of test results, however, so we should keep this possibility in mind.

Teaching test-taking strategies is a second way to accommodate students with disabilities (Mastropieri & Scruggs, 2018).

These strategies include:

- Learning to use separate multiple-choice bubble answer sheets.
- Sorting problems by type and difficulty level and beginning with easier ones first.
- Underlining key words in problems and drawing diagrams and pictures.
- Eliminating obvious wrong options and guessing where appropriate.

To be effective, we should model these strategies and provide students with a great deal of practice, well before standardized tests, and particularly high-stakes tests, are administered.

This section addresses the questions we asked in *Ed Psych and You* about your own experiences with standardized testing. We've all been in testing situations where we didn't know some of the answers or didn't even understand some questions. This may have resulted from simply not understanding the topic. At other times, however, it may have been the result of faulty items that didn't adequately assess our knowledge. Assessment bias exists, and it can negatively influence both our students and us. We describe ways to minimize these negative effects in the next section.

MyLab Education **Self-Check 15.4**

Using Educational Psychology in Teaching: Suggestions for Fulfilling Your Role in Standardized Testing

15.5 Describe your roles in standardized testing processes.

As teachers, we play a central role in ensuring that standardized test scores reflect what our students have actually learned. Given current demographic trends in the United States, we are almost certain to have students with exceptionalities as well as members of cultural minorities in our classes, and some will speak native languages other than English. In addition, we will need to communicate test results to students, their parents, and other caregivers. And we need to use the results to improve our instruction. The following suggestions can help in performing these essential functions:

- Prepare students so that test results accurately reflect what they know and can do.
- Make accommodations, if possible, for members of cultural minorities and students who are not native English speakers.
- Administer tests in ways that maximize student performance.
- Communicate results to students and their caregivers.

Preparing Students. With the emphasis on standardized tests and particularly high-stakes tests, it's our responsibility to ensure that students are as prepared as possible.

We reach this goal first with the effectiveness of our instruction, and second by providing our students with ample practice using formats similar to those they'll encounter on the test (Miller et al., 2013). For example, teachers commonly assess spelling by giving quizzes in which they say words aloud, and students are asked to correctly spell the words. However, because the overwhelming majority of standardized tests use the multiple-choice format, spelling is assessed by having students respond to items such as the following. We saw this example in Chapter 14. Let's look at it again.

Which of the following words is spelled correctly?

   a. perserve
   b. preserve
   c. pesrerve
   d. persreve

The process is similar in math. For instance, the following is an item that we might find on the math portion of a standardized test.

$\dfrac{1}{3} + \dfrac{2}{5} =$

   a. $\dfrac{3}{8}$ b. $\dfrac{11}{15}$ c. $\dfrac{3}{5}$ d. $\dfrac{3}{11}$

Providing our students with practice using this format can increase their performance on standardized tests. (This suggestion is different from "teaching to the test," which focuses on specific test items and provides practice with those items.)

Students should also be taught general test-taking strategies. These strategies are particularly important for members of cultural minorities, students whose first language isn't English, and students from low-SES backgrounds. Effective test-taking strategies for standardized tests include:

- Reading and following all directions.
- Knowing how questions will be scored, such as whether penalties exist for errors in spelling or grammar in written responses, or for guessing on multiple-choice items.

- Eliminating options on multiple-choice items and making informed guesses on remaining items (if guessing isn't penalized).
- Pacing themselves so they're sure to finish the test in the allotted time.
- Answering easier questions first and going back to check answers if time permits.
- Checking to be sure that responses on the answer sheet match the numbers in the test booklet (Brookhart & Nitko, 2015).

We can also provide our students with practice using each of these strategies.

MyLab Education Application Exercise 15.2: Preparing Students for Standardized Tests

In this exercise you will be asked to analyze suggestions for preparing students for standardized tests.

Accommodating Cultural Minorities and English Language Learners. We'll also experience pressure to ensure that subgroups of our students—members of cultural minorities, ELLs, and students with exceptionalities—perform well on these tests. As we saw in earlier sections, standardized tests often include language that isn't commonly used in everyday conversation. We can help accommodate differences in background knowledge by providing concrete examples of technical terms during instruction and emphasizing the essential characteristics of important concepts. This is particularly important for members of cultural minorities and non-native English speakers.

Providing dictionaries and allowing extra time for these students are also effective accommodations if testing procedures allow it.

Administering Tests. To ensure that standardized tests yield valid results, they must be uniformly administered. Developers typically provide detailed instructions for administering the tests (Brookhart & Nitko, 2019). Manuals specify the allotted time for each test and subtest—which should be written on the board for students—and provide scripts for introducing and describing the subtests. Again, providing students with practice taking timed tests can be helpful.

Interpreting Results. Once results are returned, we'll be responsible for explaining them to students and their caregivers, just as Mike did with David's mother. This is the reason we included the section "Understanding and Interpreting Standardized Test Scores" in this chapter.

Standardized test scores should be combined with other information about students when communicating results, and we should emphasize that the scores are only approximations of student capabilities. And, to the extent possible, avoid technical language in discussing results.

Testing experts are clear on the following point: No single test should be used as the basis for educational decisions about individual students (AERA, 2017; Miller et al., 2013). At the school level, we can help ensure that additional sources of data, such as grades, work samples, and classroom observations, are used in making decisions about individual students. At the policy level, we can advocate for the use of comprehensive assessment data in making these decisions.

Finally, when making decisions about students, we should use a variety of sources of data, such as our own quizzes, tests, homework, and informal observations, in addition to standardized test results. This is important for all students, and even more so when working with members of cultural minorities and ELLs. These sources help provide a more comprehensive and accurate picture of our students' achievements.

Classroom Connections

Effectively Using and Interpreting Standardized Tests

1. Test validity can be compromised when cultural factors unfairly affect test performance. Be aware of the potential effects that learner diversity can have on assessment performance.

   - **Elementary:** Before any of her students who are non-native English-speaking are referred for special education testing, a first-grade teacher talks with a school psychologist and describes the child's background and language patterns.

   - **Middle School:** Before administering a statewide exam, an eighth-grade math teacher explains the purpose and format of the test and gives students practice with the content covered on the test. He reads the directions for taking the test slowly and clearly and writes the amount of time remaining on the board.

   - **High School:** A high school English teacher holds sessions after school to help her students with limited English proficiency prepare for a high-stakes test. She explains test purposes and formats and provides students with timed practice on similar items.

2. Testing procedures can influence student performance and ultimately test validity. Adapt testing procedures to meet the needs of all students.

   - **Elementary:** An urban third-grade teacher states positive expectations as her students prepare for a standardized test and carefully monitors them to be sure they stay on task during the test.

   - **Middle School:** Before standardized tests are given each year, a middle school language arts teacher takes time to teach test-taking strategies. She models the strategies, discusses them with her students, and provides opportunities to practice them under test-like conditions.

   - **High School:** An algebra teacher makes a special effort to ensure that students understand the vocabulary on the state standardized test. Before the test, he carefully reviews important concepts the class has learned during the school year.

MyLab Education Self-Check 15.5

Developmentally Appropriate Practice

Standardized Testing with Learners at Different Ages

Effective assessment with standardized tests requires that teachers take learner development into account. The following sections outline suggestions for accommodating the developmental levels of your students.

Working with Students in Early Childhood Programs and Elementary Schools

The developmental characteristics of young children can have a powerful effect on the validity of standardized tests. Their short attention spans and limited language skills influence their performance, and most won't understand that the tests are important, so they often don't make efforts to perform well. For many young children, a standardized test is just one more worksheet to be completed. They also lack experience with timed tests and multiple-choice formats, which are commonly used on standardized tests. They may not follow directions, and because they tend to be impulsive, they often select the first choice that seems plausible or may rush through the test so they can return to activities they find more enjoyable.

Because of mismatches between testing requirements and students' developmental limitations, teachers of young children should treat standardized test results skeptically, particularly when they're inconsistent with a child's classroom performance. Most importantly, teachers should avoid making long-term predictions about student potential on the basis of standardized test results, and particularly on the basis of these results alone.

Working with Students in Middle Schools

Middle school students are starting to understand the importance of standardized tests, which can have both positive and negative effects; it can increase their motivation to perform well, but it can also result in test anxiety that can decrease their performance.

While generally more test-savvy than younger children in their ability to respond to standardized tests, individual development varies a great deal. Some have acquired the study habits, self-regulatory abilities, and test-taking strategies needed to navigate through timed, standardized test formats successfully, whereas others haven't.

(continued)

To accommodate these differences, middle school teachers should emphasize self-regulation and personal responsibility during tests, teach test-taking strategies, and provide ample practice with formats similar to those students will encounter on standardized tests. Emphasizing that the tests can give them valuable information about their strengths and areas that need more work, stating positive expectations about their performance, and encouraging them to do their best are also helpful with middle school students.

Working with Students in High Schools

By the time they reach high school, students have had a considerable amount of experience with standardized testing. As a result, most are familiar with test formats and procedures, but for students who have had negative experiences with standardized testing, motivation can be a problem. Motivation can be a special problem for low-performing students, and it often prevents them from performing up to their capabilities. They may have thoughts such as, "I'll probably get them wrong, so what's the point in trying so hard?"

Teachers of high school students should emphasize that standardized test results exist to provide students with information, and the results don't say anything about their intrinsic worth as human beings or determine whether they will be successful in life. Doing as well as possible is important, however, if the results are to provide the most useful information.

High school students also need help interpreting standardized test scores and how they can be used to make career decisions. Test results can be confusing, and both students and their parents need help understanding and translating them into useful information. Caring and understanding teachers are in the best position to help students understand test results because they are familiar with students' classroom performance and can help students make important decisions about their futures.

Chapter 15 Summary

1. Describe the relationships between standards, accountability, and standardized testing.
   - Standards describe what students should know or be able to do after a prescribed period of study.
   - Accountability is the process of requiring students to demonstrate that they have met standards and making teachers responsible for students' performance. Standardized testing is the process used to determine whether students have met the standards.
   - Advocates of accountability argue that standardized tests efficiently assess the educational achievements of students.
   - In a backlash against high-stakes accountability, critics assert that misuse of standardized tests discourages innovation, narrows the curriculum, and results in teaching to the test.

2. Understand standardized tests and describe their role in the total assessment process.
   - Assessing student academic progress, diagnosing strengths and weaknesses, and placing students in appropriate programs are important functions of standardized tests. Providing information for program evaluation and improvement is also an important function.
   - Achievement tests provide information about student learning; diagnostic tests provide in-depth analysis of specific student strengths and weaknesses; intelligence tests are designed to measure students' ability to acquire and use knowledge, to solve problems, and to accomplish new tasks; and aptitude tests are designed to predict potential for future learning.
   - Validity measures the appropriateness of a test for a specific purpose and includes content, predictive, and construct validity.

3. Interpret standardized test results for students, parents, and other caregivers.
   - Scaled scores help ensure that different forms of a standardized test provide uniform results.
   - The normal distribution is a set of measures that distribute themselves symmetrically in a bell-shaped curve. Standardized test results closely approximate the normal distribution.
   - Percentiles describe the rank of a score compared to others who have taken the test.

- Stanines describe an individual's standardized test performance using a scale ranging from 1 to 9 points.
- The normal curve equivalent is a measure resulting from a statistical process that standardizes scores on a test into a 0–100 scale similar to a percentile rank but preserves equal interval properties that don't exist with percentiles.
- Grade equivalent is a score determined by comparing an individual's score to the scores of students in a particular age group.
- The standard error of measurement is the range of scores within which an individual's true score is likely to fall.

4. Explain how learner diversity can influence the validity of standardized tests.
   - Learner diversity can influence the validity of standardized tests if being a member of a cultural minority or a non-native English speaker results in test bias.
   - Content bias occurs when incidental information in items discriminates against certain cultural groups.
   - Bias in testing procedures occurs when groups don't fully understand testing procedures and the implications of time limits.
   - Bias in the use of test results occurs when tests are used in isolation to make important decisions about students.

5. Describe your roles in standardized testing processes.
   - Preparing students by ensuring that they thoroughly understand the content assessed on standardized tests and providing them with practice using testing formats—usually multiple choice—will help produce standardized test scores that are valid.
   - Providing accommodations for members of cultural minorities and ELLs can also improve the validity of standardized test results.
   - Teaching and practicing test-taking strategies can help students, and particularly members of cultural minorities, ELLs, and students with exceptionalities, perform as well as possible on standardized tests.
   - Interpreting standardized test results for students, parents, and other caregivers is an important teacher role in the standardized testing process.

Preparing for Your Licensure Exam

Understanding Standardized Testing

Your licensure exam will include information related to classroom assessment, and we include the following exercises to help you practice for the exam in your state. This book and these exercises will be a resource for you as you prepare for the exam.

At the beginning of the chapter, you saw how Mike Chavez interpreted standardized test scores for a parent. Let's look now at another situation in which using standardized tests helps answer questions about learning and teaching. Read the case study and answer the questions that follow.

Peggy Barret looks up from the stack of algebra tests that she is grading as her colleague, Stan Witzel, walks into the teacher's lounge.

"How's it going?" Stan asks.

"Fine . . . I think. I'm scoring tests from my Algebra I class. That's the one where I'm trying to put more emphasis on problem solving. Quite a few kids are actually getting into the applications now, and they like the problem solving when they do small-group work. The trouble is, some of the others are really struggling. . . . So, I'm not so sure about it all."

"I wish I had your problems," Stan replies. "It sounds like your kids are learning, and at least some of them like it."

"Yeah, I know," Peggy says with a nod. "Getting these kids to like any kind of math is an accomplishment, but still I wonder. . . . It's just that I'm not sure if they're getting all that they should. I don't know whether this class is really doing better than last year's class or even my other classes this year, for that matter. The tests I give are pretty different in the different classes. I think the kids are doing better on problem solving, but to be honest about it, I see quite a few of them struggling with mechanics. I work on the mechanics, but not as much as in other classes. I'm not sure if I'm putting the right emphasis in the class."

"Good point," Stan says, shrugging. "I always wonder when I make changes. By emphasizing something more, I wonder if

they are they missing out on something else."

"As important," Peggy continues, "I wonder how they'll do when they go off to college. Quite a few of them in this class will be going. . . . Got any ideas?"

"Good question, Peggy. I wish I knew, but . . . I guess that's part of teaching."

"Yeah," she replies with her voice trailing off. "It seems as if we should be able to get some better information. I can see that some of the kids just don't seem to get it. I would say their background is weak; they seem to be trying. On the other hand, I checked out some of their old standardized test results, and their math scores weren't that bad. Maybe it's not background. Maybe they just don't belong in my class."

"Tell me about the kids who are struggling," Stan suggests.

"Well, Jacinta tries really hard. Quan is a whiz at computation but struggles when I ask him to think. Carlos seems to do fairly well with mechanics but has a hard time with word problems. For example, I tried to motivate the class the other day with several word problems involving statistics from our basketball team. Most of the class liked them and got them right. Not these three."

"Maybe you ought to talk to Yolanda," Stan suggests. "She's been in this game for a while and might know about some tests that are available that can help you answer some of your questions."

Questions for Case Analysis

Use information from this chapter and the case study to answer the following questions.

Multiple-Choice Questions

1. What type of standardized test would help Peggy determine "whether this class is really doing better than last year's class or even my other classes this year"?

   a. Achievement test

   b. Diagnostic test

   c. Intelligence test

   d. Aptitude test

2. What type of validity would be the primary concern with this test?

   a. Content validity

   b. Predictive validity

   c. Construct validity

   d. Ecological validity

Constructed Response Question

1. In investigating the problems that her students were having in math, Peggy checked out their overall test scores from past standardized tests. What else might she have done?

MyLab Education Licensure Exam 15.1

Important Concepts

accountability
achievement tests
achievement/ability comparison (AAC)
aptitude
aptitude tests
assessment bias
construct validity
content validity
criterion-referenced standardized tests
diagnostic tests
edTPA

Every Student Succeeds Act (ESSA)
grade equivalent
high-stakes tests
intelligence tests
National Assessment of Educational Progress (NAEP)
national norms
No Child Left Behind (NCLB) Act
normal curve equivalent (NCE)

normal distribution
norming group
norm-referenced standardized tests
percentile rank (PR)
predictive validity
Race to the Top
raw scores
readiness tests
scaled scores
standard deviation
standard error of measurement

standardized tests
standards
Stanford-Binet
stanine
Trends in International Mathematics and Science Study (TIMSS)
value-added modeling
Wechsler Intelligence Scale for Children

APPENDIX

Using *Educational Psychology* (11th ed.) to Prepare for the Praxis™ *Principles of Learning and Teaching* Exam

"*The Praxis Series* tests are currently required for teacher licensure in more than 40 states and U.S. territories. These tests are also used by several professional licensing agencies and by several hundred colleges and universities" (Educational Testing Service, 2014a, p. 1). Also, teacher candidates who test in one state can submit their scores for licensure in any other *Praxis®* user state (Educational Testing Service, 2014a).

Four *Principles of Learning and Teaching* (PLT) tests, one each for teachers seeking licensure in Early Childhood, or grades K–6, 5–9, and 7–12, are among the Praxis™ exams. *Educational Psychology* (11th ed.) addresses virtually all of the topics covered in the PLT tests.

Each of the four *Principles of Learning and Teaching* exams consists of 70 multiple-choice (MC) and 4 constructed-response (CR) questions organized into four sections. The four sections with the approximate number of questions in each include (Educational Testing Service, 2014b, 2014c, 2014d, 2014e):

- Students as learners—21 MC and one or two CR questions

- Instructional process—21 MC and one or two CR questions

- Assessment—14 MC and zero or one CR questions

- Professional development, leadership, and community—14 MC and zero or one CR questions

The multiple-choice questions are similar to those in the test bank that accompanies *Educational Psychology* (11th ed.). The constructed response questions are based on "case histories" (case studies), which you will be asked to read and analyze. The case histories are very similar to the case studies that appear throughout this text. Each of the constructed-response questions are scored on a scale of 0–2. Sample questions and responses that earn scores of 2, 1, and 0 can be found at the following links: http://www.ets .org/s/praxis/pdf/5025.pdf (Early Childhood); http://www .ets.org/s/praxis/pdf/5622.pdf (Grades K–6); http://www .ets.org/s/praxis/pdf/5623.pdf (Grades 5–9); http://www .ets.org/s/praxis/pdf/5624.pdf (Grades 7–12). Sample multiple-choice questions can also be found at these links.

We have designed this text to help you succeed on the Praxis™ *Principles of Learning and Teaching* exam by including case studies at the end of each chapter, which are followed by multiple-choice and short-answer questions. The case studies and questions help you prepare for your licensure exam by providing you with items similar to those that will appear on the exam. We provide feedback for all the items.

Topics Covered on the Praxis™ Exam (Educational Testing Service, 2014b, 2014c, 2014d, 2014e)	Chapter Content in *Educational Psychology* (11th ed.) Aligned with Topics Covered on the Praxis™ Exam

I. Students as Learners

Student Development and the Learning Process

- Understands the theoretical foundations of how students learn (such as how knowledge is constructed, how skills are acquired, and the cognitive processes involved)
- Knows the contributions of foundational theorists in education (such as Piaget, Vygotsky, Kohlberg, Skinner, and Bandura)
- Understands concepts and terms related to a variety of learning theories (such as schema, metacognition, transfer, zone of proximal development, and classical and operant conditioning)
- Knows the distinguishing characteristics of the stages in each domain of human development (i.e., cognitive, social, and moral)
- Understands how learning theory and human development impact the instructional process (such as using learning and development theory to design instruction and solve educational problems)

Chapter 2: Cognitive and Language Development

- Principles of development (p. 36)
- Bronfenbrenner's bioecological model of development (pp. 36–39)
- Piaget's theory of cognitive development (pp. 46–56)
- Neo-Piagetian views of cognitive development (p. 57)
- Educational psychology and teaching: Applying Piaget's theory with your students (pp. 57–59)
- Vygotsky's sociocultural theory of cognitive development (pp. 60–65)
- Educational psychology and teaching: Applying Vygotsky's theory with your students (pp. 65–69)

Chapter 3: Personal, Social, and Moral Development

- Social development (pp. 108–111)
- Development of morality, social responsibility, and self-control

Chapter 6: Behaviorism and Social Cognitive Theory (Entire chapter)

Chapter 7: Cognitive Views of Learning (Entire chapter)

Chapter 8: Complex Cognitive Processes (Entire chapter)

Chapter 9: Knowledge Construction in Social Contexts

- Knowledge construction (pp. 386–390)
- Knowledge construction and the learning sciences (pp. 390–393)
- Educational psychology and teaching: Guiding your students' knowledge constructions (pp. 398–405)

Students as Diverse Learners

- Understands that a number of variables affect how individual students perform (such as culture, gender, socioeconomic status, motivation, cognitive development, prior knowledge and experience, and language)
- Recognizes areas of exceptionality and their potential impact on student learning (such as cognitive, speech/language, and behavioral)
- Understands the implications and application of legislation relating to students with exceptionalities in classroom practice
- Recognizes the traits, behaviors, and needs of intellectually gifted students
- Recognizes that the process of English language acquisition affects the educational experience of English learners (ELs)
- Knows a variety of approaches for accommodating students with exceptionalities in each phase of the educational process

Chapter 2: Cognitive and Language Development

- How experiences advance development (pp. 49–50)
- Stages of development (pp. 51–56)
- Learning and development in a cultural context (pp. 61–63)
- Diversity: Culture and development (p. 65)
- Language development (pp. 70–76)

Chapter 4: Learner Diversity (Entire chapter)

Chapter 5: Learners with Exceptionalities

- The legal basis for working with students with exceptionalities (pp. 195–203)
- Exceptionalities and learning problems (pp. 203–214)
- Students who are gifted and talented (pp. 214–217)
- Teachers' responsibilities in inclusive classrooms (pp. 218–223)

Chapter 10: Motivation and Learning (Entire chapter)

Chapter 11: A Classroom Model for Promoting Student Motivation (Entire chapter)

Chapter 14: Increasing Learning Through Assessment

- Diversity: Effective assessment practices with students from diverse backgrounds (pp. 653–654)

Chapter 15: Standardized Testing and Learning

- Diversity and standardized testing (pp. 681–684)

Student Motivation and Learning Environment

- Knows the major contributions of foundational behavioral theorists to education (such as Skinner, Maslow, and Erikson)
- Understands the implications of foundational motivation theories for instruction, learning, and classroom management (such as extrinsic and intrinsic motivation, self-determination, attribution, classic and operant conditioning, and positive and negative reinforcers)
- Knows principles and strategies for classroom management (such as routines and procedures, rules, and ways of promoting a positive learning environment)

Chapter 3: Personal, Social, and Moral Development

- Erikson's theory of psychosocial development (pp. 96–97)

Chapter 6: Behaviorism and Social Cognitive Theory

- Classical conditioning (pp. 232–234)
- Operant conditioning (pp. 237–246)

Chapter 10: Motivation and Learning (Entire chapter)

Chapter 11: A Classroom Model for Promoting Student Motivation (Entire chapter)

Chapter 12: Classroom Management: Developing Self-Regulated Learners (Entire chapter)

(continued)

Topics Covered on the Praxis™ Exam (Educational Testing Service, 2014b, 2014c, 2014d, 2014e)	Chapter Content in *Educational Psychology* (11th ed.) Aligned with Topics Covered on the Praxis™ Exam
II. Instructional Process **Planning Instruction** • Understands the role of district, state, and national standards in instructional planning • Knows how to apply the basic concepts of predominant educational theories • Knows how to select content to achieve lesson and unit objectives • Knows how to develop objectives in the cognitive, affective, and psychomotor domains • Is aware of the need for and is able to identify various resources for planning enrichment and remediation activities	Chapter 1: Educational Psychology: Understanding Learning and Teaching • Standards and accountability (p. 24) Chapter 2: Cognitive and Language Development • Educational psychology and teaching: Applying Piaget's theory with your students (pp. 57–59) • Educational psychology and teaching: Applying Vygotsky's theory with your students (pp. 65–69) Chapter 6: Behaviorism and Social Cognitive Theory • Educational psychology and teaching: Applying classical conditioning with your students (pp. 235–236) • Educational psychology and teaching: Applying operant conditioning with your students (pp. 246–250) • Educational psychology and teaching: Using social cognitive theory to increase your students' learning (pp. 268–271) Chapter 7: Cognitive Views of Learning • Educational psychology and teaching: Applying information processing and the model of human memory with your students (pp. 321–328) Chapter 9: Knowledge Construction in Social Contexts • Educational psychology and teaching: Guiding your students' knowledge construction (pp. 398–405) Chapter 13: Learning and Effective Teaching • Identifying topics (pp. 549–550) • Specifying learning objectives (pp. 550–552) • Preparing and organizing learning activities (pp. 553–554) • Planning in a standards-based environment (pp. 554–559)
Instructional Strategies • Understands the cognitive processes associated with learning (such as critical and creative thinking, questioning, and problem solving) • Understands the distinguishing features of different instructional models (such as direct instruction, guided discovery, and cooperative learning) • Knows a variety of instructional strategies associated with each instructional model • Knows a variety of strategies for encouraging complex cognitive processes • Knows a variety of strategies for supporting student learning (such as modeling, developing self-regulation, and differentiated instruction) • Understands the use and implications of different grouping techniques and strategies	Chapter 6: Behaviorism and Social Cognitive Theory • Self-regulation (pp. 264–268) Chapter 7: Cognitive Views of Learning • Cognitive processes (pp. 301–315) Chapter 8: Complex Cognitive Processes (Entire chapter) Chapter 12: Classroom Management: Developing Self-Regulated Learners • Developing learner self-regulation (pp. 499–502) Chapter 13: Learning and Effective Teaching • Models of instruction (pp. 572–585) • Cooperative learning (pp. 585–589) • Flipped instruction (pp. 589–591) • Differentiated instruction (pp. 591–592)
Questioning Techniques • Knows the components of effective questioning (such as wait time, handling incorrect answers, and encouraging participation) • Understands the uses of questioning (such as increasing motivation, reviewing previous lessons, and summarizing information) • Knows strategies for promoting a safe and open forum for discussion	Chapter 11: A Classroom Model for Promoting Student Motivation • The teacher–student relationship (pp. 466–467) • Order and safety (pp. 475–476) Chapter 12: Classroom Management: Developing Self-Regulated Learners • Creating a community of caring and trust Chapter 13: Learning and Effective Teaching • Review (p. 564) • Questioning (pp. 564–565) • Feedback (p. 568) • Closure (p. 570)

Topics Covered on the Praxis™ Exam (Educational Testing Service, 2014b, 2014c, 2014d, 2014e)	Chapter Content in *Educational Psychology* (11th ed.) Aligned with Topics Covered on the Praxis™ Exam

Communication Techniques

- Understands various verbal and nonverbal communication models
- Is aware of how culture and gender can affect communication
- Knows how to use various communication tools to enrich the learning environment

Chapter 4: Learner Diversity

- Cultural differences in adult–child interactions (pp. 147–148)
- School-related gender differences (pp. 160–162)
- Boys' and girls' classroom behavior (pp. 160–161)

Chapter 12: Classroom Management: Developing Self-Regulated Learners

- Keep verbal and nonverbal behaviors congruent (pp. 525–526)

Chapter 13: Learning and Effective Teaching

- Communication (pp. 570–571)

III. Assessment

Assessment and Evaluation Strategies

- Understands the role of formal and informal assessment in informing the instructional process
- Understands the distinctions among the different types of assessment
- Knows how to create and select an appropriate assessment format to meet instructional objectives
- Knows how to select from a variety of assessment tools to evaluate student performance
- Understands the rationale behind and the uses of students' self and peer assessment

Chapter 9: Knowledge Construction in Social Contexts

- Promote learning with assessment

Chapter 11: A Classroom Model for Promoting Student Motivation

- Assessing students and providing feedback: Providing information about learning progress (p. 486)

Chapter 13: Learning and Effective Teaching

- Planning for assessment (pp. 552–553)
- Assessment and learning: Using assessment as a learning tool (pp. 598–599)

Chapter 14: Increasing Learning Through Assessment (Entire chapter)

Assessment Tools

- Understands the types and purposes of standardized tests
- Understands the distinction between norm-referenced and criterion-referenced scoring
- Understands terminology related to testing and scoring (such as validity, reliability, raw score, scaled score, percentile, mean, mode, median, and grade equivalent scores)
- Knows how to interpret assessment results and communicate the meaning of those results to students, parents/caregivers, and school personnel

Chapter 14: Increasing Learning Through Assessment

- Validity: Making accurate assessment decisions (p. 616)
- Reliability: Consistency in assessment (p. 616)
- Norm-referenced and criterion-referenced grading systems (p. 649)

Chapter 15: Standardized Testing and Learning

- Functions of standardized tests (p. 669–670)
- Norm- versus criterion-referenced standardized tests (p. 670)
- Types of standardized tests (pp. 670–674)
- Evaluating standardized tests: Validity revisited (pp. 674–675)
- Understanding and interpreting standardized test scores (pp. 675–680)
- Educational psychology and teaching: Your role in standardized testing (pp. 684–686)

IV. Professional Development, Leadership, and Community

- Is aware of a variety of professional development practices and resources (such as professional literature, professional associations, mentors, and study groups)
- Understands the implications of research, views, ideas, and debates on teaching practices
- Recognizes the role of reflective practice for professional growth
- Is aware of school support personnel who assist students, teachers, and families (such as guidance counselors, IEP team members, and special education teachers)
- Understands the role of teachers and schools as educational leaders in the greater community
- Knows basic strategies for developing collaborative relationships with colleagues, administrators, other school personnel, parents/caregivers, and the community to support the educational process
- Understands the implications of major legislation and court decisions relating to students and teachers

Chapter 1: Educational Psychology: Understanding Learning and Teaching

- The preeminence of teachers (pp. 5–6)
- Educational psychology, professional knowledge, and expert teaching (pp. 6–13)
- Professional knowledge and reflective practice (p. 18)
- The role of research in acquiring professional knowledge (pp. 19–23)

Chapter 5: Learners with Exceptionalities

- The legal basis for working with students with exceptionalities (pp. 195–203)
- Individualized education program (pp. 200–201)
- Collaborating with other professionals (pp. 221–222)

Chapter 12: Classroom Management: Developing Self-Regulated Learners

- Communicating with parents (pp. 515–517)

Glossary

Ability grouping. The process of placing students of similar abilities into groups and attempting to match instruction to the needs of these groups.

Academic learning time. The amount of time students are successful while engaged in learning activities.

Acceleration. Programs for students who are gifted and talented that keep the curriculum the same but allow students to move through it more quickly.

Accommodation. The process of creating new schemes or adjusting old ones when they can no longer explain new experiences.

Accountability. The process of requiring students to demonstrate that they have met specified standards and holding teachers responsible for students' performance.

Achievement tests. Standardized tests designed to assess how much students have learned in specified content areas.

Achievement/ability comparison (AAC). A representation of students' average performance compared to the total norm group.

Action research. Applied research designed to answer a specific school- or classroom-related question.

Adaptive behavior. A person's ability to perform the functions of everyday living.

Affective domain. The area of learning that focuses on people's feelings, attitudes, and emotions.

Algorithm. A specific step or set of steps for finding the solution to a problem.

Allocated time. The amount of time a teacher or school designates for a content area or topic.

Alternative assessment. Form of assessment that includes projects and performance assessments.

Analogies. Descriptions of relationships that are similar in some but not all respects.

Antecedents. Stimuli that precede and induce behaviors.

Anxiety. A general uneasiness and feeling of tension relating to a situation with an uncertain outcome.

Application. The process of having students use the information they have acquired in the lesson in a new context.

Applied behavior analysis (ABA). The process of systematically implementing the principles of operant conditioning to change student behavior.

Appropriating understanding. The process of individually internalizing understanding after it has first been socially constructed.

Aptitude. The ability to acquire knowledge.

Aptitude tests. Standardized tests designed to predict the potential for future learning and measure general abilities developed over long periods of time.

Assessment. The process of gathering information and making decisions about students' learning progress.

Assessment bias. A form of discrimination that occurs when a test or other assessment instrument unfairly penalizes a group of students because of their gender, ethnicity, race, or socioeconomic status.

Assimilation. The process of using existing schemes to interpret new experiences.

Assistive technology. A set of adaptive tools that support students with disabilities in learning activities and daily life tasks.

Attainment value. The importance an individual attaches to doing well on a task.

Attention. The process of consciously focusing on a stimulus.

Attention-deficit/hyperactivity disorder (ADHD). A specific type of learning disability, characterized by inattention, hyperactivity, and impulsiveness.

Attribution theory. A cognitive theory of motivation that attempts to systematically describe learners' beliefs about the causes of their successes and failures and how these beliefs influence motivation to learn.

Attributions. Explanations or beliefs about the causes of performance.

Autism spectrum disorder. A description of a cluster of disorders characterized by impaired social relationships and skills and often associated with highly unusual behavior.

Automaticity. The ability to perform mental operations with little awareness or conscious effort.

Autonomous morality. A stage of moral development characterized by the belief that fairness and justice is the reciprocal process of treating others as they would want to be treated.

Autonomy. Independence and the ability to alter the environment when necessary.

Axons. Longer branches that extend from the cell body of neurons and transmit messages to other neurons.

Backward design. A systematic approach to instructional planning that identifies learning objectives, assessments, and learning experiences—in that order—during the planning process.

Behaviorism. A theory that explains learning in terms of observable behaviors and how they are influenced by stimuli from the environment.

Belief. A cognitive idea we accept as true without necessarily having definitive evidence to support it.

Between-class grouping. An ability grouping process that divides students in a certain grade into levels, such as high, medium, and low.

Bidialectalism. The ability to switch back and forth between a dialect and Standard English.

Bilingualism. The ability to speak, read, and write in two languages.

Bipolar disorder. A condition characterized by alternative episodes of depressive and manic states.

Bullying. A form of peer aggression that involves a systematic or repetitious abuse of power between students.

Caring. A teacher's empathy and investment in the protection and development of young people.

Central executive. A supervisory component of working memory that controls the flow of information to and from the other components.

Centration. The tendency to focus on the most perceptually obvious aspect of an object or event, neglecting other important aspects.

Characteristics. A concept's essential, or defining, elements.

Checklists. Written descriptions of dimensions that must be present in an acceptable performance.

Child abuse. An act or failure to act by a parent or other caregiver, which can result in death, serious physical or emotional harm, sexual abuse, or exploitation, or an act or failure to act which presents an imminent risk of serious harm.

Chunking. The process of mentally combining separate items into larger, more meaningful units.

Classical conditioning. A component of behaviorism that explains how we learn to display involuntary emotional or physiological responses that are similar to instinctive or reflexive responses.

Classification. The process of grouping objects on the basis of common characteristics.

Classroom assessment. All the processes involved in making decisions about our students' learning progress.

Classroom climate. The shared beliefs, values, and attitudes that set the parameters for acceptable behavior and shape interactions between students and teachers, and students with each other.

Classroom management. All the actions teachers take to establish an environment that supports academic learning, self-regulation, and social and emotional development.

Closure. A summary that occurs at the end of lessons.

Coding. The process of using the languages programmers employ to design applications, websites, and software.

Cognition. Thinking, including beliefs, perceptions, and expectations, that is influenced by experience, prior knowledge, practice, and feedback.

Cognitive activity. The process of focusing our thinking on the learning task in which we are involved and the factors related to the task.

Cognitive apprenticeships. Social learning processes that occur when less-skilled learners work alongside experts in developing cognitive skills.

Cognitive behavior modification. A procedure that promotes behavioral change and self-regulation in students through self-talk and self-instruction.

Cognitive constructivism. A view that describes knowledge construction as an individual, internal process.

Cognitive development. Changes in our thinking that occur as a result of maturation and experience.

Cognitive domain. The area of learning that focuses on students' thinking and the processes involved in acquiring, applying, and analyzing knowledge.

Cognitive learning theories. Theories that explain learning in terms of the changes in the mental structures and processes involved in acquiring, organizing, and using knowledge.

Cognitive load. The amount of mental activity imposed on working memory.

Cognitive modeling. The process of performing a demonstration combined with verbalizing the thinking behind the actions.

Cognitive tools. The concepts and symbols (numbers and language) together with the real tools that allow people to think, solve problems, and function in a culture.

Collaboration. The process of working with other professionals to solve common problems.

Collaborative consultation. The process of general and special-education teachers working together to create effective learning experiences for learners with exceptionalities.

Collective efficacy. Beliefs that the faculty as a whole in a school can have a positive effect on student learning.

Collective self-esteem. Individuals' perceptions of the relative worth of the groups to which they belong.

Common Core State Standards Initiative (CCSSI). A state-led effort initiated in 2009 designed to establish a single set of clear educational standards for all states in mathematics and English-language arts, together with literacy in history/social studies, science, and technical subjects, that states can share and voluntarily adopt.

Communication disorders. Exceptionalities that interfere with students' abilities to receive and understand information from others and express their own ideas.

Community of learners. A learning environment in which the teacher and students work together to help everyone learn.

Competence. The ability to function effectively in the environment.

Completion. Also called "short answer," an assessment format that includes a question or incomplete statement requiring learners to write a short—often one word—answer.

Comprehension monitoring. The process of checking to see if we understand what we have read or heard.

Concept map. A visual representation of the relationships among concepts that includes the concepts themselves, sometimes enclosed in circles or boxes, together with relationships among concepts indicated by lines linking the concepts.

Concepts. Mental representations of categories that allow us to identify examples and nonexamples of those categories.

Conceptual hierarchies. Types of concept maps that visually illustrate superordinate, subordinate, and coordinate relationships among concepts.

Conditioned response (CR). A learned physiological or emotional response that is similar to the unconditioned response.

Conditioned stimuli (CS). A formerly neutral stimulus that becomes associated with an unconditioned stimulus.

Confirmation bias. People's tendency to focus only on evidence that supports their beliefs.

Consequences. Events (stimuli) that occur following a behavior that influence the probability of the behavior recurring.

Conservation. The idea that the "amount" of some substance stays the same regardless of its shape or the number of pieces into which it is divided.

Conspiracy theory. An explanation for an event that invokes plots or schemes by governments or other powerful actors for nefarious motives.

Construct validity. An indicator of the logical connection between a test and what it is designed to measure.

Constructive assertiveness. The process of communicating concerns clearly, insisting that misbehavior be corrected, and resisting being coerced or manipulated.

Constructivism. A view of learning which says that learners do not acquire knowledge directly from others; rather they construct it for themselves as they attempt to make sense of their experiences.

Content validity. A test's ability to accurately sample the content taught and to measure the extent to which learners understand it.

Continuous reinforcement schedule. A schedule of reinforcement in which every desired behavior is reinforced.

Conventional domain. The domain of moral development that addresses societal norms and ways of behaving in specific situations.

Conventional level of morality. A moral orientation linked to uncritical acceptance of society's conventions about right and wrong.

Cooperative learning. A set of instructional strategies in which students work in mixed ability groups to reach specific cognitive and social development objectives.

Corporal punishment. A form of physical punishment that involves the deliberate infliction of pain in response to misbehavior.

Cost. The consideration of what a person must give up to engage in an activity.

Creativity. The ability to produce original works or solutions to problems that are productive and task appropriate.

Criterion-referenced grading. The process of making grading decisions according to a predetermined standard, such as 90–100 for an A, 80–89 for a B, and so on.

Criterion-referenced standardized tests. Standardized tests that compare performance against a set performance standard.

Critical thinking. An individual's ability and inclination to make and assess conclusions based on evidence.

Crystallized intelligence. Culture-specific mental ability, heavily dependent on experience and schooling.

Cultural intelligence. An individual's ability to adjust and effectively adapt to diverse cultural situations.

Cultural mismatch. A clash between a child's home culture and the culture of the school that creates conflicting expectations for students and their behavior.

Culturally responsive classroom management. Classroom management that combines cultural knowledge with teachers' awareness of possible personal biases.

Culturally responsive teaching. An approach to education that attempts to understand the cultures of the students we teach, communicate positive attitudes about cultural diversity, and employ a variety of instructional approaches that build on students' cultural backgrounds.

Culture. The knowledge, attitudes, values, and customs that characterize a social group.

Curriculum-based assessment. Measurement of learners' performance in specific areas of the curriculum.

Cyberbullying. A form of bullying that occurs when students use electronic media to harass or intimidate other students.

Data-driven instruction. An approach to teaching that relies on information about student performance to inform teaching and learning.

Deaf. A hearing impairment that requires the use of other senses, usually sight, to communicate.

Declarative knowledge. Knowledge of facts, concepts, procedures, and rules.

Deficiency needs. Needs that energize people to meet them if they are unfulfilled.

Delay of gratification. The ability to forgo an immediate pleasure or reward in order to gain a more substantial one later.

Deliberate practice. An approach to the development of a wide range of abilities that is goal directed, frequent, and systematic; is conducted in real-world contexts; focuses on understanding instead of rote drill; and includes feedback about learning progress.

Dendrites. Relatively short, branchlike structures that extend from the cell body of neurons and receive messages from other neurons.

Design-based research. Research that is designed to impact classroom practice and contribute to theory by focusing on educational interventions that are conducted in real-world contexts using mixed methods, multiple iterations, and a partnership between researchers and practitioners.

Desist. A verbal or nonverbal communication that teachers use to stop a behavior.

Detention. Taking away students' free time (typically a half hour or more) by keeping them in school either before or after hours.

Development. The changes that occur in human beings as they grow from infancy to adulthood.

Developmental differences. Changes in students' thinking, personalities, and social skills that result from maturation and experience.

Developmentally appropriate practice. Instruction that matches teacher actions to the capabilities and needs of learners at different developmental levels.

Diagnostic tests. Standardized tests designed to provide a detailed description of learners' strengths and weaknesses in specific skill areas.

Dialect. A variation of Standard English that is associated with a particular regional or social group and is distinct in vocabulary, grammar, or pronunciation.

Differentiating instruction. The process of adapting instruction to meet the needs of students who vary in background knowledge, skills, needs, and motivations.

Direct instruction. A teaching model designed to help students acquire well-defined knowledge and skills needed for later learning.

Disabilities. Functional limitations or an inability to perform a certain act.

Discipline. Teachers' responses to student misbehavior.

Discrepancy model of identification. A method of identifying students with learning problems that focuses on differences between achievement and intelligence tests or subtests.

Discrimination. The process that occurs when a person gives different responses to related but not identical stimuli.

Disorder. A general malfunction of mental, physical, or psychological processes.

Distractors. Statements—when using the multiple-choice format—that are designed to identify students who do not understand the content the item is measuring.

Distributed practice. The process of spacing practice sessions over time.

Drawing analogies. A heuristic used to solve unfamiliar problems by comparing them with those already solved.

edTPA. *Educational Teacher Performance Assessment*—a high-stakes preservice assessment process designed to answer the question, "Is a new teacher ready for the job?"

Educational psychology. The academic discipline that focuses on human teaching and learning.

Effective teaching. Instruction that promotes as much learning as possible in all students.

Egocentrism. The inability to see objects and events from others' perspectives.

Elaboration. An encoding strategy that increases the meaningfulness of new information by connecting it to existing knowledge.

Elaborative questioning. The process of drawing inferences, identifying examples, and forming relationships.

Embodied cognition. The idea that cognition (our thinking) depends on characteristics of our physical bodies, and our bodies significantly influence the way we process information.

Emotion. A feeling that is often short-lived, intense, and specific.

Emotional and behavior disorder. Serious and persistent age-inappropriate behaviors that result in social conflict, personal unhappiness, and often school failure.

Emotional intelligence. A form of intelligence that involves the accurate perception and expression of emotion and the ability to adapt emotions and use emotional knowledge in thought processes.

Emotional self-regulation. The ability to manage our emotions so we can cope with the environment and accomplish goals.

Empathy. The ability to experience the same emotion someone else is feeling.

Emphasis. Verbal and vocal cues that alert students to important information in a lesson.

Encoding. The process of representing information in long-term memory.

Engaged time. The amount of time students are paying attention and involved in learning activities.

English language learners (ELLs). Students whose first or home language is not English.

Equilibrium. A cognitive state in which we are able to explain new experiences by using existing understanding.

Equitable distribution. The process of calling on all the students in a class as equally as possible, whether or not they have their hands raised.

Essay. An assessment format that requires students to make extended written responses to questions or problems.

Essential teaching skills. Basic abilities that all teachers, including those in their first year of teaching, should possess to maximize student learning.

Ethnic identity. An awareness of ethnic group membership and a commitment to the attitudes, values, and behaviors of that group.

Ethnicity. A person's ancestry and the way individuals identify with the nation from which they or their ancestors came.

Every Student Succeeds Act (ESSA). A federal effort, passed in 2015, designed to improve education in our country and replace its predecessor, No Child Left Behind.

Executive functioning. An umbrella term used to describe the cognitive processes responsible for purposeful, goal-directed behavior.

Exemplars. The most highly typical examples of a concept.

Exosystem. In bioecological theory, societal influences that affect both the micro- and mesosystems.

Expectancy x value theory. A theory that explains motivation by saying that learners will be motivated to engage in a task to the extent that they expect to succeed on a task times the value they place on the success.

Expectation. A belief about a future outcome. The influence of expectations on motivation is often described using expectancy x value theory.

Expert. An individual who highly skilled or knowledgeable in a domain, such as math, athletics, or teaching.

External morality. A stage of moral development in which individuals view rules as fixed and permanent and enforced by authority figures.

Extinction (classical conditioning). The process that occurs when the conditioned stimulus occurs often enough in the absence of the unconditioned stimulus so that it no longer elicits the conditioned response.

Extinction (operant conditioning). The disappearance of a behavior as a result of nonreinforcement.

Extrinsic motivation. Motivation to engage in an activity as a means to an end.

Fake news. Deliberate misinformation that uses exaggerated and attention-grabbing headlines for political, economic, or social gain.

Feedback. Information teachers provide to students that helps students determine whether or not the knowledge they are constructing is accurate and valid.

Fixed mindset. The belief that abilities are relatively fixed, stable, and unchanging over time and task conditions.

Flipped instruction. An approach to instruction that has students study new content online by watching video lectures, usually at home, and do problems, exercises, and other activities that apply the content in class. Also commonly called the "flipped classroom."

Flow. An intense form of intrinsic motivation in which an individual is in a state of complete absorption, focus, and concentration in a challenging activity.

Fluid intelligence. The flexible, culture-free mental ability to adapt to new situations and acquire knowledge quickly.

Focus. The essential teaching skill teachers use to capture and maintain students' attention and interest throughout the lesson.

Forgetting. The loss of, or inability to retrieve, information from long-term memory.

Formative assessment. The collection of formal and informal processes teachers and students use to gather evidence for the purpose of informing next steps in learning.

Functional analysis. The strategy used to identify antecedents and consequences that influence behavior.

Gender identity. Culturally and socially constructed conceptions of what it is like to be female or male and how each behaves, that is, things girls do and things boys do.

General pedagogical knowledge. A type of professional knowledge that involves an understanding of instructional and classroom management strategies that apply to all topics and subject matter areas.

General transfer. The ability to apply knowledge or skills learned in one context to a variety of different contexts.

Generalization. The process that occurs when stimuli similar, but not identical, to a conditioned stimulus elicit the conditioned responses by themselves.

Gifts and talents. Abilities at the upper end of the continuum that require additional support to reach full potential.

Goal. An outcome an individual hopes to attain.

Goodness of fit. Matching what we do as teachers to each student's personalities.

Grade equivalent. A score that is determined by comparing an individual's score on a standardized test to the scores of students in a particular age group.

Grammar. A subcategory of syntax that includes punctuation and capitalization.

Grit. The ability to develop and sustain passion and commitment to achieving long-term goals.

Growth mindset. The belief that intelligence or ability can be increased with effort.

Growth needs. Needs in intellectual achievement and aesthetic appreciation that increase as people have experiences with them.

Guided discovery. A model of instruction that involves teachers scaffolding students' constructions of concepts and the relationships among them.

Guided notes. Teacher-prepared handouts that "guide" students with cues and space available for writing key ideas and relationships in a written passage or presentation.

Guilt. The uncomfortable feeling people get when they know they have caused distress for someone else.

Handicap. A condition imposed on a person's functioning that restricts the individual's abilities.

Heuristics. General, widely applicable problem-solving strategies.

High-quality examples. Examples for which all the information students need to understand a topic is observable in the examples.

High-stakes tests. Standardized tests used to make important decisions that affect students, teachers, schools, and school districts.

Holophrases. One- and two-word utterances that carry as much meaning for the child as complete sentences.

Homeless students. Students who lack a fixed, regular, and adequate nighttime residence.

Hostile attribution bias. A tendency to view others' behaviors as hostile or aggressive.

Human capital. People's professional knowledge and skills, social abilities, and personality attributes that contribute to a nation's cultural and economic advancement.

Identity. Individuals' self-constructed definition of who they are, what their existence means, and what they want in life.

Ill-defined problem. A problem that has an ambiguous goal, more than one acceptable solution, and no generally agreed-upon strategy for reaching a solution.

Imagery. An encoding strategy that involves the process of forming mental pictures of an idea.

Immigrants. People who migrate to another country, typically with the intent of living there permanently.

Implementing instruction. The process of putting decisions made during planning into action.

Inclusion. The process of placing students with exceptionalities in the school's academic curriculum, extracurricular activities, and other experiences alongside students not having exceptionalities.

Individualized education program (IEP). A written statement that provides a framework for delivering a free and appropriate education (FAPE) to every eligible student with a disability.

Information processing theory. A theory that describes how information enters our memory system, is organized, and is finally stored.

Inhibition. A self-imposed restriction on one's behavior.

Instructional alignment. The match between learning objectives, learning activities, and assessments.

Instructional time. The amount of time left for teaching after routine management and administrative tasks are completed.

Instrumental aggression. An aggressive act aimed at gaining an object or privilege.

Intellectual disability. A disability characterized by significant limitations both in intellectual functioning and in adaptive behavior.

Intellectual functioning. General mental capacity, such as the ability to learn, reason, and solve problems. Also simply called intelligence.

Intelligence. The ability to acquire and use knowledge, solve problems and reason in the abstract, and adapt to new situations in the environment.

Intelligence tests. Standardized tests designed to measure an individual's capacity to acquire and use knowledge, to solve problems, and to accomplish new tasks.

Interactive whiteboard. A device including a display screen connected to a computer and projector that allows information displayed on the screen to be manipulated with special pens or hands, stored in the computer, and recovered later for further use.

Interference. The loss of information because something learned either before or after detracts from understanding.

Intermittent reinforcement schedule. A schedule of reinforcement in which some, but not all, of the desired behaviors are reinforced.

Internalization. The process through which learners incorporate external, society-based activities into internal cognitive processes.

Interpersonal harmony. A stage of moral reasoning in which conclusions are based on loyalty, living up to the expectations of others, and social conventions.

Interspersed practice. The process of mixing the practice of different skills, such as practicing word problems that sometimes require addition and at other times require subtraction.

Interval schedule of reinforcement. An intermittent reinforcement schedule in which behaviors are reinforced after a predictable (fixed) or unpredictable (variable) time interval.

Intrinsic motivation. Motivation to be involved in an activity for its own sake.

Introductory focus. A lesson beginning that attracts student attention and provides a conceptual framework for the lesson.

Involvement. The extent to which people are actively participating in an activity.

Knowledge of learners and learning. An understanding of the learning process and how students learn and develop.

Language disorders (receptive disorders). Problems with understanding language or using language to express ideas.

Law and order. A stage of moral reasoning in which conclusions are based on following laws and rules for their own sake.

Learned helplessness. Th debilitating belief that one is incapable of accomplishing tasks and has little control of the environment.

Learner diversity. The group and individual differences in our students.

Learners with exceptionalities. Students who need special help and resources to reach their full potential.

Learning (behaviorism). A relatively enduring change in observable behavior that occurs as a result of experience.

Learning (cognitive). A change in mental processes that creates the capacity to demonstrate different behaviors.

Learning activities. All the experiences we provide and actions we take to help our students reach our learning objectives.

Learning disabilities. Difficulty in acquiring and using reading, writing, reasoning, listening, or mathematical abilities.

Learning objectives. Statements that specify what students should know or be able to do with respect to a topic.

Learning sciences. A field of study that focuses on learning as it exists in real-world settings and how learning may be facilitated both with and without technology.

Learning styles. Students' personal approaches to learning, problem solving, and processing information.

Least restrictive environment (LRE). A policy that places students in as typical an educational setting as possible while still meeting the students' special needs.

Lecture–discussion. An instructional model designed to help students acquire organized bodies of knowledge through short teacher presentations followed by interactive discussions.

LGBTQ. An acronym that refers to lesbian, gay, bisexual, transgender, and individuals who are exploring or questioning their identities.

Logical consequences. Outcomes that are conceptually related to misbehavior; they help learners make sense of an intervention by creating a link between their actions and the consequences.

Long-term memory. The permanent information store in our memory system.

Macrosystem. Bronfenbrenner's fourth level, which includes cultural influences on development.

Market exchange. A stage of moral reasoning in which conclusions are based on an act of reciprocity on someone else's part.

Mastery goals. Goals that focus on accomplishing tasks, improving, and increasing understanding.

Mastery-focused classroom. A classroom environment that emphasizes effort, continuous improvement, and understanding.

Matching format. A selected-response assessment format that requires learners to classify a series of statements using the same alternatives.

Maturation.   Genetically controlled, age-related changes in individuals.

Meaningfulness.   The extent to which individual items of information are linked and related to each other.

Means–ends analysis.   A heuristic that breaks a problem into subgoals and works successively on each.

Memory stores.   Repositories—sensory memory, working memory, and long-term memory—that hold information, both in a raw state and in organized, meaningful form.

Mesosystem.   In Bronfenbrenner's model, the interactions and connections between the different elements of children's immediate settings.

Meta-attention.   Knowledge and regulation of attention.

Metacognition.   Knowledge and regulation of our cognition—commonly described as "thinking about thinking."

Metamemory.   Knowledge and regulation of memory strategies.

Microsystem.   In Bronfenbrenner's bioecological theory, the people and activities in a child's immediate surroundings.

Misconceptions.   Ideas we construct that make sense to us but are inconsistent with evidence or commonly accepted explanations.

Mixed methods research.   A research design that combines quantitative and qualitative methods.

Mnemonics.   Memory strategies that create associations that do not exist naturally in the content.

Model.   A representation that we use to help visualize what we cannot observe directly.

Modeling.   A general term that refers to behavioral, cognitive, and affective changes deriving from observing the actions of others.

Models of instruction.   Prescriptive approaches to teaching designed to help students acquire a deep understanding of specific forms of knowledge.

Moral development.   Advances in people's conceptions of right and wrong and prosocial behaviors and traits such as honesty, fairness, and respect for others.

Moral dilemma.   An ambiguous, conflicting situation that requires a person to make a moral decision.

Moral domain.   The domain of moral development that deals with basic principles of right, wrong, and justice.

Motivation to learn.   Students' tendencies to find academic activities meaningful and worthwhile and to try to get the intended learning benefits from them.

Motivation.   The process whereby goal-directed activity is instigated and sustained.

Motivational zone of proximal development.   The match between a learning activity and learners' prior knowledge and experiences that is close enough to stimulate interest and perceived value in the activity but not so familiar that learners are satiated by it.

Multiple choice.   A selected-response assessment format that consists of a stem, a correct answer choice and a series of additional answer choices called distractors.

Multitasking.   The process of engaging in two or more activities at the same time.

Myelination.   The process that occurs when cells grow around neurons to give them structural support, and a fatty coating of myelin, called the myelin sheath, develops to insulate axons and enable them to conduct electrical charges quickly and efficiently.

National Assessment of Educational Progress (NAEP).   Commonly called the "Nation's Report Card," a battery of achievement tests administered periodically to carefully selected samples of students and designed to provide a comprehensive picture of achievement in students across our country.

National norms.   Scores on standardized tests earned by representative groups of students from around the nation to which an individual's score is compared.

Nature view of intelligence.   The assertion that intelligence is essentially determined by genetics.

Need.   An internal force or drive to attain or to avoid a certain state or object.

Negative reinforcement.   The process of increasing behavior by removing or avoiding an aversive stimulus.

Negligence.   The failure of teachers or schools to exercise sufficient care in protecting students from injury.

Neo-Piagetian theories of development.   A theory of cognitive development that accepts Piaget's stages but uses the acquisition of specific processing strategies to explain movement from one stage to the next.

Neuromyth.   A misconception generated by a misunderstanding, a misreading, or a misquoting of facts scientifically established by brain research.

Neurons.   Nerve cells composed of cell bodies, dendrites, and axons, which make up the learning capability of the brain.

Neuroplasticity.   The brain's ability to physically remodel itself in response to experience.

Neuroscience.   The study of how the nervous system develops, how it is structured, and what it does.

Neutral stimulus.   An object or event that does not initially influence behavior one way or the other.

No Child Left Behind (NCLB).   Federal legislation requiring states to create standards in math and reading and to construct tests to measure every student's attainment of those standards.

Non-exclusionary timeout.   Seating a student near the teacher or on the edge of the classroom to prevent him or her from receiving reinforcers.

Normal curve equivalent (NCE).   A measure resulting from a statistical process that standardizes scores on a test into a 0–100 scale similar to a percentile rank but preserves equal interval properties that do not exist with percentiles.

Normal distribution.   A distribution of scores in which the mean, median, and mode are equal and the scores distribute themselves symmetrically in a bell-shaped curve.

Norming group.   The representative group of individuals whose standardized test scores are compiled for the purpose of national comparisons.

Norm-referenced grading.   The process of making grading decisions based on an individual's performance compared to the performance of peers.

Norm-referenced standardized tests.   Standardized tests that compare (reference) a student's performance to the performance of others.

Nurture view of intelligence.   The assertion that emphasizes the influence of the environment on intelligence.

Object permanence.   The understanding that objects exist even when out of sight.

Open-ended questions.   Questions for which a variety of answers are acceptable.

Operant conditioning.   A behaviorist form of learning that occurs when an observable behavior changes in frequency or duration as the result of a consequence.

Oppositional peer cultures.   Alleged cultures that devalue academic efforts, such as doing homework, studying, and participating in class, as "acting White."

Order and safety. A learning climate variable that creates a predictable learning environment and supports learner autonomy together with a sense of physical and emotional security.

Organization. An encoding strategy that clusters related items of content into categories that illustrate relationships.

Organized bodies of knowledge. Topics that connect facts, concepts, and generalizations and make the relationships among them explicit.

Overgeneralization. A language pattern that occurs when a child uses a word to refer to a broader class of objects than is appropriate.

Overlapping. The ability to intervene in cases of misbehavior without disrupting the flow of a lesson.

Parenting style. General patterns of interacting with and disciplining children.

Partial hearing impairment. An impairment that allows a student to use a hearing aid to hear well enough to be taught through auditory channels.

Pedagogical content knowledge. An understanding of how to represent topics in ways that make them understandable to learners, as well as an understanding of what makes specific topics easy or hard to learn.

Peer aggression. Words or physical actions that hurt, humiliate, or place other students at a disadvantage.

People-first language. Language in which a student's disability is identified after the student is named.

Percentile rank (PR). The percentage of students in the norming sample that scored at or below a particular raw score.

Perception. The process people use to find meaning in stimuli.

Performance assessments. The process of directly examining student performance on tasks relevant to life outside of school.

Performance goals. Goals that focus on demonstrating ability and competence and how learners compare to others.

Performance-approach goals. Goals that emphasize looking competent and receiving favorable judgments from others.

Performance-avoidance goal. A goal that emphasizes attempts to avoid looking incompetent and being judged unfavorably.

Performance-focused classroom. A classroom environment that emphasizes high grades, public displays of ability, and performance compared to others.

Personal domain. The domain of moral development that refers to decisions that are not socially regulated and do not harm or violate others' rights.

Personal interest. A person's ongoing affinity, attraction, or liking for a domain, subject area, topic, or activity.

Personal teaching efficacy. Teachers' beliefs that they can help all students learn, regardless of their prior knowledge, ability, or personal backgrounds.

Personal, social, and emotional development. Changes in our personality, the ways we interact with others, and our ability to manage our feelings.

Personality. A comprehensive term that describes our attitudinal, emotional, and behavioral responses to experiences in our environment.

Personalization. The process of using intellectually and/or emotionally relevant examples to illustrate a topic.

Personalized learning. Instruction in which the pace of learning and the instructional approach are optimized for the needs of each learner.

Perspective taking. The ability to understand the thoughts and feelings of others.

Phonological loop. In working memory, a short-term storage component for words and sounds.

Physical aggression. An aggressive act that can cause bodily injury.

Physical development. Changes in the size, shape, and functioning of our bodies.

Pop quizzes. Unannounced quizzes.

Portfolio assessment. The process of selecting collections of student work that both teachers and students evaluate using preset criteria.

Positive behavior support. The process of using interventions that replace problem behaviors with behaviors serving the same purpose for the student but which are more appropriate.

Positive learning climate. A classroom climate in which the teacher and students work together as a community of learners to help everyone achieve.

Positive reinforcement. The process of increasing the frequency or duration of a behavior as the result of presenting a reinforcer.

Postconventional morality. A moral orientation that views moral issues in terms of abstract and self-developed principles of right and wrong.

Post-truth. Circumstances in which objective facts are less influential in shaping public opinion than appeals to emotion and personal belief.

Poverty. The lack of enough material possessions or money to maintain an adequate quality of life.

Precise language. Teacher language that omits vague terms from explanations and responses to students' questions.

Preconventional morality. An egocentric orientation lacking any internalized standards for right and wrong.

Predictive validity. The measure of a test's ability to gauge future performance.

Prefrontal cortex. A portion of the cortex near the forehead that monitors and guides other parts of the brain's activities, including planning, maintaining attention, reasoning, decision making, emotional control, and the inhibition of unhealthy thoughts and behaviors.

Premack principle. The principle suggesting that a more desired activity can serve as a positive reinforcer for a less-desired activity.

Presentation punishment. The process of decreasing a behavior that occurs when a stimulus (punisher) is presented.

Presentation software. Computer software designed to display text, images, audio, and video information in a slideshow format.

Primary reinforcers. Consequences that satisfy basic biological needs.

Principles (laws). Statements about an area of study that are generally accepted as true.

Private speech. Self-talk that guides thinking and action.

Proactive aggression. A deliberate aggressive act initiated toward another.

Probing questions. Questions that require students to explain or provide evidence.

Problem. A condition in which a goal exists but no obvious way of reaching the goal is apparent.

Problem-based learning. A teaching strategy that uses problems as the focus for developing content, skills, and self-regulation.

Procedural knowledge. Knowledge of how to perform tasks, such as solving problems or composing essays.

Procedures. Guidelines for accomplishing recurring tasks, such as lining up for lunch or turning in papers.

Professional knowledge. The body of information and skills that are unique to a particular area of study.

Prompting.   An additional question or statement used to elicit an appropriate student response after a student fails to answer correctly.

Psychometric view of intelligence.   A view of intelligence that describes it as a unitary trait measurable with a well-crafted instrument.

Psychomotor domain.   The area of learning that focuses on physical skills.

Punishers.   Consequences that weaken behaviors or decrease the likelihood of the behaviors' recurring.

Punishment.   The process of using punishers to decrease behavior.

Punishment–obedience.   A stage of moral reasoning in which conclusions are based on the chances of getting caught and being punished.

Qualitative research.   A type of research that attempts to describe a complex educational phenomenon in a holistic fashion using non-numeric data.

Quantitative research.   The systematic, empirical investigation of phenomena using numerical data and statistical techniques.

Questioning frequency.   The process of asking large numbers of questions during learning activities.

Race.   A socially constructed category composed of people who share important biologically transmitted traits.

Race to the Top.   A competitive grant program encouraging individual states and districts to design comprehensive accountability programs that include merit pay plans for teachers based on student performance on standardized tests.

Racial macroaggressions.   Subtle insults suggesting that a particular minority is in some way inferior.

Rating scales.   Written descriptions of the dimensions of an acceptable performance together with scales of values on which each dimension is rated.

Ratio schedule of reinforcement.   An intermittent reinforcement schedule where specific behaviors are reinforced either predictably (fixed) or unpredictably (variable).

Raw scores.   The number of items an individual answered correctly on a standardized test or subtest.

Reactive aggression.   An aggressive act committed in response to frustration or another aggressive act.

Readiness tests.   Standardized tests designed to assess the degree to which children are prepared for an academic or pre-academic program.

Reciprocal causation.   The interdependence of the environment, behavior, and personal factors in learning.

Reflective practice.   The process of conducting a critical self-examination of one's teaching.

Refugees.   Special groups of immigrants who are fleeing unsafe conditions in their home countries.

Rehearsal.   The process of repeating information over and over without altering it.

Reinforcement schedules.   Patterns in the frequency and predictability of reinforcers that have differential effects on behavior.

Reinforcement.   The process of applying reinforcers to increase behavior.

Reinforcer.   A consequence that increases the likelihood of a behavior recurring.

Relatedness.   The feeling of being connected to others in one's social environment and feeling worthy of love and respect.

Relational aggression.   An aggressive act that can adversely affect interpersonal relationships.

Relationship skills.   The ability to establish and maintain healthy and rewarding relationships with diverse individuals and groups.

Reliability.   The extent to which assessments are able to provide consistent results.

Removal punishment.   The process of decreasing a behavior that occurs when a stimulus is removed or when an individual cannot receive positive reinforcement.

Research.   The process of systematically gathering information in an attempt to answer professional questions.

Resilience.   A learner characteristic that, despite adversity, increases the likelihood of success in school and later life.

Response cost.   The process of removing reinforcers already given.

Response-to-intervention model of identification.   A method of identifying a learning problem that focuses on the specific classroom instructional adaptations that teachers use and their success.

Responsible decision making.   The ability to make constructive choices about personal behavior and interactions with others, based on an understanding of the consequences for our actions.

Retrieval.   The process of pulling information from long-term memory into working memory.

Review.   A summary that helps students link what they have already learned to new information in the learning activity.

Rote learning.   Learning that involves storing information in isolated pieces, most commonly through memorization.

Rubric.   A scoring scale that explicitly describes criteria for grading.

Rules.   Descriptions of standards for acceptable behavior.

Satiation.   The process of using a reinforcer so frequently that it loses its ability to strengthen behaviors.

Scaffolding.   Assistance that helps children complete tasks they cannot complete independently.

Scaled scores.   Statistically adjusted and converted scores on standardized tests designed to accommodate differences in difficulty for different forms of the test.

Schema activation.   An encoding strategy that involves activating relevant prior knowledge so that new knowledge can be connected to it.

Schemas (schemata).   Cognitive structures that represent the way information is organized in our long-term memories.

Schemes.   Mental operations that represent our constructed understanding of the world.

School connectedness.   The belief by students that adults and peers in the school care about their learning as well as about them as individuals.

Secondary reinforcers.   Consequences that become reinforcing over time through their association with other reinforcers.

Selected-response items.   Assessment items that require learners to select the correct answer from a list of alternatives.

Self-actualization.   Reaching one's full potential and becoming all that one is capable of being.

Self-awareness.   The ability of individuals to understand their own thoughts and emotions and how both influence their responses to their environments.

Self-concept.   A cognitive assessment of our physical, social, and academic competence.

Self-determination.   The need to act on and control one's environment.

Self-efficacy.   The belief that one is capable of accomplishing a specific task.

Self-esteem (self-worth).   An emotional reaction to, or an evaluation of, the self.

Self-fulfilling prophecy. A phenomenon that occurs when a person's performance results from and confirms beliefs about his or her capabilities.

Self-management. The ability of people to regulate their emotions, thoughts, and behaviors in a variety of contexts.

Self-regulated learning. The process of setting personal goals, combined with the motivation, thought processes, strategies, and behaviors that lead to reaching the goals.

Self-regulation. The ability to direct and control our actions, thoughts, and emotions to reach academic and personal goals.

Self-worth. An emotional reaction to or an evaluation of the self. Also, commonly called self-esteem.

Semantics. A branch of linguistics that examines the meaning of words.

Sensory memory. The memory store that briefly holds incoming stimuli from the environment in a raw, unorganized state until they can be processed.

Seriation. The ability to order objects according to increasing or decreasing length, weight, or volume.

Sex. Physical characteristics, including sex organs, chromosomes, and hormones, that determine one of two major groups of individuals in most species.

Sexual assault. A form of sexual violence involving non-consensual sexual touching or a forced sex act, such as rape, forced oral sex, or sodomy.

Sexual harassment. Unwanted attention or conduct of a sexual nature that can include sexual touching, comments, jokes, or gestures that are directly sexual or have sexual overtones; displaying or distributing sexually explicit pictures, drawings, or written text; or spreading sexual rumors.

Sexual identity. Students' self-constructed definition of who they are with respect to gender orientation.

Sexual orientation. The gender to which an individual is romantically and sexually attracted.

Shame. The painful emotion aroused when people recognize that they have failed to act or think in ways they believe are good.

Shaping. The process of reinforcing successive approximations of a behavior.

Short-term memory. Historically described as the memory store that serves the same functions as the phonological loop and visual-spatial sketchpad in working memory.

Simulation. Imitations of real-world processes or systems.

Situated cognition. A view of learning suggesting that learning depends on, and cannot be separated from, the context in which it occurs.

Situational interest. A person's current enjoyment, pleasure, or satisfaction generated by the immediate context.

Social awareness. An understanding of social and ethical norms for behavior as well as the ability to take others' perspectives and feel empathy for people from a variety of backgrounds and cultures.

Social cognition. The ability to use cues to understand social interactions.

Social cognitive theory. A theory of learning that focuses on changes in behavior, thinking, and emotions that result from observing others.

Social constructivism. A view of knowledge construction that suggests that learners first construct knowledge in a social context and then individually internalize it.

Social contract. A stage of moral reasoning in which conclusions are based on socially agreed-upon principles.

Social experience. The process of interacting with others. In Piaget's theory social experience promotes development by having learners compare their schemes to those of others.

Social goals. Goals to achieve particular social outcomes or interactions.

Social intelligence. The ability to understand and work with people.

Social referencing. The ability to use vocal and nonverbal cues to evaluate ambiguous events and regulate our behaviors accordingly.

Social-emotional learning. The ability to recognize and manage emotions, set and achieve positive goals, understand and establish positive relationships with others, and make responsible decisions.

Sociocultural theory. A form of social constructivism that emphasizes the social dimensions of learning, but places greater emphasis on the larger cultural contexts in which learning occurs.

Sociocultural theory of development. A theory of cognitive development that emphasizes the influence of social interactions and language, embedded within a cultural context, on cognitive development.

Socioeconomic status (SES). The combination of parents' income, occupation, and level of education that describes families' or individuals' relative standing in society.

Sound bite. Sentences or short phrases intended to attract the attention of readers or viewers and capture the essence of what a speaker or writer is trying to say.

Special education. Instruction designed to meet the unique needs of students with exceptionalities.

Specific transfer. The ability to apply information in a context similar to the one in which it was originally learned.

Speech disorders (expressive disorders). Problems in forming and sequencing sounds.

Stages of development. General patterns of thinking for children at different ages or with different amounts of experience.

Standard deviation. A statistical measure of the way scores spread out in a distribution.

Standard error of measurement. The range of scores within which an individual's true score is likely to fall.

Standardized tests. Assessment instruments given to large samples of students under uniform conditions and scored and reported according to uniform procedures.

Standards. Statements that describe what students should know or be able to do at the end of a prescribed period of study.

Standards-based grading. A grading practice that targets specific standards and the extent to which students have met them.

Stanford-Binet. Currently called the *Stanford-Binet Intelligence Scales, Fifth Edition*, or *SB5*, an individually administered intelligence test composed of several subtests.

Stanine. A description of an individual's standardized test performance that uses a scale ranging from 1 to 9 points.

Stem. A statement that introduces a multiple-choice item that presents a problem to be solved, a question to be answered, or an incomplete statement.

Stereotype threat. The anxiety felt by members of a group resulting from concern that their behavior might confirm a stereotype.

Strategies. Cognitive operations intended to increase learning that exceed the normal activities required to carry out a task.

Students at risk. Students who fail to complete their education with the skills necessary to succeed in today's society.

Study strategies. Specific techniques students use to increase their understanding of written materials and teacher presentations.

Summarizing.   The process of preparing a concise description of verbal or written passages.

Summative assessment.   The process of gathering information used to make conclusions about the level of learner achievement.

Synapses.   The tiny spaces between neurons that allow messages to be transmitted from one neuron to another.

Synaptic pruning.   The process of eliminating synapses that are unused or unnecessary.

Syntax.   The set of rules that we use to put words together into meaningful sentences.

Systematic observation.   The process of specifying criteria for acceptable performance and taking notes based on the criteria.

Table of specifications.   A matrix that helps organize learning objectives by topic and cognitive level and helps link instruction and assessment to objectives and standards.

Task analysis.   The process of breaking content into component parts and sequencing the parts.

Task comprehension.   Learners' awareness of what they are supposed to be learning and an understanding of why the task is important and worthwhile.

Teacher evaluation.   The process of assessing teachers' classroom performance and providing feedback they can use to increase their expertise.

Temperament.   Genetically determined and relatively consistent tendencies to respond to events in the environment in particular ways.

Test anxiety.   An unpleasant emotional reaction to testing situations that can lower performance.

Text signals.   Elements included in written materials that communicate text organization and key ideas.

Theories.   Comprehensive sets of related patterns, derived from observations, that researchers use to explain and predict events in the world.

Theory of mind.   Insights into other people's minds and reasoning about how mental states influence behavior.

Tracking.   The process of placing students in different classes or curricula on the basis of achievement.

Transfer.   The ability to apply understanding acquired in one context to a different context.

Transgender students.   Students whose sense of personal identity does not correspond with the gender assigned to them at birth.

Transition signals.   Verbal statements indicating that one idea is ending and another is beginning.

Transitivity.   The ability to infer a relationship between two objects based on knowledge of their relationship with a third object.

Trends in International Mathematics and Science Study (TIMSS).   A series of international standardized assessments designed to measure the mathematics and science knowledge of students around the world.

True–false.   A selected-response assessment format that includes statements learners judge as being correct or incorrect.

Unconditional positive regard.   Treating individuals as if they are innately worthy regardless of their behavior.

Unconditioned response (UCR).   The instinctive or reflexive (unlearned) physiological or emotional response caused by the unconditioned stimulus.

Unconditioned stimulus (UCS).   An object or event that causes an instinctive or reflex (unlearned) emotional or physiological response.

Undergeneralization.   A language pattern that occurs when a child uses a word too narrowly.

Universal design.   The design of buildings, environments, and products to ensure that all people can access the building or environment, or use the product.

Universal design for learning (UDL).   The process of designing instructional materials and activities to ensure that content is accessible to all learners.

Universal principles.   A stage of moral reasoning in which conclusions are based on abstract and general principles that transcend or exceed society's laws.

Utility value.   The belief that a topic, activity, or course of study will be useful for meeting future goals, including career goals.

Validity.   The process of making accurate inferences from assessment information and using the inferred information appropriately.

Value.   The benefits and advantages individuals believe can result from participating in an activity.

Value-added modeling.   A method of teacher evaluation that measures a teacher's contribution to student learning in a given year by comparing the current test scores of their students to the scores of those same students in previous school years, and to the scores of other students in the same grade.

Vicarious learning.   The process of observing the consequences of others' actions and adjusting our own behavior accordingly.

Virtual field trips.   Visits to Internet sites that allow students to experience locations that they are unlikely to see in real life.

Virtual manipulatives.   Replicas of physical manipulatives that are accessed using technology and manipulated with a keyboard or mouse.

Visual handicap.   An uncorrectable visual impairment that interferes with learning.

Visual-spatial sketchpad.   In working memory, a short-term storage system for visual and spatial information.

Wait-time.   A period of silence, both before and after calling on a student, that gives students time to think about their answer to a question.

Wechsler Intelligence Scale for Children.   Individually administered intelligence tests for children between the ages of 6 and 16. The most widely used intelligence test in use today.

Well-defined problem.   A problem that has a clear goal, only one correct solution, and a defined method for finding it.

Within-class grouping.   A grouping process that divides students in a single class into groups, typically based on reading and math scores.

Withitness.   A teacher's awareness of what is going on in all parts of the classroom at all times and communicating this awareness to students.

Work-avoidance goal.   The absence of an achievement goal; a goal that defines success in terms of minimal work expenditure rather than any measure of competence.

Worked examples.   Problems with completed solutions that provide students with one way of learning to solve problems.

Working memory.   The conscious component of our memory system; the memory store that holds and organizes information as we try to make sense of it.

Written-response items.   Assessment items that require learners to produce, instead of select, a response.

Zone of proximal development.   A range of tasks that an individual cannot yet do alone but can accomplish when assisted by the guidance of others.

References

Aaron J., Auger, R. W., & Pepperell, J. L. (2013). "If we're ever in trouble they're always there." A qualitative study of teacher-student caring. *The Elementary School Journal, 114*, 100–117.

Abdulkadiroglu, A., Angrist, J. D., & Pathak, P. A. (2011). *The elite illusion: Achievement effects at Boston and New York exam schools.* National Bureau of Economic Research Working Paper Series, No. 17264.

Abe, J. A., & Izzard, C. E. (1999). Compliance, noncompliance strategies, and the correlates of compliance in 5-year-old Japanese and American children. *Social Development, 8*, 1–20.

Abedi, J., & Gándara, P. (2006). Performance of English language learners as a subgroup in large-scale assessment: Interaction of research and policy. *Educational Measurement: Issues and Practice, 25*(4), 36–46.

Aboud, F., & Skerry, S. (1984). The development of ethnic attitudes: A critical review. *Journal of Cross-Cultural Psychology, 15*, 3–34.

Abrams, L., Varier, D., & Jackson, L. (2016). Unpacking instructional alignment: The influence of teachers' use of assessment data on instruction. *Perspectives in Education, 34*, 15–28.

Absher, J. R. (2016). Hypersexuality and neuroimaging personality, social cognition, and character. In J. R. Absher & J. Cloutier (Eds.), *Neuroimaging personality, social cognition, and character* (pp. 3–22). New York: Academic Press.

Acar, I. H., & Ucus, S. (2017). The characteristics of elementary school teachers' lifelong-learning competencies: A convergent mixed-methods study. *Educational Sciences: Theory & Practice, 17*, 1833–1852.

Ackerman, P., & Lohman, D. (2006). Individual differences in cognitive function. In P. A. Alexander & P. H. Winne (Eds.), *Handbook of educational psychology* (2nd ed., pp. 139–162). Mahwah, NJ: Erlbaum.

Adams, W. K., & Willis, C. (2015). Sparking curiosity: How do you know what your students are thinking? *Physics Teacher, 53*, 469–472.

Adamski, A., Fraser, B. J., & Peiro, M. M. (2013). Parental involvement in schooling, classroom environment and student outcomes. *Learning Environments Research, 16*, 315–328.

Adesope, O., Lavin, T., Thompson, R., & Ungerleider, C. (2010). A systematic review and meta-analysis of the cognitive correlates of bilingualism. *Review of Educational Research, 80*, 207–245.

Adeyemo, S. A. (2013). The relationship between effective classroom management and students' academic achievement in physics. *Journal of Applied Sciences Research, 9*, 1032–1042.

Adkins, A., Haynes, M., Pringle, B, Renner, N. B., & Robinson, S. (2013). *Ensuring readiness to teach: EdTPA support and assessment* [Webinar]. Retrieved from http://all4ed.org/webinar-event/oct-9–2013/

Adkins, A., Spesia, T., & Snakenborg, J. (2015). Rebuttal to Dover et al. *Teachers College Record.* Retrieved from http://www.tcrecord.org/Content.asp?ContentID=18041

Aelenei, C., Lewis, N. A., Jr., & Oyserman, D. (2017). No pain, no gain? Social demographic correlates and identity consequences of interpreting experienced difficulty as importance. *Contemporary Educational Psychology, 48*, 43–55. http://dx.doi.org/10.1016/j.cedpsych.2016.08.004

Afflerbach, P., & Cho, B.-Y. (2010). Determining and describing reading strategies: Internet and traditional forms of reading. In H. Waters & W. Schneider (Eds.), *Metacognition, strategy use, and instruction* (pp. 201–225). New York: Guilford.

Afifi, T. O., Mota, N., Sareen, J., & MacMillan, H. L. (2017). The relationships between harsh physical punishment and child maltreatment in childhood and intimate partner violence in adulthood. *BMC Public Health, 17*, 1–10.

Ahmad, I., Said, H., & Khan, F. (2013). Effect of corporal punishment on students' motivation and classroom learning. *Review of European Studies, 5*, 130–134.

Ahn, R., Ingham, S., & Mendez, T. (2016). Socially constructed learning activity: Communal note-taking as a generative tool to promote active student engagement. *Transformative Dialogues: Teaching & Learning Journal, 8*, 1–15.

Ahrens, L. M., Pauli, P., Reif, A., Mühlberger, A., Langs, G., Aalderink, T., & Wieser, M. J. (2016). Fear conditioning and stimulus generalization in patients with social anxiety disorder. *Journal of Anxiety Disorders, 44*, 36–46.

Akcay, H. (2017). Learning from dealing with real world problems. *Education, 137*, 413–417.

Akers, R. (2017). A journey to increase student engagement. *Technology and Engineering Teacher, 76*, 28–32.

Alarcon, A. L., & Luckasson, R. (2017). Aligning IEP goals to standards without standardizing: Avoiding the legal risks associated with aligning each goal with an individual content standard. *Journal of Special Education Leadership, 30*, 82–87.

Alberto, P. A., & Troutman, A. C. (2017). *Applied behavioral analysis for teachers* (Interactive 9th ed.) Boston: Pearson.

Alexander, J. M., Johnson, K. E., & Leibham, M. E. (2005). Constructing domain-specific knowledge in kindergarten: Relations among knowledge, intelligence, and strategic performance. *Learning and Individual Differences, 15*, 35–52.

Alexander, L. (2012). NCLB lessons: It is time for Washington to get out of the way. *Education Week, 31*(15), 40.

Alexander, P. (2006). *Psychology in learning and instruction.* Upper Saddle River, NJ: Pearson.

Alghazo, Y. M., & Alghazo, R. (2017). Exploring common misconceptions and errors among college students about fractions in Saudi Arabia. *International Education Studies, 10*, 133–140.

Alibali, M. W., Spencer, R. C., Knox, L., & Kita, S. (2011). Spontaneous gestures influence strategy choices in problem solving. *Psychological Science, 22*, 1138–1144.

Alizadeh, S., KarimiMoonaghi, H., Haghir, R., JafaeiDalooei, R., & Saadatyar, F. S. (2014). Effect of pop quiz on learning of medical students in neuroanatomy course. *Journal of Medical Education and Development, 9*, 10–17.

Alkadhi, K. A. (2018). Exercise as a positive modulator of brain function. *Molecular Neurobiology, 55*, 3112–3130.

Allen, R., & Steed, E. A. (2016). Culturally responsive pyramid model practices: Program-wide positive behavior support for young children. *Topics in Early Childhood Special Education, 36*, 165–175.

Almasy, S., Segal, K., & Couwels, J. (2013). Sheriff: Taunting post leads to arrests in Rebecca Sedwick bullying death. CNN Justice. Retrieved from http://www.cnn.com/2013/10/15/justice/rebecca-sedwick-bullying-death-arrests/

Aloe, A. M., Amo, L. C., & Shanahah, M. E. (2014). Classroom management self-efficacy and burnout: A multivariate meta-analysis. *Educational Psychology Review, 26*, 101–126.

Alter, A. (2017). *Irresistible: The rise of addictive technology and the business of keeping us hooked.* New York: Penguin Press.

Alvarez, L. (2013). Seeing the toll, schools revise zero tolerance. *The New York Times.* Retrieved from http://www.nytimes.com/2013/12/03/education/seeing-the-toll-schools-revisit-zero-tolerance.html?partner=rss&emc=rss&_r=0&pagewanted=print

Alvear, S. (2015). Learning more than language: An examination of student achievement in English immersion and bilingual programs. *Conference Papers—American Sociological Association,* 1–36. Retrieved from http://eds.b.ebscohost.com.dax.lib.unf.edu/eds/pdfviewer/pdfviewer?vid=2&sid=0de275c5–29f6–4038–8e1e-737640c0fbd5%40sessionmgr4009

Ambrose, D., (2017). Interdisciplinary exploration supports Sternberg's expansion of giftedness. *Roeper Review, 39*, 178–182.

American Academy of Pediatrics. (2011). Where we stand: Spanking. Retrieved from http://www.healthychildren.org/English/familylife/family-dynamics/communication-discipline/Pages/Where-We-Stand-Spanking.aspx

American Association of Colleges of Teacher Education (AACTE). (2017). *edTPA*. Retrieved from http://edtpa.aacte.org/state-policy#page

American Association on Intellectual and Developmental Disabilities (AAIDD). (2017a). *Definition of intellectual disability*. Retrieved from http://aaidd.org/intellectual-disability/definition#.WeyYC7pFyzc. Used with permission.

American Association on Intellectual and Developmental Disabilities (AAIDD). (2017b). *Diagnostic Adaptive Behavior Scale*. Retrieved from http://aaidd.org/intellectual-disability/diagnostic-adaptive-behavior-scale#.WeoKObpFyzc

American Educational Research Association, American Psychological Association, & National Council on Measurement in Education. (2014). *Standards for educational and psychological testing*. Washington, DC: American Educational Research Association.

American Educational Research Association. (2017). *Position statement on high-stakes testing*. Retrieved from http://www.aera.net/About-AERA/AERA-Rules-Policies/Association-Policies/Position-Statement-on-High-Stakes-Testing

American Psychiatric Association. (2013). *Diagnostic and statistical manual of mental disorders* (5th ed.). Washington, DC: Author.

American Psychological Association, Coalition for Psychology in Schools and Education. (2015). *Top 20 principles from psychology for preK–12 teaching and learning*. Retrieved from http://www.apa.org/ed/schools/cpse/top-twenty-principles.pdf. Used with permission of American Psychological Association.

American Psychological Association. (2014). *Teen suicide is preventable*. Retrieved from https://www.apa.org/research/action/suicide.aspx

American Psychological Association. (2018). *Education and socioeconomic status*. Retrieved from http://www.apa.org/pi/ses/resources/publications/education.aspx

American Psychological Association. (2018). *Who we are*. Retrieved from http://www.apa.org/about/apa/index.aspx

American Society for the Positive Care of Children. (2016). *Statistics and facts about child abuse in the U.S.* Retrieved from http://americanspcc.org/child-abuse-statistics/

Amrein-Beardsley, A., Pivovarova, M., & Geiger, T. J. (2016). Value-added models: What experts say. *Phi Delta Kappan, 98*, 35–40.

Anderman, E. M., & Anderman, L. H. (2014). *Classroom motivation* (2nd ed.). Boston: Pearson.

Anderman, E. M., & Maehr, M. (1994). Motivation and schooling in the middle grades. *Review of Educational Research, 64*, 287–309.

Anderman, E. M., & Wolters, C. A. (2006). Goals, values, and affect: Influences on motivation. In P. A. Alexander & P. H. Winne (Eds.), *Handbook of educational psychology* (2nd ed., pp. 369–389). Mahwah, NJ: Erlbaum.

Anderson, L., & Krathwohl, D. (Eds.). (2001). *A taxonomy for learning, teaching, and assessing: A revision of Bloom's taxonomy of educational objectives*. New York: Addison Wesley Longman.

Anderson, M. A. (2015). Where teachers are still allowed to spank students. *The Atlantic*. Retrieved from https://www.theatlantic.com/education/archive/2015/12/corporal-punishment/420420/

Anderson, P. M., & Summerfield, J. P. (2004). Why is urban education different from suburban and rural education? In S. R. Steinberg & J. L. Kincheloe (Eds.), *19 urban questions: Teaching in the city* (pp. 29–39). New York: Peter Lang.

Anderson, T., & Shattuck, J. (2012). Design-based research: A decade of progress in education research? *Educational Researcher, 41*, 16–25. doi:10.3102/0013189X11428813

Andrew, L. (2007). Comparison of teacher educators' instructional methods with the constructivist ideal. *The Teacher Educator, 42*, 157–184.

Anguera, J. A., Boccanfuso, J., Rintoul, J. L., Al-Hashimi, O., Faraji, O., Janowich, J., . . . Gazzaley, A. (2013). Video game training enhances cognitive control in older adults. *Nature, 501*(7465), 97–101.

Annenberg Public Policy Center. (2016). *Americans' knowledge of the branches of government is declining*. Retrieved from http://www.prnewswire.com/news-releases/americans-knowledge-of-the-branches-of-government-is-declining-300325968.html

Ansari, A., & Winsler, A. (2016). Kindergarten readiness for low-income and ethnically diverse children attending publically funded preschool programs in Miami. *Early Childhood Research Quarterly, 37*, 69–80.

Ansari, F., Fathi, M., & Seidenberg, U. (2016). Problem-solving approaches in maintenance cost management: A literature review. *Journal of Quality in Maintenance Engineering, 22*, 334–353.

Antil, L., Jenkins, J., Wayne, S., & Vadasy, P. (1998). Cooperative learning: Prevalence, conceptualizations, and the relation between research and practice. *American Educational Research Journal, 35*(3), 419–454.

Apple.Inc. (2017). *Swift Playgrounds: A new way to learn to code with Swift on iPad*. Retrieved from https://developer.apple.com/swift/playgrounds/

Araujo, M. C., Carneiro, P., Cruz-Aguayo, Y. Y., & Shady, N. (2016). Teacher quality and learning outcomes in kindergarten. *Quarterly Journal of Economics, 131*, 1415–1453.

Arbuckle, D. (2017). What is the average adult male height and weight? *Livestrong.com*. Retrieved from https://www.livestrong.com/article/289265-what-is-the-average-adult-male-height/

Archambault, I., Vandenbossche-Makombo, J., & Fraser, S. (2017). Students' oppositional behaviors and engagement in school: The differential role of the student-teacher relationship. *Journal of Child and Family Studies, 26*, 1702–1712.

Arnon, I., & Ramscar, M. (2012). Granularity and the acquisition of grammatical gender: How order-of-acquisition affects what gets learned. *Cognition, 122*, 292–305.

Aronson, E., Wilson, T. D., Akert, R. M., & Sommers, S. R. (2016). *Social psychology* (9th ed.). Boston: Pearson.

Aronson, J., & Juarez, L. (2012). Growth mindsets in the laboratory and the real world. In R. F. Subotnik, A. Robinson, C. M. Callahan, & E. J. Gubbins (Eds.), *Malleable minds: Translating insights from psychology and neuroscience to gifted education* (pp. 19–36). Storrs, CT: National Research Center on the Gifted and Talented.

Artiles, A., Kozleski, E., Trent, S., Osher, D., & Ortiz, A. (2010). Justifying and explaining disproportionality, 1968–2008: A critique of underlying views of culture. *Exceptional Children, 76*(3), 279–299.

Astur, R., S., Palmisano, A. N., Carew, A. W., Deaton, B. E., Khuney, F. S., Niezrecki, R. N., Hudd, E. C., Mendicino, K. L., & Ritter, C. J. (2016). Conditioned place preferences in humans using secondary reinforcers. *Behavioural Brain Research, 297*, 15–19.

Atkinson, J., & Braddick, O. (2012). Visual attention in the first years: Typical development and developmental disorders. *Developmental Medicine and Child Neurology, 54*, 589–595.

Atkinson, R., & Shiffrin, R. (1968). Human memory: A proposed system and its control processes. In K. Spence & J. Spence (Eds.), *The psychology of learning and motivation: Advances in research and theory* (Vol. 2). San Diego, CA: Academic Press.

Au, W. (2016). Meritocracy 2.0: High-stakes, standardized testing as a racial project of neoliberal multiculturalism. *Educational Policy, 30*, 39–62.

Ausubel, D. P. (1977). The facilitation of meaningful verbal learning in the classroom. *Educational Psychologist, 12*, 162–178.

Autor, D., Figlio, D., Karbownik, K., Roth, J., & Wasserman, M. (2016). Family disadvantage and the gender gap in behavioral and educational outcomes. *National Bureau of Economic Research*. Retrieved from http://economics.mit.edu/files/11558

Avery, R. E., Smillie, L. D., & Fife-Schaw, C. R. (2015). Employee achievement orientations and personality as predictors of job satisfaction facets. *Personality and Individual Differences, 76*, 56–61.

Ayers, C. A. (2018). A first step toward a practice-based theory of pedagogical content knowledge in secondary economics. *Journal of Social Studies Research, 42*, 61–79.

Ayers, S. L., Kulis, S., & Tsethlikai, M. (2017). Assessing parenting and family functioning measures for urban American Indians. *Journal of Community Psychology, 45*, 230–249.

Baş, G. (2017). Homework and academic achievement: A meta-analytic review of research. *Issues in Educational Research, 27*, 31–50.

Babad, E., Bernieri, F., & Rosenthal, R. (1991). Students as judges of teachers' verbal and nonverbal behavior. *American Educational Research Journal, 28*(1), 211–234.

Back, L., Polk, E., Keys, C., & McMahon, S. (2016). Classroom management, school staff relations, school climate, and academic achievement: Testing a model with urban high schools. *Learning Environments Research, 19*, 397–410.

Baddeley, A. D. (1986). *Working memory: Theory and practice.* London, UK: Oxford University Press.

Baddeley, A. D. (2001). Is working memory still working? *American Psychologist, 56*, 851–864.

Baeten, M., Struyven, K., & Dochy, F. (2013). Student-centred teaching methods: Can they optimise students' approaches to learning in professional higher education? *Studies in Educational Evaluation, 39*, 14–22.

Bain, S. K., & Allin, J. D. (2005). Book review: Stanford-Binet intelligence scales, fifth edition. *Journal of Psychoeducational Assessment, 23*, 87–95.

Baines, L. (2007). Learning from the world: Achieving more by doing less. *Phi Delta Kappan, 89*, 98–100.

Baio, J., Wiggins, L., Christiansen, D. L., Maenner, M. J., Daniels, J., Warren, Z., . . . Dowling, N. F. (2018). Prevalence of Autism Spectrum Disorder Among Children Aged 8 Years—Autism and Developmental Disabilities Monitoring Network, 11 Sites, United States, 2014. *Centers for Disease Control and prevention.* Retrieved from https://www.cdc.gov/mmwr/volumes/67/ss/ss6706a1.htm

Baker, C. E., & Rimm-Kaufman, S. E. (2014). How homes influence schools: Early parenting predicts African American children's classroom social-emotional functioning. *Psychology in the Schools, 51*, 722–735.

Baker, D. (2006). For Navajo, science and tradition intertwine. *Salt Lake Tribune*, pp. D1, D5.

Bakke, S., & Henry, R. M. (2015). Unraveling the mystery of new technology use: An investigation into the interplay of desire for control, computer self-efficacy, and personal innovativeness. *AIS Transactions on Human-Computer Interaction, 7*, 270–293.

Balagna, R. M., Young, E. L., & Smith, T. B. (2013). School experiences of early adolescent Latinos/as at risk for emotional and behavioral disorders. *School Psychology Quarterly, 28*, 101–121.

Balcetis, E., & Dunning, D. (2007). Cognitive dissonance and the perception of natural environments. *Psychological Science, 18*, 917–921.

Balf, T. (2014). The story behind the SAT overhaul. *The New York Times.* Retrieved from http://www.nytimes.com/2014/03/09/magazine/the-story-behind-the-sat-overhaul.html?_r=0

Balkin, R. S., Heard, C. C., ShinHwa, L., & Wines, L. A. (2014). A primer for evaluating test bias and test fairness: Implications for multicultural assessment. *Journal of Professional Counseling: Practice, Theory & Research, 41*, 42–52.

Ball, D. (1992). Magical hopes: Manipulatives and the reform of math education. *American Educator*, 28–33.

Baloche, L., & Brody, C. M. (2017). Cooperative learning: exploring challenges, crafting innovations. *Journal of Education for Teaching, 43*, 274–283.

Balu, R., Zhu, P., Doolittle, F., Schiller, E., Jenkins, J., & Gersten, R. (2015). *Evaluation of response to intervention practices for elementary school reading.* Institute of Education Sciences, U.S. Department of Education. Retrieved from http://ies.ed.gov/ncee/pubs/20164000/pdf/20164000.pdf

Bandura, A. (1986). *Social foundations of thought and action: A social cognitive theory.* Upper Saddle River, NJ: Prentice Hall.

Bandura, A. (1997). *Self-efficacy: The exercise of control.* New York: Freeman.

Bandura, A. (2001). Social cognitive theory. In *Annual Review of Psychology.* Palo Alto, CA: Annual Review.

Bandura, A. (2004, May). *Toward a psychology of human agency.* Paper presented at the meeting of the American Psychological Society, Chicago.

Banks, J. A. (2015). *Cultural diversity and education: Foundations, curriculum, and teaching* (6th ed.). Boston: Pearson.

Banks, J. A. (2019). *An introduction to multicultural education* (6th ed.). Boston: Pearson.

Baş, G. (2016). The effect of multiple intelligences theory-based education on academic achievement: A meta-analytic review. *Educational Sciences: Theory & Practice, 16*, 1833–1864.

Barak, M. (2017). Science teacher education in the twenty-first century: A pedagogical framework for technology-integrated social constructivism. *Research in Science Education, 47*, 283–303.

Barford, K., & Smillie, L. D. (2016). Openness and other Big Five traits in relation to dispositional mixed emotions. *Personality and Individual Differences, 102*, 118–122.

Barlett, C. P., Prot, S. Anderson, C. A., & Gentile, D. A. (2017). An empirical examination of the Strength Differential Hypothesis in cyberbullying behavior. *Psychology of Violence, 7*, 22–32.

Barnes, S. P., Torrens, A., & George, V. (2007). The use of portfolios in coordinated school health programs: Benefits and challenges to implementation. *The Journal of School Health, 77*, 171–179.

Barnett, S. M., & Ceci, S. J. (2002). When and where do we apply what we learn? A taxonomy for far transfer. *Psychological Bulletin, 128*, 612–637.

Barrett, L. F. (2016). The varieties of anger. *The New York Times.* Retrieved from https://www.nytimes.com/2016/11/13/opinion/sunday/the-varieties-of-anger.html

Barrow, L., & Markman-Pithers, L. (2016). Supporting young English learners in the United States. *Future of Children, 26*, 159–183.

Barrs, M. (2016). Vygotsky's "thought and word." *Changing English: Studies in Culture & Education, 23*, 241–256.

Bartholomew, D. (2004). *Measuring intelligence.* New York: Cambridge University Press.

Bartik, T. J., & Hershbein, B. (2018). Degrees of poverty: The relationship between family income background and the returns to education. *Upjohn Institute Working Paper 18-284.* Kalamazoo, MI: W.E. Upjohn Institute for Employment Research. Retrieved from https://doi.org/10.17848/wp18-284

Bar-Yam, Y. (2016). The limits of phenomenology: From behaviorism to drug testing and engineering design. *Complexity, 21*, 181–189.

Bauerlein, M. (2008). *The dumbest generation: How the digital age stupefies young Americans and jeopardizes our future.* New York: Penguin.

Baumrind, D. (2005). Patterns of parental authority. *New Directions in Child Adolescent Development, 108*, 61–69.

Baumrind, D., Larzelere, R., & Owens, E. (2010). Effects of preschool parents' power assertive patterns and practices on adolescent development. *Parent, 10*, 157–201.

Bausell, R. B. (2013). Probing the science of value-added evaluation. *Education Week.* Retrieved from https://www.edweek.org/ew/articles/2013/01/16/17bausell.h32.html

Beck, S. W. (2017). Educational innovation as re-mediation: A sociocultural perspective. *English Teaching: Practice & Critique, 16*, 29–39.

Beghetto, R., & Kaufman, J. C. (2013). Fundamentals of creativity. *Educational Leadership, 70*, 10–15.

Begley, S. (2010, June 28 and July 5). This is your brain. Aging. *Newsweek*, 64–68.

Belfi, B., Gielen, S., De Fraine, B., Verschueren, K., & Meredith, C. (2015). School-based social capital: The missing link between schools' socioeconomic composition and collective teacher efficacy. *Teaching and Teacher Education, 45*, 33–44.

Belo, R., Ferreira, P., & Telang, R. (2010). *The effects of broadband in schools: Evidence from Portugal.* Retrieved from http://papers.ssrn.com/sol3/papers.cfm?abstract_id=1636584

Bembenutty, H. (2009). Test anxiety and academic delay of gratification. *College Student Journal, 43*, 10–21.

Ben-Eliyahu, A., Linnenbrink-Garcia. L., & Putallaz, M. (2017). The intertwined nature of adolescents' social and academic lives: Social and academic goal orientations. *Journal of Advanced Academics, 28*, 66–93.

Bennett, C. (2019). *Comprehensive multicultural education: Theory and practice* (9th ed.). Boston: Pearson.

Bennett, S., & Kalish, N. (2006). *The Case Against Homework: How Homework Is Hurting our Children and What We Can Do About It.* New York: Crown Publishers.

Benson, J. (2016). The power of positive regard. *Educational Leadership, 73,* 22–26.

Bental, B., & Tirosh, E. (2007). The relationship between attention, executive functions and reading domain abilities in attention deficit hyperactivity disorder and reading disorder: A comparative study. *The Journal of Child Psychology and Psychiatry and Allied Disciplines, 48,* 455–463.

Berger, K. (2012). *The developing person through the life span* (8th ed.). New York: Worth.

Berk, L. E. (2019a). *Exploring child and adolescent development.* Boston: Pearson.

Berk, L. E. (2019b). *Exploring child development.* Boston: Pearson.

Berkowicz, J., & Myers, A. (2017). Developing the courage to report sexual abuse begins in schools. *Education Week.* http://blogs. edweek.org/edweek/leadership_360/2017/11/developing_the_ courage_to_report_sexual_abuse_begins_in_schools .html?cmp=eml-enl-eu-news3&M=58274248&U=27557

Berliner, D. C. (2006). Educational psychology: Searching for essence throughout a century of influence. In P. A. Alexander & P. H. Winne (Eds.), *Handbook of educational psychology* (2nd ed., pp. 3–42). Mahwah, NJ: Erlbaum.

Berliner, D. C. (2014). Exogenous variables and value-added assessments: A fatal flaw. *Teachers College Record, 116.* Retrieved from http://www.tcrecord.org/Content.asp?ContentID=17293

Beuker, K. T., Rommelse, N. N., Donders, R., & Buitelaar, J. K. (2013). Development of early communication skills in the first two years of life. *Infant Behavior and Development, 36,* 71–83.

Bhutto, M. I. (2011). Effects of social reinforcers on students' learning outcomes at secondary school level. *International Journal of Academic Research in Business and Social Sciences, 1,* 71–86.

Biag, M. (2016). A descriptive analysis of school connectedness: The views of school personnel. *Urban Education, 51,* 32–59.

Bialystok, E. (2011). Coordination of executive functions in monolingual and bilingual children. *Journal of Experimental Child Psychology, 110,* 461–468.

Bian, L., Leslie, S-J., & Cimpian, A. (2017). Gender stereotypes about intellectual ability emerge early and influence children's interests. *Science, 355,* 389–391. DOI: 10.1126/science.aah6524

Binyamin, G., & Carmeli, A. (2017). Fostering members' creativity in teams: The role of structuring of human resource management processes. *Psychology of Aesthetics, Creativity, and the Arts, 11,* 18–33.

Bishop, K., & Johnson, D. E. (2011). The effects of ability, perceptions of ability, and task characteristics on proximal and distal performance outcomes over time. *Human Performance, 24,* 173–189.

Bjorklund, D. (2012). *Children's thinking* (5th ed.). Belmont, CA: Cengage.

Bjorklund, D. F., & Causey, K. B. (2018). *Children's thinking: Cognitive development and individual differences* (6th ed.). Los Angeles: Sage.

Blad, E. (2017). Is your child showing grit? School report cards rate students' soft skills. *Education Week.* Retrieved from http://www .edweek.org/ew/articles/2017/05/31/is-your-child-showing-grit-school-report.html?r=1886653370

Blad, E. (2017). When it comes to sexual harassment, schools are not immune. *Education Week.* Retrieved from https:// www.edweek.org/ew/articles/2017/11/29/when-it-comes-to-sexual-harassment-schools.html?cmp=eml-enl-eu-news1&M=58291011&U=27557

Blair, C., & McKinnona, R. D. (2016). Moderating effects of executive functions and the teacher–child relationship on the development of mathematics ability in kindergarten. *Learning and Instruction, 41,* 85–93.

Blair, K. S., Otero, M., Teng, C., Geraci, M., Lewis, E., Hollon, N., Blair, R. J. R., Ernst M., Grillon, C., & Pine, D. S. (2016). Learning from other people's fear: Amygdala-based social reference learning in social anxiety disorder. *Psychological Medicine, 46,* 2943–2953.

Blatný, M., Millová, K., Jelínek, M., & Osecká, T. (2015). Personality predictors of successful development: toddler temperament and adolescent personality traits predict well-being and career stability in middle adulthood., *PLoS ONE, 10,* 1–21.

Bleidorn, W. (2012). Hitting the road to adulthood: Short-term personality development during a major life transition. *Personality and Social Psychology Bulletin, 38,* 12, 1594–1608. doi:10.1177/0146167212456707

Block, M. (2007). Climate changes lives of whalers in Alaska. *All Things Considered.* National Public Radio. Retrieved from http:// www.npr.org/templates/story/story.php?storyId=14428086

Bloom, B., Englehart, M., Furst, E., Hill, W., & Krathwohl, O. (1956). *Taxonomy of educational objectives: The classification of educational goals: Handbook 1. The cognitive domain.* White Plains, NY: Longman.

Bloom, P. (2010). The moral life of babies. *New York Times Magazine.* Retrieved from http://www.nytimes.com/2010/05/09/ magazine/09babies-t.html?_r=0

Bobbitt, K. C., & Gershoff, E. T. (2016). Chaotic experiences and low-income children's social-emotional development. *Children and Youth Services Review, 70,* 19–29.

Boehm, K. (2012). Left brain, right brain: An outdated argument. *Yale Scientific.* Retrieved from http://www.yalescientific.org/2012/04/ left-brain-right-brain-an-outdated-argument/

Boersma, A., Dam, G., Wardekker, W., & Volman, M. (2016). Designing innovative learning environments to foster communities of learners for students in initial vocational education. *Learning Environments Research, 19,* 107–131.

Bootsman, N. J. M., Skinner, T., Lal, R., Glindermann, D., Lagasca, C., & Peeters, G. M. E. E. (2018). The relationship between physical activity, and physical performance and psycho-cognitive functioning in older adults living in residential aged care facilities. *Journal of Science and Medicine in Sport, 21,* 173–178.

Borko, H., & Putnam, R. (1996). Learning to teach. In D. Berliner & R. Calfee (Eds.), *Handbook of educational psychology* (pp. 673–708). New York: Macmillan.

Bosman, J., & Saulfeb, S. (2018). 'Teachers are educators, not security guards': Educators respond to Trump proposal. *The New York Times.* Retrieved from https://www.nytimes.com/2018/02/22/ us/arming-teachers-trump.html

Botma, Y., Van Rensburg, G. H., Coetzee, I. M., Heyns, T. (2015). A conceptual framework for educational design at modular level to promote transfer of learning. *Innovations in Education & Teaching International, 52,* 499–509.

Bouchard, K. L., & Smith, J. D. (2017). Teacher–student relationship quality and children's bullying experiences with peers: Reflecting on the Mesosystem. *The Educational Forum, 81,* 108–125.

Bowell, T. (2017). Response to the editorial "Education in a post-truth world." *Educational Philosophy & Theory, 49,* 582–585.

Bower, E. (2016). American deaths in terrorism vs. gun violence in one graph. *CNN.* Retrieved from http://www.cnn.com/2016/10/03/ us/terrorism-gun-violence/index.html

Bowman, N. A., & Stewart, D-L. (2014). Precollege exposure to racial/ ethnic difference and first-year college students' racial attitudes. *Teachers College Record.* Retrieved from http://www.tcrecord.org/ Content.asp?ContentID=17607

Boyle, J. R. (2013). Strategic note-taking for inclusive middle school science classrooms. *Remedial and Special Education, 34,* 78–90.

Bozkurt, G. (2017). Social constructivism: Does it succeed in reconciling individual cognition with social teaching and learning practices in mathematics? *Journal of Education and Practice, 8,* 210–218.

Bradbury, B., Corak, M., Waldfogel, J., & Washbrook, E. (2016). *Too many children left behind. The U.S. achievement gap in comparative perspective.* New York: The Russell Sage Foundation.

Brady, S. T., Reeves, S. L., Garcia, J., Purdie-Vaughns, V., Cook, J. E., Taborsky-Barba, S., ... Cohen, G. L. (2016). The psychology of the affirmed learner: Spontaneous self-affirmation in the face of stress. *Journal of Educational Psychology, 108,* 353–373.

Brannon, L. (2017). *Gender: Psychological perspective* (7th ed.). New York: Taylor and Francis.

Bransford, J. D., & Schwartz, D. L. (1999). Rethinking transfer: A simple proposal with multiple implications. *Review of Research in*

Education, 24, 61–100. Washington, DC: American Educational Research Association.

Bransford, J. D., & Stein, B. S. (1993). *The ideal problem solver* (2nd ed.). New York: Freeman.

Bransford, J., Brown, A., & Cocking, R. (Eds.). (2000). *How people learn: Brain, mind, experience, and school.* Washington, DC: National Academies Press.

Braun, H., Kirsch, I., & Yamamoto, K. (2011). An experimental study of the effects of monetary incentives on performance on the 12th-grade NAEP reading assessment. *Teachers College Record, 113,* 2309–2344. Retrieved from http://www.tcrecord.org/Content.asp?ContentID=16008.

Bray, B., & McClaskey, K. (2015). *Making learning personal: The what, who, WOW, where, and why.* Thousand Oaks, CA: Corwin.

Brehmer, Y., & Li, S-C. (2007). Memory plasticity across the life span: Uncovering children's latent potential. *Developmental Psychology, 43,* 465–478.

Brimley, V., Verstegen, D., & Garfield, R. (2012). *Financing education in a climate of change* (11th ed.). Boston: Allyn & Bacon.

Brinck, I., & Liljenfors, R. (2013). The developmental origin of metacognition. *Infant and Child Development, 22,* 85–101.

Brittian, A. S., Umaña-Taylor, A. J., & Derlan, C. L. (2013). An examination of biracial college youths' family ethnic socialization, ethnic identity, and adjustment: Do self-identification labels and university context matter? *Cultural Diversity and Ethnic Minority Psychology, 19,* 177–189.

Broekhuizen, M. L., Slot, P. L., van Aken, M. A. G., & Dubas, J. S. (2017). Teachers' emotional and behavioral support and preschoolers' self-regulation: Relations with social and emotional skills during play. *Early Education and Development, 28,* 135–153.

Bronfenbrenner, U. (1979). The ecology of human development: Experiments by nature and design. Cambridge, MA: Harvard University Press.

Bronfenbrenner, U. (2005). Making human beings human: Bioecological perspectives on human development. Thousand Oaks, CA: Sage.

Bronfenbrenner, U., & Morris, P. (2006). The bioecological model of human development. In R. Lerner (Ed.), *Handbook of child psychology: Vol. 1 Theoretical models of human development* (6th ed., pp. 793–828). Hoboken, NJ: Wiley.

Brook, J., Zhang, C., Finch, S., & Brook, D. (2010). Adolescent pathways to adult smoking: Ethnic identity, peer substance use, and antisocial behavior. *American Journal on Addictions, 19*(2), 178–186.

Brookhart, S. (2013). *How to create and use rubrics for formative assessment and grading.* Baltimore: American Society for Curriculum Developers.

Brookhart, S. M., & Nitko, A. J. (2019). *Educational assessment of students* (8th ed.). Boston: Pearson.

Brooks, D. (2013). Beyond the brain. *The New York Times.* Retrieved from http://www.nytimes.com/2013/06/18/opinion/brooks-beyond-the-brain.html?_r=0

Brooks, D. (2017a). How evil is Tech? *The New York Times.* Retrieved from https://www.nytimes.com/2017/11/20/opinion/how-evil-is-tech.html

Brooks, D. (2017b). When life asks for everything. *The New York Times.* Retrieved from https://www.nytimes.com/2017/09/19/opinion/when-life-asks-for-everything.html

Brophy, J. (2006). Observational research on generic aspects of classroom teaching. In P. A. Alexander & P. H. Winne (Eds.), *Handbook of educational psychology* (2nd ed., pp. 755–780). Mahwah, NJ: Erlbaum.

Brophy, J. (2006a). Graham Nuttall and social constructivist teaching; Research-based cautions and qualifications. *Teaching and Teacher Education, 22,* 529–537.

Brophy, J. (2006b). Observational research on generic aspects of classroom teaching. In P. A. Alexander & P. H. Winne (Eds.), *Handbook of educational psychology* (2nd ed., pp. 755–780). Mahwah, NJ: Erlbaum.

Brophy, J. (2010). *Motivating students to learn* (3rd ed.). New York: Routledge.

Brown, E. (2013). D.C. report: Teachers in 18 classrooms cheated on students' high-stakes tests in 2012. *The Washington Post.* Retrieved from http://www.washingtonpost.com/local/education/memo-could-revive-allegations-of-cheating-in-dc-public-schools/2013/04/12/9ddb2bb6-a35e-11e2-9c03-6952ff305f35_story.html

Brown, H., & Ciuffetelli, D. C. (Eds.). (2009). *Foundational methods: Understanding teaching and learning.* Toronto: Pearson Education.

Brown, R. (2013, June 8). A swiveling proxy that will even wear a tutu. *New York Times.* Retrieved from http://www.nytimes.com/2013/06/08/education/for-homebound-students-a-robot-proxy-in-theclassroom.html?nl=todaysheadlines&emc=edit_th_20130608&_r=0

Brown-Chidsey, R. (2007). No more "Waiting to fail." *Educational Leadership, 65*(2), 40–46.

Brugman, D. (2010). Moral reasoning competence and the moral judgment-action discrepancy in young adolescents. In W. Koops, D. Brugman, T. Ferguson, & A. Sanders (Eds.), *The development and structure of conscience* (pp. 119–133). New York: Psychology Press.

Brummelman, E., Thomaes, S., Overbeek, G., Orobio de Castro, B., van den Hout, M. A., & Bushman, B. J. (2013, February 18). On feeding those hungry for praise: Person praise backfires in children with low self-esteem. *Journal of Experimental Psychology: General.* Advance online publication. doi:10.1037/a0031917

Bruner, J. S. (1966). *Toward a theory of instruction.* New York: Norton.

Bruner, J., Goodnow, J., & Austin, G. (1956). *A study of thinking.* New York: Wiley.

Bruning, R. H., Schraw, G. J., & Norby, M. M. (2011). *Cognitive psychology and instruction* (5th ed.). Boston: Pearson.

Bryk, A., Sebring, P., Allensworth, E., Luppescu, S., & Easton, J. (2010). *Organizing schools for improvement: Lessons from Chicago.* Chicago: University of Chicago Press.

Buchholtz, N. F. (2017). The acquisition of mathematics pedagogical content knowledge in university mathematics education courses: Results of a mixed methods study on the effectiveness of teacher education in Germany. *ZDM: The International Journal of Mathematics Education, 49,* 249–264.

Buchs, C., Filippou, D., Volpé, Y., & Pulfrey, C. (2017). Challenges for cooperative learning implementation: Reports from elementary school teachers. *Journal of Education for Teaching, 43,* 296–306.

Buck, G., Kostin, I., & Morgan, R. (2002). *Examining the relationship of content to gender-based performance difference in advanced placement exams.* (Research Report No. 2002–12). New York: College Board.

Budwig, N. (2015). Concepts and tools from the learning sciences for linking research, teaching and practice around sustainability issues *Sustainability science, Current Opinion in Environmental Sustainability, 16,* 99–104.

Bui, D. C., & Myerson, J. (2014). The role of working memory abilities in lecture note-taking. *Learning and Individual Differences, 33,* 12–22.

Bui, D. C., Myerson, J., & Hale, S. (2013). Note-taking with computers: Exploring alternative strategies for improved recall. *Journal of Educational Psychology, 105,* 299–309.

Bui, S. A., Craig, S. G., & Imberman, S. A. (2011). *Is gifted education a bright idea? Assessing the impact of gifted and talented programs on achievement.* National Bureau of Economic Research Working Paper Series, No. 17089.

Bullough, R., Jr. (1989). *First-year teacher: A case study.* New York: Teachers College Press.

Bump. B. (2017). Albany schools agree to $400,000 settlement in sexual harassment case. *Albany Times Union.* Retrieved from http://www.timesunion.com/7day-breaking/article/Albany-schools-agree-to-400-000-settlement-in-11209267.php

Bushman, B. J., Moeller, S. J., & Crocker. J. (2010). Sweets, sex, or self-esteem? Comparing the value of self-esteem boosts with other pleasant rewards. *Journal of Personality.* Accepted article. doi:10.1111/j.1467-6494.2010.00712.x

Butani, L., Bannister, S. L., Rubin, A., & Forbes, K. L. (2017). Research in pediatric education: How educators conceptualize and teach reflective practice: A survey of North American pediatric medical educators. *Academic Pediatrics, 17,* 303–309.

Butler, D. L., Schnellert, L., & Perry, N. E. (2017). *Developing self-regulating learners.* Toronto: Pearson.

Byrnes, J. (2007). Some ways in which neuroscientific research can be relevant to education. In D. Coch, J. Fischer, & G. Dawson (Eds.), *Human behavior, learning, and the developing brain: Typical development* (pp. 30–49). New York: Guilford Press.

Callan, G. L., Marchant, G. J., Finch, W., H., & German, R. L. (2016). Metacognition, strategies, achievement, and demographics: Relationships across countries. *Educational Sciences: Theory and Practice, 16*, 1485–1502.

Calzada, E., Huang, K., Anicama, C., Fernandez, Y., & Brotman, L. (2012). Test of a cultural framework of parenting with Latino families of young children. *Cultural Diversity & Ethnic Minority Psychology, 18*, 285–296.

Cameron, J., Pierce, W. D., & Banko, K. M. (2005). Achievement-based rewards and intrinsic motivation: A test of cognitive mediators. *Journal of Educational Psychology, 97*, 641–655.

Campos, C., Leon, Y., Sleiman, A., & Urcuyo, B. (2017). Further evaluation of the use of multiple schedules for behavior maintained by negative reinforcement. *Behavior Modification, 41*, 269 –285.

Canter, A. (2004). A problem-solving model for improving student achievement. *Principal Leadership, 5*, 11–15.

Cantin, R. H., Gnaedinger, E. K., Gallaway, K. C., Hesson-McInnis, M. S., & Hund, A. M. (2016). Executive functioning predicts reading, mathematics, and theory of mind during the elementary years. *Journal of Experimental Child Psychology, 146*, 66–78.

Carey, B. (2010). Forget what you know about good study habits. *The New York Times.* Retrieved from http://www.nytimes.com/2010/09/07/health/views/07mind.html?_r=1&th=&emc=th&pagewanted=print

Carlo, G., Mestre, M., Samper, P., Tur, A., & Armenta, B. (2011). The longitudinal relations among dimensions of parenting styles, sympathy, prosocial moral reasoning, and prosocial behaviors. *International Journal of Behavioral Development, 35*, 116–124.

Carlson, J. F., Geisinger, K. F., & Jonson, J. L. (Eds.). (2017). *The twentieth mental measurements yearbook.* Lincoln, NE: Buros Institute of Mental Measurements.

Carlson, N. (2011). *Foundations of behavioral neuroscience* (8th ed.). Boston: Allyn & Bacon.

Carlsson, J., Wängqvist, M., & Frisén, A. (2015). Identity development in the late twenties: A never ending story. *Developmental Psychology, 51*, 334–345.

Carlsson, J., Wängqvist, M., & Frisén, A. (2016). Life on hold: Staying in identity diffusion in the late twenties. *Journal of Adolescence, 47*, 220–229.

Carmichael, C., Callingham, R., & Watt, H. (2017). Classroom motivational environment influences on emotional and cognitive dimensions of student interest in mathematics. *ZDM, 49*, 449–460.

Carnahan, C. D., Crowley, K., & Holness, P. (2016). Implementing universal design for learning. *Global Education Journal, 2016*, 10–19.

Carnine, D., W., Silbert, J., Kame'enui, E. J., Slocum, T. A., & Travers, P. A. (2017). *Direct instruction reading* (6th ed.). Boston: Pearson.

Carpenter, S. K., Pashler, H., & Cepeda, N. J. (2009). Using tests to enhance 8th grade students' retention of US history facts. *Applied Cognitive Psychology, 23*, 760–771.

Carr, N. (2010). *The shallows: What the Internet is doing to our brains.* New York: W. W. Norton.

Carr, N. S. (2013). Increasing the effectiveness of homework for all learners in the inclusive classroom. *School Community Journal, 23*, 169–182.

Carter, K., & Doyle, W. (2006). Classroom management in early childhood and elementary classrooms. In C. M. Evertson & C. S. Weinstein (Eds.), *Handbook of classroom management: Research, practice, and contemporary issues* (pp. 373–406). Mahwah, NJ: Erlbaum.

Cartwright, K. (2012). Insights from cognitive neuroscience: The importance of executive function for early reading development and education. *Early Education & Development, 23*, 24–26.

Casasola, T., Tutrang, N., Warschauer, M., & Schenke, K. (2017). Can flipping the classroom work? Evidence from undergraduate

chemistry. *International Journal of Teaching & Learning in Higher Education, 29*, 421–435.

Case, R. (1992). *The mind's staircase: Exploring the conceptual underpinnings of children's thought and knowledge.* Hillsdale, NJ: Erlbaum.

Case, R. (1998). The development of central conceptual structures. In D. Kuhn & R. Siegler (Eds.), *Handbook of child psychology: Vol. 2. Cognition, perception, and language* (5th ed., pp. 745–800). New York: Wiley.

Casey, B. J., Jones, R. M., & Somerville, L. H. (2011). Braking and accelerating of the adolescent brain. *Journal of Research on Adolescence, 21*(1), 21–33.

Caspi, J. (2012). *Sibling aggression: Assessment and treatment.* New York: Springer.

Cassady, J. (2010). Test anxiety: Contemporary theories and implications for learning. In J. Cassady (Ed.), *Anxiety in the schools: The causes, consequences, and solutions for academic anxieties* (pp. 7–26). New York: Peter Lang.

Cassano, M., & Zeman, J. (2010). Parental socialization of sadness regulation in middle childhood: The role of expectations and gender. *Developmental Psychology 35*(5),1214–1226.

Castle Heatly, M., & Votruba-Drzal, E. (2017). Parent- and teacher-child relationships and engagement at school entry: Mediating, interactive, and transactional associations across contexts. *Developmental Psychology, 53*, 1042–1062.

Catalano, T., & Gatti, L. (2017). Representing teachers as criminals in the news: a multimodal critical discourse analysis of the Atlanta schools' "Cheating Scandal." *Social Semiotics, 27*, 59–80.

Cattell, R. (1963). Theory of fluid and crystallized intelligence: A critical experiment. *Journal of Educational Psychology, 54*, 1–22.

Cattell, R. (1987). *Intelligence: Its structure, growth, and action.* Amsterdam: North-Holland.

Cavanagh, S. (2014). What is 'personalized learning'? Educators seek clarity. *Education Week.* Retrieved from https://www.edweek.org/ew/articles/2014/10/22/09pl-overview.h34.html

Çengel, M., & Türkoğlu, A. (2016). Analysis through hidden curriculum of peer relations in two different classes with positive and negative classroom climates. *Educational Sciences: Theory & Practice, 16*, 1893–1919.

Center for Behavioral Health Statistics and Quality. (2015). *2014 National Survey on Drug Use and Health: Detailed Tables.* Substance Abuse and Mental Health Services Administration, Rockville, MD.

Centers for Disease Control. (2015). *Trends in the prevalence of behaviors that contribute to violence National YRBS: 1991—2015.* Retrieved from https://www.cdc.gov/healthyyouth/data/yrbs/pdf/trends/2015_us_violence_trend_yrbs.pdf

Centers for Disease Control and Prevention. (2016). *Morbidity and mortality weekly report.* U.S. Department of Health and Human Services. Retrieved from https://www.cdc.gov/healthyyouth/data/yrbs/pdf/2015/ss6506_updated.pdf

Centers for Disease Control and Prevention. (2016a). Sexual Identity, Sex of sexual contacts, and health-risk behaviors among students in grades 9–12: *Youth Risk Behavior Surveillance.* Atlanta, GA: U.S. Department of Health and Human Services.

Centers for Disease Control and Prevention. (2016b). *Understanding school violence: Fact sheet.* Retrieved from https://www.cdc.gov/violenceprevention/pdf/School_Violence_Fact_Sheet-a.pdf

Centers for Disease Control and Prevention. (2017a). *Attention deficit/hyperactivity disorder* (ADHD). Retrieved from https://www.cdc.gov/ncbddd/adhd/data.html#ref

Centers for Disease Control and Prevention. (2017b). *Hearing loss in children.* Retrieved from https://www.cdc.gov/ncbddd/hearingloss/data.html

Centers for Disease Control and Prevention. (2017c). *Leading Causes of Death Reports, 1999–2015.* Retrieved from https://webappa.cdc.gov/sasweb/ncipc/leadcause.html

Cerasoli, C., Nicklin, J., & Nassrelgrgawi, A. (2016). Performance incentives and needs for autonomy, competence, and relatedness: A meta-analysis. *Motivation and Emotion, 40*, 781–813.

Chaffen, R., & Imreh, G. (2002). Practicing perfection: Piano performance and expert memory. *Psychological Science, 13*, 342–349.

Chang, R., & Coward, F. L. (2015). More recess time, please! *Phi Delta Kappan, 97*, 14–17.

Chang, Y.-K., Chen, S., Tu, K-W., & Chi, T L.-K. (2016). Effect of autonomy support on self-determined motivation in elementary physical education. *Journal of Sports Science & Medicine, 15*, 460–467.

Chappuis, J., & Stiggins, R. (2017). *An introduction to student-involved assessment FOR learning* (7th ed.). New York: Pearson.

Character Growth Card. (2017). Character lab. Retrieved from https://cdn.characterlab.org/assets/Character-Growth-Card-cad815b0b3ba79c794bcfd3a89e2a8d5ac3057963fff02cee539d8d9af1b9777.pdf

Chatera, N., & Loewenstein, G. (2016). The under-appreciated drive for sense-making. *Journal of Economic Behavior & Organization, 126*, 137–154.

Chatzisarantis, N. L. D., Ada, E. N., Bing, Q., Papaioannou, A., Prpa, N., & Hagger, M. S. (2016). Clarifying the link between mastery goals and social comparisons in classroom settings. *Contemporary Educational Psychology, 46*, 61–72.

Chauvet-Geliniera, J-C., & Bonina, B. (2017). Stress, anxiety and depression in heart disease patients: A major challenge for cardiac rehabilitation. *Annals of Physical and Rehabilitation Medicine, 60*, 6–12.

Cheek, C., Piercy, K. W., & Kohlenberg, M. (2015). Have I ever done anything like this before? Older adults solving ill-defined problems in intensive volunteering. *International Journal of Aging and Human Development, 80*, 184–207.

Chen, J. (2004). Theory of multiple intelligences: Is it a scientific theory? *Teachers College Record, 106*, 17–23.

Chen, J., Moran, S., & Gardner, H. (2009). *Multiple intelligences around the world*. San Francisco: Jossey-Bass.

Chen, L-X., & Sun, C-T. (2016). Self-regulation influence on game play flow state. *Computers in Human Behavior, 54*, 341–350.

Chen, N-S., Teng, D. C-E., Lee, C-H., & Kinshuk. (2011). Augmenting paper-based reading activity with direct access to digital materials and scaffolded questioning. *Computers & Education, 57*, 1705–1715.

Chen, Q., & Yan, Z. (2016). Review: Does multitasking with mobile phones affect learning? *Computers in Human Behavior, 54*, 34–42.

Chen, X., & Eisenberg, N. (2012). Understanding cultural issues in child development: Introduction. *Child Development Perspectives, 6*, 1–4.

Chen, X., & Trommsdorff, G. (Eds.). (2012). *Values, religion, and culture in adolescent development*. Cambridge, UK: Cambridge University Press.

Chen, X., & Wang, I. (2010). China. In M. H. Bornstein (Ed.), *Handbook of cultural development science* (pp. 429–444). New York: Psychology Press.

Cherry, K. (2017). Gardner's theory of multiple intelligences. *Verywell*. Retrieved from https://www.verywell.com/gardners-theory-of-multiple-intelligences-2795161

Chetty, R., Friedman, J. N., & Rockoff, J. E. (2014). Measuring the impacts of teachers II: Teacher value-added and student outcomes in adulthood. *The American Economic Review, 104*, 2633–2679.

Cheung, A. C. K., & Slavin, R. E. (2012). Effective reading programs for Spanish-dominant English language learners (ELLs) in the elementary grades: A synthesis of research. *Review of Educational Research. 82*, 351–395.

Chiang, F-K., & Chen, C. (2017). Modified flipped classroom instructional model in "Learning Sciences" course for graduate students. *Asia-Pacific Education Researcher, 26*, 1–10.

Child Welfare Information Gateway. (2016). *Definitions of child abuse and neglect*. Retrieved from https://www.childwelfare.gov/pubPDFs/define.pdf.

Choi, Y., Kim, Y. S., Kim, S. Y., & Park, I. J. (2013). Is Asian American parenting controlling and harsh? Empirical testing of relationships between Korean American and Western parenting measures. *Asian American Journal of Psychology, 4*, 19–29.

Chomsky, N. (1959). Review of B. F. Skinner's *Verbal Behavior*. *Language, 35*, 26–58.

Chomsky, N. (2006). *Language and the mind* (3rd ed.). Cambridge, UK: Cambridge University Press.

Chorzempa, B., & Graham, S. (2006). Primary-grade teachers' use of within-class ability grouping in reading. *Journal of Educational Psychology, 98*(3), 529–541.

Choukas-Bradley, S., Giletta, M., Cohen, G. L., & Prinstein, M. J. (2015). Peer influence, peer status, and prosocial behavior: An experimental investigation of peer socialization of adolescents' intentions to volunteer. *Journal of Youth & Adolescence , 44*, 2197–2210.

Chow, S. J. (2015). Many meanings of 'heuristic'. *British Journal for the Philosophy of Science, 66*, 977–1016.

Christensen, J. (2016). A critical reflection of Bronfenbrenner's development ecology model. *Problems of Education in the 21st Century, 69*, 22–28.

Chu, J. Y., & Gilligan, C. (2015). *When boys become boys: Development, relationships, and masculinity*. New York: New York University Press.

Cihon, T. M., Cihon, J. H., & Bedient, G. M. (2016). Establishing a common vocabulary of key concepts for the effective implementation of applied behavioral analysis. *International Electronic Journal of Elementary Education, 9*, 337–348.

Cimpian, J. R., Lubienski, S. T., Timmer, J. D., Makowski, M. B., & Miller, E. K. (2016). Have gender gaps in math closed? Achievement, teacher perceptions, and learning behaviors across two ECLS-K cohorts. *AERA Open, 2*, 1–19.

Cingel, D. P., & Sundar, S. S. (2012). Texting, techspeak, and tweens: The relationship between text messaging and English grammar skills. *New Media & Society, 14*, 1304–1320.

Cipriano, E., & Stifter, C. (2010). Predicting preschool effortful control from toddler temperament and parenting behavior. *Journal of Applied Developmental Psychology, 31*, 221–230.

Cismaru, M. (2014). Using the extended parallel process model to understand texting while driving and guide communication campaigns against it. *Social Marketing Quarterly, 20*, 66–82.

Clarey, C. (2014, February 22). Olympians use imagery as mental training. *New York Times*. Retrieved from http://www.nytimes.com/2014/02/23/sports/olympics/olympians-use-imagery-as-mental-training.html?hpw&rref=sports&_r=0

Clariana, R., Rysavy, M., & Taricani, E. (2015). Text signals influence team artifacts. *Educational Technology Research & Development, 63*, 35–52.

Clark, J., & Paivio, A. (1991). Dual coding theory and education. *Educational Psychology Review, 3*, 149–210.

Clark, K., & Clark, M. (1939). The development of consciousness of self and the emergence of racial identification in Negro preschool children. *Journal of Social Psychology, 10*, 591–599.

Clark, R. C. (2010). *Evidence-based training methods: A guide for training professionals*. Alexandria, VA: ASTD Press.

Clark, R. C., & Mayer, R. E. (2003). *e-Learning and the science of instruction: Proven guidelines for consumers and designers of multimedia learning*. San Francisco: Pfeiffer/Wiley.

Clark, R. E., Kirschner, P. A., & Sweller, J. (2012). Putting students on the path to learning: The case for fully guided instruction. *American Educator, 36*, 6–11.

Clarke, A., & Bautista, D. (2017). Critical reflection and arts-based action research for the educator self. *Canadian Journal of Action Research, 18*, 52–70.

Class and Family in America. (2015). Minding the nurture gap. *The Economist*. Retrieved from http://www.economist.com/news/books-and-arts/21646708-social-mobility-depends-what-happens-first-years-life-minding-nurture-gap

Clay, R. (2013). Easing ADHD without meds. *American Psychological Association, 44*(2), 44.

Cleary, T. J., & Kitsantas, A. (2017). Motivation and self-regulated learning influences on middle school mathematics achievement. *School Psychology Review, 2017, 46*, 88–107.

Clinchot, M., Ngai, C., Huie, R., Talanquer, V., Lambertz, J., Banks, G., Weinrich, M., Lewis, R., Pelletier, P., & Sevian, H. (2017). Better formative assessment. *Science Teacher, 84*, 69–75.

Code.org. (2017). *Code.org 2016 annual report*. Retrieved from https://code.org/about/2016

Coffield, F., Moseley, D., Hall, E., & Ecclestone, K. (2004). *Learning styles and pedagogy in post-16 learning: A systematic and critical review.* London: Learning and Skills Research Centre/University of Newcastle upon Tyne.

Cohen, E. (1994). Restructuring the classroom: Conditions for productive small groups. *Review of Educational Research, 64,* 1–35.

Cohen, E., & Lotan, R. (2014). *Designing Groupwork: Strategies for the Heterogeneous Classroom.* 3rd ed. New York: Teachers College Press.

Cohen, M. T. (2012). The importance of self-regulation for college student learning. *College Student Journal, 46,* 892–902.

Colangelo, N., & Davis, G. (Eds.). (2003). *Handbook of gifted education* (3rd ed.). Boston: Allyn & Bacon.

Colangelo, N., & Wood, S. M. (2015). Counseling the gifted: Past, present, and future directions. *Journal of Counseling and Development, 93,* 133–142.

Cole, M., & Packer, M. (2011). Culture in development. In M. Bornstein & M. Lamb (Eds.), *Developmental science: An advanced textbook* (6th ed., pp. 51–107). New York: Psychology Press.

Cole, S., Balcetis, E., & Zhang, S. (2013). Visual perception and regulatory conflict: Motivation and physiology influence distance perception. *Journal of Experimental Psychology, 142,* 18–22.

Collaborative for Academic, Social, and Emotional Learning (CASEL). (2013). *CASEL Guide: Effective Social and Emotional Learning Programs.* ttp://static.squarespace.com/static/513f79f9e4b05ce7b70e9673/t/526a 220de4b00a92c90436 ba/1382687245993/2013-casel-guide.pdf

College Board. (2017). *SAT suite of assessments annual report.* Retrieved from https://reports.collegeboard.org/pdf/2017-total-group-sat-suite-assessments-annual-report.pdf

Collins, M. (2010). ELL preschoolers' English vocabulary acquisition from storybook reading. *Early Childhood Research Quarterly, 25*(1), 84–97.

Collins, R. (2011). Content analysis of gender roles in media: Where are we now and where should we go? *Sex Roles, 64,* 290–298.

Colvin, G. (2010). *Talent is overrated: What really separates world-class performers from everybody else.* New York: Penguin Group.

Common Core State Standards Initiative. (2018a). English Language Arts Standards, Language, Grade 1, 1, c. Use singular and plural nouns with matching verbs in basic sentences (e.g., He hops; We hop). Retrieved from http://www.corestandards.org/ELA-Literacy/L/1/

Common Core State Standards Initiative. (2018b). Grade 6, Ratios & Proportional Relationships, Understand ratio concepts and use ratio reasoning to solve problems, 3, c. Find a percent of a quantity as a rate per 100 (e.g., 30% of a quantity means 30/100 times the quantity); solve problems involving finding the whole, given a part and the percent. Retrieved from http://www.corestandards.org/Math/Content/6/RP/A/3/c/

Common Core State Standards Initiative. (2018c). English Language Arts Standards, History/Social Studies, Grade 9–10, 8. Assess the extent to which the reasoning and evidence in a text support the author's claims. Retrieved from http://www.corestandards.org/ELA-Literacy/RH/9-10/8/

Common Core State Standards Initiative. (2018d). About the standards: Development process. Retrieved from http://www.corestandards.org/about-the-standards/

Common Core State Standards Initiative. (2018e). *Grade 5, Geometry, Classify two-dimensional figures into categories based on their properties, 4.* Retrieved from http://www.corestandards.org/Math/Content/5/G/B/4/

Common Core State Standards Initiative. (2018f). *Grade 6, Ratios & Proportional Relationships, Understand ratio concepts and use ratio reasoning to solve problems, 3, b.* Retrieved from http://www.corestandards.org/Math/Content/6/RP/A/3/b/.

Common Core State Standards Initiative. (2018g). *English Language Arts Standards, Reading: Literature, Grade 9–10, 4.* Retrieved from http://www.corestandards.org/ELA-Literacy/RL/9–10/4/

Common Core State Standards Initiative. (2018h). *English Language Arts Standards, Reading: Literature, Grade 11–12, 3.* Retrieved from http://www.corestandards.org/ELA-Literacy/RL/11–12/3/

Common Core State Standards Initiative. (2018i). *English Language Arts Standards, History/Social Studies, Grade 6–8, 8.* Retrieved from http://www.corestandards.org/ELA-Literacy/RH/6–8/8/.

Common Core State Standards Initiative. (2018j). Grade 2, Measurement & Data, Represent and interpret data, 10. Retrieved from http://www.corestandards.org/lo-que-los-padres-deben-saber/

Common Core State Standards Initiative. (2018k). Grade 5, Number & Operations—Fractions, Use equivalent fractions as a strategy to add and subtract fractions, 1. Retrieved from http://www.corestandards.org/Math/Content/5/NF/A/1/.

Common Core State Standards Initiative. (2018l). English Language Arts Standards, Reading: Informational Text, Grade 7, 2. Retrieved from http://www.corestandards.org/ELA-Literacy/RI/7/2/.

Common Core State Standards Initiative (2018m). Grade 1, Operations & Algebraic Thinking, Understand and apply properties of operations and the relationship between addition and subtraction, 3. Retrieved from http://www.corestandards.org/Math/Content/1/OA/B/3/

Common Core State Standards Initiative. (2018n). Grade 2, Operations & Algebraic Thinking. Retrieved from http://www.corestandards.org/Math/Content/2/OA/

Common Core State Standards Initiative. (2018o). English Language Arts Standards, Language, Grade 3, 1, f. Retrieved from http://www.corestandards.org/ELA-Literacy/L/3/1/f/

Common Core State Standards Initiative. (2018p). Grade 1, Operations & Algebraic Thinking, Understand and apply properties of operations and the relationship between addition and subtraction. 3. Retrieved from http://www.corestandards.org/Math/Content/1/OA/B/3/

Common Core State Standards Initiative. (2018q). English Language Arts Standards, History/Social Studies, Grade 9–10, 8. Retrieved from http://www.corestandards.org/ELA-Literacy/RH/9-10/8/

Common Core State Standards Initiative. (2018r). English Language Arts Standards, Language, Grade 8, 1, a. Retrieved from http://www.corestandards.org/ELA-Literacy/L/8/1/a/

Common Core State Standards Initiative. (2018s). English Language Arts Standards, History/Social Studies, Grade 9–10, 3. Retrieved from http://www.corestandards.org/ELA-Literacy/RH/9-10/3/

Common Core State Standards Initiative. (2018t). English Language Arts Standards, Science & Technical Subjects, Grade 6–8, 4. Retrieved from http://www.corestandards.org/ELA-Literacy/RST/6-8/4/

Common Core State Standards Initiative. (2018u). Standards in your state. Retrieved from http://www.corestandards.org/standards-in-your-state/

Common Core State Standards Initiative. (2018v). English Language Arts Standards, History/Social Studies, Grade 9–10, 7. Retrieved from http://www.corestandards.org/ELA-Literacy/RH/9-10/7/

Common Core State Standards Initiative. (2018w). *Grade 5, Number & Operations—Fractions.* Retrieved from http://www.corestandards.org/Math/Content/5/NF/

Conley, M., & Garner, G. (2015). The edTPA and the (de)skilling of America's teachers? *Teachers College Record.* Retrieved from http://www.tcrecord.org/Content.asp?ContentID=18037

Cook, A. N., Fielding, K. S., & Louis, W. R. (2016). *Environmental Education Research, 22,* 631–657.

Cook, A., & Polgar, J. (2012). *Essentials of assistive technology.* Waltham, MA: Elsevier.

Cooper, H., Robinson, I. C., & Patall, E. A. (2006). Does homework improve academic achievement? A synthesis of research, 1987–2003. *Review of Educational Research, 76,* 1–62.

Cooper, K. S. (2013). Safe, affirming, and productive spaces: Classroom engagement among Latina high school students. *Urban Education, 48,* 490–528.

Cooper, L., & Nickerson, A. (2013). Parent retrospective recollections of bullying and current views, concerns, and strategies to cope with children's bullying. *Journal of Child & Family Studies, 22,* 526–540.

Cooper, P., & Olsen, J. (2014). *Dealing with disruptive students in the classroom.* Hoboken, NJ: Routledge.

Coppinger, M. (2017). Jerry Sandusky's son arrested, charged with child sexual abuse. *USA Today*. Retrieved from http://www.usatoday.com/story/sports/ncaaf/2017/02/13/jerry-sandusky-son-jeffrey-sandusky-charged-child-sexual-abuse/97859942/

Cornelius-White, J. (2007). Learner-centered teacher-student relationships are effective: A meta-analysis. *Review of Educational Research, 77*, 113–143.

Cosgrove, H. E., & Nickerson, A. B. (2017). Anti-bullying/harassment legislation and educator perceptions of severity, effectiveness, and school climate: A cross-sectional analysis. *Educational Policy, 31*, 518–545.

Council for Exceptional Children. (2014). *A primer on the IDEA 2004 regulations*. Retrieved from http://www.cec.sped.org/Policy-and-Advocacy/Current-Sped-Gifted-Issues/Individuals-with-Disabilities-Education-Act/A-Primer-on-the-IDEA-2004-RegulationsIDEA

Covington, M. (1992). *Making the grade: A self-worth perspective on motivation and school reform*. Cambridge, MA: Harvard University Press.

Covington, M. (1998). *The will to learn: A guide for motivating young people*. New York: Cambridge University Press.

Coyne, M., Carnine, D., & Kame'enui, E. (2011). *Effective teaching strategies that accommodate diverse learners* (4th ed). Boston: Pearson.

Coyne, R. D., Lee, J., & Petrova, D. (2017). Re-visiting the flipped classroom in a design context. *Journal of Learning Design, 10*, 1–13.

Craig, W. M., & Pepler, D. J. (2007). Understanding bullying: From research to practice. *Canadian Psychology, 48*, 86–93.

Cranston, S., & Keller, S. (2013). Increasing the "meaning quotient" of work. *McKinsey Quarterly, 1*, 48–59.

Credé, M., Tynan, M. C., & Harms, P. D. (2016). Much ado about grit: A meta-analytic synthesis of the grit literature. *Journal of Personality and Social Psychology*. Advance online publication. http://dx.doi.org/10.1037/pspp0000102

Creswell, J. W., & Poth, C. N. (2018). *Qualitative inquiry and research design: Choosing among five approaches* (4th ed.). Thousand Oaks, CA: Sage.

Crooks, T. (1988). The impact of classroom evaluation practices on students. *Review of Educational Research, 58*, 438–481.

Cross, J. R., Bugaj, S. J., & Mammadov, S. (2016). Accepting a scholarly identity: Gifted students, academic crowd membership, and identification with school. *Journal for Education of the Gifted, 39*, 23–48.

Crossley, C. D., Cooper, C. D., & Wernsing, T. S. (2013). Making things happen through challenging goals: Leader proactivity, trust, and business-unit performance. *Journal of Applied Psychology, 98*, 540–549.

Crowne, K. A. (2013). An empirical analysis of three intelligences. *Canadian Journal of Behavioural Science / Revue canadienne des sciences du comportement, 45*, 105–114.

Crystal, D., Killen, M., & Ruck, M. (2010). Fair treatment by authorities is related to children's and adolescents' evaluations of interracial exclusion. *Applied Developmental Science, 14*, 125–136.

Csikszentmihalyi, M. (1990). *Flow*. New York: Harper and Row.

Csikszentmihalyi, M. (1996). *Creativity: Flow and the psychology of discovery and invention*. New York: Harper Collins.

Csikszentmihalyi, M. (1999). If we are so rich, why aren't we happy? *American Psychologist, 54*, 821–827.

Cuban, L. (1982). Persistence of the inevitable: the teacher-centered classroom. *Education & Urban Society, 15*, 26–41.

Cuban, L. (1993). *How teachers taught: Constancy and change in American classrooms: 1890–1990* (2nd ed.). New York: Teachers College Press.

Cuban, L. (2004). Assessing the 20-year impact of multiple intelligences on schooling. *Teachers College Record, 106*(1), 140–146.

Cuevas, R., García-López, L. M., & Serra-Olivares, J. (2016). Sport education model and self-determination theory: An intervention in secondary school children. *Kinesiology, 48*, 30–38.

Cunningham, C. E., Mapp, C., Rimas, H. R., Cunningham, L. Mielko, S. M., & Vaillancourt, T. (2016). What limits the effectiveness of anti-bullying programs? A thematic analysis of the perspective of students. *Psychology of Violence, 6*, 596–606.

Cunningham, C. E., Rimas, H., Mielko, S., Mapp, C., Cunningham, L., Buchanan, D., Vaillancourt, T., Chen, Y., Deal, K., & Marcus, M. (2016). What limits the effectiveness of antibullying programs? A thematic analysis of the perspective of teachers. *Journal of School Violence, 15*, 460–482.

Cuéllar, J. M., & Lanman, T. H. (2017). "Text neck": an epidemic of the modern era of cell phones? *The Spine Journal, 17*, 901–902.

D'Amico, D. (2017). High school students crack the code at Stockton competition. *Education*. Retrieved from http://www.pressofatlanticcity.com/education/high-school-students-crack-the-code-at-stockton-competition/article_e47ce35a-46de-57f3–94ad-4d688305b087.html

Dake, J. A., Price, J. H., & Telljohann, S. K. (2003). The nature and extent of bullying at school. *Journal of School Health, 73*, 173–180.

Dalland, C. P., & Klette, K. (2016). Individual teaching methods: Work plans as a tool for promoting self-regulated learning in lower secondary classrooms? *Education Inquiry, 7*, 381–404.

Dalton, J. D. (2013). Mobility and student achievement in high poverty schools. *Electronic Theses and Dissertations*. Paper 1159. Retrieved from http://dc.etsu.edu/etd/1159

Daniel, B., Shabani, D. B., & Lam, W. Y. (2013). A review of comparison studies in applied behavior analysis. *Behavioral Interventions, 28*, 158–183.

Danielsson, M., & Bengtsson, H. (2016). Global self-esteem and the processing of positive information about the self. *Personality and Individual Differences, 99*, 325–330.

Darling-Hammond, L. (2012). Value-added teacher evaluation: The harm behind the hype. *Education Week, 31*(24), 32.

Darling-Hammond, L., & Baratz-Snowden, J. (Eds.). (2005). *A good teacher in every classroom: Preparing the highly qualified teachers our children deserve*. San Francisco: Jossey-Bass/Wiley.

Darling-Hammond, L., Amrein-Beardsley, A., Haertel, E., & Rothstein, J. (2012). Evaluating teacher evaluation. *Phi Delta Kappan, 93*, 8–15.

Daugherty, M. (2015). 21 top presentation tools for teachers. *More Than a Tech*. Retrieved from https://morethanatech.com/2015/07/21/21-top-presentation-tools-for-teachers/

Davidse, N., de Jong, M., Bus, A., Huijbregts, S., & Swaab, H. (2011). Cognitive and environmental predictors of early literacy skills. *Reading and Writing, 24*(4), 395–412.

Davidson, C. A. (2012). *Now you see it: How the brain science of attention will transform the way we live, work, and learn*. New York: Penguin.

Davidson, J., & Sternberg, R. (Eds.). (2003). *The psychology of problem solving*. Cambridge: Cambridge University.

Dawes, M., & Xie, H. (2017). The trajectory of popularity goal during the transition to middle school. *Journal of Early Adolescence, 37*, 852–883.

Day, J. K., Snapp, S. D., & Russell, S. T. (2016). Supportive, not punitive, practices reduce homophobic bullying and improve school connectedness. *Psychology of Sexual Orientation and Gender Diversity, 3*, 416–425.

De Castella, K., Byrne, D., & Covington, M. (2013). Unmotivated or motivated to fail? A cross-cultural study of achievement motivation, fear of failure, and student disengagement. *Journal of Educational Psychology, 105*, 861–880.

de Jong, N., Verstegen, D. M., & Tan, F. E. (2013). Comparison of classroom and online asynchronous problem-based learning for students undertaking statistics training as part of a public health masters degree. *Advances in Health Sciences Education, 18*, 245–264.

de Posada, C. V., & Vargas-Trujillo, E. (2015). Moral reasoning and personal behavior: A meta-analytical review. *Review of General Psychology, 19*, 408–424.

Deci, E., & Ryan, R. (2008). Facilitating optimal motivation and psychological well-being across life's domains. *Canadian Psychology, 49*, 14–23.

Deci, E., & Ryan, R. (Eds.). (2002). *Handbook of self-determination research*. Rochester, NY: University of Rochester Press.

Deddeh, H., Main, E., & Fulkerson, S. (2010). Eight steps to meaningful grading. *Phi Delta Kappan, 91*, 53–58.

Dee, T. S., & Penner, E. K. (2017). The causal effects of cultural relevance: Evidence from an ethnic studies curriculum. *American Educational Research, 2017, 54*, 127–166.

Dees, L., Moore, E., & Hoggan, C. (2016). Reflective practice and North Carolina's developmental reading and English redesign efforts. *NADE Digest, 9*, 8–15.

Dekker, S., Krabbendam, L., Lee, N. C., Boschloo, A., de Groot, R., & Jolles, J. (2013). Sex differences in goal orientation in adolescents aged 10–19: The older boys adopt work-avoidant goals twice as often as girls. *Learning and Individual Differences, 26*, 196–200.

Delazer, M., Ischebeck, A., Domahs, F., Zamarian, L., Koppelstaetter, F., Siednetoph, C., . . . Felber, S. (2005). Learning by strategies and learning by drill: Evidence from an fMRI study. *NeuroImage, 25*, 838–849.

Delisle, J. R. (2015). Differentiation doesn't work. *Education Week.* http://www.edweek.org/ew/articles/2015/01/07/differentiation-doesnt-work.html

Deming, D. J. (2015). *The growing importance of social skills in the labor market.* Harvard University. Retrieved from https://scholar.harvard.edu/files/ddeming/files/deming_socialskills_august2015.pdf

Denig, S. J. (2003, April). *A proposed relationship between multiple intelligences and learning styles.* Paper presented at the annual meeting of the American Educational Research Association, Chicago.

Denworth, L. (2013). Brain-changing games. *Scientific American Mind, 23*(6), 28–35.

Depaepe, F., & König, J. (2018). General pedagogical knowledge, self-efficacy and instructional practice: Disentangling their relationship in pre-service teacher education. *Teaching and Teacher Education, 69*, 177–190.

Dermotte, E., & Pomati, M. (2016). Good parenting practices: How important are poverty, education, and time pressure? *Sociology, 50*, 125–142.

DeSteno, D., Gross, J. J., & Kubzansky, L. (2013). Affective science and health: The importance of emotion and emotion regulation. *Health Psychology, 32*, 474–486.

Devaney, J. (2018). Former NYPD boss Bratton: Arming teachers 'height of lunacy.' *Newsmax.com.* Retrieved from https://www.newsmax.com/us/nypd-bill-bratton-arm-teachers-lunacy/2018/02/22/id/844946/?ns_mail_uid=97466633&ns_mail_job=1780379_02232018&s=al&dkt_nbr=010104n2pztb

Devine, R. T., & Hughes, C. (2013). Silent films and strange stories: Theory of mind, gender, and social experiences in middle childhood. *Child Development, 84*, 989–1003.

Dewar, D. L., Lubans, D. R., Morgan, P. J., & Plotnikoff, R. C. (2013). Development and evaluation of social cognitive measures related to adolescent physical activity. *Journal of Physical Activity and Health, 10*, 544–555.

DeWitt, P. (2015). 3 reasons why high-stakes testing matters. *Education Week.* Retrieved from http://blogs.edweek.org/edweek/finding_common_ground/2014/12/3_reasons_why_high_stakes_testing_matters.html

DeWitt, P. (2016). Why Ability Grouping Doesn't Work. *Education Week.* Retrieved from http://blogs.edweek.org/edweek/finding_common_ground/2016/02/why_ability_grouping_doesnt_work.html

Deyhle, D. (1987). Learning failure: Tests as gatekeepers and the culturally different child. In H. Trueba (Ed.), *Success or failure?* (pp. 85–108). Cambridge, MA: Newbury House.

Dhaem, J. (2012). Responding to minor misbehavior through verbal and nonverbal responses. *Beyond Behavior, 21*, 29–34.

Diamond, J. B., & Huguley, J. P. (2014). Testing the oppositional culture explanation in desegregated schools: The impact of racial differences in academic orientations on school performance. *Social Forces, 93*, 747–777.

Diaz-Rico, L. (2013). *Strategies for teaching English learners* (3rd ed.). Boston: Pearson.

Diaz-Rico, L. (2014). *Crosscultural, language, & academic development handbook* (5th ed.). Boston: Pearson.

Dicke, T., Elling, J., Schmeck, A., & Leutner, D. (2015). Reducing reality shock: The effects of classroom management skills training on beginning teachers. *Teachers and Teacher Education, 48*, 1–12.

Dickerson, K. (2015). Scientists tried to redo 38 climate change-denying studies and it didn't go very well. *Business Insider.* Retrieved from http://www.businessinsider.com/global-warming-denier-studies-not-replicable-2015–9

DiDonato, M, & Berenbaum, S. (2013). Predictors and consequences of gender typicality: The mediating role of communality. *Archives of Sexual Behavior, 42*, 429–436.

DiMartino, J., & Castaneda, A. (2007). Assessing applied skills. *Educational Leadership, 64*, 38–42.

DiSalvo, D. (2011). *What makes your brain happy & why you should do the opposite.* Amherst, NY: Prometheus.

Dishion, T. J. (2016). From dynamics to function: Negative reinforcement as an amplifying mechanism. *Assessment, 23*, 518–523.

Dobbie, W., & Fryer, R. G., Jr. (2011). *Exam high schools and academic achievement: Evidence from New York City.* National Bureau of Economic Research Working Paper Series, No. 17286.

Donaldson, C.D., Handren, L.M. & Crano, W.D. (2016). The enduring impact of parents' monitoring, warmth, expectancies, and alcohol use on their children's future binge drinking and arrests: a longitudinal analysis. *Prevention Science, 17*, 606–614.

Donoghue, C., & Raia-Hawrylak, A. (2016). Moving beyond the emphasis on bullying: A generalized approach to peer aggression in high school. *Children and Schools, 38*, 30–39.

Donovan, M. S., & Bransford, J. D. (2005). Introduction. In M. S. Donovan & J. D. Bransford (Eds.), *How students learn: History, mathematics, and science in the classroom* (pp. 1–26). Washington, DC: National Academies Press.

Doty, J., Gower, A., Rudi, J., McMorris, B., & Borowsky, I. (2017). Patterns of bullying and sexual harassment: Connections with parents and teachers as direct protective factors. *Journal of Youth and Adolescence, 46*, 2289–2304.

Dougherty, D., & Sharkey, J. (2017). Reconnecting youth: Promoting emotional competence and social support to improve academic achievement. *Children and Youth Services Review, 74*, 28–34.

Dougherty, J. L., Custer, R. L., & Dixon, R. A. (2012). Mapping concepts for learning and assessment. *Technology & Engineering Teacher, 71*, 10–14.

Douthat, R. (2017). Resist the Internet. *The New York Times.* Retrieved from https://www.nytimes.com/2017/03/11/opinion/sunday/resist-the-internet.html?_r=0

Dover, A. G., Schultz, B. D., Smith, K., & Duggan, T. J. (2015a). Who's preparing our candidates? edTPA, localized knowledge, and the outsourcing of teacher evaluation. *Teachers College Record.* Retrieved from http://www.tcrecord.org/Content.asp?ContentId=17914

Dover, A. G., Shultz, B. D., Smith, K., & Duggan, T. J. (2015b). Embracing the controversy: edTPA, corporate influence, and the cooptation of teacher education. *Teachers College Record.* Retrieved from http://www.tcrecord.org/Content.asp?ContentID=18109

Downey, M. (2016). What teens resent: Classrooms controlled by students rather than teachers. *The Atlanta Journal Constitution.* Retrieved from http://getschooled.blog.myajc.com/2016/06/02/what-teens-resent-classrooms-controlled-by-students-rather-than-teachers/

Doyle, W. (2006). Ecological approaches to classroom management. In C. M. Evertson & C. S. Weinstein (Eds.), *Handbook of classroom management: Research, practice, and contemporary issues* (pp. 97–125). Mahwah, NJ: Erlbaum.

Droe, K. L. (2013). Effect of verbal praise on achievement goal orientation, motivation, and performance attribution. *Journal of Music Teacher Education, 23*, 63–78.

Dubinsky, J. M., Roehrig, G., & Varma, S. (2013). Infusing neuroscience into teacher professional development. *Educational Researcher, 42*, 317–329.

Duckworth, A. (2016). *Grit: The power of passion and perseverance.* New York: Scribner.

Duckworth, A. L., Peterson, C., Matthews, M. D., & Kelly, D. R. (2007). Grit: Perseverance and passion for long term goals. *Journal of Personality and Social Psychology*, 92, 1087–1101.

Duckworth, A. L., White, R. E., Matteucci, A. J., Shearer, A., & Gross, J. J. (2016). A stitch in time: Strategic self-control in high school and college students. *Journal of Educational Psychology*, 108, 329–341.

Duke, N., K., Cervetti, G. N., & Wise, C. N. (2016). The Teacher and the Classroom. *Journal of Education*, 196, 35–43.

Duranton, C., Bedossa, T., & Gaunet, F. (2016). When facing an unfamiliar person, pet dogs present social referencing based on their owners' direction of movement alone, *Animal Behaviour*, 113, 147–156.

Durmaz, M., & Akkus, R. (2016). Mathematics anxiety, motivation and the basic psychological needs from the perspective of self-determination theory. *Education and Science*, 41, 111–127.

Dweck, C. (1975). The role of expectations and attributions in the alleviation of learned helplessness. *Journal of Personality and Social Psychology*, 31, 674–685.

Dweck, C. S. (2008). Can personality be changed? The role of beliefs in personality and change. *Current Directions in Psychological Science*, 17, 391–394. doi:10.1111/j.1467–8721.2008.00612.x

Dweck, C. S. (2016). *Mindset: The new psychology of success*. New York: Random House.

Early, D. M., Rogge, R. D., & Deci, E. L. (2014). Engagement, alignment, and rigor as vital signs of high-quality instruction: A classroom visit protocol for instructional improvement and research. *The High School Journal*, 97, 219–239.

eBiz. (2017). *Top 15 most popular search engines*. Retrieved from http://www.ebizmba.com/articles/search-engines

Eccles, J. S., Wigfield, A., & Schiefele, U. (1998). Motivation to succeed. In W. Damon (Series Ed.) & N. Eisenberg (Vol. Ed.), *Handbook of child psychology: Vol. 3. Social, emotional, and personality development* (5th ed., pp. 1017–1095). New York: Wiley.

Echevarria, J., & Graves, A. (2015). *Sheltered content instruction: Teaching English learners with diverse abilities* (5th ed.). Boston: Pearson.

Echevarria, J., Vogt, M., & Short, D. J. (2018a). *Making content comprehensible for elementary English learners: The SIOP model* (3rd ed.). Boston: Pearson.

Echevarria, J., Vogt, M., & Short, D. J. (2018b). *Making content comprehensible for secondary English learners: The SIOP model* (3rd ed.). Boston: Pearson.

Ediger, M. (2016). Quality parent teacher conferences. *College Student Journal*, 50, 614–616.

Edsall, T. (2017). The increasing significance of the decline of men. *The New York Times*. Retrieved from https://www.nytimes.com/2017/03/16/opinion/the-increasing-significance-of-the-decline-of-men.html

EdSurge. (2017). *Teaching kids to code*. Retrieved from https://www.edsurge.com/research/guides/teaching-kids-to-code#

Educational Testing Service. (2018a). *About the Praxis® Tests*. Retrieved from https://www.ets.org/praxis/about. Used with permission from Educational Testing Service.

Educational Testing Service (2018b). *Praxis® Subject Assessments Test Content and Structure*. Retrieved from https://www.ets.org/praxis/about/subject/content/

Educational Testing Service. (2018c). *State requirements*. Retrieved from https://www.ets.org/praxis/states/

Edwards, T., Catling, J. C., & Parry, E. (2016). Identifying predictors of resilience in students. *Psychology Teaching Review*, 22, 26–34.

Eggen, P., & Kauchak, D. (2012). *Strategies and models for teachers: Teaching content and thinking skills* (6th ed.). Boston: Pearson.

Eggen, P., & Kauchak, D. (2013, April). *Educational leaders' conceptions of effective instruction: A nine-year study*. Paper presented at the annual meeting of the American Educational Research Association, San Francisco.

Egula, J. X. (2017). Discrimination and assimilation at school. *Journal of Public Economics*, 156, 48–58.

Eisenstein, J., O'Connor, B., Smith, N., & Xing, E. (2011). *A latent variable model for geographical lexical variation*. Paper presented at the Linguistic Society of America, Pittsburgh.

Eklund, K., Tanner, N., Stoll, K., & Anway, L. (2015). Identifying emotional and behavioral risk among gifted and nongifted children: a multi-gate, multi-informant approach. *School Psychology Quarterly 30*, 197–211.

El, R. P., Tillema, H., & van Koppen, S. W. M. (2012). Effects of formative feedback on intrinsic motivation: Examining ethnic differences. *Learning and Individual Differences*, 22, 449–454.

Elhai, J. D., Hall, B. J., & Erwin, M. C. (2018). Emotion regulation's relationships with depression, anxiety, and stress do to imagined smartphone and social media loss. *Psychiatry Research*, 261, 28–34.

Elliott, A. (2013). Girl in the shadows: Dasani's homeless life. *New York Times*. Retrieved from http://www.nytimes.com/projects/2013/invisible-child/#/?chapt=1

Ellis, J., Fitzsimmons, S., & Small-McGinley, J. (2010). Encouraging the discouraged: Students' views for elementary classrooms. In G. S. Goodman (Ed.), *Educational psychology reader: The art and science of how people learn* (pp. 251–272). New York: Peter Lang.

Emdin, C. A., Odutayo, A., Wong, C. X., Tran, J., Hsiao, A. J., & Hunn, B. H. M. (2016). Meta-analysis of anxiety as a risk factor for cardiovascular disease *The American Journal of Cardiology*, 118, 511–519.

Emery, A., Heath, N., & Mills, D. (2016). Basic psychological need satisfaction, emotion dysregulation, and non-suicidal self-injury engagement in young adults: An application of Self-Determination theory. *Journal of Youth and Adolescence*, 45, 612–623.

Emmer, E. T., & Evertson, C. M. (2017). *Classroom management for middle and high school teachers* (10th ed.). Boston: Pearson.

Engber, D. (2016). Is "Grit" Really the Key to Success? *Slate*. Retrieved from http://www.slate.com/articles/health_and_science/cover_story/2016/05/angela_duckworth_says_grit_is_the_key_to_success_in_work_and_life_is_this.html

Engel, M. (2013). Problematic preferences: A mixed method examination of principals' preferences for teacher characteristics in Chicago. *Educational Administration Quarterly*, 49, 52–91.

Englander, F., Terregrossa, R. A., & Wang, Z. (2017). Are their different patterns of learning styles among science majors? *International Journal of Education Research*, 12, 15–33.

Englert, C., & Bertrams, A. (2013). The role of self-control strength in the development of state anxiety in test situations. *Psychological Reports*, 112, 976–991.

Forte, E. (2010). Examining the assumptions underlying the NCLB federal accountability policy on school improvement. *Journal of Educational Psychology*, 102, 76–88.

English, A. R. (2016). Dialogic teaching and moral learning: Self-critique, narrativity, community and "blind spots." *Journal of Philosophy of Education*, 50, 150–176.

Erickson, K., Voss, M., Prakash, R., Basak, C., Szabo, A., Chaddock, L., . . . Kramer, A. (2011). Exercise training increases the size of hippocampus and improves memory. *Neuroscience*, 108, 3017–3022.

Ericsson, K. A., & Pool, R. (2016). *Peak: Secrets from the new science of expertise*. New York: Houghton Mifflin Harcourt.

Ericsson, K. A., Krampe, R., & Tesch-Romer, C. (1993). The role of deliberate practice in the acquisition of expert performance. *Psychological Review*, 100, 363–406.

Erikson, E. (1968). *Identity: Youth and crisis*. New York: Norton.

Erikson, E. (1980). *Identity and the life cycle* (2nd ed.). New York: Norton.

Eriksson, T., Adawi, T., & Stöhr, C. (2017). "Time is the bottleneck": A qualitative study exploring why learners drop out of MOOCS. *Journal of Computing in Higher Education*, 29, 133–146.

Ertem, I. S. (2013). The influence of personalization of online texts on elementary school students' reading comprehension and attitudes toward reading. *International Journal of Progressive Education*, 9, 218–228.

Eskreis-Winkler, L., Shulman, E. P., Young, V., Tsukayama, E., Brunwasser, S. M., & Duckworth, A. L. (2016). Using wise interventions to motivate deliberate practice. *Journal of Personality and Social Psychology*, 111, 728–744.

Essary, J. N. (2012). Teaching strategies: Teaching beyond the basics—young children participate in a cognitive apprenticeship. *Childhood Education*, 88, 331–334.

Evans, C., Kirby, U., & Fabrigar, L. (2003). Approaches to learning, need for cognition, and strategic flexibility among university students. *The British Journal of Educational Psychology, 73*, 507–528.

Evertson, C.M., & Emmer, E. T. (2017). *Classroom management for elementary teachers* (10th ed.). Boston: Pearson.

Ewing, W., M., Martínez, D. E., & Rumbaut, R. G. (2015). The criminalization of immigration in the United States. *American Immigration Council.* Retrieved from https://www.americanimmigrationcouncil.org/research/criminalization-immigration-united-states

Exline, R. (1962). Need affiliation and initial communication behavior in problem solving groups characterized by low interpersonal visibility. *Psychological Reports, 10*, 405–411.

FairTest. (2008). *SAT I: A faulty instrument for predicting college success.* FairTest: The National Center for Fair and Open Testing. Retrieved from http://www.fairtest.org

FairTest. (2014). FairTest questions the College Board on plans for "New" SAT. Retrieved from http://www.fairtest.org/fairtest-questions-college-board-plans-new-sat

FairTest. (2017). *950+ accredited colleges and universities that do not use ACT/SAT scores to admit substantial numbers of students into bachelor-degree programs.* Retrieved from http://fairtest.org/university/optional

Fanselow, M. S., & Sterlace, S. R. (2014). Pavlovian fear conditioning: Function, cause, and treatment. In F. K. McSweeney & E. S. Murphy (Eds.), *The Wiley Blackwell handbook of operant and classical conditioning* (pp. 117–142). Malden, MA: John Wiley & Sons.

Farkas, R. (2003). Effects of traditional versus learning-styles instructional methods on middle school students. *Journal of Educational Research, 97*(1), 42–51.

Federal Safety Net. (2017). U.S. poverty statistics. *U.S. Census Bureau.* Retrieved from http://federalsafetynet.com/us-poverty-statistics.html

Feeding America. (2013). *Hunger & poverty statistics.* Retrieved from http://feedingamerica.org/hunger-in-america/hunger-facts/hunger-and-poverty-statistics.aspx

Fein, D., Barton, M., Eigsti, I., Kelly, E. Naigles, L., Schultz, R., . . . Tyson, K. (2013). Optimal outcomes in individuals with a history of autism. *Journal of Child Psychology, 54*(2), 195–205.

Feldman, R. S. (2014). *Development across the life span* (7th ed.). Boston: Pearson.

Feldman, R. S. (2017). *Development across the lifespan* (books a la carte, 8th ed.). Boston: Pearson.

Feldon, D. F. (2007). Cognitive load and classroom teaching: The double-edged sword of automaticity. *Educational Psychologist, 42*, 123–137.

Fernandez, M., Blinder, A., & Chokshi, N. (2018). 10 dead in Santa Fe, Texas, school shooting; suspect used shotgun and revolver. *The New York Times.* https://www.nytimes.com/2018/05/18/us/school-shooting-santa-fe-texas.html

Fernbach, P., & Sloman, S. (2017). Why we believe obvious untruths. *The New York Times.* Retrieved from https://www.nytimes.com/2017/03/03/opinion/sunday/why-we-believe-obvious-untruths.html?ref=opinion&_r=0

Fiala, B., Rhodes, R. E., Blanchard, C., & Anderson, J. (2013). Using social–cognitive constructs to predict preoperative exercise before total joint replacement. *Rehabilitation Psychology, 58*, 137–147.

Fisher, C., Berliner, D., Filby, N., Marliave, R., Cahen, L., & Dishaw, M. (1980). Teaching behaviors, academic learning time, and student achievement: An overview. In C. Denham & A. Lieberman (Eds.), *Time to learn* (pp. 7–32). Washington, DC: National Institute of Education.

Fisher, O., & Oyserman, D. (2017). Assessing interpretations of experienced ease and difficulty as motivational constructs. *Motivation Science, 3*, 133–163.

Fishman, E. J., & Husman, J. (2017). Extending attribution theory: Considering students' perceived control of the attribution process. *Journal of Educational Psychology, 109*, 559–573.

Flavell, J., Miller, P., & Miller, S. (2002). *Cognitive development* (4th ed.). Upper Saddle River, NJ: Prentice Hall.

Fleming, P. J., Villa-Torres, L., Taboada, A., Richards, C., & Barrington, C. (2017). Marginalisation, discrimination, and the health of Latino immigrant day labourers in a central North Carolina community. *Health and Social Care in the Community, 25*, 527–537.

Flores, A. R., Herman, J. L., Gates, G. J., & Brown, T. N. T. (2016). How many adults identify as transgender in the United States. *The Williams Institute.* Retrieved from https://williamsinstitute.law.ucla.edu/wp-content/uploads/How-Many-Adults-Identify-as-Transgender-in-the-United-States.pdf

Flowerday, T., & Shell, D. F. (2015). Disentangling the effects of interest and choice on learning, engagement, and attitude. *Learning and Individual Differences, 40*, 134–140.

Flynn, J. (1999). Searching for justice: The discovery of IQ gains over time. *American Psychologist, 54*, 5–20.

Fogarty, M. (2011). *Grammar girl presents the ultimate writing guide for students.* New York: Henry Holt & Company.

Fond-Harmant, L., & Gavrilă-Ardelean, M. (2016). The contribution of the human development theory for the education and mental health of the child. *Journal Plus Education, 14*, 174–181.

Fong, C. J., Davis, C. W., Kim, Y., Kim, Y. W., Marriott, L., & Kim, S-Y. (2017). Psychosocial factors and community college student success: A meta-analytic investigation. *Review of Educational Research, 87*, 388–424.

Ford, C., McNally, D., & Ford, K. (2017). Using design-based research in higher education innovation. *Online Learning, 21*, 50–67.

Ford, P. (2015). Flipping a math content course for pre-service elementary school teachers. *PRIMUS, 25*, 369–380.

Forte, E. (2010). Examining the assumptions underlying the NCLB federal accountability policy on school improvement. *Journal of Educational Psychology, 102*, 76–88.

Fougnie, D., Cormiea, S. M., Kanabar, A., & Alvarez, G. A. (2016). Strategic trade-offs between quantity and quality in working memory. *Journal of Experimental Psychology: Human Perception and Performance, 42*, 1231–1240.

Friedman, I. A. (2006). Classroom management and teacher stress and burnout. In C. M. Evertson & C. S. Weinstein (Eds.), *Handbook of classroom management: Research, practice, and contemporary issues* (pp. 925–944). Mahwah, NJ: Erlbaum.

Friend, M. (2018). *Special education: Contemporary perspectives for school professionals* (5th ed.). Boston: Pearson.

Friesen, N. (2011). The lecture as a transmedial pedagogical form: A historical analysis. *Educational Researcher, 40*, 95–102.

Fryar, C. D., Gu, Q., Ogden, C. L., & Flegal, K. M. (2016). Anthropometric reference data for children and adults: United States, 2011–2014. *National Center for Health Statistics. Vital Health Stat 3*(39). Retrieved from https://www.cdc.gov/nchs/data/series/sr_03/sr03_039.pdf

Frye, J. (2018). From politics to policy: Turning the corner on sexual harassment. *Center for American Progress.* Retrieved from https://www.americanprogress.org/issues/women/news/2018/01/31/445669/politics-policy-turning-corner-sexual-harassment/

Fuhs, M. W., Hornburg, C. B., & McNeil, N. M. (2016). Specific early number skills mediate the association between executive functioning skills and mathematics achievement. *Developmental Psychology, 52*, 1217–1235.

Fukuzawa, S., Boyd, C., & Cahn, J. (2017). Student motivation in response to problem-based learning. *Collected Essays on Learning & Teaching, 10*, 175–187.

Furukawa, E., Alsop, B., Sowerby, P., Jensen, S., & Tripp, G. (2017). Evidence for increased behavioral control by punishment in children with attention-deficit hyperactivity disorder. *Journal of Child Psychology & Psychiatry, 58*, 248–257.

Gage, N. A., Larson, A., Sugai, G., & Chafouleas, S. M. (2016). Student perceptions of school climate as predictors of office discipline referrals. *American Educational Research Journal, 53*, 492–515.

Gagné, N., & Parks, S. (2013). Cooperative learning tasks in a grade 6 intensive ESL class: Role of scaffolding. *Language Teaching Research, 17*, 188–209.

Gagnon, J., McDuff, P., Daelman, S., & Fourmier, S. (2015). Is hostile attributional bias associated with negative urgency and impulsive behaviors? A social-cognitive conceptualization of impulsivity. *Personality and Individual Differences, 72*, 18–23.

Gall, M., D., Gall, J. P., & Borg, W. R. (2015). *Applying educational research: How to read, do, and use research to solve problems of practice* (7th ed.). Boston: Pearson.

Gamo, S., Sander, E., & Richard, J. (2010). Transfer of strategy use by semantic recoding in arithmetic problem solving. *Learning and Instruction, 20*, 400–410.

Ganotice, F. A., Datu, J. A. D., & King, R. B. (2016). Which emotional profiles exhibit the best learning outcomes? A person-centered analysis of students' academic emotions. *School Psychology International, 37*, 498–518.

García, E. (2015). Inequalities at the starting gate: Cognitive and noncognitive skills gaps between 2010–2011 kindergarten classmates. Retrieved from http://www.epi.org/publication/inequalities-at-thestarting-gate-cognitive-and-noncognitive-gaps-in-the-2010–2011-kindergarten-class/

Garcia-Navarro, L. (2017). Sexual harassment: Have we reached a cultural turning point? NPR. Retrieved from https://www.npr.org/2017/11/19/564987076/special-report-a-cultural-turning-point-on-sexual-harassment

Gardner, H. (1983). *Frames of mind: The theory of multiple intelligences.* New York: Basic Books.

Gardner, H. (1995). Reflections on multiple intelligences: Myths and messages. *Phi Delta Kappan, 77*, 200–209.

Gardner, H., & Hatch, T. (1989). Multiple intelligences go to school. *Educational Researcher, 18*(8), 4–10.

Gardner, H., & Moran, S. (2006). The science of multiple intelligences theory: A response to Lynn Waterhouse. *Educational Psychologist, 41*(4), 227–232.

Garren, M. V., Sexauer, S. B., & Page, T. L. (2013). Effect of circadian phase on memory acquisition and recall: Operant conditioning vs. classical conditioning. *PLoS ONE, 8*, 1–8. doi:10.1371/journal.pone.0058693

Geno, J. A. (2014). Using tests to improve student achievement. *Techniques: Connecting Education and Careers, 89*, 50–53.

Gentile, D. (2011). The multiple dimensions of video game effects. *Child Development Perspectives, 5*(2), 75–81.

Gentile, J. (1996). Setbacks in the advancement of learning. *Educational Researcher, 25*, 37–39.

Geraci, J., Palmerini, M., Cirillo, P., & McDougald, V. (2017). *What teens want from their schools: A national survey of high school student engagement.* Thomas B. Fordham Institute. Retrieved from www.edexcellence.net/publications/what-teens-want-from-their-schools

Gershenson, S., Holt, S. B., & Papageorge, N. W. (2016). Who believes in me? The effect of student-teacher demographic match on teacher expectations. *Economics of Education Review, 52*, 209–224.

Gershoff, E. T., & Grogan-Kaylor, A. (2016). Spanking and child outcomes: Old controversies and new meta-analyses. *Journal of Family Psychology, 30*, 453–469. http://dx.doi.org/10.1037/fam0000191

Ghahraman, V., & Tamimy, M. (2017). The role of culture in cooperative learning. *International Journal of Language Studies, 11*, 89–120.

Ghitis, F. (2017). A turning point in war on sexual harassment. CNN. Retrieved from http://www.cnn.com/2017/10/26/opinions/turning-point-in-war-on-sexual-harassment-ghitis/index.html

Gibb, Z. G., & Devereux, P. G. (2016). Missing link: Exploring repetition and intentionality of distress in cyberbullying behaviors within a college population. *Translational Issues in Psychological Science, 2*, 313–322.

Gibbs, J. C. (2014). *Moral development and reality: Beyond the theories of Kohlberg, Hoffman, and Haidt* (3rd ed.). New York: Oxford University Press.

Gieri, M. J., Bulut, O., Guo, Q., & Zhang, X. (2017). Developing, analyzing, and using distractors for multiple-choice tests in education: A comprehensive review. *Review of Educational Research, 87*, 1082–1116.

Gillies, R. (2014). Cooperative learning: Developments in research. *International Journal of Educational Psychology, 3*(2), 125–140.

Gilligan, C. (1977). In a different voice: Women's conceptions of the self and of morality. *Harvard Educational Review, 47*, 481–517.

Gilligan, C. (1982). *In a different voice: Psychological theory and women's development.* Cambridge, MA: Harvard University Press.

Gilligan, C. (1998). *Minding women: Reshaping the education realm.* Cambridge, MA: Harvard University Press.

Gilligan, C. (2008). Moral orientation and moral development. In A. Bailey & C. J. Cuomo (Eds.), *The feminist philosophy reader* (pp. 467–477). Boston: McGraw-Hill.

Gilligan, C., & Attanucci, J. (1988). Two moral orientations: Gender differences and similarities. *Merrill-Palmer Quarterly, 34*, 223–237.

Gini, G., & Pozzoli, T. (2013). Bullied children and psychosomatic problems: A meta-analysis. *Pediatrics, 132*, 720–730.

Gläscher, J., Rudrauf, D., Colom, R., Paul, L., Tranel, D., Damasio, H., & Adolphs, R. (2010). Distributed neural system for general intelligence revealed by lesion mapping. *Proceedings of the National Academy of Sciences of the United States of America, 107*, 4705–4709.

Gladwell, M. (2008). *Outliers: The story of success.* New York: Little, Brown, and Company.

Gloria, C. T., & Steinhardt, M. A. (2016). Relationships among positive emotions, coping, resilience and mental health. *Stress & Health, 32*, 145–156.

Glover, S., & Dixon, P. (2013). Context and vision effects on real and imagined actions: Support for the common representation hypothesis of motor imagery. *Journal of Experimental Psychology: Human Perception and Performance.* doi:10.1037/a0031276

Gluszek, A., & Dovidio, J. (2010). The way they speak: A social psychological perspective on the stigma of nonnative accents in communication. *Personality and Social Psychology Review, 14*(2), 214–237.

Gold, H. (2018). The persistence of Parkland: How the Florida shooting stayed in the media spotlight. *CNN Media.* Retrieved from http://money.cnn.com/2018/02/22/media/parkland-florida-shooting-media-coverage/index.html

Goldhaber, D. (2016). In schools, teacher quality matters most. *Education Next, 16*, 56–62.

Goldhaber, D. Lavery, L., & Theobald, R. (2015). Uneven playing field? Assessing the teacher quality gap between advantaged and disadvantaged students. *Educational Researcher, 44*, 293–307.

Goldsmith, W. (2013). Enhancing classroom conversation for all students. *Phi Delta Kappan, 94*, 48–53.

Göllner, R., Damian, R. I., Rose, N., Spengler, M., Trautwein, U., Nagengast, B., & Roberts, B. W. (2017). Is doing your homework associated with becoming more conscientious?, *Journal of Research in Personality.* doi: http://dx.doi.org/10.1016/j.jrp.2017.08.007

Goleman, D. (1995). *Emotional intelligence.* New York: Bantam.

Gollnick, D., & Chinn, P. (2017). *Multicultural education in a pluralistic society* (10th ed.). Boston: Pearson.

Goman, C. K. (2017). Body language tells your team how you really feel: Be careful! *Personal Excellence Essentials, 22*, 10–11.

Goncalves, T., Niemivirta, M., & Semos, M. S. (2017). Identification of students' multiple achievement and social goal profiles and analysis of their stability and adaptability. *Learning and Individual Differences, 54*, 149–159.

Gong, Y., Wu, J., Song, L. J., & Zhang, Z. (2017). Dual tuning in creative processes: Joint contributions of intrinsic and extrinsic motivational orientations. *Journal of Applied Psychology, 102*, 829–844.

González, A., Fernández, M-V., & Paoloni, P-V. (2017). Hope and anxiety in physics class: Exploring their motivational antecedents and influence on metacognition and performance. *Journal of Research in Science Teaching, 54*, 558–585.

Gonzalez, C. M., & Eggen, P. (2017, April). *The impact of frequent assessment and feedback on university students' understanding of educational psychology.* Poster presented at the annual meeting of the American Educational Research Association, San Antonio.

Good, T. L., & Lavigne, A. L. (2018). *Looking in classrooms* (11th ed.). New York: Routledge.

Good, T., & Brophy, J. (2008). *Looking in classrooms* (10th ed.). Boston: Allyn & Bacon.

Goodboy, A. K., Bolkan, S., & Baker, J. P. (2018): Instructor misbehaviors impede students' cognitive learning: testing the causal assumption. *Communication Education.* https://doi.org/10.1080/03634523.2018.1465192

Goodnow, J. (2010). Culture. In M. Bornstein (Ed.), *Handbook of cultural developmental science* (pp. 207–221). New York: Psychology Press.

Goodwin, B. (2014). Curiosity is fleeting, but teachable. *Educational Leadership, 72*, 73–74.

Gootman, E., & Gebeloff, R. (2008). Gifted programs in the city are less diverse. *The New York Times.* Retrieved from http://www.nytimes.com/2008/06/19/nyregion/19gifted.html?pagewanted=all&_r=0

Government Accountability Office. (2016). *EMERGENCY MANAGEMENT: Improved Federal Coordination Could Better Assist K–12 Schools Prepare for Emergencies.* Retrieved from https://www.gao.gov/assets/680/675737.pdf

Gragg, C. I. (1940). Because wisdom can't be told. *Harvard Alumni Bulletin* (October 19), 78–84.

Graham, S. (2010). What educators need to know about bullying behaviors. *Phi Delta Kappan, 92*, 66–69.

Graham, S., & Weiner, B. (1996). Theories and principles of motivation. In D. Berliner & R. Calfee (Eds.), *Handbook of educational psychology* (pp. 63–84). New York: Macmillan.

Grant, L. W. (2006). Persistence and self-efficacy: A key to understanding teacher turnover. *The Delta Kappa Gamma Bulletin, 72*(2), 50–54.

Graziano, P. A., & Hart, K. (2016). Beyond behavior modification: Benefits of social–emotional/self-regulation training for preschoolers with behavior problems. *Journal of School Psychology, 58*, 91–111.

Gredler, M. (2012). Understanding Vygotsky for the classroom: Is it too late? *Educational Psychology Review, 24*, 113–131.

Green, A. M., & Muñoz, M. A. (2016). Predictors of new teacher satisfaction in urban schools. *Journal of School Leadership, 26*, 92–123.

Greenberg, J., Putman, H., & Walsh, K. (2014). *Training our future teachers: Classroom management.* National Council on Teacher Quality. Retrieved from http://www.nctq.org/dmsView/Future_Teachers_Classroom_Management_NCTQ_Report

Gregg, M. T. (2018). The long-term effects of American Indian boarding schools. *Journal of Development Economics, 130*, 17–32.

Gregg, N. (2009). *Adolescents and adults with learning disability and ADHD: Assessment and accommodation.* New York: Guilford.

Gregory, A., Skiba, R. J., & Mediratta, K. (2017). Eliminating disparities in school discipline: A framework for intervention. In M. T. Winn & M. Souto-Manning (Eds.). *Review of Research in Education, 41*, 253–278.

Gregory, A., Skiba, R. J., & Noguera, P. A. (2010). The achievement gap and the discipline gap: Two sides of the same coin. *Educational Researcher, 39*, 59–68.

Gregory, S. E. A., & Jackson, M. C. (2017). Joint attention enhances visual working memory. *Journal of Experimental Psychology: Learning, Memory, and Cognition, 43*, 237–249.

Griffin, A. S., Guillette, L. M., & Healy, S. D. (2015). Cognition and personality: an analysis of an emerging field. *Trends in Ecology & Evolution, 30*, 207–214.

Griffin, R., MacKewn, A., Moser, E., & VanVuren, K. W. (2013). Learning skills and motivation: Correlates to superior academic performance. *Business Education & Accreditation, 5*, 53–65.

Griffiths, M. (2010). Online video gaming: What should educational psychologists know? *Educational Psychology in Practice, 26*(1), 35–40.

Grigorenko, E., Jarvin, L., Diffley, R., Goodyear, J., Shanahan, E., & Sternberg, R. (2009). Are SSATs and GPA enough? A theory-based approach to predicting academic success in secondary school. *Journal of Education Psychology, 101*(4), 964–981.

Grissom, J. A., & Redding, C. (2016). Discretion and disproportionality: Explaining the underrepresentation of high-achieving students of color in gifted programs. *AERA Open, 2*, 1–25.

Gstalter, M. (2018). Teachers protest push for guns in schools with #ArmMeWith movement. *The Hill.* Retrieved from https://www.msn.com/en-us/news/us/teachers-protest-push-for-guns-in-schools-with-supernumberarmmewith-movement/ar-BBJtesU?li=BBmkt5R&ocid=spartandhp

Guan, J., Xiang, P., McBride, R., & Keating, X. D. (2013). Achievement goals, social goals, and students' reported persistence and effort in high school athletic settings. *Journal of Sport Behavior, 36*, 149–170.

Guess, M. N., McCardell, M. J., & Stefanucci, J. K. (2016). Fear similarly alters perceptual estimates of and actions over gaps. *PloS ONE, 11*, 1–19.

Guillot, A., Moschberger, K., & Collet, C. (2013). Coupling movement with imagery as a new perspective for motor imagery practice. *Behavioral and Brain Functions, 9*, 1–8. doi:10.1186/1744-9081-9-8

Hacker, D., Bol, L., Horgan, D., & Rakow, E. (2000). Test prediction and performance in a classroom context. *Journal of Education Psychology, 92*, 160–170.

Hagen, K. (2018). Conspiracy theories and the paranoid style: Do conspiracy theories posit implausibly vast and evil conspiracies? *Social Epistemology, 32*, 24–40.

Hall, G., & Rodríguez, G. (2017). Habituation and conditioning: Salience change in associative learning. *Journal of Experimental Psychology: Animal Learning and Cognition, 43*, 48–61.

Hallahan, D. P., Kaufman, J. M., & Pullen, P. C. (2015). *Exceptional learners: An introduction to special education* (13th ed.). Boston: Pearson.

Halpern, D. (2006). Assessing gender gaps in learning and academic achievement. In P. A. Alexander & P. H. Winne (Eds.), *Handbook of educational psychology* (2nd ed., pp. 635–653). Mahwah, NJ: Erlbaum.

Hamlen, K. (2011). Children's choices and strategies in video games. *Computers in Human Behavior, 27*(1), 532–539.

Hammond, Z. (2015). *Culturally responsive teaching and the brain: Promoting authentic engagement and rigor among culturally and linguistically diverse students.* Thousand Oaks, CA: Corwin.

Handren, L. M., Donaldson, C.D. & Crano, W.D. (2016). Adolescent alcohol use: Protective and predictive parent, peer, and self-related factors. *Prevention Science, 17*, 862–871.

Hanna, J., & McLaughlin, E. C. (2017). North Carolina repeals 'bathroom bill." CNN Politics. Retrieved from https://www.cnn.com/2017/03/30/politics/north-carolina-hb2-agreement/index.html

Hansberry, L. (1959). *A raisin in the sun.* New York: Random House.

Hao, Z., & Cowan, B. W. (2017). The effects of graduation requirements on risky health behaviors of high school students. *American Journal of Health Economics.* https://doi.org/10.1162/ajhe_a_00112

Hardin, J., & Wille, D. (2017). The homeless individual's viewpoint: Causes of homelessness and resources needed to leave the sheltered environment. *Social Work and Social Sciences Review, 19*, 33–48.

Hardman, M. L., Egan, M. W., & Drew, C. J. (2017). *Human exceptionality: School, community, and family* (12th ed.). Boston: Cengage Learning.

Harmon, A. (2017). Climate science meets a stubborn obstacle: Students. *The New York Times.* Retrieved from https://www.nytimes.com/2017/06/04/us/education-climate-change-science-class-students.html

Harris, A. L. (2011). *Kids don't want to fail: Oppositional culture and the black-white achievement gap.* Cambridge, MA: Harvard University Press.

Harris, C. B., Barnier, A. J., & Sutton, J. (2013). Shared encoding and the costs and benefits of collaborative recall. *Journal of Experimental Psychology: Learning, Memory, and Cognition, 39*, 183–195.

Harris, C. M., & Shenghua, Z. (2017). Concept mapping for critical thinking: Efficacy, timing, & type. *Education, 137*, 277–280.

Harris, F., & Curtis, A. (2018). *Healing our divided society: Investing in America fifty years after the Kerner report*. Philadelphia: Temple University Press.

Harris, J. A., & Andrew, B. J. (2017). Time, trials, and extinction. *Journal of Experimental Psychology: Animal Learning and Cognition, 43*, 15–29.

Hart, R., Casserly, M., Uzzell, R., Palacios, M., Corcoran, A., & Spurgeon, L. (2015). *Student Testing in America's Great City Schools: An Inventory and Preliminary Analysis*. Council of the Great City Schools. Retrieved from http://www.cgcs.org/cms/lib/DC00001581/Centricity/Domain/87/Testing%20Report.pdf

Haskill, A., & Corts, D. (2010). Acquiring language. In E. Sandberg & B. Spritz (Eds.), *A clinician's guide to normal cognitive development in childhood* (pp. 23–41). New York: Routledge/Taylor & Francis.

Hattie, J. (2012). *Visible learning for teachers. Maximizing impact on learning*. New York: Routledge.

Hattie, J. A. C., & Timperley, H. (2007). The power of feedback. *Review of Educational Research, 77*, 81–112. doi:10.3102/003465430298487

Hattie, J., & Gan, M. (2011). Instruction based on feedback. In R. E. Mayer & P. A. Alexander (Eds.), *Handbook of research on learning and instruction* (pp. 249–271). New York: Routledge.

Haught-Tromp, C. (2017). The green eggs and ham hypothesis: How constraints facilitate creativity. *Psychology of Aesthetics, Creativity, and the Arts, 11*, 10–17.

Hauser, M. D. (2017). The essential and interrelated components of evidence-based IEPs: A user's guide. *Teaching Exceptional Children, 49*, 420–428.

Hämäläinen, R., De Wever, B., Malin, A., & Cincinnato, S. (2015). Education and working life: VET adults' problem-solving skills in technology-rich environments. *Computers and Education, 88*, 38–47.

He, W., Holton, A., Farkas, G., & Warschauer, M. (2016). The effects of flipped instruction on out-of-class study time, exam performance, and student perceptions. *Learning and Instruction, 45*, 61–71.

Heck, N. C., Mirabito, L. A., LeMaire, K, Livingston, N. A., & Flentje, A. (2017). Omitted data in randomized controleed trials for anxiety and depression: A systematic review of the inclusion of sexual orientation and gender identity. *Journal of Consulting and Clinical Psychology, 85*, 72–76.

Heckman, J. J., & Kautz, T. (2012). Hard evidence on soft skills. *Labour Economics, 19*, 451–464.

Helgeson, V. S. (2017). *Psychology of gender* (5th ed.). New York: Taylor and Francis.

Henderson, N. (2013). Havens of resilience. *Educational Leadership, 71*, 22–27.

Hernandez, I., & Preston, J. L. (2013). Disfluency disrupts the confirmation bias. *Journal of Experimental Social Psychology, 49*, 178–182.

Herold, B. (2015). Why Ed tech is not transforming how teachers teach. *Education Week*. Retrieved from http://www.edweek.org/ew/articles/2015/06/11/why-ed-tech-is-not-transforming-how.html

Herold, B. (2017). The cases(s) against personalized learning. *Education Week*. Retrieved from https://www.edweek.org/ew/articles/2017/11/08/the-cases-against-personalized-learning.html

Hess, F. M., & McShane, M. Q. (2013). Common core in the real world. *Phi Delta Kappan, 95*, 61–66.

Hessels-Schlatter, C., Hessels, M. G. P., Godin, H., Spillmann-Rojas, H. (2017). Fostering self-regulated learning: From clinical to whole class interventions. *Educational & Child Psychology, 34*, 110–125.

Heward, W. L., Alber-Morgan, S. R., & Konrad, M. (2017). *Exceptional children: An introduction to special education* (11th ed.). Boston: Pearson.

Hidi, S. (2001). Interest, reading, and learning: Theoretical and practical considerations. *Educational Psychology Review, 13*, 191–209.

Higgins, S., Kokotsaki, D., & Coe, R. (2011). Toolkit of strategies to improve learning. *The Sutton Trust*. Retrieved from https://www.scribd.com/document/114336010/Sutton-Trust-Spending-the-Pupil-Premium-and-Strategies-to-Improve-Learning-2011

Hill, A., Arford, T., Lubitow, A., & Smollin, L. M. (2012). "I'm ambivalent about it": The dilemmas of PowerPoint. *Teaching Sociology, 40*, 242–256.

Hill, C., & Kearl, H. (2011). *Crossing the line: Sexual harassment at school*. American Association of University Women. Washington, DC. Retrieved from https://secure.edweek.org/media/crossingtheline-11harass.pdf

Hillebrandt, A., & Barclay, L. J. (2017). Comparing integral and incidental emotions: Testing insights from emotions as social information theory and attribution theory. *Journal of Applied Psychology, 102*, 732–752.

Hirsch, E. (2006). *Knowledge deficit: Closing the shocking education gap for American children*. Boston: Houghton Mifflin.

Hirvikoski, T., Waaler, E., Alfredsson, J., Pihlgren, C., Holmström, A., Johnson, A., . . . Nordström, A. (2011). Reduced ADHD symptoms in adults with ADHD after structured skills training group: Results from a randomized controlled trial. *Behavioural Research and Therapy, 49*, 175–185.

Hobson, W. (2017). Former USA Gymnastics team doctor Larry Nassar pleads guilty to three more sexual assault charges. *The Washington Post*. Retrieved from https://www.washingtonpost.com/news/sports/wp/2017/11/29/former-usa-gymnastics-team-doctor-larry-nassar-pleads-guilty-to-more-sexual-assault-charges/?utm_term=.9779c9f0ef42

Hobson, W. (2018). Larry Nassar, former USA Gymnastics doctor, sentenced to 40–175 years for sex crimes. *The Washington Post*. Retrieved from https://www.washingtonpost.com/sports/olympics/larry-nassar-former-usa-gymnastics-doctor-due-to-be-sentenced-for-sex-crimes/2018/01/24/9acc22f8-0115-11e8-8acf-ad2991367d9d_story.html?utm_term=.08c42559d19c

Hochweber, J., Hosenfeld, I., & Klieme, E. (2013, August 12). Classroom composition, classroom management, and the relationship between student attributes and grades. *Journal of Educational Psychology*. Advance online publication. doi:10.1037/a0033829

Hodges, M. (2016). Largest transgender survey ever in U.S. reveals high rates of sexual assault, suicide, HIV, prostitution. *Life Site*. Retrieved from https://www.lifesitenews.com/news/transgender-survey-reveals-high-rates-of-sexual-assault-suicide-hiv-prostit

Hofer, M. (2010). Adolescents' development of individual interests: A product of multiple goal regulation? *Educational Psychologist, 45*, 149–166.

Hofferth, S. (2010). Home media and children's achievement and behavior. *Child Development, 81*, 1598–1619.

Hoffman, J. (2016). As attention grows, transgender children's numbers are elusive. *The New York Times*. Retrieved from https://www.nytimes.com/2016/05/18/science/transgender-children.html?_r=0

Hogan, T., Rabinowitz, M., & Craven, J. (2003). Representation in teaching: Inference from research on expert and novice teachers. *Educational Psychologist, 38*, 235–247.

Høgheim, S., & Reber, R. (2015). Supporting interest of middle school students in mathematics through context personalization and example choice. *Contemporary Educational Psychology, 42*, 17–25.

Hohnen, B., & Murphy, T. (2016). The optimum context for learning: drawing on neuroscience to inform best practice in the classroom. *Educational & Child Psychology, 33*, 75–90.

Holding, M., Denton, R., Kulesza, A., & Ridgway, J. (2014). Confronting scientific misconceptions by fostering a classroom of scientists in the introductory biology lab. *American Biology Teacher, 76*(8), 518–523.

Holeywell, R. (2015). New study shows benefits of two-way, dual-language education. *The Urban Edge: Kinder Institute for Urban Research at Rice University*. Retrieved from http://kinder.rice.edu/blog/holeywell060315/

Holland, G. W. O., & Holden, G. W. (2016). Changing orientations to corporal punishment: A randomized, control trial of the efficacy of a motivational approach to psycho-education. *Psychology of Violence, 6*, 233–242.

Holloway-Libell, J. (2015). Evidence of grade and subject-level bias in value-added measures. *Teachers College Record*. Retrieved from http://www.tcrecord.org/Content.asp?ContentID=17987

Holzberger, D., Philipp, A., & Kunter, M. (2013). How teachers' self-efficacy is related to instructional quality: A longitudinal analysis. *Journal of Educational Psychology, 105*, 774–786.

Honke, G., Cavagnetto, A. R., Kurtz, K., Patterson, J. D., Conoway, N., Tao, Y., & Marr, J. C. (2015, April). *Promoting transfer and mastery of evolution concepts with category construction.* Paper presented at the annual meeting of the American Educational Research Association, Chicago.

Horak, A. K., & Galluzzo, G. R. (2017). Gifted middle school students' achievement and perceptions of science classroom quality during problem-based learning. *Journal of Advanced Academics, 28*, 28–50.

Horn, J. (2008). Spearman, *g*, expertise, and the nature of human cognitive capability. In P. Kyllonen, R. Roberts, & L. Stankov (Eds.), *Extending intelligence: Enhancement and new constructs* (pp. 185–230). New York: Erlbaum/Taylor & Francis.

Horst, S. J., Finney, S. J., & Barron, K. E. (2007). Moving beyond academic achievement goal measures: A study of social achievement goals. *Contemporary Educational Psychology, 32*, 667–698.

Houdé, O., Pineau, A., Leroux, G., Poirel, N., Perchey, G., Lanoë, C., . . . Mazoyer, B. (2011). Functional MRI study of Piaget's conservation-of-number task in preschool and school-age children: A neo-Piagetian approach. *Journal of Experimental Child Psychology, 110*, 332– 346. doi: 10.1016/j.jecp.2011.04.008

Houkes-Hommes, A., ter Weel, B., & van der Wiel, K. (2016). Measuring the contribution of primary-school teachers to education outcomes in the Netherlands. *De Economist, 164*, 357–364.

Howard-Jones, P. A. (2014). Neuroscience and education: Myths and messages. *Nature Reviews Neuroscience, 15*, 817–824.

Howe, C. (2009). Collaborative group work in middle childhood. *Human Development, 52*, 215–239.

Howe, C. (2010). *Peer groups and children's development.* Malden, MA: Wiley-Blackwell.

Howe, M. L. (2004). The role of conceptual recoding in reducing children's retroactive interference. *Developmental Psychology, 40*, 131–139.

Howell, W. G. (2015). Results of President Obama's Race to the Top. *Education Next, 15*, 58–66.

Hritcu, M. S. (2016). The importance of educational software in improving the quality of education for children with special educational needs. *eLearning & Software for Education, 2*, 95–100.

Huan, V. S., Yeo, L. S., & Ang, R. P. (2006). The influence of dispositional optimism and gender on adolescents' perception of academic stress. *Adolescence, 41*, 533–546.

Hubbard, J., Morrow, M., Romano, L., & McAuliffe, M. (2010). The role of anger in children's reactive versus proactive aggression: Review of findings, issues of measurement, and implications for intervention. In W. Arsenio & E. Lemerise (Eds.), *Emotions, aggression, and morality in children: Bridging development and psychopathology* (pp. 201–217). Washington, DC: American Psychological Association. doi:10.1037/12129–01

Huesmann, L., Dubow, E., & Boxer, P. (2011). The transmission of aggressiveness across generations: Biological, contextual, and social learning processes. In P. Shaver & M. Mikulincer (Eds.), *Human aggression and violence: Causes, manifestations, and consequences. Herzliya series on personality and social psychology* (pp. 123–142). doi:10.1037/12346–007

Hughes, J. N., Wu, J-Y., Kwok, O., Villarreal, V., & Johnson, A. Y. (2012). Indirect effects of child reports of teacher–student relationship on achievement. *Journal of Educational Psychology, 104*, 350–365.

Hulac, D., Benson, N., Nesmith, M. C., & Shervey, S. W. (2016). Using variable interval reinforcement schedules to support students in the classroom: An introduction with illustrative examples. *Journal of Educational Research and Practice 2016, 6*, 90–96.

Hull, M. C. (2017). The academic progress of Hispanic immigrants. *Economics of Education Review, 57*, 91–110.

Human Rights Campaign. (2016). *Growing up LGBT in America.* Retrieved from http://hrc-assets.s3-website-us-east-1.amazonaws.com//files/assets/resources/Growing-Up-LGBT-in-America_Report.pdf

Hung, C-Y., Sun, J. C-Y., & Yu, P-T. (2015). The benefits of a challenge: Student motivation and flow experience in tablet-PC-game-based learning. *Interactive Learning Environments, 23*, 172–190.

Hunt, J. H., & Empson, S. B. (2015). Exploratory study of informal strategies for equal sharing problems of students with learning disabilities. *Learning Disability Quarterly, 38*, 208–220.

Igielnik, R., & Krogstad, J. M. (2017). Where refugees to the U.S. come from. *Pew Research Center*. Retrieved from http://www.pewresearch.org/fact-tank/2017/02/03/where-refugees-to-the-u-s-come-from/

Igo, L. B., Kiewra, K., & Bruning, R. (2004). Removing the snare from the pair: Using pictures to learn confusing word pairs. *Journal of Experimental Education, 72*(3), 165–178.

İlhan, İ. (2017). Concept-teaching practices in social studies classrooms: Teacher support for enhancing the development of students' vocabulary. *Educational Sciences: Theory & Practice, 17*, 1135–1164.

Im, S-H., Cho, J-Y., Dubinsky, J. M., & Varma, S. (2018). Taking an educational psychology course improves neuroscience literacy but does not reduce belief in neuromyths. *PLoS ONE, 13*, 1–19.

Imuta, K., Henry, J. D., Slaughter, V., Selcuk, B., & Ruffman, T. (2016). Theory of mind and prosocial behavior in childhood: A meta-analytic review. *Developmental Psychology, 52*, 1192–1205.

Inan, F. A., Lowther, D. L., Ross, S. M., & Strahl, D. (2010). Pattern of classroom activities during students' use of computers: Relations between instructional strategies and computer applications. *Teaching and Teacher Education, 26*, 540–546.

Indicators of school crime and safety. (2018). Indicator 1: Violent deaths at home and away from school. *National Center for Education Statistics.* Retrieved from https://nces.ed.gov/programs/crimeindicators/ind_01.asp

Informer Technologies, Inc. (2017). *The Geometers' Sketchpad*. Retrieved from http://en.informer.com/geometer-s-sketchpad/

Ingersoll, R., & Smith, T. (2004). What are the effects of induction and mentoring on beginning teacher turnover? *American Educational Research Journal, 41*(3), 681–714.

Ingraham, N., & Nuttall, S. (2016). The story of an arts integration school on English-Language-Learner development: A qualitative study of collaboration, integrity, and confidence. *International Journal of Education & the Arts, 17*, 1–18.

Inhelder, B., & Piaget, J. (1958). *The growth of logical thinking from childhood to adolescence* (A. Parsons & S. Milgram, Trans.). New York: Basic Books.

Insurance Institute for Highway Safety (2017). *General statistics.* Retrieved from http://www.iihs.org/iihs/topics/t/general-statistics/fatalityfacts/state-by-state-overview

Insurance Institutes for Highway Safety. (2017). *Distracted Driving: Cellphones and texting.* Retrieved from: http://www.iihs.org/iihs/topics/laws/cellphonelaws

International Society of the Learning Sciences. (2017). *Welcome to ISLS.* Retrieved from https://www.isls.org/

Ion, A., Mindu, A., & Gorbănescu, A. (2017). Grit in the workplace: Hype or ripe? *Personality and Individual Differences, 111*, 163–168.

Isaacson, A. (2009, March 5). Riding the rails. *New York Times. Retrieved from* http://travel.nytimes.com/2009/03/08/travel/08amtrak.html

Isseks, M. (2011). How PowerPoint is killing education. *Educational Leadership, 68*, 74–76.

Ivcevic, Z., & Brackett, M. (2014). Predicting school success: Comparing conscientiousness, grit, and emotion regulation ability. *Journal of Research in Personality, 52*, 29–36.**

IXL Learning. (2013). *Estimation and rounding.* Retrieved from http://www.ixl.com/math/grade-3

Jabeen, F., Anis-ul-Haque, M., & Riaz, M. N. (2013). Parenting styles as predictors of emotion regulation among adolescents. *Pakistan Journal of Psychological Research, 28,* 85–105.

Jack, F., Simcock, G., & Hayne, H., (2012). Magic memories: Young children's verbal recall after a 6-year delay. *Child Development, 83,* 159–172.

Jackson, M. (2009). *Distracted: The erosion of attention and the coming dark age.* Amherst, NY: Prometheus Books.

Jackson, P. (1968). *Life in classrooms.* New York: Holt, Rinehart & Winston.

Jackson, S. L., & Cunningham, S. A. (2015). Social competence and obesity in elementary school. *American Journal of Public Health, 105,* 153–158.

Jansen, A., & Bartell, T. (2013). Caring mathematics instruction: Middle school students' and teachers' perspectives. *Middle Grades Research Journal, 8,* 33–49.

Janssen, F., Westbroek, H., & Driel, J. (2014). How to make guided discovery learning practical for student teachers. *Instructional Science, 42,* 67–90.

Jarick, M., Laidlaw, K., Nasiopoulos, E., & Kingstone, A. (2016). Eye contact affects attention more than arousal as revealed by prospective time estimation. *Attention, Perception and Psychophysics, 78,* 1302–1307.

Jarrett, C. (2012). Why the left-brain right-brain myth will probably never die. *Psychology Today.* Retrieved from http://www.psychologytoday.com/blog/brain-myths/201206/why-the-leftbrain-right-brain-myth-will-probably-never-die

Jarrett, M. A. (2016). Attention-deficit/hyperactivity disorder (ADHD) symptoms, anxiety symptoms, and executive functioning in emerging adults. *Psychological Assessment, 28,* 245–250.

Jarrold, C., & Citroën, R. (2013). Reevaluating key evidence for the development of rehearsal: Phonological similarity effects in children are subject to proportional scaling artifacts. *Developmental Psychology, 49,* 837–847.

Jaschik, S. (2014). A new SAT. *Inside Higher Ed.* Retrieved from http://www.insidehighered.com/news/2014/03/05/college-board-unveils-new-sat-major-overhaul-writing-exam

Jaspal, R., & Cinnirella, M. (2012). The construction of ethnic identity: Insights from identity process theory. *Ethnicities, 12* (5), 503–530.

Jennings, P. A., Frank, J. L., Snowberg, K. E., Coccia, M. A., & Greenberg, M. T. (2013). Improving classroom learning environments by cultivating awareness and resilience in education (CARE): Results of a randomized controlled trial. *School Psychology Quarterly, 28,* 374–390.

Jeno, L. M., Grytnes, J-A., & Vandvik, V. (2017). The effect of a mobile-application tool on biology students' motivation and achievement in species identification: A Self-Determination Theory perspective. *Computers and Education, 107,* 1–12.

Jette, A. (2014). 10 tips for edTPA success. *Education Week.* Retrieved from http://www.edweek.org/tm/articles/2014/07/29/ctq_jette_edtpa.html

Jiang, Y. H. V., Swallow, K. M., & Rosenbaum, G. M. (2013). Guidance of spatial attention by incidental learning and endogenous cuing. *Journal of Experimental Psychology—Human Perception and Performance, 39,* 285–297.

Jiménez-Castellanos, O. H., & García, D. (2017). School expenditures and academic achievement differences between high-ELL-performing and low-ELL-performing high schools. *Bilingual Research Journal, 40,* 318–330.

Jitendra, A., Haria, P., Griffin, C., Leh, J., Adams, A., & Kaduvettoor, A. (2007). A comparison of single and multiple strategy instruction on third-grade students' mathematical problem solving. *Journal of Educational Psychology, 99*(1), 115–127.

Joe, H-K., Hiver, P., & Al-Hoorie, A. H. (2017). Classroom social climate, self-determined motivation, willingness to communicate, and achievement: A study of structural relationships in instructed second language settings. *Learning and Individual Differences, 53,* 133–144.

Johnson, D. W., & Johnson, R. T. (2017). The use of cooperative procedures in teacher education and professional development. *Journal of Education for Teaching, 43,* 284–295.

Johnson, H. B. (2015). Word play: How "Black English" coarsens culture. *Teachers College Record.* Retrieved from http://www.tcrecord.org/Content.asp?ContentID=18829

Johnson, I. (2017). Female faculty role models, self-efficacy, and student achievement. *College Student Journal, 51,* 151–173.

Johnson, L. (2004). Down with detention. *Education Week, 24*(14), 39–40.

Johnson, M., & Sinatra, G. (2014). The influence of approach and avoidance goals on conceptual change. *Journal of Educational Research, 107*(4), 312–325.

Johnson, N., & Parker, A. T. (2013). Effects of wait time when communicating with children who have sensory and additional disabilities. *Journal of Visual Impairment & Blindness, 107,* 363–74.

Johnson, S., & Birkeland, S. (2003, April). *Pursuing a "sense of success:" New teachers explain their career decisions.* Paper presented at the annual meeting of the American Educational Research Association, New Orleans, LA.

Johnson, W., & Bouchard, T. (2005). The structure of human intelligence: It is verbal, perceptual, and image rotation (VPR), not fluid and crystallized. *Intelligence, 33,* 393–416.

Johnston, L. D., O'Malley, P. M., Miech, R. A., Bachman, J. G., & Schulenberg, J. E. (2017). *Monitoring the Future national survey results on drug use, 1975–2016: Overview, key findings on adolescent drug use.* Ann Arbor: Institute for Social Research, The University of Michigan. Retrieved from http://www.monitoringthefuture.org//pubs/monographs/mtf-overview2016.pdf

Jolstead, K. A., Caldarella, P., Hansen, B., Korth, B. B., Williams, L., & Kamps, D. (2017). Implementing positive behavior support in preschools: An exploratory study of CW-FIT tier I. *Journal of Positive Behavior Interventions, 19,* 48–60.

Jonas, M. E. (2016). Plato's anti-Kohlbergian program for moral education. *Journal of Philosophy of Education, 50,* 205–217.

Jones, D. E., Greenberg, M., & Crowley, M. (2015). Early social-emotional functioning and public health: The relationship between kindergarten social competence and future wellness. *American Journal of Public Health, 105,* 2283–2290.

Jones, K. A., Jones, J. L., & Vermete, P. J. (2013). Exploring the complexity of classroom management: 8 components of managing a highly productive, safe, and respectful urban environment. *American Secondary Education, 41,* 21–33.

Jones, M. H. (2017). The relationship among achievement goals, standardized test scores, and elementary students' focus in school. *Psychology in the Schools, 54,* 979–990.

Jones, S. (2016). 1,301,239: Homeless students in public schools up 38% since 2009–10. CNSNews.com. Retrieved from https://www.cnsnews.com/news/article/susan-jones/1301239-number-homeless-students-nations-public-schools-38–2009–10

Jones, V., & Jones, L. (2016). *Comprehensive classroom management: Creating communities of support and solving problems* (11th ed.). Boston: Pearson.

Jordan, L., & Papp, R. (2013). PowerPoint™: It's not "yes" or "no"—it's "when" and "how." *Research in Higher Education Journal, 22,* 1–12.

Jordan, M. R., Amir, D., & Bloom, P. (2016). Are empathy and concern psychologically distinct? *Emotion, 16,* 1107–1116.

Josephs, M., & Rakoczy, H. (2016). Young children think you can opt out of social-conventional but not moral practices. *Cognitive Development, 39,* 197–204.

Josephson Institute Center for Youth Ethics. (2010). *The ethics of American youth: 2010.* Retrieved from http://charactercounts.org/programs/reportcard/2010/index.html

Jurow, A. (2016). Kris Gutiérrez: designing with and for diversity in the learning sciences. *Cultural Studies of Science Education, 11,* 81–88.

Jussim. L., Robustelli, S., & Cain, T. (2009). Teacher expectations and self-fulfilling prophecies. In A. Wigfield & K. Wentzel (Eds.), *Handbook of motivation at school* (pp. 349–380). Mahwah, NJ: Erlbaum.

Justice, L. M., Logan, J. A., Lin, T. J., & Kaderavek, J. N. (2014). Peer effects in early childhood education: Testing the assumptions of special-education inclusion. *Psychological Science, 25,* 1722–1729.

Juvonen, J. (2006). Sense of belonging, social bonds, and school functioning. In P. A. Alexander & P. H. Winne (Eds.), *Handbook of educational psychology* (2nd ed., pp. 655–674). Mahwah, NJ: Erlbaum.

Juvonen, J., Schacter, H. L., Sainio, M., & Salmivalli, C. (2016). Can a school-wide bullying prevention program improve the plight of victims? Evidence for risk x intervention effects. *Journal of Consulting and Clinical Psychology, 84,* 334–344.

Kaddoura, M. A. (2011). Critical thinking skills of nursing students in lecture-based teaching and case-based learning. *International Journal for the Scholarship of Teaching & Learning, 5,* 1–18.

Kafai, Y. (2006). Constructionism. In R. K. Sawyer (Ed.), *The Cambridge handbook of the learning sciences* (pp. 35–46). New York: Cambridge University Press.

Kahlenberg, S., & Hein, M. (2010). Progression on Nickelodeon? Gender-role stereotypes in toy commercials. *Sex Roles, 62,* 830–847.

Kahn, E. (2016). The schools transgender students need. *Educational Leadership, 74,* 70–73.

Kahneman, D. (2011). *Thinking fast and slow.* New York: Farrar, Straus and Giroux.

Kalyuga, S. (2010). Schema acquisition and sources of cognitive load. In J. L. Plass, R. Moreno, & R. Brünken (Eds.), *Cognitive load theory* (pp. 48–64). Cambridge, England: Cambridge University Press.

Kaminski, J. A., Sloutsky, V. M., & Heckler, A. F. (2013). The cost of concreteness: The effect of nonessential information on analogical transfer. *Journal of Experimental Psychology: Applied, 19,* 14–29.

Kanazawa, S. (2010). Evolutionary psychology and intelligence research. *American Psychologist, 65*(4), 279–289.

Kanfer, R., Frese, M., & Johnson, R. E. (2017). Motivation related to work: A century of progress. *Journal of Applied Psychology, 102,* 338–355.

Kanive, R., Nelson, P. M., Burns, M. K., & Ysseldyke, J. (2014). Comparison of the effects of computer-based practice and conceptual understanding interventions on mathematics fact retention and generalization. *The Journal of Educational Research, 107,* 83–89.

Kaplan, K., & Johnson, M. A. (2012). Sandusky convicted of 45 counts, plans to appeal. *NBC News.* Retrieved from http://usnews. nbcnews.com/_news/2012/06/22/12363955-sandusky-convicted-of-45-counts-plans-to-appeal?lite.

Kaplan, R. M., & Saccuzzo, D. P. (2018). *Psychological testing: Principles, applications, and issues* (9th ed.). Boston: Cengage.

Kar, Am. K., & Kar, Aj. K. (2017). How to walk your talk: Effective use of body language for business professionals. *IUP Journal of Soft Skills, 11,* 16–28.

Karatekin, C. (2004). A test of the integrity of the components of Baddeley's model of working memory in attention-deficit/hyperactivity disorder (ADHD). *The Journal of Child Psychology and Psychiatry and Allied Disciplines, 45*(5), 912–926.

Karssemeijer, E. G. A., Aaronson, J. A., Bossers, W. J., Smits, T., Olde Rikkert, M. G. M., & Kessels, R. P. C. (2017). Positive effects of combined cognitive and physical exercise training on cognitive function in older adults with mild cognitive impairment or dementia: A meta-analysis. *Ageing Research Reviews, 40,* 75–83.

Kaspar, K., & Stelz, H. (2013). The paradoxical effect of praise and blame: Age-related differences. *Europe's Journal of Psychology, 9,* 304–318.

Kassin, S. M., Dror, I. E., & Kukucka, J. (2013). The forensic confirmation bias: Problems, perspectives, and proposed solutions. *Journal of Applied Research in Memory and Cognition, 2,* 42–52.

Kastens, K., & Liben, L. (2007). Eliciting self-explanations improves children's performance on a field-based map skills task. *Cognition and Instruction, 25*(1), 45–74.

Katz, J. M. (2016). What happened to North Carolina? *The New York Times.* Retrieved from https://www.nytimes.com/2016/10/07/magazine/what-happened-to-north-carolina.html

Katz, J. M. (2017). Drug deaths in America are rising faster than ever. *The New York Times.* Retrieved from https://www.nytimes.com/interactive/2017/06/05/upshot/opioid-epidemic-drug-overdose-deaths-are-rising-faster-than-ever.html?_r=5

Kauchak, D., & Eggen, P. (2012). *Learning and teaching: Research-based methods* (6th ed.). Boston: Pearson.

Kearney, W. S., Smith, P. A., & Maika, S. (2016). Asking students their opinions of the learning environment: An empirical analysis of elementary classroom climate. *Educational Psychology in Practice, 32,* 310–320.

Keller, M. M., Goetz, T., Becker, E. S., Morger, V., & Hensley, L. (2014). Feeling and showing: A new conceptualization of dispositional teacher enthusiasm and its relation to students' interest. *Learning and Instruction, 33,* 29–38.

Keller, M., Hoy, A., Goetz, T., & Frensel, A. (2016). Teacher enthusiasm: Reviewing and redefining a complex construct. *Educational Psychology Review, 28,* 743–769.

Kelly, D., & Donaldson, D. I. (2016). Investigating the complexities of academic success: Personality constrains the effects of metacognition. *Psychology of Education Review, 40,* 17–23.

Kennedy Root, A., & Denham, S. (2010). The role of gender in the socialization of emotion: Key concepts and critical issues. In A. Kennedy Root & S. Denham (Eds.), *The role of gender in the socialization of emotion: Key concepts and critical issues. New Directions for Child and Adolescent Development, 128,* 1–9. San Francisco: Jossey-Bass.

Kennedy, F., Carroll, B., & Francoeur, J. (2013). Mindset not skill set: Evaluating in new paradigms of leadership development. *Advances in Developing Human Resources, 15,* 10–26.

Kennedy-Lewis, B. L., & Murphy, A. S. (2016). Listening to "frequent flyers": What persistently disciplined students have to say about being labeled as "bad." *Teachers College Record, 118,* 1–40. Retrieved from http://www.tcrecord.org/Content .asp?ContentID=18222

Kerman, S. (1979). Teacher expectations and student achievement. *Phi Delta Kappan, 60,* 70–72.

Kertz, S., & Woodruff-Borden, J. (2013). The role of metacognition, intolerance of uncertainty, and negative problem orientation in children's worry. *Behavioural and Cognitive Psychotherapy, 41,* 243–248.

Khamsi, R. (2013). Going to pot. *Scientific American, 308,* 34–36.

Khasnabis, D., Goldin, S., & Ronfeldt, M. (2018).The practice of partnering: Simulated parent-teacher conferences as a tool for teacher education. *Action in Teacher Education, 40,* 77–95.

Khodadady, E., & Hezareh, O. (2016). Social and emotional intelligences: Empirical and theoretical relationship. *Journal of Language Teaching and Research, 7,* 128–136.

Kibby, M. Y., Marks, W., & Morgan, S. (2004). Specific impairment in developmental reading disabilities: A working memory approach. *Journal of Learning Disabilities, 37,* 349–363.

Kidron, Y., & Fleischman, S. (2006). Promoting adolescents' prosocial behavior. *Educational Leadership, 63*(7), 90–91.

Kieffer, J., Lesaux, N., Rivera, M., & Francis, D. (2009). Accommodations for English language learners taking large-scale assessments: A meta-analysis on effectiveness and validity. *Review of Educational Research, 79,* 1168–1201.

Kiemer, K., Gröschner, A., Pehmer, A-K., & Seidel, T. (2015). Effects of a classroom discourse intervention on teachers' practice and students' motivation to learn mathematics and science. *Learning and Instruction, 35,* 94–103.

Kiewra, K. (2016). Note taking on trial: A legal application of note-taking research. *Educational Psychology Review, 28,* 377–384.

Kim, S. Y., Wang, Y., Orozco-Lapray, D., Shen, Y., & Murtuza, M. (2013). Does "tiger parenting" exist? Parenting profiles of Chinese

Americans and adolescent developmental outcomes. *Asian American Journal of Psychology, 4,* 7–18.

Kim, S., & Hill, N. E. (2015). Including fathers in the picture: A meta-analysis of parental involvement and students' academic achievement. *Journal of Educational Psychology, 107,* 919–934.

Kim, T., & Schallert, D. L. (2014). Mediating effects of teacher enthusiasm and peer enthusiasm on students' interest in the college classroom. *Contemporary Educational Psychology, 39,* 134–144.

Kimmel, M., (2018). *Manhood in America: A cultural history* (4th ed.). New York: Oxford University Press.

King, R. (2014). The dark cycle of work avoidance goals and disengagement: A cross-lagged analysis. *Psychological Studies, 59,* 268–277.

King, R. B., & McInerney, D. M. (2014). The work avoidance goal construct: Examining its structure, antecedents, and consequences. *Contemporary Educational Psychology, 39,* 42–58.

King, R. B., McInerney, D. M., & Nasser, R. (2017). Different goals for different folks: A cross-cultural study of achievement goals across nine cultures. *Social Psychology of Education: An International Journal, 20,* 619–642.

Kirbas, A. (2017). Effects of cooperative learning method on the development of listening comprehension and listening skills. *International Journal of Languages' Education and Teaching, 5,* 1–17.

Kirschner, P. A., Sweller, J., & Clark, R. E. (2006). Why minimal guidance during instruction does not work: An analysis of the failure of constructivist, discovery, problem-based, experiential, and inquiry-based teaching. *Educational Psychologist, 41,* 75–86.

Kirylo, J. D., Thirumurthy, V., & Spezzini, S. (2010). Children were punished: Not for what they said, but for what their teachers heard. *Childhood Education, 86,* 130–131.

Kitsantas, A., Zimmerman, B., & Cleary, T. (2000). The role of observation and emulation in the development of athletic self-regulation. *Journal of Educational Psychology, 92*(4), 811–817.

Kiyonaga, A., & Egner, T. (2013). Working memory as internal attention: Toward an integrative account of internal and external selection processes. *Psychonomic Bulletin and Review, 20,* 228–242.

Klein, A. (2018). Trump: Nation should consider arming teachers to prevent school shootings. *Education Week.* Retrieved from http://blogs.edweek.org/edweek/campaign-k-12/2018/02/trump_says_nation_should_consi.html?cmp=eml-enl-eu-news2&M=58389726&U=27557

Klein, D. O., & Wueller, J. R. (2017). Fake news: A legal perspective. *Journal of Internet Law, 20,* 1–13.

Knight, J. (2002). Crossing the boundaries: What constructivists can teach intensive-explicit instructors and vice versa. *Focus on Exceptional Children, 35,* 1–14, 16.

Kohlberg, L. (1963). The development of children's orientation toward moral order: Sequence in the development of human thought. *Vita Humana, 6,* 11–33.

Kohlberg, L. (1969). Stage and sequence: The cognitive-developmental approach to socialization. In D. Goslin (Ed.), *Handbook of socialization theory and research.* Chicago: Rand McNally.

Kohlberg, L. (1981). *Philosophy of moral development.* New York: Harper & Row.

Kohlberg, L. (1984). *The psychology of moral development: The nature and validity of moral stages.* San Francisco: Harper & Row.

Kohli, R. & Solórzano, D. (2012). Teachers, please learn our names!: Racial microaggressions and the K–12 classroom. *Race, Ethnicity and Education. 15,* 41–462.

Kohli, S. (2015). America is failing its children by not teaching code in every high school. *Quartz Media.* Retrieved from https://qz.com/340551/america-is-failing-its-children-by-not-teaching-code-in-every-high-school/

Kohn, A. (1993). *Punished by rewards: The trouble with gold stars, incentive plans, A's, praise, and other bribes.* Boston: Houghton Mifflin.

Kohn, A. (2005a). *Unconditional parenting: Moving from rewards and punishments to love and reason.* New York: Atria Books.

Kohn, A. (2005b). Unconditional teaching. *Educational Leadership, 63,* 20–24.

Kohn, A. (2007). *The Homework Myth: Why Our Kids Get Too Much of a Bad Thing.* Cambridge, MA: Da Capo Life Long.

Kohn, A. (2016). Why punishment won't stop a bully. *Education Week.* Retrieved from http://www.edweek.org/ew/articles/2016/09/07/why-punishment-wont-stop-a-bully.html?cmp=eml-enl-eu-news1-RM

Kok, B. E., Coffey, K. A., Cohn, M. A., Catalino, L. I., Vacharkulksemsuk, T., Algoe, S. B., . . . Fredrickson, B. L. (2013). How positive emotions build physical health: Perceived positive social connections account for the upward spiral between positive emotions and vagal tone. *Psychological Science, 24,* 1123–1132.

König, J., & Pflanzl, B. (2016). Is teacher knowledge associated with performance? On the relationship between teachers' general pedagogical knowledge and instructional quality. *European Journal of Teacher Education, 39,* 419–436.

Koppelman, K. L. (2017). *Understanding human differences: Multicultural education for a diverse America* (5th ed.). Boston: Pearson.

Kornhaber, M., Fierros, E., & Veenema, S. (2004). *Multiple intelligences: Best ideas from research and practice.* Boston: Allyn & Bacon.

Kornienko, O., Santos, C. E., Martin, C. L., & Granger, K. L. (2016). Peer influence on gender identity development in adolescence. *Developmental Psychology, 52,* 1578–1592.

Korpershoek, H. Harms, T., de Boer, H., van Kuijk, M., & Doolaard, S. (2016). A meta-analysis of the effects of classroom management strategies and classroom management programs on students' academic, behavioral, emotional, and motivational outcomes. *Review of Educational Research, 86,* 643–680.

Koul, R., Roy, L., & Lerdpornkulrat, T. (2012). Motivational goal orientation, perceptions of biology and physics classroom learning environments, and gender. *Learning Environments Research, 15,* 217–229.

Kounang, N. (2017). Teen drug overdose death rate climbed 19% in one year. *CNN.* Retrieved from http://www.cnn.com/2017/08/16/health/teen-overdose-death-rate/index.html

Kounin, J. (1970). *Discipline and group management in classrooms.* New York: Holt, Rinehart & Winston.

Kovacs, L., & Corrie, S. (2017). Building reflective capability to enhance coaching practice. *Coaching Psychologist, 13,* 4–12.

Kozol, J. (2005). *The shame of the nation: The restoration of apartheid schooling in America.* New York: Crown.

Kraft, M. A. (2010). From ringmaster to conductor: 10 simple techniques that can turn an unruly class into a productive one. *Phi Delta Kappan, 91,* 44–47.

Kraft, M. A. (2016). The underutilized potential of teacher-parent communication. *Communities and Banking, 27,* 15–17.

Kraft, M. A., & Rogers, T. (2015). The underutilized potential of teacher-to-parent communication: Evidence from a field experiment. *Economics of Education Review, 47,* 49–63.

Krätzig, G., & Arbuthnott, K. (2006). Perceptual learning style and learning proficiency: A test of the hypothesis. *Journal of Educational Psychology, 98*(1), 238–246.

Krendle, A., Gainsburg, I., & Ambady, N. (2012). The effects of stereotypes and observer pressure on athletic performance. *Journal of Sport and Exercise Psychology, 34,* 3–15.

Kretz, L. (2015). Teaching being ethical. *Teaching Ethics, 15,* 151–172.

Kriegbaum, K, Villarreal, B., Wu, V. C., & Heckhausen, J. (2016). Parents still matter: Patterns of shared agency with parents predict college students' motivation and achievement. *Motivation Science, 2,* 97–115.

Kroger, J., & Marcia, J. E. (2011). The identity statuses: Origins, meanings, interpretations. In S. J. Schwartz, K. Luyckx, & V. L. Vignoles (Eds.), *Handbook of identity theory and research* (pp. 31–53). New York: Springer.

Kroger, J. Martinussen, M., & Marcia, J. (2010). Identity status change during adolescence and young adulthood: A meta-analysis. *Journal of Adolescence, 33,* 683–698.

Krueger, A. B. (2016, October). *Where Have All the Workers Gone?* Paper presented at the Boston Federal Reserve Bank's 60th Economic Conference, Boston, MA.

Kuhl, P. (2004). Early language acquisition: Cracking the speech code. *Nature Reviews Neuroscience, 5*, 831–843.

Kuhl, R., (2017). The six relationships that characterize great schools. *Education Week.* Retrieved from http://blogs.edweek.org/edweek/learning_deeply/2017/06/the_six_relationships_that_characterize_great_schools.html?cmp=eml-enl-eu-news2-RM

Kuhn, D. (2009). Adolescent thinking. In R. Lerner & L. Steinberg (Eds.), *Handbook of adolescent psychology, Vol. 1: Individual bases of adolescent development* (3rd ed., pp. 152–186). Hoboken, NJ: Wiley.

Kuhn, D., & Park, S. H. (2005). Epistemological understanding and the development of intellectual values. *International Journal of Educational Research, 43*, 111–124.

Kuhn, D., Pease, M., & Wirkala, C. (2009). Coordinating the effects of multiple variables: A skill fundamental to scientific thinking. *Journal of Experimental Child Psychology, 103*(3), 268–284.

Kulasegaram, K., Chaudhary, Z., Woods, N., Dore, K., Neville, A., & Norman, G. (2017). Contexts, concepts, and cognition: Principles for the transfer of basic science knowledge. *Medical Education, 51*, 184–195.

Kulik, J. A., & Kulik, C.-L. C. (1984). Effects of accelerated instruction on students. *Review of Educational Research, 54*, 409–425.

Kulik, J. A., & Kulik, C.-L. C. (1992). Meta-analytic findings on grouping programs. *Gifted Child Quarterly, 36*, 73–77.

Kull, R. M., Kosciw, J. G., & Greytak, E. A. (2015). From statehouse to schoolhouse: Anti-bullying policy efforts in U.S. states and school districts: *The Gay, Lesbian & Straight Education Network.* Retrieved from http://www.glsen.org/sites/default/files/GLSEN%20-%20From%20Statehouse%20to%20Schoolhouse%202015_0.pdf

Kunter, M., Klusmann, U., Baumert, J., Richter, D., Voss, T., & Hachfeld, A. (2013). Professional competence of teachers: Effects on instructional quality and student development. *Journal of Educational Psychology, 105*, 805–820.

Kuppens, S., Laurent, L., Heyvaert, W., & Onghena, P. (2013). Associations between parental psychological control and relational aggression in children and adolescents: A multilevel and sequential meta-analysis. *Developmental Psychology, 49*, 1697–1712.

Kurzweil, R. (2012). *How to create a mind.* New York: Viking.

López, F. A. (2017). Altering the trajectory of the self-fulfilling prophecy: Asset-based pedagogy and classroom dynamics. *Journal of Teacher Education, 68*, 193–212.

Lacey, R. E., Kumari,M., & Bartley, M. (2014). Social isolation in childhood and adult inflammation: Evidence from the National Child Development Study. *Psychoneuroendocrinology, 50*, 85–94.

Lack, C. W., & Rousseau, J. (2016). *Critical thinking, science, and pseudoscience: Why we can't trust our brains.* New York: Springer.

Lamson, M. (2010). *No such thing as small talk: 7 keys to understanding German business culture.* Cupertino, CA: Happy About.

Lancioni, G., Sigafoos, M., & Nirbhay, S. (2013). *Assistive technology.* New York: Springer.

Langer Research Associates. (2016). *The 48th annual PDK poll of the public's attitudes toward the public schools.* Retrieved from http://pdkpoll2015.pdkintl.org/wp-content/uploads/2016/08/pdkpoll48_2016.pdf

Langer Research Associates. (2017). *The 49th annual PDK poll of the public's attitudes toward the public schools.* Retrieved from http://pdkpoll.org/assets/downloads/PDKnational_poll_2017.pdf

Langley, P., Pearce, C., Barley, M., & Emery, M. (2014). Bounded rationality in problem solving: Guiding search with domain-independent heuristics. *Mind & Society, 13*, 85–93.

Lansford, J. E., Cappa, C., Putnick, D. L., Bornstein, M. H., Deater-Deckard, K., & Bradley, R. H. (2016). Research article: Change over time in parents' beliefs about and reported use of corporal punishment with and without legal bans. *Child Abuse & Neglect.* doi: 10.1016/j.chiabu.2016.10.016

Lapidot-Lefler, N., & Dolev-Cohen, M. (2015). Comparing cyberbullying and school bullying among school students:

Prevalence, gender, and grade level differences. *Social Psychology of Education, 18*, 1–6.

Larkin, W., Hawkins, R. O., & Collins, T. (2016). Using trial-based functional analysis to design effective interventions for students diagnosed with autism spectrum disorder. *School Psychology Quarterly, 31*, 534–547.

Latif, E., & Miles, S. (2013). Students' perceptions of effective teaching. *Journal of Economics and Economic Education Research, 14*, 121–129.

Lauermann, F., & König, J. (2016). Teachers' professional competence and wellbeing: Understanding the links between general pedagogical knowledge, self-efficacy and burnout. *Learning and Instruction, 45*, 9–19.

Lavigne, A. L. (2014). Exploring the intended and unintended consequences of high-stakes teacher evaluation on schools, teachers, and students. *Teachers College Record, 116*, Retrieved from http://www.tcrecord.org/content.asp?contentid=17294

Lavy, V. (2016). What makes an effective teacher? Quasi-experimental evidence. *CESifo Economic Studies. 62*, 88–125.

Lawson, G. W. (2013). Eliminate PowerPoint in the classroom to facilitate active learning. *Global Education Journal, 2013*, 1–8.

Lawyer, G. (2018). The dangers of separating social justice from multicultural education: Applications in higher education. *International Journal of Multicultural Education, 20*, 86–101.

Layton, L. (2015). Nation's largest labor union: We want 2016 hopefuls talking about schools. *The Washington Post.* Retrieved from https://www.washingtonpost.com/local/education/nations-largest-labor-union-we-want-2016-hopefuls-talking-about-schools/2015/03/25/2715929e-d301-11e4-ab77-9646eea6a4c7_story.html?utm_term=.ab5fbbb9f921

Lazonder, A. W., & Harmsen, R. (2016). Meta-analysis of inquiry-based learning: Effects of guidance. *Review of Educational Research, 86*, 681–718.

Leatherdale, S. T. (2013). A cross-sectional examination of school characteristics associated with overweight and obesity among grade 1 to 4 students. *BMC Public Health, 13*, 1–21.

Leavell, A., Tamis-LeMonda, C., Ruble, D., Zosuls, K., & Cabrera, N. (2012). African-American, White and Latino fathers' activities with their sons and daughters in early childhood. *Sex Roles, 66*, 53–66.

Lee, C-Y., & Chen, M-J. (2016). Effects of worked examples using manipulatives on fifth graders' learning performance and attitude toward mathematics. *Journal of Educational Technology & Society, 18*, 264–275.

Lee, E. H., Zhou, Q., Ly, J., Main, A., Tao, A., & Chen, S. H. (2013, September 16). Neighborhood characteristics, parenting styles, and children's behavioral problems in Chinese American immigrant families. *Cultural Diversity and Ethnic Minority Psychology.* Advance online publication. doi:10.1037/a0034390

Lee, H. (1960). *To kill a mockingbird.* New York: J. B. Lippincott.

Lee, J., & Shute, V. (2010). Personal and social-contextual factors in K–12 academic performance: An integrative perspective on student learning. *Educational Psychologist, 45*, 185–202.

Lee, P. C., & Stewart, D. E. (2013). Does a socio-ecological school model promote resilience in primary schools? *Journal of School Health, 83*, 795–804.

Lee, V. (2000). Using hierarchical linear modeling to study social contexts: The case of school effects. *Educational Psychologist, 35*, 125–141.

Leff, S. S., Waasdorp, T. E., & Paskewich, B. S. (2016). The broader impact of friend to friend (R2F): Effects on teacher-student relationships, prosocial behaviors, and relationally and physically aggressive behaviors. *Behavior Modification, 40*, 589–610.

Legault, L., & Inzlicht, M. (2013). Self-determination, self-regulation, and the brain: Autonomy improves performance by enhancing neuroaffective responsiveness to self-regulation failure. *Journal of Personality and Social Psychology, 105*, 123–138.

Lemov, D. (2015). *Teach like a champion 2.0: 62 techniques that put students on the path to college.* San Francisco: Jossey-Bass.

Lenta, P. (2012). Corporal punishment of children. *Social Theory & Practice, 38*, 689–716.

Lereya, S. T., Copeland, W. E., Costello, E. J., & Wolke, D. (2015). Adult mental health consequences of peer bullying and maltreatment in childhood: Two cohorts in two countries. *Lancet Psychiatry, 2,* 524–531.

Lerman, R. I. (2016). Reinvigorate apprenticeships in America to expand good jobs, and reduce inequality. *Challenge (05775132), 59,* 372–389.

Lesaux, N. K., & Jones, S. M. (Eds.). (2016). *The leading edge of early childhood education: Linking science to policy for a new generation of prekindergarten.* Cambridge, MA: Harvard Education Publishing Group.

Lessne, D., & Cidade, M. (2015). Student reports of bullying and cyber-bullying: Results from the 2013 school crime supplement to the national crime victimization survey. *National Center for Educational Statistics.* Retrieved from http://nces.ed.gov/pubs2015/2015056.pdf

Lester, F. K. (2013). Thoughts about research on mathematical problem-solving instruction. *The Mathematics Enthusiast, 10,* 245–278.

Lester, R. R., Allanson, P. B., & Notar, C. E. (2017). Routines are the foundation of classroom management. *Education, 137,* 398–412.

Levesque, C., Stanek, L., Zuehlke, A. N., & Ryan, R. (2004). Autonomy and competence in German and American university students: A comparative study based on self-determination theory. *Journal of Educational Psychology, 96*(1), 68–84.

Lewin, T. (2014). A new SAT aims to realign with schoolwork. *The New York Times.* Retrieved from http://www.nytimes.com/2014/03/06/education/major-changes-in-sat-announced-by-college-board.html?_r=0

Lewis D., Madison-Harris, R., Muoneke, A., & Times, C. (2017). Using data to guide instruction and improve student learning. *American Institutes for Research.* Retrieved from http://www.sedl.org/pubs/sedl-letter/v22n02/using-data.html

Lewis, C. (2015). What is improvement science? Do we need it in education? *Educational Researcher, 44,* 54–61. Retrieved from http://dx.doi.org/10.3102/0013189X15570388

Lewis, N. A., & Sekaquaptewa, D. (2016). Beyond test performance: A broader view of stereotype threat. *Intergroup Relations, Current Opinion in Psychology, 11,* 40–43.

Lewis, R., Romi, S., & Roache, J. (2012). Excluding students from classroom: Teacher techniques that promote student responsibility. *Teaching and Teacher Education, 28,* 870–878.

Lewis, T. J., Mitchell, B. S., Trussell, R., & Newcomer, L. (2015). School-wide positive behavior support: Building systems to prevent problem behavior and maintain appropriate social behavior. In E. T. Emmer & E. J. Sabornie (Eds.), *Handbook of classroom management* (2nd ed., pp. 40–59). New York: Routledge.

Lezotte, L. W., & Snyder, K. M. (2011). *What effective schools do: Re-envisioning the correlates.* Bloomington, IN: Solution Tree Press.

Li, J. (2005). Mind or virtue: Western and Chinese beliefs about learning. *Current Directions in Psychological Science, 14,* 190–194.

Li, Y., Anderson, R., Nguyen-Jahiel, K., Dong, T., Archodidou, A., Kim, I., . . . Miller, B. (2007). Emergent leadership in children's discussion groups. *Cognition and Instruction, 25,* 75–111.

Li, Y., Dai, S., Zheng, Y., Tian, F., & Yan, X. (2018). Modeling and kinematics simulation of a Mecanum Wheel in RecurDyn. *Journal of Robotics, 2018,* 1–7.

Lidstone, J., Meins, E., & Fernyhough, C. (2010). The roles of private speech and inner speech in planning during middle childhood: Evidence from a dual task paradigm. *Journal of Experimental Child Psychology, 10,* 438–451.

Lieberman, M. D. (2013). *Social: Why our brains are wired to connect.* New York: Crown Publishers.

Liew, J., Chen, Q., & Hughes, J. N. (2010). Child effortful control, teacher-student relationships, and achievement in academically at-risk children: Additive and interactive effects. *Early Childhood Research Quarterly, 25,* 51–64.

Lin, C. F., Yeh, Y., Hung, Y. H., & Chang, R.I. (2013). Data mining for providing a personalized learning path in creativity: An application of decision trees. *Computers and Education, 68,* 199–210.

Lin, J.-R. (2007). Responses to anomalous data obtained from repeatable experiments in the laboratory. *Journal of Research in Science Teaching, 44*(3), 506–528.

Lin, L-Y, Cherng, R-J., Chen, Y-Jung., Chen, Y-Jen, & Yang, H-M. (2015). Effects of television exposure on developmental skills among young children. *Infant Behavior and Development, 38,* 20–26.

Linder Gunnoe, M. (2013). Associations between parenting style, physical discipline, and adjustment in adolescents' reports. *Psychological Reports, 112,* 933–975.

Linebarger, D., & Piotrowski, J. (2010). Structure and strategies in children's educational television: The roles of program type and learning strategies in children's learning. *Child Development, 81,* 1582–1597.

Linnenbrink-Garcia, L., & Pekrun, R. (Eds.). (2011). Students' emotions and academic engagement: Introduction to the special issue [Special issue]. *Contemporary Educational Psychology, 36,* 1–3. doi:10.1016/j.cedpsych.2010.11.004

Liptak, A. (2016). Supreme Court blocks order allowing transgender student restroom choice. *The New York Times.* Retrieved from https://www.nytimes.com/2016/08/04/us/politics/supreme-court-blocks-order-allowing-transgender-student-restroom-choice.html

Lo, C., Hopson, L., Simpson, G., & Cheng, T. (2017). Racial/ethnic differences in emotional health: A longitudinal study of immigrants' adolescent children. *Community Mental Health Journal, 53,* 92–101.

Locke, J., Shih, W., Kretzmann, M., & Kasari, C. (2016). Examining playground engagement between elementary school children with and without autism spectrum disorder. *Autism , 20,* 653–662.

Lohman, D. (2001, April). *Fluid intelligence, inductive reasoning, and working memory: Where the theory of multiple intelligences falls short.* Paper presented at the annual meeting of the American Educational Research Association, Seattle.

Loman, M., & Gunnar, M. (2010). Early experience and the development of stress reactivity and regulation in children. *Neuroscience & Biobehavioral Reviews, 34,* 867–876.

London, R. A., Westrich, L., Stokes-Guinan, K., & McLaughlin, M. (2015). Playing fair: The contribution of high-functioning recess to overall school climate in low-income elementary schools. *Journal of School Health, 85,* 53–60.

Lovelace, M. (2005). Meta-analysis of experimental research based on the Dunn and Dunn Model. *Journal of Educational Research, 98*(3), 176–183.

Loveland, J. L. (2014). Traditional lecture versus an activity approach for teaching statistics: A comparison of outcomes. *All Graduate Theses and Dissertations.* 2086. http://digitalcommons.usu.edu/etd/2086

Low, S., & Espelage, D. (2013). Differentiating cyber bullying perpetration from non-physical bullying: Commonalities across race, individual, and family predictors. *Psychology of Violence, 3,* 39–52.

Loyens, S. M., Gijbels, D., & Coertjens, L., & Côté, D. J. (2013). Students' approaches to learning in problem-based learning: Taking into account professional behavior in tutorial groups, self-study time, and different assessment aspects. *Studies in Educational Evaluation, 39,* 23–32.

Lumeng, J. C., & Cardinal, T. M. (2007). Providing information about a flavor to preschoolers: Effects on liking and memory for having tasted it. *Chemical Senses, 32,* 505–513.

Luna, B., Garver, K. E., Urban, T. A., Lazar, N. A., & Sweeney, J. A. (2004). Maturation of cognitive processes from late childhood to adulthood. *Child Development, 75,* 1357–1372.

Luong, K. T., & Knobloch-Westerwick, S. (2017). Can the media help women be better at math? Stereotype threat, selective exposure, media effects, and women's math performance. *Human Communication Research, 43,* 193–213.

Luria, A. R. (1976). *Cognitive development: Its cultural and social foundations.* Cambridge, MA: Harvard University Press.

Luyckx, K., Tildesley, E., Soenens, B., & Andrews, J. (2011). Parenting and trajectories of children's maladaptive behaviors: A 12-

year prospective community study. *Journal of Clinical Child and Adolescent Psychology, 40*, 468–478.

Lynch, M. P. (2016). Googling is believing: Trumping the informed citizen. *New York Times.* Retrieved from http://opinionator.blogs.nytimes.com/2016/03/09/googling-is-believingtrumping-the-informed-citizen/

Mızrak, E., & Öztekin, I. (2016). Relationship between emotion and forgetting. *Emotion, 16*, 33–42.

Macionis, J. (2015). *Society: The basics* (13th ed.). Boston: Pearson.

Macionis, J. (2017). *Society: The basics* (14th ed.). Boston: Pearson.

Macionis, J., & Parrillo, V. (2017). *Cities and urban life* (7th ed.). Boston: Pearson.

Macnamara, B. N., Hambrick, D. Z., & Oswald, F. L. (2014). Deliberate practice and performance in music, games, sports, education, and professions: A meta-analysis. *Psychological Science*, 2014; DOI: 10.1177/0956797614535810

MacPherson, E., Kerr, G., & Stirling, A. (2016). The influence of peer groups in organized sport on female adolescents' identity development. *Psychology of Sport & Exercise, 23*, 73–81.

MacWhinney, B. (2011). Language development. In M. Bornstein & M. Lamb (Eds.), *Developmental science: An advanced textbook* (6th ed., pp. 389–424). New York: Psychology Press.

Magen, H. (2017). The relations between executive functions, media multitasking and polychronicity. *Computers in Human Behavior, 67*, 1–9.

Magnusson, P., Westjohn, S. A., Semenov, A. V., Randrianasolo, A. A., & Zdravkovic, S. (2013). The role of cultural intelligence in marketing adaptation and export performance. *Journal of International Marketing, 21*, 44–61.

Maguire, E., Gadian, D., Johnsrude, I., Good, C., Ashburner, J., Frackowiak, R., & Frith, C. (2000). Navigation-related structural change in the hippocampi of taxi drivers. *Proceedings of the National Academy of Science, USA, 97*(8), 4398–4403.

Mahatmya, D., Lohman, B. J., Brown, E. L., & Conway-Turner, J. (2016). The role of race and teachers' cultural awareness in predicting low-income, Black and Hispanic students' perceptions of educational attainment. *Social Psychology of Education, 19*, 427–449.

Malamud, O., & Pop-Eleches, C. (2010). *Home computer use and the development of human capital* (National Bureau of Economic Research Working Paper No. 15814).

Malouff, J. M., Schutte, N. S., & Thorsteinsson, E. B. (2014). Trait emotional intelligence and romantic relationship satisfaction: A meta-analysis. *American Journal of Family Therapy, 42*, 53–66.

Malycha, C. P., & Maier, G. W. (2017). Enhancing creativity on different complexity levels by eliciting mental models. *Psychology of Aesthetics, Creativity, and the Arts 11*, 187–201.

Mandelman, S. D., & Grigorenko, E. L. (2013). Questioning the unquestionable: Reviewing the evidence for the efficacy of gifted education. *Talent Development & Excellence, 5*, 125–137.

Mandinach, E., & Gummer, E. (2016). Every teacher should succeed with data literacy. *Phi Delta Kappan, 97*(8), 43–46.

Mann, T., de Ridder, D., & Fujita, K. (2013). Self-regulation of health behavior: Social psychological approaches to goal setting and goal striving. *Health Psychology, 32*, 487–498.

Manning, F., Lawless, K., Goldman, S., & Braasch, J. (2011, April). *Evaluating the usefulness of multiple sources with respect to an inquiry question: Middle school students' analysis and ranking of Internet search results.* Paper presented at the American Educational Research Association, New Orleans.

Manolitsis, G., Georgiou, G., & Parrila, R. (2011). Revisiting the home literacy model of reading development in an orthographically consistent language. *Learning & Instruction, 21*(4), 496–505.

March of Dimes Foundation. (2016). *2016 premature birth report card.* Retrieved from https://www.marchofdimes.org/materials/premature-birth-report-card-united-states.pdf

March, S. M., Abate, P., Spear, N. E., & Molina, J. C. (2013). The role of acetaldehyde in ethanol reinforcement assessed by Pavlovian conditioning in newborn rats. *Psychopharmacology, 226*, 491–499. doi:10.1007/s00213-012-2920-9

Marchand, G., & Skinner, E. A. (2007). Motivational dynamics of children's academic help-seeking and concealment. *Journal of Educational Psychology, 99*, 65–82.

Marchand, H. (2012). Contributions of Piagetian and post-Piagetian theories to education. *Educational Research Review, 7*, 165–176.

Marcia, J. (1980). Identity in adolescence. In J. Adelson (Ed.), *Handbook of adolescent psychology.* New York: Wiley.

Marcia, J. (1987). The identity status approach to the study of ego identity development. In T. Honess & K. Yardley (Eds.), *Self and identity: Perspectives across the life span.* London: Routledge & Kegan Paul.

Marcia, J. (1999). Representational thought in ego identity, psychotherapy, and psychosocial development. In I. E. Sigel (Ed.), *Development of mental representation: Theories and applications.* Mahwah, NJ: Lawrence Erlbaum.

Marcia, J. (2010). Life transitions and stress in the context of psychosocial development. In T. Miller (Ed.), *Handbook of stressful transitions across the lifespan* (pp. 19–34). New York: Springer Science & Business Media.

Mardanparvar, H., Sabohi, F., & Rezaei, D. A. (2016). Comparison of the effect of teaching by group guided discovery learning, questions and answers and lecturing methods on the level of learning and information durability of students. *Education Strategies in Medical Sciences, 8*, 35–41.

Margoni, F., & Surian, L. (2017). Children's intention-based moral judgments of helping agents. *Cognitive Development, 41*, 46–64.

Marinellie, S. & Kneile, L. (2012). Acquiring knowledge of derived nominals and derived adjectives in context. *Language, Speech, and Hearing Services in Schools, 43*, 53–65.

Markoff, J. (2013). Device from Israeli start-up gives the visually impaired a way to read. *The New York Times.* Retrieved from http://www.nytimes.com/2013/06/04/science/israeli-start-up-gives-visually-impaired-a-way-to-read.html

Marois, R., & Ivanoff, J. (2005). Capacity limits of information processing in the brain. *Trends in Cognitive Sciences, 9*, 296–305.

Martin, C., & Ruble, D. (2010). Patterns of gender development. *Annual Review of Psychology, 61*, 353–381.

Martin, J. (2006). Social cultural perspectives in educational psychology. In P. A. Alexander & P. H. Winne (Eds.), *Handbook of educational psychology* (2nd ed., pp. 595–614). Mahwah, NJ: Erlbaum.

Martocci, L. (2015). *Bullying: The social destruction of self.* Philadelphia: Temple University Press.

Marx, G. (2015). We are all poorer for neglecting students in poverty. *Education Week.* Retrieved from http://blogs.edweek.org/edweek/authors_corner_education_week_press/2015/06/we_are_all_poorer_for_neglecting_students_in_poverty.html?cmp=ENL-EU-NEWS3

Marzano, R. J. (2003). *What works in schools: Translating research into action.* Alexandria, VA: Association for Supervision and Curriculum Development.

Marzano, R. J. (2007). *Classroom assessment and grading that work.* Alexandria VA: Association for Supervision and Curriculum Development.

Marzano, R. J., & Pickering, D. J. (2007). Errors and allegations about research on homework. *Phi Delta Kappan, 88*, 507–513.

Maslow, A. (1968). *Toward a psychology of being* (2nd ed.). New York: Van Nostrand.

Maslow, A. (1970). *Motivation and personality* (2nd ed.). New York: Harper & Row. (Original work published 1954).

Maslow, A. H. (1987). *Motivation and personality* (3rd ed.). New York: Harper & Row.

Masson, S., & Sarrasin, J. B. (2015). Neuromyths in education: It's time to bust these widely held myths about the brain. *Education Canada, 55*, 28–35.

Mastropieri, M. A., & Scruggs, T. E. (2018). *The inclusive classroom: Strategies for effective differentiated instruction* (6th ed.). Boston: Pearson.

Matlen, B. J., & Klahr, D. (2013). Sequential effects of high and low instructional guidance on children's acquisition of experimentation skills: Is it all in the timing? *Instructional Science: An International Journal of the Learning Sciences, 41*, 621–634.

Matsumoto, D., & Juang, L. (2012). Culture, self, and identity. In D. Matsumoto & L. Juang (Eds.), *Culture and psychology* (pp. 342–365). Independence, KY: Cengage Learning.

Maxwell, L. (2013). Consortia struggle with ELL provisions. *Education Week, 32*(27), 1, 16, 17.

Mayer, R. (2008). *Learning and instruction* (2nd ed.). Boston: Pearson.

Mayer, R. E. (2002). *The promise of educational psychology: Volume II. Teaching for meaningful learning.* Upper Saddle River, NJ: Merrill/Pearson.

Mayer, R. E. (2004). Should there be a three-strikes rule against pure discovery learning? *American Psychologist, 59*, 14–19.

Mayer, R. E. (2008). *Learning and instruction* (2nd ed.). Upper Saddle River, NJ: Pearson.

Mayer, R. E., & Wittrock, M. C. (2006). Problem solving. In P. A. Alexander & P. H. Winne (Eds.), *Handbook of educational psychology* (2nd ed., pp. 287–303). Mahwah, NJ: Erlbaum.

Mayer, R., & Massa, L. (2003). Three facts of visual and verbal learners: Cognitive ability, cognitive style, and learning preference. *Journal of Educational Psychology, 95*, 833–846.

Mayeux, L., Houser, J., & Dyches, K. (2011). Social acceptance and popularity: Two distinct forms of peer status. In A. Cillessen, D., Schwartz, & L. Mayeux (Eds.), *Popularity in the peer system* (pp. 79–102). New York: Guilford.

Mayor, J., & Plunkett, K. (2010). A neurocomputational account of taxonomic responding and fast mapping in early word learning. *Developmental Review, 117*(1), 1–31.

Martínez, V., Justicia, F. J., & Fernández, H. E. (2016). Teacher assertiveness in the development of students' social competence. *Electronic Journal of Research in Educational Psychology, 14*, 310–332.

McBride, A. M., Chung, S., & Robertson, A. (2016). Preventing academic disengagement through a middle school–based social and emotional learning program. *Journal of Experiential Education, 39*, 370 –385.

McCarthy, Peter, Sithole, A., McCarthy, Paul, Cho, J., & Gyan, E. (2016). Teacher questioning strategies in mathematical classroom discourse: A case study of two grade eight teachers in Tennessee, USA. *Journal of Education and Practice, 7*, 80–89.

McCoy, D. C. (2016). Early adversity, self-regulation, and child development. In N. K. Lesaux & S. M. Jones (Eds.). (2016). *The leading edge of early childhood education: Linking science to policy for a new generation of prekindergarten* (pp. 29–44). Cambridge, MA: Harvard Education Publishing Group.

McCrudden, M. T., & McNamara, D. S. (2018). *Cognition in education.* New York: Routledge.

McCutchen, D. (2000). Knowledge, processing, and working memory: Implications for a theory of writing. *Educational Psychologist, 35*(1), 13–23.

McDaniel, B. T., Drouin, M., & Cravens, J. D. (2017). Do you have anything to hide? Infidelity-related behaviors on social media sites and marital satisfaction. *Computers in Human Behavior, 66*, 88–95.

McDaniel, M. A., Agarwal, P. K., Huelser, B. J., McDermott, K. B., & Roediger, H. L. (2011). Test-enhanced learning in a middle school science classroom: The effects of quiz frequency and placement. *Journal of Educational Psychology, 103*(2), 399–414.

McDonald, D. R. (2016). Concept formation. *Salem Press Encyclopedia of Health.* Ipswich, MA: Salem Press.

McDougall, D., & Granby, C. (1996). How expectation of questioning method affects undergraduates' preparation for class. *Journal of Experimental Education, 65*, 43–54.

McEvoy, P. M., Moulds, M. L., & Mahoney, A. E. (2013). Mechanisms driving pre- and post-stressor repetitive negative thinking: Metacognitions, cognitive avoidance, and thought control. *Journal of Behavior Therapy and Experimental Psychiatry, 44*, 84–93.

McGregor, J. (2016). Why Angela Duckworth thinks "gritty" leaders are people to emulate. *The Washington Post.* Retrieved from https://www.washingtonpost.com/news/on-leadership/wp/2016/05/12/why-angela-duckworth-thinks-gritty-leaders-are-people-to-emulate/?utm_term=.b13566eccc78

McHugh, J. E., & Lawlor, B. A. (2016). Executive functioning independently predicts self-rated health and improvement in self-rated health over time among community-dwelling older adults. *Aging & Mental Health, 20*, 415–422.

McInerney, D. M., Walker, R. A., & Liem, G. A. D. (Eds.). (2011). *Sociocultural theories of learning and motivation: Looking back, looking forward.* Charlotte, N.C.: Information Age Publishing.

McIntyre, L. (2015). The attack on truth. *The Chronicle of Higher Education.* Retrieved from http://m.chronicle.com/article/The-Attack-on-Truth/230631

McIntyre, N. A., Mainhard, M. T., & Klassen, R. M. (2017). Are you looking to teach? Cultural, temporal and dynamic insights into expert teacher gaze. *Learning and Instruction, 49*, 41–53.

McKeachie, W., & Kulik, J. (1975). Effective college teaching. In F. Kerlinger (Ed.), *Review of research in education*: Vol. 3 (pp. 24–39). Washington, DC: American Educational Research Association.

McKenney, S., & Reeves, T. C. (2014). Educational design research. In J. M. Spector, M.D. Merrill, J. Elen, & M. J. Bishop (Eds.), Handbook of research on educational communications and technology (pp. 131–140). New York, NY: Springer. Retrieved from http://dx.doi.org/10.1007/978-1-4614-3185-5_11

McLaughlin, M., & Rank, M. R. (2018). Estimating the Economic Cost of Childhood Poverty in the United States. *Social Work Research.* Retrieved from https://doi.org/10.1093/swr/svy007.

McMahon, S., Rose, D., & Parks, M. (2004). Multiple intelligences and reading achievement; An examination of the Teele Inventory of Multiple Intelligences. *Journal of Experimental Education, 73*(1), 41–52.

McMorris, T. (Ed.) (2016). *Exercise-cognition interaction: Neuroscience perspectives.* Amsterdam: Academic Press.

McWhorter, J. (2013). Is texting killing the English language? *Time Ideas.* Retrieved from http://ideas.time.com/2013/04/25/is-texting-killing-the-english-language/

McWilliams, S. A. (2016). Cultivating constructivism: Inspiring intuition and promoting process and pragmatism. *Journal of Constructivist Psychology, 29*, 1–29.

Medina, M. S., Castleberry, A. N., & Persky, A. M. (2017). Strategies for improving learner metacognition in health professional education. *American Journal of Pharmaceutical Education, 81*, 1–14.

Meek, C. (2006). From the inside out: A look at testing special education students. *Phi Delta Kappan, 88*, 293–297.

Meichenbaum, D. (2000). *Cognitive behavior modification: An integrative approach.* Dordrecht, Netherlands: Kluwer Academic.

Melanko, S., & Larkin, K. T. (2013). Preference for immediate reinforcement over delayed reinforcement: Relation between delay discounting and health behavior. *Journal of Behavioral Medicine, 36*, 34–43. doi:10.1007/s10865-012-9399-z

Mendez, M., Durtschi, J., Neppl, T. K., & Stith, S. M. (2016). Corporal punishment and externalizing behaviors in toddlers: The moderating role of positive and harsh parenting. *Journal of Family Psychology, 30*, 887–895.

Meng, L., Muñoz, M., King, K., & Liu, S. (2016). Effective teaching factors and student reading strategies as predictors of student achievement in PISA 2009: The case of China and the United States. *Educational Review, 69*, 68–84.

Mercer, J. (1973). *Labeling the mentally retarded.* Berkeley: University of California Press.

Merk, S., Rosman, T., Rueß, J., Syring, M., & Schneider, J. (2017). Pre-service teachers' perceived value of general pedagogical knowledge for practice: Relations with epistemic beliefs and source beliefs. *PLoS ONE, 12*, 1–25.

Merrell, K., Gueldner, B., Ross, S., & Isava, D. (2008). How effective are school bullying intervention programs? A meta-analysis of intervention research. *School Psychology Quarterly, 23*, 26–42.

Merrotsy, P. (2013). Invisible gifted students. *Talent Development & Excellence, 5*, 31–42.

Mertz, E., & Yovel, J. (2010). Metalinguistic awareness. In J. Ostman, J. Verschureren, J. Blommaert, & C. Bulcaen (Eds.), *Handbook of pragmatics* (pp. 122–144). New York: Kluwer.

Metcalfe, J., & Finn, B. (2013). Metacognition and control of study choice in children. *Metacognition and Learning, 8*, 19–46. doi:10.1007/s11409-013-9094-7

Michael, N. A., & Libarkin, J. C. (2016). Understanding by design: Mentored implementation of backward design methodology at the university level. *Bioscene: Journal of College Biology Teaching, 42*, 44–52.

Miller, A. (2013). How to teach a teen to have impulse control. *GlobalPost*. Retrieved from http://everydaylife.globalpost.com/teach-teen-impulse-control-11045.html

Miller, A. C. (2016). Confronting confirmation bias: Giving truth a fighting chance in the information age. *Social education, 80*, 276–279.

Miller, B. (2016). *Cultural anthropology* (8th ed.). Boston: Pearson.

Miller, G. (1956). The magical number seven, plus or minus two: Some limits on our capacity for processing information. *Psychological Review, 63*, 81–97.

Miller, G. (2012). Equal opportunity: A landmark law for children and education. *Education Week, 31*(15), 40.

Miller, M. E. (2016). N.C. transgender bathroom ban is a 'national embarrassment,' state attorney general says. *The Washington Post*. Retrieved from https://www.washingtonpost.com/news/morning-mix/wp/2016/03/30/nc-transgender-bathroom-ban-is-a-national-embarrassment-says-ag-as-pilloried-law-becomes-key-election-issue/?utm_term=.55d4afe17aec

Miller, M., Linn, R., & Gronlund, N. (2013). *Measurement and assessment in teaching* (11th ed.). Boston: Pearson.

Miller, P. H. (2017). *Theories of developmental psychology* (6th ed.). New York: Worth.

Miller, R., M., Marriot, D., Trotter, J., Hammond, T., Lyman, D., Call, T., . . . Edwards, J. G. (2018). Running exercise mitigates the negative consequences of chronic stress on dorsal hippocampal long-term potentiation in male mice. *Neurobiology of Learning and Memory, 149*, 28–38. doi: 10.1016/j.nlm.2018.01.008

Miller-Cotto, D., & Byrnes, J. P. (2016). Ethnic/racial identity and academic achievement: A meta-analytic review. *Developmental Review, 41*, 51–70.

Mills, G. E. (2018). *Action research: A guide for the teacher researcher* (6th ed.). New York: Pearson.

Mills, G. E., & Gay, L. R. (2016). *Educational research: Competencies for analysis and application* (11th ed.). Boston: Pearson.

Miltenberger, R. G. (2012). *Behavior modification: Principles and procedures* (5th ed.). Belmont, CA: Cengage.

Mirpuri, D. (2014). Right brain vs left brain: Find out how the left brain and the right brain influence our personalities. *About.com Toys*. Retrieved from http://toys.about.com/od/babydvdsandmusic/qt/leftrightbrain.htm

Mitchell, M. M., & Bradshaw, C. P. (2013). Examining classroom influences on student perceptions of school climate: The role of classroom management and exclusionary discipline strategies. *Journal of School Psychology, 51*, 599–610.

Mittleman, J. (2018). Sexual orientation and school discipline: New evidence from a population-based sample. *Educational Researcher, 47*, 181–190.

Modecki, K., Minchin, J., Harbaugh, A. G., Guerra, N. G., & Runions, K. C. (2014). Bullying prevalence across contexts: A meta-analysis measuring cyber and traditional bullying. *Journal of Adolescent Health, 55*, 602–611.

Moreno, R., & Duran, R. (2004). Do multiple representations need explanations?: The role of verbal guidance and individual differences in multimedia mathematics learning. *Journal of Educational Psychology, 96*, 492–503.

Moreno, R., & Mayer, R. (2000). Engaging students in active learning: The case for personalized multimedia messages. *Journal of Educational Psychology, 92*(4), 724–733.

Moreno, R., & Mayer, R. (2005). Role of guidance, reflection, and interactivity in an agent-based multimedia game. *Journal of Educational Psychology, 97*(1), 117–128.

Morgan, B. (2017). Situated cognition and the study of culture: An introduction. *Poetics Today, 38*, 213–233.

Morgan, H. (2016). Relying on high-stakes standardized tests to evaluate schools and teachers: A bad idea. *Clearing House: A Journal of Educational Strategies, Issues and Ideas, 89*, 67–72.

Morgan, P. L., Farkas, G., Hillemeier, M. M., & Maczuga, S. (2017). Replicated evidence of racial and ethnic disparities in disability identification in U.S. schools. *Educational Researcher, 46*, 305–322.

Morgan, P., Staff, J., Hillemeier, M., Farkas, G., & Maczuga, S. (2013). Racial and ethnic disparities in ADHD diagnosis from kindergarten to eighth grade. *Pediatrics*. Retrieved from http://pediatrics.aappublications.org/content/early/2013/06/19/peds.2012-2390

Morgan, S. L., & Mehta, J. D. (2004). Beyond the laboratory: Evaluating the survey evidence for the disidentification explanation of black–white differences in achievement. *Sociology of Education, 77*(1), 82–101.

Morra, S., Gobbo, C., Marini, Z., & Sheese, R. (2008). *Cognitive development: Neo-Piagetian perspectives*. New York: Erlbaum.

Morris, A. K., & Hiebert, J. (2017). Effects of teacher preparation courses: Do graduates use what they learned to plan mathematics lessons? *American Educational Research Journal, 54*, 524–567.

Morris, P., Lloyd, C. M., Millenky, M., Leacock, N., Raver, C. C., & Bangser, M. (2013). *Using classroom management to improve preschoolers' social and emotional skills: Final impact and implementation findings from the Foundations of Learning Demonstration in Newark and Chicago*. New York: MDRC. Retrieved from http://www.eric.ed.gov.dax.lib.unf.edu/PDFS/ED540680.pdf

Morsy, L., & Rothstein, R. (2015). Five social disadvantages that depress student performance: Why schools can't close achievement gaps. *Economic Policy Institute*. Retrieved from http://www.epi.org/publication/five-social-disadvantages-that-depress-student-performance-why-schools-alone-cant-close-achievement-gaps/

Moser, L., Berlie, H., Salinitri, F., McCuistion, M, & Slaughter, R. (2015). Enhancing academic success by creating a community of learners. *American Journal of Pharmaceutical Education, 79*, 1–9.

Mosher, J., Gjerde, C. L., Wilhelm, M., Srinivasan, S., & Hagen, S. (2017). Interactive discussion versus lecture for learning and retention by medical students. *Focus on Health Professional Education (2204–7662), 18*, 16–26.

Motamedi, J. G. (2015). Time to reclassification: How long does it take English learner students in Washington Roadmap districts to develop English proficiency? *National Center for Educational Evaluation and Regional Assistance*. Retrieved from http://www.scribd.com/doc/273821952/English-language-Learner-Proficiency-Study.

Mulvey, K.L. & Killen, M. (2016). Keeping quiet just wouldn't be right: Children's and adolescents' evaluations of challenges to peer relational and physical aggression. *Journal of Youth and Adolescence, 45*, 1824–1835.

Munk, D. D., & Dempsey, T. L. (2010). *Leadership strategies for successful schoolwide inclusion: The STAR approach*. Baltimore: Brookes.

Murphy, E. S., & Lupfer, G. J. (2014). Basic principles of operant conditioning. In F. K. McSweeney & E. S. Murphy (Eds.), *The Wiley Blackwell handbook of operant and classical conditioning* (pp. 167–194). Malden, MA: John Wiley & Sons.

Murphy, M. C., & Dweck, C. S. (2016). Research dialogue: Mindsets shape consumer behavior *Journal of Consumer Psychology, 26*, 127–136.

Müller, E., Cannon, L. R., Kornblum, C., Clark, J., & Powers, M. (2016). Description and preliminary evaluation of a curriculum for teaching conversational skills to children with high-functioning autism and other social cognition challenges. *Language, Speech, and Hearing Services in Schools, 47*, 191–208.

Musu-Gillette, L., Zhang, A., Wang, K., Zhang, J., and Oudekerk, B.A. (2017). *Indicators of school crime and safety: 2016 (NCES 2017-064/NCJ 250650)*. National Center for Education Statistics, U.S. Department of Education, and Bureau of Justice Statistics, Office of Justice Programs, U.S. Department of Justice. Washington, DC. Retrieved from https://www.bjs.gov/content/pub/pdf/iscs16.pdf

Myers, C. G. (2016). Antecedents and performance benefits of reciprocal vicarious learning in teams. *Academy of Management Annual Meeting Proceedings, 30*–135. doi: 10.5465/AMBPP.2016.55

NACE. (2016). The Attributes Employers Seek on a Candidate's Resume. *National Association of Colleges and Employers.* Retrieved from http://www.naceweb.org/talent-acquisition/candidate-selection/the-attributes-employers-seek-on-a-candidates-resume/

Naci, J. C. (2013). Process inquiry: Analysis of oral problem-solving skills in mathematics of engineering students. *US-China Education Review A, 3*, 73–82.

Nahigian, K. (2017). Behaviorism. *Humanist, 77*, 36–37.

Nair, S., Sagar, M., Sollers, J., Consedine, N., & Broadbent, E. (2015). Do slumped and upright postures affect stress responses? A randomized trial. *Health Psychology, 34*, 632–641.

Najdowski, C. J., Bottoms, B. L., & Goff, P. A. (2015). Stereotype threat and racial differences in citizens experiences of police encounters. *Law and Human Behavior, 39*, 463–477.

Narciss, S., Sosnovsky, S., Schnaubert, L., Andrès, E., Eichelmann, A., Goguadze, G., & Melis, E. (2014). Exploring feedback and student characteristics relevant for personalizing feedback strategies. *Computers and Education, 71*, 56–76.

Nasir, N., Rosebery, A., Warren, B., & Lee, C. (2006). Learning as a cultural process: Achieving equity through diversity. In R. K. Sawyer (Ed.), *The Cambridge handbook of the learning sciences* (pp. 489–504). New York: Cambridge University Press.

National Aeronautics and Space Administration. (2017). *Global climate change: Vital signs of the planet.* Retrieved from https://climate.nasa.gov/evidence/

National Assessment of Educational Progress. (2014). New results show eighth-graders' knowledge of U.S. history, geography, and civics. Retrieved from http://www.nationsreportcard.gov/hgc_2014/

National Assessment of Educational Progress. (2015). *Mathematics and reading assessments.* Retrieved from https://www.nationsreportcard.gov/reading_math_2015/#mathematics?grade=4

National Association for the Education of Homeless Children and Youth. (2016). New federal policies for education of homeless children to take effect next year; decision impacts every school district nationwide. Retrieved from https://www.prnewswire.com/news-releases/new-federal-policies-for-education-of-homeless-children-to-take-effect-next-year-decision-impacts-every-school-district-nationwide-300246419.html#continue-jump

National Association of School Psychologists. (2013). *A framework for safe and successful schools.* Retrieved from www.nasponline.org.

National Center for Education Statistics. (2015). Percentage of public school students enrolled in gifted and talented programs, by sex, race/ethnicity, and state: 2004, 2006, and 2011–12. *U.S. Department of Education.* Retrieved from https://nces.ed.gov/programs/digest/d15/tables/dt15_204.90.asp

National Center for Education Statistics. (2016). *Student reports of bullying: Results from the 2015 School Crime Supplement to the National Crime Victimization Survey.* U.S. Department of Education. Retrieved from https://nces.ed.gov/pubs2017/2017015.pdf

National Center for Education Statistics. (2017a). *2015 | Mathematics & Reading Assessments.* https://www.nationsreportcard.gov/reading_math_2015/#?grade=4

National Center for Education Statistics. (2017a). Children and youth with disabilities. *U. S. Department of Education* Retrieved from https://nces.ed.gov/programs/coe/indicator_cgg.asp

National Center for Education Statistics. (2017b). *NAEP Overview.* Retrieved from https://nces.ed.gov/nationsreportcard/about/

National Center for Education Statistics. (2017b). English language learners in public schools. *U.S. Department of Education.* Retrieved from https://nces.ed.gov/programs/coe/indicator_cgf.asp

National Center for Education Statistics. (2017c). Racial/Ethnic Enrollment in Public Schools.

National Center for Education Statistics. (2017d). Undergraduate enrollment. *U.S. Department of Education.* Retrieved from https://nces.ed.gov/programs/coe/indicator_cha.asp

National Center for Education Statistics. (2017e). Undergraduate retention and graduation rates. *U.S. Department of Education.* Retrieved from https://nces.ed.gov/programs/coe/indicator_ctr.asp

National Center for Learning Disabilities. (2017). *The state of LD: Executive summary.* Retrieved from https://www.ncld.org/executive-summary

National Center on Universal Design for Learning. (2014a). *The three principles of UDL.* Retrieved from http://www.udlcenter.org/aboutudl/whatisudl/3principles

National Center on Universal Design for Learning. (2014b). *UDL and technology.* Retrieved from http://www.udlcenter.org/aboutudl/udltechnology

National Commission on Excellence in Education. (1983). *A nation at risk: The imperative for educational reform.* Washington, DC: Government Printing Office. Retrieved from https://www.edreform.com/wp-content/uploads/2013/02/A_Nation_At_Risk_1983.pdf

National Conference of State Legislatures. (2017). *State minimum wages.* Retrieve from http://www.ncsl.org/research/labor-and-employment/state-minimum-wage-chart.aspx

National Council on Disability. (2011). *National disabilities policy: A progress report—October 2011.* Retrieved from http://www.ncd.gov/progress_reports/Oct312011

National Highway Traffic Safety Administration. (2017). *Traffic safety facts.* U.S. Department of Transportation. Retrieved from https://www.nhtsa.gov/sites/nhtsa.dot.gov/files/documents/812_381_distracteddriving2015.pdf

National Institute on Drug Abuse. (2017). Overdose death rates. National Institutes of Health. Retrieved from https://www.drugabuse.gov/related-topics/trends-statistics/overdose-death-rates

National Society for the Gifted and Talented. (2014). *Giftedness defined.* Retrieved from http://www.nsgt.org/giftedness-defined/

Neisser, U. (1967). *Cognitive psychology.* New York: Appleton-Century-Crofts.

Nelson, C., Thomas, K., & de Haan, M. (2006). Neural bases of cognitive development. In D. Kuhn, R. Siegler (Vol. Eds.), W. Damon, & R. Lerner (Series Eds.), *Handbook of child psychology. Vol. 2: Cognition, perception, and language* (6th ed., pp. 3–57). New York: Wiley.

Netcoh, S. (2017). Research paper: Balancing freedom and limitations: A case study of choice provision in a personalized learning class. *Teaching and Teacher Education, 66*, 383–392.

Nettelbeck, T., & Wilson, C. (2010). Intelligence and IQ. In K. Wheldall (Ed.), *Developments in educational psychology* (2nd ed., pp. 30–52). New York: Routledge.

Neuenschwander, R., Cimeli, P., Röthlisberger, M., & Roebers, C. M. (2013). Personality factors in elementary school children: Contributions to academic performance over and above executive functions? *Learning and Individual Differences, 25*, 118–125.

Neuhauser, A. (2015). 2015 STEM index shows gender, racial gaps widen. *U.S. News.* Retrieved from https://www.usnews.com/news/stem-index/articles/2015/06/29/gender-racial-gaps-widen-in-stem-fields

Neuman, S. (2014). 1 in 4 Americans thinks the Sun goes around the Earth, survey says. *National Public Radio.* http://www.npr.org/sections/thetwo-way/2014/02/14/277058739/1-in-4-americans-think-the-sun-goes-around-the-earth-survey-says

Neuman, S. B. (2016). The danger of data-driven instruction. *Educational Leadership, 74*, 24–29.

Neuman, S. B., & Celano, D. C. (2012). *Giving our children a fighting chance: Poverty, literacy, and the development of information capital.* New York: Teachers College Press.

Neuman, S. B., Pinkham, A., & Kaefer, T. (2016). Improving low-income preschoolers' word and world knowledge: The effects of content-rich instruction. *Elementary School Journal, 116*, 652–674.

Newport, F. (2018). In U.S., estimate of LGBT population rises to 4.5%. *Gallup.* Retrieved from http://news.gallup.com/poll/234863/estimate-lgbt-population-rises.aspx?utm_source=alert&utm_medium=email&utm_content=morelink&utm_campaign=syndication

Ngu, B. H., & Yeung, A. S. (2013). Algebra word problem solving approaches in a chemistry context: Equation worked examples versus text editing. *The Journal of Mathematical Behavior, 32,* 197–208.

Nie, Y., & Liem, G. A. D. (2013). Extending antecedents of achievement goals: The double-edged sword effect of social-oriented achievement motive and gender differences. *Learning and Individual Differences, 23,* 249–255.

Nierengarten, M. B. (2015). Bipolar disorder in children: Assessment and diagnosis. *Contemporary Pediatrics, 32,* 34–38.

Nikou, S. A., & Economides, A. A. (2017). Mobile-based assessment: Integrating acceptance and motivational factors into a combined model of self-determination theory and technology acceptance. *Computers in Human Behavior, 68,* 83–95.

Niu, L., Behar-Horenstein, L. S., & Garvan, C. W. (2013). Do instructional interventions influence college students' critical thinking skills? A meta-analysis. *Educational Research Review, 9,* 114–128.

Noddings, N. (1992). *The challenge to care in schools: An alternative approach to education.* New York, NY: Teachers College Press.

Noddings, N. (2002). *Educating moral people: A caring alternative approach to education.* New York: Teachers College Press.

Noddings, N. (2008). Caring and moral education. In L. P. Nucci & D. Narváez (Eds.), *Handbook of moral and character education* (pp. 161–174). New York: Routledge.

Noddings, N. (2013). *Caring: A relational approach to ethics and moral education* (2nd ed.). Berkley, CA: University of California Press.

NoKidHungry. (2016). *No child should grow up hungry.* Retrieved from https://www.nokidhungry.org/pdfs/nkh-briefing-book-2016.pdf

Nowrasteh, A. (2015). Immigration and crime—what the research says. *The Cato Institute.* Retrieved from https://www.cato.org/blog/immigration-crime-what-research-says

Nucci, L. (2006). Classroom management for moral and social development. In C. Evertson & C. Weinstein (Eds.), *Handbook of classroom management: Research, practice, and contemporary issues* (pp. 711–731). Mahwah, NJ: Erlbaum.

Null, R. (2013). *Universal design: Principles and models.* Boca Raton: FL. CRC Press.

Nutter, S. Russell-Mayhew, S., Alberga, A. S., Arthur, N., Kassan, A. Lund, D. E., Sesma-Vazquez, M., & Williams. E. (2016). Positioning of weight bias: Moving towards social justice. *Journal of Obesity, 2016,* 1–10.

O'Brien, T. (1999). Parrot math. *Phi Delta Kappan, 80,* 434–438.

O'Connor, E. E., Dearing, E., & Collins, B. A. (2011). Teacher-child relationship and behavior problem trajectories in elementary school. *American Educational Research Journal, 48,* 120–162.

O'Connor, K. (2011). *A repair kit for grading: 15 fixes for broken grades* (2nd ed.). Boston: Pearson Assessment Training Institute.

O'Leary, A. P., & Sloutsky, V. M. (2017). Carving metacognition at its joints: Protracted development of component processes. *Child Development, 88,* 1015–1032.

O'Meara, J. (2011). *Beyond differentiated instruction.* Thousand Oaks, CA: Corwin Press.

O'Neil, J. (2012, March 27). Roadblocks to a rite of passage. *New York Times,* pp. D1, D6.

Oakes, J. (2005). *Keeping track: How schools structure inequality* (2nd ed.). New Haven, CT: Yale University Press.

Obamacare.net. (2017). 2017 Federal Poverty Level. Retrieved from https://obamacare.net/2017-federal-poverty-level/

OECD (2015). *The ABC of gender equality in education: Aptitude, behaviour, confidence.* PISA, OECD Publishing. http://dx.doi.org/10.1787/9789264229945-en

OECD (2018). Poverty gap (indicator). Retrieved from https://data.oecd.org/inequality/poverty-gap.htm#indicator-chart doi: 10.1787/349eb41b-en.

Office of Educational Technology. (2017). Reimagining the role of technology in education: 2017 national education technology plan update. *U.S. Department of Education.* Retrieved from https://tech.ed.gov/files/2017/01/NETP17.pdf

Office of Special Education and Rehabilitative Services. (2016). 38th annual report to Congress on the implementation of the Individuals with Disabilities Education Act, 2016. *U.S. Department of Education.* Retrieved from https://www2.ed.gov/about/reports/annual/osep/2016/parts-b-c/38th-arc-for-idea.pdf

Ogbu, J. (1992). Understanding cultural diversity and learning. *Educational Researcher, 21*(8), 5–14.

Ogbu, J. (2003). *Black American students in an affluent suburb: A study of academic disengagement.* Mahwah, NJ: Erlbaum.

Ogbu, J. U. (2008). Collective identity and the burden of "acting White" in Black history, community, and education. In J. U. Ogbu (Ed.), *Minority status, oppositional culture, and schooling* (pp. 29–63). New York: Routledge.

Öğmen, H., & Herzog, M. H. (2016). A new conceptualization of human visual sensory-memory. *Frontiers in Psychology.* doi. org/10.3389/fpsyg.2016.00830

Ok, M. W., Rao, K., Bryant, B. R., & McDougall, D. (2017). Universal design for learning in Pre-K to 12 classrooms: A systematic review of research. *Exceptionality, 25,* 116–138.

Okagaki, L. (2006). Ethnicity, learning. In P. A. Alexander & P. H. Winne (Eds.), *Handbook of educational psychology* (2nd ed., pp. 615–634). Mahwah, NJ: Erlbaum.

Okonofua, J. A., & Eberhardt, J. L. (2015). Two strikes: Race and the disciplining of young students. *Psychological Science, 26,* 617–624.

Okonofua, J. A., Paunesku, D., & Walton, G. M. (2016). Brief intervention to encourage empathic discipline cuts suspension rates in half among adolescents. *PNAS, 113,* 5221–5226. doi: 10.1073/pnas.1523698113

Olakanmi, E. E. (2017). The effects of a flipped classroom model of instruction on students' performance and attitudes toward chemistry. *Journal of Science Education and Technology, 26,* 127–137.

Olive, T., & Barbier, M-L. (2017). Processing time and cognitive effort of longhand note taking when reading and summarizing a structured or linear text. *Written Communication, 34,* 224–246.

Otto, B. (2018). *Language development in early childhood education* (5th ed.). Boston: Pearson.

Oudiette, D., Antony, J. W., Creery, J. C., & Paller, K. A. (2013). The role of memory reactivation during wakefulness and sleep in determining which memories endure. *Journal of Neuroscience, 33,* 6672–6678.

Owens, R. E. (2016). *Language development: An introduction* (9th ed.). Boston: Pearson.

Oyserman, D., & Destin, M. (2010). Identity-based motivation: Implications for intervention. *The Counseling Psychologist, 38,* 1001–1043.

Paas, F., Renkl, A., & Sweller, J. (2004). Cognitive load theory: Instructional implications of the interaction between information structures and cognitive architecture. *Instructional Science, 32*(1), 1–8.

Pace, A., Hirsh-Pasek, K., & Golinkoff, R. M. (2016). High-quality language leads to high-quality learning. In N. K. Lesaux & S. M. Jones (Eds.). (2016). *The leading edge of early childhood education: Linking science to policy for a new generation of prekindergarten* (pp. 45–60). Cambridge, MA: Harvard Education Publishing Group.

Padgett, S., & Notar, C. E. (2013). Anti-bullying programs for middle/high schools. *National Social Science Journal, 40,* 88–93.

Page, L. C., & Scott-Clayton, J. (2016). Improving college access in the United States: Barriers and policy responses. *Economics of Education Review, 51,* 4–22.

Paivio, A. (1986). *Mental representations: A dual-coding approach.* New York: Oxford University.

Paivio, A. (1991). Dual coding theory: Retrospect and current status. *Canadian Journal of Psychology, 45,* 255–287.

Pajares, F. (2009). Toward a positive psychology of academic motivation. The role of self-efficacy beliefs. In R. Gilman, F. S. Huebner, & M. J. Furlong (Eds.), *Handbook of positive psychology in schools* (pp. 149–160). New York: Routledge.

Palmer, E. (2018). Teachers rally against guns: #ArmMeWith better tools. *Newsweek.* Retrieved from https://www.msn.com/en-us/

news/msn/teachers-rally-against-guns-%23armmewith-better-tools/ar-BBJsZpM

Palmer, K. (2015). Flipping a calculus class: One instructor's experience. *PRIMUS, 25,* 886–891.

Paluck, E. L., Shepherd, H., & Aronow, P. M. (2016). Changing climates of conflict: A social network experiment in 56 schools. *PNAS, 113,* 566–571.

Panahon, C. J., & Martens, B. K. (2013). A comparison of noncontingent plus contingent reinforcement to contingent reinforcement alone on students' academic performance. *Journal of Behavioral Education, 22,* 37–49. doi:10.1007/s10864–012–9157-x

Pane, J. F., Steiner, E. D., Baird, M. D., Hamilton, L. S., & Pane, J. D. (2017). Informing progress: Insights on personalized learning implementation and effects. *The Rand Corporation.* Retrieved from https://www.rand.org/content/dam/rand/pubs/research_reports/RR2000/RR2042/RAND_RR2042.pdf

Panero, N. S. (2016). Progressive mastery through deliberate practice: A promising approach for improving writing. *Improving Schools, 19,* 229–245.

Pant, B. (2016). Different cultures see deadlines differently. *Harvard Business Review.* Retrieved from https://hbr.org/2016/05/different-cultures-see-deadlines-differently

Papagno, C., Comi, A., Riva, M., Bizzi, A., Vernice, M., Casarotti, A., Fava, E., & Bello, L., (2017). Mapping the brain network of the phonological loop. *Human Brain Mapping, 38,* 3011–3024.

Paradise, R., & Rogoff, B. (2009). Side by side: Learning by observing and pitching in. *Ethos, 27,* 102–138.

Park, R., & Jang, S. J. (2017). Mediating role of perceived supervisor support in the relationship between job autonomy and mental health: Moderating role of value-means fit. *International Journal of Human Resource Management, 28,* 703–723.

Park, V., & Datnow, A. (2017). Ability grouping and differentiated instruction in an era of data-driven decision making. *American Journal of Education, 123,* 281–306.

Parke, R., & Clarke-Stewart, A. (2011). *Social development.* Hoboken, NJ: Wiley.

Parker, J. D. A., Saklofske, D. H., & Keefer, K. V. (2017). Giftedness and academic success in college and university: Why emotional intelligence matters. *Gifted Education International, 33,* 183–194.

Parker, P. D., Van Zanden, B., & Parker, R. B., (2017). Girls get smart, boys get smug: Historical changes in gender differences in math, literacy, and academic social comparison and achievement. *Learning and Instruction.* https://doi.org/10.1016/j.learninstruc.2017.09.002

Parker-Pope, T. (2010, July 20). Attention disorders can take a toll on marriage. *The New York Times.* Retrieved from https://well.blogs.nytimes.com/2010/07/19/attention-disorders-can-take-a-toll-on-marriage/

Parks, F. R., & Kennedy, J. H. (2007). The impact of race, physical attractiveness, and gender on education majors' and teachers' perceptions of student competence. *Journal of Black Studies, 37,* 936–943.

Parsons, S. A., Dodman, S. L., & Burrowbridge, S. C. (2013). Broadening the view of differentiated instruction. *Phi Delta Kappan, 95,* 38–42.

Parsons, S. A., Vaughn, M., Scales, R. Q., Gallagher, M. A., Parsons, A. W., Davis, S. G., Pierczynski, M., & Allen, M. (2018). Teachers' instructional adaptations: A research synthesis. *Review of Educational Research, 88,* 205–242.

Pascual-Leone, A., Amedi, A., Fregni, F., & Merabet, L. B. (2005). The plastic human brain cortex. *Annual Review of Neuroscience, 28,* 377–401. doi 10.1146/annurev.neuro.27.070203.144216

Pashler, H., & Carrier, M. (1996). Structures, processes, and the flow of information. In E. Bjork & R. Bjork (Eds.), *Memory* (pp. 3–29). San Diego, CA: Academic Press.

Pashler, H., McDaniel, M., Rohrer, D., & Bjork, R. (2008). Learning Styles: Concepts and Evidence. *Psychological Science in the Public Interest, 9,* 105–119.

Patall, E. A., Vasquez, A. C., Steingut, R. R., Trimble, S. S., & Pituch, K. A. (2016). Empirical study: Daily interest, engagement, and autonomy support in the high school science classroom. *Contemporary Educational Psychology, 46,* 180–194.

Patterson, E. (2011). Texting: An old language habit in a new media. *International Journal of the Humanities, 9,* 235–242.

Pearson, B., Velleman, S., Bryant, T., & Charko, T. (2009). Phonological milestones for African American English-speaking children learning mainstream American English as a second dialect. *Language, Speech, and Hearing Services in School, 40*(3), 229–244.

Pekrun, R., Goetz, T., Frenzel, A. C., Barchfeld, P., & Perry, R. P. (2011). Measuring emotions in students' learning and performance: The Achievement Emotions Questionnaire (AEQ). *Contemporary Educational Psychology, 36,* 36–48. doi:10.1016/j.cedpsych.2010.10.002

Pellegrini, A. (2011). "In the eye of the beholder": Sex bias in observations and ratings of children's aggression. *Educational Researcher, 40,* 281–286.

Pellegrino, A. M. (2010). Pre-service teachers and classroom authority. *American Secondary Education, 38,* 62–78.

Pemberton, B. (2017). SCARED OF FLYING? The number of people who died in plane crashes in 2016 will surprise you . . . and not for the reason you think. *The Sun.* Retrieved from https://www.thesun.co.uk/living/2535002/the-number-of-people-who-died-in-plane-crashes-in-2016-will-surprise-you-and-not-for-the-reason-you-think/

Pence Turnbull, K. L., & Justice, L. M. (2012). *Language development from theory to practice* (2nd ed.). Upper Saddle River, NJ: Merrill/Pearson Education.

Peng, J., Mo, L., Huang, P., & Zhou, Y. (2017). The effects of working memory training on improving fluid intelligence of children during early childhood. *Cognitive Development, 43,* 224–234.

Pennebaker J. W., Gosling S. D., & Ferrell J. D. (2013). Daily online testing in large classes: Boosting college performance while reducing achievement gaps. *PLoS ONE, 8*(11), e79774. doi:10.1371/journal.pone.0079774. Retrieved from http://www.plosone.org/article/info%3Adoi%2F10.1371%2Fjournal.pone.0079774

Pentimonti, J., & Justice, L. (2010). Teachers' use of scaffolding strategies during read alouds in the preschool classroom. *Early Childhood Education, 37,* 241–248.

Penuel, W. R., Bell, P., Bevan, B., Buffington, P., & Falk, J. (2016). Enhancing use of learning sciences research in planning for and supporting educational change: Leveraging and building social networks. *Journal of Educational Change, 17,* 251–278.

Peregoy, S., & Boyle, O. (2017). *Reading, writing, and learning in ESL: A resource book for teaching K–12 English learners* (7th ed.). Boston: Pearson.

Perle, J. G. (2016). Teacher-provided positive attending to improve student behavior. *Teaching Exceptional Children, 48,* 250–257.

Perron, T. (2013). Peer victimisation: Strategies to decrease bullying in schools. *British Journal of School Nursing, 8,* 25–29.

Perry, N. E., Turner, J. C., & Meyer, D. K. (2006). Classrooms as contexts for motivating learning. In P. A. Alexander & P. H. Winne (Eds.), *Handbook of educational psychology* (2nd ed., pp. 327–348). Mahwah, NJ: Erlbaum.

Pescetelli, N., Rees, G., & Bahrami, B. (2016). The perceptual and social components of metacognition. *Journal of Experimental Psychology: General, 145,* 949–965.

Peters, M. A. (2017). Education in a post-truth world. *Educational Philosophy and Theory, 49,* 563–566. https://doi.org/10.1080/00131857.2016.1264114

Peters, R., Bradshaw, A., Petrunka, K., Nelson, G., Herry, Y., Craig, W., . . . Rossiter, M. (2010). The Better Beginnings, Better Futures Project: Findings from grade 3 to grade 9. *Monographs of the Society for Research in Child Development, 75*(3, Serial No. 297).

Peters-Burton, E., Merz, S., Ramirez, E., & Saroughi, M. (2015). The effect of cognitive apprenticeship-based professional development on teacher self-efficacy of science teaching, motivation, knowledge calibration, and perceptions of inquiry-based teaching. *Journal of Science Teacher Education, 26,* 525–548.

Peterson, A. M., Harper, F. W., Albrecht, T. L., Taub, J. W., Orom, H., Phipps, S., & Penner, L. A. (2014). Parent caregiver self-efficacy and child reactions to pediatric cancer treatment procedures. *Journal of Pediatric Oncology Nursing, 31,* 18–27.

Peterson, J. S. (2009). Myth 17: Gifted and talented individuals do not have unique social and emotional needs. *Gifted Child Quarterly, 53,* 280–282.

Petitto, L. (2009). New discoveries from the bilingual brain and mind across the life span: Implications for education. *Brain, Mind, & Education, 3,* 185–197.

Petrilli, M. J. (2011). All together now? Education high and low achievers in the same classroom. *Education Next, 11.* Retrieved from http://educationnext.org/all-together-now/

Peverly, S. T., Vekaria, P. C., Reddington, L. A., Sumowski, J. F., Johnson, K. R., & Ramsay, C. M. (2013). The relationship of handwriting speed, working memory, language comprehension and outlines to lecture note-taking and test-taking among college students. *Applied Cognitive Psychology, 27,* 115–126.

Péladeau, N., Forget, J., & Gagné, F. (2003). Effect of paced and unpaced practice on skill application and retention: How much is enough? *American Educational Research Journal, 40*(3), 769–801.

Pérez-Peña, R. (2017). Contrary to Trump's claims, immigrants are less likely to commit crimes. *The New York Times.* Retrieved from https://www.nytimes.com/2017/01/26/us/trump-illegal-immigrants-crime.html

Pfafman, T. M., & McEwan, B. (2014). Polite women at work: Negotiating professional identity through strategic assertiveness. *Women's Studies in Communication, 37,* 202–219.

Phelps, R. (Ed.). (2005). *Defending standardized testing.* Mahwah, NJ: Erlbaum.

Phillips, D. A. (2016). Stability, security, and social dynamics in early childhood environments. In N. K. Lesaux & S.M. Jones (Eds.). (2016). *The leading edge of early childhood education: Linking science to policy for a new generation of prekindergarten* (pp. 7–28). Cambridge, MA: Harvard Education Publishing Group.

Phillipson, S., & Phillipson, S. N. (2012). Children's cognitive ability and their academic achievement: The mediation effects of parental expectations. *Asia Pacific Education Review 13,* 495–508.

Piaget, J. (1952). *Origins of intelligence in children.* New York: International Universities Press.

Piaget, J. (1959). *Language and thought of the child* (M. Grabain, Trans.). New York: Humanities Press.

Piaget, J. (1965). *The moral judgment of the child.* New York: Free Press. (Original work published 1932.)

Piaget, J. (1970). *The science of education and the psychology of the child.* New York: Orion Press.

Piaget, J. (1977). Problems in equilibrium. In M. Appel & L. Goldberg (Eds.), *Topics in cognitive development: Vol. 1. Equilibration: Theory, research, and application* (pp. 3–13). New York: Plenum Press.

Piaget, J. (1980). *Adaptation and intelligence: Organic selection and phenocopy* (S. Eames, Trans.). Chicago: University of Chicago Press.

Piaget, J., & Inhelder, B. (1956). *The child's conception of space.* Boston: Routledge and Kegan-Paul.

Pianta, R., Belsky, J., Houts, R., & Morrison, F. (2007). Opportunities to learn in America's elementary classrooms. *Science, 315,* 1795–1796.

Picard, M., & Velautham, L. (2016). Developing independent listening skills for English as an additional language students. *International Journal of Teaching and Learning in Higher Education, 28,* 52–65.

Pierce, S. (2014). Examining the relationship between collective teacher efficacy and the emotional intelligence of elementary school principals. *Journal of School Leadership, 24,* 311–335.

Pillet-Shore, D. (2016). Criticizing another's child: How teachers evaluate students during parent-teacher conferences. *Language in Society, 45,* 33–58.

Pilon, M. (2013, January 16). Forging path to starting line for younger disabled athletes. *The New York Times.* Retrieved from http://www.nytimes.com/2013/01/16/sports/disabled-athletes-suit-up-raising-questions-of-logistics-and-fairness.html

Pinker, S. (2010, June 11). Mind over mass media. *New York Times.* Retrieved from http://www.nytimes.com/2010/06/11/opinion/11Pinker.html

Pinter, A. (2012). Children learning second languages. *English Language Teaching Journal, 66,* 261–263.

Platt, R. (2004). Standardized tests: Whose standards are we talking about? *Phi Delta Kappan, 85*(5), 381–382.

Plemmons, G., Hall, M., Doupnik, S., Gay, J., Brown, C., Browning, W., . . . Williams, D. (2018). Hospitalization for suicide ideation or attempt: 2008–2015. *Pediatrics.* Retrieved from http://pediatrics.aappublications.org/content/early/2018/05/14/peds.2017-2426

Plotnikoff, R. C., Costigan, S. A., Karunamuni, N., & Lubans, D. R. (2013). Social cognitive theories used to explain physical activity behavior in adolescents: A systematic review and meta-analysis. *Preventive Medicine, 56,* 245–253. doi:10.1016/j.ypmed.2013.01.013

Poirier, T. I. (2017). Is lecturing obsolete? Advocating for high value transformative lecturing. *American Journal of Pharmaceutical Education, 81,* 1–2.

Pomerance, L., Greenberg, J., & Walsh, K. (2016). *Learning about learning: What every new teacher needs to know.* National Council on Teacher Quality. Retrieved from http://www.nctq.org/dmsView/Learning_About_Learning_Report.

Pomerantz, E. M., & Kempner, S. G. (2013). Mothers' daily person and process praise: Implications for children's theory of intelligence and motivation. *Developmental Psychology.* Advance online publication. doi:10.1037/a0031840

Poole, I. R., & Evertson, C. M. (2013). Elementary classroom management. In J. Hattie & E. M. Anderman (Eds.), *International guide to student achievement* (pp. 188–191). New York: Routledge.

Pop, E. I., Negru-Subtirica, O., Crocetti, E., Opre, A, & Meeus. W. (2016). On the interplay between academic achievement and educational identity: A longitudinal study. *Journal of Adolescence, 47,* 135–144.

Pope, N. G. (2016). The marginal effect of K–12 English language development programs: Evidence from Los Angeles schools. *Economics of Education Review, 53,* 311–328.

Popescu, A. (2018). Keep your head up: How smartphone addiction kills manners and moods. *The New York Times.* Retrieved from https://www.nytimes.com/2018/01/25/smarter-living/bad-text-posture-neckpain-mood.html

Popham, W. J. (2017). *Classroom assessment: What teachers need to know* (8th ed.). Boston: Pearson.

Poulou, M. (2015). Teacher-student relationships, social and emotional skills, and emotional and behavioural difficulties. *International Journal of Educational Psychology, 4,* 84–108.

Pólya, G. (1957). *How to solve it.* Garden City, NY: Doubleday.

Prati, G. (2012). A social cognitive learning theory of homophobic aggression among adolescents. *School Psychology Review, 41,* 413–428.

Prawat, R. (1989). Promoting access to knowledge, strategy, and disposition in students: A research synthesis. *Review of Educational Research, 59,* 1–41.

Prelli, G. E. (2016). How school leaders might promote higher levels of collective teacher efficacy at the level of school and team. *English Language Teaching, 9,* 174–180.

Premack, D. (1965). Reinforcement theory. In D. Levine (Ed.), *Nebraska Symposium on Motivation* (Vol. 13, pp. 3–41). Lincoln: University of Nebraska Press.

Pressley, M., & Harris, K. R. (2006). Cognitive strategies instruction: From basic research to classroom instruction. In P. A. Alexander & P. H. Winne (Eds.), *Handbook of educational psychology* (2nd ed., pp. 265–286). Mahwah, NJ: Erlbaum.

Pressley, M., & Hilden, K. (2006). Cognitive strategies. In D. Kuhn & R. Siegler (Eds.), *Handbook of child psychology* (6th ed., Vol. 2, pp. 511–556). Hoboken, NJ: John Wiley & Sons.

Primak, B. A., Shensa, A., Escobar-Viera, C. G., Barrett, E. L., Sidani, J. E., Colditz, J. B., & James, A. E. (2017). Use of multiple social media platforms and symptoms of depression and anxiety: A nationally-representative study among U.S. young adults. *Computers in Human Behavior, 69,* 1–9.

Pritchard, R. (1990). The effects of cultural schemata on reading processing strategies. *Reading Research Quarterly, 25,* 273–295.

Proffitt, D. R. (2006). Embodied perception and the economy of action. *Perspectives on Psychological Science, 1,* 110–122.

Program for International Student Assessment (PISA). (2012). *Results in focus: What 15-year-olds know and what they can do with what they know*. Retrieved from http://www.oecd.org/pisa/keyfindings/pisa-2012-results-overview.pdf

Prooijen, J. W. (2017). Why education predicts decreased belief in conspiracy theories. *Applied Cognitive Psychology, 31,* 50–58.

Provasnik, S., Malley, L., Stephens, M., Landeros, K., Perkins, R., & Tang, J. H. (2016). Highlights from TIMSS and TIMSS Advanced 2015: Mathematics and science achievement of U.S. Students in Grades 4 and 8 and in advanced courses at the end of high school in an international context (NCES 2017–002). *U.S. Department of Education, National Center for Education Statistics.* Washington, DC. Retrieved from https://nces.ed.gov/pubs2017/2017002.pdf

Przymus, S. D. (2016). Imagining and moving beyond the ESL bubble: Facilitating communities of practice through the ELL Ambassadors program. *Journal of Language, Identity and Education, 15,* 265–279.

Pulfrey, C., Buchs, C., & Butera, F. (2011). Why grades engender performance-avoidance goals: The mediating role of autonomous motivation. *Journal of Educational Psychology, 103,* 683–700.

Purpura, D. J., Baroody, A. J., Eiland, M. D., & Reid, E. E. (2016). Fostering first graders' reasoning strategies with basic sums: The value of guided instruction. *Elementary School Journal, 117,* 72–100.

Puryear, J. S., Kettler, T., & Rinn, A. N. (2017). Relationships of personality to differential conceptions of creativity: A systematic review. *Psychology of Aesthetics, Creativity, and the Arts, 11,* 59–68.

Putnam, R. D. (2016). *Our kids: The American dream in crisis.* New York: Simon and Schuster.

Qian, G., & Pan, J. (2002). A comparison of epistemological beliefs and learning from science text between American and Chinese high school students. In B. K Hofer & P. R. Pintrich (Eds.), *Personal epistemology: The psychology of beliefs about knowledge and knowing* (pp. 365–385). Mahwah: NJ; Erlbaum.

Quinn, D. M., & Polikoff, M. (2017). Summer learning loss: What is it, and what can we do about it? *Brookings.* Retrieved from https://www.brookings.edu/research/summer-learning-loss-what-is-it-and-what-can-we-do-about-it/

Quiroga, R., Fried, I., & Koch, C. (2013). Brain cells for grandmother. *Scientific American, 308*(2), 30–5.

Radesky, J. S., & Christaskis, D. A. (2016). Increased screen time: Implications for early childhood development and behavior. *Childhood Development and Behavior, 63,* 826–839.

Radnitz, S., & Underwood, P. (2017). Is belief in conspiracy theories pathological? A survey experiment on the cognitive roots of extreme suspicion. *British Journal of Political Science, 47,* 113–129.

Radvansky, G. A., & Ashcraft, M. H. (2014). *Cognition* (6th ed.). Boston: Pearson.

Rainie, L., & Zickuhr, K. (2015). Americans' views on mobile etiquette. *Pew Research Center.* Retrieved from http://www.pewinternet.org/2015/08/26/americans-views-on-mobile-etiquette/

Ramey, D. (2015). The social structure of criminalized and medicalized school discipline. *Sociology of Education, 88,* 181–201.

Ramirez, G., & Beilock, S. L. (2011, January 14). Writing about testing worries boosts exam performance in the classroom. *Science, 331*(6014), 211–213.

Ramos, A., (2017). Piecing together ideas on sociocultural psychology and methodological approaches. *Integrative Psychological & Behavioral Science, 51,* 279–284.

Ramsletter, C., & Murray, R. (2017). Time to play: Recognizing the benefits of recess. *American Educator, 41,* 17–23.

Rank, M. R. (2018). The cost of keeping children poor. *The New York Times.* Retrieved from https://www.nytimes.com/2018/04/15/opinion/children-poverty-cost.html

Rappleye, E. (2015). Gender ratio of nurses across 50 states. *Becker's Hospital Review.* Retrieved from https://www.beckershospitalreview.com/human-capital-and-risk/gender-ratio-of-nurses-across-50-states.html

Ravitch, D. (2010). *The death and life of the great American school system.* New York: Basic Books.

Rawson, K., Thomas, R., & Jacoby, L. (2015). The power of examples: Illustrative examples enhance conceptual learning of declarative concepts. *Educational Psychology Review, 27,* 483–504.

Reardon, S. F. (2016). School segregation and racial achievement gaps. *RSF: The Russell Sage Foundation Journal of the Social Sciences, 2,* 34–57.

Reichert, M. C. (2010). Hopeful news on regarding the crisis in U.S. education: Exploring the human element in teaching boys. *Education Week, 30*(12), 27.

Renkl, A. (2011). Instruction based on examples. In R. E. Mayer & P. A. Alexander (Eds.), *Handbook of research on learning and instruction* (pp. 272–295). New York: Routledge.

Renninger, K. A. (2000). Individual interest and its implications for understanding intrinsic motivation. In J. M. Harackiewicz & C. Sansone (Eds.), *Intrinsic and extrinsic motivation: The search for optimal motivation and performance* (pp. 373–404). San Diego, CA: Academic Press.

Renzulli, J., & Reis, S. (2003). The schoolwide enrichment model: Developing creative and productive giftedness. In N. Colangelo & G. Davis (Eds.), *Handbook of gifted education* (3rd ed., pp. 184–203). Boston: Allyn & Bacon.

Resnick, L., Asterhan, C., & Clarke, S. (2015). Socializing intelligence through academic talk and dialogue. Washington, DC: American Educational Research Association.

Retting, R. (2018). Pedestrian traffic fatalities by state: 2017 preliminary data. *Governors Highway Safety Association.* Retrieved from https://www.ghsa.org/sites/default/files/2018-02/pedestrians18.pdf

Reutzel, D. R., & Cooter, R. B. (2015). *Teaching children to read: The teacher makes the difference* (7th ed.). Boston: Pearson.

Reynolds, H. L., & Kearns, K. D. (2017). A planning tool for incorporating backward design, active learning, and authentic assessment in the college classroom. *College Teaching, 65,* 17–27.

Rhodewalt, F., & Vohs, K. D. (2005). Defensive strategies, motivation, and the self: A self-regulatory process view. In A. J. Elliot & C. S. Dweck (Eds.), *Handbook of competence and motivation* (pp. 548–565). New York: Guilford.

Ribar, D. C. (2015). Why marriage matters for child wellbeing. *Future of Children, 25,* 11–27.

Rice, P. C. (2017). Pronouncing students' names correctly should be a big deal. *Education Week.* Retrieved from https://www.edweek.org/tm/articles/2017/11/15/pronouncing-students-names-correctly-should-be-a.html?cmp=eml-enl-tu-news1-rm&M=58277832&U=27557

Rich, P. R., Van Loon, M. H., Dunlosky, J., & Zaragoza, M. S. (2017). Belief in Corrective Feedback for Common Misconceptions: Implications for Knowledge Revision. *Journal of Experimental Psychology: Learning, Memory, and Cognition, 43,* 492–501.

Richey, S. (2017). A Birther and a Truther: The influence of the authoritarian personality on Conspiracy beliefs. *Politics & Policy, 45,* 465–485.

Richtel, M. (2012, May 30). Wasting time is new divide in digital era. *New York Times.* Retrieved from http://www.nytimes.com/2012/05/30/us/new-digital-divide-seen-in-wasting-time-online.html?pagewanted=all&_r=0

Rideout, V. (2015). *The common sense census: Media use by tweens and teens.* Common Sense Media. Retrieved from https://www.commonsensemedia.org/sites/default/files/uploads/research/census_researchreport.pdf

Riener, C., & Willingham, D. (2010). The myth of learning styles. *Change: The Magazine of Higher Learning.* Retrieved from https://www.researchgate.net/publication/249039450_The_Myth_of_Learning_Styles

Riley, B., & Hernandez, A. (2015). Should personalization be the future of learning? *Education Next.* Retrieved from http://educationnext.org/personalization-future-learning/

Riley, J. L. (2015). The mythical connection between immigrants and crime. *The Wall Street Journal.* Retrieved from https://www.wsj.com/articles/the-mythical-connection-between-immigrants-and-crime-1436916798

Riley, J., & Ward, K. (2017). Active learning, cooperative active learning, and passive learning methods in an accounting information systems course. *Issues in Accounting Education, 32*, 1–16.

Rimm, S. B., Siegle, D., & Davis, G. A. (2018). *Education of the gifted and talented* (7th ed.). Boston: Pearson.

Rinke, E. M. (2016). The impact of sound-bite journalism on public argument. *Journal of Communication, 66*, 625–645.

Rispoli, M., Zaini, S., Mason, R., Brodhead, M., Burke, M. D., & Gregori, E. (2017). A systematic review of teacher self-monitoring on implementation of behavioral practices. *Teaching and Teacher Education, 63*, 58–72.

Ritts, V., Patterson, M. L., & Tubbs, M. E. (1992). Expectations, impressions, and judgments of physically attractive students: A review. *Review of Educational Research, 62*, 413–426.

Robbins, P., & Aydede, M. (2009). A short primer on situated cognition. In P. Robbins & M. Aydede (Eds.), *The Cambridge handbook of situated cognition* (pp. 3–10). New York: Cambridge University Press.

Robertson, J. (2000). Is attribution training a worthwhile classroom intervention for K–12 students with learning difficulties? *Educational Psychology Review, 12*(1), 111–134.

Robinson, J. (2010). The effects of test translation on young English learners' mathematics performance. *Educational Researcher, 39*, 582–593.

Roblyer, M. D., & Hughes, J. (2019). *Integrating educational technology into teaching* (8th ed.). Boston: Pearson.

Rocha Lopes, D., van Putten, K., & Moormann, P. P. (2015). The impact of parental styles on the development of psychological complaints. *Europe's Journal of Psychology, 11*, 155–168.

Roeser, R. W., Peck, S. C., & Nasir, N. S. (2006). Self and identity processes in school motivation, learning and achievement. In P. A. Alexander & P. H. Winne (Eds.), *Handbook of educational psychology* (2nd ed., pp. 391–424). Mahwah, NJ: Erlbaum.

Rogeberg, O. (2013). Correlations between cannabis use and IQ change in the Dunedin cohort are consistent with confounding from socioeconomic status. *Proceedings of the National Academy of Sciences of the United States of America, 110*, 4251–4254.

Rogers, C. (1963). Actualizing tendency in relation to motives and to consciousness. In M. Jones (Ed.), *Nebraska Symposium on Motivation* (Vol. 11, pp. 1–24). Lincoln: University of Nebraska Press.

Rogers, C., & Freiberg, H. J. (1994). *Freedom to learn* (3rd ed.). Upper Saddle River, NJ: Merrill/Pearson.

Rogers, J. C., & DeBrito, S. A. (2016). Cortical and subcortical gray matter volume in youths with conduct problems: A meta-analysis. *JAMA Psychiatry, 73*, 64–72. doi: 10.1001/jamapsychiatry.2015.2423

Rogers, K. B. (1991). *The relationship of grouping practices to the education of the gifted and talented learner (RBDM 9102).* Storrs, CT: The National Research Center on the Gifted and Talented, University of Connecticut.

Rogoff, B. (2003). *The cultural nature of human development.* New York, NY: Oxford University Press.

Rohr, D., & Pashler, H. (2010). Recent research on human learning challenges conventional instructional strategies. *Educational Researcher, 39*, 406–412.

Rohrer, D., & Pashler, H. (2010). Recent research on human learning challenges conventional instructional strategies. *Educational Researcher, 39*, 406–412.

Rohrer, D., Taylor, K., & Sholar, B. (2010). Tests enhance the transfer of learning. *Journal of Experimental Psychology, 36*, 233–239.

Roid, G. (2003). *Stanford-Binet Intelligence Scales, Fifth Edition.* Itasca, IL: Riverside.

Romano, A. (2011, March 28). How dumb are we? *Newsweek,* 56–60.

Rosa, E. M., & Tudge, J. (2013). Urie Bronfenbrenner's theory of human development: Its evolution from ecology to bioecology. *Journal of Family Theory & Review, 5*, 243–258.

Rosen, L. D. (2012). *iDisorder: Understanding our obsession with technology and overcoming its hold on us.* New York: Palgrave/Macmillan.

Rosen, L. D., Whaling, K., Rab, S., Carrier, L. M., & Cheever, N. A. (2013). Is Facebook creating "iDisorders"? The link between clinical symptoms of psychiatric disorders and technology use, attitudes and anxiety. *Computers in Human Behavior, 29,* 1243–1254.

Rosen, R., & Parise, L. M. (2017). Using evaluation systems for teacher improvement: Are school districts ready to meet new federal goals? *MDRC,* 1–7, ERIC Number: ED574046

Rosenberg, T. (2013). Turning education upside down. *The New York Times.* Retrieved from http://opinionator.blogs.nytimes.com/2013/10/09/turning-education-upside-down/?_r=0

Rosenshine, B. (1987). Explicit teaching. In D. Berliner & B. Rosenshine (Eds.), *Talks to teachers.* New York: Random House.

Roseth, C., Akcaoglu, M., & Zellner, A. (2013). Blending synchronous face-to-face and computer-supported cooperative learning in a hybrid doctoral seminar. *TechTrends: Linking Research and Practice to Improve Learning, 57*, 54–59.

Rossetti, Z., Sauer, J. S., Bui, O., & Ou, S. (2017). Developing collaborative partnerships with culturally and linguistically diverse families during the IEP process. *Teaching Exceptional Children, 49*, 328–338.

Roth, G., Kanat-Maymon, Y., & Assor, A. (2016). The role of unconditional parental regard in autonomy-supportive parenting. *Journal of Personality, 84*, 716–725.

Rothbart, M. (2011). *Becoming who we are: Temperament and personality in development.* New York: Guilford.

Rowe, D., Mazzotti, V. L., Ingram, A., & Lee, S. (2017). Effects of goal-setting instruction on academic engagement for students at risk. *Career Development and Transition for Exceptional Individuals, 40*, 25–35.

Rowe, M. (1986). Wait-time: Slowing down may be a way of speeding up. *Journal of Teacher Education, 37*(1), 43–50.

Rubin, K., Cheah, C., & Menzer, M. (2010). Peers. In M. Bornstein (Ed.), *Handbook of cultural developmental science* (pp. 223–237). New York: Psychology Press.

Rudasill, K., Gallagher, K., & White, J. (2010). Temperamental attention and activity, classroom emotional support, and academic achievement in third grade. *Journal of School Psychology, 48*(2), 113–134.

Ruscheweyh, R., Willemer, C., Krüger, K., Duning, T., Warnecke, T., Sommer, J., . . . Flöel, A. (2009). Physical activity and memory functions: An interventional study. *Neurobiology of Aging, 32*, 1304–1319.

Russ, A. C., Moffit, D. M., & Mansell, J. L. (2017). Sexual harassment and internships: How do we protect our students and program? *Kinesiology Review, 6*, 391–394.

Russo, M., Islam, G., & Koyuncu, B. (2017). Non-native accents and stigma: How self-fulfilling prophesies can affect career outcomes. *Human Resource Management Review, 27*, 507–520.

Rutter, M., Maughan, B., Mortimore, P., Ouston, J., & Smith, A. (1979). *Fifteen thousand hours. Secondary schools and their effects on children.* Cambridge, MA: Harvard University Press.

Ryan, J. B., Katsiyannis, A., & Peterson, R. (2007). IDEA 2004 and disciplining students with disabilities. *NASSP Bulletin, 91*, 130–140.

Ryan, J. B., Peterson, R. L., & Rozalski, M. (2007). State policies concerning the use of seclusion timeout in schools. *Education and Treatment of Children, 30*, 215–239.

Ryan, J. B., Sanders, S., Katsiyannis, A., & Yell, M. L. (2007). Using time-out effectively in the classroom. *Teaching Exceptional Children, 39*, 60–67.

Ryan, K. E., & Ryan, A. M. (2005). Psychological processes of stereotype threat and standardized math test performance. *Educational Psychologist, 40*(1), 53–63.

Ryan, K. E., Ryan, A. M., Arbuthnot, K., & Samuels, M. (2007). Students' motivation for standardized math exams. *Educational Researcher, 36*(1), 5–13.

Ryan, R., & Deci, E. (1996). When paradigms clash: Comments on Cameron and Pierce's claim that rewards do not undermine intrinsic motivation. *Review of Educational Research, 66*, 33–38.

Ryan, R., & Deci, E. (2000). Intrinsic and extrinsic motivations: Classic definitions and new directions. *Contemporary Educational Psychology, 25*, 54–67.

Ryan, S. V., von der Embse, N. P., Pendergast, L. L., Saeki, E., Segool, N., & Schwing, S. (2017). Research paper: Leaving the teaching profession: The role of teacher stress and educational accountability policies on turnover intent. *Teaching and Teacher Education, 66*, 1–11.

Rye, J., Landenberger, R., & Warner, T. A. (2013). Incorporating concept mapping in project-based learning: Lessons from watershed investigations. *Journal of Science Education and Technology, 22*, 379–392. doi:10.1007/s10956–012–9400–1

Sackett, P. R., & Walmsley, P. T. (2014). Which personality attributes are most important in the workplace? *Perspectives on Psychological Science, 9*, 538–551.

Sack-Min, J. (2007). The issues of IDEA. *American School Board Journal, 194*(3), 20–25.

Saddler, B., Asaro-Saddler, K., Moeyaert, M., & Ellis-Robinson, T. (2017). Effects of a summarizing strategy on written summaries of children with emotional and behavioral disorders. *Remedial and Special Education, 38*, 87–97.

Sadler, P. M., Sonnert, G., Coyle, H. P., Cook-Smith, N., & Miller, J. I. (2013). The influence of teachers' knowledge on student learning in middle school physical science classrooms. *American Educational Research Journal, 50*, 1020–1049.

Sadoski, M., & Paivio, A. (2001). *Imagery and text: A dual coding theory of reading and writing.* Mahwah, NJ: Erlbaum.

Saewcy, E. M., Konishi C., Rose, H. A., & Homma, Y. (2014). School-based strategies to reduce suicidal ideation, suicide attempts, and discrimination among sexual minority and heterosexual adolescents in Western Canada. *International Journal of Child, Youth and Family Studies 1*, 89–112.

Safer, N., & Fleischman, S. (2005). How student progress monitoring improves instruction. *Educational Leadership, 62*(5), 81–83.

Sakr, S. (2013). Charlie Rose interviews 'Bill Gates 2.0' on 60 Minutes: The man after Microsoft. *60 Minutes.* Retrieved from http://www.engadget.com/2013/05/13/bill-gates-60-minutes/?utm_medium=feed&utm_source=Feed_Classic&utm_campaign=Engadget

Saksvik, I., & Hetland, H. (2011). The role of personality in stress perception across different vocational types. *Journal of Employment Counseling, 48*, 3–16.

Salam. M. (2017). The opioid epidemic: A crisis years in the making. *The New York Times.* Retrieved from https://www.nytimes.com/2017/10/26/us/opioid-crisis-public-health-emergency.html

Saleh, M., Lazonder, A. W., & de Jong, T. (2007). Structuring collaboration in mixed-ability groups to promote verbal interaction, learning, and motivation of average-ability students. *Contemporary Educational Psychology, 32*, 314–331.

Salvia, J., Ysseldyke, J., & Bolt, S. (2017). *Assessment in special and inclusive education* (13th ed.). Boston: Cengage.

Samuels, C. (2013). Test rules differ between groups of special ed. *Education Week, 32*(27), 1, 16, 17.

Samuels, C. (2017). Minority students still missing out on special education. *Education Week.* Retrieved from http://blogs.edweek.org/edweek/speced/2017/08/minorities_underrolled_special_education.html?M=58168360&U=19028

Sana, F., Yan, V. X., & Kim, J. A. (2017). Study sequence matters for the inductive learning of cognitive concepts. *Journal of Educational Psychology, 109*, 84–98.

Sapacz, M., Rockman, G., & Clark, J. (2016). Are we addicted to our cell phones? *Computers in Human Behavior, 57*, 153–159.

Sarzyńska, J., Żelechowska, D., Falkiewicz, M., & Nęcka, E. (2017). Attention training in schoolchildren improves attention but fails to enhance fluid intelligence. *Studia Psychologica, 59*, 50–65.

Satel, S., & Lilienfeld, S. (2013). *Brainwashed: The seductive appeal of mindless neuroscience.* New York: Basic Books.

Satsangi, R., Bouck, E. C., Taber-Doughty, T., Bofferding, L., & Roberts, C. A. (2016). Comparing the effectiveness of virtual and concrete manipulatives to teach algebra to secondary students with learning disabilities. *Learning Disability Quarterly, 39*, 240–253.

Savage, C. (2017). In shift, Justice Dept. says law doesn't bar transgender discrimination. *The New York Times.* Retrieved from https://www.nytimes.com/2017/10/05/us/politics/transgender-civil-rights-act-justice-department-sessions.html

Savolainen, R. (2013). Approaching the motivators for information seeking: The viewpoint of attribution theories. *Library & Information Science Research, 35*, 63–68.

Sawchuk, S. (2012). Access to teacher evaluations divides advocates. *Education Week, 31*(26), 1, 18.

Sawchuk, S. (2017). Even when states revise standards, the core of the Common Core remains. *Education Week.* Retrieved from https://www.edweek.org/ew/articles/2017/11/13/even-when-states-revise-standards-the-core.html

Sawyer, R. K. (2006). Introduction: The new science of learning. In R. K. Sawyer (Ed.), *The Cambridge handbook of the learning sciences* (pp. 1–18). New York: Cambridge University Press.

Scaffidi, A. C., Boca, S., & Gendolla, G. H. E. (2016). Self-awareness, perspective-taking, and egocentrism. *Self & Identity, 15*, 371–380.

Scalise, K., & Felde, M. (2017). *Why neuroscience matters in the classroom: Principles of brain-based instructional design for teacher.* Boston: Pearson.

Schacter, D. (2001). *The seven deadly sins of memory.* Boston: Houghton Mifflin.

Schaefer, J., Velly, S. A., Allen, M. S., & Magee, C. A. (2016). Competition anxiety, motivation, and mental toughness in golf. *Journal of Applied Sport Psychology, 28*, 309–321.

Scheuermann, B. K., & Hall, J. A. (2016). *Positive behavioral supports for the classroom* (3rd ed.). Boston: Pearson.

Schimmel, D., Stellman, L., Conlon, C., & Fischer, L (2015). *Teachers and the law* (9th ed.). New York: Longman.

Schlinger, H. D. (2008). The long good-bye: Why B. F. Skinner's verbal behavior is alive and well on the 50th anniversary of its publication. *The Psychological Record, 58*, 329–337.

Schmoker, M. (2010). When pedagogic fads trump priorities. *Education Week,* Retrieved from http://www.edweek.org/ew/articles/2010/09/29/05schmoker.h30.html.

Schneider, W. (2010). Metacognition and memory development in childhood and adolescence. In H. Waters & W. Schneider (Eds.), *Metacognition, strategy use, and instruction* (pp. 54–81). New York: Guilford.

Schraw, G. (2006). Knowledge structures and processes. In P. A. Alexander & P. H. Winne (Eds.), *Handbook of educational psychology* (2nd ed., pp. 245–263). Mahwah, NJ: Erlbaum.

Schraw, G., & Lehman, S. (2001). Situational interest: A review of the literature and directions for future research. *Educational Psychology Review, 13*(1), 23–52.

Schroder, H. S., Fisher, M. E., Lin, Y., Lo, S. L., Danovitch, J. H., & Moser, J. S. (2017). Neural evidence for enhanced attention to mistakes among school-aged children with a growth mindset. *Developmental Cognitive Neuroscience, 24*, 42–50.

Schunk, D. (2016). *Learning theories: An educational perspective* (7th ed.). Boston: Pearson.

Schunk, D. H., & Ertmer, P. A. (2000). Self-regulation and academic learning: Self-efficacy enhancing interventions. In M. Boekaerts, P. R. Pintrich, & M. Zeidner (Eds.), *Handbook of self-regulation* (pp. 631–649). San Diego: Academic Press.

Schunk, D. H., & Pajares, F. (2004). Self-efficacy in education revisited: Empirical and applied evidence. In D. M. McInerney & S. Van Etten (Eds.), *Sociocultural influences on motivation and learning: Vol. 4. Big theories revisited* (pp. 115–138). Greenwich, CT: Information Age.

Schunk, D. H., & Zimmerman, B. J. (2006). Competence and control beliefs: Distinguishing the means and the ends. In P. A. Alexander & P. H. Winne (Eds.), *Handbook of educational psychology* (2nd ed., pp. 349–367). Mahwah, NJ: Erlbaum.

Schunk, D. H., Meece, J. L., & Pintrich, P. R. (2014). *Motivation in education: Theory, research, and applications* (4th ed.) Boston: Pearson.

Schwab, Y., & Elias, M. J. (2015). From compliance to responsibility: Social-emotional learning and classroom management. In E. T. Emmer & E. J. Sabornie (Eds.), *Handbook of classroom management* (2nd ed., pp. 94–115). New York: Routledge.

Schwartz, D., & Heiser, J. (2006). Spatial representations and imagery in learning. In R. K. Sawyer (Ed.), *The Cambridge handbook of the learning sciences* (pp. 283–298). New York: Cambridge University Press.

Schwartz, D., Bransford, J., & Sears, D. (2005). Efficiency and innovation in transfer. In J. Mestre (Ed.), *Transfer of learning from a modern multi-disciplinary perspective* (pp. 1–51). Greenwich, CT: Information Age Publishing.

Schwartz, S. J., Luyckx, K., & Crocetti, E. (2015). What have we learned since Schwartz (2001)?: A reappraisal of the field of identity development. In K. McLean & M. Syed (Eds.), *Oxford handbook of identity development* (pp. 539–561). New York, NY: Oxford University Press.

Scogin, S. C. (2016). Identifying the factors leading to success: How an innovative science curriculum cultivates student motivation. *Journal of Science Education and Technology, 25*, 375–393.

Sedikides, C., & Gregg, A. P. (2008). Self-enhancement: Food for thought. *Perspectives on Psychological Science, 3*, 102–116.

Segalowitz, S. J. (2016). Exercise and pediatric brain development: A call to action. *Pediatric Exercise Science, 28*, 217–226.

Segev, A. (2017). Does classic school curriculum contribute to morality? Integrating school curriculum with moral and intellectual education. *Educational Philosophy and Theory, 49*, 89–98.

Seli, H., Dembo, M. H., & Crocker, S. (2009). Self in self-worth protection: The relationship of possible selves and self-protective strategies. *College Student Journal, 43*, 832–842.

Semega, J. L., Fontenot, K. R., & Kollar, M. A. (2017). Income and poverty in the United States: 2016: Current population reports. *United States Census Bureau.* Retrieved from https://www.census.gov/content/dam/Census/library/publications/2017/demo/P60-259.pdf

Servant, V. F. C., & Schmidt, H. G. (2016). Revisiting 'Foundations of problem-based learning: Some explanatory notes. *Medical Education, 50*, 698–701.

Seung, S. (2012). *Connectome.* Boston: Houghton Mifflin.

Sewell, A., St. George, A., & Cullen, J. (2013). The distinctive features of joint participation in a community of learners. *Teaching and Teacher Education, 31*, 46–55.

Shearer, C. B., & Karanian, J. M. (2017). The neuroscience of intelligence: Empirical support for the theory of multiple intelligences? *Trends in Neuroscience and Education, 6*, 211–223.

Shelton, J. T., Elliott, E. M., Matthews, R. A., Hill, B. D., & Gouvier, W. D. (2010). The relationships of working memory, secondary memory, and general fluid intelligence: Working memory is special. *Journal of Experimental Psychology. Learning, Memory and Cognition, 36*, 813–820.

Sheppard, A. B., Gross, S. C., Pavelka, S. A., Hall, M. J., & Palmatier, M. I. (2012). Caffeine increases the motivation to obtain non-drug reinforcers in rats. *Drug and Alcohol Dependence, 124*, 216–222.

Sherblom, S. A. (2015). A moral experience feedback loop: Modeling a system of moral self-cultivation in everyday life. *Journal of Moral Education, 44*, 364–381.

Shierholz, H. (2014). Wage inequality has dramatically increased among both men and women over the last 35 years. *Economic Policy Institute.* Retrieved from http://www.epi.org/publication/wage-inequality-dramatically-increased-men/

Shin, J., Lee, Y-K., & Seo, E. (2017). The effects of feedback on students' achievement goals: Interaction between reference of comparison and regulatory focus. *Learning and Instruction, 49*, 21–31.

Shin, M., Bryant, D. P., Bryant, B. R., McKenna, J. W., Hou, F., & Ok, M. W. (2017). Virtual manipulatives. *Intervention in School & Clinic, 52*, 148–153.

Shiner, R. L., Buss, K. A., McClowry, S. G., Putnam, S. P., Saudino, K. J., & Zentner, M. (2012). What is temperament now? Assessing progress in temperament research on the twenty-fifth anniversary of Goldsmith et al. (1987). *Child Development Perspectives, 6*, 436–444.

Shipstead, Z., & Engle, R. W. (2013). Interference within the focus of attention: Working memory tasks reflect more than temporary maintenance. *Journal of Experimental Psychology: Learning, Memory, and Cognition, 39*, 277–289.

Shulevitz, J. (2016). "Grit," by Angela Duckworth. *New York Times.* Retrieved from https://www.nytimes.com/2016/05/08/books/review/grit-by-angela-duckworth.html?_r=0

Shulman, L. (1987). Knowledge and teaching: Foundations of the new reform. *Harvard Educational Review, 57*, 1–22.

Shulman, R. G. (2013). *Brain imaging: What it can (and cannot) tell us about consciousness.* New York: Oxford University Press.

Shyman, E. (2016). The reinforcement of ableism: Normality, the medical model of disability, and humanism in applied behavior analysis and ASD. *Intellectual and Developmental Disabilities, 54*, 366–376.

Siegler, R. (2000). The rebirth of children's learning. *Child Development, 71*, 26–35.

Siegler, R. (2006). Microgenetic analyses of learning. In D. Kuhn & R. Siegler (Vol. Eds.), *Handbook of child psychology: Vol. 2. Cognition, perception, and language* (6th ed., pp. 464–510). Hoboken, NJ: Wiley.

Siegler, R. (2012). From theory to application and back: Following in the giant footsteps of David Klahr. In J. Shrager & S. Carver (Eds.), *The journey from child to scientist: Integrating cognitive development and the education sciences.* Washington, DC: American Psychological Association.

Siegler, R., & Alibali, M. (2005). *Children's thinking* (4th ed.). Upper Saddle River, NJ: Prentice Hall.

Siegler, R., & Lin, X. (2010). Self-explanations promote children's learning. In H. Waters & W. Schneider (Eds.), *Metacognition, strategy use, and instruction* (pp. 85–112). New York: Guilford Press.

Simons, L. G., Simons, R. L., & Su, X. L. (2013). Consequences of corporal punishment among African Americans: The importance of context and outcome. *Journal of Youth and Adolescence, 42*, 1273–1285.

Simons, R., & Burt, C. (2011). Learning to be bad: Adverse social conditions, social schemas, and crime. *Criminology, 49*, 553–597.

Sinatra, G. M., & Pintrich, P. R. (2003). The role of intentions in conceptual change learning. In G. M. Sinatra & P. R. Pintrich (Eds.), *Intentional conceptual change* (pp. 1–18). Mahwah, NJ: Erlbaum.

Singer, N. (2017). How Silicon Valley pushed coding into American classrooms. *New York Times.* Retrieved from https://www.nytimes.com/2017/06/27/technology/education-partovi-computer-science-coding-apple-microsoft.html

Sipes, S. M. (2016). Development of a problem-based learning matrix for data collection. *Interdisciplinary Journal of Problem-Based Learning, 11*, 1–12.

Sisson, S., Broyles, S., Newton, R., Jr., Baker, B., & Chernausek, S. (2011). TVs in the bedrooms of children: Does it impact health and behavior? *Preventive Medicine, 52*, 104–108.

Skatova, A., & Ferguson, E. (2013). Individual differences in behavioral inhibition explain free riding in public good games when punishment is expected but not implemented. *Behavioral and Brain Functions, 9*, 1–11. Retrieved from http://www.behavioralandbrainfunctions.com/content/9/1/3

Skeide, M. A., Kumar, U., Mishra, R. K., Tripathi, V. N., Guleria, A., Singh, J. P., Eisner, F., & Huettig, F. (2017). Learning to read alters cortico-subcortical cross-talk in the visual system of illiterates. *Science Advances, 3*, e1602612 DOI: 10.1126/sciadv.1602612

Skiba, R. J., & Raush, M. K. (2015). Reconsidering exclusionary discipline: The efficacy and equity of out-of-school suspension and expulsion. In E. T. Emmer & E. J. Sabornie (Eds.), *Handbook of classroom management* (2nd ed., pp. 116–138). New York: Routledge.

Skiba, R. J., Aritles, A. J., Kozleski, E. B., Losen, D. J., & Harry, E. G. (2016). Risks and consequences of oversimplifying educational inequities: A response to Morgan et al. (2015). *Educational Researcher, 45*, 221–225.

Skinner, B. F. (1953). *Science and human behavior*. New York: Macmillan.

Skinner, B. F. (1954). The science of learning and the art of teaching. *Harvard Educational Review, 24*, 86–97.

Skulmowski, A., & Günter, D. R. (2017). Bodily effort enhances learning and metacognition: Investigating the relation between physical effort and cognition using dual-process model of embodiment. *Advances in Cognitive Psychology, 13*, 3–10.

Skvorak, M. (2013). *Resistant students: Reach me before you teach me*. Lantham, MD: Rowman and Littlefield Education.

Slagt, M., Dubas, J. S., Deković, M., & van Aken, M. A. G. (2016). Differences in sensitivity to parenting depending on child temperament: A meta-analysis. *Psychological Bulletin, 142*, 1068–1110.

Slavin, R. E. (1987). Ability grouping and student achievement in elementary schools: A best evidence synthesis. *Review of Educational Research, 57*, 293–336.

Slavin, R. E. (1990). Achievement effects of ability grouping in secondary schools: A best evidence synthesis. *Review of Educational Research, 60*, 471–499.

Slavin, R. E. (2011). Instruction based on cooperative learning. In R. E. Mayer & P. A. Alexander (Eds.), *Handbook of research on learning and instruction* (pp. 344–360). New York: Routledge.

Slavin, R. E. (2014). Making cooperative learning powerful. *Educational Leadership, 72*, 22–26.

Slavin, R. E. (2015). Cooperative learning in elementary schools. *Education 3-13, 43*, 5–14.

Sloman, S. A., & Rabb, N. (2016). Your understanding is my understanding: Evidence for a community of knowledge. *Psychological Science, 27*, 1451–1460.

Slotter, E. B., & Winger, L. (2015). Lost without each other: The influence of group identity loss on the self-concept. *Group Dynamics: Theory, Research, and Practice, 19*, 15–30.

Slusher, A. L., Patterson, V. T., Schwartz, C. S., & Acevedo, E. O. (2018). Impact of high intensity interval exercise on executive function and brain derived neurotrophic factor in healthy college aged males. *Physiology & Behavior, 191*, 116–122.

Smart, K. L., Hicks, N., & Melton, J. (2013). Using problem-based scenarios to teach writing. *Business Communication Quarterly, 76*, 72–81. doi:10.1177/1080569912466256

Smetana, J. G., & Gettman, D. C. (2006). Autonomy and relatedness with parents and romantic development in African American adolescents. *Developmental Psychology, 42*, 1347–1351.

Smiley, D. (2014). School grades to stay, Florida education chief says. *The Miami Herald*. Retrieved from http://www.miamiherald.com/2014/01/21/3884176/florida-education-commissioner.html

Smith, D. W. (2015). Teacher perceptions of parent involvement in middle school. *Journal of Public Relations, 36*, 393–403.

Smith, H. L., Summers, B. J., Dillon, K. H., Macatee, R. J., & Cougle, J. R. (2016). Hostile interpretation bias in depression. *Journal of Affective Disorders, 203*, 9–13.

Smith, L., & King, J. (2017). A dynamic systems approach to wait time in the second language classroom. *System, 68*, 1–14.

Smith, S. M., Glenberg, A., & Bjork, R. A. (1978). Environmental context and human memory. *Memory & Cognition, 6*, 342–353.

Smith, T. E. C., Polloway, E., A., Doughty, T. T., Patton, J. R., & Dowdy, C. A. (2016). *Teaching students with special needs in inclusive settings* (7th ed.). Boston: Pearson.

Society of Health and Physical Educators. (2016). *Shape of the nation: Status of physical education in the USA*. Retrieved from http://www.shapeamerica.org/advocacy/son/2016/upload/Shape-of-the-Nation-2016_web.pdf

Sommet, N., Darnon, C., & Butera. F. (2015). To confirm or to conform? Performance goals as a regulator of conflict with more-competent others. *Journal of Educational Psychology, 107*, 580–598.

Sommet, N., Pillaud, V., Meuleman, B., & Butera, F. (2017). Empirical study: The socialization of performance goals. *Contemporary Educational Psychology, 49*, 337–354.

Sorhagen, N. S. (2013). Early teacher expectations disproportionately affect poor children's high school performance. *Journal of Educational Psychology, 105*, 465–477.

Sorrenti, L., Filippello, P., Costa, S., & Buzzai, C. (2015). A psychometric examination of the learned helplessness questionnaire in a sample of Italian school students. *Psychology in the Schools, 52*, 923–941.

Soslau, E., Kotch-Jester, S., & Jornlin, A. (2015). The dangerous message teacher candidates infer: "If the edTPA does not assess it, I don't have to do it." *Teachers College Record*. Retrieved from http://www.tcrecord.org/Content.asp?ContentId=18835

Southerland, S. A., & Sinatra, G. M. (2003). Learning about biological evolution: A special case of intentional conceptual change. In G. M. Sinatra & P. R. Pintrich (Eds.), *Intentional conceptual change* (pp. 317–345). Mahwah, NJ: Erlbaum.

Sparks, S. D. (2011). Lectures are homework in schools following Khan Academy lead. *Education Week*. Retrieved from http://www.edweek.org/ew/articles/2011/09/28/05khan_ep.h31.html

Sparks, S. D. (2015). Differentiated instruction: A primer. *Education Week*. Retrieved from http://www.edweek.org/ew/articles/2015/01/28/differentiated-instruction-a-primer.html

Sparks, S. D. (2016). Summing up results from TIMSS, PISA. *Education Week*. Retrieved from http://www.edweek.org/ew/section/multimedia/summing-up-results-from-timss-pisa.html

Sparks, S., & Harwin, A. (2016). Corporal punishment found in schools in 21 states. *Education Week*. Retrieved from http://www.edweek.org/ew/articles/2016/08/23/corporal-punishment-use-found-in-schools-in.html

Spearman, C. (1904). General intelligence, objectively determine and measured. *American Journal of Psychology, 15*, 201–293.

Spearman, C. (1927). *The abilities of man: Their nature and measurement*. New York: Macmillan.

Spicer, P., LaFramboise, T., Markstrom, C., Niles, M., West, M., Fehringer, K., . . . Sarche, M. (2012). Toward an applied developmental science for native children, families, and communities. *Child Development Perspectives, 6*, 49–54.

Sprouls, K., Mathur, S, R., & Upreti, G. (2015). Is positive feedback a forgotten classroom practice? Findings and implications for at-risk students. *Preventing School Failure, 59*, 153–160.

Standage, M., Treasure, D. C., Hooper, K., & Kuczka, K. (2007). Self-handicapping in school physical education: The influence of the motivational climate. *The British Journal of Educational Psychology, 77*, 81–99.

Stanford Achievement Test Series, Tenth Edition. (2009). *Score report sampler*. Boston: Pearson Education, Inc. Retrieved from http://images.pearsonassessments.com/images/assets/sat10/SAT10ScoreReportSampler.pdf

Stanford History Education Group. (2016). *Evaluating information: The cornerstone of civic online reasoning*. Stanford University. Retrieved from https://sheg.stanford.edu/upload/V3LessonPlans/Executive%20Summary%2011.21.16.pdf

Stanhope, D., & Rectanus, K. (2015). Current realities of edtech use: Research brief. *Lea(R)n, Inc*. Retrieved from http://www.learntrials.com/wp-content/uploads/2015/09/CurrentRealitiesOfEdTechUse_Infographic_ResearchBrief.pdf

Staples, M. (2007). Supporting whole-class collaborative inquiry in a secondary mathematics classroom. *Cognition and Instruction, 25*, 161–217.

Star, J. (2004, April). *The development of flexible procedural knowledge in equation solving*. Paper presented at the annual meeting of the American Educational Research Association, San Diego.

Starcher, D., & Allen, S. L. (2016). A global human potential movement and a rebirth of humanistic psychology. *The Humanistic Psychologist, 44*, 227–241.

State of Obesity. (2017). *Adult obesity in the United States*. Trust for America's Health and the Robert Wood Johnson Foundation. Retrieved from http://stateofobesity.org/adult-obesity/

Staub, M. E. (2016). The other side of the brain: The politics of split-brain research in the 1970s–1980s. *History of Psychology, 19*, 259–273.

Steenbergen-Hu, S., & Moon, S. M. (2011). The effects of acceleration on high-ability learners: A meta-analysis. *Gifted Child Quarterly, 55*, 39–53.

Stein, M., Kinder, D., Rolf, K., Silbert, J. & Carnine, D. W. (2018). *Direct instruction mathematics* (5th ed.). New York: Pearson.

Stenberg, G. (2017). Does contingency in adults' responding influence 12-month-old infants' social referencing? *Infant Behavior and Development, 46*, 67–79.

Stenlund, T., Eklöf, H., & Lyrén, P-E. (2017). Group differences in test-taking behavior: An example from a high-stakes testing program. *Assessment in Education: Principles, Policy & Practice, 24*, 4–20.

Stephens-Davidowitz. S (2014). Google, tell me. Is my son a genius? *The New York Times*. Retrieved from https://www.nytimes.com/2014/01/19/opinion/sunday/google-tell-me-is-my-son-a-genius.html

Sternberg, R. (1998a). Applying the triarchic theory of human intelligence in the classroom. In R. Sternberg & W. Williams (Eds.), *Intelligence, instruction, and assessment* (pp. 1–16). Mahwah, NJ: Erlbaum.

Sternberg, R. (1998b). Metacognition, abilities, and developing expertise: What makes an expert student? *Instructional Science, 26*(1–2), 127–140.

Sternberg, R. (2003a). *Cognitive psychology* (3rd ed.). Belmont, CA: Wadsworth.

Sternberg, R. (2003b). *Wisdom, intelligence, and creativity synthesized.* Cambridge: Cambridge University Press.

Sternberg, R. (2004). Culture and intelligence. *American Psychologist, 59*, 325–338.

Sternberg, R. (2006). Recognizing neglected strengths. *Educational Leadership, 64*(1), 30–35.

Sternberg, R. (2007). Who are bright children? The cultural context of being and acting intelligent. *Educational Researcher, 36*(3), 148–155.

Sternberg, R. (2009). Foreword. In S. Tobias & T. Duffy (Eds.), *Constructivist instruction: Success or failure* (pp. x–xi). New York: Routledge.

Sternberg, R. (2017a). ACCEL: A new model for identifying the gifted. *Roeper Review, 39*, 152–169.

Sternberg, R. (2017b). *Cognitive psychology* (7th ed.). Cengage Learning.

Sternberg, R., & Grigorenko, E. (2001). Learning disabilities, schooling, and society. *Phi Delta Kappan, 83*(4), 335–338.

Sterzing, P., Shattuck, P., Narendorf, S., Wagner, M., & Cooper, B. (2012). Bullying involvement and autism spectrum disorders: Prevalence and correlates of bullying involvement among adolescents with an autism spectrum disorder. *JAMA Pediatrics (formerly Archives of Pediatric & Adolescent Medicine)*. Retrieved from http://archpedi.jamanetwork.com/article.aspx?articleid=1355390

Stoilescu, D. (2016). Aspects of theories, frameworks and paradigms in mathematics education research. *European Journal of Science and Mathematics Education, 4*, 140–154.

Storage D., Horne Z., Cimpian A., & Leslie, S-J. (2016). The frequency of "brilliant" and "genius" in teaching evaluations predicts the representation of women and African Americans across fields. *PLoSONE, 11*:e0150194.doi:10.1371/journal

Strack, J., Lopes, P., Esteves, F., & Fernandez-Berrocal, P. (2017). Must we suffer to succeed? When anxiety boosts motivation and performance. *Journal of Individual Differences, 38*, 113–124.

Stringfield, S., Teddlie, C., & Suarez, S. (2017). Classroom interaction in effective and ineffective schools: Preliminary results from Phase III of the Louisiana School Effectiveness study. *Journal of Classroom Interaction, 52*, 4–14.

Strohschein, L., Ploubidis, G. B., Silverwood, R., DeStavola, B., & Grundy, E. (2016). Do men really benefit more from marriage than women? *American Journal of Public Health, 106*, 2–3.

Stross, R. (2010). Computers at home: Educational hope vs. teenage reality. *New York Times*. Retrieved from http://www.nytimes.com/2010/07/11/business/11digi.html

Su, H. F. H., Ricci, F. A., & Mnatsakanian, M. (2016). Mathematical teaching strategies: Pathways to critical thinking and metacognition. *International Journal of Research in Education and Science, 2*, 190–200.

Suarez-Orozco, C., Pimentel, A., & Martin, M. (2009). The significance of relationships: Academic engagement and achievement among newcomer immigrant youth. *Teachers College Record Volume, 111*, 712–749. Retrieved from http://www.tcrecord.org/Content.asp?ContentID=15342

Summers, J. J., Davis, H. A., & Woolfolk Hoy, A. (2017). The effects of teachers' efficacy beliefs on students' perceptions of teacher relationship quality. *Learning and Individual Differences, 53*, 17–25.

Superville, D. R. (2017). Absences, trauma, and orphaned children: How the opioid crisis Is ravaging schools. *Education Week*. Retrieved from https://www.edweek.org/ew/articles/2017/11/20/absences-trauma-and-orphaned-children-how-the.html?cmp=eml-enl-eu-news1&M=58283990&U=27557

Sutherland, M. R., McQuiggan, D. A., Ryan, J. D., & Mather, M. (2017). Perceptual salience does not influence emotional arousal's impairing effects on top-down attention. *Emotion, 17*, 700–706.

Swami, V., Funham, A., Smyth, N., Weis, L., Lay, A., & Clow, A. (2016). Putting the stress on conspiracy theories: Examining associations between psychological stress, anxiety, and belief in conspiracy theories. *Personality and Individual Differences, 99*, 72–76.

Sweller, J. (2003). Evolution of human cognitive architecture. *The Psychology of Learning and Motivation, 43*, 215–266.

Sweller, J., van Merrienboer, J., & Paas, F. (1998). Cognitive architecture and instructional design. *Educational Psychology Review, 10*, 251–296.

Talamas, S. N., Mayor, K. I., & Perrett, D. I. (2016). Blinded by beauty: Attractiveness bias and accurate perceptions of academic performance. *PloS ONE, 11*, 1–18.

Tan, X., & Michel, R. (2011). Why do standardized testing programs report scaled scores? *Educational Testing Service*. Retrieved from http://www.ets.org/Media/Research/pdf/RD_Connections16.pdf

Tanel, R. (2013). Prospective physics teachers' self-efficacy beliefs about teaching and conceptual understandings for the subjects of force and motion. *Journal of Baltic Science Education, 12*, 6–20.

Tang, Y., Zhang, W., Chen, K., Feng, S., Ji, Y., Shen, J., Reiman, E., & Liu, Y. (2006). Arithmetic processing in the brain shaped by culture. *Proceedings of the National Academy of Sciences USA, 103*, 10775–10780.

Tangen, J. L., & Borders, L. D. (2017). Applying information processing theory to supervision: an initial exploration. *Counselor Education and Supervision, 56*, 98–111.

Taraban, R., Anderson, E. E., DeFinis, A., Brown, A. G., Weigold, A., & Sharma, M. P. (2007). First steps in understanding engineering students' growth of conceptual and procedural knowledge in an interactive learning context. *Journal of Engineering Education, 96*, 57–68.

Tartaglia, S., & Rollero, C. (2015). The effects of attractiveness and status on personality evaluation. *Europe's Journal of Psychology, 11*, 677–690.

Tatera, K. (2015). Left-brained vs. right-brained? Myth debunked. *The Science Explorer*. Retrieved from http://thescienceexplorer.com/brain-and-body/left-brained-vs-right-brained-myth-debunked

Taylor, K., & Rohrer, D. (2010). The effects of interleaved practice. *Applied Cognitive Psychology, 24*, 837–848.

Temkin, D. (2015). All 50 states now have a bullying law. Now What? *The Huffington Post*. Retrieved from http://www.huffingtonpost.com/deborah-temkin/all-50-states-now-have-a_b_7153114.html

ter Vrugte, J., de Jong, T., Vandercruysse, S., Wouters, P., van Oostendorp, H., & Elen, J. (2017). Computer game-based mathematics education: Embedded faded worked examples facilitate knowledge acquisition. *Learning and Instruction, 50*, 44–53.

Terhune, K. (1968). Studies of motives, cooperation, and conflict within laboratory microcosms. In G. Snyder (Ed.), *Studies in international conflict* (Vol. 4, pp. 29–58). Buffalo, NY: SUNY Buffalo Council on International Studies.

Terman, L., & Oden, M. (1947). The gifted child grows up. In L. Terman (Ed.), *Genetic studies of genius* (Vol. 4). Stanford, CA: Stanford University Press.

Terman, L., & Oden, M. (1959). The gifted group in mid-life. In L. Terman (Ed.), *Genetic studies of genius* (Vol. 5). Stanford, CA: Stanford University Press.

Terman, L., Baldwin, B., & Bronson, E. (1925). Mental and physical traits of a thousand gifted children. In L. Terman (Ed.), *Genetic studies of genius* (Vol. 1). Stanford, CA: Stanford University Press.

Thaler, R. H., & Sunstein, C. R. (2008). *Nudge: Improving decisions about health, wealth, and happiness.* New Haven, CT: Yale University Press.

The Associated Press. (2017). AP investigation reveals hidden horror of sex assaults by K–12 students. *Education Week.* Retrieved from http://www.edweek.org/ew/articles/2017/05/01/ap-reveals-hidden-horror-of-sex_ap.html?print=1

The Associated Press. (2018). These are the companies that have cut ties with the NRA. *Los Angeles Times.* Retrieved from http://www.latimes.com/nation/nationnow/la-na-nra-companies-boycott-20180224-htmlstory.html

The Pell Institute. (2018). *Indicators of higher education equity in the United States: 2018 historical trend report.* Retrieved from http://blogs.edweek.org/edweek/high_school_and_beyond/COE-18-Pell-Indicators-f.pdf

The Pew Charitable Trusts. (2012). *Pursuing the American Dream: Economic mobility across generations.* Retrieved from http://www.pewtrusts.org/~/media/legacy/uploadedfiles/pcs_assets/2012/PursuingAmericanDreampdf.pdf

Thibodeaux, A. K., Labat, M. B., Lee, D. E., & Labat, C. A. (2015). The effects of leadership and high-stakes testing on teacher retention. *Academy of Educational Leadership Journal, 19,* 227–249.

Thomas, A. E. (2017). Gender differences in students' physical science motivation: Are teachers' implicit cognitions another piece of the puzzle? *American Educational Research Journal, 54,* 35–58.

Thomas, R. C., & Jacoby, L. L. (2013). Diminishing adult egocentrism when estimating what people know. *Journal of Experimental Psychology: Learning, Memory, and Cognition, 39,* 473–486.

Thomas-Tate, S., Connor, C. M., & Johnson, L. (2013). Design Experiments: Developing and Testing an Intervention for Elementary School-Age Students Who Use Non-Mainstream American English Dialects. *Society for Research on Educational Effectiveness.* Retrieved from http://files.eric.ed.gov/fulltext/ED563056.pdf

Thommessen, S., & Todd, B. (2010, April). *Revisiting sex differences in play: Very early evidence of stereotypical preferences in infancy.* Paper presented at the annual meeting of the British Psychological Society, Stratford-upon-Avon, UK.

Thompson, B. C., Mazer, J. P., & Flood, G. E. (2015). The changing nature of parent-teacher communication: Mode selection in the smartphone era. *Communication Education, 64,* 187–207.

Thompson, C. (2013). *Smarter than you think: How technology is changing our minds for the better.* New York: Penguin Press.

Thompson, R., & Newton, E. (2010). Emotion in early conscience. In W. Arsenio & E. Lemerise (Eds.), *Emotions, aggression, and morality in children: Bridging development and psychopathology* (pp. 13–31). Washington, DC: American Psychological Association.

Thornberg, R. (2010). A study of children's conceptions of school rules by investigating their judgments of transgressions in the absence of rules. *Educational Psychology, 30*(5), 583–603. doi:10.1080/01443410.2010.492348

Thorndike, E. (1924). Mental discipline in high school studies. *Journal of Educational Psychology, 15,* 1–2, 83–98.

Tiantong, M., & Teemuangsai, S. (2013). The four scaffolding modules for collaborative problem-based learning through the computer network on Moodle LMS for the computer programming course. *International Education Studies, 6,* 47–55.

Tichenor, M., Welsh, A., Corcoran, C., Piechura, K., & Heins, E. (2016). Elementary girls' attitudes toward mathematics in mixed-gender and single-gender classrooms. *Education, 137,* 93–100.

Tichy, M. (2017). Maslow illuminates resilience in students placed at risk. *Journal of Education and Social Justice, 5,* 94–103.

Tiedt, P., & Tiedt, I. (2010). *Multicultural teaching* (8th ed.). Boston: Allyn & Bacon.

Tillema, H., & Smith, K. (2007). Portfolio appraisal: In search of criteria. *Teaching and Teacher Education, 23,* 442–456.

Time 4 Learning. (2018). *Standardized tests by state.* Retrieved from https://www.time4learning.com/testprep/

Todd, A., R., Simpson, A. J., & Tamir, D. I. (2016). Active perspective taking induces flexible use of self-knowledge during social inference. *Journal of Experimental Psychology: General, 145,* 1583–1588.

Tofade, T., Elsner, J., & Haines, S. T. (2013). Best practice strategies for effective use of questions as a teaching tool. *American Journal of Pharmaceutical Education, 77,* 1–9.

Toga, A., & Thompson, P. (2005). Genetics of brain structure and intelligence. *Annual Review of Neuroscience, 28,* 1–23.

Toldson, I. A. (2012). Editor's comment: When standardized tests miss the mark. *Journal of Negro Education, 81,* 181–185.

Tomasello, M. (2006). Acquiring linguistic constructions. In D. Kuhn & R. Siegler (Vol. Eds.), *Handbook of child psychology: Vol. 2. Cognition, perception, and language* (6th ed., pp. 255–298). Hoboken, NJ: Wiley.

Tomasello, M. (2011). Language development. In U. Goswami (Ed.), *Wiley-Blackwell handbook of childhood cognitive development* (2nd ed., pp. 239–257). Malden, MA: Wiley-Blackwell.

Tomlinson, C. A. (2014). *The Differentiated Classroom: Responding to the Needs of All Learners* (2nd ed.). Alexandria, VA: ASCD.

Tomlinson, C. A. (2015). Differentiation does, in fact, work. *Education Week.* Retrieved from http://www.edweek.org/ew/articles/2015/01/28/differentiation-does-in-fact-work.html

Tomlinson, C. A., & McTighe, J. (2006). *Integrating differentiated instruction and understanding by design: Connecting content and kids.* Alexandria, VA: Association for Supervision and Curriculum Development.

Tomlinson, C. A., & Moon, T. R. (2013). *Assessment and Student Success in a Differentiated Classroom.* Alexandria, VA: ASCD.

Tomoda, A., Suzuki, H., Rabi, K., Yi-Shin S., Polcari, A., Teicher, M. H. (2010). Reduced prefrontal cortical gray matter volume in young adults exposed to harsh corporal punishment. *Neuroimage, 47,* T66-T71. doi: 10.1016/j.neuroimage.2009.03.005

Tompkins, G. (2018). *Literacy for the 21st century: A balanced approach* (7th ed.). Boston: Pearson.

Torelli, J. N., Lloyd, B. P., Diekman, C. A., & Wehby, J. H. (2017). Teaching stimulus control via class-wide multiple schedules of reinforcement in public elementary school classrooms. *Journal of Positive Behavior Interventions, 19,* 14 –25.

Torrez-Guzman, M. (2011). Methodologies and teacher stances: How do they interact in classrooms? *International Journal of Bilingual Education and Bilingualism, 14*(2), 225–241. doi: 10.1080/13670050.2010.539675

Toshalis, E. (2015). Five practices that provoke misbehavior. *Educational Leadership, 73,* 34–40.

Tracy, J. L., Hart J., & Martens J. P. (2011). Death and science: The existential underpinnings of belief in intelligent design and discomfort with evolution. *PLoS ONE, 6,* e17349. doi:10.1371/journal.pone.0017349

Tran, S. K. (2017). GOOGLE: A reflection of culture, leader, and management. *International Journal of Corporate Social Responsibility, 10.* https://doi.org/10.1186/s40991–017–0021–0

Trautwein, U., Lüdtke, O., & Schnyder, I. (2006). Predicting homework effort: Support for a domain-specific, multilevel homework model. *Journal of Educational Psychology, 98,* 438–456.

Trawick-Smith, J. (2014). *Early childhood development: A multicultural perspective* (6th ed.). Upper Saddle River, NJ: Merrill/Pearson.

Tritt, A. (2017). 7 young people on their views of gender. *The New York Times.* Retrieved from https://www.nytimes.com/2017/01/23/health/trans-gender-children-youth.html

Tsay, M., & Brady, M. (2010). A case study of cooperative learning and communication pedagogy; Does working in teams make a difference? *Journal of the Scholarship of Teaching and Learning, 10,* 78–89.

Tucker, M. (2014). The federal role in state education accountability systems. *Education Week.* Retrieved from http://blogs.edweek.org/edweek/top_performers/2014/04/the_federal_role_in_state_education_accountability_systems.html

Tucker, M. (2015). Why have American education standards collapsed? *Education Week.* Retrieved from http://blogs.edweek.

org/edweek/top_performers/2015/04/why_have_american_education_standards_collapsed.html?cmp=ENL-EU-MOSTPOP

Tullis, J. G., Finley, J. R., & Benjamin, A. S. (2013). Metacognition of the testing effect: Guiding learners to predict the benefits of retrieval. *Memory and Cognition, 41,* 429–442. doi:10.3758/s13421–012–0274–5

Tullis, M., & Fulmer, S. M. (2013). Students' motivational and emotional experiences and their relationship to persistence during academic challenge in mathematics and reading. *Learning and Individual Differences, 27,* 35–46.

Tuncel, G. (2017). Improving the cultural responsiveness of prospective social studies teachers: An action research. *Educational Sciences: Theory and Practice, 17,* 1317–1344.

Turkle, S. (2015). *Reclaiming conversation: The power of talk in a digital age.* New York: Penguin Press.

Turnbull, A., Turnbull, H. R., Wehmeyer, M. L., & Shogren, K. A. (2016). *Exceptional lives: Special education in today's schools* (8th ed.). Boston: Pearson.

Turner, W. D., Solis, O. J., & Kincade, D. H. (2017). Differentiating instruction for large classes in higher education. *International Journal of Teaching & Higher Learning in Higher Education, 29,* 490–500.

Twenge, J. M. (2017). Have smartphones destroyed a generation? *The Atlantic.* Retrieved from https://www.theatlantic.com/magazine/archive/2017/09/has-the-smartphone-destroyed-a-generation/534198/

Tyler, K. M. (2015). Examining cognitive predictors of academic cheating among urban middle school students: The role of home-school dissonance. *Middle Grades Research Journal, 10,* 77–93.

U.S. Department of Education. (2017). *U.S. Secretary of Education DeVos issues statement on new Title IX guidance.* Retrieved from https://content.govdelivery.com/accounts/USED/bulletins/1890330

U.S. Department of Education, National Center for Education Statistics. (2017). *The Condition of Education 2017* (NCES 2017–144), Status Dropout Rates. Retrieved from https://nces.ed.gov/fastfacts/display.asp?id=16

U.S. Department of Education. (2008). *Foundations for success: The final report of the National Mathematics Advisory Council.* Retrieved from https://nces.ed.gov/programs/coe/indicator_cgg.asp

U.S. Department of Education. (2009). *Race to Top executive summary.* Retrieved from http://www2.ed.gov/programs/racetothetop/executive-summary.pdf

U.S. Department of Education. (2016). *Equity in IDEA Rule. Assistance to states for the education of children with disabilities; preschool grants for children with disabilities.* Retrieved from: https://www.gpo.gov/fdsys/pkg/FR-2016–03–02/pdf/2016–03938.pdf

U.S. Department of Justice. (2016). Indicators of school crime and safety: 2015. *National Center for Education Statistics.* Retrieved from http://nces.ed.gov/pubs2016/2016079.pdf

Ukrainetz, T., Nuspl, J., Wilderson, K., & Beddes, S. (2011). The effects of syllable instruction on phonemic awareness in preschoolers. *Early Childhood Research Quarterly, 26,* 50–60.

Ullén, F., de Manzano, O., Almeida, R., Magnusson, P. K. E., Pedersen, N. L., Nakamura, J., . . . Madison, G. (2012). Proneness for psychological flow in everyday life: Associations with personality and intelligence. *Personality and individual differences, 52,* 167–172.

UNESCO Institute for Statistics. (2017). *Percentage of female teachers by teaching level of education.* Retrieved from http://data.uis.unesco.org/index.aspx?queryid=178

United States Census Bureau. (2016). Most popular surnames in the United States. U.S. Department of Commerce. Retrieved from https://www.census.gov/newsroom/press-releases/2016/cb16-tps154.html

United States Department of Agriculture. (2017). The national school lunch program. Retrieved from https://fns-prod.azureedge.net/sites/default/files/cn/NSLPFactSheet.pdf

Urban, S. (2014). 7 Sneaky Supermarket Marketing Strategies to Stop Falling For. *Organic Authority.* Retrieved from http://www.organicauthority.com/7-sneaky-supermarket-marketing-strategies-to-stop-falling-for/

Vacca, R. T., Vacca, J. L., & Mraz, M. (2014). *Content area reading: Literacy and learning across the curriculum* (11th ed.). Boston: Allyn & Bacon.

Vaksvik T., Ruijs, A., Røkkum, M., & Holm, I. (2016). Evaluation of a home treatment program for cold hypersensitivity using a classical conditioning procedure in patients with hand and arm injuries. *Journal of Hand Therapy: Official Journal of the American Society of Hand Therapists, 29,* 14–22.

Valdez, A. (2013). Multimedia learning from PowerPoint: Use of adjunct questions. *Psychology Journal, 10,* 35–44.

Valenzuela, K. A. V., Shields, J., & Drolet. J. (2018). Settling immigrants in neoliberal times: NGOs and immigrant well-being in comparative context. *Alternate Routes, 29,* 65–89.

Van Dam, N. (2013). Inside the learning brain. *T+D, 67,* 30–35.

van der Linden, D., Pekaar, K. A., Bakker, A. B., Schermer, J. A., Vernon, P. A., Dunkel, C. S., & Petrides, K. V. (2017). Overlap between the general factor of personality and emotional intelligence: A meta-analysis. *Psychological Bulletin, 143,* 36–52.

van der Niet, A. G., Smith, J., Oosterlaan, J., Scherder, E. J. A., Hartman, E., & Visscher, C. (2016). Effects of a cognitively demanding aerobic intervention during recess on children's physical fitness and executive functioning. *Pediatric Exercise Science, 28,* 64–71.

van Geel, M., Goemans, A., Toprak, F., & Vedder, P. (2017). Which personality traits are related to traditional bullying and cyberbullying? A study with the Big Five, Dark Triad and sadism. *Personality and Individual Differences, 106,* 231–235.

van Hek, M., Kraaykamp, G., & Pelzer, B. (2017): Do schools affect girls' and boys' reading performance differently? A multilevel study on the gendered effects of school resources and school practices, *School Effectiveness and School Improvement.* DOI:10.1080/09243453.2017.1382540

van Hoorn, J., Fuligni, A. J., Crone, E. A., & Galván . A. (2016). Peer influence effects on risk-taking and prosocial decision-making in adolescence: insights from neuroimaging studies. *Current Opinion in Behavioral Sciences, 10,* 59–64.

van Tubergen, F., & van Gaans, M. (2016). Is there an oppositional culture among immigrant adolescents in the Netherlands? *Youth and Society, 48,* 202–219.

Vandenbroucke, L., Split, J., Verschueren, K., Piccinin, C., & Baeyens, D. (2018). The classroom as a developmental context for cognitive development: A meta-analysis on the importance of teacher-student interactions for children's executive functioning. *Review of Educational Research, 88,* 125–164.

Vansteenkiste, M., Zhou, M., Lens, W., & Soenens, B. (2005). Experiences of autonomy and control among Chinese learners: Vitalizing or immobilizing. *Journal of Educational Psychology, 97,* 468–483.

Vatterott, C. (2014). Student-owned homework. *Educational Leadership, 71,* 39–42.

Vaughn, S., Bos, C., & Schumm, J. (2018). *Teaching students who are exceptional, diverse, & at risk in the general education classroom* (7th ed.). Boston: Pearson.

Vedantam, S. (2010). *The hidden brain: How unconscious minds elect presidents, control markets, wage wars, and save our lives.* New York: Spiegel & Grau.

Veenstra, R., Lindenberg, S., Oldehinkel, A. J., De Winter, A. F., Verhulst, F. C., & Ormel, J. (2005). Bullying and victimization in elementary schools: A comparison of bullies, victims, and bully/victims, and uninvolved preadolescents. *Developmental Psychology, 41,* 672–682.

Velasquez-Manoff, M. (2013). Status and stress. *The New York Times.* Retrieved from http://opinionator.blogs.nytimes.com/2013/07/27/status-and-stress/?nl=todaysheadlines&emc=edit_20130728

Verschueren, K., Doumen, S., & Buyse, E. (2012). Relationships with mother, teacher, and peers: Unique and joint effects on young children's self-concept. *Attachment & Human Development, 14,* 233–248.

Vigdor, J., & Ladd, H. (2010). *Scaling the digital divide: Home computer technology and student achievement.* Retrieved from http://www.urban.org/uploadedpdf/1001433-digital-divide.pdf

Visser, T. A. W. (2017). Frozen in time: Concurrent task performance interferes with temporal shifts of attention. *Journal of Experimental Psychology: Human Perception and Performance. 43,* 1057–1064.

Vlassova, A., & Pearson, J. (2013). Look before you leap: Sensory memory improves decision making. *Psychological Science, 24,* 1635–1643. doi:10.1177/0956797612474321

Voight, A., Hanson, T., O'Malley, M., & Adekanye, L. (2015). The racial school climate gap: Within-school disparities in students' experiences of safety, support, and connectedness. *American Journal of Community Psychology, 56,* 252–267.

Von Culin, K., R., Tsukayama. E., & Duckworth, A. L. (2014). Unpacking grit: Motivational correlates of perseverance and passion for long-term goals. *The Journal of Positive Psychology, 9,* 306–312.

von der Embse, N. P., Pendergast, L. L., Segool, N., Saeki, E., & Ryan, S. (2016). The influence of test-based accountability policies on school climate and teacher stress across four states. *Teaching and Teacher Education, 59,* 492–502.

Vosniadou, S. (2007). The cognitive-situative divide and the problem of conceptual change. *Educational Psychologist, 42*(1), 55–66.

Voyer, D., & Voyer, S. D. (2014). Gender differences in scholastic achievement: a meta-analysis. *Psychological Bulletin, 140,* 1174–1204. doi: 10.1037/a0036620

Vygotsky, L. (1978). *Mind in society: The development of higher psychological processes* (M. Cole, V. John-Steiner, S. Scribner, & E. Souberman, Eds. & Trans.). Cambridge, MA: Harvard University Press.

Vygotsky, L. (1986). *Thought and language.* Cambridge, MA: MIT Press.

Vygotsky, L. (1987). The problem and the method of investigation. In R. Rieber & A. Carton (Eds.), *Collected works of L. S. Vygotsky: Vol. 1. Problems of general psychology* (pp. 167–241). New York: Plenum Press.

Vygotsky, L. (1997). Analysis of higher mental functions. In R. Rieber & A. Carton (Eds.), *Collected works of L. S. Vygotsky: Vol. 4. The history of the development of higher mental functions* (pp. 65–82). New York: Plenum Press.

Wadsworth, B. J. (2004). *Piaget's theory of cognitive and affective development* (5th ed.). Boston: Pearson Education.

Walker, D. J., Del Bellow, M. P., Landry, J., D'Souza, D. N., & Detke, H. C. (2017). Quality of life in children and adolescents with bipolar 1 depression treated with olanzapine/fluoxetine combination. *Child & Adolescent Psychiatry & Mental Health, 11,* 1–11.

Walker, E., Shapiro, D., Esterberg, M., & Trotman, H. (2010). Neurodevelopment and schizophrenia: Broadening the focus. *Current Trends in Psychological Science, 19,* 204–208.

Walker, J. M. T., & Hoover-Dempsey, K. V. (2015). Parental engagement and classroom management: Unlocking the potential of family-school interactions and relationships. In E. T. Emmer & E. J. Sabornie (Eds.), *Handbook of classroom management* (2nd ed., pp. 459–478). New York: Routledge.

Walker, J. M. T., & Legg, A. M. (2018). Parent-teacher conference communication: a guide to integrating family engagement through simulated conversations about student academic progress. *Journal of Education for Teaching, 44,* 366–380.

Walker, O. L., & Henderson, H. A. (2012). Temperament and social problem solving competence in preschool: Influences on academic skills in early elementary school. *Social Development, 21,* 761–779.

Walkington, C., & Bernacki, M. (2015). Students authoring personalized "algebra stories": Problem-posing in the context of out-of-school interests. *The Journal of Mathematical Behavior, 40,* 171–191.

Walsh, B. (2004). *The Elephants of Style: A Trunkload of Tips on the Big Issues and Gray Areas of Contemporary American English.* New York: McGraw Hill.

Wang, A. B. (2016). 'Post-truth' named 2016 word of the year by Oxford Dictionaries. *The Washington Post.* Retrieved from https://www.washingtonpost.com/news/the-fix/wp/2016/11/16/post-truth-named-2016-word-of-the-year-by-oxford-dictionaries/?utm_term=.4922927c717e

Wang, K., & Wang, X. (2013). Promoting knowledge construction and cognitive development: A case study of teacher's questioning. *Theory and Practice in Language Studies, 3,* 1387–1392.

Wang, M-T., Hill, N. E., & Hofkens, T. (2014). Parental involvement and African American and European American adolescents' academic, behavioral, and emotional development in secondary school. *Child Development, 85,* 2151–2168.

Wang, M. (2017). Harsh parenting and peer acceptance in Chinese early adolescents: Three child aggression subtypes as mediators and child gender as moderator. *Child Abuse and Neglect, 63,* 30–40.

Wang, T., Ren, X., & Schweizer, K. (2017). Learning and retrieval processes predict fluid intelligence over and above working memory. *Intelligence, 61,* 29–36.

Wang, W. (2015). Interracial marriage: Who is 'marrying out'? *Pew Research Center.* Retrieved from http://www.pewresearch.org/fact-tank/2015/06/12/interracial-marriage-who-is-marrying-out/

Ward, Z. J., Long, M. W., Resch, S. C., Giles, C. M., Cradock, A. L., & Gortmaker, S. L. (2017). Simulation of growth trajectories of childhood obesity into adulthood. *New England Journal of Medicine, 377,* 2145–2153. DOI: 10.1056/NEJMoa1703860

Wardley, C. S., Applegate, E. B., & Van Rhee, J. A. (2013). A comparison of student knowledge acquisition by organ system and skills in parallel problem-based and lecture-based curricula. *The Journal of Physician Assistant Education, 24,* 5–14.

Ware, H., & Kitsantas, A. (2007). Teacher and collective efficacy beliefs as predictors of professional commitment. *Journal of Educational Research, 100*(5), 303–310.

Ware, L. (2017). Discriminatory discipline: The racial crisis in America's public schools. *UMKC Law Review, 85,* 739–772.

Warschauer, M. (2011). *Learning in the cloud: How (and why) to transform schools with digital media.* New York: Teachers College Press.

Warshof, A., & Rappaport, N. (2013). Staying connected with troubled students. *Educational Leadership, 71,* 34–38.

Waterhouse, L. (2006). Multiple intelligences, the Mozart effect, and emotional intelligence: A critical review. *Educational Psychologist, 41*(4), 217–225.

Watson, M., & Battistich, V. (2006). Building and sustaining caring communities. In C. M. Evertson & C. S. Weinstein (Eds.), *Handbook of classroom management: Research, practice, and contemporary issues* (pp. 253–279). Mahwah, NJ: Erlbaum.

Watson, M., & Ecken, L. (2003). *Learning to trust: Transforming difficult elementary classrooms through developmental discipline.* San Francisco: Jossey-Bass.

Waugh, C., & Gronlund, N. (2013). *Assessing student achievement* (10th ed.). Needham Heights, MA: Allyn & Bacon.

Way, N., Reddy, R., & Rhodes, J. (2007). Students' perceptions of school climate during the middle school years: Associations with trajectories of psychological and behavioral adjustment. *American Journal of Community Psychology, 40,* 194–213.

Wechsler, D. (2014). *Wechsler intelligence scale for children* (5th ed.). Bloomington, MN: Pearson.

Wedell-Wedellsborg, T., (2017). Are you solving the right problems? *Harvard Business Review, 95,* 76–83.

Weil, L. G., Fleming, S. M., Dumontheil, I., Kilford, E. J., Weil, R. S., Rees, G., . . . & Blakemore, S-J. (2013). The development of metacognitive ability in adolescence. *Consciousness and Cognition, 22,* 264–271.

Weiland, A., & Coughlin, R. (1979). Self-identification and preferences: A comparison of White and Mexican American first and third graders. *Journal of Social Psychology, 10,* 356–365.

Weiner, B. (1992). *Human motivation: Metaphors, theories, and research.* Newbury Park, CA: Sage.

Weiner, B. (2000). Interpersonal and intrapersonal theories of motivation from an attributional perspective. *Educational Psychology Review, 12,* 1–14.

Weiner, B. (2001). Intrapersonal and interpersonal theories of motivation from an attribution perspective. In F. Salili, C. Chiu, & Y. Hong (Eds.), *Student motivation: The culture and context of learning* (pp. 17–30). New York: Kluwer Academic/Plenum.

Weinstein, C. S., & Romano, M. E. (2015). *Elementary classroom management: Lessons from research and practice* (6th ed.). New York: McGraw-Hill.

Weinstock, J. (2007). Don't call my kid smart. *T.H.E. Journal, 34*, 6.

Weisgram, E., Bigler, R., & Liben, L. (2010). Gender, values, and occupational interests among children, adolescents, and adults. *Child Development, 81*(3), 778–796. doi:10.1111/j.1467–8624.2010.01433.x

Weisleder, A., & Fernald, A. (2013). Talking to children matters. *Psychological Science, 24*(11), 2143–2152.

Weiss, J., & Hess, F. M. (2015). What did Race to the Top accomplish? *Education Next, 15*, 50–56.

Weiss, J., & McGuinn, P. (2016). States as change agents under ESSA. *Phi Delta Kappan, 97*(8), 28–33.

Wellisch, M., & Brown, J. (2012). An integrated identification and intervention model for intellectually gifted children. *Journal of Advanced Academics 23*, 145–167.

Wentzel, K. R. (2005). Peer relationships, motivation, and academic performance at school. In A. J. Elliot & C.S. Dweck (Eds.), *Handbook of competence and motivation* (pp. 279–296). New York: Guilford Press.

Wentzel, K. R. (2009). Peers and academic functioning at school. In K. H. Rubin, W. M. Bukowski, & B. Laursen (Eds.), *Handbook of peer interactions, relationships, and groups* (pp. 531–547). New York: Guilford.

Wentzel, K. R. (2010). Students' relationships with teachers. In J. L. Meece & J. S. Eccles (Eds.), *Handbook of research on schools, schooling, and human development* (pp. 75–91). New York: Routledge.

Wentzel, K. R., & Watkins, D. E. (2011). Instruction based on peer interactions. In R. E. Mayer & P. A. Alexander (Eds.), *Handbook of research on learning and instruction* (pp. 322–343). New York: Routledge.

Wentzel, K. R., & Wigfield, A. (2007). Motivational interventions that work: Themes and remaining issues. *Educational Psychologist, 42*, 261–271.

Wentzel, K. R., Russell, S., & Baker, S. (2016). Emotional support and expectations from parents, teachers, and peers predict adolescent competence at school. *Journal of Educational Psychology, 108*, 242–255.

Wentzel, K., Battle, A., Russell, S., & Looney, L. (2010). Social supports from teachers and peers as predictors of academic and social motivation. *Contemporary Educational Psychology, 35*, 193–202.

West, M. (2012). *Is retaining students in the early grade self-defeating?* Brookings Institute. Retrieved from http://www.brookings.edu/research/papers/2012/08/16-student-retention-west

West, M. R., Kraft, M. A., Finn, A. S., Martin, R. E., Duckworth, A. L., Gabrieli, C. F. O., & Gabrieli, J. D. E. (2016). Promise and paradox: Measuring students' non-cognitive skills and the impact of schooling. *Educational Evaluation and Policy Analysis, 38*, 148–170. http://dx.doi.org/10.3102/0162373715597298

Whippman, R. (2016). *America the anxious: How our pursuit of happiness is creating a nation of nervous wrecks.* New York: St. Martin's Press.

Whippman, R. (2017). Happiness is other people. *The New York Times.* Retrieved from https://www.nytimes.com/2017/10/27/opinion/sunday/happiness-is-other-people.html?ref=todayspaper&_r=0

Whitaker, B. G., & Godwin, L. N. (2013). The antecedents of moral imagination in the workplace: A social cognitive theory perspective. *Journal of Business Ethics, 114*, 61–73.

White, R. (1959). Motivation reconsidered: The concept of competence. *Psychological Review, 66*, 297–333.

Whitehead, P. M. (2017). Goldstein's self-actualization: A biosemiotic view. *The Humanistic Psychologist, 45*, 71–83.

Whittaker, E., & Kowalski, R. M. (2015). Cyberbullying via social media. *Journal of School Violence, 14*, 11–29.

Wiedeman, R. (2016). The Sandy Hook hoax. *New York Magazine.* Retrieved from http://nymag.com/daily/intelligencer/2016/09/the-sandy-hook-hoax.html

Wigfield, A. (1994). Expectancy-value theory of achievement motivation: A developmental perspective. *Educational Psychology Review, 6*, 49–78.

Wigfield, A., & Eccles, J. (1992). The development of achievement task values: A theoretical analysis. *Developmental Review, 12*, 265–310.

Wigfield, A., & Eccles, J. (2000). Expectancy-value theory of achievement motivation. *Contemporary Educational Psychology, 25*, 68–81.

Wigfield, A., & Eccles, J. S. (2002). The development of competence beliefs, expectancies for success, and achievement values from childhood through adolescence. In A. Wigfield & J. S. Eccles (Eds.), *Development of achievement motivation. A volume in the educational psychology series* (pp. 91–120). San Diego, CA: Academic Press.

Wiggins, G., & McTighe, J. (2006). *Understanding by design* (2nd ed.). Upper Saddle River, NJ: Pearson.

Wiliam, D. (2014). What do teachers need to know about the new *Standards* for educational and psychological testing? *Educational Measurement: Issues and Practice, 33*, 20–30.

Wilkinson, M. (2016). Kids' lead levels high in many Michigan cities. Retrieved from http://www.detroitnews.com/story/news/michigan/flint-water-crisis/2016/01/27/many-michigan-cities-higher-lead-levels-flint/79438144/

Will, M. (2016). High school students say student-led discussions and group work often go awry. *Education Week.* Retrieved from http://blogs.edweek.org/teachers/teaching_now/2016/06/high_school_group_work_student_led_discussions.html

Will, M. (2018). 'I worry every day': Lockdown drills prompt fear, self-reflection after school shooting. *Education Week.* Retrieved from https://www.edweek.org/ew/articles/2018/02/20/theyre-coming-for-me-and-my-kids.html?cmp=eml-enl-eu-news2&M=58388145&U=27557

Williams, C., & Zacks, R. (2001). Is retrieval-induced forgetting an inhibitory process? *American Journal of Psychology, 114*, 329–354.

Williams, J. D., Wallace, T. L., & Sung, H. C. (2016). Providing choice in middle grade classrooms: An exploratory study of enactment variability and student reflection. *Journal of Early Adolescence, 36*, 527–550.

Williams, K., Swift, J., Williams, H., & Van Daal, V. (2017). Raising children's self-efficacy through parental involvement in homework. *Educational Research, 59*, 316–334.

Williamson, H. C., Hanna, M. A., Lavner, J. A., Bradbury, T. N., & Karney, B. R. (2013). Discussion topic and observed behavior in couples' problem-solving conversations: Do problem severity and topic choice matter? *Journal of Family Psychology, 27*, 330–335.

Williamson, P. O. (2016). Situated cognition principles increase students' likelihood of knowledge transfer in an online information literacy course. *Evidence Based Library and Information Practice, 11*, 66–68.

Willingham, D. T. (2007). *Cognition: The thinking animal* (3rd ed.). Upper Saddle River, NJ: Merrill/Pearson.

Willingham, D. T. (2009). *Why don't students like school? A cognitive scientist answers questions about how the mind works and what it means in your classroom.* San Francisco: Jossey-Bass.

Willis, S. L., Tennstedt, S. L, Marsiske, M., Ball, K., Elias, J., Koepke, K. M., . . . Wright, E. (2006). Long-term effects of cognitive training on everyday functional outcomes in older adults. *The Journal of the American Medical Association, 296.* Retrieved from http://jama.ama-assn.org/cgi/content/full/296/23/2805#AUTHINFO

Willson V. (2013). *Encyclopedia of Special Education: A Reference for the Education of Children, Adolescents, and Adults with Disabilities and Other Exceptional Individuals.* New York: Wiley.

Wilson, M. B. (2014). *Teasing, tattling, defiance, and more . . .: Positive approaches to 10 common classroom behaviors.* Turner Falls, MA: Center for Responsive Schools, Inc.

Winerip, M. (2010). Equity of test is debated as children compete for gifted kindergarten. *The New York Times.* Retrieved from http://www.nytimes.com/2010/07/26/education/26winerip.html?pagewanted=all&_r=0

Winerip, M. (2013). Ex-schools chief in Atlanta is indicted in testing scandal. *The New York Times.* Retrieved from http://www.nytimes.com/2013/03/30/us/former-school-chief-in-atlanta-indicted-in-cheating-scandal.html?hp&pagewanted=all&_r=2&

Wingfield, N., & Wakabayashijan, D. (2017). Tech companies fight Trump immigration order in court. *The New York Times.* Retrieved from https://www.nytimes.com/2017/01/30/technology/technology-companies-fight-trump-immigration-order-in-court.html

Winitzky, N. (1994). Multicultural and mainstreamed classrooms. In R. Arends (Ed.), *Learning to teach* (3rd ed., pp. 132–170). New York: McGraw-Hill.

Winston, C. N. (2016). An existential-humanistic-positive theory of human motivation. *The Humanistic Psychologist, 44,* 142–163.

Wolf, R. (2017). Supreme Court could pull plug on transgender case. *USA Today.* Retrieved from https://www.usatoday.com/story/news/politics/2017/02/23/education-department-transgender-bathroom-guidance/98322176/

Wolff, F., Nagy, N., Helm, F., & Möller, J. (2018). Testing the internal/external frame of reference model of academic achievement and academic self-concept with open self-concept reports. *Learning and Instruction, 55,* 58–66.

Wong, T. T-Y., & Ho, C. S-H. (2017). Component processes in Arithmetic Word-Problem Solving and Their Correlates. *Journal of Educational Psychology, 109,* 520–531.

Wood, L., & Hawley, A. (2012). Dividing at an early age: The hidden digital divide in Ohio elementary schools. *Learning, Media, & Technology, 37,* 20–39.

Wood, S. G., Hart, S. A., Little, C. W., & Phillips, B. M. (2016). Test anxiety and a high-stakes standardized reading comprehension test: A behavioral genetics perspective. *Merrill-Palmer Quarterly, 62,* 233–251.

Woods, S. A., Lievens, F., Fruyt, F. D., & Wille, B. (2013). Personality across working life: The longitudinal and reciprocal influences of personality on work. *Journal of Organizational Behavior, 34,* S7–S25.

World Health Organization. (2017). Preterm birth. Retrieved from http://www.who.int/mediacentre/factsheets/fs363/en/

Wright, F. (2012). Difference in metacognitive thinking as a cultural barrier to learning. *Journal of the Australia and New Zealand Student Services Association, 40,* 16–22.

Wubbels, T., Brekelmans, M., den Brok, P., Wijsman, L., Mainhard, T., & van Tartwijk, J. (2015). Teacher-student relationships and classroom management. In E. T. Emmer & E. J. Sabornie (Eds.), *Handbook of classroom management* (2nd ed., pp. 363–386). New York: Routledge.

Wurthmann, K. (2013). A social cognitive perspective on the relationships between ethics education, moral attentiveness, and PRESOR. *Journal of Business Ethics, 114,* 131–153.

Xu, J. & Metcalfe, J. (2016). Studying in the region of proximal learning reduces mind wandering. *Memory and Cognition, 44,* 681–695.

Xu, J., & Wu, H. (2013). Self-regulation of homework behavior: Homework management at the secondary school level. *Journal of Educational Research, 106,* 1–13.

Yacek, D. (2018). America's armed teachers: An ethical analysis. *Teachers College Record, 120.* Retrieved from http://www.tcrecord.org/content.asp?contentid=22289

Yadav, A., & Cooper, S. (2017). Fostering creativity through computing. *Communications of the ACM, 60,* 31–33.

Yan, Z. (2018). Student self-assessment practices: The role of gender, school level and goal orientation. *Assessment in Education: Principles, Policy & Practice, 25,* 183–199.

Yang, L. (2016). Interpersonal relationships and the development of student interest in science. *Electronic Journal of Science Education, 20,* 18–38.

Yee, V. (2013). Grouping students by ability regains favor in classroom. *The New York Times.* Retrieved from http://www.nytimes.com/2013/06/10/education/grouping-students-by-ability-regains-favor-with-educators.html

Yigit, C., & Bagceci, B. (2017). Teachers' opinions regarding the usage of action research in professional development. *Journal of Education and Training Studies, 5,* 243–252.

Yoo, J., Miyamoto, Y., & Ryff, C. D. (2016). Positive affect, social connectedness, and healthy biomarkers in Japan and the U.S. *Emotion, 16,* 1137–1146.

Yoon, E., Adams, K., Clawson, A., Chang, H., Surya, S., & Jérémie-Brink, G. (2017). East Asian adolescents' ethnic identity development and cultural integration: A qualitative investigation. *Journal of Counseling Psychology, 64,* 65–79.

Yoon, J. C., & Sungok, S. S. (2013). Predicting teachers' achievement goals for teaching: The role of perceived school goal structure and teachers' sense of efficacy. *Teaching and Teacher Education, 32,* 12–21.

Youssef-Shalala, A., Ayres, P., Schubert, C., & Sweller, J. (2014). Using a general problem-solving strategy to promote transfer. *Journal of Experimental Psychology: Applied, 20,* 215–231.

Yow, W., & Markman, E. (2011). Bilingualism and children's use of paralinguistic cues to interpret emotion in speech. *Bilingualism: Language & Cognition, 14,* 562–569.

Ysseldyke, J., Scerra, C., Stickney, E., Beckler, A., Dituri, J., & Ellis, K. (2017). Academic growth expectations for students with emotional and behavior disorders. *Psychology in the Schools, 54,* 792–807.

Yudin, M.K., & Musgrove, M. (2015, November 16). *Dear colleague letter.* Washington, DC: U.S. Department of Education, Office of Special Education and Rehabilitative Services.

Yuliana, Y., Tasari, T., & Wijayanti, S. (2017). The effectiveness of guided discovery learnng to teach integral calculus for the mathematics students of mathematics education Widya Dharma University. *Infinity, 6,* 1–10.

Zagorski, N. (2017). Using many social media platforms linked with depression, anxiety risk. *American Psychiatric Association.* Retrieved from https://psychnews.psychiatryonline.org/doi/full/10.1176/appi.pn.2017.1b16

Zee, M., & de Bree, E. (2017). Students' self-regulation and achievement in basic reading and math skills: The role of student-teacher relationships in middle school. *European Journal of Developmental Psychology, 14,* 265–280.

Zeller, F., Wang, T., Reiß, S., & Schweizer, K. (2017). Does the modality of measures influence the relationship among working memory, learning and fluid intelligence? *Personality and Individual Differences, 105,* 275–279.

Zentall, S. R., & Morris, B. J. (2012). A critical eye: Praise directed toward traits increases children's eye fixations on errors and decreases motivation. *Psychonomic Bulletin & Review, 19,* 1073–1077.

Zero to Three. (2015). State of America's babies: 2015. Retrieved from http://www.zerotothree.org/public-policy/state-community-policy/baby-facts/related-docs/state-of-america-s-babies-4-15-final.pdf

Zhang, D., Katsiyannis, A., Ju, S., & Roberts, E. (2014). Minority representation in special education: 5-year trends. *Journal of Child and Family Studies, 23,* 118–127.

Zhao, Q., & Li, W. (2016). Measuring perceptions of teachers' caring behaviors and their relationship to motivational responses in physical education among middle school students. *The Physical Educator, 73,* 510–529.

Zhou, J., & Urhahne, D. (2013). Teacher judgment, student motivation, and the mediating effect of attributions. *European Journal of Psychology of Education, 28,* 275–295.

Zimmerman, B. J., & Schunk, D. H. (Eds.). (2013). *Self-regulated learning and academic achievement: Theory, research, and practice.* New York: Springer.

Zingoni, M., & Corey, C. M. (2017). How mindset matters: The direct and indirect effects of employees' mindsets on job performance. *Journal of Personnel Psychology, 16,* 36–45.

Zink, C. F., Pagnoni, G., Martin-Skurski, M. E., Chappelow, J. C., & Berns, G. S. (2004). Human striatal responses to monetary reward depend on saliency. *Neuron, 42,* 509–517.

Zoder-Martell, K. A., & Dieringer, S. T. (2016). Introduction to the special issue: The use of applied behavioral analysis to address student academic referral concerns. *Psychology in the Schools, 53*, 5–7.

Zong, J., Batalova, J., & Hallock, J. (2018). Frequently requested statistics on immigrants and immigration in the United States. *Migration Policy Institute.* Retrieved from https://www.migrationpolicy.org/article/frequently-requested-statistics-immigrants-and-immigration-united-states

Zubrzycki, J. (2012). Single-gender schools scrutinized. *Education Week, 31*(17), 1, 12–13.

Zuffianò, A., Alessandri, G., Gerbino, M., Kanacri, B. P., Di Giunta, L., Milioni, M., & Caprara, G. V. (2013). Academic achievement: The unique contribution of self-efficacy beliefs in self-regulated learning beyond intelligence, personality traits, and self-esteem. *Learning and Individual Differences, 23*, 158–162.

Zyphur, M. J., Chaturvedi, S., & Arvey, R. D. (2008). Job performance over time is a function of latent trajectories and previous performance. *Journal of Applied Psychology, 93*, 217–224. doi:10.1037/0021–9010.93.1.217

Name Index

Subject Index

B

Background knowledge
  class discussions, 371
  creativity, 350
  how to develop it?, 325–326, 326t
  learner diversity, 315
  strategy use, 360
  worked examples, 354
Backward design, 609
  defined, 549
  determining acceptable evidence, 552–553
  identifying desired results, 550–552
  learning objectives, 550–551
  planning learning activities, 553–554
  traditional planning, compared, 549–550
Baseline data, 615
Behavior management strategies, 211
Behavior modification, 251
Behavior problems, 522–541
  applying consequences, 531t, 532–533
  behavioral interventions, 527–533
  behavioral management system, 529–530, 530t
  bullying, 539–541
  cognitive interventions, 523–527, 536
  congruency between verbal/ nonverbal behaviors, 525–526, 526t
  consistency in dealing with problems, 524–525
  constructive assertiveness, 526–527
  corporal punishment, 528–529
  defiant students, 538–539
  desists, 531t, 532
  detention, 528
  emotional factors, 522–523
  eye contact, 526, 526t
  fighting, 539
  follow-through, 525
  ignoring inappropriate behavior, 531–532, 531t
  indirect cues, 531t, 532
  intervention continuum, 531t, 536
  logical consequences, 527
  overlapping, 536
  positive behavior support, 530–531
  praising desired behavior, 531, 531t
  punishers, 528
  removing student from classroom, 529
  timeout, 528
  vicarious reinforcement, 532
  zero-tolerance policies, 540
Behavioral consequences, 238f
Behavioral disorders, 209–211
Behavioral interventions, 527–533
Behavioral management system, 529–530, 530t
Behaviorism, 206, 232–256
  applied behavior analysis (ABA), 251–254

classical conditioning, 232–237. See Classical conditioning
contributions/criticisms, 255–256, 256t
cultural minorities, 254–255
defined, 232
developmentally appropriate practice, 273–274
learning, 232, 280–281
motivation, 419f, 420
operant conditioning, 237–251. See also Operant conditioning
overview, 256t
Behaviorist views of learning, 232–256. See also Behaviorism
Belief, 433. See also Learner beliefs
Belongingness needs, 423, 423f, 425
Bernoulli's principle, 555f
Between-class grouping, 192
Bias
  assessment, 681–683
  confirmation, 368, 370
  content, 682
  gender, 167. See also Gender issues
  hostile attribution, 119
  unconscious, 320–321, 534
Bidialectalism, 158
"Big Five" personality traits, 86–87
Bilingualism, 151
Bioecological systems theory. See Bronfenbrenner's bioecological systems theory
Bipolar disorder, 210–211
Blindness, 211–212
Bloom's taxonomy, 551
Bodily-kinesthetic intelligence, 189t
Bolded text, 362
Boredom, 452
Brain
  basic information, 40–41
  cerebral cortex, 43, 44f
  Chinese vs. English speakers, 299
  complex organ, 40
  effective teaching, 596–597
  myelination, 43
  neurons, 41, 42f
  neuroplasticity, 41, 45
  pattern-seeking organ, 596
  permanent change in wiring, 42
  physical activity, 45, 299
  practice, 42f, 43
  prefrontal cortex, 43, 44f
  right-brain–left-brain dominance, 9, 394, 396
  synaptic pruning, 43
  teenagers, 43–44
Brain-based instruction, 45
Bronfenbrenner's bioecological systems theory, 36–40
  exosystem, 38, 38f, 40t
  implications of, for teaching, 39
  macrosystem, 38, 38f, 40t
  mesosystem, 37, 38f, 40t

microsystem, 37, 38f, 40t
overview, 40t
weaknesses/strengths of Bronfenbrenner's theory, 39, 40t
Bulleted lists, 361, 362
Bullying, 119–121, 539–541

C

California Achievement Test, 671
Cardiovascular disease, 110
Caring, 469–470, 473
Case studies, 10. See also Classroom lessons
CCSSI. See Common Core State Standards Initiative (CCSSI)
Celebrity endorsements, 262
Cell phone use while driving, 303
Central executive, 289f, 290
Centration (centering), 54–55
Cerebral cortex, 43, 44f
Chalkboard, 489–490
Challenging tasks, 476–477, 480–481
Characteristics, 338
Charts, 312, 328
Cheating, 126, 127
Checklists, 636, 636f
Child abuse, 89–90
Choice
  personalized learning, 593
  self-regulated learning, 266
Choral responding, 157
Chunking, 293–294
Cinco de Mayo, 66
Classical conditioning, 232–237
  association, 233
  "Classroom Connections" feature, 236–237
  defined, 233
  discrimination, 234
  extinction, 234
  generalization, 234
  operant conditioning, compared, 237t
  overview, 237t
  teaching strategies, 235–236
  unconditioned and conditioned responses, 233, 234t
  unconditioned and conditioned stimuli, 233, 234t
Classification, 55
Classroom assessment, 16, 608. See also Assessment
Classroom climate, 502–504
"Classroom Connections" feature
  ability differences, 194
  classical conditioning, 236–237
  classroom interventions, 537–538
  cognitive processes, 315–316
  communicating with parents, 521–522
  concept learning, 344
  cultural and linguistic diversity, 159–160

Improvement drills, 489, 490*t*
Impulse control, 265, 266*f*
"In the zone," 418
Inclusion, 196–197, 535
Income inequality, 167, 171
Incremental view of intelligence, 434
Independent practice, 573*t*, 576
Indirect cues, 531*t*, 532
Individual work spaces, 490*t*
Individualized education program
    (IEP), 196, 200–201
Individuals with Disabilities
    Education Act (IDEA), 195–196,
    196*t*, 684
Inductive sequences, 489*t*
Industry-inferiority crisis, 106
Industry vs. inferiority, 96*t*
Information processing and model of
    human memory. *See also* Model of
    human memory
    contributions/criticisms, 320–321,
        322*t*
    overview, 322*t*
    "Preparing for Your Licensure
        Exam" feature, 331–332
    teaching strategies, 321–328
Information processing theory, 287
Information stores, 322*t*. *See also*
    Memory stores
Inhibition, 261
Inhibitory control, 291
Initiative vs. guilt, 96*t*
Instructional alignment, 554
Instructional scaffolding, 65*t*
Instructional strategies, 11. *See also*
    Models of instruction
Instructional time, 504
Instructional variables, 482–492
    "Classroom Connections" feature,
        491–492
    feedback, 486, 490–491
    introductory focus, 483, 487–488,
        489*t*
    involvement, 485, 488–490, 490*t*
    overview, 483*f*
    personalization, 484–485, 488, 489*t*
    teaching strategies, 486–491
Instrumental aggression, 119
Integration, 196, 578*t*, 581
Integrity vs. despair, 96*t*
Intellectual achievement, 423, 423*f*
Intellectual disabilities, 208–209
Intellectual functioning, 208
Intellectually handicapped, 208
Intelligence, 186–195
    ability grouping, 192–193
    "Classroom Connections" feature,
        194
    comparing theories, 190–191, 191*t*
    defined, 673
    fluid/crystallized, 188
    Gardner's theory, 188–189, 191*t*
    IQ, 186–187

learning styles, 193–195
multi-trait views, 187–190
nature vs. nurture, 187
psychometric view, 186–187, 191*t*
Sternberg's triarchic theory, 190,
    190*t*, 191*t*
types, 188
Intelligence quotient (IQ), 186–187
Intelligence tests, 672–673
Interaction, 326–327, 400–403
    active cognitive processing, 343
    feedback, 402
    group work, 327, 402
    open-ended discussions, 402–403
    positive and supportive classroom,
        402
    questioning, 327
Interactive teaching abilities, 403
Interactive whiteboard, 27, 351
Interference, 313
Intermittent reinforcement schedule,
    241, 242*f*
Internalization, 62
Internalizing emotional and behavior
    disorder, 210
Internet, 367
Interpersonal harmony, 129, 129*t*
Interpersonal intelligence, 189*t*
Interpretive exercises
    completion items, 627
    de-emphasizing low levels of
        thinking, 631
    efficiency of assessment practices, 647
    higher-order multiple-choice items,
        620
    matching format, 625
    teacher workload, 621, 647
    true-false items, 623–624
    when used, 656
Interspersed practice, 357
Interval reinforcement schedule, 241,
    242*f*
Intervention continuum, 531*t*, 536
Interventions. *See* Behavior problems
Intimacy vs. isolation, 96*t*
Intrapersonal intelligence, 189*t*
Intrinsic motivation, 417–418, 418*f*
Introductory focus, 483, 487–488, 489*t*
Intuitive appeal, 396
Involvement, 455, 485, 488–490, 490*t*
Iowa Test of Basic Skills, 671
IQ. *See* Intelligence quotient (IQ)
Italicized text, 362
Item file, 647–648

J
Jigsaw II, 586*t*

K
Key-word method, 308*t*
Key words, 358
Keynote, 590, 593
Knowledge construction, 384–413.
    See also Constructivism

APA Top 20 Principles, 385
appropriating understanding, 388
"Classroom Connections" feature,
    409–410
cognitive apprenticeship, 389–390
cognitive learning theory, 282–285
community of learners, 389
contributions/criticisms, 408, 409*t*
developmentally appropriate
    practice, 406
embodied cognition, 392
feedback, 486
learning sciences, 390–393
misconceptions, 394–398
NCTQ teaching strategies, 385
overview, 409*t*
situated cognition, 392–393
sociocultural theory, 389
student diversity, 393
teaching strategies, 398–408
Knowledge of content, 8, 9
Knowledge of learners and learning,
    12–13
Kohlberg's theory of moral
    development, 128–131
    contributions/criticisms, 131*t*
    conventional ethics, 129–130, 129*t*
    evaluating Kohlberg's theory,
        130–131
    interpersonal harmony, 129, 129*t*
    law and order, 129–130, 129*t*
    market exchange, 129, 129*t*
    moral dilemmas, 128
    overview, 131*t*
    postconventional ethics, 129*t*, 130
    preconventional ethics, 129, 129*t*
    punishment-obedience, 129, 129*t*
    social contract, 129*t*, 130
    stages of moral reasoning, 129*t*
    universal principles, 129*t*, 130

L
Labeling controversy, 203–204
Language development, 70–79
    children's first words, 72
    "Classroom Connections" feature, 79
    examples, 78–79
    fluency, 78
    grammar, 73
    gurgling/cooing, 72
    interdependence between cognitive/
        language development, 70, 79
    listening, 74, 78–79
    overgeneralization/
        undergeneralization, 72
    reading, 74, 78–79
    school years, in, 72–74
    semantics, 73
    speaking, 74, 77–78
    syntax, 73
    vocabulary development,
        72–73
    writing, 74, 77